The Princeton Review®

PrincetonReview.com

THE K&W GUIDE TO
COLLEGES

FOR STUDENTS
WITH LEARNING DIFFERENCES

16TH EDITION

MARYBETH KRAVETS, MA

AND IMY F. WAX, MS

Penguin
Random
House

The Princeton Review
110 East 42nd Street, 7th Floor
New York, NY 10017

Published in the United States by Penguin Random House LLC, New York.

ISBN: 978-0-593-51740-6
ISSN: 1934-4775

The Princeton Review is not affiliated with Princeton University.

If there are any important late-breaking developments, changes, or corrections to the materials in this book, we will post that information online in the Student Tools. Register your book and check your Student Tools to see if there are any updates posted there.

Editors: Aaron Riccio and Laura Rose
Production Editors: Liz Dacey, Nina Mozes, Emmeline Parker, Heidi Torres, Emily Epstein White, and Sarah Litt
Production Artist: Deborah Weber
Printed in the United States of America.

10 9 8 7 6 5 4 3 2 1

16th Edition

The Princeton Review Publishing Team
Rob Franek, Editor-in-Chief
David Soto, Senior Director, Data Operations
Stephen Koch, Senior Manager, Data Operations
Deborah Weber, Director of Production
Jason Ullmeyer, Production Design Manager
Jennifer Chapman, Senior Production Artist
Selena Coppock, Director of Editorial
Orion McBean, Senior Editor
Aaron Riccio, Senior Editor
Meave Shelton, Senior Editor
Chris Chimera, Editor
Patricia Murphy, Editor
Laura Rose, Editor
Isabelle Appleton, Editorial Assistant

Penguin Random House Publishing Team
Tom Russell, VP, Publisher
Alison Stoltzfus, Senior Director, Publishing
Brett Wright, Senior Editor
Emily Hoffman, Assistant Managing Editor
Ellen Reed, Production Manager
Suzanne Lee, Designer
Eugenia Lo, Publishing Assistant

For customer service, please contact **editorialsupport@review.com**, and be sure to include:

- full title of the book

- ISBN

- page number

From the Authors of The K&W Guide......

We proudly introduce our 16th edition of *The K&W Guide to Colleges for Students with Learning Differences*. We once again dedicate this guide to every student who dreams of attending college. It represents our nearly 40-year labor of love, commitment, and respect for the many students who learn differently. Fortunately, many of the early barriers to college and obstacles that previously existed have given rise to services and accommodations that embrace those students who simply may learn differently.

Today, there are a growing number of colleges that are encouraging and welcoming to students who may need accommodations and support. They are also embracing the growing number and variety of assistive technologies that are leveling the college experience. The scene has improved dramatically over the years and continues to do so.

Disclosing one's learning differences no longer carries the "stigma" it once did. In fact, it is quite the opposite. One out of five students (20 percent) currently entering college has been diagnosed with a learning difference. While there are mandates that require colleges to provide reasonable support services, many more colleges are recognizing and appreciating how the value of their structured support enhances the transition to college and improves student retention and graduation rates.

We genuinely hope that our guide will serve to inform students and their families, assisting in the college selection process and providing confidence in their subsequent school choices. We trust, as well, that for parents and professionals, our guide will help in identifying a college that will be a good match, one that will provide an appropriate and enriching experience that not only satisfies whatever may be the student's unique needs but one that nurtures their potential.

It is important that students not only understand their learning differences but be able to articulate them comfortably and with confidence. We encourage you to "open the door" to our K&W Guide. We hope that it will help you prioritize your needs and better appreciate the various levels of support that may be offered, guiding you to those that you may need or desire. If we have done nothing more than help you discover that you have the potential to turn your dreams into a college reality, we have happily done our job.

Marybeth Kravets and Imy F. Wax
Co-authors of the *K&W Guide*

Dedication & Acknowledgments

This book is a labor of love. It is written to help individuals throughout the world with Attention-Deficit/Hyperactivity Disorder, Autism Spectrum Disorder, or any other Learning Difference who are seeking the right higher education match and fit for life after high school. The *K&W Guide* is an educational tool for all families, professionals, and friends who know someone with a learning difference or other learning issues.

Our gratitude to the families of Marybeth Kravets and Imy Wax for their patience and support in this continued endeavor: Wendy, Steve, Allison, Andy, Connor, Isabel, Cooper, Ginkgo, Mark, Sara, David, Robbie, Bennett, Carly, Cathy (in loving memory), Dan, Andrea, BJ, Matthew, Leia, Stella, Maizie, Blue, Dr. Jack, Howard, Lisa, Bill, Niaya, Ellis, Gary, Tamar, Jordan, Eli, Debrah, Greg, Jamie, Joey, Benji, and Goldie. Thanks also to all of the colleges that provide services and programs to promote the educational endeavors and dreams of students with learning differences or attention deficit hyperactivity disorder or who are on the autism spectrum.

We would also like to thank all of the contributors in the *K&W Guide* who share their thoughts and experiences with learning differences and attention-deficit/hyperactivity disorder. Our appreciation also goes to Dr. Miriam Pike, head of school for Wolcott College Prep High School, Chicago, Illinois, and our amazing research team, Stephanie Degodny, Marilyn Engleman, Ann Hayward, Elizabeth McGhee, Wendy Perlin, and Carol Sharp, for their support in our endeavor. Finally, we want to thank The Princeton Review and Penguin Random House for their continued confidence in the publication of the *K&W Guide to Colleges for Students with Learning Differences*.

Contents

Get More (Free) Content
at **PrincetonReview.com/cracking**

As easy as 1•2•3

1 Go to PrincetonReview.com/guidebooks or scan the **QR code** and enter the following ISBN for your book: **9780593517406**

2 Answer a few simple questions to set up an exclusive Princeton Review account. *(If you already have one, you can just log in.)*

3 Enjoy access to your **FREE** content!

Once you've registered, you can...

- Take a full-length practice SAT and ACT

- Access additional online resources, such as tips on getting ready for college and a college interview preparation form

- Use our searchable rankings from *The Best 389 Colleges* to find out more information about your dream school

- Get valuable advice about the college application process, including tips for writing a great essay and where to apply for financial aid

- Check for late-breaking updates or corrections to this edition

LET'S GO MOBILE! Access all of these free, additional resources by downloading the new Princeton Review app at www.princetonreview.com/mobile/apps/highschool or scan the QR Code to the right.

Need to report a potential **content** issue?

Contact **EditorialSupport@review.com** and include:

- full title of the book
- ISBN
- page number

Need to report a **technical** issue?

Contact **TPRStudentTech@review.com** and provide:

- your full name
- email address used to register the book
- full book title and ISBN
- Operating system (Mac/PC) and browser (Chrome, Firefox, Safari, etc.)

Foreword

College Readiness Is More Than Academic Achievement
by Daniel Linden III and Kasey Urquídez

The K&W Guide to Colleges for Students with Learning Differences is an incredible resource for students and families embarking on the college search process. In our years of professional experience at the University of Arizona, we have read hundreds of resources and guides and assisted thousands of students in finding their best college "fit." This resource will help students (as well as their families and other supporters) find the right college to meet their individual needs.

Readiness and self-awareness are sometimes more critical than academic skills, and it is important to note that those skills are often ignored as students enter college. When we look at students who demonstrate overall competence, a through line can be drawn connecting the constructs of self-awareness (What do I know about myself?), self-efficacy (What do I believe about myself?), self-regulation (Do my thoughts control my actions?), and persistence (Do I keep trying, even if I fail?). The constant sharpening of these skills is the best way to build not only academic success but life success.

The University of Arizona is dedicated to supporting students with learning challenges and believes in the success of ALL students. In 1980, Eleanor Harner, a tenacious employee in our Student Counseling Center, noticed the increasing needs of students with diagnosed learning disabilities, such as dyslexia and dysgraphia. Her efforts promoted self-advocacy among students and made instructors aware that not all students learn the same way. Eventually, Eleanor took this model of academic support and founded the SALT Program. Today, it is known as the SALT Center, and it is one of the nation's leading academic support units for college students that learn differently. We receive hundreds of inquiries about our organization each year based on the information from the *K&W Guide*—we commend the work put into this amazing Guide.

There has been an exponential increase in the number of students, with and without learning challenges, entering college with higher rates of mental health concerns such as anxiety, depression, etc. These co-occurring challenges, and sometimes primary diagnoses, have only been magnified by the COVID-19 pandemic, and as higher education professionals, we find ourselves working with students and families to circumvent these anxieties. Having the resource of the *K&W Guide* really helps to alleviate those concerns for neurodiverse students. This book has already done the research to help students determine the right school for them—one that fulfills their social and emotional, as well as academic needs.

The most important advice we can offer to help prepare these students for this phase of emerging adulthood would be for students to assume a more active role during their annual review or IEP meetings. *They* should be involved with the annual goal-setting process so they understand why those specific goals were selected. Let *them* ask questions about how their specific challenges manifest and which resources will help them at the next level of education. Practicing awareness and advocacy will benefit them when they enter higher education and will move the student from bystander to the driver of their academic development.

The goal is graduation—but that road is long, and it's important to understand that just because a student has been admitted to a university, it does not necessarily mean they are ready. These proactive measures of helping students become comfortable and confident in themselves, coupled with the constant practice of sharpening their academic and life skills, directly support a university's goals of recruiting more diverse populations, increasing retention, and fostering both intellectual and nonacademic skills.

Daniel Linden III, M.S.
Director, Student Support Services, SALT Center
University of Arizona

Kasey Urquídez, EdD
Vice President, Enrollment Management and
Dean, Undergraduate Admissions
University of Arizona

Introduction

The Rights of College Students with Disabilities: Myth vs. Reality

by Matt Cohen

Myth: Colleges and universities are covered by the same disability laws as elementary and secondary schools.

Reality: The Individuals with Disabilities Education Act (IDEA) does not apply to colleges and universities. The IEP is specific to K–12. However, Section 504 applies to all colleges and universities that receive federal financial assistance, and the Americans with Disabilities Act (ADA) applies to all colleges and universities unless they are religiously controlled.

Myth: I must disclose my medical conditions or disability in my college admissions application.

Reality: You do not have to disclose, and you can't be required to disclose, your disability prior to admission.

Myth: I should/should not disclose that I have a disability on my application.

Reality: There is no definite rule or strategy regarding how disclosure will affect a student's application for admission. If you feel it will be helpful to disclose your disability and possibly write about it in your application, you may do so. However, if you feel it will hurt your chances of acceptance, then you may choose not to disclose. A student may not be denied admission based on their disability, but may be denied should they fail to meet other qualifications.

Myth: My college must determine if I have a disability.

Reality: Colleges and universities are not responsible for discovering if a student has a disability, unlike public elementary and secondary schools. The burden is on you to self-identify that you have a disability: you must notify the college disability services office, provide documentation that confirms the disability and its impact on you, and request accommodations.

Myth: If I had an IEP or 504 Plan in high school, I am automatically entitled to accommodations in college.

Reality: An IEP terminates when a student graduates from high school. Colleges use 504 Plans to provide accommodations. Prior eligibility doesn't automatically make you eligible for accommodations in college, but it does support the need for ongoing accommodations. Colleges have a right to review your clinical documentation and history of prior support. It is possible to get accommodations based on a late diagnosed disability, particularly if it is due to a NEW medical or psychological problem but can occur even if the disability is alleged to have been present over time, though undiagnosed. If that is the case, a strong explanation for why it was not diagnosed and how the student managed to progress without formal services under 504 or an IEP would be needed. For example, the student might show that for their early educational experience they were receiving extensive tutoring outside of school and spent many extra hours on homework, which could be a basis to explain the absence of formal recognition of the disability.

Myth: Colleges must provide accommodations to students with disabilities.

Reality: Entitlement to reasonable accommodations is not as broad at the college level as in elementary and secondary school. You must meet a number of criteria. First, you must have a physical or mental impairment that substantially limits a major life activity, such as physical activity, emotional regulation, learning, reading, concentrating, thinking, or communicating. Second, you must meet the general qualifications for participation in the program or activity that you are applying for, either with or without accommodations. Third, you must establish that: (1) you have a physical, emotional, or learning impairment; (2) you need specific accommodations; and (3) these accommodations are "reasonable." A college may deny eligibility if they feel you have not adequately documented either the presence of a disability or that it is substantially limiting in the major life activities you identified. They may deny a specific accommodation request if providing the accommodation would fundamentally change the nature of an academic program or the school's curriculum or is perceived as being unduly burdensome.

Myth: I am entitled to the same accommodations and services in college that I received in high school.

Reality: You may not be entitled to the same level of services in college that they were eligible for in elementary and secondary school. You are only entitled to "reasonable accommodations," those that are not unduly burdensome and do not result in a fundamental alteration of the college's programs. Some examples of accommodations include extended time on deadlines and tests, preferential seating, access to lecture notes, or use of assistance technology. Reasonable accommodations may also be required to address the actual physical accessibility of the campus, including sidewalks and parking facilities if these are required for the student to access the school setting. Colleges must engage in an interactive process with you in determining if a requested accommodation is reasonable.

The reasonable accommodations requirement also applies to campus housing. Accommodations may include being issued a single dorm room at the same cost as having a roommate and the ability to have an emotional support animal in campus housing.

Myth: The absence of eligibility for an IEP or 504 Plan in high school disqualifies me from receiving accommodations in college.

Reality: Not having an IEP or 504 Plan in high school does not disqualify you from receiving accommodations in college, but it may make it harder to obtain eligibility for accommodations. You will need to provide current clinical documentation of the disability along with an explanation of why the disability was not diagnosed and/or accommodated previously. Generally, you will need to provide recent testing that documents the presence of your disability and its impact on your functioning, especially if you have learning disabilities, ADHD, or other disabilities that may change in impact over time.

Myth: Students whose mental health may pose a risk to others can be automatically excluded from college.

Reality: In a previous case in which a student was dismissed on the basis of campus safety, a district court found that an analysis of whether a student with a mental health disability represents a direct threat must be individualized and include consideration of reasonable accommodations likely to reduce the level of risk to others.

Myth: There is nothing more I can do if a college denies that I have a disability or refuses my request for a specific accommodation.

Reality: If the school denies accommodations, you have a right to file a grievance or appeal within the college. You can also file a complaint with the U.S. Department of Education Office of Civil Rights or the U.S. Department of Justice Civil Rights Division, Disability Rights Unit. In some cases, you may also be able to file suit in federal court.

Matt Cohen is the founder of Matt Cohen and Associates, a Chicago-based disability rights law firm, and has over 40 years of experience advocating on behalf of people with disabilities. Matt can be reached at 866-787-9270 or mdcspedlaw@gmail.com. His website is www.mattcohenandassociates.com.

General Guidelines for Documentation of a Learning Disability

1. A comprehensive psychoeducational or neuropsychological evaluation that provides a diagnosis of a learning disability must be submitted. The report should indicate the current status and impact of the learning disability in an academic setting. If another diagnosis is applicable (e.g., ADHD, mood disorder), it should be stated.

2. The evaluation must be conducted by a professional who is certified/licensed in the area of learning disabilities, such as a clinical or educational psychologist, school psychologist, neuropsychologist, or learning disabilities specialist. The evaluator's name, title, and professional credentials and affiliation should be provided.

3. The evaluation must be based on a comprehensive assessment battery:

    Aptitude: Average broad cognitive functioning must be demonstrated on an individually administered intelligence test, preferably administered during high school or beyond, such as the WAIS, WISC, Woodcock-Johnson, and Cognitive Battery. Subtest scores, regular and scaled, should be listed.

    Academic Achievement: A comprehensive academic achievement battery, such as the Woodcock-Johnson Tests of Achievement, Wechsler Individual Achievement Test, and Kaufman Tests of Educational Achievement, should document achievement deficits relative to potential. The battery should include current levels of academic functioning in relevant areas, such as reading, oral and written language, and mathematics. Standard scores and percentiles for administered subtests should be stated. Specific achievement tests can also be included, such as the Nelson-Denny Reading Test and Test of Written Language (TOWL), as well as informal measures (e.g., informal reading inventories and writing samples).

    Information Processing: Specific areas of information processing (e.g., short- and long-term memory, auditory and visual perception/processing, executive functioning) should be assessed with tests such as Wide Range Assessment of Learning and Memory, Delis-Kaplan Executive Function System, and/or a checklist such as Behavior Rating Inventory of Executive Function.

    Social-Emotional Assessment: To rule out a primary emotional basis for learning difficulties and provide information needed to establish appropriate services, a social-emotional assessment (using formal assessment instruments and/or clinical interview) should be conducted.

    Clinical Summary: A diagnostic summary should present a diagnosis of a specific learning disability; provide impressions of the testing situation; interpret the testing data; and indicate how patterns in the student's cognitive ability, achievement, and information processing reflect the presence of a learning disability. Recommendations should be provided for specific accommodations based on disability-related deficits. For students just graduating high school, an evaluation reflecting current levels of academic skills should have been administered while in high school; for students who have been out of school for a number of years, documentation will be considered on a case-by-case basis. Additional documents that do not constitute sufficient documentation, but that may be submitted in addition to a psychological, psychoeducational or neuropsychological evaluation include an individualized education plan (IEP), a 504 Plan, and/or an educational assessment.

General Guidelines for Documentation of Attention-Deficit/Hyperactivity Disorder (ADHD)

Students requesting accommodations and services on the basis of an Attention-Deficit/ Hyperactivity Disorder (ADHD) are required to submit documentation that establishes a disability and supports the need for the accommodations recommended and requested.

1. A *qualified* professional must conduct the evaluation. Those who conduct the assessment, make the diagnosis of ADHD, detail symptoms, provide relevant history, determine functional limitations, and provide recommendations for accommodation must be licensed mental health professionals. Primary care or general practice physicians are not considered qualified to complete an ADHD evaluation.

2. Documentation must be current (typically within three years). The provision of accommodations is based upon an assessment of the current impact of the student's disability on learning in the college setting.

3. Documentation *must* be comprehensive. Requirements for any diagnostic report are:

   - A medical or clinical diagnosis of ADHD based on DSM criteria
   - Assessment/testing profile and interpretation of the assessment instruments used that supports the diagnosis. Acceptable measures include objective measures of attention and discrimination or valid and reliable observer or self-report, such as the following:
     - Conner's Continuous Performance Task (CPT)
     - Test of Variables of Attention (TOVA)
     - Behavioral Assessment System for Children
     - Conner's Adult ADHD Rating Scale (CAARS)
     - CAARS-L; the long version of the self-report form
     - CARRS-O; the observer form
     - Brown Attention Deficit Disorder Scale

   - A clear description of the functional limitations in the educational setting, specifying the major life activities that are affected to a substantial degree because of the disability
   - Relevant history, including developmental, family, medical, psychosocial, pharmacological, educational and employment (ADHD is by definition first exhibited in childhood, so the assessment should include historical information establishing symptoms of ADHD throughout childhood, adolescence, and into adulthood)
   - A description of the specific symptoms manifesting themselves at the present time that may affect the student's academic performance
   - Medications the student is currently taking, as well as a description of any limitations that may persist even with medication
   - Co-existing conditions, including medical and learning disabilities that should be considered in determining reasonable accommodations

General Guidelines for Documentation of Autism Spectrum Disorder

Students requesting accommodations and services on the basis of an Autism Spectrum Disorder (ASD) are required to submit documentation that establishes a disability and supports the need for the accommodations recommended and requested.

A. Persistent deficits in social communication and social interaction across multiple contexts, as manifested by the following, currently or by history:

1. Deficits in social-emotional reciprocity, such as abnormal social approach and failure of normal back-and-forth conversation; reduced sharing of interests, emotions, or affect; and failure to initiate or respond to social interactions.

2. Deficits in nonverbal communicative behaviors used for social interaction, such as poorly integrated verbal and nonverbal communication; abnormalities in eye contact and body language or deficits in understanding and use of gestures; and a total lack of facial expressions and nonverbal communication.

3. Deficits in developing, maintaining, and understanding relationships, such as difficulty adjusting behavior to suit various social contexts; difficulty in sharing imaginative play or in making friends; and absence of interest in peers.

4. In addition to early history of social pragmatic weaknesses, sensory issues, and lack of emotions, the following instruments are helpful in diagnosing ASD: Autism Diagnostic Observation Schedule (ADOS), Social Responsiveness Scale (SRS).

Specify current severity:

Severity is based on social communication impairments and restricted, repetitive patterns of behavior.

B. Restricted, repetitive patterns of behavior, interests, or activities, as manifested by at least two of the following, currently or by history (examples are illustrative, not exhaustive; see text):

1. Stereotyped or repetitive motor movements, use of objects, or speech (e.g., simple motor stereotypes, lining up toys or flipping objects, echolalia, idiosyncratic phrases).

2. Insistence on sameness, inflexible adherence to routines, or ritualized patterns of verbal or nonverbal behavior (e.g., extreme distress at small changes, difficulties with transitions, rigid thinking patterns, greeting rituals, need to take same route or eat same food every day).

3. Highly restricted, fixated interests that are abnormal in intensity or focus (e.g., strong attachment to or preoccupation with unusual objects, excessively circumscribed or perseverative interests).

4. Hyper- or hyporeactivity to sensory input or unusual interest in sensory aspects of the environment (e.g., apparent indifference to pain/temperature, adverse response to specific sounds or textures, excessive smelling or touching of objects, visual fascination with lights or movement).

Specify current severity:

Severity is based on social communication impairments and restricted, repetitive patterns of behavior.

C. Symptoms must be present in the early developmental period (but may not become fully manifest until social demands exceed limited capacities or may be masked by learned strategies in later life).

D. Symptoms cause clinically significant impairment in social, occupational, or other important areas of current functioning.

E. These disturbances are not better explained by intellectual disability (intellectual developmental disorder) or global developmental delay. Intellectual disability and Autism Spectrum Disorder frequently co-occur; to make comorbid diagnoses of Autism Spectrum Disorder and intellectual disability, social communication should be below that expected for general developmental level.

Note: Individuals with a well-established DSM diagnosis of autistic disorder, Asperger's disorder, or pervasive developmental disorder not otherwise specified should be given the diagnosis of Autism Spectrum Disorder. Individuals who have marked deficits in social communication, but whose symptoms do not otherwise meet criteria for Autism Spectrum Disorder, should be evaluated for social (pragmatic) communication disorder.

Specify if:

■ With or without accompanying intellectual impairment
■ With or without accompanying language impairment
■ Associated with a known medical or genetic condition or environmental factor
■ Associated with another neurodevelopmental, mental, or behavioral disorder
■ With catatonia (refer to the criteria for catatonia associated with another mental disorder)

How to Use This Guide

The *K&W Guide to Colleges for Students with Learning Differences* includes information on colleges and universities that offer services to students with learning differences such as specific Learning Disabilities, Attention-Deficit/Hyperactivity Disorder, and Autism Spectrum Disorder.

Learning Disability (LD): A learning disability is a neurological condition that interferes with an individual's ability to store, process, or produce information.

Attention Deficit Hyperactive Disorder (ADHD): A learning disability in which affected individuals generally have challenges paying attention or concentrating. Individuals with ADHD may exhibit inattention, inability to focus, hyperfocus, hyperactivity, and impulsivity.

Autism Spectrum Disorder (ASD): A group of developmental disabilities that can cause significant social, communication, and behavioral challenges.

Disability: For the purpose of this book, a disability is a mental, cognitive, or developmental condition.

Conditional Admission: Acceptance to a college or university on the condition that the student complete additional specified requirements.

No two colleges are identical in the programs or services they provide, but there are some similarities. For this guide, the services and programs at the various colleges have been grouped into the following three Levels of Support.

Structured Programs (SP)

Colleges with Structured Programs offer the most comprehensive services for students with learning disabilities. The director and/or staff are certified in learning disabilities or related areas. The director is actively involved in the admission decision and, often, the criteria for admission may be more flexible than general admission requirements. Services are highly structured, and students are involved in developing plans to meet their particular learning styles and needs. Often students in Structured Programs sign a contract agreeing to actively participate in the program. There is usually an additional fee for the enhanced services. Students who have participated in a Structured Program or Structured Services in high school, such as the Learning Disabilities Resource Program, individualized or modified coursework, tutorial assistance, academic monitoring, notetakers, test accommodations, or skill classes might benefit from exploring colleges with Structured Programs or Coordinated Services.

Coordinated Services (CS)

Coordinated Services differ from Structured Programs in that the services are not as comprehensive. These services are provided by at least one certified learning disability specialist. The staff is knowledgeable and trained to provide assistance to students to develop strategies for their individual needs. The director of the program or services may be involved in the admission decision, be in a position to offer recommendations to the admissions office on the potential success of the applicant, or to assist the students with an appeal if denied admission to the college. Receiving these services generally requires specific documentation of the learning disability—students are encouraged to self-identify prior to entry. Students voluntarily request accommodations or services in the Coordinated Services category, and there may be specific skills courses or remedial classes available or required for students with learning disabilities who are admitted probationally or conditionally. High school students who may have enrolled in some modified or remedial courses, utilized test accommodations, or required tutorial assistance but who typically requested services only as needed might benefit from exploring colleges with Coordinated Services or Services.

Services (S)

Services are the least comprehensive of the three categories. Colleges offering Services generally comply with the federal mandate requiring reasonable accommodations to all students with appropriate and current documentation. These colleges routinely require documentation of the disability in order for the students with LD/ADHD/ASD to receive accommodations. Staff and faculty actively support the students by providing basic services to meet the needs of the students. Services are requested on a voluntary basis, and there may be some limitations as to what is reasonable and the degree of services available. Sometimes, just the small size of the student body allows for the necessary personal attention to help students with learning disabilities succeed in college. High school students who require minimum accommodations but who would find comfort in knowing that services are available, knowing who the contact person is, and knowing that this person is sensitive to students with learning disabilities might benefit from exploring colleges providing Services or Coordinated Services.

College Profiles Explained

The K&W Guide to Colleges for Students with Learning Differences includes information on colleges and universities that offer services to students with learning differences such as specific Learning Disabilities, Attention-Deficit/Hyperactivity Disorder, and Autism Spectrum Disorder.

Each college in the book is profiled on two pages and is arranged alphabetically by state. The first page of each spread includes level of Support, Programs/Services for Students with Learning Differences, Admissions, Additional Information, and a sidebar with Accommodations and Graduation Requirements.

SUPPORT: SP, CS, or **S**

PROGRAMS/SERVICES FOR STUDENTS WITH LEARNING DIFFERENCES describes the learning disability programs or services offered by the school

ADMISSIONS details the requirements for ALL students while including other factors the school considers when determining admission, conditional admission, and alternative admission routes that may be applicable to students with special needs; required academic courses are listed on the second page under General Admissions

ADDITIONAL INFORMATION may include more detailed information on the programs and services for students with learning differences, services available to all students that LD students should know about, and clubs or groups specific to LD students

- **ACCOMMODATIONS** and services offered by the school and individually listed
- **COLLEGE GRADUATION REQUIREMENTS** states whether course waivers and substitutions are allowed

On the second page of each school profile, you'll see both a map and a tab that pinpoint which state the school is located in and what cities are in the immediate area. This page also covers General Admissions information, Financial Aid, and Campus Life offerings.

GENERAL ADMISSIONS includes the most important factors considered and the recommended or required academic units

FINANCIAL AID lists the forms required and the need-based scholarships or grants offered

CAMPUS LIFE describes the various activities, organizations, and athletics

In the grey sidebar on this page, where reported, you'll find relevant facts and figures about:

- **CAMPUS**
  - Rural (in or near a rural community, population under 5,000)
  - Village (in or near a small town, population 5,000–24,999)
  - Town (in or near a large town, population 25,000–74,999)
  - City (in the metropolitan area of a small/medium city, population 75,000–299,999)
  - Metropolis (in the metropolitan area of a major city, population 300,000+)

- **STUDENTS**
  - demographics

- **FINANCIAL FACTS**
  - tuition, fees, room and board

- **GENERAL ADMISSIONS INFO**
  - application fees and registration dates
  - testing policy and common ACT/SAT score ranges
  - per the College Board, the digital SAT scores and ranges correspond to pre-Fall 2024 SAT scoring
  - **Test Flexible**: students choose which type of test(s) to submit; check with those schools on a case-by-case basis
  - **Test Free** (sometimes referred to as Test Blind): the school will not look at or consider scores in any capacity
  - **Test Optional:** schools will consider scores if submitted

- **ACADEMICS**
  - class size and student/faculty ratio

At the bottom of the second page, **REQUESTING SERVICES FOR STUDENTS WITH LEARNING DIFFERENCES** emphasizes what documentation is required and where it needs to be submitted.

The authors have made a conscientious effort to provide the most current information possible. However, names, costs, dates, policies, and other information are always subject to change, and colleges of particular interest or importance to the reader should be contacted directly for verification of the data. Some schools may be temporarily test-optional, so you should always check with the school to make sure of their current requirements.

College Profiles

Auburn University

The Quad Center Auburn, AL 36849-5149 • Admissions: 334-844-6425 • www.auburn.edu

Support: S

ACCOMMODATIONS

Allowed in exams:

Calculators	Yes
Dictionary	N/A
Computer	Yes
Spell-checker	Yes
Extended test time	Yes
Scribe	Yes
Proctors	Yes
Oral exams	Yes
Note-takers	Yes

Support services for students with:

LD	Yes
ADHD	Yes
ASD	Yes
Distraction-reduced environment	Yes
Recording of lecture allowed	Yes
Reading technology	Yes
Audio books	Yes
Other assistive technology	Yes
Priority registration	Yes

Added costs of services:

For LD	No
For ADHD	No
For ASD	No
LD specialists	No
ADHD & ASD coaching	No
ASD specialists	No
Professional tutors	No
Peer tutors	Yes
Max. hours/week for services	Varies
How professors are notified of student approved accommodations	Student

COLLEGE GRADUATION REQUIREMENTS

Course waivers allowed	No
Course substitutions allowed	Yes
In what courses: Math	

PROGRAMS/SERVICES FOR STUDENTS WITH LEARNING DIFFERENCES

Auburn's Office of Accessibility (OOA) provides appropriate accommodations and services for students with disabilities. Once a student is admitted to Auburn, they should complete an application, submit documentation to OAA, and request an appointment to discuss prior accommodations and explore accommodations found to be reasonable for current functional limitations. These may include academic accommodations and access to assistive technology training. OOA can also introduce students to Access Academy— AU's Web Accessibility Initiative and scholarships available for students with disabilities. AU SKILLS Program is a fee-for-service academic support program for students with learning differences. Students who sign up for SKILLS receive support scheduling courses and with their exams through time management skills, tutoring, coaching, and more. SKILLS staff coordinate with OOA to offer support to students. The Education to Accomplish Growth in Life Experiences for Success (EAGLES) program is a nondegree, post-secondary education, comprehensive transition program (CTP) for students with intellectual disabilities. The program focuses on (1) academic enrichment, (2) personal and social skills, (3) independent living skills, (4) health and wellness, and (5) integrated work experiences. In a two- or four-year campus experience, students can achieve their employment and independent living goals.

ADMISSIONS

For all applicants to Auburn, high school transcripts are the primary criteria for determining academic preparedness. Each first-year applicant must complete the core curriculum requirements by the end of their high school senior year. The admissions review committee considers GPA, grades earned in core curriculum courses, quality and rigor of coursework, pattern of grades and marked improvement in academic performance, class rank (if provided), and outstanding performance in one or more subject areas. The university may use the academic area of interest in determining admission.

Additional Information

The First Year Experience (FYE) offers Camp War Eagle (CWE), a summer orientation for incoming first-year students and their guests. The program familiarizes students with Auburn's campus, traditions, student services, and programs. FYE's Ace That Class series connects students with faculty, staff, and campus departments, and with educational panels and interactive workshops throughout the year. First Year Seminars (FYS) are semester-long courses to help new students acclimate to AU life and learn about academic and personal resources on campus, relevant social issues, time management, critical-thinking skills, study strategies, test prep, note-taking, goal setting, and other topics and skills for college success. Study Partners offers free peer tutoring sessions in core courses, and Supplemental Instruction (SI) is a free program to help students succeed in traditionally difficult courses.

Since 1892, all of Auburn's athletics teams (men's and women's) have been named the Tigers. The name comes from a line in Oliver Goldsmith's poem, "The Deserted Village," published in May 1770, "where crouching tigers await their hapless prey." It's said of mascot Aubie the Tiger: women love him, children adore him, and men want to be him.

Auburn University

GENERAL ADMISSIONS

Very important factors include: academic GPA, standardized test scores (if submitted). *Important factors include:* rigor of secondary school record. High school diploma is required and GED is accepted. Institution is test-flexible for entering Fall 2024. Check admissions website for updates. *Academic units required:* 4 English, 3 math, 2 science (1 lab), 3 social studies. *Academic units recommended:* 1 foreign language, 4 social studies.

FINANCIAL AID

Students should submit: FAFSA. *Need-based scholarships/grants offered:* College/university scholarship or grant aid from institutional funds; Federal Pell; Private scholarships; SEOG; State scholarships/grants. *Loan aid offered:* Direct PLUS loans; Direct Subsidized Loans; Direct Unsubsidized Loans. Federal Work-Study Program available. Institutional employment available.

CAMPUS LIFE

Activities: Campus Ministries; Choral groups; Concert band; Dance; Drama/theater; International Student Organization; Jazz band; Literary magazine; Marching band; Music ensembles; Musical theater; Opera; Pep band; Radio station; Student government; Student newspaper; Student-run film society; Symphony orchestra; Television station; Yearbook. **Organizations:** 550 registered organizations, 41 honor societies, 42 religious organizations, 21 fraternities, 29 sororities. **Athletics (Intercollegiate):** *Men:* baseball, basketball, crew/rowing, cross-country, golf, ice hockey, lacrosse, martial arts, racquetball, rugby, softball, swimming, table tennis, track/field (indoor), ultimate frisbee, volleyball, water polo, wrestling. *Women:* basketball, crew/rowing, cross-country, equestrian sports, golf, gymnastics, ice hockey, lacrosse, martial arts, racquetball, softball, swimming, table tennis, track/field (indoor), ultimate frisbee, volleyball, water polo, wrestling.

CAMPUS	
Type of school	Public
Environment	Town

STUDENTS	
Undergrad enrollment	24,782
% male/female	50/50
% from out of state	40
% frosh live on campus	62

FINANCIAL FACTS	
Annual in-state tuition	$10,080
Annual out-of-state tuition	$30,240
Room and board	$14,596
Required fees	$1,746

GENERAL ADMISSIONS INFO	
Application fee	$50
Regular application deadline	2/1
Nonfall registration	Yes

Fall 2024 testing policy	Test Flexible
Range SAT EBRW	590–670
Range SAT Math	580–680
Range ACT Composite	24–30

ACADEMICS	
Student/faculty ratio	20:1
% students returning for sophomore year	93
Most classes have 20–29 students.	

REQUESTING SERVICES FOR STUDENTS WITH LEARNING DIFFERENCES

Phone: 334-844-2096 • accessibility.auburn.edu • Email: accessibility@auburn.edu

Documentation submitted to: Office of Accessibility
Separate application required for Services: Yes

Documentation required for:
 LD: Psychoeducational evaluation
 ADHD: Psychoeducational evaluation
 ASD: Psychoeducational evaluation

Auburn University at Montgomery

P.O. Box 244023, Montgomery, AL 36124-4023 • Admissions: 334-244-3615 • www.aum.edu

(Support: S)

ACCOMMODATIONS

Allowed in exams:	
Calculators	Yes
Dictionary	Yes
Computer	Yes
Spell-checker	Yes
Extended test time	Yes
Scribe	Yes
Proctors	Yes
Oral exams	Yes
Note-takers	Yes
Support services for students with:	
LD	Yes
ADHD	Yes
ASD	Yes
Distraction-reduced environment	Yes
Recording of lecture allowed	Yes
Reading technology	Yes
Audio books	Yes
Other assistive technology	Yes
Priority registration	Yes
Added costs of services:	
For LD	No
For ADHD	No
For ASD	No
LD specialists	No
ADHD & ASD coaching	Yes
ASD specialists	No
Professional tutors	No
Peer tutors	Yes
Max. hours/week for services	Varies
How professors are notified of student approved accommodations	Student

COLLEGE GRADUATION REQUIREMENTS

Course waivers allowed	No
Course substitutions allowed	Yes
In what courses: Math	

PROGRAMS/SERVICES FOR STUDENTS WITH LEARNING DIFFERENCES

The Center for Disability Services (CDS) provides students with documented disabilities reasonable accommodations or auxiliary aids to participate in all educational programs and activities of AUM. To receive accommodations, students who have been accepted for an upcoming semester must register with CDS and submit current documentation. After the paperwork has been reviewed, the CDS sets an intake appointment to discuss and begin the appropriate services, such as priority registration, specialized equipment, interpreter services, note-taking assistance, one-on-one assistive technology training, and testing accommodations. The CDS uses the secure cloud-based online portal Accommodate, an ADA compliant interface, to help students directly submit requests, coordinate support, connect with notetakers/transcribers, check out assistive devices, communicate with faculty and CDS, and be proactive.

ADMISSIONS

For all applicants, high school transcripts are the primary criteria used by the admissions review committee. The review committee will be evaluating the overall academic performance of each application, GPA (minimum 2.3 unweighted), standardized test scores if submitting (minimum ACT of 18 or SAT of 940), class rank if provided, grades earned in core curriculum courses, quality of coursework, grade trends, improvement in academic performance, and exceptional work in one or more specific subject areas. Students who are not submitting test scores should have a GPA of at least 3.6 and lack of scores may limit scholarships and other opportunities. Applicants who do not meet all requirements for admission may qualify for the Bridge Program. This one-semester program provides extra academic support from faculty and staff—"bridging the gap"—prior to gaining full admission to AUM.

Additional Information

The Experiential Education and Engagement Center (EEEC) is an on-campus resource that connects students to the campus and the community with services, including peer mentoring, undergraduate research opportunities, internships, and service-learning. The Math Placement Program (aka Math Boot Camp) is a free noncredit, web-based math placement preparation course for undergraduates seeking to save tuition and time by starting at AUM in a higher-level math course. At the Warhawk Academic Success Center (WASC), students can meet with their Student Success Advisor and develop, free of charge, a plan for academic success. WASC has two tutoring centers: The Learning Center provides tutoring services related mainly to writing, liberal arts, and other core curriculum. The Instructional Support Lab offers tutoring focused on math, science, computer technology, nursing, and other science-related subjects.

A university whose chosen colors are orange and black can't help but celebrate Halloween with the fright and fun of Shriek Week. It's an October week with spook-tacular events that include decorating and costume contests, creepy crafts, themed trick-or-treating, and a haunted house for ghoulishly good times.

Auburn University at Montgomery

GENERAL ADMISSIONS

Very important factors include: rigor of secondary school record, academic GPA, standardized test scores (if submitted). High school diploma is required and GED is accepted. Institution is test-optional for entering Fall 2024. Check admissions website for updates. *Academic units recommended:* 3 English, 3 math, 2 science (2 labs), 2 foreign language, 2 social studies, 2 history, 2 academic electives.

FINANCIAL AID

Students should submit: FAFSA. *Need-based scholarships/grants offered:* College/university scholarship or grant aid from institutional funds; Federal Pell; Private scholarships; SEOG; State scholarships/grants. *Loan aid offered:* Direct PLUS loans; Direct Subsidized Loans; Direct Unsubsidized Loans. Federal Work-Study Program available. Institutional employment available.

CAMPUS LIFE

Activities: Campus Ministries; Choral groups; Dance; Drama/theater; International Student Organization; Literary magazine; Musical theater; Student government; Student newspaper. **Organizations:** 110 registered organizations, 25 honor societies, 6 religious organizations, 3 fraternities, 7 sororities. **Athletics (Intercollegiate):** *Men:* baseball, basketball, cross-country, softball, table tennis, ultimate frisbee, volleyball. *Women:* basketball, cross-country, softball, table tennis, ultimate frisbee, volleyball.

CAMPUS	
Type of school	Public
Environment	City

STUDENTS	
Undergrad enrollment	4,318
% male/female	34/66
% from out of state	5
% frosh live on campus	39

FINANCIAL FACTS	
Annual in-state tuition	$7,992
Annual out-of-state tuition	$17,952
Room and board	$6,980
Required fees	$868

GENERAL ADMISSIONS INFO	
Application fee	No fee
Regular application deadline	8/1
Nonfall registration	Yes

Fall 2024 testing policy	Test Optional
Range SAT EBRW	473–588
Range SAT Math	430–515
Range ACT Composite	18–23

ACADEMICS	
Student/faculty ratio	16:1
% students returning for sophomore year	70
Most classes have 10–19 students.	

REQUESTING SERVICES FOR STUDENTS WITH LEARNING DIFFERENCES

Phone: 334-244-3631 • www.aum.edu/center-for-disability-services • Email: cds@aum.edu

Documentation submitted to: Center for Disability Services
Separate application required for Services: Yes

Documentation required for:
LD: Psychoeducational evaluation
ADHD: Psychoeducational evaluation
ASD: Psychoeducational evaluation

The University of Alabama

P.O. Box 870132, Tuscaloosa, AL 35487-0132 • Admissions: 205-348-5666 • www.ua.edu

Support: CS

ACCOMMODATIONS

Allowed in exams:	
Calculators	Yes
Dictionary	Yes
Computer	Yes
Spell-checker	Yes
Extended test time	Yes
Scribe	Yes
Proctors	Yes
Oral exams	Yes
Note-takers	Yes
Support services for students with:	
LD	Yes
ADHD	Yes
ASD	Yes
Distraction-reduced environment	Yes
Recording of lecture allowed	Yes
Reading technology	Yes
Audio books	Yes
Other assistive technology	Yes
Priority registration	Yes
Added costs of services:	
For LD	No
For ADHD	No
For ASD	No
LD specialists	No
ADHD & ASD coaching	No
ASD specialists	Yes
Professional tutors	Yes
Peer tutors	Yes
Max. hours/week for services	Varies
How professors are notified of student approved accommodations	Student

COLLEGE GRADUATION REQUIREMENTS

Course waivers allowed	No
Course substitutions allowed	Yes
In what courses: Case-by-case basis	

PROGRAMS/SERVICES FOR STUDENTS WITH LEARNING DIFFERENCES

The Office of Disability Services (ODS) works with students who request academic accommodations. Students are encouraged to begin the registration process once accepted and committed to attend U of Alabama. Students will complete an online ODS application and submit disability documentation, then an accommodations specialist will meet with the student to talk about the impact of their disability and any necessary accommodations. Once accommodations have been determined, students will receive an accommodations letter for their professors and are expected to meet with them to discuss the plan for using the accommodations. Common accommodations include priority registration, testing alternatives, note-taking, e-text and alternative formats for course material, and assistive technology and apps.

ADMISSIONS

For admission to U of Alabama, all applicants must complete the required academic course units. Social studies must include world history or a comparable course (a second foreign language will satisfy one of the four required social science/social studies units), mathematics must include algebra I, algebra II, and one unit of either geometry, trigonometry, or calculus, and the five units of other academic courses should include fine arts or computer literacy, and additional courses in math, natural sciences, and foreign language. ACT and SAT scores are not required for admission but can be used for merit scholarship consideration.

Additional Information

Crimson Edge (Education Guarantees Excellence) is a student success program to help incoming first-year students. It provides direct access to academic advising, success coaches and plans, tutoring, and intentional connection to academic support, as well as access to community and social opportunities. The Learning Commons offers subject tutors, academic coaches to help students identify challenges and set goals, learn effective study skills, time management, handle test anxiety, work on self-esteem, and better understand expectations at the college level.

The University of Alabama has had a football rivalry with the nearby Auburn Tigers since 1893. This feud grew so contentious that they did not play one another from 1908 to 1947, but it is now a much-anticipated yearly event between schools.

The University of Alabama

GENERAL ADMISSIONS

Very important factors include: rigor of secondary school record, academic GPA, standardized test scores (if submitted). *Important factors include:* class rank. *Other factors considered include:* application essay, recommendations. High school diploma is required and GED is accepted. Institution is test-optional for entering Fall 2024. Check admissions website for updates. *Academic units required:* 4 English, 3 math, 3 science (2 labs), 1 foreign language, 4 social studies, 5 academic electives. *Academic units recommended:* 2 foreign language.

FINANCIAL AID

Students should submit: FAFSA. *Need-based scholarships/grants offered:* College/university scholarship or grant aid from institutional funds; Federal Nursing Scholarships; Federal Pell; Private scholarships; SEOG; State scholarships/grants. *Loan aid offered:* Direct PLUS loans; Direct Subsidized Loans; Direct Unsubsidized Loans. Federal Work-Study Program available. Institutional employment available.

CAMPUS LIFE

Activities: Campus Ministries; Choral groups; Concert band; Dance; Drama/theater; International Student Organization; Jazz band; Literary magazine; Marching band; Model UN; Music ensembles; Musical theater; Opera; Pep band; Radio station; Student government; Student newspaper; Student-run film society; Symphony orchestra; Television station; Yearbook. **Organizations:** 600 registered organizations, 51 honor societies, 78 religious organizations, 43 fraternities, 25 sororities. **Athletics (Intercollegiate):** *Men:* baseball, basketball, crew/rowing, cross-country, golf, ice hockey, lacrosse, rugby, swimming, table tennis, track/field (indoor), ultimate frisbee, volleyball, water polo, wrestling. *Women:* basketball, crew/rowing, cross-country, equestrian sports, field hockey, golf, gymnastics, lacrosse, rugby, softball, swimming, table tennis, track/field (indoor), ultimate frisbee, volleyball, water polo.

CAMPUS

Type of school	Public
Environment	City

STUDENTS

Undergrad enrollment	31,360
% male/female	44/56
% from out of state	60
% frosh live on campus	94

FINANCIAL FACTS

Annual in-state tuition	$11,100
Annual out-of-state tuition	$31,460
Room and board	$12,296
Required fees	$840

GENERAL ADMISSIONS INFO

Application fee	$40
Regular application deadline	Rolling
Nonfall registration	Yes

Fall 2024 testing policy	Test Optional
Range SAT EBRW	550–680
Range SAT Math	530–690
Range ACT Composite	22–31

ACADEMICS

Student/faculty ratio	19:1
% students returning for sophomore year	87

Most classes have 10–19 students.

REQUESTING SERVICES FOR STUDENTS WITH LEARNING DIFFERENCES

Phone: 205-348-4285 • www.ods.ua.edu • Email: ods@ua.edu

Documentation submitted to: Office of Disability Services
Separate application required for Services: Yes

Documentation required for:
LD: Psychoeducational evaluation
ADHD: Psychoeducational evaluation
ASD: Psychoeducational evaluation

The University of Alabama in Huntsville

UAH Office of Admissions Huntsville, AL 35899 • Admissions: 256-824-2773 • www.uah.edu

Support: S

ACCOMMODATIONS

Allowed in exams:

Calculators	Yes
Dictionary	Yes
Computer	Yes
Spell-checker	Yes
Extended test time	Yes
Scribe	Yes
Proctors	Yes
Oral exams	Yes
Note-takers	Yes

Support services for students with:

LD	Yes
ADHD	Yes
ASD	Yes
Distraction-reduced environment	Yes
Recording of lecture allowed	Yes
Reading technology	Yes
Audio books	No
Other assistive technology	Yes
Priority registration	Yes

Added costs of services:

For LD	No
For ADHD	No
For ASD	No
LD specialists	No
ADHD & ASD coaching	Yes
ASD specialists	No
Professional tutors	No
Peer tutors	Yes
Max. hours/week for services	Varies
How professors are notified of student approved accommodations	Student and Director

COLLEGE GRADUATION REQUIREMENTS

Course waivers allowed	Yes

In what courses: Individual case-by-case decisions

Course substitutions allowed	Yes

In what courses: Individual case-by-case decisions

PROGRAMS/SERVICES FOR STUDENTS WITH LEARNING DIFFERENCES

The University of Alabama provides access and support to students who have documented disabilities through its Disability Support Services (DSS) office. Enrolled students must first complete the DSS online application and include relevant documentation that confirms their disability, indicates how that disability impacts their education, and requests specific accommodations to address it. Students then contact DSS to schedule an intake appointment. After the meeting, which can be in person, by phone, or via Zoom, students will receive a link to activate the approved accommodations for each class. DSS will then notify the course professors, and students should meet with each professor to discuss the accommodations being used.

ADMISSIONS

UAH does not require letters of recommendation or an essay for admission consideration. High school coursework and test scores, if submitted, are the main factors for consideration but not the entire admission decision. An applicant with a grade point average of 2.9 and a composite score of 20 on the ACT or an equivalent SAT score is considered a strong candidate for admission. Applicants with required high school course deficiencies may be admitted in good standing. However, deficiencies must be remedied during the first year of enrollment in a manner approved by the department, and these courses cannot be used to satisfy degree requirements.

Additional Information

The Student Success Center (SSC) Academic Coaching Program offers services to help students develop new study, learning, and self-management strategies in and out of the classroom. Academic Coaching appointments are available in person or online. SSC offers tutoring for nearly all first- and second-level courses. Content tutors are available for one-on-one and small group sessions for a variety of subjects by appointment, either online or in person. Writing Tutors are available by appointment for any stage of a writing assignment to help students become more confident and successful writers and identify and develop their writing process. Students can communicate with a tutor or academic coach live from any location via desktop, laptop, iPhone, iPad, or Android device. The SSC PASS (Peer Assisted Study Sessions) program offers weekly study sessions focusing on courses like calculus, chemistry, and economics. PASS tutors sit in on courses they've already taken and succeeded in and offer class-specific study sessions out of the classroom.

In 1961, Dr. Wernher von Braun, director of the Marshall Space Flight Center in Huntsville and later known as the "Father of the American Space Program," spoke to the Alabama legislature about the need to create an environment where professors could teach and do research. Three million dollars for the Research Institute was eventually approved, and 200 acres of land were purchased for the UAH campus. Today von Braun's legacy—UAH—has 17 Research Centers and Institutes.

The University of Alabama in Huntsville

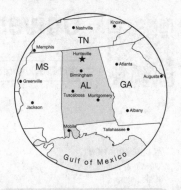

GENERAL ADMISSIONS

Very important factors include: academic GPA, standardized test scores (if submitted). High school diploma is required and GED is accepted. Institution is test-optional for entering Fall 2024. Check admissions website for updates. *Academic units required:* 4 English, 3 math, 3 science, 4 social studies, 6 academic electives. *Academic units recommended:* 4 math, 4 science (2 labs), 2 foreign language.

FINANCIAL AID

Students should submit: FAFSA. *Need-based scholarships/grants offered:* College/university scholarship or grant aid from institutional funds; Federal Nursing Scholarships; Federal Pell; Private scholarships; SEOG; State scholarships/grants. *Loan aid offered:* Direct PLUS loans; Direct Subsidized Loans; Direct Unsubsidized Loans. Federal Work-Study Program available. Institutional employment available.

CAMPUS LIFE

Activities: Campus Ministries; Choral groups; Concert band; Dance; Drama/theater; International Student Organization; Jazz band; Model UN; Music ensembles; Musical theater; Opera; Pep band; Student government; Student newspaper. **Organizations:** 125 registered organizations, 15 honor societies, 9 religious organizations, 6 fraternities, 6 sororities. **Athletics (Intercollegiate):** *Men:* baseball, basketball, crew/rowing, cross-country, cycling, ice hockey, table tennis, track/field (indoor). *Women:* basketball, crew/rowing, cross-country, cycling, softball, table tennis, track/field (indoor), volleyball.

CAMPUS
Type of school	Public
Environment	City

STUDENTS
Undergrad enrollment	6,338
% male/female	58/42
% from out of state	16
% frosh live on campus	62

FINANCIAL FACTS
Annual in-state tuition	$8,996
Annual out-of-state tuition	$19,766
Room and board	$9,603
Required fees	$846

GENERAL ADMISSIONS INFO
Application fee	$30
Regular application deadline	8/20
Nonfall registration	Yes
Fall 2024 testing policy	Test Optional
Range SAT EBRW	520–650
Range SAT Math	540–680
Range ACT Composite	25–31

ACADEMICS
Student/faculty ratio	17:1
% students returning for sophomore year	83
Most classes have 20–29 students.	

REQUESTING SERVICES FOR STUDENTS WITH LEARNING DIFFERENCES

Phone: 256-824-1997 • www.uah.edu/dss • Email: dssproctor@uah.edu

Documentation submitted to: Disability Support Services
Separate application required for Services: Yes

Documentation required for:
LD: Psychoeducational evaluation
ADHD: Psychoeducational evaluation
ASD: Psychoeducational evaluation

University of Alaska Anchorage

3211 Providence Drive, Anchorage, AK 99508-8046 • Admissions: 907-786-1480 • uaa.alaska.edu

Support: S

PROGRAMS/SERVICES FOR STUDENTS WITH LEARNING DIFFERENCES

University of Alaska Disability Support Services (DSS) provides services for students with disabilities. Students with disabilities are encouraged to be their own advocates and should make an appointment with DSS to establish eligibility and discuss their needs and reasonable accommodations supported by documentation. Once eligibility has been established, students receive information about their accommodation requests and authorize DSS to notify course faculty about them. Accommodations may vary by semester and may include alternate-format class material, assistive technology, note-taking, and testing alterations. Students are encouraged to participate in the annual high school transition event coordinated by DSS. In the spring, incoming students come to campus for a tour, pizza lunch, and a chance to hear from current UAA students, staff, and faculty. Students are also encouraged to attend the new student orientation and enroll in University Studies 150 (UNIV A150): College Survival Skills. Both opportunities strengthen connections to important student resources.

ADMISSIONS

All students complete the same application process. Applicants must have earned a high school diploma or GED and have a minimum GPA of 2.5. Students with a 2.0-2.5 GPA may be admitted to certain BA programs with academic advising as a requirement. Standardized test scores are not used as part of the admission decision for most programs but may be used to determine placement for math and writing courses. Students should consult their academic advisor before registration to discuss placement scores, course prerequisites, and testing criteria.

Additional Information

The Academic Coach Center helps students develop skills and knowledge for college success, including basic study skills, learning strategies, note-taking, textbook reading skills, and time management. Coaching services coordinate with tutoring, advising, and mentoring to complement the classroom instructional experience. They are offered as individualized sessions or group workshops led by peer coaches, staff, and faculty. First-time, first-year students who live in student housing will be automatically assigned a room in the First-Year Residential Experience (FYRE) Program. The FYRE Program integrates campus and college life: social engagement, academic success, resources and support systems, civic engagement, and professional development opportunities. Additionally, through the Learning Commons Program, students can schedule tutoring help from the Writing Center, Math Lab, Language Learning Center, Science Lab, Communication Coaching Center, and Nursing Tutoring. Students have 24-hour access to peer-created tutorial videos and free resources through the Learning Commons YouTube channel.

Anchorage is as far west as Honolulu and is the northernmost city in the United States. On a clear day, you can see Denali, the tallest peak in North America, and six other mountain ranges. Anchorage sits on a triangular peninsula surrounded by the Cook Inlet, the northernmost reach of the Pacific Ocean. UAA is surrounded by an environment that is both urban and wild, where culture, innovation and adventure converge.

University of Alaska Anchorage

General Admissions

Very important factors include: rigor of secondary school record. *Other factors considered include:* class rank, standardized test scores (if submitted). High school diploma is required and GED is accepted. Institution is test-optional for entering Fall 2024. Check admissions website for updates.

Financial Aid

Students should submit: FAFSA; Institution's own financial aid form. *Need-based scholarships/grants offered:* College/university scholarship or grant aid from institutional funds; Federal Pell; Private scholarships; SEOG; State scholarships/grants. *Loan aid offered:.* Federal Work-Study Program available. Institutional employment available.

Campus Life

Activities: Campus Ministries; Choral groups; Dance; Drama/theater; International Student Organization; Jazz band; Literary magazine; Model UN; Music ensembles; Musical theater; Opera; Radio station; Student government; Student newspaper; Student-run film society. **Organizations:** 70 registered organizations, 5 honor societies, 5 religious organizations, 1 fraternities, 2 sororities. **Athletics (Intercollegiate):** *Men:* basketball, cross-country, ice hockey, skiing (nordic/cross-country). *Women:* basketball, cross-country, gymnastics, skiing (nordic/cross-country), volleyball.

CAMPUS

Type of school	Public
Environment	City

STUDENTS

Undergrad enrollment	13,390
% male/female	42/58
% from out of state	10

FINANCIAL FACTS

Annual in-state tuition	$4,950
Annual out-of-state tuition	$17,400
Room and board	$9,827
Required fees	$832

GENERAL ADMISSIONS INFO

Application fee	$50
Regular application deadline	7/1
Nonfall registration	Yes

Fall 2024 testing policy	Test Optional
Range SAT EBRW	500–630
Range SAT Math	520–630
Range ACT Composite	17–25

ACADEMICS

Student/faculty ratio	12:1
% students returning for sophomore year	73

Most classes have 10–19 students.

REQUESTING SERVICES FOR STUDENTS WITH LEARNING DIFFERENCES

Phone: 907-786-4530 • www.uaa.alaska.edu/students/disability-support-services/
Email: uaa_dss@alaska.edu

Documentation submitted to: Disability Support Services
Separate application required for Services: Yes

Documentation required for:
LD: Psychoeducational evaluation
ADHD: Psychoeducational evaluation
ASD: Psychoeducational evaluation

University of Alaska Fairbanks

P.O. Box 757480 Fairbanks, AK 99775-7480 • Admissions: 907-474-7500 • www.uaf.edu

Support: S

ACCOMMODATIONS

Allowed in exams:	
Calculators	Yes
Dictionary	Yes
Computer	Yes
Spell-checker	Yes
Extended test time	Yes
Scribe	Yes
Proctors	Yes
Oral exams	Yes
Note-takers	Yes
Support services for students with:	
LD	Yes
ADHD	Yes
ASD	Yes
Distraction-reduced environment	Yes
Recording of lecture allowed	Yes
Reading technology	Yes
Audio books	No
Other assistive technology	Yes
Priority registration	Yes
Added costs of services:	
For LD	No
For ADHD	No
For ASD	No
LD specialists	No
ADHD & ASD coaching	No
ASD specialists	No
Professional tutors	No
Peer tutors	Yes
Max. hours/week for services	Varies
How professors are notified of student approved accommodations	Student

COLLEGE GRADUATION REQUIREMENTS

Course waivers allowed	No
Course substitutions allowed	Yes
In what courses: Individual case-by-case basis	

PROGRAMS/SERVICES FOR STUDENTS WITH LEARNING DIFFERENCES

University of Alaska Fairbanks Disability Services (UAFDS) provides students with accommodations so they can access academic classes and course materials. Students with a disability must first complete and submit an application for accommodations along with comprehensive documentation of their disability. Once UAFDS has reviewed these materials, students participate in an interview with the director of Disability Services. After UAFDS determines eligibility for services and reasonable accommodations, students are sent letters of accommodation to share with their course instructors. Accommodations may include note-taking assistance, classroom accommodations, and testing accommodations that include a quiet space to take tests, having tests read aloud and/or scribed, or additional testing time. Students with documented disabilities are eligible for Student Support Services (SSS), where they can access tutoring, peer mentors, specialized advising, exposure to cultural events and unique academic programs, help with course selections, and other support.

ADMISSIONS

Applicants seeking admission to a bachelor's degree program must have a high school diploma, have taken the required high school core curriculum, and have at least a cumulative GPA of 2.5. Unofficial transcripts may be submitted with the application; however, acceptance is not final until the official transcripts with a posted graduation date are received. Students, with some exceptions, must take the ALEKS PPL test for placement into the correct mathematics, statistics, and other quantitative courses.

Additional Information

Accounting, chemistry, math, engineering, foreign language, and math and stats labs all assist students with understanding concepts, courses, and homework. Additionally, the Speaking Center assists students in preparing and presenting speech-related assignments. In addition to these resources, the Nook offers a learning space that helps students focus while also creating, developing, and sharing new ideas.

Since 1923, Starvation Gulch, an annual festival, has passed the torch of knowledge to new students at a huge bonfire. It's changed over the years; no more drunken brawls or shotgun blasts, but there's still fierce competition for trophies given to the most creative wood pile sculpture possible, and it's still a symbol of the power of knowledge and UAF's history.

University of Alaska Fairbanks

GENERAL ADMISSIONS

Very important factors include: academic GPA, standardized test scores (if submitted). High school diploma is required and GED is accepted. Institution is test-optional for entering Fall 2024. Check admissions website for updates *Academic units required:* 4 English, 3 math, 3 science (1 labs), 3 social studies. *Academic units recommended:* 4 math, 4 science, 4 social studies, 2 foreign language.

FINANCIAL AID

Students should submit: FAFSA; Institution's own financial aid form. *Need-based scholarships/grants offered:* College/university scholarship or grant aid from institutional funds; Federal Pell; Private scholarships; SEOG; State scholarships/grants. *Loan aid offered:* Direct PLUS loans; Direct Subsidized Loans; Direct Unsubsidized Loans. Federal Work-Study Program available. Institutional employment available.

CAMPUS LIFE

Activities: Campus Ministries; Choral groups; Dance; Drama/theater; International Student Organization; Jazz band; Literary magazine; Model UN; Music ensembles; Radio station; Student government; Student newspaper; Symphony orchestra. **Organizations:** 134 registered organizations, 7 honor societies, 7 religious organizations, 1 fraternities, 1 sororities. **Athletics (Intercollegiate):** *Men:* basketball, cross-country, ice hockey, skiing (nordic/cross-country). *Women:* basketball, cross-country, skiing (nordic/cross-country), swimming, volleyball.

CAMPUS	
Type of school	Public
Environment	City

STUDENTS	
Undergrad enrollment	4,266
% male/female	43/57
% from out of state	16
% frosh live on campus	79

FINANCIAL FACTS	
Annual in-state tuition	$8,460
Annual out-of-state tuition	$25,440
Room and board	$10,540
Required fees	$2,355

GENERAL ADMISSIONS INFO	
Application fee	$50
Regular application deadline	6/15
Nonfall registration	Yes
Fall 2024 testing policy	Test Optional
Range SAT EBRW	520–630
Range SAT Math	510–620
Range ACT Composite	17–26

ACADEMICS	
Student/faculty ratio	7:1
% students returning for sophomore year	78
Most classes have 2–9 students.	

Alaska

REQUESTING SERVICES FOR STUDENTS WITH LEARNING DIFFERENCES

Phone: 907-474-5655 • www.uaf.edu/disabilityservices • Email: uaf-disabilityservices@alaska.edu

Documentation submitted to: UAF Office of Disability Services
Separate application required for Services: Yes

Documentation required for:
LD: Psychoeducational evaluation
ADHD: Psychoeducational evaluation
ASD: Psychoeducational evaluation

Arizona State University

1151 S. Forest Avenue, Tempe, AZ 85287-1004 • Admissions: 480-965-7788 • www.asu.edu

Support: CS

PROGRAMS/SERVICES FOR STUDENTS WITH LEARNING DIFFERENCES

Student Accessibility and Inclusive Learning Services is the central campus resource for students with disabilities. Students seeking accommodations must submit a new student registration form and schedule a meeting with their assigned accessibility consultant. Submitting current documentation is optional, but it may expedite the process. Accommodations may include but are not limited to, alternative testing, alternative formatted materials, captioning, note-taking, classroom laboratory aides, and assistive technology.

ADMISSIONS

All applicants are expected to meet the same admission criteria. First-year applicants must also meet at least one of the following: 3.0 GPA in the competency courses; top 25 percent in high school graduating class; an ACT score of 22 for Arizona residents (24 nonresidents); or an SAT score of 1120 for Arizona residents (1180 nonresidents). SAT or ACT scores are optional, but they may be submitted for competency requirements, course placement, or supplemental information. Specific programs may have additional requirements. Students who do not meet these requirements may be reviewed individually before a final admission decision is made. Admission may be granted with one deficiency in no more than two competency areas. Deficiencies cannot be in both math and laboratory science. Students must earn a minimum 2.0 GPA in each subject area.

Additional Information

Academic advisors and success coaches are among the most important student services available to first-year students. They assist in course registration, goal setting, defining an academic path, and connecting with other resources offered by ASU. University Academic Success Programs (UASP) provide a variety of free in-person and online services: subject area tutoring, writing tutoring, and workshops; review sessions are offered for a variety of subject areas before exams; and mini concept refresher videos are designed to prepare students for review sessions or exams. Prep review sessions are offered at the start of the semester, providing a refresher for key math concepts used in math, science, business, and engineering courses. Supplemental Instruction (SI) provides peer-led group sessions to improve student retention in courses that traditionally have high rates of D's, F's, and withdrawals. Sessions are live streamed or offered in person and are designed to be interactive. UASP's How-to-School program provides online resources to help first-year students succeed.

DID YOU KNOW?

Palm Walk is the most popular corridor on the Tempe campus, and it's lined on both sides with palm trees reaching heights of more than 70 feet. In 2016, the 100th anniversary of Palm Walk, the 110 standing Mexican fan palms were replaced with date palms to provide more shade and an annual date harvest.

Arizona State University

GENERAL ADMISSIONS

Very important factors include: class rank, academic GPA. *Important factors include:* rigor of secondary school record. High school diploma is required and GED is accepted. Institution is test-optional for entering Fall 2024. Check admissions website for updates. *Academic units required:* 4 English, 4 math, 3 science (3 labs), 2 foreign language, 1 social studies, 1 U.S. history, 1 fine arts or career and technical education.

FINANCIAL AID

Students should submit: FAFSA. *Need-based scholarships/grants offered:* College/university scholarship or grant aid from institutional funds; Federal Nursing Scholarships; Federal Pell; Private scholarships; SEOG; State scholarships/grants; United Negro College Fund. *Loan aid offered:* Direct PLUS loans; Direct Subsidized Loans; Direct Unsubsidized Loans. Federal Work-Study Program available. Institutional employment available.

CAMPUS LIFE

Activities: Campus Ministries; Choral groups; Concert band; Dance; Drama/theater; International Student Organization; Jazz band; Literary magazine; Marching band; Model UN; Music ensembles; Musical theater; Opera; Pep band; Radio station; Student government; Student newspaper; Student-run film society; Symphony orchestra; Television station. **Organizations:** 987 registered organizations, 26 honor societies, 70 religious organizations, 38 fraternities, 28 sororities. **Athletics (Intercollegiate):** *Men:* baseball, basketball, crew/rowing, cross-country, cycling, equestrian sports, golf, ice hockey, lacrosse, martial arts, racquetball, rugby, swimming, table tennis, track/field (indoor), ultimate frisbee, volleyball, water polo, wrestling. *Women:* basketball, crew/rowing, cross-country, cycling, equestrian sports, golf, gymnastics, ice hockey, lacrosse, martial arts, racquetball, rugby, softball, swimming, table tennis, track/field (indoor), ultimate frisbee, volleyball, water polo, wrestling.

CAMPUS

Type of school	Public
Environment	Metropolis

STUDENTS

Undergrad enrollment	64,778
% male/female	51/49
% from out of state	29
% frosh live on campus	71

FINANCIAL FACTS

Annual in-state tuition	$10,978
Annual out-of-state tuition	$29,952
Room and board	$14,718
Required fees	$640

GENERAL ADMISSIONS INFO

Application fee	$50
Regular application deadline	Rolling
Nonfall registration	Yes
Fall 2024 testing policy	Test Optional

ACADEMICS

Student/faculty ratio	18:1
% students returning for sophomore year	85

Most classes have 10–19 students.

REQUESTING SERVICES FOR STUDENTS WITH LEARNING DIFFERENCES

Phone: 480-965-1234 • eoss.asu.edu/accessibility • Email: student.accessibility@asu.edu

Documentation submitted to: Student Accessibility and Inclusive Learning Services
Separate application required for Services: Yes

Documentation required for:
LD: Psychoeducational evaluation
ADHD: Psychoeducational evaluation
ASD: Psychoeducational evaluation

Northern Arizona University

P.O. Box 4084, Flagstaff, AZ 86011-4084 • Admissions: 928-523-5511 • nau.edu

Support: CS

ACCOMMODATIONS

Allowed in exams:

Calculators	Yes
Dictionary	Yes
Computer	Yes
Spell-checker	Yes
Extended test time	Yes
Scribe	Yes
Proctors	Yes
Oral exams	Yes
Note-takers	Yes

Support services for students with:

LD	Yes
ADHD	Yes
ASD	Yes
Distraction-reduced environment	Yes
Recording of lecture allowed	Yes
Reading technology	Yes
Audio books	Yes
Other assistive technology	Yes
Priority registration	Yes

Added costs of services:

For LD	No
For ADHD	No
For ASD	No
LD specialists	Yes
ADHD & ASD coaching	Yes
ASD specialists	No
Professional tutors	No
Peer tutors	Yes
Max. hours/week for services	Varies
How professors are notified of student approved accommodations	Student

COLLEGE GRADUATION REQUIREMENTS

Course waivers allowed	N/A
Course substitutions allowed	Yes

In what courses: Whatever courses necessary based on the disability, granted it does not fundamentally alter the program.

PROGRAMS/SERVICES FOR STUDENTS WITH LEARNING DIFFERENCES

Disability Resources (DR) offers services and accommodations at no cost to all NAU students with disabilities. As soon as possible, before attending NAU, new students must complete a form to request accommodations from DR and include, if possible, documentation describing the impact the disability is likely to have at NAU. The third and most important step is a required initial intake interview. This interview is not dependent on the receipt of documentation; any information students share during or prior to the first meeting is helpful and can save the need for follow-up. Students will receive a letter regarding their eligibility status, accommodation determinations, and further instructions for the process. Some accommodations that may be provided include priority registration, access to assistive technology devices and software, printed material in an alternate format, note-taking, alternative testing consideration, and tutorial and informational videos. As a service to prospective NAU students, Disability Resources will review disability-related information/documentation regardless of a prospective student's current admission status. NAU has an ADHD support group and an autism support group.

ADMISSIONS

To be admitted as a first-year student at NAU, applicants must have completed the Arizona Board of Regents coursework competencies. A second language is not required. Applicants can be admitted with a 3.0 GPA or higher using the core academic courses of science, English, math, fine arts, and social studies with no more than two deficiencies in these core courses. If the deficiencies are in math and science together, then the applicant is not admissible. Deficiencies are a result of not enrolling in the required number of courses in an academic core area or earning a grade of "F" in the course or having a GPA below 2.0.

Additional Information

The Academic Success Centers (ASC) provide personalized peer support and resources to build confidence and develop independent learning. Peer academic coaches are current NAU students who work one-on-one with students to develop strong learning strategies both in and out of the classroom. Learning Specialists meet with students one-on-one to improve learning strategies and help develop an individualized plan for success. ASC-supported tutoring, in-person and online, is available in over 100 courses. Supplemental Instruction (SI) is a series of peer-facilitated weekly review sessions for students taking challenging courses. SI Leaders are current students who have previously taken the course, performed well, and want to help others succeed.

DID YOU KNOW?

In 1932, the Copper Ax was adopted as the symbol of Lumberjack sports. When two ASU students stole the ax, classes were dismissed, roadblocks set by police and sheriff, and students and faculty joined the chase. When these thieves were caught, the student council punished them by shaving their heads, painting their faces, and parading them from campus through downtown Flagstaff.

Northern Arizona University

GENERAL ADMISSIONS

Very important factors include: academic GPA. *Important factors include:* rigor of secondary school record. *Other factors considered include:* class rank, standardized test scores (if submitted). High school diploma is required and GED is accepted. Institution is test-optional for entering Fall 2024. Check admissions website for updates. *Academic units required:* 4 English, 4 math, 3 science, 1 social studies, 1 U.S. history, 1 fine arts. *Academic units recommended:* 2 foreign language.

FINANCIAL AID

Students should submit: FAFSA. *Need-based scholarships/grants offered:* College/university scholarship or grant aid from institutional funds; Federal Pell; Private scholarships; SEOG; State scholarships/grants. *Loan aid offered:* Direct PLUS loans; Direct Subsidized Loans; Direct Unsubsidized Loans. Federal Work-Study Program available. Institutional employment available.

CAMPUS LIFE

Activities: Campus Ministries; Choral groups; Concert band; Dance; Drama/theater; International Student Organization; Jazz band; Literary magazine; Marching band; Model UN; Music ensembles; Musical theater; Opera; Pep band; Radio station; Student government; Student newspaper; Student-run film society; Symphony orchestra; Television station. **Organizations:** 380 registered organizations, 17 honor societies, 29 religious organizations, 14 fraternities, 12 sororities. **Athletics (Intercollegiate):** *Men:* baseball, basketball, cross-country, equestrian sports, gymnastics, ice hockey, lacrosse, racquetball, rugby, softball, swimming, track/field (indoor), ultimate frisbee, volleyball, water polo. *Women:* baseball, basketball, cross-country, equestrian sports, golf, gymnastics, ice hockey, lacrosse, racquetball, rugby, softball, swimming, track/field (indoor), ultimate frisbee, volleyball, water polo.

CAMPUS

Type of school	Public
Environment	City

STUDENTS

Undergrad enrollment	23,090
% male/female	37/63
% from out of state	31
% frosh live on campus	83

FINANCIAL FACTS

Annual in-state tuition	$11,024
Out-of-state tuition	$26,286
Room and board	$11,728
Required fees	$1,250

GENERAL ADMISSIONS INFO

Application fee	$25
Regular application deadline	8/1
Nonfall registration	Yes

Fall 2024 testing policy	Test Optional
Range SAT EBRW	530–640
Range SAT Math	520–630
Range ACT Composite	19–25

ACADEMICS

Student/faculty ratio	20:1
% students returning for sophomore year	76

Most classes have 20–29 students.

REQUESTING SERVICES FOR STUDENTS WITH LEARNING DIFFERENCES

Phone: 928-523-8773 • nau.edu/disability-resources • Email: DR@nau.edu

Documentation submitted to: Disability Resources
Separate application required for Services: Yes

Documentation required for:
LD: Psychoeducational evaluation
ADHD: Psychoeducational evaluation
ASD: Psychoeducational evaluation

University of Arizona

P.O. Box 210073, Tucson, AZ 85721-0073 • Admissions: 520-621-3237 • www.arizona.edu

Support: SP

ACCOMMODATIONS

Allowed in exams:

Calculators	Yes
Dictionary	Yes
Computer	Yes
Spell-checker	Yes
Extended test time	Yes
Scribe	Yes
Proctors	Yes
Oral exams	Yes
Note-takers	Yes

Support services for students with:

LD	Yes
ADHD	Yes
ASD	Yes
Distraction-reduced environment	Yes
Recording of lecture allowed	Yes
Reading technology	Yes
Audio books	Yes
Other assistive technology	Yes
Priority registration	No

Added costs of services:

For LD	Yes
For ADHD	Yes
For ASD	Yes
LD specialists	Yes
ADHD & ASD coaching	Yes
ASD specialists	Yes
Professional tutors	Yes
Peer tutors	Yes
Max. hours/week for services	Varies
How professors are notified of student approved accommodations	Student and Disability Resources

COLLEGE GRADUATION REQUIREMENTS

Course waivers allowed	No
Course substitutions allowed	Yes
In what courses: Case-by-case basis.	

DID YOU KNOW?

In 1885, Tucson delegates to the 13th Arizona Territorial Legislature in Prescott arrived late due to a snowstorm. At this legislative session, institutions were being divvied up. Prescott remained the capital, Phoenix got the insane asylum, and Yuma the prison. Tucson got the last pick—a university. Forty acres of rural land were donated by two gamblers and a saloon owner so the town wouldn't lose the bonding needed.

PROGRAMS/SERVICES FOR STUDENTS WITH LEARNING DIFFERENCES

The Disability Resource Center (DRC) provides accommodations for students with disabilities. Students request accommodations and submit the online affiliation form to DRC, which DRC will review. Then, the student will receive an email to schedule a meeting with an Access Consultant to discuss accommodations. The decision of what are equitable accommodations and services is made by DRC, some faculty, and the student. Along with in-class experiences, DRC considers accessibility for exams/learning assessments, all class related-activities, labs, field trips, internships, and study abroad. The renowned Strategic Alternative Learning Techniques (SALT) Center is a fee-based program that provides a comprehensive range of services to students with learning and attention differences, including content-specific tutoring, workshops, educational technology, and access to psychological and wellness services. Weekly sessions with peer tutors create an optimal learning environment that facilitates independent and lifelong learning. Current documentation and a separate application to the SALT program are required.

ADMISSIONS

Applicants have assured admission to the University of Arizona if they attended a regionally accredited high school, rank in the top 25 percent of their graduating class, and have a 3.0 unweighted GPA through their sixth semester in the core competency requirements. The SAT and ACT are not required, but if submitted, they may be used to assist with class placement at orientation or help fulfill UofA core competency requirements. Applicants who do not meet the requirements for Assured Admission may still be admitted based on the admission review process. The UofA looks for applicants who will bring unique life experiences and personal achievements to the campus community. On the general application for admission, applicants can indicate an interest in applying to SALT, and once they submit their general application, a link will be sent to the student to access the SALT application.

Additional Information

The THINK TANK offers an array of services: academic coaching, academic skills tutoring, workshops on a range of topics (managing time effectively, adapting study strategies, how to navigate online classes), individual meetings with professional Learning Specialists on topics such as balancing and prioritizing time, success in courses, and test preparation. The THINK TANK also offers course-specific tutoring for business, science, math, statistics, language, writing, and technology. Please note that tutoring may be free or fee-based. The THINK TANK has a library of online modules and paper handouts about time management, reading, learning, exam strategies, and even on well-being. Supplemental Instruction (SI) is a free service that provides regularly scheduled, out-of-class study sessions led by trained students who have completed the course and attended every lecture. SI sessions are open to all students in the class and are a place to review course concepts, develop test prep strategies, and discuss readings.

University of Arizona

GENERAL ADMISSIONS

Very important factors include: rigor of secondary school record, academic GPA. *Other factors considered include:* class rank, standardized test scores (if submitted), application essay, recommendations. High school diploma is required and GED is accepted. Institution is test-optional for entering Fall 2024. Check admissions website for updates. *Academic units required:* 4 English, 4 math, 3 science (3 labs), 2 foreign language, 2 social studies.

FINANCIAL AID

Students should submit: FAFSA; Institution's own financial aid form. *Need-based scholarships/grants offered:* College/university scholarship or grant aid from institutional funds; Federal Pell; Private scholarships; SEOG; State scholarships/grants. *Loan aid offered:* Direct PLUS loans; Direct Subsidized Loans; Direct Unsubsidized Loans. Federal Work-Study Program available. Institutional employment available.

CAMPUS LIFE

Activities: Campus Ministries; Choral groups; Concert band; Dance; Drama/theater; International Student Organization; Jazz band; Literary magazine; Marching band; Model UN; Music ensembles; Musical theater; Opera; Pep band; Radio station; Student government; Student newspaper; Symphony orchestra; Television station; Yearbook. **Organizations:** 933 registered organizations, 62 honor societies, 68 religious organizations, 27 fraternities, 20 sororities. **Athletics (Intercollegiate):** *Men:* baseball, basketball, bowling, cross-country, cycling, equestrian sports, golf, ice hockey, lacrosse, martial arts, racquetball, rugby, swimming, table tennis, track/field (indoor), ultimate frisbee, volleyball, water polo, wrestling. *Women:* basketball, bowling, cross-country, cycling, equestrian sports, golf, gymnastics, lacrosse, martial arts, racquetball, rugby, softball, swimming, table tennis, track/field (indoor), ultimate frisbee, volleyball, water polo.

CAMPUS
Type of school	Public
Environment	Metropolis

STUDENTS
Undergrad enrollment	37,241
% male/female	44/56
% from out of state	39
% frosh live on campus	66

FINANCIAL FACTS
Annual in-state tuition	$10,990
Annual out-of-state tuition	$33,739
Room and board	$13,450
Required fees	$1,414

GENERAL ADMISSIONS INFO
Application fee	$50
Regular application deadline	5/2
Nonfall registration	Yes

Fall 2024 testing policy	Test Optional
Range SAT EBRW	560–680
Range SAT Math	560–690
Range ACT Composite	21–29

ACADEMICS
Student/faculty ratio	17:1
% students returning for sophomore year	84

Most classes have 20–29 students.

Arizona

REQUESTING SERVICES FOR STUDENTS WITH LEARNING DIFFERENCES

Phone: 520-621-3268 • salt.arizona.edu • Email: uasaltcenter@email.arizona.edu

Documentation submitted to: Strategic Alternative Learning Techniques (SALT) Center
Separate application required for Services: Yes

Documentation required for:
LD: Psychoeducational evaluation
ADHD: Psychoeducational evaluation
ASD: Psychoeducational evaluation

Arkansas State University

P.O. Box 1570 State University, Jonesboro, AR 72467 • Admissions: 870-972-3024 • www.astate.edu

Support: CS

ACCOMMODATIONS

Allowed in exams:

Calculators	Yes
Dictionary	Yes
Computer	Yes
Spell-checker	Yes
Extended test time	Yes
Scribe	Yes
Proctors	Yes
Oral exams	Yes
Note-takers	Yes

Support services for students with:

LD	Yes
ADHD	Yes
ASD	Yes
Distraction-reduced environment	Yes
Recording of lecture allowed	Yes
Reading technology	Yes
Audio books	Yes
Other assistive technology	Yes
Priority registration	Yes

Added costs of services:

For LD	No
For ADHD	No
For ASD	No
LD specialists	Yes
ADHD & ASD coaching	Yes
ASD specialists	Yes
Professional tutors	No
Peer tutors	Yes
Max. hours/week for services	Varies
How professors are notified of student approved accommodations	Student and Access and Accommodation Services

COLLEGE GRADUATION REQUIREMENTS

Course waivers allowed	Yes

In what courses: Accommodations for Physical Education requirement.

Course substitutions allowed	Yes

In what courses: Algebra and Foreign Language.

PROGRAMS/SERVICES FOR STUDENTS WITH LEARNING DIFFERENCES

Access and Accommodation Services (A&AS) recommends that students request accommodations as soon as possible. Documentation is not required with the initial application and may be submitted later. Students can contact the A&AS office to schedule an appointment via Zoom, phone, or in person. The meeting will serve to determine the student's accommodations, which may include priority registration, alternative-format material and assistive technology, note-taking, interpreter services, testing alternatives, and classroom alterations. Additional campus resources include guidance and counseling. Each semester, students request accommodations through an online process, and A&AS sends their accommodation letters to the appropriate faculty. A&AS also has disability-specific scholarship information.

ADMISSIONS

All applicants are automatically admitted to A-State if they meet one of the following criteria: a 3.0 cumulative high school GPA (or GED test score equivalent); a 19 minimum ACT superscore or a minimum 990 combined SAT superscore; or a class rank in the top 20 percent of their graduating class. Admitted students with less than a 3.0 cumulative high school GPA are required to participate in the Transition Studies (TS) leadership-based support program. TS students have access to the STEM lab, writing center, and general education tutoring, as well as intensive advising services by the faculty/academic coaches and staff of the Transition Studies department. All applicants who do not meet automatic admission standards may appeal by submitting, in addition to a transcript and ACT/SAT scores, two letters of recommendation and a personal essay. The essay should address the following: Why A-State is a good fit, the student's academic and personal strengths, and their educational goals and plans to grow as a student. Students should also describe the experiences outside of the classroom that impact their academic performance. If approved by the Undergraduate Admissions Appeal Committee, students will participate in the Transition Studies leadership-based support program.

Additional Information

A-State has nine tutoring centers that provide support to students across disciplines. Especially challenging classes offer peer or graduate assistant-led learning groups. Graduate assistant Academic Success coaches help students create study and time management plans and also help identify specific resources in Learning Support Services. Located in the library, the Learning Commons is designed for formal and informal study groups, and provides immediate access to computer labs, reference material, and the library and learning assistance staff. The Writing Center also serves as a resource to students who want to improve a specific project or improve their skills in the long term.

At dusk, following Spring Commencement, the clock tower of the Dean B. Ellis Library is lit a scarlet color to salute the newest A-State graduates. A-State also lights the tower with the local high schools' colors to salute them in their graduation ceremonies.

Arkansas State University

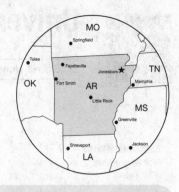

GENERAL ADMISSIONS

Very important factors include: rigor of secondary school record, standardized test scores (if submitted). *Important factors include:* class rank. *Other factors considered include:* recommendations. High school diploma is required and GED is accepted. Institution is test-flexible for entering Fall 2024. Check admissions website for updates. *Academic units required:* 4 English, 4 math, 3 science (3 labs), 3 social studies. *Academic units recommended:* 2 foreign language.

FINANCIAL AID

Students should submit: FAFSA; Institution's own financial aid form. *Need-based scholarships/grants offered:* College/university scholarship or grant aid from institutional funds; Federal Pell; Private scholarships; SEOG; State scholarships/grants. *Loan aid offered:* Direct PLUS loans; Direct Subsidized Loans; Direct Unsubsidized Loans. Federal Work-Study Program available. Institutional employment available.

CAMPUS LIFE

Activities: Campus Ministries; Choral groups; Concert band; Dance; Drama/theater; International Student Organization; Jazz band; Marching band; Model UN; Music ensembles; Musical theater; Opera; Pep band; Radio station; Student government; Student newspaper; Symphony orchestra; Television station; Yearbook. **Organizations:** 200 registered organizations, 10 honor societies, 25 religious organizations, 15 fraternities, 11 sororities. **Athletics (Intercollegiate):** *Men:* baseball, basketball, cross-country, golf, rugby, track/field (indoor). *Women:* basketball, bowling, cross-country, golf, rugby, track/field (indoor), volleyball.

CAMPUS
Type of school	Public
Environment	Town

STUDENTS
Undergrad enrollment	8,909
% male/female	43/57
% from out of state	11
% frosh live on campus	72

FINANCIAL FACTS
Annual in-state tuition	$6,060
Annual out-of-state tuition	$12,120
Room and board	$8,540
Required fees	$2,140

GENERAL ADMISSIONS INFO
Application fee	$15
Regular application deadline	8/24
Nonfall registration	Yes
Fall 2024 testing policy	Test Flexible
Range SAT EBRW	400–540
Range SAT Math	470–540
Range ACT Composite	21–26

ACADEMICS
Student/faculty ratio	17:1
% students returning for sophomore year	76
Most classes have 2–9 students.	

Arkansas

REQUESTING SERVICES FOR STUDENTS WITH LEARNING DIFFERENCES

Phone: 870-972-3964 • www.astate.edu/a/disability • Email: dowhite@astate.edu

Documentation submitted to: Access and Accommodation Services
Separate application required for Services: Yes

Documentation required for:
LD: Psychoeducational evaluation
ADHD: Psychoeducational evaluation
ASD: Psychoeducational evaluation

University of Arkansas

232 Silas H. Hunt Hall, Fayetteville, AR 72701 • Admissions: 479-575-5346 • www.uark.edu

Support: CS

ACCOMMODATIONS

Allowed in exams:

Calculators	Yes
Dictionary	Yes
Computer	Yes
Spell-checker	Yes
Extended test time	Yes
Scribe	Yes
Proctors	Yes
Oral exams	Yes
Note-takers	Yes

Support services for students with:

LD	Yes
ADHD	Yes
ASD	Yes
Distraction-reduced environment	Yes
Recording of lecture allowed	Yes
Reading technology	Yes
Audio books	Yes
Other assistive technology	Yes
Priority registration	Yes

Added costs of services:

For LD	No
For ADHD	No
For ASD	Yes
LD specialists	No
ADHD & ASD coaching	No
ASD specialists	Yes
Professional tutors	No
Peer tutors	No
Max. hours/week for services	Varies

How professors are notified
of student approved
accommodations — **Student**

COLLEGE GRADUATION REQUIREMENTS

Course waivers allowed	No
Course substitutions allowed	Yes

In what courses: Math and Foreign
Language

PROGRAMS/SERVICES FOR STUDENTS WITH LEARNING DIFFERENCES

The Center for Educational Access (CEA) supports students with disabilities. If students have an accommodation request, they are asked to submit an online request form to schedule an access plan meeting. Documentation supporting each accommodation request is required but may be provided before, during, or after the access plan meeting. The meeting is optional for students if their sole request is extended test time, distraction-free testing, or permission to audio record lectures. After registration is complete, students receive instructions on how to access accommodation letters to share with course instructors. For students age 18–24 with mild cognitive disabilities (who do not demonstrate significant behavioral or emotional challenges), the school offers EMPOWER (Educate, Motivate, Prepare, Opportunity, Workplace readiness, Employment, Responsibility)—a four-year, nondegree college experience that focuses on practical academics, independent living, wellness, employment, and interpersonal skills to help students feel capable and self-sufficient. Admission to the program requires an application form and housing request, three letters of recommendation, an IEP, documentation of cognitive disability, and an interview with EMPOWER staff.

ADMISSIONS

The university review process considers an applicant's GPA the best predictor for success in college. Students with a GPA below 3.2 should submit ACT/SAT scores with their application. For students earning a 3.2 GPA and greater, test scores are optional during the application process, but must be submitted later for placement and enrollment purposes. The admission review committee also considers the rigor of each student's course load compared to the classes available, whether their grades showed trends or improvement over time, and their involvement in and beyond the classroom. Exceptions may be made for applicants with extenuating circumstances, special talents, or if they are interested in programs with space available. Out-of-state applicants may be required to meet higher standards and provide additional academic materials for review. Students who are denied admission may reapply after successfully improving their academic record with the completion of college-level coursework at a community college. Denied students may also appeal their admissions decision and submit updated credentials, such as updated transcripts or new test scores.

Additional Information

The Student Success Center (SSC) at the Cordia Harrington Center for Excellence (CORD) provides students with academic initiatives, such as tutoring, writing studios, Supplemental Instruction, and peer academic coaching. The SSC Peer Academic Coaches assist in developing skills and strategies for learning effectively, while SSC Peer Tutors enrich students' comprehension of course content and key foundational concepts.

Senior Walk is six miles of campus sidewalks engraved with the names of graduates dating back to 1876. Names were stamped by hand until 1986, when the Physical Plant employees invented the Sand Hog—a device made specifically for etching names in the Senior Walk. From the first graduating class of nine, there are now over 200,000 graduates listed, including generations of families.

University of Arkansas

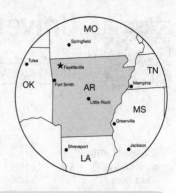

GENERAL ADMISSIONS

Very important factors include: academic GPA. *Important factors include: Other factors considered include:* rigor of secondary school record, class rank, application essay, recommendations. High school diploma is required and GED is accepted. Institution is test-optional for entering Fall 2024. Check admissions website for updates. *Academic units required:* 4 English, 4 math, 3 science (2 labs), 3 social studies, 2 academic electives. *Academic units recommended:* 2 foreign language.

FINANCIAL AID

Students should submit: FAFSA. *Need-based scholarships/grants offered:* College/university scholarship or grant aid from institutional funds; Federal Pell; Private scholarships; SEOG; State scholarships/grants. *Loan aid offered:* Direct PLUS loans; Direct Subsidized Loans; Direct Unsubsidized Loans. Federal Work-Study Program available. Institutional employment available.

CAMPUS LIFE

Activities: Campus Ministries; Choral groups; Concert band; Dance; Drama/theater; International Student Organization; Jazz band; Literary magazine; Marching band; Model UN; Music ensembles; Opera; Pep band; Radio station; Student government; Student newspaper; Student-run film society; Symphony orchestra; Television station; Yearbook. **Organizations:** 422 registered organizations, 55 honor societies, 19 fraternities, 15 sororities. **Athletics (Intercollegiate):** *Men:* baseball, basketball, cross-country, cycling, golf, ice hockey, lacrosse, racquetball, rugby, track/field (indoor), ultimate frisbee, volleyball. *Women:* basketball, cross-country, cycling, golf, gymnastics, lacrosse, racquetball, rugby, softball, swimming, track/field (indoor), ultimate frisbee, volleyball.

CAMPUS

Type of school	Public
Environment	City

STUDENTS

Undergrad enrollment	25,998
% male/female	44/56
% from out of state	52
% frosh live on campus	94

FINANCIAL FACTS

Annual in-state tuition	$7,666
Annual out-of-state tuition	$25,420
Room and board	$12,368
Required fees	$1,990

GENERAL ADMISSIONS INFO

Application fee	$40
Regular application deadline	8/1
Nonfall registration	Yes

Fall 2024 testing policy	Test Optional
Range SAT EBRW	520–610
Range SAT Math	510–610
Range ACT Composite	21–28

ACADEMICS

Student/faculty ratio	20:1
% students returning for sophomore year	86

Most classes have 10–19 students.

Arkansas

REQUESTING SERVICES FOR STUDENTS WITH LEARNING DIFFERENCES

Phone: 479-575-3104 • cea.uark.edu • Email: ada@uark.edu

Documentation submitted to: Center for Educational Access
Separate application required for Services: Yes

Documentation required for:
LD: Psychoeducational evaluation
ADHD: Psychoeducational evaluation
ASD: Psychoeducational evaluation

University of the Ozarks

415 N College Avenue, Clarksville, AR 72830 • Admissions: 479-979-1227 • www.ozarks.edu

Support: SP

ACCOMMODATIONS

Allowed in exams:

Calculators	Yes
Dictionary	No
Computer	Yes
Spell-checker	Yes
Extended test time	Yes
Scribe	Yes
Proctors	Yes
Oral exams	Yes
Note-takers	Yes

Support services for students with:

LD	Yes
ADHD	Yes
ASD	Yes
Distraction-reduced environment	Yes
Recording of lecture allowed	Yes
Reading technology	Yes
Audio books	Yes
Other assistive technology	Yes
Priority registration	Yes

Added costs of services:

For LD	Yes
For ADHD	Yes
For ASD	Yes
LD specialists	Yes
ADHD & ASD coaching	Yes
ASD specialists	Yes
Professional tutors	Yes
Peer tutors	Yes
Max. hours/week for services	Varies
How professors are notified of student approved accommodations	Student and Disability Services

COLLEGE GRADUATION REQUIREMENTS

Course waivers allowed	No
Course substitutions allowed	Yes

In what courses: Foreign Language, Math

PROGRAMS/SERVICES FOR STUDENTS WITH LEARNING DIFFERENCES

Within the Student Success Center is Disability Services, which provides support and services to students with a documented disability. Students have access to tutoring, writing and math support, and workshops. Students diagnosed with learning disabilities, ADHD, or ASD may receive additional support by enrolling in a comprehensive, fee-based program at the Jones Learning Center (JLC). The JLC staff includes writing specialists and a specialist specifically dedicated to students with ASD. Peer tutors are available for all classes for an additional fee. The JLC serves a limited number of students per semester.

ADMISSIONS

In addition to review of the high school transcript and application, the admissions committee considers motivation and work ethic to be key factors in determining acceptance. Most admitted applicants have a minimum 3.0 GPA. Students applying to the Jones Learning Center who meet the general admissions criteria and have a learning disability, ADHD, or ASD, are also admitted to the JLC. If the student does not meet the general admission criteria, the director will closely review the file and any additional information provided to make a decision about admission.

Additional Information

The JLC offers students two tracks of support. The comprehensive program track includes daily meetings with an academic program coordinator who coordinates services and acts as an academic coach to help students plan and organize their time. Students in the Track 2 program meet twice a week with an academic program coordinator and receive class notes, testing accommodations, and access to two professional writing specialists. Additional support in Track 2 can be included on a fee-for-service basis. The Jones Learning Center promotes various social activity groups each semester based on student interests.

In 1933, 50 students earned their tuition by working construction on the Munger Chapel, dedicated to the memory of Raymond Munger with a $75,000 gift from his daughter, Miss Jesse Munger. An extensive $2.75 million renovation was completed in 2015 with a gift from Frances E. Wilson in memory of her late husband, Thomas D. Wilson. In 2016, it was rededicated as the Munger-Wilson Chapel.

University of the Ozarks

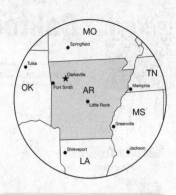

GENERAL ADMISSIONS

Important factors include: standardized test scores (if submitted). *Other factors considered include:* rigor of secondary school record, academic GPA, application essay, recommendations. High school diploma is required and GED is accepted. Institution is test-optional for entering Fall 2024. Check admissions website for updates. *Academic units recommended:* 4 English, 4 math, 3 science (2 labs), 2 foreign language, 3 social studies.

FINANCIAL AID

Students should submit: FAFSA. *Need-based scholarships/grants offered:* College/university scholarship or grant aid from institutional funds; Federal Nursing Scholarships; Federal Pell; Private scholarships; SEOG; State scholarships/grants; United Negro College Fund. *Loan aid offered:.* Federal Work-Study Program available. Institutional employment available.

CAMPUS LIFE

Activities: Campus Ministries; Choral groups; Drama/theater; International Student Organization; Literary magazine; Music ensembles; Radio station; Student government; Student-run film society; Television station; Yearbook. **Organizations:** 40 registered organizations, 6 honor societies, 7 religious organizations, 0 fraternities, 0 sororities. **Athletics (Intercollegiate):** *Men:* baseball, basketball, cross-country, swimming, track/field (indoor), wrestling. *Women:* basketball, cross-country, softball, swimming, track/field (indoor).

CAMPUS

Type of school	Private (nonprofit)
Environment	Village

STUDENTS

Undergrad enrollment	615
% male/female	45/55
% from out of state	29
% frosh live on campus	86

FINANCIAL FACTS

Annual tuition	$21,450
Room and board	$6,500
Required fees	$600

GENERAL ADMISSIONS INFO

Application fee	$30
Regular application deadline	Rolling
Nonfall registration	Yes
Fall 2024 testing policy	Test Optional
Range SAT EBRW	450–570
Range SAT Math	443–560
Range ACT Composite	19–25

ACADEMICS

Student/faculty ratio	11:1
% students returning for sophomore year	64

REQUESTING SERVICES FOR STUDENTS WITH LEARNING DIFFERENCES

Phone: 479-979-1403 • www.ozarks.edu • Email: jlc@ozarks.edu

Documentation submitted to: Disability Services
Separate application required for Services: Yes

Documentation required for:
LD: Psychoeducational evaluation
ADHD: Psychoeducational evaluation
ASD: Psychoeducational evaluation

California Polytechnic State University

Admissions Office, San Luis Obispo, CA 93407-0031 • Admissions: 805-756-2311 • www.calpoly.edu

Support: S

ACCOMMODATIONS

Allowed in exams:	
Calculators	Yes
Dictionary	Yes
Computer	Yes
Spell-checker	Yes
Extended test time	Yes
Scribe	Yes
Proctors	Yes
Oral exams	Yes
Note-takers	Yes
Support services for students with:	
LD	Yes
ADHD	Yes
ASD	Yes
Distraction-reduced environment	Yes
Recording of lecture allowed	Yes
Reading technology	Yes
Audio books	Yes
Other assistive technology	Yes
Priority registration	Yes
Added costs of services:	
For LD	No
For ADHD	No
For ASD	No
LD specialists	No
ADHD & ASD coaching	No
ASD specialists	No
Professional tutors	No
Peer tutors	Yes
Max. hours/week for services	Varies
How professors are notified of student approved accommodations	Student

COLLEGE GRADUATION REQUIREMENTS

Course waivers allowed	No
Course substitutions allowed	Yes
In what courses: Case-by-case basis	

PROGRAMS/SERVICES FOR STUDENTS WITH LEARNING DIFFERENCES

The Disability Resource Center (DRC) offers information, resources, and accommodations to students with disabilities. Eligible students should submit the student request for services form along with any current documentation of their disability and set up a meeting with the DRC to discuss accommodations. Upon approval, students will receive an electronic letter with a list of specific accommodations that can be sent to their instructors. The student decides which accommodations they want to use for each course. Possible accommodations may include early registration, alternative media, assistive technology, classroom or testing accommodations, note-taking, interpreters, a reduced course load, on-campus transportation, housing, and campus dining meal plans. Students can apply to Access Allies for a peer mentor through the DRC. These mentors are experienced students who help new students with disabilities navigate Cal Poly and the community. Mentors offer knowledge on accessibility, academic and social resources, and emotional support. The DRC has a Quick Response Form for students to use with any questions they may have; a staff member will respond within five business days.

ADMISSIONS

All applicants submit the same application and must apply to a major. Applications are reviewed based on their chosen major, high school coursework, GPA, extracurricular activities, work experience, and other factors the committee considers important to the Cal Poly campus. Cal Poly accepts coursework taken in 7th and 8th grade as long as it is not repeated in the 9th grade. ACT and SAT scores are not used for admission decisions but may be used for placement in a first-year mathematics/quantitative reasoning course. Because all majors are competitive, it isn't possible to predict an applicant's chances of admission.

Additional Information

Getting Good Grades with Gadgets is a 24-hour resource that teaches students how to use general and/or assistive technology. Some of the gadgets are software, apps, and built-in utilities that students can download for free. The gadgets work for note-taking, reading, writing, studying, research, time management, organization, and math. The Office of Writing and Learning is the primary academic support center on campus that offers free peer-to-peer tutoring. Undergraduate and graduate tutors are available for one-on-one or small groups to help with any activity, assignment, or exam. The center's tutoring sessions are student-driven, which means that learning is based on specific questions and individual needs the student brings to the session. Drop-in learning support is also available through subject-specific Help Hubs.

DID YOU KNOW?

Since 2013, a bronze bench with a seated Einstein has sat outside the Baker Center. Students rub his head for luck. The dedication plaque reads: "Imagination is more important than knowledge. Education is not the learning of facts, but the training of the mind to think. If you can't explain it simply, you don't understand it well enough."

California Polytechnic State University

GENERAL ADMISSIONS

Very important factors include: rigor of secondary school record, academic GPA. High school diploma is required and GED is accepted. Institution is test-free for entering Fall 2024. Check admissions website for updates. *Academic units required:* 4 English, 3 math, 2 science (2 labs), 2 foreign language, 1 social studies, 1 U.S. history, 1 academic elective, 1 visual/performing arts. *Academic units recommended:* 4 math, 4 science (2 labs), 4 foreign language, 2 visual/performing arts.

FINANCIAL AID

Students should submit: FAFSA. *Need-based scholarships/grants offered:* College/university scholarship or grant aid from institutional funds; Federal Pell; Private scholarships; SEOG; State scholarships/grants. *Loan aid offered:* Direct PLUS loans; Direct Subsidized Loans; Direct Unsubsidized Loans. Federal Work-Study Program available. Institutional employment available.

CAMPUS LIFE

Activities: Campus Ministries; Choral groups; Concert band; Dance; Drama/theater; International Student Organization; Jazz band; Literary magazine; Marching band; Model UN; Music ensembles; Musical theater; Opera; Pep band; Radio station; Student government; Student newspaper; Student-run film society; Symphony orchestra; Television station. **Organizations:** 384 registered organizations, 12 honor societies, 20 religious organizations, 21 fraternities, 15 sororities. **Athletics (Intercollegiate):** *Men:* baseball, basketball, bowling, cross-country, cycling, field hockey, golf, lacrosse, rugby, swimming, ultimate frisbee, volleyball, water polo, wrestling. *Women:* basketball, bowling, cross-country, cycling, field hockey, golf, lacrosse, rugby, softball, swimming, ultimate frisbee, volleyball, water polo.

CAMPUS

Type of school	Public
Environment	Town

STUDENTS

Undergrad enrollment	20,899
% male/female	51/49
% from out of state	16
% frosh live on campus	98

FINANCIAL FACTS

Annual in-state tuition	$5,742
Annual out-of-state tuition	$264
Room and board	$16,449
Required fees	$5,440

GENERAL ADMISSIONS INFO

Application fee	$70
Regular application deadline	11/30
Nonfall registration	No
Fall 2024 testing policy	Test Free

ACADEMICS

Student/faculty ratio	18:1
% students returning for sophomore year	94

Most classes have 20–29 students.

REQUESTING SERVICES FOR STUDENTS WITH LEARNING DIFFERENCES

Phone: 805-756-1395 • drc.calpoly.edu • Email: drc@calpoly.edu

Documentation submitted to: Disability Resource Center
Separate application required for Services: Yes

Documentation required for:
LD: Psychoeducational evaluation
ADHD: Psychoeducational evaluation
ASD: Psychoeducational evaluation

California

California State Polytechnic University, Pomona

3801 West Temple Avenue, Pomona, CA 91768 • Admissions: 909-869-5299 • www.cpp.edu

Support: CS

ACCOMMODATIONS

Allowed in exams:

Calculators	Yes
Dictionary	Yes
Computer	Yes
Spell-checker	Yes
Extended test time	Yes
Scribe	Yes
Proctors	Yes
Oral exams	Yes
Note-takers	Yes

Support services for students with:

LD	Yes
ADHD	Yes
ASD	Yes
Distraction-reduced environment	Yes
Recording of lecture allowed	Yes
Reading technology	Yes
Audio books	No
Other assistive technology	Yes
Priority registration	Yes

Added costs of services:

For LD	No
For ADHD	No
For ASD	No
LD specialists	No
ADHD & ASD coaching	No
ASD specialists	Yes
Professional tutors	No
Peer tutors	No
Max. hours/week for services	Varies
How professors are notified of student approved accommodations	Student and Disability Resource Center

COLLEGE GRADUATION REQUIREMENTS

Course waivers allowed	No
Course substitutions allowed	Yes
In what courses: Case-by-case basis	

PROGRAMS/SERVICES FOR STUDENTS WITH LEARNING DIFFERENCES

The Disability Resource Center (DRC) offers assistance to students with disabilities. Once a student has been accepted and decides to attend CPP, they can complete an online application form for services and submit disability documentation. If documentation isn't available, students should still submit their application and make an appointment with a DRC access specialist for a welcome meeting where any documentation needed can be discussed. The meeting is to learn first-hand the barriers and limitations the student faces and determine the accommodations needed to relieve those barriers. Accommodations that are class specific can be requested as soon as students receive their class schedule.

ADMISSIONS

To be eligible for admission to CPP, California residents must have a 2.50 GPA or higher in the required academic courses, with no grade lower than a C–. Non-California residents must have a 3.00 GPA or higher in the required courses, with no grade lower than a C–. Applicants not meeting the minimum GPA requirement will be evaluated for admission based on CPP's multifactor admissions (MFA) evaluation process. First-year applicants must declare a major on their application and are encouraged to add an alternate major in case their primary major has reached student enrollment capacity.

Additional Information

The Learning Resource Center offers subject tutoring for courses in math, science, engineering, business, social sciences, and liberal arts and can be one-on-one or small group tutoring by appointment, Zoom, or drop-in. The LRC also offers course-specific workshops, review sessions for exams, and help with course concepts, writing, and more. The Writing Center offers one-on-one, small group, and Zoom tutoring services by appointment and drop-in for research papers, job applications, and many other writing assignments. Supplemental Instruction (SI) is a voluntary non-remedial approach to learning offered to all students for certain historically difficult courses. SI has regularly scheduled, out of class, group study sessions driven by student needs and peer-to-peer interaction. SI sessions are led by SI peer leaders who consult with the academic departments.

 DID YOU KNOW?

The breakfast pioneer, W.K. Kellogg deeded the northern edge of Cal Poly Pomona in 1949 to CSU requesting it be used for education and that the horse shows he started in 1926 continue. It preserved his love for horses and belief that "education offers the greatest opportunity for really improving one generation over another."

California State Polytechnic University, Pomona

General Admissions

Very important factors include: rigor of secondary school record, academic GPA. High school diploma is required and GED is accepted. Institution is test-free for entering Fall 2024. Check admissions website for updates. *Academic units required:* 4 English, 3 math, 2 science (2 labs), 2 foreign language, 1 social studies, 1 U.S. history, 1 academic elective, 1 visual/performing arts. *Academic units recommended:* 4 math.

Financial Aid

Students should submit: FAFSA. *Need-based scholarships/grants offered:* Federal Pell; Private scholarships; SEOG; State scholarships/grants. *Loan aid offered:* Direct PLUS loans; Direct Subsidized Loans; Direct Unsubsidized Loans. Federal Work-Study Program available. Institutional employment available.

Campus Life

Activities: Campus Ministries; Choral groups; Concert band; Dance; Drama/theater; International Student Organization; Jazz band; Literary magazine; Model UN; Music ensembles; Musical theater; Opera; Pep band; Student government; Student newspaper; Symphony orchestra; Yearbook. **Organizations:** 596 registered organizations, 31 honor societies, 8 religious organizations, 6 fraternities, 5 sororities. **Athletics (Intercollegiate):** *Men:* baseball, basketball, cross-country, martial arts, ultimate frisbee, volleyball. *Women:* basketball, cross-country, martial arts, track/field (indoor), ultimate frisbee, volleyball.

CAMPUS

Type of school	Public
Environment	City

STUDENTS

Undergrad enrollment	25,041
% male/female	55/45
% from out of state	1
% frosh live on campus	41

FINANCIAL FACTS

Annual in-state tuition	$5,742
Annual out-of-state tuition	$17,622
Room and board	$16,682
Required fees	$1,696

GENERAL ADMISSIONS INFO

Application fee	$70
Regular application deadline	11/30
Nonfall registration	No
Fall 2024 testing policy	Test Free

ACADEMICS

Student/faculty ratio	25:1
% students returning for sophomore year	87

Most classes have 30–39 students.

REQUESTING SERVICES FOR STUDENTS WITH LEARNING DIFFERENCES

Phone: 909-869-3333 • cpp.edu/drc • Email: drc@cpp.edu

Documentation submitted to: Disability Resource Center
Separate application required for Services: Yes

Documentation required for:
  LD: Psychoeducational evaluation
  ADHD: Psychoeducational evaluation
  ASD: Psychoeducational evaluation

California State University, Fresno

5150 North Maple Ave. M/S JA 57, Fresno, CA 93740-8026 • Admissions: 559-278-2261 • www.csufresno.edu

Support: CS

ACCOMMODATIONS

Allowed in exams:

Calculators	Yes
Dictionary	Yes
Computer	Yes
Spell-checker	Yes
Extended test time	Yes
Scribe	Yes
Proctors	Yes
Oral exams	Yes
Note-takers	Yes

Support services for students with:

LD	Yes
ADHD	Yes
ASD	Yes
Distraction-reduced environment	Yes
Recording of lecture allowed	Yes
Reading technology	Yes
Audio books	Yes
Other assistive technology	Yes
Priority registration	Yes

Added costs of services:

For LD	No
For ADHD	No
For ASD	No
LD specialists	Yes
ADHD & ASD coaching	Yes
ASD specialists	Yes
Professional tutors	Yes
Peer tutors	Yes
Max. hours/week for services	Varies
How professors are notified of student approved accommodations	Student

COLLEGE GRADUATION REQUIREMENTS

Course waivers allowed	No
Course substitutions allowed	No

PROGRAMS/SERVICES FOR STUDENTS WITH LEARNING DIFFERENCES

The Office of Services for Students with Disabilities (SSD) offers services and accommodations for students with learning disabilities. Students should complete the online registration to SSD for accommodations. Disability documentation may be uploaded with the application. Formal documentation may not be necessary but can be helpful to determine appropriate accommodations. Once registration is complete, students make an appointment with an SSD Access Specialist (AS) to discuss the functional limitations they face on campus and accommodations that may be helpful, as well as any orientation or training needed to use the accommodations. The AS can assist with accommodations, disability-related concerns, and professor concerns, as well as some general academic advising, such as how to add or drop a class.

ADMISSIONS

All first-time applicants will be reviewed for admission based on high school coursework and GPA. A high school diploma or equivalent is required. A California high school student or resident with a GPA of 2.5 or higher in the required academic coursework is eligible for admission. A non-California high school graduate or resident is required to have a GPA of 3.0 or higher in the required coursework for eligibility. Final admission decisions are based on the space available in each program (major). For the academic course requirements, ASL (American Sign Language) counts for the non-English language requirement. All students must meet the required standards for admission, however, for students with documented disabilities, there are circumstances where substitution of course requirements may be appropriate.

Additional Information

Dog Days: New Student Orientation is a mandatory program designed to help new students transition to CSUF life. During orientation, students meet with an academic counselor and a major advisor, register for classes, learn about campus programs, and participate in a resource fair. The College of Science and Mathematics Mentorship Alliance for Student Success (MASS) Program uses volunteer peer mentors who provide first-year students exclusive support navigating CSUF and campus resources. Peer mentors help students connect academically and socially in order to reach their academic goals. The Learning Center offers free peer tutoring to students in a variety of subjects. Some departments, such as psychology, English, and chemistry, offer free tutoring labs for students. The Writing Center offers free help with planning, researching, and referencing for class papers and projects.

The Bulldogs football team wears a green "V" on the back of their helmets, signifying their commitment to the Valley community, a 250-mile portion of California served exclusively by Fresno State.

California State University, Fresno

GENERAL ADMISSIONS

Very important factors include: rigor of secondary school record, academic GPA. High school diploma is required and GED is accepted. Institution is test-free for entering Fall 2024. Check admissions website for updates. *Academic units required:* 4 English, 3 math, 2 science (2 labs), 2 foreign language, 1 social studies, 1 U.S. history, 1 academic elective, 1 visual/performing arts. *Academic units recommended:* 4 math.

FINANCIAL AID

Students should submit: FAFSA. *Need-based scholarships/grants offered:* College/university scholarship or grant aid from institutional funds; Federal Pell; Private scholarships; SEOG; State scholarships/grants. *Loan aid offered:* Direct PLUS loans; Direct Subsidized Loans; Direct Unsubsidized Loans. Federal Work-Study Program available. Institutional employment available.

CAMPUS LIFE

Activities: Choral groups; Concert band; Dance; Drama/theater; International Student Organization; Jazz band; Marching band; Music ensembles; Musical theater; Radio station; Student government; Student newspaper; Symphony orchestra; Television station; Yearbook. **Organizations:** 250 registered organizations, 21 honor societies, 11 religious organizations, 19 fraternities, 13 sororities. **Athletics (Intercollegiate):** *Men:* baseball, basketball, bowling, cross-country, golf, ice hockey, rugby, swimming, table tennis. *Women:* basketball, bowling, cross-country, equestrian sports, golf, lacrosse, softball, swimming, table tennis, volleyball, water polo.

CAMPUS

Type of school	Public
Environment	Metropolis

STUDENTS

Undergrad enrollment	18,784
% male/female	43/57
% from out of state	2
% frosh live on campus	22

FINANCIAL FACTS

Annual in-state tuition	$5,742
Out-of-state tuition	$17,622
Room and board	$10,758
Required fees	$911

GENERAL ADMISSIONS INFO

Application fee	$70
Regular application deadline	11/30
Nonfall registration	No
Fall 2024 testing policy	Test Free

ACADEMICS

Student/faculty ratio	22:1
% students returning for sophomore year	86

Most classes have 20–29 students.

REQUESTING SERVICES FOR STUDENTS WITH LEARNING DIFFERENCES

Phone: 559-278-2811 • studentaffairs.fresnostate.edu/ssd • Email: ssdstaff@csufresno.edu

Documentation submitted to: Services for Students with Disabilities
Separate application required for Services: Yes

Documentation required for:
LD: Psychoeducational evaluation
ADHD: Psychoeducational evaluation
ASD: Psychoeducational evaluation

California State University, Fullerton

P.O. Box 6900, Fullerton, CA 92834-6900 • Admissions: 657-278-7788 • www.fullerton.edu

Support: CS

ACCOMMODATIONS

Allowed in exams:

Calculators	Yes
Dictionary	Yes
Computer	Yes
Spell-checker	Yes
Extended test time	Yes
Scribe	Yes
Proctors	Yes
Oral exams	Yes
Note-takers	Yes

Support services for students with:

LD	Yes
ADHD	Yes
ASD	Yes
Distraction-reduced environment	Yes
Recording of lecture allowed	Yes
Reading technology	Yes
Audio books	Yes
Other assistive technology	Yes
Priority registration	Yes

Added costs of services:

For LD	No
For ADHD	No
For ASD	No
LD specialists	Yes
ADHD & ASD coaching	No
ASD specialists	No
Professional tutors	No
Peer tutors	Yes
Max. hours/week for services	Varies
How professors are notified of student approved accommodations	Student

COLLEGE GRADUATION REQUIREMENTS

Course waivers allowed	No
Course substitutions allowed	No

PROGRAMS/SERVICES FOR STUDENTS WITH LEARNING DIFFERENCES

Once a student is accepted to CSU Fullerton and makes the decision to attend, they should complete the online Disability Support Services (DSS) form and upload their most current disability documentation. If recent documentation is not available, a health care provider can complete CSU's online disability verification form. The next step is a welcome meeting with a disability specialist to discuss the barriers a student faces in the academic setting and the accommodations that will provide an equal opportunity for them. When accommodations are determined, students receive instruction on using the DSS online portal and activating accommodations each semester. Students are encouraged to keep in contact with their disability specialist to discuss any challenges or concerns. Along with accommodations, such as accessible technology, text box format, testing alternatives, interpreting/caption, note-taking, and classroom accommodations, DSS offers a series of online study skills workshops on note-taking strategies, organization and time management, and test-taking strategies.

ADMISSIONS

All applicants are expected to meet the same admission criteria. To be eligible for admission, first-year applicants must be high school graduates or GED equivalent and have completed the academic courses required by CUSF. To be considered for admission, California high school graduates or residents must have a minimum GPA of 2.49 and non-California high school graduates or residents must have a minimum GPA of 2.99.

Additional Information

All of CSUF's eight colleges, the Office of Graduate Studies, and the Academic Advisement Center have Student Success Teams. Teams include associate deans, faculty and staff major advisors, graduation specialists, retention specialists, assistant deans, and career specialists who help students navigate the transition to college and prepare for graduation and life after college. The University Learning Center (ULC) focuses on undergraduate 100 & 200 level high-impact courses with certified tutors supporting students in most undergraduate general education courses. Tutoring can be one-to-one or in groups of three from the same course. The ULC also offers downloadable workshops, podcasts and videos, printouts, and other online tools. The Writing Center offers 30-minute, one-on-one peer-tutoring sessions and workshops for all written assignments and helps students with writing concerns in all disciplines. Supplemental Instruction (SI) provides weekly, peer-led study groups for historically difficult courses. Pollak Library provides a vast array of research guides and services on the library website and in person.

In 1959, students voted for "Titan" as their nickname, but it took until 1962 to decide on a mascot. It started as a practical joke with the "First Intercollegiate Elephant Race in Human History," which attracted universities across the country and more than 10,000 people to watch five different elephant races. An elephant named Tuffy the Titan appeared on sweatshirts to advertise the event and was adopted as the official mascot.

California State University, Fullerton

GENERAL ADMISSIONS
Very important factors include: academic GPA. High school diploma is required and GED is accepted. Institution is test-free for entering Fall 2024. Check admissions website for updates. *Academic units required:* 4 English, 3 math, 2 science (2 labs), 2 foreign language, 1 social studies, 1 U.S. history, 1 academic elective, 1 visual/performing arts.

FINANCIAL AID
Students should submit: FAFSA. *Need-based scholarships/grants offered:* College/university scholarship or grant aid from institutional funds; Federal Pell; Private scholarships; SEOG; State scholarships/grants. *Loan aid offered:* Direct PLUS loans; Direct Subsidized Loans; Direct Unsubsidized Loans. Federal Work-Study Program available. Institutional employment available.

CAMPUS LIFE
Activities: Choral groups; Concert band; Dance; Drama/theater; International Student Organization; Jazz band; Model UN; Music ensembles; Musical theater; Radio station; Student government; Student newspaper; Symphony orchestra; Television station. **Organizations:** 374 registered organizations, 17 honor societies, 29 religious organizations, 14 fraternities, 11 sororities. **Athletics (Intercollegiate):** *Men:* baseball, basketball, bowling, cross-country, equestrian sports, golf, ice hockey, lacrosse, racquetball, rugby, softball, swimming, table tennis, ultimate frisbee, volleyball, water polo. *Women:* basketball, bowling, cross-country, equestrian sports, golf, ice hockey, lacrosse, racquetball, rugby, softball, swimming, table tennis, track/field (indoor), ultimate frisbee, volleyball, water polo.

CAMPUS

Type of school	Public
Environment	City

STUDENTS

Undergrad enrollment	36,669
% male/female	42/58
% from out of state	1
% frosh live on campus	3

FINANCIAL FACTS

Annual in-state tuition	$5,742
Out-of-state tuition	$17,622
Room and board	$16,703
Required fees	$1,234

GENERAL ADMISSIONS INFO

Application fee	$70
Regular application deadline	11/30
Nonfall registration	No
Fall 2024 testing policy	Test Free

ACADEMICS

Student/faculty ratio	26:1
% students returning for sophomore year	89

Most classes have 20–29 students.

REQUESTING SERVICES FOR STUDENTS WITH LEARNING DIFFERENCES

Phone: 657-278-3112 • www.fullerton.edu/dss • Email: dsservices@fullerton.edu

Documentation submitted to: Disability Support Services
Separate application required for Services: Yes

Documentation required for:
LD: Psychoeducational evaluation
ADHD: Psychoeducational evaluation
ASD: Psychoeducational evaluation

California

California State University, Long Beach

1250 Bellflower Boulevard, Long Beach, CA 90840 • Admissions: 562-985-5471 • www.csulb.edu

Support: CS

ACCOMMODATIONS

Allowed in exams:

Calculators	Yes
Dictionary	Yes
Computer	Yes
Spell-checker	Yes
Extended test time	Yes
Scribe	Yes
Proctors	Yes
Oral exams	Yes
Note-takers	Yes

Support services for students with:

LD	Yes
ADHD	Yes
ASD	Yes
Distraction-reduced environment	Yes
Recording of lecture allowed	Yes
Reading technology	Yes
Audio books	Yes
Other assistive technology	Yes
Priority registration	Yes

Added costs of services:

For LD	No
For ADHD	No
For ASD	No
LD specialists	Yes
ADHD & ASD coaching	Yes
ASD specialists	Yes
Professional tutors	No
Peer tutors	Yes
Max. hours/week for services	Varies
How professors are notified of student approved accommodations	Student

COLLEGE GRADUATION REQUIREMENTS

Course waivers allowed	Varies
In what courses: Case-by-case basis	
Course substitutions allowed	Yes
In what courses: Case-by-case basis	

On September 29, 1949, CSU Long Beach (then Los Angeles–Orange County State College) opened with 169 junior and senior students, mostly women and veterans, in a converted apartment building at 5401 East Anaheim Street. Large classes were held in living rooms, medium classes in dining rooms, and the smallest classes were in kitchens. The bathrooms stored music and instruments.

PROGRAMS/SERVICES FOR STUDENTS WITH LEARNING DIFFERENCES:

The Bob Murphy Access Center (BMAC) provides support services, resources, and equipment, and is the liaison with campus and community agencies to assist students with disabilities. Students should complete a BMAC application, upload supporting documentation specifying their disability, and attend a welcome meeting with a BMAC specialist to determine reasonable accommodations, services, and resources needed. Accommodations include note-taking support, sign language interpreters, alternate-format course material, mobility assistance, tutorial support, assistive technology, test-taking alternatives, accessible materials and furniture, and other support necessary to accommodate a student's specific disability. The Stephen Benson Learning Disability Program (SBP) offers psychoeducational evaluations for specific learning disorders to enrolled students and provides individualized writing support for students struggling with their writing skills. The Learning Independence for Empowerment (LIFE) Project's coordinator and peer coaches meet weekly with students with autism to help them successfully transition to college and promote their independence through social interactions, workshops, and role play. The WorkAbility IV (WAIV) Program helps students with disabilities acquire skills and resources to secure and retain successful employment. WAIV offers internship assistance, employment preparation, and job development, placement, and retention.

ADMISSIONS

First-year applicants must meet the minimum academic requirements to be considered for admission, and some majors have additional requirements. Applicants should have completed college preparatory courses with a grade of C or higher prior to high school graduation. For the academic course requirements, ASL (American Sign Language) can be used for the non-English language requirement. Students offered admission may submit test scores for course placement purposes. CSULB makes admission decisions based on intended majors; applicants may select a major or apply undeclared. Applying undeclared is not a route to an intended major and is not an advantage in the admission decisions.

Additional Information

The Learning Center has numerous resources for students, including tutors for one-on-one or Zoom appointments. Peer academic coaches work with students to help with their academic and personal transition to CSULB. Peer coaches also provide workshops on various academic success topics for all students. The Learning Center offers Supplemental Instruction (SI), a support service offered for specific courses. SI Leaders attend class lectures with the students and lead two or three weekly sessions for hands-on learning and a better understanding of course material. The Writing Center has a variety of tutoring services, from one-on-one in-depth consultations to drop-in hours for quick answers to writing questions and writing workshops.

California State University, Long Beach

GENERAL ADMISSIONS

Very important factors include: class rank, academic GPA. High school diploma is required and GED is accepted. Institution is test-free for entering Fall 2024. Check admissions website for updates. *Academic units required:* 4 English, 3 math, 2 science (2 labs), 2 foreign language, 1 social studies, 1 U.S. history, 1 academic elective, 1 visual/performing arts.

FINANCIAL AID

Students should submit: FAFSA. *Need-based scholarships/grants offered:* College/university scholarship or grant aid from institutional funds; Federal Pell; Private scholarships; SEOG; State scholarships/grants; United Negro College Fund. *Loan aid offered:* Direct PLUS loans; Direct Subsidized Loans; Direct Unsubsidized Loans. Federal Work-Study Program available. Institutional employment available.

CAMPUS LIFE

Activities: Choral groups; Concert band; Dance; Drama/theater; Jazz band; Literary magazine; Music ensembles; Musical theater; Opera; Radio station; Student newspaper; Student-run film society; Symphony orchestra; Television station; Yearbook. **Organizations:** 300 registered organizations, 25 honor societies, 20 religious organizations, 16 fraternities, 15 sororities. **Athletics (Intercollegiate):** *Men:* baseball, basketball, cross-country, golf, volleyball, water polo. *Women:* basketball, cross-country, golf, softball, volleyball, water polo.

CAMPUS

Type of school	Public
Environment	City

STUDENTS

Undergrad enrollment	31,447
% male/female	43/57
% from out of state	1
% frosh live on campus	31

FINANCIAL FACTS

Annual in-state tuition	$5,742
Annual out-of-state tuition	$16,038
Room and board	$13,158
Required fees	$1,056

GENERAL ADMISSIONS INFO

Application fee	$70
Regular application deadline	Rolling
Nonfall registration	Yes
Fall 2024 testing policy	Test Free

ACADEMICS

Student/faculty ratio	26:1
% students returning for sophomore year	87
Most classes have 20–29 students.	

REQUESTING SERVICES FOR STUDENTS WITH LEARNING DIFFERENCES

Phone: 562-985-5401 • www.csulb.edu/faculty-center/disability-services • Email: dss@csulb.edu

Documentation submitted to: Bob Murphy Access Center (BMAC)
Separate application required for Services: Yes

Documentation required for:
LD: Psychoeducational evaluation
ADHD: Psychoeducational evaluation
ASD: Psychoeducational evaluation

California

California State University, Northridge

Admissions and Records, Northridge, CA 91330-8207 • Admissions: 818-677-3700 • www.csun.edu

Support: CS

ACCOMMODATIONS

Allowed in exams:

Calculators	Yes
Dictionary	Yes
Computer	Yes
Spell-checker	Yes
Extended test time	Yes
Scribe	Yes
Proctors	Yes
Oral exams	Yes
Note-takers	Yes

Support services for students with:

LD	Yes
ADHD	Yes
ASD	Yes
Distraction-reduced environment	Yes
Recording of lecture allowed	Yes
Reading technology	Yes
Audio books	Yes
Other assistive technology	Yes
Priority registration	Yes

Added costs of services:

For LD	No
For ADHD	No
For ASD	No
LD specialists	Yes
ADHD & ASD coaching	No
ASD specialists	No
Professional tutors	No
Peer tutors	Yes
Max. hours/week for services	Varies
How professors are notified of student approved accommodations	Student

COLLEGE GRADUATION REQUIREMENTS

Course waivers allowed	No
Course substitutions allowed	No

PROGRAMS/SERVICES FOR STUDENTS WITH LEARNING DIFFERENCES

Disability Resources and Educational Services (DRES) supports students with disabilities. Students are encouraged to register with DRES as soon as possible to ensure accommodations are established before the semester begins. DRES reviews each student's documentation so that they may hold an intake appointment where a counselor can tailor accommodations to the individual's needs. Accommodations may include assistive technology, alternate-format texts, alternative testing, and registration assistance. Students registered with DRES may be eligible to receive services such as academic coaching, specialized workshops, strengths assessments, and career assistance through the Thriving and Achieving Program (TAP).

ADMISSIONS

The admission requirements are the same for all students. Students must earn a C grade or better in the required core academic courses. ACT and SAT scores are not considered for admission; they are used only for student placement in math or English courses. California residents receive priority whenever admission space is limited. If a student applies to the university and is rejected, they may appeal the decision.

Additional Information

The Thriving and Achieving Program (TAP) aims to empower students with disabilities by fostering independence, identifying and setting academic and career goals, and guiding them to realize their full potential. New students meet with a transition specialist, who introduces them to available programs that support their goals with coaching, counseling, and training sessions.

In January 1994, the 6.7 magnitude Northridge earthquake epicenter was less than two miles from CSUN and caused $400 million (today approx. $775 million) in damages to campus buildings, but no fatalities or serious injuries. It was the worst natural disaster (based on damage and costs) to hit an American college.

California State University, Northridge

GENERAL ADMISSIONS

Very important factors include: High school diploma is required and GED is accepted. Institution is test-free for entering Fall 2024. Check admissions website for updates. *Academic units required:* 4 English, 3 math, 2 science (2 labs), 2 foreign language, 1 social studies, 1 U.S. history, 1 visual or performing art, 1 academic elective.

FINANCIAL AID

Students should submit: FAFSA. *Need-based scholarships/grants offered:* College/university scholarship or grant aid from institutional funds; Federal Nursing Scholarships; Federal Pell; Private scholarships; SEOG; State scholarships/grants. *Loan aid offered:.* Federal Work-Study Program available. Institutional employment available.

CAMPUS LIFE

Activities: Choral groups; Concert band; Dance; Drama/theater; International Student Organization; Jazz band; Literary magazine; Marching band; Music ensembles; Musical theater; Radio station; Student government; Student newspaper; Yearbook. **Organizations:** 323 registered organizations, 15 honor societies, 17 religious organizations, 24 fraternities, 12 sororities. **Athletics (Intercollegiate):** *Men:* baseball, basketball, cross-country, golf, swimming, track/field (indoor), volleyball. *Women:* basketball, cross-country, golf, softball, swimming, track/field (indoor), volleyball.

CAMPUS	
Type of school	Public
Environment	City

STUDENTS	
Undergrad enrollment	31,957
% male/female	46/54
% from out of state	1

FINANCIAL FACTS	
Annual in-state tuition	$6,564
Annual out-of-state tuition	$11,028
Room and board	$9,962

GENERAL ADMISSIONS INFO	
Application fee	$70
Regular application deadline	Rolling
Nonfall registration	Yes
Fall 2024 testing policy	Test Free

ACADEMICS	
Student/faculty ratio	23:1
% students returning for sophomore year	78

REQUESTING SERVICES FOR STUDENTS WITH LEARNING DIFFERENCES

Phone: 818-677-2684 • www.csun.edu/dres • Email: dres@csun.edu

Documentation submitted to: Disability Resources and Educational Services
Separate application required for Services: Yes

Documentation required for:
LD: Psychoeducational evaluation
ADHD: Psychoeducational evaluation
ASD: Psychoeducational evaluation

California State University, San Bernardino

5500 University Parkway, San Bernardino, CA 92407-2397 • Admissions: 909-537-5188 • www.csusb.edu

Support: CS

ACCOMMODATIONS

Allowed in exams:

Calculators	Yes
Dictionary	Yes
Computer	Yes
Spell-checker	Yes
Extended test time	Yes
Scribe	Yes
Proctors	Yes
Oral exams	Yes
Note-takers	Yes

Support services for students with:

LD	Yes
ADHD	Yes
ASD	Yes
Distraction-reduced environment	Yes
Recording of lecture allowed	Yes
Reading technology	Yes
Audio books	Yes
Other assistive technology	Yes
Priority registration	Yes

Added costs of services:

For LD	No
For ADHD	No
For ASD	No
LD specialists	Yes
ADHD & ASD coaching	No
ASD specialists	No
Professional tutors	No
Peer tutors	Yes
Max. hours/week for services	Varies
How professors are notified of student approved accommodations	Student and SSD

COLLEGE GRADUATION REQUIREMENTS

Course waivers allowed	No
Course substitutions allowed	Yes

In what courses: General Ed Math for verified dyscalculia only

PROGRAMS/SERVICES FOR STUDENTS WITH LEARNING DIFFERENCES

The Services to Students with Disabilities (SSD) office is dedicated to supporting students with learning disabilities. Once a student has completed an assessment, the staff of SSD works with the student to develop compensatory methods for handling their course load. Services and accommodations for students may include the use of computers during exams, extended time on tests, distraction-free testing environments, oral exams, notetakers, proctors, scribes, priority registration, and audiobooks.

ADMISSIONS

Admission requires a minimum 15 units of courses to be admitted as a first-year student, with each unit equal to a year of study in a subject area. A grade of C (GPA 2.0) or better is required for each course to count toward any subject requirement. The ACT and SAT are not used for admission. When space is limited, California residents are given priority in the admission process.

Additional Information

Coyote First STEP (Student Transition Enrichment Program) is a free program that allows incoming CSUSB first-years to take their fall semester math course in the summer, before the year officially begins. The Early Start program is available for incoming first-years who require skills development in writing, mathematics, and quantitative reasoning. The program helps students acquire new learning skills, formulate and implement specific note-taking strategies, and develop techniques to manage written materials. The Early Start program may be completed at CSUSB or any other CSU.

DID YOU KNOW?

The original, unofficial mascot of CSUSB in the 1960s was Professor DeRemer's St. Bernard dog, who attended every event. After years of debate, the coyote became the official mascot in 1984. In 1998, he was named Cody. Today, Cody has his own Instagram and events—Coyote Fest, Coyote Hour, Coyote Walk, Coyote Cares Day, and the Howl at the Moon dance. He can be spotted at activities and around campus.

California State University, San Bernardino

General Admissions

Very important factors include: academic GPA. High school diploma is required and GED is accepted. Institution is test-free for entering Fall 2024. Check admissions website for updates. *Academic units required:* 4 English, 3 math, 2 science (2 labs), 2 foreign language, 1 social studies, 1 U.S. history, 1 academic elective, 1 visual/performing arts.

Financial Aid

Students should submit: FAFSA. *Need-based scholarships/grants offered:* College/university scholarship or grant aid from institutional funds; Federal Pell; Private scholarships; SEOG; State scholarships/grants. *Loan aid offered:* Direct PLUS loans; Direct Subsidized Loans; Direct Unsubsidized Loans. Federal Work-Study Program available. Institutional employment available.

Campus Life

Activities: Campus Ministries; Choral groups; Concert band; Dance; Drama/theater; International Student Organization; Jazz band; Model UN; Music ensembles; Musical theater; Radio station; Student government; Student newspaper; Television station. **Organizations:** 100 registered organizations, 6 honor societies. **Athletics (Intercollegiate):** *Men:* baseball, basketball, golf. *Women:* basketball, cross-country, softball, volleyball.

CAMPUS
Type of school	Public
Environment	City

STUDENTS
Undergrad enrollment	17,123
% male/female	38/62
% from out of state	<2
% frosh live on campus	16

FINANCIAL FACTS
Annual in-state tuition	$5,742
Out of state tuition	$10,494
Room and board	$12,996
Required fees	$1,683

GENERAL ADMISSIONS INFO
Application fee	$70
Regular application deadline	Rolling
Nonfall registration	Yes
Fall 2024 testing policy	Test Free

ACADEMICS
Student/faculty ratio	26:1
% students returning for sophomore year	85
Most classes have 20–29 students.	

REQUESTING SERVICES FOR STUDENTS WITH LEARNING DIFFERENCES

Phone: 909-537-5238 • csusb.edu/ssd • Email: SSD@csusb.edu

Documentation submitted to: Services to Students with Disabilities
Separate application required for Services: Yes

Documentation required for:
LD: Psychoeducational evaluation
ADHD: Psychoeducational evaluation
ASD: Psychoeducational evaluation

California

Loyola Marymount University

1 LMU Drive, Los Angeles, CA 90045-2659 • Admissions: 310-338-2750 • www.lmu.edu

(Support: CS)

ACCOMMODATIONS

Allowed in exams:

Calculators	Yes
Dictionary	Yes
Computer	Yes
Spell-checker	Yes
Extended test time	Yes
Scribe	Yes
Proctors	Yes
Oral exams	Yes
Note-takers	Yes

Support services for students with:

LD	Yes
ADHD	Yes
ASD	Yes
Distraction-reduced environment	Yes
Recording of lecture allowed	Yes
Reading technology	Yes
Audio books	Yes
Other assistive technology	Yes
Priority registration	Yes

Added costs of services:

For LD	No
For ADHD	No
For ASD	No
LD specialists	Yes
ADHD & ASD coaching	No
ASD specialists	No
Professional tutors	No
Peer tutors	Yes
Max. hours/week for services	Varies
How professors are notified of student approved accommodations	Student

COLLEGE GRADUATION REQUIREMENTS

Course waivers allowed	No
Course substitutions allowed	No

PROGRAMS/SERVICES FOR STUDENTS WITH LEARNING DIFFERENCES

The Disability Support Services Office works with students with documented disabilities to provide accommodations. Students may request services that include notetakers, readers, transcribers, and alternate testing conditions. The specialists at the DSS office are available to advocate for students who request additional support and ensure that their accommodations are provided. To begin the process of establishing accommodations, students apply online through their admitted student portal, submit eligible documentation, and meet with the DSS specialist to discuss their history of accommodations and the potential resources to support them at LMU. Trained notetakers are hired from the class in which the DSS student is enrolled. The student receiving these notes is required to be in attendance in the class. As an accommodation, some students can request to reduce their course load and take fewer credit hours than a full-time student and still maintain full-time student status.

ADMISSIONS

Loyola Marymount University prioritizes a student's academic record when making admission decisions. There is no minimum GPA or test score required for admission to LMU, but admission is selective. Applicants should be able to demonstrate the ability to write at the college level, demonstrate talent in areas such as artistic and athletic accomplishments, have volunteer experience, and have shown interest in the university. The middle 50 percent of students who elect to submit test scores have ACT scores of 29–32 or SAT scores of 1300–1400.

Additional Information

The Academic Resource Center acts as the academic success hub at Loyola Marymount. Services include academic tutoring and free peer-to-peer writing support. Workshops invite small groups to learn about time management, test-taking skills, study techniques, and organizational skills. The Writing Center offers support with writing assignments.

Sacred Heart Chapel was built in 1953 and the tower was completed in 1954, with the clock and chimes added later. Each of the 27 stained glass windows, brought from Europe, includes the seal of one of the 27 Jesuit colleges and universities in the United States, starting with Georgetown (1789) and ending with Le Moyne (1946). Sacred Heart Chapel serves as the iconic structure of the LMU campus, representing its nature and purpose without words.

Loyola Marymount University

GENERAL ADMISSIONS

Very important factors include: academic GPA. *Important factors include:* rigor of secondary school record, application essay. *Other factors considered include:* class rank, standardized test scores (if submitted), recommendations. High school diploma is required and GED is accepted. Institution is test-optional for entering Fall 2024. Check admissions website for updates. *Academic units recommended:* 4 English, 3 math, 2 science (2 labs), 3 foreign language, 3 social studies, 1 academic elective.

FINANCIAL AID

Students should submit: FAFSA. *Need-based scholarships/grants offered:* College/university scholarship or grant aid from institutional funds; Federal Pell; Private scholarships; SEOG; State scholarships/grants. *Loan aid offered:* Direct PLUS loans; Direct Subsidized Loans; Direct Unsubsidized Loans. Federal Work-Study Program available. Institutional employment available.

CAMPUS LIFE

Activities: Campus Ministries; Choral groups; Dance; Drama/theater; International Student Organization; Jazz band; Literary magazine; Model UN; Music ensembles; Opera; Radio station; Student government; Student newspaper; Television station; Yearbook. **Organizations:** 222 registered organizations, 21 honor societies, 6 religious organizations, 10 fraternities, 11 sororities. **Athletics (Intercollegiate):** *Men:* baseball, basketball, crew/rowing, cross-country, golf, ice hockey, lacrosse, rugby, ultimate frisbee, volleyball, water polo. *Women:* basketball, crew/rowing, cross-country, softball, swimming, ultimate frisbee, volleyball, water polo.

CAMPUS
Type of school	Private (nonprofit)
Environment	Town

STUDENTS
Undergrad enrollment	7,138
% male/female	47/53
% from out of state	34
% frosh live on campus	93

FINANCIAL FACTS
Annual tuition	$54,630
Room and board	$18,262
Required fees	$811

GENERAL ADMISSIONS INFO
Application fee	$60
Regular application deadline	1/15
Nonfall registration	Yes

Fall 2024 testing policy	Test Optional
Range SAT EBRW	640–720
Range SAT Math	630–730
Range ACT Composite	28–32

ACADEMICS
Student/faculty ratio	11:1
% students returning for sophomore year	88

REQUESTING SERVICES FOR STUDENTS WITH LEARNING DIFFERENCES

Phone: 310-338-4216 • academics.lmu.edu/dss • Email: dsslmu@lmu.edu

Documentation submitted to: Disability Support Services
Separate application required for Services: Yes

Documentation required for:
LD: Psychoeducational evaluation
ADHD: Psychoeducational evaluation
ASD: Psychoeducational evaluation

California

Menlo College

1000 El Camino Real, Atherton, CA 94027 • Admissions: 650-543-3753 • www.menlo.edu

Support: CS

ACCOMMODATIONS

Allowed in exams:

Calculators	Yes
Dictionary	Yes
Computer	Yes
Spell-checker	Yes
Extended test time	Yes
Scribe	Yes
Proctors	Yes
Oral exams	Yes
Note-takers	Yes

Support services for students with:

LD	Yes
ADHD	Yes
ASD	Yes
Distraction-reduced environment	Yes
Recording of lecture allowed	Yes
Reading technology	Yes
Audio books	Yes
Other assistive technology	Yes
Priority registration	No

Added costs of services:

For LD	No
For ADHD	No
For ASD	No
LD specialists	Yes
ADHD & ASD coaching	No
ASD specialists	Yes
Professional tutors	Yes
Peer tutors	Yes
Max. hours/week for services	Varies
How professors are notified of student approved accommodations	Student and Disability Services

COLLEGE GRADUATION REQUIREMENTS

Course waivers allowed	Yes

In what courses: Foreign Language and Math (for some majors)

Course substitutions allowed	Yes

In what courses: Foreign Language and Math (for some majors)

PROGRAMS/SERVICES FOR STUDENTS WITH LEARNING DIFFERENCES

Disability Services is part of Menlo Academic Success Center (ASC), and students are encouraged to meet with ASC early to arrange for accommodations. ASC provides a one-stop center for information and resources that are key to academic and career success. Services include advising, advocacy, note-taking, books on tape, assistive technology, a tutoring lab, and a writing center. There is also a faculty liaison for students with disabilities.

ADMISSIONS

Menlo does not follow a specific formula when making admission decisions. Each applicant is individually reviewed, and acceptance decisions are based on the strength of high school courses and grades. In addition, Menlo considers extracurricular activities, community involvement, employment, and leadership roles. One supplemental essay regarding reasons for seeking a college education is required.

Additional Information

ASC also helps students improve test performance, note-taking, and many other skills crucial to academic success. The Gullard Family ASC Peer Tutoring Center is staffed by excellent peer tutors who tutor nearly all subjects. Study Slam is held every Tuesday night in the Russell Center Great Room. This study event includes peer tutors, faculty, and staff, who are available to help students with homework and studying.

DID YOU KNOW?

Menlo was founded in 1927 as a two-year program for young men to complete lower-division courses before transferring to an upper-division school. Stanford was considering dropping its first- and second-year classes, imagining Menlo as the junior college division of Stanford. Menlo's fate rested with Stanford's Board of Trustees until 1932, when Stanford decided to remain a four-year university with graduate schools. In 1949, Menlo introduced its first four-year program, the School of Business Administration (SBA).

Menlo College

General Admissions

Very important factors include: rigor of secondary school record, academic GPA. *Important factors include:* class rank, application essay, recommendations. High school diploma is required and GED is accepted. Institution is test-free for entering Fall 2024. Check admissions website for updates. *Academic units recommended:* 4 English, 3 math, 3 science, 2 foreign language, 3 social studies.

Financial Aid

Students should submit: FAFSA; State aid form. *Need-based scholarships/ grants offered:* College/university scholarship or grant aid from institutional funds; Federal Pell; SEOG; State scholarships/grants. *Loan aid offered:* Direct PLUS loans; Direct Subsidized Loans; Direct Unsubsidized Loans. Federal Work-Study Program available. Institutional employment available.

Campus Life

Activities: Dance; International Student Organization; Student government; Student newspaper; Student-run film society. **Organizations:** 38 registered organizations, 3 honor societies, 0 religious organizations, 0 fraternities, 0 sororities. **Athletics (Intercollegiate):** *Men:* baseball, basketball, cross-country, golf, rugby, ultimate frisbee, volleyball, wrestling. *Women:* basketball, cross-country, golf, rugby, softball, ultimate frisbee, volleyball, wrestling.

CAMPUS
Type of school	Private (nonprofit)
Environment	Town

STUDENTS
Undergrad enrollment	774
% male/female	55/45
% from out of state	19
% frosh live on campus	86

FINANCIAL FACTS
Annual tuition	$50,190
Room and board	$15,510
Required fees	$880

GENERAL ADMISSIONS INFO
Application fee	$40
Regular application deadline	4/1
Nonfall registration	Yes
Fall 2024 testing policy	Test Free

ACADEMICS
Student/faculty ratio	14:1
% students returning for sophomore year	77

Most classes have 20–29 students.

REQUESTING SERVICES FOR STUDENTS WITH LEARNING DIFFERENCES

Phone: 650-543-3720 • menlo.edu/academics/academic-support-services/disability-services
Email: disabilityservices@menlo.edu

Documentation submitted to: Disability Services
Separate application required for Services: Yes

Documentation required for:
  LD: Psychoeducational evaluation
  ADHD: Psychoeducational evaluation
  ASD: Psychoeducational evaluation

California

Occidental College

1600 Campus Road, Los Angeles, CA 90041-3314 • Admissions: 800-825-5262 • www.oxy.edu

Support: CS

ACCOMMODATIONS

Allowed in exams:

Calculators	Yes
Dictionary	Yes
Computer	Yes
Spell-checker	Yes
Extended test time	Yes
Scribe	Yes
Proctors	Yes
Oral exams	Yes
Note-takers	Yes

Support services for students with:

LD	Yes
ADHD	Yes
ASD	Yes
Distraction-reduced environment	Yes
Recording of lecture allowed	Yes
Reading technology	Yes
Audio books	Yes
Other assistive technology	Yes
Priority registration	Yes

Added costs of services:

For LD	No
For ADHD	No
For ASD	No
LD specialists	Yes
ADHD & ASD coaching	Yes
ASD specialists	Yes
Professional tutors	No
Peer tutors	Yes
Max. hours/week for services	Varies
How professors are notified of student approved accommodations	Student

COLLEGE GRADUATION REQUIREMENTS

Course waivers allowed	No
Course substitutions allowed	Yes

In what courses: Math, Foreign Languages

PROGRAMS/SERVICES FOR STUDENTS WITH LEARNING DIFFERENCES

The Disability Service Office is committed to enhancing academic development and independence and creating a supportive community that promotes awareness, sensitivity, and understanding of students with disabilities. Documentation must be provided to access accommodations, which are determined on a case-by-case basis. Students with documented learning disabilities meet with staff in the Disability Services Office to determine eligibility for accommodations and services. Accommodations may include extended testing time, use of a computer or assistive technology, reduced-distraction testing environments, use of a calculator or spell-checker, a notetaker/recorder during lectures, or a reduced course load.

ADMISSIONS

Occidental utilizes a comprehensive review process when considering students for admission. The college values academic performance, extracurricular achievement, and personal attributes when evaluating applicants. Occidental places the most emphasis on course rigor and classroom performance. Interviews are not required but are highly recommended and are offered virtually. The median GPA for admitted applicants is 3.75, and the middle 50 percent for the SAT is 1470–1510 or 31–34 for the ACT of applicants who submit scores.

Additional Information

The Scientific Scholars Achievement Program is student-led, promotes community building between students and faculty, and offers free tutoring to students. All questions and learning styles are welcomed and encouraged in this program. The Academic Mastery Program provides workshops to promote excellence in science and math, and the Center for Digital Liberal Arts provides technical support to students. Academic coaching and peer tutoring are also available.

Occidental's Diplomacy and World Affairs (DWA) U.N. program founded in 1987, now the William and Elizabeth Kahane United Nations Program, is open to all DWA students and offers the opportunity to spend the fall semester in New York. Students take two courses on international issues with Occidental professors and an independent study seminar while holding a full-time internship at a U.N.-related agency.

Occidental College

General Admissions

Very important factors include: rigor of secondary school record, academic GPA, application essay. *Important factors include:* class rank, recommendations. *Other factors considered include:* standardized test scores (if submitted). High school diploma is required and GED is accepted. Institution is test-optional for entering Fall 2024. Check admissions website for updates. *Academic units recommended:* 4 English, 4 math, 3 science, 3 foreign language, 3 social studies.

Financial Aid

Students should submit: CSS/Financial Aid Profile; FAFSA; Noncustodial Profile; State aid form. *Need-based scholarships/grants offered:* College/university scholarship or grant aid from institutional funds; Federal Pell; Private scholarships; SEOG; State scholarships/grants. *Loan aid offered:* Direct PLUS loans; Direct Subsidized Loans; Direct Unsubsidized Loans. Federal Work-Study Program available. Institutional employment available.

Campus Life

Activities: Campus Ministries; Choral groups; Concert band; Dance; Drama/theater; International Student Organization; Jazz band; Literary magazine; Music ensembles; Musical theater; Radio station; Student government; Student newspaper; Student-run film society; Symphony orchestra; Television station; Yearbook. **Organizations:** 100 registered organizations, 8 honor societies, 4 religious organizations, 2 fraternities, 3 sororities. **Athletics (Intercollegiate):** *Men:* baseball, basketball, cross-country, golf, lacrosse, rugby, swimming, ultimate frisbee, water polo. *Women:* basketball, cross-country, golf, lacrosse, rugby, softball, swimming, ultimate frisbee, volleyball, water polo.

CAMPUS

Type of school	Private (nonprofit)
Environment	Metropolis

STUDENTS

Undergrad enrollment	1,935
% male/female	41/59
% from out of state	59
% frosh live on campus	100

FINANCIAL FACTS

Annual tuition	$59,970
Room and board	$17,330
Required fees	$596

GENERAL ADMISSIONS INFO

Application fee	$70
Regular application deadline	1/10
Nonfall registration	No

Fall 2024 testing policy	Test Optional
Range SAT EBRW	690–750
Range SAT Math	680–760
Range ACT Composite	31–34

ACADEMICS

Student/faculty ratio	9:1
% students returning for sophomore year	89

Most classes have 10–19 students.

REQUESTING SERVICES FOR STUDENTS WITH LEARNING DIFFERENCES

Phone: 323-259-2969 • www.oxy.edu/offices-services/disability-services • Email: accessibility@oxy.edu

Documentation submitted to: Disability Services
Separate application required for Services: Yes

Documentation required for:
LD: Psychoeducational evaluation
ADHD: Psychoeducational evaluation
ASD: Psychoeducational evaluation

California

San Diego State University

5500 Campanile Drive, San Diego, CA 92182-7455 • Admissions: 619-594-6336 • www.sdsu.edu

Support: S

ACCOMMODATIONS

Allowed in exams:

Calculators	Yes
Dictionary	Yes
Computer	Yes
Spell-checker	Yes
Extended test time	Yes
Scribe	Yes
Proctors	Yes
Oral exams	Yes
Note-takers	Yes

Support services for students with:

LD	Yes
ADHD	Yes
ASD	Yes
Distraction-reduced environment	Yes
Recording of lecture allowed	Yes
Reading technology	Yes
Audio books	Yes
Other assistive technology	Yes
Priority registration	Yes

Added costs of services:

For LD	No
For ADHD	No
For ASD	No
LD specialists	No
ADHD & ASD coaching	No
ASD specialists	No
Professional tutors	Yes
Peer tutors	Yes
Max. hours/week for services	Varies
How professors are notified of student approved accommodations	Student

COLLEGE GRADUATION REQUIREMENTS

Course waivers allowed	No
Course substitutions allowed	Yes
In what courses: Mathematics; Foreign Language	

PROGRAMS/SERVICES FOR STUDENTS WITH LEARNING DIFFERENCES

The Student Ability Success Center (SASC) at San Diego State University offers support and accommodations to students with documented disabilities. Students should provide appropriate documentation to SASC to determine eligibility. Services and accommodations may include note-taking, accommodated testing, real-time captioning, and textbooks in accessible formats. Students may also have access to an assistive technology lab and a grant-funded project that supports enhanced academic and personal growth. The High Tech Center is an assistive computer technology lab where students with disabilities can work independently or with trained consultants. The center provides access to various assistive software and hardware technologies for qualified students.

ADMISSIONS

All applicants must meet the admission criteria for California State University and San Diego State University. Admission is major-specific, which means applicants must elect a major and cannot change their major during the application process. Applicants are ranked within each major rather than overall. All majors are competitive; there are more applicants than there are spaces and the popularity of majors changes every year based on the applicant pool. Specific majors will have additional requirements that must be met for admission to that major and the university, such as dance, music, nursing, and theater performance. Students who are denied admission may submit a letter of appeal to have their application reviewed that details extenuating circumstances that impacted their academic record.

Additional Information

The EOP BEST Summer Bridge Program is an intensive five-week academic preparation program designed to enhance student educational achievement and successful transition to the university. Students are provided with the fundamental academic skills, social networks, and personal development essential to be successful at SDSU.

DID YOU KNOW?

On June 6, 1963, as part of his visit to the Marine Corps Recruit Depot, President John F. Kennedy gave the SDSU commencement address and spoke on the importance of education for all. He accepted the first honorary doctoral degree awarded by any California State University campus during commencement.

San Diego State University

GENERAL ADMISSIONS

Very important factors include: rigor of secondary school record, academic GPA. High school diploma is required and GED is accepted. Institution is test-free for entering Fall 2024. Check admissions website for updates. *Academic units required:* 4 English, 3 math, 2 science (2 labs), 2 foreign language, 1 social studies, 1 U.S. history, 1 academic elective, 1 visual/performing arts. *Academic units recommended:* 4 math, 3 science (3 labs).

FINANCIAL AID

Students should submit: FAFSA; State aid form. *Need-based scholarships/grants offered:* College/university scholarship or grant aid from institutional funds; Federal Pell; Private scholarships; SEOG; State scholarships/grants. *Loan aid offered:* Direct PLUS loans; Direct Subsidized Loans; Direct Unsubsidized Loans. Federal Work-Study Program available. Institutional employment available.

CAMPUS LIFE

Activities: Campus Ministries; Choral groups; Concert band; Dance; Drama/theater; International Student Organization; Jazz band; Literary magazine; Marching band; Model UN; Music ensembles; Musical theater; Opera; Pep band; Radio station; Student government; Student newspaper; Student-run film society; Symphony orchestra; Television station. **Organizations:** 274 registered organizations, 26 honor societies, 15 religious organizations, 15 fraternities, 15 sororities. **Athletics (Intercollegiate):** *Men:* baseball, basketball, crew/rowing, cycling, golf, ice hockey, lacrosse, rugby, ultimate frisbee, volleyball, water polo. *Women:* basketball, crew/rowing, cross-country, cycling, golf, lacrosse, softball, swimming, track/field (indoor), ultimate frisbee, volleyball, water polo.

CAMPUS
Type of school	Public
Environment	Metropolis

STUDENTS
Undergrad enrollment	31,656
% male/female	43/57
% from out of state	14
% frosh live on campus	75

FINANCIAL FACTS
Annual in-state tuition	$5,742
Annual out-of-state tuition	$17,622
Room and board	$20,500
Required fees	$2,432

GENERAL ADMISSIONS INFO
Application fee	$70
Regular application deadline	11/30
Nonfall registration	No
Fall 2024 testing policy	Test Free

ACADEMICS
Student/faculty ratio	24:1
% students returning for sophomore year	89

Most classes have 20–29 students.

REQUESTING SERVICES FOR STUDENTS WITH LEARNING DIFFERENCES

Phone: 619-594-6473 • www.sdsu.edu/sasc • Email: sascinfo@sdsu.edu

Documentation submitted to: Student Ability Success Center

Separate application required for Services: Yes

Documentation required for:
LD: Psychoeducational evaluation
ADHD: Psychoeducational evaluation
ASD: Psychoeducational evaluation

California

San Francisco State University

1600 Holloway Avenue, San Francisco, CA 93132 • Admissions: 415-338-6486 • www.sfsu.edu

Support: CS

ACCOMMODATIONS

Allowed in exams:

Calculators	Yes
Dictionary	Yes
Computer	Yes
Spell-checker	Yes
Extended test time	Yes
Scribe	Yes
Proctors	Yes
Oral exams	No
Note-takers	Yes

Support services for students with:

LD	Yes
ADHD	Yes
ASD	Yes
Distraction-reduced environment	Yes
Recording of lecture allowed	Yes
Reading technology	Yes
Audio books	Yes
Other assistive technology	Yes
Priority registration	Yes

Added costs of services:

For LD	No
For ADHD	No
For ASD	No
LD specialists	Yes
ADHD & ASD coaching	No
ASD specialists	No
Professional tutors	Yes
Peer tutors	Yes
Max. hours/week for services	Varies
How professors are notified of student approved accommodations	Student

COLLEGE GRADUATION REQUIREMENTS

Course waivers allowed	Yes

In what courses: Case-by-case basis

Course substitutions allowed	Yes

In what courses: Case-by-case basis

PROGRAMS/SERVICES FOR STUDENTS WITH LEARNING DIFFERENCES

The Disability Program and Resource Center (DPRC) is available to provide services and advocacy for students with disabilities. All students registered with DPRC are eligible for disability management advice, which consists of helping students access and manage DPRC services, problem-solving conflicts and concerns that are disability-related, and understanding reasonable accommodations under the law. The DPRC also arranges for testing accommodations and notetakers and has a drop-in center for tutoring. Students with disabilities may seek course substitutions for graduation requirements by consulting with the DPRC. Course substitutions may limit later enrollment in certain majors. For students with autism, there is the Autism Social Group which discusses topics such as personal and academic skill-building, disability identity, and campus and community resources. The group has guest speakers and plenty of opportunities to play games, socialize and share experiences with peers.

ADMISSIONS

All first-year applicants are encouraged to complete 15 units of college prep subjects. If a student is admissible but has not completed specific course requirements because of a learning disability, the student can appeal to admissions. The appeal should include documentation that supports the disability and explains why the student was unable to complete specific requirements. California residents must have a 2.5 GPA, and out-of-state applicants must have a 3.0 GPA for admission.

Additional Information

The Women with Hidden Disabilities Discussion Group is a group for female students to engage in weekly discussions about identifying as a woman with a hidden disability and learning about self-advocacy.

SFSU is the home of the waterbed. The inventor Charles Hall was working on his thesis project in industrial design, designing furniture that would eliminate pressure points that cut off circulation and cause discomfort. His trials included a cornstarch chair that weighed over 300 pounds and a Jell-O filler. In 1971, Mr. Hall was granted a U.S. patent for "Liquid Support for Human Bodies," i.e., the waterbed.

San Francisco State University

GENERAL ADMISSIONS

Very important factors include: rigor of secondary school record, academic GPA. High school diploma is required and GED is accepted. Institution is test-free for entering Fall 2024. Check admissions website for updates. *Academic units required:* 4 English, 3 math, 2 science (2 labs), 2 foreign language, 1 social studies, 1 U.S. history, 1 academic elective, 1 visual/performing arts. *Academic units recommended:* 4 math.

FINANCIAL AID

Students should submit: FAFSA. *Need-based scholarships/grants offered:* College/university scholarship or grant aid from institutional funds; Federal Pell; Private scholarships; SEOG; State scholarships/grants. *Loan aid offered:* Direct PLUS loans; Direct Subsidized Loans; Direct Unsubsidized Loans. Federal Work-Study Program available. Institutional employment available.

CAMPUS LIFE

Activities: Choral groups; Concert band; Dance; Drama/theater; International Student Organization; Jazz band; Literary magazine; Music ensembles; Musical theater; Opera; Radio station; Student government; Student newspaper; Student-run film society; Symphony orchestra; Television station. **Organizations:** 127 registered organizations, 8 honor societies, 11 religious organizations, 14 fraternities, 21 sororities. **Athletics (Intercollegiate):** *Men:* baseball, basketball, cross-country, cycling, ice hockey, martial arts, rugby, ultimate frisbee, volleyball, water polo, wrestling. *Women:* basketball, cross-country, cycling, ice hockey, martial arts, rugby, softball, track/field (indoor), ultimate frisbee, volleyball, water polo.

CAMPUS

Type of school	Public
Environment	Metropolis

STUDENTS

Undergrad enrollment	23,386
% male/female	45/55
% from out of state	1
% frosh live on campus	6

FINANCIAL FACTS

Annual in-state tuition	$5,742
Annual out-of-state tuition	$17,622
Room and board	$17,334
Required fees	$1,742

GENERAL ADMISSIONS INFO

Application fee	$70
Regular application deadline	11/30
Nonfall registration	Yes
Fall 2024 testing policy	Test Free

ACADEMICS

Student/faculty ratio	20:1
% students returning for sophomore year	81

Most classes have 20–29 students.

REQUESTING SERVICES FOR STUDENTS WITH LEARNING DIFFERENCES

Phone: 415-338-2472 • access.sfsu.edu • Email: dprc@sfsu.edu

Documentation submitted to: Disability Programs and Resource Center
Separate application required for Services: Yes

Documentation required for:
 LD: Psychoeducational evaluation
 ADHD: Psychoeducational evaluation
 ASD: Psychoeducational evaluation

California

San Jose State University

One Washington Square, San Jose, CA 95192-0016 • Admissions: 408-283-7500 • www.sjsu.edu

Support: CS

ACCOMMODATIONS

Allowed in exams:

Calculators	Yes
Dictionary	Yes
Computer	Yes
Spell-checker	Yes
Extended test time	Yes
Scribe	Yes
Proctors	Yes
Oral exams	Yes
Note-takers	Yes

Support services for students with:

LD	Yes
ADHD	Yes
ASD	Yes
Distraction-reduced environment	Yes
Recording of lecture allowed	Yes
Reading technology	Yes
Audio books	Yes
Other assistive technology	Yes
Priority registration	Yes

Added costs of services:

For LD	No
For ADHD	No
For ASD	No
LD specialists	Yes
ADHD & ASD coaching	No
ASD specialists	No
Professional tutors	No
Peer tutors	Yes
Max. hours/week for services	Varies
How professors are notified of student approved accommodations	Student and Accessible Education Center

COLLEGE GRADUATION REQUIREMENTS

Course waivers allowed	No
Course substitutions allowed	Yes
In what courses: Case-by-case basis	

PROGRAMS/SERVICES FOR STUDENTS WITH LEARNING DIFFERENCES

The Accessible Education Center (AEC) provides services and accommodations to students with documented disabilities. AEC advocates for students, connects them to resources, and ensures accessibility to the curriculum. Disability-management workshops are offered on a variety of topics, including time management, note-taking skills, test-taking strategies, and how to incorporate assistive technology into study habits. Assistive technology resources may include audio note-taking software, training for all built-in accessibility systems, and dictation and reading programs such as Read and Write or Natural Reader. To receive accommodations, students meet with an AEC professional counselor to review their documentation before implementing a plan. Once a determination has been made, an online portal alerts faculty via email of the student's accommodations. There is no foreign language requirement for SJSU, and students may petition for a math substitution.

ADMISSIONS

All first-year applicants must meet the same requirements for admission. Applicants must have a C or better in the core academic requirements. Meeting minimum admission requirements does not guarantee admission, and SJSU gives preference to local applicants from Santa Clara County. Admission to majors varies, and applicants are encouraged to choose their major and alternate major very carefully. Applicants cannot change their major during the application process once the application has been submitted.

Additional Information

Academic resources for students include the Student Technology Training Center and Writing Center, department-offered tutoring, individual and small-group peer tutoring, peer mentors, and the Advising Hub.

The annual Bulwer-Lytton fiction contest was founded in 1982 by Professor Scott Rice of SJSU's Department of English and Comparative Literature. The competition celebrates purposefully bad writing. Contestants worldwide submit opening, single-sentence lines of fictional novels. Winners are announced in mid-August. Dr. Rice retired in 2014 but affectionately continues to run the contest.

San Jose State University

GENERAL ADMISSIONS

Very important factors include: rigor of secondary school record, academic GPA. High school diploma is required and GED is accepted. Institution is test-free for entering Fall 2024. Check admissions website for updates. *Academic units required:* 4 English, 3 math, 2 science (2 labs), 2 foreign language, 2 social studies, 1 academic elective, 1 visual/performing arts. *Academic units recommended:* 4 math, 3 science (3 labs).

FINANCIAL AID

Students should submit: FAFSA; State aid form. *Need-based scholarships/grants offered:* College/university scholarship or grant aid from institutional funds; Federal Pell; Private scholarships; SEOG; State scholarships/grants. *Loan aid offered:* Direct PLUS loans; Direct Subsidized Loans; Direct Unsubsidized Loans. Federal Work-Study Program available. Institutional employment available.

CAMPUS LIFE

Activities: Campus Ministries; Choral groups; Concert band; Dance; Drama/theater; International Student Organization; Jazz band; Literary magazine; Marching band; Model UN; Music ensembles; Musical theater; Opera; Pep band; Radio station; Student government; Student newspaper; Student-run film society; Symphony orchestra. **Organizations:** 450 registered organizations, 21 honor societies, 13 religious organizations, 12 fraternities, 15 sororities. **Athletics (Intercollegiate):** *Men:* baseball, basketball, bowling, cross-country, cycling, golf, ice hockey, lacrosse, rugby, swimming, volleyball, water polo. *Women:* basketball, bowling, cross-country, cycling, golf, gymnastics, ice hockey, lacrosse, rugby, softball, swimming, volleyball, water polo.

CAMPUS

Type of school	Public
Environment	Metropolis

STUDENTS

Undergrad enrollment	27,680
% male/female	50/50
% from out of state	1
% frosh live on campus	11

FINANCIAL FACTS

Annual in-state tuition	$5,742
Annual out-of-state tuition	$15,246
Room and board	$17,360
Required fees	$2,110

GENERAL ADMISSIONS INFO

Application fee	$70
Regular application deadline	1/8
Nonfall registration	No
Fall 2024 testing policy	Test Free

ACADEMICS

Student/faculty ratio	26:1
% students returning for sophomore year	86

Most classes have 20–29 students.

REQUESTING SERVICES FOR STUDENTS WITH LEARNING DIFFERENCES

Phone: 408-924-6000 • www.sjsu.edu/aec • Email: aec-info@sjsu.edu

Documentation submitted to: Accessible Education Center
Separate application required for Services: Yes

Documentation required for:
LD: Psychoeducational evaluation
ADHD: Psychoeducational evaluation
ASD: Psychoeducational evaluation

Santa Clara University

500 El Camino Real, Santa Clara, CA 95053 • Admissions: 408-554-4700 • www.scu.edu

(Support: S)

ACCOMMODATIONS

Allowed in exams:

Calculators	Yes
Dictionary	Yes
Computer	Yes
Spell-checker	Yes
Extended test time	Yes
Scribe	Yes
Proctors	Yes
Oral exams	Yes
Note-takers	Yes

Support services for students with:

LD	Yes
ADHD	Yes
ASD	Yes
Distraction-reduced environment	Yes
Recording of lecture allowed	Yes
Reading technology	Yes
Audio books	Yes
Other assistive technology	Yes
Priority registration	Yes

Added costs of services:

For LD	No
For ADHD	No
For ASD	No
LD specialists	No
ADHD & ASD coaching	No
ASD specialists	No
Professional tutors	No
Peer tutors	Yes
Max. hours/week for services	Varies
How professors are notified of student approved accommodations	Student and Office of Accessible Education

COLLEGE GRADUATION REQUIREMENTS

Course waivers allowed	No
Course substitutions allowed	Yes
In what courses: Math and Foreign Language	

PROGRAMS/SERVICES FOR STUDENTS WITH LEARNING DIFFERENCES

To register with the Office of Accessible Education (OAE), students must complete an online application as well as submit appropriate documentation of the disability from a qualified professional. The office will email the student to schedule a meeting with an OAE advisor to discuss requested accommodations. Services may include priority registration, tutoring, academic counseling, and workshops on self-advocacy.

ADMISSIONS

Students must apply to one of the following: the College of Arts and Sciences, the Leavey School of Business, or the School of Engineering. While the selectivity between schools and programs does not vary greatly, academic readiness for the program of interest will be gauged based on the student's expressed interest. The average GPA for admitted students is 3.73 and varies depending on the major.

Additional Information

CONVERT is a self-service, computer-automated document conversion tool that allows students to convert documents into a variety of alternative formats. The Drahmann Center offers tutoring at no cost for many undergraduate courses and is available both in-person and via Zoom. All tutors are current undergraduate students who have been recommended by the faculty of the courses they tutor.

The Mission Santa Clara de Asís was established in 1777 and was the eighth of the 21 original California missions. Named for Saint Clare of Assisi, it was the first California mission to be named in honor of a woman. Santa Clara University, established in 1851, was built around the mission, and it remains the historical and spiritual center. It's the only mission located on a university campus.

Santa Clara University

GENERAL ADMISSIONS

Very important factors include: rigor of secondary school record, academic GPA, application essay. *Important factors include:* class rank, recommendations. *Other factors considered include:* standardized test scores (if submitted). High school diploma is required and GED is accepted. Institution is test-optional for entering Fall 2024. Check admissions website for updates. *Academic units required:* 4 English, 3 math, 2 science, 2 foreign language, 3 social studies. *Academic units recommended:* 4 math, 3 science, 3 foreign language, 1 visual/performing arts.

FINANCIAL AID

Students should submit: CSS/Financial Aid Profile; FAFSA. *Need-based scholarships/grants offered:* College/university scholarship or grant aid from institutional funds; Federal Pell; Private scholarships; SEOG; State scholarships/grants; United Negro College Fund. *Loan aid offered:* Direct PLUS loans; Direct Subsidized Loans; Direct Unsubsidized Loans. Federal Work-Study Program available. Institutional employment available.

CAMPUS LIFE

Activities: Campus Ministries; Choral groups; Concert band; Dance; Drama/theater; International Student Organization; Jazz band; Literary magazine; Model UN; Music ensembles; Musical theater; Opera; Pep band; Radio station; Student government; Student newspaper; Student-run film society; Symphony orchestra; Yearbook. **Organizations:** 177 registered organizations, 27 honor societies, 9 religious organizations, 0 fraternities, 0 sororities. **Athletics (Intercollegiate):** *Men:* baseball, basketball, crew/rowing, cross-country, cycling, equestrian sports, golf, ice hockey, lacrosse, martial arts, rugby, swimming, ultimate frisbee, volleyball, water polo. *Women:* basketball, crew/rowing, cross-country, cycling, equestrian sports, field hockey, golf, lacrosse, martial arts, rugby, softball, swimming, ultimate frisbee, volleyball, water polo.

CAMPUS
Type of school	Private (nonprofit)
Environment	City

STUDENTS
Undergrad enrollment	6,103
% male/female	52/48
% from out of state	44
% frosh live on campus	92

FINANCIAL FACTS
Annual tuition	$58,587
Room and board	$17,967
Required fees	$654

GENERAL ADMISSIONS INFO
Application fee	$70
Regular application deadline	1/7
Nonfall registration	Yes

Fall 2024 testing policy	Test Optional
Range SAT EBRW	640–720
Range SAT Math	650–760
Range ACT Composite	29–33

ACADEMICS
Student/faculty ratio	12:1
% students returning for sophomore year	92

Most classes have 20–29 students.

REQUESTING SERVICES FOR STUDENTS WITH LEARNING DIFFERENCES

Phone: 408-554-4109 • www.scu.edu/OAE • Email: oae@scu.edu

Documentation submitted to: Office of Accessible Education
Separate application required for Services: Yes

Documentation required for:
LD: Psychoeducational evaluation
ADHD: Psychoeducational evaluation
ASD: Psychoeducational evaluation

Sonoma State University

1801 East Cotati Avenue, Rohnert Park, CA 94928 • Admissions: 707-664-2778 • www.sonoma.edu

(**Support: S**)

ACCOMMODATIONS

Allowed in exams:

Calculators	Yes
Dictionary	Yes
Computer	Yes
Spell-checker	Yes
Extended test time	Yes
Scribe	Yes
Proctors	Yes
Oral exams	Yes
Note-takers	Yes

Support services for students with:

LD	Yes
ADHD	Yes
ASD	Yes
Distraction-reduced environment	Yes
Recording of lecture allowed	Yes
Reading technology	Yes
Audio books	Yes
Other assistive technology	Yes
Priority registration	Yes

Added costs of services:

For LD	No
For ADHD	No
For ASD	No
LD specialists	No
ADHD & ASD coaching	No
ASD specialists	No
Professional tutors	No
Peer tutors	Yes
Max. hours/week for services	Varies
How professors are notified of student approved accommodations	Student

COLLEGE GRADUATION REQUIREMENTS

Course waivers allowed	No
Course substitutions allowed	Yes
In what courses: Case-by-case basis	

PROGRAMS/SERVICES FOR STUDENTS WITH LEARNING DIFFERENCES

The Disability Services for Students office (DSS) provides accommodations to students with disabilities. Students are responsible for contacting DSS, completing and submitting the online DSS form, and providing disability documentation supporting their eligibility and appropriate level for accommodations. After submitting the registration material, students schedule a meeting with a DSS advisor to discuss their accommodation history and determine appropriate accommodations. Students receive an accommodations letter to share and discuss with their course instructors the implementation of the accommodations. Accommodations often used include priority registration, course material in an alternate format, assistive technology and software, note-taking, and test-taking alternatives. DSS will meet with prospective students to provide a broad overview of services.

ADMISSIONS

The California State University (CSU) system requires that first-time first-year applicants complete the required academic college prep courses with a grade of C or better. Applicants with disabilities who are unable to fulfill a specific course requirement because of a disability may qualify for substitutions based on a review and recommendation of the applicant's academic advisor or guidance counselor and the director of DSS. Applicants will still be held to the 15 units of college prep courses, and substitutions may limit enrollment in some majors. The admission review also considers work, community service, and extracurricular activities. A qualified applicant not admitted due to overcapacity in a program may be redirected to another CSU campus.

ADDITIONAL INFORMATION

The Learning and Academic Resource Center (LARC) has three academic support programs: the Tutorial Program, Supplemental Instruction (SI), and the Writing Center. Tutoring and SI are peer-led individual and small group sessions in a variety of subjects. Students can find group sessions and make tutoring appointments on the LARC web page. The Writing Center peer tutors provide support to student writers of all disciplines and abilities. Mathematics, Engineering, Science, Achievement (MESA) is part of a nationally recognized California academic support program with a goal of increasing the number of historically underrepresented students in STEM-related degrees. Students in the program receive academic support and personal advising and are involved in undergraduate research, tutoring, mentoring, and leadership development. There are MESA weekly meetings to learn and connect to resources and information. MESA has a peer mentor program, summer undergraduate research opportunities with SSU Faculty, and members receive free school supplies.

SSU is known for its beautiful location on the outskirts of Napa Valley wine county. But SSU has a fondness for "Peanuts." Charles Schulz (the Peanuts comic strip creator) and his wife Jean (1965 SSU alum) donated $5 million to the university in 1996—the largest in CSU system history. SSU has the Jean and Charles Schulz Information Center, a regional resource for the entire SSU community, Schroeder Hall, named for the Beethoven-loving piano player, and a 5-foot, 500-pound statue of Lucy in her Seawolf colors.

Sonoma State University

General Admissions

Very important factors include: academic GPA. High school diploma is required and GED is accepted. Institution is test-free for entering Fall 2024. Check admissions website for updates. *Academic units required:* 4 English, 3 math, 2 science (2 labs), 2 foreign language, 1 social studies, 1 U.S. history, 1 academic elective, 1 visual/performing arts. *Academic units recommended:* 4 math.

Financial Aid

Students should submit: FAFSA. *Need-based scholarships/grants offered:* College/university scholarship or grant aid from institutional funds; Federal Pell; Private scholarships; SEOG; State scholarships/grants; United Negro College Fund. *Loan aid offered:* Direct PLUS loans; Direct Subsidized Loans; Direct Unsubsidized Loans. Federal Work-Study Program available. Institutional employment available.

Campus Life

Activities: Choral groups; Dance; Drama/theater; Jazz band; Literary magazine; Music ensembles; Musical theater; Opera; Pep band; Radio station; Student government; Student newspaper; Symphony orchestra. **Organizations:** 109 registered organizations, 2 honor societies, 4 religious organizations, 8 fraternities, 10 sororities. **Athletics (Intercollegiate):** *Men:* baseball, basketball, golf, lacrosse, martial arts, skiing (nordic/cross-country), softball, volleyball. *Women:* basketball, cross-country, golf, lacrosse, martial arts, skiing (nordic/cross-country), softball, volleyball, water polo.

CAMPUS

Type of school	Public
Environment	Town

STUDENTS

Undergrad enrollment	8,532
% male/female	39/61
% from out of state	2
% frosh live on campus	86

FINANCIAL FACTS

Annual in-state tuition	$5,742
Annual out-of-state tuition	$17,622
Room and board	$13,960
Required fees	$2,056

GENERAL ADMISSIONS INFO

Application fee	$55
Regular application deadline	11/30
Nonfall registration	Yes
Fall 2024 testing policy	Test Free

ACADEMICS

Student/faculty ratio	23:1
% students returning for sophomore year	80

Most classes have 20–29 students.

REQUESTING SERVICES FOR STUDENTS WITH LEARNING DIFFERENCES

Phone: 707-664-2677 • dss.sonoma.edu • Email: disability.services@sonoma.edu

Documentation submitted to: Disability Services for Students
Separate application required for Services: Yes

Documentation required for:
LD: Psychoeducational evaluation
ADHD: Psychoeducational evaluation
ASD: Psychoeducational evaluation

Stanford University

Undergraduate Admission, Stanford, CA 94305-6106 • Admissions: 650-723-2091 • www.stanford.edu

Support: CS

ACCOMMODATIONS

Allowed in exams:

Calculators	Yes
Dictionary	Yes
Computer	Yes
Spell-checker	Yes
Extended test time	Yes
Scribe	Yes
Proctors	No
Oral exams	No
Note-takers	Yes

Support services for students with:

LD	Yes
ADHD	Yes
ASD	Yes
Distraction-reduced environment	Yes
Recording of lecture allowed	Yes
Reading technology	Yes
Audio books	Yes
Other assistive technology	Yes
Priority registration	No

Added costs of services:

For LD	No
For ADHD	No
For ASD	No
LD specialists	Yes
ADHD & ASD coaching	No
ASD specialists	Yes
Professional tutors	Yes
Peer tutors	Yes
Max. hours/week for services	10
How professors are notified of student approved accommodations	Student

COLLEGE GRADUATION REQUIREMENTS

Course waivers allowed	No
Course substitutions allowed	Yes
In what courses: Case-by-case basis	

PROGRAMS/SERVICES FOR STUDENTS WITH LEARNING DIFFERENCES

Once accepted to Stanford, incoming students with disabilities requiring accommodations are advised to contact the Office of Accessible Education (OAE) as soon as possible. To start the process, students should register with OAE and include current documentation of their learning disability. When registered, students are assigned a disability advisor, who will arrange an initial meeting to determine their needed accommodations and to review the process for requesting them. The advisor will then prepare an accommodation letter for the student to share with their course instructors. Although specific accommodations are determined after admission to Stanford, OAE can meet with prospective students to provide a broad overview of the OAE's services. Students can schedule a visit to OAE during their campus tour.

ADMISSIONS

All applicants are expected to meet the same admission criteria, and an official high school transcript is required. Applicants apply to the university, not a particular major. A personal essay and a Stanford essay are required. A counselor's school report and recommendation and letters of recommendation from two 11th or 12th grade classroom teachers are required. One optional letter of recommendation will be accepted, and interviews are optional.

Additional Information

The Stanford Learning Lab hosts online academic work sessions (aka Power Hours) for students four nights a week. Students can sign up online to join a group of peers to address their academic goals. Together, the students share goals before and after the session and wrap up by identifying the next steps to further advance their projects. The Center for Teaching and Learning (CTL) offers free tutoring for any student; their website contains information on the programs and policies. CTL can also refer students to professionals within the community for individual tutoring at the student's expense. CTL offers a range of other services to help students optimize their learning potential, including academic coaching, language conversation practice, technology support, and more.

Leland Stanford Junior University, still the legal name, was founded by Jane and Leland Stanford in 1885, and the first classes were held in 1891. Shortly after the death of their only child, a 15-year-old son, to typhoid, the Stanford's memorialized their son by deeding a large fortune (including 8,180 acres in Palo Alto) to establish a coeducational, nondenominational, and affordable university for young people. Until the mid-1930s, it was free to attend the university.

Stanford University

GENERAL ADMISSIONS

Very important factors include: rigor of secondary school record, class rank, academic GPA, standardized test scores (if submitted), application essay, recommendations. High school diploma is required and GED is accepted. Institution is test-optional for entering Fall 2024. Check admissions website for updates. *Academic units recommended:* 4 English, 4 math, 3 science (3 labs), 3 foreign language, 3 social studies.

FINANCIAL AID

Students should submit: CSS/Financial Aid Profile; FAFSA; Noncustodial Profile. *Need-based scholarships/grants offered:* College/university scholarship or grant aid from institutional funds; Federal Pell; Private scholarships; SEOG; State scholarships/grants. *Loan aid offered:* Direct PLUS loans; Direct Subsidized Loans; Direct Unsubsidized Loans. Federal Work-Study Program available. Institutional employment available.

CAMPUS LIFE

Activities: Campus Ministries; Choral groups; Concert band; Dance; Drama/theater; International Student Organization; Jazz band; Literary magazine; Marching band; Model UN; Music ensembles; Musical theater; Opera; Pep band; Radio station; Student government; Student newspaper; Student-run film society; Symphony orchestra; Television station; Yearbook. **Organizations:** 650 registered organizations, 30 religious organizations, 16 fraternities, 12 sororities. **Athletics (Intercollegiate):** *Men:* baseball, basketball, crew/rowing, cross-country, cycling, equestrian sports, golf, gymnastics, ice hockey, lacrosse, martial arts, racquetball, rugby, swimming, table tennis, ultimate frisbee, volleyball, water polo, wrestling. *Women:* basketball, crew/rowing, cross-country, cycling, equestrian sports, field hockey, golf, gymnastics, lacrosse, martial arts, racquetball, rugby, softball, swimming, table tennis, ultimate frisbee, volleyball, water polo.

CAMPUS

Type of school	Private (nonprofit)
Environment	City

STUDENTS

Undergrad enrollment	7,645
% male/female	49/51
% from out of state	61
% frosh live on campus	100

FINANCIAL FACTS

Annual tuition	$55,473
Room and board	$17,860
Required fees	$696

GENERAL ADMISSIONS INFO

Application fee	$90
Regular application deadline	1/2
Nonfall registration	No

Fall 2024 testing policy	Test Optional
Range SAT EBRW	720–770
Range SAT Math	750–800
Range ACT Composite	34–35

ACADEMICS

Student/faculty ratio	5:1
% students returning for sophomore year	98

Most classes have 10–19 students.

REQUESTING SERVICES FOR STUDENTS WITH LEARNING DIFFERENCES

Phone: 650-723-1066 • oae.stanford.edu • Email: oae-contactus@stanford.edu

Documentation submitted to: Office of Accessible Education

Separate application required for Services: Yes

Documentation required for:
LD: Psychoeducational evaluation
ADHD: Psychoeducational evaluation
ASD: Psychoeducational evaluation

California

University of California, Berkeley

110 Sproul Hall, Berkeley, CA 94720-5800 • Admissions: 510-642-3175 • www.berkeley.edu

Support: CS

ACCOMMODATIONS

Allowed in exams:

Calculators	Yes
Dictionary	Yes
Computer	Yes
Spell-checker	Yes
Extended test time	Yes
Scribe	Yes
Proctors	Yes
Oral exams	No
Note-takers	Yes

Support services for students with:

LD	Yes
ADHD	Yes
ASD	Yes
Distraction-reduced environment	Yes
Recording of lecture allowed	Yes
Reading technology	Yes
Audio books	Yes
Other assistive technology	Yes
Priority registration	Yes

Added costs of services:

For LD	No
For ADHD	No
For ASD	No
LD specialists	Yes
ADHD & ASD coaching	No
ASD specialists	No
Professional tutors	No
Peer tutors	Some individual tutoring is available through the TRIO grant.
Max. hours/week for services	Varies
How professors are notified of student approved accommodations	Student

COLLEGE GRADUATION REQUIREMENTS

Course waivers allowed	Yes

In what courses: Math waivers are considered on a case-by-case basis.

Course substitutions allowed	Yes

In what courses: Math substitutions are considered on a case-by-case basis.

Programs/Services for Students with Learning Differences

The Disabled Students Program (DSP) provides accommodations for students with disabilities. Eligible students must complete an online application, submit disability documentation, and contact DSP to set up an intake meeting. Services will be determined based on the limitations identified in the documentation, which should show a connection between the impact of the disability, the described barrier, and the accommodation request. DSP holds a new student orientation that provides information about disability programs, how to obtain services, resources for students, disability activism at Berkeley, and self-advocacy. There are breakout sessions to focus on specific interests for students and parents, and of course an opportunity to meet other students. DSP learning specialists offer workshops, academic coaching, and a course called Access & Self-Advocacy: An Intro to UC Berkeley for Students with Disabilities. Spectrum Connect provides students with autism support transitioning to campus at no additional charge. Spectrum Connect offers services as needed, including academic support, social and community involvement, and career readiness resources. Students work with a disability specialist throughout their time at UCB. The Disability Cultural Community Center provides a safe and social space for the UCB disability community to build authentic connections and support one another. The space serves as a platform to advocate, educate, and work and connect with other students, faculty, and staff living with a disability.

Admissions

The UC Berkeley applicant pool is highly competitive. Applicants are selected on the basis of academic performance, pattern of grades over time, and college preparatory courses (AP, IB, honors) and the level of achievement in those courses compared with other UC applicants at your school. UC Berkeley expects the reported grades, extracurricular activities, personal insight questions, and additional comments to give a full picture of a student's experience and aspirations.

Additional Information

The Student Learning Center (SLC) provides tutoring and guidance for new students. The SLC has a wide range of classes, programs, and events that push traditional learning boundaries and empower undergraduates. The SLC consists of professional staff, trained undergraduate tutors, and graduate student instructors who provide a rigorous and inclusive space for undergraduates to collaborate, learn, and grow. The SLC's Summer Bridge Program includes summer courses that are designed to introduce new first-year students to university coursework and to campus support services before the school year begins.

Berkeley's most iconic symbol may be the Sather Tower (1914), known as the Campanile, it was inspired by a tower in Venice, Italy. The clock was added in 1926. Whether lit with UCB colors or glowing from the sunset, at 307 feet tall, it's visible for miles. The 61-bell carillon is played three times a day and is used as a practice and teaching instrument. An elevator ride and 38 steps take visitors to the observation deck.

University of California, Berkeley

GENERAL ADMISSIONS
Very important factors include: rigor of secondary school record, academic GPA, application essay. *Other factors considered include:* standardized test scores (if submitted), recommendations. High school diploma is required and GED is accepted. Institution is test-free for entering Fall 2024. Check admissions website for updates. *Academic units required:* 4 English, 3 math, 2 science (2 labs), 2 foreign language, 2 history, 1 academic elective, 1 visual/performing arts. *Academic units recommended:* 4 math, 3 science (3 labs), 3 foreign language.

FINANCIAL AID
Students should submit: FAFSA; State aid form. *Need-based scholarships/grants offered:* College/university scholarship or grant aid from institutional funds; Federal Pell; Private scholarships; SEOG; State scholarships/grants. *Loan aid offered:* Direct PLUS loans; Direct Subsidized Loans; Direct Unsubsidized Loans. Federal Work-Study Program available. Institutional employment available.

CAMPUS LIFE
Activities: Campus Ministries; Choral groups; Concert band; Dance; Drama/theater; International Student Organization; Jazz band; Literary magazine; Marching band; Model UN; Music ensembles; Musical theater; Pep band; Radio station; Student government; Student newspaper; Student-run film society; Symphony orchestra; Television station; Yearbook. **Organizations:** 300 registered organizations, 6 honor societies, 28 religious organizations, 38 fraternities, 19 sororities. **Athletics (Intercollegiate):** *Men:* baseball, basketball, crew/rowing, cross-country, field hockey, golf, gymnastics, ice hockey, lacrosse, rugby, swimming, volleyball, water polo. *Women:* basketball, crew/rowing, cross-country, field hockey, golf, gymnastics, ice hockey, lacrosse, rugby, softball, swimming, volleyball, water polo.

CAMPUS	
Type of school	Public
Environment	City

STUDENTS	
Undergrad enrollment	32,211
% male/female	44/56
% from out of state	15
% frosh live on campus	93

FINANCIAL FACTS	
Annual in-state tuition	$11,928
Annual out-of-state tuition	$42,954
Room and board	$21,168
Required fees	$3,031

GENERAL ADMISSIONS INFO	
Application fee	$70
Regular application deadline	11/30
Nonfall registration	Yes
Fall 2024 testing policy	Test Free

ACADEMICS	
Student/faculty ratio	20:1
% students returning for sophomore year	96
Most classes have 10–19 students.	

REQUESTING SERVICES FOR STUDENTS WITH LEARNING DIFFERENCES

Phone: 510-642-0518 • dsp.berkeley.edu • Email: dsp@berkeley.edu

Documentation submitted to: Disabled Students Program
Separate application required for Services: Yes

Documentation required for:
LD: Psychoeducational evaluation
ADHD: Psychoeducational evaluation
ASD: Psychoeducational evaluation

California

University of California, Los Angeles

1147 Murphy Hall, Los Angeles, CA 90095-1436 • Admissions: 310-825-3101 • www.ucla.edu

Support: CS

ACCOMMODATIONS

Allowed in exams:

Calculators	Yes
Dictionary	Yes
Computer	Yes
Spell-checker	Yes
Extended test time	Yes
Scribe	Yes
Proctors	Yes
Oral exams	No
Note-takers	Yes

Support services for students with:

LD	Yes
ADHD	Yes
ASD	Yes
Distraction-reduced environment	Yes
Recording of lecture allowed	Yes
Reading technology	Yes
Audio books	No
Other assistive technology	Yes
Priority registration	Yes

Added costs of services:

For LD	No
For ADHD	No
For ASD	No
LD specialists	Yes
ADHD & ASD coaching	No
ASD specialists	No
Professional tutors	No
Peer tutors	Yes
Max. hours/week for services	Varies
How professors are notified of student approved accommodations	Student and Center for Accessible Education

COLLEGE GRADUATION REQUIREMENTS

Course waivers allowed	No
Course substitutions allowed	Yes
In what courses: Case-by-case basis	

PROGRAMS/SERVICES FOR STUDENTS WITH LEARNING DIFFERENCES

The Center for Accessible Education (CAE) supports students with disabilities and serves as a central resource on disability-related information, procedures, and services for the student community. Students are required to register with the CAE office by completing the CAE academic accommodations application and are encouraged to do so as early as possible. If needed, documentation can be uploaded with a student's application. The student's assigned CAE disability specialist will review the application and documents and let them know when to schedule an appointment. The meeting with the disability specialist will cover a lot of ground, including CAE available support, determining a student's approved accommodations, how to request accommodation letters for course instructors, and how to use the CAE student portal. CAE provides a wide variety of services to meet disability academic needs: priority registration, assistive technology, assisted note-taking, proctoring and test-taking arrangements, and more. Pathway at UCLA Extension is a fee-based, two-year certificate program with the goal of preparing young adults with developmental disabilities for independent living, employment, and lifelong learning. The program includes a curriculum of core courses, audit courses on UCLA's main campus, UCLA Extension courses, and internships. Life skills instruction takes place both in the residential setting and in the community. Students who successfully complete the program receive an award of completion in Learning and Life Skills.

ADMISSIONS

For admission to UCLA, applicants must complete 15 college preparatory courses, and at least 11 of those courses must be completed prior to the beginning of their senior year of high school. Standardized test scores may be used as an alternative method of fulfilling minimum requirements for eligibility or course placement after enrollment. UCLA considers an applicant's qualifications based on all information provided, with the goal of understanding an applicant personally as well as academically.

Additional Information

The First Year Experience (FYE) website was created to equip all first-year students with the skills, tools, and knowledge to successfully transition to college life at UCLA, whether it's information on orientation, top 10 tips for first-year students, academic advising, major selection, specific tutoring, work-study programs, career advising, events and organizations, health, or finance. UCLA Residential Life offers 11 Living Learning Communities where students find a safe, supportive, and inclusive living-learning environment.

DID YOU KNOW?

Friday, October 29, 1969, at 10:30 p.m., the first Internet message was sent from the computer science lab at UCLA to a computer at Stanford Research Institute. It was also the first network system crash and the first repair. The letters "LO" were sent, but it took an hour for the entire word (LOGIN) to be transmitted. You'll get to see the room where this happened on a UCLA tour if you can stop texting long enough to pay attention (just kidding!)

University of California, Los Angeles

GENERAL ADMISSIONS

Very important factors include: rigor of secondary school record, academic GPA, application essay. High school diploma is required and GED is accepted. Institution is test-free for entering Fall 2024. Check admissions website for updates. *Academic units required:* 4 English, 3 math, 2 science (2 labs), 2 foreign language, 2 history, 1 academic elective, 1 visual/performing arts. *Academic units recommended:* 4 math, 3 science (3 labs), 3 foreign language.

FINANCIAL AID

Students should submit: FAFSA; State aid form. *Need-based scholarships/grants offered:* College/university scholarship or grant aid from institutional funds; Federal Pell; Private scholarships; SEOG; State scholarships/ grants. *Loan aid offered:* Direct PLUS loans; Direct Subsidized Loans; Direct Unsubsidized Loans; College/university loans from institutional funds; State Loans. Federal Work-Study Program available. Institutional employment available.

CAMPUS LIFE

Activities: Campus Ministries; Choral groups; Concert band; Dance; Drama/theater; International Student Organization; Jazz band; Literary magazine; Marching band; Model UN; Music ensembles; Musical theater; Opera; Pep band; Radio station; Student government; Student newspaper; Student-run film society; Symphony orchestra; Television station; Yearbook. **Organizations:** 850 registered organizations, 21 honor societies, 35 fraternities, 35 sororities. **Athletics (Intercollegiate):** *Men:* baseball, basketball, crew/rowing, cross-country, cycling, equestrian sports, golf, gymnastics, ice hockey, lacrosse, martial arts, racquetball, rugby, skiing (nordic/cross-country), swimming, table tennis, track/field (indoor), ultimate frisbee, volleyball. *Women:* basketball, crew/rowing, cross-country, cycling, equestrian sports, golf, gymnastics, lacrosse, martial arts, racquetball, rugby, skiing (nordic/cross-country), softball, swimming, table tennis, track/field (indoor), ultimate frisbee, volleyball, water polo, wrestling.

CAMPUS	
Type of school	Public
Environment	Metropolis

STUDENTS	
Undergrad enrollment	32,065
% male/female	40/60
% from out of state	14
% frosh live on campus	97

FINANCIAL FACTS	
Annual in-state tuition	$12,522
Annual out-of-state tuition	$45,096
Room and board	$17,148
Required fees	$1,230

GENERAL ADMISSIONS INFO	
Application fee	$70
Regular application deadline	11/30
Nonfall registration	No
Fall 2024 testing policy	Test Free

ACADEMICS	
Student/faculty ratio	18:1
% students returning for sophomore year	96
Most classes have 2–9 students.	

REQUESTING SERVICES FOR STUDENTS WITH LEARNING DIFFERENCES

Phone: 310-825-1501 • www.cae.ucla.edu • Email: caeintake@saonet.ucla.edu

Documentation submitted to: Center for Accessible Education
Separate application required for Services: Yes

Documentation required for:
LD: Psychoeducational evaluation
ADHD: Psychoeducational evaluation
ASD: Psychoeducational evaluation

University of California, San Diego

9500 Gilman Drive, La Jolla, CA 92093-0021 • Admissions: 858-534-4831 • www.ucsd.edu

Support: CS

ACCOMMODATIONS

Allowed in exams:

Calculators	Yes
Dictionary	Yes
Computer	Yes
Spell-checker	Yes
Extended test time	Yes
Scribe	Yes
Proctors	Yes
Oral exams	Yes
Note-takers	Yes

Support services for students with:

LD	Yes
ADHD	Yes
ASD	Yes
Distraction-reduced environment	Yes
Recording of lecture allowed	Yes
Reading technology	Yes
Audio books	Yes
Other assistive technology	Yes
Priority registration	No

Added costs of services:

For LD	No
For ADHD	No
For ASD	No
LD specialists	Yes
ADHD & ASD coaching	Yes
ASD specialists	No
Professional tutors	Yes
Peer tutors	Yes
Max. hours/week for services	Varies
How professors are notified of student approved accommodations	Student

COLLEGE GRADUATION REQUIREMENTS

Course waivers allowed	No
Course substitutions allowed	No

PROGRAMS/SERVICES FOR STUDENTS WITH LEARNING DIFFERENCES

The Office for Students with Disabilities (OSD) provides reasonable accommodations for students with documented disabilities. After class registration, students must register with OSD to initiate the accommodations process. Before their first appointment, students should complete the online intake and consent forms. Previous documentation can also be submitted prior to intake. After intake, OSD completes a review to determine accommodations. Some of the most requested accommodations are adaptive technology, alternative-format class material, note-taking, classroom/lab accommodations, and test accommodations. In addition, OSD offers weekly or bi-monthly check-ins to help students adjust to life at UCSD. OSD hosts a job fair for students with disabilities, and its Academic Internship Program connects students with opportunities where they can earn academic credit while learning real-world skills. In addition, students with disabilities can work for OSD in customer service, front and back-office management, team building, and universal design in physical and electronic environments.

ADMISSIONS

To be eligible for admission to UCSD, California residents must earn a GPA of 3.0 or higher with no grade lower than a "C." Non-California residents must earn a GPA of 3.4 or higher; no grade may be lower than a "C." Personal insight questions on the application are considered an important part of the review process. Applicants should pick questions that reveal the most about themselves and best reflect their experiences.

Additional Information

Prospective students can learn more about USCD from Triton Talk webinars, available on USCD online and on YouTube. To learn about resources, programs, and opportunities at UCSD, prospective students can also attend the Fall Academic Support Fair, where over 50 academic and student services departments are represented. Each UCSD college offers a 2 unit First Year Experience (FYE) to assist students with the transition to a large research university. In these courses, faculty lead weekly lectures and undergraduate leaders host smaller discussions. By participating, FYE students gain skills such as effective research, strong time management, enhanced communication, and increased confidence when interacting with faculty. UCSD also offers tutoring and study assistance programs by subject or class, most at no charge. In addition, many departments offer private tutoring at no charge.

The southernmost of the 10 UC campuses, UCSD is home to an estimated 230,000 trees and 137 species. While there's no formal inventory, an estimated 90 percent of the eucalyptus trees date from a 112-acre grove planted in the early 20th century. Originally grown for railroad ties, shipbuilding, and fuel, the eucalyptus trees on the UCSD campus are said to have inspired Dr. Seuss's *The Lorax*.

University of California, San Diego

GENERAL ADMISSIONS

Very important factors include: rigor of secondary school record, academic GPA, application essay. *Other factors considered include:* class rank. High school diploma is required and GED is accepted. Institution is test-free for entering Fall 2024. Check admissions website for updates. *Academic units required:* 4 English, 3 math, 2 science (2 labs), 2 foreign language, 2 history, 1 academic elective, 1 visual/performing arts. *Academic units recommended:* 4 math, 3 science (3 labs), 3 foreign language.

FINANCIAL AID

Students should submit: FAFSA; State aid form. *Need-based scholarships/grants offered:* College/university scholarship or grant aid from institutional funds; Federal Pell; Private scholarships; SEOG; State scholarships/grants. *Loan aid offered:* Direct PLUS loans; Direct Subsidized Loans; Direct Unsubsidized Loans. Federal Work-Study Program available. Institutional employment available.

CAMPUS LIFE

Activities: Campus Ministries; Choral groups; Concert band; Dance; Drama/theater; International Student Organization; Jazz band; Literary magazine; Marching band; Model UN; Music ensembles; Musical theater; Opera; Pep band; Radio station; Student government; Student newspaper; Student-run film society; Symphony orchestra; Television station. **Organizations:** 509 registered organizations, 4 honor societies, 36 religious organizations, 16 fraternities, 12 sororities. **Athletics (Intercollegiate):** *Men:* baseball, basketball, crew/rowing, cross-country, cycling, equestrian sports, field hockey, golf, gymnastics, ice hockey, lacrosse, racquetball, rugby, swimming, table tennis, ultimate frisbee, volleyball, water polo. *Women:* basketball, crew/rowing, cross-country, cycling, equestrian sports, field hockey, gymnastics, lacrosse, racquetball, rugby, softball, swimming, table tennis, ultimate frisbee, volleyball, water polo.

CAMPUS

Type of school	Public
Environment	Metropolis

STUDENTS

Undergrad enrollment	32,456
% male/female	48/52
% from out of state	9
% frosh live on campus	88

FINANCIAL FACTS

Annual in-state tuition	$11,928
Annual out-of-state tuition	$42,954
Room and board	$16,713
Required fees	$5,401

GENERAL ADMISSIONS INFO

Application fee	$70
Regular application deadline	11/30
Nonfall registration	No
Fall 2024 testing policy	Test Free

ACADEMICS

Student/faculty ratio	19:1
% students returning for sophomore year	93

Most classes have 10–19 students.

REQUESTING SERVICES FOR STUDENTS WITH LEARNING DIFFERENCES

Phone: 858-534-4382 • disabilities.ucsd.edu • Email: osd@ucsd.edu

Documentation submitted to: Office for Students with Disabilities
Separate application required for Services: Yes

Documentation required for:
LD: Psychoeducational evaluation
ADHD: Psychoeducational evaluation
ASD: Psychoeducational evaluation

University of California, Santa Barbara

1210 Cheadle Hall, Santa Barbara, CA 93106-2014 • Admissions: 805-893-2881 • www.ucsb.edu

(Support: CS)

ACCOMMODATIONS

Allowed in exams:

Calculators	Yes
Dictionary	Yes
Computer	Yes
Spell-checker	Yes
Extended test time	Yes
Scribe	Yes
Proctors	Yes
Oral exams	Yes
Note-takers	Yes

Support services for students with:

LD	Yes
ADHD	Yes
ASD	Yes
Distraction-reduced environment	Yes
Recording of lecture allowed	Yes
Reading technology	Yes
Audio books	Yes
Other assistive technology	Yes
Priority registration	Yes

Added costs of services:

For LD	No
For ADHD	No
For ASD	No
LD specialists	Yes
ADHD & ASD coaching	No
ASD specialists	No
Professional tutors	No
Peer tutors	Yes
Max. hours/week for services	Varies
How professors are notified of student approved accommodations	Student and Disabilities Service Program

COLLEGE GRADUATION REQUIREMENTS

Course waivers allowed	No
Course substitutions allowed	No

PROGRAMS/SERVICES FOR STUDENTS WITH LEARNING DIFFERENCES

The Disabilities Service Program (DSP) works with students with disabilities. The DSP has an extensive list of standard services available and additional services that may be considered on a case-by-case basis. Students should contact the DSP and make them aware of their accommodation needs by completing a statement of intent to register (SIR) and including documentation of their disabilities. After a disability specialist has reviewed the documentation, students are contacted for an in-person interview. At the appointment, the disability specialist will review the accommodation services with the student, provide an overview of how to use the DSP online portal and how to request and use DSP services. The Workforce Recruitment Program (WRP) provides access to opportunities that run the gamut from summer internships to full-time positions by connecting motivated students with disabilities to federal government and private-sector employers nationwide.

ADMISSIONS

All applications are judged by the same eligibility requirements and selection criteria. The minimum GPA required for California students is 3.0 (3.4 for non-California residents) in all college preparatory courses. To meet minimum course requirements, students must complete 15 year-long high school courses with a letter grade of a "C" or better; at least 11 of the courses must be completed prior to the last year of high school. Students may also meet course requirements by completing college courses. During the review process, myriad traits and projects are considered: special talents, achievements, awards, special skills, completion of special projects, significant community service, and personal insight questions. UCSB can offer admission to a few students who do not meet all the course or minimum GPA requirements. Students can use the personal insight questions or additional comments section of the admission application to explain their unique story.

Additional Information

Campus Learning Assistance Services (CLAS) or Come-Learn-Achieve-Succeed is available to all registered students looking to better understand course concepts and the learning process and who wish to discover solutions to problems. CLAS Groups require regular attendance and participation, are led by peer tutors or full-time staff, and cover an assortment of topics: biology, chemistry, math, physics, economics, and statistics. In addition, CLAS offers CLAS peer tutors for languages, writing, and various math and science courses. CLAS Workshops are one-time workshops during the semester where students can work on academic skills and try out new study strategies. Finally, CLAS Academic Skills Counselors host individual appointments focused on specific issues but can also address general topics to fit student needs.

Near UCSB's Campus Point, on Lagoon Island, there's a large labyrinth surrounded by green vegetation overlooking the Pacific Ocean. It's modeled after the Chartres Cathedral labyrinth (France, early 13th century). It's the work of Ms. Carol Geer, who retired from UCSB in 2000 after 21 years as director of Counseling and Career Services. It's where students can find peace, de-stress, and have a quiet place to think. The labyrinth was built to ADA specifications, with wide paths to accommodate wheelchairs.

University of California, Santa Barbara

GENERAL ADMISSIONS

Very important factors include: academic GPA, application essay. *Important factors include:* rigor of secondary school record. High school diploma is required and GED is accepted. Institution is test-free for entering Fall 2024. Check admissions website for updates. *Academic units required:* 4 English, 3 math, 2 science (2 labs), 2 foreign language, 2 history, 1 academic elective, 1 visual/performing arts. *Academic units recommended:* 4 math, 3 science (3 labs), 3 foreign language.

FINANCIAL AID

Students should submit: FAFSA. *Need-based scholarships/grants offered:* College/university scholarship or grant aid from institutional funds; Federal Pell; Private scholarships; SEOG; State scholarships/grants. *Loan aid offered:* Direct PLUS loans; Direct Subsidized Loans; Direct Unsubsidized Loans. Federal Work-Study Program available. Institutional employment available.

CAMPUS LIFE

Activities: Campus Ministries; Choral groups; Concert band; Dance; Drama/theater; International Student Organization; Jazz band; Literary magazine; Model UN; Music ensembles; Musical theater; Opera; Pep band; Radio station; Student government; Student newspaper; Student-run film society; Symphony orchestra; Television station; Yearbook. **Organizations:** 566 registered organizations, 13 honor societies, 30 religious organizations, 41 fraternities, 41 sororities. **Athletics (Intercollegiate):** *Men:* baseball, basketball, bowling, crew/rowing, cross-country, cycling, equestrian sports, golf, gymnastics, lacrosse, racquetball, rugby, softball, swimming, ultimate frisbee, volleyball, water polo. *Women:* basketball, bowling, crew/rowing, cross-country, cycling, equestrian sports, field hockey, golf, gymnastics, lacrosse, racquetball, softball, swimming, ultimate frisbee, volleyball, water polo.

CAMPUS
Type of school	Public
Environment	City

STUDENTS
Undergrad enrollment	22,956
% male/female	44/56
% from out of state	8
% frosh live on campus	90

FINANCIAL FACTS
Annual in-state tuition	$11,834
Annual out-of-state tuition	$42,611
Room and board	$16,883
Required fees	$1,166

GENERAL ADMISSIONS INFO
Application fee	$70
Regular application deadline	11/30
Nonfall registration	No
Fall 2024 testing policy	Test Free

ACADEMICS
Student/faculty ratio	17:1
% students returning for sophomore year	92

Most classes have 2–9 students.

REQUESTING SERVICES FOR STUDENTS WITH LEARNING DIFFERENCES

Phone: 805-893-2668 • dsp.sa.ucsb.edu • Email: DSP.help@sa.ucsb.edu

Documentation submitted to: Disabilities Service Program
Separate application required for Services: Yes

Documentation required for:
LD: Psychoeducational evaluation
ADHD: Psychoeducational evaluation
ASD: Psychoeducational evaluation

California

University of San Francisco

2130 Fulton Street, San Francisco, CA 94117 • Admissions: 415-422-6563 • www.usfca.edu

Support: CS

PROGRAMS/SERVICES FOR STUDENTS WITH LEARNING DIFFERENCES

Student Disability Services (SDS) serves students with documented disabilities and works to create an environment that facilitates equal access and inclusivity, strives for the full participation of all students, and views disability as a valued aspect of diversity. SDS provides and assists in coordinating a wide array of supports, such as note-taking, assistive technology, alternative-format media, examination accommodations, and more. Recent documentation is requested, but students may submit documentation that may be considered outdated if there is no current information. During the intake and registration process, the student will meet with a specialist at SDS and participate in an individualized assessment based on the student's expressed needs and the documentation of disability. The specialist will work with the student to develop a reasonable accommodation plan. Modifications that do not fundamentally alter a course or program are made on a case-by-case basis. SDS also offers support groups or workshops based on the current interests and needs of the student population receiving services. These may include career planning, advocacy skills, or other focuses for students with similar disabilities. Learning support specialists are also available to assist with organizational, writing, and study skills.

ADMISSIONS

All applicants must meet the same general admission requirements. The average GPA for admitted students is 3.5. For admitted applicants who submit test scores, the middle 50 percent scored 1200–1370 on the SAT or 26–31 on the ACT. The essay prompt asks applicants to describe how they see themselves becoming part of the Jesuit mission. USF is a Jesuit university that welcomes students of any faith or no faith.

Additional Information

The Center for Academic and Student Achievement (CASA) has success coaches to help students achieve their academic goals.

In 2015, Pope Francis embraced sustainability with his publication *Laudato Si'* (subtitle: "On Care for Our Common Home"). It was the inspiration for USF Star Route Farms, which opened in 2017. It's a self-sustaining 40-acre organic farm and 60 acres of mixed woodland habitat, riparian forest, and Pine Gulch Creek. Students, faculty, and staff can escape urban life and participate in a new learning experience through courses, research, retreats, and workshops.

University of San Francisco

GENERAL ADMISSIONS

Very important factors include: rigor of secondary school record, academic GPA. *Important factors include:* application essay. *Other factors considered include:* class rank, standardized test scores (if submitted), recommendations. High school diploma is required and GED is accepted. Institution is test-optional for entering Fall 2024. Check admissions website for updates. *Academic units required:* 4 English, 3 math, 2 science (2 labs), 2 foreign language, 3 social studies, 6 academic electives.

FINANCIAL AID

Students should submit: FAFSA; State aid form. *Need-based scholarships/grants offered:* College/university scholarship or grant aid from institutional funds; Federal Pell; Private scholarships; SEOG; State scholarships/grants. *Loan aid offered:* Direct PLUS loans; Direct Subsidized Loans; Direct Unsubsidized Loans. Federal Work-Study Program available. Institutional employment available.

CAMPUS LIFE

Activities: Campus Ministries; Choral groups; Dance; Drama/theater; International Student Organization; Jazz band; Literary magazine; Marching band; Model UN; Music ensembles; Musical theater; Pep band; Radio station; Student government; Student newspaper; Student-run film society; Television station; Yearbook. **Organizations:** 152 registered organizations, 7 honor societies, 4 religious organizations, 4 fraternities, 6 sororities. **Athletics (Intercollegiate):** *Men:* baseball, basketball, cross-country, golf, lacrosse, martial arts, rugby, softball, swimming, volleyball. *Women:* basketball, cross-country, golf, martial arts, rugby, softball, swimming, volleyball.

CAMPUS

Type of school	Private (nonprofit)
Environment	Metropolis

STUDENTS

Undergrad enrollment	5,980
% male/female	35/65
% from out of state	33
% frosh live on campus	86

FINANCIAL FACTS

Annual tuition	$57,670
Room and board	$19,536
Required fees	$552

GENERAL ADMISSIONS INFO

Application fee	$70
Regular application deadline	1/15
Nonfall registration	Yes

Fall 2024 testing policy	Test Optional
Range SAT EBRW	610–700
Range SAT Math	600–710
Range ACT Composite	27–31

ACADEMICS

Student/faculty ratio	13:1
% students returning for sophomore year	81

Most classes have 10–19 students.

REQUESTING SERVICES FOR STUDENTS WITH LEARNING DIFFERENCES

Phone: 415-422-2613 • www.usfca.edu/student-disability-services • Email: sds@usfca.edu

Documentation submitted to: Student Disability Services
Separate application required for Services: Yes

Documentation required for:
LD: Psychoeducational evaluation
ADHD: Psychoeducational evaluation
ASD: Psychoeducational evaluation

California

University of Southern California

University Park Campus, Los Angeles, CA 90089-0911 • Admissions: 213-740-1111 • www.usc.edu

Support: CS

ACCOMMODATIONS

Allowed in exams:

Calculators	Yes
Dictionary	No
Computer	Yes
Spell-checker	Yes
Extended test time	Yes
Scribe	Yes
Proctors	Yes
Oral exams	Yes
Note-takers	Yes

Support services for students with:

LD	Yes
ADHD	Yes
ASD	Yes
Distraction-reduced environment	Yes
Recording of lecture allowed	Yes
Reading technology	Yes
Audio books	Yes
Other assistive technology	Yes
Priority registration	Yes

Added costs of services:

For LD	No
For ADHD	No
For ASD	No
LD specialists	No
ADHD & ASD coaching	Yes
ASD specialists	No
Professional tutors	Yes
Peer tutors	Yes
Max. hours/week for services	Varies
How professors are notified of student approved accommodations	Student

COLLEGE GRADUATION REQUIREMENTS

Course waivers allowed	No
Course substitutions allowed	Yes

In what courses: Students must be registered with OSAS to request a Foreign Language substitution.

PROGRAMS/SERVICES WITH STUDENTS WITH LEARNING DIFFERENCES

The Office of Student Accessibility Services (OSAS) serves the USC community by ensuring equal access, removing obstacles, and advocating for students with disabilities to increase education and awareness. Students must complete an online application to OSAS and provide appropriate documentation. Support most often involves one-on-one attention for academic planning, scheduling, organization, and methods of compensation. Students are offered standing appointments with learning assistants and subject tutors. Accommodations could include attendance modification, a reduced course load, note-taking, alternative-format materials, assistive technology, priority registration, testing accommodations, and advocacy. A peer mentorship program, Balancing LIFE (Learning, Independence, Friendship, and Empowerment), is offered through OSAS from August to May. Both mentees and mentors are USC students registered with OSAS. The program provides students an opportunity to enhance their social experience and increase their sense of community at USC. Mentors receive specialized training and meet one-on-one with mentees to explore areas of interest, such as communication and interpersonal skills.

ADMISSIONS

All applicants are expected to meet the same admission criteria and admitted students typically pursued the most rigorous program available to them. Some majors do require a portfolio or an audition, and faculty from these programs provide feedback to the admission committee. Applicants can be considered for a second-choice major or can be admitted as "undecided/undeclared."

Additional Information

The Kortschak Center for Learning and Creativity provides resources for support with study skills, organization, and learning strategies. USC also has a club for neurodiverse students and a support group for students with life-long struggles around making friends and understanding unwritten social norms and rules of social communication.

Many think that USC's mascot is Tommy Trojan, the warrior riding the white horse. The Trojan tradition originated in 1912, with an article about the team's fighting spirit. But the official mascot is Traveler, the noble White Horse. Traveler made his first appearance in 1961 and has been as far as Miami. He's at Trojan events, grade schools, high schools, charity events, and parades. In 1940, USC had a canine mascot named George Tirebiter I, who was famous for chasing cars through the USC campus.

University of Southern California

GENERAL ADMISSIONS
Very important factors include: rigor of secondary school record, academic GPA, standardized test scores (if submitted), application essay, recommendations. High school diploma is required and GED is not accepted. Institution is test-optional for entering Fall 2024. Check admissions website for updates. *Academic units required:* 4 English, 3 math, 2 science (2 labs), 2 foreign language, 2 social studies, 3 academic electives. *Academic units recommended:* 4 math, 3 science (3 labs), 3 foreign language, 3 social studies.

FINANCIAL AID
Students should submit: Business/Farm Supplement; CSS/Financial Aid Profile; FAFSA; Noncustodial Profile. *Need-based scholarships/grants offered:* College/university scholarship or grant aid from institutional funds; Federal Pell; Private scholarships; SEOG; State scholarships/grants. *Loan aid offered:* Direct PLUS loans; Direct Subsidized Loans; Direct Unsubsidized Loans. Federal Work-Study Program available. Institutional employment available.

CAMPUS LIFE
Activities: Campus Ministries; Choral groups; Concert band; Dance; Drama/theater; International Student Organization; Jazz band; Literary magazine; Marching band; Model UN; Music ensembles; Musical theater; Opera; Pep band; Radio station; Student government; Student newspaper; Student-run film society; Symphony orchestra; Television station; Yearbook. **Organizations:** 850 registered organizations, 46 honor societies, 87 religious organizations, 32 fraternities, 26 sororities. **Athletics (Intercollegiate):** *Men:* baseball, basketball, crew/rowing, cross-country, cycling, golf, ice hockey, lacrosse, martial arts, racquetball, rugby, swimming, table tennis, ultimate frisbee, volleyball, water polo. *Women:* basketball, crew/rowing, cross-country, cycling, equestrian sports, field hockey, golf, gymnastics, ice hockey, lacrosse, martial arts, racquetball, rugby, softball, swimming, table tennis, ultimate frisbee, volleyball, water polo.

CAMPUS
Type of school	Private (nonprofit)
Environment	Metropolis

STUDENTS
Undergrad enrollment	20,619
% male/female	48/52
% from out of state	39
% frosh live on campus	98

FINANCIAL FACTS
Annual tuition	$60,446
Room and board	$16,732
Required fees	$1,057

GENERAL ADMISSIONS INFO
Application fee	$85
Regular application deadline	1/15
Nonfall registration	Yes
Fall 2024 testing policy	Test Optional
Range SAT EBRW	650–740
Range SAT Math	670–780
Range ACT Composite	30–34

ACADEMICS
Student/faculty ratio	9:1
% students returning for sophomore year	96

Most classes have 10–19 students.

REQUESTING SERVICES FOR STUDENTS WITH LEARNING DIFFERENCES

Phone: 213-740-0776 • osas.usc.edu • Email: osasfrontdesk@usc.edu

Documentation submitted to: Office of Student Accessibility Services
Separate application required for Services: Yes

Documentation required for:
LD: Psychoeducational evaluation
ADHD: Psychoeducational evaluation
ASD: Psychoeducational evaluation

California

University of the Pacific

3601 Pacific Avenue, Stockton, CA 95211 • Admissions: 209-946-2211 • www.pacific.edu

Support: CS

ACCOMMODATIONS

Allowed in exams:

Calculators	Yes
Dictionary	Yes
Computer	Yes
Spell-checker	Yes
Extended test time	Yes
Scribe	Yes
Proctors	Yes
Oral exams	Yes
Note-takers	Yes

Support services for students with:

LD	Yes
ADHD	Yes
ASD	Yes
Distraction-reduced environment	Yes
Recording of lecture allowed	Yes
Reading technology	Yes
Audio books	Yes
Other assistive technology	Yes
Priority registration	Yes

Added costs of services:

For LD	No
For ADHD	No
For ASD	No
LD specialists	No
ADHD & ASD coaching	Yes
ASD specialists	Yes
Professional tutors	Yes
Peer tutors	Yes
Max. hours/week for services	Varies
How professors are notified of student approved accommodations	SSD

COLLEGE GRADUATION REQUIREMENTS

Course waivers allowed	No
Course substitutions allowed	Yes
In what courses: Math Fundamental Skills and Foreign Language	

PROGRAMS/SERVICES WITH STUDENTS WITH LEARNING DIFFERENCES

Services for Students with Disabilities (SSD) provides assistance to all students with documented disabilities. Once admitted, students may register for services by contacting SSD and submitting documentation of a disability. SSD determines accommodations on a case-by-case basis. Available services include diagnostic assessment and accommodations for academic needs and assistive technology, which ranges from e-books and alternate formatting to the Kurzweil Reading Program and note-taking apps.

ADMISSIONS

All applicants must meet the same admission criteria. The school uses a holistic approach to application review. Any student may enroll in summer session university courses, but students should not assume that participation in Pacific Summer will lead to admission for enrollment in the regular academic year.

Additional Information

Peer tutors have taken the courses they tutor and completed training before joining the peer-to-peer tutoring program. Students can meet with mentors at the writing center and take for-credit skills courses in reading, study strategies, writing, and math. Student Academic Support Services offers students individual coaching and workshops to help with time management, study skills, test prep, and sustained motivation strategies.

DID YOU KNOW?

The naturalist John Muir (1838–1914) is considered one of California's most important historical figures. University of the Pacific has housed this legend's manuscripts, personal papers, personal library, furniture from his Martinez home, and other materials since 1970. In 1989, the John Muir Center was established to encourage the use of the collection through the Muir symposium, seminars, and a semester-long course on his life, his conservation crusades, and his global legacy.

University of the Pacific

GENERAL ADMISSIONS
Very important factors include: rigor of secondary school record, academic GPA, application essay, recommendations. *Other factors considered include:* class rank, standardized test scores (if submitted). High school diploma is required and GED is accepted. Institution is test-optional for entering Fall 2024. Check admissions website for updates. *Academic units recommended:* 4 English, 4 math, 3 science, 2 foreign language, 2 social studies, 1 visual/performing arts.

FINANCIAL AID
Students should submit: FAFSA. *Need-based scholarships/grants offered:* College/university scholarship or grant aid from institutional funds; Federal Pell; Private scholarships; SEOG; State scholarships/grants. *Loan aid offered:* Direct PLUS loans; Direct Subsidized Loans; Direct Unsubsidized Loans.

CAMPUS LIFE
Activities: Campus Ministries; Choral groups; Drama/theater; International Student Organization; Model UN; Music ensembles; Radio station; Student government; Student newspaper. **Organizations:** 100 registered organizations, 14 honor societies, 10 religious organizations, 8 fraternities, 7 sororities. **Athletics (Intercollegiate):** *Men:* baseball, basketball, crew/rowing, cycling, golf, lacrosse, martial arts, rugby, swimming, volleyball, water polo. *Women:* basketball, crew/rowing, cross-country, cycling, field hockey, lacrosse, martial arts, softball, swimming, volleyball, water polo.

CAMPUS
Type of school	Private (nonprofit)
Environment	City

STUDENTS
Undergrad enrollment	3,260
% male/female	46/54
% from out of state	9
% frosh live on campus	75

FINANCIAL FACTS
Annual tuition	$52,918
Room and board	$14,420
Required fees	$764

GENERAL ADMISSIONS INFO
Application fee	$55
Regular application deadline	Rolling
Nonfall registration	Yes

Fall 2024 testing policy	Test Optional
Range SAT EBRW	560–680
Range SAT Math	560–743
Range ACT Composite	25–33

ACADEMICS
Student/faculty ratio	13:1
% students returning for sophomore year	88

Most classes have 20–29 students.

REQUESTING SERVICES FOR STUDENTS WITH LEARNING DIFFERENCES

Phone: 209-946-3221 • www.pacific.edu/disabilities • Email: ssd@pacific.edu

Documentation submitted to: Services for Students with Disabilities
Separate application required for Services: Yes

Documentation required for:
LD: Psychoeducational evaluation
ADHD: Psychoeducational evaluation
ASD: Psychoeducational evaluation

California

Whittier College

13406 E. Philadelphia Street, Whittier, CA 90608 • Admissions: 562-907-4238 • www.whittier.edu

Support: CS

ACCOMMODATIONS

Allowed in exams:

Calculators	Yes
Dictionary	Yes
Computer	Yes
Spell-checker	Yes
Extended test time	Yes
Scribe	Yes
Proctors	Yes
Oral exams	No
Note-takers	Yes

Support services for students with:

LD	Yes
ADHD	Yes
ASD	Yes
Distraction-reduced environment	Yes
Recording of lecture allowed	Yes
Reading technology	Yes
Audio books	Yes
Other assistive technology	Yes
Priority registration	Yes

Added costs of services:

For LD	No
For ADHD	No
For ASD	No
LD specialists	Yes
ADHD & ASD coaching	Yes
ASD specialists	Yes
Professional tutors	No
Peer tutors	Yes
Max. hours/week for services	Varies
How professors are notified of student approved accommodations	Student and Student Accessibility Services

COLLEGE GRADUATION REQUIREMENTS

Course waivers allowed	Yes

In what courses: Foreign Language, Math

Course substitutions allowed	Yes

In what courses: Foreign Language, Math

PROGRAMS/SERVICES FOR STUDENTS WITH LEARNING DIFFERENCES

Student Accessibility Services provides reasonable and appropriate accommodations to students with learning disabilities, ADHD, and ASD. After students submit documentation, requests are considered based on the student's disability, the impact of the disability on the student's academic and social life, and the type and extent of the requested accommodation. With proper documentation, accommodations may include extended test time, use of a computer or assistive technology, and a reduced distraction-testing environment, as well as notetakers, printed material in an electronic or alternate format, permission to record lectures, and attendance modifications.

ADMISSIONS

All applicants are expected to meet the same admission criteria. Students who apply as test-optional with a GPA under 3.0 could be required to provide test scores to be considered for admission. The average weighted GPA for admitted applicants is 3.39–4.0. For students submitting test scores, the mid-50 percent ACT score range is 24–31 and 1190–1400 for the SAT. Two letters of recommendation are required. One letter must be written by a teacher from a STEM, language arts, or social sciences class. The other letter may be from a teacher in any discipline or a counselor, coach, clergy, or employer.

Additional Information

The Center for Advising & Academic Success (CAAS) provides academic guidance, peer tutoring, workshops, and academic coaching for all students. All students have access to a math lab, writing center, learning lab, and academic counseling. The Academic Success Program utilizes a combination of academic support services to help students be successful. It is available to all students but required for those on academic probation and warning. The program offers meetings with a CAAS advisor throughout the semester, Academic Success Workshops, tutoring appointments, and academic coaching.

DID YOU KNOW?

Former President Richard Nixon graduated summa cum laude from Whittier in 1934 with a bachelor's degree in history. He spent his undergraduate years as a well-liked student body president, a strong performer in the debate club, a football player, and founding president of the Orthogonian Society. Whittier's annual Richard M. Nixon Fellowship competition honors Nixon's domestic and foreign policy legacy.

Whittier College

GENERAL ADMISSIONS

Very important factors include: rigor of secondary school record, academic GPA, application essay, recommendations. *Other factors considered include:* class rank, standardized test scores (if submitted). High school diploma is required and GED is accepted. Institution is test-optional for entering Fall 2024. Check admissions website for updates. *Academic units required:* 3 English, 2 math, 1 science (1 labs), 2 foreign language, 1 social studies. *Academic units recommended:* 4 English, 3 math, 2 science, 3 foreign language, 2 social studies.

FINANCIAL AID

Students should submit: FAFSA. *Need-based scholarships/grants offered:* College/university scholarship or grant aid from institutional funds; Federal Pell; Private scholarships; SEOG; State scholarships/grants. *Loan aid offered:* Direct PLUS loans; Direct Subsidized Loans; Direct Unsubsidized Loans. Federal Work-Study Program available.

CAMPUS LIFE

Activities: Campus Ministries; Choral groups; Dance; Drama/theater; International Student Organization; Jazz band; Literary magazine; Model UN; Music ensembles; Radio station; Student government; Student newspaper; Student-run film society; Television station; Yearbook. **Organizations:** 60 registered organizations, 17 honor societies, 6 religious organizations, 4 fraternities, 5 sororities. **Athletics (Intercollegiate):** *Men:* baseball, basketball, cross-country, equestrian sports, golf, lacrosse, rugby, swimming, water polo. *Women:* basketball, cross-country, equestrian sports, lacrosse, softball, swimming, volleyball, water polo.

CAMPUS

Type of school	Private (nonprofit)
Environment	City

STUDENTS

Undergrad enrollment	1,131
% male/female	44/56
% from out of state	24
% frosh live on campus	77

FINANCIAL FACTS

Annual tuition	$48,924
Room and board	$15,272
Required fees	$590

GENERAL ADMISSIONS INFO

Application fee	No fee
Regular application deadline	Rolling
Nonfall registration	Yes

Fall 2024 testing policy	Test Optional
Range SAT EBRW	550–650
Range SAT Math	590–690
Range ACT Composite	24–30

ACADEMICS

Student/faculty ratio	12:1
% students returning for sophomore year	69
Most classes have 10–19 students.	

REQUESTING SERVICES FOR STUDENTS WITH LEARNING DIFFERENCES

Phone: 562-907-4825 • whittier.edu/accessibility • Email: sas@whittier.edu

Documentation submitted to: Student Accessibility Services

Separate application required for Services: Yes

Documentation required for:
LD: Psychoeducational evaluation
ADHD: Psychoeducational evaluation
ASD: Psychoeducational evaluation

California

Colorado State University Pueblo

2200 Bonforte Boulevard, Pueblo, CO 81001 • Admissions: 719-549-2461 • www.csupueblo.edu

Support: S

ACCOMMODATIONS

Allowed in exams:	
Calculators	Yes
Dictionary	Yes
Computer	Yes
Spell-checker	Yes
Extended test time	Yes
Scribe	Yes
Proctors	Yes
Oral exams	Yes
Note-takers	Yes
Support services for students with:	
LD	Yes
ADHD	Yes
ASD	Yes
Distraction-reduced environment	Yes
Recording of lecture allowed	Yes
Reading technology	Yes
Audio books	Yes
Other assistive technology	Yes
Priority registration	Yes
Added costs of services:	
For LD	No
For ADHD	No
For ASD	No
LD specialists	No
ADHD & ASD coaching	No
ASD specialists	No
Professional tutors	No
Peer tutors	Yes
Max. hours/week for services	As needed
How professors are notified of student approved accommodations	Student

COLLEGE GRADUATION REQUIREMENTS

Course waivers allowed	No
Course substitutions allowed	Yes
In what courses: Case-by-case basis	

PROGRAMS/SERVICES FOR STUDENTS WITH LEARNING DIFFERENCES

The Disability Resource and Support Center (DRSC) provides reasonable academic accommodations and support for students with documented disabilities. Students are encouraged to provide DRSC with documentation that specifically identifies the disability and need for accommodations. Once requests are granted, professors are notified by email. The request for the use of a dictionary, computer, or spell check during exams will depend on the student's documented needs and permission from the professor. For required graduation requirements like math or a foreign language, there is a substitution process that DRSC can facilitate.

ADMISSIONS

CSU Pueblo's admission committee evaluates student preparation, high school GPA, and academic rigor. Most students with a 2.0 GPA are considered for admission. Applicants who do not meet admission standards are encouraged to submit personal statements explaining their circumstances and evidence of academic progress throughout high school. Students may submit ACT or SAT scores, but they are not required for admission. Determining eligibility for some scholarships may still require official test scores.

Additional Information

Student and Academic Services provides free peer tutoring to all CSU Pueblo students. Skills classes are available to develop strategies in note-taking, textbook-reading, and studying. The Writing Room offers one-on-one writing assistance. Students who are on academic probation can receive help identifying ways to improve and develop an action plan with the Academic Improvement Program.

DID YOU KNOW?

CSU Pueblo is part of an urban legend in entertainment. In the 1980s, Van Halen's performance contract included a rider with the request: "M&M's (warning: absolutely no brown ones)." Frontman David Lee Roth's autobiography explained that this was included to make sure the contract was read. Performing in the CSU Pueblo Massari Arena and discovering a brown M&M, the group did $12,000 of damage. Added to the legend was $80,000 of damage to the new basketball floor that couldn't support the band's heavy stage.

Colorado State University Pueblo

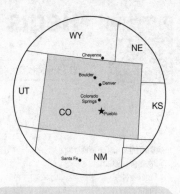

GENERAL ADMISSIONS

Very important factors include: rigor of secondary school record, academic GPA, standardized test scores (if submitted). *Important factors include:* class rank. *Other factors considered include:* application essay, recommendations. High school diploma is required and GED is accepted. Institution is test-optional for entering Fall 2024. Check admissions website for updates. *Academic units required:* 4 English, 4 math, 3 science, 1 foreign language, 3 social studies, 2 academic electives.

FINANCIAL AID

Students should submit: FAFSA; Institution's own financial aid form. *Need-based scholarships/grants offered:* College/university scholarship or grant aid from institutional funds; Federal Pell; Private scholarships; SEOG; State scholarships/grants. *Loan aid offered:* Direct PLUS loans; Direct Subsidized Loans; Direct Unsubsidized Loans. Federal Work-Study Program available. Institutional employment available.

CAMPUS LIFE

Activities: Choral groups; Concert band; Dance; Jazz band; Literary magazine; Music ensembles; Pep band; Student government; Student newspaper; Symphony orchestra; Television station. **Organizations:** 24 registered organizations, 6 honor societies, 4 religious organizations, 2 fraternities, 1 sororities. **Athletics (Intercollegiate):** *Men:* baseball, basketball, golf, lacrosse, wrestling. *Women:* basketball, cross-country, golf, softball, volleyball.

CAMPUS	
Type of school	Public
Environment	City

STUDENTS	
Undergrad enrollment	4,109
% male/female	43/57
% from out of state	7
% frosh live on campus	90

FINANCIAL FACTS	
Annual in-state tuition	$10,702
Annual out-of-state tuition	$19,042
Room and board	$11,592

GENERAL ADMISSIONS INFO	
Application fee	$25
Regular application deadline	8/1
Nonfall registration	Yes

Fall 2024 testing policy	Test Optional
Range SAT EBRW	470–570
Range SAT Math	470–560
Range ACT Composite	18–25

ACADEMICS	
Student/faculty ratio	15:1
% students returning for sophomore year	63
Most classes have 10–19 students.	

REQUESTING SERVICES FOR STUDENTS WITH LEARNING DIFFERENCES

Phone: 719-549-2648 • www.csupueblo.edu/disability-resource-and-support-center
Email: DRO@csupueblo.edu

Documentation submitted to: Disability Resource and Support Center
Separate application required for Services: Yes

Documentation required for:
LD: Psychoeducational evaluation
ADHD: Psychoeducational evaluation
ASD: Psychoeducational evaluation

Regis University

3333 Regis Boulevard, Denver, CO 80221-1099 • Admissions: 303-458-4900 • www.regis.edu

Support: S

ACCOMMODATIONS

Allowed in exams:

Calculators	Yes
Dictionary	Yes
Computer	Yes
Spell-checker	Yes
Extended test time	Yes
Scribe	Yes
Proctors	Yes
Oral exams	Yes
Note-takers	Yes

Support services for students with:

LD	Yes
ADHD	Yes
ASD	Yes
Distraction-reduced environment	Yes
Recording of lecture allowed	Yes
Reading technology	Yes
Audio books	Yes
Other assistive technology	Yes
Priority registration	Yes

Added costs of services:

For LD	No
For ADHD	No
For ASD	No
LD specialists	No
ADHD & ASD coaching	No
ASD specialists	No
Professional tutors	No
Peer tutors	Yes
Max. hours/week for services	Varies
How professors are notified of student approved accommodations	Student

COLLEGE GRADUATION REQUIREMENTS

Course waivers allowed	No
Course substitutions allowed	Yes
In what courses: Math and Foreign Language	

PROGRAMS/SERVICES FOR STUDENTS WITH LEARNING DIFFERENCES

Student Disability Services and University Testing (SDS/UT) provides support to students with disabilities. Students requesting reasonable accommodations must complete an application, submit documentation of a disability, and participate in an intake appointment. It is strongly recommended that students complete the application as early as possible. Students should request accommodations through the AIM system, allowing them to select both their registered courses and desired accommodations, which may include extended time for tests, distraction-reduced test environments, and note-taking assistance. Accommodations are determined on a case-by-case basis and students must request them at the start of each term.

ADMISSIONS

All applicants are expected to meet the same admission criteria. Recommendations and extracurricular activities will be considered, and interviews are not required. Students need to show sufficient evidence of motivation and ability to succeed in college, even though they may not have met the required GPA. Students can be admitted on a probation period and will need a 2.0 GPA to return for the second semester if admitted on probation.

Additional Information

Regis University offers students a broad range of resources to help ensure academic success. The Learning Commons has a writing center and coaches provide one-on-one appointments to guide students through any stage of writing in any discipline. Tutoring services and academic success workshops are also available through The Learning Commons. These services provide support in writing and a range of subjects through one-to-one and group sessions to promote student confidence and success.

Founded in 1877, Regis University is the only Jesuit Catholic university in the Rocky Mountains and one of 27 Jesuit colleges and universities in the U.S. Its name honors St. John Francis Regis, who was known for his service to at-risk women and youth, providing them stable incomes and independence.

Regis University

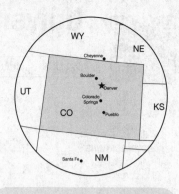

GENERAL ADMISSIONS

Very important factors include: rigor of secondary school record, academic GPA. *Important factors include:* application essay, recommendations. *Other factors considered include:* standardized test scores (if submitted). High school diploma is required and GED is accepted. Institution is test-optional for entering Fall 2024. Check admissions website for updates. *Academic units recommended:* 4 English, 3 math, 3 science, 2 foreign language, 3 social studies.

FINANCIAL AID

Students should submit: FAFSA. *Need-based scholarships/grants offered:* College/university scholarship or grant aid from institutional funds; Federal Pell; Private scholarships; SEOG; State scholarships/grants. *Loan aid offered:* Direct PLUS loans; Direct Subsidized Loans; Direct Unsubsidized Loans. Federal Work-Study Program available. Institutional employment available.

CAMPUS LIFE

Activities: Campus Ministries; Choral groups; Concert band; Dance; Drama/theater; International Student Organization; Jazz band; Literary magazine; Music ensembles; Musical theater; Radio station; Student government; Student newspaper; Yearbook. **Organizations:** 30 registered organizations, 7 honor societies, 2 religious organizations. **Athletics (Intercollegiate):** *Men:* baseball, basketball, cross-country, golf, lacrosse, rugby, volleyball. *Women:* basketball, cross-country, golf, lacrosse, rugby, softball, volleyball.

CAMPUS

Type of school	Private (nonprofit)
Environment	Metropolis

STUDENTS

Undergrad enrollment	2,513
% male/female	35/65
% from out of state	35
% frosh live on campus	65

FINANCIAL FACTS

Annual tuition	$40,830
Room and board	$13,416
Required fees	$870

GENERAL ADMISSIONS INFO

Application fee	No fee
Regular application deadline	8/1
Nonfall registration	Yes

Fall 2024 testing policy	Test Optional
Range SAT EBRW	520–640
Range SAT Math	510–630
Range ACT Composite	21–28

ACADEMICS

Student/faculty ratio	10:1
% students returning for sophomore year	79

Most classes have 10–19 students.

REQUESTING SERVICES FOR STUDENTS WITH LEARNING DIFFERENCES

Phone: 303-458-4941 • www.regis.edu/academics/student-success/disability-testing-services
Email: disability@regis.edu

Documentation submitted to: Student Disability Services
Separate application required for Services: Yes

Documentation required for:
LD: Psychoeducational evaluation
ADHD: Psychoeducational evaluation
ASD: Psychoeducational evaluation

University of Colorado Boulder

552 UCB, Boulder, CO 80309-0552 • Admissions: 303-492-6301 • www.colorado.edu

Support: S

ACCOMMODATIONS

Allowed in exams:	
Calculators	Yes
Dictionary	Yes
Computer	Yes
Spell-checker	Yes
Extended test time	Yes
Scribe	Yes
Proctors	Yes
Oral exams	Yes
Note-takers	Yes
Support services for students with:	
LD	Yes
ADHD	Yes
ASD	Yes
Distraction-reduced environment	Yes
Recording of lecture allowed	Yes
Reading technology	Yes
Audio books	Yes
Other assistive technology	Yes
Priority registration	No
Added costs of services:	
For LD	No
For ADHD	No
For ASD	No
LD specialists	No
ADHD & ASD coaching	No
ASD specialists	No
Professional tutors	No
Peer tutors	Yes
Max. hours/week for services	Varies
How professors are notified of student approved accommodations	Student

COLLEGE GRADUATION REQUIREMENTS

Course waivers allowed	No
Course substitutions allowed	No

PROGRAMS/SERVICES FOR STUDENTS WITH LEARNING DIFFERENCES

The Disability Services office provides housing accommodations, communication and interpreting services, as well as course accommodations that include assignment and attendance flexibility, note-taking services, and testing and text-formatting alternatives. Once students have submitted the online application for accommodations with appropriate documentation, they are notified and meet with a member of the Disability Services office. After the meeting, students receive a notice of determination with their accommodation and registration status. Each semester, students may submit requests to send accommodation letters to their course instructors and are encouraged to discuss the arrangements of approved accommodations with their instructors. Students with testing accommodations have access to the Student Testing Center, which provides testing environments to suit designated needs. All university library computers run assistive technology software, and the Alternate Format Production and Access Center (AFPAC) is a computer lab equipped with adaptive software designed to serve students registered with Disability Services. Additional resources offered by Disability Services include workshops and training sessions throughout the year.

ADMISSIONS

The review committee is looking for highly qualified, curious students who demonstrate maturity, personal integrity, and a commitment to servicing the community. Application requirements include a letter of recommendation, a personal essay, and short answer questions, as well the specific college and major in which the student intends to enroll. The review committee looks closely at high school GPA, and the quality and rigor of coursework completed in the context of what is available to the student. Any grade below a C, especially in the junior or senior year, should be addressed in the application. While the Office of Admissions does not host interviews, its staff is happy to talk to students by phone, email, or during a school visit.

Additional Information

The Office of Undergraduate Education (OUE) oversees a variety of academic resources and student support programs. It is home to advising initiatives, like the Academic Success & Achievement Program (ASAP), which supports students living on campus with peer tutoring and connections to additional resources. The Student Academic Success Center (SASC) provides dedicated support to low-income and first-generation students through academic skills development, math and writing courses, and tutoring.

DID YOU KNOW?

The Colorado Shakespeare Festival begins at CU Boulder. Plays are performed beneath summer night skies in the historic Mary Rippon Outdoor Theater, named in 1939 to honor Mary Rippon. Mary Rippon joined the faculty in January 1878 as one of the first professors hired at CU, teaching French and German, some math, and English grammar. She's thought to be the first female faculty at any state university.

University of Colorado Boulder

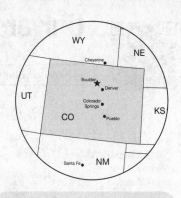

GENERAL ADMISSIONS

Very important factors include: rigor of secondary school record, academic GPA. *Important factors include:* application essay, recommendations. *Other factors considered include:* class rank, standardized test scores (if submitted). High school diploma is required and GED is accepted. Institution is test-optional for entering Fall 2024. Check admissions website for updates. *Academic units required:* 4 English, 4 math, 3 science (2 labs), 1 foreign language, 3 social studies, 2 academic electives.

FINANCIAL AID

Students should submit: FAFSA. *Need-based scholarships/grants offered:* College/university scholarship or grant aid from institutional funds; Federal Pell; Private scholarships; SEOG; State scholarships/grants. *Loan aid offered:* Direct PLUS loans; Direct Subsidized Loans; Direct Unsubsidized Loans. Federal Work-Study Program available. Institutional employment available.

CAMPUS LIFE

Activities: Campus Ministries; Choral groups; Concert band; Dance; Drama/theater; International Student Organization; Jazz band; Literary magazine; Marching band; Model UN; Music ensembles; Musical theater; Opera; Pep band; Radio station; Student government; Student newspaper; Student-run film society; Symphony orchestra. **Organizations:** 550 registered organizations, 29 honor societies, 27 religious organizations, 13 fraternities, 16 sororities. **Athletics (Intercollegiate):** *Men:* baseball, basketball, crew/rowing, cross-country, cycling, equestrian sports, field hockey, golf, ice hockey, lacrosse, martial arts, rugby, skiing (nordic/cross-country), swimming, table tennis, track/field (indoor), ultimate frisbee, volleyball, water polo. *Women:* basketball, crew/rowing, cross-country, cycling, equestrian sports, field hockey, golf, ice hockey, lacrosse, martial arts, rugby, skiing (nordic/cross-country), softball, swimming, table tennis, track/field (indoor), ultimate frisbee, volleyball, water polo.

CAMPUS
Type of school	Public
Environment	City

STUDENTS
Undergrad enrollment	30,671
% male/female	54/46
% from out of state	45
% frosh live on campus	94

FINANCIAL FACTS
Annual in-state tuition	$11,040
Annual out-of-state tuition	$37,642
Room and board	$16,146
Required fees	$1,586

GENERAL ADMISSIONS INFO
Application fee	$50
Regular application deadline	1/15
Nonfall registration	Yes

Fall 2024 testing policy	Test Optional
Range SAT EBRW	590–690
Range SAT Math	570–700
Range ACT Composite	26–31

ACADEMICS
Student/faculty ratio	18:1
% students returning for sophomore year	88

Most classes have 10–19 students.

REQUESTING SERVICES FOR STUDENTS WITH LEARNING DIFFERENCES

Phone: 303-492-8671 • www.colorado.edu/disabilityservices • Email: dsinfo@colorado.edu

Documentation submitted to: Disability Services
Separate application required for Services: Yes

Documentation required for:
  LD: Psychoeducational evaluation
  ADHD: Psychoeducational evaluation
  ASD: Psychoeducational evaluation

University of Colorado at Colorado Springs

1420 Austin Bluffs Parkway, Colorado Springs, CO 80918 • Admissions: 719-255-3084 • www.uccs.edu

Support: CS

ACCOMMODATIONS

Allowed in exams:

Calculators	Yes
Dictionary	Yes
Computer	Yes
Spell-checker	Yes
Extended test time	Yes
Scribe	Yes
Proctors	Yes
Oral exams	Yes
Note-takers	No

Support services for students with:

LD	Yes
ADHD	Yes
ASD	Yes
Distraction-reduced environment	Yes
Recording of lecture allowed	Yes
Reading technology	Yes
Audio books	Yes
Other assistive technology	Yes
Priority registration	No

Added costs of services:

For LD	No
For ADHD	No
For ASD	No
LD specialists	Yes
ADHD & ASD coaching	No
ASD specialists	Yes
Professional tutors	No
Peer tutors	Yes
Max. hours/week for services	Varies
How professors are notified of student approved accommodations	Student

COLLEGE GRADUATION REQUIREMENTS

Course waivers allowed	No
Course substitutions allowed	Yes
In what courses: Case-by-case basis	

Main Hall and Cragmor Hall are buildings from the 1905 Cragmor Sanitarium, a "luxurious palace for well-to-do consumptives." UC assumed custody of the buildings for $1 in 1964. In the 1880s, sheep grazed on the campus bluffs, and 30 sites used by Plains Indians from approximately 100–1400 A.D. have been identified on campus.

PROGRAMS/SERVICES FOR STUDENTS WITH LEARNING DIFFERENCES

Disability Services provides students with disabilities reasonable accommodations for classroom and online learning, including assistive technology, assistive listening services, a peer notetaker program, and testing accommodations. Students initiate the process by completing an online application for accommodations, providing documentation of their disability, and scheduling a meeting with Disability Services for an Intake interview. Once registration and accommodations have been determined, students use the Disability Services portal, Accommodate, to send accommodation letters to faculty for each course. The Office of Inclusive Services at UCCS provides students with intellectual disabilities the support to access academic, career, and social activities on campus. Inclusive Services students receive individualized services from trained mentors, peer volunteers, and faculty to meet their learning needs. Students take two to three courses, set goals, develop their path to their career choice, and participate in internships. They also join clubs and participate in campus activities, create a personal portfolio, develop opportunities for off-campus employment, and receive a nationally recognized certificate. The program is tuition-based.

ADMISSIONS

All applicants are expected to meet the same general admission criteria, but minimum GPA requirements vary based on the college selected within the university. The university is test-optional if students meet the GPA requirement of the college to which they are applying. For admission, the review committee considers high school GPA, academic course rigor, ACT or SAT scores if submitted, extracurricular activities including internships, work, and sports, and an explanation of extenuating circumstances or any information unique to an individual's situation. The mid-50 percent GPA range of students admitted to UCCS is 3.13–3.90.

Additional Information

The Office of First-Year Experience assists students through their first year at UCCS with their academic and personal goals by offering a variety of interactive online workshops, including the popular "Study Smarter Not Harder." The workshops help students find effective and efficient ways to manage their time and discuss best practices for studying and retaining information. Students have access to five Excel Centers for Academic Excellence that focus on communication, languages, science, math, and writing. The centers provide tutoring and academic support with a variety of free tutoring and extra instruction for specific courses. The UCCS Gallogly Recreation and Wellness Center offers health and mental health services to all actively enrolled students. Professional staff and student volunteers coordinate inclusive and socially aware cross-departmental events, workshops, presentations, and one-on-one conversations on various topics, including mental health, stress management, body image, eating disorders, sleep, nutrition, and healthy relationships.

University of Colorado at Colorado Springs

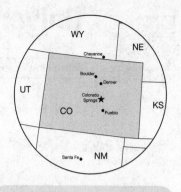

GENERAL ADMISSIONS

Very important factors include: rigor of secondary school record, class rank, academic GPA, standardized test scores (if submitted). *Other factors considered include:* application essay, recommendations. High school diploma is required and GED is accepted. Institution is test-optional for entering Fall 2024. Check admissions website for updates. *Academic units required:* 4 English, 4 math, 3 science (2 labs), 1 foreign language, 3 social studies, 2 academic electives.

FINANCIAL AID

Students should submit: FAFSA. *Need-based scholarships/grants offered:* College/university scholarship or grant aid from institutional funds; Federal Pell; Private scholarships; SEOG; State scholarships/grants. *Loan aid offered:* Direct PLUS loans; Direct Subsidized Loans; Direct Unsubsidized Loans. Federal Work-Study Program available. Institutional employment available.

CAMPUS LIFE

Activities: Choral groups; Dance; Drama/theater; International Student Organization; Literary magazine; Pep band; Radio station; Student government; Student newspaper; Television station. **Organizations:** 55 registered organizations, 4 honor societies, 7 religious organizations, 0 fraternities, 1 sororities. **Athletics (Intercollegiate):** *Men:* basketball, cross-country, golf, track/field (indoor). *Women:* basketball, cross-country, golf, softball, track/field (indoor), volleyball.

CAMPUS
Type of school	Public
Environment	Metropolis

STUDENTS
Undergrad enrollment	8,868
% male/female	47/53
% from out of state	11
% frosh live on campus	48

FINANCIAL FACTS
Annual in-state tuition	$9,129
Out-of-state tuition	$22,041
Room and board	$11,400

GENERAL ADMISSIONS INFO
Application fee	$50
Regular application deadline	Rolling
Nonfall registration	Yes

Fall 2024 testing policy	Test Optional
Range SAT EBRW	470–590
Range SAT Math	472–600
Range ACT Composite	21–25

ACADEMICS
Student/faculty ratio	17:1
% students returning for sophomore year	71

Most classes have 10–19 students.

REQUESTING SERVICES FOR STUDENTS WITH LEARNING DIFFERENCES

Phone: 719-255-3653 • disability.uccs.edu • Email: dservice@uccs.edu

Documentation submitted to: Disability Services
Separate application required for Services: Yes

Documentation required for:
 LD: Psychoeducational evaluation
 ADHD: Psychoeducational evaluation
 ASD: Psychoeducational evaluation

University of Denver

Office of Admission, Denver, CO 80208 • Admissions: 303-871-2036 • www.du.edu

Support: SP

ACCOMMODATIONS

Allowed in exams:	
Calculators	Yes
Dictionary	Yes
Computer	Yes
Spell-checker	Yes
Extended test time	Yes
Scribe	Yes
Proctors	Yes
Oral exams	Yes
Note-takers	Yes
Support services for students with:	
LD	Yes
ADHD	Yes
ASD	Yes
Distraction-reduced environment	Yes
Recording of lecture allowed	Yes
Reading technology	Yes
Audio books	Yes
Other assistive technology	Yes
Priority registration	Yes
Added costs of services:	
For LD	Yes
For ADHD	Yes
For ASD	Yes
LD specialists	Yes
ADHD & ASD coaching	No
ASD specialists	Yes
Professional tutors	Yes
Peer tutors	No
Max. hours/week for services	Varies
How professors are notified of student approved accommodations	Student

COLLEGE GRADUATION REQUIREMENTS

Course waivers allowed	No
Course substitutions allowed	Yes
In what courses: Foreign Language	

PROGRAMS/SERVICES FOR STUDENTS WITH LEARNING DIFFERENCES

The Disability Services Program (DSP) helps students with disabilities participate in courses, programs, and activities. Students are responsible for initiating contact with the DSP office by submitting an online request for accommodations along with the appropriate supporting documentation. Once accommodations have been approved by the DSP specialist, students receive their eligibility notification and a list of all accommodations that have been approved. Students are referred to the DSP Student Handbook for information on the process and procedure for using approved accommodations. Accommodations may include, but are not limited to, early registration, alternate-format texts and materials, audio recordings, peer notetakers, test accommodations, and referrals to other services and programs. The Learning Effectiveness Program (LEP) provides academic resources and individualized support to neurodiverse learners, students with diagnosed learning differences, ADHD, and students on the autism spectrum. Students enrolled in LEP receive college transition support, academic counseling, tutoring services, executive function support, and social skills support. The LEP is a student-directed program, meaning students are expected to take the lead in using the resources and support available through the LEP. There is a fee associated with the program.

ADMISSIONS

All applicants are expected to meet the same admission criteria. The admissions review committee considers a student's academic performance in high school the most important factor for admission. DU does not have a minimum GPA requirement for admission. The review committee also considers personal essays, letters of recommendation, extracurricular activities, contributions to the school and community, and taking on new challenges outside the classroom as important factors of the decision-making process.

Additional Information

DU offers support services to help students complete courses and stay on track toward graduation. Support services, offered by appointment, drop in, and online, include academic advising, academic coaching, help from the Math Learning Center and the Writing Center, science and engineering tutoring, support for online courses, technology and IT support, a laptop loaner program, a range of free software, use of the Career Center and the Health and Counseling Center, and many other services.

DID YOU KNOW?

The DU Rose is a special variety known as "Rosa Denvera." Ira Cutler, a botanist who received a master of arts degree from DU in 1907 and served as a faculty member for over 30 years, received a rose bush as a gift in 1912 from DU. Discovering the blossoms were unlike any other, he propagated the rose and planted them around campus; the red and yellow Rosa Denvera is now the DU Rose.

University of Denver

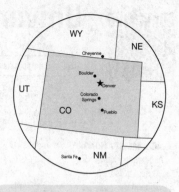

GENERAL ADMISSIONS

Very important factors include: rigor of secondary school record, academic GPA. *Important factors include:* standardized test scores (if submitted), application essay, recommendations. High school diploma is required and GED is accepted. Institution is test-optional for entering Fall 2024. Check admissions website for updates. *Academic units recommended:* 4 English, 4 math, 4 science (2 labs), 4 foreign language, 4 social studies.

FINANCIAL AID

Students should submit: CSS/Financial Aid Profile; FAFSA; Noncustodial Profile. *Need-based scholarships/grants offered:* College/university scholarship or grant aid from institutional funds; Federal Pell; Private scholarships; SEOG; State scholarships/grants. *Loan aid offered:* Direct PLUS loans; Direct Subsidized Loans; Direct Unsubsidized Loans. Federal Work-Study Program available. Institutional employment available.

CAMPUS LIFE

Activities: Campus Ministries; Choral groups; Concert band; Dance; Drama/theater; International Student Organization; Jazz band; Literary magazine; Marching band; Model UN; Music ensembles; Musical theater; Opera; Pep band; Radio station; Student government; Student newspaper; Student-run film society; Symphony orchestra; Television station. **Organizations:** 110 registered organizations, 7 fraternities, 7 sororities. **Athletics (Intercollegiate):** *Men:* baseball, basketball, crew/rowing, cycling, golf, gymnastics, ice hockey, lacrosse, martial arts, rugby, skiing (nordic/cross-country), swimming, ultimate frisbee, volleyball, water polo. *Women:* basketball, crew/rowing, cycling, field hockey, golf, gymnastics, ice hockey, lacrosse, martial arts, rugby, skiing (nordic/cross-country), swimming, ultimate frisbee, volleyball, water polo.

CAMPUS

Type of school	Private (nonprofit)
Environment	Metropolis

STUDENTS

Undergrad enrollment	5,987
% male/female	45/55
% from out of state	70
% frosh live on campus	95

FINANCIAL FACTS

Annual tuition	$58,032
Room and board	$17,049
Required fees	$1,179

GENERAL ADMISSIONS INFO

Application fee	$65
Regular application deadline	1/15
Nonfall registration	Yes

Fall 2024 testing policy	Test Optional
Range SAT EBRW	620–710
Range SAT Math	600–690
Range ACT Composite	28–32

ACADEMICS

Student/faculty ratio	8:1
% students returning for sophomore year	88

Most classes have 10–19 students.

REQUESTING SERVICES FOR STUDENTS WITH LEARNING DIFFERENCES

Phone: 303-871-2372 • studentaffairs.du.edu/disability-services-program • Email: dsp@du.edu

Documentation submitted to: Disability Services Program
Separate application required for Services: Yes

Documentation required for:
LD: Psychoeducational evaluation
ADHD: Psychoeducational evaluation
ASD: Psychoeducational evaluation

University of Northern Colorado

UNC Admissions, Greeley, CO 80639 • Admissions: 970-351-2881 • www.unco.edu

Support: S

ACCOMMODATIONS

Allowed in exams:

Calculators	Yes
Dictionary	Yes
Computer	Yes
Spell-checker	Yes
Extended test time	Yes
Scribe	Yes
Proctors	Yes
Oral exams	Yes
Note-takers	Yes

Support services for students with:

LD	Yes
ADHD	Yes
ASD	Yes
Distraction-reduced environment	Yes
Recording of lecture allowed	Yes
Reading technology	Yes
Audio books	Yes
Other assistive technology	Yes
Priority registration	Yes

Added costs of services:

For LD	No
For ADHD	No
For ASD	No
LD specialists	No
ADHD & ASD coaching	No
ASD specialists	No
Professional tutors	No
Peer tutors	Yes
Max. hours/week for services	Varies
How professors are notified of student approved accommodations	Student and Disability Resource Center

COLLEGE GRADUATION REQUIREMENTS

Course waivers allowed	No
Course substitutions allowed	No

PROGRAMS/SERVICES FOR STUDENTS WITH LEARNING DIFFERENCES

The University of Northern Colorado provides resources, education, and direct services through the Disability Resource Center (DRC). The DRC offers adaptive and assistive technologies, materials in alternative formats, notetakers, test accommodations, a reader program, and more. Services and accommodations are determined on the basis of the completed request for accommodations form, supporting documentation, and an interview with DRC. DRC can connect students without documentation to other resources on and off campus. The DRC also offers workshops on learning strategies, organizational skills, self-advocacy, study strategies, and time management.

ADMISSIONS

The admission process is the same for all students. Applicants are expected to have a minimum 2.5 GPA. Students applying to theater arts, dance, and music programs must submit additional materials. The School of Art and Design does not require an additional portfolio, but students are welcome to submit one for review.

Additional Information

The DRC identifies specific faculty members for the Faculty Ambassador Program to serve as liaisons between the DRC and academic programs.

In 1914, a graduate sent the school a Tlingit totem pole from Alaska. "Totem Teddy" became the symbol of UNC for 88 years, and athletic teams adopted a bear mascot after the carving at the top of the totem. In 2002, another alum recognized the totem in an 1890 photo at a museum in Sitka. It is still unclear whether a smallpox epidemic or profiteers brought the totem from Alaska, but by 2004, the totem was returned to its home with the Tlingit in Angoon. UNC now signals its bear pride with a bronze bear sculpture named Northern Vision.

University of Northern Colorado

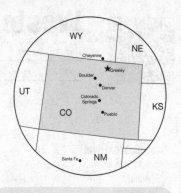

GENERAL ADMISSIONS

Very important factors include: academic GPA. *Important factors include:* rigor of secondary school record. *Other factors considered include:* class rank, standardized test scores (if submitted), application essay, recommendations. High school diploma is required and GED is accepted. Institution is test-optional for entering Fall 2024. Check admissions website for updates. *Academic units recommended:* 4 English, 4 math, 3 science (2 labs), 1 foreign language, 3 social studies, 2 academic electives.

FINANCIAL AID

Students should submit: FAFSA. *Need-based scholarships/grants offered:* College/university scholarship or grant aid from institutional funds; Federal Pell; Private scholarships; SEOG; State scholarships/grants. *Loan aid offered:* Direct PLUS loans; Direct Subsidized Loans; Direct Unsubsidized Loans. Federal Work-Study Program available. Institutional employment available.

CAMPUS LIFE

Activities: Campus Ministries; Choral groups; Concert band; Dance; Drama/theater; International Student Organization; Jazz band; Literary magazine; Marching band; Music ensembles; Musical theater; Opera; Student government; Student newspaper; Student-run film society; Symphony orchestra; Television station. **Organizations:** 97 registered organizations, 3 honor societies, 8 religious organizations, 9 fraternities, 13 sororities. **Athletics (Intercollegiate):** *Men:* baseball, basketball, cross-country, cycling, golf, ice hockey, lacrosse, martial arts, rugby, swimming, track/field (indoor), ultimate frisbee, volleyball, wrestling. *Women:* basketball, cross-country, cycling, golf, lacrosse, martial arts, rugby, softball, swimming, track/field (indoor), ultimate frisbee, volleyball.

CAMPUS
Type of school	Public
Environment	City

STUDENTS
Undergrad enrollment	6,681
% male/female	32/68
% from out of state	15
% frosh live on campus	85

FINANCIAL FACTS
Annual in-state tuition	$7,994
Annual out-of-state tuition	$20,066
Room and board	$11,684
Required fees	$2,430

GENERAL ADMISSIONS INFO
Application fee	$50
Regular application deadline	8/1
Nonfall registration	Yes

Fall 2024 testing policy	Test Optional
Range SAT EBRW	490–620
Range SAT Math	480–590
Range ACT Composite	19–27

ACADEMICS
Student/faculty ratio	14:1
% students returning for sophomore year	69

Most classes have 2–9 students.

REQUESTING SERVICES FOR STUDENTS WITH LEARNING DIFFERENCES

Phone: 970-351-2289 • go.unco.edu/drc • Email: DRC@unco.edu

Documentation submitted to: Disability Resource Center (DRC)
Separate application required for Services: Yes

Documentation required for:
LD: Psychoeducational evaluation
ADHD: Psychoeducational evaluation
ASD: Psychoeducational evaluation

Colorado

Western Colorado University

1 Western Way, Gunnison, CO 81231 • Admissions: 970-943-2119 • www.western.edu

Support: CS

ACCOMMODATIONS

Allowed in exams:

Calculators	Yes
Dictionary	Yes
Computer	Yes
Spell-checker	Yes
Extended test time	Yes
Scribe	Yes
Proctors	Yes
Oral exams	Yes
Note-takers	Yes

Support services for students with:

LD	No
ADHD	No
ASD	No
Distraction-reduced environment	Yes
Recording of lecture allowed	Yes
Reading technology	Yes
Audio books	Yes
Other assistive technology	Yes
Priority registration	Yes

Added costs of services:

For LD	No
For ADHD	No
For ASD	No
LD specialists	No
ADHD & ASD coaching	Yes
ASD specialists	Yes
Professional tutors	No
Peer tutors	Yes
Max. hours/week for services	Varies
How professors are notified of student approved accommodations	Disability Services

COLLEGE GRADUATION REQUIREMENTS

Course waivers allowed	No
Course substitutions allowed	No

PROGRAMS/SERVICES FOR STUDENTS WITH LEARNING DIFFERENCES

Disability Services coordinates support for all qualified students with disabilities. Students submit documentation online to be reviewed and once approved, there is an intake meeting to discuss accommodations. Then an accommodations plan is determined and sent to instructors. Disability Services offers a variety of resources and accommodations to assist students, including assistive technology such as eBooks, audiobooks, smart pens, and digital note-taking support. Testing accommodations may also be provided. Assistance and accommodations for housing and dining may also be available, including allowances for emotional support animals and meal plan modifications. While providing a supportive environment, Western State encourages students to develop independence and take responsibility for their academic experiences. Personal consultation and workshops are available to help students improve their learning, problem-solving, and self-advocacy skills.

ADMISSIONS

Admission to Western Colorado University depends on academic performance and background, standardized test scores if submitted, and personal attributes. In addition to general admission requirements, Western State recommends a personal essay and letter of recommendation from teachers or counselors. Applicants may also submit an essay on why they are applying to Western, a personal statement to explain specific information, and a résumé. Other factors used in admission decisions include the trend in grades, potential for success, leadership roles, volunteerism, and any situations impacting the student during high school. Academic preparation, however, is the key to admission. Interviews are not required.

Additional Information

There are no foreign language requirements at Western Colorado University, and students will be placed in the appropriate math class based on their ALEKS score. Western Colorado provides academic success advising, which includes test-taking and note-taking strategies. The Lamda Learning Center provides free peer-tutoring services for all math classes. There is also a Writing Center in the library, which offers Supplemental Instruction, including peer tutoring for traditionally difficult courses.

Western Mountain Rescue Team (WMRT), now under the jurisdiction of the Gunnison County Sheriff's Office, was initially established in 1967 by a group of Western students organizing a search for a missing professor. WMRT was the first college-based, nationally accredited Mountain Rescue Association team in the U.S. and has been MRA certified since 1987. Today, WMRT is a volunteer organization with a vast majority of members from Western's WMRT Club.

Western Colorado University

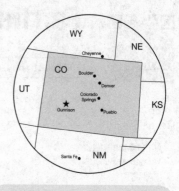

GENERAL ADMISSIONS

Very important factors include: rigor of secondary school record, academic GPA. *Important factors include:* application essay. *Other factors considered include:* class rank, standardized test scores (if submitted), recommendations. High school diploma is required and GED is accepted. Institution is test-optional for entering Fall 2024. Check admissions website for updates. *Academic units required:* 4 English, 4 math, 3 science, 1 foreign language, 3 social studies, 2 academic electives.

FINANCIAL AID

Students should submit: FAFSA. *Need-based scholarships/grants offered:* College/university scholarship or grant aid from institutional funds; Federal Pell; Private scholarships; SEOG; State scholarships/grants. *Loan aid offered:* Direct PLUS loans; Direct Subsidized Loans; Direct Unsubsidized Loans. Federal Work-Study Program available. Institutional employment available.

CAMPUS LIFE

Activities: Campus Ministries; Choral groups; Concert band; Dance; Drama/theater; International Student Organization; Jazz band; Literary magazine; Model UN; Music ensembles; Pep band; Radio station; Student government; Student newspaper; Symphony orchestra. **Organizations:** 60 registered organizations, 2 honor societies, 5 religious organizations, 0 fraternities, 0 sororities. **Athletics (Intercollegiate):** *Men:* baseball, basketball, cross-country, cycling, ice hockey, lacrosse, rugby, skiing (nordic/cross-country), track/field (indoor), volleyball, wrestling. *Women:* basketball, cross-country, cycling, ice hockey, rugby, skiing (nordic/cross-country), swimming, track/field (indoor), volleyball.

CAMPUS

Type of school	Public
Environment	Rural

STUDENTS

Undergrad enrollment	1,720
% male/female	59/41
% from out of state	28
% frosh live on campus	96

FINANCIAL FACTS

Annual in-state tuition	$6,816
Annual out-of-state tuition	$18,600
Room and board	$9,990
Required fees	$3,847

GENERAL ADMISSIONS INFO

Application fee	$30
Regular application deadline	Rolling
Nonfall registration	Yes

Fall 2024 testing policy	Test Optional
Range SAT EBRW	530–630
Range SAT Math	510–600
Range ACT Composite	21–25

ACADEMICS

Student/faculty ratio	18:1
% students returning for sophomore year	74

Most classes have 10–19 students.

REQUESTING SERVICES FOR STUDENTS WITH LEARNING DIFFERENCES

Phone: 970-943-7056 • western.edu/academics/academic-resource-center/disability-services
Email: disability@western.edu

Documentation submitted to: Disability Services
Separate application required for Services: Yes

Documentation required for:
 LD: Psychoeducational evaluation
 ADHD: Psychoeducational evaluation
 ASD: Psychoeducational evaluation

Fairfield University

1073 North Benson Road, Fairfield, CT 06824 • Admissions: 203-254-4100 • www.fairfield.edu

Support: S

PROGRAMS/SERVICES FOR STUDENTS WITH LEARNING DIFFERENCES

The Office of Accessibility (OA) at Fairfield University facilitates reasonable academic accommodations for students with disabilities. Students may request accommodations with OA by completing the online intake form on the Accessibility and Accommodations portal. Students are responsible for discussing exam arrangements and implementation with their instructors, and for confirming the arrangements for their accommodations in advance of the exams.

ADMISSIONS

All students must meet the same admission criteria for admission. The admission committee reviews each applicant's academic achievements and extracurricular activities. Most eligible applicants have earned A-/B+ grades in a college prep curriculum. The middle 50 percent of students who submitted test results scored 27–31 on the ACT or 1240–1370 on the SAT. Applicants who do not wish to submit test scores are encouraged to schedule an interview. Fairfield seeks students who embrace the Jesuit Catholic mission and vision of the school.

Additional Information

The Office of Academic Support and Retention provides academic skills training and peer tutoring services, which extend to the math and writing centers.

ACCOMMODATIONS

Allowed in exams:

Calculators	Yes
Dictionary	No
Computer	Yes
Spell-checker	Yes
Extended test time	Yes
Scribe	Yes
Proctors	Yes
Oral exams	Yes
Note-takers	Yes

Support services for students with:

LD	No
ADHD	No
ASD	No
Distraction-reduced environment	Yes
Recording of lecture allowed	Yes
Reading technology	Yes
Audio books	Yes
Other assistive technology	Yes
Priority registration	Yes

Added costs of services:

For LD	No
For ADHD	No
For ASD	No
LD specialists	No
ADHD & ASD coaching	No
ASD specialists	No
Professional tutors	No
Peer tutors	Yes
Max. hours/week for services	4
How professors are notified of student approved accommodations	Student

COLLEGE GRADUATION REQUIREMENTS

Course waivers allowed	Yes

In what courses: Foreign Language and Math

Course substitutions allowed	Yes

In what courses: Foreign Language and Math

Spectators flock to the Rec Complex pool for the annual Walk On Water competition, where first-year engineering students design, build, and race contraptions that allow them to "walk on water," using only a budget of $100 and lessons learned from their Fundamentals of Engineering course.

Fairfield University

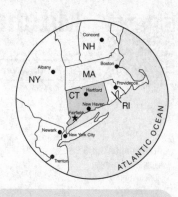

General Admissions

Very important factors include: rigor of secondary school record, academic GPA, application essay, recommendations. *Other factors considered include:* class rank, standardized test scores (if submitted). High school diploma is required and GED is accepted. Institution is test-optional for entering Fall 2024. Check admissions website for updates. *Academic units required:* 4 English, 3 math, 3 science (3 labs), 2 foreign language, 3 social studies. *Academic units recommended:* 4 math, 4 science (4 labs), 4 foreign language, 4 social studies.

Financial Aid

Students should submit: Business/Farm Supplement; CSS/Financial Aid Profile; FAFSA; Noncustodial Profile. *Need-based scholarships/grants offered:* College/university scholarship or grant aid from institutional funds; Federal Pell; SEOG; State scholarships/grants. *Loan aid offered:* Direct PLUS loans; Direct Subsidized Loans; Direct Unsubsidized Loans. Federal Work-Study Program available. Institutional employment available.

Campus Life

Activities: Campus Ministries; Choral groups; Concert band; Dance; Drama/theater; International Student Organization; Jazz band; Literary magazine; Model UN; Music ensembles; Musical theater; Pep band; Radio station; Student government; Student newspaper; Student-run film society; Symphony orchestra; Television station; Yearbook. **Organizations:** 94 registered organizations, 21 honor societies, 25 religious organizations, 0 fraternities, 0 sororities. **Athletics (Intercollegiate):** *Men:* baseball, basketball, crew/rowing, cross-country, equestrian sports, field hockey, golf, ice hockey, lacrosse, martial arts, rugby, swimming, ultimate frisbee, volleyball, wrestling. *Women:* basketball, crew/rowing, cross-country, equestrian sports, field hockey, golf, lacrosse, martial arts, rugby, softball, swimming, ultimate frisbee, volleyball, wrestling.

CAMPUS

Type of school	Private (nonprofit)
Environment	Town

STUDENTS

Undergrad enrollment	4,706
% male/female	42/58
% from out of state	81
% frosh live on campus	96

FINANCIAL FACTS

Annual tuition	$53,630
Room and board	$16,750
Required fees	$825

GENERAL ADMISSIONS INFO

Application fee	$60
Regular application deadline	1/15
Nonfall registration	Yes

Fall 2024 testing policy	Test Optional
Range SAT EBRW	620–680
Range SAT Math	620–690
Range ACT Composite	28–31

ACADEMICS

Student/faculty ratio	12:1
% students returning for sophomore year	91

Most classes have 20–29 students.

REQUESTING SERVICES FOR STUDENTS WITH LEARNING DIFFERENCES

Phone: 203-254-4000 ext.2615 • www.fairfield.edu/undergraduate/academics/resources/academic-commons/accessibility • Email: OOA@fairfield.edu

Documentation submitted to: The Office of Accessibility
Separate application required for Services: Yes

Documentation required for:
LD: Psychoeducational evaluation
ADHD: Psychoeducational evaluation
ASD: Psychoeducational evaluation

Mitchell College

437 Pequot Avenue, New London, CT 06320 • Admissions: 860-701-5011 • www.mitchell.edu

Support: SP

ACCOMMODATIONS

Allowed in exams:

Calculators	Yes
Dictionary	Yes
Computer	Yes
Spell-checker	Yes
Extended test time	Yes
Scribe	Yes
Proctors	Yes
Oral exams	Yes
Note-takers	Yes

Support services for students with:

LD	Yes
ADHD	Yes
ASD	Yes
Distraction-reduced environment	Yes
Recording of lecture allowed	Yes
Reading technology	Yes
Audio books	Yes
Other assistive technology	Yes
Priority registration	Yes

Added costs of services:

For LD	Yes
For ADHD	Yes
For ASD	Yes
LD specialists	Yes
ADHD & ASD coaching	Yes
ASD specialists	No
Professional tutors	Yes
Peer tutors	No
Max. hours/week for services	Varies
How professors are notified of student approved accommodations	Student

COLLEGE GRADUATION REQUIREMENTS

Course waivers allowed	No
Course substitutions allowed	Yes
In what courses: Case-by-case basis	

PROGRAMS/SERVICES FOR STUDENTS WITH LEARNING DIFFERENCES

The Accessibility Services (AS) office provides support to students with disabilities. To apply for services, students submit a request form and documentation and meet with Accessibility Services to determine specific needs. The Bentsen Learning Center (BLC) comprehensive program assists students with diagnosed learning differences and ADHD in developing study and self-advocacy strategies. This fee-based academic support program continually assesses students' progress in developing academic skills in self-advocacy, time management, organization, comprehension, writing, research, study skills, and test prep. BLC offers three tiers of academic support: Comprehensive, Enhanced, and Transition. Students begin in the Comprehensive Strategic Learning Tier or Enhanced Strategic Learning Tier, which provides the maximum time to develop and practice new strategies. As students demonstrate independence, they move to the Transition tier with fewer support sessions. Thames at Mitchell College is a residential transition program that helps students with learning differences increase self-confidence, improve study skills and executive function, and strengthen academic preparedness while earning up to 15 college credits over two semesters. This fee-based program offers a full year of academic preparation that students take between the end of high school and beginning of college. Mitchell also offers the Mystic Program—a fee-based program for first-year students that focuses on self-awareness, responsible decision-making, building relationships, social awareness, and self-management. Students who are admitted to the college and need an additional year of development typically benefit from the Mystic Program.

ADMISSIONS

Mitchell College follows a rolling admission policy. Applications will be reviewed as they become complete. Students can use the Common App or the Unique Minds application for both regular admission to Mitchell and admission to the Thames program. To apply for Thames, students submit a copy of their most recent IEP or 504 Plan, high school transcripts, one letter of recommendation, a comprehensive diagnostic assessment, and a parent statement.

Additional Information

The Tutoring Center offers free tutoring to all Mitchell College students in subjects across the curriculum. All of the tutors in Mitchell's Tutoring Center are trained professionals with advanced degrees.

Dale Earnhardt Jr. is one of the most popular race car drivers in the world. For most of his NASCAR career, he drove the #8 and the #88 cars. He earned his associate degree in automotive technology at Mitchell Community College and serviced cars in his dad's dealership before he began racing.

Mitchell College

GENERAL ADMISSIONS

Very important factors include: academic GPA. *Important factors include:* rigor of secondary school record, application essay, recommendations. *Other factors considered include:* standardized test scores (if submitted). High school diploma is required and GED is accepted. Institution is test-optional for entering Fall 2024. Check admissions website for updates. *Academic units recommended:* 4 English, 3 math, 3 science, 2 social studies, 2 history, 2 academic electives.

FINANCIAL AID

Students should submit: FAFSA. *Need-based scholarships/grants offered:* College/university scholarship or grant aid from institutional funds; Federal Pell; Private scholarships; SEOG; State scholarships/grants. *Loan aid offered:* Direct PLUS loans; Direct Subsidized Loans; Direct Unsubsidized Loans. Federal Work-Study Program available. Institutional employment available.

CAMPUS LIFE

Activities: Dance; Drama/theater; Radio station; Student government. **Organizations:** 30 registered organizations, 8 honor societies. **Athletics (Intercollegiate):** *Men:* baseball, basketball, cross-country, golf, lacrosse, wrestling. *Women:* basketball, cross-country, golf, softball, volleyball, wrestling.

CAMPUS

Type of school	Private (nonprofit)
Environment	Town

STUDENTS

Undergrad enrollment	526
% male/female	58/42
% from out of state	34
% frosh live on campus	80

FINANCIAL FACTS

Annual tuition	$36,050
Room and board	$15,540
Required fees	$3,000

GENERAL ADMISSIONS INFO

Application fee	$0
Regular application deadline	Rolling
Nonfall registration	Yes
Fall 2024 testing policy	Test Optional

ACADEMICS

Student/faculty ratio	13:1
% students returning for sophomore year	64

Most classes have 10–19 students.

Connecticut

REQUESTING SERVICES FOR STUDENTS WITH LEARNING DIFFERENCES

Phone: 860-701-5790 • mitchell.edu/access • Email: accessibility@mitchell.edu

Documentation submitted to: Accessibility Services
Separate application required for Services: Yes

Documentation required for:
LD: Psychoeducational evaluation
ADHD: Psychoeducational evaluation
ASD: Psychoeducational evaluation

Southern Connecticut State University

SCSU-Admissions House, New Haven, CT 06515-1202 • Admissions: 203-392-5644 • www.southernct.edu

Support: CS

ACCOMMODATIONS

Allowed in exams:

Calculators	Yes
Dictionary	Yes
Computer	Yes
Spell-checker	Yes
Extended test time	Yes
Scribe	Yes
Proctors	Yes
Oral exams	Yes
Note-takers	Yes

Support services for students with:

LD	Yes
ADHD	Yes
ASD	Yes
Distraction-reduced environment	Yes
Recording of lecture allowed	Yes
Reading technology	Yes
Audio books	Yes
Other assistive technology	Yes
Priority registration	Yes

Added costs of services:

For LD	No
For ADHD	No
For ASD	No
LD specialists	Yes
ADHD & ASD coaching	Yes
ASD specialists	Yes
Professional tutors	Yes
Peer tutors	Yes
Max. hours/week for services	Varies
How professors are notified of student approved accommodations	Student

COLLEGE GRADUATION REQUIREMENTS

Course waivers allowed	No
Course substitutions allowed	Yes
In what courses: Foreign Language	

PROGRAMS/SERVICES FOR STUDENTS WITH LEARNING DIFFERENCES

The Center for Academic Success and Accessibility Services (CASAS) provides accommodations for students with documented disabilities. Once students have enrolled and registered for classes, they are eligible to request accommodations by providing documentation along with a completed intake form. They then meet with Accessibility Services staff to discuss and determine appropriate accommodations. Once accommodations are approved, students can access an online portal for an official letter to share with course instructors each semester. Available accommodations include access to assistive computer technology and alternate-format course material, testing accommodations and auxiliary aids, readers, notetakers, and guided referrals to services and resources on campus, in the community, and the state.

ADMISSIONS

All applicants are expected to meet the same general admission requirements. A strong candidate will have a minimum cumulative GPA of 2.7 and a class rank in the top 50 percent of their graduating class. Applicants are required to submit an official copy of their high school transcript or high school equivalency diploma. A personal essay is required. SCSU does not require letters of recommendation or an interview but may request them for additional information, or to clarify details on application materials if a student appeals denial.

Additional Information

CASAS offers academic support to all students. Academic and writing specialists are available for tutoring by appointment, in-person, or virtually, for 30- or 60-minute sessions. Math tutoring is also offered on a drop-in basis during peak times in the CASAS Math Zone. Tutoring for higher-level scientific writing is available to students for assistance with lab reports and papers. CASAS offers peer-led, weekly one-hour study groups in challenging courses each semester. Any student enrolled in one of the courses can attend that study group. CASAS also offers PALS (Peer Academic Leaders), a non-remedial approach to learning that helps students integrate *what* to learn with *how* to learn. PALS embeds students in each section of certain courses to act as peer leaders who work to facilitate peer-to-peer interaction in small groups.

The Multicultural Center sponsors many events like the Chinese Mid-Autumn Festival with music and traditional eats, the Cultural Fest with worldwide foods, crafts, and performances, and the Heritage Ball to celebrate different cultures and heritages.

Southern Connecticut State University

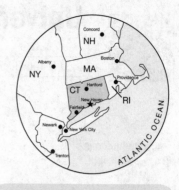

GENERAL ADMISSIONS

Very important factors include: rigor of secondary school record, academic GPA. *Important factors include:* class rank, standardized test scores (if submitted), application essay, recommendations. High school diploma is required and GED is accepted. Institution is test-optional for entering Fall 2024. Check admissions website for updates. *Academic units recommended:* 9 humanities, 9 STEM, 1 foreign language, 1 health.

FINANCIAL AID

Students should submit: FAFSA. *Need-based scholarships/grants offered:* College/university scholarship or grant aid from institutional funds; Federal Pell; SEOG; State scholarships/grants. *Loan aid offered:* Direct PLUS loans; Direct Subsidized Loans; Direct Unsubsidized Loans. Federal Work-Study Program available. Institutional employment available.

CAMPUS LIFE

Activities: Campus Ministries; Choral groups; Dance; Drama/theater; International Student Organization; Literary magazine; Music ensembles; Musical theater; Pep band; Radio station; Student government; Student newspaper; Television station; Yearbook. **Organizations:** 63 registered organizations, 12 honor societies, 4 religious organizations, 5 fraternities, 6 sororities. **Athletics (Intercollegiate):** *Men:* baseball, basketball, cross-country, golf, gymnastics, ice hockey, rugby, softball, swimming, track/field (indoor), volleyball, wrestling. *Women:* basketball, cross-country, field hockey, golf, gymnastics, rugby, softball, swimming, track/field (indoor), volleyball.

CAMPUS

Type of school	Public
Environment	Village

STUDENTS

Undergrad enrollment	8,525
% male/female	40/60
% from out of state	4
% frosh live on campus	62

FINANCIAL FACTS

Annual in-state tuition	$6,162
Out-of-state tuition	$18,436
Room and board	$13,666
Required fees	$5,720

GENERAL ADMISSIONS INFO

Application fee	$50
Regular application deadline	4/1
Nonfall registration	Yes

Fall 2024 testing policy	Test Optional
Range SAT EBRW	420–520
Range SAT Math	410–530
Range ACT Composite	17–22

ACADEMICS

Student/faculty ratio	12:1
% students returning for sophomore year	72

Most classes have 20–29 students.

REQUESTING SERVICES FOR STUDENTS WITH LEARNING DIFFERENCES

Phone: 203-392-6828 • www.southernct.edu/student-life/disability-resource-center
Email: DRC@southernct.edu

Documentation submitted to: Center for Academic Success and Accessibility Services
Separate application required for Services: Yes

Documentation required for:
 LD: Psychoeducational evaluation
 ADHD: Psychoeducational evaluation
 ASD: Psychoeducational evaluation

Connecticut

University of Connecticut

2131 Hillside Road, Storrs, CT 06268-3088 • Admissions: 860-486-3137 • www.uconn.edu

Support: SP

ACCOMMODATIONS

Allowed in exams:

Calculators	Yes
Dictionary	Yes
Computer	Yes
Spell-checker	Yes
Extended test time	Yes
Scribe	Yes
Proctors	Yes
Oral exams	Yes
Note-takers	Yes

Support services for students with:

LD	Yes
ADHD	Yes
ASD	Yes
Distraction-reduced environment	Yes
Recording of lecture allowed	Yes
Reading technology	Yes
Audio books	Yes
Other assistive technology	Yes
Priority registration	Yes

Added costs of services:

For LD	Yes
For ADHD	Yes
For ASD	Yes
LD specialists	Yes
ADHD & ASD coaching	No
ASD specialists	No
Professional tutors	Yes
Peer tutors	Yes
Max. hours/week for services	Varies
How professors are notified of student approved accommodations	Student and CSD

COLLEGE GRADUATION REQUIREMENTS

Course waivers allowed	No
Course substitutions allowed	Yes
In what courses: Case-by-case basis	

PROGRAMS/SERVICES FOR STUDENTS WITH LEARNING DIFFERENCES

The Center for Students with Disabilities (CSD) ensures students with disabilities have equal access to programs, activities, and opportunities. Students must register online with the CSD and provide evidence of their disability. This can be self-reported or may include documentation from a professional. Students meet in person or virtually with a disability service professional (DSP) to discuss the request. A DSP will be assigned to the student to assist them throughout their time at UConn. Once approved, students can request accommodation letters for their professors. Accommodations may begin with priority registration and continue with assistive technology, alternate media, alternate assignments, attendance flexibility, exam accommodations, lab or discussion assistants, and note-taking. Beyond Access (BA) is a fee-based program geared toward students with disabilities. All students enrolled in BA work with their strategy instructor to create their own program and can choose what they want to be their focus or order of focus: academic support, personal growth, or career readiness. Each student meets weekly with their strategy instructor, and students with executive functioning challenges can meet two to three times a week if desired. Students are invited to BA group activities and have connections to campus partners for tutoring, career services, and more. Beyond Access's UConn GPS program gives first-year students an opportunity to move on campus early for a three-day workshop and activities to support student success.

ADMISSIONS

The Office of Undergraduate Admissions recalculates grade point averages for first-year applicants as a part of the review process. The final selection is based on a review of all academic and personal information provided. A personal essay is required and two letters of recommendation are optional.

Additional Information

UConn First Summer is a five-week summer program opportunity for all incoming first-year students who plan to begin in the fall semester. First Summer students live on campus, take two courses, and gain a strong start to coursework and the UConn experience. First Year Experience (FYE) programs offer 1 credit courses to help students transition to college, develop skills, explore, learn, and research in small 19-seat seminar sections. Through the Academic Support Center (ASC), academic advisors help students with course placement, majors, and career exploration. The ASC offers free walk-in tutoring for writing, language, economics, engineering, physics, and research help. The ASC also provides an extensive list of tools and resources for academic and nonacademic support.

DID YOU KNOW?

Many traditions, like the Horse Rush, the Rope Pull, and the Pied Piper Parade, are part of UConn's history. To start the Huskie journey, students can pick up or download the list of "81 Things to Do Before You Graduate." There are eighty-one items listed as a nod to the university's inception in 1881. The list, created by the UConn Student Alumni Association, is the bucket list for "how to be a student now and become a Huskie for life."

University of Connecticut

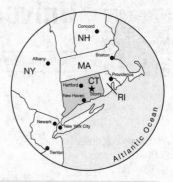

GENERAL ADMISSIONS
Very important factors include: rigor of secondary school record, class rank, academic GPA, standardized test scores (if submitted). *Important factors include:* application essay, recommendations. High school diploma is required and GED is accepted. Institution is test-optional for entering Fall 2024. Check admissions website for updates. *Academic units required:* 4 English, 3 math, 2 science (2 labs), 2 foreign language, 2 social studies, 3 academic electives. *Academic units recommended:* 3 foreign language.

FINANCIAL AID
Students should submit: FAFSA. *Need-based scholarships/grants offered:* College/university scholarship or grant aid from institutional funds; Federal Pell; Private scholarships; SEOG; State scholarships/grants. *Loan aid offered:* Direct PLUS loans; Direct Subsidized Loans; Direct Unsubsidized Loans. Federal Work-Study Program available. Institutional employment available.

CAMPUS LIFE
Activities: Campus Ministries; Choral groups; Concert band; Dance; Drama/theater; International Student Organization; Jazz band; Literary magazine; Marching band; Model UN; Music ensembles; Musical theater; Opera; Pep band; Radio station; Student government; Student newspaper; Student-run film society; Symphony orchestra; Television station; Yearbook. **Organizations:** 765 registered organizations, 23 honor societies, 30 religious organizations, 23 fraternities, 13 sororities. **Athletics (Intercollegiate):** *Men:* baseball, basketball, bowling, crew/rowing, cross-country, cycling, equestrian sports, field hockey, golf, ice hockey, lacrosse, martial arts, racquetball, rugby, swimming, track/field (indoor), ultimate frisbee, volleyball, water polo, wrestling. *Women:* basketball, bowling, crew/rowing, cross-country, cycling, equestrian sports, field hockey, gymnastics, ice hockey, lacrosse, martial arts, racquetball, rugby, softball, swimming, track/field (indoor), ultimate frisbee, volleyball, water polo.

CAMPUS

Type of school	Public
Environment	Town

STUDENTS

Undergrad enrollment	19,030
% male/female	50/50
% from out of state	22
% frosh live on campus	97

FINANCIAL FACTS

Annual in-state tuition	$13,798
Annual out-of-state tuition	$36,466
Room and board	$13,258
Required fees	$3,428

GENERAL ADMISSIONS INFO

Application fee	$80
Regular application deadline	1/15
Nonfall registration	Yes

Fall 2024 testing policy	Test Optional
Range SAT EBRW	600–680
Range SAT Math	610–710
Range ACT Composite	26–31

ACADEMICS

Student/faculty ratio	16:1
% students returning for sophomore year	92

Most classes have 10–19 students.

REQUESTING SERVICES FOR STUDENTS WITH LEARNING DIFFERENCES

Phone: 860-486-2020 • csd.uconn.edu • Email: csd@uconn.edu

Documentation submitted to: Center for Students with Disabilities
Separate application required for Services: Yes

Documentation required for:
LD: Psychoeducational evaluation
ADHD: Psychoeducational evaluation
ASD: Psychoeducational evaluation

University of Hartford

200 Bloomfield Avenue, West Hartford, CT 06117 • Admissions: 860-768-4296 • www.hartford.edu

Support: CS

ACCOMMODATIONS

Allowed in exams:

Calculators	Yes
Dictionary	Yes
Computer	Yes
Spell-checker	Yes
Extended test time	Yes
Scribe	Yes
Proctors	Yes
Oral exams	Yes
Note-takers	Yes

Support services for students with:

LD	Yes
ADHD	Yes
ASD	Yes
Distraction-reduced environment	Yes
Recording of lecture allowed	Yes
Reading technology	Yes
Audio books	Yes
Other assistive technology	Yes
Priority registration	Yes

Added costs of services:

For LD	No
For ADHD	No
For ASD	No
LD specialists	Yes
ADHD & ASD coaching	No
ASD specialists	No
Professional tutors	No
Peer tutors	Yes
Max. hours/week for services	Varies
How professors are notified of student approved accommodations	Student and AAS

COLLEGE GRADUATION REQUIREMENTS

Course waivers allowed	Yes

In what courses: Math and Foreign Language

Course substitutions allowed	Yes

In what courses: Math and Foreign Language

PROGRAMS/SERVICES FOR STUDENTS WITH LEARNING DIFFERENCES

Access-Ability Services (AAS) provides accommodations and services to students with disabilities. Documentation required by Access-Ability Services is separate from the admissions application. After registering and submitting documentation, students meet with an AAS staff member for an intake interview to discuss the student's disability, history, experience, requests, and any unique needs of each course and program. At the end of the meeting, the student will be advised of all approved accommodations, and AAS will send an accommodations letter to their professors. Students need to speak with their professors to activate accommodations. Students have the right to use or waive accommodations each semester. AAS academic coaches are available by appointment to meet with students weekly to help with organizational skills, stress management, note-taking for lectures and readings, test prep and test-taking, self-advocacy, and personal accountability.

ADMISSIONS

The Office of Admissions pays close attention to academic achievements, coursework, community service, and extracurricular activities in their review process. High school GPA and class rank are not required but are considered if recorded on the official high school transcript. A letter of recommendation from a teacher or counselor is required, and an interview is encouraged.

Additional Information

Hillyer College, one of UHart's seven schools and colleges, provides the first two years of a four-year undergraduate degree. Students admitted to Hillyer are able to pursue their major with the advantage of smaller class sizes, academic advisors who are also their professors, faculty mentors, courses tailored for different learning styles, a dedicated study center, a math lab, and a faculty-led writing center. The Center for Student Success (CSS) provides students with academic and personal guidance. The CSS offers support in study skills, health and wellness, technology resources, online learning, career exploration, internships, financial aid and scholarships, student clubs, activities, and reminders for important deadlines. The Tutoring Center offers free peer-to-peer content-based tutoring in most subject areas and writing tutors for students who want to improve their writing skills and strategies.

In 1959, Martin Luther King Jr. came to UHart as a speaker for a new lecture series. He began by recalling the summer of 1944 that he spent working in the nearby tobacco fields, and he delivered his famous speech, "The Future of Integration," based on the U.S. Supreme Court's ruling five years earlier that state laws of separate public schools for Black and white students were unconstitutional.

University of Hartford

GENERAL ADMISSIONS

Very important factors include: rigor of secondary school record. *Important factors include:* class rank, academic GPA, standardized test scores (if submitted). *Other factors considered include:* application essay, recommendations. High school diploma is required and GED is accepted. Institution is test-optional for entering Fall 2024. Check admissions website for updates. *Academic units required:* 4 English, 2 math, 2 science, 2 social studies, 4 academic electives. *Academic units recommended:* 3 math, 3 science, 2 foreign language.

FINANCIAL AID

Students should submit: FAFSA. *Need-based scholarships/grants offered:* College/university scholarship or grant aid from institutional funds; Federal Pell; Private scholarships; SEOG; State scholarships/grants. *Loan aid offered:* Direct PLUS loans; Direct Subsidized Loans; Direct Unsubsidized Loans.

CAMPUS LIFE

Activities: Campus Ministries; Choral groups; Concert band; Dance; Drama/theater; International Student Organization; Jazz band; Literary magazine; Music ensembles; Musical theater; Pep band; Radio station; Student government; Student newspaper; Student-run film society; Symphony orchestra; Television station; Yearbook. **Organizations:** 93 registered organizations, 22 honor societies, 7 religious organizations, 16 fraternities, 14 sororities. **Athletics (Intercollegiate):** *Men:* baseball, basketball, cross-country, cycling, golf, lacrosse, racquetball, rugby, track/field (indoor), volleyball. *Women:* basketball, cross-country, cycling, golf, racquetball, rugby, softball, track/field (indoor), volleyball.

CAMPUS

Type of school	Private (nonprofit)
Environment	Metropolis

STUDENTS

Undergrad enrollment	4,378
% male/female	46/54
% from out of state	48
% frosh live on campus	78

FINANCIAL FACTS

Annual tuition	$41,704
Room and board	$13,353
Required fees	$3,181

GENERAL ADMISSIONS INFO

Application fee	$35
Regular application deadline	Rolling
Nonfall registration	Yes

Fall 2024 testing policy	Test Optional
Range SAT EBRW	510–610
Range SAT Math	510–600
Range ACT Composite	22–29

ACADEMICS

Student/faculty ratio	8:1
% students returning for sophomore year	81

Most classes have 10–19 students.

REQUESTING SERVICES FOR STUDENTS WITH LEARNING DIFFERENCES

Phone: 860-768-4312 • www.hartford.edu/academics/academic-support/accessibility-services
Email: tlopez@hartford.edu

Documentation submitted to: Access-Ability Services
Separate application required for Services: Yes

Documentation required for:
LD: Psychoeducational evaluation
ADHD: Psychoeducational evaluation
ASD: Psychoeducational evaluation

University of New Haven

300 Boston Post Road, West Haven, CT 06516 • Admissions: 203-932-7000 • www.newhaven.edu

Support: S

ACCOMMODATIONS

Allowed in exams:	
Calculators	Yes
Dictionary	Yes
Computer	Yes
Spell-checker	Yes
Extended test time	Yes
Scribe	Yes
Proctors	Yes
Oral exams	No
Note-takers	Yes
Support services for students with:	
LD	Yes
ADHD	Yes
ASD	Yes
Distraction-reduced environment	Yes
Recording of lecture allowed	Yes
Reading technology	Yes
Audio books	Yes
Other assistive technology	Yes
Priority registration	No
Added costs of services:	
For LD	No
For ADHD	No
For ASD	No
LD specialists	No
ADHD & ASD coaching	No
ASD specialists	No
Professional tutors	No
Peer tutors	Yes
Max. hours/week for services	Varies
How professors are notified of student approved accommodations	Student

COLLEGE GRADUATION REQUIREMENTS

Course waivers allowed	No
Course substitutions allowed	Yes
In what courses: Case-by-case basis	

PROGRAMS/SERVICES FOR STUDENTS WITH LEARNING DIFFERENCES

The University of New Haven's Accessibility Resources Center (ARC) provides comprehensive support and a range of services that promote educational equity for students with learning differences. Some of the services coordinated through ARC include assistive technology, exam proctoring, notetakers, and learning assistants to assist with time and organization management, academic progress monitoring, and limited tutoring. ARC also facilitates special orientation programming for incoming students, as well as specific support for students diagnosed with nonverbal learning disabilities or who are on the autism spectrum. Registered students are strongly encouraged to participate in D.R.E.A.M. (Defeating Roadblocks in Education through Awareness and Mentoring), an early move-in orientation program for new students with disabilities. This program connects students with ARC as well as learning assistants and peers. More Than Access is a support program for students with autism, nonverbal learning disabilities, and pervasive developmental disorders. Students meet twice weekly with graduate staff and once weekly with professional staff who provide academic coaching and advising, assist with organization and time management, and help build communication and social skills. There is no fee for the More Than Access program, but space is limited.

ADMISSIONS

The University of New Haven is test-optional for all applicants except those applying to the forensic science major program or the honors college. Each applicant is assigned a personal admission counselor to aid during the application process. If applicants are using the Common Application, they will be required to answer the general essay prompt. Applicants who are applying Early Decision must have an interview. Foreign language courses are not required for admission. Students with learning disabilities may self-disclose if they feel that it would positively affect the admission decision. Students with conditional admits are limited to four classes for the first semester.

Additional Information

The Center for Learning Resources (CLR) offers free tutoring for all students, including students with disabilities. These tutors are available more than 60 hours a week and can help students in more than 30 different subject areas.

DID YOU KNOW?

Dr. Henry Lee retired in 2020 "...to enable the next generation of forensic science professors to step to the forefront." Dr. Lee joined UNH in 1975 and helped build the forensic science program from a small classroom with a single fingerprint kit into an internationally recognized academic program. He founded the Henry C. Lee Institute of Forensic Science and has assisted in the investigations of more than 8,000 criminal cases across the globe and continues to serve UHN as professor emeritus.

University of New Haven

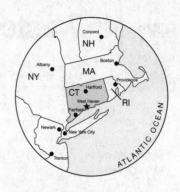

GENERAL ADMISSIONS

Very important factors include: academic GPA. *Important factors include:* application essay, recommendations. *Other factors considered include:* rigor of secondary school record, class rank, standardized test scores (if submitted). High school diploma is required and GED is accepted. Institution is test-optional for entering Fall 2024. Check admissions website for updates. *Academic units recommended:* 4 English, 3 math, 3 science (2 labs), 2 foreign language, 3 social studies.

FINANCIAL AID

Students should submit: FAFSA. *Need-based scholarships/grants offered:* College/university scholarship or grant aid from institutional funds; Federal Pell; Private scholarships; SEOG; State scholarships/grants. *Loan aid offered:* Direct PLUS loans; Direct Subsidized Loans; Direct Unsubsidized Loans. Federal Work-Study Program available. Institutional employment available.

CAMPUS LIFE

Activities: Campus Ministries; Dance; Drama/theater; International Student Organization; Marching band; Model UN; Music ensembles; Pep band; Radio station; Student government; Student newspaper; Television station; Yearbook. **Organizations:** 210 registered organizations. **Athletics (Intercollegiate):** *Men:* baseball, basketball, cross-country, field hockey, golf, gymnastics, ice hockey, lacrosse, rugby, swimming, track/field (indoor), ultimate frisbee, volleyball, wrestling. *Women:* basketball, cross-country, field hockey, golf, gymnastics, ice hockey, lacrosse, rugby, softball, swimming, track/field (indoor), ultimate frisbee, volleyball.

Connecticut

CAMPUS
Type of school	Private (nonprofit)
Environment	Town

STUDENTS
Undergrad enrollment	4,970
% male/female	44/56
% from out of state	57
% frosh live on campus	74

FINANCIAL FACTS
Annual tuition	$42,610
Room and board	$17,778
Required fees	$1,574

GENERAL ADMISSIONS INFO
Application fee	$50
Regular application deadline	3/1
Nonfall registration	Yes

Fall 2024 testing policy	Test Optional
Range SAT EBRW	560–650
Range SAT Math	550–630

ACADEMICS
Student/faculty ratio	16:1
% students returning for sophomore year	76

Most classes have 10–19 students.

REQUESTING SERVICES FOR STUDENTS WITH LEARNING DIFFERENCES

Phone: 203-932-7332 • newhaven.edu/student-life/diversity-inclusion/accessibility-resources-center
Email: ARC@newhaven.edu

Documentation submitted to: Accessibility Resources Center
Separate application required for Services: Yes

Documentation required for:
  LD: Psychoeducational evaluation
  ADHD: Psychoeducational evaluation
  ASD: Psychoeducational evaluation

Western Connecticut State University

Undergraduate Admissions Office, Danbury, CT 06810-6855 • Admissions: 203-837-9000 • www.wcsu.edu

Support: CS

ACCOMMODATIONS

Allowed in exams:

Calculators	Yes
Dictionary	Yes
Computer	Yes
Spell-checker	Yes
Extended test time	Yes
Scribe	Yes
Proctors	Yes
Oral exams	Yes
Note-takers	Yes

Support services for students with:

LD	Yes
ADHD	Yes
ASD	Yes
Distraction-reduced environment	Yes
Recording of lecture allowed	Yes
Reading technology	Yes
Audio books	Yes
Other assistive technology	Yes
Priority registration	Yes

Added costs of services:

For LD	No
For ADHD	No
For ASD	No
LD specialists	Yes
ADHD & ASD coaching	No
ASD specialists	No
Professional tutors	Yes
Peer tutors	Yes
Max. hours/week for services	Varies
How professors are notified of student approved accommodations	Student and AccessAbility

COLLEGE GRADUATION REQUIREMENTS

Course waivers allowed	Yes
In what courses: Case-by-case basis	
Course substitutions allowed	Yes
In what courses: Math and Foreign Language	

PROGRAMS/SERVICES FOR STUDENTS WITH LEARNING DIFFERENCES

AccessAbility Services (AAS) provides accommodations and support services to students with documented disabilities. Under the umbrella of Student Affairs, AAS collaborates with all departments within the university. AAS is proactive in providing institutional planning to ensure that the university meets the diverse needs of students. Each student who requests accommodations from AAS is considered on a case-by-case basis. The goal is to provide reasonable accommodations and services while supporting each student in developing the skills necessary to be independent learners. Students must request accommodation letters each semester; these are then emailed to the professors. Some of the services available include priority registration, tutoring, testing accommodations, advocacy, and counseling. Assistive technology includes, but is not limited to, smart pens, iPads, Read & Write, Kurzweil, Dragon, and Jaws. Academic Coaching and Educational Support (ACES) offers one-on-one academic coaching with professional learning specialists on a first-come, first-served basis; this is offered in the areas of time management, organization, study preparation, stress management, and academic strategies. Students are encouraged to schedule weekly or biweekly meetings at the beginning of the semester as space is limited. Substitutions for a foreign language are allowed, and math substitutions depend on the student's major.

ADMISSIONS

Students applying to Western Connecticut State should rank in the top third of their class and have at least a B average in the core academic courses. Western Connecticut State University is test-optional for students with at least a 3.0 GPA and a ranking in the top 35 percent of their class. The recommended minimum test scores are 1080 for the SAT and 21 for the ACT. If students choose not to submit test scores, the following must also be submitted: first quarter fourth-year grades, a résumé of activities, and/or two letters of recommendation. Students applying to the nursing department must submit SAT or ACT scores for consideration.

Additional Information

All students have access to free peer tutoring.

In 1995, the Jane Goodall Center for Excellence in Environmental Studies opened on campus as a partnership between WCSU and the Jane Goodall Institute. The center's focus is environmental stewardship, conservation, wildlife education, and research. The center offers events, programs, classes, and workshops; it also fosters service-learning projects for students in afterschool programs, animal shelters, environmental causes, nursing homes, and food pantries.

Western Connecticut State University

GENERAL ADMISSIONS

Very important factors include: rigor of secondary school record, standardized test scores (if submitted). *Important factors include:* class rank, academic GPA. *Other factors considered include:* application essay, recommendations. High school diploma is required and GED is accepted. Institution is test-optional for entering Fall 2024. Check admissions website for updates. *Academic units required:* 4 English, 3 math, 2 science (2 labs), 1 social studies, 1 U.S. history. *Academic units recommended:* 2 foreign language.

FINANCIAL AID

Students should submit: FAFSA; Institution's own financial aid form. *Need-based scholarships/grants offered:* College/university scholarship or grant aid from institutional funds; Federal Pell; Private scholarships; SEOG; State scholarships/grants. *Loan aid offered:* Direct PLUS loans; Direct Subsidized Loans; Direct Unsubsidized Loans. Federal Work-Study Program available. Institutional employment available.

CAMPUS LIFE

Activities: Campus Ministries; Choral groups; Concert band; Dance; Drama/theater; International Student Organization; Jazz band; Literary magazine; Music ensembles; Musical theater; Opera; Pep band; Radio station; Student government; Student newspaper; Symphony orchestra. **Organizations:** 79 registered organizations, 8 honor societies, 3 religious organizations, 3 fraternities, 4 sororities. **Athletics (Intercollegiate):** *Men:* baseball, basketball, cross-country, golf, ice hockey, lacrosse, rugby, swimming. *Women:* basketball, cross-country, field hockey, lacrosse, softball, swimming, volleyball.

CAMPUS

Type of school	Public
Environment	City

STUDENTS

Undergrad enrollment	4,451
% male/female	48/52
% from out of state	22
% frosh live on campus	47

FINANCIAL FACTS

Annual in-state tuition	$12,763
Annual out-of-state tuition	$16,095
Room and board	$15,131

GENERAL ADMISSIONS INFO

Application fee	$50
Regular application deadline	Rolling
Nonfall registration	Yes

Fall 2024 testing policy	Test Optional
Range SAT EBRW	510–610
Range SAT Math	510–590
Range ACT Composite	20–26

ACADEMICS

Student/faculty ratio	13:1
% students returning for sophomore year	76

Most classes have 20–29 students.

Connecticut

REQUESTING SERVICES FOR STUDENTS WITH LEARNING DIFFERENCES

Phone: 203-837-8225 • www.wcsu.edu/accessability • Email: aas@wcsu.edu

Documentation submitted to: AccessAbility Services
Separate application required for Services: Yes

Documentation required for:
 LD: Psychoeducational evaluation
 ADHD: Psychoeducational evaluation
 ASD: Psychoeducational evaluation

University of Delaware

Undergraduate Admissions., Newark, DE 19716 • Admissions: 302-831-8123 • www.udel.edu

(Support: CS)

ACCOMMODATIONS

Allowed in exams:

Calculators	Yes
Dictionary	No
Computer	Yes
Spell-checker	Yes
Extended test time	Yes
Scribe	Yes
Proctors	Yes
Oral exams	No
Note-takers	Yes

Support services for students with:

LD	Yes
ADHD	Yes
ASD	Yes
Distraction-reduced environment	Yes
Recording of lecture allowed	Yes
Reading technology	Yes
Audio books	Yes
Other assistive technology	Yes
Priority registration	Yes

Added costs of services:

For LD	No
For ADHD	No
For ASD	No
LD specialists	Yes
ADHD & ASD coaching	Yes
ASD specialists	No
Professional tutors	No
Peer tutors	Yes
Max. hours/week for services	Varies
How professors are notified of student approved accommodations	Student and DSS

COLLEGE GRADUATION REQUIREMENTS

Course waivers allowed	No
Course substitutions allowed	Yes
In what courses: Case-by-case basis	

PROGRAMS/SERVICES FOR STUDENTS WITH LEARNING DIFFERENCES

The Office of Disability Support Services (DSS) provides services for students with documented disabilities. Students should register with DSS once they accept admission to the university. Students will schedule a meeting with an accommodation coordinator to discuss their learning disability, past accommodations, and academic goals to decide reasonable accommodations. Accommodations include academic aids, alternate formats, assistive technology, note-taking, and test-taking accommodations. The Spectrum Scholars program is available to students with autism who want to develop and pursue their goals, increase self-awareness, and become effective self-advocates. Spectrum Scholars participate in weekly coaching, mentoring, workshops to build skills, progressive internships, and career development. Students not selected as Spectrum Scholars may still be eligible to receive group-based or other specialized support. The fee-based Career and Life Studies Certificate (CLSC) Program offers students with intellectual disabilities academic, career, and independent-living skills to help prepare for further education or employment. Students in this program will participate in classes, clubs, campus events, internships, and work experiences. Twelve students who have completed high school or are in their final year are selected for the program each year. These are students who want to step out of their comfort zone, continue their education, live independently, make new friendships, and prepare for careers.

ADMISSIONS

Applicants self-report academic records and GPAs with their application. Applicants who do not submit test scores may submit any additional evidence of academic skills in the area of their intended major. UD requires a school report from a high school counselor. Other letters of recommendation are not required but will be considered. Students conditionally admitted to UD are automatically registered in the Get Ready Program. This is a five-week summer session for students to receive close advising and tutoring while earning college credits for at least two online courses. Get Ready students arrive on campus one week early to meet their peers and participate in special orientation activities.

Additional Information

The Student Support Services Program (SSSP) adds to a student's university academic, cultural, and social experience with an assigned academic program coordinator. Students can take advantage of free individual and group tutoring, peer mentoring, free social and cultural programs, and lots of referrals. The Office of Academic Enrichment offers individual tutoring by appointment or drop-in, or students can add a tutor to their study groups.

UD's early history contains many years of tall tales and legends, reality and rumors: closure in 1777 with the British approaching, alumni signers of the Declaration of Independence, an 1843 lecture and antics of Edgar Allen Poe, starting and stopping female enrollment, a 0.01-watt nuclear reactor installed in the '50s, riots and fires, a secret society, the kissing arch, and the beloved Blue Hen. Fact or fiction, UD embraces all of its past.

University of Delaware

General Admissions
Very important factors include: rigor of secondary school record, academic GPA. *Important factors include:* standardized test scores (if submitted), application essay, recommendations. *Other factors considered include:* class rank. High school diploma is required and GED is accepted. Institution is test-optional for entering Fall 2024. Check admissions website for updates. *Academic units required:* 4 English, 3 math, 3 science (2 labs), 2 foreign language, 4 social studies, 2 academic electives. *Academic units recommended:* 4 math, 4 science (3 labs), 4 foreign language.

Financial Aid
Students should submit: FAFSA. *Need-based scholarships/grants offered:* College/university scholarship or grant aid from institutional funds; Federal Pell; Private scholarships; SEOG; State scholarships/grants. *Loan aid offered:* Direct PLUS loans; Direct Subsidized Loans; Direct Unsubsidized Loans. Federal Work-Study Program available. Institutional employment available.

Campus Life
Activities: Campus Ministries; Choral groups; Concert band; Dance; Drama/theater; International Student Organization; Jazz band; Literary magazine; Marching band; Model UN; Music ensembles; Musical theater; Opera; Pep band; Radio station; Student government; Student newspaper; Student-run film society; Symphony orchestra; Television station. **Organizations:** 350 registered organizations, 16 honor societies, 20 religious organizations, 24 fraternities, 19 sororities. **Athletics (Intercollegiate):** *Men:* baseball, basketball, bowling, crew/rowing, cross-country, cycling, equestrian sports, golf, ice hockey, lacrosse, rugby, swimming, track/field (indoor), ultimate frisbee, volleyball, water polo, wrestling. *Women:* basketball, bowling, crew/rowing, cross-country, cycling, equestrian sports, field hockey, golf, ice hockey, lacrosse, rugby, softball, swimming, track/field (indoor), ultimate frisbee, volleyball, water polo, wrestling.

CAMPUS

Type of school	Public
Environment	Town

STUDENTS

Undergrad enrollment	17,968
% male/female	41/59
% from out of state	62
% frosh live on campus	93

FINANCIAL FACTS

Annual in-state tuition	$13,370
Annual out-of-state tuition	$35,890
Room and board	$14,234
Required fees	$2,040

GENERAL ADMISSIONS INFO

Application fee	$75
Regular application deadline	1/15
Nonfall registration	Yes
Fall 2024 testing policy	Test Optional
Range SAT EBRW	590–670
Range SAT Math	580–680
Range ACT Composite	26–31

ACADEMICS

Student/faculty ratio	12:1
% students returning for sophomore year	92
Most classes have 20–29 students.	

Delaware

REQUESTING SERVICES FOR STUDENTS WITH LEARNING DIFFERENCES

Phone: 302-831-4643 • sites.udel.edu/dss • Email: dssoffice@udel.edu

Documentation submitted to: Disability Support Services
Separate application required for Services: Yes

Documentation required for:
LD: Psychoeducational evaluation
ADHD: Psychoeducational evaluation
ASD: Psychoeducational evaluation

American University

4400 Massachusetts Ave. NW, Washington, DC 20016 · Admissions: 202-885-6000 · american.edu

Support: SP

ACCOMMODATIONS

Allowed in exams:

Calculators	Yes
Dictionary	Yes
Computer	Yes
Spell-checker	Yes
Extended test time	Yes
Scribe	Yes
Proctors	Yes
Oral exams	Yes
Note-takers	Yes

Support services for students with:

LD	Yes
ADHD	Yes
ASD	Yes
Distraction-reduced environment	Yes
Recording of lecture allowed	Yes
Reading technology	Yes
Audio books	Yes
Other assistive technology	Yes
Priority registration	Yes

Added costs of services:

For LD	Yes
For ADHD	Yes
For ASD	Yes
LD specialists	Yes
ADHD & ASD coaching	Yes
ASD specialists	No
Professional tutors	No
Peer tutors	Yes
Max. hours/week for services	Varies
How professors are notified of student approved accommodations	Student

COLLEGE GRADUATION REQUIREMENTS

Course waivers allowed	No
Course substitutions allowed	No

PROGRAMS/SERVICES FOR STUDENTS WITH LEARNING DIFFERENCES

The Academic Support and Access Center (ASAC) serves students with disabilities. Students complete a questionnaire, submit documentation, and meet with their assigned disability access advisor to discuss their accommodation requests. Once determined, students receive an accommodation letter for the year stating the services that have been approved. Accommodations can include assistive technology, course material in an alternate format, ASL interpreters, accessible classrooms, alternatives to test taking, and housing accommodations. Also available to first-year students with learning disabilities is a Learning Services Program (LSP)—a one-year, one-time fee-based program to help students cope with the demands of college-level courses. Participants are assisted with course selection, registration, and developing new and more efficient study skills. LSP application materials must be submitted at the same time as the admission application.

ADMISSIONS

Academic performance is the most important factor in the review process. All applicants are expected to meet the same admission criteria. The admission committee also requires and looks closely at the personal essay, letters of recommendation, extracurricular activities, and midyear report and grades. Admission applications may also serve as applications for merit scholarships.

Additional Information

ASAC offers academic support and resources in individual and group settings. The Peer-Assisted Student Support (PASS) program offers free individual tutoring in courses such as accounting, biology, chemistry, finance, government, and psychology. The Supplemental Instruction (SI) Program has free, weekly small-group tutoring sessions geared toward students' needs. SI is a non-remedial approach to historically difficult courses combining *what to learn* with *how to learn*. The sessions are led by trained SI Leaders who consult with academic staff. The ASAC Writing Center is a resource for students to strengthen their writing skills and receive insight and feedback on their work.

At the 1963 American University's 49th Commencement, President John F. Kennedy called on the Soviet Union to work with the United States on a nuclear test ban treaty. The famous speech became known as "A Strategy of Peace."

American University

GENERAL ADMISSIONS

Very important factors include: rigor of secondary school record, academic GPA. *Important factors include:* application essay, recommendations. *Other factors considered include:* standardized test scores (if submitted). High school diploma is required and GED is accepted. Institution is test-optional for entering Fall 2024. Check admissions website for updates. *Academic units required:* 4 English, 3 math, 2 science (2 labs), 2 foreign language, 2 social studies, 3 academic electives. *Academic units recommended:* 4 math, 4 science, 3 foreign language, 4 social studies, 4 academic electives.

FINANCIAL AID

Students should submit: CSS/Financial Aid Profile; FAFSA. *Need-based scholarships/grants offered:* College/university scholarship or grant aid from institutional funds; Federal Pell; Private scholarships; SEOG; State scholarships/grants. *Loan aid offered:* Direct PLUS loans; Direct Subsidized Loans; Direct Unsubsidized Loans. Federal Work-Study Program available. Institutional employment available.

CAMPUS LIFE

Activities: Campus Ministries; Choral groups; Concert band; Dance; Drama/theater; International Student Organization; Jazz band; Literary magazine; Model UN; Music ensembles; Musical theater; Opera; Pep band; Radio station; Student government; Student newspaper; Student-run film society; Symphony orchestra; Television station; Yearbook. **Organizations:** 200 registered organizations. **Athletics (Intercollegiate):** *Men:* baseball, basketball, crew/rowing, cross-country, cycling, equestrian sports, field hockey, golf, gymnastics, ice hockey, lacrosse, rugby, swimming, track/field (indoor), ultimate frisbee, volleyball, wrestling. *Women:* basketball, crew/rowing, cross-country, cycling, equestrian sports, field hockey, golf, gymnastics, ice hockey, lacrosse, rugby, softball, swimming, track/field (indoor), ultimate frisbee, volleyball.

CAMPUS
Type of school	Private (nonprofit)
Environment	Metropolis

STUDENTS
Undergrad enrollment	7,669
% male/female	36/64
% from out of state	81

FINANCIAL FACTS
Annual tuition	$55,724
Room and board	$16,432
Required fees	$819

GENERAL ADMISSIONS INFO
Application fee	$75
Regular application deadline	1/15
Nonfall registration	Yes
Fall 2024 testing policy	Test Optional
Range SAT EBRW	660–730
Range SAT Math	630–700
Range ACT Composite	29–32

ACADEMICS
Student/faculty ratio	12:1
% students returning for sophomore year	86
Most classes have 10–19 students.	

District of Columbia

REQUESTING SERVICES FOR STUDENTS WITH LEARNING DIFFERENCES

Phone: 202-885-3360 • www.american.edu/ocl/asac/learning-services-program.cfm
Email: asac@american.edu

Documentation submitted to: Academic Support and Access Center
Separate application required for Services: Yes

Documentation required for:
LD: Psychoeducational evaluation
ADHD: Psychoeducational evaluation
ASD: Psychoeducational evaluation

The Catholic University of America

Undergraduate Admissions, Washington, DC 20064 • Admissions: 202-319-5305 • catholic.edu

Support: CS

ACCOMMODATIONS

Allowed in exams:

Calculators	Yes
Dictionary	N/A
Computer	Yes
Spell-checker	Yes
Extended test time	Yes
Scribe	Yes
Proctors	Yes
Oral exams	No
Note-takers	Yes

Support services for students with:

LD	Yes
ADHD	Yes
ASD	Yes
Distraction-reduced environment	Yes
Recording of lecture allowed	Yes
Reading technology	Yes
Audio books	Yes
Other assistive technology	Yes
Priority registration	Yes

Added costs of services:

For LD	No
For ADHD	No
For ASD	No
LD specialists	Yes
ADHD & ASD coaching	Yes
ASD specialists	Yes
Professional tutors	No
Peer tutors	Yes
Max. hours/week for services	Varies
How professors are notified of student approved accommodations	Student

COLLEGE GRADUATION REQUIREMENTS

Course waivers allowed	No
Course substitutions allowed	Yes
In what courses: Foreign Language and Math	

PROGRAMS/SERVICES FOR STUDENTS WITH LEARNING DIFFERENCES

The Catholic University of America provides programs and services for students with disabilities through the Office of Disability Support Services (DSS). Once admitted, students should contact DSS and request an intake packet. DSS reviews each student's application and documentation to determine appropriate accommodations and services. Students must complete a request form each semester to obtain an accommodations letter to give to their professors. DSS staff is available to answer questions concerning accommodations and available services, or offer information about admissions, registration, financial aid, and more. DSS promotes partnerships among faculty, students, and staff to ensure that students achieve independence and recognition for their abilities, not disabilities. Once they have enrolled, students with learning disabilities can apply for a math and/or foreign language substitution. Students who have documented disabilities are eligible to participate in Smart Start, an optional pre-orientation program offered by DSS that takes place before the annual new student orientation and allows students more time to transition to college life. Students may bring up to two additional individuals to this program. The 248 Model is a program created by DSS to provide students with the necessary skills to successfully transition to college life. All first-year students registered with DSS meet individually with a learning specialist three times during the first semester, in weeks 2, 4, and 8.

ADMISSIONS

All applicants are expected to meet the same admission criteria. Prospective students with disabilities are encouraged to write an additional personal statement but should not include any documentation of disabilities with their application. The university recommends that students take additional science and math courses if they are applying to the School of Engineering, School of Nursing, or departments of the physical sciences.

Additional Information

DSS staff ensures students have the necessary tools to address areas of difficulty, improve their academic and study skills, and make the most of their accommodations. Learning specialists help students achieve their goals by advising them on topics such as time management, organization, test-taking, note-taking, and stress management. Additionally, writing center consultants and tutors are available to work with students.

CUA was established in 1887 by U.S. bishops. On May 24, 1888, the cornerstone for Caldwell Hall was laid. President Grover Cleveland, members of Congress, and the U.S. Cabinet were in attendance. On March 7, 1889, Pope Leo XIII formally approved CUA statutes with his apostolic letter *Magni Nobis Gaudii.* Bishops remain on the board of trustees to this day. Bylaws stipulate that 24 of the 48 members must be of the cleric, with 18 from the bishop's conference.

The Catholic University of America

GENERAL ADMISSIONS

Very important factors include: rigor of secondary school record, academic GPA. *Important factors include:* application essay, recommendations. *Other factors considered include:* class rank. High school diploma is required and GED is accepted. Institution is test-free for entering Fall 2024. Check admissions website for updates. *Academic units recommended:* 4 English, 4 math, 3 science (2 labs), 2 foreign language, 4 social studies.

FINANCIAL AID

Students should submit: FAFSA; Noncustodial Profile. *Need-based scholarships/ grants offered:* College/university scholarship or grant aid from institutional funds; Federal Pell; Private scholarships; SEOG; State scholarships/grants. *Loan aid offered:* Direct PLUS loans; Direct Subsidized Loans; Direct Unsubsidized Loans. Federal Work-Study Program available. Institutional employment available.

CAMPUS LIFE

Activities: Campus Ministries; Choral groups; Concert band; Dance; Drama/theater; International Student Organization; Jazz band; Literary magazine; Model UN; Music ensembles; Musical theater; Opera; Radio station; Student government; Student newspaper; Student-run film society; Symphony orchestra. **Organizations:** 96 registered organizations, 16 honor societies, 10 religious organizations, 2 fraternities, 1 sororities. **Athletics (Intercollegiate):** *Men:* baseball, basketball, crew/rowing, cross-country, golf, ice hockey, lacrosse, rugby, swimming, track/field (indoor), ultimate frisbee. *Women:* basketball, crew/rowing, cross-country, field hockey, golf, lacrosse, rugby, softball, swimming, track/field (indoor), ultimate frisbee, volleyball.

CAMPUS
Type of school	Private (nonprofit)
Environment	Metropolis

STUDENTS
Undergrad enrollment	2,885
% male/female	44/56
% from out of state	95
% frosh live on campus	89

FINANCIAL FACTS
Annual tuition	$53,040
Room and board	$16,670
Required fees	$1,146

GENERAL ADMISSIONS INFO
Application fee	No fee
Regular application deadline	1/15
Nonfall registration	Yes
Fall 2024 testing policy	Test Free

ACADEMICS
Student/faculty ratio	10:1
% students returning for sophomore year	88

Most classes have 10–19 students.

District of Columbia

REQUESTING SERVICES FOR STUDENTS WITH LEARNING DIFFERENCES

Phone: 202-319-5211 • dss.catholic.edu • Email: cua-dss@cua.edu

Documentation submitted to: Office of Disability Support Services
Separate application required for Services: Yes

Documentation required for:
LD: Psychoeducational evaluation
ADHD: Psychoeducational evaluation
ASD: Psychoeducational evaluation

The George Washington University

800 21st Street NW Suite 100, Washington, DC 20052 • Admissions: 202-994-6040 • gwu.edu

Support: CS

ACCOMMODATIONS

Allowed in exams:

Calculators	Yes
Dictionary	Yes
Computer	Yes
Spell-checker	Yes
Extended test time	Yes
Scribe	Yes
Proctors	Yes
Oral exams	Yes
Note-takers	Yes

Support services for students with:

LD	Yes
ADHD	Yes
ASD	Yes
Distraction-reduced environment	Yes
Recording of lecture allowed	Yes
Reading technology	Yes
Audio books	Yes
Other assistive technology	Yes
Priority registration	Yes

Added costs of services:

For LD	No
For ADHD	No
For ASD	No
LD specialists	Yes
ADHD & ASD coaching	No
ASD specialists	No
Professional tutors	No
Peer tutors	No
Max. hours/week for services	Varies
How professors are notified of student approved accommodations	Student

COLLEGE GRADUATION REQUIREMENTS

Course waivers allowed	Yes
In what courses: Case-by-case basis	
Course substitutions allowed	Yes
In what courses: Case-by-case basis	

PROGRAMS/SERVICES FOR STUDENTS WITH LEARNING DIFFERENCES

Disability Support Services (DSS) at GW works collaboratively with students, faculty, and staff. Students seeking academic accommodations must complete the DSS registration form in SharePoint and provide documentation of a disability. Students then meet with a DSS representative via telephone, Zoom, or Webex to determine their eligibility for services. Once this registration process is complete, students receive an electronic eligibility letter and email detailing the steps required to secure accommodations in their classes. The eligibility letter outlines the student's approved accommodations and directs the student on how to request official letters of accommodation for their professors. Accommodations may include registration assistance, reading services, assistive technology, learning specialists, note-taking assistance, testing accommodations, and referrals.

ADMISSIONS

Admission to GW is competitive, and most admitted students are academically strong. GW takes a holistic approach to the application review process and has no minimum GPA requirements for admission. GW is test-optional for first-year and transfer applicants. GW does however require standardized test scores from students applying to the accelerated seven-year BA/MD program, recruited NCAA Division I athletes, students of home-schooling or online high schools, and graduates of secondary schools that provide narrative evaluations in lieu of grades.

Additional Information

Content tutoring is available on a fee basis from campus resources outside of DSS. Enrolled students who have not yet been identified with a learning disability or ADHD, but are interested in consulting a learning specialist, may do so at DSS.

The George Washington University

GENERAL ADMISSIONS

Very important factors include: rigor of secondary school record, academic GPA. *Important factors include:* application essay, recommendations. *Other factors considered include:* standardized test scores (if submitted). High school diploma is required and GED is accepted. Institution is test-optional for entering Fall 2024. Check admissions website for updates. *Academic units required:* 4 English, 2 math, 2 science (1 labs), 2 foreign language, 2 social studies. *Academic units recommended:* 4 English, 4 math, 4 science, 4 foreign language, 4 social studies.

FINANCIAL AID

Students should submit: CSS/Financial Aid Profile; FAFSA; Noncustodial Profile. *Need-based scholarships/grants offered:* College/university scholarship or grant aid from institutional funds; Federal Pell; SEOG; State scholarships/grants. *Loan aid offered:* Direct PLUS loans; Direct Subsidized Loans; Direct Unsubsidized Loans. Federal Work-Study Program available. Institutional employment available.

CAMPUS LIFE

Activities: Choral groups; Concert band; Dance; Drama/theater; International Student Organization; Jazz band; Literary magazine; Marching band; Model UN; Music ensembles; Musical theater; Pep band; Radio station; Student government; Student newspaper; Student-run film society; Symphony orchestra; Television station; Yearbook. **Organizations:** 220 registered organizations, 3 honor societies, 5 religious organizations, 12 fraternities, 9 sororities. **Athletics (Intercollegiate):** *Men:* baseball, basketball, crew/rowing, cross-country, golf, swimming, water polo. *Women:* basketball, crew/rowing, cross-country, gymnastics, lacrosse, softball, swimming, volleyball, water polo.

CAMPUS

Type of school	Private (nonprofit)
Environment	Metropolis

STUDENTS

Undergrad enrollment	10,929
% male/female	37/63
% from out of state	97
% frosh live on campus	97

FINANCIAL FACTS

Annual tuition	$59,780
Room and board	$18,000
Required fees	$90

GENERAL ADMISSIONS INFO

Application fee	$80
Regular application deadline	1/5
Nonfall registration	Yes

Fall 2024 testing policy	Test Optional
Range SAT EBRW	660–740
Range SAT Math	650–750
Range ACT Composite	30–34

ACADEMICS

Student/faculty ratio	13:1
% students returning for sophomore year	91

Most classes have 10–19 students.

District of Columbia

REQUESTING SERVICES FOR STUDENTS WITH LEARNING DIFFERENCES

Phone: 202-994-8250 • disabilitysupport.gwu.edu • Email: dss@gwu.edu

Documentation submitted to: Disability Support Services
Separate application required for Services: Yes

Documentation required for:
LD: Psychoeducational evaluation
ADHD: Psychoeducational evaluation
ASD: Psychoeducational evaluation

Barry University

11300 NE 2nd Avenue, Miami Shores, FL 33161-6695 • Admissions: 305-899-3100 • www.barry.edu

Support: SP

ACCOMMODATIONS

Allowed in exams:

Calculators	Yes
Dictionary	Yes
Computer	Yes
Spell-checker	Yes
Extended test time	Yes
Scribe	Yes
Proctors	Yes
Oral exams	Yes
Note-takers	Yes

Support services for students with:

LD	Yes
ADHD	Yes
ASD	Yes
Distraction-reduced environment	Yes
Recording of lecture allowed	Yes
Reading technology	Yes
Audio books	Yes
Other assistive technology	Yes
Priority registration	No

Added costs of services:

For LD	Yes
For ADHD	Yes
For ASD	Yes
LD specialists	Yes
ADHD & ASD coaching	Yes
ASD specialists	No
Professional tutors	Yes
Peer tutors	No
Max. hours/week for services	Varies
How professors are notified of student approved accommodations	Student and OAS

COLLEGE GRADUATION REQUIREMENTS

Course waivers allowed	No
Course substitutions allowed	Yes
In what courses: Case-by-case basis	

PROGRAMS/SERVICES FOR STUDENTS WITH LEARNING DIFFERENCES

The Office of Accessibility Services (OAS) ensures that students with disabilities receive reasonable accommodations. Students must submit a request and supporting documentation. Eligible students then meet with the OAS director to create an individual accommodation plan based on their specific disability and individual needs. Accommodations may include priority registration, textbooks in an alternate format, a reduced course load, course substitutions, notetakers, assistive technology software, extended time on exams, or alternative testing locations. The OAS is committed to assist students in obtaining the educational materials in the form they need and will offset any additional costs this incurs.

ADMISSIONS

All applicants must submit high school transcripts or the GED equivalent for general admission. A GPA above 2.3 may be considered for test-optional admission for most majors. Personal essays are optional, and letters of recommendation are not used. Applicants should have earned at least 18 units of college preparatory courses. All prospective students are encouraged to attend a Recruitment and Admissions Event or schedule a phone, online, or in-person campus visit. Some majors have specific requirements beyond that of general admission. Every student is considered for academic scholarships when they apply for admission.

Additional Information

The Center for Academic Success and Advising (CASA) includes academic advising for every first-year student, from individual academic success coaching and professional tutoring to financial aid counseling and connecting students to needed resources. The Glenn Hubert Learning Center (GHLC) has professional tutors available to support students in writing, math, and reading. GHLC conducts workshops and seminars on various writing topics throughout the year. GHLC professional tutors work 1:1 with students to help develop reading strategies and study techniques needed for college-level texts. The Math Lab has a reference library, handouts, computer software, video tapes, and tutors for additional support.

Held the day before graduation, the Rose and Candle Ceremony is one of the oldest student traditions. To symbolize the bonds of friendship that developed between students, graduating students give a candle, a symbol of knowledge and wisdom, to an undergraduate of their choice. In return, they receive a red rose, a symbol of love and friendship.

Barry University

GENERAL ADMISSIONS

Very important factors include: academic GPA, standardized test scores (if submitted). *Other factors considered include:* rigor of secondary school record, class rank, recommendations. High school diploma is required and GED is accepted. Institution is test-optional for entering Fall 2024. Check admissions website for updates. *Academic units recommended:* 4 English, 3 math, 3 science, 3 social studies, 2 foreign language, 3 academic electives.

FINANCIAL AID

Students should submit: FAFSA. *Need-based scholarships/grants offered:* College/university scholarship or grant aid from institutional funds; Federal Nursing Scholarships; Federal Pell; Private scholarships; SEOG; State scholarships/grants. *Loan aid offered:* Direct PLUS loans; Direct Subsidized Loans; Direct Unsubsidized Loans. Federal Work-Study Program available. Institutional employment available.

CAMPUS LIFE

Activities: Campus Ministries; Dance; Drama/theater; International Student Organization; Literary magazine; Music ensembles; Musical theater; Opera; Radio station; Student government; Student newspaper; Television station; Yearbook. **Organizations:** 60 registered organizations, 20 honor societies, 1 religious organizations, 2 fraternities, 2 sororities. **Athletics (Intercollegiate):** *Men:* baseball, basketball, golf. *Women:* basketball, crew/rowing, golf, softball, volleyball.

CAMPUS

Type of school	Private (nonprofit)
Environment	Metropolis

STUDENTS

Undergrad enrollment	3,368
% male/female	38/62
% from out of state	20
% frosh live on campus	70

FINANCIAL FACTS

Annual tuition	$29,700
Room and board	$11,100
Required fees	$150

GENERAL ADMISSIONS INFO

Application fee	No fee
Regular application deadline	Rolling
Nonfall registration	Yes

Fall 2024 testing policy	Test Optional
Range SAT EBRW	480–560
Range SAT Math	460–540
Range ACT Composite	17–22

ACADEMICS

Student/faculty ratio	11:1
% students returning for sophomore year	62

Most classes have 10–19 students.

REQUESTING SERVICES FOR STUDENTS WITH LEARNING DIFFERENCES

Phone: 305-899-3488 • www.barry.edu/en/academic-affairs/accessibility-services
Email: accessibilityservices@barry.edu

Documentation submitted to: Office of Accessibility Services
Separate application required for Services: Yes

Documentation required for:
LD: Psychoeducational evaluation
ADHD: Psychoeducational evaluation
ASD: Psychoeducational evaluation

Florida

Beacon College

105 E. Main Street, Leesburg, FL 34748 • Admissions: 352-638-9731 • www.beaconcollege.edu

Support: SP

ACCOMMODATIONS

Allowed in exams:

Calculators	Yes
Dictionary	Yes
Computer	Yes
Spell-checker	Yes
Extended test time	Yes
Scribe	Yes
Proctors	Yes
Oral exams	Yes
Note-takers	Yes

Support services for students with:

LD	Yes
ADHD	Yes
ASD	Yes
Distraction-reduced environment	Yes
Recording of lecture allowed	Yes
Reading technology	Yes
Audio books	Yes
Other assistive technology	Yes
Priority registration	Yes

Added costs of services:

For LD	No
For ADHD	No
For ASD	No
LD specialists	Yes
ADHD & ASD coaching	Yes
ASD specialists	Yes
Professional tutors	Yes
Peer tutors	Yes
Max. hours/week for services	Varies
How professors are notified of student approved accommodations	Both student and program

COLLEGE GRADUATION REQUIREMENTS

Course waivers allowed	Yes
In what courses: Math	
Course substitutions allowed	Yes
In what courses: Math	

"A World of Difference" PBS TV is produced by Beacon College. Episodes examine neurodiversity issues related to learning disabilities, ADHD, dyslexia, and autistic spectrum disorders through storytelling, viewer Q&As, conversations with experts, and interviews with successful or famous people with learning differences.

PROGRAMS/SERVICES FOR STUDENTS WITH LEARNING DIFFERENCES

Beacon College awards bachelor's and associate degrees exclusively to students who learn differently, including those diagnosed with LD, ADHD, Dyslexia, and ASD. All programs include all the support services needed for college and beyond. Beacon offers developmental courses for college-level learning skills, trained learning specialists to provide individual academic mentoring, faculty who tailor teaching to each student's learning style and unique needs, specialty courses for critical thinking and problem-solving ability, and advanced technology and/or assistive technology integrated into all coursework. Essential support services are included in the cost of tuition. Most students entering Beacon College participate in one of the College Readiness programs: Navigator PREP, Navigator PREP Jr., Summer for Success, or Beacon Foundations. These programs work closely with students and families on developing self-awareness, executive functioning, emotional regulation, social skills, and self-advocacy skills. Through the Center for Student Success (the Center) every student is assigned a learning specialist at the time of enrollment. First-year students meet with their learning specialist once or twice a week for a total of 60 minutes. Learning specialists are educational and developmental mentors, student advocates, and academic advisors. First-year students are also assigned a resident director to support social engagement and a transition counselor who oversees their overall adjustment to college life. These two individuals collaborate with the student's learning specialist to monitor performance and overall engagement. The Math Lab provides individual instruction and the computerized Math Lab assists students with memory deficits with repetition of material and continuous practice formats. The Writing Center offers one-on-one assistance as well as through assistive reading and writing technology for every phase of the writing process.

ADMISSIONS

Application requirements include a completed application, an official high school transcript or GED equivalent (enrollment is contingent upon receipt of an official and final high school transcript), and documentation of a diagnosis of a specific learning disability or attention-deficit/hyperactivity disorder (ADHD). Two letters of recommendation are required, up to four will be accepted. A personal essay is optional. ACT/SAT scores are not required or recommended. A personal interview, in person or by video conferencing is required. Students who do not meet admission standards may be provisionally accepted pending completion in a college readiness program, including Navigator PREP, Summer for Success, or Beacon Foundations.

Additional Information

Peer tutors are an important part of the Center for Student Success. Peer tutors are current Beacon students, nominated by faculty and trained in tutoring strategies. They provide individual and small group tutoring throughout the semester. The Travel Abroad program, offered during summer term, lasts three weeks and emphasizes out-of-classroom learning. The focus can be cultural, historical, environmental, or scientific exploration.

Beacon College

GENERAL ADMISSIONS

Very important factors include: recommendations. *Important factors include:* rigor of secondary school record, application essay. *Other factors considered include:* class rank, academic GPA. High school diploma is required and GED is accepted. Institution is test-optional for entering Fall 2024. Check admissions website for updates. *Academic units required:* 4 English, 1 math, 1 science, 1 social studies, 2 history, 3 academic electives.

FINANCIAL AID

Students should submit: FAFSA; Institution's own financial aid form; State aid form. *Need-based scholarships/grants offered:* College/university scholarship or grant aid from institutional funds; Federal Pell; Private scholarships; SEOG; State scholarships/grants. *Loan aid offered:.* Federal Work-Study Program available.

CAMPUS LIFE

Activities: Choral groups; Drama/theater; Literary magazine; Student government; Student newspaper; Yearbook. **Organizations:** 13 registered organizations, 1 honor societies, 1 fraternities, 1 sororities. **Athletics (Intercollegiate):** *Men:* basketball, golf, softball. *Women:* golf, softball.

CAMPUS
Type of school	Private (nonprofit)
Environment	Village

STUDENTS
Undergrad enrollment	460
% male/female	67/33
% from out of state	82
% frosh live on campus	99

FINANCIAL FACTS
Annual tuition	$48,510
Room and board	$14,842
Required fees	$720

GENERAL ADMISSIONS INFO
Application fee	$50
Regular application deadline	8/1
Nonfall registration	Yes

Fall 2024 testing policy	Test Optional

ACADEMICS
Student/faculty ratio	11:1
% students returning for sophomore year	73

Most classes have 10–19 students.

REQUESTING SERVICES FOR STUDENTS WITH LEARNING DIFFERENCES

Phone: 855-220-5376 • www.beaconcollege.edu/admissions • Email: admissions@beaconcollege.edu

Documentation submitted to: Office of Admissions
Separate application required for Services: No

Documentation required for:
LD: Psychoeducational evaluation
ADHD: Psychoeducational evaluation
ASD: Psychoeducational evaluation

Eckerd College

4200 54th Avenue South, St. Petersburg, FL 33711 • Admissions: 727-864-8331 • www.eckerd.edu

Support: S

ACCOMMODATIONS

Allowed in exams:

Calculators	Yes
Dictionary	Yes
Computer	Yes
Spell-checker	Yes
Extended test time	Yes
Scribe	Yes
Proctors	Yes
Oral exams	Yes
Note-takers	Yes

Support services for students with:

LD	Yes
ADHD	Yes
ASD	Yes
Distraction-reduced environment	Yes
Recording of lecture allowed	Yes
Reading technology	Yes
Audio books	Yes
Other assistive technology	Yes
Priority registration	Yes

Added costs of services:

For LD	No
For ADHD	No
For ASD	No
LD specialists	No
ADHD & ASD coaching	No
ASD specialists	No
Professional tutors	No
Peer tutors	Yes
Max. hours/week for services	Varies
How professors are notified of student approved accommodations	Student

COLLEGE GRADUATION REQUIREMENTS

Course waivers allowed	No
Course substitutions allowed	No

PROGRAMS/SERVICES FOR STUDENTS WITH LEARNING DIFFERENCES

Eckerd College's Office of Accessibility provides support services to students with disabilities. The Office of Accessibility is part of the Center for Academic Excellence. Staff members review documentation and determine the accommodations that are appropriate. Students are instructed on the process of logging in and managing their accommodations, signing up for a place to take tests, and renewing their accommodations each semester. Professors are notified by email, but the nature of the disability is not disclosed without permission from the student. Typical accommodations may include extended testing time, reduced-distraction testing, and note-taking assistance.

ADMISSIONS

Eckerd College seeks applicants who have taken rigorous high school courses. The average GPA for an entering first-year student is 3.5, and most students graduate in the top 20 percent of their high school class. Applicants should demonstrate leadership and be involved in school or community activities.

Additional Information

The John M. Bevan Center for Academic Excellence (BCAE) offers peer mentoring and academic coaching. Peer mentors help incoming students develop academic skills and transition successfully into the Eckerd community. Peer tutoring is available in many subjects, including behavioral sciences, communication, computer science, world language, natural sciences, and quantitative sciences/mathematics. Academic coaches work one-on-one with students and offer several workshops on study strategies, organization, and time management skills.

Eckerd College Search and Rescue (EC-SAR) program was founded in 1971 to provide safety services for the college's watersports activities. The EC-SAR's team was one of the first rescue units to respond to the Skyway Bridge disaster in May of 1980. The program is a respected search and rescue organization working with the U.S. Coast Guard, 911 EMR, and other agencies, answering more than 500 maritime distress calls per year.

Eckerd College

General Admissions

Very important factors include: rigor of secondary school record, academic GPA. *Important factors include:* standardized test scores (if submitted), application essay, recommendations. *Other factors considered include:* class rank. High school diploma is required and GED is accepted. Institution is test-optional for entering Fall 2024. Check admissions website for updates. *Academic units recommended:* 4 English, 3 math, 3 science (2 labs), 2 foreign language, 3 social studies, 3 academic electives.

Financial Aid

Students should submit: FAFSA. *Need-based scholarships/grants offered:* College/university scholarship or grant aid from institutional funds; Federal Pell; SEOG; State scholarships/grants. *Loan aid offered:* Direct PLUS loans; Direct Subsidized Loans; Direct Unsubsidized Loans. Federal Work-Study Program available. Institutional employment available.

Campus Life

Activities: Campus Ministries; Choral groups; Concert band; Dance; Drama/theater; International Student Organization; Jazz band; Literary magazine; Music ensembles; Musical theater; Radio station; Student government; Student newspaper; Yearbook. **Organizations:** 85 registered organizations, 14 honor societies, 5 religious organizations, 0 fraternities, 0 sororities. **Athletics (Intercollegiate):** *Men:* baseball, basketball, equestrian sports, golf, lacrosse, martial arts, rugby, swimming, ultimate frisbee, volleyball. *Women:* baseball, basketball, equestrian sports, golf, martial arts, rugby, softball, swimming, ultimate frisbee, volleyball.

CAMPUS
Type of school	Private (nonprofit)
Environment	City

STUDENTS
Undergrad enrollment	1,986
% male/female	30/70
% from out of state	79
% frosh live on campus	98

FINANCIAL FACTS
Annual tuition	$48,220
Room and board	$13,854
Required fees	$680

GENERAL ADMISSIONS INFO
Application fee	$40
Regular application deadline	7/25
Nonfall registration	Yes
Fall 2024 testing policy	Test Optional
Range SAT EBRW	570–670
Range SAT Math	540–630
Range ACT Composite	23–29

ACADEMICS
Student/faculty ratio	11:1
% students returning for sophomore year	77

Most classes have 20–29 students.

REQUESTING SERVICES FOR STUDENTS WITH LEARNING DIFFERENCES

Phone: 727-864-7723 • www.eckerd.edu/aes • Email: accessibility@eckerd.edu

Documentation submitted to: Office of Accessibility
Separate application required for Services: Yes

Documentation required for:
  LD: Psychoeducational evaluation
  ADHD: Psychoeducational evaluation
  ASD: Psychoeducational evaluation

Flagler College

74 King Street, Augustine, FL 32085-1027 • Admissions: 904-819-6220 • www.flagler.edu

> **Support: CS**

ACCOMMODATIONS

Allowed in exams:

Calculators	Yes
Dictionary	Yes
Computer	Yes
Spell-checker	Yes
Extended test time	Yes
Scribe	Yes
Proctors	Yes
Oral exams	Yes
Note-takers	Yes

Support services for students with:

LD	Yes
ADHD	Yes
ASD	Yes
Distraction-reduced environment	Yes
Recording of lecture allowed	Yes
Audio books	Yes
Other assistive technology	Yes
Priority registration	Yes

Added costs of services:

For LD	No
For ADHD	No
For ASD	No
LD specialists	Yes
ADHD & ASD coaching	Yes
ASD specialists	Yes
Professional tutors	No
Peer tutors	Yes
Max. hours/week for services	Varies
How professors are notified of student approved accommodations	Student

COLLEGE GRADUATION REQUIREMENTS

Course waivers allowed	No
Course substitutions allowed	Yes
In what courses: Case-by-case basis	

PROGRAMS/SERVICES FOR STUDENTS WITH LEARNING DIFFERENCES

The Disability Resource Center (DRC) provides accommodations to students with disabilities to ensure they have full access to the college and its programs. Students complete the DRC intake form and submit supporting documentation as part of their application for accommodations. Students may request academic accommodations as soon as they are admitted to Flagler. DRC offers the Learning Community with Canvas software to provide students with learning strategies, time management skills, and other resources to maximize their learning potential.

ADMISSIONS

Students may apply to Flagler using the Flagler College Application or the Common Application; each application has unique essay prompts. The average GPA for admitted students is 3.5. Flagler College allows applicants to self-report their grades and courses. Students are under no obligation to disclose a learning disability on their application; however, they are more than welcome to self-disclose if they feel it allows them to better describe personal experiences and challenges, and if they require certain accommodations. Students who require accommodations to complete the general admission application should contact the DRC.

Additional Information

The Learning Resource Center offers peer tutoring in one-on-one and small-group settings, and by appointment. The Academic Success Lab helps students develop effective studying and test-taking strategies, as well as practice time management, critical thinking, speaking, and listening skills. The Lab also helps students improve their reading comprehension and speed, vocabulary, learning styles, and develop tools to manage their stress and mental health.

Railroad pioneer, entrepreneur, and cofounder of the Standard Oil Co., Henry Morrison Flagler, built the luxurious Ponce de Leon Hotel in 1888. Louis C. Tiffany, famous for his stained-glass lamps, designed the interior of this building, one of the first in the nation to convert to electricity. During WWII, the hotel was taken over by the federal government to be used as a Coast Guard Training Centre, and permanently closed in 1967. In 1968, the Ponce de Leon Hotel became the centerpiece for the newly established Flagler College.

Flagler College

GENERAL ADMISSIONS

Very important factors include: academic GPA. *Important factors include:* rigor of secondary school record, standardized test scores (if submitted), application essay, recommendations. High school diploma is required and GED is accepted. Institution is test-optional for entering Fall 2024. Check admissions website for updates. *Academic units recommended:* 4 English, 4 math, 3 science (1 lab), 4 social studies, 4 academic electives.

FINANCIAL AID

Students should submit: FAFSA; State aid form. *Need-based scholarships/grants offered:* College/university scholarship or grant aid from institutional funds; Federal Pell; Private scholarships; SEOG; State scholarships/grants. *Loan aid offered:* Direct PLUS loans; Direct Subsidized Loans; Direct Unsubsidized Loans. Federal Work-Study Program available. Institutional employment available.

CAMPUS LIFE

Activities: Campus Ministries; Choral groups; Dance; Drama/theater; International Student Organization; Literary magazine; Model UN; Musical theater; Radio station; Student government; Student newspaper; Student-run film society. **Organizations:** 30 registered organizations, 2 honor societies, 4 religious organizations, 1 fraternities, 2 sororities. **Athletics (Intercollegiate):** *Men:* baseball, basketball, cross-country, golf, lacrosse, volleyball. *Women:* basketball, cross-country, golf, lacrosse, softball, volleyball.

CAMPUS

Type of school	Private (nonprofit)
Environment	Village

STUDENTS

Undergrad enrollment	2,571
% male/female	32/68
% from out of state	41
% frosh live on campus	91

FINANCIAL FACTS

Annual tuition	$25,710
Room and board	$14,350
Required fees	$900

GENERAL ADMISSIONS INFO

Application fee	$50
Regular application deadline	3/1
Nonfall registration	Yes
Fall 2024 testing policy	Test Optional

ACADEMICS

Student/faculty ratio	14:1
% students returning for sophomore year	69
Most classes have 10–19 students.	

REQUESTING SERVICES FOR STUDENTS WITH LEARNING DIFFERENCES

Phone: 904-819-6460 • www.flagler.edu/student-support-services/disability-resource-center
Email: ppownall@flagler.edu

Documentation submitted to: Disability Resource Center
Separate application required for Services: Yes

Documentation required for:
LD: Psychoeducational evaluation
ADHD: Psychoeducational evaluation
ASD: Psychoeducational evaluation

Florida A&M University

Room 204, Tallahassee, FL 32307-3200 • Admissions: 850-599-3796 • www.famu.edu

Support: CS

ACCOMMODATIONS

Allowed in exams:

Calculators	Yes
Dictionary	Yes
Computer	Yes
Spell-checker	Yes
Extended test time	Yes
Scribe	Yes
Proctors	Yes
Oral exams	Yes
Note-takers	Yes

Support services for students with:

LD	Yes
ADHD	Yes
ASD	Yes
Distraction-reduced environment	Yes
Recording of lecture allowed	Yes
Reading technology	Yes
Audio books	Yes
Other assistive technology	No
Priority registration	No

Added costs of services:

For LD	No
For ADHD	No
For ASD	No
LD specialists	Yes
ADHD & ASD coaching	No
ASD specialists	No
Professional tutors	Yes
Peer tutors	Yes
Max. hours/week for services	Varies
How professors are notified of student approved accommodations	Student

COLLEGE GRADUATION REQUIREMENTS

Course waivers allowed	Yes
In what courses: Case-by-case basis	
Course substitutions allowed	Yes
In what courses: Case-by-case basis	

PROGRAMS/SERVICES FOR STUDENTS WITH LEARNING DIFFERENCES

The Center for Disability Access and Resources (CeDAR) provides accommodations and support services to students with disabilities to help promote their personal, academic, and professional growth. Students can apply for services, request accommodations, and set up testing appointments using the online portal Accessible Information Management (AIM). AIM also emails approved accommodations to the appropriate faculty or professors. Eligible CeDAR participants receive note-taking support via Glean, a web and mobile app that empowers students to take notes independently and improves their learning outcomes.

ADMISSIONS

General admission at FAMU expects a 3.0 GPA and requires ACT or SAT scores. Students wishing to enroll in the summer or spring may have a lower GPA. Applicants who do not meet the standard admission criteria may be admitted to FAMU under alternate criteria, based on the applicant's disability. Students who wish to request an alternate review must do so in writing and provide documentation that certifies the existence of a disability and verifies functional limitations. These applicants are forwarded to CeDAR admissions for review, and their staff makes a recommendation to the admissions office.

Additional Information

The Writing Resource Center (WRC) offers peer-to-peer writing consultations to all students in individual and group settings, as well as writing-related workshops to classes, student organizations, and other university-related groups. Florida A&M was founded in 1887 and is a public, historically Black university.

DID YOU KNOW?

The Carnegie Library was built in 1908 with a donation from Andrew Carnegie. It was the first Carnegie library built on a Black land grant college campus, and the first building with modern amenities: electricity, indoor plumbing, and city-supplied water. In 1976, the library became the home of the Black Archives Research Center and Museum. James Nathaniel Eaton, Sr. spent the next 30 years as archivist, curator, and director, compiling one of the region's largest collections of history, culture, and contributions of people of African descent living in the U.S.

Florida A&M University

GENERAL ADMISSIONS

Very important factors include: rigor of secondary school record, academic GPA, standardized test scores, application essay, recommendations. High school diploma is required and GED is accepted. Institution requires SAT/ACT scores for entering Fall 2024. Check admissions website for updates. *Academic units required:* 4 English, 4 math, 3 science (2 labs), 2 foreign language, 3 social studies, 2 academic electives.

FINANCIAL AID

Students should submit: FAFSA. *Need-based scholarships/grants offered:* College/university scholarship or grant aid from institutional funds; Federal Pell; Private scholarships; SEOG; State scholarships/grants; United Negro College Fund. *Loan aid offered:* Direct PLUS loans; Direct Subsidized Loans; Direct Unsubsidized Loans. Federal Work-Study Program available. Institutional employment available.

CAMPUS LIFE

Activities: Campus Ministries; Choral groups; Concert band; Dance; Drama/theater; International Student Organization; Jazz band; Literary magazine; Marching band; Music ensembles; Musical theater; Pep band; Radio station; Student government; Student newspaper; Symphony orchestra; Television station; Yearbook. **Organizations:** 169 registered organizations, 9 honor societies, 5 religious organizations, 5 fraternities, 3 sororities. **Athletics (Intercollegiate):** *Men:* baseball, basketball, cross-country, golf, swimming, table tennis, track/field (indoor), wrestling. *Women:* basketball, bowling, cross-country, golf, softball, swimming, table tennis, track/field (indoor), volleyball.

CAMPUS	
Type of school	Public
Environment	City

STUDENTS	
Undergrad enrollment	7,365
% male/female	35/65
% from out of state	13
% frosh live on campus	81

FINANCIAL FACTS	
Annual in-state tuition	$5,645
Annual out-of-state tuition	$17,585
Room and board	$10,058
Required fees	$140

GENERAL ADMISSIONS INFO	
Application fee	$30
Regular application deadline	5/15
Nonfall registration	Yes
Fall 2024 testing policy	SAT or ACT Required
Range SAT EBRW	460–550
Range SAT Math	440–530
Range ACT Composite	19–24

ACADEMICS	
Student/faculty ratio	15:1
% students returning for sophomore year	83
Most classes have 20–29 students.	

REQUESTING SERVICES FOR STUDENTS WITH LEARNING DIFFERENCES

Phone: 850-599-3180 • famu.edu/students/student-resources/center-for-disability-access-and-resources
Email: cedar@famu.edu

Documentation submitted to: Center for Disability Access and Resources (CeDAR)
Separate application required for Services: Yes

Documentation required for:
LD: Psychoeducational evaluation
ADHD: Psychoeducational evaluation
ASD: Psychoeducational evaluation

Florida

Florida Atlantic University

777 Glades Road, Boca Raton, FL 33431-0991 • Admissions: 561-297-3040 • www.fau.edu

Support: CS

ACCOMMODATIONS

Allowed in exams:

Calculators	Yes
Dictionary	Yes
Computer	Yes
Spell-checker	Yes
Extended test time	Yes
Scribe	Yes
Proctors	Yes
Oral exams	Yes
Note-takers	Yes

Support services for students with:

LD	Yes
ADHD	Yes
ASD	Yes
Distraction-reduced environment	Yes
Recording of lecture allowed	Yes
Reading technology	Yes
Audio books	Yes
Other assistive technology	No
Priority registration	No

Added costs of services:

For LD	No
For ADHD	No
For ASD	No
LD specialists	Yes
ADHD & ASD coaching	No
ASD specialists	No
Professional tutors	No
Peer tutors	Yes
Max. hours/week for services	Varies
How professors are notified of student approved accommodations	Student

COLLEGE GRADUATION REQUIREMENTS

Course waivers allowed	Yes

In what courses: Varies

Course substitutions allowed	Yes

In what courses: Math and Foreign Language

PROGRAMS/SERVICES FOR STUDENTS WITH LEARNING DIFFERENCES

Student Accessibility Services (SAS) provides academic support through advocacy, academic accommodations, and access to and training in assistive technology and learning strategies. Additional resources include an assistive-technology computer lab and an active student organization. SAS has offices and services across three FAU campuses, including Boca Raton, Davey, and Jupiter. The FAU Academy for Community Inclusion is a college program for high school graduates with intellectual and developmental disabilities. Students can earn certificates in supported employment, supported community living, and supported community access. These certificates are offered in an inclusive college environment on both the Jupiter and Boca Raton campuses. Students in the program can participate in the same college organizations, clubs, activities, and events that are available to all students.

ADMISSIONS

The application process is the same for all students. For automatic admission, FAU requires a minimum 3.3 GPA. The mid-50 percent of admitted applicants have a GPA of 3.8 to 4.5. Some colleges require additional courses beyond the general admission requirements, and an audition is required for music majors. An essay submission is required only with applications to the honors college.

Additional Information

Students receive online support with writing, library resources, and math. Online and in-person tutoring is available.

FAU has its own student-run recording label. Hoot/Wisdom Recordings is part of the Commercial Music Program and Department of Music in FAU's Dorothy F. Schmidt College of Arts and Letters. Students get hands-on experience in all aspects of the label, from content creation to production and marketing.

Florida Atlantic University

GENERAL ADMISSIONS

Very important factors include: academic GPA, standardized test scores. *Important factors include:* rigor of secondary school record, class rank. *Other factors considered include:* application essay, recommendations. High school diploma is required and GED is accepted. Institution requires SAT/ACT scores for entering Fall 2024. Check admissions website for updates. *Academic units required:* 4 English, 4 math, 3 science (2 labs), 2 foreign language, 3 social studies, 3 academic electives.

FINANCIAL AID

Students should submit: FAFSA. *Need-based scholarships/grants offered:* College/university scholarship or grant aid from institutional funds; Federal Nursing Scholarships; Federal Pell; Private scholarships; SEOG; State scholarships/grants. *Loan aid offered:* Direct PLUS loans; Direct Subsidized Loans; Direct Unsubsidized Loans. Federal Work-Study Program available. Institutional employment available.

CAMPUS LIFE

Activities: Campus Ministries; Choral groups; Concert band; Dance; Drama/theater; International Student Organization; Jazz band; Literary magazine; Marching band; Model UN; Music ensembles; Musical theater; Opera; Pep band; Radio station; Student government; Student newspaper; Student-run film society; Symphony orchestra; Television station. **Organizations:** 300 registered organizations, 11 honor societies, 6 religious organizations, 16 fraternities, 12 sororities. **Athletics (Intercollegiate):** *Men:* baseball, basketball, cross-country, equestrian sports, golf, ice hockey, lacrosse, rugby, swimming, ultimate frisbee, wrestling. *Women:* basketball, cross-country, equestrian sports, golf, lacrosse, rugby, softball, swimming, track/field (indoor), ultimate frisbee, volleyball.

CAMPUS

Type of school	Public
Environment	City

STUDENTS

Undergrad enrollment	24,228
% male/female	43/57
% from out of state	5
% frosh live on campus	69

FINANCIAL FACTS

Annual in-state tuition	$6,099
Annual out-of-state tuition	$21,655
Room and board	$12,536

GENERAL ADMISSIONS INFO

Application fee	$30
Regular application deadline	5/1
Nonfall registration	Yes
Fall 2024 testing policy	SAT or ACT Required
Range SAT EBRW	480–570
Range SAT Math	490–580
Range ACT Composite	21–25

ACADEMICS

Student/faculty ratio	20:1
% students returning for sophomore year	81

Most classes have 20–29 students.

REQUESTING SERVICES FOR STUDENTS WITH LEARNING DIFFERENCES

Phone: 561-297-3880 • www.fau.edu/sas/ • Email: fau.edu/sas/about/contact_us.php

Documentation submitted to: Student Accessibility Services

Separate application required for Services: Yes

Documentation required for:
LD: Psychoeducational evaluation
ADHD: Psychoeducational evaluation
ASD: Psychoeducational evaluation

Florida

Florida State University

P.O. Box 3062400, Tallahassee, FL 32306-2400 • Admissions: 850-644-6200 • www.fsu.edu

Support: S

ACCOMMODATIONS

Allowed in exams:

Calculators	Yes
Dictionary	Yes
Computer	Yes
Spell-checker	Yes
Extended test time	Yes
Scribe	Yes
Proctors	Yes
Oral exams	Yes
Note-takers	Yes

Support services for students with:

LD	Yes
ADHD	Yes
ASD	Yes
Distraction-reduced environment	Yes
Recording of lecture allowed	Yes
Reading technology	Yes
Audio books	Yes
Other assistive technology	Yes
Priority registration	Yes

Added costs of services:

For LD	No
For ADHD	No
For ASD	No
LD specialists	No
ADHD & ASD coaching	No
ASD specialists	No
Professional tutors	No
Peer tutors	Yes
Max. hours/week for services	Varies
How professors are notified of student approved accommodations	Student

COLLEGE GRADUATION REQUIREMENTS

Course waivers allowed	No
Course substitutions allowed	Yes
In what courses: Math and Foreign Language	

PROGRAMS/SERVICES FOR STUDENTS WITH LEARNING DIFFERENCES

At Florida State University, academic accommodations and services for students with disabilities are coordinated by the Office of Accessibility Services (OAS). OAS staff determines necessary accommodations based on individual documentation submitted by the student. Once accommodations are implemented, they are monitored by OAS disability specialists. OAS also provides assistive technology equipment and services free of charge. Academic accommodations may include alternate-format texts, alternative testing locations, extended time, a reader and/or scribe, and in-class notetakers. OAS teaches students study skills, memory enhancement techniques, organizational skills, test-taking strategies, stress management techniques, and skills for self-advocacy to communicate their needs and accommodations to instructors.

ADMISSIONS

Criteria for admission include the written essay, the rigor and quality of courses and curriculum, grade trends, class rank, strength of the senior schedule and academic subjects, math level in the senior year, and the number of years in a sequential foreign language. ACT or SAT scores are required for admission. The middle 50 percent of enrolled first-year students scored between 26–31 on the ACT or 1200–1340 on the SAT.

Additional Information

The University of Choice is a student-led advocacy group at Florida State University that enhances relationships, builds community relations, and advocates for the needs of individuals with disabilities.

There's been a Sod Cemetery at FSU since 1962. After an unlikely 18-0 away-game victory over the University of Georgia, the football team brought grass from the UGA stadium back home with them. They buried the grass under a plaque commemorating the score of the game. It was the first "Sod Game," and to this day, anytime FSU has an unlikely win on the road, they take sod from the stadium to bury in the FSU Sod Cemetery.

Florida State University

GENERAL ADMISSIONS

Very important factors include: rigor of secondary school record. *Important factors include:* class rank, academic GPA, standardized test scores, application essay. High school diploma is required and GED is accepted. Institution requires SAT/ACT scores for entering Fall 2024. Check admissions website for updates. *Academic units required:* 4 English, 4 math, 3 science (2 labs), 2 foreign language, 3 social studies, 3 academic electives. *Academic units recommended:* 4 science (2 labs), 4 foreign language, 4 social studies.

FINANCIAL AID

Students should submit: FAFSA; State aid form. *Need-based scholarships/grants offered:* College/university scholarship or grant aid from institutional funds; Federal Pell; Private scholarships; SEOG; State scholarships/grants; United Negro College Fund. *Loan aid offered:* Direct PLUS loans; Direct Subsidized Loans; Direct Unsubsidized Loans. Federal Work-Study Program available. Institutional employment available.

CAMPUS LIFE

Activities: Campus Ministries; Choral groups; Concert band; Dance; Drama/theater; International Student Organization; Jazz band; Literary magazine; Marching band; Model UN; Music ensembles; Musical theater; Opera; Pep band; Radio station; Student government; Student newspaper; Student-run film society; Symphony orchestra; Television station; Yearbook. **Organizations:** 763 registered organizations, 63 honor societies, 56 religious organizations, 24 fraternities, 24 sororities. **Athletics (Intercollegiate):** *Men:* baseball, basketball, bowling, crew/rowing, cross-country, cycling, equestrian sports, field hockey, golf, gymnastics, ice hockey, lacrosse, martial arts, rugby, swimming, table tennis, track/field (indoor), ultimate frisbee, volleyball, water polo. *Women:* basketball, bowling, crew/rowing, cross-country, cycling, equestrian sports, field hockey, golf, gymnastics, lacrosse, martial arts, rugby, softball, swimming, table tennis, track/field (indoor), ultimate frisbee, volleyball, water polo.

CAMPUS

Type of school	Public
Environment	City

STUDENTS

Undergrad enrollment	32,691
% male/female	43/57
% from out of state	13
% frosh live on campus	80

FINANCIAL FACTS

Annual in-state tuition	$4,640
Annual out-of-state tuition	$19,806
Room and board	$11,472
Required fees	$1,877

GENERAL ADMISSIONS INFO

Application fee	$30
Regular application deadline	3/1
Nonfall registration	Yes
Fall 2024 testing policy	SAT or ACT Required
Range SAT EBRW	620–690
Range SAT Math	590–680
Range ACT Composite	26–31

ACADEMICS

Student/faculty ratio	21:1
% students returning for sophomore year	94

Most classes have 10–19 students.

REQUESTING SERVICES FOR STUDENTS WITH LEARNING DIFFERENCES

Phone: 850-644-9566 • dsst.fsu.edu/oas • Email: oas@fsu.edu

Documentation submitted to: Office of Accessibility Services
Separate application required for Services: Yes

Documentation required for:
LD: Psychoeducational evaluation
ADHD: Psychoeducational evaluation
ASD: Psychoeducational evaluation

Florida

Lynn University

3601 North Military Trail, Boca Raton, FL 33431-5598 • Admissions: 561-237-7900 • www.lynn.edu

(Support: SP)

ACCOMMODATIONS

Allowed in exams:

Calculators	Yes
Dictionary	No
Computer	Yes
Spell-checker	Yes
Extended test time	Yes
Scribe	Yes
Proctors	Yes
Oral exams	No
Note-takers	Yes

Support services for students with:

LD	Yes
ADHD	Yes
ASD	Yes
Distraction-reduced environment	Yes
Recording of lecture allowed	Yes
Reading technology	Yes
Audio books	Yes
Other assistive technology	Yes
Priority registration	No

Added costs of services:

For LD	Yes
For ADHD	Yes
For ASD	Yes
LD specialists	Yes
ADHD & ASD coaching	Yes
ASD specialists	No
Professional tutors	Yes
Peer tutors	No
Max. hours/week for services	10
How professors are notified of student approved accommodations	Student

COLLEGE GRADUATION REQUIREMENTS

Course waivers allowed	Yes
In what courses: Case-by-case basis	
Course substitutions allowed	Yes
In what courses: Case-by-case basis	

PROGRAMS/SERVICES FOR STUDENTS WITH LEARNING DIFFERENCES

Lynn University provides disability services through the Student Accessibility Services (SAS) office and the Institute for Achievement and Learning (IAL) program. Students may apply for free services through SAS and obtain reasonable accommodations such as extended test times, a reduced-distraction testing environment, or notetakers. Students should request these accommodations through the student portal and schedule an appointment with the academic accommodation specialist. The IAL full-service program has a separate admission process, is fee-based, and provides structured support to students with learning differences. IAL provides group and individual tutoring, study and organizational skill workshops, and sessions to determine student anxiety levels. The IAL team collaborates with SAS and the school faculty to ensure students receive the appropriate resources. As an IAL participant, students will build a strong foundation for academic excellence, receive support as they transition to college, and learn how to live independently. The faculty are trained to use an IAL style of instruction that allows the IAL staff to work in collaboration with the student's plan.

ADMISSIONS

To be considered for admission to Lynn University, all students complete the same application process. Provisional admittance may be offered to students who have a 2.5 or lower GPA. Students with a 3.0 GPA during their first semester at Lynn are invited to take an accelerated three-year bachelor's degree.

ADDITIONAL INFORMATION

The Lynn University Institute for Achievement and Learning program is free and assists all Lynn University students with coursework by offering individual and content-area tutoring, academic coaching, and a writing center.

Lynn hosted the third and final 2012 U.S. presidential debate between President Barack Obama and former Massachusetts governor and presidential hopeful Mitt Romney, and an estimated 59.2 million people tuned in to watch. It was up against Monday Night Football on ESPN (10.7 million viewers) and Game 7 of the MLB NLCS on FOX (8.1 million viewers). The debate was to only discuss foreign policy, but both candidates managed to fit in domestic policy, including education.

Lynn University

General Admissions

Very important factors include: rigor of secondary school record, academic GPA, application essay. *Important factors include:* class rank, standardized test scores (if submitted), recommendations. High school diploma is required and GED is accepted. Institution is test-optional for entering Fall 2024. Check admissions website for updates. *Academic units recommended:* 4 English, 4 math, 4 science, 2 social studies, 2 history.

Financial Aid

Students should submit: FAFSA. *Need-based scholarships/grants offered:* College/university scholarship or grant aid from institutional funds; Federal Pell; Private scholarships; SEOG; State scholarships/grants. *Loan aid offered:* Direct PLUS loans; Direct Subsidized Loans; Direct Unsubsidized Loans. Federal Work-Study Program available. Institutional employment available.

Campus Life

Activities: Campus Ministries; Dance; Drama/theater; International Student Organization; Literary magazine; Model UN; Music ensembles; Musical theater; Radio station; Student government; Student newspaper; Student-run film society; Symphony orchestra; Television station. **Organizations:** 33 registered organizations, 2 honor societies, 3 religious organizations, 3 fraternities, 2 sororities. **Athletics (Intercollegiate):** *Men:* baseball, basketball, cross-country, golf, ice hockey, lacrosse, rugby, swimming, table tennis, ultimate frisbee, volleyball. *Women:* basketball, cross-country, golf, ice hockey, lacrosse, softball, swimming, table tennis, ultimate frisbee, volleyball.

CAMPUS
Type of school	Private (nonprofit)
Environment	City

STUDENTS
Undergrad enrollment	2,632
% male/female	50/50
% from out of state	33
% frosh live on campus	76

FINANCIAL FACTS
Annual tuition	$39,800
Room and board	$13,200
Required fees	$1,750

GENERAL ADMISSIONS INFO
Application fee	No fee
Regular application deadline	8/1
Nonfall registration	Yes
Fall 2024 testing policy	Test Optional
Range SAT EBRW	510–600
Range SAT Math	515–600
Range ACT Composite	20–26

ACADEMICS
Student/faculty ratio	18:1
% students returning for sophomore year	76

Most classes have 20–29 students.

REQUESTING SERVICES FOR STUDENTS WITH LEARNING DIFFERENCES

Phone: 561-237-7028 • lynn.edu/campus-directory/departments/accessibility-services
Email: phyman@lynn.edu

Documentation submitted to: Student Accessibility Services
Separate application required for Services: Yes

Documentation required for:
LD: Psychoeducational evaluation
ADHD: Psychoeducational evaluation
ASD: Psychoeducational evaluation

New College of Florida

5800 Bay Shore Road, Sarasota, FL 34243-2109 • Admissions: 941-487-5000 • www.ncf.edu

Support: CS

ACCOMMODATIONS

Allowed in exams:

Calculators	Yes
Dictionary	Yes
Computer	Yes
Spell-checker	Yes
Extended test time	Yes
Scribe	Yes
Proctors	Yes
Oral exams	Yes
Note-takers	Yes

Support services for students with:

LD	Yes
ADHD	Yes
ASD	Yes
Distraction-reduced environment	Yes
Recording of lecture allowed	Yes
Reading technology	Yes
Audio books	Yes
Other assistive technology	Yes
Priority registration	No

Added costs of services:

For LD	No
For ADHD	No
For ASD	No
LD specialists	Yes
ADHD & ASD coaching	Yes
ASD specialists	No
Professional tutors	No
Peer tutors	Yes
Max. hours/week for services	Varies
How professors are notified of student approved accommodations	Student and AALC

COLLEGE GRADUATION REQUIREMENTS

Course waivers allowed	No
Course substitutions allowed	No

PROGRAMS/SERVICES FOR STUDENTS WITH LEARNING DIFFERENCES

The Advocacy and Accessible Learning Center (AALC) provides appropriate accommodations, services, resources, and referrals to create equal access to educational and living opportunities. The AALC works with faculty, staff, and students to provide for students with learning differences. Optional services include an alternative testing location, extended testing time, a reduced-distraction environment, interpreting services, and notetakers. To apply for accommodations, students must register using a personal (non-college) email, complete the new student request form, upload documentation, and attend an intake meeting.

ADMISSIONS

The New College of Florida (NCF) consults with the Advocacy and Accessible Learning Center to determine if a student's inability to meet the application requirements is due to their disability. The significant factors that determine admission eligibility include academic rigor, class rank (if applicable), SAT or ACT scores, ability to write at college level, leadership activities, and character. The middle 50 percent range for admitted students generally have a 3.68–4.31 GPA and an SAT score of 1100–1310.

Additional Information

The NCF Student Success Center offers one-on-one appointments with trained peer coaches, group study sessions, recurring appointments, workshops, printable resources, and referrals. During coaching sessions, students work with their coach on time management, goal setting, note-taking, presentation skills, reading comprehension study skills, and stress management.

Dating from the early 1920s, three campus buildings were once bayfront mansions. College Hall was the home of Edith and Charles Ringling and Cook Hall was the home of Hester Ringling Lancaster Sanford—of the Ringling Bros. Circus fame. Caples Hall was the home of Ellen and Ralph Caples, the first "power couple" of Sarasota and instrumental in Ringling's move to Sarasota. The buildings are used for classrooms, meeting rooms, and offices and are on the National Register of Historic Places.

New College of Florida

General Admissions

Very important factors include: rigor of secondary school record, academic GPA. *Important factors include:* class rank, standardized test scores, application essay. *Other factors considered include:* recommendations. High school diploma is required and GED is accepted. Institution requires SAT/ACT scores for entering Fall 2024. Check admissions website for updates. *Academic units required:* 4 English, 4 math, 3 science (2 labs), 2 foreign language, 3 social studies, 2 academic electives. *Academic units recommended:* 4 science (4 labs), 4 foreign language, 4 social studies, 2 visual/performing arts.

Financial Aid

Students should submit: FAFSA. *Need-based scholarships/grants offered:* College/university scholarship or grant aid from institutional funds; Federal Pell; Private scholarships; SEOG; State scholarships/grants. *Loan aid offered:* Direct PLUS loans; Direct Subsidized Loans; Direct Unsubsidized Loans. Federal Work-Study Program available. Institutional employment available.

Campus Life

Activities: Campus Ministries; Choral groups; Dance; Drama/theater; International Student Organization; Music ensembles; Musical theater; Student government; Student newspaper. **Organizations:** 74 registered organizations, 1 honor societies, 3 religious organizations, 0 fraternities, 0 sororities. **Athletics (Intercollegiate):** *Men:* basketball, crew/rowing, martial arts, swimming. *Women:* basketball, crew/rowing, martial arts, swimming.

CAMPUS
Type of school	Public
Environment	Town

STUDENTS
Undergrad enrollment	669
% male/female	32/68
% from out of state	18
% frosh live on campus	81

FINANCIAL FACTS
Annual in-state tuition	$6,916
Annual out-of-state tuition	$29,944
Room and board	$10,489

GENERAL ADMISSIONS INFO
Application fee	$30
Regular application deadline	4/15
Nonfall registration	No
Fall 2024 testing policy	SAT or ACT Required
Range SAT EBRW	580–710
Range SAT Math	523–650
Range ACT Composite	24–31

ACADEMICS
Student/faculty ratio	6:1
% students returning for sophomore year	75

Most classes have 10–19 students.

REQUESTING SERVICES FOR STUDENTS WITH LEARNING DIFFERENCES

Phone: 941-487-4844 • www.ncf.edu/departments/advocacy-accessibility • Email: aalc@ncf.edu

Documentation submitted to: Advocacy and Accessible Learning Center
Separate application required for Services: Yes

Documentation required for:
LD: Psychoeducational evaluation
ADHD: Psychoeducational evaluation
ASD: Psychoeducational evaluation

Florida

Stetson University

421 N. Woodland Boulevard, DeLand, FL 32723 • Admissions: 386-822-7100 • stetson.edu

Support: S

ACCOMMODATIONS

Allowed in exams:

Calculators	Yes
Dictionary	Yes
Computer	Yes
Spell-checker	Yes
Extended test time	Yes
Scribe	Yes
Proctors	Yes
Oral exams	Yes
Note-takers	Yes

Support services for students with:

LD	Yes
ADHD	Yes
ASD	Yes
Distraction-reduced environment	Yes
Recording of lecture allowed	Yes
Reading technology	Yes
Audio books	Yes
Other assistive technology	Yes
Priority registration	Yes

Added costs of services:

For LD	No
For ADHD	No
For ASD	No
LD specialists	No
ADHD & ASD coaching	Yes
ASD specialists	No
Professional tutors	No
Peer tutors	Yes
Max. hours/week for services	Varies
How professors are notified of student approved accommodations	Accessibility Services

COLLEGE GRADUATION REQUIREMENTS

Course waivers allowed	No
Course substitutions allowed	Yes
In what courses: Foreign Language, Math	

PROGRAMS/SERVICES FOR STUDENTS WITH LEARNING DIFFERENCES

The Accessibility Services Center (ASC) provides accommodations to students with disabilities. Once admitted, students are encouraged to contact ASC right away to request academic accommodations. Students must complete the online accommodations profile along with submitting supporting documentation. Then a meeting with an ASC staff member is scheduled to discuss appropriate accommodations. The ASC office notifies professors of a student's accommodations; however, students are encouraged to take an active role and discuss the specific accommodations with each professor. Accommodations can include priority registration, alternate-format class material, note-taking, recording of classes, assistive technology, copies of lectures or presentations, and exam accommodations.

ADMISSIONS

All applicants must meet the admission criteria. Applicants should have completed a college preparatory program in high school, and a GPA average of greater than 3.0 is typical for accepted students. A personal essay is not required, and a previously graded paper can be submitted. When applying for admission, self-reported information is accepted, but official transcripts are required for enrollment. American Sign Language (ASL) is accepted for the foreign language requirement. Students auditioning for the School of Music have a separate application type and deadline.

Additional Information

All students are assigned a faculty advisor to help guide and support students during their time at Stetson. The Advising Team in the Academic Success department provides supplemental advising services. Academic Success' peer tutoring service is provided to students free of charge. Tutors are available for one-on-one and small group tutoring for support in coursework, test prep, and study review sessions for students; by appointment or walk-in. The Stetson Peer Instruction (SPI) program assists students enrolled in certain courses, which are listed on the SPI webpage, along with a schedule for signup. SPI offers help with course content, exam preparation, and study skills. Academic Success offers online learning tools on various topics, including strategies for test-taking, memorization, time management, and note-taking, among others. Each topic has handouts and additional external website links to further discussion of the topics presented. Students can also make an in-person appointment to meet with an Academic Success staff member or a peer success coach.

The Campus Historic District was listed on the National Register of Historic Places in 1991 and contains nine historic buildings, including DeLand Hall (1884). Looking to protect the future, in 2016 students established a Revolving Green Fund, with all students paying a $5 fee each semester for environmental projects. The RGF's first project was completed in 2018—231 solar panels on the roof of the Carlton Union, expected to produce an estimated 131.2 megawatts of clean energy annually.

Stetson University

GENERAL ADMISSIONS

Very important factors include: rigor of secondary school record, academic GPA. *Important factors include:* class rank, application essay, recommendations. *Other factors considered include:* standardized test scores (if submitted). High school diploma is required and GED is accepted. Institution is test-optional for entering Fall 2024. Check admissions website for updates. *Academic units required:* 4 English, 3 math, 3 science, 2 foreign language, 2 social studies. *Academic units recommended:* 4 English, 4 math, 4 science, 2 foreign language, 4 social studies.

FINANCIAL AID

Students should submit: CSS/Financial Aid Profile; FAFSA. *Need-based scholarships/grants offered:* College/university scholarship or grant aid from institutional funds; Federal Pell; Private scholarships; SEOG; State scholarships/grants. *Loan aid offered:* Direct PLUS loans; Direct Subsidized Loans; Direct Unsubsidized Loans. Federal Work-Study Program available. Institutional employment available.

CAMPUS LIFE

Activities: Campus Ministries; Choral groups; Concert band; Dance; Drama/theater; International Student Organization; Jazz band; Literary magazine; Marching band; Music ensembles; Musical theater; Opera; Pep band; Radio station; Student government; Student newspaper; Symphony orchestra. **Organizations:** 129 registered organizations, 17 honor societies, 9 religious organizations, 9 fraternities, 6 sororities. **Athletics (Intercollegiate):** *Men:* baseball, basketball, crew/rowing, cross-country, equestrian sports, golf, martial arts, softball, table tennis, ultimate frisbee. *Women:* baseball, basketball, crew/rowing, cross-country, equestrian sports, golf, lacrosse, martial arts, softball, table tennis, ultimate frisbee, volleyball.

CAMPUS

Type of school	Private (nonprofit)
Environment	Town

STUDENTS

Undergrad enrollment	2,506
% male/female	43/57
% from out of state	25
% frosh live on campus	85

FINANCIAL FACTS

Annual tuition	$54,820
Room and board	$16,030
Required fees	$400

GENERAL ADMISSIONS INFO

Application fee	No fee
Regular application deadline	Rolling
Nonfall registration	Yes

Fall 2024 testing policy	Test Optional
Range SAT EBRW	540–650
Range SAT Math	505–620
Range ACT Composite	20–27

ACADEMICS

Student/faculty ratio	11:1
% students returning for sophomore year	68

Most classes have 10–19 students.

REQUESTING SERVICES FOR STUDENTS WITH LEARNING DIFFERENCES

Phone: 386-822-7127 • www.stetson.edu/administration/accessibility-services • Email: asc@stetson.edu

Documentation submitted to: Accessibility Services Center
Separate application required for Services: Yes

Documentation required for:
LD: Psychoeducational evaluation
ADHD: Psychoeducational evaluation
ASD: Psychoeducational evaluation

Florida

University of Central Florida

P.O. Box 160111, Orlando, FL 32816-0111 • Admissions: 407-823-3000 • www.ucf.edu

Support: S

ACCOMMODATIONS

Allowed in exams:

Calculators	Yes
Dictionary	Yes
Computer	Yes
Spell-checker	Yes
Extended test time	Yes
Scribe	Yes
Proctors	Yes
Oral exams	No
Note-takers	Yes

Support services for students with:

LD	Yes
ADHD	Yes
ASD	Yes
Distraction-reduced environment	Yes
Recording of lecture allowed	Yes
Reading technology	Yes
Audio books	Yes
Other assistive technology	Yes
Priority registration	Yes

Added costs of services:

For LD	No
For ADHD	No
For ASD	No
LD specialists	No
ADHD & ASD coaching	No
ASD specialists	No
Professional tutors	Yes
Peer tutors	Yes
Max. hours/week for services	Varies
How professors are notified of student approved accommodations	Student Accessibility Services

COLLEGE GRADUATION REQUIREMENTS

Course waivers allowed	No
Course substitutions allowed	Yes
In what courses: Generally Math and Foreign Language	

PROGRAMS/SERVICES FOR STUDENTS WITH LEARNING DIFFERENCES

Student Accessibility Services (SAS) provides accommodations for students with documented disabilities. Students should apply online to schedule a welcome meeting, where they can discuss experiences, barriers, reasonable accommodations, options, and next steps with SAS consultants. Students can upload documentation to show the history of their past accommodations prior to the meeting. However, students shouldn't worry if they don't have the right paperwork. Accommodations at a university may differ from K-12; SAS consultants will discuss specific documentation needs during the meeting. SAS does not handle housing accommodations. The Center for Autism and Related Disabilities (CARD) at UC Florida is one of seven CARD centers in Florida. UCF CARD provides Central Floridians with autism spectrum disorders individualized support from a specialist. CARD also offers services like technical assistance, professional training, and more.

ADMISSIONS

All applicants submit the same application. Admission decisions are primarily determined by applicants' academic credentials, including high school GPA, rigor of coursework, and SAT or ACT scores. Letters of recommendation are neither required nor considered. Students can describe their extracurricular activities on the application. Personal essays are optional but encouraged because they give the admissions committee the opportunity to get to know applicants outside of test scores and other quantitative data. Applicants denied admission because of their academic credentials will have the right to appeal the decision. Each year, some first-years will be selected by the admissions office to receive additional academic prep before their first semester through The Access Program, a six-week on-campus summer module run through SARC.

Additional Information

The Student Academic Resource Center (SARC) provides workshops, study sessions, and tutoring. Students are paired with peer advisors and coaches who help them develop study skills, including preparing for tests, textbook reading, and note-taking. They also promote motivation, persistence, and wellness and can help students effectively manage their time. Students can sign up for one-on-one tutoring sessions for course-specific material. Each semester, SARC provides students with an opportunity to enhance their learning and study skills through a series of Academic Success Workshops. Topics include test preparation, time management, textbook reading, note-taking, and more. Workshops are live streamed and can be rewatched on the SARC YouTube channel. SARC Supplemental Instruction (SI) provides weekly study sessions for students taking difficult courses.

In 1970, a murky, mud-filled pit was transformed into The Reflecting Pond at the heart of campus. Every year for the homecoming tradition "Spirit Splash," students try and catch rubber ducks in The Reflecting Pond while UCF cheerleaders and the Marching Knights cheer them on.

University of Central Florida

GENERAL ADMISSIONS

Very important factors include: rigor of secondary school record, academic GPA, standardized test scores. *Important factors include:* application essay. *Other factors considered include:* class rank. High school diploma is required and GED is accepted. Institution requires SAT/ACT scores for entering Fall 2024. Check admissions website for updates. *Academic units required:* 4 English, 4 math, 3 science (2 labs), 2 foreign language, 3 social studies, 2 academic electives.

FINANCIAL AID

Students should submit: FAFSA. *Need-based scholarships/grants offered:* College/university scholarship or grant aid from institutional funds; Federal Pell; Private scholarships; SEOG; State scholarships/grants. *Loan aid offered:* Direct PLUS loans; Direct Subsidized Loans; Direct Unsubsidized Loans. Federal Work-Study Program available. Institutional employment available.

CAMPUS LIFE

Activities: Campus Ministries; Choral groups; Concert band; Dance; Drama/theater; International Student Organization; Jazz band; Literary magazine; Marching band; Model UN; Music ensembles; Musical theater; Opera; Pep band; Radio station; Student government; Student newspaper; Student-run film society; Symphony orchestra; Television station. **Organizations:** 606 registered organizations, 24 honor societies, 46 religious organizations, 22 fraternities, 23 sororities. **Athletics (Intercollegiate):** *Men:* baseball, basketball, bowling, crew/rowing, cycling, equestrian sports, golf, ice hockey, lacrosse, martial arts, racquetball, rugby, swimming, table tennis, ultimate frisbee, volleyball, water polo, wrestling. *Women:* basketball, bowling, crew/rowing, cross-country, cycling, equestrian sports, golf, lacrosse, martial arts, racquetball, rugby, softball, swimming, table tennis, track/field (indoor), ultimate frisbee, volleyball, water polo, wrestling.

CAMPUS

Type of school	Public
Environment	City

STUDENTS

Undergrad enrollment	58,400
% male/female	45/55
% from out of state	7
% frosh live on campus	69

FINANCIAL FACTS

Annual in-state tuition	$6,368
Annual out-of-state tuition	$22,467
Room and board	$10,000
Required fees	$212

GENERAL ADMISSIONS INFO

Application fee	$30
Regular application deadline	5/1
Nonfall registration	Yes
Fall 2024 testing policy	SAT or ACT Required
Range SAT EBRW	610–680
Range SAT Math	590–680
Range ACT Composite	25–29

ACADEMICS

Student/faculty ratio	29:1
% students returning for sophomore year	93

Most classes have 20–29 students.

REQUESTING SERVICES FOR STUDENTS WITH LEARNING DIFFERENCES

Phone: 407-823-2371 • sas.sdes.ucf.edu • Email: sas@ucf.edu

Documentation submitted to: Student Accessibility Services

Separate application required for Services: Yes

Documentation required for:
LD: Psychoeducational evaluation
ADHD: Psychoeducational evaluation
ASD: Psychoeducational evaluation

Florida

University of Florida

201 Criser Hall, Gainesville, FL 32611-4000 • Admissions: 352-392-1365 • www.ufl.edu

(Support: CS)

ACCOMMODATIONS

Allowed in exams:

Calculators	Yes
Dictionary	Yes
Computer	Yes
Spell-checker	Yes
Extended test time	Yes
Scribe	Yes
Proctors	Yes
Oral exams	Yes
Note-takers	Yes

Support services for students with:

LD	Yes
ADHD	Yes
ASD	Yes
Distraction-reduced environment	Yes
Recording of lecture allowed	Yes
Reading technology	Yes
Audio books	Yes
Other assistive technology	Yes
Priority registration	Yes

Added costs of services:

For LD	No
For ADHD	No
For ASD	No
LD specialists	Yes
ADHD & ASD coaching	Yes
ASD specialists	Yes
Professional tutors	No
Peer tutors	Yes
Max. hours/week for services	Varies
How professors are notified of student approved accommodations	Student

COLLEGE GRADUATION REQUIREMENTS

Course waivers allowed	No
Course substitutions allowed	Yes
In what courses: Foreign Language and Math	

PROGRAMS/SERVICES FOR STUDENTS WITH LEARNING DIFFERENCES

The Disability Resource Center (DRC) provides a variety of reasonable accommodations for students with learning disabilities. Students submit a preregistration form and schedule a meeting with an assigned accessibility specialist to explore previous educational experiences, past use of accommodations, what has been effective, and current appropriate accommodations and housing needs. Students will need to submit an online accommodation letter of request for each course (accommodations may vary course to course). Students are responsible for informing their instructors and discussing their approved accommodations. Accommodations may include access to PowerPoints, alternate-format textbooks, audio recordings of lectures, and more. Scholarships are available for current students registered with the Disability Resource Center; each scholarship has distinct qualifications and application criteria.

ADMISSIONS

UF is competitive, and students should have a C or better in academic core courses. SAT or ACT scores are required. Regardless of academic qualifications, a record of good conduct is also required. All applications are reviewed at least twice by the admissions committee. Due to the thorough review process, appeals will only be considered if they provide new and compelling information. Qualified first-year applicants may be selected by the admissions office for the Pathway to Campus Enrollment (PaCE) and given the opportunity to start their degree through UFonline. After meeting specific requirements, students transition to campus to complete an undergraduate degree. During the admissions review process, applicants may be selectively chosen for the UF Promise Program. These are students who might benefit from additional academic support and campus experience. Promise students begin their first semester on campus during the summer before school starts. Promise students have access to exclusive resources such as priority options for smaller class sizes during Summer B, and advanced registration and advising, free tutoring through Knack tutoring services, personal and professional workshops, and peer coaching. They must also complete a mandatory First-Year Florida course with sections dedicated specifically for Promise students.

Additional Information

All students can take advantage of the Office of Academic Support (OAS), offering students a variety of free resources, workshops, peer coaching test review throughout the semester, and a video library accessible anytime. OAS tutoring is offered by appointment and there are drop-in hours for biology, chemistry, mathematics, physics, and statistics courses within the College of Liberal Arts and Sciences.

UF's first intercollegiate football game was in 1906; the squad was called "Pee Wee's Boys," led by 24-year-old coach Jack "Pee Wee" Forsythe. The name "Gators" was adopted in 1911. Today more gator statues are on UF's campus than statues of people in the city of Gainesville. The football field is known as the "Swamp," the student section is the "Rowdy Reptiles." "Go Gators" can be used as a greeting and a way to end any speech or conversation.

University of Florida

GENERAL ADMISSIONS

Very important factors include: rigor of secondary school record, academic GPA, application essay. *Important factors include:* standardized test scores. *Other factors considered include:* class rank. High school diploma is required and GED is accepted. Institution requires SAT/ACT scores for entering Fall 2024. Check admissions website for updates. *Academic units required:* 4 English, 4 math, 3 science (2 labs), 3 social studies, 2 foreign language. *Academic units recommended:* 4 science, 4 foreign language.

FINANCIAL AID

Students should submit: FAFSA. *Need-based scholarships/grants offered:* College/university scholarship or grant aid from institutional funds; Federal Pell; Private scholarships; SEOG; State scholarships/grants; United Negro College Fund. *Loan aid offered:* Direct PLUS loans; Direct Subsidized Loans; Direct Unsubsidized Loans. Federal Work-Study Program available. Institutional employment available.

CAMPUS LIFE

Activities: Campus Ministries; Choral groups; Concert band; Dance; Drama/theater; International Student Organization; Jazz band; Literary magazine; Marching band; Model UN; Music ensembles; Musical theater; Opera; Pep band; Radio station; Student government; Student newspaper; Student-run film society; Symphony orchestra; Television station; Yearbook. **Organizations:** 1058 registered organizations, 30 honor societies, 49 religious organizations, 36 fraternities, 28 sororities. **Athletics (Intercollegiate):** *Men:* baseball, basketball, bowling, crew/rowing, cross-country, cycling, equestrian sports, field hockey, golf, ice hockey, lacrosse, martial arts, rugby, swimming, table tennis, track/field (indoor), ultimate frisbee, volleyball, water polo, wrestling. *Women:* basketball, bowling, crew/rowing, cross-country, cycling, equestrian sports, field hockey, golf, gymnastics, lacrosse, martial arts, rugby, softball, swimming, table tennis, track/field (indoor), ultimate frisbee, volleyball, water polo, wrestling.

CAMPUS
Type of school	Public
Environment	City

STUDENTS
Undergrad enrollment	33,673
% male/female	44/56
% from out of state	10
% frosh live on campus	77

FINANCIAL FACTS
Annual in-state tuition	$6,381
Annual out-of-state tuition	$28,658
Room and board	$10,400

GENERAL ADMISSIONS INFO
Application fee	$30
Regular application deadline	3/1
Nonfall registration	Yes
Fall 2024 testing policy	SAT or ACT Required
Range SAT EBRW	650–730
Range SAT Math	650–760
Range ACT Composite	28–33

ACADEMICS
Student/faculty ratio	17:1
% students returning for sophomore year	97

REQUESTING SERVICES FOR STUDENTS WITH LEARNING DIFFERENCES

Phone: 352-392-8565 • www.disability.ufl.edu • Email: jenna04@ufl.edu

Documentation submitted to: Disability Resource Center
Separate application required for Services: Yes

Documentation required for:
LD: Psychoeducational evaluation
ADHD: Psychoeducational evaluation
ASD: Psychoeducational evaluation

University of Tampa

401 West Kennedy Boulevard, Tampa, FL 33606-1490 • Admissions: 813-253-6211 • www.ut.edu

Support: S

ACCOMMODATIONS

Allowed in exams:

Calculators	Yes
Dictionary	Yes
Computer	Yes
Spell-checker	Yes
Extended test time	Yes
Scribe	Yes
Proctors	Yes
Oral exams	Yes
Note-takers	Yes

Support services for students with:

LD	Yes
ADHD	Yes
ASD	Yes
Distraction-reduced environment	Yes
Recording of lecture allowed	Yes
Reading technology	Yes
Audio books	N/A
Other assistive technology	Yes
Priority registration	No

Added costs of services:

For LD	No
For ADHD	No
For ASD	No
LD specialists	No
ADHD & ASD coaching	No
ASD specialists	No
Professional tutors	No
Peer tutors	Yes
Max. hours/week for services	Varies
How professors are notified of student approved accommodations	Student and SAS

COLLEGE GRADUATION REQUIREMENTS

Course waivers allowed	Yes
In what courses: Math	
Course substitutions allowed	Yes
In what courses: Math	

PROGRAMS/SERVICES FOR STUDENTS WITH LEARNING DIFFERENCES

Student Accessibility Services (SAS), through the Office of Student Accessibility and Academic Support, serves students with learning differences. A wide array of academic supports and accommodations are available, including coaching, tutoring, testing services, assistive technology, and alternative media formats. Students must complete an online accommodation request and submit documentation. A high school IEP or 504 Plan is an acceptable form of documentation but does not guarantee services.

ADMISSIONS

All applicants must meet the same general admission requirements. Some majors (such as athletic training, education, nursing, music, performing arts, and theater) require an additional application, portfolio, or audition. In certain instances, students may be eligible for a waiver of the math requirement based on a disability. The average GPA for admitted applicants is 3.45.

Additional Information

The Academic Success Center is available to provide students with strategies to be successful in college. Within Student Accessibility and Academic Support is the SOAR program (Students Overcoming Academic Roadblocks). SOAR provides individualized academic support focusing on campus engagement, study skills, and goal setting. Peer tutoring and peer-assisted study sessions are also available. The Dickey Health and Wellness Center provides an array of supports, including counseling and social wellness. The Center for Public Speaking helps students improve communication skills by providing one-to-one tutoring and small group workshops with peer tutors and experienced professionals. The university does not have a foreign language requirement.

To be inspired, students visit the seven pillars of the Sticks of Fire campus sculpture, which represents the Native American meaning of the word Tampa: "bringing light of knowledge and warmth of feeling to a people who don't just wish to exist, but to excel." Students can also visit the Sykes Chapel—for meditation and celebration of all faiths—with an organ that has 3,184 pipes and stands 55 feet tall. Or take a walk around UT's 105 acres—with river views, Tampa skyline, Plant Park (with cannons from the original harbor fort), and beautiful old oak trees.

University of Tampa

GENERAL ADMISSIONS

Very important factors include: rigor of secondary school record, academic GPA. *Important factors include:* application essay, recommendations. *Other factors considered include:* class rank. High school diploma is required and GED is accepted. Institution is test-optional for entering Fall 2024. Check admissions website for updates. *Academic units required:* 4 English, 3 math, 3 science (2 labs), 2 foreign language, 3 social studies, 3 academic electives.

FINANCIAL AID

Students should submit: FAFSA. *Need-based scholarships/grants offered:* College/university scholarship or grant aid from institutional funds; Federal Pell; Private scholarships; SEOG; State scholarships/grants. *Loan aid offered:* Direct PLUS loans; Direct Subsidized Loans; Direct Unsubsidized Loans. Federal Work-Study Program available. Institutional employment available.

CAMPUS LIFE

Activities: Campus Ministries; Choral groups; Concert band; Dance; Drama/theater; International Student Organization; Jazz band; Literary magazine; Model UN; Music ensembles; Musical theater; Pep band; Radio station; Student government; Student newspaper; Student-run film society; Symphony orchestra; Television station; Yearbook. **Organizations:** 240 registered organizations, 15 honor societies, 8 religious organizations, 13 fraternities, 14 sororities. **Athletics (Intercollegiate):** *Men:* baseball, basketball, crew/rowing, cross-country, field hockey, golf, ice hockey, lacrosse, swimming. *Women:* basketball, crew/rowing, cross-country, equestrian sports, field hockey, golf, lacrosse, softball, swimming, volleyball.

CAMPUS

Type of school	Private (nonprofit)
Environment	Metropolis

STUDENTS

Undergrad enrollment	9,593
% male/female	41/59
% from out of state	73
% frosh live on campus	94

FINANCIAL FACTS

Annual tuition	$30,036
Room and board	$12,332
Required fees	$2,182

GENERAL ADMISSIONS INFO

Application fee	$40
Regular application deadline	Rolling
Nonfall registration	Yes
Fall 2024 testing policy	Test Optional
Range SAT EBRW	540–640
Range SAT Math	540–640
Range ACT Composite	22–28

ACADEMICS

Student/faculty ratio	17:1
% students returning for sophomore year	81

Most classes have 20–29 students.

REQUESTING SERVICES FOR STUDENTS WITH LEARNING DIFFERENCES

Phone: 813-257-3266 • www.ut.edu/academics/academic-support/academic-excellence-programs/student-accessibility-services • Email: accessibility.services@ut.edu

Documentation submitted to: Student Accessibility Services
Separate application required for Services: Yes

Documentation required for:
LD: Psychoeducational evaluation
ADHD: Psychoeducational evaluation
ASD: Psychoeducational evaluation

University of West Florida

11000 University Parkway, Pensacola, FL 32514-5750 • Admissions: 850-474-2230 • uwf.edu

ACCOMMODATIONS

Allowed in exams:

Calculators	Yes
Dictionary	No
Computer	Yes
Spell-checker	Yes
Extended test time	Yes
Scribe	Yes
Proctors	Yes
Oral exams	No
Note-takers	Yes

Support services for students with:

LD	Yes
ADHD	Yes
ASD	Yes
Distraction-reduced environment	Yes
Recording of lecture allowed	Yes
Reading technology	Yes
Audio books	Yes
Other assistive technology	Yes
Priority registration	Yes

Added costs of services:

For LD	No
For ADHD	No
For ASD	Yes
LD specialists	No
ADHD & ASD coaching	Yes
ASD specialists	Yes
Professional tutors	No
Peer tutors	Yes
Max. hours/week for services	Varies
How professors are notified of student approved accommodations	Students

COLLEGE GRADUATION REQUIREMENTS

Course waivers allowed	Yes

In what courses: Case-by-case basis

Course substitutions allowed	Yes

In what courses: Case-by-case basis

PROGRAMS/SERVICES FOR STUDENTS WITH LEARNING DIFFERENCES

Student Accessibility Resources (SAR) offers a variety of accommodations and services for students with documented disabilities. Students may register with SAR soon after admission to the university; appointments for incoming students are typically scheduled no earlier than one month before the start of the first semester. Accommodations and services provided by SAR include assistive technology, audiobooks, housing accommodations, interpretive services, note-taking support, scribes, readers, enlarged text, preferential seating, a reduced course load, and testing accommodations. SAR also assists students who need to request substitutions or waivers for graduation requirements, such as foreign language. SAR and the UWF Center for Behavior Analysis offer the Argos Autism Program (AAP), which helps students build life skills through social and academic coaching. SAR staff aids students in navigating campus resources, academic challenges, and career planning. AAP hosts the Early Arrival Program for students with ASD to allow students to acclimate to campus life prior to the official start of school. There is a fee for this two-day program.

ADMISSIONS

All students must meet the same admission criteria. Applications are reviewed holistically, with consideration for test scores, rigor of academics, GPA, personal essay, letters of recommendation, extracurricular activities, and volunteerism. The middle 50 percent of admitted students have a 3.6–4.2 high school GPA and 1060–1240 on the SAT or 21–27 on the ACT. Students who do not meet the standards for admission may still be accepted through the Argo's Pathway to Success program. Such students demonstrate the potential to succeed in college, but their academic profile suggests they would benefit from transitional support during their first semester. Following completion of the first semester, Pathway participants can enroll as full-time students and graduate in four years.

Additional Information

Through the Center for Academic Success, first-year students are assigned to a specific advisor in First Year Advising to assist with academic goal setting, degree planning, and initial course registration before transitioning to academic advisors in the major departments. Tutoring and Learning Resources provides strategies to build learning and study skills and has subject-based free tutoring for all UWF students.

The Library Green became Cannon Green after former UWF student Bob Annin found the cannon at the mouth of Pensacola Pass in February 1970 and donated it to UWF. The markings on the cannon showed that it had been cast in England circa 1760 and may have been used during British control of Pensacola. It's an iconic part of UWF and the inspiration for Cannon Fest, the Cannon Party, and Cannon Citations.

University of West Florida

GENERAL ADMISSIONS

Very important factors include: rigor of secondary school record, academic GPA, standardized test scores. *Other factors considered include:* application essay, recommendations. High school diploma is required and GED is accepted. Institution requires SAT/ACT scores for entering Fall 2024. Check admissions website for updates. *Academic units required:* 4 English, 3 math, 3 science (2 labs), 2 foreign language, 3 social studies, 4 academic electives.

FINANCIAL AID

Students should submit: FAFSA. *Need-based scholarships/grants offered:* College/university scholarship or grant aid from institutional funds; Federal Pell; Private scholarships; SEOG; State scholarships/grants. *Loan aid offered:* Direct PLUS loans; Direct Subsidized Loans; Direct Unsubsidized Loans. Federal Work-Study Program available. Institutional employment available.

CAMPUS LIFE

Activities: Campus Ministries; Choral groups; Concert band; Dance; Drama/theater; International Student Organization; Jazz band; Music ensembles; Musical theater; Pep band; Radio station; Student government; Student newspaper; Symphony orchestra; Television station. **Organizations:** 154 registered organizations, 7 honor societies, 10 religious organizations, 9 fraternities, 7 sororities. **Athletics (Intercollegiate):** *Men:* baseball, basketball, cross-country, cycling, golf, lacrosse, martial arts, racquetball, rugby, swimming, table tennis, wrestling. *Women:* basketball, cross-country, cycling, golf, lacrosse, martial arts, racquetball, rugby, softball, swimming, table tennis, volleyball, wrestling.

CAMPUS	
Type of school	Public
Environment	City

STUDENTS	
Undergrad enrollment	9,786
% male/female	43/57
% from out of state	9
% frosh live on campus	54

FINANCIAL FACTS	
Annual in-state tuition	$4,319
Annual out-of-state tuition	$16,587
Room and board	$11,268
Required fees	$2,041

GENERAL ADMISSIONS INFO	
Application fee	$30
Regular application deadline	6/30
Nonfall registration	Yes
Fall 2024 testing policy	SAT or ACT Required
Range SAT EBRW	530–630
Range SAT Math	510–600
Range ACT Composite	21–27

ACADEMICS	
Student/faculty ratio	21:1
% students returning for sophomore year	84
Most classes have 20–29 students.	

REQUESTING SERVICES FOR STUDENTS WITH LEARNING DIFFERENCES

Phone: 850-474-2387 • uwf.edu/academic-engagement-and-student-affairs/departments/student-accessibility-resources • Email: sar@uwf.edu

Documentation submitted to: Student Accessibility Resources

Separate application required for Services: Yes

Documentation required for:
LD: Psychoeducational evaluation
ADHD: Psychoeducational evaluation
ASD: Psychoeducational evaluation

Brenau University

500 Washington Street SE, Gainesville, GA 30501 • Admissions: 770-534-6100 • www.brenau.edu

Support: CS

ACCOMMODATIONS

Allowed in exams:

Calculators	Yes
Dictionary	Yes
Computer	Yes
Spell-checker	Yes
Extended test time	Yes
Scribe	Yes
Proctors	Yes
Oral exams	Yes
Note-takers	No

Support services for students with:

LD	Yes
ADHD	Yes
ASD	Yes
Distraction-reduced environment	Yes
Recording of lecture allowed	Yes
Reading technology	Yes
Audio books	Yes
Other assistive technology	Yes
Priority registration	Yes

Added costs of services:

For LD	No
For ADHD	No
For ASD	No
LD specialists	Yes
ADHD & ASD coaching	Yes
ASD specialists	No
Professional tutors	Yes
Peer tutors	Yes
Max. hours/week for services	Varies
How professors are notified of student approved accommodations	Student

COLLEGE GRADUATION REQUIREMENTS

Course waivers allowed	No
Course substitutions allowed	No

PROGRAMS/SERVICES FOR STUDENTS WITH LEARNING DIFFERENCES

The Office of Accessibility Services (OAS) provides accommodations and guidance for students with documented disabilities. To request accommodations, students provide current documentation to OAS and then have a one-on-one meeting with the OAS director. Once students are approved for accommodations, they will receive an official letter stating their specific needs. OAS provides reasonable accommodations such as a distraction-free environment for testing, extended time on tests, note-taking, and guidance in navigating the accommodations process. OAS also helps students access other resources, such as academic coaching and peer support. Students with a diagnosed learning difference can access tutoring support, reading remediation, study strategies, and academic advising through the Center for Academic Success. The staff from the OAS and the Center for Academic Success offices collaborate to manage cases and provide the individual support needed.

ADMISSIONS

Applicants taking college prep courses in high school and have a minimum GPA of 2.5 will generally be admitted to Brenau. SAT and ACT scores are not required; however, if submitted, they can be used for scholarships and English placement. Applicants seeking admission in the performing arts, nursing, occupational therapy, or education must submit supplemental applications. Applicants who do not meet the minimum admission requirements may be granted admission on a probationary status.

Additional Information

The Center for Academic Success offers tutoring and coaching for all students at Brenau. The center is staffed with faculty who are experts in their disciplines, as well as professional and peer tutors. Students can make an appointment or drop in for help. The Writing Center has peer tutors who help students with writing and speaking skills, computer-based tutorials, and group workshops.

During R.A.T.T (Remember All The Traditions) Week, second-year students test the first-year class on their school history knowledge. If they answer incorrectly, students receive a fun task to complete to redeem themselves. During the Gold Refined by Fire ceremony, first-year students write down their goals and then drop them in a fire pit. The significance is to let students know that when they graduate, their goals will be "gold refined by fire."

Brenau University

GENERAL ADMISSIONS

Very important factors include: academic GPA. *Important factors include:* rigor of secondary school record. *Other factors considered include:* class rank, standardized test scores (if submitted), application essay, recommendations. High school diploma is required and GED is accepted. Institution is test-optional for entering Fall 2024. Check admissions website for updates. *Academic units required:* 4 English, 4 math, 3 science, 2 foreign language, 3 social studies.

FINANCIAL AID

Students should submit: FAFSA; State aid form. *Need-based scholarships/grants offered:* College/university scholarship or grant aid from institutional funds; Federal Pell; Private scholarships; SEOG; State scholarships/grants. *Loan aid offered:* Direct PLUS loans; Direct Subsidized Loans; Direct Unsubsidized Loans. Federal Work-Study Program available. Institutional employment available.

CAMPUS LIFE

Activities: Choral groups; Dance; Drama/theater; International Student Organization; Literary magazine; Music ensembles; Musical theater; Opera; Radio station; Student government; Student newspaper. **Organizations:** 26 registered organizations, 20 honor societies, 1 religious organizations, 0 fraternities, 7 sororities. **Athletics (Intercollegiate):** *Women:* basketball, cross-country, golf, lacrosse, softball, swimming, track/field (indoor), volleyball.

CAMPUS

Type of school	Private (nonprofit)
Environment	Town

STUDENTS

Undergrad enrollment	1,183
% male/female	7/93
% from out of state	5
% frosh live on campus	55

FINANCIAL FACTS

Annual tuition	$31,000
Room and board	$12,900
Required fees	$1,685

GENERAL ADMISSIONS INFO

Application fee	No fee
Regular application deadline	Rolling
Nonfall registration	Yes

Fall 2024 testing policy	Test Optional
Range SAT EBRW	490–590
Range SAT Math	480–570
Range ACT Composite	18–23

ACADEMICS

Student/faculty ratio	12:1
% students returning for sophomore year	55

Most classes have 2–9 students.

REQUESTING SERVICES FOR STUDENTS WITH LEARNING DIFFERENCES

Phone: 770-534-6133 • intranet.brenau.edu/office-of-accessibility-services
Email: accommodations@brenau.edu

Documentation submitted to: Office of Accessibility Services

Separate application required for Services: Yes

Documentation required for:
LD: Psychoeducational evaluation
ADHD: Psychoeducational evaluation
ASD: Psychoeducational evaluation

Emory University

Boiseuillet Jones Center, Atlanta, GA 30322 • Admissions: 404-727-6036 • www.emory.edu

ACCOMMODATIONS

Allowed in exams:

Calculators	Yes
Dictionary	Yes
Computer	Yes
Spell-checker	Yes
Extended test time	Yes
Scribe	Yes
Proctors	Yes
Oral exams	Yes
Note-takers	No

Support services for students with:

LD	Yes
ADHD	Yes
ASD	Yes
Distraction-reduced environment	Yes
Recording of lecture allowed	Yes
Reading technology	Yes
Audio books	Yes
Other assistive technology	Yes
Priority registration	Yes

Added costs of services:

For LD	No
For ADHD	No
For ASD	No
LD specialists	No
ADHD & ASD coaching	No
ASD specialists	No
Professional tutors	No
Peer tutors	Yes
Max. hours/week for services	Varies
How professors are notified of student approved accommodations	Student

COLLEGE GRADUATION REQUIREMENTS

Course waivers allowed	No
Course substitutions allowed	No

PROGRAMS/SERVICES FOR STUDENTS WITH LEARNING DIFFERENCES

The Department of Accessibility Services (DAS), part of the Office of Institutional Equity and Compliance, assists qualified students with obtaining various services and reasonable accommodations. The needs of students with learning disabilities are met through academic accommodations and a variety of support services. Qualified students must register with DAS and request services. DAS staff provides information for students about how to access specific accommodation needs once they've been accepted.

ADMISSIONS

Admission is the same for all students; however, teacher and/or counselor recommendations may be weighted more heavily in the admission process. All applicants are evaluated individually and admitted based on their potential for success. All first-year applicants are required to submit strong grades and have taken rigorous courses. Be aware that if submitting test scores, high board scores will not make up for an applicant's weak course selection or grades.

Additional Information

Tutoring is offered by Emory college in most subjects on a one-on-one basis or in small groups. Learning specialists are available to assist students in developing skills and strategies to define learning goals and individualized plans to reach their academic potential.

Dooley Week is a long-standing spring tradition at Emory. A skeleton used in the 1899 biology department became the unofficial mascot and guardian of school spirit, so, during Dooley Week, an unidentified student dresses up as Dooley and creates a little mischief. Dooley has the ability to end a class early just by walking in and proclaiming the class over. Students enjoy a week of fun activities, food, and end the week with a concert called Dooleypalooza—a musical extravaganza with food and activity stations and an after party. All events are free.

Emory University

GENERAL ADMISSIONS

Very important factors include: rigor of secondary school record, academic GPA, recommendations. *Important factors include:* standardized test scores (if submitted), application essay. *Other factors considered include:* class rank. High school diploma is required and GED is not accepted. Institution is test-optional for entering Fall 2024. Check admissions website for updates. *Academic units recommended:* 4 English, 4 math, 4 science (2 labs), 4 foreign language, 2 social studies, 2 history, 1 visual/performing arts.

FINANCIAL AID

Students should submit: CSS/Financial Aid Profile; FAFSA; Noncustodial Profile. *Need-based scholarships/grants offered:* College/university scholarship or grant aid from institutional funds; Federal Pell; Private scholarships; SEOG. *Loan aid offered:* Direct PLUS loans; Direct Subsidized Loans; Direct Unsubsidized Loans. Federal Work-Study Program available. Institutional employment available.

CAMPUS LIFE

Activities: Campus Ministries; Choral groups; Concert band; Dance; Drama/theater; International Student Organization; Jazz band; Literary magazine; Model UN; Music ensembles; Musical theater; Opera; Radio station; Student government; Student newspaper; Student-run film society; Symphony orchestra; Television station. **Organizations:** 28 honor societies. **Athletics (Intercollegiate):** *Men:* baseball, basketball, crew/rowing, cross-country, cycling, equestrian sports, field hockey, golf, lacrosse, martial arts, rugby, softball, swimming, track/field (indoor). *Women:* basketball, crew/rowing, cross-country, cycling, equestrian sports, field hockey, golf, gymnastics, lacrosse, martial arts, rugby, softball, swimming, track/field (indoor), ultimate frisbee, volleyball, water polo.

CAMPUS
Type of school	Private (nonprofit)
Environment	City

STUDENTS
Undergrad enrollment	7,022
% male/female	43/57
% from out of state	84
% frosh live on campus	99

FINANCIAL FACTS
Annual tuition	$54,660
Room and board	$16,302
Required fees	$808

GENERAL ADMISSIONS INFO
Application fee	$75
Regular application deadline	1/1
Nonfall registration	No

Fall 2024 testing policy	Test Optional
Range SAT EBRW	700–760
Range SAT Math	730–790
Range ACT Composite	32–34

ACADEMICS
Student/faculty ratio	9:1
% students returning for sophomore year	95

Most classes have 10–19 students.

REQUESTING SERVICES FOR STUDENTS WITH LEARNING DIFFERENCES

Phone: 404-727-9877 • accessibility.emory.edu • Email: accessibility@emory.edu

Documentation submitted to: Department of Accessibility Services
Separate application required for Services: Yes

Documentation required for:
 LD: Psychoeducational evaluation
 ADHD: Psychoeducational evaluation
 ASD: Psychoeducational evaluation

Georgia Southern University

P.O. Box 8024, Statesboro, GA 30460 • Admissions: 912-478-5391 • www.georgiasouthern.edu

Support: CS

ACCOMMODATIONS

Allowed in exams:

Calculators	Yes
Dictionary	Yes
Computer	Yes
Spell-checker	Yes
Extended test time	Yes
Scribe	Yes
Proctors	Yes
Oral exams	Yes
Note-takers	Yes

Support services for students with:

LD	Yes
ADHD	Yes
ASD	Yes
Distraction-reduced environment	Yes
Recording of lecture allowed	Yes
Reading technology	Yes
Audio books	No
Other assistive technology	Yes
Priority registration	Yes

Added costs of services:

For LD	No
For ADHD	No
For ASD	No
LD specialists	Yes
ADHD & ASD coaching	Yes
ASD specialists	Yes
Professional tutors	No
Peer tutors	Yes
Max. hours/week for services	Varies
How professors are notified of student approved accommodations	Student

COLLEGE GRADUATION REQUIREMENTS

Course waivers allowed	Yes
In what courses: Foreign Language and Math	
Course substitutions allowed	Yes
In what courses: Foreign Language and Math	

PROGRAMS/SERVICES FOR STUDENTS WITH LEARNING DIFFERENCES

Georgia Southern University offers a variety of services specifically tailored to students with learning disabilities. Students with identified learning disabilities should register with the Student Accessibility Resource Center (SARC). Through SARC, students may be eligible for special registration, academic assistance, and support and strategy-building services to help with time management, note-taking, studying, and boosting self-confidence. SARC professional staff members are available to meet with students individually to help ensure their specific needs and goals are being addressed. A support group is also available, designed to help students manage any personal and academic challenges related to their disabilities.

ADMISSIONS

All applicants must meet the same requirements for admission. A 2.5 GPA is recommended; however, the Office of Admissions may admit new first-years as long as they've earned a high school diploma. Students admitted without meeting the required admission criteria for the Statesboro and Armstrong campuses must complete 30 or more credit hours with a cumulative 2.0 or higher GPA, as well as make up any previously incomplete high school requirements before transitioning to another Georgia Southern campus.

Additional Information

The Academic Success Center (ASC) offers a variety of services, including academic success coaching, consultations, workshops, peer mentoring, peer tutoring, and testing services. As part of the ASC, the Learning Support Program provides students with additional support to develop skills in reading, composition, and mathematics. Students are enrolled in the Learning Support Program based on placement test results. The Peer Mentoring Program offers students guidance on courses and campus life from trained upper-level students.

The Smithsonian Museum of Natural History has a National Tick Collection (USNTC). Since 1990, GSU's James H. Oliver, Jr., Institute for Coastal Plain Science has been home to the collection of over one million specimens, their data, and an extensive library. USNTC contains specimens from all continents: most of the 860 known species and a quarter of primary tick types. Because of the impact on human and veterinary medicine, the USNTC is significant to public health officials, as well as tick taxonomists.

Georgia Southern University

GENERAL ADMISSIONS

Very important factors include: rigor of secondary school record, academic GPA, standardized test scores (if submitted). *Other factors considered include:* class rank. High school diploma is required and GED is not accepted. Institution is test-optional for entering Fall 2024. Check admissions website for updates. *Academic units required:* 4 English, 4 math, 4 science (2 labs), 2 foreign language, 3 social studies.

FINANCIAL AID

Students should submit: FAFSA. *Need-based scholarships/grants offered:* College/university scholarship or grant aid from institutional funds; Federal Pell; Private scholarships; SEOG; State scholarships/grants. *Loan aid offered:* Direct PLUS loans; Direct Subsidized Loans; Direct Unsubsidized Loans. Federal Work-Study Program available. Institutional employment available.

CAMPUS LIFE

Activities: Campus Ministries; Choral groups; Concert band; Dance; Drama/theater; International Student Organization; Jazz band; Literary magazine; Marching band; Music ensembles; Musical theater; Opera; Radio station; Student government; Student newspaper; Student-run film society; Symphony orchestra. **Organizations:** 280 registered organizations, 17 honor societies, 24 religious organizations, 48 fraternities, 12 sororities. **Athletics (Intercollegiate):** *Men:* baseball, basketball, bowling, cross-country, equestrian sports, golf, lacrosse, rugby, swimming, table tennis, ultimate frisbee, volleyball, wrestling. *Women:* basketball, bowling, cross-country, equestrian sports, golf, lacrosse, rugby, softball, swimming, table tennis, ultimate frisbee, volleyball.

CAMPUS
Type of school	Public
Environment	Town

STUDENTS
Undergrad enrollment	22,242
% male/female	46/54
% from out of state	6
% frosh live on campus	81

FINANCIAL FACTS
Annual in-state tuition	$5,330
Annual out-of-state tuition	$18,812
Room and board	$10,070
Required fees	$2,092

GENERAL ADMISSIONS INFO
Application fee	$30
Regular application deadline	5/1
Nonfall registration	Yes

Fall 2024 testing policy	Test Optional
Range SAT EBRW	540–610
Range SAT Math	520–590
Range ACT Composite	21–25

ACADEMICS
Student/faculty ratio	21:1
% students returning for sophomore year	80

Most classes have 20–29 students.

REQUESTING SERVICES FOR STUDENTS WITH LEARNING DIFFERENCES

Phone: 912-478-1566 • students.georgiasouthern.edu/sarc • Email: sarcboro@georgiasouthern.edu

Documentation submitted to: Student Accessibility Resource Center
Separate application required for Services: Yes

Documentation required for:
LD: Psychoeducational evaluation
ADHD: Psychoeducational evaluation
ASD: Psychoeducational evaluation

Georgia State University

P.O. Box 4009, Atlanta, GA 30302-4009 • Admissions: 404-413-2500 • www.gsu.edu

Support: CS

PROGRAMS/SERVICES FOR STUDENTS WITH LEARNING DIFFERENCES

Georgia State University provides accommodations for students with disabilities on an individualized basis. To receive accommodations, students are expected to self-identify with the Access and Accommodations Center (AACE) by completing and returning the AACE registration form and submitting documentation of their disability. Resources for students with diagnosed disabilities may include assistive technology, foreign language substitutions, math course substitutions, and note-taking software. Accommodated testing for students requiring extended time or a distraction-reduced environment may also be available. Eligibility for priority registration is determined during the orientation meeting with an AACE coordinator. Student Support Services (SSS) is provided at no cost to eligible students, which include students with learning disabilities and/or ADHD. Services of SSS include academic advice, individual and group tutoring, and workshops.

ADMISSIONS

All students must meet the same admission criteria. Substitutions for the foreign language requirement are permitted if the student has documentation that supports the substitution. If students are denied admission, they may appeal; probationary admission can be granted with an appeal.

Additional Information

The Academic Coaching Experience offers academic support services to all students at Georgia State University. The coach and student begin by assessing the student's academic strengths, weaknesses, and other factors that may be impeding academic progress. Students can also find assistance remotely. The Learning & Tutoring Center (LTC) provides free tutoring online in mathematics, reading, writing, science, and more.

GSU's Sports Arena hosted the 1996 Summer Olympic Games badminton matches. The first campus dormitories, The Village, were also part of the 1996 Olympic Village. Some of the Atlanta venues for the Olympics still remain, but with new purpose. Centennial Olympic Stadium, host of the opening and closing ceremonies of the Olympics, was converted to Turner Field, for MLB's Atlanta Braves. After the Braves moved to SunTrust Park, Turner Field and the surrounding grounds were purchased by GSU, and is now recognized as Center Parc Stadium, home to GSU's Panther football team.

Georgia State University

GENERAL ADMISSIONS

Very important factors include: rigor of secondary school record, academic GPA, standardized test scores (if submitted). *Other factors considered include:* application essay, recommendations. High school diploma is required and GED is not accepted. Institution is test-optional for entering Fall 2024. Check admissions website for updates. *Academic units required:* 4 English, 4 math, 4 science (2 labs), 2 foreign language, 3 social studies. *Academic units recommended:* 4 English, 4 math, 4 science (2 labs), 2 foreign language, 3 social studies.

FINANCIAL AID

Students should submit: FAFSA. *Need-based scholarships/grants offered:* College/university scholarship or grant aid from institutional funds; Federal Pell; Private scholarships; SEOG; State scholarships/grants; United Negro College Fund. *Loan aid offered:* Direct PLUS loans; Direct Subsidized Loans; Direct Unsubsidized Loans. Federal Work-Study Program available. Institutional employment available.

CAMPUS LIFE

Activities: Campus Ministries; Choral groups; Concert band; Dance; Drama/theater; International Student Organization; Jazz band; Literary magazine; Marching band; Model UN; Music ensembles; Musical theater; Opera; Pep band; Radio station; Student government; Student newspaper; Student-run film society; Symphony orchestra; Television station. **Organizations:** 520 registered organizations, 19 honor societies, 37 religious organizations, 15 fraternities, 15 sororities. **Athletics (Intercollegiate):** *Men:* baseball, basketball, crew/rowing, cycling, equestrian sports, golf, ice hockey, lacrosse, martial arts, rugby, swimming, table tennis, ultimate frisbee, volleyball, wrestling. *Women:* basketball, crew/rowing, cross-country, cycling, equestrian sports, golf, ice hockey, lacrosse, martial arts, softball, swimming, table tennis, track/field (indoor), ultimate frisbee, volleyball, wrestling.

CAMPUS

Type of school	Public
Environment	Metropolis

STUDENTS

Undergrad enrollment	28,425
% male/female	40/60
% from out of state	6
% frosh live on campus	49

FINANCIAL FACTS

Annual in-state tuition	$8,948
Annual out-of-state tuition	$27,986
Room and board	$15,109
Required fees	$2,128

GENERAL ADMISSIONS INFO

Application fee	$60
Regular application deadline	4/1
Nonfall registration	Yes
Fall 2024 testing policy	Test Optional
Range SAT EBRW	485–590
Range SAT Math	490–630
Range ACT Composite	19–27

ACADEMICS

Student/faculty ratio	27:1
% students returning for sophomore year	73
Most classes have 20–29 students.	

REQUESTING SERVICES FOR STUDENTS WITH LEARNING DIFFERENCES

Phone: 404-413-1560 • access.gsu.edu • Email: access@gsu.edu

Documentation submitted to: Access and Accommodations Center
Separate application required for Services: Yes

Documentation required for:
LD: Psychoeducational evaluation
ADHD: Psychoeducational evaluation
ASD: Psychoeducational evaluation

Kennesaw State University

3391 Town Point Drive, Suite 1000, Kennesaw, GA 30144 • Admissions: 770-423-6300 • kennesaw.edu

Support: S

ACCOMMODATIONS

Allowed in exams:

Calculators	Yes
Dictionary	Yes
Computer	Yes
Spell-checker	Yes
Extended test time	Yes
Scribe	Yes
Proctors	Yes
Oral exams	Yes
Note-takers	Yes

Support services for students with:

LD	Yes
ADHD	Yes
ASD	Yes
Distraction-reduced environment	Yes
Recording of lecture allowed	Yes
Reading technology	Yes
Audio books	Yes
Other assistive technology	Yes
Priority registration	Yes

Added costs of services:

For LD	No
For ADHD	No
For ASD	No
LD specialists	No
ADHD & ASD coaching	Yes
ASD specialists	No
Professional tutors	No
Peer tutors	Yes
Max. hours/week for services	Varies
How professors are notified of student approved accommodations	Student

COLLEGE GRADUATION REQUIREMENTS

Course waivers allowed	No
Course substitutions allowed	Yes

In what courses: Math and Foreign Language, on a case-by-case basis

PROGRAMS/SERVICES FOR STUDENTS WITH LEARNING DIFFERENCES

Kennesaw State University offers academic accommodations through the Student Disability Services Office (DSO). To be considered for services, admitted students complete an intake form, provide eligible documentation (within the last three years), and meet with a Disability Services Provider (DSP). The DSP will determine appropriate accommodations and coordinate with the student to ensure access. Some services include relaxed attendance, notetakers, alternative-format textbooks, and academic coaching. Through academic coaching sessions, students learn strategies to address academic challenges. The DSO will share accessibility letters with faculty and work with the students and staff to support them in accessing eligible services. The letter provides details that help the faculty determine how to create an inclusive classroom environment.

ADMISSIONS

Kennesaw State University (KSU) does not require ACT or SAT scores for applicants with a GPA of 3.2 or higher. Students may submit scores to be considered for departmental scholarships and a higher math course placement. For admitted applicants, the average GPA is 3.36, and for those submitting test scores, the average SAT writing is 579, SAT math is 563, ACT English is 23, ACT reading is 25, and ACT math is 22. Students may request accommodations after being accepted through the general admission process.

Additional Information

Students are encouraged to register for classes four weeks prior to beginning school in the fall. There are no additional fees for services offered through the Disability Services Office (DSO) and they do not offer scholarships. If the students disclose their disability on the application, they may be recommended to apply for services.

DID YOU KNOW?

The Bentley Rare Book Museum is Georgia's first rare book museum and the state's third-largest museum-grade rare book collection. The museum holds over 10,000 items, from Sumerian clay tablets and medieval manuscript leaves to modern fine press books and literary first editions. The collection supports teaching at KSU and allows undergraduates the opportunity to study original works firsthand. The Virtual Coffee with a Curator program is a fall/spring semester monthly opportunity to engage in conversations about rare books and book collecting.

Kennesaw State University

General Admissions

Very important factors include: academic GPA, standardized test scores (if submitted). High school diploma is required and GED is not accepted. Institution is test-optional for entering Fall 2024. Check admissions website for updates. *Academic units recommended:* 4 English, 4 math, 4 science (2 labs), 2 foreign language, 1 social studies, 2 history.

Financial Aid

Students should submit: FAFSA. *Need-based scholarships/grants offered:* College/university scholarship or grant aid from institutional funds; Federal Pell; Private scholarships; SEOG; State scholarships/grants; United Negro College Fund. *Loan aid offered:* Direct PLUS loans; Direct Subsidized Loans; Direct Unsubsidized Loans. Federal Work-Study Program available. Institutional employment available.

Campus Life

Activities: Campus Ministries; Choral groups; Concert band; Dance; Drama/theater; International Student Organization; Jazz band; Literary magazine; Marching band; Music ensembles; Musical theater; Opera; Pep band; Radio station; Student government; Student newspaper; Symphony orchestra. **Organizations:** 411 registered organizations, 19 honor societies, 27 religious organizations, 19 fraternities, 13 sororities. **Athletics (Intercollegiate):** *Men:* baseball, basketball, cross-country, cycling, equestrian sports, golf, ice hockey, lacrosse, martial arts, rugby, softball, swimming, table tennis, track/field (indoor), ultimate frisbee, volleyball, water polo, wrestling. *Women:* baseball, basketball, cross-country, cycling, equestrian sports, golf, ice hockey, lacrosse, martial arts, rugby, softball, swimming, table tennis, track/field (indoor), ultimate frisbee, volleyball, water polo, wrestling.

CAMPUS

Type of school	Public
Environment	Town

STUDENTS

Undergrad enrollment	37,755
% male/female	50/50
% from out of state	8
% frosh live on campus	38

FINANCIAL FACTS

Annual in-state tuition	$5,562
Annual out-of-state tuition	$19,630
Room and board	$12,497
Required fees	$1,336

GENERAL ADMISSIONS INFO

Application fee	$40
Regular application deadline	6/1
Nonfall registration	Yes

Fall 2024 testing policy	Test Optional
Range SAT EBRW	530–630
Range SAT Math	520–620
Range ACT Composite	20–26

ACADEMICS

Student/faculty ratio	21:1
% students returning for sophomore year	74

Most classes have 20–29 students.

REQUESTING SERVICES FOR STUDENTS WITH LEARNING DIFFERENCES

Phone: 470-578-2666 • sds.kennesaw.edu • Email: sds@kennesaw.edu

Documentation submitted to: Student Disability Services
Separate application required for Services: Yes

Documentation required for:
LD: Psychoeducational evaluation
ADHD: Psychoeducational evaluation
ASD: Psychoeducational evaluation

Reinhardt University

7300 Reinhardt Circle, Waleska, GA 30183 • Admissions: 770-720-5526 • www.reinhardt.edu

Support: SP

ACCOMMODATIONS

Allowed in exams:

Calculators	Yes
Dictionary	No
Computer	Yes
Spell-checker	Yes
Extended test time	Yes
Scribe	Yes
Proctors	Yes
Oral exams	Yes
Note-takers	Yes

Support services for students with:

LD	Yes
ADHD	Yes
ASD	Yes
Distraction-reduced environment	Yes
Recording of lecture allowed	Yes
Reading technology	Yes
Audio books	Yes
Other assistive technology	Yes
Priority registration	Yes

Added costs of services:

For LD	Yes
For ADHD	Yes
For ASD	Yes
LD specialists	Yes
ADHD & ASD coaching	Yes
ASD specialists	No
Professional tutors	Yes
Peer tutors	No
Max. hours/week for services	Varies
How professors are notified of student approved accommodations	Student and Academic Support Office

COLLEGE GRADUATION REQUIREMENTS

Course waivers allowed	No
Course substitutions allowed	No

PROGRAMS/SERVICES FOR STUDENTS WITH LEARNING DIFFERENCES

The Academic Support Office (ASO) assists students with specific learning disabilities and ADHD. To receive services from ASO, students must have a diagnosed disability that requires academic accommodations and request an ASO admission packet. Each semester, students who are registered with ASO must get accommodation letters from their ASO advisors to give to their professors. Reasonable accommodations may include extended time on tests, copies of class lecture notes taken by selected students, coordinated access to appropriate assistive learning technology, one-on-one academic advising, counseling, and coaching. ASO provides specialized programs, academic advising, group tutoring, tutoring sessions led by an ASO faculty member for an additional fee, assistance in writing assignments, testing accommodations, note-taking, and coordination of assistive technology. The Building Opportunities for Students with Learning Disabilities (B.O.L.D.) and Strategic Education for Students with Autism Spectrum Disorders (S.E.A.D.) are two of the programs offered by ASO. The B.O.L.D. program anticipates the needs of students with learning disabilities and offers services that are individualized and go beyond standard accommodations. The S.E.A.D. program helps students develop social skills, transition smoothly to college life, and supports them throughout their college experience.

ADMISSIONS

Admission requirements are the same for all applicants. SAT and ACT scores are not required for first-year applicants with a GPA of 2.5 or higher. The middle 50 percent of students submitting scores have a 940–1160 SAT.

Additional Information

There are several scholarship opportunities available for students with ADHD, language-related learning differences, autism, and other learning disabilities.

Established in the early 1880s, Reinhardt was governed by strict social rules. Study hours were from 7-9 p.m., it was forbidden to be out after dark, and male and female students were forbidden to visit each other's dorm. Alcohol (except prescribed "health tonics"), bad public behavior, cheating, dishonesty, falsehoods, fighting, gambling, malicious mischief, quarreling, playing cards, profanity, social dancing, tattling, and the use of tobacco—except for boys with parental permission—were prohibited. Girls were not allowed to tilt their chairs or cross their feet.

Reinhardt University

GENERAL ADMISSIONS

Very important factors include: academic GPA, standardized test scores (if submitted). *Important factors include:* rigor of secondary school record, class rank. High school diploma is required and GED is accepted. Institution is test-optional for entering Fall 2024. Check admissions website for updates. *Academic units required:* 4 English, 4 math, 3 science, 3 social studies. *Academic units recommended:* 2 foreign language.

FINANCIAL AID

Students should submit: FAFSA; State aid form. *Need-based scholarships/grants offered:* College/university scholarship or grant aid from institutional funds; Federal Pell; Private scholarships; SEOG; State scholarships/grants. *Loan aid offered:* Direct PLUS loans; Direct Subsidized Loans; Direct Unsubsidized Loans. Federal Work-Study Program available.

CAMPUS LIFE

Activities: Campus Ministries; Choral groups; Concert band; Drama/theater; International Student Organization; Jazz band; Literary magazine; Music ensembles; Musical theater; Student government; Student newspaper; Student-run film society; Symphony orchestra; Television station; Yearbook. **Organizations:** 40 registered organizations, 12 honor societies, 5 religious organizations, 0 fraternities, 0 sororities. **Athletics (Intercollegiate):** *Men:* baseball, basketball, cross-country, golf, lacrosse. *Women:* basketball, cross-country, golf, lacrosse, softball, volleyball.

CAMPUS

Type of school	Private (nonprofit)
Environment	Rural

STUDENTS

Undergrad enrollment	1,096
% male/female	52/48
% from out of state	8
% frosh live on campus	50

FINANCIAL FACTS

Annual tuition	$27,300
Room and board	$12,300

GENERAL ADMISSIONS INFO

Application fee	$25
Regular application deadline	Rolling
Nonfall registration	Yes
Fall 2024 testing policy	Test Optional
Range SAT EBRW	410–540
Range SAT Math	430–530
Range ACT Composite	17–22

ACADEMICS

Student/faculty ratio	12:1
% students returning for sophomore year	61

Most classes have 10–19 students.

REQUESTING SERVICES FOR STUDENTS WITH LEARNING DIFFERENCES

Phone: 770-720-5567 • www.reinhardt.edu/academic-resources/academic-support-office
Email: AAA@reinhardt.edu

Documentation submitted to: Academic Support Office
Separate application required for Services: Yes

Documentation required for:
LD: Psychoeducational evaluation
ADHD: Psychoeducational evaluation
ASD: Psychoeducational evaluation

Savannah College of Art and Design

P.O. Box 3146, Savannah, GA 31402-3146 • Admissions: 912-525-5100 • www.scad.edu

Support: CS

ACCOMMODATIONS

Allowed in exams:

Calculators	Yes
Dictionary	Yes
Computer	Yes
Spell-checker	Yes
Extended test time	Yes
Scribe	Yes
Proctors	Yes
Oral exams	Yes
Note-takers	Yes

Support services for students with:

LD	Yes
ADHD	Yes
ASD	Yes
Distraction-reduced environment	Yes
Recording of lecture allowed	Yes
Reading technology	Yes
Audio books	Yes
Other assistive technology	Yes
Priority registration	Yes

Added costs of services:

For LD	No
For ADHD	No
For ASD	No
LD specialists	Yes
ADHD & ASD coaching	Yes
ASD specialists	No
Professional tutors	No
Peer tutors	Yes
Max. hours/week for services	8
How professors are notified of student approved accommodations	Student

COLLEGE GRADUATION REQUIREMENTS

Course waivers allowed	Yes
In what courses: Math and Foreign Language	
Course substitutions allowed	Yes
In what courses: Math and Foreign Language	

PROGRAMS/SERVICES FOR STUDENTS WITH LEARNING DIFFERENCES

Students admitted to Savannah College of Art and Design (SCAD) receive additional information about disability services and an invitation to the disability services orientation. There are a variety of services and accommodations available to students who have a disability that may impact their ability to learn. Accommodations may include academic accommodations, housing accommodations, course load accommodations, and assistive technology accommodations. To access accommodations, students should contact the Counseling and Student Support Services Department. All reasonable accommodations are determined for students on an individual basis. Jump Start is a special program occurring before the general SCAD Savannah orientation for students who qualify for accommodations. It is designed to ease the transition to college life, increase awareness of the services and resources available to students with disabilities, and provide strategies for academic success.

ADMISSIONS

Applications for SCAD are accepted at any time throughout the year. There are no deadlines to apply; however, students are encouraged to apply at least six months in advance to allow time to arrange for financial aid and no later than 30 days prior to the start of their first quarter. It usually takes between two and four weeks for admission results. Applicants who do not meet the standard criteria for admission are encouraged to submit supplementary materials. An exception to the general rules of admission may be made for applicants with exceptional drive and a passion for the arts. Supplementary materials may include one to three recommendations and a statement of purpose. Portfolios and auditions are not required. Portfolios are, however, encouraged to be considered for achievement scholarships.

Additional Information

Each student is assigned a success advisor based on the student's declared or intended major. Students receive their advisor assignment and contact information at orientation. Success advisors help students assess and match their interests, skills, and abilities to SCAD programs and help students decide their major, course selection, and course registration. During the First Year Experience course, success advisors work closely with incoming first-year students to help them understand their responsibilities and roles in the educational process.

SCAD's flagship campus, spread through Savannah, is in one of the renowned National Historic Landmark districts. In 1979, the school purchased the 1893 Savannah Volunteer Guards Armory for $250,000 and renovated it as its first classroom and administration building. SCAD worked with the city to preserve its architectural heritage, including restoring buildings for use as college facilities. The campus includes 67 buildings, many in the 22 squares of Old Town.

Savannah College of Art and Design

GENERAL ADMISSIONS

Very important factors include: academic GPA. *Important factors include:* rigor of secondary school record, standardized test scores (if submitted). *Other factors considered include:* class rank, application essay, recommendations. High school diploma is required and GED is accepted. Institution is test-optional for entering Fall 2024. Check admissions website for updates.

FINANCIAL AID

Students should submit: FAFSA; State aid form. *Need-based scholarships/grants offered:* College/university scholarship or grant aid from institutional funds; Federal Pell; Private scholarships; SEOG; State scholarships/grants; United Negro College Fund. *Loan aid offered:* Direct PLUS loans; Direct Subsidized Loans; Direct Unsubsidized Loans. Federal Work-Study Program available. Institutional employment available.

CAMPUS LIFE

Activities: Campus Ministries; Choral groups; Dance; Drama/theater; International Student Organization; Literary magazine; Music ensembles; Musical theater; Radio station; Student newspaper; Television station. **Organizations:** 105 registered organizations, 2 honor societies, 5 religious organizations, 0 fraternities, 0 sororities. **Athletics (Intercollegiate):** *Men:* basketball, bowling, cross-country, equestrian sports, golf, lacrosse, swimming, table tennis, volleyball. *Women:* basketball, bowling, cross-country, equestrian sports, golf, lacrosse, swimming, table tennis, volleyball.

CAMPUS

Type of school	Private (nonprofit)
Environment	City

STUDENTS

Undergrad enrollment	10,483
% male/female	33/67
% from out of state	79
% frosh live on campus	84

FINANCIAL FACTS

Annual tuition	$40,095
Room and board	$17,493

GENERAL ADMISSIONS INFO

Application fee	$40
Regular application deadline	Rolling
Nonfall registration	Yes

Fall 2024 testing policy	Test Optional
Range SAT EBRW	490–610
Range SAT Math	460–580
Range ACT Composite	21–27

ACADEMICS

Student/faculty ratio	19:1
% students returning for sophomore year	85
Most classes have 10–19 students.	

REQUESTING SERVICES FOR STUDENTS WITH LEARNING DIFFERENCES

Phone: 912-525-6233 • scad.edu/life/health-and-wellness/counseling-and-student-support-services
Email: disability@scad.edu

Documentation submitted to: SCAD Counseling and Student Support Services
Separate application required for Services: Yes

Documentation required for:
LD: Psychoeducational evaluation
ADHD: Psychoeducational evaluation
ASD: Psychoeducational evaluation

University of Georgia

Terrell Hall, 210 South Jackson Street, Athens, GA 30602-1633 • Admissions: 706-542-8776 • www.uga.edu

Support: S

ACCOMMODATIONS

Allowed in exams:

Calculators	Yes
Dictionary	No
Computer	Yes
Spell-checker	Yes
Extended test time	Yes
Scribe	Yes
Proctors	Yes
Oral exams	Yes
Note-takers	Yes

Support services for students with:

LD	Yes
ADHD	Yes
ASD	Yes
Distraction-reduced environment	Yes
Recording of lecture allowed	Yes
Reading technology	Yes
Audio books	Yes
Other assistive technology	Yes
Priority registration	Yes

Added costs of services:

For LD	No
For ADHD	No
For ASD	No
LD specialists	No
ADHD & ASD coaching	No
ASD specialists	No
Professional tutors	Yes
Peer tutors	Yes
Max. hours/week for services	Varies
How professors are notified of student approved accommodations	Student

COLLEGE GRADUATION REQUIREMENTS

Course waivers allowed	No
Course substitutions allowed	Yes
In what courses: Foreign Language; Math	

DID YOU KNOW?

When the UGA Bulldogs win a home football game, the Chapel Bell traditionally rings until midnight. When Georgia beats Georgia Tech, the bell rings all night! In the old days, freshmen did the hard work of ringing the bell. Today, fans, students, and alums all line up to wait their turns. This cherished and oldest UGA tradition was first recorded on December 1, 1894.

PROGRAMS/SERVICES FOR STUDENTS WITH LEARNING DIFFERENCES

The Disability Resource Center (DRC) serves students with disabilities who have been accepted to the university. As soon as possible, students should register with DRC by completing the online application and submitting any supporting documentation. Accommodations are determined in a meeting between the student and DRC coordinator and may include alternative-format text, assistive technology, academic assistance, note-taking, classroom accommodations, and alternate testing. Students who have registered with DRC and have completed at least one semester of classes with a minimum 2.5 GPA may be eligible for awards and scholarships through DRC. The Institute on Human Development and Disability offers Destination Dogs, a two-year certificate program for students between 18–25 with intellectual disabilities (IDD) who want to gain skills for independent living and career development. With individualized support from the Destination Dogs team, students are involved in four program areas: academic courses, work-based experiential learning, social and campus involvement, and building independence. Destination Dogs is certified by the Department of Education as a Comprehensive Transition Postsecondary (CTP) program for youth with IDD.

ADMISSIONS

The application process is the same for all applicants. Demonstrated academic achievement is the primary factor in first-year admission decisions and centers on GPA in core academic courses (calculated by UGA), the rigor of course selection, and the best combination of scores on the SAT or ACT, which is required. All first-year applicants should have counselors submit a secondary school report and an optional letter of recommendation from a teacher. Factors that also will be considered include school activities, intellectual pursuits, creative efforts, understanding and respect for intellectual, social, and cultural differences, and a significant commitment to public service, community involvement, leadership, integrity, and personal maturity. All applications are reviewed for conduct issues.

Additional Information

Each school and college have an advising office for students within that school or college. The Division of Academic Enhancement (DAE) provides academic coaching, free peer tutoring through the Academic Resource Center and Peer Learning and Teaching Others (PLaTO), student success workshops, online resources, and a mobile app warehouse. DAE offers a wide variety of courses (prefix "UNIV") to help students become better learners, and that count as elective degree credits. Students can meet with a peer tutor who has successfully completed the course to discuss class content, ask questions, and get study tips and resources. Tutoring is available as one-on-one appointments and in-person and online study pods across campus and online via Zoom.

University of Georgia

GENERAL ADMISSIONS

Very important factors include: rigor of secondary school record, academic GPA. *Important factors include:* standardized test scores. *Other factors considered include:* application essay, recommendations. High school diploma is required and GED is accepted. Institution is SAT/ACT required for entering Fall 2024. Check admissions website for updates. *Academic units required:* 4 English, 4 math, 4 science (2 labs), 2 foreign language, 3 social studies. *Academic units recommended:* 4 English, 4 math, 4 science (2 labs), 3 foreign language, 3 social studies, 1 academic elective.

FINANCIAL AID

Students should submit: FAFSA. *Need-based scholarships/grants offered:* College/university scholarship or grant aid from institutional funds; Federal Pell; Private scholarships; SEOG; State scholarships/grants. *Loan aid offered:* Direct PLUS loans; Direct Subsidized Loans; Direct Unsubsidized Loans. Federal Work-Study Program available. Institutional employment available.

CAMPUS LIFE

Activities: Campus Ministries; Choral groups; Concert band; Dance; Drama/theater; International Student Organization; Jazz band; Literary magazine; Marching band; Model UN; Music ensembles; Musical theater; Opera; Pep band; Radio station; Student government; Student newspaper; Student-run film society; Symphony orchestra; Yearbook. **Organizations:** 832 registered organizations, 28 honor societies, 57 religious organizations, 37 fraternities, 29 sororities. **Athletics (Intercollegiate):** *Men:* baseball, basketball, crew/rowing, cross-country, cycling, field hockey, golf, gymnastics, ice hockey, lacrosse, martial arts, racquetball, rugby, swimming, table tennis, track/field (indoor), ultimate frisbee, volleyball, water polo, wrestling. *Women:* basketball, crew/rowing, cross-country, cycling, equestrian sports, field hockey, golf, gymnastics, ice hockey, lacrosse, martial arts, racquetball, rugby, softball, swimming, table tennis, track/field (indoor), ultimate frisbee, volleyball, water polo.

CAMPUS

Type of school	Public
Environment	City

STUDENTS

Undergrad enrollment	30,507
% male/female	42/58
% from out of state	15
% frosh live on campus	98

FINANCIAL FACTS

Annual in-state tuition	$9,790
Annual out-of-state tuition	$28,830
Room and board	$10,940
Required fees	$1,390

GENERAL ADMISSIONS INFO

Application fee	$70
Regular application deadline	1/1
Nonfall registration	Yes
Fall 2024 testing policy	SAT/ACT Required
Range SAT EBRW	620–710
Range SAT Math	600–720
Range ACT Composite	26–32

ACADEMICS

Student/faculty ratio	17:1
% students returning for sophomore year	94

Most classes have 10–19 students.

REQUESTING SERVICES FOR STUDENTS WITH LEARNING DIFFERENCES

Phone: 706-542-8719 • drc.uga.edu • Email: drc@uga.edu

Documentation submitted to: Disability Resource Center
Separate application required for Services: Yes

Documentation required for:
LD: Psychoeducational evaluation
ADHD: Psychoeducational evaluation
ASD: Psychoeducational evaluation

Aurora University

347 South Gladstone Avenue, Aurora, IL 60606-4892 • Admissions: 630-844-5533 • www.aurora.edu

Support: CS

PROGRAMS/SERVICES FOR STUDENTS WITH LEARNING DIFFERENCES

The Disability Resource Office (DRO) provides accommodations for students with documented disabilities. Once admitted, students should register with the DRO by submitting an accommodations request and disability documentation. Eligible students will then meet with the DRO to discuss their background, needs, and barriers. They'll establish expectations and develop a strategy with reasonable accommodations. Accommodations include alternative-format textbooks, audio recording lectures, assistive technology, and a distraction-reduced testing environment. AU's Pathways is a fee-based program for students with autism. Pathways helps students with ASD get accustomed to college life, reach their learning potential, and prepares them for their careers with a two-year career exploration experience. Students first meet general admission requirements and then apply to the Pathways Program. In the program, they will engage in weekly meetings, structured study sessions, peer mentoring, social and recreation experiences, access sensory-supportive spaces, and receive support from faculty and staff. Pathways Programs also offers high school students with autism an opportunity to learn more about attending college with a two-week day camp open to all campers or 12-night residential camp for rising seniors and recent high school graduates.

ADMISSIONS

All applicants for admission are required to submit transcripts from an accredited high school with a college preparatory curriculum or a completed GED credential. Applications are considered based on academic ability, character, activities, and motivation. Personal essays and letters of recommendation are optional. Prospective students who want to attend Aurora are encouraged to apply early in their senior year. Admission to specific programs may have additional requirements. Students who do not meet the criteria for regular admission may be admitted at the discretion of the admission review committee on a conditional basis and are required to enroll in two first-year seminar courses to support academic success and assist in their transition to college.

Additional Information

AU's First-Year Experience program can help ease the transition from high school to college, guiding student success in and out of the classroom. The FYE begins at the AU4U and Welcome U event the summer before first semester and continues until the end of that semester. Students have access to their FYE facilitator for guidance and advice throughout this time. The Academic Support Center offers content-specific tutoring through study sessions and individual appointments with staff and peer tutors. Writing specialists are also available online and in person to guide students through the entire writing process. The Kimberly and James Hill Center for Student Success offers quiet spaces to study, guidance in work and life, and free snacks.

ACCOMMODATIONS

Allowed in exams:

Calculators	Yes
Dictionary	Yes
Computer	Yes
Spell-checker	Yes
Extended test time	Yes
Scribe	Yes
Proctors	Yes
Oral exams	Yes
Note-takers	Yes

Support services for students with:

LD	Yes
ADHD	Yes
ASD	Yes
Distraction-reduced environment	Yes
Recording of lecture allowed	Yes
Reading technology	Yes
Audio books	Yes
Other assistive technology	Yes
Priority registration	Yes

Added costs of services:

For LD	No
For ADHD	No
For ASD	No
LD specialists	No
ADHD & ASD coaching	Yes
ASD specialists	Yes
Professional tutors	Yes
Peer tutors	Yes
Max. hours/week for services	Varies
How professors are notified of student approved accommodations	Disability Resource Office

COLLEGE GRADUATION REQUIREMENTS

Course waivers allowed	No
Course substitutions allowed	No

Colonel Harland S. Sanders, the founder of Kentucky Fried Chicken Corp., visited in 1967 and made AU a permanent recipient of scholarship funds from his foundation to support charitable, religious, and educational institutions. The bells on top of Eckhart Hall, donated by the Colonel, can be heard on campus throughout the day.

Aurora University

GENERAL ADMISSIONS

Very important factors include: rigor of secondary school record, class rank, academic GPA, standardized test scores (if submitted). *Other factors considered include:* application essay, recommendations. High school diploma is required and GED is accepted. Institution is test-optional for entering Fall 2024. Check admissions website for updates. *Academic units required:* 4 English, 3 math, 3 science, 3 social studies, 3 academic electives.

FINANCIAL AID

Students should submit: FAFSA. *Need-based scholarships/grants offered:* College/university scholarship or grant aid from institutional funds; Federal Pell; Private scholarships; SEOG; State scholarships/grants. *Loan aid offered:* Direct PLUS loans; Direct Subsidized Loans; Direct Unsubsidized Loans. Federal Work-Study Program available. Institutional employment available.

CAMPUS LIFE

Activities: Campus Ministries; Choral groups; Dance; Drama/theater; Literary magazine; Music ensembles; Musical theater; Opera; Pep band; Radio station; Student government; Student newspaper; Television station. **Organizations:** 50 registered organizations, 2 honor societies, 1 religious organizations, 1 fraternities, 4 sororities. **Athletics (Intercollegiate):** *Men:* baseball, basketball, cross-country, golf, lacrosse, track/field (indoor). *Women:* basketball, cross-country, golf, softball, track/field (indoor), volleyball.

CAMPUS

Type of school	Private (nonprofit)
Environment	City

STUDENTS

Undergrad enrollment	3,944
% male/female	35/65
% from out of state	11
% frosh live on campus	43

FINANCIAL FACTS

Annual tuition	$24,800
Room and board	$11,700
Required fees	$260

GENERAL ADMISSIONS INFO

Application fee	No fee
Regular application deadline	Rolling
Nonfall registration	Yes

Fall 2024 testing policy	Test Optional
Range SAT EBRW	490–580
Range SAT Math	480–570
Range ACT Composite	19–23

ACADEMICS

Student/faculty ratio	19:1
% students returning for sophomore year	75

Most classes have 20–29 students.

Illinois

REQUESTING SERVICES FOR STUDENTS WITH LEARNING DIFFERENCES

Phone: 630-844-4225 • aurora.edu/academics/resources/ada • Email: disabilityresources@aurora.edu

Documentation submitted to: Disability Resource Office
Separate application required for Services: Yes

Documentation required for:
LD: Psychoeducational evaluation
ADHD: Psychoeducational evaluation
ASD: Psychoeducational evaluation

Bradley University

1501 W. Bradley Avenue, Peoria, IL 61625 • Admissions: 309-677-1000 • www.bradley.edu

Support: CS

ACCOMMODATIONS

Allowed in exams:

Calculators	Yes
Dictionary	Yes
Computer	Yes
Spell-checker	Yes
Extended test time	Yes
Scribe	Yes
Proctors	Yes
Oral exams	Yes
Note-takers	Yes

Support services for students with:

LD	No
ADHD	No
ASD	No
Distraction-reduced environment	Yes
Recording of lecture allowed	Yes
Reading technology	Yes
Audio books	Yes
Other assistive technology	Yes
Priority registration	Yes

Added costs of services:

For LD	No
For ADHD	No
For ASD	No
LD specialists	No
ADHD & ASD coaching	Yes
ASD specialists	Yes
Professional tutors	Yes
Peer tutors	Yes
Max. hours/week for services	Varies
How professors are notified of student approved accommodations	Student and Student Access Services

COLLEGE GRADUATION REQUIREMENTS

Course waivers allowed	Yes

In what courses: Case-by-case basis

Course substitutions allowed	Yes

In what courses: Case-by-case basis

PROGRAMS/SERVICES FOR STUDENTS WITH LEARNING DIFFERENCES

The Office of Student Access Services (SAS) provides reasonable and appropriate accommodations for qualified students with documented disabilities. Students must submit a registration and accommodation request form to the SAS office and include documentation of their disability. Students meet with the director for a final determination of approved accommodations. Once appropriate accommodations have been approved, and with the student's permission, a faculty notification letter is used to communicate with faculty and staff about the accommodations needed for each course. Students are responsible for talking to each instructor about the accommodations and any adjustments during the semester. Accommodations may include priority registration, assistive technology, alternate formats for course material, note-taking assistance, reader or scribe services, and testing alternatives.

ADMISSIONS

All applicants are expected to meet the same general academic and extracurricular admission requirements. An official copy of high school transcripts must be sent directly to Bradley. Letters of recommendation are not required, but applicants may include up to three from a teacher, school counselor, coach, or school activity advisor. A personal essay is required. Applicants lacking admission requirements may be admitted but will be required to take preparatory courses in addition to the program. Bradley University encourages all prospective new first-year and transfer students and their families to visit campus.

Additional Information

The Academic Success Center (ASC) Math Success Center tutors help students by appointment, providing clarification on mathematical concepts. The Writing Center offers online and in-person help with writing projects, from formatting to creative, technical, or STEM presentations and group writing projects. ASC also offers free, one-on-one, in-person tutoring appointments (up to 3 hours per week) available for a variety of select courses, including languages. Students will find ASC professional academic coaching staff available to help students identify and address barriers and create strategies and resources for more effective learning. Students can also sign up for ASC's workshops on time management and goal setting to ease test anxiety and prepare for exams.

A statue of Lydia Moss Bradley, the founder of the university, is located in front of Bradley Hall in the Founder's Circle. During finals week, students ask for wisdom and luck by rubbing her shoulder before each exam. That's why her shoulder is a slightly different color than the rest of the statue.

Bradley University

General Admissions

Very important factors include: rigor of secondary school record, academic GPA. *Other factors considered include:* class rank, standardized test scores (if submitted), application essay, recommendations. High school diploma is required and GED is accepted. Institution is test-optional for entering Fall 2024. Check admissions website for updates. *Academic units required:* 4 English, 3 math, 2 science (2 labs), 2 social studies. *Academic units recommended:* 4 math, 3 science (3 labs), 2 foreign language, 3 social studies.

Financial Aid

Students should submit: FAFSA. *Need-based scholarships/grants offered:* College/university scholarship or grant aid from institutional funds; Federal Pell; Private scholarships; SEOG; State scholarships/grants; United Negro College Fund. *Loan aid offered:* Direct PLUS loans; Direct Subsidized Loans; Direct Unsubsidized Loans. Federal Work-Study Program available. Institutional employment available.

Campus Life

Activities: Campus Ministries; Choral groups; Concert band; Dance; Drama/theater; International Student Organization; Jazz band; Literary magazine; Music ensembles; Musical theater; Pep band; Radio station; Student government; Student newspaper; Student-run film society; Symphony orchestra; Television station. **Organizations:** 216 registered organizations, 16 honor societies, 9 religious organizations, 17 fraternities, 12 sororities. **Athletics (Intercollegiate):** *Men:* baseball, basketball, cross-country, golf, ice hockey, lacrosse, table tennis, track/field (indoor), ultimate frisbee, volleyball, water polo, wrestling. *Women:* basketball, cross-country, golf, lacrosse, softball, track/field (indoor), ultimate frisbee, volleyball, water polo.

CAMPUS

Type of school	Private (nonprofit)
Environment	City

STUDENTS

Undergrad enrollment	4,133
% male/female	49/51
% from out of state	15
% frosh live on campus	88

FINANCIAL FACTS

Annual tuition	$37,380
Room and board	$12,196
Required fees	$420

GENERAL ADMISSIONS INFO

Application fee	No fee
Regular application deadline	Rolling
Nonfall registration	Yes
Fall 2024 testing policy	Test Optional
Range SAT EBRW	580–670
Range SAT Math	490–610
Range ACT Composite	24–30

ACADEMICS

Student/faculty ratio	12:1
% students returning for sophomore year	83
Most classes have 10–19 students.	

Illinois

REQUESTING SERVICES FOR STUDENTS WITH LEARNING DIFFERENCES

Phone: 309-677-3654 • www.bradley.edu/offices/student/sas • Email: sas@bradley.edu

Documentation submitted to: Student Access Services
Separate application required for Services: Yes

Documentation required for:
LD: Psychoeducational evaluation
ADHD: Psychoeducational evaluation
ASD: Psychoeducational evaluation

DePaul University

1 East Jackson Boulevard, Chicago, IL 60604-2287 • Admissions: 312-362-8300 • www.depaul.edu

Support: CS

PROGRAMS/SERVICES FOR STUDENTS WITH LEARNING DIFFERENCES

The Center for Students with Disabilities (CSD) provides support and services to all students with disabilities, including learning disabilities and ADHD. Once accepted to the university, each student requesting accommodations submits documentation to CSD, and attends a one-on-one meeting where CSD determines the student's needs and whether a Learning Specialist is appropriate. Once students are approved for accommodations, they may go online and allow professors to view their relevant accommodations. Course waivers may be determined on an individual basis. Both campuses have private test-taking rooms to accommodate eligible students. About 10 percent of students with accommodations enroll in the Learning Specialist Clinician Services program—an intensive, one-on-one, fee-based service where learning specialists meet with students regularly to develop academic and executive functioning skills and self-advocacy strategies. There is a per-quarter cost for this program based on weekly or twice-weekly meetings. The School Success group was created specifically for students with ASD, who can attend weekly meetings led by CSD clinicians to develop social skills and community in a safe space. DePaul has a chapter of Delta Alpha Pi, a merit-based honor society for students with disabilities.

ADMISSIONS

All applicants are expected to meet the same admission criteria. Official high school transcripts are required, and students are strongly advised to complete the recommended academic courses. Advanced coursework credit may be given for Advanced Placement, International Baccalaureate, College Level Examination Program, or dual enrollment programs. Credit is evaluated by the Office of Admission. DePaul's School of Music and The Theatre School require additional application steps, including auditions, interviews, and application fees. Students applying to the Animation BA or Animation BFA degree programs are required to submit a creative statement and a creative portfolio.

Additional Information

The student-run Success Coaching program provides a support network to all second-year students. Success Coaches conduct outreach, make connections with students in-person or on Zoom, and follow up throughout the year.

Ray Meyer served as the head coach of men's basketball, 1942-1984, with a record of 724-354. Following his retirement, Meyer served as special assistant to the President of DePaul until 1997. He was the fourth active coach to be elected to the Naismith Memorial Basketball Hall of Fame, and is remembered beyond the court as leader, mentor, a champion of education, and a beloved symbol of DePaul values.

DePaul University

GENERAL ADMISSIONS

Very important factors include: rigor of secondary school record, academic GPA, standardized test scores (if submitted). *Important factors include:* class rank, recommendations. *Other factors considered include:* application essay. High school diploma is required and GED is accepted. Institution is test-optional for entering Fall 2024. Check admissions website for updates. *Academic units recommended:* 4 English, 3 math, 3 science (2 labs), 2 foreign language, 2 social studies.

FINANCIAL AID

Students should submit: FAFSA. *Need-based scholarships/grants offered:* College/university scholarship or grant aid from institutional funds; Federal Pell; Private scholarships; SEOG; State scholarships/grants. *Loan aid offered:* Direct PLUS loans; Direct Subsidized Loans; Direct Unsubsidized Loans. Federal Work-Study Program available. Institutional employment available.

CAMPUS LIFE

Activities: Campus Ministries; Choral groups; Concert band; Dance; Drama/theater; International Student Organization; Jazz band; Literary magazine; Model UN; Music ensembles; Musical theater; Opera; Pep band; Radio station; Student government; Student newspaper; Student-run film society; Symphony orchestra; Television station. **Organizations:** 314 registered organizations, 26 honor societies, 21 religious organizations, 10 fraternities, 17 sororities. **Athletics (Intercollegiate):** *Men:* baseball, basketball, bowling, cross-country, golf, ice hockey, lacrosse, rugby, swimming, track/field (indoor), ultimate frisbee, volleyball, water polo. *Women:* baseball, basketball, bowling, cross-country, golf, ice hockey, lacrosse, rugby, softball, swimming, track/field (indoor), ultimate frisbee, volleyball, water polo.

Illinois

CAMPUS
Type of school	Private (nonprofit)
Environment	Metropolis

STUDENTS
Undergrad enrollment	13,948
% male/female	45/55
% from out of state	26
% frosh live on campus	50

FINANCIAL FACTS
Annual tuition	$42,189
Room and board	$16,068
Required fees	$651

GENERAL ADMISSIONS INFO
Application fee	No fee
Regular application deadline	2/1
Nonfall registration	Yes
Fall 2024 testing policy	Test Optional
Range SAT EBRW	550–660
Range SAT Math	520–640

ACADEMICS
Student/faculty ratio	17:1
% students returning for sophomore year	84
Most classes have 20–29 students.	

REQUESTING SERVICES FOR STUDENTS WITH LEARNING DIFFERENCES

Phone: 773-325-1677 • offices.depaul.edu/student-affairs/about/departments/Pages/csd.aspx
Email: csd@depaul.edu

Documentation submitted to: Center for Students with Disabilities
Separate application required for Services: Yes

Documentation required for:
LD: Psychoeducational evaluation
ADHD: Psychoeducational evaluation
ASD: Psychoeducational evaluation

Eastern Illinois University

600 Lincoln Avenue, Charleston, IL 61920 • Admissions: 217-581-2223 • www.eiu.edu

Support: SP

ACCOMMODATIONS

Allowed in exams:

Calculators	Yes
Dictionary	Yes
Computer	Yes
Spell-checker	Yes
Extended test time	Yes
Scribe	No
Proctors	Yes
Oral exams	Yes
Note-takers	Yes

Support services for students with:

LD	Yes
ADHD	Yes
ASD	Yes
Distraction-reduced environment	Yes
Recording of lecture allowed	No
Reading technology	Yes
Audio books	Yes
Other assistive technology	Yes
Priority registration	Yes

Added costs of services:

For LD	No
For ADHD	No
For ASD	Yes
LD specialists	Yes
ADHD & ASD coaching	Yes
ASD specialists	Yes
Professional tutors	No
Peer tutors	Yes
Max. hours/week for services	Varies
How professors are notified of student approved accommodations	Student

COLLEGE GRADUATION REQUIREMENTS

Course waivers allowed	No
Course substitutions allowed	No

PROGRAMS/SERVICES FOR STUDENTS WITH LEARNING DIFFERENCES

Student Disability Services (SDS) supports students with learning disabilities and ADHD. SDS provides academic accommodations based on submitted documentation and an in-person discussion with the student to discuss their needs. A media specialist is available to work with students to arrange assistive technology. Students who have been admitted to Eastern Illinois University (EIU) may apply to the Students with Autism Transitional Education Program (STEP). STEP provides enhanced support to improve academic, social, and daily living skills. The program is fee-based and limited to 20 students. Students who have enrolled in STEP for at least one semester can transition to STEP-Maintenance (STEP-M) at the discretion of the STEP administrators. STEP-M participants continue to receive support services on a level that permits greater independence. Students admitted to STEP find growth opportunities through individualized peer mentorships, social skills groups focusing on interpersonal skills in the classroom and the campus community, regularly scheduled academic study tables, daily-living skills trainings, personalized fitness programs, social events that cultivate friendships, active involvement on campus, and vocational skills. Single-room options, pending availability, can be provided for an additional fee, and allow students to decompress and regulate, along with early move-in dates for calmer transitions. The program encourages regular contact with parents to allow optimum teamwork between the individual, campus supports, and the family.

ADMISSIONS

EIU required a high school grade GPA of 2.5 on a 4.0 unweighted scale. Students who fall slightly below this criterion or demonstrate a noticeable semester decrease are strongly encouraged to include a personal statement or explanation and letter of recommendation. Additional materials may be requested and used in the decision process. If a student with a language-based disability meets criteria in other areas, the foreign language requirement could be substituted with American Sign Language or waived entirely.

Additional Information

Free peer tutoring is available for all EIU students.

Old Main is one of the five "Altgeld's castles" built on Illinois state college campuses in the 1890s. Governor John Peter Altgeld was instrumental in funding the Illinois university system and was fond of Gothic architecture. Originally named the Livingston C. Lord Administration Building in honor of the first EIU president, Old Main's outline of heavy Gothic Revival style with turrets, towers, and battlements is instantly recognizable as the official symbol of EIU.

Eastern Illinois University

GENERAL ADMISSIONS

Very important factors include: rigor of secondary school record, academic GPA. *Other factors considered include:* standardized test scores (if submitted), application essay, recommendations. High school diploma is required and GED is accepted. Institution is test-optional for entering Fall 2024. Check admissions website for updates. *Academic units required:* 4 English, 3 math, 3 science (3 labs), 3 social studies, 2 academic electives. *Academic units recommended:* 2 foreign language.

FINANCIAL AID

Students should submit: FAFSA. *Need-based scholarships/grants offered:* College/university scholarship or grant aid from institutional funds; Federal Pell; Private scholarships; SEOG; State scholarships/grants. *Loan aid offered:* Direct PLUS loans; Direct Subsidized Loans; Direct Unsubsidized Loans. Federal Work-Study Program available. Institutional employment available.

CAMPUS LIFE

Activities: Campus Ministries; Choral groups; Concert band; Dance; Drama/theater; International Student Organization; Jazz band; Literary magazine; Marching band; Music ensembles; Musical theater; Pep band; Radio station; Student government; Student newspaper; Symphony orchestra; Television station; Yearbook. **Organizations:** 101 registered organizations, 10 honor societies, 9 religious organizations, 12 fraternities, 12 sororities. **Athletics (Intercollegiate):** *Men:* baseball, basketball, cross-country, equestrian sports, golf, ice hockey, racquetball, softball, swimming, track/field (indoor), ultimate frisbee. *Women:* baseball, basketball, cross-country, equestrian sports, golf, ice hockey, racquetball, softball, swimming, track/field (indoor), ultimate frisbee, volleyball.

CAMPUS	
Type of school	Public
Environment	Village

STUDENTS	
Undergrad enrollment	4,616
% male/female	39/61
% from out of state	9
% frosh live on campus	90

FINANCIAL FACTS	
Annual in-state tuition	$9,472
Annual out-of-state tuition	$11,840
Room and board	$10,548
Required fees	$3,090

GENERAL ADMISSIONS INFO	
Application fee	No fee
Regular application deadline	8/15
Nonfall registration	Yes

Fall 2024 testing policy	Test Optional
Range SAT EBRW	460–580
Range SAT Math	440–560
Range ACT Composite	17–23

ACADEMICS	
Student/faculty ratio	14:1
% students returning for sophomore year	73
Most classes have 10–19 students.	

Illinois

REQUESTING SERVICES FOR STUDENTS WITH LEARNING DIFFERENCES

Phone: 217-581-6583 • www.eiu.edu/disability • Email: studentdisability@eiu.edu

Documentation submitted to: Student Disability Services
Separate application required for Services: Yes

Documentation required for:
LD: Psychoeducational evaluation
ADHD: Psychoeducational evaluation
ASD: Psychoeducational evaluation

Illinois State University

Office of Admissions, Normal, IL 61790-2200 • Admissions: 309-438-2181 • illinoisstate.edu

Support: CS

ACCOMMODATIONS

Allowed in exams:

Calculators	Yes
Dictionary	No
Computer	Yes
Spell-checker	Yes
Extended test time	Yes
Scribe	Yes
Proctors	Yes
Oral exams	Yes
Note-takers	Yes

Support services for students with:

LD	Yes
ADHD	Yes
ASD	Yes
Distraction-reduced environment	Yes
Recording of lecture allowed	Yes
Reading technology	Yes
Audio books	Yes
Other assistive technology	Yes
Priority registration	Yes

Added costs of services:

For LD	No
For ADHD	No
For ASD	No
LD specialists	Yes
ADHD & ASD coaching	No
ASD specialists	No
Professional tutors	No
Peer tutors	Yes
Max. hours/week for services	Varies
How professors are notified of student approved accommodations	Student

COLLEGE GRADUATION REQUIREMENTS

Course waivers allowed	No
Course substitutions allowed	Yes

In what courses: Case-by-case basis.

PROGRAMS/SERVICES FOR STUDENTS WITH LEARNING DIFFERENCES

The Office of Student Access and Accommodation Services (SAAS) provides one-on-one academic support and alternative resources to students with learning disabilities. Students must submit formal documentation to request accommodations. Depending on the diagnosis, documentation may include a full psychoeducational assessment, Individualized Education Plans (IEP), and/or 504 Plans. Students are encouraged to contact SAAS to learn more about the resources that can be offered as they complete the ISU application. Once the documentation has been verified, students participate in access training and obtain eligibility for services. Students then receive a faculty verification letter and are responsible for discussing the accommodations with each of their professors.

ADMISSIONS

The general admission process is the same for all students. The middle 50 percent of admitted students have a 3.30–4.02 GPA. ISU requires a personal statement, which should share additional details about what makes ISU a good fit.

Additional Information

First- and second-year students taking 100-level courses can attend scheduled or drop-in tutoring sessions at the Julia N. Visor Academic Center. The center also hosts writing and math workshops for all students, and special "Blitz-style" sessions to review materials for classes prior to finals. This allows students to have two hours of dedicated time to be coached through reviews of each of their classes' materials to be prepared for the final exam.

Prairie Grove is a collection of native trees planted at ISU's Horticulture Center in collaboration with the Children and Elders Forest (CEF). Each tree is planted by at least one child and one elder in an effort to deepen the bonds between generations. Many of the Prairie Grove trees are dedicated to loved ones with a connection to ISU, and CEF trees continue to be planted to honor others.

Illinois State University

GENERAL ADMISSIONS

Very important factors include: academic GPA. *Other factors considered include:* standardized test scores (if submitted), application essay. High school diploma is required and GED is accepted. Institution is test-optional for entering Fall 2024. Check admissions website for updates. *Academic units required:* 4 English, 3 math, 2 science (2 labs), 2 foreign language, 2 social studies, 2 academic electives, 2 visual/performing arts.

FINANCIAL AID

Students should submit: FAFSA. *Need-based scholarships/grants offered:* College/university scholarship or grant aid from institutional funds; Federal Nursing Scholarships; Federal Pell; Private scholarships; SEOG; State scholarships/grants. *Loan aid offered:* Direct PLUS loans; Direct Subsidized Loans; Direct Unsubsidized Loans. Federal Work-Study Program available. Institutional employment available.

CAMPUS LIFE

Activities: Campus Ministries; Choral groups; Concert band; Dance; Drama/theater; International Student Organization; Jazz band; Literary magazine; Marching band; Model UN; Music ensembles; Musical theater; Opera; Pep band; Radio station; Student government; Student newspaper; Student-run film society; Symphony orchestra; Television station. **Organizations:** 375 registered organizations, 17 honor societies, 28 religious organizations, 20 fraternities, 20 sororities. **Athletics (Intercollegiate):** *Men:* baseball, basketball, bowling, cross-country, equestrian sports, golf, ice hockey, lacrosse, rugby, table tennis, track/field (indoor), ultimate frisbee, volleyball, water polo. *Women:* basketball, bowling, cross-country, equestrian sports, golf, gymnastics, ice hockey, lacrosse, rugby, softball, swimming, table tennis, track/field (indoor), volleyball, water polo.

CAMPUS

Type of school	Public
Environment	City

STUDENTS

Undergrad enrollment	17,632
% male/female	43/57
% from out of state	3

FINANCIAL FACTS

Annual in-state tuition	$11,524
Annual out-of-state tuition	$23,048
Room and board	$10,146
Required fees	$3,233

GENERAL ADMISSIONS INFO

Application fee	$50
Regular application deadline	4/1
Nonfall registration	Yes

Fall 2024 testing policy	Test Optional
Range SAT EBRW	510–610
Range SAT Math	490–590
Range ACT Composite	21–27

ACADEMICS

Student/faculty ratio	19:1
% students returning for sophomore year	83

Most classes have 20–29 students.

REQUESTING SERVICES FOR STUDENTS WITH LEARNING DIFFERENCES

Phone: 309-438-5853 • studentaccess.illinoisstate.edu • Email: ableisu@ilstu.edu

Documentation submitted to: Student Access and Accommodation Services
Separate application required for Services: Yes

Documentation required for:
LD: Psychoeducational evaluation
ADHD: Psychoeducational evaluation
ASD: Psychoeducational evaluation

Loyola University Chicago

820 North Michigan Avenue, Chicago, IL 60611 • Admissions: 312-915-6500 • www.luc.edu

Support: S

ACCOMMODATIONS

Allowed in exams:

Calculators	Yes
Dictionary	Yes
Computer	Yes
Spell-checker	Yes
Extended test time	Yes
Scribe	Yes
Proctors	Yes
Oral exams	Yes
Note-takers	Yes

Support services for students with:

LD	Yes
ADHD	Yes
ASD	Yes
Distraction-reduced environment	Yes
Recording of lecture allowed	Yes
Reading technology	Yes
Audio books	Yes
Other assistive technology	Yes
Priority registration	Yes

Added costs of services:

For LD	No
For ADHD	No
For ASD	No
LD specialists	No
ADHD & ASD coaching	Yes
ASD specialists	No
Professional tutors	No
Peer tutors	Yes
Max. hours/week for services	Varies
How professors are notified of student approved accommodations	Director of SAC

COLLEGE GRADUATION REQUIREMENTS

Course waivers allowed	No
Course substitutions allowed	Yes
In what courses: Math and Foreign Language	

PROGRAMS/SERVICES FOR STUDENTS WITH LEARNING DIFFERENCES

Loyola University Chicago offers services and resources for students with intellectual and learning differences through the Student Accessibility Center (SAC). Students with documented disabilities may request accommodations by submitting an application and meeting with the SAC staff. The documentation should provide clear details about the disability. All students are evaluated on a case-by-case basis.

ADMISSIONS

All students complete the same admissions process for consideration at Loyola University. The average GPA of recently admitted students is a 3.6. Applicants must submit at least one letter of recommendation, but an essay and résumé are optional. Engineering applicants should complete a 4th year of math, including calculus. After receiving an acceptance, students are encouraged to contact the SAC as soon as possible to obtain reasonable accommodations.

Additional Information

Loyola offers first-year courses that help students build a strong foundation for academic excellence. Through services at the Tutoring Center, students can obtain Supplemental Instruction, individual tutoring, and success coaching. The UNIV-112 Strategies for Learning course is a one-semester experience where students can earn 1 credit, learn study skills, practice effective test-taking strategies, and learn final exam preparation. This course will also help students to develop a tangible plan for success.

DID YOU KNOW?

In 1926, the football team traveled a lot, "rambling" from place to place for games. Football was dropped in 1930, but the nickname Ramblers stuck for athletic teams. Today the Rambler Rowdies support men's and women's basketball along with the mascot, LU Wolf. The Rowdies have been recognized as the best student section for outstanding support of basketball.

Loyola University Chicago

GENERAL ADMISSIONS

Very important factors include: rigor of secondary school record, academic GPA. *Important factors include:* application essay, recommendations. *Other factors considered include:* class rank, standardized test scores (if submitted). High school diploma is required and GED is accepted. Institution is test-optional for entering Fall 2024. Check admissions website for updates. *Academic units required:* 4 English, 3 math, 3 science, 2 foreign language, 3 social studies. *Academic units recommended:* 4 math.

FINANCIAL AID

Students should submit: FAFSA. *Need-based scholarships/grants offered:* College/university scholarship or grant aid from institutional funds; Federal Pell; Private scholarships; SEOG; State scholarships/grants. *Loan aid offered:* Direct PLUS loans; Direct Subsidized Loans; Direct Unsubsidized Loans. Federal Work-Study Program available. Institutional employment available.

CAMPUS LIFE

Activities: Campus Ministries; Choral groups; Concert band; Dance; Drama/theater; International Student Organization; Jazz band; Literary magazine; Model UN; Music ensembles; Musical theater; Opera; Pep band; Radio station; Student government; Student newspaper; Student-run film society; Symphony orchestra; Television station. **Organizations:** 230 registered organizations, 7 honor societies, 8 religious organizations, 8 fraternities, 12 sororities. **Athletics (Intercollegiate):** *Men:* baseball, basketball, cross-country, field hockey, golf, lacrosse, rugby, swimming, table tennis, track/field (indoor), ultimate frisbee, volleyball, water polo. *Women:* basketball, cross-country, field hockey, golf, ice hockey, lacrosse, rugby, softball, swimming, table tennis, track/field (indoor), ultimate frisbee, volleyball, water polo.

CAMPUS
Type of school	Private (nonprofit)
Environment	Metropolis

STUDENTS
Undergrad enrollment	11,739
% male/female	32/68
% from out of state	41
% frosh live on campus	84

FINANCIAL FACTS
Annual tuition	$48,100
Room and board	$15,180
Required fees	$1,088

GENERAL ADMISSIONS INFO
Application fee	No fee
Regular application deadline	Rolling
Nonfall registration	Yes

Fall 2024 testing policy	Test Optional
Range SAT EBRW	590–690
Range SAT Math	570–670
Range ACT Composite	27–32

ACADEMICS
Student/faculty ratio	14:1
% students returning for sophomore year	88

Most classes have 10–19 students.

Illinois

REQUESTING SERVICES FOR STUDENTS WITH LEARNING DIFFERENCES

Phone: 773-508-3700 • www.luc.edu/sac • Email: sac@luc.edu

Documentation submitted to: Student Accessibility Center

Separate application required for Services: Yes

Documentation required for:
LD: Psychoeducational evaluation
ADHD: Psychoeducational evaluation
ASD: Psychoeducational evaluation

Northern Illinois University

1425 Lincoln Hwy, DeKalb, IL 60115 • Admissions: 815-753-0446 • www.niu.edu

Support: CS

ACCOMMODATIONS

Allowed in exams:	
Calculators	Yes
Dictionary	Yes
Computer	Yes
Spell-checker	Yes
Extended test time	Yes
Scribe	Yes
Proctors	Yes
Oral exams	Yes
Note-takers	Yes
Support services for students with:	
LD	Yes
ADHD	Yes
ASD	Yes
Distraction-reduced environment	Yes
Recording of lecture allowed	Yes
Reading technology	Yes
Audio books	Yes
Other assistive technology	Yes
Priority registration	Yes
Added costs of services:	
For LD	No
For ADHD	No
For ASD	No
LD specialists	No
ADHD & ASD coaching	Yes
ASD specialists	Yes
Professional tutors	No
Peer tutors	Yes
Max. hours/week for services	Varies
How professors are notified of student approved accommodations	Student

COLLEGE GRADUATION REQUIREMENTS

Course waivers allowed	Yes
In what courses: Waivers rarely granted	
Course substitutions allowed	Yes
In what courses: Foreign Language	

PROGRAMS/SERVICES FOR STUDENTS WITH LEARNING DIFFERENCES

The Disability Resource Center (DRC) provides accommodations, resources, and guidance to students with disabilities. Appropriate and reasonable accommodations for students may include texts in alternative formats, closed captions, exam accommodations, extended time on assignments, flexible attendance, receiving class materials in advance, an assistant in lab and non-lecture settings, notetakers, and adaptive technology. The DRC works closely with faculty and department staff, so accommodations are understood and implemented for student access and success. New students seeking access and accommodations participate in an initial interview before developing an accommodation plan. The DRC promotes communication skills and self-advocacy and focuses on helping students collaborate with faculty and staff.

ADMISSIONS

All students complete the same admissions process for consideration at NIU. Students may also be admitted through the McKinley "Deacon" Davis CHANCE Program, which selects students who holistically demonstrate a commitment to learning and leadership despite challenges or extenuating circumstances. Applicants can be recruited, may self-nominate, or be nominated by their high school counselor for the CHANCE program. Students admitted with a GPA of 2.0–2.49 will be automatically selected to enroll in CHANCE.

Additional Information

The CHANCE program provides academic, financial, and social support. Students selected may have disabilities, face financial hardship, or be first generation students. CHANCE offers participants access to academic coaching, one-on-one support, peer mentoring, and a study lounge. Comprehensive academic services and resources for all students, including tutoring sessions, writing assistance, and academic skills development, are offered at the Huskie Academic Support Center.

In 1973, former Paralympian Dr. John Britton joined the faculty at NIU. Britton drew on his personal experience and competitive spirit to remove physical barriers on campus. "Project Britton" made water fountains and telephone booths physically accessible for wheelchairs, installed curb cuts and ramps, and created parking for disabled persons. Dr. Britton became an advisor to the DeKalb City Council and helped to implement similar accessibility throughout the city and across continents.

Northern Illinois University

GENERAL ADMISSIONS

Very important factors include: rigor of secondary school record, class rank. *Other factors considered include:* application essay, recommendations. High school diploma is required and GED is accepted. Institution is test-free for entering Fall 2024. Check admissions website for updates. *Academic units required:* 4 English, 3 math, 2 science (1 labs), 1 foreign language, 2 social studies. *Academic units recommended:* 4 math, 4 science (2 labs), 2 foreign language, 3 social studies.

FINANCIAL AID

Students should submit: FAFSA; Institution's own financial aid form; Noncustodial Profile. *Need-based scholarships/grants offered:* College/university scholarship or grant aid from institutional funds; Federal Nursing Scholarships; Federal Pell; Private scholarships; SEOG; State scholarships/grants. *Loan aid offered:.* Federal Work-Study Program available. Institutional employment available.

CAMPUS LIFE

Activities: Campus Ministries; Choral groups; Concert band; Dance; Drama/theater; International Student Organization; Jazz band; Marching band; Model UN; Music ensembles; Musical theater; Opera; Pep band; Radio station; Student government; Student newspaper; Student-run film society; Symphony orchestra; Television station. **Organizations:** 355 registered organizations, 23 religious organizations, 27 fraternities, 19 sororities. **Athletics (Intercollegiate):** *Men:* baseball, basketball, equestrian sports, golf, gymnastics, ice hockey, lacrosse, martial arts, racquetball, rugby, swimming, track/field (indoor), ultimate frisbee, volleyball, water polo, wrestling. *Women:* baseball, basketball, cross-country, equestrian sports, golf, gymnastics, ice hockey, lacrosse, martial arts, racquetball, rugby, softball, swimming, track/field (indoor), ultimate frisbee, volleyball, water polo, wrestling.

CAMPUS	
Type of school	Public
Environment	Village

STUDENTS	
Undergrad enrollment	11,834
% male/female	47/53
% from out of state	7
% frosh live on campus	91

FINANCIAL FACTS	
Annual in-state tuition	$9,790
Annual out-of-state tuition	$9,790
Room and board	$11,420
Required fees	$2,872

GENERAL ADMISSIONS INFO	
Application fee	$40
Regular application deadline	8/1
Nonfall registration	Yes
Fall 2024 testing policy	Test Free

ACADEMICS	
Student/faculty ratio	15:1
% students returning for sophomore year	67
Most classes have 20–29 students.	

Illinois

REQUESTING SERVICES FOR STUDENTS WITH LEARNING DIFFERENCES

Phone: 815- 753-1303 • niu.edu/disability • Email: drc@niu.edu

Documentation submitted to: Disability Resource Center
Separate application required for Services: Yes

Documentation required for:
LD: Psychoeducational evaluation
ADHD: Psychoeducational evaluation
ASD: Psychoeducational evaluation

Northwestern University

1801 Hinman Avenue, Evanston, IL 60204 • Admissions: 847-491-7271 • www.northwestern.edu

Support: CS

PROGRAMS/SERVICES FOR STUDENTS WITH LEARNING DIFFERENCES

AccessibleNU provides students with learning disabilities, ADHD, and other disabilities tools, reasonable accommodations, and support services. It is the responsibility of the student to provide documentation of disability, to inform the AccessibleNU office, and to request accommodations and services if needed. A student who has a disability but has not registered with AccessibleNU is not entitled to services or accommodations.

ADMISSIONS

All applicants must meet the general admission criteria. Most students have taken AP and honors courses in high school and have been very successful in these competitive college prep courses. Foreign language substitutions may be allowed and are decided on a case-by-case basis.

Additional Information

Undergraduate Program for Advanced Learning (UPAL) and Peer Academic Coaching is available through the office of Academic Support and Learning Advancement. UPAL provides sustained support during each quarter through a small-group experience with peer mentoring. Individual Academic Coaching pairs trained undergraduate coaches with students to help refine a student's approach to studying and learning, including time management, organizational skills, and accessing campus resources for success. SPS Learning Studios are self-paced, self-directed, noncredit, individualized online tutorials offered at no cost.

In 2022, NU got marathon fever—Dance Marathon fever, that is. The 48th annual NU 30-hour Dance Marathon raised more than half a million dollars for two local nonprofits. Hundreds of students took a break from studies to dance the night and day away: Friday night to early Sunday morning. Even the high winds that evacuated the tent in the final hours didn't spoil the mood. The NU entirely student-run Dance Marathon has raised over $16 million since its founding in 1975 and is one of the largest student-run philanthropies in the U.S.

Northwestern University

General Admissions

Very important factors include: rigor of secondary school record, class rank, academic GPA, application essay, recommendations. *Other factors considered include:* standardized test scores (if submitted). High school diploma is required and GED is accepted. Institution is test-optional for entering Fall 2024. Check admissions website for updates. *Academic units required:* 4 English, 3 math, 2 science (2 labs), 2 foreign language, 2 social studies. *Academic units recommended:* 4 math, 3 science (3 labs), 6 academic electives.

Financial Aid

Students should submit: CSS/Financial Aid Profile; FAFSA; Noncustodial Profile. *Need-based scholarships/grants offered:* College/university scholarship or grant aid from institutional funds; Federal Pell; SEOG; State scholarships/grants. *Loan aid offered:* Direct PLUS loans; Direct Subsidized Loans; Direct Unsubsidized Loans. Federal Work-Study Program available. Institutional employment available.

Campus Life

Activities: Campus Ministries; Choral groups; Concert band; Dance; Drama/theater; International Student Organization; Jazz band; Literary magazine; Marching band; Model UN; Music ensembles; Musical theater; Opera; Pep band; Radio station; Student government; Student newspaper; Student-run film society; Symphony orchestra; Television station; Yearbook. **Organizations:** 500 registered organizations. **Athletics (Intercollegiate):** *Men:* baseball, basketball, crew/rowing, cross-country, cycling, equestrian sports, golf, gymnastics, ice hockey, lacrosse, martial arts, rugby, skiing (nordic/cross-country), swimming, ultimate frisbee, volleyball, water polo, wrestling. *Women:* basketball, crew/rowing, cross-country, cycling, equestrian sports, field hockey, golf, gymnastics, ice hockey, lacrosse, martial arts, rugby, skiing (nordic/cross-country), softball, swimming, ultimate frisbee, volleyball, water polo.

Illinois

CAMPUS

Type of school	Private (nonprofit)
Environment	City

STUDENTS

Undergrad enrollment	8,847
% male/female	46/54
% from out of state	73
% frosh live on campus	99

FINANCIAL FACTS

Annual tuition	$62,391
Room and board	$19,440
Required fees	$1,077

GENERAL ADMISSIONS INFO

Application fee	$75
Regular application deadline	1/2
Nonfall registration	No

Fall 2024 testing policy	Test Optional
Range SAT EBRW	730–770
Range SAT Math	760–800
Range ACT Composite	33–35

ACADEMICS

Student/faculty ratio	6:1
% students returning for sophomore year	99

Most classes have 2–9 students.

REQUESTING SERVICES FOR STUDENTS WITH LEARNING DIFFERENCES

Phone: 847-467-5530 • www.northwestern.edu/accessiblenu • Email: accessiblenu@northwestern.edu

Documentation submitted to: AccessibleNU
Separate application required for Services: Yes

Documentation required for:
  LD: Psychoeducational evaluation
  ADHD: Psychoeducational evaluation
  ASD: Psychoeducational evaluation

Roosevelt University

430 South Michigan Avenue, Chicago, IL 60605 • Admissions: 877-277-5978 • www.roosevelt.edu

Support: CS

ACCOMMODATIONS

Allowed in exams:

Calculators	Yes
Dictionary	Yes
Computer	Yes
Spell-checker	Yes
Extended test time	Yes
Scribe	Yes
Proctors	Yes
Oral exams	No
Note-takers	Yes

Support services for students with:

LD	Yes
ADHD	Yes
ASD	Yes
Distraction-reduced environment	Yes
Recording of lecture allowed	Yes
Reading technology	Yes
Audio books	Yes
Other assistive technology	Yes
Priority registration	No

Added costs of services:

For LD	No
For ADHD	No
For ASD	No
LD specialists	Yes
ADHD & ASD coaching	Yes
ASD specialists	No
Professional tutors	No
Peer tutors	Yes
Max. hours/week for services	Varies
How professors are notified of student approved accommodations	Student

COLLEGE GRADUATION REQUIREMENTS

Course waivers allowed	Yes
In what courses: Case-by-case basis	
Course substitutions allowed	Yes
In what courses: Case-by-case basis	

PROGRAMS/SERVICES FOR STUDENTS WITH LEARNING DIFFERENCES

Disability Services (DS) is a branch of the Learning Commons and is available to all students with documented disabilities. Students are responsible for disclosing their disability and providing documentation to receive academic accommodations. Once appropriate documentation is provided, students will attend an intake meeting with a Learning Commons staff member to discuss reasonable accommodations, which may include extended time on quizzes and tests, alternative testing environments, extended time on some assignments, occasional absences, in-class breaks, notetakers, use of a recorder in class, and use of a calculator, reader, scribe, and word processor for tests and assignments.

ADMISSIONS

All applicants are expected to meet the same admission criteria. Although not initially required, a personal statement, essay, letters of recommendation, and/or official transcripts may be requested after an initial review of a student's application. Applicants who do not meet the admission requirements of a 2.0 GPA can be reconsidered for admission based on a final high school transcript. Students admitted through academic review are not eligible for merit-based scholarships. Auditions are required for music and theater majors.

Additional Information

The Writing Center helps empower students to become confident writers. The Peer Tutoring Program provides students feedback and individualized revision strategies for improving writing. Tutoring sessions are collaborative, and the tutors work with students to identify strengths and weaknesses in their writing. Writing strategies addressed in these sessions may include developing ideas, revising a draft, editing, and proofreading. Students can participate in workshops on specific writing strategies and skills and in small group discussions about writing assignments. Online tutoring is available for distance learners and students on the Schaumburg campus.

DID YOU KNOW?

Edward Sparling, president of Central YMCA College, resigned under protest when the college board proposed a quota to limit the number of Black and Jewish students. Sparling left and took many faculty and students with him to start a new college. Roosevelt University was founded in 1945 with backing from Marshall Field III, the Julius Rosenwald Foundation, the International Ladies' Garment Workers Union, and others. Early advisory board members included Eleanor Roosevelt, Albert Einstein, Marian Anderson, Pearl Buck, Ralph Bunche, Thomas Mann, Gunnar Myrdal, Draper Daniels, and Albert Schweitzer.

Roosevelt University

GENERAL ADMISSIONS

Very important factors include: academic GPA, standardized test scores (if submitted). *Other factors considered include:* rigor of secondary school record, class rank, application essay, recommendations. High school diploma is required and GED is accepted. Institution is test-optional for entering Fall 2024. Check admissions website for updates. *Academic units required:* 4 English, 3 math, 2 science (2 labs), 2 social studies. *Academic units recommended:* 3 science (3 labs), 2 foreign language, 3 social studies, 2 history, 2 academic electives.

FINANCIAL AID

Students should submit: FAFSA; Institution's own financial aid form. *Need-based scholarships/grants offered:* College/university scholarship or grant aid from institutional funds; Federal Pell; Private scholarships; SEOG; State scholarships/grants. *Loan aid offered:* Direct PLUS loans; Direct Subsidized Loans; Direct Unsubsidized Loans. Federal Work-Study Program available. Institutional employment available.

CAMPUS LIFE

Activities: Choral groups; Concert band; Dance; Drama/theater; International Student Organization; Jazz band; Literary magazine; Music ensembles; Musical theater; Opera; Pep band; Radio station; Student government; Student newspaper; Symphony orchestra. **Organizations:** 60 registered organizations, 6 honor societies, 3 religious organizations, 2 fraternities, 5 sororities. **Athletics (Intercollegiate):** *Men:* baseball, basketball, cross-country, golf, track/field (indoor). *Women:* basketball, cross-country, softball, track/field (indoor), volleyball.

CAMPUS

Type of school	Private (nonprofit)
Environment	Metropolis

STUDENTS

Undergrad enrollment	2,710
% male/female	36/64
% from out of state	15
% frosh live on campus	71

FINANCIAL FACTS

Annual tuition	$31,493
Room and board	$14,675

GENERAL ADMISSIONS INFO

Application fee	$25
Regular application deadline	Rolling
Nonfall registration	Yes
Fall 2024 testing policy	Test Optional
Range SAT EBRW	455–595
Range SAT Math	450–550
Range ACT Composite	19–24

ACADEMICS

Student/faculty ratio	11:1
% students returning for sophomore year	52

Most classes have 10–19 students.

Illinois

REQUESTING SERVICES FOR STUDENTS WITH LEARNING DIFFERENCES

Phone: 312-341-3629 • roosevelt.edu/current-students/support-services/learning-commons/disability-services • Email: nyoon@roosevelt.edu

Documentation submitted to: Disability Services
Separate application required for Services: Yes

Documentation required for:
  LD: Psychoeducational evaluation
  ADHD: Psychoeducational evaluation
  ASD: Psychoeducational evaluation

Southern Illinois University Carbondale

Undergraduate Admissions, Mailcode 4710, Carbondale, IL 62901 • Admissions: 618-536-4405 • siu.edu

Support: SP

ACCOMMODATIONS

Allowed in exams:

Calculators	Yes
Dictionary	Yes
Computer	Yes
Spell-checker	Yes
Extended test time	Yes
Scribe	Yes
Proctors	Yes
Oral exams	Yes
Note-takers	Yes

Support services for students with:

LD	Yes
ADHD	Yes
ASD	Yes
Distraction-reduced environment	Yes
Recording of lecture allowed	Yes
Reading technology	Yes
Audio books	Yes
Other assistive technology	Yes
Priority registration	Yes

Added costs of services:

For LD	Yes
For ADHD	Yes
For ASD	Yes
LD specialists	Yes
ADHD & ASD coaching	No
ASD specialists	Yes
Professional tutors	Yes
Peer tutors	Yes
Max. hours/week for services	Varies
How professors are notified of student approved accommodations	Student

COLLEGE GRADUATION REQUIREMENTS

Course waivers allowed	Yes
In what courses: Case-by-case basis	
Course substitutions allowed	Yes
In what courses: Many options	

PROGRAMS/SERVICES FOR STUDENTS WITH LEARNING DIFFERENCES

The Office of Disability Support Services (DSS) provides accommodations and services for students with disabilities. Students should complete a new student application online, submit documentation, and make an appointment with DSS staff. Students who do not have documentation can still complete the application and set a meeting with DSS to discuss services and accommodations. When accommodations are established, students use the DSS student portal to request and send faculty accommodation notification letters each term and then should speak with faculty about implementing accommodations. Accommodations include alternative testing, note-taking services and technology, alternate-format course materials, lab assistance, and assistive technology and training. The Achieve Program is a fee-for-service program that serves students with ADD, ADHD, ASD, dyslexia, processing disorders, and many other learning difficulties. The Achieve team of experienced staff advisors, case managers, test proctors, academic coaches, and content-specific tutors work with students one-on-one. Each student is assigned a case manager and meets weekly. The Center for Autism Spectrum Disorder offers social communication skills training to help with the challenges of navigating college life and support and counseling to improve independent living skills.

ADMISSIONS

Applicants who submit official high school transcripts and complete the academic course requirements are eligible for automatic general admission if they meet one of the following three criteria: a 2.75 GPA, rank in the top 10 percent of their graduating class, or an ACT score of 23 or SAT score of 1130. If not eligible for automatic admission, then coursework, GPA, letters of recommendation, and extracurricular activities in school and the community will be reviewed. Direct entry into some SIU programs exceed the general admission requirements. ACT and SAT scores are not required for applicants with a GPA of 2.75 or above.

Additional Information

The Center for Learning Support Services (CLSS) offers free tutoring for first-year students and students in lower-level courses. Group study sessions, academic coaching, and math tutoring are also available in the CLSS tutoring center. The Writing Center offers free tutoring services and writing sessions to help improve overall writing skills. The Math Lab has free tutoring, and the math department's graduate students have scheduled help sessions in the lower-level courses. Math instructors are also available during their office hours.

SIU has quite a history of presidential speakers, including presidents William Howard Taft, Harry S. Truman, Richard Nixon, John F. Kennedy, Jimmy Carter, George H. W. Bush, Barack Obama, Donald Trump, and Joe Biden in 2020. Bill Clinton, who was the first sitting president to speak at SIU, advocated for direct student loan programs and against cuts to higher education financial aid in 1995.

Southern Illinois University Carbondale

GENERAL ADMISSIONS

Very important factors include: academic GPA. *Important factors include:* rigor of secondary school record, class rank, standardized test scores (if submitted). *Other factors considered include:* application essay, recommendations. High school diploma is required and GED is accepted. Institution is test-optional for entering Fall 2024. Check admissions website for updates. *Academic units required:* 4 English, 3 math, 3 science (3 labs), 3 social studies, 2 academic electives. *Academic units recommended:* 4 math.

FINANCIAL AID

Students should submit: FAFSA. *Need-based scholarships/grants offered:* College/university scholarship or grant aid from institutional funds; Federal Pell; Private scholarships; SEOG; State scholarships/grants. *Loan aid offered:* Direct PLUS loans; Direct Subsidized Loans; Direct Unsubsidized Loans. Federal Work-Study Program available. Institutional employment available.

CAMPUS LIFE

Activities: Campus Ministries; Choral groups; Concert band; Dance; Drama/theater; International Student Organization; Jazz band; Literary magazine; Marching band; Model UN; Music ensembles; Musical theater; Opera; Pep band; Radio station; Student government; Student newspaper; Student-run film society; Symphony orchestra; Television station. **Organizations:** 319 registered organizations, 12 honor societies, 16 religious organizations, 17 fraternities, 10 sororities. **Athletics (Intercollegiate):** *Men:* baseball, basketball, cross-country, equestrian sports, golf, gymnastics, lacrosse, martial arts, racquetball, rugby, swimming, table tennis, track/field (indoor), volleyball, water polo. *Women:* basketball, cross-country, equestrian sports, golf, gymnastics, martial arts, racquetball, rugby, softball, swimming, table tennis, track/field (indoor), volleyball, water polo.

CAMPUS

Type of school	Public
Environment	Town

STUDENTS

Undergrad enrollment	7,922
% male/female	50/50
% from out of state	19
% frosh live on campus	86

FINANCIAL FACTS

Annual in-state tuition	$9,638
Annual out-of-state tuition	$9,638
Room and board	$10,622
Required fees	$5,602

GENERAL ADMISSIONS INFO

Application fee	$40
Regular application deadline	Rolling
Nonfall registration	Yes
Fall 2024 testing policy	Test Optional
Range SAT EBRW	480–590
Range SAT Math	450–570
Range ACT Composite	20–28

ACADEMICS

Student/faculty ratio	10:1
% students returning for sophomore year	75

Most classes have 10–19 students.

REQUESTING SERVICES FOR STUDENTS WITH LEARNING DIFFERENCES

Phone: 618-453-5738 • disabilityservices.siu.edu • Email: disabilityservices@siu.edu

Documentation submitted to: Office of Disability Support Services
Separate application required for Services: Yes

Documentation required for:
LD: Psychoeducational evaluation
ADHD: Psychoeducational evaluation
ASD: Psychoeducational evaluation

Southern Illinois University Edwardsville

SIUE Office of Admissions, Edwardsville, IL 62026-1047 • Admissions: 618-650-3705 • www.siue.edu

Support: CS

ACCOMMODATIONS

Allowed in exams:

Calculators	Yes
Dictionary	Yes
Computer	Yes
Spell-checker	No
Extended test time	Yes
Scribe	Yes
Proctors	Yes
Oral exams	Yes
Note-takers	Yes

Support services for students with:

LD	Yes
ADHD	Yes
ASD	Yes
Distraction-reduced environment	Yes
Recording of lecture allowed	Yes
Reading technology	Yes
Audio books	Yes
Other assistive technology	Yes
Priority registration	Yes

Added costs of services:

For LD	No
For ADHD	No
For ASD	No
LD specialists	Yes
ADHD & ASD coaching	No
ASD specialists	Yes
Professional tutors	No
Peer tutors	No
Max. hours/week for services	Varies
How professors are notified of student approved accommodations	Student

COLLEGE GRADUATION REQUIREMENTS

Course waivers allowed	No
Course substitutions allowed	Yes
In what courses: Math and Foreign Language	

With 2,660 acres of trees and lakes, SIUE is one of the largest U.S. campuses by land area. The campus core center, Stratton Quadrangle, is named after William Stratton, a governor of Illinois and first commencement speaker in 1960. The quadrangle design has no direct pathway between buildings, providing students with exposure to nature during the walk between buildings.

PROGRAMS/SERVICES FOR STUDENTS WITH LEARNING DIFFERENCES

The Office for Accessible Campus Community & Equitable Student Support (ACCESS) provides reasonable curricular and cocurricular accommodations for students with learning disabilities. Students register online, submit appropriate documentation, and are contacted to schedule an intake meeting with an ACCESS staff member to discuss the accommodations request. Students who do not have documentation should still register and can discuss assistance or referral at the intake appointment. After accommodations have been determined, ACCESS notifies the student and instructors of the approved accommodations, including the role of the student and instructor going forward. The Bridging Universal Inclusion & Leadership Development (BUILD) program is a mentoring program that works with neurodiverse learners from admission to graduation with early outreach to discuss the transition to college, college-level accommodations, and skill-development exercises. Students are paired with mentors based on criteria such as academic discipline or personal interests and take part in activities to create a successful partnership. BUILD mentors aid students in goal setting, self-advocacy, academic preparedness, and self-care.

ADMISSIONS

All applicants are required to meet the same minimum requirements for admission. Priority consideration is given to students whose applications are complete by the priority deadline, while applications received after the deadline are subject to additional review. Applicants are automatically admitted with one of the following criteria: 2.75 GPA, rank in top 10 percent of their class, or have a minimum ACT score of 23 or SAT of 1130. Students with a 2.0–2.59 GPA will be considered by the Admission Review Committee and must submit a seventh-semester transcript and a personal statement detailing any challenges that have impacted their academic record, how they navigated those challenges, and how they plan to succeed at SIUE. The committee may also consider a graded writing sample, letters of recommendation, admission counselor recommendation, a personal interview with selected committee members, or the success rates of previous students enrolled from the candidate's high school.

Additional Information

Learning Support Services (LSS) offers three academic development courses that can be elective credit for graduation credit, including AD 115 Study Skills, AD 116 Reading Speed and Efficiency, and AD 117 Career Planning and Development. LSS is home to the Tutoring Resource Center, Writing Center, and Supplemental Instruction (SI). The Tutoring Resource Center welcomes walk-ins or scheduled appointments. The Writing Center works with students to help them become stronger writers. SI is a non-remedial program with regularly scheduled, out-of-class, peer-led study groups targeting traditionally difficult academic courses.

Southern Illinois University Edwardsville

GENERAL ADMISSIONS

Very important factors include: academic GPA. *Important factors include:* rigor of secondary school record, class rank. High school diploma is required and GED is accepted. Institution is test-optional for entering Fall 2024. Check admissions website for updates. *Academic units required:* 4 English, 3 math, 3 science (3 labs), 3 social studies, 2 academic electives. *Academic units recommended:* 2 foreign language.

FINANCIAL AID

Students should submit: FAFSA. *Need-based scholarships/grants offered:* College/university scholarship or grant aid from institutional funds; Federal Nursing Scholarships; Federal Pell; Private scholarships; SEOG; State scholarships/grants. *Loan aid offered:* Direct PLUS loans; Direct Subsidized Loans; Direct Unsubsidized Loans. Federal Work-Study Program available. Institutional employment available.

CAMPUS LIFE

Activities: Campus Ministries; Choral groups; Concert band; Dance; Drama/theater; International Student Organization; Jazz band; Literary magazine; Music ensembles; Musical theater; Opera; Pep band; Radio station; Student government; Student newspaper; Symphony orchestra. **Organizations:** 302 registered organizations, 18 honor societies, 10 religious organizations, 13 fraternities, 9 sororities. **Athletics (Intercollegiate):** *Men:* baseball, basketball, bowling, cross-country, cycling, golf, ice hockey, lacrosse, martial arts, racquetball, softball, swimming, table tennis, track/field (indoor), ultimate frisbee, volleyball, wrestling. *Women:* basketball, bowling, cross-country, cycling, golf, lacrosse, martial arts, racquetball, softball, swimming, table tennis, track/field (indoor), ultimate frisbee, volleyball, wrestling.

CAMPUS

Type of school	Public
Environment	Town

STUDENTS

Undergrad enrollment	11,339
% male/female	47/53
% from out of state	12
% frosh live on campus	72

FINANCIAL FACTS

Annual in-state tuition	$9,576
Annual out-of-state tuition	$9,576
Room and board	$10,561
Required fees	$3,346

GENERAL ADMISSIONS INFO

Application fee	$40
Regular application deadline	7/19
Nonfall registration	Yes

Fall 2024 testing policy	Test Optional
Range SAT EBRW	485–625
Range SAT Math	495–600
Range ACT Composite	20–26

ACADEMICS

Student/faculty ratio	20:1
% students returning for sophomore year	73

Most classes have 10–19 students.

REQUESTING SERVICES FOR STUDENTS WITH LEARNING DIFFERENCES

Phone: 618-650-3726 • siue.edu/access • Email: myaccess@siue.edu

Documentation submitted to: Office for Accessible Campus Community & Equitable Student Support (ACCESS)

Separate application required for Services: Yes

Documentation required for:
 LD: Psychoeducational evaluation
 ADHD: Psychoeducational evaluation
 ASD: Psychoeducational evaluation

University of Illinois Springfield

One University Plaza, Springfield, IL 62703-5407 • Admissions: 217-206-4847 • www.uis.edu

(Support: CS)

ACCOMMODATIONS

Allowed in exams:

Calculators	Yes
Dictionary	Yes
Computer	No
Spell-checker	Yes
Extended test time	Yes
Scribe	Yes
Proctors	Yes
Oral exams	Yes
Note-takers	Yes

Support services for students with:

LD	Yes
ADHD	Yes
ASD	Yes
Distraction-reduced environment	Yes
Recording of lecture allowed	Yes
Reading technology	Yes
Audio books	Yes
Other assistive technology	Yes
Priority registration	Yes

Added costs of services:

For LD	No
For ADHD	No
For ASD	No
LD specialists	Yes
ADHD & ASD coaching	No
ASD specialists	Yes
Professional tutors	Yes
Peer tutors	Yes
Max. hours/week for services	Varies
How professors are notified of student approved accommodations	Student

COLLEGE GRADUATION REQUIREMENTS

Course waivers allowed	Yes

In what courses: Math and Foreign Language

Course substitutions allowed	Yes

In what courses: Math and Foreign Language

PROGRAMS/SERVICES FOR STUDENTS WITH LEARNING DIFFERENCES

The Office of Disability Services (ODS) provides reasonable accommodations to students with disabilities. Once admitted to UIS, students contact ODS for an initial interview with an ODS specialist to register, complete paperwork, provide documentation, and discuss past academic accommodations and which accommodations are appropriate for the student. Once accommodations are determined, students receive a letter of accommodations that they give to professors and discuss implementation. Accommodations are based on underlying medical and cognitive conditions and may include priority registration, adaptive technology and training, alternative-format text, peer notetakers, ASL interpreters, recording devices, the computer lab, extended exam time and alternate exam location, housing/dining accommodations, and transportation.

ADMISSIONS

Admission standards are the same for all students. Applications are evaluated based on college prep curricula and academic coursework; GPA and class rank are considered, and a personal essay is required. Students lacking some of the academic coursework requirements may be conditionally admitted, provided they can complete the requirements prior to enrollment.

Additional Information

The Center for Teaching and Learning (CTL) offers a free peer tutoring program to help students improve skills in writing, grammar and usage, math and statistics, science, reading, studying, and test-taking. The Learning Hub offers free in-person and online peer tutoring and in-class workshops for academic skills, writing, math, accounting, economics, science, exercise science, and computer science. The Hub provides Supplemental Instruction, a program offering small group study sessions for historically challenging courses. The Center for Academic Success & Advising (CASA) has a Peer Advisor/Peer Mentor Program to help new students transition to college life through individual and small group interactions. CASA's professional academic advisors help students select semester courses, prepare for a major course of study, and connect students with other services on campus.

Most streets on the UIS campus are named after writers with a connection to Illinois, such as Ernest Hemingway, born and raised in Oak Park; Carl Sandburg, born and raised in Galesburg; and Gwendolyn Brooks, who lived in Chicago and attended four different racially diverse schools.

University of Illinois Springfield

GENERAL ADMISSIONS

Very important factors include: rigor of secondary school record, class rank, academic GPA. *Important factors include:* application essay. *Other factors considered include:* recommendations. High school diploma is required and GED is accepted. Institution is test-optional for entering Fall 2024. Check admissions website for updates. *Academic units required:* 4 English, 3 math, 3 science (2 labs), 3 social studies, 2 foreign language or visual/performing arts. *Academic units recommended:* 4 math, 4 science, 2 foreign language, 4 social studies.

FINANCIAL AID

Students should submit: FAFSA. *Need-based scholarships/grants offered:* College/university scholarship or grant aid from institutional funds; Federal Pell; Private scholarships; SEOG; State scholarships/grants. *Loan aid offered:* Direct PLUS loans; Direct Subsidized Loans; Direct Unsubsidized Loans. Federal Work-Study Program available. Institutional employment available.

CAMPUS LIFE

Activities: Campus Ministries; Choral groups; Concert band; Dance; Drama/theater; International Student Organization; Jazz band; Model UN; Music ensembles; Pep band; Radio station; Student government; Student newspaper; Student-run film society. **Organizations:** 81 registered organizations, 7 honor societies, 6 religious organizations, 5 fraternities, 5 sororities. **Athletics (Intercollegiate):** *Men:* baseball, basketball, cross-country, golf, table tennis, track/field (indoor), volleyball. *Women:* basketball, cross-country, golf, softball, table tennis, track/field (indoor), volleyball.

CAMPUS	
Type of school	Public
Environment	City

STUDENTS	
Undergrad enrollment	2,503
% male/female	47/53
% from out of state	8
% frosh live on campus	74

FINANCIAL FACTS	
Annual in-state tuition	$9,503
Annual out-of-state tuition	$19,118
Room and board	$10,410
Required fees	$2,408

GENERAL ADMISSIONS INFO	
Application fee	No fee
Regular application deadline	Start of Term
Nonfall registration	Yes

Fall 2024 testing policy	Test Optional
Range SAT EBRW	510–640
Range SAT Math	480–610
Range ACT Composite	21–27

ACADEMICS	
Student/faculty ratio	12:1
% students returning for sophomore year	67
Most classes have 10–19 students.	

Illinois

REQUESTING SERVICES FOR STUDENTS WITH LEARNING DIFFERENCES

Phone: 217-206-6666 • uis.edu/disability • Email: ods@uis.edu

Documentation submitted to: Office of Disability Services (ODS)
Separate application required for Services: Yes

Documentation required for:
 LD: Psychoeducational evaluation
 ADHD: Psychoeducational evaluation
 ASD: Psychoeducational evaluation

University of Illinois at Urbana-Champaign

901 West Illinois Street, Urbana, IL 61801-3028 • Admissions: 217-333-0302 • illinois.edu

Support: CS

ACCOMMODATIONS

Allowed in exams:

Calculators	Yes
Dictionary	Yes
Computer	Yes
Spell-checker	Yes
Extended test time	Yes
Scribe	Yes
Proctors	Yes
Oral exams	Yes
Note-takers	Yes

Support services for students with:

LD	Yes
ADHD	Yes
ASD	Yes
Distraction-reduced environment	Yes
Recording of lecture allowed	Yes
Reading technology	Yes
Audio books	Yes
Other assistive technology	Yes
Priority registration	Yes

Added costs of services:

For LD	No
For ADHD	No
For ASD	No
LD specialists	Yes
ADHD & ASD coaching	Yes
ASD specialists	Yes
Professional tutors	Yes
Peer tutors	Yes
Max. hours/week for services	Varies
How professors are notified of student approved accommodations	Student

COLLEGE GRADUATION REQUIREMENTS

Course waivers allowed	No
Course substitutions allowed	Yes
In what courses: Case-by-case basis	

PROGRAMS/SERVICES FOR STUDENTS WITH LEARNING DIFFERENCES

Accommodations, adjustments, and support services for students with disabilities are available through Disability Resources and Educational Services (DRES). Once accepted to UI-UC, students with disabilities can apply to DRES, then are assigned an access specialist who will work with the student and faculty to determine appropriate classroom accommodations and services. Registered DRES students have access to academic coaching (for organization, time management, structure, prioritizing, and motivation), group therapy, and individual therapy appointments without session limits at no cost to the student. DRES has an extensive list of resources and strategies available as well as career development coaching, workshops, and networking.

ADMISSIONS

Each college and program or major have specific requirements. High school students should have strong grades in the core academic courses. Test scores will be considered, if submitted, and may be used for course placement, academic advising, scholarship, and aid decisions. Applicants are asked to reply to supplemental questions. Admissions committees also look at the quality of accomplishments in activities outside the classroom that show passion, strengths, skills, perseverance, determination, motivation, generosity, creativity, leadership ability, and intellectual curiosity. UI-UC does not accept letters of recommendation. Applicants who do not meet all the criteria required will need to document why in a personal statement, where they can also emphasize why they should still be considered.

Additional Information

The ACES Collaborative Learning Center (ACLC) provides academic assistance and peer tutoring in accounting, economics, finance, statistics, math, chemistry, history, biology, psychology, and more. The Student Assistance Center in the Office of the Dean of Students is the first point of contact for tutoring and academic support resources throughout the colleges. Each college offers tutoring, peer advisors, workshops, and exam prep opportunities. The Writers Workshop provides writing support including individual consultations and workshops, which can be used for any writing assignment.

The Division of Disability Resources and Educational Services (DRES) was the first higher-education disability support program in the world. Founded in 1948 by Dr. Tim Nugent, DRES began from his belief that veterans injured in WWII should be able to take advantage of the GI bill. From those early days came more than 60 years of breakthroughs and "firsts" in accessibility.

University of Illinois at Urbana-Champaign

GENERAL ADMISSIONS

Very important factors include: rigor of secondary school record, academic GPA. *Important factors include:* standardized test scores (if submitted), application essay. *Other factors considered include:* class rank. High school diploma is required and GED is accepted. Institution is test-optional for entering Fall 2024. Check admissions website for updates. *Academic units required:* 4 English, 3 math, 2 science (2 labs), 2 foreign language, 2 social studies, 2 academic electives. *Academic units recommended:* 4 math, 4 science (4 labs), 4 foreign language, 4 social studies, 4 academic electives.

FINANCIAL AID

Students should submit: FAFSA. *Need-based scholarships/grants offered:* College/university scholarship or grant aid from institutional funds; Federal Pell; Private scholarships; SEOG; State scholarships/grants; United Negro College Fund. *Loan aid offered:* Direct PLUS loans; Direct Subsidized Loans; Direct Unsubsidized Loans. Federal Work-Study Program available. Institutional employment available.

CAMPUS LIFE

Activities: Choral groups; Concert band; Dance; Drama/theater; International Student Organization; Jazz band; Literary magazine; Marching band; Music ensembles; Musical theater; Opera; Pep band; Radio station; Student government; Student newspaper; Student-run film society; Symphony orchestra; Television station; Yearbook. **Organizations:** 1400 registered organizations. **Athletics (Intercollegiate):** *Men:* baseball, basketball, cross-country, golf, gymnastics, track/field (indoor), wrestling. *Women:* basketball, cross-country, golf, gymnastics, softball, swimming, track/field (indoor), volleyball.

CAMPUS	
Type of school	Public
Environment	City

STUDENTS	
Undergrad enrollment	32,884
% male/female	54/46
% from out of state	14
% frosh live on campus	99

FINANCIAL FACTS	
Annual in-state tuition	$12,036
Annual out-of-state tuition	$27,658
Room and board	$11,308
Required fees	$3,832

GENERAL ADMISSIONS INFO	
Application fee	$50
Regular application deadline	1/5
Nonfall registration	No

Fall 2024 testing policy	Test Optional
Range SAT EBRW	580–690
Range SAT Math	700–790
Range ACT Composite	26–32

ACADEMICS	
Student/faculty ratio	21:1
% students returning for sophomore year	92
Most classes have 10–19 students.	

Illinois

REQUESTING SERVICES FOR STUDENTS WITH LEARNING DIFFERENCES

Phone: 217-333-4603 • www.disability.illinois.edu • Email: disability@illinois.edu

Documentation submitted to: Disability Resources and Educational Services (DRES)
Separate application required for Services: Yes

Documentation required for:
LD: Psychoeducational evaluation
ADHD: Psychoeducational evaluation
ASD: Psychoeducational evaluation

University of St. Francis

500 Wilcox Street, Joliet, IL 60435 • Admissions: 800-735-7500 • www.stfrancis.edu

Support: S

ACCOMMODATIONS

Allowed in exams:

Calculators	Yes
Dictionary	Yes
Computer	Yes
Spell-checker	Yes
Extended test time	Yes
Scribe	Yes
Proctors	Yes
Oral exams	Yes
Note-takers	Yes

Support services for students with:

LD	Yes
ADHD	Yes
ASD	Yes
Distraction-reduced environment	Yes
Recording of lecture allowed	Yes
Reading technology	Yes
Audio books	Yes
Other assistive technology	Yes
Priority registration	Yes

Added costs of services:

For LD	No
For ADHD	No
For ASD	No
LD specialists	No
ADHD & ASD coaching	No
ASD specialists	No
Professional tutors	Yes
Peer tutors	Yes
Max. hours/week for services	Varies
How professors are notified of student approved accommodations	Office of Disability Services

COLLEGE GRADUATION REQUIREMENTS

Course waivers allowed	Yes
In what courses: Case-by-case basis	
Course substitutions allowed	Yes
In what courses: Case-by-case basis	

PROGRAMS/SERVICES FOR STUDENTS WITH LEARNING DIFFERENCES

The Office of Disability Services, as part of the Academic Resource Center (ACR), supports students with learning differences. Students can also receive accommodations such as extended time on tests, assistive technology, alternative texts, note-taking, readers, scribes, and preferential seating. Students are responsible for self-disclosure and requesting accommodations.

ADMISSIONS

All applicants must meet the same criteria for admission. Students are automatically admissible with a 2.5 GPA or higher. Admitted applicants who submit test scores typically have an ACT between 20–25 or an SAT between 1030–1230.

Additional Information

Supplemental Instruction (SI) is offered by the university, which includes scheduled reviews, discussions, study strategies, and exam preparation. Each session is guided by an SI leader who has taken the course and is familiar with the professor's requirements. SI is offered in small, informal groups, and tutoring is offered to all students free of charge. The Center for Academic Success provides guidance for first-year students, including registration and tracking at-risk students. ACR provides tutoring that focuses on course content and study habits.

DID YOU KNOW?

In 2019, USF expanded the Bee and Butterfly Garden in the Quad with a second garden and a solar-powered birdbath. The Monarch Waystations provide the necessary resources for the butterflies to produce successive generations and sustain their migration. Plants in the garden include black-eyed Susan, butterfly weed, cleome, purple coneflower, coreopsis, and more. The garden was certified as a Monarch Waystation through Monarch Watch. USF is committed to making a positive environmental impact on campus.

University of St. Francis

GENERAL ADMISSIONS

Very important factors include: rigor of secondary school record, academic GPA. *Other factors considered include:* standardized test scores (if submitted). High school diploma is required and GED is accepted. Institution is test-optional for entering Fall 2024. Check admissions website for updates. *Academic units required:* 4 English, 3 math, 2 science (1 lab), 2 social studies, 3 academic electives.

FINANCIAL AID

Students should submit: FAFSA; Institution's own financial aid form. *Need-based scholarships/grants offered:* College/university scholarship or grant aid from institutional funds; Federal Pell; Private scholarships; SEOG; State scholarships/grants. *Loan aid offered:* Direct PLUS loans; Direct Subsidized Loans; Direct Unsubsidized Loans. Federal Work-Study Program available. Institutional employment available.

CAMPUS LIFE

Activities: Campus Ministries; Choral groups; Dance; Drama/theater; International Student Organization; Jazz band; Music ensembles; Musical theater; Opera; Pep band; Radio station; Student government; Student newspaper; Symphony orchestra; Television station. **Organizations:** 65 registered organizations, 19 honor societies, 2 religious organizations, 1 fraternities, 1 sororities. **Athletics (Intercollegiate):** *Men:* baseball, basketball, bowling, cross-country, golf, track/field (indoor). *Women:* basketball, bowling, cross-country, golf, softball, track/field (indoor), volleyball.

CAMPUS

Type of school	Private (nonprofit)
Environment	City

STUDENTS

Undergrad enrollment	1,519
% male/female	31/69
% from out of state	8
% frosh live on campus	38

FINANCIAL FACTS

Annual tuition	$36,000
Room and board	$11,430
Required fees	Varies

GENERAL ADMISSIONS INFO

Application fee	No fee
Regular application deadline	Rolling
Nonfall registration	Yes
Fall 2024 testing policy	Test Optional
Range SAT EBRW	470–580
Range SAT Math	450–590
Range ACT Composite	20–25

ACADEMICS

Student/faculty ratio	13:1
% students returning for sophomore year	73
Most classes have 10–19 students.	

REQUESTING SERVICES FOR STUDENTS WITH LEARNING DIFFERENCES

Phone: 815-740-3204 • www.stfrancis.edu/student-affairs/academic-resource-center
Email: salag@stfrancis.edu

Documentation submitted to: Office of Disability Services
Separate application required for Services: Yes

Documentation required for:
 LD: Psychoeducational evaluation
 ADHD: Psychoeducational evaluation
 ASD: Psychoeducational evaluation

Western Illinois University

1 University Circle, Sherman Hall 115, Macomb, IL 61455-1390 • Admissions: 309-298-3157 • www.wiu.edu

Support: CS

ACCOMMODATIONS

Allowed in exams:

Calculators	Yes
Dictionary	Yes
Computer	Yes
Spell-checker	Yes
Extended test time	Yes
Scribe	Yes
Proctors	Yes
Oral exams	Yes
Note-takers	Yes

Support services for students with:

LD	Yes
ADHD	Yes
ASD	Yes
Distraction-reduced environment	Yes
Recording of lecture allowed	Yes
Reading technology	Yes
Audio books	No
Other assistive technology	Yes
Priority registration	Yes

Added costs of services:

For LD	No
For ADHD	No
For ASD	No
LD specialists	Yes
ADHD & ASD coaching	No
ASD specialists	No
Professional tutors	Yes
Peer tutors	Yes
Max. hours/week for services	Varies
How professors are notified of student approved accommodations	Student and SDSC

COLLEGE GRADUATION REQUIREMENTS

Course waivers allowed	Yes
In what courses: Case-by-case basis	
Course substitutions allowed	Yes
In what courses: Case-by-case basis	

PROGRAMS/SERVICES FOR STUDENTS WITH LEARNING DIFFERENCES

The Student Development and Success Center (SDSC) works with students to determine disability and reasonable accommodations. Disability Resources in the SDSC encourages students to provide documentation of their disability by completing an online accommodation request form and requesting a meeting to discuss their disability and the modifications and accommodations they seek. Disability Resources staff work with the student to determine what accommodations would be reasonable, and all requests must be reasonable both at the institutional level and at the individual level. Some students may be asked for additional documentation. Once students have been approved for accommodations, they will be trained on how to notify their professors and how to schedule to take exams in the SDSC.

ADMISSIONS

Applicants should have a minimum 2.75 GPA. Applicants with a 2.0–2.74 GPA are reviewed holistically and encouraged to submit a personal statement addressing their circumstances. Students in the top 10 percent of their class at an accredited Illinois high school are automatically admitted. Students can still apply even if they have not met all the course requirements. The Reach Program is an alternative admission program for students not meeting the regular admission criteria. Selection is based on a student's academic GPA in core classes, recommendations, and goal statements. Reach advisors serve as advocates and guide, support, and impact the student's experience as they navigate their first year. There is no separate application for the Reach Program.

Additional Information

The Linkages Program is a concurrent enrollment program where students enroll at Western Illinois University and a participating community college. Students take courses at both colleges and lock in the tuition to pay less for the first two years. The Turning Point Peer Mentor program offers students practical advice addressing issues such as best approaches in working with faculty members, study skills, time management, and staying organized. Peer mentors also offer a social connection. The academic advisors in the First Year Advising Center are full-time professionals who help students establish and reach their academic, personal, and career goals. Academic Success Coaching is a one-on-one opportunity for students to get help identifying challenges, connecting with resources, creating action plans, and getting referrals for campus services. Once students sign up with a success coach, they are committing to regularly scheduled meetings for the semester.

DID YOU KNOW?

WIU's purple and gold school colors date back to 1902. First-year student Mary Jarvis submitted the colors for a schoolwide contest inspired by the "vast golden prairie strewn with purple coneflowers." Her original ribbons and diploma are in the library archives. The men's and women's athletics teams are known as The Fighting Leathernecks; WIU is the only public school in the United States with permission to use the nickname.

Western Illinois University

General Admissions
Very important factors include: academic GPA. High school diploma is required and GED is accepted. Institution is test-optional for entering Fall 2024. Check admissions website for updates. *Academic units required:* 4 English, 3 math, 3 science, 3 social studies, 2 academic electives.

Financial Aid
Students should submit: FAFSA. *Need-based scholarships/grants offered:* College/university scholarship or grant aid from institutional funds; Federal Pell; Private scholarships; SEOG; State scholarships/grants. *Loan aid offered:* Direct PLUS loans; Direct Subsidized Loans; Direct Unsubsidized Loans. Federal Work-Study Program available. Institutional employment available.

Campus Life
Activities: Campus Ministries; Choral groups; Concert band; Dance; Drama/theater; International Student Organization; Jazz band; Literary magazine; Marching band; Model UN; Music ensembles; Musical theater; Opera; Pep band; Radio station; Student government; Student newspaper; Student-run film society; Symphony orchestra; Television station. **Organizations:** 245 registered organizations, 11 honor societies, 8 religious organizations, 15 fraternities, 11 sororities. **Athletics (Intercollegiate):** *Men:* baseball, basketball, bowling, cross-country, equestrian sports, golf, lacrosse, martial arts, swimming, table tennis, track/field (indoor), ultimate frisbee, volleyball, water polo, wrestling. *Women:* basketball, bowling, cross-country, equestrian sports, golf, martial arts, rugby, softball, swimming, table tennis, track/field (indoor), ultimate frisbee, volleyball, water polo.

CAMPUS

Type of school	Public
Environment	Village

STUDENTS

Undergrad enrollment	5,394
% male/female	44/56
% from out of state	13
% frosh live on campus	83

FINANCIAL FACTS

Annual in-state tuition	$9,238
Annual out-of-state tuition	$9,238
Room and board	$10,192
Required fees	$4,431

GENERAL ADMISSIONS INFO

Application fee	$30
Regular application deadline	Rolling
Nonfall registration	Yes

Fall 2024 testing policy	Test Optional
Range SAT EBRW	460–580
Range SAT Math	440–550
Range ACT Composite	19–26

ACADEMICS

Student/faculty ratio	13:1
% students returning for sophomore year	72
Most classes have 10–19 students.	

REQUESTING SERVICES FOR STUDENTS WITH LEARNING DIFFERENCES

Phone: 309-298-1884 • www.wiu.edu/student_services/sdsc • Email: sdsc@wiu.edu

Documentation submitted to: Student Development and Success Center
Separate application required for Services: Yes

Documentation required for:
LD: Psychoeducational evaluation
ADHD: Psychoeducational evaluation
ASD: Psychoeducational evaluation

Wheaton College

501 College Avenue, Wheaton, IL 60187 • Admissions: 630-752-5011 • www.wheaton.edu

Support: CS

ACCOMMODATIONS

Allowed in exams:

Calculators	Yes
Dictionary	Yes
Computer	Yes
Spell-checker	Yes
Extended test time	Yes
Scribe	Yes
Proctors	Yes
Oral exams	Yes
Note-takers	Yes

Support services for students with:

LD	Yes
ADHD	Yes
ASD	Yes
Distraction-reduced environment	Yes
Recording of lecture allowed	Yes
Reading technology	Yes
Audio books	Yes
Other assistive technology	Yes
Priority registration	No

Added costs of services:

For LD	No
For ADHD	No
For ASD	No
LD specialists	No
ADHD & ASD coaching	Yes
ASD specialists	Yes
Professional tutors	No
Peer tutors	Yes
Max. hours/week for services	Varies
How professors are notified of student approved accommodations	Student and LAS

COLLEGE GRADUATION REQUIREMENTS

Course waivers allowed	No
Course substitutions allowed	Yes

In what courses: Foreign Language and in rare cases Public Speaking

PROGRAMS/SERVICES FOR STUDENTS WITH LEARNING DIFFERENCES

Learning and Accessibility Services (LAS) provides resources to students with learning differences. Students can request accommodations by filling out the appropriate section on their enrollment confirmation form or by contacting the LAS director. Through one-on-one strategic meetings, peer coaching, and academic seminars, students develop new strategies, build existing skills, and better understand how to maximize their personal learning experience. Students can make appointments for academic accountability coaching, advocacy, and accommodation approval. Assistive technology is determined on a case-by-case basis. LAS hosts a series of development workshops that foster community and create spaces for students with disabilities to connect. Workshop topics include time management, reading and note-taking strategies, paper writing and research skills, test preparation, overcoming procrastination and perfectionism, and more.

ADMISSIONS

Admission requirements are the same for all students; however, foreign language waivers are available for students with learning disabilities. Accepted students demonstrate strong academic abilities and have an average GPA of 3.7. The middle 50 percent of admitted students who submitted SAT scores had between a 1240 and 1550. Students for whom English is not their first language are encouraged to submit standardized test scores. Wheaton College seeks applicants with a committed Christian experience, strong moral character, personal integrity, and concern for others.

Additional Information

General academic support services through LAS are available for all students. Services include academic-life coaching and peer coaching, which provide accountability support. Wheaton College believes that peer coaching allows for more frequent check-ins and creates a comfortable environment. Students may choose to meet with the same coach or try different ones.

Wheaton College Crew is the official collegiate rowing club. Established in 1989, both the men's and women's teams are members of the American Collegiate Rowing Association (ACRA) in the Great Lakes Region. The Wheaton Crew Cheer is a long-standing oral tradition when launching boats at regattas. As a strictly oral tradition, it cannot be written down for any purpose. Memorizing the cheer is a rite of passage for rowers.

Wheaton College

GENERAL ADMISSIONS

Very important factors include: rigor of secondary school record, academic GPA, application essay, recommendations. *Other factors considered include:* class rank, standardized test scores (if submitted). High school diploma is required and GED is accepted. Institution is test-optional for entering Fall 2024. Check admissions website for updates. *Academic units required:* 4 English, 3 math, 3 science, 2 foreign language, 3 social studies. *Academic units recommended:* 4 math, 3 foreign language, 4 social studies.

FINANCIAL AID

Students should submit: FAFSA. *Need-based scholarships/grants offered:* College/university scholarship or grant aid from institutional funds; Federal Pell; Private scholarships; SEOG; State scholarships/grants. *Loan aid offered:* Direct PLUS loans; Direct Subsidized Loans; Direct Unsubsidized Loans. Federal Work-Study Program available. Institutional employment available.

CAMPUS LIFE

Activities: Campus Ministries; Choral groups; Concert band; Dance; Drama/theater; International Student Organization; Jazz band; Literary magazine; Music ensembles; Musical theater; Opera; Pep band; Student government; Student newspaper; Student-run film society; Symphony orchestra. **Organizations:** 95 registered organizations, 13 honor societies, 16 religious organizations, 0 fraternities, 0 sororities. **Athletics (Intercollegiate):** *Men:* baseball, basketball, crew/rowing, cross-country, golf, ice hockey, lacrosse, martial arts, swimming, track/field (indoor), wrestling. *Women:* basketball, crew/rowing, cross-country, golf, lacrosse, martial arts, softball, swimming, track/field (indoor), volleyball.

CAMPUS

Type of school	Private (nonprofit)
Environment	Town

STUDENTS

Undergrad enrollment	2,156
% male/female	44/56
% from out of state	75
% frosh live on campus	99

FINANCIAL FACTS

Annual tuition	$43,670
Room and board	$13,512
Required fees	$260

GENERAL ADMISSIONS INFO

Application fee	$50
Regular application deadline	8/1
Nonfall registration	Yes

Fall 2024 testing policy	Test Optional
Range SAT EBRW	610–710
Range SAT Math	640–720
Range ACT Composite	28–33

ACADEMICS

Student/faculty ratio	10:1
% students returning for sophomore year	90

Most classes have 10–19 students.

REQUESTING SERVICES FOR STUDENTS WITH LEARNING DIFFERENCES

Phone: 630-752-5615 • wheaton.edu/academics/services/learning-and-accessibility-services
Email: las@wheaton.edu

Documentation submitted to: Learning and Accessibility Services
Separate application required for Services: No

Documentation required for:
LD: Psychoeducational evaluation
ADHD: Psychoeducational evaluation
ASD: Psychoeducational evaluation

Anderson University

1100 East Fifth Street, Anderson, IN 46012-3495 • Admissions: 765-641-4080 • www.anderson.edu

Support: CS

ACCOMMODATIONS

Allowed in exams:

Calculators	Yes
Dictionary	No
Computer	Yes
Spell-checker	Yes
Extended test time	Yes
Scribe	Yes
Proctors	Yes
Oral exams	No
Note-takers	Yes

Support services for students with:

LD	Yes
ADHD	Yes
ASD	Yes
Distraction-reduced environment	Yes
Recording of lecture allowed	Yes
Reading technology	Yes
Audio books	Yes
Other assistive technology	Yes
Priority registration	No

Added costs of services:

For LD	No
For ADHD	No
For ASD	No
LD specialists	Yes
ADHD & ASD coaching	No
ASD specialists	No
Professional tutors	Yes
Peer tutors	Yes
Max. hours/week for services	Varies
How professors are notified of student approved accommodations	Student

COLLEGE GRADUATION REQUIREMENTS

Course waivers allowed	No
Course substitutions allowed	Yes
In what courses: Case-by-case basis	

PROGRAMS/SERVICES FOR STUDENTS WITH LEARNING DIFFERENCES

Student Accessibility Services (SAS) is available for students with learning disabilities. Incoming students who have special accessibility needs should contact SAS as soon as possible, identify the disability, provide appropriate documentation, and request specific accommodations. During the first semester, the Bridges Program at AU offers additional help to students with specific learning disabilities and/or ADHD. This program provides an extra layer of support during the transition from high school to college. Students who are accepted into the Bridges Program take a 2 credit required college survival skills/study skills course. First-year students enrolled in the program are fully integrated into the university and follow the regular curriculum and requirements for graduation but are typically limited to a lighter course load during their first semester.

ADMISSIONS

Anderson University admits students who are interested in higher education from a Christian faith perspective with the potential to complete the degree they plan to pursue. The admission review committee considers academic performance in high school by GPA (weighted if provided), class rank (if provided), GPA college prep curriculum (or academic ability by SAT/ACT scores if submitted), character, work ethic, community/school/church involvement, time management, leadership potential, and other personal or extenuating circumstances. Final high school transcripts showing the date of graduation are required. Admission decisions may include a director review for applicants with a GPA under 2.0. Academic program-specific admission is handled separately by respective departments.

Additional Information

The Kissinger Academic Center for Excellence (KACE) offers a wide variety of services, including hosting regular Academic Success Skills Workshops. Students who attend the entire workshop series receive a mini course in learning strategies. KACE offers one-hour study groups that connect course content with study strategies, and it offers peer tutors with set schedules for walk-in help when workshops are not quite enough. KACE also has audio tapes, videos, study guides, and other resources for students to use at their own pace. Additionally, the Writing Center's tutors can help students with writing projects in any academic course.

Candles and Carols began in 1965 to showcase the music department's ensembles and sing along to traditional Christmas Carols. Today hundreds of students from the School of Music, Theater, and Dance perform in one of the biggest campus events of the year, drawing a crowd of thousands of students, faculty, and the local community.

Anderson University

GENERAL ADMISSIONS

Very important factors include: rigor of secondary school record, recommendations. *Important factors include:* class rank, academic GPA, standardized test scores (if submitted). *Other factors considered include:* application essay. High school diploma is required and GED is accepted. Institution is test-optional for entering Fall 2024. Check admissions website for updates. *Academic units required:* 4 English, 3 math, 3 science (3 labs), 2 foreign language, 1 social studies, 1 history. *Academic units recommended:* 4 math, 4 science (4 labs), 3 foreign language, 2 social studies, 2 history, 5 academic electives, 1 visual/performing arts.

FINANCIAL AID

Students should submit: FAFSA. *Need-based scholarships/grants offered:* College/university scholarship or grant aid from institutional funds; Federal Pell; Private scholarships; SEOG; State scholarships/grants. *Loan aid offered:* Direct PLUS loans; Direct Subsidized Loans; Direct Unsubsidized Loans. Federal Work-Study Program available.

CAMPUS LIFE

Activities: Campus Ministries; Choral groups; Concert band; Dance; Drama/theater; International Student Organization; Jazz band; Literary magazine; Model UN; Music ensembles; Musical theater; Opera; Pep band; Radio station; Student government; Student newspaper; Symphony orchestra; Yearbook. **Organizations:** 42 registered organizations, 16 honor societies, 15 religious organizations, 0 fraternities, 0 sororities. **Athletics (Intercollegiate):** *Men:* baseball, basketball, cross-country, golf, rugby, swimming, track/field (indoor), volleyball. *Women:* basketball, cross-country, golf, softball, swimming, track/field (indoor), volleyball.

CAMPUS
Type of school	Private (nonprofit)
Environment	Town

STUDENTS
Undergrad enrollment	1,392
% male/female	40/60
% from out of state	23
% frosh live on campus	88

FINANCIAL FACTS
Annual tuition	$29,950
Room and board	$9,890
Required fees	$500

GENERAL ADMISSIONS INFO
Application fee	$25
Regular application deadline	7/1
Nonfall registration	Yes
Fall 2024 testing policy	Test Optional
Range SAT EBRW	500–590
Range SAT Math	500–570
Range ACT Composite	19–25

ACADEMICS
Student/faculty ratio	10:1
% students returning for sophomore year	65
Most classes have 10–19 students.	

Indiana

REQUESTING SERVICES FOR STUDENTS WITH LEARNING DIFFERENCES

Phone: 765-641-4223 • anderson.edu/kissinger/accessibility-services • Email: tjcoplin@anderson.edu

Documentation submitted to: Student Accessibility Services
Separate application required for Services: Yes

Documentation required for:
LD: Psychoeducational evaluation
ADHD: Psychoeducational evaluation
ASD: Psychoeducational evaluation

Earlham College

801 National Road, West Richmond, IN 47374-4095 • Admissions: 765-983-1600 • www.earlham.edu

(Support: S)

ACCOMMODATIONS

Allowed in exams:

Calculators	Yes
Dictionary	Yes
Computer	Yes
Spell-checker	Yes
Extended test time	Yes
Scribe	Yes
Proctors	Yes
Oral exams	Yes
Note-takers	Yes

Support services for students with:

LD	No
ADHD	No
ASD	No
Distraction-reduced environment	Yes
Recording of lecture allowed	Yes
Reading technology	Yes
Audio books	Yes
Other assistive technology	Yes
Priority registration	Yes

Added costs of services:

For LD	No
For ADHD	No
For ASD	No
LD specialists	No
ADHD & ASD coaching	No
ASD specialists	No
Professional tutors	No
Peer tutors	Yes
Max. hours/week for services	10
How professors are notified of student approved accommodations	Student

COLLEGE GRADUATION REQUIREMENTS

Course waivers allowed	No
Course substitutions allowed	Yes
In what courses: Foreign Language	

PROGRAMS/SERVICES FOR STUDENTS WITH LEARNING DIFFERENCES

Earlham College ensures equal access to its programs and services through the Academic Enrichment Center (AEC). The director of the AEC coordinates accommodations for students with learning disabilities through an individualized and interactive process. Earlham expects students with disabilities to take an active role in communicating their needs and believes it is most effective when disabilities are disclosed prior to students arriving on campus.

ADMISSIONS

The application process for admission is the same for all students. Each applicant must submit an original piece of writing that demonstrates writing skills and style and highlights the student's thinking process. Earlham evaluates each candidate holistically, and there is no required minimum GPA.

Additional Information

AEC provides group tutoring for a variety of courses, and individual tutoring for courses not supported by group tutoring sessions. Students may also meet with the director of AEC to develop time management and study skills. The Writing Center provides drop-in services as well as individual consultations. AEC pairs students with faculty to encourage collaboration. All services are offered free of charge.

Founded in 1847 by Indiana Quakers, Earlham's 800-acre campus includes 600 acres of woods, streams, ponds, old fields, and prairie. Earlham and Quakers have a history of being progressive; the Quakers of North Carolina petitioned against slavery to the U.S. Congress as early as 1838, and Earlham was the second Quaker college in the world and the first coeducational.

Earlham College

GENERAL ADMISSIONS

Very important factors include: rigor of secondary school record, academic GPA. *Important factors include:* application essay. *Other factors considered include:* class rank, standardized test scores (if submitted), recommendations. High school diploma is required and GED is accepted. Institution is test-flexible for entering Fall 2024. Check admissions website for updates. *Academic units required:* 4 English, 3 math, 2 science, 2 foreign language, 2 social studies. *Academic units recommended:* visual/performing arts.

FINANCIAL AID

Students should submit: FAFSA. *Need-based scholarships/grants offered:* College/university scholarship or grant aid from institutional funds; Federal Pell; Private scholarships; SEOG; State scholarships/grants. *Loan aid offered:* Direct PLUS loans; Direct Subsidized Loans; Direct Unsubsidized Loans. Federal Work-Study Program available. Institutional employment available.

CAMPUS LIFE

Activities: Campus Ministries; Choral groups; Concert band; Dance; Drama/theater; International Student Organization; Jazz band; Literary magazine; Model UN; Music ensembles; Musical theater; Radio station; Student government; Student newspaper. **Organizations:** 39 registered organizations, 1 honor societies, 9 religious organizations, 0 fraternities, 0 sororities. **Athletics (Intercollegiate):** *Men:* baseball, basketball, cross-country, equestrian sports, golf, lacrosse, martial arts, rugby, table tennis, track/field (indoor), ultimate frisbee. *Women:* basketball, cross-country, equestrian sports, field hockey, golf, lacrosse, martial arts, rugby, table tennis, track/field (indoor), ultimate frisbee, volleyball.

CAMPUS
Type of school	Private (nonprofit)
Environment	Town

STUDENTS
Undergrad enrollment	567
% male/female	48/52
% from out of state	73
% frosh live on campus	88

FINANCIAL FACTS
Annual tuition	$48,218
Room and board	$12,448
Required fees	$840

GENERAL ADMISSIONS INFO
Application fee	No fee
Regular application deadline	3/1
Nonfall registration	Yes
Fall 2024 testing policy	Test Flexible
Range SAT EBRW	590–710
Range SAT Math	540–670
Range ACT Composite	24–32

ACADEMICS
Student/faculty ratio	6:1
% students returning for sophomore year	80

Most classes have 2–9 students.

Indiana

REQUESTING SERVICES FOR STUDENTS WITH LEARNING DIFFERENCES

Phone: 765-983-1341 • earlham.edu/academics/academic-enrichment-center/accessibility-services
Email: odas@earlham.edu

Documentation submitted to: Academic Enrichment Center
Separate application required for Services: Yes

Documentation required for:
LD: Psychoeducational evaluation
ADHD: Psychoeducational evaluation
ASD: Psychoeducational evaluation

Indiana University Bloomington

940 E. Seventh Street, Bloomington, IN 47405 • Admissions: 812-855-0661 • www.indiana.edu

Support: S

ACCOMMODATIONS

Allowed in exams:

Calculators	Yes
Dictionary	Yes
Computer	Yes
Spell-checker	Yes
Extended test time	Yes
Scribe	Yes
Proctors	Yes
Oral exams	Yes
Note-takers	Yes

Support services for students with:

LD	Yes
ADHD	Yes
ASD	Yes
Distraction-reduced environment	Yes
Recording of lecture allowed	Yes
Reading technology	Yes
Audio books	Yes
Other assistive technology	Yes
Priority registration	Yes

Added costs of services:

For LD	No
For ADHD	No
For ASD	No
LD specialists	No
ADHD & ASD coaching	No
ASD specialists	No
Professional tutors	Yes
Peer tutors	Yes
Max. hours/week for services	Varies
How professors are notified of student approved accommodations	Student

COLLEGE GRADUATION REQUIREMENTS

Course waivers allowed	Yes
In what courses: Case-by-case basis	
Course substitutions allowed	No

PROGRAMS/SERVICES FOR STUDENTS WITH LEARNING DIFFERENCES

Indiana University's Office of Disability Services for Students (DSS) provides support and services to students with disabilities. Students receive accommodations by registering with DSS, submitting a request form, and meeting with the case coordinator. During the meeting, the case coordinator reviews documentation and discusses with the student available ways to best support their classroom experience. Students must follow up with DSS to obtain an accommodations letter to share with professors. Available accommodations include test modifications, notetakers, and priority registration. Students are encouraged to contact DSS during the admissions process to learn about services. Services and accommodations are free.

ADMISSIONS

All applications are submitted through the general IU admission process. The university is currently test-optional; however, students who are homeschooled or are being considered for athletic scholarships are encouraged to submit test scores. For the most recent admission period, 44 percent of admitted students applied test-optional. The middle 50 percent of admitted students had a GPA of 3.62–4.0, an ACT score of 27–32 or 1230–1420 for the SAT.

Additional Information

DSS can refer students to campus resources such as academic coaching, peer tutoring, and Peer Assisted Study Sessions (PASS). There are a variety of for-credit college success classes available as well, in which students learn skills and strategies to better navigate their college experience.

Howdy Wilcox, Jr., IU alum and son of Howdy Wilcox, winner of the 1919 Indianapolis 500, founded the Little 500 bicycle race in 1951. Riders compete in four-person teams around a 0.25-mile cinder track for 100 or 200 laps, or 25 or 50 miles, respectively. Proceeds of the Little 500 help fund scholarships for undergraduates.

Indiana University Bloomington

GENERAL ADMISSIONS

Very important factors include: rigor of secondary school record, class rank, academic GPA. *Important factors include:* standardized test scores (if submitted), application essay. *Other factors considered include:* recommendations. High school diploma is required and GED is accepted. Institution is test-optional for entering Fall 2024. Check admissions website for updates. *Academic units required:* 4 English, 3.5 math, 3 science, 2 science labs, 2 foreign language, 2 social studies, 1 history, 1.5 academic electives.

FINANCIAL AID

Students should submit: FAFSA. *Need-based scholarships/grants offered:* College/university scholarship or grant aid from institutional funds; Federal Pell; Private scholarships; SEOG; State scholarships/grants. *Loan aid offered:* Direct PLUS loans; Direct Subsidized Loans; Direct Unsubsidized Loans. Federal Work-Study Program available. Institutional employment available.

CAMPUS LIFE

Activities: Campus Ministries; Choral groups; Concert band; Dance; Drama/theater; International Student Organization; Jazz band; Literary magazine; Marching band; Model UN; Music ensembles; Musical theater; Opera; Pep band; Radio station; Student government; Student newspaper; Symphony orchestra; Television station; Yearbook. **Organizations:** 791 registered organizations, 19 honor societies, 59 religious organizations, 34 fraternities, 33 sororities. **Athletics (Intercollegiate):** *Men:* baseball, basketball, cross-country, cycling, equestrian sports, field hockey, golf, gymnastics, ice hockey, lacrosse, martial arts, rugby, swimming, track/field (indoor), ultimate frisbee, volleyball, water polo, wrestling. *Women:* baseball, basketball, crew/rowing, cross-country, cycling, equestrian sports, field hockey, golf, gymnastics, ice hockey, lacrosse, martial arts, rugby, softball, swimming, track/field (indoor), ultimate frisbee, volleyball, water polo.

CAMPUS

Type of school	Public
Environment	City

STUDENTS

Undergrad enrollment	35,401
% male/female	50/50
% from out of state	40
% frosh live on campus	98

FINANCIAL FACTS

Annual in-state tuition	$10,012
Annual out-of-state tuition	$37,685
Room and board	$12,228
Required fees	$1,435

GENERAL ADMISSIONS INFO

Application fee	$65
Regular application deadline	Rolling
Nonfall registration	Yes

Fall 2024 testing policy	Test Optional
Range SAT EBRW	590–690
Range SAT Math	590–710
Range ACT Composite	27–32

ACADEMICS

Student/faculty ratio	17:1
% students returning for sophomore year	90
Most classes have 20–29 students.	

Indiana

REQUESTING SERVICES FOR STUDENTS WITH LEARNING DIFFERENCES

Phone: 812-855-7578 • studentaffairs.indiana.edu/student-support/disability-services
Email: iubdss@indiana.edu

Documentation submitted to: Disability Services for Students
Separate application required for Services: Yes

Documentation required for:
LD: Psychoeducational evaluation
ADHD: Psychoeducational evaluation
ASD: Psychoeducational evaluation

Indiana University—Purdue University Indianapolis

425 University Boulevard, Indianapolis, IN 46202 • Admissions: 317-274-4591 • www.iupui.edu

Support: S

ACCOMMODATIONS

Allowed in exams:

Calculators	Yes
Dictionary	Yes
Computer	Yes
Spell-checker	Yes
Extended test time	Yes
Scribe	Yes
Proctors	Yes
Oral exams	Yes
Note-takers	Yes

Support services for students with:

LD	Yes
ADHD	Yes
ASD	Yes
Distraction-reduced environment	Yes
Recording of lecture allowed	Yes
Reading technology	Yes
Audio books	Yes
Other assistive technology	Yes
Priority registration	Yes

Added costs of services:

For LD	No
For ADHD	No
For ASD	No
LD specialists	No
ADHD & ASD coaching	No
ASD specialists	No
Professional tutors	Yes
Peer tutors	Yes
Max. hours/week for services	Varies
How professors are notified of student approved accommodations	Student

COLLEGE GRADUATION REQUIREMENTS

Course waivers allowed	Yes

In what courses: Case-by-case basis

Course substitutions allowed	Yes

In what courses: Case-by-case basis

PROGRAMS/SERVICES FOR STUDENTS WITH LEARNING DIFFERENCES

The disability services office at IUPUI is known as Adaptive Educational Services (AES). Students may apply for services by submitting an accommodations request form and supporting medical documentation and attending an intake appointment to discuss their academic needs. Once AES has confirmed eligibility, the staff facilitates collaboration between students and faculty to ensure that accommodations are accessible. While most services are available through the AES office, students may be directed to additional campus resources, including the Bepko Learning Center for additional academic coaching, mentoring, and tutoring services.

ADMISSIONS

All students must complete the same general application process. Indiana residents must meet the Indiana Core 40 courses, while out-of-state applicants have core academic course requirements. Applicants who do not meet the requirements may still be reviewed holistically for admission. Students are required to submit a 200- to 400-word personal essay describing why they believe IUPUI is a good fit. Accepted applicants who submit test scores have an average of 1120 on the SAT and 22 on the ACT.

Additional Information

The Bepko Learning Center (BLC) is available to all students on campus. At BLC, students are encouraged to set goals and discover career options. Small group sessions allow students to explore topics including time management, balancing academic and campus life, and study strategies.

DID YOU KNOW?

Indiana University-Purdue University Indianapolis has the longest name of any NCAA Division I school—a fact that was once a clue on Jeopardy!

Indiana University—Purdue University Indianapolis

GENERAL ADMISSIONS
Very important factors include: rigor of secondary school record, academic GPA. *Other factors considered include:* class rank, standardized test scores (if submitted), application essay. High school diploma is required and GED is accepted. Institution is test-optional for entering Fall 2024. Check admissions website for updates. *Academic units required:* 4 English, 3 math, 3 science (3 labs), 3 social studies.

FINANCIAL AID
Students should submit: FAFSA. *Need-based scholarships/grants offered:* College/university scholarship or grant aid from institutional funds; Federal Pell; Private scholarships; SEOG; State scholarships/grants. *Loan aid offered:* Direct PLUS loans; Direct Subsidized Loans; Direct Unsubsidized Loans. Federal Work-Study Program available. Institutional employment available.

CAMPUS LIFE
Activities: Campus Ministries; Choral groups; Dance; Drama/theater; International Student Organization; Jazz band; Literary magazine; Model UN; Music ensembles; Pep band; Student government; Student newspaper; Student-run film society; Symphony orchestra. **Organizations:** 410 registered organizations, 11 honor societies, 22 religious organizations, 9 fraternities, 15 sororities. **Athletics (Intercollegiate):** *Men:* baseball, basketball, crew/rowing, cross-country, cycling, equestrian sports, golf, ice hockey, lacrosse, rugby, swimming, track/field (indoor), ultimate frisbee, volleyball. *Women:* baseball, basketball, crew/rowing, cross-country, cycling, equestrian sports, golf, ice hockey, lacrosse, rugby, softball, swimming, track/field (indoor), ultimate frisbee, volleyball.

CAMPUS
Type of school	Public
Environment	Metropolis

STUDENTS
Undergrad enrollment	17,278
% male/female	41/59
% from out of state	7
% frosh live on campus	41

FINANCIAL FACTS
Annual in-state tuition	$8,972
Annual out-of-state tuition	$31,410
Room and board	$11,019
Required fees	$1,172

GENERAL ADMISSIONS INFO
Application fee	$65
Regular application deadline	5/15
Nonfall registration	Yes
Fall 2024 testing policy	Test Optional
Range SAT EBRW	530–630
Range SAT Math	520–620
Range ACT Composite	21–27

ACADEMICS
Student/faculty ratio	13:1
% students returning for sophomore year	71
Most classes have 10–19 students.	

REQUESTING SERVICES FOR STUDENTS WITH LEARNING DIFFERENCES

Phone: 317-274-3241 • diversity.iupui.edu/offices/aes • Email: aes@iupui.edu

Documentation submitted to: Adaptive Educational Services
Separate application required for Services: Yes

Documentation required for:
LD: Psychoeducational evaluation
ADHD: Psychoeducational evaluation
ASD: Psychoeducational evaluation

Manchester University

604 E. College Avenue, North Manchester, IN 46962 • Admissions: 260-982-5055 • www.manchester.edu

Support: CS

ACCOMMODATIONS

Allowed in exams:

Calculators	Yes
Dictionary	No
Computer	Yes
Spell-checker	Yes
Extended test time	Yes
Scribe	Yes
Proctors	Yes
Oral exams	Yes
Note-takers	Yes

Support services for students with:

LD	Yes
ADHD	Yes
ASD	Yes
Distraction-reduced environment	Yes
Recording of lecture allowed	Yes
Reading technology	Yes
Audio books	No
Other assistive technology	Yes
Priority registration	No

Added costs of services:

For LD	No
For ADHD	No
For ASD	No
LD specialists	Yes
ADHD & ASD coaching	No
ASD specialists	No
Professional tutors	Yes
Peer tutors	Yes
Max. hours/week for services	Unlimited
How professors are notified of student approved accommodations	Student and Disability Services Office

COLLEGE GRADUATION REQUIREMENTS

Course waivers allowed	No
Course substitutions allowed	No

PROGRAMS/SERVICES FOR STUDENTS WITH LEARNING DIFFERENCES

Manchester University's Disability Services Office (DSO) provides support and services to all students with disabilities. The Disability Services coordinator works with students with documented disabilities to determine reasonable accommodations, including extended exam time, distraction-reduced testing, and assistive technology. Accommodations cannot change the curriculum of a course. Students initiate the process of obtaining services by disclosing their disability to the DSO. Students are able to receive assistance with time management, note-taking strategies, study skills, and test-taking strategies. Manchester does not have a specific program for students with learning disabilities.

ADMISSIONS

All students who are interested in earning a degree from Manchester will need to complete the general admissions process and meet the requirements to be considered for admissions. While the application process includes submitting an application and transcripts, students are strongly encouraged to provide supplemental information that gives details about the student's interests and abilities. The minimum GPA for admission is a 3.0.

Additional Information

The Student Success Center is designed for students at every stage of their academics, including students with specific challenges or disabilities. The services at SSC target various aspects of navigating the academic journey to college completion. The available services include academic support, disability services, experiential learning, and the Writing Center. Writing consultants help students think critically about their goals and practice writing strategies. The SSC schedules workshops that cover time management, note-taking, vocabulary, and study skills. Academic coaches are available to work with students to improve learning strategies. Peer tutoring is available in course-specific study sessions. Peer tutors are recommended by professors and work with students to help them better understand the course material.

DID YOU KNOW?

Since 1939, Camp Mack Day has been a tradition and a surprise day in September. Students receive an email at 5 A.M. with a schedule of the day's adventures. They grab their go-bags and take off to Camp Mack, on the shores of Lake Waubee, for boating, kayaking, hiking, sand volleyball, archery, a climbing tower, hayrides, basketball, kick ball, yards games like corn hole, ladder ball, gaga ball, or 9-square-in-the-air, plus roasting s'mores, and more. It's definitely a day for students to relax, have fun, and try things they've never done before.

Manchester University

General Admissions

Very important factors include: rigor of secondary school record, class rank, academic GPA, recommendations. *Other factors considered include:* standardized test scores (if submitted). High school diploma is required and GED is accepted. Institution is test-optional for entering Fall 2024. Check admissions website for updates. *Academic units required:* 4 English, 2 math, 2 science (2 labs), 1 social studies, 1 history, 2 academic electives. *Academic units recommended:* 3 math, 3 science (2 labs), 2 foreign language, 2 social studies, 2 history, 2 academic electives, 1 visual/performing arts.

Financial Aid

Students should submit: FAFSA. *Need-based scholarships/grants offered:* College/university scholarship or grant aid from institutional funds; Federal Pell; Private scholarships; SEOG; State scholarships/grants. *Loan aid offered:* Direct PLUS loans; Direct Subsidized Loans; Direct Unsubsidized Loans. Federal Work-Study Program available. Institutional employment available.

Campus Life

Activities: Campus Ministries; Choral groups; Concert band; Dance; Drama/theater; International Student Organization; Jazz band; Literary magazine; Model UN; Music ensembles; Opera; Pep band; Radio station; Student government; Student newspaper; Symphony orchestra; Yearbook. **Organizations:** 61 registered organizations, 5 honor societies, 4 religious organizations, 0 fraternities, 0 sororities. **Athletics (Intercollegiate):** *Men:* baseball, basketball, cross-country, golf, swimming, track/field (indoor), wrestling. *Women:* basketball, cross-country, golf, softball, swimming, track/field (indoor), volleyball.

CAMPUS
Type of school	Private (nonprofit)
Environment	Rural

STUDENTS
Undergrad enrollment	981
% male/female	51/49
% from out of state	18
% frosh live on campus	95

FINANCIAL FACTS
Annual tuition	$35,800
Room and board	$11,154
Required fees	$1,290

GENERAL ADMISSIONS INFO
Application fee	No fee
Regular application deadline	Rolling
Nonfall registration	Yes

Fall 2024 testing policy	Test Optional

ACADEMICS
Student/faculty ratio	14:1
% students returning for sophomore year	59

Most classes have 10–19 students.

Indiana

REQUESTING SERVICES FOR STUDENTS WITH LEARNING DIFFERENCES

Phone: 260-982-5499 • www.manchester.edu/academics/student-success-center/academic-support/services-for-students-with-disabilities • Email: anhampshire@manchester.edu

Documentation submitted to: Disability Services
Separate application required for Services: Yes

Documentation required for:
 LD: Psychoeducational evaluation
 ADHD: Psychoeducational evaluation
 ASD: Psychoeducational evaluation

University of Indianapolis

1400 East Hanna Avenue, Indianapolis, IN 46227-3697 • Admissions: 317-788-3216 • www.uindy.edu

Support: SP

ACCOMMODATIONS

Allowed in exams:

Calculators	Yes
Dictionary	Yes
Computer	Yes
Spell-checker	Yes
Extended test time	Yes
Scribe	Yes
Proctors	Yes
Oral exams	Yes
Note-takers	Yes

Support services for students with:

LD	Yes
ADHD	Yes
ASD	Yes
Distraction-reduced environment	Yes
Recording of lecture allowed	Yes
Reading technology	Yes
Audio books	Yes
Other assistive technology	Yes
Priority registration	Yes

Added costs of services:

For LD	Yes
For ADHD	Yes
For ASD	Yes
LD specialists	Yes
ADHD & ASD coaching	No
ASD specialists	No
Professional tutors	No
Peer tutors	Yes
Max. hours/week for services	Varies
How professors are notified of student approved accommodations	Student

COLLEGE GRADUATION REQUIREMENTS

Course waivers allowed	No
Course substitutions allowed	No

PROGRAMS/SERVICES FOR STUDENTS WITH LEARNING DIFFERENCES

The Services for Students with Disabilities office (SSD) provides reasonable and appropriate accommodations to students with documented learning differences. Students accepted for admission to UIndy submit an accommodation request form to SSD along with appropriate disability documentation. SSD staff meets with the student to discuss the student's disability, goals, and needs, and what the university can provide. Only accommodations that specifically address identified functional limitations of a student's disability are approved. Students with disabilities who meet UIndy admission criteria may apply to the Baccalaureate for University of Indianapolis Learning Disabled program (BUILD). BUILD is a fee-based, full-support program for students with learning-related disabilities with dedicated professors, smaller classes, specialized study skills courses, general education courses designed for the program, tutoring, and adaptive test-taking. BUILD's capacity is typically 75 students, and students with autism are accepted to the program. High school students, accompanied by a parent or guardian, may attend a virtual or in-person BUILD preview day.

ADMISSIONS

General requirements to be considered for admission are a high school transcript through the sixth semester and a good mix of A's and B's with very few C's. An applicant with a GED or equivalent program may be considered for admission. Students may submit any evidence of their college preparedness for review. Some applicants will be asked to submit a personal statement, letters of recommendation, or a graded writing sample. Some UIndy programs or majors such as nursing, health sciences, music, education, and physical therapist assistant have designated prerequisites for admission.

Additional Information

UIndy partners with Mentor Collective to offer all first-year students a peer mentor, at no cost, to help students identify goals and prepare for their future. Mentors are upper-division students and are determined by similar interests, areas of study, needs, identities, and preferences. The Academic Success Center (ASC) is a collection of services and programs to assist first-year students in developing skills to become independent learners. Individualized academic assistance helps students customize their goals based on academic needs. ASC coaching provides support and study strategies. Secrets of Success Workshops are offered each semester, covering a variety of topics. ASC offers tutoring by appointment through the Writing Lab, Math Lab, and Physics/Engineering.

The Celebration of Flags, like the Olympics opening, celebrates UIndy's diversity honoring students, faculty, and staff from 93 countries. Flag bearers carry the national colors and wear traditional clothing of their country. An International Exposition follows in the student center. UIndy student-athletes have represented the United States in multiple Olympics and Special Olympics sports.

University of Indianapolis

GENERAL ADMISSIONS

Very important factors include: rigor of secondary school record, academic GPA. *Important factors include:* standardized test scores (if submitted). *Other factors considered include:* class rank, recommendations. High school diploma is required and GED is accepted. Institution is test-optional for entering Fall 2024. Check admissions website for updates. *Academic units required:* 4 English, 3 math, 2 science (1 labs), 2 foreign language, 2 social studies, 1 history, 3 academic electives, 2 visual/performing arts. *Academic units recommended:* 3 science (2 labs), 3 foreign language.

FINANCIAL AID

Students should submit: FAFSA; Institution's own financial aid form. *Need-based scholarships/grants offered:* College/university scholarship or grant aid from institutional funds; Federal Pell; Private scholarships; SEOG; State scholarships/grants. *Loan aid offered:* Direct PLUS loans; Direct Subsidized Loans; Direct Unsubsidized Loans. Federal Work-Study Program available. Institutional employment available.

CAMPUS LIFE

Activities: Campus Ministries; Choral groups; Concert band; Dance; Drama/theater; International Student Organization; Jazz band; Literary magazine; Music ensembles; Musical theater; Opera; Pep band; Radio station; Student government; Student newspaper; Television station; Yearbook. **Organizations:** 53 registered organizations, 14 honor societies, 4 religious organizations, 0 fraternities, 0 sororities. **Athletics (Intercollegiate):** *Men:* baseball, basketball, cross-country, golf, swimming, wrestling. *Women:* basketball, cross-country, golf, softball, swimming, volleyball.

CAMPUS
Type of school	Private (nonprofit)
Environment	Metropolis

STUDENTS
Undergrad enrollment	4,138
% male/female	32/68
% from out of state	9
% frosh live on campus	79

FINANCIAL FACTS
Annual tuition	$23,590
Room and board	$9,090
Required fees	$240

GENERAL ADMISSIONS INFO
Application fee	$25
Regular application deadline	Rolling
Nonfall registration	Yes

Fall 2024 testing policy	Test Optional
Range SAT EBRW	450–560
Range SAT Math	460–570
Range ACT Composite	19–25

ACADEMICS
Student/faculty ratio	15:1
% students returning for sophomore year	74

Most classes have 10–19 students.

Indiana

REQUESTING SERVICES FOR STUDENTS WITH LEARNING DIFFERENCES

Phone: 317-788-2140 • uindy.edu/ssd • Email: dspinney@uindy.edu

Documentation submitted to: Services for Students with Disabilities
Separate application required for Services: Yes

Documentation required for:
LD: Psychoeducational evaluation
ADHD: Psychoeducational evaluation
ASD: Psychoeducational evaluation

University of Notre Dame

McKenna Hall, Notre Dame, IN 46556 • Admissions: 574-631-7505 • www.nd.edu

Support: CS

ACCOMMODATIONS

Allowed in exams:

Calculators	Yes
Dictionary	Yes
Computer	No
Spell-checker	Yes
Extended test time	Yes
Scribe	Yes
Proctors	Yes
Oral exams	Yes
Note-takers	Yes

Support services for students with:

LD	Yes
ADHD	Yes
ASD	Yes
Distraction-reduced environment	Yes
Recording of lecture allowed	Yes
Reading technology	Yes
Audio books	Yes
Other assistive technology	Yes
Priority registration	Yes

Added costs of services:

For LD	No
For ADHD	No
For ASD	No
LD specialists	Yes
ADHD & ASD coaching	No
ASD specialists	No
Professional tutors	No
Peer tutors	Yes
Max. hours/week for services	Varies
How professors are notified of student approved accommodations	Student

COLLEGE GRADUATION REQUIREMENTS

Course waivers allowed	No
Course substitutions allowed	No

PROGRAMS/SERVICES FOR STUDENTS WITH LEARNING DIFFERENCES

Sara Bea Accessibility Services (SBAS) serves students with learning differences. Students request services by registering with SBAS and submitting information documenting their disability. Individual assistance is provided to select appropriate services, resources, and accommodations for the student. Services for students with learning disabilities, ADHD, or autism spectrum disorder include alternative text format, assistive technology, notetakers, exam modifications, and screening and referral for diagnostic testing. The services provided do not lower course standards or alter essential degree requirements. SBAS can assist in coordinating content tutoring through other resources on campus, and students may substitute American Sign Language for foreign language requirements. There are times when Sara Bea staff may contact students to review a request for accommodations. Students may be required to discuss their diagnosis and verbalize what services are being requested. If the student does not respond to the outreach within two weeks, the staff may rescind the accommodations, and the student will need to submit a supplemental request.

ADMISSIONS

All applicants must meet the same admission criteria, and interviews are not offered. Students intending to major in engineering must have a year of chemistry. The university will count math and foreign language courses taken in 8th grade.

Additional Information

The Center for Student Support and Care offers a Skills Mentoring program allowing all students to receive one-on-one mentoring to improve learning strategies, self-regulation, and time management.

Built in 1888 and named after Father Edward Sorin, Notre Dame's founder, Sorin was the first Catholic College residence hall in the U.S. to offer private quarters rather than barracks-style rooms. In 1969, protesting the Vietnam War, the Sorin Otters symbolically seceded from the university. Professors and students held classes in the dorm, boycotted campus events, and declared the dorm "Sorin College." It's still a symbol of honor and unity and a sacred tradition to refer to it only as Sorin College.

University of Notre Dame

GENERAL ADMISSIONS

Very important factors include: rigor of secondary school record. *Important factors include:* class rank, academic GPA, application essay, recommendations. *Other factors considered include:* standardized test scores (if submitted). High school diploma is required and GED is accepted. Institution is test-optional for entering Fall 2024. Check admissions website for updates. *Academic units required:* 4 English, 3 math, 2 science (2 labs), 2 foreign language, 2 social studies. *Academic units recommended:* 4 math, 4 science (2 labs), 4 foreign language, 4 social studies.

FINANCIAL AID

Students should submit: CSS/Financial Aid Profile; FAFSA; Noncustodial Profile. *Need-based scholarships/grants offered:* College/university scholarship or grant aid from institutional funds; Federal Pell; Private scholarships; SEOG; State scholarships/grants. *Loan aid offered:* Direct PLUS loans; Direct Subsidized Loans; Direct Unsubsidized Loans. Federal Work-Study Program available. Institutional employment available.

CAMPUS LIFE

Activities: Campus Ministries; Choral groups; Concert band; Dance; Drama/theater; Jazz band; Literary magazine; Marching band; Model UN; Music ensembles; Musical theater; Opera; Pep band; Radio station; Student government; Student newspaper; Student-run film society; Symphony orchestra; Television station; Yearbook. **Organizations:** 440 registered organizations, 10 honor societies, 9 religious organizations, 0 fraternities, 0 sororities. **Athletics (Intercollegiate):** *Men:* baseball, basketball, bowling, crew/rowing, cross-country, equestrian sports, golf, gymnastics, ice hockey, lacrosse, martial arts, racquetball, rugby, skiing (nordic/cross-country), swimming, track/field (indoor), ultimate frisbee, volleyball, water polo. *Women:* basketball, bowling, crew/rowing, cross-country, equestrian sports, field hockey, golf, gymnastics, ice hockey, lacrosse, martial arts, racquetball, rugby, skiing (nordic/cross-country), softball, swimming, track/field (indoor), ultimate frisbee, volleyball, water polo.

CAMPUS

Type of school	Private (nonprofit)
Environment	City

STUDENTS

Undergrad enrollment	8,917
% male/female	51/49
% from out of state	93
% frosh live on campus	100

FINANCIAL FACTS

Annual tuition	$59,794
Room and board	$16,710
Required fees	$507

GENERAL ADMISSIONS INFO

Application fee	$75
Regular application deadline	1/1
Nonfall registration	Yes

Fall 2024 testing policy	Test Optional
Range SAT EBRW	700–760
Range SAT Math	720–790
Range ACT Composite	32–35

ACADEMICS

Student/faculty ratio	9:1
% students returning for sophomore year	97

Most classes have 10–19 students.

Indiana

REQUESTING SERVICES FOR STUDENTS WITH LEARNING DIFFERENCES

Phone: 574-631-7833 • supportandcare.nd.edu • Email: sarabeacenter@nd.edu

Documentation submitted to: Sara Bea Accessibility Services
Separate application required for Services: Yes

Documentation required for:
LD: Psychoeducational evaluation
ADHD: Psychoeducational evaluation
ASD: Psychoeducational evaluation

The University of Saint Francis

2701 Spring Street, Fort Wayne, IN 46808 • Admissions: 260-399-8000 • www.sf.edu

Support: CS

ACCOMMODATIONS

Allowed in exams:

Calculators	Yes
Dictionary	Yes
Computer	Yes
Spell-checker	Yes
Extended test time	Yes
Scribe	Yes
Proctors	Yes
Oral exams	Yes
Note-takers	Yes

Support services for students with:

LD	Yes
ADHD	Yes
ASD	Yes
Distraction-reduced environment	Yes
Recording of lecture allowed	Yes
Reading technology	Yes
Audio books	Yes
Other assistive technology	Yes
Priority registration	Yes

Added costs of services:

For LD	No
For ADHD	No
For ASD	No
LD specialists	No
ADHD & ASD coaching	No
ASD specialists	Yes
Professional tutors	Yes
Peer tutors	Yes
Max. hours/week for services	Varies
How professors are notified of student approved accommodations	Student

COLLEGE GRADUATION REQUIREMENTS

Course waivers allowed	No
Course substitutions allowed	Yes
In what courses: Math and Foreign Language	

PROGRAMS/SERVICES FOR STUDENTS WITH LEARNING DIFFERENCES

The Academic and Career Development Center is home to the Student Accessibility Services office, which accommodates students with documented disabilities. Students may submit a registration form with documentation and then meet with the Student Accessibility Services coordinator to discuss and determine accommodations. Students will receive a confidential student summary of their accommodations and are encouraged to meet with their professors to discuss them. The Student Accessibility Services Coordinator is available for questions during the registration process, and encourages students with disabilities to visit campus during their application process.

ADMISSIONS

All applicants must complete an application for admission. The academic review committee is equally interested in understanding who the student is outside the classroom—their interests, passions, ideas, extracurricular activities, etc. Applicants who do not meet the criteria for admission may be asked to submit an essay addressing past academic performance and their plans to improve and succeed as a student at USF. Homeschooled students must submit additional documentation.

Additional Information

First-Year Experience (FYE) is a program designed to help students transition to academic and social life at USF by developing a key support network. During the spring semester, students are assigned a faculty advisor in their area of study. These mentors keep their students on track throughout their time at USF. The Academic and Career Development Center is available to all students, and offers free services including tutoring, study skill resources, and the Mentoring for Academic Progress (MAP) program.

DID YOU KNOW?

RED Day (Reaching Every Door) is a day in October when faculty, staff, and students say "thank you" to the community by volunteering for clean-up and painting projects, working at local animal rescues, assisting the elderly, and more. Year-round, students can earn service-learning hours as volunteers with the Jesters Program, which provides arts-education activities to those with intellectual/developmental disabilities, ages 8 and over.

The University of Saint Francis

GENERAL ADMISSIONS

Very important factors include: academic GPA. *Important factors include:* class rank. *Other factors considered include:* rigor of secondary school record, standardized test scores (if submitted), application essay, recommendations. High school diploma is required and GED is accepted. Institution is test-optional for entering Fall 2024. Check admissions website for updates. *Academic units recommended:* 4 English, 4 math, 4 science, 4 social studies, 4 academic electives.

FINANCIAL AID

Students should submit: FAFSA. *Need-based scholarships/grants offered:* College/university scholarship or grant aid from institutional funds; Federal Pell; Private scholarships; SEOG; State scholarships/grants. *Loan aid offered:* Direct PLUS loans; Direct Subsidized Loans; Direct Unsubsidized Loans. Federal Work-Study Program available. Institutional employment available.

CAMPUS LIFE

Activities: Campus Ministries; Choral groups; Concert band; Dance; Drama/theater; Jazz band; Literary magazine; Marching band; Music ensembles; Musical theater; Pep band; Student government; Student-run film society. **Organizations:** 36 registered organizations, 6 honor societies, 1 religious organizations, 0 fraternities, 0 sororities. **Athletics (Intercollegiate):** *Men:* baseball, basketball, cross-country, golf, track/field (indoor). *Women:* basketball, cross-country, golf, softball, track/field (indoor), volleyball.

CAMPUS

Type of school	Private (nonprofit)
Environment	City

STUDENTS

Undergrad enrollment	1,724
% male/female	30/70
% from out of state	10
% frosh live on campus	38

FINANCIAL FACTS

Annual tuition	$32,870
Room and board	$10,910
Required fees	$1,180

GENERAL ADMISSIONS INFO

Application fee	No fee
Regular application deadline:	
By Wednesday of the week immediately preceding the first day of classes	
Nonfall registration	Yes

Fall 2024 testing policy	Test Optional
Range SAT EBRW	480–580
Range SAT Math	480–570
Range ACT Composite	19–24

ACADEMICS

Student/faculty ratio	11:1
% students returning for sophomore year	74

Most classes have 10–19 students.

Indiana

REQUESTING SERVICES FOR STUDENTS WITH LEARNING DIFFERENCES

Phone: 260-399-8065 • accessibility.sf.edu • Email: gburgess@sf.edu

Documentation submitted to: Student Accessibility Services

Separate application required for Services: Yes

Documentation required for:
LD: Psychoeducational evaluation
ADHD: Psychoeducational evaluation
ASD: Psychoeducational evaluation

University of Southern Indiana

8600 University Boulevard, Evansville, IN 47712 • Admissions: 812-464-1765 • www.usi.edu

Support: CS

ACCOMMODATIONS

Allowed in exams:

Calculators	Yes
Dictionary	Yes
Computer	Yes
Spell-checker	Yes
Extended test time	Yes
Scribe	Yes
Proctors	Yes
Oral exams	Yes
Note-takers	Yes

Support services for students with:

LD	Yes
ADHD	Yes
ASD	Yes
Distraction-reduced environment	Yes
Recording of lecture allowed	Yes
Reading technology	Yes
Audio books	Yes
Other assistive technology	Yes
Priority registration	Yes

Added costs of services:

For LD	No
For ADHD	No
For ASD	No
LD specialists	Yes
ADHD & ASD coaching	No
ASD specialists	Yes
Professional tutors	No
Peer tutors	Yes
Max. hours/week for services	Varies
How professors are notified of student approved accommodations	Student

COLLEGE GRADUATION REQUIREMENTS

Course waivers allowed	No
Course substitutions allowed	Yes
In what courses: Case-by-case basis	

PROGRAMS/SERVICES FOR STUDENTS WITH LEARNING DIFFERENCES

Disability Resources (DR) coordinates services and academic accommodations for USI students with disabilities. Through direct support and coordination with other departments, DR can provide students with testing accommodations, note-taking assistance, alternative-format textbooks, tutoring, academic coaching, study-skills development, and peer support. Students must submit a verification of disability form from an appropriately licensed professional and supporting documentation. TIES (Together Inspiring Educational Success) is a peer-support program designed to connect students with similar backgrounds or challenges, allowing them to share common experiences, develop meaningful connections, and foster mutual empowerment.

ADMISSIONS

Admission criteria are the same for all students; however, the admissions office will work with students individually if needed. Students should have a minimum cumulative GPA of 2.5. USI has rolling admissions.

Additional Information

DR works very closely with Academic Skills and Student Support Services to provide testing, coaching, and study skills support and development.

The Annual Flowers on the Lake Ceremony is hosted by USI's Sexual Assault and Gender Violence Prevention Committee during Domestic Violence Awareness Month. The ceremony is in memory of those who have lost their lives to domestic violence, honors those who have survived, and hopes to raise awareness of the warning signs of relationship abuse. Students speak during a short presentation, share a moment of silence, and scatter flower petals over the Reflection Lake.

University of Southern Indiana

GENERAL ADMISSIONS

Very important factors include: academic GPA, standardized test scores (if submitted). *Important factors include:* class rank. *Other factors considered include:* rigor of secondary school record, application essay, recommendations. High school diploma is required and GED is accepted. Institution is test-optional for entering Fall 2024. Check admissions website for updates. *Academic units recommended:* 4 English, 3 math, 3 science, 3 social studies, 4 academic electives.

FINANCIAL AID

Students should submit: FAFSA. *Need-based scholarships/grants offered:* College/university scholarship or grant aid from institutional funds; Federal Nursing Scholarships; Federal Pell; Private scholarships; SEOG; State scholarships/grants; United Negro College Fund. *Loan aid offered:* Direct PLUS loans; Direct Subsidized Loans; Direct Unsubsidized Loans. Federal Work-Study Program available. Institutional employment available.

CAMPUS LIFE

Activities: Campus Ministries; Choral groups; Dance; Drama/theater; International Student Organization; Jazz band; Literary magazine; Pep band; Radio station; Student government; Student newspaper; Television station. **Organizations:** 151 registered organizations, 9 honor societies, 11 religious organizations, 6 fraternities, 7 sororities. **Athletics (Intercollegiate):** *Men:* baseball, basketball, cross-country, golf, rugby, track/field (indoor), ultimate frisbee, wrestling. *Women:* basketball, cross-country, golf, rugby, softball, track/field (indoor), ultimate frisbee, volleyball.

CAMPUS	
Type of school	Public
Environment	City

STUDENTS	
Undergrad enrollment	7,476
% male/female	38/62
% from out of state	15
% frosh live on campus	70

FINANCIAL FACTS	
Annual in-state tuition	$8,349
Annual out-of-state tuition	$19,437
Room and board	$9,102
Required fees	$520

GENERAL ADMISSIONS INFO	
Application fee	$40
Regular application deadline	8/15
Nonfall registration	Yes

Fall 2024 testing policy	Test Optional
Range SAT EBRW	490–590
Range SAT Math	490–590
Range ACT Composite	19–25

ACADEMICS	
Student/faculty ratio	16:1
% students returning for sophomore year	72
Most classes have 20–29 students.	

Indiana

REQUESTING SERVICES FOR STUDENTS WITH LEARNING DIFFERENCES

Phone: 812-464-1961 • www.usi.edu/disabilities • Email: rfstone@usi.edu

Documentation submitted to: Disability Resources
Separate application required for Services: Yes

Documentation required for:
LD: Psychoeducational evaluation
ADHD: Psychoeducational evaluation
ASD: Psychoeducational evaluation

Wabash College

P.O. Box 352, Crawfordsville, IN 47933 • Admissions: 765-361-6225 • www.wabash.edu

Support: S

ACCOMMODATIONS

Allowed in exams:

Calculators	Yes
Dictionary	Yes
Computer	Yes
Spell-checker	Yes
Extended test time	Yes
Scribe	Yes
Proctors	Yes
Oral exams	Yes
Note-takers	Yes

Support services for students with:

LD	No
ADHD	No
ASD	No
Distraction-reduced environment	Yes
Recording of lecture allowed	Yes
Reading technology	No
Audio books	Yes
Other assistive technology	No
Priority registration	No

Added costs of services:

For LD	No
For ADHD	No
For ASD	No
LD specialists	No
ADHD & ASD coaching	No
ASD specialists	No
Professional tutors	No
Peer tutors	Yes
Max. hours/week for services	Varies
How professors are notified of student approved accommodations	Student and Disability Resources

COLLEGE GRADUATION REQUIREMENTS

Course waivers allowed	No
Course substitutions allowed	No

PROGRAMS/SERVICES FOR STUDENTS WITH LEARNING DIFFERENCES

Students with learning disabilities are encouraged to register with Disability Services before classes begin if they wish to request accommodations. It is the student's responsibility to provide the appropriate documentation and notify relevant staff members. Disability Services finds that it benefits students when their advisors and professors are aware of their disabilities. To learn more about services and support, students are welcome to contact the Associate Dean for Student Engagement and Success.

ADMISSIONS

Wabash enrolls approximately 250 first-years. Admitted students earned an average high school GPA of 3.86 and, of those who submitted SAT scores, the middle 50 percent ranged from 1150 to 1320. Students who choose not to submit standardized test scores will still be considered for merit-based scholarships. As such, reviews will place additional weight on the rigor of the applicant's high school curriculum and performance in college preparatory courses.

Additional Information

The Academic Centers for Excellence serve all students on campus. Wabash men are offered one-on-one mentoring in time management, test preparation, test-taking, note-taking, study skills, and use of sources through the Office of Student Enrichment (OSE). The OSE also aids international students with English language skills and cultural adaptation. Students may visit the OSE as often as needed for assistance planning their semester or to work more intensely on projects. Supplemental Instruction (SI) is a structured, peer-led group study that is facilitated by a student leader who has previously taken and excelled in the course. The SI program is neither tutoring nor remedial; it is designed to give all students additional ways of processing course material and constructing new knowledge.

The oldest and strongest tradition at this men's college is living the Gentleman's Rule of Conduct. Students are expected to conduct themselves on and off campus as gentlemen and responsible citizens. Students follow the examples of past generations and become examples for future generations, each preparing the next to take the lead.

Wabash College

GENERAL ADMISSIONS

Very important factors include: rigor of secondary school record, class rank, academic GPA. *Important factors include:* recommendations. *Other factors considered include:* standardized test scores (if submitted), application essay. High school diploma is required and GED is accepted. Institution is test-optional for entering Fall 2024. Check admissions website for updates. *Academic units required:* 4 English, 3 math, 2 science (2 labs), 2 foreign language, 2 social studies. *Academic units recommended:* 4 math, 4 science (2 labs), 4 foreign language.

FINANCIAL AID

Students should submit: FAFSA. *Need-based scholarships/grants offered:* College/university scholarship or grant aid from institutional funds; Federal Pell; Private scholarships; SEOG; State scholarships/grants; United Negro College Fund. *Loan aid offered:* Direct PLUS loans; Direct Subsidized Loans; Direct Unsubsidized Loans. Federal Work-Study Program available. Institutional employment available.

CAMPUS LIFE

Activities: Campus Ministries; Choral groups; Dance; Drama/theater; International Student Organization; Jazz band; Literary magazine; Music ensembles; Pep band; Radio station; Student government; Student newspaper; Student-run film society; Symphony orchestra; Yearbook. **Organizations:** 68 registered organizations, 9 honor societies, 3 religious organizations, 10 fraternities, 0 sororities. **Athletics (Intercollegiate):** *Men:* baseball, basketball, cross-country, golf, lacrosse, rugby, swimming, track/field (indoor), ultimate frisbee, volleyball, wrestling.

CAMPUS
Type of school	Private (nonprofit)
Environment	Village

STUDENTS
Undergrad enrollment	835
% male/female	100/0
% from out of state	24
% frosh live on campus	100

FINANCIAL FACTS
Annual tuition	$48,200
Room and board	$13,300
Required fees	$925

GENERAL ADMISSIONS INFO
Application fee	No fee
Regular application deadline	Rolling
Nonfall registration	Yes

Fall 2024 testing policy	Test Optional
Range SAT EBRW	560–650
Range SAT Math	562–670
Range ACT Composite	22–30

ACADEMICS
Student/faculty ratio	9:1
% students returning for sophomore year	88

Most classes have 10–19 students.

Indiana

REQUESTING SERVICES FOR STUDENTS WITH LEARNING DIFFERENCES

Phone: 765-361-6347 • www.wabash.edu/studentlife/disability • Email: thrushh@wabash.edu

Documentation submitted to: Disability Services
Separate application required for Services: Yes

Documentation required for:
LD: Psychoeducational evaluation
ADHD: Psychoeducational evaluation
ASD: Psychoeducational evaluation

Cornell College

600 First Street SW, Mount Vernon, IA 52314 • Admissions: 319-895-4477 • cornellcollege.edu

Support: S

ACCOMMODATIONS

Allowed in exams:

Calculators	Yes
Dictionary	Yes
Computer	Yes
Spell-checker	Yes
Extended test time	Yes
Scribe	No
Proctors	Yes
Oral exams	Yes
Note-takers	Yes

Support services for students with:

LD	Yes
ADHD	Yes
ASD	Yes
Distraction-reduced environment	Yes
Recording of lecture allowed	Yes
Reading technology	Yes
Audio books	Yes
Other assistive technology	Yes
Priority registration	No

Added costs of services:

For LD	No
For ADHD	No
For ASD	No
LD specialists	No
ADHD & ASD coaching	No
ASD specialists	No
Professional tutors	No
Peer tutors	Yes
Max. hours/week for services	Varies
How professors are notified of student approved accommodations	Student and Disability Services

COLLEGE GRADUATION REQUIREMENTS

Course waivers allowed	No
Course substitutions allowed	Yes
In what courses: Foreign Language	

PROGRAMS/SERVICES FOR STUDENTS WITH LEARNING DIFFERENCES

Disability Services coordinates accommodations for students with disabilities at Cornell. To receive services, students must provide documentation that describes their learning disability and the recommended accommodations. Students then meet in person with the coordinator of Disability Services for an intake meeting to finalize their designated services. It is imperative that students notify the coordinator of Disability Services of any disability-related accommodations they require within the first three days of the term. Cornell College's unique block schedule, one course at a time for 18 days, is fast paced. As a result, students must communicate with their professors regarding the implementation of their accommodations as early in the block as possible. NSO+ is an early new student orientation for students with ASD or generalized anxiety associated with big transitions. They are invited to campus a few days early to get acclimated before the hustle and bustle of new student orientation begins.

ADMISSIONS

Requirements for admission include a high school transcript, a personal essay or writing sample, and short-answer questions if the student chooses not to submit standardized test scores. Teacher recommendations are optional and students have the option to submit a portfolio that showcases skills, talents, and the ways in which they can and will excel at Cornell. Examples include unique creative endeavors such as portfolios of paintings or drawings, photography journals, and performance recordings.

Additional Information

The Center for Teaching and Learning and the Student Success Center supports all students in both the academic and social capacities. Staff at the Student Success Center are each specialized and trained in various areas, including working with students with accommodations and students struggling with their workload. Students are welcome to walk in, email, or can be referred by a professor to develop strategies in time management, test-taking, note-taking, and acclimating to campus life. Academic support includes, workshops, peer tutoring, and math and writing studios.

DID YOU KNOW?

Cornell T. Moose has hung in the Law Hall since 1925. In the 1970s, he disappeared for a short time. Math professor Ed Hill found him at a Cornell yard sale and returned him to his rightful place. During a year of renovation, Cornell T. Moose went on a vacation, sending postcards from around the world. He got a makeover, a Facebook account, and is back to looking over the Law Hall's Moosehead Lounge.

Cornell College

GENERAL ADMISSIONS

Very important factors include: academic GPA. *Important factors include:* application essay. *Other factors considered include:* rigor of secondary school record, class rank, recommendations. High school diploma is required and GED is accepted. Institution is test-optional for entering Fall 2024. Check admissions website for updates. *Academic units recommended:* 4 English, 3 math, 3 science (2 labs), 2 foreign language, 3 social studies.

FINANCIAL AID

Students should submit: FAFSA. *Need-based scholarships/grants offered:* College/university scholarship or grant aid from institutional funds; Federal Pell; SEOG; State scholarships/grants. *Loan aid offered:* Direct PLUS loans; Direct Subsidized Loans; Direct Unsubsidized Loans. Federal Work-Study Program available. Institutional employment available.

CAMPUS LIFE

Activities: Campus Ministries; Choral groups; Concert band; Dance; Drama/theater; International Student Organization; Jazz band; Literary magazine; Model UN; Music ensembles; Musical theater; Radio station; Student government; Student newspaper; Symphony orchestra; Yearbook. **Organizations:** 36 registered organizations, 14 honor societies, 6 religious organizations, 5 fraternities, 6 sororities. **Athletics (Intercollegiate):** *Men:* baseball, basketball, cross-country, lacrosse, martial arts, track/field (indoor), ultimate frisbee, volleyball, wrestling. *Women:* basketball, cross-country, lacrosse, martial arts, softball, track/field (indoor), ultimate frisbee, volleyball, wrestling.

CAMPUS

Type of school	Private (nonprofit)
Environment	Rural

STUDENTS

Undergrad enrollment	1,010
% male/female	54/46
% from out of state	78
% frosh live on campus	98

FINANCIAL FACTS

Annual tuition	$49,970
Room and board	$11,198
Required fees	$644

GENERAL ADMISSIONS INFO

Application fee	No fee
Regular application deadline	Rolling
Nonfall registration	Yes

Fall 2024 testing policy	Test Optional
Range SAT EBRW	600–690
Range SAT Math	570–690
Range ACT Composite	23–90

ACADEMICS

Student/faculty ratio	13:1
% students returning for sophomore year	80

Most classes have 10–19 students.

Iowa

REQUESTING SERVICES FOR STUDENTS WITH LEARNING DIFFERENCES

Phone: 319-895-4207 • cornellcollege.edu/student-success-center/disabilities
Email: hganzel@cornellcollege.edu

Documentation submitted to: Disability Services
Separate application required for Services: Yes

Documentation required for:
 LD: Psychoeducational evaluation
 ADHD: Psychoeducational evaluation
 ASD: Psychoeducational evaluation

Drake University

2507 University Avenue, Des Moines, IA 50311-4505 • Admissions: 515-271-3181 • www.drake.edu

Support: S

ACCOMMODATIONS

Allowed in exams:

Calculators	Yes
Dictionary	Yes
Computer	Yes
Spell-checker	Yes
Extended test time	Yes
Scribe	Yes
Proctors	Yes
Oral exams	Yes
Note-takers	Yes

Support services for students with:

LD	Yes
ADHD	Yes
ASD	Yes
Distraction-reduced environment	Yes
Recording of lecture allowed	Yes
Reading technology	Yes
Audio books	Yes
Other assistive technology	Yes
Priority registration	No

Added costs of services:

For LD	No
For ADHD	No
For ASD	No
LD specialists	No
ADHD & ASD coaching	No
ASD specialists	No
Professional tutors	No
Peer tutors	Yes
Max. hours/week for services	Varies
How professors are notified of student approved accommodations	Student

COLLEGE GRADUATION REQUIREMENTS

Course waivers allowed	No
Course substitutions allowed	No

PROGRAMS/SERVICES FOR STUDENTS WITH LEARNING DIFFERENCES

The Access and Success (A&S) disability services program provides individualized assessments of accommodations and resource needs. Students must be admitted and enrolled in the university prior to seeking accommodations or services for a learning disability. It is the student's responsibility to self-identify a learning disability, provide documentation of their disability, and request the accommodations that they need. Drake University uses an online platform called Starfish to notify professors via email that a student has received accommodations from A&S. From there, it is the student's responsibility to connect with their professor to discuss how those accommodations will be implemented. A&S also provides one-on-one, professional academic coaching, and hosts weekly meetings to encourage accountability. Drake has accountability groups that are geared towards students with ASD, but open to all. Additional coaching is also provided for students working to manage their academic and executive functioning, time management, and help design plans to reach their goals. Academic waivers and course substitutions may be available and are decided by each department. Drake has no foreign language requirements and for some majors, students may be able to substitute a computational math requirement with Spirit of Mathematics, which focuses on theory-based math.

ADMISSIONS

All applicants are expected to meet the same admission criteria. Each application for admission is reviewed individually; there are no set, inflexible criteria that students are required to meet. First-year students may choose between the Standard Application or Test-Flexible Application. The Standard Application is reviewed based on traditional admission measurements, including the transcript, ACT or SAT score, and essay. The Test-Flexible Application path is similar, but requires an interview in lieu of test scores. First-year students may only apply via the Test-Flexible path if they have a cumulative GPA of 3.0 or higher (on a weighted or unweighted scale) and are not pursuing pre-pharmacy, pre-athletic training, pre-occupational therapy, or the National Alumni Scholarship.

Additional Information

Professors can use the online platform Starfish to identify students who are struggling and refer them to Access & Success for tutoring, counseling, or academic coaching.

The first Drake Relays track and field meet was help in 1910 during a blizzard with a crowd of nearly 100 in attendance. Today, the meet draws 220 schools and more than 40,000 spectators. Participants are often Olympic competitors. Students have free access to this week of excitement, which includes a pageant with contestants from across the country and honors the Beautiful Bulldog Contest winner as the official mascot of Drake Relays.

Drake University

GENERAL ADMISSIONS

Very important factors include: rigor of secondary school record, academic GPA. *Important factors include:* standardized test scores (if submitted), application essay. *Other factors considered include:* class rank, recommendations. High school diploma is required and GED is accepted. Institution is test-flexible for entering Fall 2024. Check admissions website for updates. *Academic units recommended:* 4 English, 3 math, 2 science (1 lab), 2 foreign language, 4 social studies.

FINANCIAL AID

Students should submit: FAFSA. *Need-based scholarships/grants offered:* College/university scholarship or grant aid from institutional funds; Federal Pell; Private scholarships; SEOG; State scholarships/grants. *Loan aid offered:* Direct PLUS loans; Direct Subsidized Loans; Direct Unsubsidized Loans. Federal Work-Study Program available. Institutional employment available.

CAMPUS LIFE

Activities: Campus Ministries; Choral groups; Concert band; Dance; Drama/theater; International Student Organization; Jazz band; Literary magazine; Marching band; Model UN; Music ensembles; Musical theater; Pep band; Radio station; Student government; Student newspaper; Symphony orchestra. **Organizations:** 160 registered organizations, 24 honor societies, 10 religious organizations, 9 fraternities, 5 sororities. **Athletics (Intercollegiate):** *Men:* basketball, cross-country, golf, track/field (indoor), ultimate frisbee. *Women:* basketball, crew/rowing, cross-country, golf, softball, track/field (indoor), volleyball.

CAMPUS

Type of school	Private (nonprofit)
Environment	Metropolis

STUDENTS

Undergrad enrollment	2,857
% male/female	40/60
% from out of state	63
% frosh live on campus	93

FINANCIAL FACTS

Annual tuition	$47,564
Room and board	$11,570
Required fees	$146

GENERAL ADMISSIONS INFO

Application fee	No fee
Regular application deadline	Rolling
Nonfall registration	Yes

Fall 2024 testing policy	Test Flexible
Range SAT EBRW	600–710
Range SAT Math	590–700
Range ACT Composite	25–31

ACADEMICS

Student/faculty ratio	11:1
% students returning for sophomore year	84

Most classes have 20–29 students.

REQUESTING SERVICES FOR STUDENTS WITH LEARNING DIFFERENCES

Phone: 515-271-1835 • drake.edu/access-success/disability-services • Email: michelle.laughlin@drake.edu

Documentation submitted to: Access and Success
Separate application required for Services: Yes

Documentation required for:
 LD: Psychoeducational evaluation
 ADHD: Psychoeducational evaluation
 ASD: Psychoeducational evaluation

Grand View University

1200 Grandview Avenue, Des Moines, IA 50316 • Admissions: 515-263-2810 • grandview.edu

Support: CS

ACCOMMODATIONS

Allowed in exams:

Calculators	Yes
Dictionary	Yes
Computer	Yes
Spell-checker	Yes
Extended test time	Yes
Scribe	Yes
Proctors	Yes
Oral exams	Yes
Note-takers	Yes

Support services for students with:

LD	Yes
ADHD	Yes
ASD	Yes
Distraction-reduced environment	Yes
Recording of lecture allowed	Yes
Reading technology	Yes
Audio books	Yes
Other assistive technology	Yes
Priority registration	No

Added costs of services:

For LD	No
For ADHD	No
For ASD	No
LD specialists	Yes
ADHD & ASD coaching	No
ASD specialists	No
Professional tutors	No
Peer tutors	Yes
Max. hours/week for services	Varies
How professors are notified of student approved accommodations	Student and Disability Support Services

COLLEGE GRADUATION REQUIREMENTS

Course waivers allowed	No
Course substitutions allowed	Yes
In what courses: Student works with institution to determine course substitutions	

PROGRAMS/SERVICES FOR STUDENTS WITH LEARNING DIFFERENCES

At Grand View University (GVU), student accommodations are processed through Disability Support Services (DSS). Students may schedule an appointment with DSS so that the administration may assess their learning difficulties and needs, develop an accommodation plan, review policies and procedures, and discuss personal advocacy issues. Accommodations may include the use of computers, scribes, proctors, oral exams, notetakers, extended testing time, recording lectures, and a distraction-free environment for tests.

ADMISSIONS

Admission requirements are the same for all students. Admission consideration is given to academic performance, including class rank, test scores if submitted, and quality of high school curriculum, as well as cocurricular achievement, and character and maturity as displayed through church, community, school, work, and family activities.

Additional Information

GVU partners with GEAR UP (Gaining Early Awareness and Readiness for Undergraduate Programs) to provide a summer bridge program. Applicants must be admitted to Grand View University and attend a Gear Up school district. Academic Success I is a 1 credit class designed to encourage students to build motivation and productive academic habits. Topics covered include goal setting, anti-procrastination techniques, habit building, study strategies, and self-care. The Academic Learning & Teaching Center (ALT) offers support with both academic content and skills development. ALT resources include study and time-management skills, math and writing instruction, and peer tutoring and workshops.

According to the rumors, a large iron eagle, nicknamed Bud the Bird, was stolen from a nearby business in 1933, and students began to hide and find him around campus. After Bud was donated to the World War II effort as scrap metal, a 200-pound replica, Bud Jr., took his place. Bud was buried on campus in the 1940s, not to be found until 1994 by crews digging for fiber optic cables. Bud Jr. and other Bud replicas have been created to continue the tradition to this day.

Grand View University

GENERAL ADMISSIONS

Very important factors include: rigor of secondary school record, class rank, academic GPA. *Important factors include:* standardized test scores (if submitted). High school diploma is required and GED is accepted. Institution is test-optional for entering Fall 2024. Check admissions website for updates. *Academic units recommended:* 4 English, 3 math, 3 science, 2 foreign language, 3 social studies.

FINANCIAL AID

Students should submit: FAFSA. *Need-based scholarships/grants offered:* College/university scholarship or grant aid from institutional funds; Federal Pell; Private scholarships; SEOG; State scholarships/grants. *Loan aid offered:.* Federal Work-Study Program available. Institutional employment available.

CAMPUS LIFE

Activities: Campus Ministries; Choral groups; Concert band; Dance; Drama/theater; International Student Organization; Jazz band; Literary magazine; Music ensembles; Pep band; Radio station; Student government; Student newspaper; Television station. **Organizations:** 28 registered organizations, 1 religious organizations. **Athletics (Intercollegiate):** *Men:* baseball, basketball, cross-country, golf. *Women:* basketball, cross-country, golf, softball, volleyball.

CAMPUS
Type of school	Private (nonprofit)
Environment	City

STUDENTS
Undergrad enrollment	1,561
% male/female	48/52
% from out of state	13
% frosh live on campus	85

FINANCIAL FACTS
Annual tuition	$30,224
Room and board	$10,520
Required fees	$640

GENERAL ADMISSIONS INFO
Application fee	No fee
Regular application deadline	8/15
Nonfall registration	Yes

Fall 2024 testing policy	Test Optional
Range SAT EBRW	470–530
Range SAT Math	450–550
Range ACT Composite	17–22

ACADEMICS
Student/faculty ratio	12:1
% students returning for sophomore year	71

Most classes have 10–19 students.

Iowa

REQUESTING SERVICES FOR STUDENTS WITH LEARNING DIFFERENCES

Phone: 515-263-2971 • www.grandview.edu/student-life/services/disability-services
Email: cfierro @ grandview.edu

Documentation submitted to: Disability Support Services
Separate application required for Services: Yes

Documentation required for:
LD: Psychoeducational evaluation
ADHD: Psychoeducational evaluation
ASD: Psychoeducational evaluation

Grinnell College

1227 Park Street, 1st Floor, Grinnell, IA 50112-1690 • Admissions: 641-269-3600 • www.grinnell.edu

Support: CS

ACCOMMODATIONS

Allowed in exams:

Calculators	Yes
Dictionary	Yes
Computer	Yes
Spell-checker	Yes
Extended test time	Yes
Scribe	Yes
Proctors	Yes
Oral exams	Yes
Note-takers	Yes

Support services for students with:

LD	Yes
ADHD	Yes
ASD	Yes
Distraction-reduced environment	Yes
Recording of lecture allowed	Yes
Reading technology	Yes
Audio books	Yes
Other assistive technology	Yes
Priority registration	Yes

Added costs of services:

For LD	No
For ADHD	No
For ASD	No
LD specialists	Yes
ADHD & ASD coaching	Yes
ASD specialists	No
Professional tutors	No
Peer tutors	Yes
Max. hours/week for services	Varies
How professors are notified of student approved accommodations	Student and Accessibility and Student Disability Resources

COLLEGE GRADUATION REQUIREMENTS

Course waivers allowed	No
Course substitutions allowed	Yes
In what courses: Case-by-case basis	

PROGRAMS/SERVICES FOR STUDENTS WITH LEARNING DIFFERENCES

The coordinator for Accessibility and Student Disability Resources is the primary contact for students with disabilities and advises students about Grinnell's disability-related policies, procedures, and resources. The staff also provides day-to-day support and accommodations for academic needs. Students should contact disability resources as soon as possible, provide the appropriate documentation, and complete the process for requesting accommodations, including talking to faculty when needed. All accommodations are reviewed and approved by the coordinator for disability resources, who will work with students and others on campus to get the necessary accommodations. Assistive technology software for students with dyslexia, dysgraphia, and other learning differences, is available on all public computers in the Burling and Kistle Libraries. Programs include text-to-speech programs like Read and Write Gold 11, and literacy solutions, including Kurzweil 3K.

ADMISSIONS

Admission criteria are the same for all students. While no single factor guarantees admission, the selection process is highly competitive, and Grinnell emphasizes the importance of a challenging and balanced high school curriculum. Interviews are not required, but high school students are welcome to interview beginning in February of their junior year, until mid-December of senior year.

Additional Information

Students can address any academic concerns with the Academic Advising Office, which offers help with study skills and time management, and provides individual and peer tutoring for all subjects in humanities and social studies.

DID YOU KNOW?

The *Scarlet & Black* campus newspaper was first published on September 12, 1894. Its 16 tabloid pages are written by students, with an occasional letter from alumni or faculty. The S&B has been digitally archived and is available online, so it serves not only as a source of up-to-date news on campus, but a rich historical resource of Grinnell. For lighter reading, the B&S is the bi-weekly satirical campus paper that comments on social and political issues through articles, graphics, and crosswords.

Grinnell College

GENERAL ADMISSIONS

Very important factors include: rigor of secondary school record, class rank, academic GPA, recommendations. *Important factors include:* standardized test scores (if submitted), application essay. High school diploma is required and GED is accepted. Institution is test-optional for entering Fall 2024. Check admissions website for updates. *Academic units recommended:* 4 English, 4 math, 4 science (2 labs), 3 foreign language, 3 social studies.

FINANCIAL AID

Students should submit: CSS/Financial Aid Profile; FAFSA; Noncustodial Profile; State aid form. *Need-based scholarships/grants offered:* College/university scholarship or grant aid from institutional funds; Federal Pell; Private scholarships; SEOG; State scholarships/grants. *Loan aid offered:* Direct PLUS loans; Direct Subsidized Loans; Direct Unsubsidized Loans. Federal Work-Study Program available. Institutional employment available.

CAMPUS LIFE

Activities: Campus Ministries; Choral groups; Concert band; Dance; Drama/theater; International Student Organization; Jazz band; Literary magazine; Model UN; Music ensembles; Musical theater; Radio station; Student government; Student newspaper; Student-run film society; Symphony orchestra; Yearbook. **Organizations:** 109 registered organizations, 2 honor societies, 5 religious organizations, 0 fraternities, 0 sororities. **Athletics (Intercollegiate):** *Men:* baseball, basketball, cross-country, golf, swimming, track/field (indoor), ultimate frisbee, water polo. *Women:* basketball, cross-country, golf, softball, swimming, track/field (indoor), ultimate frisbee, volleyball, water polo.

CAMPUS

Type of school	Private (nonprofit)
Environment	Village

STUDENTS

Undergrad enrollment	1,759
% male/female	47/53
% from out of state	91
% frosh live on campus	100

FINANCIAL FACTS

Annual tuition	$64,342
Room and board	$15,878
Required fees	$520

GENERAL ADMISSIONS INFO

Application fee	No fee
Regular application deadline	1/15
Nonfall registration	No

Fall 2024 testing policy	Test Optional
Range SAT EBRW	680–750
Range SAT Math	700–780
Range ACT Composite	31–34

ACADEMICS

Student/faculty ratio	9:1
% students returning for sophomore year	93

Most classes have 10–19 students.

Iowa

REQUESTING SERVICES FOR STUDENTS WITH LEARNING DIFFERENCES

Phone: 641-269-3089 • grinnell.edu/about/leadership/offices-services/accessibility-disability/students
Email: wilkeaut@grinnell.edu

Documentation submitted to: Accessibility and Student Disability Services
Separate application required for Services: Yes

Documentation required for:
LD: Psychoeducational evaluation
ADHD: Psychoeducational evaluation
ASD: Psychoeducational evaluation

Iowa State University

100 Enrollment Services Center, Ames, IA 50011-2011 · Admissions: 515-294-5836 · www.iastate.edu

Support: CS

ACCOMMODATIONS

Allowed in exams:

Calculators	Yes
Dictionary	Yes
Computer	Yes
Spell-checker	Yes
Extended test time	Yes
Scribe	Yes
Proctors	Yes
Oral exams	Yes
Note-takers	Yes

Support services for students with:

LD	Yes
ADHD	Yes
ASD	Yes
Distraction-reduced environment	Yes
Recording of lecture allowed	Yes
Reading technology	Yes
Audio books	Yes
Other assistive technology	Yes
Priority registration	No

Added costs of services:

For LD	No
For ADHD	No
For ASD	No
LD specialists	No
ADHD & ASD coaching	Yes
ASD specialists	No
Professional tutors	No
Peer tutors	Yes
Max. hours/week for services	Varies
How professors are notified of student approved accommodations	Student

COLLEGE GRADUATION REQUIREMENTS

Course waivers allowed	No
Course substitutions allowed	No

PROGRAMS/SERVICES FOR STUDENTS WITH LEARNING DIFFERENCES

The Student Accessibility Services (SAS) office at Iowa State University provides developmental services to students with documented disabilities. To apply for services, students must complete a registration form and schedule a welcome meeting with the accessibility coordinator. The meeting allows students the opportunity to share details about their needs and gain a general understanding of the available resources. In preparation for the meeting, students are required to submit appropriate documentation of their disability. Once students have been approved for services, the SAS staff works with the college staff to support students in obtaining reasonable accommodations.

ADMISSIONS

For applicants submitting test scores, admission is based on the Regent Admissions Index (RAI.) The RAI is a mathematical equation that considers a student's ACT scores, GPA, and the number of core courses in high school. Students who score a 245 RAI and meet the high school course requirements are automatically admitted. Applicants who do not submit test scores will be evaluated based on their GPA and high school core courses and must have an Alternative Admission Index score of 176 or higher and meet the core academic units required. Students without test scores or applicants who would like an opportunity to share more about themselves outside of their application can receive an individual review. And students who intend to request support services through the SAS office should submit a letter to the admissions office requesting an individual review and provide additional details about how their academics have impacted their learning or intellectual difference.

Additional Information

The SAS office is in the Student Success Center (SSC), where all students have access to individual tutoring and study skills, time management, and reading support. The Academic Success Center is also located in the SSC and provides a Supplemental Instruction program that helps students with traditionally difficult courses. Additionally, there are college success workshops and specialized academic coaching.

From 1942-1945, ISU played a role in developing the atomic bomb during World War II. The ISU Ames Project developed the Ames Process, a uranium purification method necessary for a self-sustaining atomic reaction. The team of chemists produced more than 2 million pounds of high-purity uranium metal for the Manhattan Project, which produced the first atomic bombs during WWII. Iowa State is one of only four universities contracted to manage a U.S. DOE national laboratory, and the Ames Laboratory is the only program physically located on a university campus.

Iowa State University

GENERAL ADMISSIONS

Very important factors include: rigor of secondary school record, academic GPA, standardized test scores (if submitted). *Other factors considered include:* class rank, application essay, recommendations. High school diploma is required and GED is accepted. Institution is test-optional for entering Fall 2024. Check admissions website for updates. *Academic units required:* 4 English, 3 math, 3 science (2 labs), 2 foreign language, 2 social studies. *Academic units recommended:* 4 math, 4 science (3 labs), 3 foreign language, 4 social studies.

FINANCIAL AID

Students should submit: FAFSA. *Need-based scholarships/grants offered:* College/university scholarship or grant aid from institutional funds; Federal Pell; SEOG. *Loan aid offered:* Direct PLUS loans; Direct Subsidized Loans; Direct Unsubsidized Loans. Federal Work-Study Program available. Institutional employment available.

CAMPUS LIFE

Activities: Campus Ministries; Choral groups; Concert band; Dance; Drama/theater; International Student Organization; Jazz band; Literary magazine; Marching band; Model UN; Music ensembles; Musical theater; Pep band; Radio station; Student government; Student newspaper; Student-run film society; Symphony orchestra; Television station. **Organizations:** 809 registered organizations, 28 honor societies, 31 religious organizations, 37 fraternities, 25 sororities. **Athletics (Intercollegiate):** *Men:* baseball, basketball, bowling, crew/rowing, cross-country, cycling, equestrian sports, golf, ice hockey, lacrosse, martial arts, racquetball, rugby, skiing (nordic/cross-country), swimming, table tennis, track/field (indoor), ultimate frisbee, volleyball, water polo, wrestling. *Women:* basketball, bowling, crew/rowing, cross-country, cycling, equestrian sports, golf, gymnastics, ice hockey, lacrosse, martial arts, racquetball, rugby, skiing (nordic/cross-country), softball, swimming, table tennis, track/field (indoor), ultimate frisbee, volleyball, water polo.

CAMPUS
Type of school	Public
Environment	Town

STUDENTS
Undergrad enrollment	25,241
% male/female	56/44
% from out of state	38
% frosh live on campus	89

FINANCIAL FACTS
Annual in-state tuition	$8,678
Annual out-of-state tuition	$25,162
Room and board	$9,358
Required fees	$1,455

GENERAL ADMISSIONS INFO
Application fee	$40
Regular application deadline	Rolling
Nonfall registration	Yes

Fall 2024 testing policy	Test Optional
Range SAT EBRW	540–660
Range SAT Math	550–620
Range ACT Composite	21–28

ACADEMICS
Student/faculty ratio	18:1
% students returning for sophomore year	86

Most classes have 20–29 students.

Iowa

REQUESTING SERVICES FOR STUDENTS WITH LEARNING DIFFERENCES

Phone: 515-294-7220 • sas.dso.iastate.edu • Email: accessibility@iastate.edu

Documentation submitted to: Student Accessibility Services
Separate application required for Services: Yes

Documentation required for:
 LD: Psychoeducational evaluation
 ADHD: Psychoeducational evaluation
 ASD: Psychoeducational evaluation

Loras College

1450 Alta Vista, Dubuque, IA 52001 • Admissions: 563-588-7236 • www.loras.edu

> **Support: SP**

ACCOMMODATIONS

Allowed in exams:

Calculators	Yes
Dictionary	Yes
Computer	Yes
Spell-checker	Yes
Extended test time	Yes
Scribe	Yes
Proctors	Yes
Oral exams	Yes
Note-takers	Yes

Support services for students with:

LD	Yes
ADHD	Yes
ASD	Yes
Distraction-reduced environment	Yes
Recording of lecture allowed	Yes
Reading technology	Yes
Audio books	Yes
Other assistive technology	Yes
Priority registration	Yes

Added costs of services:

For LD	Yes
For ADHD	Yes
For ASD	Yes
LD specialists	Yes
ADHD & ASD coaching	Yes
ASD specialists	Yes
Professional tutors	No
Peer tutors	Yes
Max. hours/week for services	Varies
How professors are notified of student approved accommodations	Student

COLLEGE GRADUATION REQUIREMENTS

Course waivers allowed	Yes
In what courses: Case-by-case basis	
Course substitutions allowed	No

PROGRAMS/SERVICES FOR STUDENTS WITH LEARNING DIFFERENCES

The Lynch Disability Resources & Cultural Center (LDRCC) offers a variety of services, including an Enhanced Program option and the Autism Resources for Career in Higher Education Program (ARCH). Reasonable accommodations for students with documented disabilities are provided through the Lynch Disability Resource & Cultural Center at no additional cost. Students are encouraged to provide diagnostic testing within the last three years. The Enhanced Program is a comprehensive fee-based program designed to provide additional academic support for students with a primary learning disability or attention deficit disorder. The program includes a 2 credit Learning Strategies class in the first year, weekly meetings with an LDRCC staff member, and peer tutors, as needed. Students considering the Enhanced Program should apply by December of their senior year of high school. Once students are part of the Enhanced Program, they can request to stay in the program beyond their first year. The ARCH program is a four-year, fee-based program designed to help students with ASD thrive emotionally, academically, and socially. Students admitted into the ARCH program work directly with Loras College certified autism specialists and develop skills ranging from self-advocacy and organization to stress management and socialization.

ADMISSIONS

The Loras College Admissions Committee reviews applications for college preparedness. Applicants with a GPA of 2.75 or higher will automatically be admitted to Loras College. Students whose GPA is less than 2.75 will engage in a director's review process that includes an interview to discuss academic readiness and identify potential resources to assist with the transition to college, as well as a conversation with two teachers who can speak to the students' academic experience.

Additional Information

The Writing Center, located in the Learning Commons, offers one-on-one sessions with trained tutors to help students with their writing projects. The Math Lab is also located in the Learning Commons.

Hall of Fame baseball pitcher, Red Faber, attended Loras in 1909. Mr. Faber set a college record by striking out 24 St. Ambrose University batters in a 1909 game. His major league career, from 1914 through 1933, was played entirely with the Chicago White Sox. He was not involved in the 1919 "Black Sox" scandal and missed the World Series due to injury and illness. He was inducted into the Baseball Hall of Fame in 1964. Farber-Clark Field, home of Loras College softball, still carries his name.

Loras College

GENERAL ADMISSIONS

Very important factors include: rigor of secondary school record, academic GPA. *Other factors considered include:* class rank, application essay, recommendations. High school diploma is required and GED is accepted. Institution is test-optional for entering Fall 2024. Check admissions website for updates. *Academic units recommended:* 4 English, 4 math, 3 science (2 labs), 3 social studies, 2 academic electives.

FINANCIAL AID

Students should submit: FAFSA. *Need-based scholarships/grants offered:* College/university scholarship or grant aid from institutional funds; Federal Pell; Private scholarships; SEOG; State scholarships/grants. *Loan aid offered:* Direct PLUS loans; Direct Subsidized Loans; Direct Unsubsidized Loans. Federal Work-Study Program available. Institutional employment available.

CAMPUS LIFE

Activities: Campus Ministries; Choral groups; Concert band; Dance; Drama/theater; International Student Organization; Jazz band; Literary magazine; Music ensembles; Pep band; Radio station; Student government; Student newspaper; Television station; Yearbook. **Organizations:** 67 registered organizations, 3 honor societies, 7 religious organizations, 1 fraternities, 1 sororities. **Athletics (Intercollegiate):** *Men:* baseball, basketball, cross-country, golf, ice hockey, martial arts, racquetball, rugby, softball, swimming, track/field (indoor), ultimate frisbee, volleyball, wrestling. *Women:* basketball, cross-country, golf, ice hockey, lacrosse, martial arts, racquetball, rugby, softball, swimming, track/field (indoor), ultimate frisbee, volleyball.

CAMPUS

Type of school	Private (nonprofit)
Environment	Town

STUDENTS

Undergrad enrollment	1,256
% male/female	57/43
% from out of state	60
% frosh live on campus	91

FINANCIAL FACTS

Annual tuition	$33,500
Room and board	$8,760
Required fees	$1,768

GENERAL ADMISSIONS INFO

Application fee	No fee
Regular application deadline	Rolling
Nonfall registration	Yes
Fall 2024 testing policy	Test Optional
Range SAT EBRW	480–580
Range SAT Math	493–590
Range ACT Composite	19–25

ACADEMICS

Student/faculty ratio	12:1
% students returning for sophomore year	79

Most classes have 20–29 students.

Iowa

REQUESTING SERVICES FOR STUDENTS WITH LEARNING DIFFERENCES

Phone: 563-588-7134 • www.loras.edu/academics/academic-support/lynch-learning-center/
Email: lynch.learningcenter@loras.edu

Documentation submitted to: Lynch Disability Resources & Cultural Center
Separate application required for Services: Yes

Documentation required for:
  LD: Psychoeducational evaluation
  ADHD: Psychoeducational evaluation
  ASD: Psychoeducational evaluation

Morningside University

1501 Morningside Avenue, Sioux City, IA 51106 • Admissions: 712-274-5511 • morningside.edu

Support: S

ACCOMMODATIONS

Allowed in exams:	
Calculators	Yes
Dictionary	Yes
Computer	Yes
Spell-checker	Yes
Extended test time	Yes
Scribe	Yes
Proctors	Yes
Oral exams	Yes
Note-takers	Yes
Support services for students with:	
LD	Yes
ADHD	Yes
ASD	Yes
Distraction-reduced environment	Yes
Recording of lecture allowed	Yes
Reading technology	Yes
Audio books	Yes
Other assistive technology	No
Priority registration	No
Added costs of services:	
For LD	No
For ADHD	No
For ASD	No
LD specialists	No
ADHD & ASD coaching	No
ASD specialists	No
Professional tutors	Yes
Peer tutors	Yes
Max. hours/week for services	Varies
How professors are notified of student approved accommodations	Associate Dean of Advising and Coordinator of Disability Services

COLLEGE GRADUATION REQUIREMENTS

Course waivers allowed	No
Course substitutions allowed	No

PROGRAMS/SERVICES FOR STUDENTS WITH LEARNING DIFFERENCES

The Disability Services Office works with qualified students—in collaboration with university staff and faculty, as necessary—to identify, facilitate, and provide appropriate academic accommodations and auxiliary aids and services. Accommodations generally offered include classroom accessibility, copies of instructors' notes, preferential seating, and test taking accommodations. Students initiate the process by applying for accommodations with the Disability Services coordinator. To apply for services, students submit documentation and complete an intake meeting.

ADMISSIONS

Morningside University maintains a selective admission process with consideration for GPA, ACT or SAT scores, and course rigor. Test scores are not required for admission purposes, but they could impact the applicant's consideration for academic scholarships. The general academic standards for admission are a 2.5 GPA, a 20 ACT score, or a 1410 SAT score. Students who have been out of college for more than five years are not required to submit scores, but they are required to take a placement test.

Additional Information

The Academic Support Center provides all students with access to supplemental aid to achieve academic goals. Staff tutors are available to help with writing techniques, math, and science courses. Student tutors help in areas such as accounting, chemistry, economics, religion, nursing, and physics. Tutors are available online and in person.

Identical twin sisters Pauline Phillips and Eppie Lederer graduated from Morningside, where they studied journalism and psychology and wrote a joint gossip column for the school's newspaper, the *Collegian Reporter*. They later became the notable newspaper columnists "Dear Abby" (Pauline) and "Ann Landers" (Eppie). "Dear Abby" was syndicated in 1,400 newspapers with 110 million readers, while a 1978 World Almanac survey named Eppie the most influential woman in the United States.

Morningside University

GENERAL ADMISSIONS

Very important factors include: rigor of secondary school record, class rank, academic GPA, standardized test scores (if submitted), recommendations. *Other factors considered include:* application essay. High school diploma is required and GED is accepted. Institution is test-optional for entering Fall 2024. Check admissions website for updates. *Academic units recommended:* 3 English, 2 math, 2 science, 3 social studies.

FINANCIAL AID

Students should submit: FAFSA. *Need-based scholarships/grants offered:* College/university scholarship or grant aid from institutional funds; Federal Pell; Private scholarships; SEOG; State scholarships/grants. *Loan aid offered:.* Federal Work-Study Program available. Institutional employment available.

CAMPUS LIFE

Activities: Campus Ministries; Choral groups; Concert band; Dance; Drama/theater; International Student Organization; Jazz band; Literary magazine; Marching band; Music ensembles; Musical theater; Pep band; Radio station; Student government; Student newspaper; Television station; Yearbook. **Organizations:** 40 registered organizations, 15 honor societies, 10 religious organizations, 2 fraternities, 1 sororities. **Athletics (Intercollegiate):** *Men:* baseball, basketball, cross-country, golf, swimming, track/field (indoor), wrestling. *Women:* basketball, cross-country, golf, softball, swimming, track/field (indoor), volleyball.

CAMPUS	
Type of school	Private (nonprofit)
Environment	City

STUDENTS	
Undergrad enrollment	1,245
% male/female	50/50
% from out of state	46
% frosh live on campus	94

FINANCIAL FACTS	
Annual tuition	$35,100
Room and board	$10,720
Required fees	$1,510

GENERAL ADMISSIONS INFO	
Application fee	$25
Regular application deadline	Rolling
Nonfall registration	Yes
Fall 2024 testing policy	Test Optional

ACADEMICS	
Student/faculty ratio	13:1
% students returning for sophomore year	66
Most classes have 10–19 students.	

REQUESTING SERVICES FOR STUDENTS WITH LEARNING DIFFERENCES

Phone: 712-274-5034 • www.morningside.edu/campus-life-and-arts/disability-services
Email: boettcherb@morningside.edu

Documentation submitted to: Disability Services
Separate application required for Services: Yes

Documentation required for:
LD: Psychoeducational evaluation
ADHD: Psychoeducational evaluation
ASD: Psychoeducational evaluation

St. Ambrose University

310 West Locust Street, Davenport, IA 52803-2898 • Admissions: 563-333-6300 • www.sau.edu

Support: CS

ACCOMMODATIONS

Allowed in exams:

Calculators	Yes
Dictionary	Yes
Computer	Yes
Spell-checker	Yes
Extended test time	Yes
Scribe	Yes
Proctors	Yes
Oral exams	Yes
Note-takers	Yes

Support services for students with:

LD	Yes
ADHD	Yes
ASD	Yes
Distraction-reduced environment	Yes
Recording of lecture allowed	Yes
Reading technology	Yes
Audio books	Yes
Other assistive technology	Yes
Priority registration	No

Added costs of services:

For LD	No
For ADHD	No
For ASD	No
LD specialists	Yes
ADHD & ASD coaching	Yes
ASD specialists	Yes
Professional tutors	No
Peer tutors	Yes
Max. hours/week for services	Varies
How professors are notified of student approved accommodations	Student

COLLEGE GRADUATION REQUIREMENTS

Course waivers allowed	No
Course substitutions allowed	Yes
In what courses: Foreign Language	

PROGRAMS/SERVICES FOR STUDENTS WITH LEARNING DIFFERENCES

The Accessibility Resource Center (ARC) offers a variety of services and reasonable accommodations for students with disabilities. While disclosing a student's disability is voluntary, students must self-identify and submit documentation to determine eligibility and request accommodations. ARC staff will meet with the student to discuss and determine if the student meets the requirements for their requested accommodations. Some of the accommodations available include alternate testing time and testing arrangements, assistive and adaptive technology, books and course material in alternate formats, notetakers, and course substitution options. Academic advisors in the ARC can help students with course selection and advise students on academic and nonacademic course requirements. ARC supports students in practicing self-advocacy with faculty and others when discussing approved accommodations. ARC offers one-on-one sessions for skills instruction strategies to compensate for a student's disability. Individual needs and staff availability determine the number of sessions.

ADMISSIONS

Applicants to St. Ambrose University are expected to have a cumulative, unweighted GPA of 2.5 or above (on a 4.0 unweighted scale) from an accredited high school. ACT and SAT scores are optional; however, test scores are required for admission to specific programs and eligibility for top academic scholarships. If test scores are sent, they should be on the official school transcript or sent directly from the testing service. A personal essay is optional, and counselor and teacher evaluations are not used. Applicants may be admitted on a provisional basis if they do not meet the full eligibility requirements. Minimum requirements for provisional status include an unweighted 2.0 GPA from an accredited high school and, if submitted, a minimum ACT composite score of 18 or a minimum SAT score of 950. Students admitted on a provisional basis will have their progress monitored each semester by the Board of Studies.

Additional Information

The Student Success Center offers small-group tutoring and study group sessions for 100- and 200-level courses. Peer tutors can help with course content comprehension and developing study strategies. Writing peer tutors can help with all phases of the writing process, from organizing ideas to drafting and revising. Students can get one-on-one appointments or submit writing projects online. Peer tutors can also help with developing learning skills for the demands of college. Supplemental Instruction (SI) peer leaders offer help with traditionally difficult courses, such as organic chemistry or anatomy.

Legend has it that as a baby, Saint Ambrose was found covered with bees, not stung but with a drop of honey on his tongue—the bee is a symbol of work, creative activity, cooperation, obedience, orderliness, and diligence. St. Ambrose's mascot, the Fighting Bee, inspires its athletes and fans. Spirit Day is the first Friday of each month when it's bee-wear day at Ambrose.

St. Ambrose University

General Admissions

Very important factors include: rigor of secondary school record, class rank, academic GPA, standardized test scores (if submitted). *Other factors considered include:* application essay, recommendations. High school diploma is required and GED is accepted. Institution is test-optional for entering Fall 2024. Check admissions website for updates. *Academic units recommended:* 4 English, 3 math, 2 science (2 labs), 1 foreign language, 1 social studies, 1 U.S. history, 4 academic electives.

Financial Aid

Students should submit: FAFSA. *Need-based scholarships/grants offered:* College/university scholarship or grant aid from institutional funds; Federal Pell; Private scholarships; SEOG; State scholarships/grants. *Loan aid offered:* Direct PLUS loans; Direct Subsidized Loans; Direct Unsubsidized Loans. Federal Work-Study Program available. Institutional employment available.

Campus Life

Activities: Campus Ministries; Choral groups; Concert band; Dance; Drama/theater; International Student Organization; Jazz band; Literary magazine; Marching band; Model UN; Music ensembles; Musical theater; Pep band; Radio station; Student government; Student newspaper; Television station. **Organizations:** 84 registered organizations, 15 honor societies, 3 religious organizations, 0 fraternities, 0 sororities. **Athletics (Intercollegiate):** *Men:* baseball, basketball, bowling, cross-country, golf, ice hockey, lacrosse, martial arts, racquetball, rugby, swimming, track/field (indoor), ultimate frisbee, volleyball. *Women:* basketball, bowling, cross-country, golf, ice hockey, lacrosse, martial arts, racquetball, rugby, softball, swimming, track/field (indoor), ultimate frisbee, volleyball.

CAMPUS

Type of school	Private (nonprofit)
Environment	City

STUDENTS

Undergrad enrollment	2,248
% male/female	45/55
% from out of state	66
% frosh live on campus	95

FINANCIAL FACTS

Annual tuition	$32,478
Room and board	$11,354
Required fees	$280

GENERAL ADMISSIONS INFO

Application fee	No fee
Regular application deadline	Rolling
Nonfall registration	Yes

Fall 2024 testing policy	Test Optional
Range SAT EBRW	490–590
Range SAT Math	580–680
Range ACT Composite	20–25

ACADEMICS

Student/faculty ratio	11:1
% students returning for sophomore year	76

Most classes have 10–19 students.

Iowa

REQUESTING SERVICES FOR STUDENTS WITH LEARNING DIFFERENCES

Phone: 563-333-6275 • www.sau.edu/academics/academic-resources/accessibility-resource-center
Email: ARC@sau.edu

Documentation submitted to: Accessibility Resource Center
Separate application required for Services: Yes

Documentation required for:
LD: Psychoeducational evaluation
ADHD: Psychoeducational evaluation
ASD: Psychoeducational evaluation

University of Iowa

108 Calvin Hall, Iowa City, IA 52242 • Admissions: 319-335-3847 • www.uiowa.edu

Support: CS

ACCOMMODATIONS

Allowed in exams:	
Calculators	Yes
Dictionary	No
Computer	Yes
Spell-checker	Yes
Extended test time	Yes
Scribe	Yes
Proctors	Yes
Oral exams	No
Note-takers	Yes
Support services for students with:	
LD	Yes
ADHD	Yes
ASD	Yes
Distraction-reduced environment	Yes
Recording of lecture allowed	Yes
Reading technology	Yes
Audio books	Yes
Other assistive technology	Yes
Priority registration	Yes
Added costs of services:	
For LD	No
For ADHD	No
For ASD	No
LD specialists	Yes
ADHD & ASD coaching	No
ASD specialists	No
Professional tutors	No
Peer tutors	Yes
Max. hours/week for services	Varies
How professors are notified of student approved accommodations	Student

COLLEGE GRADUATION REQUIREMENTS

Course waivers allowed	No
Course substitutions allowed	Yes
In what courses: World Language	

PROGRAMS/SERVICES FOR STUDENTS WITH LEARNING DIFFERENCES

Student Disability Services (SDS) is the resource to help students find and implement academic accommodations. Once admitted, students can register and submit documentation to SDS. During an initial interview with an access consultant, students receive an orientation to the accommodations process, learn how SDS supports students, and discuss specific accommodations in detail. SDS has information on disability-related scholarships and a wide variety of campus resources. All students who have completed their SDS initial meeting qualify for priority course registration. Accommodation for housing, dining, and assistance animals are referred to the Medical (ADA) Accommodations webpage through University Housing and Dining.

ADMISSIONS

The university follows the Iowa Board of Regent Admission Index (RAI). For a liberal arts degree, applicants must have taken or plan to take a minimum of 15 college-prep courses including core academic courses. The Colleges of Engineering, Public Health, Business, and Education have additional high school course requirements. Students who do not provide test scores may be required to submit additional academic documents, transcripts, or a personal statement to receive an admission decision. Applicants who are not admitted after the first review process may submit additional personal statements, official high school transcripts, and/or new test scores.

Additional Information

Tutor Iowa provides online videos that give academic tips on succeeding in specific classes, how to use academic support, how to study and prepare for exams, and how to develop good learning tools. Tutor Iowa's information worksheets cover academic skills and study strategies, communication, time management, stress management, subject-specific success, test taking, and virtual learning. Campus Help Centers offer one-on-one tutoring sessions, tech services, and more. Supplemental Instruction (SI) is a free resource in which students work with an SI leader to better understand course material and study smarter. Private tutors, approved by Tutor Iowa Administration, are available to undergraduates in a variety of courses. The Office of Academic Support & Retention organizes academic workshops that are available to student groups, student organizations, as well as university departments and course instructors.

DID YOU KNOW?

Old Capitol represents the pioneering spirit of Iowa and the university. It was the last capitol building of the Iowa territory and the first Iowa state capitol (1846 to 1857). When the state government moved to Des Moines in 1857, Old Capitol became the university's first building. In 1976, Old Capitol became a National Historic Landmark and public museum. Today it's a vital cultural and educational resource.

University of Iowa

GENERAL ADMISSIONS

Very important factors include: rigor of secondary school record, class rank, academic GPA, standardized test scores (if submitted). *Other factors considered include:* recommendations. High school diploma is required and GED is accepted. Institution is test-flexible for entering Fall 2024. Check admissions website for updates. *Academic units required:* 4 English, 3 math, 3 science, 2 foreign language, 3 social studies. *Academic units recommended:* 4 math.

FINANCIAL AID

Students should submit: FAFSA. *Need-based scholarships/grants offered:* College/university scholarship or grant aid from institutional funds; Federal Pell; Private scholarships; SEOG; State scholarships/grants. *Loan aid offered:* Direct PLUS loans; Direct Subsidized Loans; Direct Unsubsidized Loans. Federal Work-Study Program available. Institutional employment available.

CAMPUS LIFE

Activities: Campus Ministries; Choral groups; Concert band; Dance; Drama/theater; International Student Organization; Jazz band; Literary magazine; Marching band; Model UN; Music ensembles; Musical theater; Opera; Pep band; Radio station; Student government; Student newspaper; Student-run film society; Symphony orchestra; Television station. **Organizations:** 500 registered organizations, 18 honor societies, 21 religious organizations, 27 fraternities, 23 sororities. **Athletics (Intercollegiate):** *Men:* baseball, basketball, bowling, cross-country, cycling, golf, gymnastics, ice hockey, lacrosse, martial arts, rugby, table tennis, track/field (indoor), ultimate frisbee, volleyball, water polo, wrestling. *Women:* basketball, bowling, crew/rowing, cross-country, cycling, field hockey, golf, gymnastics, ice hockey, lacrosse, martial arts, rugby, softball, swimming, table tennis, track/field (indoor), ultimate frisbee, volleyball, water polo, wrestling.

CAMPUS

Type of school	Public
Environment	City

STUDENTS

Undergrad enrollment	21,198
% male/female	44/56
% from out of state	32
% frosh live on campus	89

FINANCIAL FACTS

Annual in-state tuition	$8,356
Annual out-of-state tuition	$30,319
Room and board	$11,780
Required fees	$1,533

GENERAL ADMISSIONS INFO

Application fee	$40
Regular application deadline	5/1
Nonfall registration	Yes
Fall 2024 testing policy	Test Flexible
Range SAT EBRW	570–680
Range SAT Math	560–670
Range ACT Composite	22–29

ACADEMICS

Student/faculty ratio	15:1
% students returning for sophomore year	88

Most classes have 10–19 students.

REQUESTING SERVICES FOR STUDENTS WITH LEARNING DIFFERENCES

Phone: 319-335-1462 • sds.studentlife.uiowa.edu • Email: sds-info@uiowa.edu

Documentation submitted to: Student Disability Services
Separate application required for Services: Yes

Documentation required for:
 LD: Psychoeducational evaluation
 ADHD: Psychoeducational evaluation
 ASD: Psychoeducational evaluation

University of Northern Iowa

1227 West 27th Street, Cedar Falls, IA 50614-0018 • Admissions: 319-273-2281 • www.uni.edu

(Support: CS)

ACCOMMODATIONS

Allowed in exams:

Calculators	Yes
Dictionary	No
Computer	Yes
Spell-checker	Yes
Extended test time	Yes
Scribe	Yes
Proctors	Yes
Oral exams	Yes
Note-takers	Yes

Support services for students with:

LD	Yes
ADHD	Yes
ASD	Yes
Distraction-reduced environment	Yes
Recording of lecture allowed	Yes
Reading technology	Yes
Audio books	Yes
Other assistive technology	Yes
Priority registration	Yes

Added costs of services:

For LD	No
For ADHD	No
For ASD	No
LD specialists	No
ADHD & ASD coaching	Yes
ASD specialists	Yes
Professional tutors	No
Peer tutors	Yes
Max. hours/week for services	2
How professors are notified of student approved accommodations	Student

COLLEGE GRADUATION REQUIREMENTS

Course waivers allowed	No
Course substitutions allowed	Yes
In what courses: Case-by-case basis	

PROGRAMS/SERVICES FOR STUDENTS WITH LEARNING DISABILITIES

The Student Accessibility Services (SAS) office works collaboratively with students, faculty, and staff to create an accessible educational environment for students. The SAS staff determines accommodations on a case-by-case basis after reviewing the student's request and supporting documentation. Once SAS has received both pieces of information, the student will be invited to have a one-on-one meeting with one of the professional staff to finalize eligibility for services. SAS offers executive function skills training to students registered for academic accommodations. This program helps students with time management, prioritization, goal setting, and other academic success strategies. The student organization ACCESS (Awareness, Community, Collaboration, Empowerment, Support, and Success) provides a welcoming and engaging environment for students who identify as having a disability and those who support the disability community.

ADMISSIONS

All students follow the same admission process, which is based on the Regent Admission Index (RAI). Applicants who achieve at least a 245 RAI score and meet the minimum high school course requirements are guaranteed admission. Applicants with an RAI score lower than 245 but who meet the minimum course requirements will be considered for admission on an individual basis. Applicants may be admitted conditionally if they do not meet the RAI; these students should provide a written explanation for not meeting the criteria.

Additional Information

Tutoring, academic coaching, and peer mentoring are provided through the Learning Center.

On Aug. 21, 1865, the old American House Hotel was renovated and became the Soldiers' Orphan's Home to support and educate 100+ children, ages 2–16, who were orphans of Iowa's dead Civil War soldiers. In 1876, the remaining children were transferred to a Davenport home. Through state legislation, the Iowa State Normal School was established in its place and opened with 88 students. After several name changes, in 1967, it became the University of Northern Iowa.

University of Northern Iowa

GENERAL ADMISSIONS

Very important factors include: rigor of secondary school record, academic GPA. *Other factors considered include:* class rank, standardized test scores (if submitted), application essay, recommendations. High school diploma is required and GED is accepted. Institution is test-optional for entering Fall 2024. Check admissions website for updates. *Academic units required:* 4 English, 3 math, 3 science, 3 social studies, 2 academic electives. *Academic units recommended:* 2 foreign language.

FINANCIAL AID

Students should submit: FAFSA. *Need-based scholarships/grants offered:* College/university scholarship or grant aid from institutional funds; Federal Pell; Private scholarships; SEOG; State scholarships/grants. *Loan aid offered:* Direct PLUS loans; Direct Subsidized Loans; Direct Unsubsidized Loans. Federal Work-Study Program available. Institutional employment available.

CAMPUS LIFE

Activities: Campus Ministries; Choral groups; Concert band; Dance; Drama/theater; International Student Organization; Jazz band; Literary magazine; Marching band; Model UN; Music ensembles; Musical theater; Opera; Pep band; Radio station; Student government; Student newspaper; Symphony orchestra; Yearbook. **Organizations:** 235 registered organizations, 12 honor societies, 12 religious organizations, 5 fraternities, 6 sororities. **Athletics (Intercollegiate):** *Men:* baseball, basketball, bowling, cross-country, cycling, golf, ice hockey, martial arts, rugby, swimming, table tennis, track/field (indoor), ultimate frisbee, volleyball, wrestling. *Women:* basketball, bowling, cross-country, cycling, golf, martial arts, rugby, softball, swimming, table tennis, track/field (indoor), ultimate frisbee, volleyball.

CAMPUS
Type of school	Public
Environment	Town

STUDENTS
Undergrad enrollment	7,819
% male/female	39/61
% from out of state	7
% frosh live on campus	88

FINANCIAL FACTS
Annual in-state tuition	$7,780
Annual out-of-state tuition	$18,480
Room and board	$9,160
Required fees	$1,273

GENERAL ADMISSIONS INFO
Application fee	$40
Regular application deadline	Rolling
Nonfall registration	Yes
Fall 2024 testing policy	Test Optional
Range SAT EBRW	490–580
Range SAT Math	490–610
Range ACT Composite	20–26

ACADEMICS
Student/faculty ratio	16:1
% students returning for sophomore year	81

Most classes have 20–29 students.

Iowa

REQUESTING SERVICES FOR STUDENTS WITH LEARNING DIFFERENCES

Phone: 319-273-2332 • sas.uni.edu • Email: accessibilityservices@uni.edu

Documentation submitted to: Student Accessibility Services
Separate application required for Services: Yes

Documentation required for:
LD: Psychoeducational evaluation
ADHD: Psychoeducational evaluation
ASD: Psychoeducational evaluation

Kansas State University

119 Anderson Hall, Manhattan, KS 66506 • Admissions: 785-532-6250 • www.k-state.edu

Support: CS

ACCOMMODATIONS

Allowed in exams:

Calculators	Yes
Dictionary	No
Computer	Yes
Spell-checker	Yes
Extended test time	Yes
Scribe	Yes
Proctors	Yes
Oral exams	No
Note-takers	Yes

Support services for students with:

LD	Yes
ADHD	Yes
ASD	Yes
Distraction-reduced environment	Yes
Recording of lecture allowed	Yes
Reading technology	Yes
Audio books	Yes
Other assistive technology	Yes
Priority registration	Yes

Added costs of services:

For LD	No
For ADHD	No
For ASD	No
LD specialists	Yes
ADHD & ASD coaching	Yes
ASD specialists	No
Professional tutors	No
Peer tutors	Yes
Max. hours/week for services	2
How professors are notified of student approved accommodations	Student and Student Access Center

COLLEGE GRADUATION REQUIREMENTS

Course waivers allowed	Yes
In what courses: Math and Foreign Language	
Course substitutions allowed	Yes
In what courses: Math and Foreign Language	

PROGRAMS/SERVICES FOR STUDENTS WITH LEARNING DIFFERENCES

Kansas State University provides resources for students with learning differences through its Student Access Center (SAC). The center collaborates with students, faculty, and staff to create equal access to on-campus programs and services. New students requesting services should register with SAC and provide eligible documentation prior to the initial interview. Educational Opportunity Funds and private scholarships are available through SAC each year. Students complete the K-State Scholarship Network application, an essay describing how their learning or physical difference has impacted them, along with an explanation of financial need and supporting documentation from a licensed professional.

ADMISSIONS

All applicants are expected to meet the same admission criteria. General admission to the university requires either a GPA of 3.25 or higher (weighted or unweighted) or an ACT composite score of at least 21 (1060 or higher SAT). To gain admission through qualified admission, applicants must have the following: a GPA of at least 2.0 (2.5 for non-Kansas residents) and an ACT score of 21 or higher, or an SAT score of 1060 or higher, or graduate in the top third of their class. Students who do not meet these standards will be considered for admission on a case-by-case basis. Some students may be asked to send additional information and documentation. If KSU is a top school of interest, students are encouraged to visit the campus and apply early to strengthen their admissions application.

Additional Information

The Academic Achievement Center (AAC) is a campus resource center that connects students with like-minded interests and provides tutoring and academic coaching. Students can request an appointment for tutoring at AAC to practice learning strategies to avoid dropping, failing, or withdrawing from classes. Academic coaches support the creation of time management and organizational skills and help students develop a plan for achieving short- and long-term goals. Services at AAC are free to all students.

Wabash Cannon Bowl, the Union's bowling center, is a Kansas State campus fun spot. The name is based on the unofficial, widely known fight song, "The Wabash Cannonball." In 1968, an arsonist set fire to Nichols Hall, home to the radio station and music department. The building and everything in it were lost except the one piece of music the band director had taken home to work on. For over 50 years, the Wabash Cannonball song has been a symbol of Wildcat unity during the pregame warmup.

Kansas State University

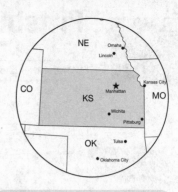

GENERAL ADMISSIONS

Very important factors include: academic GPA. *Important factors include:* standardized test scores (if submitted). *Other factors considered include:* application essay, recommendations. High school diploma is required and GED is accepted. Institution is test-optional for entering Fall 2024. Check admissions website for updates. *Academic units recommended:* 4 English, 4 math, 3 science, 2 foreign language, 3 social studies.

FINANCIAL AID

Students should submit: FAFSA. *Need-based scholarships/grants offered:* College/university scholarship or grant aid from institutional funds; Federal Pell; Private scholarships; SEOG; State scholarships/grants. *Loan aid offered:* Direct PLUS loans; Direct Subsidized Loans; Direct Unsubsidized Loans. Federal Work-Study Program available. Institutional employment available.

CAMPUS LIFE

Activities: Campus Ministries; Choral groups; Concert band; Dance; Drama/theater; International Student Organization; Jazz band; Marching band; Model UN; Music ensembles; Musical theater; Pep band; Radio station; Student government; Student newspaper; Symphony orchestra; Television station; Yearbook. **Organizations:** 594 registered organizations, 36 honor societies, 37 religious organizations, 28 fraternities, 16 sororities. **Athletics (Intercollegiate):** *Men:* baseball, basketball, crew/rowing, cross-country, golf, rugby, track/field (indoor), wrestling. *Women:* basketball, crew/rowing, cross-country, golf, lacrosse, rugby, softball, track/field (indoor), ultimate frisbee, volleyball.

CAMPUS

Type of school	Public
Environment	Town

STUDENTS

Undergrad enrollment	14,749
% male/female	50/50
% from out of state	23
% frosh live on campus	81

FINANCIAL FACTS

Annual in-state tuition	$9,489
Annual out-of-state tuition	$25,560
Room and board	$10,100
Required fees	$959

GENERAL ADMISSIONS INFO

Application fee	$40
Regular application deadline	Rolling
Nonfall registration	Yes
Fall 2024 testing policy	Test Optional
Range ACT Composite	20–27

ACADEMICS

Student/faculty ratio	18:1
% students returning for sophomore year	86

Most classes have 10–19 students.

REQUESTING SERVICES FOR STUDENTS WITH LEARNING DIFFERENCES

Phone: 785-532-6441 • www.k-state.edu/accesscenter • Email: accesscenter@k-state.edu

Documentation submitted to: Student Access Center
Separate application required for Services: Yes

Documentation required for:
  LD: Psychoeducational evaluation
  ADHD: Psychoeducational evaluation
  ASD: Psychoeducational evaluation

Pittsburg State University

1701 South Broadway, Pittsburg, KS 66762 • Admissions: 620-235-4251 • www.pittstate.edu

Support: CS

ACCOMMODATIONS

Allowed in exams:

Calculators	Yes
Dictionary	Yes
Computer	Yes
Spell-checker	Yes
Extended test time	Yes
Scribe	Yes
Proctors	Yes
Oral exams	Yes
Note-takers	Yes

Support services for students with:

LD	Yes
ADHD	Yes
ASD	Yes
Distraction-reduced environment	Yes
Recording of lecture allowed	Yes
Reading technology	Yes
Audio books	Yes
Other assistive technology	Yes
Priority registration	No

Added costs of services:

For LD	No
For ADHD	No
For ASD	No
LD specialists	Yes
ADHD & ASD coaching	Yes
ASD specialists	No
Professional tutors	No
Peer tutors	Yes
Max. hours/week for services	Varies
How professors are notified of student approved accommodations	Student Accommodations

COLLEGE GRADUATION REQUIREMENTS

Course waivers allowed	No
Course substitutions allowed	No

PROGRAMS/SERVICES FOR STUDENTS WITH LEARNING DIFFERENCES

Student Accommodations provides reasonable accommodations to students with a diagnosed disability. Once students are admitted and enrolled, they must contact Student Accommodations to schedule an appointment, complete the application, and submit documentation of their disability. Students must contact Student Accommodations at the beginning of each semester to set up accommodations. Services may include testing accommodations, notetakers, readers, and assistive technology.

ADMISSIONS

Kansas and out-of-state first-year students under the age of 21 may be granted automatic admission with a 2.25 or higher GPA on a 4.0 scale or if submitting test scores, an ACT composite score of 21 or higher (SAT of 1060 or higher).

Additional Information

Gorilla Warmup is a required pre-semester activity for new students designed to familiarize them with the campus, as well as the resources and activities available. First-year students enroll in Gorilla Gateway—a 2 credit hour course that is part of the Pitt State Pathway. The goal is to provide students with good work habits, critical analysis, and thinking skills. Gorilla Gateway also gives students the opportunity to explore the services PSU offers and how and where to obtain them. Student Success programming also includes Academic Success Workshops and tutoring.

In 1907, a delegation lobbied the state legislature for money for Pitt State's first building. One delegate broke a rule, and in good humor, the delegates were fined a barrel of apples and awarded the appropriation. Students hearing the story found it so funny they also fined the men a barrel of apples for truancy (missing work and classes). In 1908, classes were dismissed for the day in honor of the first Apple Day, now the longest-running tradition at Pitt State.

Pittsburg State University

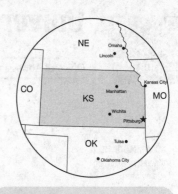

General Admissions

Very important factors include: rigor of secondary school record, class rank, academic GPA, standardized test scores (if submitted). High school diploma is required and GED is accepted. Institution is test-optional for entering Fall 2024. Check admissions website for updates. *Academic units required:* 4 English, 4 math, 3 science, 3 social studies, 3 academic electives.

Financial Aid

Students should submit: CSS/Financial Aid Profile; FAFSA. *Need-based scholarships/grants offered:* College/university scholarship or grant aid from institutional funds; Federal Nursing Scholarships; Federal Pell; Private scholarships; SEOG; State scholarships/grants. *Loan aid offered:* Direct PLUS loans; Direct Subsidized Loans; Direct Unsubsidized Loans. Federal Work-Study Program available. Institutional employment available.

Campus Life

Activities: Campus Ministries; Choral groups; Dance; Drama/theater; International Student Organization; Literary magazine; Marching band; Music ensembles; Musical theater; Opera; Radio station; Student government; Student newspaper; Symphony orchestra; Television station; Yearbook. **Organizations:** 150 registered organizations, 19 honor societies, 5 religious organizations, 7 fraternities, 3 sororities. **Athletics (Intercollegiate):** *Men:* baseball, basketball, cross-country, cycling, golf, lacrosse, martial arts, rugby, track/field (indoor), ultimate frisbee. *Women:* basketball, cross-country, cycling, lacrosse, martial arts, softball, track/field (indoor), ultimate frisbee, volleyball.

CAMPUS

Type of school	Public
Environment	Village

STUDENTS

Undergrad enrollment	5,067
% male/female	52/48
% from out of state	29

FINANCIAL FACTS

Annual in-state tuition	$5,836
Annual out-of-state tuition	$17,180
Room and board	$8,196
Required fees	$1,908

GENERAL ADMISSIONS INFO

Application fee	$30
Regular application deadline	Rolling
Nonfall registration	Yes

Fall 2024 testing policy	Test Optional
Range ACT Composite	17–24

ACADEMICS

Student/faculty ratio	15:1
% students returning for sophomore year	75

Most classes have 10–19 students.

REQUESTING SERVICES FOR STUDENTS WITH LEARNING DIFFERENCES

Phone: 620-235-6578 • www.pittstate.edu/office/center-for-student-accommodations
Email: csa@pittstate.edu

Documentation submitted to: Center for Student Accommodations
Separate application required for Services: Yes

Documentation required for:
LD: Psychoeducational evaluation
ADHD: Psychoeducational evaluation
ASD: Psychoeducational evaluation

Kansas

University of Kansas

Office of Admissions, Lawrence, KS 66045-7576 • Admissions: 785-864-3911 • www.ku.edu

Support: CS

PROGRAMS/SERVICES FOR STUDENTS WITH LEARNING DIFFERENCES

The Student Access Center (SAC) coordinates accommodations for students with disabilities. Typically, students submit requests for accommodations within the first week of classes. However, with time-intensive requests like sign language interpreting or books in an alternate format, students should request services as soon as they register for classes. Students attend an intake meeting with a SAC access specialist, where they will discuss and determine appropriate accommodations, which are then authorized during that meeting. Students receive copies of memos of their accommodations that are sent to course faculty. SAC can also arrange housing and dining accommodations. The KU Career Center supports students with disabilities in the Workforce Recruitment Program (WRP), a program that brings new talent into the federal government. Students with disabilities can explore careers in federal service, find an internship or permanent position at federal agencies, and gain interviewing experience.

ADMISSIONS

All applicants are expected to meet the same admission criteria. KU encourages in- and out-of-state students to complete a college prep curriculum similar to the Kansas Scholars Curriculum by the Board of Regents. For the recommended world language course, Latin and American Sign Language (ASL) are also accepted. First-year applicants to the College of Liberal Arts & Sciences or School of Social Welfare with a GPA of 3.25 are assured admission. Schools and programs considered selective may have additional requirements for direct admission.

Additional Information

Academic Learning Center (ALC) Success Guides can be accessed online with tips on time management, study skills, test-taking, managing stress, and learning skills development. Student groups can also request in-person workshops. ALC's Supplemental Instruction (SI) program is available to all students and targets historically difficult courses that may be required or prerequisites. All students are encouraged to attend SI sessions. ALC offers small group (five max) course-specific tutoring, or one-on-one tutoring is also available by appointment. The KU Writing Center is available to all undergraduate writers who would like help developing their writing skills. Students can schedule a face-to-face session at the Writer's Roost, schedule an online consultation, or receive written feedback via eTutoring.

During a solar eclipse in 1868, helium was detected as a yellow line surrounding the Sun but considered rare on Earth for years to come. In 1905, after two years of analysis of natural gas samples from Dexter, Kansas, chemists Hamilton P. Cady and David F. McFarland, working in Bailey Hall, discovered the large amounts of a non-burning gas in the samples was helium. Bailey Hall is a National Chemical Historical Landmark.

University of Kansas

GENERAL ADMISSIONS

Very important factors include: academic GPA. *Other factors considered include:* standardized test scores (if submitted). High school diploma is required and GED is accepted. Institution is test-optional for entering Fall 2024. Check admissions website for updates. *Academic units recommended:* 4 English, 4 math, 3 science, 2 foreign language, 3 social studies.

FINANCIAL AID

Students should submit: FAFSA. *Need-based scholarships/grants offered:* College/university scholarship or grant aid from institutional funds; Federal Nursing Scholarships; Federal Pell; Private scholarships; SEOG; State scholarships/grants. *Loan aid offered:* Direct PLUS loans; Direct Subsidized Loans; Direct Unsubsidized Loans. Federal Work-Study Program available. Institutional employment available.

CAMPUS LIFE

Activities: Choral groups; Concert band; Dance; Drama/theater; International Student Organization; Jazz band; Literary magazine; Marching band; Model UN; Music ensembles; Musical theater; Opera; Pep band; Radio station; Student government; Student newspaper; Student-run film society; Symphony orchestra; Television station. **Organizations:** 494 registered organizations, 17 honor societies, 36 religious organizations, 25 fraternities, 17 sororities. **Athletics (Intercollegiate):** *Men:* baseball, basketball, crew/rowing, cross-country, cycling, equestrian sports, golf, gymnastics, ice hockey, lacrosse, martial arts, racquetball, rugby, swimming, table tennis, track/field (indoor), ultimate frisbee, volleyball, water polo. *Women:* basketball, crew/rowing, cross-country, cycling, equestrian sports, golf, gymnastics, ice hockey, lacrosse, martial arts, racquetball, rugby, softball, swimming, table tennis, track/field (indoor), ultimate frisbee, volleyball, water polo.

CAMPUS

Type of school	Public
Environment	City

STUDENTS

Undergrad enrollment	18,539
% male/female	46/54
% from out of state	32
% frosh live on campus	72

FINANCIAL FACTS

Annual in-state tuition	$10,092
Annual out-of-state tuition	$26,960
Room and board	$10,136
Required fees	$1,075

GENERAL ADMISSIONS INFO

Application fee	$40
Regular application deadline	One week before classes start
Nonfall registration	Yes
Fall 2024 testing policy	Test Optional
Range SAT EBRW	550–670
Range SAT Math	540–670
Range ACT Composite	21–28

ACADEMICS

Student/faculty ratio	17:1
% students returning for sophomore year	85

Most classes have 10–19 students.

REQUESTING SERVICES FOR STUDENTS WITH LEARNING DIFFERENCES

Phone: 785-864-4064 • access.ku.edu • Email: access@ku.edu

Documentation submitted to: Student Access Center
Separate application required for Services: Yes

Documentation required for:
 LD: Psychoeducational evaluation
 ADHD: Psychoeducational evaluation
 ASD: Psychoeducational evaluation

Kansas

Eastern Kentucky University

SSB CPO 54, Richmond, KY 40475 • Admissions: 859-622-2106 • www.eku.edu

(Support: CS)

ACCOMMODATIONS

Allowed in exams:

Calculators	Yes
Dictionary	Yes
Computer	Yes
Spell-checker	Yes
Extended test time	Yes
Scribe	Yes
Proctors	Yes
Oral exams	Yes
Note-takers	Yes

Support services for students with:

LD	Yes
ADHD	Yes
ASD	Yes
Distraction-reduced environment	Yes
Recording of lecture allowed	Yes
Reading technology	Yes
Audio books	Yes
Other assistive technology	Yes
Priority registration	Yes

Added costs of services:

For LD	No
For ADHD	No
For ASD	No
LD specialists	Yes
ADHD & ASD coaching	No
ASD specialists	No
Professional tutors	No
Peer tutors	Yes
Max. hours/week for services	6
How professors are notified of student approved accommodations	Student

COLLEGE GRADUATION REQUIREMENTS

Course waivers allowed	Yes
In what courses: Case-by-case basis	
Course substitutions allowed	Yes
In what courses: Case-by-case basis	

PROGRAMS/SERVICES FOR STUDENTS WITH LEARNING DIFFERENCES

The Center for Student Accessibility (CSA) offers resources to students with disabilities. Students are welcome to submit documentation or accommodation inquiries to CSA prior to enrollment. Once CSA has reviewed a student's documentation, a coordinator will contact the student for a meeting to discuss accommodations. CSA offers services to students based on individualized need, including test accommodations, note-taking software, priority seating, advocacy information, auxiliary aids, assistive technology and training, digital course material, housing accommodations, classroom accommodations, and early registration. Students can also utilize CSA for academic guidance, advocacy, organization and time-management assistance, and disability outreach. The CSA student tutoring facility offers Read & Write and Ease of Access software, as well as training to utilize the technology. CSA staff can help students acquire digital books when e-books are not available. Test accommodations include quiet testing areas, assistive technology, additional test-taking time, accessible formats, noise-canceling headphones, and scribing.

ADMISSIONS

The application process is the same for all students. Students are encouraged to self-disclose their disability—many students opt to write about it in their application essay. ACT and SAT scores are not required but are a helpful tool for determining course placement. All students must have a minimum high school GPA of 2.0 on a 4.0 scale. Accepted first-years with a GPA between 2.0 and 2.49, or students required to take English and math classes with support, are enrolled in the Success First program.

Additional Information

The Success First Program works to advise, mentor, tutor, and assist students with developing learning goals.

From 1960 to 1976, Robert R. Martin was the first Eastern graduate to serve his alma mater as president. He believed it was the state's responsibility to promote higher education, so he prioritized expanding access to students from the eastern counties in Kentucky, many of whom were the first in their families to attend college. He was a firm but honest negotiator with students during a period of heightened political unrest. His tenure at the university is recognized as a time of unparalleled growth for students, faculty, campus grounds, and course studies.

Eastern Kentucky University

GENERAL ADMISSIONS

Very important factors include: rigor of secondary school record, academic GPA, standardized test scores (if submitted). High school diploma is required and GED is accepted. Institution is test-optional for entering Fall 2024. Check admissions website for updates. *Academic units required:* 4 English, 3 math, 3 science (1 labs), 2 foreign language, 3 social studies, 7 academic electives.

FINANCIAL AID

Students should submit: FAFSA. *Need-based scholarships/grants offered:* College/university scholarship or grant aid from institutional funds; Federal Pell; Private scholarships; SEOG; State scholarships/grants. *Loan aid offered:* Direct PLUS loans; Direct Subsidized Loans; Direct Unsubsidized Loans. Federal Work-Study Program available. Institutional employment available.

CAMPUS LIFE

Activities: Campus Ministries; Choral groups; Concert band; Dance; Drama/theater; International Student Organization; Jazz band; Literary magazine; Marching band; Music ensembles; Musical theater; Pep band; Radio station; Student government; Student newspaper; Student-run film society; Symphony orchestra; Yearbook. **Organizations:** 178 registered organizations, 30 honor societies, 11 religious organizations, 16 fraternities, 13 sororities. **Athletics (Intercollegiate):** *Men:* baseball, basketball, cross-country, golf, ice hockey, racquetball, rugby, softball, swimming, track/field (indoor), volleyball, wrestling. *Women:* basketball, cross-country, golf, racquetball, rugby, softball, swimming, track/field (indoor), volleyball.

CAMPUS

Type of school	Public
Environment	Town

STUDENTS

Undergrad enrollment	11,684
% male/female	41/59
% from out of state	15
% frosh live on campus	74

FINANCIAL FACTS

Annual in-state tuition	$9,452
Annual out-of-state tuition	$19,724
Room and board	$9,410
Required fees	$300

GENERAL ADMISSIONS INFO

Application fee	No fee
Regular application deadline	8/1
Nonfall registration	Yes

Fall 2024 testing policy	Test Optional
Range SAT EBRW	480–590
Range SAT Math	470–590
Range ACT Composite	18–24

ACADEMICS

Student/faculty ratio	15:1
% students returning for sophomore year	74

Most classes have 10–19 students.

REQUESTING SERVICES FOR STUDENTS WITH LEARNING DIFFERENCES

Phone: 859-622-2933 • accessibility.eku.edu • Email: accessibility@eku.edu

Documentation submitted to: Center for Student Accessibility
Separate application required for Services: Yes

Documentation required for:
LD: Psychoeducational evaluation
ADHD: Psychoeducational evaluation
ASD: Psychoeducational evaluation

Murray State University

102 Curris Center, Murray, KY 42071-0009 • Admissions: 270-809-3741 • www.murraystate.edu

Support: CS

ACCOMMODATIONS

Allowed in exams:

Calculators	Yes
Dictionary	Yes
Computer	Yes
Spell-checker	Yes
Extended test time	Yes
Scribe	Yes
Proctors	Yes
Oral exams	Yes
Note-takers	Yes

Support services for students with:

LD	Yes
ADHD	Yes
ASD	Yes
Distraction-reduced environment	Yes
Recording of lecture allowed	Yes
Reading technology	Yes
Audio books	Yes
Other assistive technology	Yes
Priority registration	Yes

Added costs of services:

For LD	No
For ADHD	No
For ASD	No
LD specialists	Yes
ADHD & ASD coaching	Yes
ASD specialists	No
Professional tutors	No
Peer tutors	Yes
Max. hours/week for services	Varies
How professors are notified of student approved accommodations	Student and SDS

COLLEGE GRADUATION REQUIREMENTS

Course waivers allowed	No
Course substitutions allowed	Yes

In what courses: Student may substitute a non-university studies program requirement for another course with approval from each of the following: academic adviser, department chair, dean of the academic college.

PROGRAMS/SERVICES FOR STUDENTS WITH LEARNING DIFFERENCES

The Office of Student Disability Services (SDS) provides accommodations and services to students with documented disabilities; students are required to request services each semester. To request accommodations, admitted students must register with SDS by submitting a completed registration form, providing current eligible documentation, and meeting with the director or associate director for an intake appointment. Project PASS (Program for Achieving Student Success) is offered through SDS and provides scheduling assistance during summer orientation, an early move-in program, specialized support classes, and Project Mentor. Project Mentor provides one-on-one support with strategies for organizing and studying for classes. Services offered through Project PASS are free.

ADMISSIONS

The admission committee accepts students with a high school GPA of 2.75 (unweighted) or higher. Admission eligibility for students with a high school GPA of 2.0–2.74 will be determined by a holistic review process. All students who are Kentucky residents must complete a state-mandated pre-college curriculum, and other applicants must complete courses that are similar.

Additional Information

Academic resources are available through the Testing Center in Applied Science, Racer Writing Center, Racer Oral Communications Center, the Math Center, and the Lowry Center, which provides free tutoring available during the fall and spring semesters.

DID YOU KNOW?

January 2022 was the 85th year of Campus Lights. Campus Lights is the longest-running entirely student-produced and performed musical in the South. The 2022 production was *Legally Blonde, the Musical*. Campus lights was started in 1938 by the Gamma Delta chapter of Phi Mu Alpha as a fundraiser to pay the chapter's chartering fees. Campus Lights is now led by the university's two music fraternities, Phi Mu Alpha Sinfonia and Sigma Alpha Iota. All proceeds from the shows are given to the department of music to fund music scholarships.

Murray State University

GENERAL ADMISSIONS

Very important factors include: rigor of secondary school record, class rank, academic GPA, standardized test scores (if submitted). High school diploma is required and GED is accepted. Institution is test-optional for entering Fall 2024. Check admissions website for updates. *Academic units required:* 4 English, 3 math, 3 science (1 lab), 2 foreign language, 3 social studies, 5 academic electives. *Academic units recommended:* 4 math, 4 science.

FINANCIAL AID

Students should submit: FAFSA. *Need-based scholarships/grants offered:* College/university scholarship or grant aid from institutional funds; Federal Pell; Private scholarships; SEOG; State scholarships/grants. *Loan aid offered:* Direct PLUS loans; Direct Subsidized Loans; Direct Unsubsidized Loans. Federal Work-Study Program available. Institutional employment available.

CAMPUS LIFE

Activities: Campus Ministries; Choral groups; Concert band; Dance; Drama/theater; International Student Organization; Jazz band; Literary magazine; Marching band; Model UN; Music ensembles; Musical theater; Opera; Pep band; Radio station; Student government; Student newspaper; Student-run film society; Symphony orchestra; Television station. **Organizations:** 162 registered organizations, 16 honor societies, 12 religious organizations, 12 fraternities, 11 sororities. **Athletics (Intercollegiate):** *Men:* baseball, basketball, bowling, crew/rowing, cross-country, cycling, equestrian sports, golf, racquetball, rugby, softball, swimming, table tennis, ultimate frisbee, volleyball, water polo. *Women:* basketball, bowling, crew/rowing, cross-country, cycling, equestrian sports, golf, racquetball, softball, swimming, table tennis, track/field (indoor), ultimate frisbee, volleyball, water polo.

CAMPUS

Type of school	Public
Environment	Village

STUDENTS

Undergrad enrollment	7,651
% male/female	38/62
% from out of state	37
% frosh live on campus	81

FINANCIAL FACTS

Annual in-state tuition	$8,040
Annual out-of-state tuition	$17,316
Room and board	$9,868
Required fees	$1,212

GENERAL ADMISSIONS INFO

Application fee	$40
Regular application deadline	Rolling
Nonfall registration	Yes

Fall 2024 testing policy	Test Optional
Range SAT EBRW	490–610
Range SAT Math	470–590
Range ACT Composite	20–27

ACADEMICS

Student/faculty ratio	16:1
% students returning for sophomore year	75

Most classes have 2-9 students.

REQUESTING SERVICES FOR STUDENTS WITH LEARNING DIFFERENCES

Phone: 270-809-2018 • murraystate.edu/about/administration/StudentAffairs/departments/StudentDisabilityServices • Email: msu.studentdisabilities@murraystate.edu

Documentation submitted to: Office of Student Disability Services
Separate application required for Services: Yes

Documentation required for:
LD: Psychoeducational evaluation
ADHD: Psychoeducational evaluation
ASD: Psychoeducational evaluation

Thomas More University

333 Thomas More Pkwy., Crestview Hills, KY 41017 • Admissions: 859-344-3332 • thomasmore.edu

Support: SP

ACCOMMODATIONS

Allowed in exams:

Calculators	Yes
Dictionary	Yes
Computer	Yes
Spell-checker	No
Extended test time	Yes
Scribe	Yes
Proctors	Yes
Oral exams	Yes
Note-takers	Yes

Support services for students with:

LD	Yes
ADHD	Yes
ASD	Yes
Distraction-reduced environment	Yes
Recording of lecture allowed	Yes
Reading technology	Yes
Audio books	Yes
Other assistive technology	Yes
Priority registration	No

Added costs of services:

For LD	Yes
For ADHD	Yes
For ASD	Yes
LD specialists	Yes
ADHD & ASD coaching	Yes
ASD specialists	Yes
Professional tutors	Yes
Peer tutors	Yes
Max. hours/week for services	Varies
How professors are notified of student approved accommodations	Student

COLLEGE GRADUATION REQUIREMENTS

Course waivers allowed	No
Course substitutions allowed	No

PROGRAMS/SERVICES FOR STUDENTS WITH LEARNING DIFFERENCES

Admitted students with disabilities must request accommodations from the Dr. Judith A. Marlowe '69 Office of Student Accessibility through online registration and include documentation of their disability. Students will then receive an email with information regarding a meeting to discuss reasonable accommodations. At the meeting, accommodations will be approved, and students will receive a letter to share with their professors regarding course accommodations. Additional supports include the Institute for Learning Differences (ILD), a fee-based per-semester program for students with documented learning differences. The ILD offers a comprehensive program of professional tutoring, academic and life coaching, and assistive technology; all coordinated through a strategic learning specialist. There is a separate application to apply to ILD, which must include copies of psychoeducational testing and diagnosis, a school history form, and a handwritten essay.

ADMISSIONS

All applicants are expected to meet the same admission criteria. An enrollment counselor may contact an applicant to request additional documents to support their application. Potential supporting documents include letters of recommendation from a teacher, principal, or coach, a résumé showing work history and extracurricular activities, or a one-page personal essay, including background information and reasons the student should be admitted to Thomas More University. First-year students admitted conditionally may be assigned developmental courses or requirements to ensure their successful transition to college.

Additional Information

The Institute for Academic Excellence (IAE) provides peer tutoring to all Thomas More University students and is set up for walk-in help, group study, or individual sessions. Additionally, academic coaches offer one-on-one sessions to cover study skills topics such as time management, learning styles, note-taking, and stress management. Study tables take place in the Benedictine Library and allow students to work together on class projects, meet as study groups, work on class assignments, or meet with a tutor.

DID YOU KNOW?

In 1958, the Perfetti Noodle Company, aka the Macaroni Factory, was purchased and converted into a temporary university spiritual center. Transforming from a factory to St. James Chapel was possible through financial support and community members working to remove the pasta-producing machines and scrubbing floors and walls to remove years of flour buildup. Mass was first celebrated in the new chapel on November 8, 1958.

Thomas More University

GENERAL ADMISSIONS

Very important factors include: academic GPA, standardized test scores (if submitted). *Important factors include:* rigor of secondary school record. *Other factors considered include:* class rank, application essay, recommendations. High school diploma is required and GED is accepted. Institution is test-optional for entering Fall 2024. Check admissions website for updates. *Academic units required:* 4 English, 3 math, 3 science (1 lab), 2 foreign language, 3 social studies. *Academic units recommended:* 2 visual/performing arts.

FINANCIAL AID

Students should submit: FAFSA; Institution's own financial aid form. *Need-based scholarships/grants offered:* College/university scholarship or grant aid from institutional funds; Federal Pell; Private scholarships; SEOG; United Negro College Fund. *Loan aid offered:* Direct PLUS loans; Direct Subsidized Loans; Direct Unsubsidized Loans.

CAMPUS LIFE

Activities: Campus Ministries; Choral groups; Dance; Drama/theater; International Student Organization; Literary magazine; Marching band; Music ensembles; Student government. **Organizations:** 40 registered organizations, 10 honor societies, 1 religious organizations, 1 fraternities, 0 sororities. **Athletics (Intercollegiate):** *Men:* baseball, basketball, bowling, cross-country, golf, rugby, track/field (indoor), wrestling. *Women:* basketball, bowling, cross-country, golf, lacrosse, rugby, softball, track/field (indoor), volleyball.

CAMPUS
Type of school	Private (nonprofit)
Environment	Village

STUDENTS
Undergrad enrollment	1,836
% male/female	47/53
% from out of state	41
% frosh live on campus	54

FINANCIAL FACTS
Annual tuition	$34,060
Room and board	$10,014
Required fees	$1,750

GENERAL ADMISSIONS INFO
Application fee	No fee
Regular application deadline	Rolling
Nonfall registration	Yes
Fall 2024 testing policy	Test Optional

ACADEMICS
Student/faculty ratio	13:1
% students returning for sophomore year	63

Most classes have 10–19 students.

REQUESTING SERVICES FOR STUDENTS WITH LEARNING DIFFERENCES

Phone: 859-344-3582 • www.thomasmore.edu/academics/student-success/office-of-student-accessibility
Email: disability@thomasmore.edu

Documentation submitted to: Dr. Judith A. Marlowe '69 Office of Student Accessibility
Separate application required for Services: Yes

Documentation required for:
LD: Psychoeducational evaluation
ADHD: Psychoeducational evaluation
ASD: Psychoeducational evaluation

University of Kentucky

100 W.D. Funkhouser Building, Lexington, KY 40506 • Admissions: 859-257-2000 • www.uky.edu

Support: S

ACCOMMODATIONS

Allowed in exams:

Calculators	No
Dictionary	No
Computer	Yes
Spell-checker	No
Extended test time	Yes
Scribe	Yes
Proctors	Yes
Oral exams	Yes
Note-takers	No

Support services for students with:

LD	Yes
ADHD	Yes
ASD	Yes
Distraction-reduced environment	Yes
Recording of lecture allowed	Yes
Reading technology	Yes
Audio books	Yes
Other assistive technology	Yes
Priority registration	Yes

Added costs of services:

For LD	No
For ADHD	No
For ASD	No
LD specialists	No
ADHD & ASD coaching	No
ASD specialists	No
Professional tutors	No
Peer tutors	Yes
Max. hours/week for services	Varies
How professors are notified of student approved accommodations	Student

COLLEGE GRADUATION REQUIREMENTS

Course waivers allowed	No
Course substitutions allowed	Yes
In what courses: Math, Statistics, and Foreign Language on a case-by-case basis	

PROGRAMS/SERVICES FOR STUDENTS WITH LEARNING DIFFERENCES

The Disability Resource Center (DRC) in the Office for Student Success provides services to students with disabilities. Students can register with DRC once admitted to the university but are also encouraged to visit DRC if taking a campus tour. Once students have registered and submitted documentation, a DRC consultant will schedule a meeting to finalize accommodations. Consultants meet with students to discuss the student's needs and how to be successful in college. Accommodations may include test-taking adaptations, alternative text for class materials, or other alternate text services. The DRC has a wide range of external partners that support individuals with disabilities. Many of these supports and services are low- or no-cost and are available to UK students regardless of their resident status or income. DRC participates in the Workforce Recruitment Program (WRP), a recruitment and referral program connecting federal sector employers nationwide with highly motivated college students and recent graduates with disabilities.

ADMISSIONS

Incoming first-year applicants must submit an official high school transcript reflecting grades through at least six semesters. To be eligible for consideration, applicants should show successful completion of the required high school college preparatory courses. First-year applicants who submit a valid High School Equivalency Certificate and General Education Development (GED) test scores will be considered. The Colleges of Business and Economics, Design, Engineering, Fine Arts, Health Sciences, Nursing, Public Health, Social Work, and Martin School of Public Policy have majors and programs that are considered selective and have separate admission requirements.

Additional Information

The UK Peer Tutoring Program offers free, drop-in tutoring for many math, science, and business core courses. UK also partners with Tutor Matching Service (TMS), an online service matching students with quality tutors for both online and in-person tutoring sessions across a broad range of academic subjects. Integrated Success Coaches (ISC) are trained to support students, working together to share disciplinary knowledge to best help each student. The Office of Undergraduate Advising and Student Success manages and assists with student support services to help ensure student satisfaction and increase retention and graduation rates.

DID YOU KNOW?

Kentucky had a women's basketball team before a men's team! The first women's team was formed in 1902, with the men organizing a team the following year in 1903. UK athletics was identified with the name Wildcats after a 6-2 football victory in 1909 when it was said that the Kentucky football team "fought like Wildcats." The name became popular with followers and the media and was adopted by the school.

University of Kentucky

GENERAL ADMISSIONS

Very important factors include: rigor of secondary school record, academic GPA, standardized test scores (if submitted), application essay. *Other factors considered include:* class rank, recommendations. High school diploma is required and GED is accepted. Institution is test-optional for entering Fall 2024. Check admissions website for updates. *Academic units required:* 4 English, 3 math, 3 science (1 labs), 2 foreign language, 3 social studies, 1 health/physical education, 1 visual/performing arts, 7 academic electives.

FINANCIAL AID

Students should submit: FAFSA. *Need-based scholarships/grants offered:* College/university scholarship or grant aid from institutional funds; Federal Pell; Private scholarships; SEOG; State scholarships/grants. *Loan aid offered:* Direct PLUS loans; Direct Subsidized Loans; Direct Unsubsidized Loans. Federal Work-Study Program available.

CAMPUS LIFE

Activities: Campus Ministries; Choral groups; Concert band; Dance; Drama/theater; International Student Organization; Jazz band; Literary magazine; Marching band; Model UN; Music ensembles; Musical theater; Opera; Pep band; Radio station; Student government; Student newspaper; Student-run film society; Symphony orchestra; Television station; Yearbook. **Organizations:** 348 registered organizations, 28 honor societies, 20 religious organizations, 19 fraternities, 16 sororities. **Athletics (Intercollegiate):** *Men:* baseball, basketball, cross-country, equestrian sports, field hockey, golf, ice hockey, martial arts, swimming, track/field (indoor), volleyball. *Women:* basketball, cross-country, equestrian sports, golf, gymnastics, martial arts, softball, swimming, track/field (indoor), volleyball.

CAMPUS	
Type of school	Public
Environment	City

STUDENTS	
Undergrad enrollment	22,075
% male/female	42/58
% from out of state	31
% frosh live on campus	86

FINANCIAL FACTS	
Annual in-state tuition	$11,496
Annual out-of-state tuition	$30,913
Room and board	$14,438
Required fees	$1,363

GENERAL ADMISSIONS INFO	
Application fee	$50
Regular application deadline	2/15
Nonfall registration	Yes
Fall 2024 testing policy	Test Optional
Range SAT EBRW	540–650
Range SAT Math	530–640
Range ACT Composite	21–28

ACADEMICS	
Student/faculty ratio	16:1
% students returning for sophomore year	85
Most classes have 20–29 students.	

REQUESTING SERVICES FOR STUDENTS WITH LEARNING DIFFERENCES

Phone: 859-257-2754 • uky.edu/DisabilityResourceCenter • Email: drc@uky.edu

Documentation submitted to: Disability Resource Center
Separate application required for Services: Yes

Documentation required for:
LD: Psychoeducational evaluation
ADHD: Psychoeducational evaluation
ASD: Psychoeducational evaluation

Western Kentucky University

Potter Hall 117, Bowling Green, KY 42101-1020 • Admissions: 270-745-2551 • www.wku.edu

Support: SP

ACCOMMODATIONS

Allowed in exams:

Calculators	Yes
Dictionary	Yes
Computer	Yes
Spell-checker	Yes
Extended test time	Yes
Scribe	Yes
Proctors	Yes
Oral exams	Yes
Note-takers	Yes

Support services for students with:

LD	Yes
ADHD	Yes
ASD	Yes
Distraction-reduced environment	Yes
Recording of lecture allowed	Yes
Reading technology	Yes
Audio books	Yes
Other assistive technology	Yes
Priority registration	Yes

Added costs of services:

For LD	Yes
For ADHD	Yes
For ASD	Yes
LD specialists	Yes
ADHD & ASD coaching	Yes
ASD specialists	Yes
Professional tutors	Yes
Peer tutors	Yes
Max. hours/week for services	20
How professors are notified of student approved accommodations	Student and SARC

COLLEGE GRADUATION REQUIREMENTS

Course waivers allowed	Yes

In what courses: Case-by-case basis

Course substitutions allowed	Yes

In what courses: Case-by-case basis

PROGRAMS/SERVICES FOR STUDENTS WITH LEARNING DIFFERENCES

The Student Accessibility Resource Center (SARC) coordinates services and accommodations for students with documented disabilities. SARC reviews disability documentation, meets with students to determine appropriate accommodations, and partners with other stakeholders on campus to implement these accommodations. Students use an online system for managing accommodations and services. This system also shares faculty notification letters and coordinates note-taking services. Testing accommodations, such as extended time, a quiet room, and assistive technology, may be provided. Students registered for note-taking accommodations can choose to use either recording devices or notetaker applications or request a notetaker for each class period. The student is responsible for working in partnership with potential classmates, course instructors, and SARC to secure a classroom notetaker. Assistive technology accommodations may include a video relay, a video phone, a captioned phone, JAWS, Read&Write Gold, Dragon Naturally Speaking, talking calculators, Intellikeys adaptive keyboard, Orbit trackball mouse, and ZoomText screen magnifier.

ADMISSIONS

Students must have at least a 2.0 unweighted GPA for admission. Students with a 2.5 unweighted GPA or greater are not required to submit ACT or SAT scores but are encouraged to do so for academic placement. Students admitted to WKU may be placed in an appropriate academic support program based on their academic needs. Students with a 2.0–2.49 unweighted GPA must submit SAT or ACT scores and have a Composite Admission Index (CAI) score of at least 60. They will be admitted to WKU via the required the Summer Scholars Program, which is a five-week summer transition program for incoming first-year students. Students in the Summer Scholars Program move to campus early, complete six hours of college credit, and receive personalized support to help them achieve success.

Additional Information

All students at WKU are assigned at least one academic advisor to assist them in course selection and help navigate their way through college.

Since 1911, WKU has sat on a hill overlooking the city of Bowling Green. The portion of campus known as College Heights overlooks the Barren River Valley and is a beautiful and distinctive city landmark. In 1924, 16-year-old Mary Frances Bradley won a campus poetry contest, and her poem became WKU's alma mater, "College Heights." Mary's father composed the melody, "College Heights on hilltop fair, with beauty all thine own."

Western Kentucky University

GENERAL ADMISSIONS

Very important factors include: academic GPA. *Other factors considered include:* standardized test scores (if submitted). High school diploma is required and GED is accepted. Institution is test-optional for entering Fall 2024. Check admissions website for updates. *Academic units required:* 4 English, 4 math, 3 science (3 labs), 3 social studies, 6 academic electives, 1 visual/performing arts. *Academic units recommended:* 2 foreign language.

FINANCIAL AID

Students should submit: FAFSA. *Need-based scholarships/grants offered:* College/university scholarship or grant aid from institutional funds; Federal Pell; Private scholarships; SEOG; State scholarships/grants; United Negro College Fund. *Loan aid offered:* Direct PLUS loans; Direct Subsidized Loans; Direct Unsubsidized Loans. Federal Work-Study Program available. Institutional employment available.

CAMPUS LIFE

Activities: Campus Ministries; Choral groups; Concert band; Dance; Drama/theater; International Student Organization; Jazz band; Literary magazine; Marching band; Model UN; Music ensembles; Musical theater; Opera; Pep band; Radio station; Student government; Student newspaper; Student-run film society; Symphony orchestra; Television station; Yearbook. **Organizations:** 250 registered organizations, 22 honor societies, 23 religious organizations, 22 fraternities, 17 sororities. **Athletics (Intercollegiate):** *Men:* baseball, basketball, cross-country, golf, lacrosse, racquetball, rugby, softball, swimming, track/field (indoor), volleyball. *Women:* basketball, cross-country, golf, lacrosse, racquetball, rugby, softball, swimming, track/field (indoor), volleyball.

CAMPUS
Type of school	Public
Environment	Town

STUDENTS
Undergrad enrollment	12,149
% male/female	38/62
% from out of state	27
% frosh live on campus	81

FINANCIAL FACTS
Annual in-state tuition	$11,112
Annual out-of-state tuition	$27,072
Room and board	$11,072

GENERAL ADMISSIONS INFO
Application fee	$50
Regular application deadline	8/1
Nonfall registration	Yes
Fall 2024 testing policy	Test Optional
Range SAT EBRW	500–590
Range SAT Math	480–580
Range ACT Composite	18–25

ACADEMICS
Student/faculty ratio	18:1
% students returning for sophomore year	77

Most classes have 10–19 students.

REQUESTING SERVICES FOR STUDENTS WITH LEARNING DIFFERENCES

Phone: 270-745-5004 • www.wku.edu/sarc • Email: sarc.connect@wku.edu

Documentation submitted to: Student Accessibility Resource Center
Separate application required for Services: Yes

Documentation required for:
LD: Psychoeducational evaluation
ADHD: Psychoeducational evaluation
ASD: Psychoeducational evaluation

Louisiana Christian University

1140 College Drive, Pineville, LA 71359-0566 • Admissions: 318-487-7259 • lcuniversity.edu

Support: CS

ACCOMMODATIONS

Allowed in exams:

Calculators	Yes
Dictionary	Yes
Computer	Yes
Spell-checker	Yes
Extended test time	Yes
Scribe	Yes
Proctors	Yes
Oral exams	Yes
Note-takers	Yes

Support services for students with:

LD	Yes
ADHD	Yes
ASD	Yes
Distraction-reduced environment	Yes
Recording of lecture allowed	Yes
Reading technology	Yes
Audio books	Yes
Other assistive technology	Yes
Priority registration	No

Added costs of services:

For LD	No
For ADHD	No
For ASD	No
LD specialists	Yes
ADHD & ASD coaching	Yes
ASD specialists	No
Professional tutors	No
Peer tutors	Yes
Max. hours/week for services	Varies
How professors are notified of student approved accommodations	Student and Student Success Center

COLLEGE GRADUATION REQUIREMENTS

Course waivers allowed	No
Course substitutions allowed	No

PROGRAMS/SERVICES FOR STUDENTS WITH LEARNING DIFFERENCES

Louisiana Christian University provides accommodations to students with disabilities through the Student Success Center (SSC). To request accommodations, students register with the Student Success Center and submit documentation of their disability from a qualified and appropriate professional. Before receiving accommodations, students must complete an SSC orientation. Students are encouraged to contact the SSC immediately after being admitted to the university.

ADMISSIONS

All students must complete the general admissions process. Louisiana Christian University provides unconditional admission to students who have completed the required academic course units and meet one of the following criteria: score a composite of 20 or above on the ACT (1030 on the SAT) with a GPA of 2.0 in academic core subjects; OR a minimum composite of 17 on the ACT (900 on the SAT) and a GPA of 2.5 in academic core subjects; OR a minimum composite of 18 on the ACT (940 on the SAT) with a GPA of 2.3 in academic core subjects; OR a minimum composite of 19 on the ACT (980 on the SAT) with a GPA of 2.2 in academic core subjects.

Additional Information

The SSC is free and available to all students on campus; it delivers numerous services, including tutoring in core courses, academic assistance, study groups, and other academic support services. Students meet with peer tutors who have excelled in the course they tutor and who have been trained to facilitate discussion on course content. The Writing Center is located within the SSC. Trained writing assistants work one-on-one with students at all phases of the writing process, beginning with brainstorming ideas to synthesizing sources, developing arguments, and editing.

Louisiana Christian University was founded as Louisiana College, October 3, 1906, in Pineville, across the Red River from Alexandria, Louisiana. The college began in tents with four professors and nineteen students. At the beginning of the fall semester in 2021, the college welcomed 350 students at the opening day of Wildcat Welcome Weekend: the largest first-year class in the school's 115-year history.

Louisiana Christian University

GENERAL ADMISSIONS

Very important factors include: academic GPA, standardized test scores. *Other factors considered include:* rigor of secondary school record. High school diploma is required and GED is accepted. Institution requires SAT/ACT scores for entering Fall 2024. Check admissions website for updates. *Academic units required:* 4 English, 4 math, 3 science, 3 social studies.

FINANCIAL AID

Students should submit: FAFSA; Institution's own financial aid form. *Need-based scholarships/grants offered:* College/university scholarship or grant aid from institutional funds; Federal Pell; Private scholarships; SEOG; State scholarships/grants. *Loan aid offered:* Direct PLUS loans; Direct Subsidized Loans; Direct Unsubsidized Loans. Federal Work-Study Program available. Institutional employment available.

CAMPUS LIFE

Activities: Campus Ministries; Choral groups; Concert band; Drama/theater; Jazz band; Marching band; Music ensembles; Musical theater; Opera; Pep band; Radio station; Student government; Symphony orchestra. **Organizations:** 12 registered organizations, 13 honor societies, 6 religious organizations, 0 fraternities, 0 sororities. **Athletics (Intercollegiate):** *Men:* baseball, basketball, cross-country, golf, track/field (indoor). *Women:* basketball, cross-country, golf, softball, track/field (indoor), volleyball.

Louisiana

CAMPUS
Type of school	Private (nonprofit)
Environment	Town

STUDENTS
Undergrad enrollment	936
% male/female	52/48
% from out of state	12
% frosh live on campus	78

FINANCIAL FACTS
Annual tuition	$17,500
Room and board	$5,646

GENERAL ADMISSIONS INFO
Application fee	$25
Regular application deadline	Rolling
Nonfall registration	Yes

Fall 2024 testing policy	SAT or ACT Required
Range SAT EBRW	460–540
Range SAT Math	450–520
Range ACT Composite	18–23

ACADEMICS
Student/faculty ratio	10:1
% students returning for sophomore year	65

Most classes have 10–19 students.

REQUESTING SERVICES FOR STUDENTS WITH LEARNING DIFFERENCES

Phone: 318-487-7629 • lcuniversity.edu/campus-life/student-services/student-success-center
Email: jolynn.mcconley@lcuniversity.edu

Documentation submitted to: Student Success Center
Separate application required for Services: Yes

Documentation required for:
LD: Psychoeducational evaluation
ADHD: Psychoeducational evaluation
ASD: Psychoeducational evaluation

Louisiana State University

Pleasant Hall, Baton Rouge, LA 70803 • Admissions: 225-578-1175 • www.lsu.edu

Support: S

PROGRAMS/SERVICES FOR STUDENTS WITH LEARNING DIFFERENCES

Disability Services (DS) at Louisiana State University (LSU) provides services to students with disabilities. A student with an eligible disability can register with the DS office by completing documentation and meeting with a Disability Services Coordinator. Services offered through DS include priority registration, tape recorders, note-taking, and extended test times.

ADMISSIONS

All applicants are expected to meet the same admission criteria. The middle 50 percent of recently admitted first-years earned a GPA between 3.5 and 4.1, an ACT score between 23 and 29, and/or an SAT score between 1140 and 1340 from those who submitted test scores. Applicants who submit scores can expect their information to be superscored for admission and scholarship consideration.

Additional Information

The Center for Academic Success (CAS) is LSU's central learning center. CAS supports academic excellence by providing innovative services and transformational experiences that support the learning process. CAS offers tutoring through programs like CAS Shell Peer Tutoring and NetTutor, Supplemental Instruction (SI) for students enrolled in traditionally challenging courses, academic coaches who provide support with effective learning strategies, and online resources.

The official capacity of Tiger Stadium is 102,321, and at full capacity, it's the 5th largest "city" in Louisiana. Nicknamed "Death Valley," poll after poll proclaims Tiger Stadium as one of the greatest sites anywhere for a football game AND the noisiest. History says fans went berserk after a winning game over Auburn and were so thunderous they caused a tremor that registered as an earthquake on a seismograph meter in LSU's Geology Department.

Louisiana State University

General Admissions

Very important factors include: rigor of secondary school record, academic GPA, standardized test scores (if submitted), recommendations. *Other factors considered include:* class rank, application essay. High school diploma is required and GED is accepted. Institution is test-optional for entering Fall 2024. Check admissions website for updates. *Academic units required:* 4 English, 4 math, 4 science, 2 foreign language, 3 social studies, 1 history, 1 visual/performing arts.

Financial Aid

Students should submit: FAFSA. *Need-based scholarships/grants offered:* College/university scholarship or grant aid from institutional funds; Federal Pell; Private scholarships; SEOG; State scholarships/grants. *Loan aid offered:* Direct PLUS loans; Direct Subsidized Loans; Direct Unsubsidized Loans. Federal Work-Study Program available. Institutional employment available.

Campus Life

Activities: Campus Ministries; Choral groups; Concert band; Dance; Drama/theater; International Student Organization; Jazz band; Literary magazine; Marching band; Music ensembles; Musical theater; Opera; Pep band; Radio station; Student government; Student newspaper; Student-run film society; Symphony orchestra; Television station; Yearbook. **Organizations:** 476 registered organizations, 10 honor societies, 19 religious organizations, 18 fraternities, 17 sororities. **Athletics (Intercollegiate):** *Men:* baseball, basketball, bowling, crew/rowing, cross-country, equestrian sports, golf, ice hockey, lacrosse, rugby, swimming, track/field (indoor), ultimate frisbee, volleyball, water polo. *Women:* basketball, bowling, crew/rowing, cross-country, equestrian sports, golf, gymnastics, ice hockey, lacrosse, rugby, softball, swimming, track/field (indoor), ultimate frisbee, volleyball, water polo.

CAMPUS

Type of school	Public
Environment	City

STUDENTS

Undergrad enrollment	26,455
% male/female	46/54
% from out of state	25
% frosh live on campus	80

FINANCIAL FACTS

Annual in-state tuition	$8,038
Annual out-of-state tuition	$24,715
Room and board	$13,154
Required fees	$3,920

GENERAL ADMISSIONS INFO

Application fee	$50
Regular application deadline	4/15
Nonfall registration	Yes

Fall 2024 testing policy	Test Optional
Range SAT EBRW	580–660
Range SAT Math	550–660
Range ACT Composite	23–29

ACADEMICS

Student/faculty ratio	22:1
% students returning for sophomore year	83

Most classes have 10–19 students.

Louisiana

REQUESTING SERVICES FOR STUDENTS WITH LEARNING DIFFERENCES

Phone: 225-578-5919 • www.lsu.edu/disability • Email: disability@lsu.edu

Documentation submitted to: Disability Services
Separate application required for Services: Yes

Documentation required for:
LD: Psychoeducational evaluation
ADHD: Psychoeducational evaluation
ASD: Psychoeducational evaluation

Loyola University New Orleans

363 St. Charles Avenue New Orleans, LA 70118-6195 Admissions: 504-865-3240 • www.loyno.edu

Support: S

ACCOMMODATIONS

Allowed in exams:	
Calculators	Yes
Dictionary	Yes
Computer	Yes
Spell-checker	Yes
Extended test time	Yes
Scribe	Yes
Proctors	Yes
Oral exams	Yes
Note-takers	Yes
Support services for students with:	
LD	Yes
ADHD	Yes
ASD	Yes
Distraction-reduced environment	Yes
Recording of lecture allowed	Yes
Reading technology	Yes
Audio books	Yes
Other assistive technology	Yes
Priority registration	Yes
Added costs of services:	
For LD	No
For ADHD	No
For ASD	No
LD specialists	No
ADHD & ASD coaching	Yes
ASD specialists	No
Professional tutors	No
Peer tutors	Yes
Max. hours/week for services	Varies
How professors are notified of student approved accommodations	Student

COLLEGE GRADUATION REQUIREMENTS

Course waivers allowed	No
Course substitutions allowed	Yes

PROGRAMS/SERVICES FOR STUDENTS WITH LEARNING DIFFERENCES

The Office for Accessible Education (OAE) in the Student Success Center collaborates with faculty and students to provide equal access to education at Loyola. Students may request accommodations that include closed captioning, alternative formatting for texts, note-taking, preferential seating, priority registration for courses, and extended time for tests and quizzes. Glean Audio Notetaker with Transcription and Kurzweil 3000 + Firefly are available systems that support delivering services. During the registration process, an OAE representative works with each student to review their request and determine reasonable accommodations.

ADMISSIONS

All applicants are expected to meet the same admission criteria. Standardized test scores are not used for admission or merit scholarships, with the only exceptions being for the TOPS scholarship and recruited student athletes for NAIA eligibility. The average GPA for admitted applicants is 3.94. Although the university encourages students to pursue a rigorous curriculum in high school, it does not require that students take AP or IB courses to be admitted. The College of Music and Media requires an audition, interview, or portfolio.

Additional Information

Additional services within the Student Success Center include career development resources, and the Office of Writing and Learning Services (OWLS). OWLS offers free peer tutoring to all full-time undergraduate students in math, science, business, writing, foreign languages, and study skills. Academic advisors guide students in transitioning from high school to college and are full-time staff members in the Office of Academic Advising and Success Coaching.

The Maroon is the weekly student-run newspaper, printed since 1923. In October 2022, the Society of Professional Journalists named The Maroon Best All-Around Student Newspaper among small college newspapers. The Maroon is also up for the Pacemaker award from the Associated College Press. Like everyone, the newsroom and reporters were working remotely for indefinite periods of time, but they managed to stay safe and still tell the campus and community the many stories of COVID-19 exile and the Hurricane Ida evacuations.

Loyola University New Orleans

GENERAL ADMISSIONS

Very important factors include: rigor of secondary school record, academic GPA. *Important factors include:* application essay, recommendations. *Other factors considered include:* class rank. High school diploma is required and GED is accepted. Institution is test-free for entering Fall 2024. Check admissions website for updates. *Academic units recommended:* 4 English, 3 math, 3 science (1 lab), 2 foreign language, 2 social studies, 2 history.

FINANCIAL AID

Students should submit: FAFSA. *Need-based scholarships/grants offered:* College/university scholarship or grant aid from institutional funds; Federal Pell; Private scholarships; SEOG; State scholarships/grants; United Negro College Fund. *Loan aid offered:* Direct PLUS loans; Direct Subsidized Loans; Direct Unsubsidized Loans. Federal Work-Study Program available. Institutional employment available.

CAMPUS LIFE

Activities: Campus Ministries; Choral groups; Concert band; Dance; Drama/theater; International Student Organization; Jazz band; Literary magazine; Music ensembles; Musical theater; Opera; Pep band; Student government; Student newspaper; Student-run film society; Symphony orchestra. **Organizations:** 115 registered organizations, 13 honor societies, 7 religious organizations, 4 fraternities, 8 sororities. **Athletics (Intercollegiate):** *Men:* baseball, basketball, cross-country, golf, martial arts, rugby, swimming, track/field (indoor), water polo. *Women:* basketball, cross-country, golf, martial arts, rugby, swimming, track/field (indoor), volleyball, water polo.

CAMPUS

Type of school	Private (nonprofit)
Environment	Metropolis

STUDENTS

Undergrad enrollment	3,231
% male/female	34/66
% from out of state	54
% frosh live on campus	81

FINANCIAL FACTS

Annual tuition	$43,160
Room and board	$13,930
Required fees	$1,870

GENERAL ADMISSIONS INFO

Application fee	No fee
Regular application deadline	Rolling
Nonfall registration	Yes
Fall 2024 testing policy	Test Free

ACADEMICS

Student/faculty ratio	14:1
% students returning for sophomore year	76

Most classes have 10–19 students.

Louisiana

REQUESTING SERVICES FOR STUDENTS WITH LEARNING DIFFERENCES

Phone: 504-865-2990 • success.loyno.edu/accessible-education • Email: oae@loyno.edu

Documentation submitted to: Student Success Center - Accessible Education
Separate application required for Services: Yes

Documentation required for:
LD: Psychoeducational evaluation
ADHD: Psychoeducational evaluation
ASD: Psychoeducational evaluation

Nicholls State University

P.O. Box 2004, Thibodaux, LA 70301 • Admissions: 985-448-4507 • www.nicholls.edu

Support: CS

ACCOMMODATIONS

Allowed in exams:

Calculators	Yes
Dictionary	Yes
Computer	Yes
Spell-checker	Yes
Extended test time	Yes
Scribe	Yes
Proctors	Yes
Oral exams	Yes
Note-takers	Yes

Support services for students with:

LD	Yes
ADHD	Yes
ASD	Yes
Distraction-reduced environment	Yes
Recording of lecture allowed	Yes
Reading technology	Yes
Audio books	Yes
Other assistive technology	Yes
Priority registration	Yes

Added costs of services:

For LD	No
For ADHD	No
For ASD	No
LD specialists	No
ADHD & ASD coaching	No
ASD specialists	Yes
Professional tutors	No
Peer tutors	No
Max. hours/week for services	Varies
How professors are notified of student approved accommodations	Student

COLLEGE GRADUATION REQUIREMENTS

Course waivers allowed	No
Course substitutions allowed	No

PROGRAMS/SERVICES FOR STUDENTS WITH LEARNING DIFFERENCES:

The Student Access Center/Disability Services provides reasonable accommodations to students with disabilities. Students are encouraged to complete the registration form and provide documentation of their disability as soon as possible. The Student Access Center (SAC) director will contact the student to schedule an intake meeting to allow the student to present their limitations, discuss past accommodations, and request reasonable accommodations to ensure equal access to all NSU programs and activities. The director will do a final review and notify the student via email with a decision and letter of accommodation (LOA). Students have the responsibility to deliver the LOA to their instructors. NSU offers the Bridge to Independence–Degree program, a traditional degree program designed to help students with autism spectrum disorder (ASD) successfully transition to college life. Once accepted to NSU through the regular admission process, students with ASD are eligible to enroll in the Bridge Degree program. Students attend weekly social skills seminars, receive monitoring of their academic, behavior, and social performance, and are provided academic coaches, peer mentors, counseling, and tutoring. NSU also offers the Bridge to Independence–Certificate program, a two-year program designed to help students with intellectual disabilities become gainfully employed through college courses and job training. Students have a program of study based on their career goals and strengths, and peer mentors attend classes with the students and help with modified class assignments. Students receive job training through internships, attend weekly social skill seminars, participate in campus activities and organizations, and receive a Nicholls State University Certificate of Achievement upon completing the program.

ADMISSIONS

All applicants are expected to meet the same general admission criteria. Louisiana high school graduates and out-of-state high school graduates have a different set of core requirements. Students are encouraged to apply even if they do not meet all requirements. These applications will be reviewed, and an admission decision will be made that considers each applicant's potential for success.

Additional Information

The Tutorial and Academic Enhancement Center (TAEC) offers peer tutoring and coaching to students, and the Tutoring Center and the Writing Center are part of TAEC. The Tutoring Center offers one-on-one sessions, and the tutors set session goals with students, provide study skills methods, and assist with homework assignments. The Writing Center offers one-on-one sessions in any writing area. Tutors brainstorm with students on how to approach subjects, clarify assignments, and explain writing and revision techniques and grammar rules.

Beginning in 1948, and continuing for almost 40 years, parishes provided free transportation to Nicholls State college students from distant bayou villages. The school bus served as a mobile student union to reinforce skills in English and math during rides of two hours or more each way—bringing a whole new meaning to the term "distance education."

Nicholls State University

GENERAL ADMISSIONS

Very important factors include: rigor of secondary school record. *Important factors include:* standardized test scores (if submitted). *Other factors considered include:* class rank, academic GPA. High school diploma is required and GED is accepted. Institution is test-optional for entering Fall 2024. Check admissions website for updates. *Academic units recommended:* 4 English, 4 math, 4 science, 2 foreign language, 4 social studies, 1 academic elective.

FINANCIAL AID

Students should submit: FAFSA; Institution's own financial aid form; Noncustodial Profile; State aid form. *Need-based scholarships/grants offered:* College/university scholarship or grant aid from institutional funds; Federal Pell; Private scholarships; SEOG; State scholarships/grants. *Loan aid offered:*. Federal Work-Study Program available. Institutional employment available.

CAMPUS LIFE

Activities: Choral groups; Concert band; Dance; Drama/theater; Jazz band; Literary magazine; Marching band; Music ensembles; Musical theater; Radio station; Student government; Student newspaper; Student-run film society; Television station; Yearbook. **Organizations:** 121 registered organizations, 24 honor societies, 6 religious organizations, 10 fraternities, 5 sororities. **Athletics (Intercollegiate):** *Men:* baseball, basketball, cross-country, golf, softball, volleyball. *Women:* basketball, cross-country, golf, softball, track/field (indoor), volleyball.

Louisiana

CAMPUS
Type of school	Public
Environment	Village

STUDENTS
Undergrad enrollment	5,567
% male/female	36/64
% from out of state	2
% frosh live on campus	46

FINANCIAL FACTS
Annual in-state tuition	$8,156
Annual out-of-state tuition	$9,249
Room and board	$10,602

GENERAL ADMISSIONS INFO
Application fee	$20
Regular application deadline	Rolling
Nonfall registration	Yes
Fall 2024 testing policy	Test Optional
Range SAT EBRW	520–605
Range SAT Math	518–623
Range ACT Composite	20–25

ACADEMICS
Student/faculty ratio	16:1
% students returning for sophomore year	70
Most classes have 20–29 students.	

REQUESTING SERVICES FOR STUDENTS WITH LEARNING DIFFERENCES

Phone: 985-448-4430 • www.nicholls.edu/student-access-center/ • Email: studentaccess@nicholls.edu

Documentation submitted to: Student Access Center - Disability Services
Separate application required for Services: Yes

Documentation required for:
LD: Psychoeducational evaluation
ADHD: Psychoeducational evaluation
ASD: Psychoeducational evaluation

Tulane University

6823 St. Charles Avenue, New Orleans, LA 70118 • Admissions: 504-865-5731 • www.tulane.edu

Support: CS

PROGRAMS/SERVICES FOR STUDENTS WITH LEARNING DIFFERENCES

Tulane University's Goldman Center for Student Accessibility provides services for students with learning disabilities. To begin the process of obtaining accommodations, students need to complete an online registration form and submit disability documentation; formal documentation is required. If a student does not have the appropriate documentation, they should still schedule a welcome meeting with Goldman Center staff to discuss the situation and the possibility of provisional accommodations. Reasonable accommodations are determined after the welcome meeting, and students will be provided information on how to activate and use their accommodations. Students who are registered with the Goldman Center can attend the optional fall new student orientation for academic accommodations. The orientation has information on using accommodations, and there are sessions with a guest speaker, a student panel, a parent session, and the "Extended Time Testing 101" overview.

ADMISSIONS

All full-time applicants are expected to have taken a rigorous high school curriculum, and official high school transcripts are required. A personal essay and a letter of recommendation should also be submitted with the application. Admitted Tulane applicants typically have a GPA of 3.56 or higher. AP or IB classes boost a weighted GPA and show the student's ability to take challenging classes.

Additional Information

Newcomb-Tulane College's (NTC) Student Success team supports students personally and academically. Student Success offers peer tutoring in math and science, accounting and business, and languages and art. Courses available for tutoring may vary each semester. The Writing Center's peer tutors can help students improve their writing skills in most courses. The Math Center provides assistance to students enrolled in difficult calculus and statistics courses. The Success Center also offers resources such as the Learning Canvas Toolkit, a series of self-guided online modules on skill building and conducts workshops and programs throughout the semester. First-Year Seminars (FYS) are a requirement for all incoming students during the first semester. These seminars bring small groups of students and faculty together to explore academics and the city of New Orleans from an interdisciplinary perspective. FYS focus is on learning by interaction and is driven by intellectual curiosity. Students also have the option to apply to live in one of seven different Residential Learning Communities (RLC). All RLCs are theme-based and offer increased interaction with staff and faculty with added out-of-classroom experiences.

Tulane's history dates back to 1834. Hurricane Katrina was the second time in history Tulane closed (four months); the first was the American Civil War (four years). Students scattered to schools around the country as provisional students for fall, but 90 percent returned for the spring semester and graduated on schedule. Former presidents George H.W. Bush and Bill Clinton were keynote speakers at their 2006 commencement.

Tulane University

General Admissions

Very important factors include: rigor of secondary school record, class rank, academic GPA, standardized test scores (if submitted). *Important factors include:* application essay, recommendations. High school diploma is required and GED is not accepted. Institution is test-optional for entering Fall 2024. Check admissions website for updates. *Academic units recommended:* 4 English, 4 math, 4 science (4 labs), 4 foreign language, 4 social studies.

Financial Aid

Students should submit: Business/Farm Supplement; CSS/Financial Aid Profile; FAFSA; Noncustodial Profile. *Need-based scholarships/grants offered:* College/university scholarship or grant aid from institutional funds; Federal Pell; Private scholarships; SEOG; State scholarships/grants. *Loan aid offered:* Direct PLUS loans; Direct Subsidized Loans; Direct Unsubsidized Loans. Federal Work-Study Program available. Institutional employment available.

Campus Life

Activities: Campus Ministries; Choral groups; Concert band; Dance; Drama/theater; International Student Organization; Jazz band; Literary magazine; Marching band; Model UN; Music ensembles; Musical theater; Pep band; Radio station; Student government; Student newspaper; Student-run film society; Symphony orchestra; Television station; Yearbook. **Organizations:** 250 registered organizations, 48 honor societies, 9 religious organizations, 9 fraternities, 14 sororities. **Athletics (Intercollegiate):** *Men:* baseball, basketball, crew/rowing, cross-country, cycling, equestrian sports, field hockey, golf, gymnastics, ice hockey, lacrosse, martial arts, racquetball, rugby, softball, swimming, ultimate frisbee, volleyball, water polo. *Women:* basketball, crew/rowing, cross-country, cycling, equestrian sports, field hockey, golf, gymnastics, lacrosse, martial arts, racquetball, rugby, softball, swimming, track/field (indoor), ultimate frisbee, volleyball, water polo.

CAMPUS

Type of school	Private (nonprofit)
Environment	Metropolis

STUDENTS

Undergrad enrollment	7,350
% male/female	39/61
% from out of state	90
% frosh live on campus	99

FINANCIAL FACTS

Annual tuition	$58,666
Room and board	$17,346
Required fees	$4,178

GENERAL ADMISSIONS INFO

Application fee	No fee
Regular application deadline	1/15
Nonfall registration	Yes

Fall 2024 testing policy	Test Optional
Range SAT EBRW	680–750
Range SAT Math	690–760
Range ACT Composite	31–33

ACADEMICS

Student/faculty ratio	8:1
% students returning for sophomore year	93

Most classes have 10–19 students.

REQUESTING SERVICES FOR STUDENTS WITH LEARNING DIFFERENCES

Phone: 504-862-8433 • accessibility.tulane.edu/ • Email: goldman@tulane.edu

Documentation submitted to: Goldman Center for Student Accessibility
Separate application required for Services: Yes

Documentation required for:
LD: Psychoeducational evaluation
ADHD: Psychoeducational evaluation
ASD: Psychoeducational evaluation

University of New Orleans

Privateer Enrollment Center, New Orleans, LA 70148 • Admissions: 504-280-6595 • www.uno.edu

Support: S

ACCOMMODATIONS

Allowed in exams:

Calculators	Yes
Dictionary	Yes
Computer	Yes
Spell-checker	Yes
Extended test time	Yes
Scribe	Yes
Proctors	Yes
Oral exams	Yes
Note-takers	Yes

Support services for students with:

LD	Yes
ADHD	Yes
ASD	Yes
Distraction-reduced environment	Yes
Recording of lecture allowed	Yes
Reading technology	Yes
Audio books	No
Other assistive technology	Yes
Priority registration	No

Added costs of services:

For LD	No
For ADHD	No
For ASD	No
LD specialists	No
ADHD & ASD coaching	No
ASD specialists	No
Professional tutors	No
Peer tutors	Yes
Max. hours/week for services	Varies
How professors are notified of student approved accommodations	Student

COLLEGE GRADUATION REQUIREMENTS

Course waivers allowed	No
Course substitutions allowed	No

PROGRAMS/SERVICES FOR STUDENTS WITH LEARNING DIFFERENCES

The Office of Disability Services (ODS) at the University of New Orleans coordinates all services and programs. In addition to serving its primary function as a liaison between the student and the university, the office provides some direct services to students. The services may include testing accommodations, note-taking assistance, attendance modification, and assistive technology. ODS works closely with The Learning Resource Center for access to tutoring and the Writing Center. Services begin when a student registered with the university contacts the ODS office, provides documentation of the disability, and requests assistance.

ADMISSIONS

All students submit the general application form and are expected to meet the admission standards. There are different requirements for in-state and out-of-state applicants. Check the website for the most updated requirements. The university may choose to admit students who do not meet all requirements.

Additional Information

Privateer Pathways is designed for students who need additional support in mathematics and/or English through tutoring, group study sessions, and support classes. Each student will be individually evaluated for program eligibility based on high school transcripts and Accuplacer exam or test scores. Participants will receive academic advising on courses required as part of the Pathways program. Bi-weekly Success Coaching is also available to first-year students.

The U.S. Navy closed its air station on the shore of Lake Pontchartrain in 1957. With renovation to existing buildings, the UNO campus opened to students in September 1958 ahead of schedule and was the first racially integrated public university in the South. Completed in 1960, the Liberal Arts Building and the Science Building are both numbered and laid out like a ship. Liberal Arts has exterior balconies for access to classrooms rather than interior hallways. Both buildings feature central courtyards.

University of New Orleans

GENERAL ADMISSIONS

Very important factors include: academic GPA, standardized test scores (if submitted). High school diploma is required and GED is accepted. Institution is test-optional for entering Fall 2024. Check admissions website for updates. *Academic units required:* 4 English, 4 math, 4 science, 2 foreign language, 4 social studies, 1 visual/performing arts.

FINANCIAL AID

Students should submit: FAFSA; Institution's own financial aid form. *Need-based scholarships/grants offered:* College/university scholarship or grant aid from institutional funds; Federal Pell; Private scholarships; SEOG; State scholarships/grants; United Negro College Fund. *Loan aid offered:* Direct PLUS loans; Direct Subsidized Loans; Direct Unsubsidized Loans. Federal Work-Study Program available. Institutional employment available.

CAMPUS LIFE

Activities: Campus Ministries; Choral groups; Concert band; Dance; Drama/theater; International Student Organization; Jazz band; Literary magazine; Model UN; Music ensembles; Musical theater; Pep band; Radio station; Student government; Student newspaper; Student-run film society. **Organizations:** 101 registered organizations, 9 honor societies, 5 religious organizations, 8 fraternities, 7 sororities. **Athletics (Intercollegiate):** *Men:* baseball, basketball, cross-country, cycling, golf, martial arts, rugby, swimming, table tennis, track/field (indoor). *Women:* basketball, cross-country, cycling, martial arts, swimming, table tennis, track/field (indoor), volleyball.

CAMPUS	
Type of school	Public
Environment	Metropolis

STUDENTS	
Undergrad enrollment	6,508
% male/female	48/52
% from out of state	7

FINANCIAL FACTS	
Annual in-state tuition	$9,172
Annual out-of-state tuition	$14,008
Room and board	$12,174

GENERAL ADMISSIONS INFO	
Application fee	$25
Regular application deadline	7/15
Nonfall registration	Yes

Fall 2024 testing policy	Test Optional
Range SAT EBRW	520–640
Range SAT Math	490–640
Range ACT Composite	18–24

ACADEMICS	
Student/faculty ratio	19:1
% students returning for sophomore year	58
Most classes have 10–19 students.	

Louisiana

REQUESTING SERVICES FOR STUDENTS WITH LEARNING DIFFERENCES

Phone: 504-280-7284 • www.uno.edu/disability-services/ • Email: aaking@uno.edu

Documentation submitted to: Office of Disability Services
Separate application required for Services: Yes

Documentation required for:
 LD: Psychoeducational evaluation
 ADHD: Psychoeducational evaluation
 ASD: Psychoeducational evaluation

University of Maine

5713 Chadbourne Hall, Orono, ME 04469-5713 • Admissions: 207-581-1561 • www.umaine.edu

(Support: S)

ACCOMMODATIONS

Allowed in exams:

Calculators	Yes
Dictionary	No
Computer	Yes
Spell-checker	Yes
Extended test time	Yes
Scribe	Yes
Proctors	Yes
Oral exams	Yes
Note-takers	Yes

Support services for students with:

LD	Yes
ADHD	No
ASD	Yes
Distraction-reduced environment	Yes
Recording of lecture allowed	Yes
Reading technology	Yes
Audio books	Yes
Other assistive technology	Yes
Priority registration	No

Added costs of services:

For LD	No
For ADHD	No
For ASD	No
LD specialists	No
ADHD & ASD coaching	No
ASD specialists	No
Professional tutors	No
Peer tutors	Yes
Max. hours/week for services	Varies
How professors are notified of student approved accommodations	Student

COLLEGE GRADUATION REQUIREMENTS

Course waivers allowed	No
Course substitutions allowed	Yes
In what courses: Case-by-case basis	

PROGRAMS/SERVICES FOR STUDENTS WITH LEARNING DIFFERENCES

The University of Maine Student Accessibility Services (SAS) provides support to students with disabilities. Students seeking accommodations should submit documentation that identifies the disability, provides a specific diagnosis, and describes the likely impact of the learning disability on the individual's participation in the learning process, as well as other campus programs and activities. Copies of IEPs and Section 504 Plans may be useful, but additional documentation, such as a neuropsychological or psychoeducational assessment and report, is often needed. Services that SAS provides include testing accommodations, ordering alternate-format texts, notetakers, and access to Glean, a note-taking and recording app. The staff of SAS promotes self-determination and personal responsibility by educating and advising students to make informed choices and meet or exceed the standards expected of all students. SAS coordinates with several other departments to provide support for additional services. Tutoring is provided to students through The Tutor Program as well as TRIO Student Support Services. TRIO SSS is a federally funded program open to students with disabilities and can provide an array of support including individual tutoring, personal counseling, peer coaching, and more.

ADMISSIONS

Admission criteria are the same for all applicants. Most programs require a minimum of a 2.0 GPA. Some programs such as nursing requires a 3.5 GPA, and some programs within education, science, and engineering require a 2.3–2.5 GPA. In addition to the core academic requirements, computer science and fine arts courses are strongly recommended. Some programs require specific science courses.

Additional Information

Tutoring is provided to all students through The Tutor Program. Students may also receive assistance in writing and math through The Writing Center and The Math Lab.

The "King of Horror" author Stephen King graduated from UMaine in 1970 with a B.A. in English. The main character in his novel, *Pet Sematary*, is a fictional head doctor at UMaine Cutler Health Center. In October 2016, UMaine created the Stephen E. King Chair in Literature in honor of his substantial body of work and creative impact.

University of Maine

General Admissions

Very important factors include: rigor of secondary school record, class rank, academic GPA, application essay, recommendations. *Other factors considered include:* standardized test scores (if submitted). High school diploma is required and GED is accepted. Institution is test-optional for entering Fall 2024. Check admissions website for updates. *Academic units required:* 4 English, 3 math, 2 science (2 labs), 2 social studies, 4 academic electives. *Academic units recommended:* 4 math, 4 science (3 labs), 2 foreign language, 3 social studies.

Financial Aid

Students should submit: FAFSA. *Need-based scholarships/grants offered:* College/university scholarship or grant aid from institutional funds; Federal Pell; Private scholarships; SEOG; State scholarships/grants. *Loan aid offered:* Direct PLUS loans; Direct Subsidized Loans; Direct Unsubsidized Loans. Federal Work-Study Program available. Institutional employment available.

Campus Life

Activities: Campus Ministries; Choral groups; Concert band; Dance; Drama/theater; International Student Organization; Jazz band; Literary magazine; Marching band; Model UN; Music ensembles; Musical theater; Opera; Pep band; Radio station; Student government; Student newspaper; Student-run film society; Symphony orchestra. **Organizations:** 205 registered organizations, 12 honor societies, 8 religious organizations, 16 fraternities, 8 sororities. **Athletics (Intercollegiate):** *Men:* baseball, basketball, crew/rowing, cross-country, equestrian sports, field hockey, ice hockey, lacrosse, martial arts, rugby, swimming, table tennis, track/field (indoor), ultimate frisbee, volleyball, wrestling. *Women:* basketball, crew/rowing, cross-country, equestrian sports, field hockey, ice hockey, lacrosse, martial arts, rugby, softball, swimming, table tennis, track/field (indoor), ultimate frisbee, volleyball, wrestling.

CAMPUS
Type of school	Public
Environment	Village

STUDENTS
Undergrad enrollment	8,374
% male/female	53/47
% from out of state	38
% frosh live on campus	90

FINANCIAL FACTS
Annual in-state tuition	$11,640
Annual out-of-state tuition	$33,240
Room and board	$12,050
Required fees	$496

GENERAL ADMISSIONS INFO
Application fee	No fee
Regular application deadline	Rolling
Nonfall registration	Yes
Fall 2024 testing policy	Test Optional
Range SAT EBRW	550–670
Range SAT Math	530–670
Range ACT Composite	24–30

ACADEMICS
Student/faculty ratio	15:1
% students returning for sophomore year	75

Most classes have 10–19 students.

Maine

REQUESTING SERVICES FOR STUDENTS WITH LEARNING DIFFERENCES

Phone: 207-581-2319 • umaine.edu/studentaccessibility • Email: um.sas@maine.edu

Documentation submitted to: Student Accessibility Services
Separate application required for Services: Yes

Documentation required for:
LD: Psychoeducational evaluation
ADHD: Psychoeducational evaluation
ASD: Psychoeducational evaluation

University of New England

11 Hills Beach Road, Biddeford, ME 04005-9599 • Admissions: 207-602-2847 • www.une.edu

Support: CS

ACCOMMODATIONS

Allowed in exams:	
Calculators	Yes
Dictionary	Yes
Computer	Yes
Spell-checker	Yes
Extended test time	Yes
Scribe	Yes
Proctors	Yes
Oral exams	No
Note-takers	Yes
Support services for students with:	
LD	Yes
ADHD	Yes
ASD	Yes
Distraction-reduced environment	Yes
Recording of lecture allowed	Yes
Reading technology	Yes
Audio books	Yes
Other assistive technology	Yes
Priority registration	Yes
Added costs of services:	
For LD	No
For ADHD	No
For ASD	No
LD specialists	No
ADHD & ASD coaching	No
ASD specialists	No
Professional tutors	Yes
Peer tutors	Yes
Max. hours/week for services	Varies
How professors are notified of student approved accommodations	Student

COLLEGE GRADUATION REQUIREMENTS

Course waivers allowed	No
Course substitutions allowed	No

PROGRAMS/SERVICES FOR STUDENTS WITH LEARNING DIFFERENCES

The University of New England supports students with learning differences through the Student Access Center (SAC). Primary services include providing testing accommodations and materials in alternative formats. SAC works closely with other departments to provide additional services such as tutoring and writing services. Students requesting accommodations for learning differences must submit current supporting documentation, complete an application, and, if accepted, attend an interview/welcome meeting. Students have access to assistive technology, including smart pens for note-taking assistance.

ADMISSIONS

All applicants are expected to meet the same admission criteria. UNE offers GradVantage, an academic designation that can be added to the undergraduate major to streamline the process of applying to and enrolling in participating UNE graduate programs. A UNE undergraduate student has a higher likelihood of being invited to interview and gaining acceptance to some of UNE's most competitive graduate programs. Qualified applicants declare their intent to pursue a graduate or professional degree by selecting an intended GradVantage designation on the Common Application or UNE's application.

Additional Information

The Student Academic Success Center (SASC) provides a comprehensive array of academic support services, including placement testing, courses, workshops, and tutoring. In SASC, professional staff members help students develop and maintain the skills they need to meet the challenges of undergraduate and graduate study through individual consultations, workshops, and classroom presentations. The SASC Learning Specialists work with students to assess progress and effectiveness of implemented strategies. SASC provides a staff of peer, graduate, and professional tutors to support a wide selection of undergraduate courses.

DID YOU KNOW?

"Do it in the Dark" is an annual residence hall energy competition. Students compete for the greatest amount of electricity reduction by turning off lights, unplugging appliances not in use, studying in common areas, and playing board games instead of video games. The UNE Facebook and Instagram pages have energy-saving tips and progress updates. The winning residence hall wins bragging rights and "Do it in the Dark" flashlights.

University of New England

General Admissions

Very important factors include: rigor of secondary school record, academic GPA. *Important factors include:* application essay. *Other factors considered include:* class rank, recommendations. High school diploma is required and GED is accepted. Institution is test-free for entering Fall 2024. Check admissions website for updates. *Academic units recommended:* 4 English, 3 math, 2 science (2 labs), 2 social studies.

Financial Aid

Students should submit: FAFSA. *Need-based scholarships/grants offered:* College/university scholarship or grant aid from institutional funds; Federal Pell; Private scholarships; SEOG; State scholarships/grants. *Loan aid offered:* Direct PLUS loans; Direct Subsidized Loans; Direct Unsubsidized Loans. Federal Work-Study Program available. Institutional employment available.

Campus Life

Activities: Campus Ministries; Choral groups; Dance; Drama/theater; International Student Organization; Literary magazine; Music ensembles; Musical theater; Student government; Student newspaper. **Organizations:** 80 registered organizations, 0 fraternities, 0 sororities. **Athletics (Intercollegiate):** *Men:* baseball, basketball, crew/rowing, cross-country, equestrian sports, field hockey, golf, gymnastics, ice hockey, lacrosse, rugby, softball, swimming, ultimate frisbee, volleyball. *Women:* baseball, basketball, crew/rowing, cross-country, equestrian sports, field hockey, gymnastics, ice hockey, lacrosse, rugby, softball, swimming, ultimate frisbee, volleyball.

CAMPUS

Type of school	Private (nonprofit)
Environment	Town

STUDENTS

Undergrad enrollment	2,272
% male/female	32/68
% from out of state	76
% frosh live on campus	97

FINANCIAL FACTS

Annual tuition	$39,510
Room and board	$16,100
Required fees	$1,440

GENERAL ADMISSIONS INFO

Application fee	$40
Regular application deadline	2/15
Nonfall registration	Yes
Fall 2024 testing policy	Test Free

ACADEMICS

Student/faculty ratio	12:1
% students returning for sophomore year	70

Most classes have 10–19 students.

Maine

REQUESTING SERVICES FOR STUDENTS WITH LEARNING DIFFERENCES

Phone: 207-602-2119 • une.edu/student-affairs/student-access-center • Email: bcstudentaccess@une.edu

Documentation submitted to: Student Access Center
Separate application required for Services: Yes

Documentation required for:
LD: Psychoeducational evaluation
ADHD: Psychoeducational evaluation
ASD: Psychoeducational evaluation

Frostburg State University

FSU, 101 Braddock Road, Frostburg, MD 21532 • Admissions: 301-687-4201 • www.frostburg.edu

Support: S

ACCOMMODATIONS

Allowed in exams:

Calculators	Yes
Dictionary	Yes
Computer	Yes
Spell-checker	Yes
Extended test time	Yes
Scribe	Yes
Proctors	Yes
Oral exams	Yes
Note-takers	Yes

Support services for students with:

LD	Yes
ADHD	Yes
ASD	Yes
Distraction-reduced environment	Yes
Recording of lecture allowed	Yes
Reading technology	Yes
Audio books	Yes
Other assistive technology	Yes
Priority registration	Yes

Added costs of services:

For LD	No
For ADHD	No
For ASD	No
LD specialists	No
ADHD & ASD coaching	Yes
ASD specialists	No
Professional tutors	Yes
Peer tutors	Yes
Max. hours/week for services	Varies
How professors are notified of student approved accommodations	Student

COLLEGE GRADUATION REQUIREMENTS

Course waivers allowed	No
Course substitutions allowed	Yes
In what courses: Case-by-case basis	

PROGRAMS/SERVICES FOR STUDENTS WITH LEARNING DIFFERENCES

The Student Accessibility Services Office (SASO) at Frostburg State University provides accommodations for students with disabilities, serves as a campus resource, and performs outreach within the FSU community. To receive services and accommodations, students must complete the disability accommodations form and submit documentation of their disability. Once SASO has reviewed the documentation and approves it, the director will contact the student to meet virtually or in person to review accommodation requests. Students must contact SASO at the beginning of each semester to request accommodations. Services provided may include extended time for testing, notetakers, advocacy, electronic texts, priority registration, readers, scribes, and assistive technology.

ADMISSIONS

Admission requirements are the same for all applicants. Admission to FSU is determined by a thorough assessment of the applicant's likelihood of success in a regular college program with support service assistance. The essay submission and recommendations are optional.

Additional Information

FSU Programs Advancing Student Success (PASS) works with students to strengthen skills in time management, studying, and test taking. PASS offers preparatory courses in pre-algebra and algebra, provides peer tutors to help with note-taking, and assists students on probation. Students on academic probation can work with the Center for Academic Advising and Retention (CAAR) to develop an academic recovery plan. The Academic Success Network includes CAAR, PASS, the Tutoring Center, and Student Success.

The Cultural Events Series (CES) programmers have a knack for finding and booking talent before they become superstars. It began in 1956, when a fledgling dance troupe arrived at FSU in a borrowed station wagon for their first-ever performance. That troupe—The Joffrey Ballet—returned to perform in 1994 at the new Performing Arts Center. Linda Ronstadt, Maroon 5, Megan Thee Stallion, and Sara Bareilles are a few of the CES's biggest acts to perform on campus before they became household names.

Frostburg State University

GENERAL ADMISSIONS

Very important factors include: rigor of secondary school record, academic GPA, standardized test scores (if submitted). *Important factors include:* recommendations. High school diploma is required and GED is accepted. Institution is test-optional for entering Fall 2024. Check admissions website for updates. *Academic units required:* 4 English, 4 math, 3 science (2 labs), 2 foreign language, 3 social studies.

FINANCIAL AID

Students should submit: FAFSA. *Need-based scholarships/grants offered:* College/university scholarship or grant aid from institutional funds; Federal Pell; Private scholarships; SEOG; State scholarships/grants. *Loan aid offered:* Direct PLUS loans; Direct Subsidized Loans; Direct Unsubsidized Loans. Federal Work-Study Program available. Institutional employment available.

CAMPUS LIFE

Activities: Campus Ministries; Choral groups; Dance; Drama/theater; International Student Organization; Jazz band; Literary magazine; Marching band; Model UN; Music ensembles; Pep band; Radio station; Student government; Student newspaper; Television station; Yearbook. **Organizations:** 95 registered organizations, 18 honor societies, 6 religious organizations, 9 fraternities, 6 sororities. **Athletics (Intercollegiate):** *Men:* baseball, basketball, cross-country, lacrosse, rugby, swimming, track/field (indoor), wrestling. *Women:* basketball, cross-country, field hockey, lacrosse, rugby, softball, swimming, track/field (indoor), volleyball.

CAMPUS

Type of school	Public
Environment	Village

STUDENTS

Undergrad enrollment	3,680
% male/female	46/54
% from out of state	15
% frosh live on campus	72

FINANCIAL FACTS

Annual in-state tuition	$6,834
Annual out-of-state tuition	$21,320
Room and board	$11,648
Required fees	$2,760

GENERAL ADMISSIONS INFO

Application fee	$45
Regular application deadline	Rolling
Nonfall registration	Yes

Fall 2024 testing policy	Test Optional
Range SAT EBRW	500–610
Range SAT Math	480–590
Range ACT Composite	17–25

ACADEMICS

Student/faculty ratio	13:1
% students returning for sophomore year	70

Most classes have 10–19 students.

Maryland

REQUESTING SERVICES FOR STUDENTS WITH LEARNING DIFFERENCES

Phone: 301-687-3064 • www.frostburg.edu/academics/academic-success-network/student-accessibility-services-home/ • Email: disability@frostburg.edu

Documentation submitted to: Student Accessibility Services Office
Separate application required for Services: Yes

Documentation required for:
LD: Psychoeducational evaluation
ADHD: Psychoeducational evaluation
ASD: Psychoeducational evaluation

Hood College

401 Rosemont Avenue, Frederick, MD 21701 • Admissions: 301-696-3400 • www.hood.edu

Support: S

ACCOMMODATIONS

Allowed in exams:

Calculators	Yes
Dictionary	Yes
Computer	Yes
Spell-checker	Yes
Extended test time	Yes
Scribe	Yes
Proctors	Yes
Oral exams	Yes
Note-takers	Yes

Support services for students with:

LD	Yes
ADHD	Yes
ASD	Yes
Distraction-reduced environment	Yes
Recording of lecture allowed	Yes
Reading technology	Yes
Audio books	Yes
Other assistive technology	Yes
Priority registration	No

Added costs of services:

For LD	No
For ADHD	No
For ASD	No
LD specialists	No
ADHD & ASD coaching	No
ASD specialists	No
Professional tutors	Yes
Peer tutors	Yes
Max. hours/week for services	Varies
How professors are notified of student approved accommodations	Student and Office of Accessibility Services

COLLEGE GRADUATION REQUIREMENTS

Course waivers allowed	No
Course substitutions allowed	Yes

In what courses: Foreign Language

PROGRAMS/SERVICES FOR STUDENTS WITH LEARNING DIFFERENCES

The Office of Accessibility Services (OAS) provides accommodations, consultations, information, and advocacy support for qualified students with disabilities. OAS works with the Testing Center to administer accommodated tests to students with approved accommodation plans. Prospective students are encouraged only to submit necessary documentation once they have enrolled in the university.

ADMISSIONS

General admission criteria include a minimum 2.75 GPA in core academic courses; substitutions for foreign language may be permitted when deemed appropriate. The average GPA of admitted students is 3.5. Admissions approaches its review of applications with a detailed look at each individual. In addition to the application, essay, transcript, and letter of recommendation, Hood strongly encourages students to submit a résumé, additional writing sample, online portfolio, letters of recommendation, and to schedule an interview.

Additional Information

Undergraduate peer tutoring at the Tutoring Center is free and available to all students in many subject areas. Students may also access 10 hours of professional online tutoring. The Writing Center staff helps students with course papers as well as nonacademic papers, such as scholarship applications. Peer tutors can help students improve their punctuation, grammar, organization, sentence structure, and spelling. The Math Center is available for students seeking extra help in math classes.

The wife of first Hood President John Apple, Gertrude Apple, spearheaded fundraising to beautify campus grounds, and in 1939 she documented over 500 trees with 48 varieties planted on campus. Past and present members of the community continue her legacy. Select trees are on the Maryland State Big Tree List; three are Frederick County Champions, and one Big Leaf Magnolia is a State Champion. The Hood College Tree Walk currently has 14 unique, large trees highlighted with name tags and QR codes.

Hood College

GENERAL ADMISSIONS

Very important factors include: rigor of secondary school record, academic GPA. *Important factors include:* application essay. *Other factors considered include:* class rank, standardized test scores (if submitted), recommendations. High school diploma is required and GED is accepted. Institution is test-optional for entering Fall 2024. Check admissions website for updates. *Academic units required:* 4 English, 3 math, 3 science (2 labs), 2 foreign language, 3 social studies, 1 academic elective. *Academic units recommended:* 4 math, 3 foreign language, 2 academic electives.

FINANCIAL AID

Students should submit: FAFSA; State aid form. *Need-based scholarships/grants offered:* College/university scholarship or grant aid from institutional funds; Federal Pell; Private scholarships; SEOG; State scholarships/grants. *Loan aid offered:* Direct PLUS loans; Direct Subsidized Loans; Direct Unsubsidized Loans. Federal Work-Study Program available. Institutional employment available.

CAMPUS LIFE

Activities: Campus Ministries; Choral groups; Dance; Drama/theater; International Student Organization; Jazz band; Literary magazine; Model UN; Music ensembles; Musical theater; Radio station; Student government; Student newspaper; Television station. **Organizations:** 50 registered organizations, 16 honor societies, 8 religious organizations, 0 fraternities, 0 sororities. **Athletics (Intercollegiate):** *Men:* baseball, basketball, cross-country, equestrian sports, golf, lacrosse, swimming, track/field (indoor). *Women:* basketball, cross-country, equestrian sports, field hockey, golf, lacrosse, softball, swimming, track/field (indoor), volleyball.

CAMPUS

Type of school	Private (nonprofit)
Environment	Town

STUDENTS

Undergrad enrollment	1,217
% male/female	36/64
% from out of state	26
% frosh live on campus	82

FINANCIAL FACTS

Annual tuition	$43,800
Room and board	$13,600
Required fees	$700

GENERAL ADMISSIONS INFO

Application fee	No fee
Regular application deadline	1/15
Nonfall registration	Yes

Fall 2024 testing policy	Test Optional
Range SAT EBRW	510–610
Range SAT Math	490–600
Range ACT Composite	19–24

ACADEMICS

Student/faculty ratio	10:1
% students returning for sophomore year	72

Most classes have 10–19 students.

Maryland

REQUESTING SERVICES FOR STUDENTS WITH LEARNING DIFFERENCES

Phone: 301-696-3421 • www.hood.edu/academics/josephine-steiner-student-success-center/accessibility-services • Email: accessibilityservices@hood.edu

Documentation submitted to: Accessibility Services
Separate application required for Services: Yes

Documentation required for:
LD: Psychoeducational evaluation
ADHD: Psychoeducational evaluation
ASD: Psychoeducational evaluation

McDaniel College

2 College Hill, Westminster, MD 21157 • Admissions: 410-857-2230 • www.mcdaniel.edu

Support: CS

ACCOMMODATIONS

Allowed in exams:

Calculators	Yes
Dictionary	No
Computer	Yes
Spell-checker	Yes
Extended test time	Yes
Scribe	Yes
Proctors	Yes
Oral exams	No
Note-takers	Yes

Support services for students with:

LD	Yes
ADHD	Yes
ASD	Yes
Distraction-reduced environment	Yes
Recording of lecture allowed	Yes
Reading technology	Yes
Audio books	Yes
Other assistive technology	Yes
Priority registration	Yes

Added costs of services:

For LD	Yes
For ADHD	Yes
For ASD	Yes
LD specialists	No
ADHD & ASD coaching	No
ASD specialists	No
Professional tutors	No
Peer tutors	Yes
Max. hours/week for services	Varies
How professors are notified of student approved accommodations	Student

COLLEGE GRADUATION REQUIREMENTS

Course waivers allowed	No
Course substitutions allowed	Yes
In what courses: Foreign Language	

PROGRAMS/SERVICES FOR STUDENTS WITH LEARNING DIFFERENCES

The Student Accessibility & Support Services (SASS) Office helps students with documented disabilities receive appropriate and individualized academic accommodations. SASS offers several program levels of support for students with documented disabilities. Students must register with SASS to receive accommodations, regardless of the level of service. The Basic Program has no fee and is available to students at all academic levels. This program includes access to applicable accommodations, use of the testing center, weekly meetings with SASS graduate assistants, use of SASS office assistive technology, and drop-in tutoring for select basic courses. In addition to the Basic Program, SASS offers fee-based levels of support—the Academic Skills Program (ASP) offers all-inclusive support services; alternatively, students can choose which services they need with the Mentorship Advantage Program (MAP), Providing Academic Support for Success (PASS), and College PRO (Prepare, Reinforce, Organize) programs. ASP for first-year students includes weekly one-on-one sessions with an academic counselor providing support in academics, time management, organizational skills, and self-advocacy techniques. Academic counselors communicate with professors, and students have access to individual peer tutoring, weekly support sessions with graduate assistants, and priority registration. PASS includes group academic support sessions run by a SASS graduate assistant. MAP includes weekly activities designed to enhance students' skills in such areas as socialization, problem solving, communication, and independence. College PRO provides one-hour weekly interactive group sessions led by SASS staff to enhance academic skills for success, including note-taking, technology, discussion boards, test preparation, organization, and time management. Step Ahead is a summer transitional program for first-year college students with disabilities and occurs each year in the five days before first-year orientation.

ADMISSIONS

The admission process is the same for all applicants. General admission criteria include a minimum of a 2.8 GPA in core academic courses; substitutions for foreign language are allowed if appropriate.

Additional Information

Student advising begins with McDaniel Local the summer before first semester. Prior to registering for fall classes, students meet one-on-one with a professional staff member for their first advising session to discuss course preferences. First-year students are advised by their First Year Seminar professor until a major is declared.

McDaniel is proud to be the first coeducational college south of the Mason-Dixon Line, and one of the first coeducational colleges in the nation. It was originally named Western Maryland College because its first board chair was the president of the Western Maryland Railroad. In 2002, the college was renamed in honor of William R. McDaniel's lifetime of service. He began as a student in 1870, then served the school as a professor, vice president, acting president, treasurer, and trustee until 1942.

McDaniel College

GENERAL ADMISSIONS

Very important factors include: rigor of secondary school record, academic GPA. *Important factors include:* application essay, recommendations. *Other factors considered include:* class rank. High school diploma is required and GED is accepted. Institution is test-optional for entering Fall 2024. Check admissions website for updates. *Academic units required:* 4 English, 3 math, 3 science (3 labs), 3 foreign language, 3 social studies. *Academic units recommended:* 4 math, 4 science, 4 foreign language.

FINANCIAL AID

Students should submit: FAFSA. *Need-based scholarships/grants offered:* College/university scholarship or grant aid from institutional funds; Federal Pell; Private scholarships; SEOG; State scholarships/grants. *Loan aid offered:* Direct PLUS loans; Direct Subsidized Loans; Direct Unsubsidized Loans. Federal Work-Study Program available. Institutional employment available.

CAMPUS LIFE

Activities: Campus Ministries; Choral groups; Concert band; Dance; Drama/theater; International Student Organization; Jazz band; Literary magazine; Marching band; Model UN; Music ensembles; Musical theater; Pep band; Radio station; Student government; Student newspaper; Student-run film society; Television station; Yearbook. **Organizations:** 90 registered organizations, 28 honor societies, 3 religious organizations, 5 fraternities, 6 sororities. **Athletics (Intercollegiate):** *Men:* baseball, basketball, cross-country, equestrian sports, golf, lacrosse, softball, swimming, track/field (indoor), ultimate frisbee, volleyball, wrestling. *Women:* basketball, cross-country, equestrian sports, field hockey, golf, lacrosse, softball, swimming, track/field (indoor), ultimate frisbee, volleyball.

CAMPUS

Type of school	Private (nonprofit)
Environment	Town

STUDENTS

Undergrad enrollment	1,744
% male/female	41/59
% from out of state	27
% frosh live on campus	92

FINANCIAL FACTS

Annual tuition	$48,672
Room and board	$13,756
Required fees	$975

GENERAL ADMISSIONS INFO

Application fee	No fee
Regular application deadline	Rolling
Nonfall registration	Yes

Fall 2024 testing policy	Test Optional
Range SAT EBRW	520–645
Range SAT Math	500–615
Range ACT Composite	23–29

ACADEMICS

Student/faculty ratio	12:1
% students returning for sophomore year	76

Most classes have 10–19 students.

Maryland

REQUESTING SERVICES FOR STUDENTS WITH LEARNING DIFFERENCES

Phone: 410-857-2504 • mcdaniel.edu/academics/academic-resources-support/student-accessibility-support-services • Email: sass@mcdaniel.edu

Documentation submitted to: Student Accessibility & Support Services
Separate application required for Services: Yes

Documentation required for:
LD: Psychoeducational evaluation
ADHD: Psychoeducational evaluation
ASD: Psychoeducational evaluation

Salisbury University

1101 Camden Avenue, Salisbury, MD 21801 • Admissions: 410-543-6161 • www.salisbury.edu

Support: S

ACCOMMODATIONS

Allowed in exams:

Calculators	Yes
Dictionary	Yes
Computer	Yes
Spell-checker	Yes
Extended test time	Yes
Scribe	Yes
Proctors	Yes
Oral exams	Yes
Note-takers	No

Support services for students with:

LD	Yes
ADHD	Yes
ASD	Yes
Distraction-reduced environment	Yes
Recording of lecture allowed	Yes
Reading technology	Yes
Audio books	Yes
Priority registration	Yes

Added costs of services:

For LD	No
For ADHD	No
For ASD	No
LD specialists	No
ADHD & ASD coaching	Yes
ASD specialists	No
Professional tutors	No
Peer tutors	Yes
Max. hours/week for services	Varies
How professors are notified of student approved accommodations	Student and Disability Resource Center

COLLEGE GRADUATION REQUIREMENTS

Course waivers allowed	Yes
In what courses: Math and Foreign Language	
Course substitutions allowed	Yes
In what courses: Math and Foreign Language	

PROGRAMS/SERVICES FOR STUDENTS WITH LEARNING DIFFERENCES

The Disability Resource Center (DRC) evaluates the submitted disability documentation and then meets with the student to discuss accommodations and academic and campus resources. Services offered by the DRC include exam and classroom accommodations, assistive technology training, alternative textbooks and course materials, academic-skill building, academic coaching, and advocacy. The DRC S.T.A.R.S. (Student Transition, Access, Retention, and Success) Program is a summer orientation program for incoming students with disabilities. It is designed to provide students with the resources, information, and services necessary to ensure a smooth transition to Salisbury University. Students are paired with a peer mentor who helps them adjust to college, identify campus resources, and get involved. Program activities include early move-in, a family advocate session, a mentor meet-and-greet, help with assistive technology, guidance with utilizing campus resources, and fun activities. There is a small fee for this program.

ADMISSIONS

All students submit the same application for admission along with their high school transcript, essay, and letters of recommendation. The university does a holistic review and considers leadership, community service, artistic talent, and athletic talent, as well as cultural, experiential, and geographic diversity. The university recommends 2 years of foreign language, which can also be satisfied with 2 courses in advanced technology.

Additional Information

The Center for Student Achievement provides coaching, academic workshops, Supplemental Instruction and tutoring for all students.

The Sea Gull Century is a nationally acclaimed bicycling event organized by The SU Foundation. The Sea Gull Century began in 1988 with a group of 68 cycling enthusiasts. The ride is now limited to 5,000 riders who have the option of the traditional 100-mile Assateague Century or the 63-mile Princess Anne Metric. In 2021, the oldest rider was 99 and rode the 100-mile route.

Salisbury University

GENERAL ADMISSIONS

Very important factors include: rigor of secondary school record, academic GPA. *Important factors include:* class rank, standardized test scores (if submitted). *Other factors considered include:* application essay, recommendations. High school diploma is required and GED is accepted. Institution is test-optional for entering Fall 2024. Check admissions website for updates. *Academic units required:* 4 English, 4 math, 3 science (2 labs), 2 foreign language, 3 social studies. *Academic units recommended:* 4 science (3 labs), 3 foreign language, 3 academic electives.

FINANCIAL AID

Students should submit: FAFSA. *Need-based scholarships/grants offered:* College/university scholarship or grant aid from institutional funds; Federal Pell; Private scholarships; SEOG; State scholarships/grants. *Loan aid offered:* Direct PLUS loans; Direct Subsidized Loans; Direct Unsubsidized Loans. Federal Work-Study Program available. Institutional employment available.

CAMPUS LIFE

Activities: Campus Ministries; Choral groups; Concert band; Dance; Drama/theater; International Student Organization; Jazz band; Literary magazine; Model UN; Music ensembles; Musical theater; Opera; Pep band; Radio station; Student government; Student newspaper; Student-run film society; Symphony orchestra; Television station. **Organizations:** 123 registered organizations, 31 honor societies, 9 religious organizations, 11 fraternities, 8 sororities. **Athletics (Intercollegiate):** *Men:* baseball, basketball, cross-country, equestrian sports, field hockey, gymnastics, ice hockey, lacrosse, rugby, softball, swimming, table tennis, track/field (indoor), ultimate frisbee, volleyball. *Women:* basketball, cross-country, equestrian sports, field hockey, gymnastics, ice hockey, lacrosse, rugby, softball, swimming, table tennis, track/field (indoor), ultimate frisbee, volleyball.

CAMPUS
Type of school	Public
Environment	Town

STUDENTS
Undergrad enrollment	6,145
% male/female	45/55
% from out of state	15
% frosh live on campus	89

FINANCIAL FACTS
Annual in-state tuition	$7,556
Annual out-of-state tuition	$18,032
Room and board	$12,990
Required fees	$2,840

GENERAL ADMISSIONS INFO
Application fee	$50
Regular application deadline	1/15
Nonfall registration	Yes

Fall 2024 testing policy	Test Optional
Range SAT EBRW	600–660
Range SAT Math	580–660
Range ACT Composite	22–27

ACADEMICS
Student/faculty ratio	13:1
% students returning for sophomore year	76

Most classes have 10–19 students.

Maryland

REQUESTING SERVICES FOR STUDENTS WITH LEARNING DIFFERENCES

Phone: 410-543-6087 • www.salisbury.edu/administration/student-affairs/disability-resource-center
Email: disabilitysupport@salisbury.edu

Documentation submitted to: Disability Resource Center
Separate application required for Services: Yes

Documentation required for:
  LD: Psychoeducational evaluation
  ADHD: Psychoeducational evaluation
  ASD: Psychoeducational evaluation

St. Mary's College of Maryland

47645 College Drive, St. Mary's City, MD 20686-3001 • Admissions: 240-895-5000 • www.smcm.edu

Support: S

ACCOMMODATIONS

Allowed in exams:

Calculators	Yes
Dictionary	Yes
Computer	Yes
Spell-checker	Yes
Extended test time	Yes
Scribe	Yes
Proctors	Yes
Oral exams	Yes
Note-takers	Yes

Support services for students with:

LD	Yes
ADHD	Yes
ASD	Yes
Distraction-reduced environment	Yes
Recording of lecture allowed	Yes
Reading technology	Yes
Audio books	Yes
Other assistive technology	Yes
Priority registration	Yes

Added costs of services:

For LD	No
For ADHD	No
For ASD	No
LD specialists	No
ADHD & ASD coaching	No
ASD specialists	No
Professional tutors	No
Peer tutors	Yes
Max. hours/week for services	Varies
How professors are notified of student approved accommodations	Student and Office of Accessibility Services

COLLEGE GRADUATION REQUIREMENTS

Course waivers allowed	No
Course substitutions allowed	Yes
In what courses: Foreign Language	

PROGRAMS/SERVICES FOR STUDENTS WITH LEARNING DIFFERENCES

The Office of Accessibility Services (OAS) determines eligibility for reasonable accommodations for students with disabilities. Students register on the OAS webpage to request accommodations and submit supporting disability documentation. Students without documentation should still complete the registration and schedule a meeting with OAS to discuss. OAS will review the information, then schedule an intake meeting so the student can provide the staff with information about their experiences and discuss which accommodations are needed during the semester. Students receive their notice of accommodation eligibility each semester to share with their instructors for each course they want to use the accommodations. The OAS webpage has guides on how to share letters of accommodation, book an exam, request additional accommodations, and other helpful guides.

ADMISSIONS

The admissions committee considers college preparation and achievement shown on a high school transcript as the most important factors in the review process. Strong applicants have taken at least the recommended core academic units, but more is better. A personal essay, school report, teacher letter of recommendation, and counselor recommendation are required. One other teacher recommendation and one letter of recommendation from another source are both optional. In-person or virtual school visits and interviews are not required or used by the admission committee, but they are encouraged as a way for the student to learn more about the college. Applicants can also schedule a phone conversation with an admissions counselor to answer any questions about the admission process, campus life, and the academics offered.

Additional Information

The Office of Student Success Services (OSSS) is the resource center for academic support and advising. Tutoring is free and can be accessed online. Departments also provide course-specific tutoring services, as well as groups like the Economics Club and the Physics Club. And students are encouraged to talk to their professors in any class about tutoring options. The Writing and Speaking Center peer tutors help with everything from brainstorming a project and draft review to revising for a finished product. The Writing and Speaking Center also assists with English courses. OSSS created the Peer Academic Success Strategies (PASS) Specialists Program to work with individual students or small groups to help learn at the college level to review course syllabi; read textbooks; take class or reading notes; manage time; avoid procrastination and get organized; prepare for and take exams; and talk with professors and academic advisors. The Seahawk Academic Improvement & Learning Strategies (SAILS) course is designed to help students learn useful study and time-management strategies as well as note-taking, test preparation, and test-taking skills. These strategies, skills, and techniques can help students improve their academic performance.

St. John's Pond is a landmark on campus, located between the Hilda C. Landers Library and Queen Anne Hall. St. John's Pond was used as a harbor for arriving colonists as early as the 1630s. Beginning in the 1930s, students started ice skating on the pond, and in 1970, the birthday tradition of "ponding" began, where students were thrown into the pond. The tradition continues, and during the warmer months, half-birthdays count, and students get a second dunk.

St. Mary's College of Maryland

GENERAL ADMISSIONS

Very important factors include: rigor of secondary school record, academic GPA, application essay, recommendations. *Important factors include:* class rank. *Other factors considered include:* standardized test scores (if submitted). High school diploma is required and GED is accepted. Institution is test-optional for entering Fall 2024. Check admissions website for updates. *Academic units recommended:* 4 English, 3 math, 2 science, 3 social studies, 2 foreign language.

FINANCIAL AID

Students should submit: FAFSA. *Need-based scholarships/grants offered:* College/university scholarship or grant aid from institutional funds; Federal Pell; Private scholarships; SEOG; State scholarships/grants. *Loan aid offered:* Direct PLUS loans; Direct Subsidized Loans; Direct Unsubsidized Loans. Federal Work-Study Program available. Institutional employment available.

CAMPUS LIFE

Activities: Campus Ministries; Choral groups; Dance; Drama/theater; Jazz band; Literary magazine; Music ensembles; Pep band; Student government; Student newspaper; Symphony orchestra. **Organizations:** 68 registered organizations, 13 honor societies, 3 religious organizations, 0 fraternities, 0 sororities. **Athletics (Intercollegiate):** *Men:* baseball, basketball, cross-country, equestrian sports, lacrosse, rugby, softball, swimming, track/field (indoor), ultimate frisbee, volleyball, wrestling. *Women:* basketball, crew/rowing, cross-country, equestrian sports, field hockey, lacrosse, rugby, softball, swimming, track/field (indoor), ultimate frisbee, volleyball, wrestling.

CAMPUS

Type of school	Public
Environment	Rural

STUDENTS

Undergrad enrollment	1,491
% male/female	41/59
% from out of state	9
% frosh live on campus	95

FINANCIAL FACTS

Annual in-state tuition	$12,116
Annual out-of-state tuition	$28,192
Room and board	$14,264
Required fees	$3,064

GENERAL ADMISSIONS INFO

Application fee	$50
Regular application deadline	1/15
Nonfall registration	Yes

Fall 2024 testing policy	Test Optional
Range SAT EBRW	590–710
Range SAT Math	540–660
Range ACT Composite	28–30

ACADEMICS

Student/faculty ratio	10:1
% students returning for sophomore year	82

Most classes have 10–19 students.

Maryland

REQUESTING SERVICES FOR STUDENTS WITH LEARNING DIFFERENCES

Phone: 240-895-2250 • www.smcm.edu/office-accessibility-services • Email: adasupport@smcm.edu

Documentation submitted to: Office of Accessibility Services
Separate application required for Services: Yes

Documentation required for:
  LD: Psychoeducational evaluation
  ADHD: Psychoeducational evaluation
  ASD: Psychoeducational evaluation

Towson University

8000 York Road, Towson, MD 21252-0001 • Admissions: 410-704-2113 • www.towson.edu

Support: CS

ACCOMMODATIONS

Allowed in exams:

Calculators	Yes
Dictionary	No
Computer	Yes
Spell-checker	Yes
Extended test time	Yes
Scribe	Yes
Proctors	Yes
Oral exams	Yes
Note-takers	Yes

Support services for students with:

LD	Yes
ADHD	Yes
ASD	Yes
Distraction-reduced environment	Yes
Recording of lecture allowed	Yes
Reading technology	Yes
Audio books	Yes
Other assistive technology	Yes
Priority registration	Yes

Added costs of services:

For LD	No
For ADHD	No
For ASD	No
LD specialists	Yes
ADHD & ASD coaching	Yes
ASD specialists	Yes
Professional tutors	No
Peer tutors	Yes
Max. hours/week for services	Varies
How professors are notified of student approved accommodations	Student

COLLEGE GRADUATION REQUIREMENTS

Course waivers allowed	No
Course substitutions allowed	Yes
In what courses: Math	

PROGRAMS/SERVICES FOR STUDENTS WITH LEARNING DIFFERENCES:

Towson University (TU) provides reasonable accommodations to students with disabilities through the Accessibility & Disability Services (ADS) office. After admission to TU, students must initiate the registration process by submitting an ADS application along with supporting documentation of their disability. Once reviewed by the office, an ADS specialist will set up an interview to determine eligibility and discuss the history of the disability, accommodations used in the past, and accommodations requested for courses at TU. Students will then receive a memo with approved accommodations, which includes how to discuss accommodations with course instructors. ADS can also help students with the transition to college, managing course loads, course selection, and priority registration. For students with autism, additional support is available through the Hussman Center for Adults with Autism, a fee-based program that provides programming, training, and resources for adults and TU students on the autism spectrum. The Hussman Center offers three types of programs: (1) group programs for neurodiverse individuals with inclusive TU student involvement, (2) College Autism Peer Support (CAPS) for TU students on the autism spectrum, and (3) Friday evening social groups for TU students and Hussman Center participants.

ADMISSIONS

Admission requirements are the same for all students. The admissions review considers the strength and rigor of the curriculum taken by the applicant, as well as the student's extracurricular involvement, personal essay, and supplemental materials. An applicant whose high school transcript does not include all of the curriculum requirements may be admitted with the understanding that select deficiencies must be completed during the first term of their first year.

Additional Information

All incoming first-year students must participate in the First Year Experience (FYE) advising program. In FYE, students are paired with an advisor based on their major or special population, who works with them on course selection, major or minor selection, academic enrichment opportunities, and study skills, as well as their general adjustment to college. More support is available with Peer-Assisted Learning Sessions (PALS)—weekly drop-in sessions led by peer tutors. During each session, a specific topic is reviewed that is related to the current course material, allowing students the opportunity to ask questions and work on examples and problems. Additionally, the Tutoring and Learning Center (TLC) offers free course tutoring, Supplemental Instruction for difficult courses, one-on-one academic coaching, and help organizing study groups. TLC also offers study skills workshops throughout the semester.

If it's fall, it's time for Family Weekend, giving parents, siblings, grandparents—the whole family—time to enjoy TU's campus. A block of Towson is taken over with black and gold pride for the annual Uptown Roar with food and live music; other festivities include a planetarium show with a telescope viewing, a Stuff-a-Tiger and movie night, Towson Tigers football games, and the largest collegiate crab feast in Maryland.

Towson University

GENERAL ADMISSIONS

Very important factors include: academic GPA. *Important factors include:* rigor of secondary school record, application essay. *Other factors considered include:* class rank, standardized test scores (if submitted). High school diploma is required and GED is accepted. Institution is test-optional for entering Fall 2024. Check admissions website for updates. *Academic units required:* 4 English, 4 math, 3 science (2 labs), 2 foreign language, 3 social studies, 6 academic electives.

FINANCIAL AID

Students should submit: FAFSA; State aid form. *Need-based scholarships/grants offered:* College/university scholarship or grant aid from institutional funds; Federal Pell; Private scholarships; SEOG; State scholarships/grants. *Loan aid offered:* Direct PLUS loans; Direct Subsidized Loans; Direct Unsubsidized Loans. Federal Work-Study Program available. Institutional employment available.

CAMPUS LIFE

Activities: Campus Ministries; Choral groups; Concert band; Dance; Drama/theater; International Student Organization; Jazz band; Literary magazine; Marching band; Model UN; Music ensembles; Musical theater; Opera; Pep band; Radio station; Student government; Student newspaper; Student-run film society; Symphony orchestra; Television station. **Organizations:** 273 registered organizations, 23 honor societies, 23 religious organizations, 22 fraternities, 20 sororities. **Athletics (Intercollegiate):** *Men:* baseball, basketball, cross-country, field hockey, golf, gymnastics, ice hockey, lacrosse, rugby, swimming, track/field (indoor), ultimate frisbee, volleyball, wrestling. *Women:* basketball, cross-country, field hockey, golf, gymnastics, ice hockey, lacrosse, rugby, softball, swimming, track/field (indoor), ultimate frisbee, volleyball, wrestling.

CAMPUS

Type of school	Public
Environment	Metropolis

STUDENTS

Undergrad enrollment	17,817
% male/female	40/60
% from out of state	9
% frosh live on campus	77

FINANCIAL FACTS

Annual in-state tuition	$7,238
Annual out-of-state tuition	$23,240
Room and board	$14,312
Required fees	$3,580

GENERAL ADMISSIONS INFO

Application fee	$45
Regular application deadline	4/1
Nonfall registration	Yes

Fall 2024 testing policy	Test Optional
Range SAT EBRW	520–620
Range SAT Math	520–600
Range ACT Composite	21–26

ACADEMICS

Student/faculty ratio	16:1
% students returning for sophomore year	85

Most classes have 20–29 students.

Maryland

REQUESTING SERVICES FOR STUDENTS WITH LEARNING DIFFERENCES

Phone: 410-704-2638 • www.towson.edu/accessibility-disability-services • Email: TUADS@towson.edu

Documentation submitted to: Accessibility & Disability Services
Separate application required for Services: Yes

Documentation required for:
  LD: Psychoeducational evaluation
  ADHD: Psychoeducational evaluation
  ASD: Psychoeducational evaluation

American International College

1000 State Street, Springfield, MA 01109-3184 • Admissions: 413-205-3201 • www.aic.edu

Support: SP

ACCOMMODATIONS

Allowed in exams:

Calculators	Yes
Dictionary	No
Computer	Yes
Spell-checker	Yes
Extended test time	Yes
Scribe	Yes
Proctors	Yes
Oral exams	Yes
Note-takers	No

Support services for students with:

LD	Yes
ADHD	Yes
ASD	Yes
Distraction-reduced environment	Yes
Recording of lecture allowed	Yes
Reading technology	Yes
Audio books	Yes
Other assistive technology	Yes
Priority registration	Yes

Added costs of services:

For LD	Yes
For ADHD	Yes
For ASD	Yes
LD specialists	Yes
ADHD & ASD coaching	Yes
ASD specialists	No
Professional tutors	Yes
Peer tutors	No
Max. hours/week for services	5
How professors are notified of student approved accommodations	Student and CASAA

COLLEGE GRADUATION REQUIREMENTS

Course waivers allowed	No
Course substitutions allowed	No

PROGRAMS/SERVICES FOR STUDENTS WITH LEARNING DIFFERENCES

The Center for Accessibility Services and Academic Accommodations (CASAA) supports students with disabilities. After submitting the required documentation, students meet with the CASAA coordinator to discuss accommodations, how to proceed, and available resources that might be appropriate. Students are welcome to participate in the fee-based program, Reaching Educational Achievements (REACH). REACH provides professional learning services to students with or without diagnosed learning challenges; the program includes both content-based tutoring and academic strategies, like study skills, organization, and time management.

ADMISSIONS

All applicants are required to meet the same academic and technical standards and must submit an official high school transcript. For students who were home-schooled or do not have a traditional transcript, please contact an admissions counselor in the admissions office. While supplemental materials like letters of recommendation and personal statements are optional, they can provide AIC useful insight into an applicant's character and ability to be a successful college student. These materials can also illustrate the student's life outside of school and provide context for any personal experience that may have impacted the student's academic performance. Applicants are encouraged to visit campus and meet with an admissions counselor. Optional one-on-one interviews in the fall are scheduled on a first-come, first-served basis. All applicants to AIC are considered for a merit scholarship upon acceptance.

Additional Information

Summer Summit Days, provides orientation to first-year and first-time students so that incoming students feel confident they have everything they need for the fall semester. The Center for Navigating Educational Success Together (aka the NEST) supports students socially and academically, from counseling and advising to tutors and study groups. Students can discover an extensive database of internships, work-study, and employment opportunities at the Saremi Center for Career Development.

AIC was founded in 1885 by Reverend Calvin E. Amaron to provide young French Canadians access to higher education. AIC was chartered by the Commonwealth of Massachusetts in 1885 with the purpose of educating immigrants coming to America through New York. Women were given access in 1892, and by World War I, AIC had established its reputation for diversity and enrolled students from 42 nations.

American International College

GENERAL ADMISSIONS

Very important factors include: academic GPA, standardized test scores (if submitted). *Important factors include:* rigor of secondary school record. *Other factors considered include:* application essay, recommendations. High school diploma is required and GED is accepted. Institution is test-optional for entering Fall 2024. Check admissions website for updates. *Academic units recommended:* 4 English, 3 math, 2 science (2 labs), 1 foreign language, 2 social studies, 4 academic electives.

FINANCIAL AID

Students should submit: FAFSA. *Need-based scholarships/grants offered:* College/university scholarship or grant aid from institutional funds; Federal Nursing Scholarships; Federal Pell; Private scholarships; SEOG; State scholarships/grants. *Loan aid offered:* Direct PLUS loans; Direct Subsidized Loans; Direct Unsubsidized Loans. Federal Work-Study Program available. Institutional employment available.

CAMPUS LIFE

Activities: Campus Ministries; Dance; Drama/theater; International Student Organization; Literary magazine; Model UN; Pep band; Student government; Student newspaper; Yearbook. **Organizations:** 45 registered organizations, 5 honor societies, 1 religious organizations, 3 fraternities, 3 sororities. **Athletics (Intercollegiate):** *Men:* baseball, basketball, cross-country, golf, ice hockey, lacrosse, rugby, track/field (indoor), wrestling. *Women:* basketball, cross-country, field hockey, golf, lacrosse, rugby, softball, track/field (indoor), volleyball.

CAMPUS

Type of school	Private (nonprofit)
Environment	City

STUDENTS

Undergrad enrollment	1,288
% male/female	42/58
% from out of state	39
% frosh live on campus	80

FINANCIAL FACTS

Annual tuition	$39,370
Room and board	$14,800

GENERAL ADMISSIONS INFO

Application fee	No fee
Regular application deadline	Rolling
Nonfall registration	Yes

Fall 2024 testing policy	Test Optional
Range SAT EBRW	470–555
Range SAT Math	470–555
Range ACT Composite	16–23

ACADEMICS

Student/faculty ratio	17:1
% students returning for sophomore year	63

Most classes have 20–29 students.

REQUESTING SERVICES FOR STUDENTS WITH LEARNING DIFFERENCES

Phone: 413-205-3037 • www.aic.edu/academics/academic-support/casaa
Email: accessibility.services@aic.edu

Documentation submitted to: Center for Accessibility Services and Academic Accommodations
Separate application required for Services: Yes

Documentation required for:
LD: Psychoeducational evaluation
ADHD: Psychoeducational evaluation
ASD: Psychoeducational evaluation

Boston College

140 Commonwealth Avenue, Chestnut Hill, MA 02467-3809 • Admissions: 617-552-3100 • www.bc.edu

Support: CS

ACCOMMODATIONS

Allowed in exams:

Calculators	Yes
Dictionary	No
Computer	Yes
Spell-checker	Yes
Extended test time	Yes
Scribe	Yes
Proctors	Yes
Oral exams	Yes
Note-takers	Yes

Support services for students with:

LD	Yes
ADHD	Yes
ASD	Yes
Distraction-reduced environment	Yes
Recording of lecture allowed	No
Reading technology	No
Audio books	Yes
Other assistive technology	No
Priority registration	Yes

Added costs of services:

For LD	No
For ADHD	No
For ASD	No
LD specialists	Yes
ADHD & ASD coaching	No
ASD specialists	No
Professional tutors	No
Peer tutors	Yes
Max. hours/week for services	3
How professors are notified of student approved accommodations	ADHD & Learning Disability Support Services

COLLEGE GRADUATION REQUIREMENTS

Course waivers allowed	No
Course substitutions allowed	Yes

In what courses: Foreign Language

PROGRAMS/SERVICES FOR STUDENTS WITH LEARNING DIFFERENCES

Students who are diagnosed with a learning disability or ADHD and require accommodations should contact ADHD and Learning Disability Support Services in the Connors Family Learning Center (CFLC). Accommodations may include alternative course material and modified deadlines for assignments and exams. Through CFLC, students can find support from professional staff, as well as tutoring services offered by undergraduates and graduates in high standing, those of whom are either certified or in the process of becoming certified by the CRLA (College Reading and Learning Association). Assistance is available in over 60 courses, along with lessons in writing development and English as a second language.

ADMISSIONS

While applicants need only declare majors for engineering and nursing, all students are required to apply to one of four undergraduate academic divisions: Morrissey College of Arts and Sciences, Carroll School of Management, Lynch School of Education and Human Development, and Connell School of Nursing. Applications are considered only for the selected division. The admissions committee is looking for prospective students who studied four years of the five main subjects: English, math, social science, natural science, and foreign language, and took the most challenging courses available. Applicants must submit an official school transcript, a counselor recommendation, two teacher evaluations, mid-year grade reports, a personal essay, and a BC writing supplement. The decision-making process looks closely at academic performance, extracurricular activities, evaluations, and the quality of self-expression in written submissions.

Additional Information

The Online Writing Lab (OWL) offers email-based feedback on works in progress and tutorials for students to improve their writing skills. The Math Department is available for tutoring in core-level courses through calculus.

BC's Red Bandana 5K Run and the Red Bandana football game honor BC alum and volunteer firefighter Welles Crowther, who passed away on 9/11. Crowther wore a red bandana around his face while guiding survivors to safety during the World Trade Center evacuations. The signature bandana is incorporated into football uniforms, runners' outfits, and fan gear.

Boston College

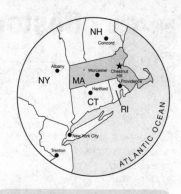

General Admissions

Very important factors include: rigor of secondary school record, academic GPA. *Important factors include:* class rank, application essay, recommendations. *Other factors considered include:* standardized test scores (if submitted). High school diploma is required and GED is accepted. Institution is test-optional for entering Fall 2024. Check admissions website for updates. *Academic units recommended:* 4 English, 4 math, 4 science (4 labs), 4 foreign language, 4 social studies.

Financial Aid

Students should submit: Business/Farm Supplement; CSS/Financial Aid Profile; FAFSA; Noncustodial Profile. *Need-based scholarships/grants offered:* College/university scholarship or grant aid from institutional funds; Federal Pell; Private scholarships; SEOG; State scholarships/grants. *Loan aid offered:* Direct PLUS loans; Direct Subsidized Loans; Direct Unsubsidized Loans. Federal Work-Study Program available. Institutional employment available.

Campus Life

Activities: Campus Ministries; Choral groups; Concert band; Dance; Drama/theater; International Student Organization; Jazz band; Literary magazine; Marching band; Model UN; Music ensembles; Musical theater; Pep band; Radio station; Student government; Student newspaper; Student-run film society; Symphony orchestra; Television station; Yearbook. **Organizations:** 300 registered organizations, 12 honor societies, 14 religious organizations, 0 fraternities, 0 sororities. **Athletics (Intercollegiate):** *Men:* baseball, basketball, crew/rowing, cross-country, cycling, equestrian sports, field hockey, golf, ice hockey, lacrosse, rugby, swimming, table tennis, track/field (indoor), ultimate frisbee, volleyball, water polo. *Women:* basketball, crew/rowing, cross-country, cycling, equestrian sports, field hockey, golf, ice hockey, lacrosse, rugby, softball, swimming, table tennis, track/field (indoor), ultimate frisbee, volleyball, water polo.

CAMPUS
Type of school	Private (nonprofit)
Environment	City

STUDENTS
Undergrad enrollment	9,484
% male/female	47/53
% from out of state	75
% frosh live on campus	99

FINANCIAL FACTS
Annual tuition	$62,950
Room and board	$16,120
Required fees	$1,226

GENERAL ADMISSIONS INFO
Application fee	$80
Regular application deadline	1/1
Nonfall registration	Yes

Fall 2024 testing policy	Test Optional
Range SAT EBRW	705–760
Range SAT Math	730–780
Range ACT Composite	33–35

ACADEMICS
Student/faculty ratio	10:1
% students returning for sophomore year	95

Most classes have 20–29 students.

REQUESTING SERVICES FOR STUDENTS WITH LEARNING DIFFERENCES

Phone: 617-552-8055 • www.bc.edu/connors • Email: farrowe@bc.edu

Documentation submitted to: The Connors Family Learning Center – ADHD & Learning Disability Support Services
Separate application required for Services: Yes

Documentation required for:
LD: Psychoeducational evaluation
ADHD: Psychoeducational evaluation
ASD: Psychoeducational evaluation

Massachusetts

Boston University

233 Bay State Road, Boston, MA 02215 • Admissions: 617-353-2300 • www.bu.edu

(**Support: CS**)

ACCOMMODATIONS

Allowed in exams:

Calculators	No
Dictionary	No
Computer	Yes
Spell-checker	Yes
Extended test time	Yes
Scribe	Yes
Proctors	Yes
Oral exams	Yes
Note-takers	Yes

Support services for students with:

LD	Yes
ADHD	Yes
ASD	Yes
Distraction-reduced environment	Yes
Recording of lecture allowed	Yes
Reading technology	No
Audio books	Yes
Other assistive technology	Yes
Priority registration	No

Added costs of services:

For LD	No
For ADHD	No
For ASD	No
LD specialists	Yes
ADHD & ASD coaching	No
ASD specialists	No
Professional tutors	No
Peer tutors	No
Max. hours/week for services	Varies
How professors are notified of student approved accommodations	Student

COLLEGE GRADUATION REQUIREMENTS

Course waivers allowed	No
Course substitutions allowed	No

PROGRAMS/SERVICES FOR STUDENTS WITH LEARNING DIFFERENCES

Disability & Access Services (DAS) provides academic and housing accommodations to students with disabilities. Accommodations are determined on a case-by-case basis; students must first submit an online intake form and provide appropriate documentation that demonstrates a significant need. They then meet with DAS staff for an intake assessment. Prospective students are encouraged to call, visit, or arrange an appointment with DAS staff at any time to ask questions or address concerns. For those deemed eligible by DAS, Strategic Education Services (SES) delivers 1:1, free weekly strategy sessions that offer practical help to students with psychiatric, attentional, and developmental disabilities. SES helps students implement their accommodations, access other resources on campus, and develop learning skills to achieve success in the university setting. The Office of Diversity and Inclusion sponsors the Learn More Series, including workshops like PACE (Peer support, Access to accommodations, Communities that care, and Educational resources), which helps students with and without disabilities learn how to navigate personal and professional challenges. PACE workshops are for small or large groups, as stand-alone workshops, or can be embedded into classes or meetings.

ADMISSIONS

Applicants are required to submit high school transcripts, a personal essay, school counselor recommendation, and a teacher evaluation. Students should submit applications that fully reflect their academic ability and potential, as illustrated by their academic record and contributions in and outside of the classroom and community. BU is test-optional; once an application is submitted, test scores cannot be added or removed.

Additional Information

The Educational Resource Center (ERC) offers academic skills advising, academic skills workshops, and the first-year course, Academic Strategies: Mastering the Art of Learning. Students can drop by the ERC for individual or group tutoring in their coursework, writing assistance from a writing fellow, or for conversation in a non-native language with Language Link. To get the most out of campus resources, students can find directions and guides at the University Service Center.

Originally named the Cottage Farm Bridge, the Boston University Bridge, built in 1928, replaced an 1850s drawbridge called the Brookline Bridge. The bridge connects Boston to Cambridge and is one of three bridges in the world where a plane can fly over a car that is driving over a train traveling over a boat.

Boston University

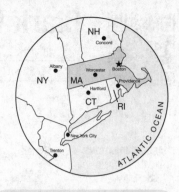

GENERAL ADMISSIONS

Very important factors include: rigor of secondary school record, academic GPA. *Important factors include:* class rank, application essay, recommendations. *Other factors considered include:* standardized test scores (if submitted). High school diploma is required and GED is accepted. Institution is test-optional for entering Fall 2024. Check admissions website for updates. *Academic units required:* 4 English, 3 math, 3 science (3 labs), 2 foreign language, 3 social studies. *Academic units recommended:* 4 English, 4 math, 4 science (4 labs), 4 foreign language, 4 social studies.

FINANCIAL AID

Students should submit: CSS/Financial Aid Profile; FAFSA; Noncustodial Profile. *Need-based scholarships/grants offered:* College/university scholarship or grant aid from institutional funds; Federal Pell; Private scholarships; SEOG; State scholarships/grants. *Loan aid offered:* Direct PLUS loans; Direct Subsidized Loans; Direct Unsubsidized Loans. Federal Work-Study Program available. Institutional employment available.

CAMPUS LIFE

Activities: Campus Ministries; Choral groups; Concert band; Dance; Drama/theater; International Student Organization; Jazz band; Literary magazine; Marching band; Model UN; Music ensembles; Musical theater; Opera; Pep band; Radio station; Student government; Student newspaper; Student-run film society; Symphony orchestra; Television station; Yearbook. **Organizations:** 450 registered organizations, 9 honor societies, 17 religious organizations, 8 fraternities, 13 sororities. **Athletics (Intercollegiate):** *Men:* baseball, basketball, crew/rowing, cross-country, cycling, equestrian sports, golf, gymnastics, ice hockey, lacrosse, martial arts, rugby, swimming, table tennis, track/field (indoor), ultimate frisbee, volleyball, water polo. *Women:* basketball, crew/rowing, cross-country, cycling, equestrian sports, field hockey, golf, gymnastics, ice hockey, lacrosse, martial arts, rugby, softball, swimming, table tennis, track/field (indoor), ultimate frisbee, volleyball, water polo.

CAMPUS
Type of school	Private (nonprofit)
Environment	Metropolis

STUDENTS
Undergrad enrollment	17,668
% male/female	42/58
% from out of state	73
% frosh live on campus	99

FINANCIAL FACTS
Annual tuition	$61,050
Room and board	$17,400
Required fees	$1,310

GENERAL ADMISSIONS INFO
Application fee	$80
Regular application deadline	1/4
Nonfall registration	Yes

Fall 2024 testing policy	Test Optional
Range SAT EBRW	660–730
Range SAT Math	690–770
Range ACT Composite	31–34

ACADEMICS
Student/faculty ratio	11:1
% students returning for sophomore year	94

Most classes have 10–19 students.

REQUESTING SERVICES FOR STUDENTS WITH LEARNING DIFFERENCES

Phone: 617-353-3658 • www.bu.edu/disability • Email: access@bu.edu

Documentation submitted to: Disability and Access Services
Separate application required for Services: Yes

Documentation required for:
LD: Psychoeducational evaluation
ADHD: Psychoeducational evaluation
ASD: Psychoeducational evaluation

Massachusetts

Clark University

950 Main Street, Worcester, MA 01610-1477 • Admissions: 508-793-7431 • www.clarku.edu

Support: CS

PROGRAMS/SERVICES FOR STUDENTS WITH LEARNING DIFFERENCES

Clark University students with learning disabilities can receive academic support and accommodations by registering with Student Accessibility Services (SAS). Students must submit appropriate documentation and meet with an SAS staff member for an intake meeting. The director of SAS works with each student to coordinate accommodations and services on campus that meet their needs. Accommodations for students with learning disabilities include extended time on tests, use of a recording device in the classroom, assistance in locating textbooks in an alternate format, and computer access for written work and essay tests. Students who register with SAS may attend SAS Early Orientation, which is an opportunity to meet other students in the program, work with student leaders, attend workshops, and use this extra time to transition to college life and practice navigating the campus. Participants move into their residence halls before most of the other first-year students. After Early Orientation concludes, students then join First-Year Orientation with the rest of the incoming class.

ADMISSIONS

All applicants must meet the standard admission requirements. Students with a GPA of 2.5 or higher are given preference. Interviews are optional, and those who wish to schedule one are encouraged to do so early in their application process.

Additional Information

Students at Clark typically take a foreign language to fulfill the Language and Culture requirement. American Sign Language (ASL) is available and can be a great option for students whose disabilities impact their potential for learning a foreign language.

Spree Day is one of Clark's oldest and most loved traditions, dating back to 1903. Classes are canceled, and students enjoy a fun-filled day before finals begin. Original festivities were rope pulls and greased pole climbs; today, activities include interclass football, canoe jousting, Jell-O wrestling, inflatable slides, concerts, dancing, and an abundance of food.

Clark University

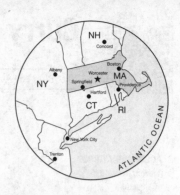

GENERAL ADMISSIONS

Very important factors include: rigor of secondary school record, academic GPA, recommendations. *Important factors include:* application essay. *Other factors considered include:* class rank, standardized test scores (if submitted). High school diploma is required and GED is accepted. Institution is test-optional for entering Fall 2024. Check admissions website for updates. *Academic units recommended:* 4 English, 3 math, 3 science (2 labs), 2 foreign language, 3 social studies.

FINANCIAL AID

Students should submit: CSS/Financial Aid Profile; FAFSA; Noncustodial Profile. *Need-based scholarships/grants offered:* College/university scholarship or grant aid from institutional funds; Federal Pell; SEOG; State scholarships/grants. *Loan aid offered:* Direct PLUS loans; Direct Subsidized Loans; Direct Unsubsidized Loans. Federal Work-Study Program available. Institutional employment available.

CAMPUS LIFE

Activities: Choral groups; Concert band; Dance; Drama/theater; International Student Organization; Jazz band; Literary magazine; Marching band; Model UN; Music ensembles; Musical theater; Pep band; Radio station; Student government; Student newspaper; Student-run film society; Symphony orchestra; Television station; Yearbook. **Organizations:** 130 registered organizations, 10 honor societies, 7 religious organizations, 0 fraternities, 0 sororities. **Athletics (Intercollegiate):** *Men:* baseball, basketball, cross-country, golf, ice hockey, lacrosse, martial arts, swimming, ultimate frisbee, volleyball. *Women:* basketball, crew/rowing, cross-country, equestrian sports, field hockey, golf, lacrosse, martial arts, softball, swimming, ultimate frisbee, volleyball.

CAMPUS

Type of school	Private (nonprofit)
Environment	City

STUDENTS

Undergrad enrollment	2,361
% male/female	41/59
% from out of state	60
% frosh live on campus	95

FINANCIAL FACTS

Annual tuition	$54,760
Room and board	$11,690
Required fees	$427

GENERAL ADMISSIONS INFO

Application fee	No fee
Regular application deadline	1/15
Nonfall registration	Yes
Fall 2024 testing policy	Test Optional
Range SAT EBRW	640–720
Range SAT Math	610–710
Range ACT Composite	28–33

ACADEMICS

Student/faculty ratio	9:1
% students returning for sophomore year	88

Most classes have 10–19 students.

REQUESTING SERVICES FOR STUDENTS WITH LEARNING DIFFERENCES

Phone: 508-798-4368 • clarku.edu/offices/student-accessibility-services
Email: accessibilityservices@clarku.edu

Documentation submitted to: Student Accessibility Services
Separate application required for Services: Yes

Documentation required for:
LD: Psychoeducational evaluation
ADHD: Psychoeducational evaluation
ASD: Psychoeducational evaluation

Massachusetts

Curry College

1071 Blue Hill Avenue, Milton, MA 02186 • Admissions: 617-333-2210 • www.curry.edu

Support: SP

ACCOMMODATIONS

Allowed in exams:

Calculators	Yes
Dictionary	Yes
Computer	Yes
Spell-checker	Yes
Extended test time	Yes
Scribe	Yes
Proctors	Yes
Oral exams	Yes
Note-takers	Yes

Support services for students with:

LD	Yes
ADHD	Yes
ASD	Yes
Distraction-reduced environment	Yes
Recording of lecture allowed	Yes
Reading technology	Yes
Audio books	Yes
Other assistive technology	Yes
Priority registration	No

Added costs of services:

For LD	Yes
For ADHD	Yes
For ASD	Yes
LD specialists	Yes
ADHD & ASD coaching	No
ASD specialists	No
Professional tutors	Yes
Peer tutors	Yes
Max. hours/week for services	2.5
How professors are notified of student approved accommodations	Student

COLLEGE GRADUATION REQUIREMENTS

Course waivers allowed	No
Course substitutions allowed	Yes
In what courses: Case-by-case basis	

PROGRAMS/SERVICES FOR STUDENTS WITH LEARNING DIFFERENCES

The Office of Disability Services offers an accessible and inclusive environment for students with disabilities, providing accommodations and auxiliary aids based on submitted documentation. Accommodations include additional time and distraction-reduced environments for exams, notetakers, alternate-format texts, assistive technologies, and housing and dining accommodations. The Program for Advancement of Learning (PAL) at Curry College is a fee-based, comprehensive individualized program specifically designed for students with diagnosed learning differences and/or ADHD. Students in PAL participate fully in college coursework and extracurricular activities. PAL helps students understand their individual learning styles and achieve independence as learners. PAL is a strength-based program, and the student's individual needs drive the curriculum. PAL students must commit to the program for at least one year, at which point they may choose to continue the following years in a full or partial capacity.

ADMISSIONS

The application for the PAL program is filed concurrently with application to Curry. Requirements that apply to all students include an official high school transcript, letter of recommendation, and essay. Students applying to PAL must also submit a recent diagnostic evaluation; a supplementary application and IEP (or equivalent) are optional, but may be requested. PAL enrolls 20 percent of the incoming Curry College first-year class. The PAL admissions coordinator helps with admission decisions and works collaboratively with the main admissions office to determine if a student is the right fit. Interviews are encouraged and, in some cases, required if the committee feels more information is needed. Space is limited in the program.

Additional Information

PAL offers a three-week residential summer program to facilitate the transition to college that can earn students 4 credits toward their degree. Students meet regularly with their designated PAL professor, who is also a learning specialist. The program focuses on using the student's strengths to improve skills in areas such as listening, speaking, reading, writing, note-taking, test-taking, organization, and time management. PAL professors review diagnostic testing to help the students understand their unique learning profiles. A full array of assistive technology is provided through PAL, and there are many collaborative spaces in the Assistive Technology Center. PAL students earn 3 credits towards graduation for the first year.

Curry College was founded in 1879 by Anna Baright Curry and Samuel Silas Curry. Alexander Melville Bell, father of Alexander Graham Bell, was a valued advisor of Silas Curry. When the elder Bell received the school's diploma of honor in 1899, it addressed him as a co-founder. Alexander Graham Bell was an Oratory teacher of Curry's. According to his daughter, Silas Curry was present in 1876 when Alexander Graham Bell made his first phone call to Mr. Watson.

Curry College

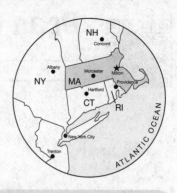

GENERAL ADMISSIONS

Very important factors include: rigor of secondary school record. *Important factors include:* academic GPA, standardized test scores (if submitted), application essay, recommendations. *Other factors considered include:* class rank. High school diploma is required and GED is accepted. Institution is test-optional for entering Fall 2024. Check admissions website for updates. *Academic units required:* 4 English, 3 math, 2 science (1 lab), 2 foreign language, 2 social studies.

FINANCIAL AID

Students should submit: FAFSA. *Need-based scholarships/grants offered:* College/university scholarship or grant aid from institutional funds; Federal Pell; Private scholarships; SEOG; State scholarships/grants. *Loan aid offered:* Direct PLUS loans; Direct Subsidized Loans; Direct Unsubsidized Loans.

CAMPUS LIFE

Activities: Campus Ministries; Choral groups; Dance; Drama/theater; International Student Organization; Literary magazine; Music ensembles; Radio station; Student government; Student newspaper; Student-run film society; Television station; Yearbook. **Organizations:** 1 honor societies, 2 religious organizations, 0 fraternities, 0 sororities. **Athletics (Intercollegiate):** *Men:* baseball, basketball, crew/rowing, ice hockey, lacrosse. *Women:* basketball, crew/rowing, cross-country, lacrosse, softball.

CAMPUS
Type of school	Private (nonprofit)
Environment	Village

STUDENTS
Undergrad enrollment	2,843
% male/female	37/63
% from out of state	22
% frosh live on campus	89

FINANCIAL FACTS
Annual tuition	$34,730
Room and board	$13,900
Required fees	$1,715

GENERAL ADMISSIONS INFO
Application fee	$50
Regular application deadline	Rolling
Nonfall registration	Yes
Fall 2024 testing policy	Test Optional
Range SAT EBRW	420–520
Range SAT Math	430–520
Range ACT Composite	18–21

ACADEMICS
Student/faculty ratio	11:1
% students returning for sophomore year	71

Most classes have 10–19 students.

REQUESTING SERVICES FOR STUDENTS WITH LEARNING DIFFERENCES

Phone: 617-333-2385 • www.curry.edu/student-life/student-services/disability-services
Email: disabilityservices@curry.edu

Documentation submitted to: Office of Disability Services
Separate application required for Services: Yes

Documentation required for:
LD: Psychoeducational evaluation
ADHD: Psychoeducational evaluation
ASD: Psychoeducational evaluation

Dean College

Office of Admission, Franklin, MA 02038-1994 Admissions: 508-541-1508 • www.dean.edu

Support: SP

ACCOMMODATIONS

Allowed in exams:	
Calculators	Yes
Dictionary	Yes
Computer	Yes
Spell-checker	Yes
Extended test time	Yes
Scribe	Yes
Proctors	Yes
Oral exams	Yes
Note-takers	Yes
Support services for students with:	
LD	Yes
ADHD	Yes
ASD	Yes
Distraction-reduced environment	Yes
Recording of lecture allowed	Yes
Reading technology	Yes
Audio books	Yes
Other assistive technology	Yes
Priority registration	Yes
Added costs of services:	
For LD	Yes
For ADHD	Yes
For ASD	Yes
LD specialists	Yes
ADHD & ASD coaching	Yes
ASD specialists	Yes
Professional tutors	Yes
Peer tutors	Yes
Max. hours/week for services	Varies
How professors are notified of student approved accommodations	Student and Office of Accessibility Services

COLLEGE GRADUATION REQUIREMENTS

Course waivers allowed	No
Course substitutions allowed	Yes
In what courses: Math	

PROGRAMS/SERVICES FOR STUDENTS WITH LEARNING DIFFERENCES

The Office of Accessibility Services offers learning and academic support to students with learning disabilities. Students need to register with Accessibility Services if they are requesting accommodations. Requests are evaluated on a case-by-case basis, based on submitted documentation and completion of the accessibility request form. Examples of qualifying disabilities include executive functioning disorder, sensory processing or nonverbal learning issues, and other learning disabilities. Once students have completed their forms, they meet with a coordinator from Accessibility Services to discuss reasonable accommodations.

ADMISSIONS

A high school transcript is required for admission. Applications are evaluated based on high school course selection, academic performance, recommendation letters, and extracurricular activities. SAT or ACT scores, letters of recommendation, and a personal statement are all optional but can add to the admission committee's understanding of the student. Dance and theater candidates are required to audition and submit a performance résumé and photo. Students applying to the Arch Learning Community program must meet certain requirements in addition to submitting the documentation and application, including the ability to live independently.

Additional Information

The Morton Family Learning Center offers a number of tutoring programs, in addition to learning support programs and facilities, such as the Arch Learning Center, the Green Family Library Learning Commons, and the Berenson Center for Writing, Mathematics and Presentation Excellence. The Arch Learning Community is a fee-based program offering cohort classroom learning, customized coaching, Arch-designated courses, and specialized success and career advising to students with diagnosed learning disabilities or differences. Students who are accepted into the Arch Learning Community can enroll for one or two years, or for the duration of their time at school, and will work to get the skills necessary to be successful in their degree program. Dean College offers free support services to all students. A full-time staff of advisors can arrange peer or faculty tutoring, formal one-on-one academic coaching, assistance with learning differences, and help through the Writing and Math Centers.

DID YOU KNOW?

Arthur W. Peirce served as headmaster from 1897-1934. His time at Dean is considered one of the most significant. His initials gave him the nickname of "Awpie"; a kind, generous man whose faith in young people earned tremendous respect and loyalty. The Arthur W. Peirce Prize was established by the Class of 1917 to honor his character, and continues to be awarded annually to a graduate who is honest, loyal, friendly, and cooperative in spirit.

Dean College

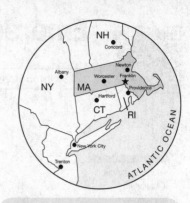

GENERAL ADMISSIONS

Other factors considered include: rigor of secondary school record, class rank, academic GPA, standardized test scores (if submitted), application essay, recommendations. High school diploma is required and GED is accepted. Institution is test-optional for entering Fall 2024. Check admissions website for updates. *Academic units recommended:* 4 English, 3 math, 3 science, 3 social studies.

FINANCIAL AID

Students should submit: FAFSA. *Need-based scholarships/grants offered:* College/university scholarship or grant aid from institutional funds; Federal Pell; Private scholarships; SEOG; State scholarships/grants. *Loan aid offered:* Direct PLUS loans; Direct Subsidized Loans; Direct Unsubsidized Loans. Federal Work-Study Program available. Institutional employment available.

CAMPUS LIFE

Activities: Dance; Drama/theater; Literary magazine; Musical theater; Radio station; Student government; Yearbook. **Organizations:** 80 registered organizations, 6 honor societies. **Athletics (Intercollegiate):** *Men:* baseball, basketball, cross-country, golf, lacrosse, volleyball. *Women:* basketball, cross-country, field hockey, golf, lacrosse, softball, volleyball.

CAMPUS
Type of school	Private (nonprofit)
Environment	Town

STUDENTS
Undergrad enrollment	1,206
% male/female	51/49
% from out of state	51
% frosh live on campus	92

FINANCIAL FACTS
Annual tuition	$44,710
Room and board	$19,192
Required fees	$550

GENERAL ADMISSIONS INFO
Application fee	No fee
Regular application deadline	Rolling
Nonfall registration	Yes
Fall 2024 testing policy	Test Optional

ACADEMICS
Student/faculty ratio	16:1
% students returning for sophomore year	75

Most classes have 10–19 students.

REQUESTING SERVICES FOR STUDENTS WITH LEARNING DIFFERENCES

Phone: 508-541-1942 • dean.edu/support-success/student-services-resources/learning-support-services/accessibility-services • Email: accessibility@dean.edu

Documentation submitted to: Office of Accessibility Services

Separate application required for Services: Yes

Documentation required for:
LD: Psychoeducational evaluation
ADHD: Psychoeducational evaluation
ASD: Psychoeducational evaluation

Emerson College

120 Boylston Street, Boston, MA 02116-4624 • Admissions: 617-824-8600 • www.emerson.edu

Support: S

ACCOMMODATIONS

Allowed in exams:

Calculators	Yes
Dictionary	Yes
Computer	Yes
Spell-checker	Yes
Extended test time	Yes
Scribe	Yes
Proctors	Yes
Oral exams	No
Note-takers	Yes

Support services for students with:

LD	Yes
ADHD	Yes
ASD	Yes
Distraction-reduced environment	Yes
Recording of lecture allowed	Yes
Reading technology	Yes
Audio books	No
Other assistive technology	Yes
Priority registration	No

Added costs of services:

For LD	No
For ADHD	No
For ASD	No
LD specialists	No
ADHD & ASD coaching	No
ASD specialists	No
Professional tutors	No
Peer tutors	Yes
Max. hours/week for services	4
How professors are notified of student approved accommodations	Student

COLLEGE GRADUATION REQUIREMENTS

Course waivers allowed	Yes
In what courses: Quantitative Reasoning (Math) and World Languages	
Course substitutions allowed	Yes
In what courses: Quantitative Reasoning (Math) and World Languages	

PROGRAMS/SERVICES FOR STUDENTS WITH LEARNING DIFFERENCES

Student Accessibility Services (SAS) provides support and accommodations to students with disabilities. Students must self-disclose, complete the initial accommodation request form, and provide documentation to SAS. Interviews are scheduled, and the director or assistant director will determine appropriate accommodations. Once approved, students receive an accommodation letter to give to their professors. Student Accessibility Services offers peer mentoring to students requesting social support.

ADMISSIONS

The general admission requirements are the same for all applicants. Emerson College accepts the Common Application with a required supplemental essay, and admission is competitive. In choosing candidates for the entering class, Emerson looks for students who present academic promise in their high school record, strong recommendations, and writing competency, as well as personal qualities as seen in extracurricular activities, community involvement, and demonstrated leadership. The average GPA for acceptance is 3.73, and for students who submit SAT scores, the middle 50 percent is between 1280 and 1410. Ninety-four percent of the first-year class ranks in the top 50 percent of their high school graduation class. Applicants to the performing arts, comedic arts, or media production have additional requirements.

Additional Information

Students can make an appointment with an Academic Success Consultant in the Writing and Academic Resource Center (WARC) to work on time management tools and organizational skills, action plans to complete a project or manage multiple projects, reading strategies, test preparation strategies, and note-taking strategies. The office of Student Success offers one-to-one sessions with staff for a meeting or ongoing support. Emerson offers a 1 credit course in Foundations of Success to help students transitioning to college.

In 1988, Emerson obtained a castle in the Netherlands called Kasteel Well, a restored 14th century moated medieval castle located in the village of Well. The village is named for the original "sweet-water" well at the castle. Nearly one hundred students call it home and campus for three months each fall, spring, and summer for Emerson's study abroad programs.

Emerson College

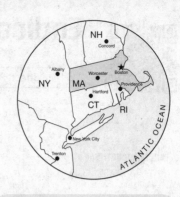

GENERAL ADMISSIONS

Very important factors include: academic GPA, application essay. *Important factors include:* rigor of secondary school record, class rank, recommendations. *Other factors considered include:* standardized test scores (if submitted). High school diploma is required and GED is accepted. Institution is test-optional for entering Fall 2024. Check admissions website for updates. *Academic units required:* 4 English, 3 math, 3 science, 3 foreign language, 3 social studies. *Academic units recommended:* 4 academic electives.

FINANCIAL AID

Students should submit: Business/Farm Supplement; CSS/Financial Aid Profile; FAFSA; Noncustodial Profile. *Need-based scholarships/grants offered:* College/university scholarship or grant aid from institutional funds; Federal Pell; Private scholarships; SEOG; State scholarships/grants. *Loan aid offered:* Direct PLUS loans; Direct Subsidized Loans; Direct Unsubsidized Loans. Federal Work-Study Program available. Institutional employment available.

CAMPUS LIFE

Activities: Campus Ministries; Choral groups; Dance; Drama/theater; International Student Organization; Literary magazine; Model UN; Music ensembles; Musical theater; Radio station; Student government; Student newspaper; Student-run film society; Television station; Yearbook. **Organizations:** 80 registered organizations. **Athletics (Intercollegiate):** *Men:* baseball, basketball, cross-country, lacrosse, volleyball. *Women:* basketball, cross-country, lacrosse, softball, volleyball.

CAMPUS
Type of school	Private (nonprofit)
Environment	Metropolis

STUDENTS
Undergrad enrollment	4,113
% male/female	36/64
% from out of state	81
% frosh live on campus	97

FINANCIAL FACTS
Annual tuition	$51,520
Room and board	$19,528
Required fees	$944

GENERAL ADMISSIONS INFO
Application fee	$65
Regular application deadline	1/15
Nonfall registration	Yes

Fall 2024 testing policy	Test Optional
Range SAT EBRW	620–710
Range SAT Math	580–690
Range ACT Composite	28–32

ACADEMICS
Student/faculty ratio	15:1
% students returning for sophomore year	87

Most classes have 10–19 students.

REQUESTING SERVICES FOR STUDENTS WITH LEARNING DIFFERENCES

Phone: 617-824-8592 • www.emerson.edu/departments/student-accessibility-services
Email: sas@emerson.edu

Documentation submitted to: Student Accessibility Services
Separate application required for Services: Yes

Documentation required for:
  LD: Psychoeducational evaluation
  ADHD: Psychoeducational evaluation
  ASD: Psychoeducational evaluation

Massachusetts

Endicott College

376 Hale Street, Beverly, MA 01915 • Admissions: 978-921-1000 • www.endicott.edu

Support: CS

ACCOMMODATIONS

Allowed in exams:

Calculators	Yes
Dictionary	Yes
Computer	Yes
Spell-checker	Yes
Extended test time	Yes
Scribe	Yes
Proctors	Yes
Oral exams	Yes
Note-takers	Yes

Support services for students with:

LD	Yes
ADHD	Yes
ASD	Yes
Distraction-reduced environment	Yes
Recording of lecture allowed	Yes
Reading technology	Yes
Audio books	Yes
Other assistive technology	Yes
Priority registration	No

Added costs of services:

For LD	No
For ADHD	No
For ASD	No
LD specialists	Yes
ADHD & ASD coaching	No
ASD specialists	No
Professional tutors	Yes
Peer tutors	Yes
Max. hours/week for services	6
How professors are notified of student approved accommodations	Center for Accessibility Services

COLLEGE GRADUATION REQUIREMENTS

Course waivers allowed	No
Course substitutions allowed	No

PROGRAMS/SERVICES FOR STUDENTS WITH LEARNING DIFFERENCES

The Center for Accessibility Services provides accommodations to qualified students. Students requesting accommodations must provide appropriate documentation of their disability. Eligibility for reasonable and appropriate accommodations will be determined on an individual basis.

ADMISSIONS

Endicott College seeks students who present academic promise in their secondary school records. They are looking for strong recommendations, writing competency, and personal qualities, as seen in extracurricular activities, community involvement, and demonstrated leadership. The average GPA is 3.4 for accepted applicants, and Endicott College believes that grades earned in high school are the most important factor in the admission decision.

Additional Information

The Division of Academic Success offers workshops on a variety of topics such as note-taking strategies, mindset and motivation, strategies for test-taking, basics of time management, and goal setting. The Center for Academic Coaching provides fee-for-service academic coaching. Students meet individually and independently with academic coaches at a mutually convenient time for up to three hours per week. Academic coaches help students develop academic self-awareness and confidence, organize course material, manage a college schedule, create work plans and study schedules, manage calendars and to-do lists, and learn test-taking strategies.

Beverly borders "Witches Woods," where accused witches fled in the 1600s during the Salem witch trials. The region is known for its witchy history and ghostly lore. Some ghost stories that students share are thought to be true; everyone has at least one. Pink Lady, Blue Lady, White Lady—the Winthrop Hall benevolent spirit goes by many names. Endicott is listed in the book *Haunted Colleges and Universities in MA* by Renee Mallet and mentioned in *Haunted Halls* by Elizabeth Tucker.

Endicott College

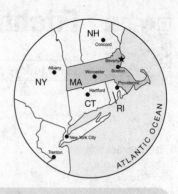

General Admissions

Very important factors include: rigor of secondary school record, academic GPA. *Important factors include:* application essay, recommendations. *Other factors considered include:* class rank, standardized test scores (if submitted). High school diploma is required and GED is accepted. Institution is test-optional for entering Fall 2024. Check admissions website for updates. *Academic units recommended:* 4 English, 3 math, 3 science, 2 foreign language, 3 social studies.

Financial Aid

Students should submit: FAFSA. *Need-based scholarships/grants offered:* College/university scholarship or grant aid from institutional funds; Federal Pell; Private scholarships; SEOG; State scholarships/grants. *Loan aid offered:* Direct PLUS loans; Direct Subsidized Loans; Direct Unsubsidized Loans. Federal Work-Study Program available. Institutional employment available.

Campus Life

Activities: Campus Ministries; Choral groups; Dance; Drama/theater; International Student Organization; Jazz band; Literary magazine; Music ensembles; Musical theater; Pep band; Radio station; Student government; Student newspaper; Television station; Yearbook. **Organizations:** 63 registered organizations, 16 honor societies, 2 religious organizations, 0 fraternities, 0 sororities. **Athletics (Intercollegiate):** *Men:* baseball, basketball, crew/rowing, cross-country, equestrian sports, golf, ice hockey, lacrosse, rugby, volleyball. *Women:* basketball, crew/rowing, cross-country, equestrian sports, field hockey, ice hockey, lacrosse, rugby, softball, track/field (indoor), volleyball.

CAMPUS
Type of school	Private (nonprofit)
Environment	Town

STUDENTS
Undergrad enrollment	3,220
% male/female	37/63
% from out of state	44
% frosh live on campus	98

FINANCIAL FACTS
Annual tuition	$36,926
Room and board	$16,948
Required fees	$850

GENERAL ADMISSIONS INFO
Application fee	$50
Regular application deadline	2/15
Nonfall registration	Yes
Fall 2024 testing policy	Test Optional
Range SAT EBRW	570–650
Range SAT Math	560–630
Range ACT Composite	24–29

ACADEMICS
Student/faculty ratio	12:1
% students returning for sophomore year	85

Most classes have 10–19 students.

REQUESTING SERVICES FOR STUDENTS WITH LEARNING DIFFERENCES

Phone: 978-998-7769 • www.endicott.edu/academics/academic-resources-support/accessibility
Email: access@endicott.edu

Documentation submitted to: Center for Accessibility Services
Separate application required for Services: Yes

Documentation required for:
LD: Psychoeducational evaluation
ADHD: Psychoeducational evaluation
ASD: Psychoeducational evaluation

Fitchburg State University

160 Pearl Street, Fitchburg, MA 01420-2697 • Admissions: 978-665-3144 • www.fitchburgstate.edu

Support: S

ACCOMMODATIONS

Allowed in exams:

Calculators	Yes
Dictionary	Yes
Computer	Yes
Spell-checker	Yes
Extended test time	Yes
Scribe	Yes
Proctors	Yes
Oral exams	Yes
Note-takers	Yes

Support services for students with:

LD	Yes
ADHD	Yes
ASD	Yes
Distraction-reduced environment	Yes
Recording of lecture allowed	Yes
Reading technology	Yes
Audio books	No
Other assistive technology	Yes
Priority registration	No

Added costs of services:

For LD	No
For ADHD	No
For ASD	No
LD specialists	No
ADHD & ASD coaching	No
ASD specialists	No
Professional tutors	Yes
Peer tutors	Yes
Max. hours/week for services	Varies
How professors are notified of student approved accommodations	Student

COLLEGE GRADUATION REQUIREMENTS

Course waivers allowed	No
Course substitutions allowed	Yes
In what courses: Case-by-case basis	

PROGRAMS/SERVICES FOR STUDENTS WITH LEARNING DIFFERENCES

Disability Services (DS) empowers students with disabilities to engage in all facets of academic, residential, and student life at FSU. To register for accommodations, students fill out a request for services form and file supporting documentation. Students must allow 7-10 business days for DS to process their application materials and schedule an orientation for services. DS assists in coordinating all approved accommodations across campus.

ADMISSIONS

All applicants are expected to meet the same admission criteria, and must submit an application and official high school transcript. For the foreign language requirement, American Sign Language (ASL) is accepted. Applicants with a GPA below 3.0 will be reviewed on a sliding scale to determine admissibility. Their GPA will be recalculated based on their college prep, honors, and AP level courses. Interviews and letters of recommendation are both optional. Students who have not met the requirements may be considered for admission through the Summer Bridge Program.

Additional Information

The Summer Bridge Program is for first-year students who have demonstrated the potential to succeed in college, but whose high school academic record fell just below the university's minimum admission criteria. To successfully complete the Summer Bridge Program, students must pass three courses in writing, math, and college preparation with a cumulative average of 2.0 or higher. Admission to the Summer Bridge program is at the discretion of the Admissions Office, and admission to the university is contingent upon successful completion of the program. The program is free, but the deposit for enrollment must be submitted to secure a spot. Housing is available if needed.

Fitchburg was originally established in 1894 as a two-year teacher-training program for women. Thompson Hall, built in 1896 and named for its first president John G. Thompson, was the first campus building, and is still in use today. Edgerly Hall, now the home of the computer science and mathematics departments, was one of the first junior high schools in America, where student-teachers-in-training could put their lessons into practice.

Fitchburg State University

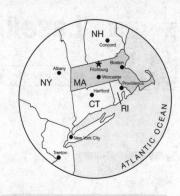

GENERAL ADMISSIONS

Very important factors include: rigor of secondary school record. *Important factors include:* academic GPA, standardized test scores (if submitted), application essay. *Other factors considered include:* recommendations. High school diploma is required and GED is accepted. Institution is test-optional for entering Fall 2024. Check admissions website for updates. *Academic units required:* 4 English, 4 math, 3 science (3 labs), 2 foreign language, 1 social studies, 1 U.S. history, 2 academic electives.

FINANCIAL AID

Students should submit: FAFSA. *Need-based scholarships/grants offered:* College/university scholarship or grant aid from institutional funds; Federal Pell; Private scholarships; SEOG; State scholarships/grants. *Loan aid offered:* Direct PLUS loans; Direct Subsidized Loans; Direct Unsubsidized Loans. Federal Work-Study Program available. Institutional employment available.

CAMPUS LIFE

Activities: Choral groups; Concert band; Dance; Drama/theater; Jazz band; Literary magazine; Model UN; Radio station; Student government; Student newspaper; Student-run film society. **Organizations:** 60 registered organizations, 12 honor societies, 1 religious organizations, 2 fraternities, 3 sororities. **Athletics (Intercollegiate):** *Men:* baseball, basketball, cross-country, ice hockey, track/field (indoor). *Women:* basketball, cross-country, field hockey, lacrosse, softball, track/field (indoor).

CAMPUS
Type of school	Public
Environment	Town

STUDENTS
Undergrad enrollment	3,958
% male/female	46/54
% from out of state	8
% frosh live on campus	70

FINANCIAL FACTS
Annual in-state tuition	$970
Annual out-of-state tuition	$7,050
Room and board	$8,256
Required fees	$7,330

GENERAL ADMISSIONS INFO
Application fee	$25
Regular application deadline	Rolling
Nonfall registration	Yes

Fall 2024 testing policy	Test Optional
Range SAT EBRW	450–560
Range SAT Math	460–560
Range ACT Composite	19–23

ACADEMICS
Student/faculty ratio	16:1
% students returning for sophomore year	73

Most classes have 20–29 students.

REQUESTING SERVICES FOR STUDENTS WITH LEARNING DIFFERENCES

Phone: 978-665-4020 • www.fitchburgstate.edu/student-support/disability-services
Email: disabilityserviceslist@fitchburgstate.edu

Documentation submitted to: Disability Services
Separate application required for Services: Yes

Documentation required for:
  LD: Psychoeducational evaluation
  ADHD: Psychoeducational evaluation
  ASD: Psychoeducational evaluation

Massachusetts

Lasell University

Undergraduate Admissions, Newton, MA 02466 • Admissions: 617-243-2225 • lasell.edu

Support: CS

ACCOMMODATIONS

Allowed in exams:

Calculators	Yes
Dictionary	Yes
Computer	Yes
Spell-checker	Yes
Extended test time	Yes
Scribe	Yes
Proctors	No
Oral exams	No
Note-takers	Yes

Support services for students with:

LD	Yes
ADHD	Yes
ASD	Yes
Distraction-reduced environment	Yes
Recording of lecture allowed	
Reading technology	Yes
Audio books	Yes
Other assistive technology	Yes
Priority registration	No

Added costs of services:

For LD	No
For ADHD	No
For ASD	No
LD specialists	Yes
ADHD & ASD coaching	No
ASD specialists	No
Professional tutors	No
Peer tutors	Yes
Max. hours/week for services	Varies
How professors are notified of student approved accommodations	Student and Accessibility Services

COLLEGE GRADUATION REQUIREMENTS

Course waivers allowed	No
Course substitutions allowed	Yes
In what courses: Foreign Language	

PROGRAMS/SERVICES FOR STUDENTS WITH LEARNING DIFFERENCES

The Office of Accessibility Services at Lasell University provides reasonable accommodations to all eligible students. Students may apply for services by completing an accommodation request form, submitting eligible documentation, and meeting with the director of Disability Services.

ADMISSIONS

Admission requirements are the same for all applicants. Eligible students may submit the LEAP application, which replaces the application essay and recommendation letters with a one-on-one interview. Both the traditional and LEAP applications are reviewed for admission consideration with the same approach. Interviews are not required but are recommended. Admitted students typically have a 2.5 GPA or higher. Students who believe that their standardized test scores will support their consideration for admission are encouraged to include them on their application.

Additional Information

The Academic Achievement Center (AAC) provides learning specialists and peer tutors to help with time management, writing skills, tutoring, study groups, academic technology, and academic success workshops. The Academic Advising Center employs three professional advisors who work with students to help them succeed academically.

Lasell was founded in 1851 as the Auburndale Female Seminary. In 1859, Lasell established a "new and most important feature"—the incorporation of physical culture. In 1888, a raised gymnasium, the nation's first-ever college swimming pool, and a bowling alley were dedicated by Lucy Hayes, first lady and wife of President Rutherford B. Hayes. Athletic clubs grew to include canoeing, archery, tennis, horseback riding, and military drills. In the 1900s, academics and athletics began to tie together. River Days, dating back to the 1900s, is still a tradition today. Men were first admitted to Lasell in 1997.

Lasell University

GENERAL ADMISSIONS

Very important factors include: rigor of secondary school record, academic GPA. *Important factors include:* application essay, recommendations. *Other factors considered include:* standardized test scores (if submitted). High school diploma is required and GED is accepted. Institution is test-optional for entering Fall 2024. Check admissions website for updates. *Academic units required:* 4 English, 3 math, 2 science (2 labs), 2 social studies. *Academic units recommended:* 4 math, 3 science (3 labs), 2 foreign language, 3 social studies.

FINANCIAL AID

Students should submit: FAFSA. *Need-based scholarships/grants offered:* College/university scholarship or grant aid from institutional funds; Federal Pell; Private scholarships; SEOG; State scholarships/grants. *Loan aid offered:* Direct PLUS loans; Direct Subsidized Loans; Direct Unsubsidized Loans. Federal Work-Study Program available. Institutional employment available.

CAMPUS LIFE

Activities: Choral groups; Dance; Drama/theater; International Student Organization; Jazz band; Literary magazine; Music ensembles; Musical theater; Radio station; Student government; Student newspaper; Television station; Yearbook. **Organizations:** 74 registered organizations, 4 honor societies, 1 religious organizations, 0 fraternities, 0 sororities. **Athletics (Intercollegiate):** *Men:* baseball, basketball, crew/rowing, cross-country, gymnastics, lacrosse, rugby, ultimate frisbee, volleyball. *Women:* basketball, crew/rowing, cross-country, field hockey, gymnastics, lacrosse, rugby, softball, ultimate frisbee, volleyball.

CAMPUS
Type of school	Private (nonprofit)
Environment	City

STUDENTS
Undergrad enrollment	1,294
% male/female	36/64
% from out of state	40
% frosh live on campus	91

FINANCIAL FACTS
Annual tuition	$40,980
Room and board	$16,500
Required fees	$1,650

GENERAL ADMISSIONS INFO
Application fee	No fee
Regular application deadline	Rolling
Nonfall registration	Yes

Fall 2024 testing policy	Test Optional
Range SAT EBRW	570–705
Range SAT Math	510–620
Range ACT Composite	24–28.5

ACADEMICS
Student/faculty ratio	14:1
% students returning for sophomore year	72

Most classes have 10–19 students.

REQUESTING SERVICES FOR STUDENTS WITH LEARNING DIFFERENCES

Phone: 617-243-2212 • www.lasell.edu/campus-life/disability-services • Email: shawthorne@lasell.edu

Documentation submitted to: Office of Accessibility Services
Separate application required for Services: Yes

Documentation required for:
LD: Psychoeducational evaluation
ADHD: Psychoeducational evaluation
ASD: Psychoeducational evaluation

Lesley University

Undergraduate Admission, Cambridge, MA 02140 • Admissions: 617-349-8800 • www.lesley.edu

Support: S

ACCOMMODATIONS

Allowed in exams:

Calculators	Yes
Dictionary	Yes
Computer	Yes
Spell-checker	Yes
Extended test time	Yes
Scribe	Yes
Proctors	No
Oral exams	No
Note-takers	

Support services for students with:

LD	Yes
ADHD	Yes
ASD	Yes
Distraction-reduced environment	Yes
Recording of lecture allowed	Yes
Reading technology	Yes
Audio books	Yes
Other assistive technology	Yes
Priority registration	Yes

Added costs of services:

For LD	No
For ADHD	No
For ASD	No
LD specialists	No
ADHD & ASD coaching	Yes
ASD specialists	No
Professional tutors	No
Peer tutors	Yes
Max. hours/week for services	Varies
How professors are notified of student approved accommodations	

COLLEGE GRADUATION REQUIREMENTS

Course waivers allowed	No
Course substitutions allowed	No

PROGRAMS/SERVICES FOR STUDENTS WITH LEARNING DIFFERENCES

Services and accommodations for students with disabilities are initiated through the Disability Services Office (DSO). Academic accommodations include deadline extensions for assignments, electronic technology, tutors, and writing assistants. Students should contact the DSO team prior to the start of each semester regarding their accommodations. Students needing more comprehensive support or having difficulty at a traditional college campus are encouraged to apply to the Threshold Program. Threshold is a non-degree, two-year certificate transition program for young adults with diverse learning, developmental, and intellectual disabilities. This fee-based program focuses on students with a specific profile of academic achievement but a wide range of backgrounds. Students may have learning, intellectual, or developmental disabilities, including (but not limited to) autism, nonverbal learning disabilities, ADHD, cerebral palsy, Down syndrome, or multiple disabilities. At Threshold, dorm living, student activities, and a curriculum focused on career training and independent living create a college experience that feels both authentic and supported. Threshold students begin with a two-year academic program, and after completion, they can choose to continue with programs that support them as they work toward independence with the Bridge Year or Transition Year.

ADMISSIONS

Admitted students have a 3.1 average GPA and have taken a college preparatory course load in high school that includes 4 years of English, 3 years of math (including algebra II), 3 years of science (including 2 or more lab courses), and 3 years of history/social sciences (including U.S. history).

Additional Information

The Center for Academic Achievement provides free academic tutoring and coaching to all students to help them with their coursework and projects.

The Lesley School was founded by Edith Lesley in 1909 at her home in Cambridge. The school began as a private women's institution that trained kindergarten (a new movement) teachers. Lesley and her husband expanded the school with an addition to their home, which is now the Office of the President. Around 1913, the Lesley School began training elementary teachers, then reorganized under a board of trustees in 1944, receiving the authority to award baccalaureate degrees, and became Lesley College. In 1954, the college began awarding graduate degrees.

Lesley University

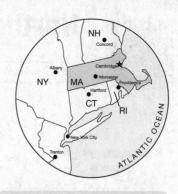

GENERAL ADMISSIONS

Very important factors include: rigor of secondary school record, academic GPA. *Important factors include:* class rank, , application essay, recommendations. High school diploma is required and GED is accepted. Institution is test-free for entering Fall 2024. Check admissions website for updates. *Academic units required:* 4 English, 3 math, 3 science (2 labs), 2 social studies, 1 U.S. history. *Academic units recommended:* 4 math, 4 science, 2 foreign language, 4 social studies.

FINANCIAL AID

Students should submit: FAFSA. *Need-based scholarships/grants offered:* College/university scholarship or grant aid from institutional funds; Federal Pell; Private scholarships; SEOG; State scholarships/grants. *Loan aid offered:* Direct PLUS loans; Direct Subsidized Loans; Direct Unsubsidized Loans. Federal Work-Study Program available. Institutional employment available.

CAMPUS LIFE

Activities: Campus Ministries; Choral groups; Dance; Drama/theater; International Student Organization; Literary magazine; Musical theater; Student government; Student newspaper. **Organizations:** 25 registered organizations, 2 honor societies, 2 religious organizations, 0 fraternities, 0 sororities. **Athletics (Intercollegiate):** *Men:* basketball, cross-country, volleyball. *Women:* basketball, crew/rowing, cross-country, softball, volleyball.

CAMPUS	
Type of school	Private (nonprofit)
Environment	Metropolis

STUDENTS	
Undergrad enrollment	1,418
% male/female	25/75
% from out of state	57
% frosh live on campus	83

FINANCIAL FACTS	
Annual tuition	$25,500
Room and board	$15,300
Required fees	$2,508

GENERAL ADMISSIONS INFO	
Application fee	No fee
Regular application deadline	Rolling
Nonfall registration	Yes
Fall 2024 testing policy	Test Free

ACADEMICS	
Student/faculty ratio	9:1
% students returning for sophomore year	78
Most classes have 10–19 students.	

REQUESTING SERVICES FOR STUDENTS WITH LEARNING DIFFERENCES

Phone: 617-349-8462 • lesley.edu/students/health-wellness-safety/disability-services
Email: kjohnso7@lesley.edu

Documentation submitted to: Disability Services
Separate application required for Services: Yes

Documentation required for:
  LD: Psychoeducational evaluation
  ADHD: Psychoeducational evaluation
  ASD: Psychoeducational evaluation

Massachusetts

Northeastern University

360 Huntington Avenue, Boston, MA 02115 • Admissions: 617-373-2200 • www.northeastern.edu

(Support: SP)

ACCOMMODATIONS

Allowed in exams:

Calculators	Yes
Dictionary	Yes
Computer	Yes
Spell-checker	Yes
Extended test time	Yes
Scribe	Yes
Proctors	Yes
Oral exams	Yes
Note-takers	Yes

Support services for students with:

LD	Yes
ADHD	Yes
ASD	Yes
Distraction-reduced environment	Yes
Recording of lecture allowed	Yes
Reading technology	Yes
Audio books	Yes
Other assistive technology	Yes
Priority registration	No

Added costs of services:

For LD	Yes
For ADHD	Yes
For ASD	Yes
LD specialists	Yes
ADHD & ASD coaching	No
ASD specialists	No
Professional tutors	Yes
Peer tutors	Yes
Max. hours/week for services	Varies
How professors are notified of student approved accommodations	Student

COLLEGE GRADUATION REQUIREMENTS

Course waivers allowed	No
Course substitutions allowed	Yes
In what courses: Foreign Language	

PROGRAMS/SERVICES FOR STUDENTS WITH LEARNING DIFFERENCES

The Disability Resource Center (DRC) determines appropriate accommodations for students with disabilities. To request accommodations, students must complete a disclosure application and submit documentation of their disability. Once the DRC committee has reviewed the information, students are invited to register with the DRC and meet to discuss accommodations, policies, and procedures for accessing accommodations, training on accommodation use, learning strategies for a specific course load, and other resources on campus that may be helpful. The Learning Disabilities Program (LDP) is a fee-based comprehensive academic support program for students with a learning disability and/or attention deficit disorder. LDP students meet one-on-one with an LDP specialist twice a week to discuss the student's learning profile, coursework, and goals. They might also address topics such as studying and test-taking strategies, the use of accommodations and campus resources, time management, organization, and monitoring progress to achieve goals. The Brian Evans Learning Disabilities Program Assistance Fund provides scholarships for three to five students each year. Students are selected by the director of the LDP, and their eligibility is determined by the Office of Student Financial Services and the senior vice president for Enrollment and Student Life.

ADMISSIONS

All applicants are expected to meet the same admission criteria. High school transcripts, midyear reports, and a letter of recommendation from a school counselor are required. One teacher recommendation is required, while any additional recommendations are optional. A personal essay is required, and applicants are encouraged to use this essay to highlight their strengths, qualities, commitment, and contributions to the community. All applicants apply to one of seven undergraduate colleges or to the Explore Program for undeclared students. All students who apply on time are considered for scholarships, and no additional applications are necessary.

Additional Information

The Peer Tutoring Program offers a variety of free tutoring services, either in-person or online, and in individual or group sessions. This program also holds weekly peer reviews—problem-solving sessions offered in selected courses and authorized by faculty. Supplemental Instruction (SI) is led by a peer tutor and designed to supplement, not replace class lectures. Designated tutors offer one-on-one sessions with students who are at potential risk of failing a course. All peer tutors are trained in accordance with College Reading & Learning Association (CRLA) tutor certification guidelines.

DID YOU KNOW?

Conveniently held on Parents' Weekend, the "Underwear Run" has become a rite of passage for several thousand Huskies who strip down to their underwear and sprint up and down Huntington Avenue, giving high-end stores and restaurants quite a show. The run ends with an icy dunk in the Reflecting Pool.

Northeastern University

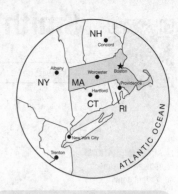

GENERAL ADMISSIONS

Very important factors include: rigor of secondary school record, academic GPA, standardized test scores (if submitted), application essay, recommendations. *Other factors considered include:* class rank. High school diploma is required and GED is accepted. Institution is test-optional for entering Fall 2024. Check admissions website for updates. *Academic units required:* 4 English, 3 math, 3 science (2 labs), 2 foreign language, 3 social studies. *Academic units recommended:* 4 math, 4 science (4 labs), 4 foreign language, 4 social studies.

FINANCIAL AID

Students should submit: CSS/Financial Aid Profile; FAFSA; Noncustodial Profile. *Need-based scholarships/grants offered:* College/university scholarship or grant aid from institutional funds; Federal Pell; Private scholarships; SEOG; State scholarships/grants. *Loan aid offered:* Direct PLUS loans; Direct Subsidized Loans; Direct Unsubsidized Loans. Federal Work-Study Program available. Institutional employment available.

CAMPUS LIFE

Activities: Choral groups; Concert band; Dance; Drama/theater; International Student Organization; Jazz band; Literary magazine; Model UN; Music ensembles; Musical theater; Pep band; Radio station; Student government; Student newspaper; Student-run film society; Symphony orchestra; Television station; Yearbook. **Organizations:** 400 registered organizations, 22 religious organizations. **Athletics (Intercollegiate):** *Men:* baseball, basketball, crew/rowing, cross-country, cycling, golf, ice hockey, lacrosse, martial arts, rugby, swimming, table tennis, track/field (indoor), ultimate frisbee, volleyball, wrestling. *Women:* basketball, crew/rowing, cross-country, cycling, field hockey, golf, ice hockey, lacrosse, martial arts, rugby, swimming, table tennis, track/field (indoor), ultimate frisbee, volleyball, wrestling.

CAMPUS

Type of school	Private (nonprofit)
Environment	Metropolis

STUDENTS

Undergrad enrollment	20,850
% male/female	45/55
% from out of state	73
% frosh live on campus	99

FINANCIAL FACTS

Annual tuition	$59,100
Room and board	$18,440
Required fees	$1,092

GENERAL ADMISSIONS INFO

Application fee	$75
Regular application deadline	1/1
Nonfall registration	Yes

Fall 2024 testing policy	Test Optional
Range SAT EBRW	700–760
Range SAT Math	740–790
Range ACT Composite	33–35

ACADEMICS

Student/faculty ratio	14:1
% students returning for sophomore year	97

Most classes have 10–19 students.

REQUESTING SERVICES FOR STUDENTS WITH LEARNING DIFFERENCES

Phone: 617-373-2675 • drc.sites.northeastern.edu • Email: drc@northeastern.edu

Documentation submitted to: Disability Resource Center
Separate application required for Services: Yes

Documentation required for:
LD: Psychoeducational evaluation
ADHD: Psychoeducational evaluation
ASD: Psychoeducational evaluation

Massachusetts

Smith College

7 College Lane, Northampton, MA 01063 • Admissions: 413-585-2500 • www.smith.edu

Support: S

ACCOMMODATIONS

Allowed in exams:

Calculators	Yes
Dictionary	No
Computer	Yes
Spell-checker	Yes
Extended test time	Yes
Scribe	Yes
Proctors	No
Oral exams	Yes
Note-takers	Yes

Support services for students with:

LD	Yes
ADHD	Yes
ASD	Yes
Distraction-reduced environment	Yes
Recording of lecture allowed	Yes
Reading technology	Yes
Audio books	Yes
Other assistive technology	Yes
Priority registration	Yes

Added costs of services:

For LD	No
For ADHD	No
For ASD	No
LD specialists	No
ADHD & ASD coaching	No
ASD specialists	No
Professional tutors	Yes
Peer tutors	Yes
Max. hours/week for services	Varies
How professors are notified of student approved accommodations	Student and Office of Disability Services

COLLEGE GRADUATION REQUIREMENTS

Course waivers allowed	No
Course substitutions allowed	Yes
In what courses: Case-by-case basic	

Julia Child, the beloved "French Chef," graduated from Smith in 1934. In 1990, she formally donated her Cambridge home to Smith College, where her famous TV series "In Julia's Kitchen with Master Chefs" was filmed. On Julia Child Day, every dining hall cooks one of her famous recipes for breakfast, lunch, and dinner, each serving a different dish.

PROGRAMS/SERVICES FOR STUDENTS WITH LEARNING DIFFERENCES

The Office of Disability Services (ODS) sources information and coordinates accommodations for students with disabilities. Following their acceptance to Smith, students can register with ODS and submit the online Disability Identification Form along with disability documentation. Students will then be contacted by ODS staff to meet and discuss their challenges and determine appropriate accommodations. Early registration may be arranged to help determine and facilitate the accommodation process. Common accommodations include extended time or a reduced-distraction environment for exams, additional time for writing assignments, notetakers, assistive technology, and books and class materials in an alternate format. Advancing Student Success in Educational Transitions at Smith (ASSETS) provides structured support for first-year students with disabilities that impact learning, such as LD, ASD, and ADHD, and helps smooth the transition to college while developing their independence and essential learning skills. At the start of the program, students and their parents are invited to an orientation that covers academic requirements and social expectations. ODS also offers weekly workshops during the first four weeks of the semester that feature guest presenters and student mentors. Students may choose to develop a peer mentorship with a student who has a similar disability.

ADMISSIONS

All applicants are held to the same standard for admission. Smith is a competitive school; on average, students enrolled at Smith had achieved a 4.0 high school GPA. The admission committee requires a secondary school report, including an official high school transcript, GPA, class rank, two teacher evaluations plus a counselor recommendation, a mid-year report, and a personal essay. These materials are reviewed in conjunction with the student's extracurricular activities. A personal interview is highly recommended and can take place on or off campus.

Additional Information

Students can access the Assistive Technology Lab during the library's regular open hours by booking a session online. The lab has specialized software, such as Dragon, Kurzweil, and Big Keys, and offers software training on both Mac and Windows machines. The Jacobson Center for Writing, Teaching, and Learning is a resource for developing a variety of skills, and is equipped to address the needs of students with learning disabilities. Students can attend workshops or individual sessions on time management, organization, and academic study skills, and meet with professional writing instructors during the day to improve their drafts or final compositions. Similar services are available evenings and weekends when they are provided by peer writing tutors at the center and other campus locations. The Lazarus Center for Career Development (or CDO—Career Development Office) is a counseling resource that prepares students for the workforce, in the form of individual or group sessions, seminars, workshops, and panels. Topics cover internships, résumé writing, interviewing, and job search techniques.

Smith College

GENERAL ADMISSIONS

Very important factors include: rigor of secondary school record, academic GPA, application essay, recommendations. *Important factors include:* class rank. *Other factors considered include:* standardized test scores (if submitted). High school diploma or equivalent is not required. Institution is test-optional for entering Fall 2024. Check admissions website for updates. *Academic units recommended:* 4 English, 3 math, 3 science (3 labs), 3 foreign language, 2 history, 1 academic elective.

FINANCIAL AID

Students should submit: CSS/Financial Aid Profile; FAFSA; Institution's own financial aid form; Noncustodial Profile. *Need-based scholarships/grants offered:* College/university scholarship or grant aid from institutional funds; Federal Pell; Private scholarships; SEOG; State scholarships/grants. *Loan aid offered:* Direct PLUS loans; Direct Subsidized Loans; Direct Unsubsidized Loans. Federal Work-Study Program available. Institutional employment available.

CAMPUS LIFE

Activities: Campus Ministries; Choral groups; Concert band; Dance; Drama/theater; International Student Organization; Jazz band; Literary magazine; Model UN; Music ensembles; Musical theater; Radio station; Student government; Student newspaper; Television station; Yearbook. **Organizations:** 100 registered organizations, 3 honor societies, 9 religious organizations, 0 fraternities, 0 sororities. **Athletics (Intercollegiate):** *Women:* basketball, crew/rowing, cross-country, equestrian sports, field hockey, golf, ice hockey, lacrosse, martial arts, rugby, softball, swimming, track/field (indoor), ultimate frisbee, volleyball, water polo.

CAMPUS
Type of school	Private (nonprofit)
Environment	Town

STUDENTS
Undergrad enrollment	2,565
% male/female	0/100
% from out of state	81
% frosh live on campus	100

FINANCIAL FACTS
Annual tuition	$55,830
Room and board	$19,420
Required fees	$284

GENERAL ADMISSIONS INFO
Application fee	No fee
Regular application deadline	1/15
Nonfall registration	Yes

Fall 2024 testing policy	Test Optional
Range SAT EBRW	690–760
Range SAT Math	680–770
Range ACT Composite	31–34

ACADEMICS
Student/faculty ratio	8:1
% students returning for sophomore year	95

Most classes have 10–19 students.

REQUESTING SERVICES FOR STUDENTS WITH LEARNING DIFFERENCES

Phone: 413-585-2071 • www.smith.edu/about-smith/disability-services • Email: ods@smith.edu

Documentation submitted to: Disability Services
Separate application required for Services: Yes

Documentation required for:
LD: Psychoeducational evaluation
ADHD: Psychoeducational evaluation
ASD: Psychoeducational evaluation

University of Massachusetts Amherst

University Admissions Center, Amherst, MA 01003 • Admissions: 413-545-0222 • www.umass.edu

Support: CS

ACCOMMODATIONS

Allowed in exams:

Calculators	Yes
Dictionary	Yes
Computer	Yes
Spell-checker	Yes
Extended test time	Yes
Scribe	Yes
Proctors	Yes
Oral exams	Yes
Note-takers	Yes

Support services for students with:

LD	Yes
ADHD	Yes
ASD	Yes
Distraction-reduced environment	Yes
Recording of lecture allowed	Yes
Reading technology	Yes
Audio books	Yes
Other assistive technology	Yes
Priority registration	Yes

Added costs of services:

For LD	No
For ADHD	No
For ASD	No
LD specialists	Yes
ADHD & ASD coaching	No
ASD specialists	No
Professional tutors	No
Peer tutors	Yes
Max. hours/week for services	Varies
How professors are notified of student approved accommodations	Disability Services

COLLEGE GRADUATION REQUIREMENTS

Course waivers allowed	No
Course substitutions allowed	Yes
In what courses: Math, Analytical Reasoning, and Foreign Language	

PROGRAMS/SERVICES FOR STUDENTS WITH LEARNING DIFFERENCES

Disability Services at the University of Massachusetts Amherst serves students with learning differences and disabilities. Students seeking accommodations must register with Disability Services, provide appropriate documentation, and meet with an access coordinator. Students who have not been diagnosed but are struggling academically may be eligible for scholarships to cover some or all of the costs of testing. Incoming students can become acquainted with Disability Services by participating in the new student orientation and transition summer sessions. Those who are unable to attend in person can attend online question-and-answer sessions. Students with ASD are eligible to participate in a networking group that is co-led by Disability Services and the Center for Counseling and Psychological Health.

ADMISSIONS

Admission criteria are the same for all applicants, and it is at the student's discretion whether they disclose a disability on their application. The admission review places importance on grade trend and courses taken that are relevant to the student's intended major. Applicants to the College of Engineering, Isenberg School of Management, or the computer science major must include an advanced math course in their high school curriculum, such as precalculus, calculus, or trigonometry. Applicants to the College of Engineering must also have taken chemistry and physics.

Additional Information

Through the Massachusetts Inclusive Concurrent Enrollment Initiative (MAICEI), Massachusetts students with significant disabilities aged 18-22 receiving IEP services from their school district can experience college while still maintaining their special education services. MAICEI students at UMass Amherst are supported by the MAICEI program coordinator, educational coaches, and peer mentors. The extensive tutoring program at UMass Amherst is accessible to all students.

There are five 22-floor towers in the Southwest residential halls. A sixth was planned, but engineers discovered the ground could not support its weight. The towers are named after U.S. presidents: George Washington and four from Massachusetts—John Adams, John Quincy Adams, Calvin Coolidge, and John F. Kennedy. The five towers and 11 smaller residence halls, with 5,500 students living in a 0.25 square mile, are often considered one of the most densely populated spots on Earth.

University of Massachusetts Amherst

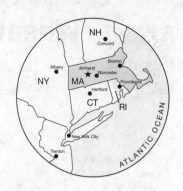

GENERAL ADMISSIONS

Very important factors include: rigor of secondary school record, academic GPA. *Important factors include:* class rank, application essay, recommendations. *Other factors considered include:* standardized test scores (if submitted). High school diploma is required and GED is accepted. Institution is test-optional for entering Fall 2024. Check admissions website for updates. *Academic units required:* 4 English, 4 math, 3 science (3 labs), 2 foreign language, 1 social studies, 1 U.S. history, 2 academic electives.

FINANCIAL AID

Students should submit: FAFSA. *Need-based scholarships/grants offered:* College/university scholarship or grant aid from institutional funds; Federal Pell; Private scholarships; SEOG; State scholarships/grants. *Loan aid offered:* Direct PLUS loans; Direct Subsidized Loans; Direct Unsubsidized Loans. Federal Work-Study Program available. Institutional employment available.

CAMPUS LIFE

Activities: Campus Ministries; Choral groups; Concert band; Dance; Drama/theater; International Student Organization; Jazz band; Literary magazine; Marching band; Model UN; Music ensembles; Musical theater; Opera; Pep band; Radio station; Student government; Student newspaper; Student-run film society; Symphony orchestra; Television station. **Organizations:** 500 registered organizations, 38 honor societies, 25 religious organizations, 27 fraternities, 19 sororities. **Athletics (Intercollegiate):** *Men:* baseball, basketball, crew/rowing, cross-country, cycling, equestrian sports, golf, gymnastics, ice hockey, lacrosse, martial arts, racquetball, rugby, swimming, table tennis, track/field (indoor), ultimate frisbee, volleyball, water polo. *Women:* basketball, crew/rowing, cross-country, cycling, equestrian sports, field hockey, golf, gymnastics, ice hockey, lacrosse, martial arts, racquetball, rugby, softball, swimming, table tennis, track/field (indoor), ultimate frisbee, water polo.

CAMPUS

Type of school	Public
Environment	Town

STUDENTS

Undergrad enrollment	24,111
% male/female	49/51
% from out of state	20
% frosh live on campus	80

FINANCIAL FACTS

Annual in-state tuition	$16,186
Annual out-of-state tuition	$37,405
Room and board	$14,776
Required fees	$766

GENERAL ADMISSIONS INFO

Application fee	$85
Regular application deadline	1/15
Nonfall registration	Yes

Fall 2024 testing policy	Test Optional
Range SAT EBRW	630–720
Range SAT Math	630–760
Range ACT Composite	29–33

ACADEMICS

Student/faculty ratio	18:1
% students returning for sophomore year	90

Most classes have 10–19 students.

REQUESTING SERVICES FOR STUDENTS WITH LEARNING DIFFERENCES

Phone: 413-545-0892 • www.umass.edu/disability • Email: disability@umass.edu

Documentation submitted to: Disability Services
Separate application required for Services: Yes

Documentation required for:
 LD: Psychoeducational evaluation
 ADHD: Psychoeducational evaluation
 ASD: Psychoeducational evaluation

Wheaton College

26 E. Main Street, Norton, MA 02766 • Admissions: 508-286-8251 • www.wheatoncollege.edu

Support: S

ACCOMMODATIONS

Allowed in exams:

Calculators	Yes
Dictionary	No
Computer	Yes
Spell-checker	No
Extended test time	Yes
Scribe	Yes
Proctors	No
Oral exams	No
Note-takers	Yes

Support services for students with:

LD	Yes
ADHD	Yes
ASD	Yes
Distraction-reduced environment	Yes
Recording of lecture allowed	Yes
Reading technology	Yes
Audio books	Yes
Other assistive technology	Yes
Priority registration	Yes

Added costs of services:

For LD	No
For ADHD	No
For ASD	No
LD specialists	No
ADHD & ASD coaching	No
ASD specialists	No
Professional tutors	No
Peer tutors	Yes
Max. hours/week for services	Varies
How professors are notified of student approved accommodations	Student

COLLEGE GRADUATION REQUIREMENTS

Course waivers allowed	No
Course substitutions allowed	Yes
In what courses: Foreign Language	

PROGRAMS/SERVICES FOR STUDENTS WITH LEARNING DIFFERENCES

The associate director of Accessibility Services (AS) is available to meet with students on an appointment basis after acceptance, before enrollment, or anytime during a student's time at Wheaton. To be considered for accommodations offered through AS, students must submit an intake form and documentation of their disability and schedule an intake interview. Academic accommodations are determined on a case-by-case basis and must be requested by the student each semester. There is a two-day pre-orientation program for students with disabilities called Abilities 1st! Pre-Orientation. Students can elect to move on campus two days early and participate in a small group orientation program. Students with disabilities may qualify for a reduced course load, and students with a language-based learning disability may petition for a modification of the foreign language college graduation requirement. If granted a substitution, students can select two courses within the same culture that are taught in English in consultation with their Student Success Advisor.

ADMISSIONS

All applicants must meet the same admission standards, and Wheaton will accept courses taken in the special education department. Students are encouraged to take AP and honors courses and visual or performing arts courses. There are general recommended academic courses, but the college emphasizes that the most competitive applicants will have also completed 4 units of math and 4 units of a foreign language. Creative portfolios are submitted through Slideroom. The average unweighted GPA for admitted students is 3.78.

Additional Information

Peer group tutoring is available and conducted by students screened by the specific academic department.

Honors Theses represent the best original research by undergraduate honors students. Wheaton's first honors thesis was prepared in 1928. The tradition of delivering a senior honors thesis involves first putting on academic robes tricked out with costume accessories: masks, beads, capes, and then parading with fellow students, professors, and staff to the tune of "The March of Acid-Free Paper." It's silly. It's fun. And it's the point of the celebration.

Wheaton College

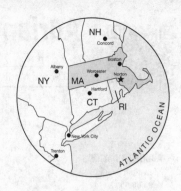

General Admissions

Very important factors include: rigor of secondary school record, academic GPA, application essay, recommendations. *Other factors considered include:* class rank, standardized test scores (if submitted). High school diploma is required and GED is accepted. Institution is test-optional for entering Fall 2024. Check admissions website for updates. *Academic units recommended:* 4 English, 3 math, 3 science (3 labs), 3 foreign language, 3 social studies.

Financial Aid

Students should submit: Business/Farm Supplement; CSS/Financial Aid Profile; FAFSA; Noncustodial Profile. *Need-based scholarships/grants offered:* College/university scholarship or grant aid from institutional funds; Federal Pell; Private scholarships; SEOG; State scholarships/grants. *Loan aid offered:* Direct PLUS loans; Direct Subsidized Loans; Direct Unsubsidized Loans. Federal Work-Study Program available. Institutional employment available.

Campus Life

Activities: Campus Ministries; Choral groups; Dance; Drama/theater; International Student Organization; Jazz band; Literary magazine; Model UN; Music ensembles; Musical theater; Radio station; Student government; Student newspaper; Student-run film society; Symphony orchestra; Yearbook. **Organizations:** 110 registered organizations, 10 honor societies, 5 religious organizations, 0 fraternities, 0 sororities. **Athletics (Intercollegiate):** *Men:* baseball, basketball, cross-country, equestrian sports, ice hockey, lacrosse, rugby, swimming, track/field (indoor), ultimate frisbee. *Women:* basketball, cross-country, equestrian sports, field hockey, ice hockey, lacrosse, rugby, softball, swimming, track/field (indoor), ultimate frisbee, volleyball.

CAMPUS

Type of school	Private (nonprofit)
Environment	Village

STUDENTS

Undergrad enrollment	1,648
% male/female	37/63
% from out of state	60

FINANCIAL FACTS

Annual tuition	$61,600
Room and board	$15,430
Required fees	$480

GENERAL ADMISSIONS INFO

Application fee	$60
Regular application deadline	1/15
Nonfall registration	Yes

Fall 2024 testing policy	Test Optional
Range SAT EBRW	630–700
Range SAT Math	630–690
Range ACT Composite	27–33

ACADEMICS

Student/faculty ratio	12:1
% students returning for sophomore year	81

REQUESTING SERVICES FOR STUDENTS WITH LEARNING DIFFERENCES

Phone: 508-286-8215 • wheatoncollege.edu/accessibility-services • Email: accessibility@wheatoncollege.edu

Documentation submitted to: Accessibility Services
Separate application required for Services: Yes

Documentation required for:
LD: Psychoeducational evaluation
ADHD: Psychoeducational evaluation
ASD: Psychoeducational evaluation

Adrian College

110 South Madison Street, Adrian, MI 49221 • Admissions: 517-265-5161 • www.adrian.edu

Support: CS

ACCOMMODATIONS

Allowed in exams:

Calculators	No
Dictionary	Yes
Computer	Yes
Spell-checker	Yes
Extended test time	Yes
Scribe	Yes
Proctors	Yes
Oral exams	Yes
Note-takers	Yes

Support services for students with:

LD	Yes
ADHD	Yes
ASD	Yes
Distraction-reduced environment	Yes
Recording of lecture allowed	Yes
Reading technology	Yes
Audio books	Yes
Other assistive technology	Yes
Priority registration	No

Added costs of services:

For LD	No
For ADHD	No
For ASD	No
LD specialists	Yes
ADHD & ASD coaching	No
ASD specialists	No
Professional tutors	No
Peer tutors	Yes
Max. hours/week for services	Varies
How professors are notified of student approved accommodations	Student and Accessibility Services

COLLEGE GRADUATION REQUIREMENTS

Course waivers allowed	No
Course substitutions allowed	No

PROGRAMS/SERVICES FOR STUDENTS WITH LEARNING DIFFERENCES

Students with disabilities should contact Accessibility Services and register, provide necessary documentation, and meet with an Accessibility Services specialist. Accommodations might include note-taking services, scribes, text scanners, voice activation software, voice recognition software, computers, and test-taking accommodations such as extended time and tutoring. Promoting the Rights of Individuals Everywhere (PRIDE) is a student organization at AC where students learn about the challenges of people with disabilities, and educate others about ways to support people with disabilities. PRIDE also arranges a Special Olympics where students and individuals with disabilities can compete in sports.

ADMISSIONS

All prospective students are held to the same requirements. Applications are reviewed and evaluated on the merits of academic credentials, rigor of curriculum, grades earned, class rank (if provided), personal character, and leadership potential based on involvement in school, community, or religious organizations. Applicants should have successfully completed a minimum of 15 units of academic coursework in English, mathematics, science, social science, and foreign language. Students may be asked to successfully complete the Nelson-Denny Reading Test as a condition of admission. Students may also be asked to take the college's mathematics placement exam.

Additional Information

All first-year students are assigned an academic advisor who assists and approves the undergraduate student's schedule of classes each semester. Small-group or individual peer tutoring is available by appointment or drop-in. Tutors offer support with coursework, study skills, identifying learning styles, developing personal learning strategies, and can offer feedback on class performance. Students visit the Don Kleinsmith Writing Center for tutors who can assist with any stage in the writing process. At the Math Lab, students can drop in for help from peer tutors and math professors.

Chartered by the Michigan Legislature in 1859, the first president of the college was abolitionist Asa Mahan. At the beginning of the Civil War, the college volunteered itself as a base camp for the soldiers of Michigan regiments on the Union side. Valade Hall sits on the site of the former camp.

Adrian College

General Admissions

Very important factors include: rigor of secondary school record, class rank. *Important factors include:* academic GPA, standardized test scores (if submitted). High school diploma is required and GED is accepted. Institution is test-optional for entering Fall 2024. Check admissions website for updates. *Academic units recommended:* 4 English, 3 math, 2 science (1 lab), 2 foreign language, 2 social studies, 2 academic electives.

Financial Aid

Students should submit: FAFSA. *Need-based scholarships/grants offered:* College/university scholarship or grant aid from institutional funds; Federal Pell; Private scholarships; SEOG; State scholarships/grants. *Loan aid offered:*. Federal Work-Study Program available. Institutional employment available.

Campus Life

Activities: Campus Ministries; Choral groups; Concert band; Dance; Drama/theater; International Student Organization; Jazz band; Literary magazine; Marching band; Music ensembles; Musical theater; Pep band; Radio station; Student government; Student newspaper; Symphony orchestra; Yearbook. **Organizations:** 68 registered organizations, 13 honor societies, 8 religious organizations, 4 fraternities, 3 sororities. **Athletics (Intercollegiate):** *Men:* baseball, basketball, cross-country, golf, ice hockey, lacrosse. *Women:* basketball, bowling, cross-country, golf, ice hockey, lacrosse, softball, volleyball.

CAMPUS
Type of school	Private (nonprofit)
Environment	Town

STUDENTS
Undergrad enrollment	1,308
% male/female	53/47
% from out of state	24
% frosh live on campus	85

FINANCIAL FACTS
Annual tuition	$23,090
Room and board	$7,600
Required fees	$300

GENERAL ADMISSIONS INFO
Application fee	No fee
Regular application deadline	Rolling
Nonfall registration	No

Fall 2024 testing policy	Test Optional
Range SAT EBRW	430–515
Range SAT Math	410–535
Range ACT Composite	20–25

ACADEMICS
Student/faculty ratio	12:1
% students returning for sophomore year	73

Most classes have 10–19 students.

REQUESTING SERVICES FOR STUDENTS WITH LEARNING DIFFERENCES

Phone: 517-265-5161 • www.adrian.edu/academics/academic-services/accessibility-services
Email: academicservices@adrian.edu

Documentation submitted to: Accessibility Services
Separate application required for Services: Yes

Documentation required for:
 LD: Psychoeducational evaluation
 ADHD: Psychoeducational evaluation
 ASD: Psychoeducational evaluation

Calvin University

3201 Burton Street SE, Grand Rapids, MI 49546 • Admissions: 800-688-0122 • www.calvin.edu

Support: CS

ACCOMMODATIONS

Allowed in exams:

Calculators	Yes
Dictionary	Yes
Computer	Yes
Spell-checker	Yes
Extended test time	Yes
Scribe	Yes
Proctors	Yes
Oral exams	Yes
Note-takers	Yes

Support services for students with:

LD	Yes
ADHD	Yes
ASD	Yes
Distraction-reduced environment	Yes
Recording of lecture allowed	Yes
Reading technology	Yes
Audio books	Yes
Other assistive technology	Yes
Priority registration	Yes

Added costs of services:

For LD	No
For ADHD	No
For ASD	No
LD specialists	No
ADHD & ASD coaching	Yes
ASD specialists	Yes
Professional tutors	Yes
Peer tutors	Yes
Max. hours/week for services	1
How professors are notified of student approved accommodations	Student

COLLEGE GRADUATION REQUIREMENTS

Course waivers allowed	No
Course substitutions allowed	Yes
In what courses: Foreign Language	

PROGRAMS/SERVICES FOR STUDENTS WITH LEARNING DIFFERENCES

Disability Services is committed to supporting students with disabilities. Students interested in receiving accommodations meet with the disability coordinator, where they will discuss the documentation necessary to support each student's unique situation.

ADMISSIONS

Admission requirements are the same for all applicants. The mid-50% GPA of accepted applicants is from 3.3 to 3.9. Students who are unable to meet all the admission standards but show promise of being successful at Calvin may be eligible for the Access Program. The program provides placement testing in math and English, special advising, and enrollment in a first-semester course that facilitates college-level thinking and learning. Depending on the outcome of placement testing, additional developmental courses may be required as a condition of admission.

Additional Information

The Center for Student Success provides services to all Calvin students, including professional academic counseling, academic tutoring, and help sessions for setting and achieving goals. The Knights Scholars Program is available to eligible students and provides tools to students so that they may smoothly transition to college life and achieve academic success. The program includes academic advising, personalized coursework, regular meetings with their professors and peer coaches, and some motivational Calvin swag. Students are admitted to the program by a committee or through direct communication with the program director.

The Calvin Knight dates back to 1926. The story is that the nickname "Knight" came from a reporter who misunderstood "Calvin-ites," and the name stuck. The values, pride, and traditions of Calvin grew around the nickname, but it was not until 2009 that the Knight officially became the Calvin mascot.

Calvin University

GENERAL ADMISSIONS

Very important factors include: rigor of secondary school record, academic GPA. *Important factors include:* standardized test scores (if submitted), application essay, recommendations. *Other factors considered include:* class rank. High school diploma is required and GED is accepted. Institution is test-optional for entering Fall 2024. Check admissions website for updates. *Academic units required:* 3 English, 2 math, 2 science, 2 social studies, 3 academic electives. *Academic units recommended:* 4 English, 3 math, 3 science, 2 foreign language, 3 social studies.

FINANCIAL AID

Students should submit: FAFSA. *Need-based scholarships/grants offered:* College/university scholarship or grant aid from institutional funds; Federal Pell; Private scholarships; SEOG; State scholarships/grants; United Negro College Fund. *Loan aid offered:* Direct PLUS loans; Direct Subsidized Loans; Direct Unsubsidized Loans. Federal Work-Study Program available. Institutional employment available.

CAMPUS LIFE

Activities: Campus Ministries; Choral groups; Concert band; Dance; Drama/theater; International Student Organization; Jazz band; Literary magazine; Music ensembles; Pep band; Student government; Student newspaper; Student-run film society; Symphony orchestra; Yearbook. **Organizations:** 75 registered organizations, 6 honor societies, 5 religious organizations, 0 fraternities, 0 sororities. **Athletics (Intercollegiate):** *Men:* baseball, basketball, crew/rowing, cross-country, cycling, equestrian sports, golf, ice hockey, lacrosse, rugby, swimming, track/field (indoor), ultimate frisbee, volleyball. *Women:* basketball, crew/rowing, cross-country, cycling, equestrian sports, golf, lacrosse, softball, swimming, track/field (indoor), volleyball.

CAMPUS
Type of school	Private (nonprofit)
Environment	Metropolis

STUDENTS
Undergrad enrollment	2,963
% male/female	47/53
% from out of state	36
% frosh live on campus	93

FINANCIAL FACTS
Annual tuition	$38,370
Room and board	$10,908
Required fees	$250

GENERAL ADMISSIONS INFO
Application fee	$35
Regular application deadline	8/15
Nonfall registration	Yes

Fall 2024 testing policy	Test Optional
Range SAT EBRW	560–670
Range SAT Math	560–670
Range ACT Composite	24–30

ACADEMICS
Student/faculty ratio	12:1
% students returning for sophomore year	86

Most classes have 20–29 students.

REQUESTING SERVICES FOR STUDENTS WITH LEARNING DIFFERENCES

Phone: 616-526-6155 • www.calvin.edu/go/disability-services • Email: disabilityservices@calvin.edu

Documentation submitted to: Disability Services
Separate application required for Services: Yes

Documentation required for:
 LD: Psychoeducational evaluation
 ADHD: Psychoeducational evaluation
 ASD: Psychoeducational evaluation

Eastern Michigan University

401 Pierce Hall, Ypsilanti, MI 48197 • Admissions: 734-487-3060 • www.emich.edu

Support: SP

ACCOMMODATIONS

Allowed in exams:

Calculators	Yes
Dictionary	Yes
Computer	Yes
Spell-checker	Yes
Extended test time	Yes
Scribe	Yes
Proctors	Yes
Oral exams	Yes
Note-takers	Yes

Support services for students with:

LD	Yes
ADHD	Yes
ASD	Yes
Distraction-reduced environment	Yes
Recording of lecture allowed	Yes
Reading technology	Yes
Audio books	Yes
Other assistive technology	Yes
Priority registration	Yes

Added costs of services:

For LD	No
For ADHD	No
For ASD	Yes
LD specialists	Yes
ADHD & ASD coaching	Yes
ASD specialists	Yes
Professional tutors	No
Peer tutors	Yes
Max. hours/week for services	Varies
How professors are notified of student approved accommodations	Student and Disability Resource Center

COLLEGE GRADUATION REQUIREMENTS

Course waivers allowed	No
Course substitutions allowed	No

PROGRAMS/SERVICES FOR STUDENTS WITH LEARNING DIFFERENCES

To register with the Disability Resource Center (DRC), students complete the DRC student intake questionnaire, provide documentation, and schedule an appointment to discuss possible accommodations. A letter of accommodation (LOA) is created and delivered to students via email to share with their professors. The Center for Adaptive Technology in Education (CATE) Lab provides resources, evaluations, and technology training for students with disabilities. The College Supports Program (CSP) increases admission, retention, and matriculation for students with autism spectrum disorder (ASD) through a fee-for-service, supportive program. This program includes assistance in academic and social-emotional growth, helps students develop the daily living skills needed for independence, and supports executive functioning skills. CSP requires parents and students to have a formal interview before applying to the university to get an overview of the program. Students are evaluated on their potential to benefit from the program and their willingness to utilize the support provided as opposed to a diagnosis or test score.

ADMISSIONS

All applicants must meet the same admission criteria. The minimum GPA requirement is 2.0. Applicants with a 2.75 GPA or higher will not be asked for ACT or SAT scores. Applicants with a 2.5–2.74 GPA are also test-optional but may be asked to submit a test score after the initial review. Applicants with a 2.49 GPA or lower are required to submit ACT or SAT scores. The average GPA for accepted applicants is 3.28, the average ACT score is 22, and the average SAT score is 1100. Students are encouraged to provide additional information to support their application.

Additional Information

The Holman Success Centers offer academic support for all students. Holman has tutoring, workshops, Supplemental Instruction, success coaching, and peer academic coaching available.

The EMU Planetarium opened January 2011. It's a sphere suspended four stories aboveground in the atrium of the Mark Jefferson Science Complex. Over 450 students studying astronomy call the planetarium their classroom.

Eastern Michigan University

GENERAL ADMISSIONS

Very important factors include: academic GPA, standardized test scores. *Important factors include:* rigor of secondary school record. *Other factors considered include:* application essay, recommendation(s). High school diploma is required and GED is accepted. Institution is test-optional for entering Fall 2024. Check admissions website for updates. *Academic units recommended:* 4 English, 4 math, 4 science, 2 foreign language, 2 social studies, 1 U.S. history, 4 electives.

FINANCIAL AID

Students should submit: FAFSA. *Need-based scholarships/grants offered:* College/university scholarship or grant aid from institutional funds; Federal Pell; Private scholarships; SEOG; State scholarships/grants. *Loan aid offered:* Direct PLUS loans; Direct Subsidized Loans; Direct Unsubsidized Loans.

CAMPUS LIFE

Activities: Campus Ministries; Choral groups; Concert band; Dance; Drama/theater; International Student Organization; Jazz band; Literary magazine; Marching band; Model UN; Music ensembles; Musical theater; Opera; Pep band; Radio station; Student government; Student newspaper; Student-run film society; Symphony orchestra; Television station. **Organizations:** 300 registered organizations, 14 honors societies, 24 religious organizations, 11 fraternities, 13 sororities. **Athletics (Intercollegiate):** *Men:* baseball, basketball, football, ice hockey, soccer, tennis. *Women:* basketball, cross-country, golf, gymnastics, soccer, softball, tennis, track/field (outdoor), track/field (indoor), volleyball.

CAMPUS	
Type of school	Public
Environment	City

STUDENTS	
Undergrad enrollment	17,256
% male/female	41/59
% from out of state	10
% frosh live on campus	65

FINANCIAL FACTS	
Annual in-state tuition	$15,060
Out-of-state tuition	$15,060
Room and board	$12,068

GENERAL ADMISSIONS INFO	
Application fee	$35
Regular application deadline	Rolling
Nonfall registration	Yes
Fall 2024 testing policy	Test Optional
Range SAT EBRW	460–550
Range SAT Math	450–570
Range ACT Composite	19–25

ACADEMICS	
Student/faculty ratio	17:1
% students returning for sophomore year	74
Most classes have 20–29 students.	

REQUESTING SERVICES FOR STUDENTS WITH LEARNING DIFFERENCES

Phone: 734-487-2470 • www.emich.edu/drc • Email: drc@emich.edu

Documentation submitted to: Disability Resource Center (DRC)
Separate application required for Services: Yes

Documentation required for:
LD: Psychoeducational evaluation
ADHD: Psychoeducational evaluation
ASD: Psychoeducational evaluation

Ferris State University

1201 South State Street, Big Rapids, MI 49307 • Admissions: 231-591-2100 • www.ferris.edu

Support: CS

ACCOMMODATIONS

Allowed in exams:

Calculators	Yes
Dictionary	Yes
Computer	Yes
Spell-checker	Yes
Extended test time	Yes
Scribe	Yes
Proctors	Yes
Oral exams	Yes
Note-takers	Yes

Support services for students with:

LD	No
ADHD	No
ASD	No
Distraction-reduced environment	Yes
Recording of lecture allowed	Yes
Reading technology	Yes
Audio books	Yes
Other assistive technology	Yes
Priority registration	Yes

Added costs of services:

For LD	No
For ADHD	No
For ASD	No
LD specialists	Yes
ADHD & ASD coaching	Yes
ASD specialists	Yes
Professional tutors	No
Peer tutors	Yes
Max. hours/week for services	Varies
How professors are notified of student approved accommodations	Student and ECDS

COLLEGE GRADUATION REQUIREMENTS

Course waivers allowed	No
Course substitutions allowed	No

PROGRAMS/SERVICES FOR STUDENTS WITH LEARNING DIFFERENCES

Educational Counseling and Disabilities Services (ECDS) facilitates accommodations for students with disabilities. Students may register with ECDS by filling out the online intake form, submitting documentation from a qualified provider, and scheduling an appointment with an ECDS counselor. Determinations are made once the counselor has met with the student and reviewed the documentation. Students must self-register each semester using the ECDS portal. Available accommodations and services include notetakers, permissible use of recording devices in class, spellcheckers, Dragon Naturally Speaking software, electronic texts, extended time on tests, reduced-distraction testing environments, calculators for exams, and educational counseling.

ADMISSIONS

All students must meet the same admission criteria. Most high school graduates are eligible for admission based on Ferris's flexible admission policy and diverse curricula offerings. The typical applicant is expected to have a minimum 2.0 GPA; specific programs may be more selective and require a higher GPA and completion of specific courses. Admissions may require an interview if the applicant's GPA does not meet admission standards. Students with learning disabilities and ADHD are encouraged to self-disclose and provide insight into their disability.

Additional Information

The Academic Support Center offers tutoring for most courses to all students.

Ferris athletic teams were unofficially called Spartans or Ferrisites, until the local *Pioneer* newspaper gave them the name that stuck: the Bulldogs. During the 1931 basketball season, the team had lost and regained players due to injury and eligibility. Watching the team turn their season around, the newspaper referred to Ferris as "immovable bulldogs," based on their ability to "hang on to their men and never let go."

Ferris State University

GENERAL ADMISSIONS

Very important factors include: rigor of secondary school record. *Important factors include:* academic GPA, standardized test scores (if submitted). *Other factors considered include:* class rank. High school diploma is required and GED is accepted. Institution is test-optional for entering Fall 2024. Check admissions website for updates. *Academic units recommended:* 4 English, 4 math, 3 science, 2 foreign language, 3 social studies, 1 academic elective, 1 visual/performing arts.

FINANCIAL AID

Students should submit: FAFSA. *Need-based scholarships/grants offered:* College/university scholarship or grant aid from institutional funds; Federal Pell; Private scholarships; SEOG; State scholarships/grants. *Loan aid offered:* Direct PLUS loans; Direct Subsidized Loans; Direct Unsubsidized Loans. Federal Work-Study Program available. Institutional employment available.

CAMPUS LIFE

Activities: Campus Ministries; Choral groups; Concert band; Dance; Drama/theater; International Student Organization; Jazz band; Music ensembles; Musical theater; Opera; Pep band; Radio station; Student government; Student newspaper; Student-run film society; Symphony orchestra; Television station; Yearbook. **Organizations:** 220 registered organizations, 19 honor societies, 10 religious organizations, 5 fraternities, 3 sororities. **Athletics (Intercollegiate):** *Men:* baseball, basketball, bowling, cross-country, equestrian sports, golf, ice hockey, lacrosse, martial arts, rugby, table tennis, track/field (indoor), ultimate frisbee, volleyball, wrestling. *Women:* basketball, bowling, cross-country, equestrian sports, golf, lacrosse, martial arts, rugby, softball, table tennis, track/field (indoor), ultimate frisbee, volleyball, wrestling.

CAMPUS
Type of school	Public
Environment	Village

STUDENTS
Undergrad enrollment	9,575
% male/female	48/52
% from out of state	5
% frosh live on campus	69

FINANCIAL FACTS
Annual in-state tuition	$13,695
Annual out-of-state tuition	$13,695
Room and board	$9,650
Required fees	$180

GENERAL ADMISSIONS INFO
Application fee	No fee
Regular application deadline	Rolling
Nonfall registration	Yes
Fall 2024 testing policy	Test Optional
Range SAT EBRW	470–580
Range SAT Math	470–580
Range ACT Composite	18–26

ACADEMICS
Student/faculty ratio	15:1
% students returning for sophomore year	79

Most classes have 10–19 students.

REQUESTING SERVICES FOR STUDENTS WITH LEARNING DIFFERENCES

Phone: 231-591-3057 • www.ferris.edu/ecds • Email: ecds@ferris.edu

Documentation submitted to: Educational Counseling & Disabilities Services
Separate application required for Services: Yes

Documentation required for:
LD: Psychoeducational evaluation
ADHD: Psychoeducational evaluation
ASD: Psychoeducational evaluation

Grand Valley State University

1 Campus Drive, Allendale, MI 49401 • Admissions: 616-331-2025 • www.gvsu.edu

Support: CS

ACCOMMODATIONS

Allowed in exams:

Calculators	Yes
Dictionary	Yes
Computer	Yes
Spell-checker	Yes
Extended test time	Yes
Scribe	Yes
Proctors	Yes
Oral exams	Yes
Note-takers	Yes

Support services for students with:

LD	Yes
ADHD	Yes
ASD	Yes
Distraction-reduced environment	Yes
Recording of lecture allowed	Yes
Reading technology	Yes
Audio books	Yes
Other assistive technology	Yes
Priority registration	Yes

Added costs of services:

For LD	No
For ADHD	No
For ASD	No
LD specialists	Yes
ADHD & ASD coaching	Yes
ASD specialists	Yes
Professional tutors	Yes
Peer tutors	Yes
Max. hours/week for services	1
How professors are notified of student approved accommodations	Student

COLLEGE GRADUATION REQUIREMENTS

Course waivers allowed	No
Course substitutions allowed	No

PROGRAMS/SERVICES FOR STUDENTS WITH LEARNING DIFFERENCES

Disability Support Resources (DSR) provides resources and accommodations to students with disabilities. Students must complete a DSR application and submit documentation of the disability. A DSR advisor then meets with the student to review the circumstances and make a determination. Following DSR's determination, students receive a DSR accommodation letter to share with their professors. Accommodations may include extended-time testing, written materials in electronic format, and note-taking aids. DSR staff has an assistive technology coordinator, and students registered with DSR can work with an advisor on learning and time-management skills, organization, and career preparation. Advisors are available and can even meet weekly. Campus Links is a peer mentoring program providing support to students with autism spectrum disorder (ASD) while they adjust to the university environment. In coordination with the Disability Support Resources office, students in the program have easy access to social, academic, and classroom support. There are two different tiers of support: residential and nonresidential. Campus Links Red is the residential program where the mentors and mentees live in the same on-campus housing, providing daily support. Campus Links Blue is the nonresidential program for students.

ADMISSIONS

Admissions considers academic performance and rigor of coursework, as well as personal data and standardized test scores, when provided. One weak academic area does not disqualify an applicant, but multiple deficiencies can put a candidate at a significant disadvantage. The middle 50 percent of admitted students have a 3.4–3.9 GPA, 21–27 ACT, or 1050–1240 SAT if submitting scores. All applicants admitted to GVSU by March 1 will be considered for merit-based scholarships, regardless of whether test scores are submitted with the application.

Additional Information

The Student Academic Success Center (SASC) assists students in achieving their educational goals. Available resources include success coaching and academic success workshops. Students can also utilize the Tutoring and Reading Center for academic tutoring and help.

The first student newspaper at GVSU was printed in 1963. Grand Valley Lanthorn printed its first issue in October 1968, and released its first online edition in 1995. In 1969, the Lanthorn made news with a freedom-of-speech scandal. Following a printing that contained vulgarities and obscenities, the county sheriff arrested the editor, and the county prosecutor closed the newspaper's office. GVSU sued both, and the Michigan attorney general ruled in favor of GVSU and free speech.

Grand Valley State University

General Admissions

Very important factors include: rigor of secondary school record, academic GPA. *Important factors include:* standardized test scores (if submitted). *Other factors considered include:* class rank, application essay, recommendations. High school diploma is required and GED is accepted. Institution is test-optional for entering Fall 2024. Check admissions website for updates. *Academic units required:* 4 English, 3 math, 3 science (2 labs), 2 foreign language, 3 social studies.

Financial Aid

Students should submit: FAFSA. *Need-based scholarships/grants offered:* College/university scholarship or grant aid from institutional funds; Federal Pell; Private scholarships; SEOG; State scholarships/grants. *Loan aid offered:* Direct PLUS loans; Direct Subsidized Loans; Direct Unsubsidized Loans. Federal Work-Study Program available. Institutional employment available.

Campus Life

Activities: Campus Ministries; Choral groups; Concert band; Dance; Drama/theater; International Student Organization; Jazz band; Literary magazine; Marching band; Music ensembles; Musical theater; Pep band; Radio station; Student government; Student newspaper; Symphony orchestra; Television station. **Organizations:** 407 registered organizations, 20 honor societies, 16 religious organizations, 14 fraternities, 14 sororities. **Athletics (Intercollegiate):** *Men:* baseball, basketball, bowling, crew/rowing, cross-country, equestrian sports, golf, ice hockey, lacrosse, martial arts, rugby, swimming, track/field (indoor), water polo, wrestling. *Women:* basketball, bowling, crew/rowing, cross-country, equestrian sports, golf, gymnastics, ice hockey, lacrosse, martial arts, rugby, softball, swimming, track/field (indoor), volleyball, water polo.

Michigan

CAMPUS

Type of school	Public
Environment	City

STUDENTS

Undergrad enrollment	19,220
% male/female	39/61
% from out of state	9
% frosh live on campus	85

FINANCIAL FACTS

Annual in-state tuition	$13,560
Annual out-of-state tuition	$19,296
Room and board	$9,200
Required fees	$0

GENERAL ADMISSIONS INFO

Application fee	$30
Regular application deadline	5/1
Nonfall registration	Yes

Fall 2024 testing policy	Test Optional
Range SAT EBRW	510–620
Range SAT Math	500–610
Range ACT Composite	21–27

ACADEMICS

Student/faculty ratio	15:1
% students returning for sophomore year	83

Most classes have 20–29 students.

REQUESTING SERVICES FOR STUDENTS WITH LEARNING DIFFERENCES

Phone: 616-331-2490 • www.gvsu.edu/dsr • Email: dsrgvsu@gvsu.edu

Documentation submitted to: Disability Support Resources
Separate application required for Services: Yes

Documentation required for:
LD: Psychoeducational evaluation
ADHD: Psychoeducational evaluation
ASD: Psychoeducational evaluation

Lake Superior State University

650 W. Easterday Avenue, Sault Sainte Marie, MI 49783-1699 • Admissions: 906-635-2231 • lssu.edu

Support: S

ACCOMMODATIONS

Allowed in exams:

Calculators	Yes
Dictionary	Yes
Computer	Yes
Spell-checker	Yes
Extended test time	Yes
Scribe	Yes
Proctors	Yes
Oral exams	Yes
Note-takers	Yes

Support services for students with:

LD	Yes
ADHD	Yes
ASD	Yes
Distraction-reduced environment	Yes
Recording of lecture allowed	Yes
Reading technology	Yes
Audio books	Yes
Other assistive technology	Yes
Priority registration	Yes

Added costs of services:

For LD	No
For ADHD	No
For ASD	No
LD specialists	No
ADHD & ASD coaching	No
ASD specialists	No
Professional tutors	Yes
Peer tutors	Yes
Max. hours/week for services	Varies
How professors are notified of student approved accommodations	Student

COLLEGE GRADUATION REQUIREMENTS

Course waivers allowed	No
Course substitutions allowed	No

PROGRAMS/SERVICES FOR STUDENTS WITH LEARNING DIFFERENCES

The Accessibility Services (AS) office supports students in compliance with ADA requirements, and with attention to the length of time an individual has had a disability, its severity, and impact. New students are encouraged to make an appointment with the AS office at least four weeks before beginning on campus. Students may request specific accommodations that are not listed, and AS will work with the university to gain access to the service or product.

ADMISSIONS

All applicants are expected to meet the same admission criteria. Students with a minimum 2.4 GPA and a college preparatory curriculum are admissible to Lake Superior State University (LSSU). ACT or SAT scores will not be used in the admissions process but, if submitted, may be used for appropriate course placement. Students requesting accommodations must complete the general admissions process.

Additional Information

The Academic Success Center at LSSU provides math and writing tutoring and small-group peer academic support. These services are open to all registered students on campus. The support groups include conversations that focus on academics and students' struggles with college life and provide resources to build confidence and prepare students for independent living.

Since 1976, LSSU has compiled an annual Banished Words List "to uphold, protect, and support excellence in language by encouraging avoidance of words and terms that are overworked, redundant, oxymoronic, clichéd, illogical, nonsensical and otherwise ineffective, baffling, or irritating." The 2022 nominations mainly came from U.S. cities but were also from Norway, Belgium, England, Scotland, Australia, and several Canadian provinces. LSSU and the judges from the English department always announce the results of the yearly compilation on December 31 to start the New Year on the right foot, er, tongue.

Lake Superior State University

GENERAL ADMISSIONS

Very important factors include: rigor of secondary school record, academic GPA, standardized test scores (if submitted). *Other factors considered include:* class rank, recommendations. High school diploma is required and GED is accepted. Institution is test-optional for entering Fall 2024. Check admissions website for updates. *Academic units recommended:* 4 English, 4 math, 3 science (3 labs), 2 foreign language, 3 social studies.

FINANCIAL AID

Students should submit: FAFSA. *Need-based scholarships/grants offered:* College/university scholarship or grant aid from institutional funds; Federal Nursing Scholarships; Federal Pell; Private scholarships; SEOG; State scholarships/grants. *Loan aid offered:* Direct PLUS loans; Direct Subsidized Loans; Direct Unsubsidized Loans.

CAMPUS LIFE

Activities: Campus Ministries; Choral groups; Dance; Drama/theater; International Student Organization; Literary magazine; Model UN; Pep band; Radio station; Student government; Student newspaper. **Organizations:** 60 registered organizations, 4 fraternities, 4 sororities. **Athletics (Intercollegiate):** *Men:* basketball, cross-country, ice hockey, track/field (indoor). *Women:* basketball, cross-country, softball, track/field (indoor), volleyball.

CAMPUS	
Type of school	Public
Environment	City

STUDENTS	
Undergrad enrollment	1,812
% male/female	44/56
% from out of state	13
% frosh live on campus	69

FINANCIAL FACTS	
Annual in-state tuition	$13,728
Annual out-of-state tuition	$13,728
Room and board	$11,516

GENERAL ADMISSIONS INFO	
Application fee	No fee
Regular application deadline	Rolling
Nonfall registration	Yes

Fall 2024 testing policy	Test Optional
Range SAT EBRW	480–590
Range SAT Math	470–570
Range ACT Composite	18–27

ACADEMICS	
Student/faculty ratio	16:1
% students returning for sophomore year	67
Most classes have 10–19 students.	

REQUESTING SERVICES FOR STUDENTS WITH LEARNING DIFFERENCES

Phone: 906-635-2355 • www.lssu.edu/academic-services/accessibility/ • Email: accessibility@lssu.edu

Documentation submitted to: Accessibility Services
Separate application required for Services: Yes

Documentation required for:
 LD: Psychoeducational evaluation
 ADHD: Psychoeducational evaluation
 ASD: Psychoeducational evaluation

Michigan State University

250 Administration Building, East Lansing, MI 48824 • Admissions: 517-355-8332 • www.msu.edu

(Support: CS)

ACCOMMODATIONS

Allowed in exams:

Calculators	Yes
Dictionary	Yes
Computer	Yes
Spell-checker	Yes
Extended test time	Yes
Scribe	Yes
Proctors	Yes
Oral exams	Yes
Note-takers	Yes

Support services for students with:

LD	Yes
ADHD	Yes
ASD	Yes
Distraction-reduced environment	Yes
Recording of lecture allowed	Yes
Reading technology	Yes
Audio books	Yes
Other assistive technology	Yes
Priority registration	Yes

Added costs of services:

For LD	No
For ADHD	No
For ASD	No
LD specialists	Yes
ADHD & ASD coaching	Yes
ASD specialists	Yes
Professional tutors	Yes
Peer tutors	Yes
Max. hours/week for services	2
How professors are notified of student approved accommodations	Student

COLLEGE GRADUATION REQUIREMENTS

Course waivers allowed	No
Course substitutions allowed	Yes

In what courses: In very rare circumstances, MSU will offer a course substitution process for a student with a disability who has repeatedly been unable to meet a math-related university requirement.

PROGRAMS/SERVICES FOR STUDENTS WITH LEARNING DIFFERENCES

The Resource Center for Persons with Disabilities (RCPD) works closely with students to coordinate accommodations. Documentation of disabilities is essential for the RCPD staff to best determine what accommodations are needed. This documentation should explain the nature and degree to which the disability affects major life activities, including learning. Students register for accommodations through MyProfile and are assigned a specialist in RCPD. The Building Opportunities for Networking and Discovery (BOND) program offers structured opportunities for social and communication development for students with autism, and students can connect with others facing similar challenges. The BOND program offers peer mentoring, skill-building events, and social outings. The Stern Tutoring and Alternative Techniques for Education (STATE) Program provides services to students with learning disabilities who are academically at risk. Services include tutoring, peer mentoring, and strategies for academic success. STATE conducts an instructional seminar on successful learning strategies, ways to utilize support services at MSU, assistive technology, and academic accommodations.

ADMISSIONS

Admission is based on academic performance in high school, strength and quality of the curriculum, recent trends in academic performance, class rank, standardized test results (if applicable), leadership, talents, conduct, and diversity of experience. The middle 50 percent of admitted students have a 3.5 to 4.0 GPA.

Additional Information

The Runge Family Endowment for Students with Learning Differences assists students with learning differences by helping to fund programming that provides structure, learning strategies, and academic tutoring.

MSU was founded in 1855. In 1863, Michigan designated MSU its land grant institution, making it the nation's first land grant college and the first institution of higher education to teach scientific agriculture. The federal funding rescued the college from possible closure due to financial difficulties, and MSU served as a model for future land grant colleges.

Michigan State University

GENERAL ADMISSIONS

Very important factors include: academic GPA, application essay. *Important factors include:* rigor of secondary school record. *Other factors considered include:* class rank, standardized test scores (if submitted), recommendations. High school diploma is required and GED is accepted. Institution is test-optional for entering Fall 2024. Check admissions website for updates. *Academic units required:* 4 English, 3 math, 2 science, 2 foreign language, 3 social studies. *Academic units recommended:* 3 science.

FINANCIAL AID

Students should submit: FAFSA. *Need-based scholarships/grants offered:* College/university scholarship or grant aid from institutional funds; Federal Pell; Private scholarships; SEOG; State scholarships/grants. *Loan aid offered:* Direct PLUS loans; Direct Subsidized Loans; Direct Unsubsidized Loans. Federal Work-Study Program available. Institutional employment available.

CAMPUS LIFE

Activities: Campus Ministries; Choral groups; Concert band; Dance; Drama/theater; International Student Organization; Jazz band; Literary magazine; Marching band; Model UN; Music ensembles; Musical theater; Opera; Pep band; Radio station; Student government; Student newspaper; Student-run film society; Symphony orchestra; Television station; Yearbook. **Organizations:** 700 registered organizations, 47 honor societies, 50 religious organizations, 38 fraternities, 23 sororities. **Athletics (Intercollegiate):** *Men:* baseball, basketball, crew/rowing, cross-country, golf, ice hockey, lacrosse, martial arts, rugby, table tennis, track/field (indoor), ultimate frisbee, volleyball, water polo, wrestling. *Women:* basketball, crew/rowing, cross-country, field hockey, golf, gymnastics, lacrosse, martial arts, rugby, softball, table tennis, track/field (indoor), ultimate frisbee, volleyball, water polo.

CAMPUS

Type of school	Public
Environment	City

STUDENTS

Undergrad enrollment	39,021
% male/female	48/52
% from out of state	15
% frosh live on campus	95

FINANCIAL FACTS

Annual in-state tuition	$16,531
Annual out-of-state tuition	$42,427
Room and board	$10,990
Required fees	$180

GENERAL ADMISSIONS INFO

Application fee	$65
Regular application deadline	4/1
Nonfall registration	Yes

Fall 2024 testing policy	Test Optional
Range SAT EBRW	550–660
Range SAT Math	550–680
Range ACT Composite	24–30

ACADEMICS

Student/faculty ratio	17:1
% students returning for sophomore year	89

Most classes have 20–29 students.

REQUESTING SERVICES FOR STUDENTS WITH LEARNING DIFFERENCES

Phone: 517-884-7273 • www.rcpd.msu.edu/services • Email: mjh@msu.edu

Documentation submitted to: Resource Center for Persons with Disabilities
Separate application required for Services: Yes

Documentation required for:
  LD: Psychoeducational evaluation
  ADHD: Psychoeducational evaluation
  ASD: Psychoeducational evaluation

Michigan Technological University

1400 Townsend Drive, Houghton, MI 49931 • Admissions: 906-487-2335 • www.mtu.edu

(**Support: CS**)

ACCOMMODATIONS

Allowed in exams:

Calculators	Yes
Dictionary	N/A
Computer	Yes
Spell-checker	Yes
Extended test time	Yes
Scribe	Yes
Proctors	Yes
Oral exams	Yes
Note-takers	Yes

Support services for students with:

LD	Yes
ADHD	Yes
ASD	Yes
Distraction-reduced environment	Yes
Recording of lecture allowed	Yes
Reading technology	Yes
Audio books	Yes
Other assistive technology	Yes
Priority registration	Yes

Added costs of services:

For LD	No
For ADHD	No
For ASD	No
LD specialists	Yes
ADHD & ASD coaching	Yes
ASD specialists	Yes
Professional tutors	No
Peer tutors	Yes
Max. hours/week for services	Varies
How professors are notified of student approved accommodations	Student and Student Disability Services

COLLEGE GRADUATION REQUIREMENTS

Course waivers allowed	No
Course substitutions allowed	No

PROGRAMS/SERVICES FOR STUDENTS WITH LEARNING DIFFERENCES

To be eligible for accommodations, students with disabilities must present professional documentation to the coordinator for Student Disability Services. Documentation should be recent, on letterhead, and should describe the current impact of the disability. Students do not need to have documentation of a disability to discuss support, resources, or strategies for college success with the coordinator of Student Disability Services. Incoming students should make an appointment with SDS as early as possible in their first semester. Accommodations may include extended time in class and on tests, a quiet environment for testing, consideration for spelling errors, instructor-provided course material, notetakers, scribes, recording of lectures, Kurzweil reader, and priority registration.

ADMISSIONS

All applicants must meet the same admission criteria. The average GPA for accepted students is 3.8. Michigan Tech does not recompute the GPA but will use either a weighted or unweighted GPA, whichever is higher. However, the university will convert any GPA not reported on a 4.0 scale.

Additional Information

Success Coaches are peer advisors who assist fellow students with time management, organizational skills, social support, and academic strategies. The Waino Wahtera Center for Student Success provides courses tailored to students on academic probation, as well as other services. Students can request formal or informal connections to mentors. Learning centers, which are staffed by students who have been successful in particular courses, are available for content tutoring, test-taking strategies, and tips on writing essays.

With approximately 140 inches of snowfall at MTU annually, the MTU Winter Carnival began in 1922. It has grown to be one of the largest annual winter festivals and is an internationally known, six-day extravaganza. Organized by Blue Key National Honor Society since 1934, it features dozens of huge, intricate snow statues all around the campus. Students participate in broomball, human bowling, snow volleyball, sleigh rides, a queen coronation, and an ice fishing competition, plus fireworks from the top of MTU Ripley Ski Area.

Michigan Technological University

GENERAL ADMISSIONS

Very important factors include: academic GPA. *Important factors include:* rigor of secondary school record, standardized test scores (if submitted). *Other factors considered include:* application essay, recommendations. High school diploma is required and GED is accepted. Institution is test-optional for entering Fall 2024. Check admissions website for updates. *Academic units required:* 3 English, 3 math, 2 science. *Academic units recommended:* 4 English, 4 math, 3 science, 2 foreign language, 3 social studies, 2 academic electives.

FINANCIAL AID

Students should submit: FAFSA. *Need-based scholarships/grants offered:* College/university scholarship or grant aid from institutional funds; Federal Pell; Private scholarships; SEOG; State scholarships/grants. *Loan aid offered:* Direct PLUS loans; Direct Subsidized Loans; Direct Unsubsidized Loans. Federal Work-Study Program available. Institutional employment available.

CAMPUS LIFE

Activities: Campus Ministries; Choral groups; Concert band; Dance; Drama/theater; International Student Organization; Jazz band; Literary magazine; Music ensembles; Musical theater; Pep band; Radio station; Student government; Student newspaper; Student-run film society; Symphony orchestra. **Organizations:** 242 registered organizations, 16 honor societies, 11 religious organizations, 11 fraternities, 7 sororities. **Athletics (Intercollegiate):** *Men:* baseball, basketball, crew/rowing, cross-country, cycling, golf, gymnastics, ice hockey, lacrosse, martial arts, racquetball, rugby, skiing (nordic/cross-country), swimming, table tennis, ultimate frisbee, volleyball, water polo, wrestling. *Women:* basketball, crew/rowing, cross-country, cycling, golf, gymnastics, ice hockey, lacrosse, martial arts, racquetball, rugby, skiing (nordic/cross-country), softball, swimming, table tennis, ultimate frisbee, volleyball, water polo, wrestling.

CAMPUS

Type of school	Public
Environment	Village

STUDENTS

Undergrad enrollment	5,643
% male/female	70/30
% from out of state	22
% frosh live on campus	95

FINANCIAL FACTS

Annual in-state tuition	$17,296
Annual out-of-state tuition	$39,256
Room and board	$12,058
Required fees	$318

GENERAL ADMISSIONS INFO

Application fee	No fee
Regular application deadline	Rolling
Nonfall registration	Yes

Fall 2024 testing policy	Test Optional
Range SAT EBRW	560–670
Range SAT Math	570–680
Range ACT Composite	24–30

ACADEMICS

Student/faculty ratio	13:1
% students returning for sophomore year	85

Most classes have 2–9 students.

REQUESTING SERVICES FOR STUDENTS WITH LEARNING DIFFERENCES

Phone: 906-487-3558 • www.mtu.edu/success/disability • Email: sds@mtu.edu

Documentation submitted to: Student Disability Services

Separate application required for Services: Yes

Documentation required for:
LD: Psychoeducational evaluation
ADHD: Psychoeducational evaluation
ASD: Psychoeducational evaluation

Northern Michigan University

1401 Presque Isle Avenue, Marquette, MI 49855 • Admissions: 906-227-2650 • www.nmu.edu

Support: S

ACCOMMODATIONS

Allowed in exams:	
Calculators	Yes
Dictionary	Yes
Computer	Yes
Spell-checker	Yes
Extended test time	Yes
Scribe	Yes
Proctors	Yes
Oral exams	Yes
Note-takers	Yes
Support services for students with:	
LD	Yes
ADHD	Yes
ASD	Yes
Distraction-reduced environment	Yes
Recording of lecture allowed	Yes
Reading technology	Yes
Audio books	Yes
Other assistive technology	Yes
Priority registration	No
Added costs of services:	
For LD	No
For ADHD	No
For ASD	No
LD specialists	No
ADHD & ASD coaching	No
ASD specialists	No
Professional tutors	No
Peer tutors	Yes
Max. hours/week for services	Varies
How professors are notified of student approved accommodations	Student

COLLEGE GRADUATION REQUIREMENTS

Course waivers allowed	No
Course substitutions allowed	No

PROGRAMS/SERVICES FOR STUDENTS WITH LEARNING DIFFERENCES

Disability Services provides resources and accommodations to students with disabilities. Accommodation requests are reviewed on an individual basis. Students are required to meet with Disability Services and provide appropriate documentation. Once students are approved for testing accommodations, they will be sent a letter that serves as verification for professors. Students are responsible for confirming that professors receive the letter and arranging accommodations. Disability Services helps students with their self-advocacy skills as well as the confidence to take responsibility for their academic success. Accommodations may include assistive technology, alternate testing sites, classroom preferential seating, advocating with professors, extended test times, test readers, test scribes, notetakers/LiveScribe pen, and alternative textbooks. Disability Services works one-on-one with students as needed and will also meet with students who do not have specific documentation if they also require assistance. Skills classes are offered in reading, writing, math, study skills, sociocultural development, and interpersonal growth. No course waivers are granted for graduation requirements; however, substitutions may be granted if appropriate.

ADMISSIONS

All students submit the same general application and are expected to have a high school GPA of at least 2.25. Applicants who do not meet the criteria will still be considered for admission. Applicants may be asked to take a pre-admission test or supply further information.

Additional Information

Student Support Services provides each student with an individual program of educational support services, including academic advising, basic skill building in reading, math, and writing, counseling, career advisement, developmental skill building, mentoring, support groups and study groups, tutoring from paraprofessionals, specialized tutors, group tutoring or Supplemental Instruction, and workshops on personal development and study skills improvement.

On March 28, 2017, Al Roker and The Today Show crew were at NMU to break a Guinness World Record for the largest game of freeze tag ever played. To break the record, the game had to be played for a minimum of 15 minutes; more than 634 NMU students (all had to be actively playing) ran around the Superior Dome turf, playing freeze tag to shatter the two-year-old record of 431. Al gave two lucky students $5,000 scholarships.

Northern Michigan University

General Admissions

Very important factors include: academic GPA. High school diploma is required and GED is accepted. Institution is test-free for entering Fall 2024. Check admissions website for updates. *Academic units recommended:* 4 English, 4 math, 4 science, 2 foreign language, 4 social studies.

Financial Aid

Students should submit: FAFSA. *Need-based scholarships/grants offered:* College/university scholarship or grant aid from institutional funds; Federal Pell; Private scholarships; SEOG; State scholarships/grants. *Loan aid offered:* Direct PLUS loans; Direct Subsidized Loans; Direct Unsubsidized Loans. Federal Work-Study Program available. Institutional employment available.

Campus Life

Activities: Campus Ministries; Choral groups; Concert band; Dance; Drama/theater; International Student Organization; Jazz band; Literary magazine; Marching band; Model UN; Music ensembles; Musical theater; Opera; Pep band; Radio station; Student government; Student newspaper; Student-run film society; Symphony orchestra; Television station. **Organizations:** 383 registered organizations, 9 honor societies, 22 religious organizations, 2 fraternities, 3 sororities. **Athletics (Intercollegiate):** *Men:* baseball, basketball, crew/rowing, cross-country, cycling, golf, ice hockey, lacrosse, rugby, skiing (nordic/cross-country), swimming, ultimate frisbee, volleyball, wrestling. *Women:* baseball, basketball, crew/rowing, cross-country, cycling, golf, ice hockey, lacrosse, rugby, skiing (nordic/cross-country), softball, swimming, track/field (indoor), ultimate frisbee, volleyball, wrestling.

CAMPUS
Type of school	Public
Environment	Village

STUDENTS
Undergrad enrollment	6,611
% male/female	41/59
% from out of state	27
% frosh live on campus	82

FINANCIAL FACTS
Annual in-state tuition	$13,028
Annual out-of-state tuition	$18,524
Room and board	$12,620

GENERAL ADMISSIONS INFO
Application fee	$35
Regular application deadline	Rolling
Nonfall registration	Yes
Fall 2024 testing policy	Test Free

ACADEMICS
Student/faculty ratio	19:1
% students returning for sophomore year	73
Most classes have 20–29 students.	

REQUESTING SERVICES FOR STUDENTS WITH LEARNING DIFFERENCES

Phone: 906-227-1737 • nmu.edu/disabilityservices • Email: disability@nmu.edu

Documentation submitted to: Disability Services
Separate application required for Services: Yes

Documentation required for:
  LD: Psychoeducational evaluation
  ADHD: Psychoeducational evaluation
  ASD: Psychoeducational evaluation

University of Michigan

515 E. Jefferson Street, Ann Arbor, MI 48109-1316 • Admissions: 734-764-7433 • umich.edu

Support: CS

ACCOMMODATIONS

Allowed in exams:

Calculators	Yes
Dictionary	Yes
Computer	Yes
Spell-checker	Yes
Extended test time	Yes
Scribe	Yes
Proctors	Yes
Oral exams	No
Note-takers	Yes
Support services for students with:	
LD	Yes
ADHD	Yes
ASD	Yes
Distraction-reduced environment	Yes
Recording of lecture allowed	Yes
Reading technology	Yes
Audio books	No
Other assistive technology	Yes
Priority registration	No
Added costs of services:	
For LD	No
For ADHD	No
For ASD	No
LD specialists	Yes
ADHD & ASD coaching	No
ASD specialists	No
Professional tutors	Yes
Peer tutors	Yes
Max. hours/week for services	Varies
How professors are notified of student approved accommodations	Student

COLLEGE GRADUATION REQUIREMENTS

Course waivers allowed	No
Course substitutions allowed	No

PROGRAMS/SERVICES FOR STUDENTS WITH LEARNING DIFFERENCES

Students with disabilities must register with the Services for Students with Disabilities office (SSD) in order to receive services. SSD engages in a collaborative process with students to best determine each individual's accommodations for their particular academic path. When submitting documentation to request accommodations, SSD suggests that it speaks specifically to the disability. The services provided by SSD include peer-assisted study sessions, testing accommodations, writing center support, science learning center support, executive functioning support, assistive technology resources, and career center access. Registered students have access to individual and group academic coaching with the Academic Support and Access Partnerships (ASAP). ASAP also offers self-directed modules to assist students with organization and executive functioning skills.

ADMISSIONS

Admission requirements are the same for all students. Applicants with learning disabilities are encouraged to disclose their disability on the application form or by writing a cover letter. Applicants are welcome to submit AP scores or IB test scores. The median GPA for accepted students is 3.9, and of the applicants who submitted test scores, the middle 50 percent scored a 1400–1540 on the SAT. Applicants cannot apply Early Action (due November 1) to the School of Music, Theater & Dance or Taubman College of Architecture and Urban Planning. Early Action does not improve chances for admission; it provides a decision in January instead of April.

Additional Information

Following admission, students must complete the student initial information form and schedule a welcome meeting with their assigned advisor. For additional academic support, students can meet with graduate student coaches on a weekly basis through Peer Assisted Study Sessions (PASS). The Science Learning Center (SLC) provides drop-in small-group tutoring and appointment-based tutoring. Students can receive writing consultation in person or online at the Sweetland Center for Writing. The Counseling and Psychological Services (CAPS) office offers services to support wellness and treat anxiety, stress, and depression.

In 1817, U-M was created in Detroit and originally named the Catholepistemiad (meaning "School of Universal Knowledge"), but in 1821, the charter was amended to the University of Michigan. In 1837, the state gave U-M permission to leave Detroit; Ann Arbor had offered free land to the university. No classes were ever held in Detroit; the first classes were 2.5 decades later in Ann Arbor in 1841. The 1845 graduating class consisted of 11 men.

University of Michigan

GENERAL ADMISSIONS

Very important factors include: rigor of secondary school record, academic GPA. *Important factors include:* standardized test scores (if submitted), application essay, recommendations. High school diploma is required and GED is accepted. Institution is test-optional for entering Fall 2024. Check admissions website for updates. *Academic units required:* 4 English, 3 math, 3 science (1 labs), 2 foreign language, 3 social studies. *Academic units recommended:* 4 math, 4 science, 4 foreign language, 4 social studies, 5 academic electives.

FINANCIAL AID

Students should submit: CSS/Financial Aid PROFILE; FAFSA. *Need-based scholarships/grants offered:* College/university scholarship or grant aid from institutional funds; Federal Pell; Private scholarships; SEOG; State scholarships/grants. *Loan aid offered:* Direct PLUS loans; Direct Subsidized Loans; Direct Unsubsidized Loans. Federal Work-Study Program available. Institutional employment available.

CAMPUS LIFE

Activities: Campus Ministries; Choral groups; Concert band; Dance; Drama/theater; International Student Organization; Jazz band; Literary magazine; Marching band; Model UN; Music ensembles; Musical theater; Opera; Pep band; Radio station; Student government; Student newspaper; Student-run film society; Symphony orchestra; Television station; Yearbook. **Organizations:** 1500 registered organizations, 85 religious organizations, 16 fraternities, 16 sororities. **Athletics (Intercollegiate):** *Men:* baseball, basketball, cross-country, golf, gymnastics, ice hockey, lacrosse, swimming, track/field (indoor), wrestling. *Women:* basketball, crew/rowing, cross-country, field hockey, golf, gymnastics, lacrosse, softball, swimming, track/field (indoor), volleyball, water polo.

CAMPUS

Type of school	Public
Environment	City

STUDENTS

Undergrad enrollment	32,448
% male/female	48/52
% from out of state	39
% frosh live on campus	97

FINANCIAL FACTS

Annual in-state tuition	$17,454
Annual out-of-state tuition	$56,941
Room and board	$13,171
Required fees	$332

GENERAL ADMISSIONS INFO

Application fee	$75
Regular application deadline	2/1
Nonfall registration	Yes

Fall 2024 testing policy	Test Optional
Range SAT EBRW	670–750
Range SAT Math	680–780
Range ACT Composite	31–34

ACADEMICS

Student/faculty ratio	15:1
% students returning for sophomore year	97

Most classes have 10–19 students.

REQUESTING SERVICES FOR STUDENTS WITH LEARNING DIFFERENCES

Phone: 734-763-3000 • ssd.umich.edu • Email: ssdoffice@umich.edu

Documentation submitted to: Services for Students with Disabilities
Separate application required for Services: Yes

Documentation required for:
LD: Psychoeducational evaluation
ADHD: Psychoeducational evaluation
ASD: Psychoeducational evaluation

Western Michigan University

1903 W. Michigan Avenue, Kalamazoo, MI 49008-5211 • Admissions: 269-387-2000 • wmich.edu

Support: SP

ACCOMMODATIONS

Allowed in exams:

Calculators	Yes
Dictionary	Yes
Computer	Yes
Spell-checker	Yes
Extended test time	Yes
Scribe	Yes
Proctors	Yes
Oral exams	Yes
Note-takers	Yes

Support services for students with:

LD	Yes
ADHD	Yes
ASD	Yes
Distraction-reduced environment	Yes
Recording of lecture allowed	Yes
Reading technology	Yes
Audio books	Yes
Other assistive technology	Yes
Priority registration	Yes

Added costs of services:

For LD	No
For ADHD	No
For ASD	Yes
LD specialists	Yes
ADHD & ASD coaching	Yes
ASD specialists	Yes
Professional tutors	No
Peer tutors	Yes
Max. hours/week for services	Varies
How professors are notified of student approved accommodations	Student

COLLEGE GRADUATION REQUIREMENTS

Course waivers allowed	No
Course substitutions allowed	No

PROGRAMS/SERVICES FOR STUDENTS WITH LEARNING DIFFERENCES

Disability Services for Students (DSS) supports students with learning disabilities. DSS promotes self-advocacy, provides resources and services, and acts on behalf of the student if necessary. After completing the DSS-Accommodate form, students should call DSS to schedule an initial appointment. Students will not be considered registered with the office until they meet with DSS to finalize registration and accommodations. Available accommodations may include various testing accommodations and alternate-format texts. Students registered with DSS can access the Mentoring for Success Program, a peer-mentoring program geared towards first- and second-year students and helps them achieve specific academic and developmental goals. Additionally, Western Michigan University's Autism Services Center (ASC) provides transition support for students with ASD and other disabilities. The fee for this program includes weekly one-on-one meetings with an ASD coordinator or graduate student, organized social events, and workshops. It also promotes increased communication between students, parents, and faculty.

ADMISSIONS

All applicants are expected to meet the same admission criteria. Admitted students typically have a 3.4 high school GPA and a minimum ACT score of 23 or an SAT score of 1090, if submitted. Western Michigan University does not require letters of recommendation, résumés, or personal statements. Although not required, students' involvement in leadership, volunteering, school activities, or work is valued in the admission review.

Additional Information

The Autism Services Center Summer Transition Program is designed for 18-year-old individuals with ASD and other disabilities. Participants in the Summer Transition Program will enroll in a 3 or 4 credit WMU course of the student's choosing; have paid on-campus employment for 10 hours per week; participate in instruction focused on pre-employment, social, study, academic, and transition skills; live in a residence hall for 7.5 weeks; meet weekly with a peer mentor and an ASC graduate point person; and engage in various social events, such as game nights, movie nights, and hanging out at the Student Recreation Center.

Originally named Western State Normal School, WMU held its first class in 1904 on East Campus with an enrollment of 107 students. Since access to the site was so steep, the Western State Normal Railroad was built in 1907 (a funicular: two counterbalanced cars attached to opposite ends of a haul cable—when one ascended, the other descended) to transport students up and down the hill. The railroad stopped operating in 1949 due to the popularity of cars.

Western Michigan University

General Admissions

Very important factors include: academic GPA. *Important factors include:* rigor of secondary school record. *Other factors considered include:* standardized test scores (if submitted), application essay, recommendations. High school diploma is required and GED is accepted. Institution is test-optional for entering Fall 2024. Check admissions website for updates. *Academic units recommended:* 4 English, 3 math, 3 science, 2 foreign language, 3 social studies.

Financial Aid

Students should submit: FAFSA. *Need-based scholarships/grants offered:* College/university scholarship or grant aid from institutional funds; Federal Pell; Private scholarships; SEOG; State scholarships/grants. *Loan aid offered:* Direct PLUS loans; Direct Subsidized Loans; Direct Unsubsidized Loans. Federal Work-Study Program available. Institutional employment available.

Campus Life

Activities: Campus Ministries; Choral groups; Concert band; Dance; Drama/theater; International Student Organization; Jazz band; Literary magazine; Marching band; Model UN; Music ensembles; Musical theater; Opera; Pep band; Radio station; Student government; Student newspaper; Student-run film society; Symphony orchestra. **Organizations:** 210 registered organizations, 11 honor societies, 18 religious organizations, 20 fraternities, 16 sororities. **Athletics (Intercollegiate):** *Men:* baseball, basketball, cross-country, golf, ice hockey, lacrosse, racquetball, rugby, swimming, ultimate frisbee, volleyball. *Women:* basketball, cross-country, equestrian sports, golf, gymnastics, lacrosse, racquetball, rugby, softball, swimming, track/field (indoor), ultimate frisbee, volleyball.

CAMPUS

Type of school	Public
Environment	City

STUDENTS

Undergrad enrollment	14,310
% male/female	50/50
% from out of state	21
% frosh live on campus	81

FINANCIAL FACTS

Annual in-state tuition	$13,334
Annual out-of-state tuition	$16,668
Room and board	$10,884
Required fees	$100

GENERAL ADMISSIONS INFO

Application fee	$40
Regular application deadline	6/1
Nonfall registration	Yes
Fall 2024 testing policy	Test Optional
Range SAT EBRW	510–620
Range SAT Math	490–600
Range ACT Composite	21–27

ACADEMICS

Student/faculty ratio	16:1
% students returning for sophomore year	77
Most classes have 10–19 students.	

REQUESTING SERVICES FOR STUDENTS WITH LEARNING DIFFERENCES

Phone: 269-387-2116 • wmich.edu/disabilityservices • Email: vpsa-dsrs@wmich.edu

Documentation submitted to: Disability Services for Students

Separate application required for Services: Yes

Documentation required for:
LD: Psychoeducational evaluation
ADHD: Psychoeducational evaluation
ASD: Psychoeducational evaluation

Augsburg University

2211 Riverside Avenue, Minneapolis, MN 55454 • Admissions: 612-330-1001 • www.augsburg.edu

Support: SP

ACCOMMODATIONS

Allowed in exams:

Calculators	Yes
Dictionary	Yes
Computer	Yes
Spell-checker	Yes
Extended test time	Yes
Scribe	Yes
Proctors	Yes
Oral exams	Yes
Note-takers	Yes

Support services for students with:

LD	Yes
ADHD	Yes
ASD	Yes
Distraction-reduced environment	Yes
Recording of lecture allowed	Yes
Reading technology	Yes
Audio books	Yes
Other assistive technology	Yes
Priority registration	No

Added costs of services:

For LD	No
For ADHD	No
For ASD	No
LD specialists	Yes
ADHD & ASD coaching	No
ASD specialists	No
Professional tutors	No
Peer tutors	Yes
Max. hours/week for services	Varies
How professors are notified of student approved accommodations	Student

COLLEGE GRADUATION REQUIREMENTS

Course waivers allowed	No
Course substitutions allowed	Yes
In what courses: Case-by-case basis	

DID YOU KNOW?

As students begin preparing for finals in November, they also look to holiday traditions. Velkommen Jul begins with chapel and worship, on to Scandinavian music and foods, handcrafted items, and a visit from St. Nicholas. It's rumored to be one of the largest gatherings of Norwegian sweaters in the country.

PROGRAMS/SERVICES FOR STUDENTS WITH LEARNING DIFFERENCES

The Franklin Groves Center for Learning and Accessible Student Services (CLASS) assists students with disability access and equity. Eligible students must schedule a meeting with a disability specialist in the CLASS office and submit documentation. At the meeting, the student and specialist will discuss the impact of the disability, discuss barriers and what CLASS can offer to minimize those barriers, and plan for any next steps and any other resources. Accommodations may include alternative-format textbooks and course materials, assistive technology, note-taking support, testing alternatives, and classroom accommodations. Disability specialists may also assist with course selection, offer individual support and learning strategies, and help with time management and organizational skills.

ADMISSIONS

All applicants are required to meet the same academic and technical standards and are accepted based on their ability to succeed in the college environment. Prospective students who have taken college prep courses, demonstrated academic success, and are active in school and their community are invited to apply. The admission committee looks at an application based on academic trends, rigor of curriculum, unweighted GPA, leadership traits, persistence, and writing skills as their most reliable predictors of success. There is no standard GPA or specific course requirements. Prospective students must submit a complete application, official high school transcripts, and a personal essay. Letters of academic recommendation are optional. For students meeting a specific GPA, Augsburg Applies To You has a fast-track admission where they will be offered direct admission, bypassing the need for submitting a general application, essays, and evaluations. This process will give counselors more time to work with students and students more time to prepare for the college experience.

Additional Information

The Gage Center for Student Success offers academic support, resources, and services to help students achieve educational goals through Academic Advising, the Academic Skills Office, Disability Resources (the CLASS Office), and TRIO/Student Support Services. Tutoring and Supplemental Instruction are coordinated through the Academic Skills Office in the Gage Center. The Gage Center also houses the Groves Accommodations Lab, which provides assistive technology and testing accommodations, and the Groves Technology Center, a fully equipped computer lab available to all students. The Writing Center offers individual tutoring for students who want help developing college-level writing skills. The center works with students on writing assignments, from brainstorming ideas to editing strategies for final drafts. The Speaking Lab is a free individual or group tutoring resource meant to help in any way it can with oral presentations, speeches, topics, outlines, and presentations.

Augsburg University

GENERAL ADMISSIONS

Very important factors include: rigor of secondary school record, class rank, academic GPA, application essay, recommendations. *Important factors include:* High school diploma is required and GED is accepted. Institution is test-free for entering Fall 2024. Check admissions website for updates. *Academic units recommended:* 4 English, 3 math, 3 science, 2 foreign language, 2 social studies.

FINANCIAL AID

Students should submit: FAFSA. *Need-based scholarships/grants offered:* College/university scholarship or grant aid from institutional funds; Federal Pell; Private scholarships; SEOG; State scholarships/grants. *Loan aid offered:* Direct PLUS loans; Direct Subsidized Loans; Direct Unsubsidized Loans. Institutional employment available.

CAMPUS LIFE

Activities: Campus Ministries; Choral groups; Concert band; Dance; Drama/theater; International Student Organization; Jazz band; Literary magazine; Music ensembles; Opera; Radio station; Student government; Student newspaper; Yearbook. **Organizations:** 35 registered organizations, 1 honor societies, 1 religious organizations, 0 fraternities, 0 sororities. **Athletics (Intercollegiate):** *Men:* baseball, basketball, cross-country, golf, ice hockey, track/field (indoor), wrestling. *Women:* basketball, cross-country, golf, ice hockey, softball, swimming, track/field (indoor), volleyball.

CAMPUS

Type of school	Private (nonprofit)
Environment	Metropolis

STUDENTS

Undergrad enrollment	3,014
% male/female	45/55
% from out of state	13
% frosh live on campus	82

FINANCIAL FACTS

Annual tuition	$29,794
Room and board	$8,072
Required fees	$624

GENERAL ADMISSIONS INFO

Application fee	$25
Regular application deadline	8/15
Nonfall registration	Yes
Fall 2024 testing policy	Test Free

ACADEMICS

Student/faculty ratio	16:1
% students returning for sophomore year	83

Most classes have 10–19 students.

REQUESTING SERVICES FOR STUDENTS WITH LEARNING DIFFERENCES

Phone: 612-330-1053 • www.augsburg.edu/class • Email: class@augsburg.edu

Documentation submitted to: CLASS Disability Resources
Separate application required for Services: Yes

Documentation required for:
LD: Psychoeducational evaluation
ADHD: Psychoeducational evaluation
ASD: Psychoeducational evaluation

Minnesota State University Moorhead

1104 7th Avenue, South Moorhead, MN 56563 • Admissions: 218-477-2161 • www.mnstate.edu

Support: CS

ACCOMMODATIONS

Allowed in exams:

Calculators	Yes
Dictionary	Yes
Computer	Yes
Spell-checker	Yes
Extended test time	Yes
Scribe	Yes
Proctors	Yes
Oral exams	Yes
Note-takers	Yes

Support services for students with:

LD	Yes
ADHD	Yes
ASD	Yes
Distraction-reduced environment	Yes
Recording of lecture allowed	Yes
Reading technology	Yes
Audio books	Yes
Other assistive technology	Yes
Priority registration	Yes

Added costs of services:

For LD	No
For ADHD	No
For ASD	No
LD specialists	Yes
ADHD & ASD coaching	No
ASD specialists	No
Professional tutors	No
Peer tutors	Yes
Max. hours/week for services	1
How professors are notified of student approved accommodations	Student and Accessibility Resources

COLLEGE GRADUATION REQUIREMENTS

Course waivers allowed	Yes

In what courses: Case-by-case basis

Course substitutions allowed	Yes

In what courses: Case-by-case basis

PROGRAMS/SERVICES FOR STUDENTS WITH LEARNING DIFFERENCES

The Accessibility Resources office works with students with disabilities to provide reasonable accommodations that include extended test time, use of assistive technology, a notetaker, and alternate-format textbooks and materials. To apply for services, students complete and submit a request for accommodations form, participate in an intake interview, and provide disability information or documentation.

ADMISSIONS

Minnesota State University Moorhead does not consider ACT or SAT scores for admission as long as applicants meet the other requirements. The automatic admission requirements are a cumulative GPA of at least 3.0, or rank in the top 50 percent of their high school class, or achieve a 21 or higher composite score on the ACT, or achieve a 1060 or higher on the SAT. Each application is reviewed for those who do not meet the automatic requirements. Applicants who have a composite ACT score of 17–20 or a 900–1050 SAT score and a GPA of 2.70–2.99 are evaluated for the strength of their high school academic record. The admission committee may request additional information, such as an updated transcript.

Additional Information

Students who do not meet the admission requirements but who the university feels have the potential to be successful in college are identified by the admission committee to participate in the Growth, Resilience, Initiative, Transformation Program (GRIT). Students work with a success coach and are mentored and given direct advice during their first year in college. Students who do not meet during their assigned times will not be able to register for the following year. All students have access to academic coaches in the Success Center to get help with their learning styles, reducing anxiety, time management, and enhancing their study, test-taking, and note-taking skills. Tutoring is also offered in groups or one-to-one.

Dane Willard Boedigheimer was a speech communications major with an emphasis in film studies. One of his final MSUM projects was a full-length feature film titled *Trash TV*, shown at the Fargo Theatre. He's better known by his stage name DaneBoe, an American Internet personality, voice actor, writer, and animator. He's the creator of the web series *The Annoying Orange* and the spin-off TV series, *The High Fructose Adventures of Annoying Orange*.

Minnesota State University Moorhead

GENERAL ADMISSIONS

Very important factors include: class rank, academic GPA, standardized test scores (if submitted). *Other factors considered include:* rigor of secondary school record, application essay, recommendations. High school diploma is required and GED is accepted. Institution is test-optional for entering Fall 2024. Check admissions website for updates. *Academic units required:* 4 English, 3 math, 3 science (1 lab), 2 foreign language, 3 social studies.

FINANCIAL AID

Students should submit: FAFSA; State aid form. *Need-based scholarships/grants offered:* College/university scholarship or grant aid from institutional funds; Private scholarships; State scholarships/grants. *Loan aid offered:* Direct PLUS loans; Direct Subsidized Loans; Direct Unsubsidized Loans. Federal Work-Study Program available. Institutional employment available.

CAMPUS LIFE

Activities: Campus Ministries; Choral groups; Concert band; Dance; Drama/theater; International Student Organization; Jazz band; Literary magazine; Model UN; Music ensembles; Musical theater; Pep band; Radio station; Student government; Student newspaper; Student-run film society; Television station. **Organizations:** 130 registered organizations, 7 honor societies, 11 religious organizations, 0 fraternities, 2 sororities. **Athletics (Intercollegiate):** *Men:* basketball, cross-country, track/field (indoor), wrestling. *Women:* basketball, cross-country, golf, softball, swimming, track/field (indoor), volleyball.

CAMPUS
Type of school	Public
Environment	City

STUDENTS
Undergrad enrollment	5,025
% male/female	40/60
% from out of state	33
% frosh live on campus	91

FINANCIAL FACTS
Annual in-state tuition	$6,898
Annual out-of-state tuition	$13,796
Room and board	$7,398
Required fees	$940

GENERAL ADMISSIONS INFO
Application fee	$20
Regular application deadline	6/15
Nonfall registration	Yes
Fall 2024 testing policy	Test Optional
Range SAT EBRW	445–520
Range SAT Math	480–570
Range ACT Composite	20–25

ACADEMICS
Student/faculty ratio	17:1
% students returning for sophomore year	73

Most classes have 20–29 students.

Minnesota

REQUESTING SERVICES FOR STUDENTS WITH LEARNING DIFFERENCES

Phone: 218-477-2167 • www.mnstate.edu/student-life/student-services/accessibility
Email: accessibility@mnstate.edu

Documentation submitted to: Accessibility Resources
Separate application required for Services: Yes

Documentation required for:
LD: Psychoeducational evaluation
ADHD: Psychoeducational evaluation
ASD: Psychoeducational evaluation

St. Catherine University

2004 Randolph Avenue, Saint Paul, MN 55105 • Admissions: 651-690-6000 • www.stkate.edu

Support: CS

ACCOMMODATIONS

Allowed in exams:

Calculators	Yes
Dictionary	Yes
Computer	Yes
Spell-checker	Yes
Extended test time	Yes
Scribe	Yes
Proctors	Yes
Oral exams	Yes
Note-takers	Yes

Support services for students with:

LD	Yes
ADHD	Yes
ASD	Yes
Distraction-reduced environment	Yes
Recording of lecture allowed	Yes
Reading technology	Yes
Audio books	Yes
Other assistive technology	Yes
Priority registration	Yes

Added costs of services:

For LD	No
For ADHD	No
For ASD	No
LD specialists	Yes
ADHD & ASD coaching	No
ASD specialists	No
Professional tutors	No
Peer tutors	Yes
Max. hours/week for services	Varies
How professors are notified of student approved accommodations	Student and Student Accessibility and Accommodations

COLLEGE GRADUATION REQUIREMENTS

Course waivers allowed	No
Course substitutions allowed	Yes
In what courses: Case-by-case basis	

PROGRAMS/SERVICES FOR STUDENTS WITH LEARNING DIFFERENCES

Student Accessibility and Accommodations (SAA) determines eligibility and accommodations for students with disabilities. Once enrolled, students start the process by contacting SAA to schedule an initial meeting. During the meeting, staff and the student will discuss reasonable accommodations and the student will learn about helpful campus and community resources. The meeting will also determine the necessary disability documentation, information, and verification needed. Once documentation has been received and accommodations finalized for each course, students receive accommodation letters to distribute to course instructors and should talk to their instructors about implementation. Accommodations are determined for each student and each class. Common accommodations include alternative testing, live transcription, textbooks in alternative formats, closed captioning, note-taking software, screen readers, and other assistive technology. Prospective students are welcome to contact SAA early in their college planning with any concerns or questions.

ADMISSIONS

All applicants submit the same general admission application and are required to submit a transcript of courses from an accredited high school or GED equivalent that indicates the applicant followed a solid college preparatory program while in high school. A counselor recommendation and a personal essay or statement are required, and teacher evaluations are not required, but up to three will be considered. St. Kate's is test-optional except in specific programs, but SAT or ACT scores are required for homeschooled applicants. The committee may defer an admission decision and inform an applicant of a request for further information, or they may request an interview with the applicant.

Additional Information

Students can sign up for one of the three Living Learning Community Housing options where they can live and participate with others who share their passions, interests, and goals. The O'Neill Center for Academic Development includes the Writing/Reading Center and Math/Science Center for one-on-one online and in-person tutoring in undergraduate writing, math, science, and health sciences. Drop-in study sessions are available for introductory math and science courses as well as selected health science courses.

St. Catherine of Alexandria is a composite of several Christian women who defied Roman authority and were punished for their faith. The Feast of St. Catherine honors the patron saint of students, scholars, and philosophers and begins the holiday season at St. Kate's, which includes the campus light tour, parade, Candlelight Christmas Concert, crafting and baking talents, and the Charity Ball raising money for Sarah's Oasis.

St. Catherine University

GENERAL ADMISSIONS

Very important factors include: rigor of secondary school record. *Important factors include:* class rank, academic GPA, standardized test scores (if submitted), application essay, recommendations. High school diploma is required and GED is accepted. Institution is test-optional for entering Fall 2024. Check admissions website for updates. *Academic units recommended:* 4 English, 3 math, 2 science, 2 social studies.

FINANCIAL AID

Students should submit: FAFSA; Institution's own financial aid form. *Need-based scholarships/grants offered:* College/university scholarship or grant aid from institutional funds; Federal Nursing Scholarships; Federal Pell; Private scholarships; SEOG; State scholarships/grants. *Loan aid offered:* Direct PLUS loans; Direct Subsidized Loans; Direct Unsubsidized Loans. Federal Work-Study Program available. Institutional employment available.

CAMPUS LIFE

Activities: Campus Ministries; Choral groups; Dance; Drama/theater; International Student Organization; Literary magazine; Music ensembles; Musical theater; Radio station; Student government; Student newspaper. **Organizations:** 40 registered organizations, 24 honor societies, 4 religious organizations, 0 fraternities, 1 sororities. **Athletics (Intercollegiate):** *Women:* basketball, cross-country, golf, ice hockey, lacrosse, softball, swimming, track/field (indoor), volleyball.

Minnesota

REQUESTING SERVICES FOR STUDENTS WITH LEARNING DIFFERENCES

Phone: 651-690-6563 • www.stkate.edu/life/student-assistance/accessibility-accommodations
Email: accessibility@stkate.edu

Documentation submitted to: Student Accessibility and Accommodations
Separate application required for Services: Yes

Documentation required for:
LD: Psychoeducational evaluation
ADHD: Psychoeducational evaluation
ASD: Psychoeducational evaluation

St. Olaf College

1520 St. Olaf Avenue, Northfield, MN 55057 • Admissions: 507-786-3025 • wp.stolaf.edu

Support: S

ACCOMMODATIONS

Allowed in exams:

Calculators	Yes
Dictionary	Yes
Computer	Yes
Spell-checker	Yes
Extended test time	Yes
Scribe	Yes
Proctors	Yes
Oral exams	Yes
Note-takers	Yes

Support services for students with:

LD	Yes
ADHD	Yes
ASD	Yes
Distraction-reduced environment	Yes
Recording of lecture allowed	Yes
Reading technology	Yes
Audio books	Yes
Other assistive technology	Yes
Priority registration	Yes

Added costs of services:

For LD	No
For ADHD	No
For ASD	No
LD specialists	No
ADHD & ASD coaching	Yes
ASD specialists	No
Professional tutors	No
Peer tutors	Yes
Max. hours/week for services	3
How professors are notified of student approved accommodations	Disability and Access

COLLEGE GRADUATION REQUIREMENTS

Course waivers allowed	No
Course substitutions allowed	Yes
In what courses: Foreign Language on a case-by-case basis	

PROGRAMS/SERVICES FOR STUDENTS WITH LEARNING DIFFERENCES

Disability and Access (DAC) serves students with disabilities. Students complete and submit the online academic accommodations request form. When the request form has been reviewed, an access specialist will set up an initial meeting. Students can email DAC documentation in advance or take it to the meeting. At the meeting, the student and access specialist will develop an accommodation plan, an accommodation letter will be prepared, and any resources that may be helpful will be discussed. DAC accommodations may include priority registration, assistive technology, alternate text formats, note-taking, extended time or other accommodations for exams, and support in breaking assignments into smaller parts with incremental due dates.

ADMISSIONS

St. Olaf's is interested in how well an applicant is prepared to thrive in a college environment. The transcript is reviewed for grade strength, trends, course rigor, and any disruptions in performance. A personal essay and additional writing supplements are required, and the university also looks for strong writing throughout the application. The average GPA of recently admitted classes is 3.68 (unweighted). One letter of recommendation from a teacher in a core academic subject is required; one other is optional. For students who submit SAT scores, St. Olaf's median range score is 1150–1400.

Additional Information

The Academic Success Center offers students tutoring, academic advising, success coaching, Supplemental Instruction, and writing tutors and support. Center for Advising and Academic Support (CAAS) gives students at least three advisors: summer registration faculty advisor, college advisor (typically first two years), and major advisor (typically junior and senior years). First-year students are assigned a success coach to facilitate academic and personal development. One-on-one peer academic tutoring is available by appointment at no cost in most 100- and 200-level courses. Writing Desk tutors provide guidance for any stage of the writing process, and some are also able to offer "speaking support" for preparing, rehearsing, and polishing presentations. Supplemental Instruction (SI) sessions are peer-led sessions to assist students in learning and retaining course material in courses that are known to be challenging. There are also Virtual Academic Strategy Workshops, which can be accessed anytime.

In 1874, a group of pioneering pastors, farmers, and businessmen laid the groundwork for St. Olaf college. As Norwegian immigrants looking for Nordic religious symbolism from the Middle Ages, they named the school for Olav II Haraldsson ("Olaf"), king of Norway, from 1016 until 1030. He was killed on July 29, 1030, at the Battle of Stiklestad, one of the most famous battles in Norway's history. The Roman Catholic Church declared Olaf a saint in 1164, making him Norway's patron saint and eternal king.

St. Olaf College

General Admissions

Very important factors include: rigor of secondary school record, academic GPA, application essay. *Important factors include:* class rank, recommendations. *Other factors considered include:* standardized test scores (if submitted). High school diploma is required and GED is accepted. Institution is test-optional for entering Fall 2024. Check admissions website for updates. *Academic units recommended:* 4 English, 4 math, 4 science (2 labs), 4 foreign language, 4 social studies.

Financial Aid

Students should submit: CSS/Financial Aid Profile; FAFSA; Noncustodial Profile. *Need-based scholarships/grants offered:* College/university scholarship or grant aid from institutional funds; Federal Pell; Private scholarships; SEOG; State scholarships/grants. *Loan aid offered:* Direct PLUS loans; Direct Subsidized Loans; Direct Unsubsidized Loans. Federal Work-Study Program available. Institutional employment available.

Campus Life

Activities: Campus Ministries; Choral groups; Concert band; Dance; Drama/theater; International Student Organization; Jazz band; Literary magazine; Music ensembles; Musical theater; Opera; Pep band; Radio station; Student government; Student newspaper; Student-run film society; Symphony orchestra. **Organizations:** 193 registered organizations, 24 honor societies, 8 religious organizations, 0 fraternities, 0 sororities. **Athletics (Intercollegiate):** *Men:* baseball, basketball, crew/rowing, cross-country, cycling, equestrian sports, golf, ice hockey, lacrosse, martial arts, rugby, skiing (nordic/cross-country), swimming, track/field (indoor), ultimate frisbee, volleyball, water polo. *Women:* basketball, crew/rowing, cross-country, cycling, equestrian sports, golf, ice hockey, martial arts, rugby, skiing (nordic/cross-country), softball, swimming, track/field (indoor), ultimate frisbee, volleyball, water polo.

CAMPUS

Type of school	Private (nonprofit)
Environment	Village

STUDENTS

Undergrad enrollment	3,003
% male/female	42/58
% from out of state	50
% frosh live on campus	100

FINANCIAL FACTS

Annual tuition	$56,970
Room and board	$13,000

GENERAL ADMISSIONS INFO

Application fee	No fee
Regular application deadline	1/15
Nonfall registration	No

Fall 2024 testing policy	Test Optional
Range SAT EBRW	660–730
Range SAT Math	640–750
Range ACT Composite	28–33

ACADEMICS

Student/faculty ratio	12:1
% students returning for sophomore year	90

Most classes have 10–19 students.

REQUESTING SERVICES FOR STUDENTS WITH LEARNING DIFFERENCES

Phone: 507-786-3288 • wp.stolaf.edu/academic-support/dac • Email: dobosel@stolaf.edu

Documentation submitted to: Disability and Access
Separate application required for Services: Yes

Documentation required for:
 LD: Psychoeducational evaluation
 ADHD: Psychoeducational evaluation
 ASD: Psychoeducational evaluation

University of Minnesota Morris

600 E. 4th Street, Morris, MN 56267 • Admissions: 320-589-6035 • www.morris.umn.edu

Support: CS

ACCOMMODATIONS

Allowed in exams:

Calculators	Yes
Dictionary	Yes
Computer	Yes
Spell-checker	Yes
Extended test time	Yes
Scribe	Yes
Proctors	Yes
Oral exams	Yes
Note-takers	Yes

Support services for students with:

LD	Yes
ADHD	Yes
ASD	Yes
Distraction-reduced environment	Yes
Recording of lecture allowed	Yes
Reading technology	Yes
Audio books	Yes
Other assistive technology	Yes
Priority registration	Yes

Added costs of services:

For LD	No
For ADHD	No
For ASD	No
LD specialists	No
ADHD & ASD coaching	Yes
ASD specialists	Yes
Professional tutors	No
Peer tutors	Yes
Max. hours/week for services	Varies
How professors are notified of student approved accommodations	Student and Disability Resource Center

COLLEGE GRADUATION REQUIREMENTS

Course waivers allowed	Yes
In what courses: Case-by-case basis	
Course substitutions allowed	Yes
In what courses: Case-by-case basis	

PROGRAMS/SERVICES FOR STUDENTS WITH LEARNING DIFFERENCES

The Disability Resource Center (DRC) coordinates with the Student Success Center to facilitate accommodations, academic advising, career services, and workshops. To receive accommodations, DRC requires proper documentation from a licensed professional or qualified health provider. Should additional information be needed, the DRC coordinator can assist students in obtaining information or further assessment. DRC does not cover provider assessment or appointment costs.

ADMISSIONS

All applicants are expected to meet the same admission criteria. Applicants who have not fulfilled the foreign language requirement will still be considered for admission if they otherwise meet the criteria. Admissions supports the submission of additional materials, such as personal statements, recommendations, portfolios, and résumés. If an extenuating circumstance has impacted a student's high school record, the student is encouraged to provide an explanation so that their application may be more accurately evaluated.

Additional Information

The Peer-Assisted Learning (PAL) program is offered in connection to particularly challenging courses. All students enrolled in these classes have the option of attending weekly meetings with PAL facilitators to build learning strategies and improve course comprehension. Workshops are also offered across departments and cover topics including stress management, wellness, social issues, and financial health.

University land was originally inhabited by the Anishinaabe and Dakota/Lakota people, and the Multi-Ethnic Resource Center building was originally a boarding school for Native Americans. The boarding school was closed in 1909, and the campus was transferred to the state with the stipulation that "American Indian students shall at all times be admitted to such school free of charge for tuition." That policy remains in place at UM Morris.

University of Minnesota Morris

GENERAL ADMISSIONS

Very important factors include: rigor of secondary school record, class rank, academic GPA, standardized test scores (if submitted). *Other factors considered include:* application essay, recommendations. High school diploma is required and GED is accepted. Institution is test-optional for entering Fall 2024. Check admissions website for updates. *Academic units required:* 4 English, 4 math, 3 science, 2 foreign language, 3 social studies.

FINANCIAL AID

Students should submit: FAFSA. *Need-based scholarships/grants offered:* College/university scholarship or grant aid from institutional funds; Federal Pell; Private scholarships; SEOG; State scholarships/grants. *Loan aid offered:* Direct PLUS loans; Direct Subsidized Loans; Direct Unsubsidized Loans. Federal Work-Study Program available. Institutional employment available.

CAMPUS LIFE

Activities: Campus Ministries; Choral groups; Concert band; Dance; Drama/theater; International Student Organization; Jazz band; Literary magazine; Music ensembles; Musical theater; Radio station; Student government; Student newspaper; Symphony orchestra. **Organizations:** 100 registered organizations, 5 honor societies, 12 religious organizations, 0 fraternities, 0 sororities. **Athletics (Intercollegiate):** *Men:* baseball, basketball, cross-country, equestrian sports, golf, ice hockey, racquetball, rugby, skiing (nordic/cross-country), softball, swimming, track/field (indoor), ultimate frisbee, volleyball. *Women:* basketball, cross-country, equestrian sports, golf, ice hockey, racquetball, rugby, skiing (nordic/cross-country), softball, swimming, track/field (indoor), ultimate frisbee, volleyball.

CAMPUS

Type of school	Public
Environment	Rural

STUDENTS

Undergrad enrollment	1,286
% male/female	43/57
% from out of state	24
% frosh live on campus	95

FINANCIAL FACTS

Annual in-state tuition	$12,804
Annual out-of-state tuition	$14,934
Room and board	$9,522
Required fees	$1,316

GENERAL ADMISSIONS INFO

Application fee	$30
Regular application deadline	8/1
Nonfall registration	Yes
Fall 2024 testing policy	Test Optional

ACADEMICS

Student/faculty ratio	11:1
% students returning for sophomore year	78

Most classes have 10–19 students.

REQUESTING SERVICES FOR STUDENTS WITH LEARNING DIFFERENCES

Phone: 320-589-6178 • morris.umn.edu/directory/disability-resource-center
Email: hoekstra@morris.umn.edu

Documentation submitted to: Disability Resource Center
Separate application required for Services: Yes

Documentation required for:
LD: Psychoeducational evaluation
ADHD: Psychoeducational evaluation
ASD: Psychoeducational evaluation

Winona State University

175 Mark Street, Morris, MN 56267 • Admissions: 507-457-5100 • www.winona.edu

Support: S

PROGRAMS/SERVICES FOR STUDENTS WITH LEARNING DIFFERENCES

The Warrior Success Center houses Access Services for students with disabilities. Students must complete the online access services registration form, submit documentation, and schedule a meeting with Access Services to receive accommodations. Accommodations provided include extended time on tests, distraction-free testing areas, scribes, audio format, note-taking, assistive technology, textbooks in an alternate format, priority registration, and advocacy.

ADMISSIONS

Admission to Winona State University is guaranteed to students with a cumulative high school GPA of 3.0 or higher on a 4.0 scale if the required high school courses are completed before the end of senior year. For the course requirements, math must include 2 years of algebra and 1 year of geometry, science must include 1 year of biological science and 1 year of chemistry or physics (all should include labs), and American Sign Language can be accepted for the world language requirement.

Additional Information

The Supplement to Instruction Program has peer leaders facilitate weekly study sessions in specific courses. The Writing Center is staffed by trained students and offers individual support in helping students plan and edit their writing assignments. The Warrior Success Center also provides free and accessible tutoring for students of all ability levels as well as individualized advising to help students identify the majors and careers best suited to their unique interests, strengths, and goals.

In May 2021, a new tradition arrived in time for graduation. The Commencement Bell is a 275-pound cast iron, 40-foot-tall bell, a project of the Student Experience Committee as a way to start a special new tradition. Each graduate switching their tassel will have the opportunity to announce the completion of their degree by ringing the bell. Director of Archives Russ Dennison, one of the longest-standing current faculty and the most knowledgeable person of WSU traditions and history, was given the honor of the very first ring.

Winona State University

GENERAL ADMISSIONS
Very important factors include: rigor of secondary school record, academic GPA, standardized test scores (if submitted). *Other factors considered include:* class rank. High school diploma is required and GED is accepted. Institution is test-flexible for entering Fall 2024. Check admissions website for updates. *Academic units required:* 4 English, 3 math, 3 science (3 labs), 2 foreign language, 2 social studies, 1 U.S. history, 1 academic elective.

FINANCIAL AID
Students should submit: FAFSA. *Need-based scholarships/grants offered:* College/university scholarship or grant aid from institutional funds; Federal Pell; Private scholarships; SEOG; State scholarships/grants. *Loan aid offered:* Direct PLUS loans; Direct Subsidized Loans; Direct Unsubsidized Loans. Federal Work-Study Program available. Institutional employment available.

CAMPUS LIFE
Activities: Campus Ministries; Choral groups; Concert band; Dance; Drama/theater; International Student Organization; Jazz band; Literary magazine; Model UN; Music ensembles; Musical theater; Pep band; Radio station; Student government; Student newspaper; Student-run film society. **Organizations:** 198 registered organizations, 9 honor societies, 8 religious organizations, 7 fraternities, 3 sororities. **Athletics (Intercollegiate):** *Men:* baseball, basketball, bowling, cross-country, cycling, golf, lacrosse, martial arts, rugby, skiing (nordic/cross-country), softball, swimming, table tennis, ultimate frisbee, volleyball, wrestling. *Women:* baseball, basketball, bowling, cross-country, cycling, golf, gymnastics, lacrosse, martial arts, rugby, skiing (nordic/cross-country), softball, swimming, table tennis, track/field (indoor), ultimate frisbee, volleyball, wrestling.

CAMPUS

Type of school	Public
Environment	Town

STUDENTS

Undergrad enrollment	6,255
% male/female	34/66
% from out of state	28
% frosh live on campus	84

FINANCIAL FACTS

Annual in-state tuition	$7,712
Annual out-of-state tuition	$13,903
Room and board	$9,310
Required fees	$2,068

GENERAL ADMISSIONS INFO

Application fee	$20
Regular application deadline	7/1
Nonfall registration	Yes

Fall 2024 testing policy	Test Flexible
Range SAT EBRW	470–570
Range SAT Math	490–560
Range ACT Composite	19–25

ACADEMICS

Student/faculty ratio	18:1
% students returning for sophomore year	74
Most classes have 20–29 students.	

Minnesota

REQUESTING SERVICES FOR STUDENTS WITH LEARNING DIFFERENCES

Phone: 507-457-5878 • www2.winona.edu/accessservices • Email: access@winona.edu

Documentation submitted to: Access Services
Separate application required for Services: Yes

Documentation required for:
LD: Psychoeducational evaluation
ADHD: Psychoeducational evaluation
ASD: Psychoeducational evaluation

Drury University

900 North Benton Avenue, Springfield, MO 65802-3712 • Admissions: 417-873-7205 • www.drury.edu

(Support: CS)

ACCOMMODATIONS

Allowed in exams:

Calculators	Yes
Dictionary	Yes
Computer	Yes
Spell-checker	Yes
Extended test time	Yes
Scribe	Yes
Proctors	Yes
Oral exams	Yes
Note-takers	Yes

Support services for students with:

LD	Yes
ADHD	Yes
ASD	Yes
Distraction-reduced environment	Yes
Recording of lecture allowed	Yes
Reading technology	No
Audio books	Yes
Other assistive technology	No
Priority registration	Yes

Added costs of services:

For LD	No
For ADHD	No
For ASD	No
LD specialists	No
ADHD & ASD coaching	Yes
ASD specialists	Yes
Professional tutors	No
Peer tutors	Yes
Max. hours/week for services	Varies
How professors are notified of student approved accommodations	Student

COLLEGE GRADUATION REQUIREMENTS

Course waivers allowed	Yes

In what courses: Case-by-case basis

Course substitutions allowed	Yes

In what courses: Case-by-case basis

PROGRAMS/SERVICES FOR STUDENTS WITH LEARNING DIFFERENCES

Accessibility and Disability Services provides support to students with learning disabilities. Services include academic accommodations and referral services for programs offered on campus and in the Springfield community. To receive accommodations, students are encouraged to submit appropriate documentation prior to the start of the first semester so that Accessibility and Disability Services may evaluate their specific needs. Academic accommodations coordinated by Accessibility and Disability Services include extended time during exams, testing in a low-distraction environment, out-of-class testing, audio textbooks and materials, student notetakers, preferential seating, and recorded lectures.

ADMISSIONS

The admissions committee believes that the application, transcript, and essay provide Drury with the necessary information to determine potential success. The application should represent the student and serve as a record of what has been accomplished during their four years of high school. The most important components the review board considers are the student's academic record, curriculum, grades, and grade trend.

Additional Information

Drury's curriculum, Your Drury Fusion (YDF), is designed in contrast to the traditional education of single majors and rigid formulas. YDF is both universal and customizable, centering around three components: first-year seminar courses, Exploration requirements, and certificates. YDF combines theoretical learning with real-world projects to help students develop intellectually and gain marketable attributes. Students are able to finish college with at least three credentials, including their major, without taking any extra time.

Drury's Pool Art Center Gallery has held the Annual Best of the Midwest High School Competitive Exhibition, open to all currently enrolled high school students in 14 states. Each student artist can submit up to three works in any medium and subject matter. Best of Show receives a $2,000 art/art history activity grant for students accepted to Drury; renewable for up to four years by maintaining the grant requirements.

Drury University

GENERAL ADMISSIONS

Very important factors include: rigor of secondary school record, academic GPA. *Important factors include:* application essay. *Other factors considered include:* class rank, standardized test scores (if submitted). High school diploma is required and GED is accepted. Institution is test-optional for entering Fall 2024. Check admissions website for updates. *Academic units required:* 4 English, 3 math, 3 science (2 labs), 2 foreign language, 4 social studies. *Academic units recommended:* 4 math, 4 science (3 labs), 3 foreign language.

FINANCIAL AID

Students should submit: FAFSA. *Need-based scholarships/grants offered:* College/university scholarship or grant aid from institutional funds; Federal Pell; Private scholarships; SEOG; State scholarships/grants. *Loan aid offered:* Direct PLUS loans; Direct Subsidized Loans; Direct Unsubsidized Loans. Federal Work-Study Program available. Institutional employment available.

CAMPUS LIFE

Activities: Campus Ministries; Choral groups; Concert band; Dance; Drama/theater; International Student Organization; Jazz band; Marching band; Model UN; Music ensembles; Musical theater; Pep band; Radio station; Student government; Student newspaper; Symphony orchestra; Television station. **Organizations:** 69 registered organizations, 9 honor societies, 5 religious organizations, 4 fraternities, 4 sororities. **Athletics (Intercollegiate):** *Men:* baseball, basketball, bowling, cross-country, golf, ice hockey, lacrosse, rugby, swimming, track/field (indoor), ultimate frisbee, wrestling. *Women:* basketball, bowling, cross-country, golf, rugby, softball, swimming, track/field (indoor), ultimate frisbee, volleyball.

CAMPUS
Type of school	Private (nonprofit)
Environment	Metropolis

STUDENTS
Undergrad enrollment	1,369
% male/female	46/54
% from out of state	24
% frosh live on campus	95

FINANCIAL FACTS
Annual tuition	$33,900
Room and board	$10,760
Required fees	$1,400

GENERAL ADMISSIONS INFO
Application fee	No fee
Regular application deadline	8/15
Nonfall registration	Yes
Fall 2024 testing policy	Test Optional
Range SAT EBRW	590–700
Range SAT Math	560–660
Range ACT Composite	22–28

ACADEMICS
Student/faculty ratio	12:1
% students returning for sophomore year	75

Most classes have 10–19 students.

Missouri

REQUESTING SERVICES FOR STUDENTS WITH LEARNING DIFFERENCES

Phone: 417-873-7267 • drury.edu/compass-center/accessibility-disability-support-services
Email: lslater002@drury.edu

Documentation submitted to: Accessibility and Disability Services
Separate application required for Services: Yes

Documentation required for:
LD: Psychoeducational evaluation
ADHD: Psychoeducational evaluation
ASD: Psychoeducational evaluation

Saint Louis University

Office of Admissions, DuBourg Hall, Saint Louis, MO 63103 • Admissions: 314-977-2500 • www.slu.edu

Support: S

ACCOMMODATIONS

Allowed in exams:

Calculators	Yes
Dictionary	Yes
Computer	Yes
Spell-checker	Yes
Extended test time	Yes
Scribe	Yes
Proctors	Yes
Oral exams	Yes
Note-takers	Yes

Support services for students with:

LD	No
ADHD	Yes
ASD	No
Distraction-reduced environment	Yes
Recording of lecture allowed	Yes
Reading technology	Yes
Audio books	No
Other assistive technology	Yes
Priority registration	Yes

Added costs of services:

For LD	No
For ADHD	No
For ASD	No
LD specialists	No
ADHD & ASD coaching	No
ASD specialists	No
Professional tutors	No
Peer tutors	Yes
Max. hours/week for services	Varies
How professors are notified of student approved accommodations	Student and CADR

COLLEGE GRADUATION REQUIREMENTS

Course waivers allowed	Yes
In what courses: Varies	
Course substitutions allowed	Yes
In what courses: Varies	

PROGRAMS/SERVICES FOR STUDENTS WITH LEARNING DIFFERENCES

Students with disabilities at Saint Louis University may apply for accommodations through the Center for Accessibility and Disability Resources (CADR). Accommodations must be renewed annually. To receive services, students must complete the application for accommodations and submit documentation of diagnosis or disability. Documentation should be as current as possible to ensure appropriate accommodations are being considered. The CADR offers academic coaching for students diagnosed with ADHD. These coaches help students improve their executive functioning skills, including organizing, planning, task completion, and time management. Registered students with disabilities also have access to a sensory room for sensory and coping needs. Prior to using the sensory room, students will work with an occupational therapy graduate student to go through an assessment.

ADMISSIONS

Saint Louis admissions are selective, with an acceptance rate of 58 percent. Students admitted to Saint Louis who submit test scores have an average SAT score between 1180–1370 and the average GPA for admitted applicants is 3.9.

Additional Information

The Student Success Center provides student success coaching, Supplemental Instruction (SI), tutoring, and writing services.

In October 2014, the clocktower plaza, a center of campus life, became the focal point for a student-led demonstration known as OccupySLU. Hundreds of students and community leaders peacefully occupied the plaza for six days, engaged in teach-ins, peaceful protest, and conversation in the aftermath of the shootings of Michael Brown and Vonderrit Myers Jr. Known as the Clocktower Accords, newly appointed President Fred Pestello promised concrete action to address the demonstrators' demands. The Clock Tower Accords commit Saint Louis University to strengthen diversity, access, and equity on campus.

Saint Louis University

GENERAL ADMISSIONS
Very important factors include: academic GPA. *Important factors include:* rigor of secondary school record, application essay. *Other factors considered include:* standardized test scores (if submitted), recommendations. High school diploma is required and GED is accepted. Institution is test-optional for entering Fall 2024. Check admissions website for updates. *Academic units recommended:* 4 English, 4 math, 3 science, 3 foreign language, 3 social studies, 3 academic electives.

FINANCIAL AID
Students should submit: FAFSA. *Need-based scholarships/grants offered:* College/university scholarship or grant aid from institutional funds; Federal Nursing Scholarships; Federal Pell; Private scholarships; SEOG; State scholarships/grants. *Loan aid offered:* Direct PLUS loans; Direct Subsidized Loans; Direct Unsubsidized Loans. Federal Work-Study Program available. Institutional employment available.

CAMPUS LIFE
Activities: Campus Ministries; Choral groups; Dance; Drama/theater; International Student Organization; Jazz band; Literary magazine; Model UN; Music ensembles; Musical theater; Pep band; Radio station; Student government; Student newspaper; Symphony orchestra. **Organizations: Athletics (Intercollegiate):** *Men:* baseball, basketball, crew/rowing, cross-country, cycling, equestrian sports, golf, ice hockey, lacrosse, racquetball, rugby, swimming, table tennis, track/field (indoor), ultimate frisbee, volleyball, water polo. *Women:* basketball, crew/rowing, cross-country, cycling, equestrian sports, field hockey, golf, lacrosse, racquetball, softball, swimming, table tennis, track/field (indoor), ultimate frisbee, volleyball, water polo.

CAMPUS

Type of school	Private (nonprofit)
Environment	Metropolis

STUDENTS

Undergrad enrollment	7,332
% male/female	39/61
% from out of state	59
% frosh live on campus	88

FINANCIAL FACTS

Annual tuition	$49,800
Room and board	$13,890
Required fees	$844

GENERAL ADMISSIONS INFO

Application fee	No fee
Regular application deadline	Rolling
Nonfall registration	Yes

Fall 2024 testing policy	Test Optional
Range SAT EBRW	570–680
Range SAT Math	570–680
Range ACT Composite	24–30

ACADEMICS

Student/faculty ratio	9:1
% students returning for sophomore year	87

Most classes have 20–29 students.

Missouri

REQUESTING SERVICES FOR STUDENTS WITH LEARNING DIFFERENCES

Phone: 314-977-3484 • www.slu.edu/life-at-slu/student-success-center/accessibility-and-disability-resources
Email: accessibility_disability@slu.edu

Documentation submitted to: Center for Accessibility and Disability Resources
Separate application required for Services: Yes

Documentation required for:
LD: Psychoeducational evaluation
ADHD: Psychoeducational evaluation
ASD: Psychoeducational evaluation

University of Missouri

230 Jesse Hall, Columbia, MO 65211 • Admissions: 573-882-7786 • www.missouri.edu

Support: CS

ACCOMMODATIONS

Allowed in exams:

Calculators	Yes
Dictionary	Yes
Computer	Yes
Spell-checker	Yes
Extended test time	Yes
Scribe	Yes
Proctors	Yes
Oral exams	Yes
Note-takers	Yes

Support services for students with:

LD	Yes
ADHD	Yes
ASD	Yes
Distraction-reduced environment	Yes
Recording of lecture allowed	Yes
Reading technology	Yes
Audio books	Yes
Other assistive technology	Yes
Priority registration	Yes

Added costs of services:

For LD	No
For ADHD	No
For ASD	No
LD specialists	Yes
ADHD & ASD coaching	Yes
ASD specialists	No
Professional tutors	Yes
Peer tutors	Yes
Max. hours/week for services	Varies
How professors are notified of student approved accommodations	Student

COLLEGE GRADUATION REQUIREMENTS

Course waivers allowed	No
Course substitutions allowed	Yes
In what courses: Case-by-case basis	

PROGRAMS/SERVICES FOR STUDENTS WITH LEARNING DIFFERENCES

The Disability Center ensures that any student with a disability will have equal access to the educational programs and activities at MU. Some accommodations include testing accommodations, assistive technology, reduced course load recommendations, flexible attendance, and faculty mentors. Additional support through tutoring, academic coaching, and advocacy are coordinated with other departments. There is no stand-alone testing center, but there are three different locations for testing support. Students are expected to complete all graduation requirements, however, there are some instances in which students may request a course substitution. Once admitted to MU, students must complete an online application to request accommodations. There is a separate online application to request housing accommodations. While a student's self-report can be considered sufficient in some cases, students should be prepared to provide third-party documentation if requested. The on-campus Mizzou Disability Coalition is a good resource for connection, activities, advocacy, and support.

ADMISSIONS

Test scores are optional, but they allow accurate course placement, maximize chances for scholarships, and may improve chances of admission. Applicants can also submit test scores at a later date. For applicants who submit test scores of at least 24 on the ACT or 1160 on the SAT, the required GPA is 2.0; those with scores as low as an ACT of 17 or SAT of 920–960 will need a 3.65 GPA.

Additional Information

The Learning Center provides tutoring and academic coaching for students wanting to improve their study skills. MU Student Health and Well Being provides group therapy for students with ADD, social/relational struggles, and anxiety.

DID YOU KNOW?

In 1908, Walter Williams founded the first School of Journalism in the United States at the University of Missouri. He envisioned a school that would positively influence the quality of journalism and advertising. The J-School today has eight buildings dedicated to journalism, operates the only NBC TV News Station at a university, an NPR Radio Station, and prints *The Missourian Newspaper* and *Vox Magazine*. At age 25, Walter Williams became the youngest-ever president of the MO Press Association, and after founding the J-School, went on to become president of the university.

University of Missouri

GENERAL ADMISSIONS

Very important factors include: class rank, academic GPA, standardized test scores (if submitted). *Other factors considered include:* rigor of secondary school record, application essay, recommendations. High school diploma is required and GED is accepted. Institution is test-optional for entering Fall 2024. Check admissions website for updates. *Academic units required:* 4 English, 4 math, 3 science (1 lab), 2 foreign language, 3 social studies.

FINANCIAL AID

Students should submit: FAFSA. *Need-based scholarships/grants offered:* College/university scholarship or grant aid from institutional funds; Federal Nursing Scholarships; Federal Pell; Private scholarships; SEOG; State scholarships/grants. *Loan aid offered:* Direct PLUS loans; Direct Subsidized Loans; Direct Unsubsidized Loans. Federal Work-Study Program available. Institutional employment available.

CAMPUS LIFE

Activities: Campus Ministries; Choral groups; Concert band; Dance; Drama/theater; International Student Organization; Jazz band; Literary magazine; Marching band; Model UN; Music ensembles; Musical theater; Opera; Pep band; Radio station; Student government; Student newspaper; Student-run film society; Symphony orchestra; Television station. **Organizations:** 600 registered organizations, 31 honor societies, 40 religious organizations, 31 fraternities, 23 sororities. **Athletics (Intercollegiate):** *Men:* baseball, basketball, bowling, crew/rowing, cross-country, cycling, golf, gymnastics, ice hockey, lacrosse, martial arts, racquetball, rugby, swimming, table tennis, track/field (indoor), ultimate frisbee, volleyball, water polo, wrestling. *Women:* basketball, bowling, crew/rowing, cross-country, cycling, field hockey, golf, gymnastics, lacrosse, martial arts, racquetball, rugby, softball, swimming, table tennis, track/field (indoor), ultimate frisbee, volleyball, water polo.

CAMPUS

Type of school	Public
Environment	City

STUDENTS

Undergrad enrollment	23,092
% male/female	46/54
% from out of state	20
% frosh live on campus	93

FINANCIAL FACTS

Annual in-state tuition	$10,020
Annual out-of-state tuition	$29,400
Room and board	$11,520
Required fees	$1,529

GENERAL ADMISSIONS INFO

Application fee	$55
Regular application deadline	Rolling
Nonfall registration	Yes
Fall 2024 testing policy	Test Optional
Range SAT EBRW	570–680
Range SAT Math	560–670
Range ACT Composite	23–30

ACADEMICS

Student/faculty ratio	18:1
% students returning for sophomore year	88

Most classes have 10–19 students.

Missouri

REQUESTING SERVICES FOR STUDENTS WITH LEARNING DIFFERENCES

Phone: 573-882-4696 • disabilitycenter.missouri.edu • Email: disabilitycenter@missouri.edu

Documentation submitted to: Disability Center
Separate application required for Services: Yes

Documentation required for:
  LD: Psychoeducational evaluation
  ADHD: Psychoeducational evaluation
  ASD: Psychoeducational evaluation

University of Missouri—Kansas City

5000 Holmes Street, Kansas City, MO 64114 • Admissions: 816-235-8652 • www.umkc.edu

Support: CS

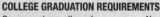

ACCOMMODATIONS

Allowed in exams:

Calculators	Yes
Dictionary	Yes
Computer	Yes
Spell-checker	Yes
Extended test time	Yes
Scribe	Yes
Proctors	Yes
Oral exams	Yes
Note-takers	Yes

Support services for students with:

LD	Yes
ADHD	Yes
ASD	Yes
Distraction-reduced environment	Yes
Recording of lecture allowed	Yes
Reading technology	Yes
Audio books	Yes
Other assistive technology	Yes
Priority registration	Yes

Added costs of services:

For LD	No
For ADHD	No
For ASD	No
LD specialists	No
ADHD & ASD coaching	Yes
ASD specialists	No
Professional tutors	No
Peer tutors	Yes
Max. hours/week for services	Varies
How professors are notified of student approved accommodations	Student

COLLEGE GRADUATION REQUIREMENTS

Course waivers allowed	No
Course substitutions allowed	Yes
In what courses: Case-by-case basis	

PROGRAMS/SERVICES FOR STUDENTS WITH LEARNING DIFFERENCES

The University of Missouri–Kansas City supports students with learning differences through the Student Disability Services office. SDS partners with students to ensure equal access to everything that UMKC has to offer. Some of the services include peer notetakers, testing accommodations, alternative text formats, flexible attendance, and flexible assignment deadlines. They also provide reasonable accommodations to help students demonstrate their abilities, knowledge, and skills. Students wishing to receive accommodations must submit supporting documentation or a disability verification form and complete an online application. Once received, an accommodation planning meeting will be scheduled.

ADMISSIONS

Admission requirements are the same for all applicants. Under the test-optional process, students with a 2.75 GPA may be fully admitted with no test score to UMKC. However, the following programs and colleges require a test score: architectural studies, the conservatory, School of Computing and Engineering, School of Dentistry, School of Medicine, School of Nursing and Health Studies, School of Pharmacy, and the honors college. Students who do not meet certain core curriculum requirements may be admitted to UMKC conditionally, pending completion of an academic support program.

Additional Information

Academic Support and Mentoring provides services to all students at UMKC. Peer tutoring and peer writing support are both free of charge. Supplemental Instruction (SI) provides non-remedial guidance to help students identify their learning styles. Sessions are voluntary and led by trained peers, and most of the SI instruction is offered in the more challenging courses. The Student Success Center is another service designed to provide an important role in student success.

When UMKC was only three years old and didn't have an athletic program, the debate team was going to compete and wanted a mascot. Across town, the Kansas City Zoo was expecting a little joey, and that inspired students to adopt the kangaroo as their mascot. In the fall of 1937, Kasey Kangaroo was born. In 1938, students asked for help illustrating Kasey from a local celebrity and Kansas City native, Walt Disney. His illustration of KC Roo may be the most well-known.

University of Missouri—Kansas City

GENERAL ADMISSIONS

Very important factors include: rigor of secondary school record, academic GPA. *Other factors considered include:* class rank, standardized test scores (if submitted), application essay, recommendations. High school diploma is required and GED is accepted. Institution is test-optional for entering Fall 2024. Check admissions website for updates. *Academic units required:* 4 English, 4 math, 3 science (1 lab), 2 foreign language, 3 social studies, 1 visual/performing arts.

FINANCIAL AID

Students should submit: FAFSA. *Need-based scholarships/grants offered:* College/university scholarship or grant aid from institutional funds; Federal Nursing Scholarships; Federal Pell; Private scholarships; SEOG; State scholarships/grants; United Negro College Fund. *Loan aid offered:* Direct PLUS loans; Direct Subsidized Loans; Direct Unsubsidized Loans. Federal Work-Study Program available. Institutional employment available.

CAMPUS LIFE

Activities: Campus Ministries; Choral groups; Concert band; Dance; Drama/theater; International Student Organization; Jazz band; Literary magazine; Music ensembles; Musical theater; Opera; Pep band; Radio station; Student government; Student newspaper; Student-run film society; Symphony orchestra. **Organizations:** 338 registered organizations, 32 honor societies, 13 religious organizations, 5 fraternities, 7 sororities. **Athletics (Intercollegiate):** *Men:* basketball, crew/rowing, cross-country, golf, racquetball, rugby, softball, swimming, table tennis, track/field (indoor), volleyball, water polo. *Women:* basketball, crew/rowing, cross-country, golf, racquetball, rugby, softball, swimming, table tennis, track/field (indoor), volleyball, water polo.

CAMPUS

Type of school	Public
Environment	Metropolis

STUDENTS

Undergrad enrollment	10,698
% male/female	41/59
% from out of state	28
% frosh live on campus	48

FINANCIAL FACTS

Annual in-state tuition	$11,287
Annual out-of-state tuition	$27,760
Room and board	$12,262

GENERAL ADMISSIONS INFO

Application fee	$45
Regular application deadline	6/15
Nonfall registration	Yes

Fall 2024 testing policy	Test Optional
Range SAT EBRW	570–743
Range SAT Math	573–763
Range ACT Composite	21–30

ACADEMICS

Student/faculty ratio	14:1
% students returning for sophomore year	72

Most classes have 10–19 students.

Missouri

REQUESTING SERVICES FOR STUDENTS WITH LEARNING DIFFERENCES

Phone: 816-235-5612 • info.umkc.edu/disability-services • Email: disability@umkc.edu

Documentation submitted to: Student Disability Services
Separate application required for Services: Yes

Documentation required for:
LD: Psychoeducational evaluation
ADHD: Psychoeducational evaluation
ASD: Psychoeducational evaluation

Washington University in St. Louis

MSC 1089-105-05, St. Louis, MO 63130-4899 • Admissions: 314-935-6000 • wustl.edu

Support: S

ACCOMMODATIONS

Allowed in exams:

Calculators	Yes
Dictionary	Yes
Computer	Yes
Spell-checker	Yes
Extended test time	Yes
Scribe	Yes
Proctors	Yes
Oral exams	Yes
Note-takers	Yes

Support services for students with:

LD	Yes
ADHD	Yes
ASD	Yes
Distraction-reduced environment	Yes
Recording of lecture allowed	Yes
Reading technology	Yes
Audio books	Yes
Other assistive technology	Yes
Priority registration	Yes

Added costs of services:

For LD	No
For ADHD	No
For ASD	No
LD specialists	No
ADHD & ASD coaching	Yes
ASD specialists	No
Professional tutors	Yes
Peer tutors	Yes
Max. hours/week for services	4
How professors are notified of student approved accommodations	Student

COLLEGE GRADUATION REQUIREMENTS

Course waivers allowed	Yes
In what courses: Case-by-case basis	
Course substitutions allowed	Yes
In what courses: Case-by-case basis	

PROGRAMS/SERVICES FOR STUDENTS WITH LEARNING DIFFERENCES

The Disability Resources (DR) office assists students with disabilities by providing guidance and accommodations. Students must submit a request with the appropriate documentation, then DR will determine eligibility and work with each student to implement accommodations. Access WashU is an online portal through which students can request accommodations and teachers can be notified of accommodations. DR will proctor most accommodated exams, but some are proctored by the course instructor.

ADMISSIONS

Admission requirements are the same for all applicants. For students considering pre-med or the natural sciences or engineering, it is recommended that they have taken chemistry and physics. The architecture, business, and engineering schools recommend that students have taken calculus. A portfolio is required for applicants to the College of Art and is strongly encouraged for those applying to the College of Architecture. For those students submitting scores, the middle 50 percent of admitted applicants have a 33–35 ACT score and a 1500–1570 SAT score.

Additional Information

The Center for Teaching and Learning provides support services to help students succeed academically. Study and test-taking skills, executive functioning, time management and study techniques, and access to peer mentors are just some of the services provided. The Writing Center provides assistance with essays, presentations, senior thesis, and more. There is no fee for help in the Writing Center. For students wanting guidance with public speaking, the Speaking Studio is offered through the Writing Center.

The university is named after the first U.S. president, George Washington. In 1897, the school seal was adopted using elements from George Washington's coat of arms and the fleurs-de-lis—the symbol of King Louis IX, patron and namesake of St. Louis. The motto, Per Veritatem Vis, "Strength through Truth," was adopted in 1915. The current version of the official seal was created in 2000, using the same elements.

Washington University in St. Louis

GENERAL ADMISSIONS

Very important factors include: rigor of secondary school record, class rank, academic GPA, standardized test scores (if submitted), application essay, recommendations. High school diploma is required and GED is accepted. Institution is test-optional for entering Fall 2024. Check admissions website for updates. *Academic units recommended:* 4 English, 4 math, 3 science (3 labs), 2 foreign language, 3 social studies.

FINANCIAL AID

Students should submit: CSS/Financial Aid Profile; FAFSA; Noncustodial Profile. *Need-based scholarships/grants offered:* College/university scholarship or grant aid from institutional funds; Federal Pell; Private scholarships; SEOG; State scholarships/grants; United Negro College Fund. *Loan aid offered:* Direct PLUS loans; Direct Subsidized Loans; Direct Unsubsidized Loans. Federal Work-Study Program available. Institutional employment available.

CAMPUS LIFE

Activities: Campus Ministries; Choral groups; Concert band; Dance; Drama/theater; International Student Organization; Jazz band; Literary magazine; Model UN; Music ensembles; Musical theater; Opera; Pep band; Radio station; Student government; Student newspaper; Student-run film society; Symphony orchestra; Television station. **Organizations:** 465 registered organizations, 8 honor societies, 22 religious organizations, 18 fraternities, 11 sororities. **Athletics (Intercollegiate):** *Men:* baseball, basketball, crew/rowing, cross-country, cycling, equestrian sports, golf, gymnastics, ice hockey, lacrosse, martial arts, rugby, swimming, table tennis, track/field (indoor), ultimate frisbee, volleyball, water polo, wrestling. *Women:* basketball, crew/rowing, cross-country, cycling, equestrian sports, field hockey, golf, gymnastics, lacrosse, martial arts, rugby, softball, swimming, table tennis, track/field (indoor), ultimate frisbee, volleyball, water polo.

CAMPUS

Type of school	Private (nonprofit)
Environment	City

STUDENTS

Undergrad enrollment	7,801
% male/female	46/54
% from out of state	89
% frosh live on campus	100

FINANCIAL FACTS

Annual tuition	$61,750
Room and board	$20,778
Required fees	$1,232

GENERAL ADMISSIONS INFO

Application fee	$75
Regular application deadline	1/3
Nonfall registration	No

Fall 2024 testing policy	Test Optional
Range SAT EBRW	730–770
Range SAT Math	770–800
Range ACT Composite	33–35

ACADEMICS

Student/faculty ratio	7:1
% students returning for sophomore year	96

Most classes have 10–19 students.

Missouri

REQUESTING SERVICES FOR STUDENTS WITH LEARNING DIFFERENCES

Phone: 314-935-5970 • students.wustl.edu/disability-resources • Email: disabilityresources@wustl.edu

Documentation submitted to: Disability Resources
Separate application required for Services: Yes

Documentation required for:
  LD: Psychoeducational evaluation
  ADHD: Psychoeducational evaluation
  ASD: Psychoeducational evaluation

Westminster College

501 Westminster Avenue, Fulton, MO 65251 • Admissions: 573-592-5251 • wcmo.edu

Support: SP

ACCOMMODATIONS

Allowed in exams:

Calculators	Yes
Dictionary	Yes
Computer	Yes
Spell-checker	Yes
Extended test time	Yes
Scribe	Yes
Proctors	Yes
Oral exams	Yes
Note-takers	Yes

Support services for students with:

LD	Yes
ADHD	Yes
ASD	Yes
Distraction-reduced environment	Yes
Recording of lecture allowed	Yes
Reading technology	Yes
Audio books	Yes
Other assistive technology	Yes
Priority registration	No

Added costs of services:

For LD	Yes
For ADHD	Yes
For ASD	Yes
LD specialists	Yes
ADHD & ASD coaching	No
ASD specialists	No
Professional tutors	No
Peer tutors	Yes
Max. hours/week for services	Varies
How professors are notified of student approved accommodations	Student and Learning Differences Program

COLLEGE GRADUATION REQUIREMENTS

Course waivers allowed	No
Course substitutions allowed	Yes
In what courses: Case-by-case basis	

PROGRAMS/SERVICES FOR STUDENTS WITH LEARNING DIFFERENCES

The Tomnitz Family Learning Opportunity Center provides accommodations to students with documented disabilities. Students requesting accommodations should submit documentation that includes a diagnosis, an explanation of the disability, and recommended accommodations. Individualized Education Plans are accepted to verify existing accommodations. Students then complete the appropriate accommodation request form and set up a meeting with the director to discuss their requested accommodations. Once they are determined, students should discuss the approved accommodations with their instructors and notify instructors of their needs. The Learning Differences Program (LDP) supports students with learning disabilities. The LDP's services meet the specific needs of these students and include one-on-one professional academic advising, enrollment in supplemental courses designed to encourage and support academic success, extended-time testing, class notes, dictation, and access to a quiet or supportive study environment. The College Transition Program (CTP) is a fee-based program designed specifically to support students with the diagnosis of autism spectrum disorder who are high functioning. Besides professional academic coaching, social skills development, and physical fitness programming, services include communication with parents and instructors. The program has a 1 credit pass/fail course for ASD students.

ADMISSIONS

There is a separate application and admissions procedure for students with learning disabilities. Students submit a completed Westminster college application form, which includes a question asking whether the student is interested in the LDP or CTP. If yes, the student receives an email with program information and a link to apply. The Common App has a similar process to generate that email. Appropriate documentation must be submitted, along with four teacher recommendations. Once all required information has been sent, students will schedule an in-person or virtual interview. For admittance into the LDP or CTP, the director and staff work as a team to review each applicant. Students with at least a 3.0 GPA gain automatic admission and those with less than 3.0 are reviewed by the admissions committee. No essay is required.

Additional Information

Assistive technology includes dictation technology with editing support and an iPad for each student at the school. There is a process by which students can petition for waivers or substitutions for math and foreign language classes.

Originally Fulton College, the college president had the courage to write an invitation for British Prime Minister Winston Churchill to speak. President Harry S. Truman endorsed the invitation, and Churchill accepted. The two traveled together to Fulton, where Churchill delivered his 1946 speech, "Sinews of Peace," a message heard around the world. History calls it the "Iron Curtain Speech," his most famous post-WWII speech.

Westminster College

GENERAL ADMISSIONS

Very important factors include: rigor of secondary school record, standardized test scores (if submitted). *Important factors include:* class rank, academic GPA, recommendations. *Other factors considered include:* application essay. High school diploma is required and GED is accepted. Institution is test-optional for entering Fall 2024. Check admissions website for updates. *Academic units required:* 4 English, 3 math, 2 science (2 labs). *Academic units recommended:* 2 foreign language, 2 social studies, 2 academic electives.

FINANCIAL AID

Students should submit: FAFSA. *Need-based scholarships/grants offered:* College/university scholarship or grant aid from institutional funds; Federal Pell; Private scholarships; SEOG; State scholarships/grants. *Loan aid offered:* Direct PLUS loans; Direct Subsidized Loans; Direct Unsubsidized Loans. Federal Work-Study Program available. Institutional employment available.

CAMPUS LIFE

Activities: Campus Ministries; Choral groups; Dance; Drama/theater; International Student Organization; Jazz band; Literary magazine; Model UN; Music ensembles; Pep band; Student government; Student newspaper. **Organizations:** 49 registered organizations, 15 honor societies, 2 religious organizations, 6 fraternities, 3 sororities. **Athletics (Intercollegiate):** *Men:* baseball, basketball, cross-country, golf, softball, volleyball. *Women:* basketball, cross-country, golf, softball, volleyball.

CAMPUS

Type of school	Private (nonprofit)
Environment	Village

STUDENTS

Undergrad enrollment	764
% male/female	56/44
% from out of state	19
% frosh live on campus	94

FINANCIAL FACTS

Annual tuition	$25,700
Room and board	$10,140
Required fees	$1,900

GENERAL ADMISSIONS INFO

Application fee	No fee
Regular application deadline	Rolling
Nonfall registration	Yes
Fall 2024 testing policy	Test Optional
Range SAT EBRW	500–600
Range SAT Math	515–575
Range ACT Composite	21–26

ACADEMICS

Student/faculty ratio	11:1
% students returning for sophomore year	73

Most classes have 10–19 students.

REQUESTING SERVICES FOR STUDENTS WITH LEARNING DIFFERENCES

Phone: 573-592-5304 • www.wcmo.edu/academics/ssc/loc • Email: westminster@westminster-mo.edu

Documentation submitted to: Learning Opportunities Center
Separate application required for Services: Yes

Documentation required for:
LD: Psychoeducational evaluation
ADHD: Psychoeducational evaluation
ASD: Psychoeducational evaluation

Montana State University Billings

1500 University Drive, Billings, MT 59101 • Admissions: 406-657-2158 • www.msubillings.edu

Support: S

ACCOMMODATIONS

Allowed in exams:

Calculators	Yes
Dictionary	Yes
Computer	Yes
Spell-checker	Yes
Extended test time	Yes
Scribe	Yes
Proctors	Yes
Oral exams	Yes
Note-takers	Yes

Support services for students with:

LD	Yes
ADHD	Yes
ASD	Yes
Distraction-reduced environment	Yes
Recording of lecture allowed	Yes
Reading technology	Yes
Audio books	Yes
Other assistive technology	Yes
Priority registration	Yes

Added costs of services:

For LD	No
For ADHD	No
For ASD	No
LD specialists	No
ADHD & ASD coaching	No
ASD specialists	No
Professional tutors	Yes
Peer tutors	Yes
Max. hours/week for services	Varies
How professors are notified of student approved accommodations	Student and Disability Support Services

COLLEGE GRADUATION REQUIREMENTS

Course waivers allowed	No
Course substitutions allowed	No

PROGRAMS/SERVICES FOR STUDENTS WITH LEARNING DIFFERENCES

Montana State University Billings (MSU Billings) Disability Support Services (DSS) is available to help students access reasonable academic accommodations that promote success across campus. Students must submit a completed application and appointment request form to apply for services. Students then meet with a counselor in the DSS office to determine necessary support services on a case-by-case basis. The College Transition Program (CTP) helps students with disabilities obtain accommodations before the start of classes. The CTP is a collaboration with MSUB and City College. Students enrolled in CTP can reserve various services, including audio textbooks or a sign language interpreter. Students are invited to campus to meet with faculty, advisors, and financial aid staff and may pre-qualify with DSS. The staff may discuss the student's transition to college with the IEP or 504 teams. Additionally, CTP students will meet with tutors at Academic Support Services and TRIO (a federal student support services program).

ADMISSIONS

Montana State University Billings has rolling admissions, and students may apply at any time. Students are encouraged to submit test scores that can be used in place of a supplemental assessment administered to determine math and English placement. The minimum admission requirements are a 2.5 GPA or a rank in the top half of the class.

Additional Information

The Academic Support Center provides qualified tutors, Supplemental Instruction (SI) leaders, Peer Navigators, and writing consultants for all students. Peer Navigators are assigned to first-year students and assist with time management, study skills, planning success strategies, and navigating college life.

The MSU Billings Foundation's Wine & Food Festival is a signature event in Montana and celebrated its 30th anniversary in 2022. The festival is three nights of fun-filled events with participants enjoying incredible food, a collection of world-class wines, wine and food pairings, and a grand gala on the last evening. The festival is instrumental in raising scholarship dollars to fulfill the needs of students. The first scholarships were awarded in the 1999-2000 academic year.

Montana State University Billings

GENERAL ADMISSIONS

Very important factors include: rigor of secondary school record, class rank, academic GPA, standardized test scores (if submitted). High school diploma is required and GED is accepted. Institution is test-optional for entering Fall 2024. Check admissions website for updates. *Academic units required:* 4 English, 3 math, 2 science (2 labs), 3 social studies.

FINANCIAL AID

Students should submit: FAFSA. *Need-based scholarships/grants offered:* College/university scholarship or grant aid from institutional funds; Federal Pell; Private scholarships; SEOG; State scholarships/grants. *Loan aid offered:* Direct PLUS loans; Direct Subsidized Loans; Direct Unsubsidized Loans. Federal Work-Study Program available. Institutional employment available.

CAMPUS LIFE

Activities: Campus Ministries; Choral groups; Concert band; Drama/theater; International Student Organization; Jazz band; Literary magazine; Music ensembles; Musical theater; Pep band; Radio station; Student government; Student newspaper; Symphony orchestra. **Organizations:** 53 registered organizations, 10 honor societies, 38 religious organizations, 0 fraternities, 0 sororities. **Athletics (Intercollegiate):** *Men:* baseball, basketball, cross-country, golf, racquetball, track/field (indoor), volleyball. *Women:* basketball, cross-country, golf, racquetball, softball, track/field (indoor), volleyball.

CAMPUS
Type of school	Public
Environment	City

STUDENTS
Undergrad enrollment	3,570
% male/female	39/61
% from out of state	9
% frosh live on campus	33

FINANCIAL FACTS
Annual in-state tuition	$4,397
Annual out-of-state tuition	$16,662
Room and board	$7,510
Required fees	$1,429

GENERAL ADMISSIONS INFO
Application fee	$30
Regular application deadline	Rolling
Nonfall registration	Yes

Fall 2024 testing policy	Test Optional
Range SAT EBRW	430–520
Range SAT Math	420–500
Range ACT Composite	18–22

ACADEMICS
Student/faculty ratio	17:1
% students returning for sophomore year	55
Most classes have 10–19 students.	

Montana

REQUESTING SERVICES FOR STUDENTS WITH LEARNING DIFFERENCES

Phone: 406-657-2283 • www.msubillings.edu/dss • Email: disability@msubillings.edu

Documentation submitted to: Disability Support Services
Separate application required for Services: Yes

Documentation required for:
LD: Psychoeducational evaluation
ADHD: Psychoeducational evaluation
ASD: Psychoeducational evaluation

Montana Technological University

1300 West Park Street, Butte, MT 59701 • Admissions: 406-496-4256 • www.mtech.edu

> **Support: S**

ACCOMMODATIONS

Allowed in exams:

Calculators	Yes
Dictionary	Yes
Computer	Yes
Spell-checker	Yes
Extended test time	Yes
Scribe	Yes
Proctors	Yes
Oral exams	Yes
Note-takers	Yes

Support services for students with:

LD	Yes
ADHD	Yes
ASD	Yes
Distraction-reduced environment	Yes
Recording of lecture allowed	Yes
Reading technology	Yes
Audio books	Yes
Other assistive technology	Yes
Priority registration	Yes

Added costs of services:

For LD	No
For ADHD	No
For ASD	No
LD specialists	No
ADHD & ASD coaching	Yes
ASD specialists	No
Professional tutors	Yes
Peer tutors	Yes
Max. hours/week for services	Varies
How professors are notified of student approved accommodations	Student and Disability and Accessibility Services

COLLEGE GRADUATION REQUIREMENTS

Course waivers allowed	No
Course substitutions allowed	Yes
In what courses: Case-by-case basis	

PROGRAMS/SERVICES FOR STUDENTS WITH LEARNING DIFFERENCES

Montana Technological University (Montana Tech) is committed to increasing campus accessibility and equitable access by providing reasonable accommodations to qualified students with disabilities. Students meet with counselors at the Disability and Accessibility Services Office (DAS) to initiate the process of obtaining services and access to resources. Counselors are responsible for providing reasonable accommodations, but students must provide current and appropriate documentation prior to receiving services.

ADMISSIONS

Applicants should have completed a college prep curriculum and have any of the following: a cumulative GPA of 2.50 or greater; a minimum ACT composite score of 22; a minimum SAT combined score of 1120; or rank in the upper half of their graduating class. Test scores are optional, however, they are used to determine course placement and eligibility for some scholarships, so they are recommended. There are also math and writing proficiency requirements.

Additional Information

Academic Success Coaches are available to all students through the Academic Center for Excellence (ACE). Coaching sessions cover a range of topics, including study skills, overcoming test anxiety, guidance on time management, and general aid in navigating being a student in a rigorous academic setting. ACE offers workshops for peer-to-peer learning. These small group sessions focus on time management, study skills, and goal setting. The combination of one-on-one and group activities help students build learning skills and strategies to create a personalized academic toolkit.

In 1910, 45 students had a goal to place an emblem of their school in the most conspicuous place—the face of Big Butte. The original M was 67 feet high by 75 feet wide. In 1912, serifs at the base of the M increased the width to 90 feet. Yearly maintenance tasks were assigned to each class, with seniors most often having supervisory duties, of course. Early M-Day kicked off with a blast behind the M, followed by a campus clean-up. It's grown yearly to M-days, a weeklong celebration of activities hosted by the Associated Students.

Montana Technological University

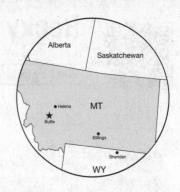

General Admissions

Very important factors include: class rank, academic GPA. High school diploma is required and GED is accepted. Institution is test-optional for entering Fall 2024. Check admissions website for updates. *Academic units required:* 4 English, 3 math, 2 science (2 labs), 3 social studies. *Academic units recommended:* 4 math.

Financial Aid

Students should submit: FAFSA. *Need-based scholarships/grants offered:* College/university scholarship or grant aid from institutional funds; Federal Pell; Private scholarships; SEOG; State scholarships/grants. *Loan aid offered:* Direct PLUS loans; Direct Subsidized Loans; Direct Unsubsidized Loans. Federal Work-Study Program available. Institutional employment available.

Campus Life

Activities: Campus Ministries; Choral groups; International Student Organization; Pep band; Student government; Student newspaper. **Organizations:** 50 registered organizations, 3 honor societies, 0 fraternities, 0 sororities. **Athletics (Intercollegiate):** *Men:* basketball, cross-country, golf, ice hockey, rugby, skiing (nordic/cross-country), softball, track/field (indoor), volleyball. *Women:* basketball, cross-country, golf, ice hockey, rugby, skiing (nordic/cross-country), softball, track/field (indoor), volleyball.

CAMPUS
Type of school	Public
Environment	Town

STUDENTS
Undergrad enrollment	1,779
% male/female	61/39
% from out of state	15
% frosh live on campus	61

FINANCIAL FACTS
Annual in-state tuition	$7,580
Annual out-of-state tuition	$23,210
Room and board	$10,741

GENERAL ADMISSIONS INFO
Application fee	No fee
Regular application deadline	Rolling
Nonfall registration	Yes

Fall 2024 testing policy	Test Optional
Range SAT EBRW	540–660
Range SAT Math	550–630
Range ACT Composite	20–27

ACADEMICS
Student/faculty ratio	13:1
% students returning for sophomore year	76
Most classes have 2–9 students.	

Montana

REQUESTING SERVICES FOR STUDENTS WITH LEARNING DIFFERENCES

Phone: 406-496-4428 • www.mtech.edu/disability • Email: sgoodell@mtech.edu

Documentation submitted to: Disability and Accessibility Services
Separate application required for Services: Yes

Documentation required for:
LD: Psychoeducational evaluation
ADHD: Psychoeducational evaluation
ASD: Psychoeducational evaluation

Rocky Mountain College

1511 Poly Drive, Billings, MT 59102-1796 • Admissions: 406-657-1026 • www.rocky.edu

Support: CS

ACCOMMODATIONS

Allowed in exams:

Calculators	Yes
Dictionary	Yes
Computer	Yes
Spell-checker	Yes
Extended test time	Yes
Scribe	Yes
Proctors	Yes
Oral exams	Yes
Note-takers	Yes

Support services for students with:

LD	Yes
ADHD	Yes
ASD	Yes
Distraction-reduced environment	Yes
Recording of lecture allowed	Yes
Reading technology	Yes
Audio books	Yes
Other assistive technology	Yes
Priority registration	No

Added costs of services:

For LD	No
For ADHD	No
For ASD	No
LD specialists	Yes
ADHD & ASD coaching	No
ASD specialists	No
Professional tutors	Yes
Peer tutors	Yes
Max. hours/week for services	Varies
How professors are notified of student approved accommodations	Student and Services for Academic Success

COLLEGE GRADUATION REQUIREMENTS

Course waivers allowed	No
Course substitutions allowed	Yes
In what courses: Case-by-case basis	

PROGRAMS/SERVICES FOR STUDENTS WITH LEARNING DIFFERENCES

Services for Academic Success (SAS) provide a comprehensive support program for students with learning disabilities. Students are responsible for self-identifying, providing appropriate documentation, and requesting reasonable accommodations as soon as possible after enrolling. The program tailors its services to meet the needs of the individual. Some of the services and accommodations for students with learning disabilities include alternative testing arrangements, recordings of lectures or textbooks, cultural and academic enrichment opportunities, and advocacy. SAS staff meet with each student to discuss the necessary support services and develop a semester plan. The small size of the college, the caring attitude of the faculty, and the excellent support program all make Rocky Mountain a learning disability-friendly college.

ADMISSIONS

All applicants must meet the same criteria for admission, which includes a minimum GPA of 2.5, and applicants may be considered for conditional admission if scores or grades are below the cut-offs. To identify and provide necessary support services as soon as possible, students with disabilities are encouraged to complete the Services for Academic Success application when they are accepted. All documentation is confidential.

Additional Information

SAS provides a variety of services to meet a student's individual needs. These services are free and include developmental coursework in reading, writing, and mathematics; study skills classes; tutoring in all subjects; academic, career, and personal counseling. Skills classes for college credit are offered in math, English, and studying techniques.

In 1909, before RMC construction was complete, classes were held in downtown Billings. By January 1910, the building was complete. Students, faculty, and staff loaded hay wagons and headed to the campus. Cold, tired, and hungry, they went to the dining hall and discovered the electricity was not on. They ate their first meal on campus by candlelight. It may not have been the most pleasant meal, but students decided it was worth commemorating. RMC has celebrated the Candlelight Dinner every winter since 1910.

Rocky Mountain College

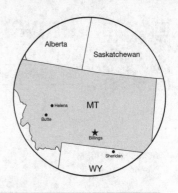

GENERAL ADMISSIONS

Very important factors include: academic GPA, standardized test scores (if submitted). *Important factors include:* rigor of secondary school record, application essay, recommendations. *Other factors considered include:* class rank. High school diploma is required and GED is accepted. Institution is test-optional for entering Fall 2024. Check admissions website for updates. *Academic units required:* 4 English, 4 math, 3 science, 3 social studies, 3 academic electives.

FINANCIAL AID

Students should submit: FAFSA. *Need-based scholarships/grants offered:* College/university scholarship or grant aid from institutional funds; Federal Pell; Private scholarships; SEOG; State scholarships/grants. *Loan aid offered:* Direct PLUS loans; Direct Subsidized Loans; Direct Unsubsidized Loans. Federal Work-Study Program available. Institutional employment available.

CAMPUS LIFE

Activities: Campus Ministries; Choral groups; Concert band; Drama/theater; International Student Organization; Jazz band; Music ensembles; Musical theater; Pep band; Student government; Student newspaper; Yearbook. **Organizations:** 13 registered organizations, 1 honor societies, 4 religious organizations, 0 fraternities, 0 sororities. **Athletics (Intercollegiate):** *Men:* basketball, cross-country, equestrian sports, golf, track/field (indoor). *Women:* basketball, cross-country, equestrian sports, golf, track/field (indoor), volleyball.

CAMPUS
Type of school	Private (nonprofit)
Environment	City

STUDENTS
Undergrad enrollment	817
% male/female	51/49
% from out of state	34
% frosh live on campus	82

FINANCIAL FACTS
Annual tuition	$30,725
Room and board	$8,855
Required fees	$610

GENERAL ADMISSIONS INFO
Application fee	$35
Regular application deadline	Rolling
Nonfall registration	Yes

Fall 2024 testing policy	Test Optional
Range SAT EBRW	500–600
Range SAT Math	475–580
Range ACT Composite	18–25

ACADEMICS
Student/faculty ratio	12:1
% students returning for sophomore year	60

Most classes have 2–9 students.

Montana

REQUESTING SERVICES FOR STUDENTS WITH LEARNING DIFFERENCES

Phone: 406-657-1129 • www.rocky.edu/academics/academic-support/disability-services
Email: lisa.laird@rocky.edu

Documentation submitted to: Services for Academic Success

Separate application required for Services: Yes

Documentation required for:
 LD: Psychoeducational evaluation
 ADHD: Psychoeducational evaluation
 ASD: Psychoeducational evaluation

University of Montana

Lommasson Center 101, Missoula, MT 59812 • Admissions: 406-243-6266 • www.umt.edu

Support: SP

ACCOMMODATIONS

Allowed in exams:

Calculators	Yes
Dictionary	No
Computer	Yes
Spell-checker	Yes
Extended test time	Yes
Scribe	Yes
Proctors	Yes
Oral exams	No
Note-takers	Yes

Support services for students with:

LD	Yes
ADHD	Yes
ASD	Yes
Distraction-reduced environment	Yes
Recording of lecture allowed	Yes
Reading technology	Yes
Audio books	Yes
Other assistive technology	Yes
Priority registration	Yes

Added costs of services:

For LD	No
For ADHD	No
For ASD	Yes
LD specialists	No
ADHD & ASD coaching	No
ASD specialists	Yes
Professional tutors	No
Peer tutors	Yes
Max. hours/week for services	Varies
How professors are notified of student approved accommodations	Student

COLLEGE GRADUATION REQUIREMENTS

Course waivers allowed	No
Course substitutions allowed	Yes
In what courses: Varies	

PROGRAMS/SERVICES FOR STUDENTS WITH LEARNING DIFFERENCES

The Office for Disability Equity (ODE) is the campus resource for disability-related information on all University of Montana campuses. Taking an intersectional approach to disability, the office provides consultation, training, and academic services to provide accessibility and inclusion for students. Once the students contacts ODE to request services, the office assigns the student to an access consultant who is knowledgeable and trained to assist students with autism, ADHD, and LD. ODE works with students collaboratively and individually to address barriers and implement reasonable and effective accommodations for equal access. Students can receive assistance with course substitution petitions from ODE.

ADMISSIONS

Admission requirements are the same for all applicants. Applicants should have a 2.5 GPA or rank in the top 50 percent of their class. Courses required include 4 years of English, 3 years of math, 3 years of social studies, 2 years of science, and 2 years of foreign language. Students not meeting the standard admission criteria may be admitted on a conditional status.

Additional Information

Approximately 1,400 students are registered with the Office for Disability Equity, and students with disabilities make up approximately 13–14 percent of the student population. The University of Montana offers various academic support services, including academic advising, registration support, tutoring services, study groups, career advising, study skill courses, and a leadership development program. The MOSSAIC program (Mentoring, Organization, and Social Support for Autism/All Inclusion on Campus) provides fee-based comprehensive support to students with autism and related disabilities.

At age 14, Michael J. Mansfield quit school and joined the navy. In 1928, he met Maureen, a Butte high school teacher who urged him to complete his education. With her moral and financial support, he earned his GED and received a master's degree at UM in 1934. He served in congress for 34 years and was the longest-serving U.S. senate majority leader in history. Maureen and Mike Mansfield were married for 68 years. The Mansfield Library is named in their honor, and a statue of the couple is nearby.

University of Montana

GENERAL ADMISSIONS

Very important factors include: rigor of secondary school record, class rank, academic GPA, standardized test scores (if submitted). High school diploma is required and GED is accepted. Institution is test-optional for entering Fall 2024. Check admissions website for updates. *Academic units required:* 4 English, 3 math, 2 science (2 labs), 3 social studies, 2 (foreign language, visual/performing arts, computer science, or vocational education).

FINANCIAL AID

Students should submit: FAFSA. *Need-based scholarships/grants offered:* College/university scholarship or grant aid from institutional funds; Federal Pell; Private scholarships; SEOG; State scholarships/grants. *Loan aid offered:* Direct PLUS loans; Direct Subsidized Loans; Direct Unsubsidized Loans. Federal Work-Study Program available. Institutional employment available.

CAMPUS LIFE

Activities: Campus Ministries; Choral groups; Concert band; Dance; Drama/theater; International Student Organization; Jazz band; Literary magazine; Marching band; Model UN; Music ensembles; Musical theater; Opera; Pep band; Radio station; Student government; Student newspaper; Symphony orchestra; Television station. **Organizations:** 150 registered organizations, 6 fraternities, 4 sororities. **Athletics (Intercollegiate):** *Men:* baseball, basketball, cross-country, cycling, equestrian sports, ice hockey, lacrosse, martial arts, rugby, track/field (indoor), ultimate frisbee. *Women:* basketball, crew/rowing, cross-country, cycling, equestrian sports, golf, ice hockey, lacrosse, martial arts, rugby, softball, track/field (indoor), ultimate frisbee, volleyball.

CAMPUS

Type of school	Public
Environment	City

STUDENTS

Undergrad enrollment	7,515
% male/female	44/56
% from out of state	30
% frosh live on campus	76

FINANCIAL FACTS

Annual in-state tuition	$5,352
Annual out-of-state tuition	$24,144
Room and board	$9,966
Required fees	$2,002

GENERAL ADMISSIONS INFO

Application fee	$30
Regular application deadline	Rolling
Nonfall registration	Yes
Fall 2024 testing policy	Test Optional
Range SAT EBRW	535–635
Range SAT Math	520–610
Range ACT Composite	20–26

ACADEMICS

Student/faculty ratio	16:1
% students returning for sophomore year	71

Most classes have 10–19 students.

Montana

REQUESTING SERVICES FOR STUDENTS WITH LEARNING DIFFERENCES

Phone: 406-243-2243 • www.umt.edu/disability • Email: ode@umontana.edu

Documentation submitted to: Office for Disability Equity
Separate application required for Services: Yes

Documentation required for:
LD: Psychoeducational evaluation
ADHD: Psychoeducational evaluation
ASD: Psychoeducational evaluation

The University of Montana Western

710 South Atlantic, Dillon, MT 59725 • Admissions: 406-683-7331 • umwestern.edu

> **Support: S**

ACCOMMODATIONS

Allowed in exams:

Calculators	Yes
Dictionary	Yes
Computer	Yes
Spell-checker	Yes
Extended test time	Yes
Scribe	Yes
Proctors	Yes
Oral exams	Yes
Note-takers	Yes

Support services for students with:

LD	Yes
ADHD	Yes
ASD	Yes
Distraction-reduced environment	Yes
Recording of lecture allowed	Yes
Reading technology	Yes
Audio books	Yes
Other assistive technology	Yes
Priority registration	Yes

Added costs of services:

For LD	No
For ADHD	No
For ASD	No
LD specialists	No
ADHD & ASD coaching	No
ASD specialists	No
Professional tutors	No
Peer tutors	Yes
Max. hours/week for services	Varies
How professors are notified of student approved accommodations	Student and Disability Support Services

COLLEGE GRADUATION REQUIREMENTS

Course waivers allowed	Yes
In what courses: General Education	
Course substitutions allowed	Yes
In what courses: General Education	

PROGRAMS/SERVICES FOR STUDENTS WITH LEARNING DIFFERENCES

Disability Support Services (DSS) provides accommodations for students with disabilities. Eligible students must submit disability documentation, and once it has been received and verified, DSS will arrange a meeting to discuss accommodations. DSS works with students to develop a reasonable academic accommodation plan and connect them with additional campus resources. Approved accommodations might include note-taking, audio books, proctored and/or orally-delivered tests, extended testing periods, and dictation services.

ADMISSIONS

Admission requirements are the same for everyone. Prospective students must earn at least a 2.5 high school GPA, or rank in the top half of their graduating class, or earn an ACT composite score of 22 or higher (SAT total score of 1120 or higher). There are also writing and math proficiency requirements. Students are encouraged to submit test scores if they are applying for MUS scholarships or UMW's Chancellor's Leadership Scholar Award. Students with learning differences who are provisionally admitted can submit a letter to the admissions office documenting a disability that prevented the student from adequately demonstrating academic proficiency due to lack of accommodations.

Additional Information

UMW offers the "Experience One" (X1) educational model. Students take one course (one block) for three hours each day for 18 days, completing one course at a time. Students generally take four blocks per semester, and class sizes average about 15 students. The faculty works very closely with their students, starting on their first day on campus through graduation. First Year Experience (FYE) classes are mandatory for all incoming first-year students with less than 30 college credits. FYE students attend one class per week that is centered around transitioning to UMW life and gaining the skills and knowledge to be successful. Professional, confidential counseling is available to help students overcome personal obstacles that may be affecting their mental health and wellness. The Learning Center provides free peer-tutoring services. They can help students with daily assignments, study habits, course writing assignments, research papers, help explain course content, and review for tests.

In 1895, Montana's legislators approved the funding for a State Normal School, now University of Montana Western, to focus on training teachers in Dillon, Montana. William Chandler Bagley, professor from 1902 to 1907, pioneered training future teachers by sending students out to local schools to gain hands-on experience. Student teaching eventually became a national standard of practice for teachers across the country.

The University of Montana Western

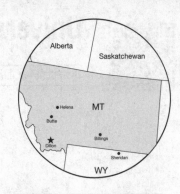

GENERAL ADMISSIONS

Very important factors include: rigor of secondary school record, class rank, academic GPA, standardized test scores (if submitted). High school diploma is required and GED is accepted. Institution is test-optional for entering Fall 2024. Check admissions website for updates. *Academic units required:* 4 English, 3 math, 2 science (2 labs), 3 social studies, 2 (foreign language, visual/performing arts, computer science, or vocational education). *Academic units recommended:* 4 math, 3 science.

FINANCIAL AID

Students should submit: FAFSA. *Need-based scholarships/grants offered:* College/university scholarship or grant aid from institutional funds; Federal Pell; Private scholarships; SEOG; State scholarships/grants. *Loan aid offered:* Direct PLUS loans; Direct Subsidized Loans; Direct Unsubsidized Loans. Federal Work-Study Program available. Institutional employment available.

CAMPUS LIFE

Activities: Campus Ministries; Choral groups; Drama/theater; Music ensembles; Musical theater; Radio station; Student government. **Organizations:** 25 registered organizations, 2 honor societies, 2 religious organizations, 0 fraternities, 0 sororities. **Athletics (Intercollegiate):** *Men:* basketball, equestrian sports, golf. *Women:* basketball, equestrian sports, golf, volleyball.

CAMPUS	
Type of school	Public
Environment	Rural

STUDENTS	
Undergrad enrollment	1,399
% male/female	33/67
% from out of state	32
% frosh live on campus	72

FINANCIAL FACTS	
Annual in-state tuition	$5,874
Annual out-of-state tuition	$17,698
Room and board	$8,588

GENERAL ADMISSIONS INFO	
Application fee	$30
Regular application deadline	Rolling
Nonfall registration	Yes

Fall 2024 testing policy	Test Optional
Range SAT EBRW	430–540
Range SAT Math	420–530
Range ACT Composite	17–22

ACADEMICS	
Student/faculty ratio	14:1
% students returning for sophomore year	73
Most classes have 10–19 students.	

Montana

REQUESTING SERVICES FOR STUDENTS WITH LEARNING DIFFERENCES

Phone: 406-683-7311 • www.umwestern.edu/section/disability-services
Email: randal.johnson@umwestern.edu

Documentation submitted to: Disability Support Services
Separate application required for Services: Yes

Documentation required for:
  LD: Psychoeducational evaluation
  ADHD: Psychoeducational evaluation
  ASD: Psychoeducational evaluation

University of Nebraska—Lincoln

1410 Q Street, Lincoln, NE 68588-0417 • Admissions: 402-472-2023 • www.unl.edu

Support: CS

ACCOMMODATIONS

Allowed in exams:

Calculators	Yes
Dictionary	Yes
Computer	Yes
Spell-checker	Yes
Extended test time	Yes
Scribe	Yes
Proctors	Yes
Oral exams	Yes
Note-takers	Yes

Support services for students with:

LD	Yes
ADHD	Yes
ASD	Yes
Distraction-reduced environment	Yes
Recording of lecture allowed	Yes
Reading technology	Yes
Audio books	Yes
Other assistive technology	Yes
Priority registration	Yes

Added costs of services:

For LD	No
For ADHD	No
For ASD	No
LD specialists	Yes
ADHD & ASD coaching	Yes
ASD specialists	Yes
Professional tutors	No
Peer tutors	Yes
Max. hours/week for services	Varies
How professors are notified of student approved accommodations	Student and Services for Students with Disabilities

COLLEGE GRADUATION REQUIREMENTS

Course waivers allowed	No
Course substitutions allowed	Yes
In what courses: Foreign Language and Math	

PROGRAMS/SERVICES FOR STUDENTS WITH LEARNING DIFFERENCES

Services for Students with Disabilities (SSD) facilitates equal and integrated access to the academic, social, cultural, and recreational programs offered at the University of Nebraska–Lincoln. Services are designed to meet the unique educational needs of enrolled students with documented disabilities. Some of the accommodations supported by SSD include priority registration, reduced course load, testing support, note-taking, and alternative media formats. The student needs to complete the SSD application to receive services and must provide supporting documentation. UNL Disability Club is a registered student organization, open to all students and community members with or without disabilities. The objective of the UNL Disability Club is to share information, resources, and advocacy for students with disabilities, as well as opportunities to socialize.

ADMISSIONS

Admissions requirements are the same for all applicants, and all students must meet the same academic standards. First-year applicants should rank in the top 50 percent of their high school class or have a 3.0 GPA. The ACT and SAT are not required for admission but are encouraged for first-year applicants.

Additional Information

The university offers free tutoring, mentoring, and consulting services to all students. University Career Services collaborates with SSD and provides individualized career coaching and resources to empower students.

November 27, 1890, was the beginning of the Nebraska football tradition; they defeated a team representing the Omaha YMCA 10-0. Their coach was a new faculty member from Harvard, primarily made coach because he owned a football. The team went through several nicknames—Tree-planters, Rattlesnake Boys, Antelopes, Old Gold Knights, and Bugeaters—until 1899, when sports editor Charles "Cy" Sherman first assigned the name Cornhuskers and later became the "father of the Cornhuskers."

University of Nebraska—Lincoln

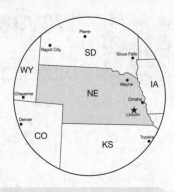

General Admissions

Important factors include: rigor of secondary school record, class rank, academic GPA, standardized test scores (if submitted). High school diploma is required and GED is accepted. Institution is test-optional for entering Fall 2024. Check admissions website for updates. *Academic units required:* 4 English, 4 math, 3 science (1 lab), 2 foreign language, 3 social studies.

Financial Aid

Students should submit: FAFSA. *Need-based scholarships/grants offered:* Federal Pell; Private scholarships; SEOG; State scholarships/grants. *Loan aid offered:* Direct PLUS loans; Direct Subsidized Loans; Direct Unsubsidized Loans. Federal Work-Study Program available. Institutional employment available.

Campus Life

Activities: Campus Ministries; Choral groups; Concert band; Dance; Drama/theater; International Student Organization; Jazz band; Literary magazine; Marching band; Model UN; Music ensembles; Musical theater; Opera; Pep band; Radio station; Student government; Student newspaper; Student-run film society; Symphony orchestra; Television station. **Organizations:** 405 registered organizations, 16 honor societies, 23 religious organizations, 31 fraternities, 22 sororities. **Athletics (Intercollegiate):** *Men:* baseball, basketball, bowling, crew/rowing, cross-country, cycling, equestrian sports, golf, gymnastics, ice hockey, lacrosse, martial arts, rugby, swimming, table tennis, track/field (indoor), ultimate frisbee, volleyball, water polo, wrestling. *Women:* baseball, basketball, bowling, crew/rowing, cross-country, cycling, equestrian sports, golf, gymnastics, ice hockey, lacrosse, martial arts, softball, swimming, table tennis, track/field (indoor), ultimate frisbee, volleyball, water polo.

CAMPUS

Type of school	Public
Environment	City

STUDENTS

Undergrad enrollment	19,097
% male/female	50/50
% from out of state	25
% frosh live on campus	86

FINANCIAL FACTS

Annual in-state tuition	$7,770
Annual out-of-state tuition	$24,900
Room and board	$11,928
Required fees	$2,084

GENERAL ADMISSIONS INFO

Application fee	$45
Regular application deadline	5/1
Nonfall registration	Yes

Fall 2024 testing policy	Test Optional
Range SAT EBRW	560–670
Range SAT Math	550–670
Range ACT Composite	22–28

ACADEMICS

Student/faculty ratio	16:1
% students returning for sophomore year	82

Most classes have 20–29 students.

REQUESTING SERVICES FOR STUDENTS WITH LEARNING DIFFERENCES

Phone: 402-472-3787 • www.unl.edu/ssd • Email: ssd@unl.edu

Documentation submitted to: Services for Students with Disabilities
Separate application required for Services: Yes

Documentation required for:
LD: Psychoeducational evaluation
ADHD: Psychoeducational evaluation
ASD: Psychoeducational evaluation

Nebraska

Wayne State College

1111 Main Street, Wayne, NE 68787 • Admissions: 402-375-7234 • www.wsc.edu

Support: S

PROGRAMS/SERVICES FOR STUDENTS WITH LEARNING DIFFERENCES

The Disability Services office provides services for students with appropriate documentation, including requests for accommodations, determination of eligibility for services, and referral to appropriate resources. Accommodations can include exam accommodations, recorded books, reader services, audio-recorded lectures, note-taking, learning strategies, support and discussion groups, and screening and referrals for evaluation.

ADMISSIONS

Admission to Wayne State College is open to all high school graduates or students with a GED or equivalent. High school special education courses are accepted. Applicants electing to apply test-optional will need to respond to two essay prompts (200 words), submit a recommendation from an academic teacher and a complete list of leadership, activities, community involvement, and job experience. Applicants should have at least a 2.5 GPA.

Additional Information

The Holland Academic Success Center offers academic resources to Wayne State students, including coaches who work one-on-one with students to create academic goals through weekly individual meetings. Academic coaches do not take the place of program advisors, but they are there to motivate students, identify goals, work on time-management skills, and encourage the use of campus resources. The Holland Peer Tutor Program offers free peer tutoring to all students. Writing tutors are also available on campus and online to help review papers before they are submitted to professors.

In the late 1960s, more than 100 Wayne State students and faculty volunteered their tutoring services weekly on the nearby Winnebago Indian reservation. Their service led to a decision to focus attention on improving Native American education by training teachers specifically to be more aware of Native American culture and issues.

Wayne State College

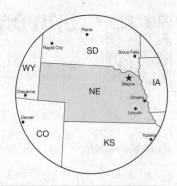

GENERAL ADMISSIONS

High school diploma is required and GED is accepted. Institution is test-optional for entering Fall 2024. Check admissions website for updates. *Academic units recommended:* 4 English, 3 math, 3 science, 2 foreign language, 3 social studies, 2 visual/performing arts.

FINANCIAL AID

Students should submit: FAFSA. *Need-based scholarships/grants offered:* College/university scholarship or grant aid from institutional funds; Federal Pell; Private scholarships; SEOG; State scholarships/grants. *Loan aid offered:* Direct PLUS loans; Direct Subsidized Loans; Direct Unsubsidized Loans. Federal Work-Study Program available. Institutional employment available.

CAMPUS LIFE

Activities: Campus Ministries; Choral groups; Concert band; Dance; Drama/theater; International Student Organization; Jazz band; Literary magazine; Marching band; Music ensembles; Musical theater; Pep band; Radio station; Student government; Student newspaper; Television station. **Organizations:** 100 registered organizations. **Athletics (Intercollegiate):** *Men:* baseball, basketball, cross-country, rugby, track/field (indoor), wrestling. *Women:* basketball, cross-country, golf, rugby, softball, track/field (indoor), volleyball.

CAMPUS
Type of school	Public
Environment	Rural

STUDENTS
Undergrad enrollment	3,766
% male/female	41/59
% from out of state	14
% frosh live on campus	95

FINANCIAL FACTS
Annual in-state tuition	$7,786
Annual out-of-state tuition	$7,786
Room and board	$8,870

GENERAL ADMISSIONS INFO
Application fee	No fee
Regular application deadline	8/22
Nonfall registration	Yes

Fall 2024 testing policy	Test Optional

ACADEMICS
Student/faculty ratio	20:1
% students returning for sophomore year	72
Most classes have 10–19 students.	

REQUESTING SERVICES FOR STUDENTS WITH LEARNING DIFFERENCES

Phone: 402-375-7451 • www.wsc.edu/disability-services • Email: disabilityservices@wsc.edu

Documentation submitted to: Student Disability Services
Separate application required for Services: Yes

Documentation required for:
LD: Psychoeducational evaluation
ADHD: Psychoeducational evaluation
ASD: Psychoeducational evaluation

Nebraska

University of Nevada, Las Vegas

4505 Maryland Parkway, Las Vegas, NV 89154-1021 · Admissions: 702-774-8658 · www.unlv.edu

Support: CS

ACCOMMODATIONS

Allowed in exams:

Calculators	Yes
Dictionary	Yes
Computer	Yes
Spell-checker	Yes
Extended test time	Yes
Scribe	Yes
Proctors	Yes
Oral exams	Yes
Note-takers	Yes

Support services for students with:

LD	Yes
ADHD	Yes
ASD	Yes
Distraction-reduced environment	Yes
Recording of lecture allowed	Yes
Reading technology	Yes
Audio books	Yes
Other assistive technology	Yes
Priority registration	Yes

Added costs of services:

For LD	No
For ADHD	No
For ASD	No
LD specialists	Yes
ADHD & ASD coaching	No
ASD specialists	No
Professional tutors	No
Peer tutors	No
Max. hours/week for services	Varies
How professors are notified of student approved accommodations	Student

COLLEGE GRADUATION REQUIREMENTS

Course waivers allowed	No
Course substitutions allowed	Yes
In what courses: Case-by-case basis	

PROGRAMS/SERVICES FOR STUDENTS WITH LEARNING DIFFERENCES

The Disability Resource Center (DRC) at the University of Nevada, Las Vegas provides academic accommodations for students with documented disabilities. Accommodations are determined after DRC reviews submitted documentation of the student's disability and meets with the student to discuss disability-related needs. If the student's documentation is insufficient or outdated, DRC can arrange for an assessment at a reduced rate with the on-campus clinic, pending eligibility. Available accommodations include note-taking, testing accommodations, materials in an alternative format, assistive technology for learning, housing adjustments, and referral to an on-campus dietitian. Campus Connections is a fee-based support program for students with disabilities. Students receive individual support for organization skills and planning, career development, soft skills, and time management. Campus Connections can also provide weekly support sessions with a coach.

ADMISSIONS

All applicants are expected to meet the same admission criteria. First-year applicants are expected to have a weighted 3.0 GPA in the required core academic courses. If a student does not have a 3.0 GPA, the student may still be admissible to UNLV if they score a minimum of 1020 on the SAT, 22 or higher on the ACT, or have obtained a Nevada Advanced High School Diploma. Applicants who do not satisfy the minimum admission requirements may still be eligible for admission via an alternative admission process.

Additional Information

All students have year-round access to psychological services through The PRACTICE (The Partnership for Research, Assessment, Counseling, Therapy, and Innovative Clinical Education).

Many UNLV Rebels show their pride with a UNLV license plate. The license plate program began in 1993 and has raised close to $2 million for student scholarships. The fund is divided between the alumni association and the athletics department, which set criteria and award yearly scholarships to deserving students.

University of Nevada, Las Vegas

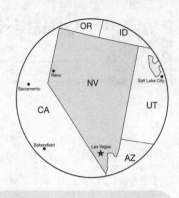

GENERAL ADMISSIONS

Very important factors include: rigor of secondary school record, academic GPA. *Important factors include:* standardized test scores (if submitted). High school diploma is required and GED is not accepted. Institution is test-optional for entering Fall 2024. Check admissions website for updates. *Academic units required:* 4 English, 3 math, 3 science (2 labs), 3 social studies.

FINANCIAL AID

Students should submit: FAFSA. *Need-based scholarships/grants offered:* College/university scholarship or grant aid from institutional funds; Federal Pell; Private scholarships; SEOG; State scholarships/grants. *Loan aid offered:* Direct PLUS loans; Direct Subsidized Loans; Direct Unsubsidized Loans. Federal Work-Study Program available. Institutional employment available.

CAMPUS LIFE

Activities: Campus Ministries; Choral groups; Concert band; Dance; Drama/theater; International Student Organization; Jazz band; Literary magazine; Marching band; Model UN; Music ensembles; Musical theater; Opera; Pep band; Radio station; Student government; Student newspaper; Student-run film society; Symphony orchestra; Television station; Yearbook. **Organizations:** 24 honor societies, 14 religious organizations, 8 fraternities, 6 sororities. **Athletics (Intercollegiate):** *Men:* baseball, basketball, cross-country, golf, softball, swimming, volleyball. *Women:* basketball, cross-country, equestrian sports, golf, softball, swimming, volleyball.

CAMPUS	
Type of school	Public
Environment	Metropolis

STUDENTS	
Undergrad enrollment	25,312
% male/female	43/57
% from out of state	14
% frosh live on campus	24

FINANCIAL FACTS	
Annual in-state tuition	$7,875
Annual out-of-state tuition	$24,831
Room and board	$12,072
Required fees	$1,268

GENERAL ADMISSIONS INFO	
Application fee	$60
Regular application deadline	6/1
Nonfall registration	Yes

Fall 2024 testing policy	Test Optional
Range SAT EBRW	510–620
Range SAT Math	490–600
Range ACT Composite	18–24

ACADEMICS	
Student/faculty ratio	18:1
% students returning for sophomore year	77

Most classes have 20–29 students.

REQUESTING SERVICES FOR STUDENTS WITH LEARNING DIFFERENCES

Phone: 702-895-0866 • www.unlv.edu/drc • Email: drc@unlv.edu

Documentation submitted to: Disability Resource Center
Separate application required for Services: Yes

Documentation required for:
LD: Psychoeducational evaluation
ADHD: Psychoeducational evaluation
ASD: Psychoeducational evaluation

Colby-Sawyer College

541 Main Street, New London, NH 03257-7835 • Admissions: 603-526-3700 • www.colby-sawyer.edu

Support: CS

ACCOMMODATIONS

Allowed in exams:

Calculators	Yes
Dictionary	Yes
Computer	Yes
Spell-checker	Yes
Extended test time	Yes
Scribe	Yes
Proctors	Yes
Oral exams	No
Note-takers	Yes

Support services for students with:

LD	Yes
ADHD	Yes
ASD	Yes
Distraction-reduced environment	Yes
Recording of lecture allowed	Yes
Reading technology	Yes
Audio books	Yes
Other assistive technology	Yes
Priority registration	No

Added costs of services:

For LD	No
For ADHD	No
For ASD	No
LD specialists	Yes
ADHD & ASD coaching	Yes
ASD specialists	Yes
Professional tutors	Yes
Peer tutors	Yes
Max. hours/week for services	Varies
How professors are notified of student approved accommodations	Student

COLLEGE GRADUATION REQUIREMENTS

Course waivers allowed	No
Course substitutions allowed	No

PROGRAMS/SERVICES FOR STUDENTS WITH LEARNING DIFFERENCES

Colby-Sawyer aims to provide an individualized learning experience for every student. Learning specialists are available to serve students with documented disabilities and offer weekly meetings. They also ensure that the students have equal access to the curriculum and the tools to develop study skills. While there are no specialized programs for students with learning disabilities, there are many academic support services available, and students are expected to self-advocate. Prior to admission, interested students and parents are welcome to schedule a meeting with Access Resources and bring documentation to review in an unofficial capacity. Official documentation is accepted only after the student is accepted and has submitted a deposit for enrollment.

ADMISSIONS

The admission process is the same for all students. In addition to the core academic course requirements, students must submit a personal essay. Colby-Sawyer encourages student involvement in leadership positions, organized clubs, employment, or volunteer services.

Additional Information

Peer Mentors are a resource to students throughout their years at Colby-Sawyer. They are in each First Year Experience (FYE) class, and share important information about thriving in college. Peer Mentors are upper-level students trained to help students problem-solve and achieve their goals, and are available to meet with students for meals, exercise, weekly talks, or study time. If a student would like to request a 1:1 Peer Mentor match, they can contact the director of Student Success and Retention. The curriculum at Colby-Sawyer College is writing intensive, requires critical reading and thinking skills, and quantitative literacy abilities. Students are also required to complete an internship related to their major.

Everyone looks forward to Mountain Day, the annual fall hike up Mt. Kearsarge, a tradition since the 1850s. The highly anticipated day is a well-kept secret until the president sends an all-school email, the bell tolls atop Colgate Hall, and classes are canceled. Over 1,000 students pile into vans to one of two trailheads wearing tie-dyed Mountain Day T-shirts, and spend the day climbing, signing a banner at the summit, and enjoying a picnic with friends.

Colby-Sawyer College

General Admissions

Very important factors include: rigor of secondary school record, academic GPA. *Important factors include:* class rank, standardized test scores (if submitted), application essay, recommendations. High school diploma is required and GED is accepted. Institution is test-optional for entering Fall 2024. Check admissions website for updates. *Academic units recommended:* 4 English, 3 math, 3 science (3 labs), 2 foreign language, 3 social studies.

Financial Aid

Students should submit: FAFSA. *Need-based scholarships/grants offered:* College/university scholarship or grant aid from institutional funds; Federal Pell; Private scholarships; SEOG; State scholarships/grants. *Loan aid offered:*. Federal Work-Study Program available. Institutional employment available.

Campus Life

Activities: Choral groups; Dance; Drama/theater; Literary magazine; Musical theater; Radio station; Student government; Student newspaper; Yearbook. **Organizations:** 40 registered organizations, 5 honor societies, 1 religious organizations, 0 fraternities, 0 sororities. **Athletics (Intercollegiate):** *Men:* baseball, basketball, cross-country, cycling, equestrian sports, golf, ice hockey, rugby, swimming. *Women:* basketball, cross-country, cycling, equestrian sports, golf, ice hockey, lacrosse, rugby, softball, swimming, volleyball.

CAMPUS
Type of school	Private (nonprofit)
Environment	Rural

STUDENTS
Undergrad enrollment	942
% male/female	35/65
% from out of state	68
% frosh live on campus	98

FINANCIAL FACTS
Annual tuition	$17,500
Room and board	$16,858
Required fees	$900

GENERAL ADMISSIONS INFO
Application fee	$45
Regular application deadline	4/1
Nonfall registration	Yes

Fall 2024 testing policy	Test Optional
Range SAT EBRW	440–540
Range SAT Math	440–530
Range ACT Composite	18–22

ACADEMICS
Student/faculty ratio	11:1
% students returning for sophomore year	71

Most classes have 10–19 students.

REQUESTING SERVICES FOR STUDENTS WITH LEARNING DIFFERENCES

Phone: 603-526-3000 • colby-sawyer.edu/access-resources • Email: accessresources@colby-sawyer.edu

Documentation submitted to: Access Resources
Separate application required for Services: Yes

Documentation required for:
 LD: Psychoeducational evaluation
 ADHD: Psychoeducational evaluation
 ASD: Psychoeducational evaluation

New England College

102 Bridge Street, Henniker, NH 03242 • Admissions: 603-428-2223 • www.nec.edu

(Support: CS)

ACCOMMODATIONS

Allowed in exams:

Calculators	Yes
Dictionary	Yes
Computer	Yes
Spell-checker	Yes
Extended test time	Yes
Scribe	No
Proctors	Yes
Oral exams	Yes
Note-takers	Yes

Support services for students with:

LD	Yes
ADHD	Yes
ASD	Yes
Distraction-reduced environment	Yes
Recording of lecture allowed	No
Reading technology	Yes
Audio books	Yes
Other assistive technology	Yes
Priority registration	No

Added costs of services:

For LD	No
For ADHD	No
For ASD	No
LD specialists	Yes
ADHD & ASD coaching	Yes
ASD specialists	No
Professional tutors	Yes
Peer tutors	Yes
Max. hours/week for services	Varies
How professors are notified of student approved accommodations	Office of Student Access and Accommodations

COLLEGE GRADUATION REQUIREMENTS

Course waivers allowed	Yes
In what courses: Basic College Math requirement	
Course substitutions allowed	Yes
In what courses: Math unless it's a major requirement	

PROGRAMS/SERVICES FOR STUDENTS WITH LEARNING DIFFERENCES

The Office of Disability Services (ODS) ensures equal access to academic programs and activities for students with disabilities. To be eligible for accommodations, students with learning disabilities need to submit current documentation to ODS. Students with disabilities other than learning should contact ODS to determine the type of documentation needed. Students meet with ODS staff to discuss their limitations and accommodation needs, which might include extra time on tests, use of a computer for testing, recording lectures, lecture notes, and books in alternative formats. Once accommodations are determined, students receive copies of an accommodation letter to share with faculty and staff.

ADMISSIONS

All students complete the same general application for admission and include a self-reported GPA. When accepted, official transcripts will be required before enrollment. A counselor report is required, and applicants may submit up to two teacher evaluations and up to three evaluations from other sources. A personal essay is optional. The nursing program requires a 3.0 GPA for admission.

Additional Information

All first-year students take the First-Year Seminar and Lab during their first semester, where they engage in workshops and activities to learn about campus resources, build a community of support, and gain skills to become successful college students. Students are expected to participate in a weekly seminar, Community Wednesday events, and a First-Year Lab. Peer Leaders (PLs) are upper-level students who begin by welcoming first-year students at orientation and continue supporting them through the semester and beyond. PLs help students connect with campus resources, build camaraderie, and help new students engage in the whole NEC community. The Writing and Academic Support Center (WASC) is available to all students, is free of charge, and provides writing and tutoring services. WASC is staffed by professional and peer tutors who work with students on a variety of academic skills. Academic tutoring is free and available to all students and is open from early morning until late at night in several locations on campus. Many tutors have college degrees and do subject tutoring, proofreading, editing, and skills and strategies development.

New students become part of the college community by crossing the Henniker Covered Bridge before being welcomed by the college. Built in 1972 in a traditional style of covered bridges, the Henniker Bridge serves New England College and the community of Henniker as a footbridge across the Contoocook River.

New England College

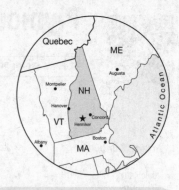

GENERAL ADMISSIONS

Very important factors include: academic GPA. *Other factors considered include:* rigor of secondary school record, class rank, application essay, recommendations. High school diploma is required and GED is accepted. Institution is test-optional for entering Fall 2024. Check admissions website for updates. *Academic units recommended:* 4 English, 3 math, 3 science (1 lab), 3 social studies.

FINANCIAL AID

Students should submit: CSS/Financial Aid Profile; FAFSA. *Need-based scholarships/grants offered:* College/university scholarship or grant aid from institutional funds; Federal Pell; Private scholarships; SEOG; State scholarships/grants. *Loan aid offered:* Direct PLUS loans; Direct Subsidized Loans; Direct Unsubsidized Loans. Federal Work-Study Program available. Institutional employment available.

CAMPUS LIFE

Activities: Drama/theater; International Student Organization; Literary magazine; Radio station; Student government; Student newspaper. **Organizations:** 26 registered organizations, 3 honor societies, 1 religious organizations, 0 fraternities, 1 sororities. **Athletics (Intercollegiate):** *Men:* baseball, basketball, cross-country, ice hockey, lacrosse, rugby, wrestling. *Women:* basketball, cross-country, field hockey, ice hockey, lacrosse, rugby, softball, volleyball.

CAMPUS

Type of school	Private (nonprofit)
Environment	Rural

STUDENTS

Undergrad enrollment	1,311
% male/female	45/55
% from out of state	61
% frosh live on campus	61

FINANCIAL FACTS

Annual tuition	$39,390
Room and board	$16,472
Required fees	$1,252

GENERAL ADMISSIONS INFO

Application fee	No fee
Regular application deadline	Rolling
Nonfall registration	Yes

Fall 2024 testing policy	Test Optional
Range SAT EBRW	430–550
Range SAT Math	420–530

ACADEMICS

Student/faculty ratio	9:1
% students returning for sophomore year	60

Most classes have 10–19 students.

REQUESTING SERVICES FOR STUDENTS WITH LEARNING DIFFERENCES

Phone: 603-428-2302 • www.nec.edu/academic-assistance#Disability_Services
Email: disabilityservices@nec.edu

Documentation submitted to: Office of Disability Services
Separate application required for Services: Yes

Documentation required for:
LD: Psychoeducational evaluation
ADHD: Psychoeducational evaluation
ASD: Psychoeducational evaluation

Plymouth State University

17 High Street Plymouth, NH 03264 • Admissions: 603-535-2237 • www.plymouth.edu

Support: CS

ACCOMMODATIONS

Allowed in exams:

Calculators	Yes
Dictionary	Yes
Computer	Yes
Spell-checker	Yes
Extended test time	Yes
Scribe	Yes
Proctors	Yes
Oral exams	Yes
Note-takers	Yes

Support services for students with:

LD	Yes
ADHD	Yes
ASD	Yes
Distraction-reduced environment	Yes
Recording of lecture allowed	Yes
Reading technology	Yes
Audio books	Yes
Other assistive technology	No
Priority registration	Yes

Added costs of services:

For LD	No
For ADHD	No
For ASD	No
LD specialists	No
ADHD & ASD coaching	No
ASD specialists	Yes
Professional tutors	No
Peer tutors	Yes
Max. hours/week for services	6
How professors are notified of student approved accommodations	Student

COLLEGE GRADUATION REQUIREMENTS

Course waivers allowed	No
Course substitutions allowed	Yes
In what courses: Foreign Language	

PROGRAMS/SERVICES FOR STUDENTS WITH LEARNING DIFFERENCES

To receive support services, students meet with a Campus Accessibility Services (CAS) advisor and provide documentation of their disability. CAS staff will manage, coordinate, implement, and evaluate accommodations and services. In addition, they serve as a resource to both students and faculty to ensure services are provided effectively. Accommodations may include extended time for tests, a quiet testing space, alternative testing formats, notetakers, and assistive technology.

ADMISSIONS

Admission requirements are the same for all applicants. Plymouth encourages students to contact an admissions counselor if they do not meet the academic course requirements. All students are considered for a merit scholarship based on their GPA at the time of admission.

Additional Information

The learning model of Plymouth State University is Integrated Clusters, where students work with students from other majors, faculty, businesses, nonprofits, and regional partners to gain real-world, résumé-boosting experience. Beginning in the first semester, students will begin tackling The Four Tools of Clusters, which include Tackling a Wicked Problem (e.g., sustainability, social justice, education, and artificial intelligence—to name just a few), Themed Courses, Open Laboratories, and Integrated Capstone (INCAP) Experience.

Rounds Hall and its clock tower were dedicated in 1891 and served as the main academic building, and it now houses a mix of classrooms and offices. Poet laureate Robert Frost taught education and psychology courses in Rounds Hall and lived on campus from 1911–1912. A statue of Robert Frost sits on a bench in front of Rounds Hall. Since 1975, an annual tradition called Pumpkins on Rounds has pumpkins mysteriously appearing on top of the two spires of the clock tower shortly before Halloween.

Plymouth State University

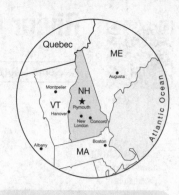

GENERAL ADMISSIONS

Very important factors include: rigor of secondary school record. *Important factors include:* academic GPA. *Other factors considered include:* application essay, recommendations. High school diploma is required and GED is accepted. Institution is test-optional for entering Fall 2024. Check admissions website for updates. *Academic units required:* 4 English, 3 math, 3 science (1 lab), 3 social studies. *Academic units recommended:* 2 foreign language.

FINANCIAL AID

Students should submit: FAFSA. *Need-based scholarships/grants offered:* College/university scholarship or grant aid from institutional funds; Federal Pell; Private scholarships; SEOG; State scholarships/grants. *Loan aid offered:* Direct PLUS loans; Direct Subsidized Loans; Direct Unsubsidized Loans. Federal Work-Study Program available. Institutional employment available.

CAMPUS LIFE

Activities: Campus Ministries; Choral groups; Concert band; Dance; Drama/theater; International Student Organization; Jazz band; Literary magazine; Model UN; Music ensembles; Musical theater; Pep band; Radio station; Student government; Student newspaper; Student-run film society; Yearbook. **Organizations:** 86 registered organizations, 15 honor societies, 4 religious organizations, 0 fraternities, 3 sororities. **Athletics (Intercollegiate):** *Men:* baseball, basketball, cross-country, golf, ice hockey, lacrosse, rugby, skiing (nordic/cross-country), track/field (indoor), ultimate frisbee, wrestling. *Women:* basketball, cross-country, field hockey, golf, ice hockey, lacrosse, rugby, skiing (nordic/cross-country), softball, swimming, track/field (indoor), ultimate frisbee, volleyball.

New Hampshire

CAMPUS

Type of school	Public
Environment	Village

STUDENTS

Undergrad enrollment	4,135
% male/female	50/50
% from out of state	53
% frosh live on campus	88

FINANCIAL FACTS

Annual in-state tuition	$11,580
Annual out-of-state tuition	$20,250
Room and board	$11,100
Required fees	$2,519

GENERAL ADMISSIONS INFO

Application fee	$50
Nonfall registration	Yes

Fall 2024 testing policy	Test Optional
Range SAT EBRW	417–611
Range SAT Math	398–592
Range ACT Composite	17–28

ACADEMICS

Student/faculty ratio	17:1
% students returning for sophomore year	70

Most classes have 10–19 students.

REQUESTING SERVICES FOR STUDENTS WITH LEARNING DIFFERENCES

Phone: 603-535-3300 • campus.plymouth.edu/accessibility-services/ • Email: lbpage@plymouth.edu

Documentation submitted to: Campus Accessibility Services

Separate application required for Services: Yes

Documentation required for:
LD: Psychoeducational evaluation
ADHD: Psychoeducational evaluation
ASD: Psychoeducational evaluation

Rivier University

420 South Main Street, Nashua, NH 03060 • Admissions: 603-897-8219 • www.rivier.edu

Support: S

PROGRAMS/SERVICES FOR STUDENTS WITH LEARNING DIFFERENCES

Rivier University provides appropriate and reasonable accommodations to students with documented disabilities. To access services, students must contact the coordinator of Disability Services before the start of each semester to discuss accommodations and services. There are many supports available through the Office of Disability Services, including counseling, preferential registration, advocacy, and the Writing Center for individualized instruction in writing. Classroom accommodations may include recorded lectures, extended time for test completion, distraction-free test environments, and notetakers.

ADMISSIONS

Admission requirements are the same for all applicants. Students should rank in the top 80 percent of their graduating class and take college-prep courses in high school. Applicants not meeting the general admission requirements may inquire about alternative admissions. The college offers a probational admit option that requires students to maintain a minimum 2.0 GPA their first semester. Foreign language substitutions are available for some students.

Additional Information

The Academic Support Center offers a variety of services to help students be successful. Professional consultants and peer tutors are available to help students overcome academic challenges and help students take their writing to the next level.

Rivier University formally opened in 1933 as a Catholic college to educate local mill workers' daughters, with seven faculty and three students; the next year, 24 students enrolled. At RU's first commencement in 1937, the original three students received degrees. In 1938, RU was granted permission to accept international students and in 1958, RU celebrated its 25th anniversary. Sister Marie-Madeleine of Jesus, founder of RU, was the guest of honor, and Mrs. Rose Kennedy was the keynote speaker. It wasn't until 1991 that RU admitted its first male student and became coeducational.

Rivier University

General Admissions

Very important factors include: rigor of secondary school record, academic GPA. *Important factors include:* class rank, standardized test scores (if submitted), application essay. *Other factors considered include:* recommendations. High school diploma is required and GED is accepted. Institution is test-optional for entering Fall 2024. Check admissions website for updates. *Academic units recommended:* 4 English, 3 math, 1 science (1 lab), 2 foreign language, 2 social studies, 4 academic electives.

Financial Aid

Students should submit: FAFSA. *Need-based scholarships/grants offered:* College/university scholarship or grant aid from institutional funds; Federal Pell; Private scholarships; SEOG; State scholarships/grants. *Loan aid offered:* Direct PLUS loans; Direct Subsidized Loans; Direct Unsubsidized Loans. Federal Work-Study Program available. Institutional employment available.

Campus Life

Activities: Campus Ministries; Choral groups; Dance; Drama/theater; International Student Organization; Model UN; Music ensembles; Student government; Television station; Yearbook. **Organizations:** 30 registered organizations, 2 honor societies, 2 religious organizations, 0 fraternities, 0 sororities. **Athletics (Intercollegiate):** *Men:* baseball, basketball, cross-country, lacrosse, volleyball. *Women:* basketball, cross-country, lacrosse, softball, volleyball.

CAMPUS

Type of school	Private (nonprofit)
Environment	City

STUDENTS

Undergrad enrollment	1,370
% male/female	15/85
% from out of state	38
% frosh live on campus	65

FINANCIAL FACTS

Annual tuition	$25,410
Room and board	$9,798
Required fees	$600

GENERAL ADMISSIONS INFO

Application fee	$25
Regular application deadline	Rolling
Nonfall registration	No

Fall 2024 testing policy	Test Optional
Range SAT EBRW	410–510
Range SAT Math	410–510
Range ACT Composite	17–21

ACADEMICS

Student/faculty ratio	17:1
% students returning for sophomore year	78

Most classes have 10–19 students.

REQUESTING SERVICES FOR STUDENTS WITH LEARNING DIFFERENCES

Phone: 603-897-8497 • www.rivier.edu/academics/support-resources/disability-services
Email: disabilityservices@rivier.edu

Documentation submitted to: Disability Services
Separate application required for Services: Yes

Documentation required for:
LD: Psychoeducational evaluation
ADHD: Psychoeducational evaluation
ASD: Psychoeducational evaluation

University of New Hampshire

UNH Office of Admissions, Durham, NH 03824 • Admissions: 603-862-1360 • www.unh.edu

Support: S

PROGRAMS/SERVICES FOR STUDENTS WITH LEARNING DIFFERENCES

Students with learning differences at the University of New Hampshire are supported by Student Accessibility Services (SAS) with coordinated services, including assistive technology support, testing accommodations through the testing center, and community support. SAS ensures that accommodations are effectively provided. Many of the services are coordinated through The Center for Academic Resources (CFAR), which offers academic mentors, study skills support, organization and time management support, and tutoring.

ADMISSIONS

All applicants are expected to meet the same admission criteria. The average GPA for accepted applicants is between a B and B+, depending on the major. Students planning to study music education, music history, music performance, or music theory are required to audition as part of the application process. Students planning to study theater acting, dance, or musical theater are also required to audition as part of the application process.

Additional Information

The Center for Academic Resources can guide students in hiring a private tutor. A skills group for students struggling with focus, attention, and other symptoms of ADHD is offered through Psychological and Counseling Services (PAC). The Beauregard Center works with all students to provide advocacy and advising services.

Wildcat Sendoff countdown to graduation begins with picking up caps and gowns. There are a variety of graduation week activities, including a trip to the Brew UNH Lab to learn all things beer, a Paint Night with friends to create an original UNH wine glass, and cornhole tournaments. The best decorating of a graduation cap receives a UNH prize.

University of New Hampshire

GENERAL ADMISSIONS

Very important factors include: rigor of secondary school record, academic GPA. *Important factors include:* recommendations. *Other factors considered include:* class rank, standardized test scores (if submitted), application essay. High school diploma is required and GED is accepted. Institution is test-optional for entering Fall 2024. Check admissions website for updates. *Academic units required:* 4 English, 3 math, 2 science (2 labs), 2 social studies, 2 academic electives. *Academic units recommended:* 4 math, 4 science (3 labs), 2 foreign language, 3 social studies.

FINANCIAL AID

Students should submit: FAFSA. *Need-based scholarships/grants offered:* College/university scholarship or grant aid from institutional funds; Federal Pell; Private scholarships; SEOG; State scholarships/grants. *Loan aid offered:* Direct PLUS loans; Direct Subsidized Loans; Direct Unsubsidized Loans. Federal Work-Study Program available. Institutional employment available.

CAMPUS LIFE

Activities: Campus Ministries; Choral groups; Concert band; Dance; Drama/theater; International Student Organization; Jazz band; Literary magazine; Marching band; Model UN; Music ensembles; Musical theater; Opera; Pep band; Radio station; Student government; Student newspaper; Student-run film society; Symphony orchestra. **Organizations:** 200 registered organizations, 12 honor societies, 10 religious organizations, 13 fraternities, 8 sororities. **Athletics (Intercollegiate):** *Men:* baseball, basketball, crew/rowing, cross-country, cycling, golf, ice hockey, lacrosse, martial arts, rugby, skiing (nordic/cross-country), track/field (indoor), ultimate frisbee, volleyball, wrestling. *Women:* basketball, crew/rowing, cross-country, cycling, field hockey, golf, gymnastics, ice hockey, lacrosse, martial arts, rugby, skiing (nordic/cross-country), softball, swimming, track/field (indoor), ultimate frisbee, volleyball, wrestling.

CAMPUS
Type of school	Public
Environment	Village

STUDENTS
Undergrad enrollment	11,396
% male/female	44/56
% from out of state	54
% frosh live on campus	97

FINANCIAL FACTS
Annual in-state tuition	$15,520
Annual out-of-state tuition	$34,430
Room and board	$12,676
Required fees	$3,504

GENERAL ADMISSIONS INFO
Application fee	$50
Regular application deadline	2/1
Nonfall registration	Yes

Fall 2024 testing policy	Test Optional
Range SAT EBRW	570–660
Range SAT Math	550–660
Range ACT Composite	26–31

ACADEMICS
Student/faculty ratio	16:1
% students returning for sophomore year	86

Most classes have 20–29 students.

REQUESTING SERVICES FOR STUDENTS WITH LEARNING DIFFERENCES

Phone: 603-862-2607 • www.unh.edu/sas • Email: sas.office@unh.edu

Documentation submitted to: Student Accessibility Services

Separate application required for Services: Yes

Documentation required for:
LD: Psychoeducational evaluation
ADHD: Psychoeducational evaluation
ASD: Psychoeducational evaluation

Drew University

Undergraduate Admissions, Madison, NJ 07940 • Admissions: 973-408-3739 • drew.edu

Support: CS

ACCOMMODATIONS

Allowed in exams:

Calculators	Yes
Dictionary	Yes
Computer	Yes
Spell-checker	Yes
Extended test time	Yes
Scribe	Yes
Proctors	Yes
Oral exams	Yes
Note-takers	Yes

Support services for students with:

LD	Yes
ADHD	Yes
ASD	Yes
Distraction-reduced environment	Yes
Recording of lecture allowed	Yes
Reading technology	Yes
Audio books	Yes
Other assistive technology	Yes
Priority registration	Yes

Added costs of services:

For LD	No
For ADHD	No
For ASD	No
LD specialists	Yes
ADHD & ASD coaching	Yes
ASD specialists	No
Professional tutors	No
Peer tutors	Yes
Max. hours/week for services	3
How professors are notified of student approved accommodations	Student

COLLEGE GRADUATION REQUIREMENTS

Course waivers allowed	Yes

In what courses: Varies

Course substitutions allowed	Yes

In what courses: Varies

PROGRAMS/SERVICES FOR STUDENTS WITH LEARNING DIFFERENCES

The Office of Accessibility Resources (OAR) provides academic accommodations based on each student's disability and individual needs. Students must submit a form that explains the nature of their needs along with supporting documentation from a licensed professional. Once OAR has all the necessary information, the director and student can review the forms together in a personal and confidential meeting to determine appropriate accommodations.

ADMISSIONS

All applicants are expected to meet the same admission criteria. Admissions takes a holistic approach to the review process, considering grades, rigor of courses, recommendations, personal essay, extracurricular involvement, and SAT/ACT scores. While Drew University is test-optional, students who choose not to submit test scores must present a strong high school transcript and display academic achievement in a challenging curriculum. Drew recommends that applicants take a college-prep curriculum in high school. The minimum GPA for admission is 2.5.

Additional Information

The Office of Academic Services connects students to coaching, peer tutoring, and specialized academic support. There are several on-campus resources for all students, including a writing center. Students have the opportunity to take a variety of workshops, including a hands-on procrastination seminar that teaches time-management skills and prepares students to set and meet deadlines.

Drew is aptly nicknamed the "University in the Forest," because of its 186-acre wooded campus. This includes an 80-acre forest preserve. Created in 1980 and named for two botany faculty, the Florence and Robert Zuck Arboretum includes native and non-native trees, flowering plants and shrubs, and two small glacial ponds that are stops for migrating birds. It's a natural laboratory for the Biology Department, as well as a retreat for students.

Drew University

GENERAL ADMISSIONS

Very important factors include: rigor of secondary school record, academic GPA. *Important factors include:* application essay, recommendations. *Other factors considered include:* class rank, standardized test scores (if submitted). High school diploma is required and GED is accepted. Institution is test-optional for entering Fall 2024. Check admissions website for updates. *Academic units recommended:* 4 English, 3 math, 2 science, 2 foreign language, 2 social studies, 2 history, 3 academic electives.

FINANCIAL AID

Students should submit: FAFSA. *Need-based scholarships/grants offered:* College/university scholarship or grant aid from institutional funds; Federal Pell; Private scholarships; SEOG; State scholarships/grants. *Loan aid offered:* Direct PLUS loans; Direct Subsidized Loans; Direct Unsubsidized Loans. Federal Work-Study Program available. Institutional employment available.

CAMPUS LIFE

Activities: Campus Ministries; Choral groups; Dance; Drama/theater; International Student Organization; Jazz band; Literary magazine; Model UN; Music ensembles; Musical theater; Pep band; Radio station; Student government; Student newspaper; Student-run film society; Symphony orchestra; Yearbook. **Organizations:** 133 registered organizations, 17 honor societies, 8 religious organizations, 0 fraternities, 0 sororities. **Athletics (Intercollegiate):** *Men:* baseball, basketball, cross-country, golf, lacrosse, rugby, swimming, ultimate frisbee, volleyball. *Women:* basketball, cross-country, equestrian sports, field hockey, golf, lacrosse, rugby, softball, swimming, ultimate frisbee, volleyball.

CAMPUS

Type of school	Private (nonprofit)
Environment	Village

STUDENTS

Undergrad enrollment	1,541
% male/female	41/59
% from out of state	30
% frosh live on campus	90

FINANCIAL FACTS

Annual tuition	$39,828
Room and board	$14,723
Required fees	$832

GENERAL ADMISSIONS INFO

Application fee	$40
Regular application deadline	2/1
Nonfall registration	Yes

Fall 2024 testing policy	Test Optional
Range SAT EBRW	560–660
Range SAT Math	540–640
Range ACT Composite	24–30

ACADEMICS

Student/faculty ratio	12:1
% students returning for sophomore year	88

Most classes have 10–19 students.

New Jersey

REQUESTING SERVICES FOR STUDENTS WITH LEARNING DIFFERENCES

Phone: 973-408-3962 • drew.edu/center-academic-excellence/cae/accessibility-resources
Email: disabilityserv@drew.edu

Documentation submitted to: Office of Accessibility Resources
Separate application required for Services: Yes

Documentation required for:
LD: Psychoeducational evaluation
ADHD: Psychoeducational evaluation
ASD: Psychoeducational evaluation

Fairleigh Dickinson University—Florham

285 Madison Avenue, Madison, NJ 07940 • Admissions: 800-338-8803 • www.fdu.edu

Support: SP

ACCOMMODATIONS

Allowed in exams:

Calculators	Yes
Dictionary	Yes
Computer	Yes
Spell-checker	Yes
Extended test time	Yes
Scribe	Yes
Proctors	Yes
Oral exams	Yes
Note-takers	Yes

Support services for students with:

LD	Yes
ADHD	Yes
ASD	Yes
Distraction-reduced environment	Yes
Recording of lecture allowed	Yes
Reading technology	Yes
Audio books	Yes
Other assistive technology	Yes
Priority registration	Yes

Added costs of services:

For LD	No
For ADHD	No
For ASD	Yes
LD specialists	Yes
ADHD & ASD coaching	No
ASD specialists	Yes
Professional tutors	Yes
Peer tutors	No
Max. hours/week for services	Varies
How professors are notified of student approved accommodations	Student and Office of Disability Support Services

COLLEGE GRADUATION REQUIREMENTS

Course waivers allowed	No
Course substitutions allowed	Yes
In what courses: Case-by-case basis	

PROGRAMS/SERVICES FOR STUDENTS WITH LEARNING DIFFERENCES

The Office of Disability Support Services provides a variety of accommodations to students with disabilities. Accommodations are determined on a case-by-case basis based on the student's documented disability-related needs and essential requirements of their academic program. Accommodations may include extended time on tests, use of a classroom computer, reduced-distraction testing, assistance with note-taking, priority course registration, preferential seating, and assistive technology. The Regional Center for Learning Disabilities is a structured program of academic support, personalized advice, and counseling services that give students the resources they need to succeed while participating in traditional college classes. Services are offered at no additional charge and include in-depth training in the use of the latest assistive technology and individualized academic counseling services. More than half of all participants earn a "B" average or higher. COMmunity Promoting Academic and Social Success (COMPASS) is an individually tailored, comprehensive, academic, and social support program for a limited number of college students with autism spectrum disorder. The goals of this two-year program are to help each student make use of existing academic and social strengths, assist in the development of new abilities, and promote a higher level of independent functioning.

ADMISSIONS

All applicants are expected to meet the same admission criteria. The university does not require ACT or SAT scores in the application process except for the nursing program. Personal essays, a résumé, and recommendations are optional but helpful. Applicants can schedule an interview, but it is not required.

Additional Information

The Academic Support Center (ASC) provides free one-on-one tutoring to all current undergraduate and graduate students at the Florham Campus. The Summer College Prep Program is a two-week program on the Metropolitan Campus for graduating high school students and rising seniors run by the Regional Center. The program introduces students to college-level work and helps them develop the specific skills and academic strategies needed to successfully transition from high school.

FDU's Florham campus is on the former grounds of Florham, the estate of early 20th-century socialites Florence Vanderbilt and Hamilton Twombly. (The estate gets its name Florham from the first names of the couple who built it.) Frederick Law Olmsted, the designer of Central Park, designed the landscape for the Twombly-Vanderbilt estate, now the Florham campus. Hennessy Hall, used for classrooms and administrative offices, was the original 100-room main house of the estate and is recognized as one of the eight largest mansions in the U.S.

Fairleigh Dickinson University— Florham

GENERAL ADMISSIONS
Very important factors include: academic GPA, standardized test scores (if submitted). *Important factors include:* rigor of secondary school record, recommendations. *Other factors considered include:* class rank, application essay. High school diploma is required and GED is accepted. Institution is test-optional for entering Fall 2024. Check admissions website for updates. *Academic units required:* 4 English, 3 math, 2 science (2 labs), 2 history, 3 academic electives. *Academic units recommended:* 3 science (2 labs), 2 foreign language, 4 academic electives.

FINANCIAL AID
Students should submit: FAFSA. *Need-based scholarships/grants offered:* College/university scholarship or grant aid from institutional funds; Federal Pell; Private scholarships; SEOG; State scholarships/grants. *Loan aid offered:* Direct PLUS loans; Direct Subsidized Loans; Direct Unsubsidized Loans. Federal Work-Study Program available. Institutional employment available.

CAMPUS LIFE
Activities: Campus Ministries; Choral groups; Dance; Drama/theater; International Student Organization; Literary magazine; Musical theater; Radio station; Student government; Student newspaper; Student-run film society. **Organizations:** 43 registered organizations, 9 honor societies, 3 religious organizations, 7 fraternities, 5 sororities. **Athletics (Intercollegiate):** *Men:* baseball, basketball, cross-country, golf, lacrosse, swimming. *Women:* basketball, cross-country, field hockey, golf, lacrosse, softball, swimming, volleyball.

CAMPUS
Type of school	Private (nonprofit)
Environment	Village

STUDENTS
Undergrad enrollment	2,320
% male/female	43/57
% from out of state	17
% frosh live on campus	79

FINANCIAL FACTS
Annual tuition	$32,000
Room and board	$15,588
Required fees	$1,114

GENERAL ADMISSIONS INFO
Application fee	$40
Regular application deadline	Rolling
Nonfall registration	Yes
Fall 2024 testing policy	Test Optional
Range SAT EBRW	510–610
Range SAT Math	500–620
Range ACT Composite	22–28

ACADEMICS
Student/faculty ratio	11:1
% students returning for sophomore year	77

New Jersey

REQUESTING SERVICES FOR STUDENTS WITH LEARNING DIFFERENCES

Phone: 973-443-8079 • www.fdu.edu/campuses/florham-campus/student-services/disability-support-services

Documentation submitted to: Disability Support Services
Separate application required for Services: Yes

Documentation required for:
LD: Psychoeducational evaluation
ADHD: Psychoeducational evaluation
ASD: Psychoeducational evaluation

Georgian Court University

900 Lakewood Avenue, Lakewood, NJ 08701-2697 • Admissions: 732-987-2700 • georgian.edu

Support: SP

ACCOMMODATIONS

Allowed in exams:	
Calculators	Yes
Dictionary	Yes
Computer	Yes
Spell-checker	Yes
Extended test time	Yes
Scribe	Yes
Proctors	Yes
Oral exams	Yes
Note-takers	Yes
Support services for students with:	
LD	Yes
ADHD	Yes
ASD	Yes
Distraction-reduced environment	Yes
Recording of lecture allowed	Yes
Reading technology	Yes
Audio books	Yes
Other assistive technology	Yes
Priority registration	Yes
Added costs of services:	
For LD	Yes
For ADHD	Yes
For ASD	Yes
LD specialists	Yes
ADHD & ASD coaching	Yes
ASD specialists	Yes
Professional tutors	Yes
Peer tutors	Yes
Max. hours/week for services	Varies
How professors are notified of student approved accommodations	Student

COLLEGE GRADUATION REQUIREMENTS

Course waivers allowed	No
Course substitutions allowed	Yes
In what courses: Math and Foreign Language	

PROGRAMS/SERVICES FOR STUDENTS WITH LEARNING DIFFERENCES

The Office of Student Success (OSS) provides services to students with documented disabilities. Students must contact OSS each semester to schedule an appointment to fill out forms, discuss the challenges the disability presents in an academic setting, and request accommodations. This should be done before the semester begins, or during the first week of classes. Students who receive testing accommodations may request to take exams in the Office of Student Success. The Learning Connection (TLC) Program is a fee-based, formally structured program designed to assist students with learning disabilities or other conditions that may impact their academic performance. TLC aims to optimize academic, personal, and life skills.

ADMISSIONS

Georgian Court University examines class rank and transcript for evidence that an applicant will succeed in college. Applicants are expected to have completed a rigorous high school curriculum and core courses including English, math, science, social studies, and foreign language. ACT and SAT scores are optional for most students; they are a requirement for students who are international, homeschooled, or applying to the nursing program. Interviews are not required, but informational interviews are available at a student's request. Students with learning disabilities who are interested in applying to the Learning Connection should indicate that on their application.

Additional Information

Performance Assistance Through Coaching and Tutoring (PACT) is a mandatory support program for first-year students who are accepted to Georgian Court University on the condition that the PACT program will provide the additional assistance necessary to transition to college life in the academic year. The student's acceptance to PACT is based on their application and supplemental data, such as GPA and SAT/ACT scores. Accepted students attend a PACT orientation during regular New Student Orientation and meet with PACT coaches to schedule weekly appointments.

DID YOU KNOW?

GSU's main campus is on the former summer estate of millionaire George Jay Gould. Built in 1899, the estate included a court tennis, or "real tennis" court. Court tennis is played indoors with a heavier, less bouncy ball and a shorter wood and tight nylon string racquet with more complex rules. GSU is one of 11 court tennis facilities in the U.S. and the only court on a university campus. About 45 real tennis courts are still in use in the world today.

Georgian Court University

General Admissions

Very important factors include: rigor of secondary school record, academic GPA. *Important factors include:* application essay, recommendations. *Other factors considered include:* class rank, standardized test scores (if submitted). High school diploma is required and GED is accepted. Institution is test-optional for entering Fall 2024. Check admissions website for updates. *Academic units required:* 4 English, 2 math, 2 science (2 labs), 2 foreign language, 2 history, 4 academic electives.

Financial Aid

Students should submit: FAFSA. *Need-based scholarships/grants offered:* College/university scholarship or grant aid from institutional funds; Federal Pell; Private scholarships; SEOG; State scholarships/grants. *Loan aid offered:* Direct PLUS loans; Direct Subsidized Loans; Direct Unsubsidized Loans. Federal Work-Study Program available. Institutional employment available.

Campus Life

Activities: Campus Ministries; Choral groups; Concert band; Dance; Drama/theater; International Student Organization; Jazz band; Literary magazine; Music ensembles; Student government; Student newspaper. **Organizations:** 60 registered organizations, 19 honor societies, 2 religious organizations. **Athletics (Intercollegiate):** *Men:* basketball, cross-country, lacrosse, track/field (indoor). *Women:* basketball, cross-country, lacrosse, softball, track/field (indoor), volleyball.

New Jersey

REQUESTING SERVICES FOR STUDENTS WITH LEARNING DIFFERENCES

Phone: 732-987-2363 • georgian.edu/academics/student-success • Email: success@georgian.edu

Documentation submitted to: Office of Student Success
Separate application required for Services: Yes

Documentation required for:
 LD: Psychoeducational evaluation
 ADHD: Psychoeducational evaluation
 ASD: Psychoeducational evaluation

Kean University

Office of Admissions -Kean Hall, Union, NJ 07083-0411 • Admissions: 908-737-7100 • www.kean.edu

> Support: CS

ACCOMMODATIONS

Allowed in exams:

Calculators	Yes
Dictionary	Yes
Computer	Yes
Spell-checker	Yes
Extended test time	Yes
Scribe	Yes
Proctors	Yes
Oral exams	Yes
Note-takers	Yes

Support services for students with:

LD	Yes
ADHD	Yes
ASD	Yes
Distraction-reduced environment	Yes
Recording of lecture allowed	Yes
Reading technology	Yes
Audio books	Yes
Other assistive technology	Yes
Priority registration	Yes

Added costs of services:

For LD	No
For ADHD	No
For ASD	No
LD specialists	No
ADHD & ASD coaching	Yes
ASD specialists	Yes
Professional tutors	No
Peer tutors	Yes
Max. hours/week for services	5
How professors are notified of student approved accommodations	Student

COLLEGE GRADUATION REQUIREMENTS

Course waivers allowed	No
Course substitutions allowed	Yes
In what courses: Varies	

PROGRAMS/SERVICES FOR STUDENTS WITH LEARNING DIFFERENCES

The Office of Accessibility Services (OAS) at Kean University provides services to students with disabilities. Students must register with OAS and provide current documentation that was done within five years of entering college. The documentation is reviewed and accommodations are provided on an individual basis. Students meet with an OAS advisor to determine accommodation needs. Resources include alternate-format texts, accessible technology, and note-taking services. Through a community partnership, Kean University offers the College Steps program to ensure that students with autism and executive functioning challenges gain access to academic enrichment resources, social engagement skills, independent living supports, and pre-employment training. The program is a wraparound service that includes both expert coordinators and peer mentors who communicate with Kean faculty and staff. College Steps is a fee-based program, providing funding when available.

ADMISSIONS

All applicants are expected to meet the same admission criteria. Academic rigor is strongly considered and the average GPA for admitted students is 3.0. Applicants must submit two letters of recommendation, a personal essay about educational and future career goals, and a complete list of their high school activities, leadership, and work. Students who are disadvantaged educationally or financially may apply through the Educational Opportunities Fund and are eligible for state-funded grants. SUPERA Spanish Speaking Program is an admissions opportunity for Spanish-speaking students whose first language is not English. SUPERA students are offered courses in Spanish during their first two years of college. Applicants can appeal a denial explaining why the college should reconsider the application.

Additional Information

The Nancy Thompson Learning Commons offers writing and speaking services, tutoring, academic coaches, and numerous workshops for all Kean University students.

Built in 1772 by William Livingston, who became a member of the first and second Continental Congress, a signatory of the Constitution, and the first governor of New Jersey, Liberty Hall Campus has a rich history of distinguished visitors from Revolutionary times to current. In 2015, one of the most extensive collections of Madeira wines in the world was uncovered at Liberty Hall, some bottles more than 200 years old. A portion of the collection comprises the "History in a Bottle" exhibit in the Liberty Hall Museum.

Kean University

GENERAL ADMISSIONS

Very important factors include: rigor of secondary school record, academic GPA. *Other factors considered include:* class rank, standardized test scores (if submitted), application essay, recommendations. High school diploma is required and GED is accepted. Institution is test-optional for entering Fall 2024. Check admissions website for updates. *Academic units required:* 4 English, 3 math, 2 science (2 labs), 2 history, 2 foreign language, 3 approved electives in social studies, science, or math.

FINANCIAL AID

Students should submit: FAFSA; State aid form. *Need-based scholarships/grants offered:* College/university scholarship or grant aid from institutional funds; Federal Pell; Private scholarships; SEOG; State scholarships/grants. *Loan aid offered:* Direct PLUS loans; Direct Subsidized Loans; Direct Unsubsidized Loans. Federal Work-Study Program available. Institutional employment available.

CAMPUS LIFE

Activities: Campus Ministries; Choral groups; Concert band; Dance; Drama/theater; International Student Organization; Jazz band; Marching band; Model UN; Music ensembles; Musical theater; Opera; Pep band; Radio station; Student government; Student newspaper; Student-run film society; Symphony orchestra; Television station; Yearbook. **Organizations:** 128 registered organizations, 31 honor societies, 9 religious organizations, 11 fraternities, 13 sororities. **Athletics (Intercollegiate):** *Men:* baseball, basketball, cross-country, lacrosse, volleyball. *Women:* basketball, cross-country, field hockey, lacrosse, softball, swimming, volleyball.

CAMPUS

Type of school	Public
Environment	City

STUDENTS

Undergrad enrollment	10,524
% male/female	39/61
% from out of state	3
% frosh live on campus	36

FINANCIAL FACTS

Annual in-state tuition	$10,758
Annual out-of-state tuition	$18,150
Room and board	$14,834
Required fees	$2,214

GENERAL ADMISSIONS INFO

Application fee	$75
Regular application deadline	8/15
Nonfall registration	Yes
Fall 2024 testing policy	Test Optional
Range SAT EBRW	450–580
Range SAT Math	450–580
Range ACT Composite	16–25

ACADEMICS

Student/faculty ratio	16:1
% students returning for sophomore year	74
Most classes have 20–29 students.	

New Jersey

REQUESTING SERVICES FOR STUDENTS WITH LEARNING DIFFERENCES

Phone: 908-737-4910 • www.kean.edu/oas • Email: accessibilityservices@kean.edu

Documentation submitted to: Office of Accessibility Services
Separate application required for Services: Yes

Documentation required for:
LD: Psychoeducational evaluation
ADHD: Psychoeducational evaluation
ASD: Psychoeducational evaluation

Monmouth University

400 Cedar Avenue, West Long Branch, NJ 07764-1898 Admissions: 732-571-3456 • www.monmouth.edu

Support: CS

ACCOMMODATIONS

Allowed in exams:

Calculators	Yes
Dictionary	Yes
Computer	Yes
Spell-checker	Yes
Extended test time	Yes
Scribe	Yes
Proctors	Yes
Oral exams	Yes
Note-takers	Yes

Support services for students with:

LD	Yes
ADHD	Yes
ASD	Yes
Distraction-reduced environment	Yes
Recording of lecture allowed	Yes
Reading technology	Yes
Audio books	Yes
Other assistive technology	Yes
Priority registration	Yes

Added costs of services:

For LD	No
For ADHD	No
For ASD	No
LD specialists	Yes
ADHD & ASD coaching	No
ASD specialists	No
Professional tutors	No
Peer tutors	Yes
Max. hours/week for services	Varies
How professors are notified of student approved accommodations	Student

COLLEGE GRADUATION REQUIREMENTS

Course waivers allowed	No
Course substitutions allowed	Yes
In what courses: Foreign Language	

PROGRAMS/SERVICES FOR STUDENTS WITH LEARNING DIFFERENCES

The Department of Disability Services (DDS) provides reasonable accommodations to students with learning differences. The DDS refers students to additional campus resources, including tutoring services, writing services, Supplemental Instruction, and the math learning center. To apply for services, students complete the confidential registration form and upload the required documentation. Students should request services in writing and should forward the required documentation as soon as they receive acceptance to the university. Academic accommodations are determined on a case-by-case basis. Monmouth University offers a course called Transition to College. This 1 credit elective course supports incoming first-year students with disabilities in their transition to college by focusing on topics that promote independent learning. This includes learning styles, self-exploration of learning strengths and weaknesses, self-advocacy, test preparation and test-taking strategies, organizational methods and time management, and study skills.

ADMISSIONS

All applicants are expected to meet the same admission requirements. The university evaluates all submitted information within a holistic review process that considers each applicant's entire achievement history. Students should pursue a rigorous academic curriculum in high school and be involved in leadership development activities.

Additional Information

The Center for Student Success offers academic advising, peer tutors, the Writing Services office, and many other resources including experiential education opportunities.

Wilson Hall is Monmouth's identifying landmark and backdrop for university festivities. It's the administrative, academic, and social hub of campus. The 130-room mansion was built in 1929 by Philadelphia architect Horace Trumbauer and his assistant Julian Abele, the first African American professional architect. Their relationship was unusual for the time, with Abele serving as the chief designer at a major Philadelphia firm. Throughout his career, Julian Abele designed more than 400 buildings.

Monmouth University

General Admissions

Very important factors include: rigor of secondary school record, academic GPA. *Important factors include:* application essay, recommendations. *Other factors considered include:* standardized test scores (if submitted). High school diploma is required and GED is accepted. Institution is test-optional for entering Fall 2024. Check admissions website for updates. *Academic units required:* 4 English, 3 math, 2 science (1 lab), 2 history, 5 academic electives. *Academic units recommended:* 2 foreign language.

Financial Aid

Students should submit: FAFSA. *Need-based scholarships/grants offered:* College/university scholarship or grant aid from institutional funds; Federal Pell; Private scholarships; SEOG; State scholarships/grants. *Loan aid offered:* Direct PLUS loans; Direct Subsidized Loans; Direct Unsubsidized Loans. Federal Work-Study Program available. Institutional employment available.

Campus Life

Activities: Campus Ministries; Choral groups; Dance; International Student Organization; Literary magazine; Model UN; Musical theater; Pep band; Radio station; Student government; Student newspaper; Television station. **Organizations:** 129 registered organizations, 31 honor societies, 6 religious organizations, 6 fraternities, 8 sororities. **Athletics (Intercollegiate):** *Men:* baseball, basketball, cross-country, golf, ice hockey, lacrosse, swimming, track/field (indoor), wrestling. *Women:* basketball, bowling, crew/rowing, cross-country, field hockey, golf, lacrosse, softball, swimming, track/field (indoor), volleyball, wrestling.

CAMPUS

Type of school	Private (nonprofit)
Environment	Village

STUDENTS

Undergrad enrollment	4,080
% male/female	38/62
% from out of state	28
% frosh live on campus	79

FINANCIAL FACTS

Annual tuition	$44,098
Room and board	$17,738
Required fees	$752

GENERAL ADMISSIONS INFO

Application fee	$50
Regular application deadline	3/1
Nonfall registration	Yes

Fall 2024 testing policy	Test Optional
Range SAT EBRW	540–630
Range SAT Math	530–620
Range ACT Composite	21–26

ACADEMICS

Student/faculty ratio	12:1
% students returning for sophomore year	84

Most classes have 20–29 students.

New Jersey

REQUESTING SERVICES FOR STUDENTS WITH LEARNING DIFFERENCES

Phone: 732-571-3460 • www.monmouth.edu/disability-services • Email: dds@monmouth.edu

Documentation submitted to: Department of Disability Services
Separate application required for Services: Yes

Documentation required for:
LD: Psychoeducational evaluation
ADHD: Psychoeducational evaluation
ASD: Psychoeducational evaluation

Montclair State University

One Normal Avenue, Montclair, NJ 07043-1624 • Admissions: 973-655-4444 • www.montclair.edu

Support: CS

ACCOMMODATIONS

Allowed in exams:

Calculators	Yes
Dictionary	Yes
Computer	Yes
Spell-checker	Yes
Extended test time	Yes
Scribe	Yes
Proctors	Yes
Oral exams	Yes
Note-takers	Yes

Support services for students with:

LD	Yes
ADHD	Yes
ASD	Yes
Distraction-reduced environment	Yes
Recording of lecture allowed	Yes
Reading technology	Yes
Audio books	Yes
Other assistive technology	Yes
Priority registration	Yes

Added costs of services:

For LD	No
For ADHD	No
For ASD	No
LD specialists	No
ADHD & ASD coaching	Yes
ASD specialists	Yes
Professional tutors	No
Peer tutors	Yes
Max. hours/week for services	Varies
How professors are notified of student approved accommodations	Student

COLLEGE GRADUATION REQUIREMENTS

Course waivers allowed	Yes

In what courses: Case-by-case basis

Course substitutions allowed	Yes

In what courses: Foreign Language, Physical Education, and Public Speaking

PROGRAMS/SERVICES FOR STUDENTS WITH LEARNING DIFFERENCES

The Disability Resource Center (DRC) provides accommodations to ensure students succeed in academic and student-life-related activities. Services available to students include additional time on exams, note-taking assistance, assistive listening devices, digital recorders, captioning or ASL interpreting, and early registration. To apply for services, students submit the registration form at the beginning of each semester and attend a meeting with a DRC staff member. Current and eligible documentation is required prior to each season to determine accommodative service needs.

ADMISSIONS

The primary factors considered for admissions include the student's high school GPA, the rigor of the courses taken, strong letters of recommendation from teachers and counselors, a well-written, thoughtful admissions essay, a commitment to extracurricular engagement, and ACT or SAT test scores (if applicable.) The strongest candidates for admission have a 3.2 or higher cumulative high school GPA on an unweighted, 4.0 scale.

Additional Information

The DRC hires graduate students as academic coaches (AC) to provide individual and group sessions. Academic coaches assist students with developing the academic, professional, and self-advocacy necessary for success in college and beyond. Some topics of interest include time management, organizational skills, note-taking, business and professional communication, and avoiding procrastination. The Center for Academic Success offers Supplemental Instruction review sessions led by peers; students who are struggling in courses are encouraged to participate.

According to documents at the time, in 1952, MSU was "undoubtedly the first" to use a non-commercial UHF channel to broadcast a full day of educational television to 13 schools. Twenty-nine students developed and produced eight ½ hour programs in a television workshop class as a result of a partnership between MSU and Allen B. DuMont, a television pioneer. A week before the broadcast, special 21-inch TV sets were put in the participating classrooms so students in classes could get used to them.

Montclair State University

General Admissions

Very important factors include: academic GPA. *Important factors include:* rigor of secondary school record, application essay, recommendations. *Other factors considered include:* class rank. High school diploma is required and GED is accepted. Institution is test-optional for entering Fall 2024. Check admissions website for updates. *Academic units required:* 4 English, 3 math, 2 science (2 labs), 2 foreign language, 2 social studies, 3 academic electives. *Academic units recommended:* 4 math, 3 science (3 labs), 3 foreign language.

Financial Aid

Students should submit: FAFSA; State aid form. *Need-based scholarships/grants offered:* College/university scholarship or grant aid from institutional funds; Federal Pell; Private scholarships; SEOG; State scholarships/grants. *Loan aid offered:* Direct PLUS loans; Direct Subsidized Loans; Direct Unsubsidized Loans. Federal Work-Study Program available. Institutional employment available.

Campus Life

Activities: Campus Ministries; Choral groups; Concert band; Dance; Drama/theater; International Student Organization; Jazz band; Literary magazine; Marching band; Model UN; Music ensembles; Musical theater; Opera; Pep band; Radio station; Student government; Student newspaper; Student-run film society; Symphony orchestra; Television station; Yearbook. **Organizations:** 103 registered organizations, 14 fraternities, 18 sororities. **Athletics (Intercollegiate):** *Men:* baseball, basketball, equestrian sports, field hockey, golf, gymnastics, ice hockey, lacrosse, rugby, softball, swimming, table tennis, track/field (indoor), volleyball, wrestling. *Women:* baseball, basketball, equestrian sports, field hockey, golf, gymnastics, ice hockey, lacrosse, rugby, softball, swimming, table tennis, track/field (indoor), volleyball, wrestling.

CAMPUS

Type of school	Public
Environment	Town

STUDENTS

Undergrad enrollment	16,902
% male/female	40/60
% from out of state	5
% frosh live on campus	41

FINANCIAL FACTS

Annual in-state tuition	$12,755
Annual out-of-state tuition	$21,465
Room and board	$16,388
Required fees	$1,007

GENERAL ADMISSIONS INFO

Application fee	$65
Regular application deadline	3/1
Nonfall registration	Yes

Fall 2024 testing policy	Test Optional
Range SAT EBRW	480–610
Range SAT Math	470–590

ACADEMICS

Student/faculty ratio	17:1
% students returning for sophomore year	81

Most classes have 20–29 students.

New Jersey

REQUESTING SERVICES FOR STUDENTS WITH LEARNING DIFFERENCES

Phone: 973-655-5431 • www.montclair.edu/disability-resource-center • Email: drc@montclair.edu

Documentation submitted to: Disability Resource Center
Separate application required for Services: Yes

Documentation required for:
LD: Psychoeducational evaluation
ADHD: Psychoeducational evaluation
ASD: Psychoeducational evaluation

New Jersey City University

2039 Kennedy Boulevard, Jersey City, NJ 07305 • Admissions: 201-200-3234 • www.njcu.edu

Support: CS

ACCOMMODATIONS

Allowed in exams:

Calculators	Yes
Dictionary	Yes
Computer	Yes
Spell-checker	Yes
Extended test time	Yes
Scribe	Yes
Proctors	Yes
Oral exams	Yes
Note-takers	Yes

Support services for students with:

LD	Yes
ADHD	Yes
ASD	Yes
Distraction-reduced environment	Yes
Recording of lecture allowed	Yes
Reading technology	Yes
Audio books	Yes
Other assistive technology	Yes
Priority registration	Yes

Added costs of services:

For LD	No
For ADHD	No
For ASD	No
LD specialists	Yes
ADHD & ASD coaching	Yes
ASD specialists	No
Professional tutors	No
Peer tutors	Yes
Max. hours/week for services	Varies
How professors are notified of student approved accommodations	Office of Specialized Services and Supplemental Instruction

COLLEGE GRADUATION REQUIREMENTS

Course waivers allowed	No
Course substitutions allowed	Yes
In what courses: Case-by-case basis	

PROGRAMS/SERVICES FOR STUDENTS WITH LEARNING DIFFERENCES

The Office of Specialized Services and Supplemental Instruction (OSS/SI) assists students with disabilities requesting reasonable accommodations supported by documentation. Students must request accommodations by submitting an OSS registration form and documentation of their disability. Once the form and documentation have been received, the OSS director and student will meet in person, by phone, or via video conference to discuss the request and determine the accommodations needed for each class. Reasonable accommodations include but are not limited to, alternative testing arrangements, adaptive/assistive technology, sign language interpreters, peer notetakers, and books in an alternate format.

ADMISSIONS

All applicants complete the same admission application and must have graduated from high school or earned a GED equivalent diploma. Official high school transcripts must be submitted by a school counselor and should show a college preparatory curriculum. NJCU accepts applicants with a GPA of at least 2.91, which should be a mix of B's and C's; lower grades suggest to the admission review that an applicant may struggle to succeed in a university environment. A personal essay and letters of recommendation are optional; applicants may submit up to two recommendations from a teacher and two from other sources. Some degree programs may have additional requirements.

Additional Information

ASCEND is a university-sponsored, six-week (July–August) academic and college preparatory program designed to help incoming first-year students transition to college. The Office of Student Outreach and Retention (SOAR) also supports students with the transition to college, and SOAR Rising Knight Peer Mentors (RKPM) are paired with new students who help navigate their first year at NJCU. SOAR Personal Development Meetings offer one-on-one meetings with SOAR staff who guide and advise students on many college topics. The Office of Centralized Tutoring and Academic Support Programming offers one-on-one and group tutoring for writing, reading, mathematics, business, and STEM subjects. For tutoring and academic coaching in other subjects, students can make online or in-person appointments via the Tutoring and Academic Support Services course on Blackboard. Academic Workshops are held throughout the fall and spring semesters with a focus on topics such as academic integrity, writing tips and strategies, grammar, time management, and study skills.

At NJCU, children go to college. Since 1982, the Children's Learning Center (fully licensed and accredited) has offered preschool, prekindergarten, and drop-in childcare services to students, faculty, and alums at competitive rates. Children enrolled full-time can receive an individualized curriculum for their developmental level. The center also serves as a training site for NJCU students to gain preprofessional childcare field experience.

New Jersey City University

GENERAL ADMISSIONS

Very important factors include: rigor of secondary school record, class rank, academic GPA. High school diploma is required and GED is accepted. Institution is test-optional for entering Fall 2024. Check admissions website for updates. *Academic units required:* 4 English, 4 math, 2 science, 4 foreign language. *Academic units recommended:* 3 science (2 labs).

FINANCIAL AID

Students should submit: FAFSA. *Need-based scholarships/grants offered:* College/university scholarship or grant aid from institutional funds; Federal Pell. *Loan aid offered:* Direct PLUS loans; Direct Subsidized Loans; Direct Unsubsidized Loans. Federal Work-Study Program available. Institutional employment available.

CAMPUS LIFE

Activities: Concert band; Drama/theater; Jazz band; Student government; Symphony orchestra; Yearbook. **Organizations:** 23 registered organizations. **Athletics (Intercollegiate):** *Men:* baseball, basketball, bowling, cross-country, golf, martial arts, racquetball, softball, swimming, table tennis, volleyball. *Women:* basketball, bowling, cross-country, martial arts, racquetball, softball, swimming, table tennis, volleyball.

CAMPUS

Type of school	Public
Environment	City

STUDENTS

Undergrad enrollment	5,262
% male/female	42/58
% from out of state	3
% frosh live on campus	21

FINANCIAL FACTS

Annual in-state tuition	$13,564
Annual out-of-state tuition	$24,163
Room and board	$15,800

GENERAL ADMISSIONS INFO

Application fee	$55
Regular application deadline	Rolling
Nonfall registration	Yes
Fall 2024 testing policy	Test Optional
Range SAT EBRW	440–570
Range SAT Math	450–570

ACADEMICS

Student/faculty ratio	14:1
% students returning for sophomore year	74

Most classes have 20–29 students.

REQUESTING SERVICES FOR STUDENTS WITH LEARNING DIFFERENCES

Phone: 201-200-2091 • www.njcu.edu/directories/offices-centers/office-specialized-services-and-supplemental-instruction • Email: jaitken@njcu.edu

Documentation submitted to: Office of Specialized Services

Separate application required for Services: Yes

Documentation required for:
LD: Psychoeducational evaluation
ADHD: Psychoeducational evaluation
ASD: Psychoeducational evaluation

Rider University

2083 Lawrenceville Road, Lawrenceville, NJ 08648-3099 • Admissions: 609-896-5042 • www.rider.edu

Support: CS

ACCOMMODATIONS

Allowed in exams:

Calculators	Yes
Dictionary	Yes
Computer	Yes
Spell-checker	Yes
Extended test time	Yes
Scribe	Yes
Proctors	Yes
Oral exams	No
Note-takers	Yes

Support services for students with:

LD	Yes
ADHD	Yes
ASD	Yes
Distraction-reduced environment	Yes
Recording of lecture allowed	Yes
Reading technology	Yes
Audio books	Yes
Other assistive technology	Yes
Priority registration	Yes

Added costs of services:

For LD	No
For ADHD	No
For ASD	No
LD specialists	Yes
ADHD & ASD coaching	Yes
ASD specialists	No
Professional tutors	Yes
Peer tutors	Yes
Max. hours/week for services	Varies
How professors are notified of student approved accommodations	Student Accessibility and Support Services

COLLEGE GRADUATION REQUIREMENTS

Course waivers allowed	No
Course substitutions allowed	Yes
In what courses: Math and Foreign Language unless they are essential to the student's major.	

PROGRAMS/SERVICES FOR STUDENTS WITH LEARNING DIFFERENCES

Student Accessibility and Support Services (SASS) helps students access academic support. To receive services, students must complete the confidential self-disclosure form, provide documentation of their disability, attend an intake meeting, and email SASS after their schedule has been finalized to receive that semester's accommodation letter. SASS will also email accommodation letters to professors. Accommodations are provided only to students whose disability significantly limits their academic functioning. In addition to accommodations, SASS offers coaching and consultation to students with documented disabilities.

ADMISSIONS

Admissions perform a holistic review of all applications. Rider University is test-optional, and ACT or SAT scores are not required for admission. Course requirements include 4 years of English, 3 years of math, and 9 year-long credits in humanities, foreign language, math, social science, or science. There is a required audition for some performing arts programs.

Additional Information

The Academic Success Center (ASC) offers all qualifying students free programs and services. The staff is made up of trained professionals, peer tutors, and peer assistants who provide tutoring and other forms of academic support both in person and remotely. Professional tutors work with students individually to improve their reading, writing, study, time management, and organizational strategies, as well as assistance with English as a second language skills. Supplemental Instruction is provided to students enrolled in targeted courses who attend sessions to review notes and assignments and prepare for exams. Some composition courses have embedded tutors, and students enrolled in specific sections are required to meet tutors on a weekly basis for writing workshops.

Cranberry Fest is held each September to welcome everyone back to campus with free barbecue, live music, games, giveaways, a beer garden (for the 21+ Broncs), and more. The festival was first held in 1979 to celebrate Andrew J. Rider, the school's namesake. According to legend, Mr. Rider introduced the cranberry to the queen of England, and she nicknamed him "The Cranberry King of New Jersey." Mr. Rider owned a horse named Cranberry, and "Cranberry King" is the basis for Rider's school colors: cranberry and white.

Rider University

GENERAL ADMISSIONS

Very important factors include: rigor of secondary school record, academic GPA, application essay, recommendations. *Other factors considered include:* standardized test scores (if submitted). High school diploma is required and GED is accepted. Institution is test-optional for entering Fall 2024. Check admissions website for updates. *Academic units required:* 4 English, 3 math, 9 academic electives. *Academic units recommended:* 4 math, 3 science, 5 academic electives.

FINANCIAL AID

Students should submit: FAFSA. *Need-based scholarships/grants offered:* College/university scholarship or grant aid from institutional funds; Federal Pell; Private scholarships; SEOG; State scholarships/grants. *Loan aid offered:* Direct PLUS loans; Direct Subsidized Loans; Direct Unsubsidized Loans. Federal Work-Study Program available. Institutional employment available.

CAMPUS LIFE

Activities: Campus Ministries; Choral groups; Concert band; Dance; Drama/theater; International Student Organization; Literary magazine; Model UN; Music ensembles; Musical theater; Pep band; Radio station; Student government; Student newspaper; Student-run film society; Television station. **Organizations:** 258 registered organizations, 15 honor societies, 8 religious organizations, 5 fraternities, 9 sororities. **Athletics (Intercollegiate):** *Men:* baseball, basketball, cross-country, equestrian sports, golf, ice hockey, lacrosse, softball, swimming, ultimate frisbee, wrestling. *Women:* baseball, basketball, cross-country, equestrian sports, field hockey, ice hockey, lacrosse, softball, swimming, ultimate frisbee, volleyball.

CAMPUS

Type of school	Private (nonprofit)
Environment	Village

STUDENTS

Undergrad enrollment	3,097
% male/female	43/57
% from out of state	24
% frosh live on campus	78

FINANCIAL FACTS

Annual tuition	$47,270
Room and board	$16,130
Required fees	$850

GENERAL ADMISSIONS INFO

Application fee	$50
Regular application deadline	Rolling
Nonfall registration	Yes
Fall 2024 testing policy	Test Optional
Range SAT EBRW	560–650
Range SAT Math	540–650
Range ACT Composite	21–29

ACADEMICS

Student/faculty ratio	10:1
% students returning for sophomore year	77

Most classes have 10–19 students.

New Jersey

REQUESTING SERVICES FOR STUDENTS WITH LEARNING DIFFERENCES

Phone: 609-895-5492 • www.rider.edu/academics/academic-support/student-accessibility-support-services • Email: accessbility@rider.edu

Documentation submitted to: Student Accessibility and Support Services
Separate application required for Services: Yes

Documentation required for:
LD: Psychoeducational evaluation
ADHD: Psychoeducational evaluation
ASD: Psychoeducational evaluation

Seton Hall University

Office of Admission, South Orange, NJ 07079 • Admissions: 973-313-6146 • shu.edu

Support: CS

PROGRAMS/SERVICES FOR STUDENTS WITH LEARNING DIFFERENCES

Students with disabilities can request services and accommodations from Disability Support Services (DSS) as soon as they are admitted to Seton Hall University. Students should contact DSS, complete the request form, and upload documentation of their disability so that DSS may review the materials and schedule an intake appointment to discuss services and determine accommodations. Following determination, a letter of accommodation is issued. DSS strongly encourages students to take ownership of their documentation and share it directly with course instructors. Additional resources to assist students with disabilities include a regularly updated directory of external scholarship opportunities, federal and state government internships and employment opportunities, and other employment resources.

ADMISSIONS

All applicants submit the same general application for review. The application must include an official high school transcript (average GPA is 3.6), a personal essay, a guidance counselor report, and a teacher or mentor recommendation. While ACT/SAT standardized test scores are optional, they may be required for specific programs, some scholarship opportunities, and could help waive certain placement tests upon enrollment. How well an applicant does in high school is of primary importance in admission decisions. However, the admissions committee also considers an applicant's personal statement, recommendations, test scores if submitted, as well as their demonstrated interest during the application review process. Visiting campus, attending an open house, and responding to all emails shows the committee that an applicant is serious about attending Seton Hall.

Additional Information

The Freshman Studies program offers personalized support and resources to adjust to campus life on the academic, social, and professional levels. Each student in the program takes the first semester for-credit course, Academic Survival Skills 101, and is assigned a program mentor who serves as an academic advisor, and a peer advisor, who encourages involvement in university life and acclimation to the environment. Seton Hall also offers Tutors-In-Residence (TIRs)—undergraduate peer tutors who live in certain residence halls and have scheduled lobby hours to assist both their resident and commuter classmates with coursework. Students can also find extra help in math, science, language, and writing at the Academic Resource Center (ARC). The ARC's workshops, one-on-one tutoring, and online resources are available to students throughout their college careers.

Elizabeth Ann Bayley Seton (1774-1821), the namesake of Seton Hall University, became a teacher in order to educate her own children. Her hopes were that all children could receive a free education. In 1809, she took vows of poverty, chastity, and obedience, and became known as Mother Seton. Mother Seton is the first American-born person to be canonized as a saint. Her banner hung over the entrance to St. Peter's Basilica in Rome before being placed on display at her national shrine in Emmitsburg, Maryland.

Seton Hall University

GENERAL ADMISSIONS

Very important factors include: rigor of secondary school record, academic GPA, application essay, recommendations. *Other factors considered include:* class rank, standardized test scores (if submitted). High school diploma is required and GED is accepted. Institution is test-optional for entering Fall 2024. Check admissions website for updates. *Academic units required:* 4 English, 3 math, 1 science (1 lab), 2 foreign language, 2 social studies, 4 academic electives.

FINANCIAL AID

Students should submit: FAFSA. *Need-based scholarships/grants offered:* College/university scholarship or grant aid from institutional funds; Federal Pell; Private scholarships; SEOG; State scholarships/grants. *Loan aid offered:* Direct PLUS loans; Direct Subsidized Loans; Direct Unsubsidized Loans. Federal Work-Study Program available. Institutional employment available.

CAMPUS LIFE

Activities: Campus Ministries; Choral groups; Concert band; Dance; Drama/theater; International Student Organization; Jazz band; Model UN; Music ensembles; Pep band; Radio station; Student government; Student newspaper; Television station. **Organizations:** 202 registered organizations, 11 honor societies, 3 religious organizations, 12 fraternities, 12 sororities. **Athletics (Intercollegiate):** *Men:* baseball, basketball, cross-country, golf, ice hockey, lacrosse, rugby, swimming. *Women:* basketball, cross-country, golf, lacrosse, softball, swimming, volleyball.

CAMPUS
Type of school	Private (nonprofit)
Environment	Village

STUDENTS
Undergrad enrollment	5,874
% male/female	45/55
% from out of state	24
% frosh live on campus	61

FINANCIAL FACTS
Annual tuition	$46,380
Room and board	$17,482
Required fees	$2,580

GENERAL ADMISSIONS INFO
Application fee	$55
Regular application deadline	Rolling
Nonfall registration	Yes
Fall 2024 testing policy	Test Optional
Range SAT EBRW	620–700
Range SAT Math	610–690
Range ACT Composite	28–31

ACADEMICS
Student/faculty ratio	15:1
% students returning for sophomore year	83
Most classes have 10–19 students.	

New Jersey

REQUESTING SERVICES FOR STUDENTS WITH LEARNING DIFFERENCES

Phone: 973-313-6003 • www.shu.edu/disability-support-services • Email: dss@shu.edu

Documentation submitted to: Office of Disability Support Services
Separate application required for Services: Yes

Documentation required for:
LD: Psychoeducational evaluation
ADHD: Psychoeducational evaluation
ASD: Psychoeducational evaluation

New Mexico Institute of Mining & Technology

Campus Station, Socorro, NM 87801 • Admissions: 575-835-5424 • www.nmt.edu

Support: S

ACCOMMODATIONS

Allowed in exams:

Calculators	Yes
Dictionary	No
Computer	Yes
Spell-checker	Yes
Extended test time	Yes
Scribe	Yes
Proctors	Yes
Oral exams	Yes
Note-takers	Yes

Support services for students with:

LD	Yes
ADHD	Yes
ASD	Yes
Distraction-reduced environment	Yes
Recording of lecture allowed	Yes
Reading technology	Yes
Audio books	Yes
Other assistive technology	Yes
Priority registration	Yes

Added costs of services:

For LD	No
For ADHD	No
For ASD	No
LD specialists	No
ADHD & ASD coaching	No
ASD specialists	No
Professional tutors	No
Peer tutors	Yes
Max. hours/week for services	Varies
How professors are notified of student approved accommodations	Student and Office of Student Access Services

COLLEGE GRADUATION REQUIREMENTS

Course waivers allowed	No
Course substitutions allowed	No

PROGRAMS/SERVICES FOR STUDENTS WITH LEARNING DIFFERENCES

The Office of Student Access Services (SAS) arranges accommodations for students who have documented disabilities. Students new to SAS must complete a student application to register and request accommodations. It's important to provide documentation that indicates a history of a disability; however, students should not delay meeting with SAS because they are not sure if they have the correct paperwork. At a welcome meeting with a SAS consultant, documentation needs can be determined, as well as discussing accommodation solutions and the next steps. Meetings last 45–50 minutes and may be in person or remote. Once accommodations are approved, students receive an accessibility letter they will deliver to their class instructors and can discuss a plan to ensure access to accommodations.

ADMISSIONS

New Mexico Tech looks to admit students who are interested in STEM. All students must meet the same minimum general requirements for admission for a first-year student: a high school GPA of at least 2.5 or a GED score of 500 or a HiSET combined score of 75+, and a minimum 21 ACT composite score or a 1070 SAT combined score. Applicants with a 3.3 GPA or higher do not need to submit ACT or SAT scores. Test scores are necessary for scholarship consideration. Applicants must submit an official high school transcript, GED score, or HiSET scores to have their application reviewed. Homeschooled students must provide documentation of all courses completed. An applicant who is not admitted may be reevaluated with an updated official high school transcript and/or test scores that satisfy the above admission requirements. Students who do not meet the admission requirements but feel they can succeed at NM Tech may appeal their admission decision.

Additional Information

The Office for Student Learning (OSL) offers free in-person drop-in tutoring across disciplines and at all levels. OSL uses Discord as an online community space where students can talk with other students, ask tutors and staff quick questions, and stay up-to-date with OSL announcements. OSL's Math & Physics Extravaganza is a huge review session to help students prepare for their final exams. Incoming new students can apply for the Summer Math Success Scholarship, which enables them to take a distance education pre-calculus, algebra, or trigonometry class the summer before they start as full-time NM Tech undergraduates. This course advances their math knowledge and math placement and introduces them to math faculty and some of their incoming classmates.

TruTV's Man vs. Cartoon (2009) featured students and researchers at NM Tech's Energetic Materials Research and Testing Center. They were shown a cartoon clip and then attempted to recreate a number of the contraptions and situations found in Wile E. Coyote and the Road Runner cartoons, trying to succeed where Wile E. Coyote had failed.

New Mexico Institute of Mining & Technology

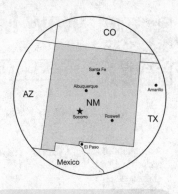

GENERAL ADMISSIONS

Very important factors include: rigor of secondary school record, academic GPA, standardized test scores (if submitted). *Other factors considered include:* class rank. High school diploma is required and GED is accepted. Institution is test-optional for entering Fall 2024. Check admissions website for updates. *Academic units required:* 4 English, 3 math, 2 science (2 labs), 2 social studies, 3 academic electives. *Academic units recommended:* 4 math, 4 science (3 labs), 2 foreign language, 3 social studies.

FINANCIAL AID

Students should submit: FAFSA. *Need-based scholarships/grants offered:* College/university scholarship or grant aid from institutional funds; Federal Pell; Private scholarships; SEOG; State scholarships/grants. *Loan aid offered:* Direct PLUS loans; Direct Subsidized Loans; Direct Unsubsidized Loans. Federal Work-Study Program available. Institutional employment available.

CAMPUS LIFE

Activities: Choral groups; Concert band; Dance; Drama/theater; International Student Organization; Jazz band; Music ensembles; Musical theater; Radio station; Student government; Student newspaper. **Organizations:** 60 registered organizations, 7 honor societies, 3 religious organizations, 0 fraternities, 0 sororities. **Athletics (Intercollegiate):** *Men:* golf, rugby. *Women:* golf, rugby.

CAMPUS	
Type of school	Public
Environment	Village

STUDENTS	
Undergrad enrollment	1,190
% male/female	71/29
% from out of state	10
% frosh live on campus	89

FINANCIAL FACTS	
Annual in-state tuition	$7,030
Annual out-of-state tuition	$22,860
Room and board	$8,624
Required fees	$1,330

GENERAL ADMISSIONS INFO	
Application fee	$15
Regular application deadline	8/1
Nonfall registration	Yes

Fall 2024 testing policy	Test Optional
Range SAT EBRW	570–670
Range SAT Math	580–700
Range ACT Composite	23–30

ACADEMICS	
Student/faculty ratio	10:1
% students returning for sophomore year	77
Most classes have 2-9 students.	

REQUESTING SERVICES FOR STUDENTS WITH LEARNING DIFFERENCES

Phone: 575-835-6209 • www.nmt.edu/student-access-services.php • Email: access@nmt.edu

Documentation submitted to: Student Access Services
Separate application required for Services: Yes

Documentation required for:
 LD: Psychoeducational evaluation
 ADHD: Psychoeducational evaluation
 ASD: Psychoeducational evaluation

New Mexico State University

P.O. Box 30001, Las Cruces, NM 88003-8001 • Admissions: 575-646-3121 • www.nmsu.edu

Support: S

ACCOMMODATIONS

Allowed in exams:

Calculators	Yes
Dictionary	No
Computer	Yes
Spell-checker	No
Extended test time	Yes
Scribe	Yes
Proctors	Yes
Oral exams	Yes
Note-takers	Yes

Support services for students with:

LD	Yes
ADHD	Yes
ASD	Yes
Distraction-reduced environment	Yes
Recording of lecture allowed	Yes
Reading technology	Yes
Audio books	Yes
Other assistive technology	Yes
Priority registration	Yes

Added costs of services:

For LD	No
For ADHD	No
For ASD	No
LD specialists	No
ADHD & ASD coaching	No
ASD specialists	No
Professional tutors	Yes
Peer tutors	Yes
Max. hours/week for services	Varies
How professors are notified of student approved accommodations	Student

COLLEGE GRADUATION REQUIREMENTS

Course waivers allowed	No
Course substitutions allowed	Yes
In what courses: Communications and Foreign Language	

PROGRAMS/SERVICES FOR STUDENTS WITH LEARNING DIFFERENCES

Disability Access Services (DAS) provides a variety of services for qualified students with documented learning disabilities. To receive accommodations, students must complete an online application, submit documentation, and set an appointment with DAS staff to discuss appropriate accommodations, which also considers the courses the student will have. Accommodations may include early registration, alternate or electronic text in several formats, readers, assistive technology, note-taking services, and testing alternatives. The TRIO STEM-H Student Support Services Program is designed to support qualified students, including students with disabilities, pursuing degrees in science, technology, engineering, math, and the health sciences. The STEM-H program includes peer mentoring, academic coaching, academic skills workshops, and more.

ADMISSIONS

All prospective students are eligible for regular general admission to NMSU if they are a graduate of an accredited high school and meet one of the following requirements: a minimum cumulative high school GPA of 2.75; an ACT score of 21 or SAT score of 1060; or rank in the top 20 percent of their graduating class. Official ACT or SAT scores are not required but are beneficial to maximize scholarship opportunities and for math and English placement once enrolled. Applicants who do not meet all the requirements may also be offered admission if their additional information indicates that the student will be successful at NMSU. Applicants who don't meet NMSU admission requirements may be eligible for the Aggie Pathway Program at NMSU and one of four community colleges. After completing 24 college-level credit hours with a minimum 2.0 GPA, students are eligible to transfer to NMSU–Las Cruces. Aggie Pathway features small, interactive courses and regular meetings with peer mentors, faculty, and staff for academic and personal guidance.

Additional Information

The Student Success Center (SSC) offers workshops throughout the year on study skills, learning styles, active listening, note-taking, overcoming procrastination, speed reading, concentration and memory, time management, stress management, critical thinking, effective communication, and effective public speaking and presentations. SSC's Student Lingo also offers over 50 on-demand interactive workshops, available 24/7, to assist in achieving personal, academic, and career goals. Campus Tutoring Services offers free, 60-minute tutoring sessions by appointment, online, and drop-in for the most in-demand courses and additional resources for math, accounting, writing, engineering, and more.

On April Fool's Day 1920, the NMSU Aggies began their tradition of Painting the "A" on the west side of Tortugas Mountain by creating a rough 100-foot letter "A." Today, the landmark "A" is 300 feet tall and 80 feet wide and is the symbol and pride of NMSU.

New Mexico State University

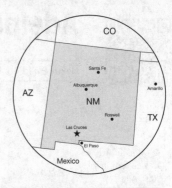

GENERAL ADMISSIONS

Very important factors include: academic GPA, standardized test scores (if submitted). *Other factors considered include:* rigor of secondary school record, class rank. High school diploma is required and GED is accepted. Institution is test-optional for entering Fall 2024. Check admissions website for updates. *Academic units required:* meet the minimum high school course requirements of the state from which the student receives their high school diploma.

FINANCIAL AID

Students should submit: FAFSA. *Need-based scholarships/grants offered:* College/university scholarship or grant aid from institutional funds; Federal Pell; Private scholarships; SEOG; State scholarships/grants. *Loan aid offered:* Direct PLUS loans; Direct Subsidized Loans; Direct Unsubsidized Loans. Federal Work-Study Program available. Institutional employment available.

CAMPUS LIFE

Activities: Campus Ministries; Choral groups; Concert band; Dance; Drama/theater; International Student Organization; Jazz band; Literary magazine; Marching band; Model UN; Music ensembles; Musical theater; Opera; Pep band; Radio station; Student government; Student newspaper; Symphony orchestra; Television station. **Organizations:** Over 400 different student organizations. **Athletics (Intercollegiate):** *Men:* baseball, basketball, cross-country, golf, rugby, softball, ultimate frisbee, volleyball. *Women:* basketball, cross-country, equestrian sports, golf, rugby, softball, swimming, ultimate frisbee, volleyball.

CAMPUS

Type of school	Public
Environment	City

STUDENTS

Undergrad enrollment	11,231
% male/female	42/58
% from out of state	28
% frosh live on campus	53

FINANCIAL FACTS

Annual in-state tuition	$8,409
Annual out-of-state tuition	$26,735
Room and board	$11,252

GENERAL ADMISSIONS INFO

Application fee	$25
Regular application deadline	Rolling
Nonfall registration	Yes

Fall 2024 testing policy	Test Optional
Range SAT EBRW	470–580
Range SAT Math	450–560
Range ACT Composite	17–23

ACADEMICS

Student/faculty ratio	15:1
% students returning for sophomore year	72

Most classes have 10–19 students.

New Mexico

REQUESTING SERVICES FOR STUDENTS WITH LEARNING DIFFERENCES

Phone: 575-646-6840 • studentlife.nmsu.edu/disability-access-services1 • Email: das@nmsu.edu

Documentation submitted to: Disability Access Services
Separate application required for Services: Yes

Documentation required for:
  LD: Psychoeducational evaluation
  ADHD: Psychoeducational evaluation
  ASD: Psychoeducational evaluation

Adelphi University

Nexus Building, Room 111, Garden City, NY 11530 • Admissions: 516-877-3050 • www.adelphi.edu

Support: SP

ACCOMMODATIONS

Allowed in exams:

Calculators	Yes
Dictionary	Yes
Computer	Yes
Spell-checker	Yes
Extended test time	Yes
Scribe	Yes
Proctors	Yes
Oral exams	Yes
Note-takers	Yes

Support services for students with:

LD	Yes
ADHD	Yes
ASD	Yes
Distraction-reduced environment	Yes
Recording of lecture allowed	Yes
Reading technology	Yes
Audio books	Yes
Other assistive technology	Yes
Priority registration	Yes

Added costs of services:

For LD	Yes
For ADHD	Yes
For ASD	Yes
LD specialists	Yes
ADHD & ASD coaching	Yes
ASD specialists	Yes
Professional tutors	Yes
Peer tutors	Yes
Max. hours/week for services	Varies
How professors are notified of student approved accommodations	Student

COLLEGE GRADUATION REQUIREMENTS

Course waivers allowed	No
Course substitutions allowed	Yes
In what courses: Math and Foreign Language	

PROGRAMS/SERVICES FOR STUDENTS WITH LEARNING DIFFERENCES

The Student Access Office (SAO) assists students with disabilities. Once students are accepted, but before registration, they should contact SAO and submit documentation of their disabilities, so that the office may designate appropriate services to meet their needs. Services and accommodations provided by SAO may include alternative textbooks, note-taking, scribes, screen readers, assistive technology, flexibility for attendance, and testing accommodations, such as a reduced-distraction environment or extended time. The Learning Resource Program (LRP) is a fee-based program for students with language-based learning disabilities and/or ADHD that keeps participants on track to earn credits and complete their degree requirements. LRP students meet weekly with a learning specialist, are offered optional group and individual counseling, receive assistance with course and vocational planning, and participate in the "Campus Ally" Program. All first-years enrolled in the program are assigned a "Campus Ally," who are experienced LRP students. Students and Allies meet throughout the first semester. LRP students may participate in the optional three-week LRP Summer Transition Program. Another program that provides individualized academic, social, and vocation support services to neurodiverse students is Bridges to Adelphi; participants include those who self-disclose an autism spectrum diagnosis or other non-verbal and neurological-social disorders.

ADMISSIONS

Applications are reviewed based on individual academic records and cocurricular activities. To be considered, applicants must be graduating or have graduated from a recognized four-year secondary school or provide official proof of the equivalent. Applicants are required to submit one or more letters of recommendation, urged to include a résumé, and encouraged to include an essay. All applicants are considered for merit scholarships with or without test scores. For some students, although their applications may not meet traditional admission requirements, their potential for academic achievement has been identified over the course of interviews with university faculty and staff. In such cases, these admitted students are enrolled in the one-year intensive program, General Studies Learning Community.

Additional Information

The Office of Academic Services and Retention offers students academic advising and support. Peer tutors at the Learning Center provide help with specific courses and classes, and at the Writing Center, with all aspects of the writing process. Additionally, the Center for Career and Professional Development presents workshops on résumé writing and interview skills and shares up-to-date information on off-campus and on-campus part-time employment, seasonal employment, and volunteer opportunities.

Adelphi's campus is registered with the American Public Gardens Association as an arboretum, and the school flower, brown-eyed Susan, grows in abundance. Its colors match the school's: brown for the arts and gold for the sciences. The brown eastern cottontail, Adelphi's unofficial mascot, can also be spotted on campus grounds.

Adelphi University

General Admissions

Very important factors include: rigor of secondary school record. *Important factors include:* class rank, academic GPA, standardized test scores (if submitted), application essay, recommendations. High school diploma is required and GED is accepted. Institution is test-optional for entering Fall 2024. Check admissions website for updates. *Academic units recommended:* 4 English, 3 math, 3 science, 2 foreign language, 2 social studies, 2 academic electives.

Financial Aid

Students should submit: FAFSA; State aid form. *Need-based scholarships/grants offered:* College/university scholarship or grant aid from institutional funds; Federal Pell; Private scholarships; SEOG; State scholarships/grants. *Loan aid offered:* Direct PLUS loans; Direct Subsidized Loans; Direct Unsubsidized Loans. Federal Work-Study Program available. Institutional employment available.

Campus Life

Activities: Campus Ministries; Dance; Drama/theater; International Student Organization; Literary magazine; Radio station; Student government; Student newspaper; Yearbook. **Organizations:** 80 registered organizations, 33 honor societies, 5 religious organizations, 8 fraternities, 10 sororities. **Athletics (Intercollegiate):** *Men:* baseball, basketball, cross-country, equestrian sports, golf, lacrosse, swimming, track/field (indoor), ultimate frisbee. *Women:* basketball, bowling, cross-country, equestrian sports, field hockey, golf, lacrosse, softball, swimming, track/field (indoor), ultimate frisbee, volleyball.

CAMPUS
Type of school	Private (nonprofit)
Environment	Metropolis

STUDENTS
Undergrad enrollment	5,004
% male/female	32/68
% from out of state	7
% frosh live on campus	32

FINANCIAL FACTS
Annual tuition	$42,085
Room and board	$17,193
Required fees	$1,715

GENERAL ADMISSIONS INFO
Application fee	$50
Regular application deadline	Rolling
Nonfall registration	Yes
Fall 2024 testing policy	Test Optional
Range SAT EBRW	560–650
Range SAT Math	550–660
Range ACT Composite	22–29

ACADEMICS
Student/faculty ratio	12:1
% students returning for sophomore year	85

Most classes have 10–19 students.

REQUESTING SERVICES FOR STUDENTS WITH LEARNING DIFFERENCES

Phone: 516-877-3806 • adelphi.edu/access-office/accessibility-support-services • Email: sao@adelphi.edu

Documentation submitted to: Student Access Office
Separate application required for Services: Yes

Documentation required for:
LD: Psychoeducational evaluation
ADHD: Psychoeducational evaluation
ASD: Psychoeducational evaluation

New York

Barnard College

3009 Broadway, New York, NY 10027 • Admissions: 212-854-2014 • www.barnard.edu

Support: CS

ACCOMMODATIONS

Allowed in exams:

Calculators	Yes
Dictionary	Yes
Computer	Yes
Spell-checker	Yes
Extended test time	Yes
Scribe	Yes
Proctors	Yes
Oral exams	No
Note-takers	Yes

Support services for students with:

LD	Yes
ADHD	Yes
ASD	Yes
Distraction-reduced environment	Yes
Recording of lecture allowed	Yes
Reading technology	No
Audio books	Yes
Other assistive technology	No
Priority registration	No

Added costs of services:

For LD	No
For ADHD	No
For ASD	No
LD specialists	Yes
ADHD & ASD coaching	Yes
ASD specialists	No
Professional tutors	No
Peer tutors	Yes
Max. hours/week for services	Varies
How professors are notified of student approved accommodations	Student and Center for Accessibility Resources & Disability Services

COLLEGE GRADUATION REQUIREMENTS

Course waivers allowed	No
Course substitutions allowed	No

PROGRAMS/SERVICES FOR STUDENTS WITH LEARNING DIFFERENCES

The Center for Accessibility Resources & Disability Services (CARDS) is available to any Barnard student living with a disability. All students with disabilities are encouraged to register with CARDS even if they feel accommodations aren't necessary at present; by doing so, there will be no delay in implementation should the need arise. To register, students complete an application, submit documentation, and request a meeting with the CARDS coordinator. The coordinator will explain CARDS policies and procedures for accessing accommodations and create a reasonable accommodation plan for each student.

ADMISSIONS

All applications for admission are thoroughly reviewed by a regional admissions representative and a second reader before the committee comes to a final decision. High school students should have a strong academic foundation in college preparatory subjects: math, science, English, history, and a foreign language. The admission committee has no preference on the submission of standardized test scores, but does require a counselor recommendation, two teacher evaluations, and a personal essay.

Additional Information

First- and second-year students consult with a faculty advisor and class dean on their college plan and academic goals. Once students declare a major, a second advisor who specializes in the chosen field steers students toward graduation and their careers. Faculty and TAs are available during office hours and regularly held review sessions. Students can also be matched with peer tutors to meet for one hour weekly to review course-specific material. Additionally, Help Rooms offer group tutoring in computer science, chemistry, economics, math, Spanish, physics, and more. Students can improve their communication and writing skills with Speaking and Writing Fellows, respectively. And all students have a personal librarian to help them develop strong research practices.

Midnight Breakfast is a tradition at Barnard. College deans, trustees, the president, and staff serve themed breakfast food to over a thousand students the night before finals begin.

Barnard College

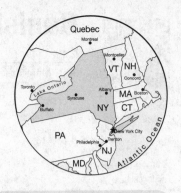

GENERAL ADMISSIONS

Very important factors include: rigor of secondary school record, academic GPA, application essay, recommendations. *Important factors include:* class rank. *Other factors considered include:* standardized test scores (if submitted). High school diploma is required and GED is accepted. Institution is test-optional for entering Fall 2024. Check admissions website for updates. *Academic units recommended:* 4 English, 3 math, 3 science, 3 foreign language, 3 history.

FINANCIAL AID

Students should submit: CSS/Financial Aid Profile; FAFSA; Noncustodial Profile. *Need-based scholarships/grants offered:* College/university scholarship or grant aid from institutional funds; Federal Pell; Private scholarships; SEOG; State scholarships/grants. *Loan aid offered:* Direct PLUS loans; Direct Subsidized Loans; Direct Unsubsidized Loans. Federal Work-Study Program available. Institutional employment available.

CAMPUS LIFE

Activities: Campus Ministries; Choral groups; Concert band; Dance; Drama/theater; International Student Organization; Jazz band; Literary magazine; Marching band; Model UN; Music ensembles; Musical theater; Opera; Pep band; Radio station; Student government; Student newspaper; Student-run film society; Symphony orchestra; Yearbook. **Organizations:** 100 registered organizations, 1 honor societies, 75 religious organizations, 10 sororities. **Athletics (Intercollegiate):** *Women:* basketball, crew/rowing, cross-country, cycling, equestrian sports, field hockey, golf, ice hockey, lacrosse, martial arts, racquetball, rugby, softball, swimming, table tennis, ultimate frisbee, volleyball, water polo.

CAMPUS

Type of school	Private (nonprofit)
Environment	Metropolis

STUDENTS

Undergrad enrollment	2,744
% male/female	0/100
% from out of state	71
% frosh live on campus	91

FINANCIAL FACTS

Annual tuition	$55,781
Room and board	$15,692
Required fees	$1,698

GENERAL ADMISSIONS INFO

Application fee	$75
Regular application deadline	1/1
Nonfall registration	No

Fall 2024 testing policy	Test Optional
Range SAT EBRW	680–747.5
Range SAT Math	670–770
Range ACT Composite	31–34

ACADEMICS

Student/faculty ratio	9:1
% students returning for sophomore year	93

Most classes have 10–19 students.

REQUESTING SERVICES FOR STUDENTS WITH LEARNING DIFFERENCES

Phone: 212-854-4634 • barnard.edu/disabilityservices • Email: cards@barnard.edu

Documentation submitted to: Center for Accessibility Resources & Disability Services
Separate application required for Services: Yes

Documentation required for:
LD: Psychoeducational evaluation
ADHD: Psychoeducational evaluation
ASD: Psychoeducational evaluation

New York

Canisius College

2001 Main Street, Buffalo, NY 14208 • Admissions: 716-888-2200 • www.canisius.edu

Support: CS

ACCOMMODATIONS

Allowed in exams:

Calculators	Yes
Dictionary	Yes
Computer	Yes
Spell-checker	Yes
Extended test time	Yes
Scribe	Yes
Proctors	Yes
Oral exams	Yes
Note-takers	Yes

Support services for students with:

LD	Yes
ADHD	Yes
ASD	Yes
Distraction-reduced environment	Yes
Recording of lecture allowed	Yes
Reading technology	Yes
Audio books	Yes
Other assistive technology	Yes
Priority registration	No
For LD	No
For ADHD	No
For ASD	No
LD specialists	Yes
ADHD & ASD coaching	Yes
ASD specialists	Yes
Professional tutors	Yes
Peer tutors	No
Max. hours/week for services	Varies
How professors are notified of student approved accommodations	Student Accessibility Services

COLLEGE GRADUATION REQUIREMENTS

Course waivers allowed	Yes
In what courses: Primarily Math and Foreign Language	
Course substitutions allowed	Yes
In what courses: Primarily Math and Foreign Languages	

PROGRAMS/SERVICES FOR STUDENTS WITH LEARNING DIFFERENCES

Located within the Griff Center for Student Success, the Student Accessibility Services (SAS) office supports individuals in need of services and accommodations. To receive services, students must register with SAS by completing the appropriate intake form and providing documentation of a disability. The student then meets with an SAS professional to discuss accommodations and review procedures. Accommodations may include alternative texts, notetakers, readers, and assistive listening devices. The Griff Center Proctor Site is a designated area for students that need testing accommodations due to a disability or to make up missed exams. Testing accommodations are determined on a case-by-case basis.

ADMISSIONS

The admission criteria are the same for all students. When reviewing applications, the admissions committee looks for students with at least a solid B average in a college preparatory program of study. Admissions considers the rigor of curriculum to be the most important factor when reviewing applications, and this includes courses being taken in their senior year.

Additional Information

The Academic Mentoring Program helps students navigate various issues that may arise during their academic careers. Students meet regularly with academic mentors to learn time management skills, how to balance coursework, and the study skills they must implement to achieve academic success.

Founded in 1870 by German Jesuits and named for St. Peter Canisius, varsity sports were considered a drain on finances. Around 1902, Andrew Carnegie's donation to Princeton University's rowing team changed opinions at Canisius and schools around the country, and the advent of soliciting philanthropic gifts for sports began. Canisius's first football team hit the field in 1918 and played until 1949 and returned from 1975-2002 with an all-time record of 241-251-26.

Canisius College

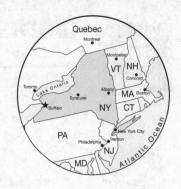

General Admissions

Very important factors include: rigor of secondary school record, academic GPA. *Important factors include:* application essay, recommendations. *Other factors considered include:* class rank. High school diploma is required and GED is accepted. Institution is test-free for entering Fall 2024. Check admissions website for updates. *Academic units required:* 4 English, 3 math, 3 science (2 labs), 2 foreign language, 4 social studies. *Academic units recommended:* 4 math, 4 science (2 labs), 4 foreign language, 4 academic electives.

Financial Aid

Students should submit: FAFSA; State aid form. *Need-based scholarships/grants offered:* College/university scholarship or grant aid from institutional funds; Federal Pell; Private scholarships; SEOG; State scholarships/grants; United Negro College Fund. *Loan aid offered:* Direct PLUS loans; Direct Subsidized Loans; Direct Unsubsidized Loans. Federal Work-Study Program available. Institutional employment available.

Campus Life

Activities: Campus Ministries; Choral groups; Concert band; Dance; Drama/theater; International Student Organization; Jazz band; Literary magazine; Marching band; Model UN; Music ensembles; Musical theater; Pep band; Radio station; Student government; Student newspaper; Student-run film society; Symphony orchestra; Television station; Yearbook. **Organizations:** 140 registered organizations, 17 honor societies, 2 religious organizations, 1 fraternities, 1 sororities. **Athletics (Intercollegiate):** *Men:* baseball, basketball, bowling, crew/rowing, cross-country, golf, ice hockey, lacrosse, martial arts, rugby, swimming, table tennis, ultimate frisbee, volleyball, wrestling. *Women:* basketball, bowling, crew/rowing, cross-country, equestrian sports, field hockey, ice hockey, lacrosse, martial arts, rugby, softball, swimming, table tennis, ultimate frisbee, volleyball.

CAMPUS

Type of school	Private (nonprofit)
Environment	Metropolis

STUDENTS

Undergrad enrollment	2,325
% male/female	50/50
% from out of state	11
% frosh live on campus	62

FINANCIAL FACTS

Annual tuition	$27,000
Room and board	$11,300
Required fees	$1,488

GENERAL ADMISSIONS INFO

Application fee	No fee
Regular application deadline	Rolling
Nonfall registration	Yes
Fall 2024 testing policy	Test Free

ACADEMICS

Student/faculty ratio	11:1
% students returning for sophomore year	83

Most classes have 10–19 students.

REQUESTING SERVICES FOR STUDENTS WITH LEARNING DIFFERENCES

Phone: 716-888-2485 • canisius.edu/student-experience/griff-center-student-success/student-accessibility-services • Email: rapones@canisius.edu

Documentation submitted to: Student Accessibility Services
Separate application required for Services: Yes

Documentation required for:
LD: Psychoeducational evaluation
ADHD: Psychoeducational evaluation
ASD: Psychoeducational evaluation

New York

Clarkson University

Holcroft House, Potsdam, NY 13699 • Admissions: 315-268-6480 • www.clarkson.edu

Support: S

ACCOMMODATIONS

Allowed in exams:

Calculators	Yes
Dictionary	Yes
Computer	Yes
Spell-checker	Yes
Extended test time	Yes
Scribe	Yes
Proctors	Yes
Oral exams	Yes
Note-takers	Yes

Support services for students with:

LD	Yes
ADHD	Yes
ASD	Yes
Distraction-reduced environment	Yes
Recording of lecture allowed	Yes
Reading technology	Yes
Audio books	Yes
Other assistive technology	Yes
Priority registration	Yes

Added costs of services:

For LD	No
For ADHD	No
For ASD	No
LD specialists	No
ADHD & ASD coaching	No
ASD specialists	No
Professional tutors	No
Peer tutors	Yes
Max. hours/week for services	Varies
How professors are notified of student approved accommodations	Student and Office of Accessibility Services

COLLEGE GRADUATION REQUIREMENTS

Course waivers allowed	Yes

In what courses: On a case-by-case basis

Course substitutions allowed	Yes

In what courses: On a case-by-case basis

PROGRAMS/SERVICES FOR STUDENTS WITH LEARNING DIFFERENCES

The Office of Accessibility Services (OAS) determines accommodations and services for students with learning disabilities on a case-by-case basis. Once a student has been admitted to the university, they may submit appropriate documentation to OAS and request accommodations online through Tutoring & Accommodations on their myCU account. OAS conducts an evaluative intake interview with each student and reviews their supplied documentation. Students may also submit their high school IEP or 504 Plan or have their health provider complete and submit the Academic Accommodation Request Form.

ADMISSIONS

The admission process and criteria are the same for all students applying to Clarkson. Counselor and teacher recommendations are required.

Additional Information

There are several no-fee services available to Clarkson University students. Student Support Services (SSS) offers academic support in the form of weekly small-group tutoring, practice exams, and workshops. SSS offers individual academic counseling to students who require assistance building study techniques, time management skills, and strategies for dealing with test-taking stress and improving motivation. The Writing Center delivers one-on-one help with essays, reports, and labs. The Counseling Center promotes the social and emotional development of students and propels students to reach their full potential.

Clarkson University was founded in 1896 and originally named Thomas S. Clarkson Memorial School of Technology, in honor of the pioneering entrepreneur and humanitarian. The school was funded by the sisters of Thomas Clarkson, who gave his life trying to save another. The main campus in Potsdam is located on the historic 640-acre wooded homestead of the Clarkson family in the foothills of Adirondack Park.

Clarkson University

GENERAL ADMISSIONS

Very important factors include: rigor of secondary school record, academic GPA. *Important factors include:* class rank, recommendations. *Other factors considered include:* standardized test scores (if submitted), application essay. High school diploma is required and GED is accepted. Institution is test-optional for entering Fall 2024. Check admissions website for updates. *Academic units required:* 4 English, 3 math, 3 science, 4 social studies. *Academic units recommended:* 4 math, 4 science, 1 foreign language.

FINANCIAL AID

Students should submit: FAFSA; State aid form. *Need-based scholarships/grants offered:* College/university scholarship or grant aid from institutional funds; Federal Pell; Private scholarships; SEOG; State scholarships/grants. *Loan aid offered:* Direct PLUS loans; Direct Subsidized Loans; Direct Unsubsidized Loans. Federal Work-Study Program available. Institutional employment available.

CAMPUS LIFE

Activities: Choral groups; Concert band; Dance; Drama/theater; International Student Organization; Jazz band; Model UN; Music ensembles; Musical theater; Pep band; Radio station; Student government; Student-run film society; Symphony orchestra; Television station; Yearbook. **Organizations:** 206 registered organizations, 26 honor societies, 5 religious organizations, 9 fraternities, 4 sororities. **Athletics (Intercollegiate):** *Men:* baseball, basketball, bowling, crew/rowing, cross-country, cycling, equestrian sports, golf, ice hockey, lacrosse, racquetball, rugby, skiing (nordic/cross-country), softball, swimming, table tennis, track/field (indoor), ultimate frisbee, volleyball, wrestling. *Women:* basketball, bowling, crew/rowing, cross-country, cycling, equestrian sports, ice hockey, lacrosse, racquetball, rugby, skiing (nordic/cross-country), softball, swimming, table tennis, track/field (indoor), ultimate frisbee, volleyball.

CAMPUS
Type of school	Private (nonprofit)
Environment	Village

STUDENTS
Undergrad enrollment	2,790
% male/female	69/31
% from out of state	33
% frosh live on campus	98

FINANCIAL FACTS
Annual tuition	$54,960
Room and board	$18,152
Required fees	$1,298

GENERAL ADMISSIONS INFO
Application fee	$50
Regular application deadline	1/15
Nonfall registration	Yes

Fall 2024 testing policy	Test Optional
Range SAT EBRW	580–680
Range SAT Math	600–700
Range ACT Composite	25–32

ACADEMICS
Student/faculty ratio	12:1
% students returning for sophomore year	84

Most classes have 10–19 students.

REQUESTING SERVICES FOR STUDENTS WITH LEARNING DIFFERENCES

Phone: 315-268-7643 • www.clarkson.edu/accessibility-services • Email: oas@clarkson.edu

Documentation submitted to: Office of Accessibility Services
Separate application required for Services: Yes

Documentation required for:
LD: Psychoeducational evaluation
ADHD: Psychoeducational evaluation
ASD: Psychoeducational evaluation

New York

Colgate University

13 Oak Drive, Hamilton, NY 13346 • Admissions: 315-228-7401 • www.colgate.edu

Support: CS

ACCOMMODATIONS

Allowed in exams:

Calculators	Yes
Dictionary	Yes
Computer	Yes
Spell-checker	Yes
Extended test time	Yes
Scribe	Yes
Proctors	Yes
Oral exams	Yes
Note-takers	Yes

Support services for students with:

LD	Yes
ADHD	Yes
ASD	Yes
Distraction-reduced environment	Yes
Recording of lecture allowed	Yes
Reading technology	Yes
Audio books	Yes
Other assistive technology	Yes
Priority registration	No

Added costs of services:

For LD	No
For ADHD	No
For ASD	No
LD specialists	Yes
ADHD & ASD coaching	Yes
ASD specialists	No
Professional tutors	Yes
Peer tutors	Yes
Max. hours/week for services	Varies
How professors are notified of student approved accommodations	Student and Office of Student Disability Services

COLLEGE GRADUATION REQUIREMENTS

Course waivers allowed	No
Course substitutions allowed	No

PROGRAMS/SERVICES FOR STUDENTS WITH LEARNING DIFFERENCES

The Office of Student Disability Services (OSDS) offers resources and services within the campus-wide support system to students with disabilities. Students can request accommodations through the online portal Accommodate, where they will complete a confidential self-assessment and provide documentation of their disabilities. The portal also allows students to notify professors of their accommodations. Approved accommodations may include notetakers, tutors, readers, assistive technology such as the Notability app, audiobooks, noise-canceling headphones, and smart pens. The director of OSDS works with students to ensure that their needs are met. Colgate believes that being proactive in seeking help and learning to self-advocate are essential skills for success. Students with executive function challenges can consult the two licensed executive function coaches on staff or attend weekly group meetings that are co-facilitated through the Counseling Center.

ADMISSIONS

Admission requirements are the same for all students. The Office of Admissions requires one counselor recommendation, a personal essay, and evidence of extracurricular and substantial academic achievement in the context of a rigorous secondary school curriculum. Colgate is competitive; the average GPA of admitted applicants is 3.95 and 91 percent rank in the top 20 percent of their graduating class. For those submitting test scores, the mid-50 percent of admitted applicants have an SAT score of 1460–1540 or an ACT score of 32–35.

Additional Information

The Writing and Speaking Center provides free, peer and professional tutoring. Students can also visit the center to develop their reading and writing skills, and hone new study strategies. Student Talking Tables bring in experts to discuss time and stress management techniques and are scheduled throughout the year.

Student schedules at Colgate have changed radically in the past 100 years. In the 1830s, students awoke at 4:30 A.M., endured two hours a day of "exercise by manual labor," in between studies, meals, chapel services, and private prayer; bedtime was at 9:30 P.M.

Colgate University

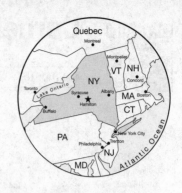

General Admissions

Very important factors include: rigor of secondary school record, class rank, academic GPA. *Important factors include:* standardized test scores (if submitted), application essay, recommendations. High school diploma is required and GED is accepted. Institution is test-optional for entering Fall 2024. Check admissions website for updates. *Academic units required:* 4 English, 3 math, 3 science (2 labs), 3 foreign language, 3 social studies. *Academic units recommended:* 4 math, 4 science (4 labs), 4 foreign language, 4 social studies.

Financial Aid

Students should submit: Business/Farm Supplement; CSS/Financial Aid Profile; FAFSA; Noncustodial Profile. *Need-based scholarships/grants offered:* College/university scholarship or grant aid from institutional funds; Federal Pell; SEOG. *Loan aid offered:* Direct PLUS loans; Direct Subsidized Loans; Direct Unsubsidized Loans. Federal Work-Study Program available. Institutional employment available.

Campus Life

Activities: Campus Ministries; Choral groups; Concert band; Dance; Drama/theater; International Student Organization; Jazz band; Literary magazine; Model UN; Music ensembles; Musical theater; Opera; Pep band; Radio station; Student government; Student newspaper; Symphony orchestra; Yearbook. **Organizations:** 196 registered organizations, 12 honor societies, 11 religious organizations, 5 fraternities, 3 sororities. **Athletics (Intercollegiate):** *Men:* baseball, basketball, bowling, crew/rowing, cross-country, equestrian sports, golf, ice hockey, lacrosse, rugby, swimming, track/field (indoor), ultimate frisbee, volleyball, water polo. *Women:* basketball, bowling, crew/rowing, cross-country, equestrian sports, field hockey, ice hockey, lacrosse, rugby, softball, swimming, track/field (indoor), ultimate frisbee, volleyball, water polo.

CAMPUS
Type of school	Private (nonprofit)
Environment	Rural

STUDENTS
Undergrad enrollment	3,124
% male/female	45/55
% from out of state	76
% frosh live on campus	100

FINANCIAL FACTS
Annual tuition	$66,622
Room and board	$16,790
Required fees	$402

GENERAL ADMISSIONS INFO
Application fee	$60
Regular application deadline	1/15
Nonfall registration	No

Fall 2024 testing policy	Test Optional
Range SAT EBRW	700–750
Range SAT Math	710–780
Range ACT Composite	32–35

ACADEMICS
Student/faculty ratio	9:1
% students returning for sophomore year	94

Most classes have 10–19 students.

REQUESTING SERVICES FOR STUDENTS WITH LEARNING DIFFERENCES

Phone: 315-228-6955 • www.colgate.edu/about/offices-centers-institutes/centers-institutes/center-learning-teaching-and-research/office • Email: elester@colgate.edu

Documentation submitted to: Office of Student Disability Services
Separate application required for Services: Yes

Documentation required for:
LD: Psychoeducational evaluation
ADHD: Psychoeducational evaluation
ASD: Psychoeducational evaluation

New York

Cornell University

410 Thurston Avenue, Ithaca, NY 14850 • Admissions: 607-255-5241 • www.cornell.edu

(Support: S)

ACCOMMODATIONS

Allowed in exams:	
Calculators	Yes
Dictionary	Yes
Computer	Yes
Spell-checker	Yes
Extended test time	Yes
Scribe	Yes
Proctors	Yes
Oral exams	Yes
Note-takers	Yes
Support services for students with:	
LD	Yes
ADHD	Yes
ASD	Yes
Distraction-reduced environment	Yes
Recording of lecture allowed	Yes
Reading technology	Yes
Audio books	Yes
Other assistive technology	Yes
Priority registration	No
Added costs of services:	
For LD	No
For ADHD	No
For ASD	No
LD specialists	No
ADHD & ASD coaching	No
ASD specialists	No
Professional tutors	No
Peer tutors	Yes
Max. hours/week for services	Varies
How professors are notified of student approved accommodations	Student

COLLEGE GRADUATION REQUIREMENTS

Course waivers allowed	No
Course substitutions allowed	No

PROGRAMS/SERVICES FOR STUDENTS WITH LEARNING DIFFERENCES

The university provides support services through Student Disabilities Services (SDS). There is no specific program designed for students with learning disabilities. Incoming first-year students should submit the Disability Self-Disclosure Form to the SDS and request accommodations as soon as possible. SDS encourages students to self-advocate and will only communicate with students, not parents, about accommodations. Depending on an individual student's needs, accommodations such as assistive technology may include text-to-speech, screen readers, speech-to-text, captions and transcriptions, and audio recordings, as well as reading, writing, and note-taking tools. Disability representatives are the liaison between SDS and other college offices involving disability issues.

ADMISSIONS

All students applying to Cornell are expected to meet the same admissions criteria. Recommendations and supplemental essays are required. Students applying to the architecture program must have an interview during the admission process. Cornell University encourages students applying to the Department of Art or Urban and Regional Studies to request an interview. Interviews are not offered to any other applicants.

Additional Information

There are several student-run organizations for students with disabilities. Access Johnson is a business club for neurodiverse students and others who self-identify. Project LETS (Let US Erase the Stigma) is a community of students with different types of disabilities, including students who identify as neurodivergent or neurotypical. Students do not need an official diagnosis to join.

Bill Nye, "the Science Guy," graduated with a BS in mechanical engineering in 1977 after studying at Cornell's Sibley School of Mechanical and Aerospace Engineering. He learned from Carl Sagan while enrolled in his astronomy class, and again, at his 10-year reunion. When Bill Nye mentioned his science TV idea to Sagan, Mr. Sagan said, "...Kids resonate to pure science rather than technology." Bill Nye The Science Guy was nominated for 23 Emmy Awards and won 19.

Cornell University

General Admissions

Very important factors include: rigor of secondary school record, academic GPA, application essay, recommendations. *Important factors include:* class rank. *Other factors considered include:* standardized test scores (if submitted). Institution is test-optional for entering Fall 2024. Check admissions website for updates. *Academic units recommended:* 4 English, 3 math, 3 science, 3 foreign language, 3 social studies.

Financial Aid

Students should submit: CSS/Financial Aid Profile; FAFSA. *Need-based scholarships/grants offered:* College/university scholarship or grant aid from institutional funds; Federal Pell; Private scholarships; SEOG; State scholarships/grants. *Loan aid offered:* Direct PLUS loans; Direct Subsidized Loans; Direct Unsubsidized Loans. Federal Work-Study Program available. Institutional employment available.

Campus Life

Activities: Campus Ministries; Choral groups; Concert band; Dance; Drama/theater; International Student Organization; Jazz band; Literary magazine; Marching band; Model UN; Music ensembles; Musical theater; Pep band; Radio station; Student government; Student newspaper; Student-run film society; Symphony orchestra; Television station; Yearbook. **Organizations:** 1296 registered organizations, 1 honor societies, 66 religious organizations, 34 fraternities, 19 sororities. **Athletics (Intercollegiate):** *Men:* baseball, basketball, bowling, crew/rowing, cross-country, cycling, equestrian sports, golf, gymnastics, ice hockey, lacrosse, martial arts, rugby, skiing (nordic/cross-country), softball, swimming, table tennis, track/field (indoor), ultimate frisbee, volleyball. *Women:* basketball, crew/rowing, cross-country, cycling, equestrian sports, field hockey, golf, gymnastics, ice hockey, lacrosse, martial arts, rugby, skiing (nordic/cross-country), softball, swimming, table tennis, track/field (indoor), ultimate frisbee, volleyball.

CAMPUS
Type of school	Private (nonprofit)
Environment	Town

STUDENTS
Undergrad enrollment	15,450
% male/female	46/54
% from out of state	63
% frosh live on campus	100

FINANCIAL FACTS
Annual tuition	$60,286
Room and board	$16,446
Required fees	$729

GENERAL ADMISSIONS INFO
Application fee	$80
Regular application deadline	1/2
Nonfall registration	Yes

Fall 2024 testing policy	Test Optional
Range SAT EBRW	700–760
Range SAT Math	750–800
Range ACT Composite	33–35

ACADEMICS
Student/faculty ratio	9:1
% students returning for sophomore year	97

Most classes have 10–19 students.

REQUESTING SERVICES FOR STUDENTS WITH LEARNING DIFFERENCES

Phone: 607-254-4545 • sds.cornell.edu/ • Email: sds_cu@cornell.edu

Documentation submitted to: Student Disability Services
Separate application required for Services: Yes

Documentation required for:
LD: Psychoeducational evaluation
ADHD: Psychoeducational evaluation
ASD: Psychoeducational evaluation

New York

Hobart and William Smith Colleges

629 South Main Street, Geneva, NY 14456 • Admissions: 315-781-3622 • www.hws.edu

Support: CS

ACCOMMODATIONS

Allowed in exams:	
Calculators	Yes
Dictionary	Yes
Computer	Yes
Spell-checker	Yes
Extended test time	Yes
Scribe	Yes
Proctors	Yes
Oral exams	Yes
Note-takers	Yes
Support services for students with:	
LD	Yes
ADHD	Yes
ASD	Yes
Distraction-reduced environment	Yes
Recording of lecture allowed	Yes
Reading technology	Yes
Audio books	Yes
Other assistive technology	Yes
Priority registration	Yes
Added costs of services:	
For LD	No
For ADHD	No
For ASD	No
LD specialists	Yes
ADHD & ASD coaching	No
ASD specialists	No
Professional tutors	No
Peer tutors	Yes
Max. hours/week for services	Varies
How professors are notified of student approved accommodations	Office of Disability Services

COLLEGE GRADUATION REQUIREMENTS

Course waivers allowed	No
Course substitutions allowed	Yes
In what courses: Foreign Language	

PROGRAMS/SERVICES FOR STUDENTS WITH LEARNING DIFFERENCES

The Office of Disability Services in the Center for Teaching and Learning supports students with disabilities through individualized accommodations and student development. Students requesting accommodations for the first time should upload supporting documentation and complete the accommodation request intake form on the Accommodate portal. Once students submit their request, they can then meet with Disability Services to discuss a personalized plan.

ADMISSIONS

The admissions process is the same as for all students. The average GPA of admitted students is 3.54, ranking (when provided) in the top 25 percent of their class. Hobart and William Smith colleges are committed to a holistic review of every applicant and welcome admission interviews when possible. Standardized test scores are not required, however, of submitted scores, 75 percent of admitted students scored 1200 or higher on the SAT, and 40 percent scored 30 or higher on the ACT.

Additional Information

Study Mentors meet one-on-one with students to collaborate on learning strategies and study practices, and ensure they are utilizing all available campus resources. Appointments can take place in the Center for Teaching and Learning (CTL) or via Zoom. Teaching Fellows (TFs) are peer-learning facilitators nominated by faculty and trained by the CTL to provide ongoing academic support to all students. TFs are available to students in a group setting during drop-in hours Sunday through Thursday evenings.

Hobart College opened in 1822 (as Geneva College), and saw a number of pioneering students in the 19th century. In 1836, Isaiah George DeGrasse was the first African American to enroll in the Medical College, though financial difficulties prevented him from graduating. Peter Wilson of the Cayuga Nation was the first Native American graduate in 1844 and became a noted orator and practitioner of medicine. In 1849, Elizabeth Blackwell was the first woman in America to receive the degree of Doctor of Medicine, graduating at the top of her class.

Hobart and William Smith Colleges

GENERAL ADMISSIONS

Very important factors include: rigor of secondary school record, academic GPA. *Important factors include:* class rank, application essay, recommendations. *Other factors considered include:* standardized test scores (if submitted). High school diploma is required and GED is accepted. Institution is test-optional for entering Fall 2024. Check admissions website for updates. *Academic units required:* 4 English, 3 math, 3 science (2 labs), 2 foreign language, 4 social studies, 2 academic electives. *Academic units recommended:* 4 math, 4 science, 3 foreign language, 4 academic electives.

FINANCIAL AID

Students should submit: FAFSA; State aid form. *Need-based scholarships/grants offered:* College/university scholarship or grant aid from institutional funds; Federal Pell; Private scholarships; SEOG; State scholarships/grants. *Loan aid offered:* Direct PLUS loans; Direct Subsidized Loans; Direct Unsubsidized Loans. Federal Work-Study Program available. Institutional employment available.

CAMPUS LIFE

Activities: Campus Ministries; Choral groups; Concert band; Dance; Drama/theater; International Student Organization; Jazz band; Literary magazine; Model UN; Music ensembles; Radio station; Student government; Student newspaper. **Organizations:** 110 registered organizations, 12 honor societies, 1 religious organizations, 8 fraternities, 1 sororities. **Athletics (Intercollegiate):** *Men:* baseball, basketball, crew/rowing, cross-country, equestrian sports, golf, ice hockey, lacrosse, rugby, swimming, ultimate frisbee, volleyball. *Women:* basketball, bowling, crew/rowing, cross-country, equestrian sports, field hockey, golf, ice hockey, lacrosse, rugby, swimming, ultimate frisbee, volleyball.

CAMPUS
Type of school	Private (nonprofit)
Environment	Village

STUDENTS
Undergrad enrollment	1,512
% male/female	49/51
% from out of state	57
% frosh live on campus	100

FINANCIAL FACTS
Annual tuition	$60,350
Room and board	$16,910
Required fees	$1,375

GENERAL ADMISSIONS INFO
Application fee	No fee
Regular application deadline	2/1
Nonfall registration	Yes

Fall 2024 testing policy	Test Optional
Range SAT EBRW	610–700
Range SAT Math	600–700
Range ACT Composite	27–32

ACADEMICS
Student/faculty ratio	9:1
% students returning for sophomore year	86
Most classes have 10–19 students.	

REQUESTING SERVICES FOR STUDENTS WITH LEARNING DIFFERENCES

Phone: 315-781-3351 • www.hws.edu/centers/ctl/disability-services.aspx • Email: ctl@hws.edu

Documentation submitted to: Disability Services
Separate application required for Services: Yes

Documentation required for:
 LD: Psychoeducational evaluation
 ADHD: Psychoeducational evaluation
 ASD: Psychoeducational evaluation

Hofstra University

100 Hofstra University, Hempstead, NY 11549 • Admissions: 516-463-6700 • www.hofstra.edu

(Support: SP)

ACCOMMODATIONS

Allowed in exams:

Calculators	Yes
Dictionary	Yes
Computer	Yes
Spell-checker	Yes
Extended test time	Yes
Scribe	Yes
Proctors	Yes
Oral exams	Yes
Note-takers	Yes

Support services for students with:

LD	Yes
ADHD	Yes
ASD	Yes
Distraction-reduced environment	Yes
Recording of lecture allowed	Yes
Reading technology	Yes
Audio books	Yes
Other assistive technology	Yes
Priority registration	No

Added costs of services:

For LD	Yes
For ADHD	Yes
For ASD	Yes
LD specialists	Yes
ADHD & ASD coaching	Yes
ASD specialists	Yes
Professional tutors	No
Peer tutors	Yes
Max. hours/week for services	Varies
How professors are notified of student approved accommodations	Student

COLLEGE GRADUATION REQUIREMENTS

Course waivers allowed	No
Course substitutions allowed	Yes
In what courses: Foreign Language	

PROGRAMS/SERVICES FOR STUDENTS WITH LEARNING DIFFERENCES

Student Access Services (SAS) arranges academic accommodations and provides support for students with disabilities. To receive services, students must formally disclose their disability, register with SAS, and submit documentation for review. By registering, current and prospective students can access all SAS forms. Students registered with SAS have the option of enrolling in the fee-based Program for Academic Learning Skills (PALS), which helps students develop their academic and study skills. Covered topics include adjusting to college life, stress management, and classroom strategies and skills. Students enrolled in PALS have regularly scheduled one-on-one meetings with a qualified SAS learning specialist.

ADMISSIONS

All students must meet the same admission criteria. The average GPA for accepted students is 3.7, and most students have a 3.0 GPA or higher. The mid-range SAT scores for students who choose to submit them is 1210–1400. Students may be requested to interview with admission staff or SAS to assess fit for the university.

Additional Information

All students have access to the tutoring program, academic workshops, and success advisors through the Center for Academic Excellence. Success advisors support students who seek to develop strategies in organization, time management, and study methods. Group tutoring is available for biology, chemistry, and physics, and one-on-one appointments can be made for tutoring in other courses. All students can participate in workshops that cover short- and long-term goal setting, mindfulness, learning styles, and note-taking tips.

Hofstra alumnus Laurence Herbert became a color matcher at Pantone® in 1956 and bought the company in 1962. In 1963, he invented the Pantone Matching System®, a global color standard. In 2013, the Laurence Herbert School of Communication was so named to honor Herbert's support of the university and his "revolutionary impact on print and design." Pantone® color chip blocks decorate the walls throughout the building.

Hofstra University

GENERAL ADMISSIONS

Very important factors include: rigor of secondary school record, class rank, academic GPA, application essay, recommendations. *Other factors considered include:* standardized test scores (if submitted). High school diploma is required and GED is accepted. Institution is test-optional for entering Fall 2024. Check admissions website for updates. *Academic units required:* 4 English, 3 math, 3 science (1 labs), 2 foreign language, 3 social studies. *Academic units recommended:* 4 math, 4 science (2 labs), 3 foreign language, 4 social studies.

FINANCIAL AID

Students should submit: FAFSA; State aid form. *Need-based scholarships/grants offered:* College/university scholarship or grant aid from institutional funds; Federal Pell; Private scholarships; SEOG; State scholarships/grants; United Negro College Fund. *Loan aid offered:* Direct PLUS loans; Direct Subsidized Loans; Direct Unsubsidized Loans. Federal Work-Study Program available. Institutional employment available.

CAMPUS LIFE

Activities: Campus Ministries; Choral groups; Concert band; Dance; Drama/theater; Literary magazine; Model UN; Music ensembles; Musical theater; Pep band; Radio station; Student government; Student newspaper; Student-run film society; Television station. **Organizations:** 223 registered organizations, 39 honor societies, 6 religious organizations, 9 fraternities, 10 sororities. **Athletics (Intercollegiate):** *Men:* baseball, basketball, bowling, cross-country, equestrian sports, golf, ice hockey, lacrosse, rugby, skiing (nordic/cross-country), swimming, table tennis, track/field (indoor), ultimate frisbee, volleyball, wrestling. *Women:* basketball, bowling, cross-country, equestrian sports, field hockey, golf, ice hockey, lacrosse, rugby, skiing (nordic/cross-country), softball, swimming, table tennis, track/field (indoor), ultimate frisbee, volleyball.

CAMPUS

Type of school	Private (nonprofit)
Environment	City

STUDENTS

Undergrad enrollment	6,051
% male/female	43/57
% from out of state	33
% frosh live on campus	57

FINANCIAL FACTS

Annual tuition	$52,215
Room and board	$17,960
Required fees	$1,115

GENERAL ADMISSIONS INFO

Application fee	$70
Regular application deadline	Rolling
Nonfall registration	Yes
Fall 2024 testing policy	Test Optional
Range SAT EBRW	600–680
Range SAT Math	590–690
Range ACT Composite	26–31

ACADEMICS

Student/faculty ratio	13:1
% students returning for sophomore year	83

Most classes have 10–19 students.

REQUESTING SERVICES FOR STUDENTS WITH LEARNING DIFFERENCES

Phone: 516-463-7075 • www.hofstra.edu/SAS • Email: SAS@hofstra.edu

Documentation submitted to: Student Access Services
Separate application required for Services: Yes

Documentation required for:
LD: Psychoeducational evaluation
ADHD: Psychoeducational evaluation
ASD: Psychoeducational evaluation

New York

Iona University

715 North Avenue, New Rochelle, NY 10801 • Admissions: 914-633-2502 • www.iona.edu

(**Support: SP**)

ACCOMMODATIONS

Allowed in exams:

Calculators	Yes
Dictionary	Yes
Computer	Yes
Spell-checker	Yes
Extended test time	Yes
Scribe	Yes
Proctors	Yes
Oral exams	Yes
Note-takers	Yes

Support services for students with:

LD	Yes
ADHD	Yes
ASD	Yes
Distraction-reduced environment	Yes
Recording of lecture allowed	Yes
Reading technology	Yes
Audio books	Yes
Other assistive technology	Yes
Priority registration	Yes

Added costs of services:

For LD	No
For ADHD	No
For ASD	No
LD specialists	Yes
ADHD & ASD coaching	Yes
ASD specialists	Yes
Professional tutors	No
Peer tutors	Yes
Max. hours/week for services	Varies
How professors are notified of student approved accommodations	Student

COLLEGE GRADUATION REQUIREMENTS

Course waivers allowed	Yes
In what courses: Foreign Language	
Course substitutions allowed	Yes
In what courses: Foreign Language	

PROGRAMS/SERVICES FOR STUDENTS WITH LEARNING DIFFERENCES

The Accessibility Services Office (ASO) provides accommodations to students with disabilities. Once students have been approved for accommodations, ASO generates letters for students to give to professors stating their academic accommodations. Iona University also provides a fee-based Comprehensive Assistance Program (CAP), which creates an individualized plan for academic, personal, and career services for students with learning disabilities, ADHD, and ASD. Students should submit an application for CAP when applying for general admission. Documentation must be submitted, and appropriate accommodations will be determined between the student and the CAP counselor. CAP provides academic coaching, and the staff works with students to help them become self-confident and effectively handle stress.

ADMISSIONS

All applicants are expected to meet the same admission criteria. Students must demonstrate a commitment to academic success by completing a college prep curriculum and maintaining a 3.0 GPA to be considered for admission to Iona. All students are considered for scholarships as part of the application review process. Students applying to CAP are encouraged to attend an informational session to learn about CAP. The application is submitted along with the general admissions application, and documentation must be submitted to support the application's details before meeting with a CAPs counselor. Students admitted to the CAPs program are required to participate in a week-long residential program on campus prior to beginning classes in the fall.

Additional Information

Students meet with CAP Counselors twice weekly to discuss self-advocacy, test strategies, time management, and note-taking. Students receive priority registration access and one-on-one support from CAP. The Office of Student Success aids all students in adjusting to college, and collaborates with CAP, the Academic Resource Center, the Accessibility Service Offices, and the Counseling and Advising Centers.

For over 40 years, Iona has chosen the week following Veterans Day to dedicate academic and cocurricular attention to peacemaking. This annual observance honors the values of peace and social justice integral to Iona's heritage and the dedication of veterans to the cause of peace, freedom, and justice. Each year, the university chooses a theme for its Week of the Peacemaker and, through lectures, films, and activities, supports the year's theme.

Iona University

General Admissions

Very important factors include: rigor of secondary school record, academic GPA. *Other factors considered include:* class rank, standardized test scores (if submitted), application essay, recommendations. High school diploma is required and GED is accepted. Institution is test-optional for entering Fall 2024. Check admissions website for updates. *Academic units recommended:* 4 English, 4 math, 3 science (2 labs), 2 foreign language, 3 social studies.

Financial Aid

Students should submit: FAFSA; State aid form. *Need-based scholarships/grants offered:* College/university scholarship or grant aid from institutional funds; Federal Pell; Private scholarships; SEOG; State scholarships/grants. *Loan aid offered:* Direct PLUS loans; Direct Subsidized Loans; Direct Unsubsidized Loans. Federal Work-Study Program available. Institutional employment available.

Campus Life

Activities: Campus Ministries; Choral groups; Concert band; Dance; Drama/theater; International Student Organization; Literary magazine; Model UN; Music ensembles; Musical theater; Pep band; Radio station; Student government; Student newspaper; Student-run film society; Television station; Yearbook. **Organizations:** 80 registered organizations, 26 honor societies, 4 fraternities, 6 sororities. **Athletics (Intercollegiate):** *Men:* baseball, basketball, crew/rowing, cross-country, golf, martial arts, rugby, swimming, track/field (indoor), water polo. *Women:* basketball, crew/rowing, cross-country, lacrosse, martial arts, softball, swimming, track/field (indoor), volleyball, water polo.

CAMPUS

Type of school	Private (nonprofit)
Environment	City

STUDENTS

Undergrad enrollment	2,633
% male/female	48/52
% from out of state	21
% frosh live on campus	56

FINANCIAL FACTS

Annual tuition	$42,128
Room and board	$17,200
Required fees	$2,200

GENERAL ADMISSIONS INFO

Application fee	No fee
Regular application deadline	2/15
Nonfall registration	Yes

Fall 2024 testing policy	Test Optional
Range SAT EBRW	520–610
Range SAT Math	510–600
Range ACT Composite	22–31

ACADEMICS

Student/faculty ratio	15:1
% students returning for sophomore year	80

REQUESTING SERVICES FOR STUDENTS WITH LEARNING DIFFERENCES

Phone: 914-633-2366 • www.iona.edu/offices/accessibility-services • Email: access@iona.edu

Documentation submitted to: Accessibility Services Office and College Assistance Program
Separate application required for Services: Yes

Documentation required for:
LD: Psychoeducational evaluation
ADHD: Psychoeducational evaluation
ASD: Psychoeducational evaluation

New York

Le Moyne College

1419 Salt Springs Road, Syracuse, NY 13214-1301 • Admissions: 315-445-4300 • lemoyne.edu

Support: S

ACCOMMODATIONS

Allowed in exams:

Calculators	Yes
Dictionary	Yes
Computer	Yes
Spell-checker	Yes
Extended test time	Yes
Scribe	No
Proctors	Yes
Oral exams	No
Note-takers	Yes

Support services for students with:

LD	No
ADHD	No
ASD	No
Distraction-reduced environment	Yes
Recording of lecture allowed	Yes
Reading technology	Yes
Audio books	Yes
Other assistive technology	Yes
Priority registration	Yes

Added costs of services:

For LD	No
For ADHD	No
For ASD	No
LD specialists	No
ADHD & ASD coaching	No
ASD specialists	No
Professional tutors	No
Peer tutors	Yes
Max. hours/week for services	Varies
How professors are notified of student approved accommodations	Student

COLLEGE GRADUATION REQUIREMENTS

Course waivers allowed	No
Course substitutions allowed	Yes
In what courses: Case-by-case basis	

PROGRAMS/SERVICES FOR STUDENTS WITH LEARNING DIFFERENCES

The director of Disability Support Services works with students to determine reasonable academic accommodations. The process includes a review of previously administered diagnostic tests and an intake meeting. Students with documented disabilities gain access to supplemental academic advising, coaching to assist students in developing self-advocacy skills, and a staff liaison and advocate who works with students and faculty or staff to ensure accommodations are being provided. Students are required to meet with the director of Disability Support each semester to reevaluate services and update the student's file to confirm the usefulness of current services or provide recommendations for alternate services.

ADMISSIONS

Student applications are reviewed for both academic rigor and leadership involvement. Admitted students have a minimum 3.6 GPA. Students who do not have 4 years of math can be admitted but will be required to complete a noncredit intermediate algebra course in college before they can take any math course for credit. Students who plan to major in biology, chemistry, math, or physics must have 4 years of high school math before enrolling at Le Moyne.

Additional Information

During the fall of their first year, students are assigned an academic advisor in the Student Success Center. Additional support offered through the Student Success Center includes tutoring, group study, learning-strategy skills, time management, testing, and note-taking.

Iggy the Dolphin has historic and current significance at Le Moyne. A dolphin was a common symbol with early Christians for its grace, swiftness, tenderness, and desire for knowledge. As a symbol and mascot of Le Moyne, Iggy inspires and guides, adds a positive environment, and gives hope. Iggy's energy is always unmatched. The saying around Le Moyne is, "Phins don't swim alone."

Le Moyne College

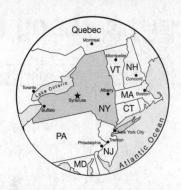

General Admissions

Very important factors include: rigor of secondary school record, academic GPA. *Important factors include:* class rank, application essay, recommendations. *Other factors considered include:* standardized test scores (if submitted). High school diploma is required and GED is accepted. Institution is test-optional for entering Fall 2024. Check admissions website for updates. *Academic units required:* 4 English, 3 math, 3 science, 3 foreign language, 4 social studies. *Academic units recommended:* 4 math, 4 science (3 labs), 4 foreign language.

Financial Aid

Students should submit: FAFSA; State aid form. *Need-based scholarships/grants offered:* College/university scholarship or grant aid from institutional funds; Federal Pell; Private scholarships; SEOG; State scholarships/grants. *Loan aid offered:* Direct PLUS loans; Direct Subsidized Loans; Direct Unsubsidized Loans. Federal Work-Study Program available. Institutional employment available.

Campus Life

Activities: Campus Ministries; Choral groups; Concert band; Dance; Drama/theater; International Student Organization; Jazz band; Literary magazine; Model UN; Music ensembles; Musical theater; Radio station; Student government; Student newspaper; Student-run film society; Symphony orchestra; Television station; Yearbook. **Organizations:** 80 registered organizations, 20 honor societies, 9 religious organizations, 0 fraternities, 0 sororities. **Athletics (Intercollegiate):** *Men:* baseball, basketball, crew/rowing, cross-country, equestrian sports, golf, ice hockey, lacrosse, martial arts, rugby, swimming, track/field (indoor), ultimate frisbee. *Women:* basketball, crew/rowing, cross-country, equestrian sports, field hockey, golf, lacrosse, martial arts, rugby, softball, swimming, track/field (indoor), ultimate frisbee, volleyball.

CAMPUS

Type of school	Private (nonprofit)
Environment	City

STUDENTS

Undergrad enrollment	2,459
% male/female	39/61
% from out of state	7
% frosh live on campus	74

FINANCIAL FACTS

Annual tuition	$36,320
Room and board	$15,050
Required fees	$1,130

GENERAL ADMISSIONS INFO

Application fee	No fee
Regular application deadline	Rolling
Nonfall registration	Yes

Fall 2024 testing policy	Test Optional
Range SAT EBRW	560–640
Range SAT Math	570–650
Range ACT Composite	26–31

ACADEMICS

Student/faculty ratio	12:1
% students returning for sophomore year	86

Most classes have 10–19 students.

REQUESTING SERVICES FOR STUDENTS WITH LEARNING DIFFERENCES

Phone: 315-445-4118 • www.lemoyne.edu/dss • Email: dss@lemoyne.edu

Documentation submitted to: Disability Support Services
Separate application required for Services: Yes

Documentation required for:
LD: Psychoeducational evaluation
ADHD: Psychoeducational evaluation
ASD: Psychoeducational evaluation

New York

Long Island University Post

720 Northern Boulevard, Brookville, NY 11548 • Admissions: 516-299-2900 • www.liu.edu

Support: CS

ACCOMMODATIONS

Allowed in exams:

Calculators	Yes
Dictionary	No
Computer	Yes
Spell-checker	Yes
Extended test time	Yes
Scribe	Yes
Proctors	Yes
Oral exams	Yes
Note-takers	Yes

Support services for students with:

LD	Yes
ADHD	Yes
ASD	Yes
Distraction-reduced environment	Yes
Recording of lecture allowed	Yes
Reading technology	Yes
Audio books	No
Other assistive technology	No
Priority registration	No

Added costs of services:

For LD	No
For ADHD	No
For ASD	No
LD specialists	Yes
ADHD & ASD coaching	Yes
ASD specialists	No
Professional tutors	No
Peer tutors	No
Max. hours/week for services	Varies
How professors are notified of student approved accommodations	Student

COLLEGE GRADUATION REQUIREMENTS

Course waivers allowed	No
Course substitutions allowed	Yes

In what courses: Math and Foreign Language

PROGRAMS/SERVICES FOR STUDENTS WITH LEARNING DIFFERENCES

Students with documented disabilities access support services through the Learning Center's Disability Support Services. Services include the tutoring program, writing center, and academic success workshops. By completing the request for accommodations, students are able to obtain testing accommodations, note-taking assistance, and technology accommodations. To maintain access to services, students must disclose their disability to the Learning Center team, submit appropriate documentation for review, participate in the intake interview with the accommodations specialist, complete the accommodation forms for each class, and renew the accommodation forms each semester.

ADMISSIONS

Long Island University Post (LIU Post) considers student academic rigor, test scores, and recommendation letters for admissions. The university is test-optional, but for students submitting scores, the minimum ACT score is 19 and 1000 for the SAT. The minimum GPA is 2.5 with college prep courses in high school.

Additional Information

LIU Promise is the Long Island University system-wide commitment that students will receive access to a success coach who will serve as a mentor and resource for every aspect of the college experience. The Learning Center and LIU Promise host Academic Success Workshops each semester that help students with general learning and academic skills, including time management, organization skills, and test-taking strategies. Additionally, LIU Promise hosts workshops each semester for career- and internship-related topics, including building a résumé and cover letter, effective networking, building a LinkedIn profile, and enhancing interview skills. The Writing Center offers free, one-to-one, student-centered conferencing on any writing project.

DID YOU KNOW?

Southampton College, the easternmost campus of LIU, closed in 2005. But in 1996, it was well known for its "green" environmental studies program, and Kermit the Frog was invited to deliver the commencement address. Of course, Kermit accepted and showed up to the ceremony dressed in his own cap and robe. He thanked the students on behalf of all animals for their dedication to saving the environment. Kermit was also awarded an honorary doctorate of amphibious letters—the very first of its kind.

Long Island University Post

GENERAL ADMISSIONS

Very important factors include: rigor of secondary school record, class rank, academic GPA, standardized test scores (if submitted). *Important factors include:* application essay. *Other factors considered include:* recommendations. High school diploma is required and GED is accepted. Institution is test-optional for entering Fall 2024. Check admissions website for updates. *Academic units recommended:* 4 English, 3 math, 3 science (3 labs), 2 foreign language, 4 social studies.

FINANCIAL AID

Students should submit: FAFSA; State aid form. *Need-based scholarships/grants offered:* College/university scholarship or grant aid from institutional funds; Federal Pell; Private scholarships; SEOG; State scholarships/grants; United Negro College Fund. *Loan aid offered:* Direct PLUS loans; Direct Subsidized Loans; Direct Unsubsidized Loans. Federal Work-Study Program available. Institutional employment available.

CAMPUS LIFE

Activities: Campus Ministries; Choral groups; Concert band; Dance; Drama/theater; International Student Organization; Jazz band; Literary magazine; Marching band; Model UN; Music ensembles; Musical theater; Pep band; Radio station; Student government; Student newspaper; Student-run film society; Symphony orchestra; Television station; Yearbook. **Organizations:** 68 registered organizations, 20 honor societies, 3 religious organizations, 5 fraternities, 4 sororities. **Athletics (Intercollegiate):** *Men:* baseball, basketball, cross-country, equestrian sports, golf, ice hockey, lacrosse, racquetball, softball, swimming, track/field (indoor), ultimate frisbee, wrestling. *Women:* basketball, bowling, cross-country, equestrian sports, field hockey, golf, gymnastics, ice hockey, lacrosse, racquetball, rugby, softball, swimming, track/field (indoor), ultimate frisbee, volleyball, water polo.

CAMPUS

Type of school	Private (nonprofit)
Environment	Metropolis

STUDENTS

Undergrad enrollment	5,751
% male/female	33/67
% from out of state	19
% frosh live on campus	40

FINANCIAL FACTS

Annual tuition	$39,458
Room and board	$17,354
Required fees	$2,034

GENERAL ADMISSIONS INFO

Application fee	$50
Regular application deadline	Rolling
Nonfall registration	Yes

Fall 2024 testing policy	Test Optional
Range SAT EBRW	550–660
Range SAT Math	550–670
Range ACT Composite	23–29

ACADEMICS

Student/faculty ratio	13:1
% students returning for sophomore year	76

Most classes have 10–19 students.

REQUESTING SERVICES FOR STUDENTS WITH LEARNING DIFFERENCES

Phone: 516-299-3057 • www.liu.edu/post/dss • Email: marie.fatscher@liu.edu

Documentation submitted to: Learning Center–Disability Support Services
Separate application required for Services: Yes

Documentation required for:
LD: Psychoeducational evaluation
ADHD: Psychoeducational evaluation
ASD: Psychoeducational evaluation

New York

Manhattanville College

2900 Purchase Street, Purchase, NY 10577 • Admissions: 914-323-5464 • www.mville.edu

Support: SP

ACCOMMODATIONS

Allowed in exams:

Calculators	Yes
Dictionary	No
Computer	Yes
Spell-checker	Yes
Extended test time	Yes
Scribe	Yes
Proctors	Yes
Oral exams	Yes
Note-takers	Yes

Support services for students with:

LD	Yes
ADHD	Yes
ASD	Yes
Distraction-reduced environment	Yes
Recording of lecture allowed	Yes
Reading technology	Yes
Audio books	Yes
Other assistive technology	Yes
Priority registration	No

Added costs of services:

For LD	Yes
For ADHD	Yes
For ASD	Yes
LD specialists	Yes
ADHD & ASD coaching	Yes
ASD specialists	Yes
Professional tutors	Yes
Peer tutors	Yes
Max. hours/week for services	4
How professors are notified of student approved accommodations	Student

COLLEGE GRADUATION REQUIREMENTS

Course waivers allowed	No
Course substitutions allowed	Yes
In what courses: Math and Second Language	

PROGRAMS/SERVICES FOR STUDENTS WITH LEARNING DIFFERENCES

The Center for Student Accessibility supports students with disabilities. There are two fee-based programs for students with learning differences: Valiant Learning Support Program and the Pathways and Connections Program. The Valiant Learning Support Program (VLSP) assists students navigating academic challenges in college. Students receive customized learning strategy sessions with professional Learning Specialists for three hours of weekly one-on-one academic support, including writing skills, reading comprehension, time management and prioritization, and study skills. Students also have the option of adding a fourth hour for an additional fee. The Pathways and Connections Program (PAC) is for students on the autism spectrum with executive functioning skills as the main focus. The program supports and helps students with ASD integrate into the Manhattanville community. Students who are enrolled in the program benefit from individual, customized meetings with the PAC Coordinator, weekly group sessions, peer mentoring, and school-coordinated social events.

ADMISSIONS

Manhattanville College admits students on a rolling basis. Applicants are encouraged to apply early action (non-binding) to receive a decision earlier than applicants who apply as regular applicants. For admitted applicants, the average GPA is 3.1, and if submitted, the average ACT score is 22 and 1190 for the SAT. A formal interview is available and encouraged for students who believe that it will strengthen their candidate profile. Students may apply to the VLSP or PAC programs after receiving admittance to Manhattanville.

Additional Information

The Academic Resource Center provides free individual and small-group peer tutoring sessions, and the Writing Center provides students with support at any stage of the writing process.

In the 1930s, with just over 200 students, the college made headlines across the nation for taking a strong position promoting racial equality. The all-female student body created the "Manhattanville Resolutions" that pledged commitment to racial justice. Alumni response was mixed and controversial. In 1938, the first African American woman was admitted. College president Grace Dammann delivered a passionate speech entitled "Principles Versus Prejudices," arguing that education is the key to rising above prejudices.

Manhattanville College

GENERAL ADMISSIONS

Very important factors include: rigor of secondary school record, academic GPA, application essay, recommendations. *Other factors considered include:* class rank. High school diploma is required and GED is accepted. Institution is test-free for entering Fall 2024. Check admissions website for updates. *Academic units required:* 4 English, 3 math, 2 science, 2 social studies, 5 academic electives.

FINANCIAL AID

Students should submit: FAFSA; State aid form. *Need-based scholarships/ grants offered:* College/university scholarship or grant aid from institutional funds; Federal Nursing Scholarships; Federal Pell; Private scholarships; SEOG; State scholarships/grants; United Negro College Fund. *Loan aid offered:* Direct PLUS loans; Direct Subsidized Loans; Direct Unsubsidized Loans. Federal Work-Study Program available. Institutional employment available.

CAMPUS LIFE

Activities: Campus Ministries; Choral groups; Concert band; Dance; Drama/theater; Music ensembles; Musical theater; Radio station; Student government; Television station. **Organizations:** 30 registered organizations, 4 honor societies, 4 religious organizations, 0 fraternities, 0 sororities. **Athletics (Intercollegiate):** *Men:* baseball, basketball, cross-country, golf, ice hockey, lacrosse, track/field (indoor). *Women:* basketball, cross-country, field hockey, golf, ice hockey, lacrosse, rugby, softball, track/field (indoor), volleyball.

CAMPUS
Type of school	Private (nonprofit)
Environment	Town

STUDENTS
Undergrad enrollment	1,274
% male/female	40/60
% from out of state	21
% frosh live on campus	65

FINANCIAL FACTS
Annual tuition	$40,850
Room and board	$15,540
Required fees	$1,700

GENERAL ADMISSIONS INFO
Application fee	$50
Regular application deadline	Rolling
Nonfall registration	Yes
Fall 2024 testing policy	Test Free

ACADEMICS
Student/faculty ratio	12:1
% students returning for sophomore year	80

Most classes have 10–19 students.

REQUESTING SERVICES FOR STUDENTS WITH LEARNING DIFFERENCES

Phone: 914-323-1434 • www.mville.edu/offices/center-for-student-accessibility.php
Email: Joseph.Gaines@mville.edu

Documentation submitted to: Center for Student Accessibility
Separate application required for Services: Yes

Documentation required for:
  LD: Psychoeducational evaluation
  ADHD: Psychoeducational evaluation
  ASD: Psychoeducational evaluation

Marist College

3399 North Road, Poughkeepsie, NY 12601-1387 • Admissions: 845-575-3226 • www.marist.edu

Support: SP

ACCOMMODATIONS

Allowed in exams:

Calculators	Yes
Dictionary	N/A
Computer	Yes
Spell-checker	Yes
Extended test time	Yes
Scribe	Yes
Proctors	Yes
Oral exams	No
Note-takers	Yes
Support services for students with:	
LD	Yes
ADHD	Yes
ASD	Yes
Distraction-reduced environment	Yes
Recording of lecture allowed	Yes
Reading technology	Yes
Audio books	Yes
Other assistive technology	Yes
Priority registration	No
Added costs of services:	
For LD	Yes
For ADHD	Yes
For ASD	Yes
LD specialists	Yes
ADHD & ASD coaching	No
ASD specialists	Yes
Professional tutors	No
Peer tutors	Yes
Max. hours/week for services	12
How professors are notified of student approved accommodations	Student

COLLEGE GRADUATION REQUIREMENTS

Course waivers allowed	No
Course substitutions allowed	No

PROGRAMS/SERVICES FOR STUDENTS WITH LEARNING DIFFERENCES

The Office of Accommodations and Accessibility (OAA) supports students with documented disabilities by providing a range of academic resources and accommodations that are individualized to meet the student's needs. The Learning Support Program is a fee-based program that emphasizes the development of compensatory strategies. Each student works one-on-one with a Learning Specialist and meets twice a week. The goals of each session are individualized, and typical sessions focus on writing skills, note-taking skills, organization skills, test-taking strategies, and time-management skills. Applicants to the Learning Support Program should possess a documented learning disability, an aptitude solidly in the average range, a college preparatory course of study, and a commitment to work with a Learning Specialist. The process for applying to the Learning Support Program requires students first be admitted to Marist through general admissions. After receiving admittance, students submit a separate application through the Office of Accommodations and Accessibility. Application materials include the results of a psychological evaluation, the student's most recent IEP/504 Plan if available, two letters of recommendation by teachers or tutors, transcripts, and a personal essay. Candidates for the program are invited to interview to receive a final admission decision.

ADMISSIONS

A student's high school transcript is a primary factor for admission consideration at Marist. Students interested in applying should have high school courses that reflect a college prep curriculum, rank in the top half of their graduating class, and hold an average GPA between 3.1 and 3.7. Leadership qualities and high school activities are also important. For applicants who choose to submit SAT scores, admitted students generally score between 1210–1360. All students are eligible for scholarships, regardless of their decision to submit test scores.

Additional Information

The Academic Learning Center provides academic support to Marist students, both undergraduate and graduate, through courses, tutoring programs, proofreading services, and academic counseling.

Since 1984, The Silver Needle Runway Show has been produced entirely by students from the School of Communications and the Arts and is now the largest event production presented by Marist. The show features garments designed and finished by senior Fashion Design students and shown in a professional runway setting. The Runway Show closes out the academic year with a community-wide celebration of growth and achievements.

Marist College

General Admissions

Very important factors include: rigor of secondary school record, academic GPA. *Important factors include:* recommendations. *Other factors considered include:* class rank, standardized test scores (if submitted), application essay. High school diploma is required and GED is accepted. Institution is test-optional for entering Fall 2024. Check admissions website for updates. *Academic units required:* 4 English, 3 math, 3 science, 2 foreign language, 3 social studies.

Financial Aid

Students should submit: FAFSA. *Need-based scholarships/grants offered:* College/university scholarship or grant aid from institutional funds; Federal Pell; Private scholarships; SEOG; State scholarships/grants. *Loan aid offered:* Direct PLUS loans; Direct Subsidized Loans; Direct Unsubsidized Loans. Federal Work-Study Program available. Institutional employment available.

Campus Life

Activities: Campus Ministries; Choral groups; Concert band; Dance; Drama/theater; International Student Organization; Jazz band; Literary magazine; Marching band; Model UN; Music ensembles; Musical theater; Pep band; Radio station; Student government; Student newspaper; Student-run film society; Symphony orchestra; Television station. **Organizations:** 81 registered organizations, 20 honor societies, 5 religious organizations, 3 fraternities, 4 sororities. **Athletics (Intercollegiate):** *Men:* baseball, basketball, crew/rowing, cross-country, equestrian sports, golf, ice hockey, lacrosse, rugby, skiing (nordic/cross-country), swimming, track/field (indoor), ultimate frisbee, volleyball. *Women:* basketball, crew/rowing, cross-country, equestrian sports, golf, lacrosse, rugby, skiing (nordic/cross-country), softball, swimming, track/field (indoor), ultimate frisbee, volleyball, water polo.

CAMPUS

Type of school	Private (nonprofit)
Environment	Town

STUDENTS

Undergrad enrollment	5,069
% male/female	41/59
% from out of state	48
% frosh live on campus	94

FINANCIAL FACTS

Annual tuition	$45,300
Room and board	$18,530
Required fees	$660

GENERAL ADMISSIONS INFO

Application fee	$50
Regular application deadline	2/15
Nonfall registration	Yes

Fall 2024 testing policy	Test Optional
Range SAT EBRW	610–690
Range SAT Math	590–670
Range ACT Composite	25–30

ACADEMICS

Student/faculty ratio	16:1
% students returning for sophomore year	86

Most classes have 20–29 students.

REQUESTING SERVICES FOR STUDENTS WITH LEARNING DIFFERENCES

Phone: 845-575-3274 • www.marist.edu/accommodations-accessibility/ • Email: accommodations@marist.edu

Documentation submitted to: The Office of Accommodations and Accessibility
Separate application required for Services: Yes

Documentation required for:
LD: Psychoeducational evaluation
ADHD: Psychoeducational evaluation
ASD: Psychoeducational evaluation

New York

Marymount Manhattan College

221 East 71 Street, New York, NY 10021 • Admissions: 212-517-0430 • www.mmm.edu

Support: SP

PROGRAMS/SERVICES FOR STUDENTS WITH LEARNING DIFFERENCES

MMC's Office of Disability Services accommodates students with documented learning, physical, medical, and/or psychological disabilities. Students who are eligible for support start by submitting an accommodations request detailing the request and uploading supporting documentation. After DS reviews the completed request and documentation, the student will be contacted for an intake meeting to discuss available options that will best meet the student's needs. Assistive technology accommodations include text-to-speech, the recording capability of classes, and study tools used for content review and paper writing. Training is provided by the assistive technology specialist for Academic Access and Disability Services. Academic Access is a fee-based program for students with learning disabilities, specifically designed to promote academic success. The program provides accommodations including extended testing time, notetakers, two hours weekly with a learning specialist, academic coaching for executive functioning skills, academic counseling for academic programs, priority registration, and monthly parent meetings during the academic year. Admission to the Academic Access Program is based on acceptance from Marymount Manhattan College's Admission Office, a diagnosis of dyslexia, primary learning disability, or ADHD, an intellectual potential within the average to the superior range, and a record that predicts a serious commitment in attitude and work habits to meet both the program and college academic requirements. Students in the Academic Access Program must spend a minimum of two consecutive semesters in the program. Provided they are in good standing at the college and show evidence of academic independence, they may then leave, but some students continue to participate for part or all of their college careers.

ADMISSIONS

Students are expected to have college prep courses in high school, but a foreign language is not required for admission. For admitted students who submitted SAT scores, 50 percent had scores of 1050–1258. One recommendation letter is required.

Additional Information

The Center for Academic Support and Tutoring (CAST) provides professional and peer tutors for various academic subjects, including math, science, and writing.

Priscilla and John Costello, married English professors, devoted a combined total of 78 years to Marymount and its students. Priscilla's career began in 1965, John's in 1966. Priscilla established the Critical Thinking Program and served as director for over 10 years, then became the assistant vice president for Academic Affairs in the late 1980s. John taught more than 70 different literature courses and created courses with colleagues in art history, history, music, philosophy, psychology, sociology, and theater.

Marymount Manhattan College

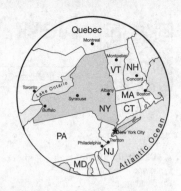

GENERAL ADMISSIONS

Very important factors include: rigor of secondary school record, academic GPA, standardized test scores (if submitted). *Important factors include:* application essay, recommendations. High school diploma is required and GED is accepted. Institution is test-optional for entering Fall 2024. Check admissions website for updates. *Academic units required:* 4 English, 3 math, 3 science, 3 social studies, 4 academic electives. *Academic units recommended:* 2 foreign language.

FINANCIAL AID

Students should submit: FAFSA; State aid form. *Need-based scholarships/grants offered:* College/university scholarship or grant aid from institutional funds; Federal Pell; Private scholarships; SEOG; State scholarships/grants. *Loan aid offered:* Direct PLUS loans; Direct Subsidized Loans; Direct Unsubsidized Loans. Federal Work-Study Program available. Institutional employment available.

CAMPUS LIFE

Activities: Campus Ministries; Choral groups; Dance; Drama/theater; International Student Organization; Musical theater; Radio station; Student government; Student newspaper; Yearbook. **Organizations:** 3 religious organizations, 0 fraternities, 0 sororities. **Athletics (Intercollegiate):** *Men:* volleyball. *Women:* volleyball.

CAMPUS

Type of school	Private (nonprofit)
Environment	Metropolis

STUDENTS

Undergrad enrollment	1,875
% male/female	23/77
% from out of state	59
% frosh live on campus	79

FINANCIAL FACTS

Annual tuition	$28,870
Room and board	$15,990
Required fees	$1,420

GENERAL ADMISSIONS INFO

Application fee	$60
Regular application deadline	Rolling
Nonfall registration	Yes

Fall 2024 testing policy	Test Optional
Range SAT EBRW	470–590
Range SAT Math	440–550
Range ACT Composite	20–26

ACADEMICS

Student/faculty ratio	11:1
% students returning for sophomore year	74
Most classes have 10–19 students.	

REQUESTING SERVICES FOR STUDENTS WITH LEARNING DIFFERENCES

Phone: 212-774-0719 • www.mmm.edu/offices/disability-services/ • Email: disabilityservices@mmm.edu

Documentation submitted to: Office of Disability Services
Separate application required for Services: Yes

Documentation required for:
LD: Psychoeducational evaluation
ADHD: Psychoeducational evaluation
ASD: Psychoeducational evaluation

New York University

383 Lafayette Street, New York, NY 10012 • Admissions: 212-998-4500 • www.nyu.edu

Support: CS

ACCOMMODATIONS

Allowed in exams:

Calculators	Yes
Dictionary	Yes
Computer	Yes
Spell-checker	Yes
Extended test time	Yes
Scribe	Yes
Proctors	Yes
Oral exams	No
Note-takers	Yes

Support services for students with:

LD	Yes
ADHD	Yes
ASD	Yes
Distraction-reduced environment	Yes
Recording of lecture allowed	Yes
Reading technology	Yes
Audio books	No
Other assistive technology	Yes
Priority registration	Yes

Added costs of services:

For LD	No
For ADHD	No
For ASD	No
LD specialists	Yes
ADHD & ASD coaching	No
ASD specialists	No
Professional tutors	Yes
Peer tutors	Yes
Max. hours/week for services	Varies
How professors are notified of student approved accommodations	Student

COLLEGE GRADUATION REQUIREMENTS

Course waivers allowed	No
Course substitutions allowed	Yes
In what courses: Case-by-case basis	

PROGRAMS/SERVICES FOR STUDENTS WITH LEARNING DIFFERENCES

The Moses Center for Student Accessibility (CSA) determines qualified disability status. Students must submit an online application and include an electronic copy of documentation if available. An accessibility specialist will set a time to complete an orientation meeting and determine reasonable accommodations. Students who feel they need accommodations, but do not have current documentation, should still contact CSA for assistance. CSA along with the Office of Financial Aid annually provide a limited number of tuition awards based on financial need, severity of disability, and academic qualifications. NYU Connections ASD is a free and optional program for NYU students with autism. The program has three main components: one-on-one student-controlled weekly meetings on academics, daily living, campus, and social life; peer group meetings to help build supportive relationships and find valuable resources (the meetings often include guest speakers with practical advice for navigating NYU, achieving success, and connecting with the autistic community); and public events that provide support for neurodiverse students and educate the NYU community on issues relating to neurodiversity and student success.

ADMISSIONS

All applicants are expected to meet the same admission criteria. In the application process, students will be asked to select academic programs of interest and campuses. Specific programs may have additional requirements. Admission requirements include a high school transcript or a GED equivalent, a mid-year academic report, a counselor evaluation, a personal essay, and one letter of recommendation from a teacher, counselor, coach, supervisor, or anyone else in a position of authority. NYU will accept up to two other optional letters of recommendation. Most admitted first-year students rank in the top 10 percent of their high school graduating class and have an average unweighted GPA of 3.7. The admissions committee in consultation with the dean of the appropriate school/college/campus, may offer conditional admission to a candidate with academic potential but who exhibits areas of academic concern.

Additional Information

The NYU Precollege Summer Program offers prospective students a six-week program with more than 100 courses to choose from. Students earn credits, try out academic majors, participate in extracurricular programming, boost college readiness, connect with other students, and gain experience living and learning at NYU's "Campus Without Walls." The Academic Resource Center offers a variety of academic support resources, cross-school advising, peer tutoring, and referrals. The University Learning Center has free one-on-one peer tutoring, group review workshops, academic skills workshops, and more.

For over a century, NYU athletes wore violet and white colors in competitions and were proudly nicknamed the Violets. Briefly in the 1980s, the school mascot was a student dressed as a violet, but unsurprisingly, it didn't instill awe or fear in NYU's opponents. The current mascot, the Bobcat, is named for the Bobst Library card catalog, aka the Bobst Catalog.

New York University

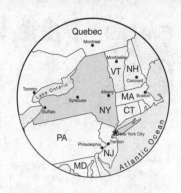

General Admissions

Very important factors include: rigor of secondary school record, class rank, academic GPA, standardized test scores (if submitted). *Important factors include:* application essay, recommendations. High school diploma is required and GED is accepted. Institution is test-flexible for entering Fall 2024. Check admissions website for updates. *Academic units required:* 4 English, 3 math, 3 science (3 labs), 3 foreign language, 3 social studies. *Academic units recommended:* 4 English, 4 math, 4 science (4 labs), 4 foreign language, 4 social studies.

Financial Aid

Students should submit: CSS/Financial Aid Profile; FAFSA; Noncustodial Profile. *Need-based scholarships/grants offered:* College/university scholarship or grant aid from institutional funds; Federal Nursing Scholarships; Federal Pell; Private scholarships; SEOG; State scholarships/grants. *Loan aid offered:* Direct PLUS loans; Direct Subsidized Loans; Direct Unsubsidized Loans. Federal Work-Study Program available. Institutional employment available.

Campus Life

Activities: Campus Ministries; Choral groups; Concert band; Dance; Drama/theater; International Student Organization; Jazz band; Literary magazine; Model UN; Music ensembles; Musical theater; Opera; Pep band; Radio station; Student government; Student newspaper; Student-run film society; Symphony orchestra; Television station; Yearbook. **Organizations:** 300 registered organizations, 3 honor societies, 46 religious organizations, 12 fraternities, 12 sororities. **Athletics (Intercollegiate):** *Men:* baseball, basketball, bowling, crew/rowing, cross-country, cycling, equestrian sports, golf, ice hockey, lacrosse, martial arts, racquetball, swimming, table tennis, track/field (indoor), ultimate frisbee, volleyball, water polo, wrestling. *Women:* basketball, bowling, crew/rowing, cross-country, cycling, equestrian sports, golf, lacrosse, martial arts, racquetball, softball, swimming, table tennis, track/field (indoor), ultimate frisbee, volleyball, water polo.

CAMPUS

Type of school	Private (nonprofit)
Environment	Metropolis

STUDENTS

Undergrad enrollment	29,136
% male/female	41/59
% from out of state	67
% frosh live on campus	83

FINANCIAL FACTS

Annual tuition	$58,128
Room and board	$20,272

GENERAL ADMISSIONS INFO

Application fee	$80
Regular application deadline	1/5
Nonfall registration	Yes

Fall 2024 testing policy	Test Flexible
Range SAT EBRW	720–770
Range SAT Math	750–800
Range ACT Composite	33–35

ACADEMICS

Student/faculty ratio	8:1
% students returning for sophomore year	95

Most classes have 10–19 students.

REQUESTING SERVICES FOR STUDENTS WITH LEARNING DIFFERENCES

Phone: 212-998-4980 • www.nyu.edu/students/communities-and-groups/student-accessibility
Email: mosescsa@nyu.edu

Documentation submitted to: The Moses Center for Student Accessibility
Separate application required for Services: Yes

Documentation required for:
LD: Psychoeducational evaluation
ADHD: Psychoeducational evaluation
ASD: Psychoeducational evaluation

Pace University

One Pace Plaza, New York, NY 10038 • Admissions: 212-346-1323 • www.pace.edu

Support: SP

ACCOMMODATIONS

Allowed in exams:

Calculators	Yes
Dictionary	Yes
Computer	Yes
Spell-checker	Yes
Extended test time	Yes
Scribe	Yes
Proctors	Yes
Oral exams	Yes
Note-takers	Yes

Support services for students with:

LD	Yes
ADHD	Yes
ASD	Yes
Distraction-reduced environment	Yes
Recording of lecture allowed	Yes
Reading technology	Yes
Audio books	Yes
Other assistive technology	Yes
Priority registration	Yes

Added costs of services:

For LD	No
For ADHD	No
For ASD	Yes
LD specialists	No
ADHD & ASD coaching	Yes
ASD specialists	Yes
Professional tutors	Yes
Peer tutors	Yes
Max. hours/week for services	Varies
How professors are notified of student approved accommodations	Student

COLLEGE GRADUATION REQUIREMENTS

Course waivers allowed	Yes
In what courses: Determined on a case-by-case basis	
Course substitutions allowed	Yes
In what courses: Determined on a case-by-case basis	

PROGRAMS/SERVICES FOR STUDENTS WITH LEARNING DIFFERENCES

To request an accommodation for a disability, students must register with the Student Accessibility Services Office. The student is responsible for providing documentation and meeting with a member of this office to discuss accommodation requests and procedures for accessing accommodations. Accommodations are determined on a case-by-case basis according to a student's documented needs. Academic adjustments may include extended time to complete examinations, a distraction-reduced testing environment, permission to record classes, course substitutions, note-taking services, and readers and/or scribes for exams. Pace University's Ongoing Academic Social Instructional Support (OASIS) program provides comprehensive support services for neurodiverse college students, including those with autism spectrum disorder and other learning disabilities. Academic coaches meet with students several times a week to help with assignments and organization. Personalized study plans are used to help students capitalize on their strengths and address challenges. Assignments are not modified, and students learn with their peers where course accommodations are provided. Campus life coordinators and social coaches help students integrate into dorm and campus life. Collaboration with Career Services and outside agencies provides opportunities for internships and future employment. OASIS students graduate with a bachelor's degree in any field of study.

ADMISSIONS

All applicants must submit the general application for admission. Applicants must provide two recommendations and a personal statement or essay. The OASIS program has a separate application process, but students must be admitted to Pace first. Applicants for OASIS go through a special admission process in which they're evaluated by the admission team during a personal interview. For all other students, the same rigorous admission and academic standards apply.

Additional Information

Academic Advisors guide students from their first semester through graduation with course selection and sequencing, major and minor information, special program opportunities, registration, and clarity on all university policies and procedures. The Learning Commons offers tutoring, academic coaching, peer mentoring, and content workshops and reviews.

An important but somber fact about the university is that on September 11, 2001, Pace NYC campus, four blocks from ground zero, was covered with debris and three inches of dust and ash. Students were evacuated, and although Pace was without electricity, the admission lobby became a triage center. An emergency call center was established on the Westchester Campus staffed by Pace employees. Memorials to the four students and 40 alums who lost their lives are on all three campuses. A statue of a German Shepherd, a gift from the American Kennel Club, stands at One Pace Plaza to commemorate Pace's support as a triage center.

Pace University

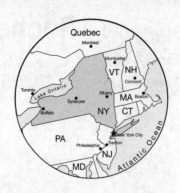

General Admissions

Very important factors include: rigor of secondary school record, application essay. *Important factors include:* class rank, academic GPA, recommendations. *Other factors considered include:* standardized test scores (if submitted). High school diploma is required and GED is accepted. Institution is test-optional for entering Fall 2024. Check admissions website for updates. *Academic units required:* 4 English, 3 math, 3 science (2 labs), 2 foreign language, 3 history, 2 academic electives.

Financial Aid

Students should submit: FAFSA; State aid form. *Need-based scholarships/ grants offered:* College/university scholarship or grant aid from institutional funds; Federal Nursing Scholarships; Federal Pell; Private scholarships; SEOG; State scholarships/grants. *Loan aid offered:* Direct PLUS loans; Direct Subsidized Loans; Direct Unsubsidized Loans. Federal Work-Study Program available. Institutional employment available.

Campus Life

Activities: Campus Ministries; Choral groups; Concert band; Dance; Drama/ theater; International Student Organization; Literary magazine; Model UN; Radio station; Student government; Student newspaper; Student-run film society; Television station; Yearbook. **Organizations:** 165 registered organizations, 10 honor societies, 1 religious organizations, 12 fraternities, 11 sororities. **Athletics (Intercollegiate):** *Men:* baseball, basketball, cross-country, lacrosse, swimming. *Women:* basketball, cross-country, field hockey, lacrosse, softball, swimming, volleyball.

CAMPUS
Type of school	Private (nonprofit)
Environment	Metropolis

STUDENTS
Undergrad enrollment	7,820
% male/female	34/66
% from out of state	49
% frosh live on campus	71

FINANCIAL FACTS
Annual tuition	$46,978
Room and board	$19,682
Required fees	$1,852

GENERAL ADMISSIONS INFO
Application fee	$50
Regular application deadline	2/15
Nonfall registration	Yes

Fall 2024 testing policy	Test Optional
Range SAT EBRW	570–660
Range SAT Math	550–650
Range ACT Composite	23–28

ACADEMICS
Student/faculty ratio	15:1
% students returning for sophomore year	75

Most classes have 10–19 students.

REQUESTING SERVICES FOR STUDENTS WITH LEARNING DIFFERENCES

Phone: 212-346-1199 • www.pace.edu/student-accessibility-services • Email: asanguinetti@pace.edu

Documentation submitted to: Student Accessibility Services
Separate application required for Services: Yes

Documentation required for:
LD: Psychoeducational evaluation
ADHD: Psychoeducational evaluation
ASD: Psychoeducational evaluation

Rochester Institute of Technology

60 Lomb Memorial Drive, Rochester, NY 14623-5604 • Admissions: 585-475-6631 • www.rit.edu

Support: SP

ACCOMMODATIONS

Allowed in exams:

Calculators	Yes
Dictionary	Yes
Computer	Yes
Spell-checker	Yes
Extended test time	Yes
Scribe	Yes
Proctors	Yes
Oral exams	Yes
Note-takers	Yes

Support services for students with:

LD	Yes
ADHD	Yes
ASD	Yes
Distraction-reduced environment	Yes
Recording of lecture allowed	Yes
Reading technology	Yes
Audio books	Yes
Other assistive technology	Yes
Priority registration	Yes

Added costs of services:

For LD	No
For ADHD	No
For ASD	No
LD specialists	Yes
ADHD & ASD coaching	Yes
ASD specialists	Yes
Professional tutors	No
Peer tutors	Yes
Max. hours/week for services	Varies
How professors are notified of student approved accommodations	Disability Services Office

COLLEGE GRADUATION REQUIREMENTS

Course waivers allowed	No
Course substitutions allowed	No

PROGRAMS/SERVICES FOR STUDENTS WITH LEARNING DIFFERENCES

The Disability Services Office (DSO) uses a collaborative process to determine and approve reasonable accommodations for students with disabilities. Students must first complete the application form and submit documentation of a disability before specific accommodations can be approved. Once DSO has reviewed all forms and documentation, the student will be contacted to schedule an initial meeting with a member of DSO. This process can take up to three weeks. Students must log into the MyDSO student portal every term to request the academic accommodations they plan to use in their classes. The Spectrum Support Program (SSP) provides support for those with autism spectrum disorder to help them achieve social, academic, and career success. Enrollment in the program averages 30 new incoming students each fall semester and continues to provide support throughout enrollment at RIT. Program participants are paired with a trained coach. SSP students will also be assigned to a Spectrum Support Program staff member who works with the students to connect them to the appropriate campus resources and departments, such as Academic Advising, Residence Life, Disability Services Office, Career Services and Co-op, Academic Success Center, and Counseling and Psychological Services. Students participating in the Spectrum Support Program can participate in pre-arrival programming before student orientation, which can include information sessions, game nights, group meals, a fall schedule walk-through, and a fall semester kick-off event.

ADMISSIONS

Most students applying to RIT choose a specific major as part of the admission process. In addition, all colleges offer undeclared options, and the University Studies program is available to applicants with interests in two or more colleges. Admission requirements, including core academic courses, and entrance exam score ranges vary from one college to another. Applicants for the Spectrum Support Program for students with ASD must meet all the academic requirements of admission to RIT and be admitted into an undergraduate program. A pre-baccalaureate studies option is also available for students who may need additional preparation before entering a bachelor's degree program. An art portfolio is required for admission to the School of Art, Design, or Film and Animation.

Additional Information

University Studies is a student-first program that meets students where they are and assists them in choosing curricular and extracurricular options that will enhance their career opportunities.

The 1965 Public Law 89-36, known as the National Technical Institute for the Deaf Act, signed by President Johnson, chose RIT as its campus. In 1968, NTID began classes providing deaf and hard-of-hearing students with technical and professional education programs. In 1971, 54 NTID's students were the first graduating class. More than 3,000 alumni attended NTID's 50th anniversary. RIT/NTID Deaf Studies Archive preserves and illustrates the history, art, culture, technology, and language of the Deaf community.

Rochester Institute of Technology

GENERAL ADMISSIONS

Very important factors include: rigor of secondary school record, academic GPA. *Important factors include:* class rank. *Other factors considered include:* standardized test scores (if submitted), application essay, recommendations. High school diploma is required and GED is accepted. Institution is test-optional for entering Fall 2024. Check admissions website for updates. *Academic units required:* 4 English, 3 math, 2 science (2 labs), 3 social studies. *Academic units recommended:* 4 math, 4 science.

FINANCIAL AID

Students should submit: FAFSA; State aid form. *Need-based scholarships/grants offered:* College/university scholarship or grant aid from institutional funds; Federal Pell; Private scholarships; SEOG; State scholarships/grants. *Loan aid offered:* Direct PLUS loans; Direct Subsidized Loans; Direct Unsubsidized Loans. Federal Work-Study Program available. Institutional employment available.

CAMPUS LIFE

Activities: Campus Ministries; Choral groups; Concert band; Dance; Drama/theater; International Student Organization; Jazz band; Literary magazine; Music ensembles; Musical theater; Pep band; Radio station; Student government; Student newspaper; Student-run film society; Symphony orchestra; Yearbook. **Organizations:** 300 registered organizations, 9 honor societies, 10 religious organizations, 19 fraternities, 10 sororities. **Athletics (Intercollegiate):** *Men:* baseball, basketball, bowling, crew/rowing, cross-country, cycling, equestrian sports, ice hockey, lacrosse, racquetball, rugby, swimming, track/field (indoor), ultimate frisbee, volleyball, water polo, wrestling. *Women:* basketball, bowling, crew/rowing, cross-country, cycling, equestrian sports, field hockey, ice hockey, lacrosse, racquetball, rugby, softball, swimming, track/field (indoor), ultimate frisbee, volleyball.

CAMPUS
Type of school	Private (nonprofit)
Environment	City

STUDENTS
Undergrad enrollment	12,489
% male/female	66/34
% from out of state	49
% frosh live on campus	88

FINANCIAL FACTS
Annual tuition	$46,964
Room and board	$13,976
Required fees	$676

GENERAL ADMISSIONS INFO
Application fee	$65
Regular application deadline	1/15
Nonfall registration	Yes
Fall 2024 testing policy	Test Optional
Range SAT EBRW	630–710
Range SAT Math	640–740
Range ACT Composite	29–33

ACADEMICS
Student/faculty ratio	13:1
% students returning for sophomore year	89

Most classes have 10–19 students.

REQUESTING SERVICES FOR STUDENTS WITH LEARNING DIFFERENCES

Phone: 585-475-2023 • www.rit.edu/disabilityservices/ • Email: dso@rit.edu

Documentation submitted to: Disability Services Office
Separate application required for Services: Yes

Documentation required for:
LD: Psychoeducational evaluation
ADHD: Psychoeducational evaluation
ASD: Psychoeducational evaluation

New York

State University of New York at Albany

Office of Undergraduate Admissions, Albany, NY 12222 • Admissions: 518-442-5435 • www.albany.edu

Support: CS

ACCOMMODATIONS

Allowed in exams:

Calculators	Yes
Dictionary	Yes
Computer	Yes
Spell-checker	Yes
Extended test time	Yes
Scribe	Yes
Proctors	Yes
Oral exams	Yes
Note-takers	Yes

Support services for students with:

LD	Yes
ADHD	Yes
ASD	Yes
Distraction-reduced environment	Yes
Recording of lecture allowed	Yes
Reading technology	Yes
Audio books	Yes
Other assistive technology	Yes
Priority registration	Yes

Added costs of services:

For LD	No
For ADHD	No
For ASD	No
LD specialists	Yes
ADHD & ASD coaching	No
ASD specialists	No
Professional tutors	No
Peer tutors	Yes
Max. hours/week for services	Varies
How professors are notified of student approved accommodations	Student

COLLEGE GRADUATION REQUIREMENTS

Course waivers allowed	No
Course substitutions allowed	Yes
In what courses: Case-by-case basis	

PROGRAMS/SERVICES FOR STUDENTS WITH LEARNING DIFFERENCES

Disability Access and Inclusion Student Services (DAISS) works with students with disabilities to find reasonable accommodations. Students are responsible for requesting accommodations by registering with DAISS and submitting documentation of their disability. Students then meet with DAISS staff to discuss past accommodations, potential new accommodations, policies and procedures, and create an accommodation letter to share with course professors each semester. Accommodations can include audio recordings of class lectures, scribes, and extended testing time. Certain accommodations are not available, including clarification of test questions, resource rooms, or accommodations that alter the exam or assignments.

ADMISSIONS

Applicants for admission to all undergraduate programs must complete a minimum of 18 units in a college preparatory program. An essay (250–600 words) and one teacher or school counselor recommendation are required, and additional recommendations are welcome. The mid-range GPA of accepted students is 3.4–3.8. In a limited number of cases, the director of admissions is authorized to apply subjective admission standards for applicants who possess unusual maturity or valuable life experiences.

Additional Information

Graduation requirements include math and foreign language; however, substitutions may be offered.

Started in 2009, UAlbany's Speaker Series is a lecture series that brings well-known guest speakers to campus to engage the campus community in conversations on important issues, including politics, global affairs, business, journalism, and popular culture. The program, started by a group of student leaders in the Student Association, is now funded by the Division of Student Affairs, the Student Association, University Auxiliary Services, and the UAlbany Alumni Association.

State University of New York at Albany

GENERAL ADMISSIONS

Very important factors include: rigor of secondary school record, academic GPA. *Other factors considered include:* class rank, standardized test scores (if submitted), application essay, recommendations. High school diploma is required and GED is accepted. Institution is test-optional for entering Fall 2024. Check admissions website for updates. *Academic units required:* 4 English, 3 math, 2 science (2 labs), 1 foreign language, 4 social studies (1 U.S. history), 4 academic electives. *Academic units recommended:* 4 math, 3 science (3 labs), 3 foreign language.

FINANCIAL AID

Students should submit: FAFSA. *Need-based scholarships/grants offered:* College/university scholarship or grant aid from institutional funds; Federal Pell; Private scholarships; SEOG; State scholarships/grants; United Negro College Fund. *Loan aid offered:* Direct PLUS loans; Direct Subsidized Loans; Direct Unsubsidized Loans. Federal Work-Study Program available. Institutional employment available.

CAMPUS LIFE

Activities: Campus Ministries; Choral groups; Concert band; Dance; Drama/theater; International Student Organization; Jazz band; Literary magazine; Marching band; Model UN; Music ensembles; Musical theater; Pep band; Radio station; Student government; Student newspaper; Student-run film society; Symphony orchestra; Television station; Yearbook. **Organizations:** 210 registered organizations, 22 honor societies, 14 religious organizations, 13 fraternities, 16 sororities. **Athletics (Intercollegiate):** *Men:* baseball, basketball, bowling, crew/rowing, cross-country, equestrian sports, field hockey, golf, ice hockey, lacrosse, martial arts, rugby, softball, swimming, table tennis, track/field (indoor), ultimate frisbee, volleyball, wrestling. *Women:* basketball, bowling, crew/rowing, cross-country, equestrian sports, field hockey, golf, ice hockey, lacrosse, martial arts, rugby, softball, swimming, table tennis, track/field (indoor), ultimate frisbee, volleyball.

CAMPUS

Type of school	Public
Environment	City

STUDENTS

Undergrad enrollment	12,175
% male/female	46/54
% from out of state	4
% frosh live on campus	92

FINANCIAL FACTS

Annual in-state tuition	$7,070
Annual out-of-state tuition	$24,910
Room and board	$15,598
Required fees	$3,338

GENERAL ADMISSIONS INFO

Application fee	$50
Regular application deadline	7/1
Nonfall registration	Yes
Fall 2024 testing policy	Test Optional
Range SAT EBRW	560–660
Range SAT Math	560–660
Range ACT Composite	22–31

ACADEMICS

Student/faculty ratio	17:1
% students returning for sophomore year	83
Most classes have 10–19 students.	

REQUESTING SERVICES FOR STUDENTS WITH LEARNING DIFFERENCES

Phone: 518-442-5501 • www.albany.edu/dean-students/disability • Email: daiss@albany.edu

Documentation submitted to: Disability Access and Inclusion Student Services
Separate application required for Services: Yes

Documentation required for:
LD: Psychoeducational evaluation
ADHD: Psychoeducational evaluation
ASD: Psychoeducational evaluation

State University of New York—Alfred State College

10 Upper College Drive, Alfred, NY 14802 • Admissions: 607-587-4215 • www.alfredstate.edu

Support: CS

ACCOMMODATIONS

Allowed in exams:

Calculators	Yes
Dictionary	Yes
Computer	Yes
Spell-checker	Yes
Extended test time	Yes
Scribe	Yes
Proctors	Yes
Oral exams	Yes
Note-takers	Yes

Support services for students with:

LD	Yes
ADHD	Yes
ASD	Yes
Distraction-reduced environment	Yes
Recording of lecture allowed	Yes
Reading technology	Yes
Audio books	Yes
Other assistive technology	Yes
Priority registration	Yes

Added costs of services:

For LD	No
For ADHD	No
For ASD	No
LD specialists	No
ADHD & ASD coaching	Yes
ASD specialists	Yes
Professional tutors	Yes
Peer tutors	Yes
Max. hours/week for services	15
How professors are notified of student approved accommodations	Office of Student Accessibilities Services

COLLEGE GRADUATION REQUIREMENTS

Course waivers allowed	No
Course substitutions allowed	No

PROGRAMS/SERVICES FOR STUDENTS WITH LEARNING DIFFERENCES

The Office of Student Accessibilities Services (OSAS) provides academic and nonacademic assistance to students with documented disabilities. Students are encouraged to register and submit disability documentation with OSAS as early as possible. Students must meet with an OSAS coordinator who will review documentation and the student's class schedule to determine appropriate accommodations. Approved accommodations are put in a letter for the student to deliver to faculty to discuss their implementation, which may include faculty conferencing, tutoring referrals, assistive technology, notetakers, and testing accommodations.

ADMISSIONS

All applicants apply to a specific program (major) of study rather than general admission. Applications are reviewed with entrance requirement considerations for the student's intended major, letters of recommendation, strength of transcript, and extracurricular activities. Three teacher letters, three other letters of recommendation, and personal essays are optional. However, applicants are encouraged to submit any supplemental materials such as a personal statement, letters of recommendation, or a résumé. Applicants who do not meet specified program requirements but show potential for success may be considered for admission through the Alfred State Opportunity Program (ASOP) or the Educational Opportunity Program (EOP). The ASOP program allows for lighter course loads and college prep and development courses. EOP is an extended program where students study full-time, enrolling in at least 12 credit hours per semester. To comply with program requirements, EOP students may be required to repeat courses in which they have earned a D or D+.

Additional Information

Alfred State Student Success Center offers free peer tutoring services for most courses. Online tutoring can be arranged through STAR-NY, an interactive whiteboard providing direct access to professional tutoring. The Math Lab and Writing Center have schedules posted for drop-in tutor times, and the Learning Lab has peer tutors available on a drop-in schedule. Supplemental Instruction (SI) offers a schedule of weekly review sessions for students taking historically difficult courses. SI is provided for students who want to improve their understanding of course material and improve grades. Most residence halls have Academic Peer Mentors (APMs) to support students with resources and assist in their studies.

DID YOU KNOW?

In April, Hot Dog Day is a celebration coordinated by Alfred State and Alfred University to bring the schools together and support local charities. At noon, there's a parade down Main Street honoring the 1972 AU founders, live music, a spring carnival, pets in costumes, vendors, and hot dog sales for charity. The weekend begins with the ASC-hosted annual regional track and field Special Olympics competition, which typically has approximately 300 participants and huge numbers of volunteers and fans.

State University of New York— Alfred State College

GENERAL ADMISSIONS

Very important factors include: rigor of secondary school record, academic GPA, standardized test scores (if submitted). *Other factors considered include:* application essay, recommendations. High school diploma is required and GED is accepted. Institution is test-optional for entering Fall 2024. Check admissions website for updates. *Academic units recommended:* 4 English, 3 math, 3 science, 1 foreign language, 4 social studies.

FINANCIAL AID

Students should submit: FAFSA; State aid form. *Need-based scholarships/grants offered:* College/university scholarship or grant aid from institutional funds; Federal Pell; Private scholarships; SEOG; State scholarships/grants. *Loan aid offered:* Direct PLUS loans; Direct Subsidized Loans; Direct Unsubsidized Loans. Federal Work-Study Program available. Institutional employment available.

CAMPUS LIFE

Activities: Campus Ministries; Choral groups; Concert band; Dance; Drama/theater; International Student Organization; Jazz band; Literary magazine; Music ensembles; Musical theater; Pep band; Radio station; Student government; Student newspaper; Symphony orchestra; Yearbook. **Organizations:** 125 registered organizations, 5 honor societies, 4 religious organizations, 6 fraternities, 6 sororities. **Athletics (Intercollegiate):** *Men:* baseball, basketball, cross-country, equestrian sports, ice hockey, lacrosse, swimming, track/field (indoor), wrestling. *Women:* basketball, cross-country, equestrian sports, softball, swimming, track/field (indoor), volleyball.

CAMPUS

Type of school	Public
Environment	Rural

STUDENTS

Undergrad enrollment	3,334
% male/female	64/36
% from out of state	4
% frosh live on campus	79

FINANCIAL FACTS

Annual in-state tuition	$7,070
Annual out-of-state tuition	$11,040
Room and board	$13,180
Required fees	$1,624

GENERAL ADMISSIONS INFO

Application fee	$50
Regular application deadline	Rolling
Nonfall registration	Yes

Fall 2024 testing policy	Test Optional
Range SAT EBRW	460–580
Range SAT Math	480–590
Range ACT Composite	19–26

ACADEMICS

Student/faculty ratio	17:1
% students returning for sophomore year	78

Most classes have 10–19 students.

REQUESTING SERVICES FOR STUDENTS WITH LEARNING DIFFERENCES

Phone: 607-587-4506 • www.alfredstate.edu/student-success-center/accessibility-services
Email: ryanma@alfredstate.edu

Documentation submitted to: Office of Student Accessibility Services
Separate application required for Services: Yes

Documentation required for:
LD: Psychoeducational evaluation
ADHD: Psychoeducational evaluation
ASD: Psychoeducational evaluation

New York

State University of New York at Binghamton University

P.O. Box 6001, Binghamton, NY 13902-6001 • Admissions: 607-777-2171 • www.binghamton.edu

Support: CS

ACCOMMODATIONS

Allowed in exams:

Calculators	Yes
Dictionary	No
Computer	Yes
Spell-checker	No
Extended test time	Yes
Scribe	Yes
Proctors	Yes
Oral exams	No
Note-takers	Yes

Support services for students with:

LD	Yes
ADHD	Yes
ASD	Yes
Distraction-reduced environment	Yes
Recording of lecture allowed	Yes
Reading technology	Yes
Audio books	Yes
Other assistive technology	Yes
Priority registration	No

Added costs of services:

For LD	No
For ADHD	No
For ASD	No
LD specialists	Yes
ADHD & ASD coaching	No
ASD specialists	Yes
Professional tutors	No
Peer tutors	No
Max. hours/week for services	Varies
How professors are notified of student approved accommodations	Student

COLLEGE GRADUATION REQUIREMENTS

Course waivers allowed	No
Course substitutions allowed	Yes

In what courses: Foreign Language on a case-by-case basis

PROGRAMS/SERVICES FOR STUDENTS WITH LEARNING DIFFERENCES

Services for Students with Disabilities (SSD) requires students to complete the online registration form and include the appropriate documentation. SSD will set an appointment for an intake meeting, where the student and a staff member will discuss accommodations. These may consist of books and course materials in an alternate format, assistive technology, note-taking, additional time for assignments or exams, and other exam alternatives. Once SSD has determined and authorized accommodation access, they will provide instructions on requesting academic accommodation letters each semester. Students are required to meet with course instructors to discuss implementing their accommodations.

ADMISSIONS

All applicants are required to complete the same general admission application and submit an official high school transcript. The middle 50 percent of accepted students have a GPA of 3.7–3.9. A personal essay and one teacher or counselor recommendation are required. Binghamton does not require interviews as part of the admissions process.

Additional Information

Tutoring appointments are available through University Tutoring Services; students may sign up for peer tutoring at the B-Successful website. At the Writing Center, students can work on their writing assignments with English-major tutors (availability is listed on the website). The math and chemistry departments have Help Room schedules with tutoring hours. The Speaking Center provides peer-to-peer consulting on public speaking and oral presentations. The Critical Thinking Lab offers individualized sessions to help students develop critical thinking for essays, summaries, formal arguments, in-class writing, speeches, presentations, and application materials. Supplemental Instruction (SI) sessions are available and promote student interaction and mutual support between classmates. Success Coaching appointments are available with both peer- and professional-level coaches to support undergraduate students with topics such as time and task management, study strategies, procrastination, motivation, and organization. Weekly Student Success Groups are available, with Success Coaches working with students to reflect on goals, progress, and plans for the week ahead.

DID YOU KNOW?

Distinguished Professor of Chemistry and Material Science M. Stanley Whittingham teaches at Binghamton. He invented the first rechargeable lithium metal battery (LMB), patented in 1977. In 2018, he was elected to the National Academy of Engineering, and in 2019, he was awarded the Nobel Prize in Chemistry. In 2020, he was named to the Carnegie Corporation of New York's 2020 list of "Great Immigrants, Great Americans."

State University of New York at Binghamton University

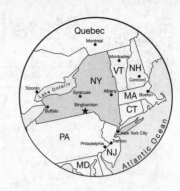

GENERAL ADMISSIONS

Very important factors include: rigor of secondary school record, academic GPA. *Important factors include:* class rank, application essay. *Other factors considered include:* standardized test scores (if submitted), recommendations. High school diploma is required and GED is accepted. Institution is test-optional for entering Fall 2024. Check admissions website for updates. *Academic units required:* 4 English, 3 math, 2 science, 2 foreign language, 2 social studies. *Academic units recommended:* 4 math, 4 science, 4 social studies.

FINANCIAL AID

Students should submit: FAFSA; State aid form. *Need-based scholarships/grants offered:* College/university scholarship or grant aid from institutional funds; Federal Pell; Private scholarships; SEOG; State scholarships/grants. *Loan aid offered:* Direct PLUS loans; Direct Subsidized Loans; Direct Unsubsidized Loans. Federal Work-Study Program available. Institutional employment available.

CAMPUS LIFE

Activities: Campus Ministries; Choral groups; Concert band; Dance; Drama/theater; International Student Organization; Jazz band; Literary magazine; Model UN; Music ensembles; Musical theater; Opera; Radio station; Student government; Student newspaper; Student-run film society; Symphony orchestra; Television station; Yearbook. **Organizations:** 373 registered organizations, 28 honor societies, 14 religious organizations, 36 fraternities, 17 sororities. **Athletics (Intercollegiate):** *Men:* baseball, basketball, bowling, crew/rowing, cross-country, cycling, equestrian sports, field hockey, golf, gymnastics, ice hockey, lacrosse, martial arts, racquetball, rugby, softball, swimming, table tennis, track/field (indoor), ultimate frisbee, volleyball, water polo, wrestling. *Women:* basketball, bowling, crew/rowing, cross-country, cycling, equestrian sports, field hockey, golf, gymnastics, ice hockey, lacrosse, martial arts, racquetball, rugby, softball, swimming, table tennis, track/field (indoor), ultimate frisbee, volleyball, water polo.

CAMPUS
Type of school	Public
Environment	City

STUDENTS
Undergrad enrollment	14,303
% male/female	49/51
% from out of state	7
% frosh live on campus	98

FINANCIAL FACTS
Annual in-state tuition	$7,070
Annual out-of-state tuition	$24,910
Room and board	$16,250
Required fees	$3,320

GENERAL ADMISSIONS INFO
Application fee	$50
Regular application deadline	Rolling
Nonfall registration	Yes
Fall 2024 testing policy	Test Optional
Range SAT EBRW	650–720
Range SAT Math	660–750
Range ACT Composite	30–33

ACADEMICS
Student/faculty ratio	19:1
% students returning for sophomore year	91

Most classes have 10–19 students.

REQUESTING SERVICES FOR STUDENTS WITH LEARNING DIFFERENCES

Phone: 607-777-2686 • www.binghamton.edu/ssd/ • Email: ssd@binghamton.edu

Documentation submitted to: Services for Students with Disabilities
Separate application required for Services: Yes

Documentation required for:
LD: Psychoeducational evaluation
ADHD: Psychoeducational evaluation
ASD: Psychoeducational evaluation

New York

State University of New York at Potsdam

44 Pierrepont Avenue, Potsdam, NY 13676 • Admissions: 315-267-2180 • www.potsdam.edu

Support: CS

ACCOMMODATIONS

Allowed in exams:

Calculators	Yes
Dictionary	Yes
Computer	Yes
Spell-checker	Yes
Extended test time	Yes
Scribe	Yes
Proctors	Yes
Oral exams	Yes
Note-takers	Yes

Support services for students with:

LD	Yes
ADHD	Yes
ASD	Yes
Distraction-reduced environment	Yes
Recording of lecture allowed	Yes
Reading technology	Yes
Audio books	Yes
Other assistive technology	Yes
Priority registration	Yes

Added costs of services:

For LD	No
For ADHD	No
For ASD	No
LD specialists	No
ADHD & ASD coaching	No
ASD specialists	Yes
Professional tutors	No
Peer tutors	Yes
Max. hours/week for services	Varies
How professors are notified of student approved accommodations	Student and Office of Accommodative Services

COLLEGE GRADUATION REQUIREMENTS

Course waivers allowed	Yes
Course substitutions allowed	Yes
In what courses: Varies	

PROGRAMS/SERVICES FOR STUDENTS WITH LEARNING DIFFERENCES

The Office of Accommodative Services provides academic accommodations for all qualified students with documented learning disabilities. New students can start the registration process and submit their documentation to OAS once they have paid their tuition deposit. OAS staff will review the information and documentation and schedule an intake meeting where the student will meet with the OAS director to discuss documentation, appropriate accommodations, and how to set them up. With student consent, accommodation plans are emailed to course professors for implementation. Accommodations can include note-taking via assistive technology, text readers, e-text, classroom relocation, foreign language substitution, alternative testing arrangements (extended time, distraction-reduced environment, exam readers, scribes, word processors with spell check), special registration, and academic advising.

ADMISSIONS

All applicants are required to meet the general application requirements. Potsdam considers high school averages, classes taken, academic rigor, and strength of coursework as the best predictors of college success. An official high school transcript is required. A personal essay and one letter of recommendation from a school counselor or teacher are required; additional teacher recommendations are optional. The Bridges program is a special program designed to provide admission to students who fall slightly below the published academic standards for regular admission but demonstrate potential for success. All new Bridges students are assigned to a Bridges Advisor as their primary contact, who will help them select and register for courses, discuss any personal, academic, social, financial, and career concerns, and meet each month to review academic progress. Bridge students are required to attend group meetings designed to help in the transition to college and cover academic and nonacademic topics.

Additional Information

All incoming first-year students have the opportunity to participate in the First-Year Connect (1YC) program before the semester begins. Students meet online for two hours a week for four weeks. 1YC is led by trained facilitators and Potsdam faculty. Sessions are semi-structured, with student participants deciding the specific topics such as identity, methods of communicating, stereotypes, social inequality, race and racism, partisan politics, gender, and immigration. Peer tutoring is free of charge and available for various lower-level and some upper-division undergraduate courses. The Writers' Block offers free writing assistance on assignments, scholarship applications, and more. The Math Lab provides help with math on a walk-in basis.

Founded in 1886, Potsdam's Crane School of Music offers as many as 300 recitals, lectures, and concerts by faculty, students, and guests each year. Crane made the largest piano order in Steinway & Sons' history—twice, with 125 pianos in 1955 and 141 in 2007. Crane School of Music provided all the music for the 1980 Winter Olympic Games in Lake Placid, New York, and the Crane Chorus performed at the unveiling of the refurbished Statue of Liberty in 1986.

State University of New York at Potsdam

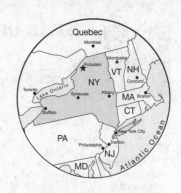

GENERAL ADMISSIONS

Very important factors include: rigor of secondary school record, academic GPA, application essay, recommendations. *Other factors considered include:* class rank. High school diploma is required and GED is accepted. Institution is test-optional for entering Fall 2024. Check admissions website for updates. *Academic units recommended:* 4 English, 3 math, 3 science, 3 foreign language, 4 social studies, 1 visual/performing arts.

FINANCIAL AID

Students should submit: FAFSA; State aid form. *Need-based scholarships/grants offered:* College/university scholarship or grant aid from institutional funds; Federal Pell; Private scholarships; SEOG; State scholarships/grants. *Loan aid offered:* Direct PLUS loans; Direct Subsidized Loans; Direct Unsubsidized Loans. Federal Work-Study Program available. Institutional employment available.

CAMPUS LIFE

Activities: Campus Ministries; Choral groups; Concert band; Dance; Drama/theater; International Student Organization; Jazz band; Literary magazine; Music ensembles; Musical theater; Opera; Pep band; Radio station; Student government; Student newspaper; Symphony orchestra. **Organizations:** 101 registered organizations, 27 honor societies, 2 religious organizations, 1 fraternities, 7 sororities. **Athletics (Intercollegiate):** *Men:* basketball, bowling, cross-country, ice hockey, lacrosse, martial arts, rugby, skiing (nordic/cross-country), swimming, track/field (indoor), volleyball. *Women:* basketball, bowling, cross-country, ice hockey, lacrosse, martial arts, rugby, skiing (nordic/cross-country), softball, swimming, track/field (indoor), volleyball.

CAMPUS	
Type of school	Public
Environment	Village

STUDENTS	
Undergrad enrollment	2,078
% male/female	39/61
% from out of state	3
% frosh live on campus	85

FINANCIAL FACTS	
Annual in-state tuition	$7,070
Annual out-of-state tuition	$16,980
Room and board	$14,600
Required fees	$1,742

GENERAL ADMISSIONS INFO	
Application fee	$50
Regular application deadline	Rolling
Nonfall registration	Yes
Fall 2024 testing policy	Test Optional

ACADEMICS	
Student/faculty ratio	10:1
% students returning for sophomore year	75
Most classes have 10–19 students.	

REQUESTING SERVICES FOR STUDENTS WITH LEARNING DIFFERENCES

Phone: 315-267-3267 • www.potsdam.edu/studentlife/support/accommodative-services
Email: burnetjj@potsdam.edu

Documentation submitted to: Accommodative Services
Separate application required for Services: Yes

Documentation required for:
 LD: Psychoeducational evaluation
 ADHD: Psychoeducational evaluation
 ASD: Psychoeducational evaluation

State University of New York—Stony Brook University

100 Nicolls Road, Stony Brook, NY 11794-1901 • Admissions: 631-632-6868 • www.stonybrook.edu

Support: S

PROGRAMS/SERVICES FOR STUDENTS WITH LEARNING DIFFERENCES

Student Accessibility Support Center (SASC) provides accommodations for eligible students with disabilities. Students begin by completing the online student intake form and submitting any documentation in support of accommodations. Once the intake form and documentation have been received, students meet with a SASC accessibility counselor to discuss and arrange reasonable accommodations. The accessibility counselor will help students communicate with course instructors to implement accommodations. Accommodation needs may vary based on course format; students are encouraged to review their syllabi and discuss the course with their instructors to help determine which accommodations they may need in their courses.

ADMISSIONS

All students are required to meet general application requirements for admission to the university and submit an official high school transcript. The admission process has no automatic cutoff for GPA, rank, or test scores. Stony Brook looks for students who have excelled in a strong college preparatory program. A personal essay on a topic of the applicant's choice is required. One letter of recommendation from a teacher or counselor are required and applicants applying to a specific major may have additional requirements.

Additional Information

The Academic Success and Tutoring Center (ASTC) provides peer tutoring at no cost for one-on-one or small-group tutoring appointments that are course-based or skill-oriented. Students can find a list of courses supported and can sign up starting at the beginning of the semester. There is also drop-in tutoring for a variety of courses. STAR-NY provides free online tutoring for various subject areas through a consortium of SUNY colleges and universities sharing resources and expertise. The Peer Academic Success Coaching Program (PASC) offers students help with time management, organizational strategies, and studying skills. Through the Peer Assisted Learning (PAL) program, PAL leaders work weekly with participating students.

Every Wednesday is a red-letter day at Stonybrook. It's called Campus Life Time, a weekly tradition since 1991. No classes are scheduled on Wednesdays between 1:00 and 2:30 P.M. so students can put down their books and get involved with student life. Campus Life Time has carnivals, concerts, student expo fairs, live entertainment, celebrity speakers, free food, giveaways, and a chance to spend time with friends or make new friends.

State University of New York— Stony Brook University

GENERAL ADMISSIONS

Very important factors include: rigor of secondary school record, academic GPA, standardized test scores (if submitted). *Important factors include:* application essay, recommendations. *Other factors considered include:* class rank. High school diploma is required and GED is accepted. Institution is test-optional for entering Fall 2024. Check admissions website for updates. *Academic units required:* 4 English, 3 math, 3 science, 4 social studies. *Academic units recommended:* 4 math, 4 science, 3 foreign language.

FINANCIAL AID

Students should submit: FAFSA; State aid form. *Need-based scholarships/grants offered:* College/university scholarship or grant aid from institutional funds; Federal Pell; Private scholarships; SEOG; State scholarships/grants. *Loan aid offered:* Direct PLUS loans; Direct Subsidized Loans; Direct Unsubsidized Loans. Federal Work-Study Program available. Institutional employment available.

CAMPUS LIFE

Activities: Campus Ministries; Choral groups; Concert band; Dance; Drama/theater; International Student Organization; Jazz band; Literary magazine; Marching band; Model UN; Music ensembles; Musical theater; Opera; Pep band; Radio station; Student government; Student newspaper; Student-run film society; Symphony orchestra; Television station. **Organizations:** 316 registered organizations, 7 honor societies, 5 religious organizations, 11 fraternities, 12 sororities. **Athletics (Intercollegiate):** *Men:* baseball, basketball, bowling, crew/rowing, cross-country, equestrian sports, field hockey, golf, ice hockey, lacrosse, martial arts, rugby, swimming, table tennis, track/field (indoor), ultimate frisbee, volleyball, wrestling. *Women:* basketball, bowling, crew/rowing, cross-country, equestrian sports, field hockey, golf, lacrosse, martial arts, rugby, softball, swimming, table tennis, track/field (indoor), ultimate frisbee, volleyball, wrestling.

CAMPUS

Type of school	Public
Environment	Town

STUDENTS

Undergrad enrollment	17,406
% male/female	49/51
% from out of state	7
% frosh live on campus	77

FINANCIAL FACTS

Annual in-state tuition	$7,070
Annual out-of-state tuition	$24,990
Room and board	$16,408
Required fees	$3,490

GENERAL ADMISSIONS INFO

Application fee	$50
Regular application deadline	1/15
Nonfall registration	Yes

Fall 2024 testing policy	Test Optional
Range SAT EBRW	640–720
Range SAT Math	680–780
Range ACT Composite	28–34

ACADEMICS

Student/faculty ratio	19:1
% students returning for sophomore year	88

Most classes have 20–29 students.

REQUESTING SERVICES FOR STUDENTS WITH LEARNING DIFFERENCES

Phone: 631-632-6748 • www.stonybrook.edu/sasc • Email: sasc@stonybrook.edu

Documentation submitted to: Student Accessibility Support Center
Separate application required for Services: Yes

Documentation required for:
LD: Psychoeducational evaluation
ADHD: Psychoeducational evaluation
ASD: Psychoeducational evaluation

St. Bonaventure University

3261 West State Road, St. Bonaventure, NY 14778 • Admissions: 716-375-2400 • www.sbu.edu

Support: S

ACCOMMODATIONS

Allowed in exams:

Calculators	Yes
Dictionary	Yes
Computer	Yes
Spell-checker	Yes
Extended test time	Yes
Scribe	Yes
Proctors	Yes
Oral exams	Yes
Note-takers	Yes

Support services for students with:

LD	Yes
ADHD	Yes
ASD	Yes
Distraction-reduced environment	Yes
Recording of lecture allowed	Yes
Reading technology	Yes
Audio books	Yes
Other assistive technology	No
Priority registration	Yes

Added costs of services:

For LD	No
For ADHD	No
For ASD	No
LD specialists	No
ADHD & ASD coaching	No
ASD specialists	No
Professional tutors	No
Peer tutors	Yes
Max. hours/week for services	1
How professors are notified of student approved accommodations	Student

COLLEGE GRADUATION REQUIREMENTS

Course waivers allowed	No
Course substitutions allowed	Yes
In what courses: Foreign Language	

Alphonsus A. Trabold, OFM, began a 45-year career at St. Bonaventure in 1958. He taught religion and a paranormal class that was so popular, there was often a wait list. The front row of seats in every class was left open for any spirits interested in his lecture. Affectionately nicknamed "Spooks" by his students, Fr. Trabold was fascinated by the paranormal. He was a frequently consulted expert in the paranormal field.

PROGRAMS/SERVICES FOR STUDENTS WITH LEARNING DIFFERENCES

The Office of Accessibility Services and Academic Support (ASAS) accommodates students with disabilities. Students begin the process by completing the online registration form with up-to-date documentation and a request for accommodations. Once received, ASAS will contact the student for an intake meeting to discuss accommodations and review policies and procedures. Upon approval, students should notify and meet with their instructors to discuss the implementation of their accommodations. ASAS offers accommodations such as extended time for testing, reduced-distraction testing rooms, note-taking assistance, and assistive technology. Students with disabilities may also attend weekly meetings offered by ASAS to develop self-advocacy and fine-tune their organizational skills, study habits, and test-taking strategies.

ADMISSIONS

All applicants are required to submit a high school transcript, personal essay or writing sample, and at least one letter of recommendation. The admission committee reviews each student's academic performance by examining their cumulative GPA, class rank if available, rigor of course schedule, and guidance counselor school report. Science, computer science, and mathematics majors should have additional coursework in science and math. Applicants who apply as test-optional will be considered for scholarships based on high school GPA and rigor of courses.

Additional Information

First-year students are required to take the 2 credit seminar, SBU 101 Community of Learners, which teaches effective learning strategies, identifies campus resources, and explores the SBU community. Students are assigned a book during orientation as part of All Bonaventure Reads that they read and then critique in writing; selected essays are published and discussed. Collegiate Opportunities to Reach Excellence (CORE) offers FRES100 seminars that meet once a week during the first semester and provide guidance to students in taking full advantage of university support services. CORE requires students to meet with their academic advisors during the first few weeks of class and encourages them to take advantage of Student Success Center programs and resources. During orientation Welcome Days, new students meet their peer coaches, who are upper-class students eager to help incoming students become immersed in the campus community. Students are encouraged to discuss academic concerns first with their professors, and then look to tutoring for assistance. The Student Success Center (SSC) offers one-on-one or small group tutoring for any class on a first-come, first-served basis. SSC Writing Lab offers help by appointment or drop-in at any stage of a writing project, from creating an outline to reviewing the final draft. Supplemental Instruction (SI) for historically difficult classes is distinct from tutoring sessions, and SI leaders encourage peer-to-peer learning.

St. Bonaventure University

General Admissions

Very important factors include: rigor of secondary school record, academic GPA, recommendations. *Important factors include:* application essay. *Other factors considered include:* class rank, standardized test scores (if submitted). High school diploma is required and GED is accepted. Institution is test-optional for entering Fall 2024. Check admissions website for updates. *Academic units recommended:* 4 English, 3 math, 3 science (3 labs), 2 foreign language, 4 social studies.

Financial Aid

Students should submit: FAFSA; State aid form. *Need-based scholarships/grants offered:* College/university scholarship or grant aid from institutional funds; Federal Pell; Private scholarships; SEOG; State scholarships/grants. *Loan aid offered:* Direct PLUS loans; Direct Subsidized Loans; Direct Unsubsidized Loans. Federal Work-Study Program available. Institutional employment available.

Campus Life

Activities: Campus Ministries; Choral groups; Concert band; Dance; Drama/theater; International Student Organization; Jazz band; Literary magazine; Model UN; Music ensembles; Pep band; Radio station; Student government; Student newspaper; Television station. **Organizations:** 65 registered organizations, 7 honor societies, 4 religious organizations, 0 fraternities, 0 sororities. **Athletics (Intercollegiate):** *Men:* baseball, basketball, bowling, cross-country, field hockey, golf, ice hockey, lacrosse, racquetball, rugby, swimming, volleyball. *Women:* basketball, bowling, cross-country, field hockey, lacrosse, racquetball, rugby, softball, swimming, volleyball.

CAMPUS

Type of school	Private (nonprofit)
Environment	Village

STUDENTS

Undergrad enrollment	1,742
% male/female	55/45
% from out of state	23
% frosh live on campus	97

FINANCIAL FACTS

Annual tuition	$37,620
Room and board	$14,450
Required fees	$1,150

GENERAL ADMISSIONS INFO

Application fee	No fee
Regular application deadline	8/15
Nonfall registration	Yes

Fall 2024 testing policy	Test Optional
Range SAT EBRW	530–630
Range SAT Math	540–640
Range ACT Composite	21–27

ACADEMICS

Student/faculty ratio	12:1
% students returning for sophomore year	73

Most classes have 20–29 students.

REQUESTING SERVICES FOR STUDENTS WITH LEARNING DIFFERENCES

Phone: 716-375-2065 • www.sbu.edu/life-at-sbu/student-services/student-success-center/accessibility-services-and-acommodations • Email: aspencer@sbu.edu

Documentation submitted to: Accessibility Services and Academic Support
Separate application required for Services: Yes

Documentation required for:
LD: Psychoeducational evaluation
ADHD: Psychoeducational evaluation
ASD: Psychoeducational evaluation

New York

St. Lawrence University

23 Romoda Drive, Canton, NY 13617 • Admissions: 315-229-5261 • www.stlawu.edu

Support: S

ACCOMMODATIONS

Allowed in exams:

Calculators	Yes
Dictionary	No
Computer	Yes
Spell-checker	Yes
Extended test time	Yes
Scribe	Yes
Proctors	Yes
Oral exams	Yes
Note-takers	Yes

Support services for students with:

LD	Yes
ADHD	Yes
ASD	Yes
Distraction-reduced environment	Yes
Recording of lecture allowed	Yes
Reading technology	Yes
Audio books	Yes
Other assistive technology	Yes
Priority registration	No

Added costs of services:

For LD	No
For ADHD	No
For ASD	No
LD specialists	No
ADHD & ASD coaching	No
ASD specialists	No
Professional tutors	No
Peer tutors	Yes
Max. hours/week for services	2
How professors are notified of student approved accommodations	Student

COLLEGE GRADUATION REQUIREMENTS

Course waivers allowed	No
Course substitutions allowed	No

PROGRAMS/SERVICES FOR STUDENTS WITH LEARNING DIFFERENCES

The Student Accessibility Services office (SAS) grants accommodations to students with documented disabilities, including neurodiversity. After completing the registration form and submitting documentation, students meet with the director or assistant director of SAS to discuss and determine reasonable accommodations. SAS works with each student to prepare an Individual Education Accommodation Plan (IEAP) based on their studies and activities. The IEAP is shared with course instructors, and students are expected to meet with their instructors to review the guidelines for implementing their accommodations. The SAS staff advocates, facilitates, and refers students to additional resources available on campus, including advisors, peer tutors, and health and counseling services.

ADMISSIONS

The admission requirements are the same for all applicants. Admissions also requires a personal essay, two letters of recommendation from high school teachers, and one recommendation from a school counselor. In the Activities Section of the application, the committee would like to see applicants detail their extracurricular and cocurricular activities, hobbies, interests, and family responsibilities.

Additional Information

The First-Year Program (FYP) is a combined academic and residential program designed to help students successfully transition from high school to college. During their first semester, students live in one of 32 residential colleges with their peers, who are enrolled in the same course. This living and learning environment emphasizes the development of social, writing, speaking, and research skills necessary for college-level courses. Students can seek additional support through Academic Advising, which offers free tutoring on a regular basis that accommodates an individual's schedule. The Word Studio is open to all students to boost their communication skills in speaking and writing, and the Peterson Quantitative Resource Center provides help with math and statistical assignments. Students can visit the Office of Academic Support to develop skills and new tools to achieve academic success.

Every fall, the Outing Club leads students of all hiking abilities into Adirondack Park to climb their choice of the 46 major Adirondack Mountains' peaks. All peaks are over 4,000 feet and vary in difficulty, but over the course of a single weekend, a St. Lawrence student will reach the top of each one. One who has climbed all 46 peaks, or an official "46er," has traversed 70,000 feet.

St. Lawrence University

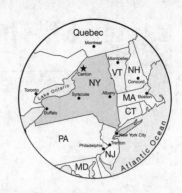

GENERAL ADMISSIONS

Very important factors include: rigor of secondary school record, academic GPA, application essay, recommendations. *Important factors include:* class rank. *Other factors considered include:* standardized test scores (if submitted). High school diploma is required and GED is accepted. Institution is test-optional for entering Fall 2024. Check admissions website for updates. *Academic units recommended:* 4 English, 3 math, 3 science, 3 foreign language, 3 social studies.

FINANCIAL AID

Students should submit: FAFSA. *Need-based scholarships/grants offered:* College/university scholarship or grant aid from institutional funds; Federal Pell; Private scholarships; SEOG; State scholarships/grants. *Loan aid offered:* Direct PLUS loans; Direct Subsidized Loans; Direct Unsubsidized Loans. Federal Work-Study Program available. Institutional employment available.

CAMPUS LIFE

Activities: Campus Ministries; Choral groups; Concert band; Dance; Drama/theater; International Student Organization; Jazz band; Literary magazine; Model UN; Music ensembles; Radio station; Student government; Student newspaper; Student-run film society; Yearbook. **Organizations:** 140 registered organizations, 24 honor societies, 4 religious organizations, 2 fraternities, 4 sororities. **Athletics (Intercollegiate):** *Men:* baseball, basketball, crew/rowing, cross-country, cycling, equestrian sports, golf, ice hockey, lacrosse, martial arts, rugby, skiing (nordic/cross-country), swimming, track/field (indoor), ultimate frisbee. *Women:* basketball, crew/rowing, cross-country, cycling, equestrian sports, field hockey, golf, ice hockey, lacrosse, martial arts, rugby, skiing (nordic/cross-country), softball, swimming, track/field (indoor), ultimate frisbee, volleyball.

CAMPUS

Type of school	Private (nonprofit)
Environment	Village

STUDENTS

Undergrad enrollment	2,130
% male/female	46/54
% from out of state	59
% frosh live on campus	100

FINANCIAL FACTS

Annual tuition	$63,450
Room and board	$16,480
Required fees	$420

GENERAL ADMISSIONS INFO

Application fee	No fee
Regular application deadline	2/1
Nonfall registration	Yes

Fall 2024 testing policy	Test Optional
Range SAT EBRW	630–700
Range SAT Math	610–710
Range ACT Composite	29–32

ACADEMICS

Student/faculty ratio	11:1
% students returning for sophomore year	85

Most classes have 10–19 students.

REQUESTING SERVICES FOR STUDENTS WITH LEARNING DIFFERENCES

Phone: 315-229-5537 • www.stlawu.edu/offices/student-accessibility-services
Email: studentaccessibility@stlawu.edu

Documentation submitted to: Student Accessibility Services
Separate application required for Services: Yes

Documentation required for:
LD: Psychoeducational evaluation
ADHD: Psychoeducational evaluation
ASD: Psychoeducational evaluation

St. Thomas Aquinas College

125 Route 340, Sparkill, NY 10976 • Admissions: 845-398-4100 • www.stac.edu

Support: CS

ACCOMMODATIONS

Allowed in exams:

Calculators	Yes
Dictionary	No
Computer	Yes
Spell-checker	Yes
Extended test time	Yes
Scribe	Yes
Proctors	Yes
Oral exams	No
Note-takers	Yes

Support services for students with:

LD	Yes
ADHD	Yes
ASD	Yes
Distraction-reduced environment	Yes
Recording of lecture allowed	Yes
Reading technology	Yes
Audio books	Yes
Other assistive technology	Yes
Priority registration	Yes

Added costs of services:

For LD	No
For ADHD	No
For ASD	No
LD specialists	Yes
ADHD & ASD coaching	No
ASD specialists	No
Professional tutors	Yes
Peer tutors	No
Max. hours/week for services	Varies
How professors are notified of student approved accommodations	Student

COLLEGE GRADUATION REQUIREMENTS

Course waivers allowed	No
Course substitutions allowed	Yes

In what courses: Foreign Language, Speech, and Math (only when math is not a requirement of the major)

DID YOU KNOW?

Oktoberfest is an annual fall event of concerts, inflatables, and Oktoberfest food. In April before the last week of classes, Springfest celebrates the end of the academic year with carnival games and a barbecue. Both events are sponsored by the Student Activities Office, are free to enjoy for students, faculty, and staff, and include contests, prizes, and a T-shirt giveaway.

PROGRAMS/SERVICES FOR STUDENTS WITH LEARNING DIFFERENCES

The Office of Disability Services (ODS) provides reasonable accommodations and services to meet the needs of students with documented disabilities. Students who choose to disclose a disability and request accommodations may register online by completing a request form and providing documentation. Accommodations provided include note-taking assistance, accessible-format textbooks, permission to use a calculator, preferential seating, extended time for timed testing, a reduced-distraction testing environment, and a scribe for testing. Eligible students with learning disabilities and attention deficit disorders may utilize the fee-based Pathways Program. The Pathways Program begins with a required summer program prior to the first semester to help transition students to college learning and the campus community. Pathway students meet with a learning specialist twice a week to review course content, build learning plans, and develop time management and organizational strategies. The learning specialists also serve as mentors to encourage self-advocacy and personal growth. In Pathway Workshops, students work with their peers on developing tools such as note-taking, assigned reading, effective communication and interview skills, and essay and résumé writing.

ADMISSIONS

All applicants follow the same general admission requirements. Applicants are required to submit a school report, résumé of extracurricular activities, a counselor recommendation, and one teacher evaluation. Students have the option to include a second teacher evaluation and up to two recommendations from other sources, if they so choose. The evaluation of applications that do not include SAT or ACT scores will place more emphasis on academic performance, the rigor of coursework, class placement, personal statements, recommendations, and cocurricular activities. If an applicant's high school coursework is lacking, they might be considered by the admissions committee if they can demonstrate a desire to pursue a college-level education and an intellectual readiness for college-level work.

Additional Information

The First Year Seminar (FYS), called STAGE 101, provides a semester-long introduction to college academics and learning skills. FYS sets expectations for class discussions, essay assignments, presentations, and defines terms that may be new to students. FYS creates a foundation of civic knowledge by posing questions concerning identity, diversity, inequality, citizenship, democracy, privilege, social responsibility, and ethical action. Every FYS has a common theme, but each section is unique to the instructor's interests and teaching style, and to the specific course topics that students choose. For more academic support, students can utilize the AQ Writing Center and the Student Success Center's peer tutoring program. The center is dedicated to sourcing tutors in every offered subject who have been trained, recommended by two faculty members, and have themselves taken the course for which they are tutoring.

St. Thomas Aquinas College

GENERAL ADMISSIONS

Very important factors include: rigor of secondary school record. *Important factors include:* recommendations. *Other factors considered include:* academic GPA, standardized test scores (if submitted), application essay. High school diploma is required and GED is accepted. Institution is test-optional for entering Fall 2024. Check admissions website for updates. *Academic units required:* 4 English, 3 math, 3 science (2 labs), 2 foreign language, 4 social studies, 1 academic elective. *Academic units recommended:* 3 foreign language.

FINANCIAL AID

Students should submit: FAFSA; State aid form. *Need-based scholarships/grants offered:* College/university scholarship or grant aid from institutional funds; Federal Pell; Private scholarships; SEOG; State scholarships/grants. *Loan aid offered:* Direct PLUS loans; Direct Subsidized Loans; Direct Unsubsidized Loans. Federal Work-Study Program available. Institutional employment available.

CAMPUS LIFE

Activities: Campus Ministries; Choral groups; Concert band; Dance; Drama/theater; Literary magazine; Music ensembles; Musical theater; Radio station; Student government; Student newspaper; Yearbook. **Organizations:** 35 registered organizations, 8 honor societies. **Athletics (Intercollegiate):** *Men:* baseball, basketball, cross-country, golf, ice hockey, lacrosse, track/field (indoor). *Women:* basketball, bowling, cross-country, field hockey, lacrosse, softball, track/field (indoor).

CAMPUS

Type of school	Private (nonprofit)
Environment	Village

STUDENTS

Undergrad enrollment	1,016
% male/female	53/47
% from out of state	18
% frosh live on campus	69

FINANCIAL FACTS

Annual tuition	$31,150
Room and board	$13,250
Required fees	$800

GENERAL ADMISSIONS INFO

Application fee	$30
Regular application deadline	Rolling
Nonfall registration	Yes
Fall 2024 testing policy	Test Optional
Range SAT EBRW	460–560
Range SAT Math	450–560
Range ACT Composite	18–25

ACADEMICS

Student/faculty ratio	14:1
% students returning for sophomore year	71

Most classes have 20–29 students.

REQUESTING SERVICES FOR STUDENTS WITH LEARNING DIFFERENCES

Phone: 845-398-4087 • stac.edu/about-stac/college-offices-directory/human-resources/disability-services
Email: aschlinc@stac.edu

Documentation submitted to: Office of Disability Services
Separate application required for Services: Yes

Documentation required for:
LD: Psychoeducational evaluation
ADHD: Psychoeducational evaluation
ASD: Psychoeducational evaluation

New York

Syracuse University

401 University Place, Syracuse, NY 13244-2130 • Admissions: 315-443-3611 • www.syracuse.edu

Support: SP

ACCOMMODATIONS

Allowed in exams:

Calculators	Yes
Dictionary	No
Computer	Yes
Spell-checker	Yes
Extended test time	Yes
Scribe	Yes
Proctors	Yes
Oral exams	Yes
Note-takers	Yes

Support services for students with:

LD	Yes
ADHD	Yes
ASD	Yes
Distraction-reduced environment	Yes
Recording of lecture allowed	Yes
Reading technology	Yes
Audio books	Yes
Other assistive technology	Yes
Priority registration	Yes

Added costs of services:

For LD	Yes
For ADHD	Yes
For ASD	Yes
LD specialists	No
ADHD & ASD coaching	Yes
ASD specialists	No
Professional tutors	Yes
Peer tutors	Yes
Max. hours/week for services	2
How professors are notified of student approved accommodations	Student

COLLEGE GRADUATION REQUIREMENTS

Course waivers allowed	No
Course substitutions allowed	Yes
In what courses: Math and Foreign Language	

PROGRAMS/SERVICES FOR STUDENTS WITH LEARNING DIFFERENCES

The Center for Disability Resources (CDR) assists students with disabilities who need accommodations and academic support. To begin the process, students must complete an online registration form and summarize their educational experience and history of using accommodations. Disability documentation can be uploaded at the same time. Students who do not have documentation should still register online and complete the form as thoroughly as possible, detailing their learning experience and request for specific accommodations. After CDR completes a review of the materials, students will receive an email with an assigned access coordinator and a guide to scheduling appointments. CDR offers services such as Academic Support Services, which provides content tutoring, assistance with learning, study, and note-taking strategies, "TimePlus" appointments to assist students with executive functioning skills related to academic priorities, and general support (non-clinical) for students experiencing frustration, anxiety with academics, and transitioning to college life. Access 'Cuse is a two-day, pre-Syracuse welcome program for students planning to seek disability-related accommodations, where students have small group discussions regarding the social, emotional, and academic expectations of the college experience. OnTrack at SU is a fee-based program for first-year students with ADHD and learning disabilities that addresses the academic, social, and emotional aspects of transitioning to college. Students meet in person twice a week with an assigned coach for structure, support, and guidance. OnTrack is focused on building independence and executive function during the first year, however, students enrolled in OnTrack during their first year have the option to continue a scaled-down version in their second year.

ADMISSIONS

All applicants complete the same application process and are reviewed the same for admission. Official high school transcripts, a senior year grade report, a school counselor report, and two academic recommendations are required. Students who choose not to submit test scores will not be disadvantaged in the application process and will remain eligible for merit scholarships. A personal essay and an additional college question are required. There are also college-specific additional requirements.

Additional Information

The Center for Learning and Student Success (CLASS) offers in-person, small-group tutoring in approximately 20 courses that have traditionally been challenging for students. Syracuse University covers tutoring costs for students by issuing tutoring vouchers that work like gift cards, covering up to a specific dollar amount.

DID YOU KNOW?

Sam Van Aken, sculptor and art professor, produced his first "Tree of 40 Fruits" in 2008 at SU on the Quad walkway. It came from an interest in grafting and natural art, and the number 40 was chosen for its historical and biblical significance. In spring, it blossoms in shades of white, pink, and crimson and then bears a variety of stone fruits. Today some of his trees are planted around the country, with more to come. His work offers creative and practical thinking about climate change and food security.

Syracuse University

General Admissions

Very important factors include: rigor of secondary school record, class rank, academic GPA, application essay, recommendations. *Other factors considered include:* standardized test scores (if submitted). High school diploma is required and GED is accepted. Institution is test-optional for entering Fall 2024. Check admissions website for updates. *Academic units recommended:* 4 English, 4 math, 4 science (4 labs), 3 foreign language, 4 social studies.

Financial Aid

Students should submit: CSS/Financial Aid Profile; FAFSA; Noncustodial Profile. *Need-based scholarships/grants offered:* College/university scholarship or grant aid from institutional funds; Federal Pell; Private scholarships; SEOG; State scholarships/grants. *Loan aid offered:* Direct PLUS loans; Direct Subsidized Loans; Direct Unsubsidized Loans. Federal Work-Study Program available. Institutional employment available.

Campus Life

Activities: Campus Ministries; Choral groups; Concert band; Dance; Drama/theater; International Student Organization; Jazz band; Literary magazine; Marching band; Model UN; Music ensembles; Musical theater; Opera; Pep band; Radio station; Student government; Student newspaper; Student-run film society; Symphony orchestra; Television station; Yearbook. **Organizations:** 311 registered organizations, 34 honor societies, 27 religious organizations, 21 fraternities, 24 sororities. **Athletics (Intercollegiate):** *Men:* baseball, basketball, bowling, crew/rowing, cross-country, equestrian sports, golf, gymnastics, ice hockey, lacrosse, martial arts, swimming, table tennis, track/field (indoor), ultimate frisbee, volleyball, water polo, wrestling. *Women:* basketball, bowling, crew/rowing, cross-country, equestrian sports, field hockey, golf, gymnastics, ice hockey, lacrosse, martial arts, softball, swimming, table tennis, track/field (indoor), ultimate frisbee, volleyball, water polo.

CAMPUS

Type of school	Private (nonprofit)
Environment	City

STUDENTS

Undergrad enrollment	15,071
% male/female	46/54
% from out of state	65
% frosh live on campus	99

FINANCIAL FACTS

Annual tuition	$58,440
Room and board	$17,170
Required fees	$1,695

GENERAL ADMISSIONS INFO

Application fee	$85
Regular application deadline	1/5
Nonfall registration	Yes

Fall 2024 testing policy	Test Optional
Range SAT EBRW	630–710
Range SAT Math	620–720
Range ACT Composite	28–32

ACADEMICS

Student/faculty ratio	15:1
% students returning for sophomore year	91

Most classes have 10–19 students.

REQUESTING SERVICES FOR STUDENTS WITH LEARNING DIFFERENCES

Phone: 315-443-4498 • disabilityresources.syr.edu/ • Email: disabilityresources@syr.edu

Documentation submitted to: Center for Disability Resources
Separate application required for Services: Yes

Documentation required for:
LD: Psychoeducational evaluation
ADHD: Psychoeducational evaluation
ASD: Psychoeducational evaluation

New York

Utica University

1600 Burrstone Road, Utica, NY 13502-4892 • Admissions: 315-792-3006 • www.utica.edu

Support: CS

ACCOMMODATIONS

Allowed in exams:	
Calculators	Yes
Dictionary	Yes
Computer	Yes
Spell-checker	Yes
Extended test time	Yes
Scribe	Yes
Proctors	Yes
Oral exams	Yes
Note-takers	Yes
Support services for students with:	
LD	Yes
ADHD	Yes
ASD	Yes
Distraction-reduced environment	Yes
Recording of lecture allowed	Yes
Reading technology	Yes
Audio books	Yes
Other assistive technology	Yes
Priority registration	Yes
Added costs of services:	
For LD	No
For ADHD	No
For ASD	No
LD specialists	Yes
ADHD & ASD coaching	No
ASD specialists	Yes
Professional tutors	Yes
Peer tutors	Yes
Max. hours/week for services	Varies
How professors are notified of student approved accommodations	Student and Office of Learning Services

COLLEGE GRADUATION REQUIREMENTS

Course waivers allowed	No
Course substitutions allowed	Yes
In what courses: Case-by-case basis	

PROGRAMS/SERVICES FOR STUDENTS WITH LEARNING DIFFERENCES

The Office of Learning Services (OLS) at Utica University provides support to students with learning disabilities. Once they are accepted to the university, students can initiate a request for accommodations by contacting OLS and submitting supporting documentation. Professional staff members at OLS meet with students to discuss accommodations and determine eligibility, coordinate auxiliary services, and assist, advise, and advocate for the students. Services may include priority registration, specific skill remediation, learning and study strategy development, referrals for diagnostic evaluation, time management strategies, and professional tutoring. Accommodations such as recording devices, notetakers, extended time on tests, alternative testing methods, and separate locations for tests are also available. Each student receives a letter outlining their accommodations and should meet with their instructors to review them.

ADMISSIONS

Admissions evaluates all students individually and holistically. Students should meet all of the academic course requirements; a foreign language is no longer required. Substitutions or waivers for math courses may be permitted but are reviewed on a case-by-case basis. A personal statement on a topic of the applicant's choosing is required. In general, the university is test-optional. However, certain nursing and health programs do require applicants to submit ACT or SAT scores. Students interested in physical and occupational therapy, nursing and pre-med programs must have taken 4 years of math and science.

Additional Information

All students have access to free student tutors and professional online tutors who hold a master's degree or higher. First-years also benefit from a peer mentoring program.

Utica's annual Squirrel Day began in September 2015 when a squirrel, later dubbed "Sparky," chewed electrical lines and caused a campus-wide power outage. Classes were canceled and students gathered on the quad to play games. Squirrel Day is now a yearly tradition for students to unwind with a zip line, planned activities, a petting zoo, and more.

Utica University

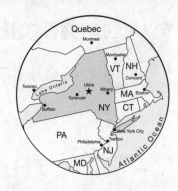

General Admissions

Very important factors include: rigor of secondary school record, academic GPA. *Important factors include:* standardized test scores (if submitted), application essay. *Other factors considered include:* class rank, recommendations. High school diploma is required and GED is accepted. Institution is test-optional for entering Fall 2024. Check admissions website for updates. *Academic units recommended:* 4 English, 3 math, 3 science, 2 foreign language, 3 social studies.

Financial Aid

Students should submit: FAFSA; State aid form. *Need-based scholarships/grants offered:* College/university scholarship or grant aid from institutional funds; Federal Pell; Private scholarships; SEOG; State scholarships/grants. *Loan aid offered:* Direct PLUS loans; Direct Subsidized Loans; Direct Unsubsidized Loans. Federal Work-Study Program available. Institutional employment available.

Campus Life

Activities: Campus Ministries; Choral groups; Concert band; Dance; Drama/theater; International Student Organization; Jazz band; Literary magazine; Music ensembles; Radio station; Student government; Student newspaper; Television station; Yearbook. **Organizations:** 80 registered organizations, 8 honor societies, 3 religious organizations, 3 fraternities, 4 sororities. **Athletics (Intercollegiate):** *Men:* baseball, basketball, cross-country, golf, ice hockey, lacrosse, martial arts, swimming, track/field (indoor). *Women:* basketball, cross-country, field hockey, ice hockey, lacrosse, martial arts, softball, swimming, track/field (indoor), volleyball, water polo.

CAMPUS
Type of school	Private (nonprofit)
Environment	City

STUDENTS
Undergrad enrollment	2,813
% male/female	42/58
% from out of state	12
% frosh live on campus	70

FINANCIAL FACTS
Annual tuition	$22,314
Room and board	$12,572
Required fees	$950

GENERAL ADMISSIONS INFO
Application fee	$40
Regular application deadline	Rolling
Nonfall registration	Yes

Fall 2024 testing policy	Test Optional
Range SAT EBRW	530–610
Range SAT Math	530–610
Range ACT Composite	24–25

ACADEMICS
Student/faculty ratio	11:1
% students returning for sophomore year	74
Most classes have 10–19 students.	

REQUESTING SERVICES FOR STUDENTS WITH LEARNING DIFFERENCES

Phone: 315-792-3032 • www.utica.edu/student/development/learning/ • Email: jcborner@utica.edu

Documentation submitted to: Learning Services Office
Separate application required for Services: Yes

Documentation required for:
LD: Psychoeducational evaluation
ADHD: Psychoeducational evaluation
ASD: Psychoeducational evaluation

Appalachian State University

Office of Admissions, Boone, NC 28608-2004 • Admissions: 828-262-2120 • www.appstate.edu

Support: CS

ACCOMMODATIONS

Allowed in exams:

Calculators	Yes
Dictionary	No
Computer	Yes
Spell-checker	Yes
Extended test time	Yes
Scribe	Yes
Proctors	Yes
Oral exams	Yes
Note-takers	Yes

Support services for students with:

LD	Yes
ADHD	Yes
ASD	Yes
Distraction-reduced environment	Yes
Recording of lecture allowed	Yes
Reading technology	Yes
Audio books	Yes
Other assistive technology	Yes
Priority registration	Yes

Added costs of services:

For LD	No
For ADHD	No
For ASD	No
LD specialists	No
ADHD & ASD coaching	Yes
ASD specialists	No
Professional tutors	No
Peer tutors	Yes
Max. hours/week for services	Varies
How professors are notified of student approved accommodations	Student

COLLEGE GRADUATION REQUIREMENTS

Course waivers allowed	Yes
In what courses: Case-by-case basis	
Course substitutions allowed	Yes
In what courses: Case-by-case basis	

PROGRAMS/SERVICES FOR STUDENTS WITH LEARNING DIFFERENCES

The Office of Disability Resources (ODR) determines and coordinates course accommodations for students with disabilities. Students are encouraged to begin the process of requesting accommodations once they are accepted and have chosen to attend Appalachian State. Accommodations are determined on a case-by-case basis, and can include priority registration, academic adjustments, alternate-format material, auxiliary aids/services, and note-taking provisions. Students admitted through the general application process may apply to As-U-R, a no-fee, intensive support program for students with executive function challenges (EFCs). The program focuses on developing successful academic skills, such as organization, prioritizing and completing tasks, and decision-making. The program has weekly one-on-one meetings with a mentoring graduate assistant, as well as access to As-U-R coordinators and learning specialists. As-U-R also offers several seminars for elective credit.

ADMISSIONS

All applicants need to have completed the minimum admission requirements of core high school-level coursework; official high school transcripts are required. The weighted GPA of the middle 50 percent of first-year applicants admitted to Appalachian State is 3.82–4.34, based on all courses taken during high school.

Additional Information

The Disco Student Learning Center offers academic resources to help students improve their ability to learn. Peer Academic Coaches (PACs) provide coaching for academic success skills, and students can schedule daily appointments with peer tutors for each course. Additionally, students may take a graded 1 credit hour elective academic success course. Other resources that promote students' success include counseling, health and wellness, and clubs and activities.

DID YOU KNOW?

Appalachian State surrounds Boone Cemetery, where the university's founders and other leading citizens have been buried. Fenced off on the east side is the old Jordan Councill Cemetery, where remains of 160 unknown enslaved Africans, members of the Junaluska community, and Union soldiers were buried. In 2017, through extraordinary collaborative efforts, 65 known names were memorialized on a single marker to recognize the site as a community treasure.

Appalachian State University

GENERAL ADMISSIONS

Very important factors include: rigor of secondary school record, class rank, academic GPA. *Important factors include:* standardized test scores (if submitted). *Other factors considered include:* application essay. High school diploma is required and GED is accepted. Institution is test-optional for entering Fall 2024. Check admissions website for updates. *Academic units required:* 4 English, 4 math, 3 science (1 lab), 2 foreign language, 1 social studies, 1 U.S. history.

FINANCIAL AID

Students should submit: FAFSA. *Need-based scholarships/grants offered:* College/university scholarship or grant aid from institutional funds; Federal Pell; Private scholarships; SEOG; State scholarships/grants. *Loan aid offered:* Direct PLUS loans; Direct Subsidized Loans; Direct Unsubsidized Loans. Federal Work-Study Program available. Institutional employment available.

CAMPUS LIFE

Activities: Campus Ministries; Choral groups; Concert band; Dance; Drama/theater; International Student Organization; Jazz band; Literary magazine; Marching band; Model UN; Music ensembles; Musical theater; Opera; Pep band; Radio station; Student government; Student newspaper; Student-run film society; Symphony orchestra; Television station. **Organizations:** 413 registered organizations, 22 honor societies, 30 religious organizations, 18 fraternities, 13 sororities. **Athletics (Intercollegiate):** *Men:* baseball, basketball, cross-country, cycling, equestrian sports, golf, ice hockey, lacrosse, rugby, swimming, ultimate frisbee, volleyball, wrestling. *Women:* basketball, cross-country, cycling, equestrian sports, field hockey, golf, ice hockey, lacrosse, rugby, softball, swimming, track/field (indoor), ultimate frisbee, volleyball.

CAMPUS

Type of school	Public
Environment	Village

STUDENTS

Undergrad enrollment	18,467
% male/female	44/56
% from out of state	8
% frosh live on campus	99

FINANCIAL FACTS

Annual in-state tuition	$4,242
Annual out-of-state tuition	$20,246
Room and board	$11,582
Required fees	$3,208

GENERAL ADMISSIONS INFO

Application fee	$65
Regular application deadline	2/1
Nonfall registration	Yes

Fall 2024 testing policy	Test Optional
Range SAT EBRW	560–650
Range SAT Math	540–620
Range ACT Composite	21–27

ACADEMICS

Student/faculty ratio	16:1
% students returning for sophomore year	83

Most classes have 20–29 students.

REQUESTING SERVICES FOR STUDENTS WITH LEARNING DIFFERENCES

Phone: 828-262-3056 • odr.appstate.edu • Email: odr@appstate.edu

Documentation submitted to: Office of Disability Resources
Separate application required for Services: Yes

Documentation required for:
LD: Psychoeducational evaluation
ADHD: Psychoeducational evaluation
ASD: Psychoeducational evaluation

Brevard College

One Brevard College Drive, Brevard, NC 28712 • Admissions: 828-884-8300 • brevard.edu

Support: CS

ACCOMMODATIONS

Allowed in exams:

Calculators	Yes
Dictionary	Yes
Computer	Yes
Spell-checker	Yes
Extended test time	Yes
Scribe	Yes
Proctors	Yes
Oral exams	Yes
Note-takers	Yes

Support services for students with:

LD	Yes
ADHD	Yes
ASD	Yes
Distraction-reduced environment	Yes
Recording of lecture allowed	Yes
Reading technology	Yes
Audio books	Yes
Other assistive technology	Yes
Priority registration	Yes

Added costs of services:

For LD	No
For ADHD	No
For ASD	No
LD specialists	Yes
ADHD & ASD coaching	Yes
ASD specialists	No
Professional tutors	No
Peer tutors	Yes
Max. hours/week for services	Varies
How professors are notified of student approved accommodations	Student

COLLEGE GRADUATION REQUIREMENTS

Course waivers allowed	No
Course substitutions allowed	Yes
In what courses: Case-by-case basis	

PROGRAMS/SERVICES FOR STUDENTS WITH LEARNING DIFFERENCES

The Accessibility and Disability Services offers support and accommodations to students with learning differences. Prior to starting the semester, students submit documentation of their disability with a request for academic accommodation form to the Accessibility and Disability Services office. Upon approval, students are invited to a welcome meeting with the director to discuss implementation. Students can forward their official academic letter from the office to each professor in the courses where accommodations will be used. In addition to providing resources for learning strategies, Accessibility and Disability Services offers other services, including computer or assistive technology, notetakers, course material in alternate formats, and extended or testing in a reduced-distraction setting.

ADMISSIONS

All applicants are expected to meet the same admission criteria. A foreign language is not required for admission. Students may apply via the test-optional route but must submit a personal essay in lieu of test scores. While teacher evaluations are not required, admissions will consider up to 10 letters of recommendation from teachers and other sources. The minimum GPA required for admission of first-year students is 2.5 (unweighted), and the average first-year class has an average unweighted GPA of 3.23. Students offered conditional admission are automatically enrolled in the Academic Progress Program for Students (APPS). This program works closely with students who may have academic challenges, and ensures they are building skills in time management, studying, and exam preparation.

Additional Information

For their first semester, all students enroll in a First Year Experience (FYE) course, which helps transition them to college life, introduce campus resources, and encourage engagement within the BC community. Each student is also assigned a Success Mentor to ensure that students are both excited and challenged by their environment. All students are offered tutoring services at the Experimental Learning Center (ELC), where they can refine their study habits, strengthen their grasp of course materials, and get feedback on their writing. Additionally, the Writing Center offers proofreading and consults for students to build writing and research skills.

Brevard celebrates and honors its students by inviting their families to visit during Family Weekend. Senior Pinning is a treasured Brevard Family Weekend tradition where seniors are presented with a special pin by a significant person of their choice.

Brevard College

GENERAL ADMISSIONS

Very important factors include: rigor of secondary school record, academic GPA. *Important factors include:* class rank, application essay. *Other factors considered include:* standardized test scores (if submitted), recommendations. High school diploma is required and GED is accepted. Institution is test-optional for entering Fall 2024. Check admissions website for updates. *Academic units recommended:* 4 English, 4 math, 3 science (1 lab), 2 social studies, 4 academic electives.

FINANCIAL AID

Students should submit: FAFSA. *Need-based scholarships/grants offered:* College/university scholarship or grant aid from institutional funds; Federal Pell; Private scholarships; SEOG; State scholarships/grants. *Loan aid offered:* Direct PLUS loans; Direct Subsidized Loans; Direct Unsubsidized Loans. Federal Work-Study Program available. Institutional employment available.

CAMPUS LIFE

Activities: Campus Ministries; Choral groups; Concert band; Dance; Drama/theater; Jazz band; Literary magazine; Music ensembles; Musical theater; Opera; Pep band; Student government; Student newspaper; Yearbook. **Organizations:** 32 registered organizations, 3 honor societies, 1 religious organizations, 0 fraternities, 0 sororities. **Athletics (Intercollegiate):** *Men:* baseball, basketball, cross-country, cycling, golf, lacrosse, softball, ultimate frisbee, volleyball. *Women:* basketball, cross-country, cycling, golf, lacrosse, softball, ultimate frisbee, volleyball.

CAMPUS

Type of school	Private (nonprofit)
Environment	Village

STUDENTS

Undergrad enrollment	770
% male/female	59/41
% from out of state	47
% frosh live on campus	87

FINANCIAL FACTS

Annual tuition	$29,400
Room and board	$13,400
Required fees	$1,850

GENERAL ADMISSIONS INFO

Application fee	No fee
Regular application deadline	Rolling
Nonfall registration	Yes

Fall 2024 testing policy	Test Optional
Range SAT EBRW	420–520
Range SAT Math	420–530
Range ACT Composite	17–22

ACADEMICS

Student/faculty ratio	10:1
% students returning for sophomore year	67

Most classes have 2–9 students.

REQUESTING SERVICES FOR STUDENTS WITH LEARNING DIFFERENCES

Phone: 828-641-0653 • brevard.edu/disability-services • Email: Kathleen.Koontz@brevard.edu

Documentation submitted to: Accessibility and Disability Services

Separate application required for Services: Yes

Documentation required for:
LD: Psychoeducational evaluation
ADHD: Psychoeducational evaluation
ASD: Psychoeducational evaluation

Davidson College

P.O. Box 7156, Davidson, NC 28035-7156 • Admissions: 704-894-2230 • www.davidson.edu

Support: CS

ACCOMMODATIONS

Allowed in exams:

Calculators	Yes
Dictionary	Yes
Computer	Yes
Spell-checker	Yes
Extended test time	Yes
Scribe	Yes
Proctors	Yes
Oral exams	No
Note-takers	Yes

Support services for students with:

LD	Yes
ADHD	Yes
ASD	Yes
Distraction-reduced environment	Yes
Recording of lecture allowed	Yes
Reading technology	Yes
Audio books	Yes
Other assistive technology	Yes
Priority registration	Yes

Added costs of services:

For LD	No
For ADHD	No
For ASD	No
LD specialists	Yes
ADHD & ASD coaching	Yes
ASD specialists	No
Professional tutors	No
Peer tutors	Yes
Max. hours/week for services	Varies
How professors are notified of student approved accommodations	Student and Academic Access and Disability Resources

COLLEGE GRADUATION REQUIREMENTS

Course waivers allowed	No
Course substitutions allowed	Yes

In what courses: Case-by-case basis

PROGRAMS/SERVICES FOR STUDENTS WITH LEARNING DIFFERENCES

The Academic Access and Disability Resources office (AADR) serves students with learning differences regarding course content, services, and programs. To receive accommodations, students must register and submit accommodation requests along with appropriate documentation as soon as possible. Accommodations are not retroactive and will only take effect once AADR staff have issued formal communication stating the approved accommodations. Academic accommodations may include extended time on tests, reduced-distraction testing, note-taking assistance, accessible course materials, and use of a computer or assistive technology. Reduced course loads and foreign language substitutions may also be considered if the student's documentation supports it. Support services include consults, referrals, and diagnostic evaluation, as well as guidance from peers and professionals.

ADMISSIONS

Admission requirements are the same for all students. However, students with learning differences are encouraged to self-disclose, as the admission office may consult with knowledgeable support staff. The process is competitive, and disclosure can help the admissions office more fairly evaluate a student's transcript. For example, a lack of foreign language or lower math grades on a student transcript could be related to learning disabilities and addressed by the applicant's acknowledgement. Interviews are neither required nor recommended.

Additional Information

Students can utilize the Peer Academic Coaching program in addition receiving one-on-one instruction in study and learning strategies from professional coaches.

Lux the Wildcat is a Davidson iconic mascot and appears at every pep rally and sporting event. His history dates back to the late 1800s, when rumor spread of a real-life wildcat roaming the campus. In the late 1890s, to play a prank, a group of students created a fake wildcat. In 1917, the Wildcat was officially adopted as mascot after an Atlanta sportswriter called the Davidson football team "Wildcats" because of their small stature and ferocious style.

Davidson College

GENERAL ADMISSIONS

Very important factors include: rigor of secondary school record, recommendations. *Important factors include:* application essay. *Other factors considered include:* class rank, academic GPA, standardized test scores (if submitted). High school diploma is required and GED is not accepted. Institution is test-optional for entering Fall 2024. Check admissions website for updates. *Academic units required:* 4 English, 3 math, 2 science, 2 social studies, 2 foreign language. *Academic units recommended:* 4 social studies, 4 math, 4 science, 4 foreign language.

FINANCIAL AID

Students should submit: CSS/Financial Aid Profile; FAFSA; Noncustodial Profile. *Need-based scholarships/grants offered:* College/university scholarship or grant aid from institutional funds; Federal Pell; Private scholarships; SEOG; State scholarships/grants. *Loan aid offered:* Direct PLUS loans; Direct Subsidized Loans; Direct Unsubsidized Loans. Federal Work-Study Program available. Institutional employment available.

CAMPUS LIFE

Activities: Campus Ministries; Choral groups; Dance; Drama/theater; International Student Organization; Jazz band; Literary magazine; Model UN; Music ensembles; Musical theater; Pep band; Radio station; Student government; Student newspaper; Symphony orchestra; Yearbook. **Organizations:** 168 registered organizations, 15 honor societies, 16 religious organizations, 8 fraternities, 6 sororities. **Athletics (Intercollegiate):** *Men:* baseball, basketball, crew/rowing, cross-country, field hockey, golf, lacrosse, rugby, swimming, wrestling. *Women:* basketball, crew/rowing, cross-country, field hockey, lacrosse, swimming, volleyball.

CAMPUS
Type of school	Private (nonprofit)
Environment	Village

STUDENTS
Undergrad enrollment	1,922
% male/female	47/53
% from out of state	78
% frosh live on campus	100

FINANCIAL FACTS
Annual tuition	$58,970
Room and board	$16,400
Required fees	$540

GENERAL ADMISSIONS INFO
Application fee	$50
Regular application deadline	1/10
Nonfall registration	No

Fall 2024 testing policy	Test Optional
Range SAT EBRW	670–740
Range SAT Math	680–760
Range ACT Composite	31–33

ACADEMICS
Student/faculty ratio	9:1
% students returning for sophomore year	94

Most classes have 10–19 students.

REQUESTING SERVICES FOR STUDENTS WITH LEARNING DIFFERENCES

Phone: 704-894-2071 • www.davidson.edu/offices-and-services/academic-access-disability-resources
Email: AADR@davidson.edu

Documentation submitted to: The Academic Access and Disability Resources Office
Separate application required for Services: Yes

Documentation required for:
LD: Psychoeducational evaluation
ADHD: Psychoeducational evaluation
ASD: Psychoeducational evaluation

Duke University

2138 Campus Drive, Durham, NC 27708 • Admissions: 919-684-3214 • www.duke.edu

Support: CS

ACCOMMODATIONS

Allowed in exams:

Calculators	Yes
Dictionary	Yes
Computer	Yes
Spell-checker	Yes
Extended test time	Yes
Scribe	Yes
Proctors	Yes
Oral exams	Yes
Note-takers	Yes

Support services for students with:

LD	Yes
ADHD	Yes
ASD	Yes
Distraction-reduced environment	Yes
Recording of lecture allowed	Yes
Reading technology	Yes
Audio books	Yes
Other assistive technology	Yes
Priority registration	No

Added costs of services:

For LD	No
For ADHD	No
For ASD	No
LD specialists	Yes
ADHD & ASD coaching	Yes
ASD specialists	No
Professional tutors	No
Peer tutors	Yes
Max. hours/week for services	Varies
How professors are notified of student approved accommodations	Student and Student Disability Access Office

COLLEGE GRADUATION REQUIREMENTS

Course waivers allowed	No
Course substitutions allowed	No

DID YOU KNOW?

In 1878, after the Civil War, Washington Duke and his children established a tobacco farm that became the American Tobacco Company. In 1890, he donated $85,000 (approximately $3 million today) to the school. The Duke Endowment was created by his sons in 1924, providing ongoing funding for Duke. Today, smoking is not permitted within 10 feet of residential buildings or dining facilities and is completely banned on the campus of the medical center.

PROGRAMS/SERVICES FOR STUDENTS WITH LEARNING DIFFERENCES

The Student Disability Access Office (SDAO) determines eligibility for services and accommodations for students with documented disabilities. Students can obtain reasonable accommodations by submitting supporting documentation to SDAO's online student portal, Accommodate, and may speak with a case manager in SDAO about the process. Documentation should address the disability and provide recommendations for appropriate accommodations. Once the request has been received, an email is sent from SDAO to schedule a meeting with a case manager to review approved accommodations. It is then the student's responsibility to request an accommodation notification letter and a meeting with their professors to discuss implementation. In addition to accommodations, the Academic Resource Center (ARC) offers specific supports for students with learning disabilities, ADHD, executive function disorders, and ASD, including coaching, consulting, and training in compensatory learning strategies. Specialized learning consultants who are well-versed in neurodiversity provide individual academic support services to students and are available for weekly meetings to cover course-specific challenges and tailored learning strategies.

ADMISSIONS

All applicants must meet the general Duke admission criteria. Most applicants are in the top 10 percent of their class and have completed a demanding curriculum that consists of many AP and honors courses. Duke requires two teacher and one counselor recommendations. Applicants have the option to submit one additional personal recommendation from a coach, a director, or a teacher of an elective. Some students choose to disclose a disability in their application because it is an important element of their experiences, or because it demonstrates how they dealt with an obstacle. Duke considers this information in understanding a student's achievements and evaluates accomplishments within the context of opportunities or challenges presented to that student. Duke does not use this information to deny admission to a student.

Additional Information

Available to all Duke students, the Academic Resource Center (ARC) has learning consultants to help with time management, test preparation, class and course strategies, problem solving, and learning alternatives. The consultants can also help students understand their unique learning styles. There are learning consultants with specific areas of expertise who can work with students to identify strategies for problem solving for a particular course. Peer tutors are available, and sessions are generally one hour in length but can be longer based on a student's needs. The ARC also hosts workshops and presentations on a range of topics, including effective studying and learning strategies, time management, and more.

Duke University

GENERAL ADMISSIONS

Very important factors include: rigor of secondary school record, academic GPA, standardized test scores (if submitted), application essay, recommendations. High school diploma is required and GED is not accepted. Institution is test-optional for entering Fall 2024. Check admissions website for updates. *Academic units recommended:* 4 English, 3 math, 3 science, 3 foreign language, 3 social studies.

FINANCIAL AID

Students should submit: Business/Farm Supplement; CSS/Financial Aid Profile; FAFSA; Noncustodial Profile. *Need-based scholarships/grants offered:* College/university scholarship or grant aid from institutional funds; Federal Pell; Private scholarships; SEOG; State scholarships/grants. *Loan aid offered:* Direct PLUS loans; Direct Subsidized Loans; Direct Unsubsidized Loans. Federal Work-Study Program available. Institutional employment available.

CAMPUS LIFE

Activities: Campus Ministries; Choral groups; Concert band; Dance; Drama/theater; International Student Organization; Jazz band; Literary magazine; Marching band; Model UN; Music ensembles; Musical theater; Opera; Pep band; Radio station; Student government; Student newspaper; Student-run film society; Symphony orchestra; Television station. **Organizations:** 200 registered organizations, 10 honor societies, 25 religious organizations, 21 fraternities, 14 sororities. **Athletics (Intercollegiate):** *Men:* baseball, basketball, crew/rowing, cross-country, golf, ice hockey, lacrosse, rugby, swimming, track/field (indoor), volleyball, water polo, wrestling. *Women:* basketball, crew/rowing, cross-country, field hockey, golf, lacrosse, softball, swimming, track/field (indoor), volleyball, water polo.

CAMPUS

Type of school	Private (nonprofit)
Environment	Metropolis

STUDENTS

Undergrad enrollment	6,596
% male/female	50/50
% from out of state	85
% frosh live on campus	100

FINANCIAL FACTS

Annual tuition	$55,880
Room and board	$15,588
Required fees	$2,051

GENERAL ADMISSIONS INFO

Application fee	$85
Regular application deadline	1/3
Nonfall registration	No

Fall 2024 testing policy	Test Optional
Range SAT EBRW	710–770
Range SAT Math	740–800
Range ACT Composite	33–35

ACADEMICS

Student/faculty ratio	6:1
% students returning for sophomore year	98

Most classes have 10–19 students.

REQUESTING SERVICES FOR STUDENTS WITH LEARNING DIFFERENCES

Phone: 919-668-1267 • access.duke.edu • Email: sdao@duke.edu

Documentation submitted to: Student Disability Access Office

Separate application required for Services: Yes

Documentation required for:
LD: Psychoeducational evaluation
ADHD: Psychoeducational evaluation
ASD: Psychoeducational evaluation

East Carolina University

Undergraduate Admissions, Greenville, NC 27858 • Admissions: 252-328-6640 • ecu.edu

Support: CS

ACCOMMODATIONS

Allowed in exams:	
Calculators	Yes
Dictionary	Yes
Computer	Yes
Spell-checker	Yes
Extended test time	Yes
Scribe	Yes
Proctors	Yes
Oral exams	Yes
Note-takers	Yes
Support services for students with:	
LD	Yes
ADHD	Yes
ASD	Yes
Distraction-reduced environment	Yes
Recording of lecture allowed	Yes
Reading technology	Yes
Audio books	Yes
Other assistive technology	Yes
Priority registration	Yes
Added costs of services:	
For LD	No
For ADHD	No
For ASD	No
LD specialists	No
ADHD & ASD coaching	Yes
ASD specialists	Yes
Professional tutors	No
Peer tutors	Yes
Max. hours/week for services	Varies
How professors are notified of student approved accommodations	Student

COLLEGE GRADUATION REQUIREMENTS

Course waivers allowed	Yes
In what courses: Case-by-case basis	
Course substitutions allowed	No

PROGRAMS/SERVICES FOR STUDENTS WITH LEARNING DIFFERENCES

Disability Support Services (DSS) provides accommodations for students with documented disabilities. Prior to receiving services, DSS requires that students attend an intake meeting and provide appropriate documentation. Once accommodations have been determined by DSS, students receive an approved accommodations letter to present to their professors. Once approved, students remain eligible for accommodations throughout their enrollment at East Carolina University (ECU), but students must come to DSS at the start of each new semester to receive new accommodations letters. The STEPP Program (Supporting Transition and Education through Planning and Partnership) at ECU provides comprehensive support for students with specific learning disabilities. Limited to 10 students each year, the program offers social, academic, and life skills support with graduate student mentors and tutors. STEPP students are required to take five STEPP courses in addition to their course load. There are required study halls, graduate student mentors, tutors in certain subjects, and ongoing advising. There is no additional fee to participate. First-year students are required to attend a boot camp with their parents to introduce them to the college experience at the university.

ADMISSIONS

The admission standards are the same for all students. It's important to ensure that applicants complete two years of the same foreign language and four years of math before graduating high school. ECU accepts American Sign Language (ASL) and Latin for the foreign language requirement. Students should begin their application to STEPP 18 months before their expected start date at ECU. While STEPP has some flexibility and alternate admissions criteria, students who meet or exceed expectations are the most competitive candidates. STEPP's application process considers traditional admission criteria and seeks to admit students who show a readiness for college and a willingness to use the support offered. If students are denied admission because they do not meet the admission standards, they may appeal that decision to Admissions.

Additional Information

There are several free tutoring resources available to all East Carolina University students. The Pirate Academic Success Center has tutors available for learning, time management, and core first-year classes. There are two writing labs on campus and a math lab as well. There are also tutors available through individual academic departments.

In 1984, Dr. Walter Randolph Chitwood, Jr., accepted a position at Brody School of Medicine at ECU as the chief of cardiothoracic and vascular surgery. In May 2000, he was the first surgeon in North America (and 2nd ever) to perform open-heart surgery using a newly developed da Vinci robotic surgical system that he helped to design. In Dr. Chitwood's surgical career, he performed over 10,000 surgical procedures, authored over 250 scientific articles, and received worldwide professional recognition.

East Carolina University

GENERAL ADMISSIONS

Very important factors include: rigor of secondary school record, academic GPA, application essay. *Important factors include:* class rank. High school diploma is required and GED is accepted. Institution is test-optional for entering Fall 2024. Check admissions website for updates. *Academic units required:* 4 English, 4 math, 3 science (1 lab), 2 foreign language, 1 social studies, 1 U.S. history. *Academic units recommended:* 1 visual/performing arts.

FINANCIAL AID

Students should submit: FAFSA. *Need-based scholarships/grants offered:* College/university scholarship or grant aid from institutional funds; Federal Nursing Scholarships; Federal Pell; Private scholarships; SEOG; State scholarships/grants. *Loan aid offered:* Direct PLUS loans; Direct Subsidized Loans; Direct Unsubsidized Loans. Federal Work-Study Program available. Institutional employment available.

CAMPUS LIFE

Activities: Campus Ministries; Choral groups; Concert band; Dance; Drama/theater; International Student Organization; Jazz band; Literary magazine; Marching band; Model UN; Music ensembles; Musical theater; Opera; Pep band; Radio station; Student government; Student newspaper; Student-run film society; Symphony orchestra; Television station; Yearbook. **Organizations:** 345 registered organizations, 19 honor societies, 26 religious organizations, 22 fraternities, 14 sororities. **Athletics (Intercollegiate):** *Men:* baseball, basketball, bowling, cross-country, equestrian sports, field hockey, golf, ice hockey, lacrosse, martial arts, rugby, softball, swimming, track/field (indoor), ultimate frisbee, volleyball, wrestling. *Women:* basketball, bowling, cross-country, equestrian sports, field hockey, golf, lacrosse, martial arts, rugby, softball, swimming, track/field (indoor), ultimate frisbee, volleyball.

CAMPUS
Type of school	Public
Environment	City

STUDENTS
Undergrad enrollment	20,385
% male/female	43/57
% from out of state	9
% frosh live on campus	92

FINANCIAL FACTS
Annual in-state tuition	$7,516
Annual out-of-state tuition	$23,793
Room and board	$11,000

GENERAL ADMISSIONS INFO
Application fee	$75
Regular application deadline	4/1
Nonfall registration	Yes

Fall 2024 testing policy	Test Optional
Range SAT EBRW	520–620
Range SAT Math	520–620
Range ACT Composite	18–24

ACADEMICS
Student/faculty ratio	18:1
% students returning for sophomore year	80

Most classes have 20–29 students.

REQUESTING SERVICES FOR STUDENTS WITH LEARNING DIFFERENCES

Phone: 252-737-1016 • accessibility.ecu.edu/students • Email: dssdept@ecu.edu

Documentation submitted to: Disability Support Services
Separate application required for Services: Yes

Documentation required for:
  LD: Psychoeducational evaluation
  ADHD: Psychoeducational evaluation
  ASD: Psychoeducational evaluation

Elon University

50 Campus Drive, Elon, NC 27244-2010 • Admissions: 336-278-3566 • www.elon.edu

(**Support: S**)

PROGRAMS/SERVICES FOR STUDENTS WITH LEARNING DIFFERENCES

Elon University's Disabilities Resources program supports students with different needs and disabilities. Faculty, staff, and administrators work together with students to identify the most effective approaches, accommodations, programs, and activities for the student. DR also facilitates connections between students and instructors to encourage the understanding of each student's needs.

ADMISSIONS

All students must meet the same admission criteria. When considering applicants, Elon University places a strong emphasis on grades and rigor of coursework. The average GPA for accepted students is 4.07 on a weighted scale. Students who submitted test scores averaged 1250 on the SAT and 27 on the ACT.

Additional Information

Substitutions for world language and mathematics courses are only permitted under certain circumstances. Students must have significant documentation describing deficits that would pose significant challenges in the course, as well as evidence that prior enrollment in similar courses yielded poor results. Courses may not be substituted if they are required for a major. If a student has not yet taken such a class, they will be asked to enroll, and their performance will be evaluated before the end of the drop/add period, at which point a decision regarding the substitution will be made.

In 2000, Elon changed its mascot from the Fighting Christian to the Phoenix to honor its resilient response to a campus fire. In 1923, a fire destroyed most of the campus, including school records, classrooms, the library, and the chapel, but a new campus was rebuilt in its place.

Elon University

GENERAL ADMISSIONS

Very important factors include: rigor of secondary school record, academic GPA, application essay, recommendations. *Other factors considered include:* class rank. High school diploma is required and GED is accepted. Institution is test-optional for entering Fall 2024. Check admissions website for updates. *Academic units required:* 4 English, 3 math, 3 science (1 lab), 2 foreign language, 2 social studies, 1 U.S. history. *Academic units recommended:* 4 math, 4 science, 3 foreign language, 4 social studies.

FINANCIAL AID

Students should submit: CSS/Financial Aid Profile; FAFSA. *Need-based scholarships/grants offered:* College/university scholarship or grant aid from institutional funds; Federal Pell; Private scholarships; SEOG; State scholarships/grants; United Negro College Fund. *Loan aid offered:* Direct PLUS loans; Direct Subsidized Loans; Direct Unsubsidized Loans. Federal Work-Study Program available. Institutional employment available.

CAMPUS LIFE

Activities: Campus Ministries; Choral groups; Concert band; Dance; Drama/theater; International Student Organization; Jazz band; Literary magazine; Marching band; Model UN; Music ensembles; Musical theater; Pep band; Radio station; Student government; Student newspaper; Student-run film society; Symphony orchestra; Television station; Yearbook. **Organizations:** 237 registered organizations, 25 honor societies, 15 religious organizations, 12 fraternities, 13 sororities. **Athletics (Intercollegiate):** *Men:* baseball, basketball, cross-country, equestrian sports, golf, ice hockey, lacrosse, martial arts, racquetball, rugby, swimming, table tennis, ultimate frisbee, volleyball. *Women:* basketball, cross-country, equestrian sports, field hockey, golf, lacrosse, martial arts, racquetball, rugby, softball, swimming, table tennis, track/field (indoor), ultimate frisbee, volleyball.

CAMPUS

Type of school	Private (nonprofit)
Environment	Town

STUDENTS

Undergrad enrollment	6,337
% male/female	41/59
% from out of state	79
% frosh live on campus	99

FINANCIAL FACTS

Annual tuition	$41,734
Room and board	$13,886
Required fees	$507

GENERAL ADMISSIONS INFO

Application fee	$60
Regular application deadline	1/10
Nonfall registration	Yes

Fall 2024 testing policy	Test Optional
Range SAT EBRW	590–680
Range SAT Math	580–680
Range ACT Composite	25–30

ACADEMICS

Student/faculty ratio	11:1
% students returning for sophomore year	90

Most classes have 20–29 students.

REQUESTING SERVICES FOR STUDENTS WITH LEARNING DIFFERENCES

Phone: 336-278-6568 • www.elon.edu/u/academics/academic-support/disabilities-services/
Email: disabilities@elon.edu

Documentation submitted to: The Office of Disabilities Resources
Separate application required for Services: Yes

Documentation required for:
LD: Psychoeducational evaluation
ADHD: Psychoeducational evaluation
ASD: Psychoeducational evaluation

Guilford College

5800 West Friendly Avenue, Greensboro, NC 27410 • Admissions: 336-316-2100 • www.guilford.edu

Support: CS

PROGRAMS/SERVICES FOR STUDENTS WITH LEARNING DIFFERENCES

The Accessibility Resource Center (ARC) provides support and accommodations for students with disabilities. Students seeking accommodations must register with ARC by completing the online registration agreement form and disclosing their disability status. Students will then meet with ARC for an intake meeting to develop an accommodation and support plan. Students who qualify for alternative testing accommodations may receive extended time on tests, reduced-distraction environments, and speech-to-text software. Classroom accommodations may include a computer for typing notes, note-taking support software, audio recording, non-punitive breaks, presentation slides and/or instructor notes, adaptive furniture, alternative-format texts (e-reader support), preferred seating, and modified attendance. Assistive technology made available by ARC includes smart pens and recording software.

ADMISSIONS

Admission criteria are the same for all students. Following admission, students who choose to self-disclose their learning differences will be connected with the ARC to initiate the accommodation process prior to campus arrival. Substitutions for foreign language requirements may be possible for students with documented disabilities.

Additional Information

Tutoring, writing support, and executive functioning tips and tools are available to all students at the Learning and Writing Center. The Guilford College Rise program is a three-week, fee-based residential summer program for rising seniors in high school. Scholarships are available, and students can earn six college credits in courses relating to international affairs and entrepreneurship. Admission to the program is competitive.

Originally founded as a small music camp on the Guilford campus in 1962, the Eastern Music Festival (EMF) is now a nationally recognized classical music festival and summer educational program. Professional and student musicians from across the country convene at Guilford for six weeks to celebrate visiting artists with more than 70 concerts, seminars, and music-related events on and off campus.

Guilford College

GENERAL ADMISSIONS

Important factors include: rigor of secondary school record, class rank, academic GPA, standardized test scores (if submitted), application essay. *Other factors considered include:* recommendations. High school diploma is required and GED is accepted. Institution is test-optional for entering Fall 2024. Check admissions website for updates. *Academic units recommended:* 4 English, 3 math, 3 science, 2 foreign language, 3 social studies.

FINANCIAL AID

Students should submit: FAFSA; Institution's own financial aid form. *Need-based scholarships/grants offered:* College/university scholarship or grant aid from institutional funds; Federal Pell; Private scholarships; SEOG; State scholarships/grants. *Loan aid offered:* Direct PLUS loans; Direct Subsidized Loans; Direct Unsubsidized Loans. Federal Work-Study Program available. Institutional employment available.

CAMPUS LIFE

Activities: Campus Ministries; Choral groups; Drama/theater; International Student Organization; Jazz band; Music ensembles; Pep band; Radio station; Student government; Student newspaper; Student-run film society; Yearbook. **Organizations:** 54 registered organizations, 1 honor societies, 5 religious organizations, 0 fraternities, 0 sororities. **Athletics (Intercollegiate):** *Men:* baseball, basketball, cross-country, golf, lacrosse, rugby, softball, table tennis, track/field (indoor), ultimate frisbee, volleyball. *Women:* basketball, cross-country, lacrosse, rugby, softball, swimming, table tennis, track/field (indoor), ultimate frisbee, volleyball.

CAMPUS
Type of school	Private (nonprofit)
Environment	City

STUDENTS
Undergrad enrollment	1,493
% male/female	46/54
% from out of state	29
% frosh live on campus	89

FINANCIAL FACTS
Annual tuition	$37,920
Room and board	$11,800
Required fees	$680

GENERAL ADMISSIONS INFO
Application fee	No fee
Regular application deadline	Rolling
Nonfall registration	Yes

Fall 2024 testing policy	Test Optional
Range SAT EBRW	440–585
Range SAT Math	463–558
Range ACT Composite	19–25

ACADEMICS
Student/faculty ratio	12:1
% students returning for sophomore year	66

Most classes have 10–19 students.

REQUESTING SERVICES FOR STUDENTS WITH LEARNING DIFFERENCES

Phone: 336-316-2243 • www.guilford.edu/academic-resources/accessibility-resource-center
Email: accessibility@guilford.edu

Documentation submitted to: Accessibility Resource Center
Separate application required for Services: Yes

Documentation required for:
 LD: Psychoeducational evaluation
 ADHD: Psychoeducational evaluation
 ASD: Psychoeducational evaluation

High Point University

One University Parkway, High Point, NC 27268 • Admissions: 336-841-9216 • www.highpoint.edu

(Support: SP)

PROGRAMS/SERVICES FOR STUDENTS WITH LEARNING DIFFERENCES

The Office of Accessibility Resources and Services (OARS) coordinates accommodations for students with disabilities. Students may complete the registration process, including submission of documentation and an appointment with an accessibility specialist, by utilizing the OARS COMPASS Portal on the High Point University website. Accommodations may include extended time on tests, testing in a distraction-reduced environment, note-taking assistance, and alternate-format texts. High Point University requires that students take one foreign language class unless the student requests and is approved for substitution by OARS.

ADMISSIONS

The average GPA for admitted students is 3.39. For admitted students who submitted scores, the average scores are 27 for the ACT and 1281 for the SAT. A letter of recommendation is required.

Additional Information

Peer tutoring is available for all students, and any student can request tutoring through Academic Tutoring Services. Learning Excellence is a fee-based program offering academic coaching in time management, note-taking skills, study strategies, problem-solving, and self-advocating. Students meet weekly with the specialist and can also meet with professional tutors. Interested students must apply directly to the program, and parents receive a weekly progress report.

To show their commitment to the community and desire for local engagement, each year, HPU offers a lineup of more than 150 cultural and athletic events for students, faculty, staff, and the community. The schedule features art exhibits, concerts, theater performances, a world-renowned campus speaker, and of course, cheering on the Panthers at one of the 16 Division 1 sports.

High Point University

GENERAL ADMISSIONS

Very important factors include: academic GPA. *Important factors include:* rigor of secondary school record, standardized test scores (if submitted), application essay, recommendations. *Other factors considered include:* class rank. High school diploma is required and GED is accepted. Institution is test-optional for entering Fall 2024. Check admissions website for updates. *Academic units recommended:* 4 English, 4 math, 3 science (1 lab), 3 foreign language, 3 social studies.

FINANCIAL AID

Students should submit: FAFSA; State aid form. *Need-based scholarships/grants offered:* College/university scholarship or grant aid from institutional funds; Federal Pell; Private scholarships; SEOG; State scholarships/grants. *Loan aid offered:* Direct PLUS loans; Direct Subsidized Loans; Direct Unsubsidized Loans. Federal Work-Study Program available. Institutional employment available.

CAMPUS LIFE

Activities: Campus Ministries; Choral groups; Concert band; Dance; Drama/theater; International Student Organization; Jazz band; Literary magazine; Marching band; Model UN; Music ensembles; Musical theater; Opera; Pep band; Radio station; Student government; Student newspaper; Student-run film society; Symphony orchestra; Television station; Yearbook. **Organizations:** 139 registered organizations, 23 honor societies, 6 religious organizations, 6 fraternities, 10 sororities. **Athletics (Intercollegiate):** *Men:* baseball, basketball, crew/rowing, cross-country, equestrian sports, golf, gymnastics, ice hockey, lacrosse, martial arts, swimming, track/field (indoor), ultimate frisbee, volleyball. *Women:* basketball, crew/rowing, cross-country, equestrian sports, field hockey, golf, gymnastics, lacrosse, martial arts, softball, swimming, track/field (indoor), volleyball.

CAMPUS

Type of school	Private (nonprofit)
Environment	City

STUDENTS

Undergrad enrollment	4,965
% male/female	45/55
% from out of state	73
% frosh live on campus	97

FINANCIAL FACTS

Annual tuition	$36,636
Room and board	$16,524
Required fees	$5,280

GENERAL ADMISSIONS INFO

Application fee	$50
Regular application deadline	3/1
Nonfall registration	Yes

Fall 2024 testing policy	Test Optional
Range SAT EBRW	563–640
Range SAT Math	540–640
Range ACT Composite	23–29

ACADEMICS

Student/faculty ratio	17:1
% students returning for sophomore year	83
Most classes have 20–29 students.	

REQUESTING SERVICES FOR STUDENTS WITH LEARNING DIFFERENCES

Phone: 336-841-9026 • www.highpoint.edu/oars/ • Email: OARS@highpoint.edu

Documentation submitted to: Office of Accessibility Resources and Services
Separate application required for Services: Yes

Documentation required for:
LD: Psychoeducational evaluation
ADHD: Psychoeducational evaluation
ASD: Psychoeducational evaluation

Lenoir–Rhyne University

524 7th Avenue NE, Hickory, NC 28603 • Admissions: 828-328-7300 • www.lr.edu

Support: S

ACCOMMODATIONS

Allowed in exams:

Calculators	Yes
Dictionary	Yes
Computer	Yes
Spell-checker	Yes
Extended test time	Yes
Scribe	Yes
Proctors	Yes
Oral exams	Yes
Note-takers	Yes

Support services for students with:

LD	Yes
ADHD	Yes
ASD	Yes
Distraction-reduced environment	Yes
Recording of lecture allowed	Yes
Reading technology	Yes
Audio books	Yes
Other assistive technology	Yes
Priority registration	No

Added costs of services:

For LD	No
For ADHD	No
For ASD	No
LD specialists	No
ADHD & ASD coaching	No
ASD specialists	No
Professional tutors	Yes
Peer tutors	Yes
Max. hours/week for services	Varies
How professors are notified of student approved accommodations	Student and Disability Services

COLLEGE GRADUATION REQUIREMENTS

Course waivers allowed	No
Course substitutions allowed	Yes
In what courses: Foreign Language	

PROGRAMS/SERVICES FOR STUDENTS WITH LEARNING DIFFERENCES

Lenoir-Rhyne University (LRU) provides services for students with learning differences through the Lohr Learning Center (LLC). The Disability Services Office (DSO) is the designated office at LLC for disability services that include extended testing time, note-taking, books on tape, alternative testing arrangements, assistive technology, preferential seating, and referrals to other campus support services. To apply for reasonable accommodations, students must provide appropriate documentation and meet with the director, shortly after being admitted to LRU. After appropriate documentation is received, the DSO director evaluates the documentation and schedules a meeting to discuss needs and determine final accommodations. Accommodation letters are sent to faculty and staff as needed.

ADMISSIONS

All applicants are expected to meet the same admission criteria. For applicants who submit scores, the average ACT is 21 and the average SAT is 1075. The typical GPA for admitted students is 3.28. Students with a lower GPA should submit their ACT or SAT scores if they demonstrate the student's academic potential.

Additional Information

The Lohr Learning Commons' Writing Center offers one-on-one support with generating ideas, editing for coherence, clarity, and correctness, and citing sources correctly. Drop-in and scheduled tutoring are available for both math and computer science courses. For additional academic support, students may schedule academic coaching sessions with a trained peer coach. During these sessions, students learn about the challenges and opportunities available on campus. They work with their peers to identify learning and study strategies and set goals for success.

Elwood "Buck" Lake Perry earned a bachelor's degree in physics and mathematics from Lenoir-Rhyne College. In 1946, he invented the spoonplug fishing lure. In 1965, he published a 31-page guide, *Spoonplugging: for fresh water bass and all game fish*. More importantly was his concern for the migration of fish, underwater topography, weather, water conditions, and more. He's credited as the father of structure fishing and was inducted into the National Freshwater Fishing Hall of Fame. His lures and books are still sold today.

Lenoir–Rhyne University

GENERAL ADMISSIONS

Very important factors include: academic GPA, standardized test scores (if submitted). *Important factors include:* rigor of secondary school record, class rank, application essay, recommendations. High school diploma is required and GED is accepted. Institution is test-optional for entering Fall 2024. Check admissions website for updates. *Academic units required:* 4 English, 4 math, 3 science (1 lab), 2 foreign language, 2 history.

FINANCIAL AID

Students should submit: FAFSA. *Need-based scholarships/grants offered:* College/university scholarship or grant aid from institutional funds; Federal Pell; Private scholarships; SEOG; State scholarships/grants. *Loan aid offered:* Direct PLUS loans; Direct Subsidized Loans; Direct Unsubsidized Loans. Federal Work-Study Program available. Institutional employment available.

CAMPUS LIFE

Activities: Campus Ministries; Choral groups; Concert band; Dance; Drama/theater; International Student Organization; Jazz band; Literary magazine; Marching band; Model UN; Music ensembles; Musical theater; Pep band; Radio station; Student government; Student newspaper; Student-run film society; Symphony orchestra; Yearbook. **Organizations:** 57 registered organizations, 12 honor societies, 7 religious organizations, 4 fraternities, 5 sororities. **Athletics (Intercollegiate):** *Men:* baseball, basketball, cross-country, equestrian sports, golf, lacrosse, swimming, track/field (indoor). *Women:* basketball, cross-country, equestrian sports, golf, lacrosse, softball, swimming, track/field (indoor), volleyball.

CAMPUS

Type of school	Private (nonprofit)
Environment	Town

STUDENTS

Undergrad enrollment	1,579
% male/female	42/58
% from out of state	16
% frosh live on campus	54

FINANCIAL FACTS

Annual tuition	$30,000
Room and board	$12,900
Required fees	$900

GENERAL ADMISSIONS INFO

Application fee	$35
Regular application deadline	Rolling
Nonfall registration	Yes
Fall 2024 testing policy	Test Optional

ACADEMICS

Student/faculty ratio	12:1
% students returning for sophomore year	62
Most classes have 20–29 students.	

REQUESTING SERVICES FOR STUDENTS WITH LEARNING DIFFERENCES

Phone: 828-328-7296 • www.lr.edu/student-life/health-wellness/disability-services • Email: proctors@lr.edu

Documentation submitted to: Disability Services Office
Separate application required for Services: Yes

Documentation required for:
  LD: Psychoeducational evaluation
  ADHD: Psychoeducational evaluation
  ASD: Psychoeducational evaluation

North Carolina State University

Box 7103, Raleigh, NC 27695 • Admissions: 919-515-2434 • www.ncsu.edu

ACCOMMODATIONS

Allowed in exams:

Calculators	Yes
Dictionary	Yes
Computer	Yes
Spell-checker	Yes
Extended test time	Yes
Scribe	Yes
Proctors	Yes
Oral exams	Yes
Note-takers	Yes

Support services for students with:

LD	No
ADHD	No
ASD	No
Distraction-reduced environment	Yes
Recording of lecture allowed	Yes
Reading technology	Yes
Audio books	Yes
Other assistive technology	Yes
Priority registration	Yes

Added costs of services:

For LD	No
For ADHD	No
For ASD	No
LD specialists	No
ADHD & ASD coaching	Yes
ASD specialists	No
Professional tutors	No
Peer tutors	Yes
Max. hours/week for services	Varies
How professors are notified of student approved accommodations	Student

COLLEGE GRADUATION REQUIREMENTS

Course waivers allowed	No
Course substitutions allowed	Yes
In what courses: Case-by-case basis	

PROGRAMS/SERVICES FOR STUDENTS WITH LEARNING DIFFERENCES

The Disability Resource Office (DRO) determines appropriate accommodations for students with disabilities. Once they have accepted admission, students are encouraged to contact DRO and complete and submit a disclosure application form. Students must submit documentation of a learning disability with the application. After review, DRO will contact the student with the next steps and determine appropriate accommodations. The use or need of the accommodation may be determined on a course-specific basis. To use approved accommodations, students receive an accommodations letter to give to their professors. Along with a long list of available accommodations, assistive technology at NC State includes screen reading and low vision, assisted listening and hearing, voice and speech recognition software, text-to-speech software, online testing environments, time management and organization, and recording and note-taking.

ADMISSIONS

All first-year applicants complete the same general application form and select one or two majors they're interested in. Accepted students are admitted to the program they've chosen. Some programs may be more competitive and may have additional requirements. In addition to the minimum high school course requirements, a personal essay is required giving students the opportunity to tell who they are outside of the classroom.

Additional Information

Summer Start is five weeks of college courses, up to 5 credit hours, before first-year students' first fall semester. Summer Start students live on campus, learn in smaller classes with other new students and student mentors, and have other optional academic, social, leadership, and service program opportunities. Additional summer opportunities for incoming first-year students are the Wolf Camp and Wolfpack Bound outdoor programs with activities like kayaking, rock climbing, zip lining, and hiking. New students can sign up for a three- or four-day trip, meet other new students during the experience, and learn about the upcoming first semester from experienced student trip leaders. The registration fee includes equipment, meals, transportation, and instruction by the Wellness and Recreation Outdoor Adventures staff. The Academic Success Center (ASC) offers weekly one-hour group tutoring and study sessions in biology, math, chemistry, and physics led by a trained tutor. The ASC also provides individual tutoring sessions by appointment. Students can request weekly sessions with an ASC peer mentor to improve their time management, organizational, and note-taking skills, study techniques, exam preparation, and more. Students can make appointments with the ASC Writing Center for help with writing or assignments that have a specific audience and purpose.

The Krispy Kreme Challenge is a yearly winter event where students run 2.5 miles to the nearest Krispy Kreme, eat 12 doughnuts, and run the 2.5 miles back—all in one hour. The race raises funds for UNC Children's Hospital.

North Carolina State University

GENERAL ADMISSIONS

Very important factors include: rigor of secondary school record, class rank, academic GPA. *Other factors considered include:* standardized test scores (if submitted), application essay, recommendations. High school diploma is required and GED is accepted. Institution is test-optional for entering Fall 2024. Check admissions website for updates. *Academic units required:* 4 English, 4 math, 3 science (1 lab), 2 foreign language, 1 social studies, 1 U.S. history.

FINANCIAL AID

Students should submit: FAFSA. *Need-based scholarships/grants offered:* College/university scholarship or grant aid from institutional funds; Federal Pell; Private scholarships; SEOG; State scholarships/grants; United Negro College Fund. *Loan aid offered:* Direct PLUS loans; Direct Subsidized Loans; Direct Unsubsidized Loans. Federal Work-Study Program available. Institutional employment available.

CAMPUS LIFE

Activities: Campus Ministries; Choral groups; Concert band; Dance; Drama/theater; International Student Organization; Jazz band; Literary magazine; Marching band; Model UN; Music ensembles; Musical theater; Pep band; Radio station; Student government; Student newspaper; Student-run film society; Symphony orchestra; Television station; Yearbook. **Organizations:** 720 registered organizations, 24 honor societies, 49 religious organizations, 28 fraternities, 19 sororities. **Athletics (Intercollegiate):** *Men:* baseball, basketball, crew/rowing, cross-country, equestrian sports, golf, gymnastics, ice hockey, lacrosse, racquetball, rugby, swimming, table tennis, track/field (indoor), ultimate frisbee, volleyball, water polo, wrestling. *Women:* basketball, crew/rowing, cross-country, equestrian sports, golf, gymnastics, lacrosse, racquetball, rugby, softball, swimming, table tennis, track/field (indoor), ultimate frisbee, volleyball, water polo.

CAMPUS	
Type of school	Public
Environment	Metropolis

STUDENTS	
Undergrad enrollment	25,108
% male/female	50/50
% from out of state	10
% frosh live on campus	62

FINANCIAL FACTS	
Annual in-state tuition	$6,535
Annual out-of-state tuition	$28,276
Room and board	$12,748
Required fees	$2,593

GENERAL ADMISSIONS INFO	
Application fee	$85
Regular application deadline	1/15
Nonfall registration	Yes

Fall 2024 testing policy	Test Optional
Range SAT EBRW	620–700
Range SAT Math	625–674
Range ACT Composite	24–31

ACADEMICS	
Student/faculty ratio	16:1
% students returning for sophomore year	94
Most classes have 20–29 students.	

REQUESTING SERVICES FOR STUDENTS WITH LEARNING DIFFERENCES

Phone: 919-515-7653 • dro.dasa.ncsu.edu/ • Email: disability@ncsu.edu

Documentation submitted to: Disability Resource Office
Separate application required for Services: Yes

Documentation required for:
LD: Psychoeducational evaluation
ADHD: Psychoeducational evaluation
ASD: Psychoeducational evaluation

St. Andrews University

1700 Dogwood Mile, Laurinburg, NC 28352 • Admissions: 910-277-5555 • sa.edu

Support: S

ACCOMMODATIONS

Allowed in exams:

Calculators	Yes
Dictionary	Yes
Computer	Yes
Spell-checker	Yes
Extended test time	Yes
Scribe	Yes
Proctors	Yes
Oral exams	Yes
Note-takers	Yes

Support services for students with:

LD	Yes
ADHD	Yes
ASD	Yes
Distraction-reduced environment	Yes
Recording of lecture allowed	Yes
Reading technology	Yes
Audio books	Yes
Other assistive technology	Yes
Priority registration	No

Added costs of services:

For LD	No
For ADHD	No
For ASD	No
LD specialists	No
ADHD & ASD coaching	No
ASD specialists	No
Professional tutors	No
Peer tutors	Yes
Max. hours/week for services	Varies
How professors are notified of student approved accommodations	Student

COLLEGE GRADUATION REQUIREMENTS

Course waivers allowed	No
Course substitutions allowed	Yes
In what courses: Case-by-case basis	

PROGRAMS/SERVICES FOR STUDENTS WITH LEARNING DIFFERENCES

The Center for Academic Services office (CAS) of Disability Services provides academic accommodations to students with documented learning disabilities. Students are asked to register by completing the accommodations request form. When the form has been received, students are sent the documentation requirements for their specific disabilities. Disability Services recommends all students with disabilities register even if they don't plan to use accommodations immediately so that their eligibility will already be determined and accommodations can be put in place without delay. Services and accommodations will be provided once the intake meeting is completed and eligibility is determined. The CAS office administers tests for students with learning disabilities that make them eligible for accommodations, including extended time, proctored testing in a separate setting, computer use for typing, readers, scribes, breaks as needed, and large print texts.

ADMISSIONS

All first-year applicants complete the same general admission requirements. ACT and SAT scores are optional in most cases, but a personal essay is required. Letters of recommendation are not required, but applicants may submit up to three teacher evaluations and up to three from other sources. No minimum GPA is required; the admission office considers past and potential future academic success, extracurricular activities, leadership opportunities, volunteerism, community service, and commitment. Prospective students are encouraged to contact St. Andrews to discuss its programs and to share personal goals. Campus visits are also encouraged.

Additional Information

CAS offers weekly study sessions and weekly tutoring sessions in various courses. CAS also offers walk-in assistance with by-appointment mentoring and tutoring sessions. The Writing Center offers students free tutoring and accepts drop-ins for appointments or online sessions. Tutors are available for any stage of a writing assignment, from organizing and developing to editing final papers.

Honoring the first Highland Scots in North Carolina (1739), the Scottish Heritage Center on campus preserves the Scottish heritage and traditions of the region with a collection of artifacts, rare books of Scottish, Scottish-American history, genealogy, culture, and a large collection of Celtic music. The annual Scottish Heritage Weekend and Scotland County Highland Games welcome the public from all over North America and Scotland.

St. Andrews University

GENERAL ADMISSIONS

Important factors include: academic GPA, standardized test scores (if submitted). *Other factors considered include:* rigor of secondary school record, class rank, application essay, recommendations. High school diploma is required and GED is accepted. Institution is test-optional for entering Fall 2024. Check admissions website for updates. *Academic units required:* 3 English, 3 math, 3 science, 1 foreign language, 3 social studies.

FINANCIAL AID

Students should submit:. *Need-based scholarships/grants offered:* College/university scholarship or grant aid from institutional funds; Federal Pell; Private scholarships; SEOG; State scholarships/grants. *Loan aid offered:* Direct PLUS loans; Direct Subsidized Loans; Direct Unsubsidized Loans. Federal Work-Study Program available. Institutional employment available.

CAMPUS LIFE

Organizations: 30 registered organizations, 3 honor societies, 1 religious organizations, 0 fraternities, 0 sororities. **Athletics (Intercollegiate):** *Men:* baseball, basketball, cross-country, equestrian sports, golf, lacrosse, ultimate frisbee, wrestling. *Women:* basketball, cross-country, equestrian sports, lacrosse, softball, ultimate frisbee, wrestling.

CAMPUS

Type of school	Private (nonprofit)
Environment	Rural

STUDENTS

Undergrad enrollment	876
% male/female	46/54
% from out of state	58

FINANCIAL FACTS

Annual tuition	$29,600
Room and board	$11,480

GENERAL ADMISSIONS INFO

Application fee	No fee
Regular application deadline	Rolling
Nonfall registration	Yes
Fall 2024 testing policy	Test Optional

ACADEMICS

Student/faculty ratio	14:1
% students returning for sophomore year	60

Most classes have 2–9 students.

REQUESTING SERVICES FOR STUDENTS WITH LEARNING DIFFERENCES

Phone: 910-277-5337 • www.sa.edu/student-services/campus-services/disability-accommodations/

Documentation submitted to: Disability Services
Separate application required for Services: Yes

Documentation required for:
LD: Psychoeducational evaluation
ADHD: Psychoeducational evaluation
ASD: Psychoeducational evaluation

University of North Carolina at Asheville

One University Heights, Asheville, NC 28804-8502 • Admissions: 828-251-6481 • www.unca.edu

Support: S

ACCOMMODATIONS

Allowed in exams:

Calculators	Yes
Dictionary	Yes
Computer	Yes
Spell-checker	Yes
Extended test time	Yes
Scribe	Yes
Proctors	Yes
Oral exams	Yes
Note-takers	Yes

Support services for students with:

LD	Yes
ADHD	Yes
ASD	Yes
Distraction-reduced environment	Yes
Recording of lecture allowed	Yes
Reading technology	Yes
Audio books	Yes
Other assistive technology	Yes
Priority registration	Yes

Added costs of services:

For LD	No
For ADHD	No
For ASD	No
LD specialists	No
ADHD & ASD coaching	No
ASD specialists	No
Professional tutors	No
Peer tutors	Yes
Max. hours/week for services	4
How professors are notified of student approved accommodations	Student

COLLEGE GRADUATION REQUIREMENTS

Course waivers allowed	No
Course substitutions allowed	Yes

In what courses: Math, Foreign Languages, and others on a case-by-case basis

PROGRAMS/SERVICES FOR STUDENTS WITH LEARNING DIFFERENCES

The Office of Academic Accessibility (OAA) works together with students with disabilities. Students apply for accommodations by submitting an online application and any documentation they feel is relevant to the application request. Some students may be asked to schedule a welcome meeting with the OAA. Students receive letters of accommodation to share with course instructors for approved accommodations for each class. The most common accommodations are for books and class materials in an alternate format, notetakers, the use of recording devices, classroom adjustments and reserved seating, and test-taking alternatives.

ADMISSIONS

The admissions committee review takes into consideration all parts of the application before making a decision with an emphasis placed on rigor of course performance, grade trends, and class rank (if provided). A personal essay, extracurricular activities, honors achieved, leadership roles, special talents and abilities are also considered. Applicants who do not meet the minimum course requirements may still apply for admission and explain in the application what circumstances prevented them from fulfilling the course requirements. Applicants who are not admitted may appeal the decision and should contact their admissions counselor who can serve as an advocate and help the student submit appropriate materials to provide the best chance for the appeal to be granted.

Additional Information

First-year students are assigned an academic advisor who assists students in planning their course schedule before class registration each semester. When students declare a major, they are assigned a faculty advisor from their department. Students can reach out to their advisors at any point in the semester. The Academic Success Center Peer Tutoring program is a good resource for students and the Writing Center offers one-on-one sessions for any writing project at any stage. Supplemental Instruction (SI) leaders are embedded in classes to provide additional student support for specific courses. Parsons Mathematics Assistance Center (aka The Math Lab) offers tutoring to support mathematics or any math-related course, statistics courses, science, or engineering courses.

Rocky the Bulldog has been the UNCA mascot since the 1930s. UNCA students have a tradition of patting the statue of Rocky for good luck and a successful year on move-in day and after attending convocation and EmBark Orientation. There are many events to welcome incoming students to UNCA, including the popular RockyPalooza, which is a night of good food, entertainment, fun, and new friends.

University of North Carolina at Asheville

GENERAL ADMISSIONS
Very important factors include: rigor of secondary school record, class rank, academic GPA, standardized test scores (if submitted), application essay, recommendations. High school diploma is required and GED is not accepted. Institution is test-optional for entering Fall 2024. Check admissions website for updates. *Academic units required:* 4 English, 4 math, 3 science (1 lab), 2 foreign language, 2 social studies.

FINANCIAL AID
Students should submit: FAFSA. *Need-based scholarships/grants offered:* College/university scholarship or grant aid from institutional funds; Federal Pell; Private scholarships; SEOG; State scholarships/grants. *Loan aid offered:* Direct PLUS loans; Direct Subsidized Loans; Direct Unsubsidized Loans. Federal Work-Study Program available. Institutional employment available.

CAMPUS LIFE
Activities: Campus Ministries; Choral groups; Concert band; Dance; Drama/theater; International Student Organization; Jazz band; Literary magazine; Model UN; Music ensembles; Musical theater; Pep band; Radio station; Student government; Student newspaper; Student-run film society. **Organizations:** 59 registered organizations, 1 honor societies, 5 religious organizations, 2 fraternities, 1 sororities. **Athletics (Intercollegiate):** *Men:* baseball, basketball, cross-country, cycling, equestrian sports, track/field (indoor), ultimate frisbee. *Women:* basketball, cross-country, cycling, equestrian sports, golf, swimming, track/field (indoor), ultimate frisbee, volleyball.

CAMPUS	
Type of school	Public
Environment	City

STUDENTS	
Undergrad enrollment	2,803
% male/female	42/58
% from out of state	12
% frosh live on campus	95

FINANCIAL FACTS	
Annual in-state tuition	$4,122
Annual out-of-state tuition	$21,470
Room and board	$9,950
Required fees	$3,122

GENERAL ADMISSIONS INFO	
Application fee	$75
Regular application deadline	7/31
Nonfall registration	Yes

Fall 2024 testing policy	Test Optional
Range SAT EBRW	600–680
Range SAT Math	540–650
Range ACT Composite	21–28

ACADEMICS	
Student/faculty ratio	11:1
% students returning for sophomore year	69
Most classes have 10–19 students.	

REQUESTING SERVICES FOR STUDENTS WITH LEARNING DIFFERENCES

Phone: 828-232-5050 • accessibility.unca.edu • Email: academicaccess@unca.edu

Documentation submitted to: Office of Academic Accessibility
Separate application required for Services: Yes

Documentation required for:
LD: Psychoeducational evaluation
ADHD: Psychoeducational evaluation
ASD: Psychoeducational evaluation

University of North Carolina at Chapel Hill

Jackson Hall, Chapel Hill, NC 27599-2200 • Admissions: 919-962-2211 • www.unc.edu

Support: CS

ACCOMMODATIONS

Allowed in exams:

Calculators	Yes
Dictionary	Yes
Computer	Yes
Spell-checker	Yes
Extended test time	Yes
Scribe	Yes
Proctors	Yes
Oral exams	Yes
Note-takers	Yes

Support services for students with:

LD	Yes
ADHD	Yes
ASD	Yes
Distraction-reduced environment	Yes
Recording of lecture allowed	Yes
Reading technology	Yes
Audio books	Yes
Other assistive technology	Yes
Priority registration	Yes

Added costs of services:

For LD	No
For ADHD	No
For ASD	No
LD specialists	Yes
ADHD & ASD coaching	Yes
ASD specialists	No
Professional tutors	No
Peer tutors	Yes
Max. hours/week for services	2
How professors are notified of student approved accommodations	Student

COLLEGE GRADUATION REQUIREMENTS

Course waivers allowed	No
Course substitutions allowed	Yes

In what courses: Math and Foreign Language

PROGRAMS/SERVICES FOR STUDENTS WITH LEARNING DIFFERENCES

Accessibility Resources & Service (ARS) provides reasonable accommodations, resources, and services to students with disabilities. Accommodations include individual testing arrangements, assistive technology, attendance adjustments, and per-assignment deadline extensions. ARS staff works with the student to determine specific accommodations, and documentation of a disability should be submitted. ARS will help contact professors to evaluate if the course can provide reasonable accommodations given how the class is taught. The Learning Center has regularly scheduled social groups and workshops for students with ADHD, and an ADHD Peer Connect Group is offered weekly. Counseling and Psychological Services offers several support groups, including a weekly Autistic Students Social Group.

ADMISSIONS

All students are expected to meet the same standards of academic admission criteria and academic performance. Applicants who have a 2.5 GPA or a minimum ACT of 19 or SAT of 1010 are eligible to be evaluated for admission by colleges in the UNC system. However, UNC Chapel Hill is very selective, and successful applicants have much higher GPAs and test scores. Applicants who have not taken U.S. History may be admitted conditionally and must pass 3 hours of U.S. History by the end of their second year in college. Ninety-two percent of admitted students rank in the top 10 percent of their class, and the middle SAT score for those submitting is 1360–1500.

Additional Information

The Learning Center provides extensive support for students, including ADHD/LD specialists that can provide one-on-one coaching. Peer tutoring as well as academic coaches to improve time management and study skills are available by appointment in person or by Zoom.

The Old Well at the heart of campus is the most enduring symbol of the school and was the primary source of water for over a century. The most revered tradition may be the belief that starting at midnight on the first day of classes, you must drink from the Old Well, or you will not get a 4.0 in any of your classes. Even in the rain, hundreds of students wait in line just for a quick sip from this drinking fountain where the water has never tasted so good.

University of North Carolina at Chapel Hill

GENERAL ADMISSIONS

Very important factors include: rigor of secondary school record, application essay, recommendations. *Important factors include:* class rank, academic GPA. *Other factors considered include:* standardized test scores (if submitted). High school diploma is required and GED is not accepted. Institution is test-optional for entering Fall 2024. Check admissions website for updates. *Academic units required:* 4 English, 4 math, 3 science (1 lab), 2 foreign language, 1 social studies, 1 U.S. history, 1 academic elective.

FINANCIAL AID

Students should submit: CSS/Financial Aid Profile; FAFSA. *Need-based scholarships/grants offered:* College/university scholarship or grant aid from institutional funds; Federal Pell; Private scholarships; SEOG; State scholarships/grants. *Loan aid offered:* Direct PLUS loans; Direct Subsidized Loans; Direct Unsubsidized Loans. Federal Work-Study Program available. Institutional employment available.

CAMPUS LIFE

Activities: Campus Ministries; Choral groups; Concert band; Dance; Drama/theater; International Student Organization; Jazz band; Literary magazine; Marching band; Model UN; Music ensembles; Musical theater; Opera; Pep band; Radio station; Student government; Student newspaper; Student-run film society; Symphony orchestra; Television station; Yearbook. **Organizations:** 824 registered organizations, 25 honor societies, 42 religious organizations, 27 fraternities, 20 sororities. **Athletics (Intercollegiate):** *Men:* baseball, basketball, crew/rowing, cross-country, equestrian sports, field hockey, golf, gymnastics, ice hockey, lacrosse, racquetball, rugby, swimming, table tennis, track/field (indoor), ultimate frisbee, volleyball, water polo, wrestling. *Women:* basketball, crew/rowing, cross-country, equestrian sports, field hockey, golf, gymnastics, lacrosse, martial arts, racquetball, rugby, softball, swimming, table tennis, track/field (indoor), ultimate frisbee, volleyball, water polo.

CAMPUS

Type of school	Public
Environment	Town

STUDENTS

Undergrad enrollment	19,931
% male/female	40/60
% from out of state	14
% frosh live on campus	100

FINANCIAL FACTS

Annual in-state tuition	$7,020
Annual out-of-state tuition	$37,360
Room and board	$13,016
Required fees	$1,978

GENERAL ADMISSIONS INFO

Application fee	$85
Regular application deadline	1/15
Nonfall registration	No

Fall 2024 testing policy	Test Optional
Range SAT EBRW	670–750
Range SAT Math	670–780
Range ACT Composite	28–33

ACADEMICS

Student/faculty ratio	17:1
% students returning for sophomore year	96

Most classes have 10–19 students.

REQUESTING SERVICES FOR STUDENTS WITH LEARNING DIFFERENCES

Phone: 919-962-8300 • ars.unc.edu • Email: ars@unc.edu

Documentation submitted to: Accessibility Resources & Service

Separate application required for Services: Yes

Documentation required for:
LD: Psychoeducational evaluation
ADHD: Psychoeducational evaluation
ASD: Psychoeducational evaluation

College Profiles ■ 483

University of North Carolina at Charlotte

Undergraduate Admissions, Charlotte, NC 28223-0001 • Admissions: 704-687-5507 • charlotte.edu

Support: S

ACCOMMODATIONS

Allowed in exams:

Calculators	Yes
Dictionary	No
Computer	Yes
Spell-checker	Yes
Extended test time	Yes
Scribe	Yes
Proctors	Yes
Oral exams	No
Note-takers	Yes

Support services for students with:

LD	Yes
ADHD	Yes
ASD	Yes
Distraction-reduced environment	Yes
Recording of lecture allowed	Yes
Reading technology	Yes
Audio books	Yes
Other assistive technology	Yes
Priority registration	Yes

Added costs of services:

For LD	No
For ADHD	No
For ASD	No
LD specialists	No
ADHD & ASD coaching	No
ASD specialists	No
Professional tutors	No
Peer tutors	Yes
Max. hours/week for services	Varies
How professors are notified of student approved accommodations	Student

COLLEGE GRADUATION REQUIREMENTS

Course waivers allowed	No
Course substitutions allowed	Yes

In what courses: Foreign Language on a case-by-case basis

PROGRAMS/SERVICES FOR STUDENTS WITH LEARNING DIFFERENCES

The office of Disability Services (DS) supports students with learning differences. DS facilitates accommodations, discourse, and engagement to promote a universally accessible learning environment for all. Some common accommodations include assistive/adaptive technology, note-taking assistance, attendance accommodation within reasonable limits, and foreign language substitution when appropriate. Students must submit documentation and register through the DS Portal. Once a student is determined eligible for accommodations, the student will be notified and required to schedule a meeting with a DS counselor.

ADMISSIONS

All applicants must meet the same admission criteria. The middle 50 percent GPA for admitted students is 3.4–3.9 unweighted or 3.8–4.4 weighted. Admission decisions are based on GPA and courses (including senior year courses) and may depend on the identified major. The business, nursing, computing and informatics, and engineering programs are more competitive.

Additional Information

The University Center for Academic Excellence provides a number of programs to assist students needing academic support. Students Obtaining Success (SOS) is a peer-based mentoring program for students experiencing academic difficulties or on academic probation. It is a semester-long program individually tailored to help students identify unique challenges and improve academic performance. Students who are placed on academic probation at the end of their first or second semester are required to participate in 49'er Rebound, a program that helps students experiencing academic difficulties. The Peer Assisted Learning (PAL) program offers students additional academic group study support led by peer leaders—current students who have completed the course successfully. Tutorial services are provided in course-specific academic subjects. There is no charge for these services.

The city of Charlotte first sought to become a public university in 1871, but over the years, it lost to Raleigh and then Chapel Hill. Finally, in 1946, the Charlotte Center of the University of North Carolina opened with 278 students. Like many universities, it owes its inception to the GI Bill and its effects on public education to serve World War II veterans. In 1949, when the state began closing the centers, the Charlotte Center was taken over by the city school district. The athletic team's nickname, the 49'ers, is based on the college being saved from permanent closure in 1949.

University of North Carolina at Charlotte

GENERAL ADMISSIONS

Very important factors include: rigor of secondary school record, academic GPA, standardized test scores (if submitted). *Other factors considered include:* application essay, recommendations. High school diploma is required and GED is accepted. Institution is test-optional for entering Fall 2024. Check admissions website for updates. *Academic units required:* 4 English, 4 math, 3 science (1 lab), 2 foreign language, 1 social studies, 1 U.S. history. *Academic units recommended:* 3 foreign language.

FINANCIAL AID

Students should submit: FAFSA. *Need-based scholarships/grants offered:* College/university scholarship or grant aid from institutional funds; Federal Pell; Private scholarships; SEOG; State scholarships/grants; United Negro College Fund. *Loan aid offered:* Direct PLUS loans; Direct Subsidized Loans; Direct Unsubsidized Loans. Federal Work-Study Program available. Institutional employment available.

CAMPUS LIFE

Activities: Campus Ministries; Choral groups; Concert band; Dance; Drama/theater; International Student Organization; Jazz band; Literary magazine; Marching band; Model UN; Music ensembles; Musical theater; Opera; Pep band; Radio station; Student government; Student newspaper; Student-run film society; Symphony orchestra; Television station. **Organizations:** 361 registered organizations, 20 fraternities, 20 sororities. **Athletics (Intercollegiate):** *Men:* baseball, basketball, cross-country, equestrian sports, golf, ice hockey, lacrosse, martial arts, rugby, swimming, table tennis, track/field (indoor), ultimate frisbee, volleyball, wrestling. *Women:* basketball, cross-country, equestrian sports, golf, lacrosse, martial arts, rugby, softball, swimming, table tennis, track/field (indoor), ultimate frisbee, volleyball, wrestling.

CAMPUS
Type of school	Public
Environment	Metropolis

STUDENTS
Undergrad enrollment	23,708
% male/female	52/48
% from out of state	5
% frosh live on campus	72

FINANCIAL FACTS
Annual in-state tuition	$3,812
Annual out-of-state tuition	$17,246
Room and board	$11,180
Required fees	$3,376

GENERAL ADMISSIONS INFO
Application fee	$75
Regular application deadline	6/1
Nonfall registration	Yes
Fall 2024 testing policy	Test Optional
Range SAT EBRW	560–650
Range SAT Math	560–670
Range ACT Composite	21–26

ACADEMICS
Student/faculty ratio	20:1
% students returning for sophomore year	85
Most classes have 20–29 students.	

REQUESTING SERVICES FOR STUDENTS WITH LEARNING DIFFERENCES

Phone: 704-687-0040 • ds.charlotte.edu/ • Email: disability@uncc.edu

Documentation submitted to: Office of Disability Services
Separate application required for Services: Yes

Documentation required for:
LD: Psychoeducational evaluation
ADHD: Psychoeducational evaluation
ASD: Psychoeducational evaluation

University of North Carolina at Greensboro

P.O. Box 26170, Greensboro, NC 27402-6170 • Admissions: 336-334-5243 • www.uncg.edu

Support: S

ACCOMMODATIONS

Allowed in exams:

Calculators	Yes
Dictionary	Yes
Computer	Yes
Spell-checker	Yes
Extended test time	Yes
Scribe	Yes
Proctors	Yes
Oral exams	Yes
Note-takers	Yes

Support services for students with:

LD	Yes
ADHD	Yes
ASD	Yes
Distraction-reduced environment	Yes
Recording of lecture allowed	Yes
Reading technology	Yes
Audio books	Yes
Other assistive technology	Yes
Priority registration	No

Added costs of services:

For LD	No
For ADHD	No
For ASD	No
LD specialists	No
ADHD & ASD coaching	Yes
ASD specialists	No
Professional tutors	No
Peer tutors	Yes
Max. hours/week for services	3
How professors are notified of student approved accommodations	Student

COLLEGE GRADUATION REQUIREMENTS

Course waivers allowed	No
Course substitutions allowed	Yes
In what courses: Case-by-case basis	

PROGRAMS/SERVICES FOR STUDENTS WITH LEARNING DIFFERENCES

The Office of Accessibility Resources and Services (OARS) helps students understand their learning needs and styles. Some of the supports offered may include testing accommodations, assistive technology, and academic and organizational assistance. Additionally, the staff serve as advocates when the student may need to explain to professors the type of accommodations needed in the classroom. OARS works closely with other departments to provide additional support where needed. Students registered with OARS have access to support to help them better understand their specific learning styles. Students with ADHD can also get support through the counseling and psychological services office. Through group counseling, students can participate in ACCESS, a cognitive behavioral therapy (CBT) program that offers students with ADHD the skills to achieve academic, personal, and social success.

ADMISSIONS

All applicants are expected to meet the same admission criteria, and an applicant's admission is based solely on academic qualifications. The University of North Carolina system has minimum admission requirements for all colleges in the system, and each college has its own admission criteria. Students not accepted could be matched with another North Carolina university with admission slots available for qualified students.

Additional Information

The Academic Achievement Center is a division of Student Success and provides services such as tutoring, academic skills, coaching, Supplemental Instruction, and workshops. The Student First Office serves as an academic one-stop-shop for assisting students with academic advising, academic recovery, academic transition, appeals, and graduation planning.

Minerva, the goddess of wisdom and women's arts, was chosen as the symbol for the school and, since 1893, has appeared on every diploma. Over time, the statue of Minerva, gifted by the class of 1907, was damaged beyond repair, so the class of '53 gave the school its current statue. At exam time, students leave apples at Minerva's feet so the goddess of wisdom will bring them good luck. Minerva isn't the only one enjoying the apples; campus squirrels also find good luck via a tasty treat during exam time.

University of North Carolina at Greensboro

GENERAL ADMISSIONS

Very important factors include: rigor of secondary school record, academic GPA. *Important factors include:* standardized test scores (if submitted). *Other factors considered include:* class rank, application essay, recommendations. High school diploma is required and GED is accepted. Institution is test-optional for entering Fall 2024. Check admissions website for updates. *Academic units required:* 4 English, 4 math, 3 science (1 lab), 2 foreign language, 2 social studies.

FINANCIAL AID

Students should submit: FAFSA. *Need-based scholarships/grants offered:* College/university scholarship or grant aid from institutional funds; Federal Pell; Private scholarships; SEOG; State scholarships/grants. *Loan aid offered:* Direct PLUS loans; Direct Subsidized Loans; Direct Unsubsidized Loans. Federal Work-Study Program available. Institutional employment available.

CAMPUS LIFE

Activities: Campus Ministries; Choral groups; Concert band; Dance; Drama/theater; International Student Organization; Jazz band; Literary magazine; Music ensembles; Musical theater; Opera; Pep band; Radio station; Student government; Student newspaper; Student-run film society; Symphony orchestra. **Organizations:** 339 registered organizations, 6 honor societies, 2 religious organizations, 12 fraternities, 12 sororities. **Athletics (Intercollegiate):** *Men:* baseball, basketball, cross-country, equestrian sports, golf, martial arts, rugby, softball, swimming, volleyball. *Women:* basketball, cross-country, equestrian sports, golf, lacrosse, martial arts, rugby, softball, swimming, volleyball.

CAMPUS	
Type of school	Public
Environment	City

STUDENTS	
Undergrad enrollment	13,862
% male/female	34/66
% from out of state	4
% frosh live on campus	79

FINANCIAL FACTS	
Annual in-state tuition	$4,422
Annual out-of-state tuition	$19,582
Room and board	$9,924
Required fees	$2,957

GENERAL ADMISSIONS INFO	
Application fee	$65
Regular application deadline	3/1
Nonfall registration	Yes

Fall 2024 testing policy	Test Optional
Range SAT EBRW	570–660
Range SAT Math	540–620
Range ACT Composite	22–27

ACADEMICS	
Student/faculty ratio	17:1
% students returning for sophomore year	73

Most classes have 20–29 students.

REQUESTING SERVICES FOR STUDENTS WITH LEARNING DIFFERENCES

Phone: 336-334-5440 • oars.uncg.edu/ • Email: oars@uncg.edu

Documentation submitted to: Office of Accessibility Resources and Services
Separate application required for Services: Yes

Documentation required for:
  LD: Psychoeducational evaluation
  ADHD: Psychoeducational evaluation
  ASD: Psychoeducational evaluation

University of North Carolina Wilmington

601 South College Road, Wilmington, NC 28403-5904 • Admissions: 910-962-3243 • www.uncw.edu

Support: CS

ACCOMMODATIONS

Allowed in exams:

Calculators	Yes
Dictionary	Yes
Computer	Yes
Spell-checker	Yes
Extended test time	Yes
Scribe	Yes
Proctors	Yes
Oral exams	Yes
Note-takers	Yes

Support services for students with:

LD	Yes
ADHD	Yes
ASD	Yes
Distraction-reduced environment	Yes
Recording of lecture allowed	Yes
Reading technology	Yes
Audio books	Yes
Other assistive technology	Yes
Priority registration	Yes

Added costs of services:

For LD	No
For ADHD	No
For ASD	No
LD specialists	No
ADHD & ASD coaching	No
ASD specialists	Yes
Professional tutors	Yes
Peer tutors	Yes
Max. hours/week for services	Varies
How professors are notified of student approved accommodations	Student and Disability Resource Center

COLLEGE GRADUATION REQUIREMENTS

Course waivers allowed	Yes

In what courses: Case-by-case basis

Course substitutions allowed	Yes

In what courses: Case-by-case basis

PROGRAMS/SERVICES FOR STUDENTS WITH LEARNING DIFFERENCES

The University of North Carolina Wilmington supports students with learning differences through the Disability Resource Center (DRC). DRC assists with accommodations such as assistive technology, alternative media formats, testing support, and coordination with other departments to support tutoring and study skills. Students are required to complete an online preregistration form, submit supporting documentation, and schedule a meeting with DRC. Students must be registered for classes prior to scheduling a meeting with DRC.

ADMISSIONS

All applicants are expected to meet the same admission criteria. The middle 50 percent weighted GPA for accepted applicants is 3.8–4.4 (A/B average). The minimum GPA for the UNC System is 2.5; however, these applicants are unlikely to be admitted. A GPA will not be recalculated, but it is reviewed, and class rank will be considered if provided (not in classes with less than 50 students).

Additional Information

The University Learning Center provides academic support through reasonable accommodations such as tutoring and study skills. The tutoring is free, and most tutoring is one-on-one. There are also small group sessions. Writing consultations are available for all academic writing. There is also Supplemental Instruction (SI), which includes peer-facilitated group review sessions hosted by students who have already taken the specific course. Math Services provides tutoring, and the STEM lab is where students can study at their own pace. The on-campus organization Disability Alliance Association offers opportunities to connect with other students.

DID YOU KNOW?

In the fall of 1972, UNCW biologists were concerned that "progress" was invading its natural areas, including a trail that had been used since 1964 to teach ecological principles in the most diverse collection of native plants found anywhere on campus. Because of these biologists' actions and the Bluethenthal family's time and donations, approximately 10 acres are "forever protected from all other uses." On November 8, 1974, the old nature trail was officially dedicated as the Herbert Bluethenthal Memorial Wildflower Preserve.

University of North Carolina Wilmington

GENERAL ADMISSIONS

Very important factors include: rigor of secondary school record, academic GPA, standardized test scores (if submitted), application essay. *Important factors include:* class rank. *Other factors considered include:* recommendations. High school diploma is required and GED is accepted. Institution is test-optional for entering Fall 2024. Check admissions website for updates. *Academic units required:* 4 English, 4 math, 3 science (1 lab), 2 foreign language, 1 social studies, 1 U.S. history.

FINANCIAL AID

Students should submit: FAFSA; Institution's own financial aid form. *Need-based scholarships/grants offered:* College/university scholarship or grant aid from institutional funds; Federal Nursing Scholarships; Federal Pell; Private scholarships; SEOG; State scholarships/grants; United Negro College Fund. *Loan aid offered:* Direct PLUS loans; Direct Subsidized Loans; Direct Unsubsidized Loans. Federal Work-Study Program available. Institutional employment available.

CAMPUS LIFE

Activities: Campus Ministries; Choral groups; Concert band; Dance; Drama/theater; International Student Organization; Literary magazine; Music ensembles; Musical theater; Pep band; Radio station; Student government; Student newspaper; Student-run film society. **Organizations:** 331 registered organizations, 9 honor societies, 20 religious organizations, 18 fraternities, 14 sororities. **Athletics (Intercollegiate):** *Men:* baseball, basketball, crew/rowing, cross-country, equestrian sports, field hockey, golf, gymnastics, ice hockey, lacrosse, rugby, softball, swimming, ultimate frisbee, volleyball, water polo. *Women:* baseball, basketball, crew/rowing, cross-country, equestrian sports, field hockey, golf, gymnastics, ice hockey, lacrosse, rugby, softball, swimming, ultimate frisbee, volleyball, water polo.

CAMPUS

Type of school	Public
Environment	City

STUDENTS

Undergrad enrollment	13,960
% male/female	35/65
% from out of state	13
% frosh live on campus	94

FINANCIAL FACTS

Annual in-state tuition	$4,443
Annual out-of-state tuition	$19,063
Room and board	$12,120
Required fees	$2,795

GENERAL ADMISSIONS INFO

Application fee	$80
Regular application deadline	2/1
Nonfall registration	Yes

Fall 2024 testing policy	Test Optional
Range SAT EBRW	620–690
Range SAT Math	600–680
Range ACT Composite	24–29

ACADEMICS

Student/faculty ratio	17:1
% students returning for sophomore year	83

Most classes have 20–29 students.

REQUESTING SERVICES FOR STUDENTS WITH LEARNING DIFFERENCES

Phone: 910-962-7555 • uncw.edu/disability • Email: DRC@uncw.edu

Documentation submitted to: Disability Resource Center
Separate application required for Services: Yes

Documentation required for:
LD: Psychoeducational evaluation
ADHD: Psychoeducational evaluation
ASD: Psychoeducational evaluation

Wake Forest University

P.O. Box 7305 Reynolda Station, Winston-Salem, NC 27109 • Admissions: 336-758-5201 • www.wfu.edu

(Support: CS)

ACCOMMODATIONS

Allowed in exams:

Calculators	No
Dictionary	Yes
Computer	Yes
Spell-checker	Yes
Extended test time	Yes
Scribe	No
Proctors	No
Oral exams	No
Note-takers	No

Support services for students with:

LD	Yes
ADHD	Yes
ASD	Yes
Distraction-reduced environment	Yes
Recording of lecture allowed	Yes
Reading technology	Yes
Audio books	Yes
Other assistive technology	Yes
Priority registration	No

Added costs of services:

For LD	No
For ADHD	No
For ASD	No
LD specialists	Yes
ADHD & ASD coaching	No
ASD specialists	No
Professional tutors	No
Peer tutors	Yes
Max. hours/week for services	Varies
How professors are notified of student approved accommodations	Student and Center for Learning Access and Student Success

COLLEGE GRADUATION REQUIREMENTS

Course waivers allowed	No
Course substitutions allowed	Yes
In what courses: Case-by-case basis	

PROGRAMS/SERVICES FOR STUDENTS WITH LEARNING DIFFERENCES

The Center for Learning, Access, and Student Success (CLASS) provides services and accommodations for students with disabilities. Once enrolled at Wake Forest, students contact CLASS and then meet to discuss accommodations, which are determined based on appropriate documentation. For students with documented disabilities, CLASS staff will notify the professors and work with the student and professors to help implement any approved course accommodations. Students with learning disabilities have a series of conferences with staff members who specialize in academic skills and will help design an overall study plan to improve scholastic performance in those areas needing assistance. Assistive technology opportunities are determined on an individual basis. Course substitutions are available for a foreign language as well as for math, on occasion.

ADMISSIONS

All applicants are expected to meet the same admission criteria. Interviews are optional. High school curriculum and classroom performance, combined with the student's writing ability, extracurricular activities, and evidence of character and talent, are the most important criteria for admission.

Additional Information

CLASS helps students develop study, organization, and time management strategies and methods for improving reading comprehension, note-taking, memory, motivation, and self-advocacy skills. Free, one-on-one tutoring is available in many academic subjects. The tutors are advanced undergraduates or graduate students who have demonstrated mastery of specific subject areas and are supervised by the CLASS staff for their tutoring activities. CLASS ambassadors are a group of students that help with student outreach and awareness of the resources offered to all students.

Sigma Pi Johnny Dawkins ('81) wanted to show that fraternities could do good and unite the campus community. The Brian Piccolo Cancer Research Fund Drive started modestly in the fall of 1980 and continues today. Brian Piccolo was an All-American running back for Wake Forest in 1964, leading the nation in rushing and touchdowns. Brian died of cancer in 1970 at age 26 and inspired the 1971 TV movie "Brian's Song."

Wake Forest University

General Admissions

Very important factors include: rigor of secondary school record, class rank, academic GPA, application essay. *Important factors include:* recommendations. *Other factors considered include:* standardized test scores (if submitted). High school diploma is required and GED is accepted. Institution is test-optional for entering Fall 2024. Check admissions website for updates. *Academic units required:* 4 English, 3 math, 1 science, 2 foreign language, 2 social studies. *Academic units recommended:* 4 math, 4 science, 4 foreign language, 4 social studies.

Financial Aid

Students should submit: CSS/Financial Aid Profile; FAFSA; Noncustodial Profile; State aid form. *Need-based scholarships/grants offered:* College/university scholarship or grant aid from institutional funds; Federal Pell; Private scholarships; SEOG; State scholarships/grants; United Negro College Fund. *Loan aid offered:* Direct PLUS loans; Direct Subsidized Loans; Direct Unsubsidized Loans. Federal Work-Study Program available. Institutional employment available.

Campus Life

Activities: Campus Ministries; Choral groups; Concert band; Dance; Drama/theater; International Student Organization; Jazz band; Literary magazine; Marching band; Model UN; Music ensembles; Musical theater; Pep band; Radio station; Student government; Student newspaper; Student-run film society; Symphony orchestra; Television station; Yearbook. **Organizations:** 168 registered organizations, 16 honor societies, 16 religious organizations, 14 fraternities, 9 sororities. **Athletics (Intercollegiate):** *Men:* baseball, basketball, bowling, crew/rowing, cross-country, cycling, equestrian sports, golf, ice hockey, lacrosse, martial arts, rugby, skiing (nordic/cross-country), swimming, track/field (indoor), ultimate frisbee, volleyball, wrestling. *Women:* basketball, bowling, crew/rowing, cross-country, cycling, equestrian sports, field hockey, golf, ice hockey, lacrosse, martial arts, rugby, skiing (nordic/cross-country), softball, swimming, track/field (indoor), ultimate frisbee, volleyball.

CAMPUS

Type of school	Private (nonprofit)
Environment	City

STUDENTS

Undergrad enrollment	5,465
% male/female	46/54
% from out of state	73
% frosh live on campus	100

FINANCIAL FACTS

Annual tuition	$58,708
Room and board	$18,014
Required fees	$1,062

GENERAL ADMISSIONS INFO

Application fee	$85
Regular application deadline	1/1
Nonfall registration	No

Fall 2024 testing policy	Test Optional
Range SAT EBRW	670–730
Range SAT Math	680–770
Range ACT Composite	30–33

ACADEMICS

Student/faculty ratio	11:1
% students returning for sophomore year	94

Most classes have 10–19 students.

REQUESTING SERVICES FOR STUDENTS WITH LEARNING DIFFERENCES

Phone: 336-758-5929 • class.wfu.edu/ • Email: class@wfu.edu

Documentation submitted to: Center for Learning, Access, and Student Success (CLASS)
Separate application required for Services: Yes

Documentation required for:
LD: Psychoeducational evaluation
ADHD: Psychoeducational evaluation
ASD: Psychoeducational evaluation

Western Carolina University

102 Camp Building, Cullowhee, NC 28723 • Admissions: 828-227-7317 • www.wcu.edu

Support: CS

ACCOMMODATIONS

Allowed in exams:

Calculators	Yes
Dictionary	Yes
Computer	Yes
Spell-checker	Yes
Extended test time	Yes
Scribe	Yes
Proctors	Yes
Oral exams	Yes
Note-takers	Yes

Support services for students with:

LD	Yes
ADHD	Yes
ASD	Yes
Distraction-reduced environment	Yes
Recording of lecture allowed	Yes
Reading technology	Yes
Audio books	No
Other assistive technology	Yes
Priority registration	Yes

Added costs of services:

For LD	No
For ADHD	No
For ASD	No
LD specialists	Yes
ADHD & ASD coaching	No
ASD specialists	No
Professional tutors	Yes
Peer tutors	Yes
Max. hours/week for services	Varies
How professors are notified of student approved accommodations	Student

COLLEGE GRADUATION REQUIREMENTS

Course waivers allowed	Yes
In what courses: Case-by-case basis	
Course substitutions allowed	Yes
In what courses: Case-by-case basis	

PROGRAMS/SERVICES FOR STUDENTS WITH LEARNING DIFFERENCES

The Office of Accessibility Resources (OAR) responds to the needs of students with learning disabilities by making services and assistive technologies available as needed. Students register for academic and testing accommodations through the online portal AIM (Accessible Information Management). Then, OAR conducts a virtual initial intake meeting with the student to review services offered and required current documentation and determine proper accommodations. Students with approved accommodations are provided an accommodation letter, which they give to their professors. Accommodations may include alternative-format textbooks and assistive technology, including Kurzweil 3000. OAR Academic Coaching employs qualified graduate assistants as coaches to help students set goals, build skills to help navigate transitions, and apply strategies for success. GETS stands for Goal Setting, Empowerment, Transitional support, Success and is the foundation of OAR Coaching Services. Coaching topics may include managing time efficiently, utilizing tools for optimizing organizational skills, planning steps toward completing goals, exploring recreation and leisure opportunities on campus and in the local community, promoting the student's self-advocacy skills, and communicating effectively with instructors, classmates, and others.

ADMISSIONS

All applicants are expected to meet the same admission criteria. The average GPA for accepted applicants is 3.7. Some students who do not meet the standard admission guidelines may be offered an opportunity to enroll through the Academic Success Program (ASP). This conditional admission program has a required five-week intensive summer program that invited students must successfully complete before beginning in the fall. Students are enrolled in 7 credit hours of courses, which count toward graduation, and they also participate in seminars, workshops, and social, academic, and transitional support events. ASP provides a full year of support to students to develop the skills to succeed in college.

Additional Information

The Writing and Learning Commons and Mathematics Tutoring Center promote student success through math and course tutoring, writing support, academic skills consultation, exam prep activities, and more.

In 1957 the landmark Brown v. Board of Education Supreme Court case made racial segregation in public places illegal. In 1957, Levern Hamlin Allen received a job offer in Mecklenburg County but needed to be certified in Special Needs. She was the first African American student to enroll at WCU. In 1987, she was invited back to WCU by the Organization of Ebony Students. The same year, she was selected to serve on the WCU Board of Trustees, which she did from 1987–1995.

Western Carolina University

GENERAL ADMISSIONS

Very important factors include: rigor of secondary school record, class rank, academic GPA, standardized test scores (if submitted). *Important factors include:* application essay, recommendations. High school diploma is required and GED is accepted. Institution is test-optional for entering Fall 2024. Check admissions website for updates. *Academic units required:* 4 English, 4 math, 3 science (1 lab), 2 foreign language, 1 social studies, 1 U.S. history, 4 academic electives.

FINANCIAL AID

Students should submit: FAFSA; Institution's own financial aid form. *Need-based scholarships/grants offered:* College/university scholarship or grant aid from institutional funds; Federal Pell; Private scholarships; SEOG; State scholarships/grants. *Loan aid offered:* Direct PLUS loans; Direct Subsidized Loans; Direct Unsubsidized Loans. Federal Work-Study Program available. Institutional employment available.

CAMPUS LIFE

Activities: Campus Ministries; Choral groups; Concert band; Dance; Drama/theater; International Student Organization; Jazz band; Literary magazine; Marching band; Model UN; Music ensembles; Musical theater; Pep band; Radio station; Student government; Student newspaper; Student-run film society; Television station. **Organizations:** 150 registered organizations, 7 honor societies, 17 religious organizations, 13 fraternities, 9 sororities. **Athletics (Intercollegiate):** *Men:* baseball, basketball, cross-country, cycling, equestrian sports, golf, lacrosse, rugby, swimming, track/field (indoor), ultimate frisbee, wrestling. *Women:* basketball, cross-country, cycling, equestrian sports, golf, lacrosse, rugby, softball, swimming, track/field (indoor), ultimate frisbee, volleyball, wrestling.

CAMPUS

Type of school	Public
Environment	Rural

STUDENTS

Undergrad enrollment	9,835
% male/female	46/54
% from out of state	9
% frosh live on campus	99

FINANCIAL FACTS

Annual in-state tuition	$1,000
Annual out-of-state tuition	$5,000
Room and board	$9,682
Required fees	$3,220

GENERAL ADMISSIONS INFO

Application fee	$65
Regular application deadline	3/1
Nonfall registration	Yes

Fall 2024 testing policy	Test Optional
Range SAT EBRW	520–620
Range SAT Math	510–600
Range ACT Composite	20–25

ACADEMICS

Student/faculty ratio	17:1
% students returning for sophomore year	80

Most classes have 20–29 students.

REQUESTING SERVICES FOR STUDENTS WITH LEARNING DIFFERENCES

Phone: 828-227-3886 • www.wcu.edu/learn/academic-services/disability-services
Email: accessibility@wcu.edu

Documentation submitted to: Office of Accessibility Resources
Separate application required for Services: Yes

Documentation required for:
  LD: Psychoeducational evaluation
  ADHD: Psychoeducational evaluation
  ASD: Psychoeducational evaluation

North Dakota State University

P.O. Box 6050 Dept 2832, Fargo, ND 58108 • Admissions: 701-231-8643 • www.ndsu.edu

Support: S

ACCOMMODATIONS

Allowed in exams:

Calculators	Yes
Dictionary	Yes
Computer	Yes
Spell-checker	Yes
Extended test time	Yes
Scribe	Yes
Proctors	Yes
Oral exams	Yes
Note-takers	Yes

Support services for students with:

LD	Yes
ADHD	Yes
ASD	Yes
Distraction-reduced environment	Yes
Recording of lecture allowed	Yes
Reading technology	Yes
Audio books	No
Other assistive technology	Yes
Priority registration	Yes

Added costs of services:

For LD	No
For ADHD	No
For ASD	No
LD specialists	No
ADHD & ASD coaching	No
ASD specialists	No
Professional tutors	No
Peer tutors	Yes
Max. hours/week for services	Varies
How professors are notified of student approved accommodations	Student

COLLEGE GRADUATION REQUIREMENTS

Course waivers allowed	Yes
In what courses: Case-by-case basis	
Course substitutions allowed	Yes
In what courses: Case-by-case basis	

PROGRAMS/SERVICES FOR STUDENTS WITH LEARNING DIFFERENCES

The Office of Disability Services (ODS) offers a range of services for students with disabilities to assist with a successful academic and campus experience. Students initiate the accommodations process through ODS by submitting an online application and securely uploading documentation of their disability. The student will then schedule an in-person meeting with a disability specialist to discuss reasonable accommodations to ensure the student has their needs met. Examples of accommodations available include alternative textbooks and course material, assistive technology, software, note-taking, recording lectures, test-taking accommodations, and housing accommodations. Students must access their online account and request course accommodations each semester.

ADMISSIONS

It is recommended that all applicants for admission to NDSU have completed the core courses with a GPA of 2.75 or higher. The academic elective course can be from an existing core subject area or world language, including foreign languages, Native American languages, or American Sign Language. A GED certificate will be accepted in place of a high school transcript. Applicants who feel their test scores show a good representation of their abilities can submit scores for consideration. If submitted, NDSU also will consider test scores for math and English placements. Students who do not meet these minimum guidelines will still be considered for admission if their high school records show evidence that they are adequately prepared to be successful in college.

Additional Information

The foundation of Student Support Services (SSS) is individual academic guidance. Students can make appointments with an SSS education specialist for assistance with determining course selection for the semester and long-term education plans. They also offer strategies for improving GPA, study skills, and help with and referrals to other campus and community services. Students can sign up for a SSS peer mentor who will help first-year students familiarize themselves with the university, identify campus resources, develop academic and personal skills, and offer information about campus organizations and more. Trained tutors are available, and promote good study habits as well as assist students with their academic needs. Free online tutoring is available to all NDSU students through Smarthinking, a national tutoring service. The Center for Writers provides free writing support with one-on-one sessions, writing courses, workshops, and a wealth of resources for writers and writing instructors. The Math Emporium provides tutors for college algebra, trigonometry, and pre-calculus.

In 1922, the Lettermen's Club voted to adopt the nickname Bison for the sports teams, discontinuing the use of Aggies. Large herds of bison once roamed the North Dakota prairie, so it seemed fitting. The mascot was named Thundar, and the Bison athletic teams soon became known as the Thundering Herd.

North Dakota State University

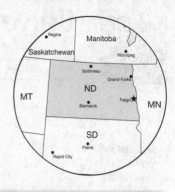

GENERAL ADMISSIONS

Very important factors include: academic GPA, standardized test scores (if submitted). High school diploma is required and GED is accepted. Institution is test-optional for entering Fall 2024. Check admissions website for updates. *Academic units required:* 4 English, 3 math, 3 science (3 labs), 3 social studies, 1 academic elective.

FINANCIAL AID

Students should submit: FAFSA. *Need-based scholarships/grants offered:* College/university scholarship or grant aid from institutional funds; Federal Pell; Private scholarships; SEOG; State scholarships/grants. *Loan aid offered:* Direct PLUS loans; Direct Subsidized Loans; Direct Unsubsidized Loans. Federal Work-Study Program available. Institutional employment available.

CAMPUS LIFE

Activities: Campus Ministries; Choral groups; Concert band; Dance; Drama/theater; International Student Organization; Jazz band; Marching band; Model UN; Music ensembles; Musical theater; Opera; Pep band; Radio station; Student government; Student newspaper; Symphony orchestra; Television station. **Organizations:** 300 registered organizations, 23 honor societies, 22 religious organizations, 12 fraternities, 3 sororities. **Athletics (Intercollegiate):** *Men:* baseball, basketball, cross-country, cycling, golf, ice hockey, lacrosse, swimming, track/field (indoor), ultimate frisbee, volleyball, wrestling. *Women:* basketball, cross-country, cycling, equestrian sports, golf, ice hockey, lacrosse, rugby, softball, swimming, track/field (indoor), volleyball.

CAMPUS

Type of school	Public
Environment	City

STUDENTS

Undergrad enrollment	11,609
% male/female	55/45
% from out of state	57
% frosh live on campus	93

FINANCIAL FACTS

Annual in-state tuition	$6,762
Annual out-of-state tuition	$18,056
Room and board	$7,502
Required fees	$1,216

GENERAL ADMISSIONS INFO

Application fee	$35
Regular application deadline	8/1
Nonfall registration	Yes

Fall 2024 testing policy	Test Optional
Range SAT EBRW	480–630
Range SAT Math	500–630
Range ACT Composite	21–26

ACADEMICS

Student/faculty ratio	17:1
% students returning for sophomore year	78

Most classes have 20–29 students.

REQUESTING SERVICES FOR STUDENTS WITH LEARNING DIFFERENCES

Phone: 701-231-8463 • www.ndsu.edu/disabilityservices/ • Email: ndsu.cadr@ndsu.edu

Documentation submitted to: Office of Disability Services

Separate application required for Services: Yes

Documentation required for:
LD: Psychoeducational evaluation
ADHD: Psychoeducational evaluation
ASD: Psychoeducational evaluation

North Dakota

University of Jamestown

6081 College Lane, Jamestown, ND 58405-0001 • Admissions: 701-252-3467 • www.uj.edu

Support: CS

ACCOMMODATIONS

Allowed in exams:

Calculators	Yes
Dictionary	Yes
Computer	Yes
Spell-checker	Yes
Extended test time	Yes
Scribe	Yes
Proctors	Yes
Oral exams	Yes
Note-takers	Yes

Support services for students with:

LD	Yes
ADHD	Yes
ASD	Yes
Distraction-reduced environment	Yes
Recording of lecture allowed	Yes
Reading technology	Yes
Audio books	Yes
Other assistive technology	Yes
Priority registration	No

Added costs of services:

For LD	No
For ADHD	No
For ASD	No
LD specialists	No
ADHD & ASD coaching	No
ASD specialists	Yes
Professional tutors	No
Peer tutors	Yes
Max. hours/week for services	Varies
How professors are notified of student approved accommodations	Student and Office of Disability Services

COLLEGE GRADUATION REQUIREMENTS

Course waivers allowed	Yes
In what courses: Varies	
Course substitutions allowed	Yes
In what courses: Varies	

PROGRAMS/SERVICES FOR STUDENTS WITH LEARNING DIFFERENCES

The Office of Disability Services offers reasonable accommodations to afford students with disabilities an equal opportunity to academic and campus life. It's the student's responsibility to register with the Office of Disability Services. Once registered, students may be asked to provide documentation describing the functional limitations of their disability in the classroom or the nonacademic setting. During a meeting with the student and staff, accommodations will be determined, which may vary according to each course's requirements and the nature of the disability. Students receive a letter from the office verifying accommodations that they can share with faculty, or they can request the letter be sent directly to their instructors. Students meet each semester with the Office of Disability Services once they have their class schedule to renew or change accommodations as needed.

ADMISSIONS

All applicants are expected to meet the same admission criteria. In addition to core academic courses, it's recommended that high school students take at least two foreign language courses, which may include American Sign Language or Native American languages. The admissions officials at UJ review applications based on high school transcripts or GED, the student's chosen program of study, and a personal essay outlining the applicant's plans for success in college. The minimum GPA required for admission is 2.5.

Additional Information

The Student Success Center offers several group study sessions each semester. Students can also register for one-on-one in-person or virtual tutoring sessions. The UJ Writing Center is a free resource for the UJ community. Writers learn to communicate effectively by sharing their thoughts with a wider audience and gain help with critical thinking skills, setting realistic goals, and understanding the writing process. In UJ Foundations, a 1 credit course, first-year students meet in small groups each week with a faculty member and an upper-level student guide to help them adjust to academic and student life. Students participate in discussions to help them set goals both inside and outside the classroom.

UJ was founded in 1883 as Jamestown College in the Dakota territories, the first private college in what's now North Dakota (statehood was granted in 1889). There were 35 students enrolled in the first classes that began on September 29, 1886. The four areas of study offered were scientific, classical, commercial, and music. The school closed during the Panic of 1893 (one of the most severe financial crises in the history of the United States), reopened in 1909, and has remained in operation ever since.

University of Jamestown

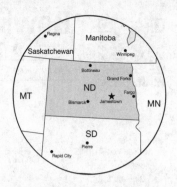

GENERAL ADMISSIONS

Very important factors include: academic GPA, standardized test scores (if submitted). *Important factors include:* rigor of secondary school record. *Other factors considered include:* class rank, application essay, recommendations. High school diploma is required and GED is accepted. Institution is test-optional for entering Fall 2024. Check admissions website for updates. *Academic units recommended:* 4 English, 3 math, 4 science, 2 foreign language, 3 social studies.

FINANCIAL AID

Students should submit: FAFSA. *Need-based scholarships/grants offered:* Federal Pell; Private scholarships; SEOG; State scholarships/grants. *Loan aid offered:* Direct PLUS loans; Direct Subsidized Loans; Direct Unsubsidized Loans. Federal Work-Study Program available. Institutional employment available.

CAMPUS LIFE

Activities: Campus Ministries; Choral groups; Concert band; Drama/theater; International Student Organization; Jazz band; Literary magazine; Music ensembles; Musical theater; Pep band; Student government; Student newspaper. **Organizations:** 26 registered organizations, 5 honor societies, 2 religious organizations, 0 fraternities, 0 sororities. **Athletics (Intercollegiate):** *Men:* baseball, basketball, cross-country, golf, ice hockey, track/field (indoor), volleyball, wrestling. *Women:* basketball, cross-country, golf, softball, track/field (indoor), volleyball, wrestling.

CAMPUS

Type of school	Private (nonprofit)
Environment	Village

STUDENTS

Undergrad enrollment	905
% male/female	55/45
% from out of state	60
% frosh live on campus	95

FINANCIAL FACTS

Annual tuition	$22,718
Room and board	$8,316
Required fees	$780

GENERAL ADMISSIONS INFO

Application fee	No fee
Regular application deadline	Rolling
Nonfall registration	Yes

Fall 2024 testing policy	Test Optional
Range SAT EBRW	480–560
Range SAT Math	470–560
Range ACT Composite	19–25

ACADEMICS

Student/faculty ratio	10:1
% students returning for sophomore year	70

Most classes have 10–19 students.

REQUESTING SERVICES FOR STUDENTS WITH LEARNING DIFFERENCES

Phone: 701-543-0114 ext 5721 • www.uj.edu/academics/academic-support/disability-services
Email: tracy.boze@uj.edu

Documentation submitted to: Office of Disability Services
Separate application required for Services: Yes

Documentation required for:
LD: Psychoeducational evaluation
ADHD: Psychoeducational evaluation
ASD: Psychoeducational evaluation

Bowling Green State University

200 University Hall, Bowling Green, OH 43403-0085 • Admissions: 419-372-2478 • www.bgsu.edu

Support: SP

ACCOMMODATIONS

Allowed in exams:

Calculators	Yes
Dictionary	No
Computer	Yes
Spell-checker	Yes
Extended test time	Yes
Scribe	Yes
Proctors	Yes
Oral exams	Yes
Note-takers	Yes

Support services for students with:

LD	Yes
ADHD	Yes
ASD	Yes
Distraction-reduced environment	Yes
Recording of lecture allowed	Yes
Reading technology	Yes
Audio books	Yes
Other assistive technology	Yes
Priority registration	Yes

Added costs of services:

For LD	No
For ADHD	No
For ASD	No
LD specialists	No
ADHD & ASD coaching	Yes
ASD specialists	Yes
Professional tutors	No
Peer tutors	Yes
Max. hours/week for services	Varies
How professors are notified of student approved accommodations	Student

COLLEGE GRADUATION REQUIREMENTS

Course waivers allowed	No
Course substitutions allowed	Yes

In what courses: Foreign Language

PROGRAMS/SERVICES FOR STUDENTS WITH LEARNING DIFFERENCES:

Accessibility Services (AS) provides assistance to students with disabilities. Accommodations are determined on a case-by-case basis once the student registers and submits documentation of their disability to AS. Students are encouraged to contact the office during the pre-admission process, and submit their documentation as soon as they know they will attend BGSU. Most students who register with AS are eligible for priority registration for classes, academic accommodations, auxiliary aids, and services. Students who are not be eligible for AS may still qualify for a variety of other services on campus. The Falcon Learning Your Way Program (FLY) is a fee-based academic support program available to students who have learning differences, such as ADHD, or students who would benefit from help with time-management and learning strategies. FLY supports students in their transition from high school with the help of a learning specialist. The Ohio College2Careers program is a partnership between Opportunities for Ohioans with Disabilities (OOD) and the Ohio higher education system that connects students with disabilities to supportive resources and Ohio businesses that help achieve vocational goals. Services can include career counseling, résumé and interview preparation, assistive technology, and assistance finding internships and permanent employment.

ADMISSIONS

For admission to BGSU, all applicants must meet the minimum requirements. Applicants must be graduates of an accredited senior high school, have a high school GED equivalency, or, if home-schooled, submit GED test results and ACT or SAT test results. The most important criteria reviewed by admissions are high school coursework and rigor of curriculum, cumulative GPA, class rank if available, and ACT or SAT scores, if submitted. ACT and SAT test scores are optional, but may allow the committee to evaluate college readiness more accurately, can also be used for math placement, and may add to scholarship consideration. BGSU also considers applicants' special talents in the arts, sciences, and athletics, and as well as identities and representation in order to diversify the student population with unique perspectives. Personal essays are optional, and letters of recommendation are not considered.

Additional Information

The Math and Stats Lab provides tutoring for all math and statistics courses. The Writing Center staff is available by appointment to help students through all stages of writing projects, with an emphasis on the development of writing skills. Students interested in science can attend the Art of Science Community gatherings to hear from guest speakers and connect with mentors, educators, and colleagues in northwest Ohio.

In 1914, Dr. Homer B. Williams, BGSU's first president, asked a committee to decide the school colors. While on a trolley ride, Dr. Winslow sat behind a woman wearing a hat with brown and orange feathers. He was so impressed by the colors that he recommended them to his committee, and the Board of Trustees approved burnt orange and seal brown. Today, BGSU is the only Division I university to have orange and brown as its school colors.

Bowling Green State University

GENERAL ADMISSIONS

Very important factors include: rigor of secondary school record, academic GPA, standardized test scores (if submitted). *Important factors include:* class rank. *Other factors considered include:* application essay, recommendations. High school diploma is required and GED is accepted. Institution is test-optional for entering Fall 2024. Check admissions website for updates. *Academic units required:* 4 English, 4 math, 3 science, 2 foreign language, 3 social studies, 1 visual/performing arts.

FINANCIAL AID

Students should submit: FAFSA. *Need-based scholarships/grants offered:* College/university scholarship or grant aid from institutional funds; Federal Pell; Private scholarships; SEOG; State scholarships/grants. *Loan aid offered:* Direct PLUS loans; Direct Subsidized Loans; Direct Unsubsidized Loans. Federal Work-Study Program available. Institutional employment available.

CAMPUS LIFE

Activities: Campus Ministries; Choral groups; Concert band; Dance; Drama/theater; International Student Organization; Jazz band; Literary magazine; Marching band; Model UN; Music ensembles; Musical theater; Pep band; Radio station; Student government; Student newspaper; Student-run film society; Symphony orchestra; Television station; Yearbook. **Organizations:** 366 registered organizations, 11 honor societies, 14 religious organizations, 22 fraternities, 17 sororities. **Athletics (Intercollegiate):** *Men:* baseball, basketball, bowling, cross-country, equestrian sports, golf, gymnastics, ice hockey, lacrosse, martial arts, racquetball, rugby, swimming, table tennis, track/field (indoor), ultimate frisbee, volleyball, water polo. *Women:* basketball, bowling, cross-country, equestrian sports, golf, gymnastics, ice hockey, lacrosse, martial arts, racquetball, rugby, softball, swimming, table tennis, track/field (indoor), ultimate frisbee, volleyball, water polo.

CAMPUS

Type of school	Public
Environment	Town

STUDENTS

Undergrad enrollment	13,853
% male/female	43/57
% from out of state	11
% frosh live on campus	87

FINANCIAL FACTS

Annual in-state tuition	$11,273
Annual out-of-state tuition	$19,261
Room and board	$11,384
Required fees	$2,367

GENERAL ADMISSIONS INFO

Application fee	$45
Regular application deadline	7/15
Nonfall registration	Yes

Fall 2024 testing policy	Test Optional
Range SAT EBRW	490–600
Range SAT Math	500–600
Range ACT Composite	19–25

ACADEMICS

Student/faculty ratio	17:1
% students returning for sophomore year	77

Most classes have 20–29 students.

Ohio

REQUESTING SERVICES FOR STUDENTS WITH LEARNING DIFFERENCES

Phone: 419-372-8495 • www.bgsu.edu/accessibility-services • Email: access@bgsu.edu

Documentation submitted to: Accessibility Services
Separate application required for Services: Yes

Documentation required for:
LD: Psychoeducational evaluation
ADHD: Psychoeducational evaluation
ASD: Psychoeducational evaluation

Case Western Reserve University

Wolstein Hall, Cleveland, OH 44106-7055 • Admissions: 216-368-4450 • www.case.edu

Support: CS

ACCOMMODATIONS

Allowed in exams:

Calculators	Yes
Dictionary	N/A
Computer	Yes
Spell-checker	Yes
Extended test time	Yes
Scribe	Yes
Proctors	Yes
Oral exams	Yes
Note-takers	Yes

Support services for students with:

LD	Yes
ADHD	Yes
ASD	Yes
Distraction-reduced environment	Yes
Recording of lecture allowed	Yes
Reading technology	Yes
Audio books	Yes
Other assistive technology	Yes
Priority registration	Yes

Added costs of services:

For LD	No
For ADHD	No
For ASD	No
LD specialists	Yes
ADHD & ASD coaching	Yes
ASD specialists	Yes
Professional tutors	No
Peer tutors	Yes
Max. hours/week for services	5
How professors are notified of student approved accommodations	Student and Disability Resources

COLLEGE GRADUATION REQUIREMENTS

Course waivers allowed	No
Course substitutions allowed	Yes
In what courses: Math	

PROGRAMS/SERVICES FOR STUDENTS WITH LEARNING DIFFERENCES

The Disability Resources department at Case Western Reserve University provides services to students with disabilities. To receive accommodations, students submit an application and documentation, and meet in person for an interview with the department. Once approved, Disability Resources works closely with students to design each individual plan for accommodations and services. Plans include the identifying of specific accommodations for each course as well as strategies for disclosing their needs to professors. Disability Resources and the Office of Accommodated Testing and Services (OATS) provide required course material in alternate formats for students with approved accommodations. Students denied eligibility or who are dissatisfied with an accommodation method may request a meeting with the director of Disability Resources to discuss the matter. Services available include notetakers, alternative formats for print materials, scheduling assistance, assistive technology, testing accommodations, and testing information. Disability Resources offers the support group Campus Connections for students with social anxiety and other social impairments, including ASD. Campus Connections assists students with their transition to residence halls and greater independence, ways to initiate and sustain healthy relationships, and how to navigate campus resources, organizations, clubs, and social media. The Hot Mess Express Group is a 10-week program for students who struggle with executive functioning.

ADMISSIONS

Standards for admission are the same for all students. Applicants who wish to pursue engineering or the sciences should have an additional year of math and laboratory science. Likewise, liberal arts majors should consider an additional year of social studies and foreign language. The admissions office considers academic performance, life experiences, and interests when determining acceptance.

Additional Information

Free academic peer tutoring is available to all CWRU students.

Did you know that in 1895, Edward W. Morley determined the atomic weight of oxygen (15.999) in his lab at CWRU? His methods of research set a new standard for chemistry and his accuracy in chemical methods have never been replaced. His work also gave insight into the atomic theory of matter. In 1995, the American Chemical Society published a commemorative booklet on his work and presented Case Western with a plaque that marks the site of his lab.

Case Western Reserve University

GENERAL ADMISSIONS

Very important factors include: rigor of secondary school record, class rank, academic GPA. *Important factors include:* application essay, recommendations. *Other factors considered include:* standardized test scores (if submitted). High school diploma is required and GED is accepted. Institution is test-optional for entering Fall 2024. Check admissions website for updates. *Academic units required:* 4 English, 3 math, 3 science (2 labs), 2 foreign language, 3 social studies. *Academic units recommended:* 4 math, 4 science (3 labs), 3 foreign language, 4 social studies.

FINANCIAL AID

Students should submit: CSS/Financial Aid Profile; FAFSA; Institution's own financial aid form; Noncustodial Profile. *Need-based scholarships/grants offered:* College/university scholarship or grant aid from institutional funds; Federal Pell; Private scholarships; SEOG; State scholarships/grants. *Loan aid offered:* Direct PLUS loans; Direct Subsidized Loans; Direct Unsubsidized Loans. Federal Work-Study Program available. Institutional employment available.

CAMPUS LIFE

Activities: Campus Ministries; Choral groups; Concert band; Dance; Drama/theater; International Student Organization; Jazz band; Literary magazine; Marching band; Model UN; Music ensembles; Musical theater; Pep band; Radio station; Student government; Student newspaper; Student-run film society; Symphony orchestra; Yearbook. **Organizations:** 249 registered organizations, 8 honor societies, 7 religious organizations, 18 fraternities, 9 sororities. **Athletics (Intercollegiate):** *Men:* baseball, basketball, crew/rowing, cross-country, cycling, ice hockey, lacrosse, martial arts, rugby, swimming, table tennis, track/field (indoor), ultimate frisbee, volleyball, water polo, wrestling. *Women:* basketball, crew/rowing, cross-country, cycling, ice hockey, lacrosse, martial arts, rugby, softball, swimming, table tennis, track/field (indoor), ultimate frisbee, volleyball, water polo.

CAMPUS
Type of school	Private (nonprofit)
Environment	Metropolis

STUDENTS
Undergrad enrollment	5,697
% male/female	53/47
% from out of state	80
% frosh live on campus	90

FINANCIAL FACTS
Annual tuition	$64,100
Room and board	$18,202
Required fees	$571

GENERAL ADMISSIONS INFO
Application fee	$70
Regular application deadline	1/15
Nonfall registration	Yes

Fall 2024 testing policy	Test Optional
Range SAT EBRW	680–740
Range SAT Math	730–790
Range ACT Composite	32–35

ACADEMICS
Student/faculty ratio	9:1
% students returning for sophomore year	94

Most classes have 10–19 students.

Ohio

REQUESTING SERVICES FOR STUDENTS WITH LEARNING DIFFERENCES

Phone: 216-368-5230 • case.edu/studentlife/disability/ • Email: disability@case.edu

Documentation submitted to: Disability Resources
Separate application required for Services: Yes

Documentation required for:
LD: Psychoeducational evaluation
ADHD: Psychoeducational evaluation
ASD: Psychoeducational evaluation

Cedarville University

251 N. Main Street, Cedarville, OH 45314 • Admissions: 937-766-7700 • www.cedarville.edu

(Support: CS)

ACCOMMODATIONS

Allowed in exams:

Calculators	Yes
Dictionary	Yes
Computer	Yes
Spell-checker	Yes
Extended test time	Yes
Scribe	Yes
Proctors	Yes
Oral exams	Yes
Note-takers	Yes

Support services for students with:

LD	Yes
ADHD	Yes
ASD	Yes
Distraction-reduced environment	Yes
Recording of lecture allowed	Yes
Reading technology	Yes
Audio books	Yes
Other assistive technology	Yes
Priority registration	Yes

Added costs of services:

For LD	No
For ADHD	No
For ASD	No
LD specialists	Yes
ADHD & ASD coaching	Yes
ASD specialists	Yes
Professional tutors	No
Peer tutors	Yes
Max. hours/week for services	2
How professors are notified of student approved accommodations	Student and Disability Services

COLLEGE GRADUATION REQUIREMENTS

Course waivers allowed	Yes

In what courses: Math and Foreign Language on a case-by-case basis

Course substitutions allowed	Yes

In what courses: Math and Foreign Language on a case-by-case basis

PROGRAMS/SERVICES FOR STUDENTS WITH LEARNING DIFFERENCES

Disability Services ensures that students with disabilities receive the access they need by evaluating all requests to determine reasonable accommodations. Disability Services is part of the Academic Enrichment Center (known as The Cove).

ADMISSIONS

Cedarville University seeks motivated students of faith who want to grow academically. For admission, the university requires a high school transcript, a Christian leader recommendation, and evidence of a personal relationship with Christ. Some academic departments require specific credentials, interviews, or auditions for admission to their programs. Admitted students who ranked close to the university's admission criteria but fell below are placed into foundation courses.

Additional Information

The Cove provides academic resources and support to all students. At the Cove, Academic Peer Coaches (APCs) lead weekly review and drop-in sessions for various courses, and work closely with professors. Students can attend these 20 weekly sessions. The Cove's Tutoring Lab also hosts more than 10 tutoring sessions each week for math and chemistry courses. APCs and tutoring labs offer group and individual tutoring. For courses that do not have either resource, students may apply for a tutor in a study group or one-on-one setting. Additionally, faculty academic coaches are available to keep students motivated with study strategies, test prep, test-taking, test anxiety, note-taking, and time management. The Cove offers courses and learning programs for students who seek to improve study habits and fundamentals, such as Foundations, Intermediate Algebra, MAP, WAVE, and Excel at Reading.

Since 1978, The Rock remains a place to exchange informative messages, Bible verses, birthday shoutouts, and even art. The idea began with Dick Walker, the leader of student-life, with the intention to promote campus community. Few things on campus have seen its longevity and visibility, and all feel empowered to paint on The Rock (probably late at night with lots of friends).

Cedarville University

GENERAL ADMISSIONS

Very important factors include: rigor of secondary school record, academic GPA, standardized test scores (if submitted), recommendations. *Important factors include:* class rank, application essay. High school diploma is required and GED is accepted. Institution is test-optional for entering Fall 2024. Check admissions website for updates. *Academic units recommended:* 4 English, 3 math, 3 science (2 labs), 3 foreign language, 3 social studies.

FINANCIAL AID

Students should submit: FAFSA. *Need-based scholarships/grants offered:* College/university scholarship or grant aid from institutional funds; Federal Nursing Scholarships; Federal Pell; Private scholarships; SEOG; State scholarships/grants. *Loan aid offered:* Direct PLUS loans; Direct Subsidized Loans; Direct Unsubsidized Loans. Federal Work-Study Program available. Institutional employment available.

CAMPUS LIFE

Activities: Campus Ministries; Choral groups; Concert band; Dance; Drama/theater; International Student Organization; Jazz band; Model UN; Music ensembles; Musical theater; Pep band; Radio station; Student government; Student newspaper; Student-run film society; Symphony orchestra; Yearbook. **Organizations:** 90 registered organizations, 5 honor societies, 12 religious organizations. **Athletics (Intercollegiate):** *Men:* baseball, basketball, cross-country, golf, rugby, swimming, track/field (indoor), ultimate frisbee. *Women:* basketball, cross-country, rugby, softball, swimming, track/field (indoor), ultimate frisbee, volleyball.

CAMPUS

Type of school	Private (nonprofit)
Environment	Rural

STUDENTS

Undergrad enrollment	3,568
% male/female	46/54
% from out of state	57
% frosh live on campus	95

FINANCIAL FACTS

Annual tuition	$33,174
Room and board	$8,120
Required fees	$200

GENERAL ADMISSIONS INFO

Application fee	$30
Regular application deadline	8/1
Nonfall registration	Yes

Fall 2024 testing policy	Test Optional
Range SAT EBRW	570–680
Range SAT Math	540–670
Range ACT Composite	23–30

ACADEMICS

Student/faculty ratio	17:1
% students returning for sophomore year	88

Most classes have 10–19 students.

REQUESTING SERVICES FOR STUDENTS WITH LEARNING DIFFERENCES

Phone: 937-766-7700 • www.cedarville.edu/Offices/Academic-Enrichment/Disabilities
Email: disabilityservices@cedarville.edu

Documentation submitted to: Disability Services at The Cove
Separate application required for Services: Yes

Documentation required for:
LD: Psychoeducational evaluation
ADHD: Psychoeducational evaluation
ASD: Psychoeducational evaluation

Central Ohio Technical College

1179 University Drive, Newark, OH 43055 • Admissions: 740-366-9494 • www.cotc.edu

Support: CS

ACCOMMODATIONS

Allowed in exams:

Calculators	Yes
Dictionary	No
Computer	Yes
Spell-checker	Yes
Extended test time	Yes
Scribe	Yes
Proctors	Yes
Oral exams	Yes
Note-takers	Yes

Support services for students with:

LD	Yes
ADHD	Yes
ASD	Yes
Distraction-reduced environment	Yes
Recording of lecture allowed	Yes
Reading technology	Yes
Audio books	Yes
Other assistive technology	Yes
Priority registration	Yes

Added costs of services:

For LD	No
For ADHD	No
For ASD	No
LD specialists	Yes
ADHD & ASD coaching	No
ASD specialists	No
Professional tutors	Yes
Peer tutors	Yes
Max. hours/week for services	Varies
How professors are notified of student approved accommodations	Student

COLLEGE GRADUATION REQUIREMENTS

Course waivers allowed	No
Course substitutions allowed	No

PROGRAMS/SERVICES FOR STUDENTS WITH LEARNING DIFFERENCES

Student Life-Disability Services (SL-DS) supports students from both Central Ohio Technical College and the Ohio State University at Newark. SL-DS provides free services and programs that help students with disabilities have full access to college life. Students should contact SL-DS early in their college planning to learn more about available accommodations. Prior to admission, SL-DS can share information with prospective students about academic support services, specialized equipment, and how to ease the transition to campus life. Students may also meet with staff counselors. At the Testing Center, students can receive testing accommodations, including a distraction-free environment.

ADMISSIONS

The application process is the same for all students, and open to all applicants with a high school diploma or GED, and there are no specific course requirements. Determining eligibility for services and accommodations is a separate process from admissions, and documentation of disabilities should be sent directly to SL-DS.

Additional Information

Learning Specialists meet in person with students to discuss their academic challenges and make recommendations tailored to their particular needs. Areas of support include planning, prioritizing, study skills, time management, goal setting, effective use of resources, assistive technology, and e-learning.

For COTC's 50th anniversary in 2021, the university partnered with locally owned Velvet® Ice Cream. Faculty, alumni, students and staff voted on flavors, and the winner, Berry Rumble (a blend of strawberry, blueberry, and blackberry), was available at every special event during the year-long anniversary celebration.

Central Ohio Technical College

GENERAL ADMISSIONS

High school diploma is required and GED is accepted. Institution is test-flexible for entering Fall 2024. Check admissions website for updates.

FINANCIAL AID

Students should submit: FAFSA. *Need-based scholarships/grants offered:* College/university scholarship or grant aid from institutional funds; Federal Pell; Private scholarships; SEOG; State scholarships/grants. *Loan aid offered:* Direct PLUS loans; Direct Subsidized Loans; Direct Unsubsidized Loans. Federal Work-Study Program available. Institutional employment available.

CAMPUS LIFE

Activities: Choral groups; Drama/theater; Music ensembles; Student government; Student newspaper.

CAMPUS

Type of school	Public
Environment	Suburb

STUDENTS

Undergrad enrollment	2,636
% male/female	30/70
% from out of state	2

FINANCIAL FACTS

Annual in-state tuition	$4,896
Annual out-of-state tuition	$7,656

GENERAL ADMISSIONS INFO

Application fee	No fee
Regular application deadline	Rolling
Nonfall registration	Yes
Fall 2024 testing policy	Test Flexible

ACADEMICS

Student/faculty ratio	14:1
% students returning for sophomore year	46

Ohio

REQUESTING SERVICES FOR STUDENTS WITH LEARNING DIFFERENCES

Phone: 740-755-7755 • www.cotc.edu/disability-services • Email: rowland.245@mail.cotc.edu

Documentation submitted to: Student Life-Disability Services
Separate application required for Services: Yes

Documentation required for:
 LD: Psychoeducational evaluation
 ADHD: Psychoeducational evaluation
 ASD: Psychoeducational evaluation

The College of Wooster

847 College Avenue, Wooster, OH 44691 • Admissions: 330-263-2322 • www.wooster.edu

Support: CS

ACCOMMODATIONS

Allowed in exams:

Calculators	Yes
Dictionary	Yes
Computer	Yes
Spell-checker	Yes
Extended test time	Yes
Scribe	Yes
Proctors	Yes
Oral exams	Yes
Note-takers	Yes

Support services for students with:

LD	Yes
ADHD	Yes
ASD	Yes
Distraction-reduced environment	Yes
Recording of lecture allowed	Yes
Reading technology	Yes
Audio books	Yes
Other assistive technology	Yes
Priority registration	Yes

Added costs of services:

For LD	No
For ADHD	No
For ASD	No
LD specialists	Yes
ADHD & ASD coaching	No
ASD specialists	No
Professional tutors	No
Peer tutors	Yes
Max. hours/week for services	Varies
How professors are notified of student approved accommodations	Student and Disability Support Services

COLLEGE GRADUATION REQUIREMENTS

Course waivers allowed	Yes
In what courses: Foreign Language	
Course substitutions allowed	Yes
In what courses: Case-by-case basis	

PROGRAMS/SERVICES FOR STUDENTS WITH LEARNING DIFFERENCES

Disability Support Services, part of the Academic Resource Center (ARC), assists students with learning disabilities. Students complete an online intake form and answer questions about their disability-related needs. Students should provide documentation issued within the last five years. If a neuropsychological/educational evaluation report is not available, students may have a qualified licensed professional complete the Disability Information and Verification Form. Students should schedule an appointment with ARC staff to review documentation, discuss the history of previous supports, and determine needed accommodations. Letters of accommodation are provided to the student's professors each semester certifying that the student has a documented disability and the determined reasonable accommodations.

ADMISSIONS

First-year applicants are not required to disclose their disability; however, students who wish to have their disability considered as a factor of admission should disclose their disability and provide an explanation of why it is a factor in the evaluation of their qualifications. It may be necessary to provide appropriate documentation of the disability. All applicants are required to complete an essay and send recommendations from two teachers and the school counselor. ACT or SAT scores are optional and are not used for merit-based scholarships. National Interview Day is a popular Wooster tradition, and all applicants are invited to participate in an interview on this day each fall; advance registration is required. An interview is not required for admission but is essential for the College Scholar Award. Interviews can be included with an in-person campus tour or scheduled virtually.

Additional Information

The center for Advising, Planning, and Experiential Learning (APEX) and the Learning Center offer Wooster 101, a series of workshops in the fall designed for first-year students to help them transition to college, learn test-taking strategies, and hone time-management, reading, and study skills. ARC offers one-on-one specific topic meetings that focus on time management, testing strategies, enhanced reading support, identifying academic goals, and organization skills. Peer tutors, trained through ARC are available for individual, weekly one-hour sessions, and many academic departments have tutors and other resources to assist students in their coursework. Students can partner with a certified Academic Life Coach for up to eight sessions per semester to explore academic thinking, the science of learning, motivation, leadership, resilience, and more.

Wooster's colors are black and old gold, and its mascot is the "Fighting Scot." In 1939, a large donation funded kilts for the marching band in the yellow-and-black MacLeod of Lewis tartan. Today, football games feature a Scottish pipe band, Highland dancers, and a traditional marching band—all wearing the MacLeod tartan. The college offers the Scottish Arts Scholarship for students who perform as pipers, drummers, or Scottish dancers.

The College of Wooster

GENERAL ADMISSIONS

Very important factors include: rigor of secondary school record, academic GPA. *Important factors include:* class rank, class rank, application essay, recommendation(s). *Other factors considered include:* standardized test scores. High school diploma is required and GED is accepted. Institution is test-optional for entering Fall 2024. Check admissions website for updates. *Academic units required:* 4 English, 3 math, 3 science (2 labs), 2 foreign language, 3 social studies, 1 academic elective.

FINANCIAL AID

Students should submit: FAFSA. *Need-based scholarships/grants offered:* College/university scholarship or grant aid from institutional funds; Federal Pell; Private scholarships; SEOG; State scholarships/grants. *Loan aid offered:* Direct PLUS loans; Direct Subsidized Loans; Direct Unsubsidized Loans.

CAMPUS LIFE

Activities: Campus Ministries; Choral groups; Concert band; Dance; Drama/theater; International Student Organization; Jazz band; Literary magazine; Marching band; Model UN; Music ensembles; Musical theater; Radio station; Student government; Student newspaper; Student-run film society; Symphony orchestra; Yearbook. **Organizations:** 125 registered organizations, 18 honors societies, 5 religious organizations, 4 fraternities, 6 sororities. **Athletics (Intercollegiate):** *Men:* baseball, basketball, crosscountry, diving, football, golf, lacrosse, soccer, swimming, tennis, track/field (outdoor), track/field (indoor). *Women:* basketball, cross-country, diving, field hockey, lacrosse, soccer, softball, swimming, tennis, track/field (outdoor), track/field (indoor), volleyball.

CAMPUS
Type of school	Private (nonprofit)
Environment	Town

STUDENTS
Undergrad enrollment	1,960
% male/female	46/54
% from out of state	50
% frosh live on campus	99

FINANCIAL FACTS
Annual tuition	$59,550
Room and board	$14,000

GENERAL ADMISSIONS INFO
Application fee	$45
Regular application deadline	2/15
Nonfall registration	Yes

Fall 2024 testing policy	Test Optional
Range SAT EBRW	620–720
Range SAT Math	600–710
Range ACT Composite	26–32

ACADEMICS
Student/faculty ratio	11:1
% students returning for sophomore year	85

Most classes have 2–9 students.

Ohio

REQUESTING SERVICES FOR STUDENTS WITH LEARNING DIFFERENCES

Phone: 330-263-2595 • inside.wooster.edu/arc/disability/ • Email: arc@wooster.edu

Documentation submitted to: Academic Resource Center/Disability Support Services
Separate application required for Services: Yes

Documentation required for:
  LD: Psychoeducational evaluation
  ADHD: Psychoeducational evaluation
  ASD: Psychoeducational evaluation

Defiance College

701 North Clinton Street, Defiance, OH 43512-1695 • Admissions: 419-783-2359 • www.defiance.edu

(Support: CS)

PROGRAMS/SERVICES FOR STUDENTS WITH LEARNING DIFFERENCES

Accessibility Services assists students with disabilities. Students are responsible for requesting necessary accommodations. To be eligible, students with a documented, psychological, or learning disability must provide appropriate documentation, meet with the Accessibility Services coordinator, and complete an intake interview to discuss adjustments specific to the student's disability. The ASD Affinity Program accepts academically qualified college applicants with autism spectrum disorders who might require help navigating the traditional college residential campus. Varying levels of academic, social, and residential support assist students in personal growth and meeting their professional goals. Participating students receive campus housing with support from trained resident advisors and peer interventionists. The program fosters independence for young adults with autism by providing a residential campus experience with numerous services in place to maximize opportunities for success and entry into the workforce.

ADMISSIONS

All applicants submit the same first-year application and an official high school transcript that demonstrates academic ability and promise. Successful applicants submit transcripts that include in-depth work in English, mathematics, foreign language, science, and social studies. The caliber of high school, difficulty of courses, and academic achievement are all considered. DC is test-optional admission except for applicants majoring in nursing, education, or pre-health profession programs who must submit ACT or SAT scores. Most admitted first-year students maintained at least a B average in high school academic coursework, scored above the national average on the ACT when submitted, and completed a college preparatory academic curriculum.

Additional Information

The First-Year Experience (FYE) Program helps first-year students transition to academic life by establishing college-level academic strategies, exposing students to academic and cocurricular opportunities, encouraging self-awareness, and teaching basic college research skills. FYE includes a required college engagement seminar course, utilization of peer leaders for each FYE 100 course section, participation in a Common Read with an annual author visit, and completion of an Inquiry Research assignment tailored to the student's experiences. The Academic Support Center (ASC) provides resources and opportunities to improve learning and focuses on assisting students with STEM-related courses. ASC provides Supplemental Instruction for select courses in math and science. Individual and group tutoring for most courses is free, and study skills development workshops are available. The Structured Study Program (SSP) offers sessions during the week to assist students in developing effective time management and college study skills. SSP is an environment free of distraction where students can do coursework, receive academic assistance, and improve their study skills. The Writing Studio consultants offer individualized help to develop strategies for approaching writing assignments through the understanding of purpose, structure, topic, and audience.

ACCOMMODATIONS

Allowed in exams:

Calculators	Yes
Dictionary	Yes
Computer	Yes
Spell-checker	Yes
Extended test time	Yes
Scribe	Yes
Proctors	Yes
Oral exams	Yes
Note-takers	Yes

Support services for students with:

LD	Yes
ADHD	Yes
ASD	Yes
Distraction-reduced environment	Yes
Recording of lecture allowed	Yes
Reading technology	Yes
Audio books	Yes
Other assistive technology	Yes
Priority registration	Yes

Added costs of services:

For LD	No
For ADHD	No
For ASD	Yes
LD specialists	Yes
ADHD & ASD coaching	Yes
ASD specialists	Yes
Professional tutors	No
Peer tutors	Yes
Max. hours/week for services	Varies
How professors are notified of student approved accommodations	Student and Accessibility Services

COLLEGE GRADUATION REQUIREMENTS

Course waivers allowed	No
Course substitutions allowed	No

President Dwight D. Eisenhower paid two visits to Defiance College. On Oct. 15, 1953, he laid the cornerstone for the Anthony Wayne Library of American Study, and on May 26, 1963, he delivered the commencement address. At that time, the college announced that one room in the library had been designated The Eisenhower Room, honoring the friendship between Eisenhower and Defiance College President Kevin C. McCann.

Defiance College

General Admissions

Very important factors include: rigor of secondary school record, academic GPA, standardized test scores. *Other factors considered include:* class rank, class rank, application essay, recommendation(s). High school diploma is required and GED is accepted. Institution is test-optional for entering Fall 2024. Check admissions website for updates. *Academic units required:* 4 English, 3 math, 3 science (2 labs), 2 foreign language, 2 social studies, 2 visual/performing arts.

Financial Aid

Students should submit: FAFSA. *Need-based scholarships/grants offered:* College/university scholarship or grant aid from institutional funds; Federal Pell; Private scholarships; SEOG; State scholarships/grants. *Loan aid offered:* Direct PLUS loans; Direct Subsidized Loans; Direct Unsubsidized Loans.

Campus Life

Activities: Campus Ministries; Choral groups; Concert band; Dance; Drama/theater; Jazz band; Literary magazine; Marching band; Music ensembles; Musical theater; Pep band; Student government; Student newspaper. **Organizations:** 36 registered organizations, 3 honors societies, 2 religious organizations, 1 fraternities, 1 sororities. **Athletics (Intercollegiate):** *Men:* baseball, basketball, cross-country, football, golf, soccer, tennis, track/field (outdoor), track/field (indoor). *Women:* basketball, cross-country, golf, soccer, softball, tennis, track/field (outdoor), track/field (indoor), volleyball.

CAMPUS

Type of school	Private (nonprofit)
Environment	Village

STUDENTS

Undergrad enrollment	195
% male/female	58/42
% from out of state	28
% frosh live on campus	84

FINANCIAL FACTS

Annual tuition	$34,556
Room and board	$11,042
Required fees	$356

GENERAL ADMISSIONS INFO

Application fee	No fee
Regular application deadline	Rolling
Nonfall registration	Yes

Fall 2024 testing policy	Test Optional
Range SAT EBRW	360–490
Range SAT Math	340–470
Range ACT Composite	18–22

ACADEMICS

Student/faculty ratio	11:1
% students returning for sophomore year	61

Most classes have 2–9 students.

Ohio

REQUESTING SERVICES FOR STUDENTS WITH LEARNING DIFFERENCES

Phone: 419-783-2445 • www.defiance.edu/student-life/accessibility-services/ • Email: kknight@defiance.edu

Documentation submitted to: Accessibility Services
Separate application required for Services: Yes

Documentation required for:
 LD: Psychoeducational evaluation
 ADHD: Psychoeducational evaluation
 ASD: Psychoeducational evaluation

Kent State University

161 Schwartz Center, Kent, OH 44242-0001 • Admissions: 330-672-2444 • www.kent.edu

(Support: CS)

ACCOMMODATIONS

Allowed in exams:

Calculators	Yes
Dictionary	Yes
Computer	Yes
Spell-checker	Yes
Extended test time	Yes
Scribe	Yes
Proctors	Yes
Oral exams	Yes
Note-takers	Yes

Support services for students with:

LD	Yes
ADHD	Yes
ASD	Yes
Distraction-reduced environment	Yes
Recording of lecture allowed	Yes
Reading technology	Yes
Audio books	Yes
Other assistive technology	Yes
Priority registration	Yes

Added costs of services:

For LD	No
For ADHD	No
For ASD	No
LD specialists	No
ADHD & ASD coaching	Yes
ASD specialists	No
Professional tutors	No
Peer tutors	Yes
Max. hours/week for services	Varies
How professors are notified of student approved accommodations	Student

COLLEGE GRADUATION REQUIREMENTS

Course waivers allowed	Yes

In what courses: Case-by-case basis

Course substitutions allowed	Yes

In what courses: Case-by-case basis

PROGRAMS/SERVICES FOR STUDENTS WITH LEARNING DIFFERENCES

Kent State University's Office of Student Accessibility Services (SAS) supports students with disabilities. Students may apply for services through a traditional or expedited process (which excludes the welcome meeting). For both options, students will need to complete an application and submit eligible documentation. The expedited process is most suitable for students looking for extended test time, access to lecture visuals, note-taking technology, and priority scheduling. For any additional accommodations, students must complete the traditional registration process. Kent State also offers the Career and Community Studies (CCS) program for students with intellectual and developmental disabilities. This nondegree, two- or four-year comprehensive program focuses on personal development, health and wellness, and preparing students to become autonomous adults. Students are helped with academics and learn strategies to prepare for life after college—the last two years of the program focus on career preparation. CCS students can select from one of three programs/tracks and earn up to 120 credits.

ADMISSIONS

Students submit an application and high school transcript to be considered for admission. Admission criteria may vary by program, and students are responsible for determining any different criteria. The average GPA of admitted students is 3.4, and for students submitting test scores, the average ACT is 23. Students who receive deferred admission may complete coursework at one of the regional Kent State campuses.

Additional Information

There is a separate tuition and cost of attendance for students participating in the CSS program. Students may be eligible for financial aid to support with fees.

DID YOU KNOW?

Since the 1950s, the campus newspaper has reported on Tray Sledding on Blanket Hill. It's easy: channel your inner child, borrow a tray from the dining hall, find a snow-covered hill around campus, and you're off. It's been on bucket lists, considered a rite of passage, or just a way to take a break from studies. Trays are available, but students have found other means of sledding, including plastic bags, trash can lids, and of course, store-bought sleds and snowboards.

Kent State University

GENERAL ADMISSIONS

Very important factors include: academic GPA. *Important factors include:* rigor of secondary school record. *Other factors considered include:* standardized test scores (if submitted), application essay, recommendations. High school diploma is required and GED is accepted. Institution is test-optional for entering Fall 2024. Check admissions website for updates. *Academic units recommended:* 4 English, 4 math, 3 science (2 labs), 2 foreign language, 3 social studies, 1 visual/performing arts.

FINANCIAL AID

Students should submit: FAFSA. *Need-based scholarships/grants offered:* College/university scholarship or grant aid from institutional funds; Federal Pell; Private scholarships; SEOG; State scholarships/grants. *Loan aid offered:* Direct PLUS loans; Direct Subsidized Loans; Direct Unsubsidized Loans. Federal Work-Study Program available. Institutional employment available.

CAMPUS LIFE

Activities: Campus Ministries; Choral groups; Concert band; Dance; Drama/theater; International Student Organization; Jazz band; Literary magazine; Marching band; Music ensembles; Musical theater; Opera; Pep band; Radio station; Student government; Student newspaper; Student-run film society; Symphony orchestra; Television station. **Organizations:** 320 registered organizations, 15 honor societies, 22 religious organizations, 22 fraternities, 11 sororities. **Athletics (Intercollegiate):** *Men:* baseball, basketball, bowling, cross-country, equestrian sports, golf, gymnastics, ice hockey, lacrosse, martial arts, rugby, track/field (indoor), ultimate frisbee, volleyball, wrestling. *Women:* basketball, bowling, cross-country, equestrian sports, field hockey, golf, gymnastics, lacrosse, martial arts, rugby, softball, track/field (indoor), ultimate frisbee, volleyball.

CAMPUS

Type of school	Public
Environment	Town

STUDENTS

Undergrad enrollment	21,133
% male/female	38/62
% from out of state	18
% frosh live on campus	80

FINANCIAL FACTS

Annual in-state tuition	$12,464
Annual out-of-state tuition	$21,570
Room and board	$12,676

GENERAL ADMISSIONS INFO

Application fee	$50
Regular application deadline	8/1
Nonfall registration	Yes

Fall 2024 testing policy	Test Optional
Range SAT EBRW	500–610
Range SAT Math	500–600
Range ACT Composite	19–25

ACADEMICS

Student/faculty ratio	19:1
% students returning for sophomore year	81
Most classes have 10–19 students.	

Ohio

REQUESTING SERVICES FOR STUDENTS WITH LEARNING DIFFERENCES

Phone: 330-672-3391 • www.kent.edu/sas • Email: sas@kent.edu

Documentation submitted to: Student Accessibility Services
Separate application required for Services: Yes

Documentation required for:
LD: Psychoeducational evaluation
ADHD: Psychoeducational evaluation
ASD: Psychoeducational evaluation

Miami University

301 S. Campus Avenue, Oxford, OH 45056 • Admissions: 513-529-2531 • www.miamioh.edu

(Support: CS)

ACCOMMODATIONS

Allowed in exams:

Calculators	Yes
Dictionary	Yes
Computer	Yes
Spell-checker	Yes
Extended test time	Yes
Scribe	Yes
Proctors	Yes
Oral exams	Yes
Note-takers	Yes

Support services for students with:

LD	Yes
ADHD	Yes
ASD	Yes
Distraction-reduced environment	Yes
Recording of lecture allowed	Yes
Reading technology	Yes
Audio books	Yes
Other assistive technology	Yes
Priority registration	Yes

Added costs of services:

For LD	No
For ADHD	No
For ASD	No
LD specialists	Yes
ADHD & ASD coaching	Yes
ASD specialists	Yes
Professional tutors	No
Peer tutors	Yes
Max. hours/week for services	Varies
How professors are notified of student approved accommodations	Student and Student Disability Services

COLLEGE GRADUATION REQUIREMENTS

Course waivers allowed	No
Course substitutions allowed	Yes

In what courses: Math and Foreign Language

PROGRAMS/SERVICES FOR STUDENTS WITH LEARNING DIFFERENCES

Student Disability Services (SDS) coordinates university resources for students with learning disabilities. Students must submit documentation and check their Miami email account for application status updates. After receiving an email from the access coordinator, students schedule an access consultation to determine accommodations. Accommodations may include preferential seating, audiotaping course lectures, advance access to presentation slides, note-taking with laptops, Livescribe Note Taking Pen, note-taking applications, and peer note-taking services. Testing accommodations may include a distraction-reduced space, extended time, assistive technology, accessible formats, access to a computer for essay exams, and readers or scribes. Under certain circumstances, a student affiliated with Student Disability Services (SDS) can apply for a course substitution for a foreign language or mathematics course requirement. While SDS approves the application for the course substitution, the specific course to be used as a substitute is determined by the academic department with the course requirement.

ADMISSIONS

All applicants are expected to meet the same admission criteria. The review process is individualized and includes class rank if provided, commitment to social service, leadership, work, extenuating circumstances, extracurriculars, first generation, GPA, grade trends, high school profile, legacy status, and letters of recommendation. The middle 50 percent GPA for admitted students is 3.59–4.18, and for students who submit SAT scores, the middle 50 percent have a 1220–1410. Applicants can substitute computer science for math or science requirements. They can also use computer coding as a substitution for the foreign language requirement.

Additional Information

The Students with Disabilities Advisory Council (SDAC) is a group of students who identify as having a disability. The group plans and implements events and programs for current and prospective Miami students and the entire disability community.

Miami University was created by an ordinance signed by President George Washington in 1795. The first 20 students enrolled in 1824, and by 1839, enrollment reached its peak of 250 students. In 1848, a student rebellion against the administration led to the "Snowball Rebellion." Students blockaded Old Main with packed snow, firewood, chairs, benches, and tables.

Miami University

GENERAL ADMISSIONS

Very important factors include: rigor of secondary school record, class rank, academic GPA, standardized test scores (if submitted), application essay, recommendations. High school diploma is required and GED is accepted. Institution is test-optional for entering Fall 2024. Check admissions website for updates. *Academic units recommended:* 4 English, 4 math, 3 science, 2 foreign language, 3 social studies, 1 visual/performing arts.

FINANCIAL AID

Students should submit: FAFSA. *Need-based scholarships/grants offered:* College/university scholarship or grant aid from institutional funds; Federal Pell; Private scholarships; SEOG; State scholarships/grants. *Loan aid offered:* Direct PLUS loans; Direct Subsidized Loans; Direct Unsubsidized Loans. Federal Work-Study Program available. Institutional employment available.

CAMPUS LIFE

Activities: Campus Ministries; Choral groups; Concert band; Dance; Drama/theater; International Student Organization; Jazz band; Literary magazine; Marching band; Model UN; Music ensembles; Musical theater; Opera; Pep band; Radio station; Student government; Student newspaper; Student-run film society; Symphony orchestra; Television station; Yearbook. **Organizations:** 656 registered organizations, 19 honor societies, 29 religious organizations, 25 fraternities, 22 sororities. **Athletics (Intercollegiate):** *Men:* baseball, basketball, crew/rowing, cross-country, equestrian sports, field hockey, golf, gymnastics, ice hockey, lacrosse, martial arts, rugby, softball, swimming, ultimate frisbee, volleyball, water polo, wrestling. *Women:* baseball, basketball, crew/rowing, cross-country, equestrian sports, field hockey, golf, gymnastics, ice hockey, lacrosse, martial arts, rugby, softball, swimming, ultimate frisbee, volleyball, water polo, wrestling.

CAMPUS
Type of school	Public
Environment	Village

STUDENTS
Undergrad enrollment	16,842
% male/female	49/51
% from out of state	33
% frosh live on campus	96

FINANCIAL FACTS
Annual in-state tuition	$12,637
Annual out-of-state tuition	$32,464
Room and board	$14,454
Required fees	$2,984

GENERAL ADMISSIONS INFO
Application fee	$50
Regular application deadline	2/1
Nonfall registration	Yes

Fall 2024 testing policy	Test Optional
Range SAT EBRW	580–680
Range SAT Math	580–690
Range ACT Composite	24–30

ACADEMICS
Student/faculty ratio	16:1
% students returning for sophomore year	89

Most classes have 20–29 students.

Ohio

REQUESTING SERVICES FOR STUDENTS WITH LEARNING DIFFERENCES

Phone: 513-529-1541 • www.miamioh.edu/SDS • Email: SDS@miamioh.edu

Documentation submitted to: Student Disability Services
Separate application required for Services: Yes

Documentation required for:
  LD: Psychoeducational evaluation
  ADHD: Psychoeducational evaluation
  ASD: Psychoeducational evaluation

Mount St. Joseph University

5701 Delhi Road, Cincinnati, OH 45233 • Admissions: 513-244-4531 • www.msj.edu

(Support: SP)

ACCOMMODATIONS

Allowed in exams:

Calculators	Yes
Dictionary	N/A
Computer	Yes
Spell-checker	Yes
Extended test time	Yes
Scribe	Yes
Proctors	Yes
Oral exams	Yes
Note-takers	Yes

Support services for students with:

LD	Yes
ADHD	Yes
ASD	Yes
Distraction-reduced environment	Yes
Recording of lecture allowed	Yes
Reading technology	Yes
Audio books	Yes
Other assistive technology	Yes
Priority registration	No

Added costs of services:

For LD	Yes
For ADHD	Yes
For ASD	No
LD specialists	Yes
ADHD & ASD coaching	Yes
ASD specialists	Yes
Professional tutors	Yes
Peer tutors	No
Max. hours/week for services	Varies
How professors are notified of student approved accommodations	Student

COLLEGE GRADUATION REQUIREMENTS

Course waivers allowed	No
Course substitutions allowed	Yes
In what courses: Foreign Language	

PROGRAMS/SERVICES FOR STUDENTS WITH LEARNING DIFFERENCES

Disability Services and the Learning Center offer accommodations and modifications to qualified students with documented disabilities. Students need to contact the director of Disability Services to schedule an intake meeting in person or by phone. Reasonable and appropriate academic accommodations for the student will be documented in an accommodations letter approved by the director. The university has a fee-based program, Project EXCEL, to help students with learning differences transition to college. The Project EXCEL program includes professional tutoring, academic counseling, scheduled consultations to promote organization and time-management skills, instruction in using technology, access to speech-recognition software, and direct instruction in academic success strategies. The cut-off date for admittance to the Project EXCEL program is two weeks before the beginning of the term, and space is limited, so students are encouraged to apply as early as possible. Each application is evaluated to determine if the student's needs match the support offered by the program. Students complete an applicant information form, submit documentation verifying the disability and a letter of recommendation, and have an interview with the Project EXCEL director.

ADMISSIONS

Applications are reviewed individually to determine college readiness. Students who are conditionally accepted to the university are required to participate in the PASS Program.

Additional Information

Mount St. Joseph's PASS Program (Path to Achieving Student Success) guides students through their first year of college. The PASS Program provides students with additional support from an advisor in the Academic Advising Resource Center (AARC). Meetings between a PASS Program student and an AARC advisor typically occur biweekly. Individualized interventions are available to help manage course loads, register for appropriate course schedules, develop and achieve first year academic goals, and to create a network of support that will be with them through their entire experience. The PASS program is available to students who receive a conditional admittance and are asked to participate.

In 2014, Lauren Hill, an incoming first-year basketball player with an inoperable brain tumor, wished to play in a college game. In a sold-out game, she scored the first and last baskets and played in three more games before her health declined. The game was the start of a charitable fundraising campaign that, by her death in April 2015, raised over $1.5 million for research for her specific pediatric cancer, DIPG. The Lauren Hill Classic continues to raise money for DIPG in the form of an annual season-opening basketball doubleheader.

Mount St. Joseph University

GENERAL ADMISSIONS
Very important factors include: rigor of secondary school record, academic GPA. *Other factors considered include:* class rank, standardized test scores (if submitted), application essay, recommendations. High school diploma is required and GED is accepted. Institution is test-optional for entering Fall 2024. Check admissions website for updates. *Academic units recommended:* 4 English, 3 math, 2 science (2 labs), 2 foreign language, 3 social studies, 1 visual/performing arts.

FINANCIAL AID
Students should submit: FAFSA. *Need-based scholarships/grants offered:* College/university scholarship or grant aid from institutional funds; Federal Pell; Private scholarships; SEOG; State scholarships/grants. *Loan aid offered:* Direct PLUS loans; Direct Subsidized Loans; Direct Unsubsidized Loans. Federal Work-Study Program available. Institutional employment available.

CAMPUS LIFE
Activities: Campus Ministries; Choral groups; Concert band; Dance; Drama/theater; Jazz band; Literary magazine; Marching band; Musical theater; Pep band; Student government; Student newspaper. **Organizations:** 44 registered organizations, 13 honor societies, 1 religious organizations, 1 fraternities, 0 sororities. **Athletics (Intercollegiate):** *Men:* baseball, basketball, cross-country, golf, lacrosse, track/field (indoor), volleyball, wrestling. *Women:* basketball, cross-country, golf, lacrosse, softball, track/field (indoor), volleyball.

CAMPUS

Type of school	Private (nonprofit)
Environment	Metropolis

STUDENTS

Undergrad enrollment	1,087
% male/female	47/53
% from out of state	19
% frosh live on campus	59

FINANCIAL FACTS

Annual tuition	$35,450
Room and board	$10,650
Required fees	$1,200

GENERAL ADMISSIONS INFO

Application fee	$25
Regular application deadline	8/17
Nonfall registration	Yes

Fall 2024 testing policy	Test Optional
Range SAT EBRW	498–580
Range SAT Math	520–613
Range ACT Composite	20–27

ACADEMICS

Student/faculty ratio	11:1
% students returning for sophomore year	72

Ohio

REQUESTING SERVICES FOR STUDENTS WITH LEARNING DIFFERENCES

Phone: 513-244-4631 • www.msj.edu/academics/disability-services • Email: heather.crabbe@msj.edu

Documentation submitted to: Disability Services
Separate application required for Services: Yes

Documentation required for:
  LD: Psychoeducational evaluation
  ADHD: Psychoeducational evaluation
  ASD: Psychoeducational evaluation

Muskingum University

163 Stormont Street, New Concord, OH 43762 • Admissions: 740-826-8137 • muskingum.edu

(Support: SP)

PROGRAMS/SERVICES FOR STUDENTS WITH LEARNING DIFFERENCES

The Disability Education Office (DEO) provides accommodations to students with disabilities. The PLUS Program is also available and is a fee-based program that uses learning strategy approaches for students with learning disabilities. Students may apply for the PLUS Opportunity Award, a need-based scholarship to help offset the costs of the program. There are four levels of service available through PLUS. The Premier level provides comprehensive academic support for up to five hours per week. The Select level provides less frequent academic support, the Transitions level supports the transition from high school to college or college to career, and the Connections level focuses on communication and social skills to foster success. The PLUS Program includes staff consultants and coordinators who have earned a bachelor's or master's degree in their field. The staff supports the student's individual learning needs, monitors academic performance, and provides content tutoring. PLUS Early Connection is a summer transition program designed to assist incoming first-year PLUS students make the transition to college. Students gain a head start on navigating classes, and assistance with strategy instruction, understanding academic platforms, making social connections, self-advocacy training, connecting with an upper-level student mentor, and developing an individual study plan.

ADMISSIONS

Applications are reviewed on an ongoing basis, and students should demonstrate the ability to succeed at the college level by completing a college preparatory curriculum.

Additional Information

The Study Center offer tutoring to all students in a variety of subjects, and the Writing Center has trained tutors to help students draft, review, and revise their work.

The first astronaut to circle the Earth, a senator for 24 years, and a presidential candidate—John Glenn studied chemistry at Muskingum, played football, and joined the Stag Club fraternity. He received his BS degree in engineering and was given an honorary Doctor of Science in Engineering. As a student, he made his first solo flight in a Naval civilian aviation training class. On live TV, Mr. Glenn announced his retirement from the U.S. Senate in Brown Chapel in 1997. Senator Glenn was a featured speaker at commencement exercises, and he and his wife participated in many other university events.

Muskingum University

GENERAL ADMISSIONS

Very important factors include: rigor of secondary school record, academic GPA. *Important factors include:* class rank, standardized test scores (if submitted). *Other factors considered include:* application essay, recommendations. High school diploma is required and GED is accepted. Institution is test-optional for entering Fall 2024. Check admissions website for updates. *Academic units required:* 4 English, 2 math, 2 science (1 lab), 2 foreign language, 2 social studies. *Academic units recommended:* 3 math, 3 science (2 labs), 3 social studies.

FINANCIAL AID

Students should submit: FAFSA. *Need-based scholarships/grants offered:* College/university scholarship or grant aid from institutional funds; Federal Pell; Private scholarships; SEOG; State scholarships/grants. *Loan aid offered:* Direct PLUS loans; Direct Subsidized Loans; Direct Unsubsidized Loans. Federal Work-Study Program available. Institutional employment available.

CAMPUS LIFE

Activities: Campus Ministries; Choral groups; Concert band; Dance; Drama/theater; International Student Organization; Jazz band; Literary magazine; Marching band; Model UN; Music ensembles; Musical theater; Pep band; Radio station; Student government; Student newspaper; Symphony orchestra; Television station. **Organizations:** 96 registered organizations, 26 honor societies, 5 religious organizations, 6 fraternities, 6 sororities. **Athletics (Intercollegiate):** *Men:* baseball, basketball, bowling, cross-country, golf, lacrosse, rugby, track/field (indoor), wrestling. *Women:* basketball, bowling, cross-country, golf, lacrosse, rugby, softball, track/field (indoor), volleyball.

CAMPUS
Type of school	Private (nonprofit)
Environment	Rural

STUDENTS
Undergrad enrollment	1,580
% male/female	46/54
% from out of state	8
% frosh live on campus	85

FINANCIAL FACTS
Annual tuition	$30,650
Room and board	$12,550
Required fees	$790

GENERAL ADMISSIONS INFO
Application fee	No fee
Regular application deadline	8/1
Nonfall registration	Yes

Fall 2024 testing policy	Test Optional
Range SAT EBRW	463–578
Range SAT Math	460–530
Range ACT Composite	18–24

ACADEMICS
Student/faculty ratio	13:1
% students returning for sophomore year	68

Most classes have 10–19 students.

Ohio

REQUESTING SERVICES FOR STUDENTS WITH LEARNING DIFFERENCES

Phone: 740-826-8280 • www.muskingum.edu/accessibility • Email: accessibility@muskingum.edu

Documentation submitted to: Disability Education Office
Separate application required for Services: Yes

Documentation required for:
LD: Psychoeducational evaluation
ADHD: Psychoeducational evaluation
ASD: Psychoeducational evaluation

Oberlin College

38 East College Street, Oberlin, OH 44074 • Admissions: 440-775-8411 • www.oberlin.edu

Support: CS

ACCOMMODATIONS

Allowed in exams:

Calculators	Yes
Dictionary	Yes
Computer	Yes
Spell-checker	Yes
Extended test time	Yes
Scribe	Yes
Proctors	Yes
Oral exams	Yes
Note-takers	Yes

Support services for students with:

LD	Yes
ADHD	Yes
ASD	Yes
Distraction-reduced environment	Yes
Recording of lecture allowed	Yes
Reading technology	Yes
Audio books	Yes
Other assistive technology	Yes
Priority registration	Yes

Added costs of services:

For LD	No
For ADHD	No
For ASD	No
LD specialists	Yes
ADHD & ASD coaching	Yes
ASD specialists	No
Professional tutors	No
Peer tutors	Yes
Max. hours/week for services	Varies
How professors are notified of student approved accommodations	Student and Office for Disability and Access

COLLEGE GRADUATION REQUIREMENTS

Course waivers allowed	No
Course substitutions allowed	Yes
In what courses: Case-by-case basis	

PROGRAMS/SERVICES FOR STUDENTS WITH LEARNING DIFFERENCES

The Office for Disability and Access (ODA) facilitates equal access to all programs, courses, and resources at Oberlin College. Students request accommodations by registering with ODA and submitting documentation from a licensed professional who is unrelated to the student and whose credentials permit the evaluation of the disability. Accommodations that ODA can arrange include quiet spaces for exams, extended time, assistive technology, books in alternative formats, and other resources and accommodations as appropriate. ODA hosts the Executive Functioning Program (EF), which provides peer coaching and tutoring for all interested students, including neurodiverse students, students with ADHD, ASD, or LD. The EF peer tutors work on fundamental skills related to executive functioning, including adaptable thinking, planning, self-monitoring, self-control, working memory, time management, and organizational skills. The EF Program also provides group workshops throughout the year.

ADMISSIONS

Admission requirements are the same for all applicants. Students attending high schools that do not offer all of the recommended courses should still consider applying to Oberlin. Admission reviews are holistic, and many factors are considered in making an admission decision. The admission committee seeks students who exhibit leadership traits and are involved in their school communities. The committee prefers to see students show a greater amount of time commitment to fewer activities rather than spend a limited time in many activities. Applicants to the Conservatory of Music may have different admission requirements.

Additional Information

The Center for Student Success (CSS) provides academic services, Learning Enhancement Across the Disciplines (LEAD) courses, and success coaching for all students at Oberlin. LEAD classes empower students to approach their education independently and to succeed as learners. LEAD helps students discover learning strategies and academic skills, develop wellness and reflective practices, and find self-advocacy, leadership, and resilience. The LEAD courses may also identify students for peer support roles and mentorship. In addition to semester and module LEAD classes, instructors offer individual studies and sponsor projects during the winter term.

Football wasn't an approved sport at Oberlin until 1891. John W. Heisman started his coaching career as Oberlin's first football coach in 1892 and led the "O" Men to their first undefeated season. Heisman enrolled in postgraduate courses, which allowed him to play for Oberlin as well, demonstrating that an intelligent coach was an integral part of the sport. Named in his honor, the Heisman Trophy is awarded annually to the season's most outstanding college football player in the nation.

Oberlin College

GENERAL ADMISSIONS

Very important factors include: rigor of secondary school record, class rank, academic GPA. *Important factors include:* application essay, recommendations. *Other factors considered include:* standardized test scores (if submitted). High school diploma is required and GED is not accepted. Institution is test-optional for entering Fall 2024. Check admissions website for updates. *Academic units recommended:* 4 English, 4 math, 3 science (3 labs), 3 foreign language, 3 social studies.

FINANCIAL AID

Students should submit: Business/Farm Supplement; CSS/Financial Aid Profile; FAFSA; Institution's own financial aid form; Noncustodial Profile. *Need-based scholarships/grants offered:* College/university scholarship or grant aid from institutional funds; Federal Pell; Private scholarships; SEOG; State scholarships/grants. *Loan aid offered:* Direct PLUS loans; Direct Subsidized Loans; Direct Unsubsidized Loans. Federal Work-Study Program available. Institutional employment available.

CAMPUS LIFE

Activities: Campus Ministries; Choral groups; Concert band; Dance; Drama/theater; International Student Organization; Jazz band; Literary magazine; Marching band; Music ensembles; Musical theater; Opera; Pep band; Radio station; Student government; Student newspaper; Student-run film society; Symphony orchestra; Yearbook. **Organizations:** 200 registered organizations, 3 honor societies, 12 religious organizations, 0 fraternities, 0 sororities. **Athletics (Intercollegiate):** *Men:* baseball, basketball, bowling, cross-country, equestrian sports, golf, ice hockey, lacrosse, martial arts, swimming, track/field (indoor), ultimate frisbee, volleyball, water polo, wrestling. *Women:* basketball, bowling, cross-country, equestrian sports, field hockey, golf, gymnastics, ice hockey, lacrosse, martial arts, rugby, softball, swimming, track/field (indoor), ultimate frisbee, volleyball, water polo.

CAMPUS	
Type of school	Private (nonprofit)
Environment	Village

STUDENTS	
Undergrad enrollment	2,942
% male/female	42/58
% from out of state	93
% frosh live on campus	100

FINANCIAL FACTS	
Annual tuition	$61,106
Room and board	$18,390
Required fees	$918

GENERAL ADMISSIONS INFO	
Application fee	No fee
Regular application deadline	1/15
Nonfall registration	No

Fall 2024 testing policy	Test Optional
Range SAT EBRW	680–750
Range SAT Math	658–710
Range ACT Composite	30–34

ACADEMICS	
Student/faculty ratio	9:1
% students returning for sophomore year	87
Most classes have 2–9 students.	

Ohio

REQUESTING SERVICES FOR STUDENTS WITH LEARNING DIFFERENCES

Phone: 440-775-5588 • www.oberlin.edu/accessibility-services • Email: ODA@oberlin.edu

Documentation submitted to: Office for Disability and Access
Separate application required for Services: Yes

Documentation required for:
  LD: Psychoeducational evaluation
  ADHD: Psychoeducational evaluation
  ASD: Psychoeducational evaluation

The Ohio State University

Undergraduate Admissions, Columbus, OH 43210 • Admissions: 614-292-3980 • www.osu.edu

Support: CS

ACCOMMODATIONS

Allowed in exams:

Calculators	Yes
Dictionary	Yes
Computer	Yes
Spell-checker	Yes
Extended test time	Yes
Scribe	Yes
Proctors	Yes
Oral exams	Yes
Note-takers	Yes

Support services for students with:

LD	Yes
ADHD	Yes
ASD	Yes
Distraction-reduced environment	Yes
Recording of lecture allowed	Yes
Reading technology	Yes
Audio books	No
Other assistive technology	Yes
Priority registration	Yes

Added costs of services:

For LD	No
For ADHD	No
For ASD	Yes
LD specialists	No
ADHD & ASD coaching	Yes
ASD specialists	Yes
Professional tutors	No
Peer tutors	Yes
Max. hours/week for services	Varies
How professors are notified of student approved accommodations	Student

COLLEGE GRADUATION REQUIREMENTS

Course waivers allowed	No
Course substitutions allowed	Yes

In what courses: Math and Foreign Language

PROGRAMS/SERVICES FOR STUDENTS WITH LEARNING DIFFERENCES

Once students have accepted an offer of admission, they can register with Disability Services to request accommodations. Students submit an online application and download any corresponding documentation; students who do not have documentation should not delay completing the application and contacting Disability Services. Prospective students are invited to contact Disability Services to schedule an appointment with an Access Specialist to learn more about the services offered and the accommodation registration process. Once the application has been reviewed, students receive an email from their assigned Access Specialist and schedule a meeting in person, via phone, or via a Zoom conference to discuss disability-related barriers experienced in academics, accommodations that best address those barriers, and how to set up accommodations. Course accessibility letters are generated to students and instructors with procedures to follow. Students with ASD can access support through the Nisonger Center, for which there is a fee.

ADMISSIONS

The admissions process and requirements are the same for all students. High school transcripts, including the senior year course schedule, are required and should be sent by a school counselor. The counselor may include one optional teacher letter of recommendation. A personal essay by the student is required, and additional consideration will be given to students who exceed the minimum required curriculum. Once an applicant is determined to be eligible for enrollment, academic records are then reviewed for enrollment in a major or pre-major program. The disclosure of a disability on the admissions application is completely voluntary. Some students choose to disclose their disability to provide context to their GPA and grade history.

Additional Information

The Transition and Academic Growth (TAG) team offers First Year Success Series workshops online through CarmenZoom or Carmen Canvas. First-year students (FYS) are expected to attend a minimum number of credit sessions during the fall semester to help students transition to college life, explore campus resources, and get answers to their questions and concerns. The TAG team includes Academic Advising, the University Exploration offices, Buckeyes First, Complete Ohio State, the Spring Forward program, and the student success platform OnCourse.

Colonel Ralph D. Mershon's bequest to OSU in 1952 founded the Mershon Center for International Security Studies, a research center. The center is home to five programs, each with a unique goal and perspective on security. The center supports faculty and student research through grants and scholarships and brings scholars, government officials, NGOs (non-governmental organizations), and business leaders from around the world to discuss research in national and international security affairs.

The Ohio State University

GENERAL ADMISSIONS

Very important factors include: rigor of secondary school record, class rank, academic GPA, standardized test scores (if submitted). *Important factors include:* application essay. *Other factors considered include:* recommendations. High school diploma is required and GED is accepted. Institution is test-optional for entering Fall 2024. Check admissions website for updates. *Academic units required:* 4 English, 3 math, 3 science (3 labs), 2 foreign language, 2 social studies, 1 academic elective, 1 visual/performing arts. *Academic units recommended:* 4 math, 4 science (3 labs), 3 foreign language, 3 social studies.

FINANCIAL AID

Students should submit: FAFSA. *Need-based scholarships/grants offered:* College/university scholarship or grant aid from institutional funds; Federal Pell; Private scholarships; SEOG; State scholarships/grants. *Loan aid offered:* Direct PLUS loans; Direct Subsidized Loans; Direct Unsubsidized Loans. Federal Work-Study Program available. Institutional employment available.

CAMPUS LIFE

Activities: Campus Ministries; Choral groups; Concert band; Dance; Drama/theater; International Student Organization; Jazz band; Literary magazine; Marching band; Model UN; Music ensembles; Musical theater; Opera; Pep band; Radio station; Student government; Student newspaper; Student-run film society; Symphony orchestra; Television station. **Organizations:** 1441 registered organizations, 28 honor societies, 58 religious organizations, 37 fraternities, 27 sororities. **Athletics (Intercollegiate):** *Men:* baseball, basketball, bowling, crew/rowing, cross-country, field hockey, golf, gymnastics, ice hockey, lacrosse, martial arts, racquetball, rugby, swimming, track/field (indoor), ultimate frisbee, volleyball, water polo, wrestling. *Women:* basketball, bowling, crew/rowing, cross-country, equestrian sports, field hockey, golf, gymnastics, ice hockey, lacrosse, martial arts, racquetball, rugby, softball, swimming, track/field (indoor), ultimate frisbee, volleyball, water polo.

CAMPUS
Type of school	Public
Environment	Metropolis

STUDENTS
Undergrad enrollment	45,140
% male/female	50/50
% from out of state	20
% frosh live on campus	92

FINANCIAL FACTS
Annual in-state tuition	$12,484
Annual out-of-state tuition	$36,720
Room and board	$13,966

GENERAL ADMISSIONS INFO
Application fee	$60
Regular application deadline	2/1
Nonfall registration	Yes

Fall 2024 testing policy	Test Optional
Range SAT EBRW	610–710
Range SAT Math	640–750
Range ACT Composite	27–32

ACADEMICS
Student/faculty ratio	17:1
% students returning for sophomore year	93

Most classes have 10–19 students.

Ohio

REQUESTING SERVICES FOR STUDENTS WITH LEARNING DIFFERENCES

Phone: 614-292-3307 • slds.osu.edu • Email: slds@osu.edu

Documentation submitted to: Student Life Disability Services
Separate application required for Services: Yes

Documentation required for:
LD: Psychoeducational evaluation
ADHD: Psychoeducational evaluation
ASD: Psychoeducational evaluation

Ohio University

120 Chubb Hall, Athens, OH 45701 • Admissions: 740-593-4100 • www.ohio.edu

Support: CS

ACCOMMODATIONS

Allowed in exams:

Calculators	Yes
Dictionary	N/A
Computer	Yes
Spell-checker	Yes
Extended test time	Yes
Scribe	Yes
Proctors	Yes
Oral exams	N/A
Note-takers	Yes

Support services for students with:

LD	Yes
ADHD	Yes
ASD	Yes
Distraction-reduced environment	Yes
Recording of lecture allowed	Yes
Reading technology	Yes
Audio books	Yes
Other assistive technology	Yes
Priority registration	Yes

Added costs of services:

For LD	No
For ADHD	No
For ASD	No
LD specialists	No
ADHD & ASD coaching	Yes
ASD specialists	Yes
Professional tutors	No
Peer tutors	Yes
Max. hours/week for services	4
How professors are notified of student approved accommodations	Student

COLLEGE GRADUATION REQUIREMENTS

Course waivers allowed	No
Course substitutions allowed	Yes
In what courses: Varies	

PROGRAMS/SERVICES FOR STUDENTS WITH LEARNING DIFFERENCES

Accessibility Services determines reasonable accommodations, assists with self-advocacy, and serves as a central point of contact for students with disabilities. Accessibility coordinators are available and will meet with students upon request; however, progress is not formally monitored by Accessibility Services. A coaching program through Accessibility Services provides an additional layer of individualized support for students on the autism spectrum throughout their transition to college by working with them on five key competency areas to develop the skills and strategies needed in college. The program's focus shifts from adjusting to college life to pursuing independence and transitioning to the workforce as the students progress.

ADMISSIONS

All applicants are expected to meet the same admission criteria. General admission students not meeting the admission criteria are encouraged to write a narrative explaining the impact of their disability. The average GPA of admitted applicants is 3.5. Admissions consider curriculum, class rank, GPA, and ACT or SAT, if submitted. Some programs have more selective criteria.

Additional Information

The Academic Achievement Center provides tutoring and writing assistance.

The 225-member marching band is still called the Marching 110 from its original number of members in 1923. Today, the 110 stands for the effort expected of its members, as their marching and choreographed dance style is known around the world. The band has played NFL halftimes and the Macy's Thanksgiving Day and the Rose parades. They've also performed in Canada, Ireland, Italy, and France. In 1976, the Marching 110 became the first marching band ever to perform at Carnegie Hall in New York City.

Ohio University

GENERAL ADMISSIONS

Very important factors include: rigor of secondary school record, academic GPA. *Important factors include:* class rank. *Other factors considered include:* standardized test scores (if submitted), application essay, recommendations. High school diploma is required and GED is accepted. Institution is test-optional for entering Fall 2024. Check admissions website for updates. *Academic units required:* 4 English, 4 math, 3 science, 2 foreign language, 3 social studies, 4 academic electives. *Academic units recommended:* 1 visual/performing arts.

FINANCIAL AID

Students should submit: FAFSA. *Need-based scholarships/grants offered:* College/university scholarship or grant aid from institutional funds; Federal Pell; Private scholarships; SEOG; State scholarships/grants. *Loan aid offered:* Direct PLUS loans; Direct Subsidized Loans; Direct Unsubsidized Loans. Federal Work-Study Program available. Institutional employment available.

CAMPUS LIFE

Activities: Campus Ministries; Choral groups; Concert band; Dance; Drama/theater; International Student Organization; Jazz band; Literary magazine; Marching band; Music ensembles; Musical theater; Opera; Pep band; Radio station; Student government; Student newspaper; Student-run film society; Symphony orchestra; Television station; Yearbook. **Organizations:** 682 registered organizations, 39 honor societies, 31 religious organizations, 17 fraternities, 12 sororities. **Athletics (Intercollegiate):** *Men:* baseball, basketball, crew/rowing, cross-country, equestrian sports, golf, gymnastics, ice hockey, lacrosse, martial arts, rugby, swimming, ultimate frisbee, volleyball, wrestling. *Women:* basketball, crew/rowing, cross-country, equestrian sports, field hockey, golf, gymnastics, lacrosse, martial arts, rugby, softball, swimming, track/field (indoor), ultimate frisbee, volleyball, water polo.

CAMPUS
Type of school	Public
Environment	Town

STUDENTS
Undergrad enrollment	18,687
% male/female	39/61
% from out of state	12
% frosh live on campus	95

FINANCIAL FACTS
Annual in-state tuition	$13,352
Annual out-of-state tuition	$23,720
Room and board	$13,656

GENERAL ADMISSIONS INFO
Application fee	$50
Regular application deadline	2/1
Nonfall registration	Yes

Fall 2024 testing policy	Test Optional
Range SAT EBRW	530–630
Range SAT Math	520–620
Range ACT Composite	21–26

ACADEMICS
Student/faculty ratio	16:1
% students returning for sophomore year	81

Most classes have 10–19 students.

Ohio

REQUESTING SERVICES FOR STUDENTS WITH LEARNING DIFFERENCES

Phone: 740-593-2620 • www.ohio.edu/accessibility • Email: access@ohio.edu

Documentation submitted to: Student Accessibility Services
Separate application required for Services: Yes

Documentation required for:
LD: Psychoeducational evaluation
ADHD: Psychoeducational evaluation
ASD: Psychoeducational evaluation

Ohio Wesleyan University

61 South Sandusky Street, Delaware, OH 43015 • Admissions: 740-368-3020 • www.owu.edu

(Support: CS)

ACCOMMODATIONS

Allowed in exams:

Calculators	Yes
Dictionary	Yes
Computer	Yes
Spell-checker	Yes
Extended test time	Yes
Scribe	Yes
Proctors	Yes
Oral exams	Yes
Note-takers	Yes

Support services for students with:

LD	Yes
ADHD	Yes
ASD	Yes
Distraction-reduced environment	Yes
Recording of lecture allowed	Yes
Reading technology	Yes
Audio books	Yes
Other assistive technology	Yes
Priority registration	Yes

Added costs of services:

For LD	No
For ADHD	No
For ASD	Yes
LD specialists	Yes
ADHD & ASD coaching	Yes
ASD specialists	Yes
Professional tutors	No
Peer tutors	Yes
Max. hours/week for services	Varies
How professors are notified of student approved accommodations	Student and Accessibility Services Office

COLLEGE GRADUATION REQUIREMENTS

Course waivers allowed	No
Course substitutions allowed	No

Programs/Services for Students with Learning Differences

The Accessibility Services Office (ASO) assists students with disabilities. To receive accommodations, students must complete the online intake form, provide requested professional documentation, and meet with the ASO coordinator for a one-hour meeting to discuss the student's need for reasonable accommodation, academic modifications, and services. Bishop ACCESS is a fee-based program that provides one-on-one academic coaching for students with executive function disabilities, including ADHD, learning disabilities, and mental health disabilities. The program supports the student's entire career at OWU. Bishop ACCESS students meet regularly with an academic coach and attend Academic Skills and Campus Life Workshops. First-year students have a peer mentor and attend daily dedicated study tables with peer mentors and coaches. The first two years prioritize adjusting to campus life and community resources, academic skills, self-advocacy skills, and service-learning opportunities. The last two years prioritize skills and strategies to use after college and working with campus partners to assist with travel-learning opportunities, internships, career planning, and transitioning from college.

Admissions

All applicants are expected to meet the same admission criteria. All student applicants, regardless of test score submission, will be considered for both admission to the OWU and merit scholarships. Successful applicants typically rank in the top quarter of their high school class, have earned a minimum B average in their academic coursework, and have demonstrated involvement and leadership in school or community organizations.

Additional Information

The Sagan Academic Resource Center is home to The Writing Center, The Academic Skills Center, and The Quantitative Skills Center. The Writing Center offers tutoring in almost any class, subject, or assignment. The Q Center offers tutoring in any class with math components. Students can also check with their professors for drop-in and scheduled departmental tutoring. The Academic Skills Center is available by appointment and walk-in. The Division of Student Engagement and Success focuses on working with students to attain competencies in community service, critical thinking, cultural awareness, sustaining relationships, conflict resolution, self-advocacy, leadership skills, time management, and public speaking.

In 1917, Mildred Elizabeth Gillars (née Sisk) majored at OWU in dramatic arts but did not meet the requirements to graduate. In 1935, she moved to Germany and later worked for Radio Berlin; GIs dubbed her "Axis Sally," a counterpart to the "Tokyo Rose." In 1949, in Washington, D.C., she was the first American woman to be charged, tried, convicted, and sentenced for treason for broadcasting Nazi propaganda for Germany. After serving a 12-year sentence, Mildred returned to study at OWU, and in 1973, she received a bachelor's degree in speech.

Ohio Wesleyan University

GENERAL ADMISSIONS

Very important factors include: rigor of secondary school record, academic GPA. *Important factors include:* application essay, recommendation(s). *Other factors considered include:* class rank, class rank. High school diploma is required and GED is accepted. Institution is test-optional for entering Fall 2024. Check admissions website for updates. *Academic units required:* 4 English, 3 math, 3 science, 2 foreign language, 3 social studies. *Academic units recommended:* 4 math, 4 science, 3 foreign language, 4 social studies.

FINANCIAL AID

Students should submit: FAFSA. *Need-based scholarships/grants offered:* College/university scholarship or grant aid from institutional funds; Federal Pell; Private scholarships; SEOG; State scholarships/grants. *Loan aid offered:* Direct PLUS loans; Direct Subsidized Loans; Direct Unsubsidized Loans.

CAMPUS LIFE

Activities: Campus Ministries; Choral groups; Concert band; Dance; Drama/theater; International Student Organization; Jazz band; Literary magazine; Marching band; Model UN; Music ensembles; Musical theater; Pep band; Student government; Student newspaper; Symphony orchestra.

CAMPUS
Type of school	Private (nonprofit)
Environment	Town

STUDENTS
Undergrad enrollment	1,399
% male/female	44/56
% from out of state	33
% frosh live on campus	90

FINANCIAL FACTS
Annual tuition	$51,711
Room and board	$14,226
Required fees	$1,006

GENERAL ADMISSIONS INFO
Application fee	No fee
Regular application deadline	3/1
Nonfall registration	Yes
Fall 2024 testing policy	Test Optional

ACADEMICS
Student/faculty ratio	11:1
% students returning for sophomore year	82

Most classes have 10–19 students.

Ohio

REQUESTING SERVICES FOR STUDENTS WITH LEARNING DIFFERENCES

Phone: 740-368-3990 • www.owu.edu/about/offices-services-directory/sagan-academic-resource-center/accessibility-services-office/ • Email: anrodenborg@owu.edu

Documentation submitted to: Accessibility Services Office

Separate application required for Services: Yes

Documentation required for:
LD: Psychoeducational evaluation
ADHD: Psychoeducational evaluation
ASD: Psychoeducational evaluation

University of Cincinnati

P.O. Box 21009, Cincinnati, OH 45221-0091 • Admissions: 513-556-1100 • www.uc.edu

Support: CS

ACCOMMODATIONS

Allowed in exams:

Calculators	Yes
Dictionary	Yes
Computer	Yes
Spell-checker	Yes
Extended test time	Yes
Scribe	Yes
Proctors	Yes
Oral exams	No
Note-takers	Yes

Support services for students with:

LD	Yes
ADHD	Yes
ASD	Yes
Distraction-reduced environment	Yes
Recording of lecture allowed	Yes
Reading technology	Yes
Audio books	Yes
Other assistive technology	Yes
Priority registration	Yes

Added costs of services:

For LD	No
For ADHD	No
For ASD	No
LD specialists	No
ADHD & ASD coaching	No
ASD specialists	Yes
Professional tutors	No
Peer tutors	Yes
Max. hours/week for services	Varies
How professors are notified of student approved accommodations	Student and Accessibility Resources

COLLEGE GRADUATION REQUIREMENTS

Course waivers allowed	No
Course substitutions allowed	Yes

In what courses: Foreign Language and sometimes Math. Case-by-case basis

PROGRAMS/SERVICES FOR STUDENTS WITH LEARNING DIFFERENCES

Accessibility Resources (AR) supports students with disabilities. Students can start the registration process by completing a new student registration form. Documentation is not required to register for services; however, if available, it can help the AR staff see the full impact of a disability, the barriers, and workable solutions for accommodations. Students meet with an accommodation coordinator (AC) after submitting the registration form; meetings are available in person, over the phone, and online. In the meeting, the AC will help determine appropriate accommodations. Services can include alternative versions of course materials and textbooks or guidance on software, hardware, apps, and learning aides. AR's digital access team offers one-on-one appointments for students who want to learn more about the resources available.

ADMISSIONS

All applicants are expected to meet the same admission criteria. Official or unofficial high school transcripts must be submitted with the application. ACT or SAT scores are optional for most programs. Letters of recommendation are optional and GPA requirements vary depending on the program.

Additional Information

All UC students participate in experience-based learning; this can include cooperative education (Co-op), internships, research, studying abroad, clinicals, service learning, and other hands-on experiences. Open to all students, the Learning Commons (LC) brings together hundreds of peer educators and faculty to provide free, centralized academic support. The LC offers both one-on-one and group-based support and also provides online tutoring appointments for over 200 courses. The LC MASS Center includes free, tutor-supported study tables for math, stats, biology, chemistry, physics, business, and engineering. The Writing Center offers free help with writing assignments; students can make an appointment or submit work for feedback. The Learning Communities Program brings groups of students and faculty together based on shared academic interests. During orientation, first-year students can join one of over 100 Learning Communities based on their major or area of interest. Benefits of joining a Learning Community include further exploring an interest, establishing relationships with professors and students, and accessing difficult-to-get-into courses. Learning Communities create a small-college feel with all the benefits of a large university.

In 1906, the dean of the College of Engineering created the first cooperative education program in the world. Twenty-seven students and 13 companies participated in the opportunity to combine classroom education with work experience. Due to the positive reception, by 1920, UC canceled its traditional engineering program and Co-op became mandatory for all engineering and business students.

University of Cincinnati

GENERAL ADMISSIONS

Very important factors include: academic GPA. *Important factors include:* rigor of secondary school record, application essay. *Other factors considered include:* class rank, standardized test scores (if submitted), recommendations. High school diploma is required and GED is accepted. Institution is test-optional for entering Fall 2024. Check admissions website for updates. *Academic units required:* 4 English, 4 math, 3 science, 3 social studies, 5 academic electives.

FINANCIAL AID

Students should submit: FAFSA. *Need-based scholarships/grants offered:* College/university scholarship or grant aid from institutional funds; Federal Pell; Private scholarships; SEOG; State scholarships/grants; United Negro College Fund. *Loan aid offered:* Direct PLUS loans; Direct Subsidized Loans; Direct Unsubsidized Loans. Federal Work-Study Program available. Institutional employment available.

CAMPUS LIFE

Activities: Campus Ministries; Choral groups; Concert band; Dance; Drama/theater; International Student Organization; Jazz band; Marching band; Model UN; Music ensembles; Musical theater; Opera; Pep band; Radio station; Student government; Student newspaper; Student-run film society; Symphony orchestra. **Organizations:** 740 registered organizations, 18 honor societies, 33 religious organizations, 37 fraternities, 13 sororities. **Athletics (Intercollegiate):** *Men:* baseball, basketball, bowling, cross-country, cycling, equestrian sports, golf, gymnastics, ice hockey, lacrosse, martial arts, racquetball, rugby, softball, swimming, table tennis, track/field (indoor), ultimate frisbee, volleyball, water polo, wrestling. *Women:* baseball, basketball, bowling, cross-country, cycling, equestrian sports, golf, gymnastics, ice hockey, lacrosse, martial arts, racquetball, rugby, softball, swimming, table tennis, track/field (indoor), ultimate frisbee, volleyball, water polo, wrestling.

Ohio

REQUESTING SERVICES FOR STUDENTS WITH LEARNING DIFFERENCES

Phone: 513-556-6823 • www.uc.edu/campus-life/accessibility-resources • Email: accessresources@uc.edu

Documentation submitted to: Accessibility Resources
Separate application required for Services: Yes

Documentation required for:
  LD: Psychoeducational evaluation
  ADHD: Psychoeducational evaluation
  ASD: Psychoeducational evaluation

University of Dayton

300 College Park, Dayton, OH 45469-1669 • Admissions: 937-229-4411 • www.udayton.edu

Support: CS

ACCOMMODATIONS

Allowed in exams:

Calculators	Yes
Dictionary	No
Computer	Yes
Spell-checker	Yes
Extended test time	Yes
Scribe	Yes
Proctors	Yes
Oral exams	Yes
Note-takers	Yes

Support services for students with:

LD	Yes
ADHD	Yes
ASD	Yes
Distraction-reduced environment	Yes
Recording of lecture allowed	Yes
Reading technology	Yes
Audio books	Yes
Other assistive technology	Yes
Priority registration	Yes

Added costs of services:

For LD	No
For ADHD	No
For ASD	No
LD specialists	Yes
ADHD & ASD coaching	Yes
ASD specialists	Yes
Professional tutors	No
Peer tutors	Yes
Max. hours/week for services	Varies
How professors are notified of student approved accommodations	Student

COLLEGE GRADUATION REQUIREMENTS

Course waivers allowed	No
Course substitutions allowed	Yes
In what courses: Case-by-case basis	

PROGRAMS/SERVICES FOR STUDENTS WITH LEARNING DIFFERENCES

The Office of Learning Resources (OLR) provides services and accommodations for students with disabilities. Students should submit an initial online accommodation request form with supporting documents and then schedule a meeting with OLR staff. At the meeting, the student will be asked to describe their disability and how the requested accommodations will solve the barriers. Students work directly with disability service staff to request and manage a wide range of accommodations that may be academic or classroom related and require assistive technology or alternative testing. OLR supports students through a variety of programs and services, including free tutoring and study resources. Prospective students touring UD are welcome to make an appointment with OLR to gather information and ask questions about OLR.

ADMISSIONS

The review committee assesses applications for admission based on the academic major or program selected. The quality of an applicant's academic record is reviewed based on GPA, grade pattern throughout high school, selection of college prep courses, class standing, and rank if provided. The admissions committee also considers the recommendation of high school guidance counselors, along with other factors, including a student's interest in UD shown by an official campus visit or an event in the applicant's area. After a thorough review of an applicant's academic quality and the requirements of the major selected, the committee may choose to approve admission but to a different academic program. Each academic division accepts a limited number of first-year students with deficiencies in their academic background as Special Admit students. The Special Admit Program may include course placement, special advising, Supplemental Instruction, study tables, and math workshops. For a limited number of students needing extra support, the Fully Integrated Resource, Support, and Transition (FIRST) Program is offered to students whose profile suggests they will benefit from a structured transition to college. This is a contractual agreement between students, parents, and UD.

Additional Information

All students are assigned an academic advisor to help create an educational plan to meet their personal and professional goals. UD students may schedule one-on-one sessions with a tutor through the Student Success Network and meet with a tutor in person or via Zoom. In addition to the usual offerings, Roesch Library also has a Dialogue Zone, Scholars' Commons, Story Studio, and Zen Den.

During the Great Dayton Flood of 1913, 800 refugees fled to (then) St. Mary's College on a hilltop south of town for shelter. It was Easter break, and the campus was well stocked with food, clean water, and provisions. The kitchen also provided meals to Miami Valley Hospital and St. Elizabeth Hospital. In 1920, the school was incorporated as the University of Dayton.

University of Dayton

General Admissions

Very important factors include: rigor of secondary school record, class rank, academic GPA, application essay. *Important factors include:* recommendations. *Other factors considered include:* standardized test scores (if submitted). High school diploma is required and GED is accepted. Institution is test-optional for entering Fall 2024. Check admissions website for updates. *Academic units recommended:* 4 English, 4 math, 4 science (1 lab), 2 foreign language, 4 social studies, 4 visual/performing arts.

Financial Aid

Students should submit: FAFSA. *Need-based scholarships/grants offered:* College/university scholarship or grant aid from institutional funds; Federal Pell; Private scholarships; State scholarships/grants. *Loan aid offered:* Direct PLUS loans; Direct Subsidized Loans; Direct Unsubsidized Loans. Federal Work-Study Program available. Institutional employment available.

Campus Life

Activities: Campus Ministries; Choral groups; Concert band; Dance; Drama/theater; International Student Organization; Jazz band; Literary magazine; Marching band; Model UN; Music ensembles; Musical theater; Opera; Pep band; Radio station; Student government; Student newspaper; Symphony orchestra; Television station; Yearbook. **Organizations:** 225 registered organizations, 16 honor societies, 10 religious organizations, 9 fraternities, 11 sororities. **Athletics (Intercollegiate):** *Men:* baseball, basketball, crew/rowing, cross-country, field hockey, golf, gymnastics, ice hockey, lacrosse, racquetball, rugby, swimming, ultimate frisbee, volleyball, water polo, wrestling. *Women:* basketball, crew/rowing, cross-country, field hockey, golf, gymnastics, lacrosse, racquetball, rugby, softball, swimming, track/field (indoor), ultimate frisbee, volleyball, water polo, wrestling.

CAMPUS

Type of school	Private (nonprofit)
Environment	City

STUDENTS

Undergrad enrollment	8,349
% male/female	52/48
% from out of state	45
% frosh live on campus	92

FINANCIAL FACTS

Annual tuition	$46,170
Room and board	$15,390

GENERAL ADMISSIONS INFO

Application fee	No fee
Regular application deadline	2/1
Nonfall registration	Yes

Fall 2024 testing policy	Test Optional
Range SAT EBRW	588–673
Range SAT Math	570–690
Range ACT Composite	24–30

ACADEMICS

Student/faculty ratio	15:1
% students returning for sophomore year	88
Most classes have 10–19 students.	

Ohio

REQUESTING SERVICES FOR STUDENTS WITH LEARNING DIFFERENCES

Phone: 937-229-2066 • udayton.edu/olr/disability • Email: disabilityservices@udayton.edu

Documentation submitted to: Office of Learning Resources
Separate application required for Services: Yes

Documentation required for:
LD: Psychoeducational evaluation
ADHD: Psychoeducational evaluation
ASD: Psychoeducational evaluation

Ursuline College

2550 Lander Road, Pepper Pike, OH 44124-4398 • Admissions: 440-449-4203 • www.ursuline.edu

Support: SP

ACCOMMODATIONS

Allowed in exams:	
Calculators	Yes
Dictionary	N/A
Computer	Yes
Spell-checker	Yes
Extended test time	Yes
Scribe	Yes
Proctors	Yes
Oral exams	Yes
Note-takers	Yes
Support services for students with:	
LD	Yes
ADHD	Yes
ASD	Yes
Distraction-reduced environment	Yes
Recording of lecture allowed	Yes
Reading technology	Yes
Audio books	Yes
Other assistive technology	Yes
Priority registration	Yes
Added costs of services:	
For LD	Yes
For ADHD	Yes
For ASD	No
LD specialists	Yes
ADHD & ASD coaching	Yes
ASD specialists	No
Professional tutors	Yes
Peer tutors	Yes
Max. hours/week for services	13
How professors are notified of student approved accommodations	Student

COLLEGE GRADUATION REQUIREMENTS

Course waivers allowed	No
Course substitutions allowed	Yes
In what courses: Case-by-case basis	

PROGRAMS/SERVICES FOR STUDENTS WITH LEARNING DIFFERENCES

The staff at Ursuline College is committed to helping students with learning disabilities and has in-service training to better understand how to accommodate students. Students requesting accommodations will meet with a disability specialist to discuss their needs. FOCUS is a fee-based program available to students with learning disabilities. Eligibility for FOCUS is determined by recent documentation of a learning disability, admission to the college, and a meeting with the LD specialist to assess fit. The program helps to provide a smooth transition to college life, identify individualized learning strategies, and teach self-advocacy skills. The FOCUS program is offered in a multi-tiered format, and all stages include an individual orientation, co-advising on academic courses and majors, priority registration, assistance connecting with tutors, academic and social support, mid-term progress monitoring, and ongoing communication with faculty. Program fees vary depending on the level of support.

ADMISSIONS

Ursuline admits candidates who demonstrate the potential for success in a rigorous academic program and show promise for making contributions to the community. Most students with learning disabilities meet the general admission requirements, but it is possible for students with lower GPAs to receive conditional admission. Students with conditional admission are limited to 12 credit-hours per semester for their first year. While Ursuline is test-optional, standardized tests are still required for students applying to the 3+4 Pharmacy Programs with Duquesne and LECOM.

Additional Information

All students at Ursuline have the support of an academic advisor. Peer and professional tutoring sessions are available to all students in one-on-one or small group settings.

DID YOU KNOW?

Ursuline College was founded in 1871 by the Ursuline Sisters of Cleveland, who arrived in Cleveland by way of France. The Ursuline ministries are called to empower others through lifelong learning, so it should come as no surprise that Ursuline is the first Catholic women's college in Ohio and one of the oldest institutions of higher education for women in the United States.

Ursuline College

GENERAL ADMISSIONS

Very important factors include: academic GPA, standardized test scores (if submitted). *Other factors considered include:* rigor of secondary school record, class rank, application essay, recommendations. High school diploma is required and GED is accepted. Institution is test-optional for entering Fall 2024. Check admissions website for updates. *Academic units recommended:* 4 English, 3 math, 3 science (2 labs), 2 foreign language, 3 social studies, 1 visual/performing arts.

FINANCIAL AID

Students should submit: FAFSA. *Need-based scholarships/grants offered:* College/university scholarship or grant aid from institutional funds; Federal Nursing Scholarships; Federal Pell; Private scholarships; SEOG; State scholarships/grants. *Loan aid offered:* Direct PLUS loans; Direct Subsidized Loans; Direct Unsubsidized Loans. Federal Work-Study Program available.

CAMPUS LIFE

Activities: Campus Ministries; Drama/theater; Literary magazine; Student government. **Organizations:** 23 registered organizations, 4 honor societies, 0 religious organizations, 0 fraternities, 0 sororities. **Athletics (Intercollegiate):** *Women:* basketball, bowling, cross-country, golf, lacrosse, softball, swimming, volleyball.

CAMPUS
Type of school	Private (nonprofit)
Environment	City

STUDENTS
Undergrad enrollment	663
% male/female	7/93
% from out of state	8
% frosh live on campus	72

FINANCIAL FACTS
Annual tuition	$37,380
Room and board	$12,284
Required fees	$380

GENERAL ADMISSIONS INFO
Application fee	No fee
Regular application deadline	Rolling
Nonfall registration	Yes

Fall 2024 testing policy	Test Optional
Range SAT EBRW	533–615
Range SAT Math	503–540
Range ACT Composite	19–26

ACADEMICS
Student/faculty ratio	7:1
% students returning for sophomore year	72

Most classes have 2–9 students.

Ohio

REQUESTING SERVICES FOR STUDENTS WITH LEARNING DIFFERENCES

Phone: 440-449-2046 • ursuline.edu/academics/academic-support-svcs/disabilities-services
Email: morgan.weber@ursuline.edu

Documentation submitted to: Disabilities Services
Separate application required for Services: Yes

Documentation required for:
LD: Psychoeducational evaluation
ADHD: Psychoeducational evaluation
ASD: Psychoeducational evaluation

Wright State University

3640 Colonel Glenn Highway, Dayton, OH 45435 • Admissions: 937-775-5700 • www.wright.edu

Support: SP

ACCOMMODATIONS

Allowed in exams:

Calculators	Yes
Dictionary	Yes
Computer	Yes
Spell-checker	Yes
Extended test time	Yes
Scribe	Yes
Proctors	Yes
Oral exams	Yes
Note-takers	Yes

Support services for students with:

LD	Yes
ADHD	Yes
ASD	Yes
Distraction-reduced environment	Yes
Recording of lecture allowed	Yes
Reading technology	Yes
Audio books	Yes
Other assistive technology	Yes
Priority registration	No

Added costs of services:

For LD	Yes
For ADHD	Yes
For ASD	Yes
LD specialists	No
ADHD & ASD coaching	Yes
ASD specialists	Yes
Professional tutors	Yes
Peer tutors	Yes
Max. hours/week for services	2
How professors are notified of student approved accommodations	Student

COLLEGE GRADUATION REQUIREMENTS

Course waivers allowed	No
Course substitutions allowed	Yes
In what courses: Case-by-case basis	

PROGRAMS/SERVICES FOR STUDENTS WITH LEARNING DIFFERENCES

The Office of Disability Services provides support to students with disabilities. Accommodations may include readers, note-taking assistance, access to teaching materials, a laptop in class for note-taking, audio recordings, a scribe, Smart Pens, extended test time, reduced-distraction testing environments, and assistive technology. To receive accommodations, students must complete the online application, submit professional documentation of their disability, and attend a college accommodation planning meeting. Raiders on the Autism Spectrum Excelling (RASE) is a fee-based program that provides support to students on the autism spectrum. Students are assigned transition coaches to work with one-on-one for up to five hours per week. The transition coaches are experienced undergraduate or graduate students who are available as a resource for students with ASD. Coaches assist them with self-advocacy skills, accessing campus resources, and problem-solving. PreFlight Summer Bridge, offered by the Office of Disability Services, gives students a chance to participate in activities to develop personal and academic skills, such as time management, study, reading, and writing skills, and accessing campus resources.

ADMISSIONS

The admission process is the same for all students. Applicants with a 2.5 GPA and the required academic courses will be admitted to the university. Applicants with the required courses and a GPA of 2.0–2.5 may be admitted if they have an ACT of 15 or higher or an SAT of 830 or higher. Applicants with a 2.0 GPA but missing the core academic requirements may be admitted if they meet certain requirements.

Additional Information

The Student Success Center includes the University Writing Center, the Math Learning Center, in-person and online tutoring, and Supplemental Instruction.

Wright State was named to honor aviation pioneers Orville and Wilbur Wright, inventors of the world's first successful airplane. They conducted early test flights at Huffman Prairie, just minutes from campus. One of the world's most complete collections of Wright brothers' materials is at the Dunbar Library's Special Collections and Archives and includes the Wrights' technical and personal library, family papers, and film documenting the invention of the airplane.

Wright State University

GENERAL ADMISSIONS

Very important factors include: rigor of secondary school record, academic GPA, standardized test scores (if submitted). *Other factors considered include:* recommendations. High school diploma is required and GED is accepted. Institution is test-optional for entering Fall 2024. Check admissions website for updates. *Academic units required:* 4 English, 4 math, 3 science (3 labs), 3 social studies. *Academic units recommended:* 2 foreign language, 1 visual/performing arts.

FINANCIAL AID

Students should submit: FAFSA. *Need-based scholarships/grants offered:* College/university scholarship or grant aid from institutional funds; Federal Nursing Scholarships; Federal Pell; Private scholarships; SEOG; State scholarships/grants; United Negro College Fund. *Loan aid offered:* Direct PLUS loans; Direct Subsidized Loans; Direct Unsubsidized Loans. Federal Work-Study Program available. Institutional employment available.

CAMPUS LIFE

Activities: Campus Ministries; Choral groups; Concert band; Dance; Drama/theater; International Student Organization; Jazz band; Literary magazine; Model UN; Music ensembles; Musical theater; Opera; Pep band; Radio station; Student government; Student newspaper; Symphony orchestra; Television station. **Organizations:** 205 registered organizations, 12 honor societies, 18 religious organizations, 9 fraternities, 11 sororities. **Athletics (Intercollegiate):** *Men:* baseball, basketball, bowling, golf, gymnastics, ice hockey, racquetball, rugby, softball, swimming, ultimate frisbee, volleyball. *Women:* basketball, bowling, golf, gymnastics, racquetball, rugby, softball, swimming, ultimate frisbee, volleyball.

CAMPUS	
Type of school	Public
Environment	City

STUDENTS	
Undergrad enrollment	7,477
% male/female	45/55
% from out of state	4
% frosh live on campus	26

FINANCIAL FACTS	
Annual in-state tuition	$10,864
Annual out-of-state tuition	$20,282
Room and board	$10,686

GENERAL ADMISSIONS INFO	
Application fee	No fee
Regular application deadline	8/23
Nonfall registration	Yes
Fall 2024 testing policy	Test Optional
Range SAT EBRW	470–640
Range SAT Math	475–610
Range ACT Composite	17–24

ACADEMICS	
Student/faculty ratio	14:1
% students returning for sophomore year	65

REQUESTING SERVICES FOR STUDENTS WITH LEARNING DIFFERENCES

Phone: 937-775-5680 • www.wright.edu/disability-services • Email: disability_services@wright.edu

Documentation submitted to: Office of Disability Services
Separate application required for Services: Yes

Documentation required for:
LD: Psychoeducational evaluation
ADHD: Psychoeducational evaluation
ASD: Psychoeducational evaluation

Xavier University

3800 Victory Parkway, Cincinnati, OH 45207-5311 • Admissions: 513-745-3301 • www.xavier.edu

Support: CS

ACCOMMODATIONS

Allowed in exams:

Calculators	Yes
Dictionary	Yes
Computer	Yes
Spell-checker	Yes
Extended test time	Yes
Scribe	Yes
Proctors	Yes
Oral exams	Yes
Note-takers	Yes

Support services for students with:

LD	Yes
ADHD	Yes
ASD	Yes
Distraction-reduced environment	Yes
Recording of lecture allowed	Yes
Reading technology	Yes
Audio books	Yes
Other assistive technology	Yes
Priority registration	Yes

Added costs of services:

For LD	No
For ADHD	No
For ASD	Yes
LD specialists	No
ADHD & ASD coaching	Yes
ASD specialists	Yes
Professional tutors	No
Peer tutors	Yes
Max. hours/week for services	1
How professors are notified of student approved accommodations	Student

COLLEGE GRADUATION REQUIREMENTS

Course waivers allowed	No
Course substitutions allowed	Yes
In what course: Math and Foreign Language	

PROGRAMS/SERVICES FOR STUDENTS WITH LEARNING DIFFERENCES

The Accessibility and Disability Resources office works with students to provide appropriate accommodations. General accommodations may include academic coaching, assistive technology, course substitutions, exam accommodations, note-taking accommodations, Read&Write software, and textbooks and class materials in alternative formats. To receive accommodations, students must submit documentation, complete the online application form, and then schedule an appointment to discuss accommodations. Students must request accommodations each semester and meet with their professors to review their accommodations. The X-Path Program is a fee-based program for students on the autism spectrum. Applicants must first be admitted to Xavier University, be registered with the Office of Accessibility and Disability Resources, and submit a completed online X-Path Program application. Applications are reviewed and interviews are required to assess whether the X-Path Program is an appropriate option for the applicant's specific needs. With the X-Path Program, support and coaching are tailored to the needs of each student to develop academic competence, social skills, and self-advocacy. Each student works with the Accommodation and Support Coordinators and is assigned a Peer Coach.

ADMISSIONS

All applicants must meet the same admission requirements. The average high school GPA for admitted applicants is 3.6. For those who submit test scores, the average SAT scores are between 1070 and 1250. The music and nursing programs have selective admission requirements.

Additional Information

Academic resources for students include the Writing Center, the Math Lab, tutoring, success coaches, and Supplemental Instruction.

D'Artagnan the Musketeer has served as the official mascot of Xavier University's athletic teams since 1925. The Musketeer was a nod to chivalry, tied with French origins and culture, and a symbol of qualities to inspire students. In 1985, the spirit squad coordinators realized the Musketeer's handlebar mustache and prop sword scared young spectators, and a friendlier furry creature, the Blue Blob, became the secondary mascot.

Xavier University

GENERAL ADMISSIONS

Very important factors include: rigor of secondary school record, academic GPA. *Important factors include:* application essay, recommendations. *Other factors considered include:* class rank, standardized test scores (if submitted). High school diploma is required and GED is accepted. Institution is test-optional for entering Fall 2024. Check admissions website for updates. *Academic units recommended:* 4 English, 3 math, 3 science, 2 foreign language, 3 social studies, 5 academic electives.

FINANCIAL AID

Students should submit: FAFSA. *Need-based scholarships/grants offered:* College/university scholarship or grant aid from institutional funds; Federal Pell; Private scholarships; SEOG; State scholarships/grants; United Negro College Fund. *Loan aid offered:* Direct PLUS loans; Direct Subsidized Loans; Direct Unsubsidized Loans. Federal Work-Study Program available. Institutional employment available.

CAMPUS LIFE

Activities: Campus Ministries; Choral groups; Concert band; Dance; Drama/theater; International Student Organization; Jazz band; Literary magazine; Music ensembles; Musical theater; Pep band; Student government; Student newspaper; Symphony orchestra; Television station. **Organizations:** 164 registered organizations, 9 honor societies, 4 religious organizations, 0 fraternities, 0 sororities. **Athletics (Intercollegiate):** *Men:* baseball, basketball, cross-country, equestrian sports, field hockey, golf, gymnastics, ice hockey, lacrosse, rugby, swimming, track/field (indoor), ultimate frisbee, volleyball, water polo. *Women:* basketball, cross-country, equestrian sports, field hockey, golf, gymnastics, lacrosse, softball, swimming, track/field (indoor), ultimate frisbee, volleyball.

CAMPUS

Type of school	Private (nonprofit)
Environment	Metropolis

STUDENTS

Undergrad enrollment	5,129
% male/female	43/57
% from out of state	57
% frosh live on campus	90

FINANCIAL FACTS

Annual tuition	$47,896
Room and board	$13,820
Required fees	$230

GENERAL ADMISSIONS INFO

Application fee	No fee
Regular application deadline	Rolling
Nonfall registration	Yes

Fall 2024 testing policy	Test Optional
SAT EBRW	570–660
SAT Math	550–650
ACT Composite range	23–30

ACADEMICS

Student/faculty ratio	11:1
% students returning for sophomore year	83

Most classes have 20–29 students.

Ohio

REQUESTING SERVICES FOR STUDENTS WITH LEARNING DIFFERENCES

Phone: 513-745-3280 • www.xavier.edu/disability-services/ • Email: disabilityservices@xavier.edu

Documentation submitted to: Accessibility and Disability Resources
Separate application required for Services: Yes

Documentation required for:
LD: Psychoeducational evaluation
ADHD: Psychoeducational evaluation
ASD: Psychoeducational evaluation

Oklahoma State University

219 Student Union, Stillwater, OK 74078 • Admissions: 405-744-5358 • www.okstate.edu

Support: S

ACCOMMODATIONS

Allowed in exams:

Calculators	Yes
Dictionary	Yes
Computer	Yes
Spell-checker	Yes
Extended test time	Yes
Scribe	Yes
Proctors	Yes
Oral exams	Yes
Note-takers	Yes

Support services for students with:

LD	No
ADHD	No
ASD	No
Distraction-reduced environment	Yes
Recording of lecture allowed	Yes
Reading technology	Yes
Audio books	Yes
Other assistive technology	Yes
Priority registration	No

Added costs of services:

For LD	No
For ADHD	No
For ASD	No
LD specialists	No
ADHD & ASD coaching	No
ASD specialists	No
Professional tutors	No
Peer tutors	Yes
Max. hours/week for services	Varies
How professors are notified of student approved accommodations	Student Accessibility Services

COLLEGE GRADUATION REQUIREMENTS

Course waivers allowed	No
Course substitutions allowed	No

PROGRAMS/SERVICES FOR STUDENTS WITH LEARNING DIFFERENCES

Student Accessibility Services (SAS) provides assistance to students with disabilities. Academic support services can include classroom and testing accommodations, accessible textbooks, assistive technology, and other services. Once the documentation has been received and reviewed, students can set up an intake meeting to discuss available accommodations and resources. For students beginning school in the fall semester, this meeting typically occurs the summer before school starts, but students can also schedule an intake meeting for the first or second week of the semester.

ADMISSIONS

Students qualify for assured admission if they meet ONE of the following criteria: 3.0 or better unweighted cumulative GPA and rank in the top 33.3 percent of their high school graduating class; or 3.0 GPA or better in 15-unit core and 21 ACT/1060 SAT or better; or a minimum 24 ACT or 1160 SAT. OSU will accept the official superscore provided directly from ACT for both admission and scholarship consideration. Consideration for most OSU scholarships will require a test score submission.

Additional Information

Tutoring at the Learning and Student Success Opportunity Center (LASSO) is open to all Oklahoma State University students at no additional charge. There are university-hired peer tutors available to students in every course. Each tutor has superior qualifications and has gone through extensive tutor training. Supplemental Instruction sessions engage students in challenging courses with innovative learning techniques.

The schedule for Muttday Monday, Tail Waggin' Tuesday, Waggin' Wednesday, Tail Thumping Thursdays, and Furry Friend Friday lets students know the time and location of Pete's Pet Posse. OSU's full-time, multi-campus pet therapy program, a wellness program since 2013, allows students to interact and de-stress with one of its 22 members.

Oklahoma State University

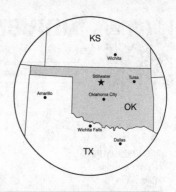

GENERAL ADMISSIONS

Other factors considered include: class rank, academic GPA, standardized test scores (if submitted), application essay, recommendations. High school diploma is required and GED is accepted. Institution is test-optional for entering Fall 2024. Check admissions website for updates. *Academic units required:* 4 English, 3 math, 3 science (3 labs), 2 social studies, 1 U.S. history.

FINANCIAL AID

Students should submit: FAFSA. *Need-based scholarships/grants offered:* College/university scholarship or grant aid from institutional funds; Federal Pell; Private scholarships; SEOG; State scholarships/grants. *Loan aid offered:* Direct PLUS loans; Direct Subsidized Loans; Direct Unsubsidized Loans. Federal Work-Study Program available. Institutional employment available.

CAMPUS LIFE

Activities: Campus Ministries; Choral groups; Concert band; Dance; Drama/theater; International Student Organization; Jazz band; Literary magazine; Marching band; Model UN; Music ensembles; Musical theater; Opera; Pep band; Radio station; Student government; Student newspaper; Student-run film society; Symphony orchestra; Television station. **Organizations:** 521 registered organizations, 32 honor societies, 24 religious organizations, 28 fraternities, 21 sororities. **Athletics (Intercollegiate):** *Men:* baseball, basketball, crew/rowing, cross-country, cycling, golf, lacrosse, rugby, track/field (indoor), ultimate frisbee, volleyball, water polo, wrestling. *Women:* basketball, crew/rowing, cross-country, cycling, equestrian sports, golf, lacrosse, rugby, softball, track/field (indoor), ultimate frisbee, volleyball, water polo.

CAMPUS

Type of school	Public
Environment	Town

STUDENTS

Undergrad enrollment	20,376
% male/female	48/52
% from out of state	28
% frosh live on campus	91

FINANCIAL FACTS

Annual in-state tuition	$5,417
Annual out-of-state tuition	$20,937
Room and board	$9,106
Required fees	$3,827

GENERAL ADMISSIONS INFO

Application fee	$40
Regular application deadline	Rolling
Nonfall registration	Yes
Fall 2024 testing policy	Test Optional
Range SAT EBRW	510–630
Range SAT Math	500–620
Range ACT Composite	20–27

ACADEMICS

Student/faculty ratio	18:1
% students returning for sophomore year	84

Most classes have 10–19 students.

Oklahoma

REQUESTING SERVICES FOR STUDENTS WITH LEARNING DIFFERENCES

Phone: 405-744-7116 • accessibility.okstate.edu/ • Email: accessibility@okstate.edu

Documentation submitted to: Student Accessibility Services
Separate application required for Services: Yes

Documentation required for:
LD: Psychoeducational evaluation
ADHD: Psychoeducational evaluation
ASD: Psychoeducational evaluation

University of Tulsa

800 South Tucker Drive, Tulsa, OK 74104 • Admissions: 918-631-2307 • utulsa.edu

Support: CS

ACCOMMODATIONS

Allowed in exams:

Calculators	Yes
Dictionary	Yes
Computer	Yes
Spell-checker	Yes
Extended test time	Yes
Scribe	Yes
Proctors	Yes
Oral exams	Yes
Note-takers	Yes

Support services for students with:

LD	Yes
ADHD	Yes
ASD	Yes
Distraction-reduced environment	Yes
Recording of lecture allowed	Yes
Reading technology	Yes
Audio books	Yes
Other assistive technology	Yes
Priority registration	Yes

Added costs of services:

For LD	No
For ADHD	No
For ASD	No
LD specialists	Yes
ADHD & ASD coaching	Yes
ASD specialists	Yes
Professional tutors	No
Peer tutors	Yes
Max. hours/week for services	Varies
How professors are notified of student approved accommodations	Student

COLLEGE GRADUATION REQUIREMENTS

Course waivers allowed	Yes

In what courses: Any applicable courses.

Course substitutions allowed	Yes

In what courses: Any applicable courses.

PROGRAMS/SERVICES FOR STUDENTS WITH LEARNING DIFFERENCES

The Student Access office offers disability accommodations, coaching groups, free peer tutoring, and workshops. Coaches partner one-on-one with students to create individualized academic success plans and establish accountability for coursework. On average, meetings last 30 minutes and take place weekly. Topics covered may include learning styles, study skills, note-taking strategies, test-taking skills, time management, prioritization, organization, test anxiety, and memory and concentration. Coaches also organize monthly small group workshops and activities. LD specialists are on staff, and free peer tutoring and mentoring services are available. Assistive technology is provided on a case-by-case basis. The library contains a designated testing center and sensory room. Students can notify their teachers of their accommodations through the online portal. The Pathfinders Program offers additional support to students with ASD or social anxiety disorders. The program's residence hall has suites with separate rooms and a shared bathroom, fewer structured social activities, and an especially quiet campus. Students can request to be placed in this residence hall through Student Access; students who wish to live in their own bedroom in another residence hall can make a request to campus housing, but this accommodation cannot be guaranteed. Pathfinders offers individualized support with social events, skill-building groups that cover time management and the transition to campus life, and additional programs like cooking classes.

ADMISSIONS

The general admission requirements are the same for all students. In some cases, first-years may be granted conditional admission, and probational admission for transfers. While interviews are not required, they are always encouraged.

Additional Information

STEM Bootcamp is a summer bridge program for students to develop their math, chemistry, and study skills before starting college. The program is by invitation and meets for eight weeks, beginning with two weeks in August and continuing into the fall semester.

In 1909, John Mabee's 160-acre homestead became an oil field and earned him a fortune. Named Oklahoma's "Mr. Philanthropy," his gifts built two residence halls: the Lottie Jane Hall for women, named after his wife, and the John Mabee ("The John") Hall for men. The John has inspired the annual Toilet Bowl flag football game, where students don Toilet Bowl T-shirts, a Toilet Bowl queen is crowned, and hot dogs and hamburgers are served in front of Lottie Jane.

University of Tulsa

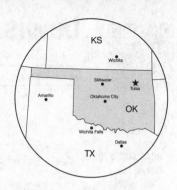

GENERAL ADMISSIONS

Very important factors include: rigor of secondary school record, academic GPA, standardized test scores (if submitted). *Important factors include:* class rank, application essay, recommendations. High school diploma is required and GED is accepted. Institution is test-optional for entering Fall 2024. Check admissions website for updates. *Academic units recommended:* 4 English, 4 math, 3 science (3 labs), 2 foreign language, 3 social studies.

FINANCIAL AID

Students should submit: FAFSA. *Need-based scholarships/grants offered:* College/university scholarship or grant aid from institutional funds; Federal Pell; Private scholarships; SEOG; State scholarships/grants. *Loan aid offered:* Direct PLUS loans; Direct Subsidized Loans; Direct Unsubsidized Loans. Federal Work-Study Program available. Institutional employment available.

CAMPUS LIFE

Activities: Campus Ministries; Choral groups; Concert band; Dance; Drama/theater; International Student Organization; Jazz band; Marching band; Music ensembles; Musical theater; Opera; Pep band; Student government; Student newspaper; Student-run film society; Symphony orchestra; Television station. **Organizations:** 196 registered organizations, 35 honor societies, 19 religious organizations, 7 fraternities, 8 sororities. **Athletics (Intercollegiate):** *Men:* basketball, crew/rowing, cross-country, golf, rugby, table tennis, track/field (indoor), volleyball. *Women:* basketball, crew/rowing, cross-country, golf, rugby, softball, table tennis, track/field (indoor), volleyball.

CAMPUS
Type of school	Private (nonprofit)
Environment	Metropolis

STUDENTS
Undergrad enrollment	2,698
% male/female	49/51
% from out of state	40
% frosh live on campus	81

FINANCIAL FACTS
Annual tuition	$46,932
Room and board	$12,782
Required fees	$1,170

GENERAL ADMISSIONS INFO
Application fee	$60
Regular application deadline	Rolling
Nonfall registration	Yes
Fall 2024 testing policy	Test Optional
Range SAT EBRW	540–680
Range SAT Math	538–670
Range ACT Composite	21–30

ACADEMICS
Student/faculty ratio	10:1
% students returning for sophomore year	85

Oklahoma

REQUESTING SERVICES FOR STUDENTS WITH LEARNING DIFFERENCES

Phone: 918-631-2315 • accessibility.utulsa.edu • Email: studentaccess@utulsa.edu

Documentation submitted to: Student Access
Separate application required for Services: Yes

Documentation required for:
LD: Psychoeducational evaluation
ADHD: Psychoeducational evaluation
ASD: Psychoeducational evaluation

Lewis & Clark College

615 S. Palatine Hill Road, Portland, OR 97219-7899 • Admissions: 503-768-7040 • www.lclark.edu

Support: CS

ACCOMMODATIONS

Allowed in exams:

Calculators	Yes
Dictionary	Yes
Computer	Yes
Spell-checker	Yes
Extended test time	Yes
Scribe	Yes
Proctors	Yes
Oral exams	Yes
Note-takers	Yes

Support services for students with:

LD	Yes
ADHD	Yes
ASD	Yes
Distraction-reduced environment	Yes
Recording of lecture allowed	Yes
Reading technology	Yes
Audio books	Yes
Other assistive technology	Yes
Priority registration	No

Added costs of services:

For LD	No
For ADHD	No
For ASD	No
LD specialists	Yes
ADHD & ASD coaching	Yes
ASD specialists	No
Professional tutors	No
Peer tutors	Yes
Max. hours/week for services	10
How professors are notified of student approved accommodations	Office of Student Accessibility

COLLEGE GRADUATION REQUIREMENTS

Course waivers allowed	No
Course substitutions allowed	Yes

In what courses: Foreign Language and Physical Education (P.E.)

PROGRAMS/SERVICES FOR STUDENTS WITH LEARNING DIFFERENCES

The Office of Student Accessibility (OSA) provides support to students with learning and intellectual differences. Students connect with OSA to obtain accommodations, education, and consultations. Resources that are generally offered include note-taking services and testing center access. The OSA team is responsible for approving all accommodations. To apply for services, students meet with a staff member, provide documentation, and discuss accommodations with faculty and staff. Student Support Services will facilitate the execution of accommodations by acting as the liaison with staff/faculty, if necessary.

ADMISSIONS

All applicants are expected to meet the same admission criteria. Successful students at Lewis & Clark have taken rigorous college preparatory curriculums and maintain at least a B average.

Additional Information

The Student Academic Affairs Board (SAAB) is a free peer-to-peer tutoring program that helps students with studying for tests, completing homework, reviewing notes, or practicing speaking skills. Students are eligible to receive two hours of tutoring per course each week. The Writing Center assists students with such things as writing a strong thesis statement, developing a clear and logical structure, finding support for an argument, proofreading skills, and proper citation. The Student Support Network has representatives from many departments who work with students who are at risk.

The L & C Festival of Scholars and Artists is a beloved annual tradition. It's a full day of celebrating and showcasing students and their academic, intellectual, scientific, scholarly, and artistic accomplishments. The community comes together for performances of original compositions, exhibitions of original art, theater and music performances, and research presentations, including international affairs, political science, religious studies, environmental studies, chemistry, mathematics, computer science, and more.

Lewis & Clark College

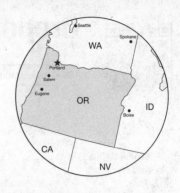

GENERAL ADMISSIONS

Very important factors include: rigor of secondary school record, academic GPA. *Important factors include:* application essay, recommendations. *Other factors considered include:* class rank, standardized test scores (if submitted). High school diploma is required and GED is accepted. Institution is test-optional for entering Fall 2024. Check admissions website for updates. *Academic units recommended:* 4 English, 4 math, 3 science (2 labs), 2 foreign language, 3 social studies, 1 visual/performing arts.

FINANCIAL AID

Students should submit: FAFSA. *Need-based scholarships/grants offered:* College/university scholarship or grant aid from institutional funds; Federal Pell; Private scholarships; SEOG; State scholarships/grants. *Loan aid offered:* Direct PLUS loans; Direct Subsidized Loans; Direct Unsubsidized Loans. Federal Work-Study Program available. Institutional employment available.

CAMPUS LIFE

Activities: Campus Ministries; Choral groups; Concert band; Dance; Drama/theater; International Student Organization; Jazz band; Literary magazine; Music ensembles; Musical theater; Radio station; Student government; Student newspaper; Symphony orchestra. **Organizations:** 130 registered organizations, 2 honor societies, 5 religious organizations, 0 fraternities, 0 sororities. **Athletics (Intercollegiate):** *Men:* baseball, basketball, crew/rowing, cross-country, golf, rugby, swimming, ultimate frisbee. *Women:* basketball, crew/rowing, cross-country, golf, lacrosse, rugby, softball, swimming, ultimate frisbee, volleyball.

CAMPUS

Type of school	Private (nonprofit)
Environment	Metropolis

STUDENTS

Undergrad enrollment	2,187
% male/female	35/65
% from out of state	86
% frosh live on campus	97

FINANCIAL FACTS

Annual tuition	$59,250
Room and board	$14,384
Required fees	$434

GENERAL ADMISSIONS INFO

Application fee	No fee
Regular application deadline	1/15
Nonfall registration	Yes

Fall 2024 testing policy	Test Optional
Range SAT EBRW	650–720
Range SAT Math	610–680
Range ACT Composite	29–32

ACADEMICS

Student/faculty ratio	13:1
% students returning for sophomore year	86

Most classes have 10–19 students.

REQUESTING SERVICES FOR STUDENTS WITH LEARNING DIFFERENCES

Phone: 503-768-7192 • www.lclark.edu/offices/student-accessibility/ • Email: access@lclark.edu

Documentation submitted to: Office of Student Accessibility
Separate application required for Services: Yes

Documentation required for:
LD: Psychoeducational evaluation
ADHD: Psychoeducational evaluation
ASD: Psychoeducational evaluation

Oregon

Oregon State University

104 Kerr Administration Building, Corvallis, OR 97331 • Admissions: 541-737-4411 • oregonstate.edu

Support: CS

ACCOMMODATIONS

Allowed in exams:

Calculators	Yes
Dictionary	No
Computer	Yes
Spell-checker	Yes
Extended test time	Yes
Scribe	Yes
Proctors	Yes
Oral exams	Yes
Note-takers	Yes

Support services for students with:

LD	Yes
ADHD	Yes
ASD	Yes
Distraction-reduced environment	Yes
Recording of lecture allowed	Yes
Reading technology	Yes
Audio books	Yes
Other assistive technology	Yes
Priority registration	Yes

Added costs of services:

For LD	No
For ADHD	No
For ASD	No
LD specialists	Yes
ADHD & ASD coaching	Yes
ASD specialists	No
Professional tutors	No
Peer tutors	Yes
Max. hours/week for services	Varies
How professors are notified of student approved accommodations	Disability Access Services

COLLEGE GRADUATION REQUIREMENTS

Course waivers allowed	No
Course substitutions allowed	Yes

In what courses: Math and Foreign Language. Substitutions for core requirements only, not major requirements.

PROGRAMS/SERVICES FOR STUDENTS WITH LEARNING DIFFERENCES

Disability Access Services (DAS) assists students with disabilities through accommodations, education, consultation, and advocacy. Accommodations are determined on a case-by-case basis, depending on the student's documentation, and DAS recommends that students meet with their academic advisor every term to discuss accommodations. DAS will notify professors each term about the student's accommodation needs. Coaching sessions are available in the Academic Success Center to students registered with DAS. Coaching provides students with individualized strategies based on the student's needs. Individual sessions focus on strategies, resources, and techniques, and common topics include time management, study skills, managing course load, and navigating the college environment as a student with a disability. There's no set number of coaching sessions, as they're based on student needs. Counseling and Psychological Services (CAPS) provides individual services that help students with ADHD develop effective habits to overcome poor focus, distractibility, disorganization, and difficulty completing tasks. They can also help with issues of poor self-esteem, lack of self-confidence, anxiety and/or depression.

ADMISSIONS

Oregon State admission requirements are the same for all students. Considerations include but are not limited to academic achievement, creativity, initiative, motivation, leadership, persistence, recognition, unusual talent or ability, substantial experience with other cultures, and the ability to overcome significant challenges. Applicants must have at least a C– GPA in all of the required courses.

Additional Information

At the Academic Success Center, students can receive tutoring, coaching, writing support, and help developing study strategies.

There are 76 colleges today that commemorate Abraham Lincoln's land grant proposal as an investment in the country's future after the Civil War. OSU, formed in 1868, was one of the original and most distant land grant universities in the United States and the first commitment to further the cultural and educational goals of the state of Oregon. OSU is backed by a land, sea, and sun grant from the U.S. government, allowing training and research in forestry, ocean science, and agricultural science.

Oregon State University

General Admissions

Very important factors include: academic GPA. *Important factors include:* rigor of secondary school record, application essay. *Other factors considered include:* class rank, standardized test scores (if submitted), recommendations. High school diploma is required and GED is accepted. Institution is test-optional for entering Fall 2024. Check admissions website for updates. *Academic units required:* 4 English, 3 math, 3 science (2 labs), 2 foreign language, 3 social studies. *Academic units recommended:* 3 science labs.

Financial Aid

Students should submit: FAFSA. *Need-based scholarships/grants offered:* College/university scholarship or grant aid from institutional funds; Federal Pell; Private scholarships; SEOG; State scholarships/grants. *Loan aid offered:* Direct PLUS loans; Direct Subsidized Loans; Direct Unsubsidized Loans. Federal Work-Study Program available. Institutional employment available.

Campus Life

Activities: Campus Ministries; Choral groups; Concert band; Dance; Drama/theater; International Student Organization; Jazz band; Literary magazine; Marching band; Model UN; Music ensembles; Musical theater; Opera; Pep band; Radio station; Student government; Student newspaper; Student-run film society; Symphony orchestra; Television station; Yearbook. **Organizations:** 400 registered organizations, 12 honor societies, 28 religious organizations, 27 fraternities, 22 sororities. **Athletics (Intercollegiate):** *Men:* baseball, basketball, crew/rowing, cycling, equestrian sports, golf, gymnastics, lacrosse, racquetball, rugby, skiing (nordic/cross-country), table tennis, ultimate frisbee, volleyball, water polo, wrestling. *Women:* basketball, crew/rowing, cross-country, cycling, equestrian sports, golf, gymnastics, lacrosse, racquetball, rugby, skiing (nordic/cross-country), softball, swimming, table tennis, ultimate frisbee, volleyball, water polo.

CAMPUS

Type of school	Public
Environment	Town

STUDENTS

Undergrad enrollment	27,564
% male/female	52/48
% from out of state	35
% frosh live on campus	91

FINANCIAL FACTS

Annual in-state tuition	$13,191
Annual out-of-state tuition	$34,983
Room and board	$14,238

GENERAL ADMISSIONS INFO

Application fee	$65
Regular application deadline	9/1
Nonfall registration	Yes

Fall 2024 testing policy	Test Optional
Range SAT EBRW	560–680
Range SAT Math	560–690
Range ACT Composite	21–28

ACADEMICS

Student/faculty ratio	18:1
% students returning for sophomore year	87

Most classes have 20–29 students.

REQUESTING SERVICES FOR STUDENTS WITH LEARNING DIFFERENCES

Phone: 541-737-4098 • ds.oregonstate.edu • Email: disability.services@oregonstate.edu

Documentation submitted to: Disability Access Services
Separate application required for Services: Yes

Documentation required for:
LD: Psychoeducational evaluation
ADHD: Psychoeducational evaluation
ASD: Psychoeducational evaluation

Oregon

University of Oregon

1217 University of Oregon, Eugene, OR 97403-1217 • Admissions: 541-346-3201 • www.uoregon.edu

Support: CS

ACCOMMODATIONS

Allowed in exams:

Calculators	Yes
Dictionary	No
Computer	Yes
Spell-checker	Yes
Extended test time	Yes
Scribe	Yes
Proctors	Yes
Oral exams	Yes
Note-takers	Yes

Support services for students with:

LD	Yes
ADHD	Yes
ASD	Yes
Distraction-reduced environment	Yes
Recording of lecture allowed	Yes
Reading technology	Yes
Audio books	Yes
Other assistive technology	Yes
Priority registration	Yes

Added costs of services:

For LD	No
For ADHD	No
For ASD	No
LD specialists	Yes
ADHD & ASD coaching	No
ASD specialists	Yes
Professional tutors	No
Peer tutors	Yes
Max. hours/week for services	Varies
How professors are notified of student approved accommodations	Student and Accessible Education Center

COLLEGE GRADUATION REQUIREMENTS

Course waivers allowed	No
Course substitutions allowed	Yes

In what courses: Math, Foreign Language, and others on a case-by-case basis

PROGRAMS/SERVICES FOR STUDENTS WITH LEARNING DIFFERENCES

The University of Oregon serves students with documented learning differences through the Accessible Education Center (AEC). Accommodations are determined on a case-by-case basis. Prospective students may meet with AEC staff to learn more about how their needs can be met once they enroll. Once admitted, students meet with an AEC advisor to review documentation of their disability, discuss educational goals, and work together to develop an accommodation plan. Students are provided with a faculty notification letter outlining the suggested accommodations and may be shared at the student's discretion. Services provided include academic and testing accommodations, adaptive technology, note-taking, and executive functioning support. Two psychoeducational groups are available for students; one for students living with ADHD to develop skills and strategies, and one for students diagnosed with ASD and related diagnoses to socialize in a safe and welcoming environment and discuss social connectedness.

ADMISSIONS

All students must meet the same admission criteria. In exceptional cases, however, students who do not meet the admission requirements due to a documented disability may request additional consideration of their application by the Disability Review Committee. Requirements for this special consideration include a completed application form, a graded writing sample, two letters of recommendation, and documentation of the disability with information about how it has influenced the student's ability to meet the minimum admission requirements. Students with a GPA below 3.0 are not typically admitted, but these students can be reviewed for admission.

Additional Information

Students may participate in the Student Voices Panel, a group committed to educating the community on disabilities and inclusivity.

Previously a UO dairy cattle pasture, Hayward Field was constructed in 1919 as a football stadium. In 1970, it was designated for track and field only, and the first all-weather urethane surface was laid. It has become one of the most famous track and field-only facilities in the world, hosting numerous U.S.A Championships, NCAA Championships, Pac-12 Championships, U.S. Olympic trials, and Olympic team trials. Hayward Field is named for track and field coach Bill Hayward, who was hired in 1904 and saw numerous athletes break world records and make Olympic teams during his 44-year tenure.

University of Oregon

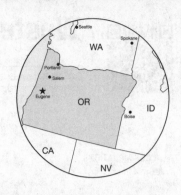

GENERAL ADMISSIONS

Very important factors include: rigor of secondary school record, academic GPA. *Important factors include:* application essay. *Other factors considered include:* class rank, standardized test scores (if submitted), recommendations. High school diploma is required and GED is accepted. Institution is test-optional for entering Fall 2024. Check admissions website for updates. *Academic units required:* 4 English, 3 math, 3 science, 2 foreign language, 3 social studies.

FINANCIAL AID

Students should submit: FAFSA. *Need-based scholarships/grants offered:* College/university scholarship or grant aid from institutional funds; Federal Pell; Private scholarships; SEOG; State scholarships/grants. *Loan aid offered:* Direct PLUS loans; Direct Subsidized Loans; Direct Unsubsidized Loans. Federal Work-Study Program available. Institutional employment available.

CAMPUS LIFE

Activities: Campus Ministries; Choral groups; Concert band; Dance; Drama/theater; International Student Organization; Jazz band; Literary magazine; Marching band; Music ensembles; Musical theater; Opera; Pep band; Radio station; Student government; Student newspaper; Student-run film society; Symphony orchestra; Television station. **Organizations:** 250 registered organizations, 21 honor societies, 18 fraternities, 15 sororities. **Athletics (Intercollegiate):** *Men:* baseball, basketball, crew/rowing, cross-country, cycling, equestrian sports, golf, ice hockey, lacrosse, martial arts, rugby, swimming, table tennis, track/field (indoor), ultimate frisbee, volleyball, water polo, wrestling. *Women:* basketball, crew/rowing, cross-country, cycling, equestrian sports, golf, ice hockey, lacrosse, martial arts, rugby, softball, swimming, table tennis, track/field (indoor), ultimate frisbee, volleyball, water polo.

CAMPUS

Type of school	Public
Environment	City

STUDENTS

Undergrad enrollment	19,376
% male/female	44/56
% from out of state	49
% frosh live on campus	93

FINANCIAL FACTS

Annual in-state tuition	$11,674
Annual out-of-state tuition	$37,363
Room and board	$14,640
Required fees	$2,438

GENERAL ADMISSIONS INFO

Application fee	$65
Regular application deadline	1/15
Nonfall registration	Yes
Fall 2024 testing policy	Test Optional
Range SAT EBRW	580–690
Range SAT Math	560–680
Range ACT Composite	24–30

ACADEMICS

Student/faculty ratio	19:1
% students returning for sophomore year	86

Most classes have 20–29 students.

REQUESTING SERVICES FOR STUDENTS WITH LEARNING DIFFERENCES

Phone: 541-346-1155 • aec.uoregon.edu/ • Email: uoaec@uoregon.edu

Documentation submitted to: Accessible Education Center
Separate application required for Services: Yes

Documentation required for:
LD: Psychoeducational evaluation
ADHD: Psychoeducational evaluation
ASD: Psychoeducational evaluation

Western Oregon University

345 N. Monmouth Avenue, Monmouth, OR 97361 • Admissions: 503-838-8211 • www.wou.edu

Support: CS

ACCOMMODATIONS

Allowed in exams:	
Calculators	Yes
Dictionary	Yes
Computer	Yes
Spell-checker	Yes
Extended test time	Yes
Scribe	Yes
Proctors	Yes
Oral exams	Yes
Note-takers	Yes
Support services for students with:	
LD	Yes
ADHD	Yes
ASD	Yes
Distraction-reduced environment	Yes
Recording of lecture allowed	Yes
Reading technology	Yes
Audio books	Yes
Other assistive technology	Yes
Priority registration	Yes
Added costs of services:	
For LD	No
For ADHD	No
For ASD	No
LD specialists	Yes
ADHD & ASD coaching	No
ASD specialists	No
Professional tutors	No
Peer tutors	Yes
Max. hours/week for services	Varies
How professors are notified of student approved accommodations	Student and Office of Disability Services

COLLEGE GRADUATION REQUIREMENTS

Course waivers allowed	No
Course substitutions allowed	Yes
In what courses: Case-by-case basis	

PROGRAMS/SERVICES FOR STUDENTS WITH LEARNING DIFFERENCES

The Office of Disability Services (ODS) provides reasonable accommodations and support services to meet the needs of students with disabilities. ODS notifies faculty of student accommodations and provides free peer-to-peer tutoring. Usually, testing accommodations are offered in the ODS Testing Center. The Student Enrichment Program (SEP) supports students with documented disabilities, as well as low-income and first-generation students. The program helps students develop communication skills and maintain a sense of self-worth. SEP provides students basic math courses, individualized instruction in reading, study skills, writing, and critical thinking, and workshops on research writing, speed reading, note-taking, and time management. Academic advising and assistance working with various departments on campus are available through SEP.

ADMISSIONS

Students with a cumulative GPA below 2.74 are encouraged, but not required, to provide ACT or SAT scores. If students are short on requirements in the core subject areas, they may be asked to submit additional items, such as a personal statement or letter of recommendation explaining the reason they have fallen short of fulfilling these requirements.

Additional Information

Skills classes are offered in academic survival strategies (no credit) and critical thinking (college credit). The university offers an expanded Summer Bridge program called Destination Western. While there is no programming specific only to students with disabilities, Destination Western gives priority admission to students with disabilities and those from other underserved communities.

Todd Hall was built in 1912 and named in honor of Jessica Todd, the first Dean of Women. She expected girls to be "worthy representatives of teaching" and was well known for her discipline (even after her retirement in 1931), traditions like family Sunday dinner, and helping girls with their social, familial, or financial hardships. Jessica Todd passed away in 1944, but there are rumors (and sometimes signs) of her spirit continuing to watch over students.

Western Oregon University

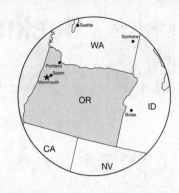

GENERAL ADMISSIONS

Very important factors include: rigor of secondary school record, class rank, academic GPA. *Important factors include:* recommendations. *Other factors considered include:* standardized test scores (if submitted), application essay. High school diploma is required and GED is accepted. Institution is test-optional for entering Fall 2024. Check admissions website for updates. *Academic units required:* 4 English, 3 math, 3 science, 2 foreign language, 3 social studies.

FINANCIAL AID

Students should submit: FAFSA. *Need-based scholarships/grants offered:* College/university scholarship or grant aid from institutional funds; Federal Pell; Private scholarships; SEOG; State scholarships/grants; United Negro College Fund. *Loan aid offered:* Direct PLUS loans; Direct Subsidized Loans; Direct Unsubsidized Loans. Federal Work-Study Program available.

CAMPUS LIFE

Activities: Campus Ministries; Choral groups; Concert band; Dance; Drama/theater; International Student Organization; Jazz band; Literary magazine; Marching band; Model UN; Music ensembles; Musical theater; Pep band; Radio station; Student government; Student newspaper. **Organizations:** 50 registered organizations, 4 honor societies, 6 religious organizations, 0 fraternities, 0 sororities. **Athletics (Intercollegiate):** *Men:* baseball, basketball, crew/rowing, cross-country, martial arts, rugby, water polo. *Women:* basketball, crew/rowing, cross-country, martial arts, rugby, softball, volleyball, water polo.

CAMPUS

Type of school	Public
Environment	Village

STUDENTS

Undergrad enrollment	3,615
% male/female	33/67
% from out of state	18
% frosh live on campus	81

FINANCIAL FACTS

Annual in-state tuition	$9,000
Annual out-of-state tuition	$28,710
Room and board	$11,601
Required fees	$2,028

GENERAL ADMISSIONS INFO

Application fee	$60
Regular application deadline	Rolling
Nonfall registration	Yes
Fall 2024 testing policy	Test Optional
Range SAT EBRW	475–595
Range SAT Math	435–575
Range ACT Composite	20–26

ACADEMICS

Student/faculty ratio	12:1
% students returning for sophomore year	65

REQUESTING SERVICES FOR STUDENTS WITH LEARNING DIFFERENCES

Phone: 503-838-8250 • wou.edu/disabilityservices/ • Email: ods@wou.edu

Documentation submitted to: Office of Disability Services
Separate application required for Services: Yes

Documentation required for:
LD: Psychoeducational evaluation
ADHD: Psychoeducational evaluation
ASD: Psychoeducational evaluation

Oregon

Bucknell University

Office of Admissions, 1 Dent Drive, Lewisburg, PA 17837 • Admissions: 570-577-3000 • www.bucknell.edu

Support: CS

ACCOMMODATIONS

Allowed in exams:

Calculators	Yes
Dictionary	No
Computer	Yes
Spell-checker	Yes
Extended test time	Yes
Scribe	Yes
Proctors	Yes
Oral exams	Yes
Note-takers	Yes

Support services for students with:

LD	Yes
ADHD	Yes
ASD	Yes
Distraction-reduced environment	Yes
Recording of lecture allowed	Yes
Reading technology	Yes
Audio books	Yes
Other assistive technology	Yes
Priority registration	No

Added costs of services:

For LD	No
For ADHD	No
For ASD	No
LD specialists	Yes
ADHD & ASD coaching	Yes
ASD specialists	Yes
Professional tutors	Yes
Peer tutors	Yes
Max. hours/week for services	Varies
How professors are notified of student approved accommodations	Student and Office of Accessibility Resources

COLLEGE GRADUATION REQUIREMENTS

Course waivers allowed	No
Course substitutions allowed	Yes
In what courses: Foreign Language	

PROGRAMS/SERVICES FOR STUDENTS WITH LEARNING DIFFERENCES

The Office of Accessibility Resources (OAR) provides support, accommodations, and academic adjustments to all eligible students with documented disabilities. Once students submit a disability request form along with documentation, they meet with the OAR director. In the meeting, students will discuss their needs and OAR will determine reasonable accommodations and communicate the procedures necessary for implementation. Accommodations may include an alternative format for printed materials, note-taking, class accessibility, testing accommodations, and resources on and off campus.

ADMISSIONS

Bucknell expects all applicants to be graduates of high school or provide evidence of a GED equivalent. All degree programs require a minimum 2 years of the same foreign language (ASL is accepted) and at least 2.5 years of college-preparatory math. Students must apply to one of three colleges: College of Arts & Sciences, College of Engineering, or the Freeman College of Management. Math and science applicants must have completed 3 years of college-prep math. Engineering applicants are required to have completed 1 year of chemistry or physics, 1 year of pre-calculus, and 3 years of college-prep math. Bucknell requires a personal essay and one teacher evaluation; a second evaluation is optional. All applicants will be considered for Bucknell's merit scholarships.

Additional Information

All students, regardless of major, must complete three writing-intensive courses to develop their written language and communication skills. Writing Center consultants work one-on-one with students on writing assignments, from planning and drafting to feedback on oral presentations and class projects. At the Teaching & Learning Center, students can find study groups, peer tutoring, individual help with learning strategies, and academic skills workshops. The Counseling & Student Development Center offers a wide range of confidential services and programs to help students grow in self-understanding, use their intellectual and emotional resources as effectively as possible, and provides a supportive safe space.

First Night is a tradition at Bucknell. It's a celebration for members of the first-year class to mark the successful completion of their first semester. The students select class colors, create a motto, and design a class crest. Each residence hall floor produces two pages of pictures, drawings, and quotes to reflect their lives as first-year students. The class presents the crest, adds hall pages to the class book, and sings the alma mater at the university president's home.

Bucknell University

GENERAL ADMISSIONS

Very important factors include: rigor of secondary school record, academic GPA, application essay. *Important factors include:* standardized test scores (if submitted), recommendations. *Other factors considered include:* class rank. High school diploma is required and GED is accepted. Institution is test-optional for entering Fall 2024. Check admissions website for updates. *Academic units required:* 4 English, 3 math, 2 science, 2 foreign language, 2 social studies, 1 academic elective. *Academic units recommended:* 4 English, 4 math, 4 science (2 labs), 4 foreign language, 4 social studies, 1 academic elective.

FINANCIAL AID

Students should submit: CSS/Financial Aid Profile; FAFSA. *Need-based scholarships/grants offered:* College/university scholarship or grant aid from institutional funds; Federal Pell; Private scholarships; SEOG; State scholarships/grants. *Loan aid offered:* Direct PLUS loans; Direct Subsidized Loans; Direct Unsubsidized Loans. Federal Work-Study Program available. Institutional employment available.

CAMPUS LIFE

Activities: Campus Ministries; Choral groups; Concert band; Dance; Drama/theater; International Student Organization; Jazz band; Literary magazine; Model UN; Music ensembles; Musical theater; Opera; Pep band; Radio station; Student government; Student newspaper; Student-run film society; Symphony orchestra; Yearbook. **Organizations:** 152 registered organizations, 22 honor societies, 9 religious organizations, 7 fraternities, 9 sororities. **Athletics (Intercollegiate):** *Men:* baseball, basketball, crew/rowing, cross-country, cycling, golf, ice hockey, lacrosse, rugby, swimming, track/field (indoor), ultimate frisbee, volleyball, water polo, wrestling. *Women:* basketball, crew/rowing, cross-country, equestrian sports, field hockey, golf, lacrosse, softball, swimming, track/field (indoor), ultimate frisbee, volleyball, water polo.

CAMPUS

Type of school	Private (nonprofit)
Environment	Village

STUDENTS

Undergrad enrollment	3,732
% male/female	48/52
% from out of state	76
% frosh live on campus	100

FINANCIAL FACTS

Annual tuition	$64,418
Room and board	$16,118
Required fees	$354

GENERAL ADMISSIONS INFO

Application fee	$50
Regular application deadline	1/15
Nonfall registration	No

Fall 2024 testing policy	Test Optional
Range SAT EBRW	590–690
Range SAT Math	580–710
Range ACT Composite	27–32

ACADEMICS

Student/faculty ratio	9:1
% students returning for sophomore year	91

Most classes have 10–19 students.

REQUESTING SERVICES FOR STUDENTS WITH LEARNING DIFFERENCES

Phone: 570-577-1188 • www.bucknell.edu/life-bucknell/diversity-equity-inclusion/accessibility-resources
Email: oar@bucknell.edu

Documentation submitted to: Office of Accessibility Resources
Separate application required for Services: Yes

Documentation required for:
  LD: Psychoeducational evaluation
  ADHD: Psychoeducational evaluation
  ASD: Psychoeducational evaluation

Chatham University

Admissions Offices, Pittsburgh, PA 15232 • Admissions: 412-365-1825 • www.chatham.edu

Support: CS

ACCOMMODATIONS

Allowed in exams:	
Calculators	Yes
Dictionary	Yes
Computer	Yes
Spell-checker	Yes
Extended test time	Yes
Scribe	Yes
Proctors	Yes
Oral exams	Yes
Note-takers	Yes
Support services for students with:	
LD	Yes
ADHD	Yes
ASD	Yes
Distraction-reduced environment	Yes
Recording of lecture allowed	Yes
Reading technology	Yes
Audio books	Yes
Other assistive technology	Yes
Priority registration	No
Added costs of services:	
For LD	No
For ADHD	No
For ASD	No
LD specialists	No
ADHD & ASD coaching	Yes
ASD specialists	No
Professional tutors	Yes
Peer tutors	Yes
Max. hours/week for services	2
How professors are notified of student approved accommodations	Student and Office of Academic and Accessibility Resources

COLLEGE GRADUATION REQUIREMENTS

Course waivers allowed	No
Course substitutions allowed	Yes
In what courses: Physical Education	

PROGRAMS/SERVICES FOR STUDENTS WITH LEARNING DIFFERENCES

The Office of Academic and Accessibility Resources (OAAR) supports all students and accommodates students with learning differences on a case-by-case basis. OAAR reviews each student's submitted documentation, and after meeting with the director, the student reviews and confirms the recommended accommodations. OAAR sends official accommodation letters to the professors, and encourages students to follow up with faculty to discuss implementation. Academic accommodations for students with disabilities may include, but are not limited to, alternate-format texts, distraction-limited testing settings, extended time for testing, note-taking services, and screen-reading software. While Chatham does not offer a specialized curriculum, OAAR collaborates with faculty, staff, and students to provide reasonable accommodations in a way that does not substantially alter course content. OAAR approaches disability support services using a student-centered academic support model that provides peer-to-peer assistance across disciplines. Additional OAAR services available for students with disabilities include academic skills coaching, procrastination management, self-advocacy development, study strategies analysis, time management planning, tutoring, and Supplemental Instruction.

ADMISSIONS

The Office of Admission carefully considers each application on the holistic level to determine whether a student will be successful at Chatham. Counselor or teacher recommendations are not required but are welcome for submission. Students are not required, but encouraged, to submit a personal essay. While Chatham is test-optional, students who choose not to submit test scores are advised to submit a letter of recommendation and a strong essay.

Additional Information

The writing center on campus is staffed by both peer and professional writing tutors.

In 2019, Chatham's Occupational Therapy department received an internal grant to create a therapeutic sensory garden on the Eden Hall Campus. The garden is a natural sensory environment that engages sight, sound, touch, taste, smell, and movement. Proven to help veterans overcome PTSD and aid special needs students, the sensory garden is a pilot endeavor to explore the potential for improving the quality of life for students.

Chatham University

GENERAL ADMISSIONS

Very important factors include: rigor of secondary school record. *Important factors include:* academic GPA, application essay. *Other factors considered include:* class rank, standardized test scores (if submitted), recommendations. High school diploma is required and GED is accepted. Institution is test-optional for entering Fall 2024. Check admissions website for updates. *Academic units required:* 4 English, 2 math, 2 science, 2 social studies. *Academic units recommended:* 3 math, 3 science, 2 foreign language, 3 social studies.

FINANCIAL AID

Students should submit: FAFSA. *Need-based scholarships/grants offered:* College/university scholarship or grant aid from institutional funds; Federal Pell; SEOG; State scholarships/grants. *Loan aid offered:* Direct PLUS loans; Direct Subsidized Loans; Direct Unsubsidized Loans. Federal Work-Study Program available. Institutional employment available.

CAMPUS LIFE

Activities: Campus Ministries; Choral groups; Drama/theater; International Student Organization; Literary magazine; Student government; Student newspaper. **Organizations:** 42 registered organizations, 6 honor societies, 3 religious organizations, 0 fraternities, 0 sororities. **Athletics (Intercollegiate):** *Men:* baseball, basketball, cross-country, cycling, golf, ice hockey, lacrosse, swimming, track/field (indoor), volleyball. *Women:* basketball, cross-country, cycling, golf, ice hockey, lacrosse, softball, swimming, track/field (indoor), volleyball.

CAMPUS

Type of school	Private (nonprofit)
Environment	Metropolis

STUDENTS

Undergrad enrollment	1,206
% male/female	30/70
% from out of state	27
% frosh live on campus	87

FINANCIAL FACTS

Annual tuition	$42,250
Room and board	$14,327
Required fees	$1,560

GENERAL ADMISSIONS INFO

Application fee	$35
Regular application deadline	8/1
Nonfall registration	Yes

Fall 2024 testing policy	Test Optional
Range SAT EBRW	550–650
Range SAT Math	510–620
Range ACT Composite	21–29

ACADEMICS

Student/faculty ratio	10:1
% students returning for sophomore year	80

Most classes have 10–19 students.

REQUESTING SERVICES FOR STUDENTS WITH LEARNING DIFFERENCES

Phone: 412-365-1523 • www.chatham.edu/academics/support-and-services/office-of-academic-accessibility-resources • Email: oaar@chatham.edu

Documentation submitted to: Office of Academic and Accessibility Resources (OAAR)
Separate application required for Services: Yes

Documentation required for:
 LD: Psychoeducational evaluation
 ADHD: Psychoeducational evaluation
 ASD: Psychoeducational evaluation

Drexel University

3141 Chestnut Street, Philadelphia, PA 19104 • Admissions: 215-895-2400 • www.drexel.edu

(Support: SP)

ACCOMMODATIONS

Allowed in exams:

Calculators	Yes
Dictionary	No
Computer	Yes
Spell-checker	Yes
Extended test time	Yes
Scribe	Yes
Proctors	Yes
Oral exams	Yes
Note-takers	Yes

Support services for students with:

LD	Yes
ADHD	Yes
ASD	Yes
Distraction-reduced environment	Yes
Recording of lecture allowed	Yes
Reading technology	Yes
Audio books	Yes
Other assistive technology	Yes
Priority registration	Yes

Added costs of services:

For LD	No
For ADHD	No
For ASD	No
LD specialists	Yes
ADHD & ASD coaching	Yes
ASD specialists	Yes
Professional tutors	Yes
Peer tutors	Yes
Max. hours/week for services	Varies
How professors are notified of student approved accommodations	Student

COLLEGE GRADUATION REQUIREMENTS

Course waivers allowed	No
Course substitutions allowed	No

PROGRAMS/SERVICES FOR STUDENTS WITH LEARNING DIFFERENCES

Drexel University serves students with learning disabilities through the Office of Disability Resources (ODR). Incoming students can contact ODR prior to their campus arrival to register for an individualized transition program offered to students with disabilities. Accommodations for students with learning disabilities include electronic books, a distraction-free testing environment, breaks during testing, extended time on tests, note-taking, and access to overhead slides and PowerPoint presentations before the beginning of class. ODR offers workshops, such as Disability Services 101, Effectively Communicating With and About People Who Have Disabilities, and Incorporating Universal Design Into All You Do. The Drexel Autism Support Program (DASP) for neurodivergent students promotes academic and social competency, interpersonal skills, independent living, self-advocacy, and social integration. It encourages participants to take advantage of university life and develop academic and social skills to achieve success in their careers and communities. Services include one-on-one peer mentoring and coaching, a 1.5 credit neurodiversity course, workshops, planned social events, and collaborations with other campus departments. The Neurodragons student organization offers social and extracurricular opportunities held in judgement-free environments. Neurodragons consist of neurodivergent and neurotypical students committed to raising awareness of the value of neurodiversity within the Drexel learning community and beyond.

ADMISSIONS

The regular admission requirements are the same for all students. The average GPA for accepted applicants is 3.4. Interviews are recommended.

Additional Information

The Dragon Scholars Program (DSP) is a summer bridge program that helps first-year students transition to college. With the help of mentors and coaches, students can acclimate to the quieter campus and classroom, adjust to residential living, experience Philadelphia, and gain college credit and insight into Drexel's resources.

In 1958, Drexel opened its computing center with an IBM 650. At the dedication, faculty and students were invited to watch a demonstration in which a human competed with the computer. In 1983, Drexel made national headlines by requiring all students and faculty to have personal computers. Then-president, William Hagerty, thought computers would be a passing fad, but figured the move would make for great publicity; enrollment at Drexel spiked.

Drexel University

GENERAL ADMISSIONS

Very important factors include: rigor of secondary school record, class rank, academic GPA, standardized test scores (if submitted). *Important factors include:* application essay, recommendations. High school diploma is required and GED is accepted. Institution is test-optional for entering Fall 2024. Check admissions website for updates. *Academic units recommended:* 4 English, 3 math, 1 science (1 lab), 1 social studies, 7 academic electives.

FINANCIAL AID

Students should submit: CSS/Financial Aid Profile; FAFSA. *Need-based scholarships/grants offered:* College/university scholarship or grant aid from institutional funds; Federal Pell; Private scholarships; SEOG; State scholarships/grants. *Loan aid offered:* Direct PLUS loans; Direct Subsidized Loans; Direct Unsubsidized Loans. Federal Work-Study Program available. Institutional employment available.

CAMPUS LIFE

Activities: Campus Ministries; Choral groups; Concert band; Dance; Drama/theater; Jazz band; Literary magazine; Model UN; Music ensembles; Musical theater; Pep band; Radio station; Student government; Student newspaper; Student-run film society; Symphony orchestra; Television station; Yearbook. **Organizations:** 367 registered organizations, 9 honor societies, 19 religious organizations, 20 fraternities, 11 sororities. **Athletics (Intercollegiate):** *Men:* baseball, basketball, crew/rowing, cycling, equestrian sports, field hockey, golf, ice hockey, lacrosse, martial arts, rugby, swimming, track/field (indoor), ultimate frisbee, volleyball, water polo, wrestling. *Women:* basketball, crew/rowing, cycling, equestrian sports, field hockey, lacrosse, martial arts, rugby, softball, swimming, track/field (indoor), ultimate frisbee, volleyball.

CAMPUS
Type of school	Private (nonprofit)
Environment	Metropolis

STUDENTS
Undergrad enrollment	13,613
% male/female	51/49
% from out of state	50
% frosh live on campus	82

FINANCIAL FACTS
Annual tuition	$56,595
Room and board	$16,980
Required fees	$2,370

GENERAL ADMISSIONS INFO
Application fee	$50
Regular application deadline	1/15
Nonfall registration	Yes

Fall 2024 testing policy	Test Optional
Range SAT EBRW	610–700
Range SAT Math	620–730
Range ACT Composite	27–32

ACADEMICS
Student/faculty ratio	9:1
% students returning for sophomore year	87

Most classes have 10–19 students.

REQUESTING SERVICES FOR STUDENTS WITH LEARNING DIFFERENCES

Phone: 215-895-1401 • drexel.edu/disability-resources • Email: disability@drexel.edu

Documentation submitted to: Office of Disability Resources

Separate application required for Services: Yes

Documentation required for:
LD: Psychoeducational evaluation
ADHD: Psychoeducational evaluation
ASD: Psychoeducational evaluation

East Stroudsburg University of Pennsylvania

200 Prospect Street East Stroudsburg, PA 18301-2999 • Admissions: 570-422-3542 • esu.edu

Support: CS

ACCOMMODATIONS

Allowed in exams:

Calculators	Yes
Dictionary	Yes
Computer	Yes
Spell-checker	Yes
Extended test time	Yes
Scribe	Yes
Proctors	Yes
Oral exams	No
Note-takers	Yes

Support services for students with:

LD	Yes
ADHD	Yes
ASD	Yes
Distraction-reduced environment	Yes
Recording of lecture allowed	Yes
Reading technology	Yes
Audio books	Yes
Other assistive technology	Yes
Priority registration	Yes

Added costs of services:

For LD	No
For ADHD	No
For ASD	No
LD specialists	Yes
ADHD & ASD coaching	Yes
ASD specialists	No
Professional tutors	Yes
Peer tutors	Yes
Max. hours/week for services	2
How professors are notified of student approved accommodations	Student

COLLEGE GRADUATION REQUIREMENTS

Course waivers allowed	No
Course substitutions allowed	No

PROGRAMS/SERVICES FOR STUDENTS WITH LEARNING DIFFERENCES

The Office of Accessible Services Individualized for Students (OASIS) determines services and accommodation for students with documented disabilities on a case-by-case basis. OASIS helps coordinate academics and housing accommodations and connects students to on- and off-campus resources. Accommodations include assistive technology, alternate-format materials, and note-taking. Note-taking support includes recorded lectures, professors' notes, peer notes, and the use of smart pens. Students with learning disabilities may work with a specialist individually or in groups. ESU is the home of the Alpha Chapter of Delta Alpha Pi International Honor Society, an organization for students with disabilities who have achieved academic success. ESU hosts the Career, Independent Living, and Learning Studies (CILLS) program—a nondegree certificate program designed to help young adults with intellectual and other developmental disabilities lead productive lives.

ADMISSIONS

Academic achievement is the primary factor considered in the selection process. ESU is interested in students' contributions to their schools and communities, activities, achievements, aspirations, and any other indicators that demonstrate potential success. Students with learning disabilities should fill out the general application and are encouraged to complete the Disabilities Information section. Students should then forward documentation of their disability to OASIS. ESU is test-optional, however, SAT/ACT scores are required for consideration to receive academic and merit-based scholarships.

Additional Information

All students enrolled in the university can take skills classes in reading, composition, and math. Other services offered include workshops in time management and test taking strategies. The Learning Center provides free individual and group peer tutoring to all ESC students. Tutors are assigned on a first-come, first-served basis, and students must complete and submit a request form to receive tutoring.

Founded in 1893, ESU hit notable milestones by 1897: students published their first newspaper, *The Conglomerate*, a pay phone was installed on campus, and 62 women and 12 men became the first graduating class.

East Stroudsburg University of Pennsylvania

GENERAL ADMISSIONS

Very important factors include: rigor of secondary school record, class rank, academic GPA, standardized test scores (if submitted). High school diploma is required and GED is accepted. Institution is test-optional for entering Fall 2024. Check admissions website for updates. *Academic units recommended:* 4 English, 4 math, 3 science (2 labs), 2 foreign language, 3 social studies.

FINANCIAL AID

Students should submit: FAFSA. *Need-based scholarships/grants offered:* College/university scholarship or grant aid from institutional funds; Federal Pell; Private scholarships; SEOG; State scholarships/grants. *Loan aid offered:* Direct PLUS loans; Direct Subsidized Loans; Direct Unsubsidized Loans. Federal Work-Study Program available. Institutional employment available.

CAMPUS LIFE

Activities: Campus Ministries; Choral groups; Concert band; Dance; Drama/theater; International Student Organization; Jazz band; Literary magazine; Marching band; Music ensembles; Musical theater; Pep band; Radio station; Student government; Student newspaper; Symphony orchestra. **Organizations:** 110 registered organizations, 28 honor societies, 3 religious organizations, 5 fraternities, 5 sororities. **Athletics (Intercollegiate):** *Men:* baseball, basketball, cross-country, golf, ice hockey, lacrosse, rugby, softball, track/field (indoor), volleyball, wrestling. *Women:* basketball, cross-country, field hockey, golf, ice hockey, lacrosse, rugby, softball, swimming, track/field (indoor), volleyball.

CAMPUS

Type of school	Public
Environment	Village

STUDENTS

Undergrad enrollment	4,320
% male/female	43/57
% from out of state	19
% frosh live on campus	80

FINANCIAL FACTS

Annual in-state tuition	$10,987
Annual out-of-state tuition	$18,953
Room and board	$11,400
Required fees	$3,271

GENERAL ADMISSIONS INFO

Application fee	$25
Regular application deadline	4/1
Nonfall registration	Yes

Fall 2024 testing policy	Test Optional
Range SAT EBRW	480–580
Range SAT Math	480–570
Range ACT Composite	20–26

ACADEMICS

Student/faculty ratio	18:1
% students returning for sophomore year	67

Most classes have 20–29 students.

REQUESTING SERVICES FOR STUDENTS WITH LEARNING DIFFERENCES

Phone: 570-422-3954 • www.esu.edu/oasis • Email: oasis@esu.edu

Documentation submitted to: OASIS (Office of Accessible Services Individualized for Students)
Separate application required for Services: Yes

Documentation required for:
LD: Psychoeducational evaluation
ADHD: Psychoeducational evaluation
ASD: Psychoeducational evaluation

Gannon University

109 University Square, Erie, PA 16541 • Admissions: 814-871-7407 • www.gannon.edu

(Support: CS)

ACCOMMODATIONS

Allowed in exams:

Calculators	Yes
Dictionary	Yes
Computer	Yes
Spell-checker	Yes
Extended test time	Yes
Scribe	Yes
Proctors	Yes
Oral exams	No
Note-takers	Yes

Support services for students with:

LD	Yes
ADHD	Yes
ASD	Yes
Distraction-reduced environment	Yes
Recording of lecture allowed	Yes
Reading technology	Yes
Audio books	Yes
Other assistive technology	Yes
Priority registration	Yes

Added costs of services:

For LD	No
For ADHD	No
For ASD	No
LD specialists	Yes
ADHD & ASD coaching	No
ASD specialists	No
Professional tutors	Yes
Peer tutors	Yes
Max. hours/week for services	Varies
How professors are notified of student approved accommodations	Student and Office of Disability Services

COLLEGE GRADUATION REQUIREMENTS

Course waivers allowed	No
Course substitutions allowed	Yes
In what courses: Case-by-case basis	

PROGRAMS/SERVICES FOR STUDENTS WITH LEARNING DIFFERENCES

The Office of Accessibility Services (OAS) helps students obtain necessary academic accommodations. Students seeking services should contact OAS once they have been accepted to the university. Students are responsible for making sure OAS receives the appropriate documentation directly from the testing source. Accommodation requests and documentation are reviewed on a case-by-case basis. Students must request accommodation letters from OAS at the start of each semester to give to their professors. OAS monitors students' exams by requiring student and teacher to complete and return a test accommodation form to OAS. Additional services available may include recording of classes, extended time on exams, and scribes.

ADMISSIONS

Admission is based on several factors, including academic courses, grades, class rank, and counselor recommendation. Students with a diagnosed learning disability are encouraged to submit a personal letter of recommendation from a teacher, counselor, or school administrator, as well as records from professionals with whom the student has worked, including medical professionals or academic specialists. Students admitted conditionally must enter as undeclared majors until they can achieve a 2.0 GPA. ACT or SAT scores may be required by some programs, such as Lecom's Medical, Pharmacy, and Dental Schools, or the Duquesne School of Law, and may also serve as an aid to increase the value of merit awards. Applicants must submit a personal statement that responds to one of the proposed topics: "How have you applied a classroom lesson to your daily life?" or "Ask and answer one question that you wish we had asked."

Additional Information

The Student Success Center (SSC) provides support for all students. This includes academic advising, career counseling, tutoring, programming, and additional resources. All SSC services are available virtually for online students as well. Gannon University has campuses in Erie, Pennsylvania, and Ruskin, Florida, as well as an online program where students can receive a degree in high-demand fields from wherever they live.

Celebrate Gannon is an annual event honoring each year's undergraduate and graduate research and academic accomplishments. Students present their scholarly and creative work in engagement, fine arts, research, and scholarship. Each project evolves out of coursework, independent research, and volunteer endeavors. Classes are canceled so that the whole community can participate. It's also Gannon's annual Day of Giving.

Gannon University

GENERAL ADMISSIONS

Very important factors include: rigor of secondary school record, academic GPA, standardized test scores (if submitted). *Other factors considered include:* class rank, application essay, recommendations. High school diploma is required and GED is accepted. Institution is test-optional for entering Fall 2024. Check admissions website for updates. *Academic units required:* 4 English, 2 math, 2 science (2 labs), 2 social studies, 3 academic electives. *Academic units recommended:* 4 math, 4 science (3 labs), 2 foreign language, 3 social studies, 1 visual/performing arts.

FINANCIAL AID

Students should submit: FAFSA. *Need-based scholarships/grants offered:* College/university scholarship or grant aid from institutional funds; Federal Nursing Scholarships; Federal Pell; Private scholarships; SEOG; State scholarships/grants. *Loan aid offered:* Direct PLUS loans; Direct Subsidized Loans; Direct Unsubsidized Loans. Federal Work-Study Program available. Institutional employment available.

CAMPUS LIFE

Activities: Campus Ministries; Choral groups; Concert band; Dance; Drama/theater; International Student Organization; Literary magazine; Model UN; Pep band; Radio station; Student government; Student newspaper. **Organizations:** 91 registered organizations, 16 honor societies, 5 religious organizations, 7 fraternities, 5 sororities. **Athletics (Intercollegiate):** *Men:* baseball, basketball, cross-country, golf, ice hockey, lacrosse, rugby, swimming, ultimate frisbee, volleyball, water polo, wrestling. *Women:* basketball, cross-country, golf, gymnastics, lacrosse, softball, swimming, ultimate frisbee, volleyball, water polo.

CAMPUS
Type of school	Private (nonprofit)
Environment	City

STUDENTS
Undergrad enrollment	3,165
% male/female	40/60
% from out of state	25
% frosh live on campus	68

FINANCIAL FACTS
Annual tuition	$36,706
Room and board	$15,410

GENERAL ADMISSIONS INFO
Application fee	$25
Regular application deadline	Rolling
Nonfall registration	Yes

Fall 2024 testing policy	Test Optional
Range SAT EBRW	500–620
Range SAT Math	490–630
Range ACT Composite	20–28

ACADEMICS
Student/faculty ratio	13:1
% students returning for sophomore year	81

Most classes have 20–29 students.

REQUESTING SERVICES FOR STUDENTS WITH LEARNING DIFFERENCES

Phone: 814-871-5522 • www.gannon.edu/student-life/student-success-center/accessibility-services
Email: ods@gannon.edu

Documentation submitted to: Office of Accessibility Services
Separate application required for Services: Yes

Documentation required for:
  LD: Psychoeducational evaluation
  ADHD: Psychoeducational evaluation
  ASD: Psychoeducational evaluation

Kutztown University of Pennsylvania

Admissions Office, Kutztown, PA 19530-0730 • Admissions: 610-683-4060 • www.kutztown.edu

(Support: SP)

ACCOMMODATIONS

Allowed in exams:

Calculators	Yes
Dictionary	N/A
Computer	Yes
Spell-checker	Yes
Extended test time	Yes
Scribe	Yes
Proctors	Yes
Oral exams	No
Note-takers	Yes

Support services for students with:

LD	No
ADHD	No
ASD	Yes
Distraction-reduced environment	Yes
Recording of lecture allowed	Yes
Reading technology	Yes
Audio books	Yes
Other assistive technology	Yes
Priority registration	Yes

Added costs of services:

For LD	No
For ADHD	No
For ASD	Yes
LD specialists	No
ADHD & ASD coaching	Yes
ASD specialists	Yes
Professional tutors	Yes
Peer tutors	Yes
Max. hours/week for services	3
How professors are notified of student approved accommodations	Student

COLLEGE GRADUATION REQUIREMENTS

Course waivers allowed	No
Course substitutions allowed	Yes

In what courses: Math and Foreign Language on a case-by-case basis

PROGRAMS/SERVICES FOR STUDENTS WITH LEARNING DIFFERENCES

Kutztown University Disability Services Office (DSO) works with students with disabilities. To apply for services, students submit an accommodations request form, submit eligible documentation, and schedule an accommodations plan meeting. While there is an individualized approach to determining services, common accommodations include extended test time, test readers, note-taking assistance, audio-recorded lectures, captioning, and preferential seating. Kutztown offers My Place, a fee-based program that provides students on the autism spectrum with additional support services. The program focuses on four main areas: executive function skills related to academics, career development, social skills, and independent college living. The program includes weekly individual coaching, group activities, and career events and gives students a supportive community while developing their self-advocacy skills. My Place students who are in the final year of the program may enroll in the transition program. The application process for My Place includes both student and parent applications, a clinical psychological evaluation, and a copy of the student's high school IEP and transcript.

ADMISSIONS

All applicants are expected to meet the same admission criteria. Students must submit an application and high school transcripts for admission consideration. Applicants are encouraged to have completed a college preparatory curriculum.

Additional Information

The My Place program is also offered to commuter students, with a less intensive meeting schedule, and at a lower cost.

KU is the home of the Pennsylvania German Cultural Heritage Center, a museum and research center dedicated to preserving and celebrating Pennsylvania's German culture, history, and language in an educational setting. The center offers exhibitions, programs, lectures, online educational resources, classes in Pennsylvania Dutch, and an extensive research library to conduct genealogical, historical, linguistic, and cultural research. The center publishes *Hiwwe wie Driwwe,* the world's only Pennsylvania German newspaper.

Kutztown University of Pennsylvania

GENERAL ADMISSIONS

Very important factors include: rigor of secondary school record, class rank, standardized test scores (if submitted). *Other factors considered include:* academic GPA, recommendations. High school diploma is required and GED is accepted. Institution is test-optional for entering Fall 2024. Check admissions website for updates. *Academic units required:* 4 English, 3 math, 3 science (2 labs), 3 social studies.

FINANCIAL AID

Students should submit: FAFSA. *Need-based scholarships/grants offered:* College/university scholarship or grant aid from institutional funds; Federal Pell; Private scholarships; SEOG; State scholarships/grants. *Loan aid offered:* Direct PLUS loans; Direct Subsidized Loans; Direct Unsubsidized Loans. Federal Work-Study Program available. Institutional employment available.

CAMPUS LIFE

Activities: Campus Ministries; Choral groups; Concert band; Dance; Drama/theater; International Student Organization; Jazz band; Literary magazine; Marching band; Model UN; Music ensembles; Musical theater; Radio station; Student government; Student newspaper; Student-run film society; Symphony orchestra; Television station; Yearbook. **Organizations:** 222 registered organizations, 13 honor societies, 6 religious organizations, 10 fraternities, 9 sororities. **Athletics (Intercollegiate):** *Men:* baseball, basketball, cross-country, equestrian sports, golf, ice hockey, lacrosse, rugby, track/field (indoor), ultimate frisbee, volleyball, wrestling. *Women:* basketball, bowling, cross-country, equestrian sports, field hockey, golf, lacrosse, rugby, softball, swimming, track/field (indoor), ultimate frisbee, volleyball.

CAMPUS
Type of school	Public
Environment	Rural

STUDENTS
Undergrad enrollment	6,485
% male/female	44/56
% from out of state	13
% frosh live on campus	87

FINANCIAL FACTS
Annual in-state tuition	$7,716
Annual out-of-state tuition	$11,574
Room and board	$10,830
Required fees	$3,404

GENERAL ADMISSIONS INFO
Application fee	$35
Regular application deadline	Rolling
Nonfall registration	Yes

Fall 2024 testing policy	Test Optional
Range SAT EBRW	500–620
Range SAT Math	490–590
Range ACT Composite	19–26

ACADEMICS
Student/faculty ratio	18:1
% students returning for sophomore year	78

Most classes have 20–29 students.

REQUESTING SERVICES FOR STUDENTS WITH LEARNING DIFFERENCES

Phone: 610-683-4108 • www.kutztown.edu/DSO • Email: DSO@kutztown.edu

Documentation submitted to: Disability Services Office (DSO)
Separate application required for Services: Yes

Documentation required for:
LD: Psychoeducational evaluation
ADHD: Psychoeducational evaluation
ASD: Psychoeducational evaluation

Lehigh University

27 Memorial Drive, West Bethlehem, PA 18015 • Admissions: 610-758-3100 • www.lehigh.edu

Support: CS

ACCOMMODATIONS

Allowed in exams:

Calculators	Yes
Dictionary	Yes
Computer	Yes
Spell-checker	Yes
Extended test time	Yes
Scribe	Yes
Proctors	Yes
Oral exams	Yes
Note-takers	Yes

Support services for students with:

LD	Yes
ADHD	Yes
ASD	Yes
Distraction-reduced environment	Yes
Recording of lecture allowed	Yes
Reading technology	Yes
Audio books	Yes
Other assistive technology	Yes
Priority registration	Yes

Added costs of services:

For LD	No
For ADHD	No
For ASD	No
LD specialists	Yes
ADHD & ASD coaching	Yes
ASD specialists	Yes
Professional tutors	No
Peer tutors	Yes
Max. hours/week for services	Varies
How professors are notified of student approved accommodations	Student

COLLEGE GRADUATION REQUIREMENTS

Course waivers allowed	No
Course substitutions allowed	N/A

PROGRAMS/SERVICES FOR STUDENTS WITH LEARNING DIFFERENCES

The Disability Support Services (DSS) office coordinates reasonable accommodations for students with learning differences. To apply for services, students submit the request form and appropriate documentation to DSS. Each file is reviewed individually, and a meeting with a coordinator is scheduled to discuss disability impacts, accommodations, and services that have been used in the past. Students may be recommended for academic coaching. This is a one-on-one process to help students examine academic concerns and barriers to success and develop individualized plans. The DSS data proves that students who participate in the academic coaching program typically have higher GPAs than their non-coached peers. The Peer Mentor Program is student led, and each year the peer mentors decide and lead the year's activities. Mentors are upper-year students with disabilities who have been very successful at Lehigh. The mentors are available to provide guidance on academic and social issues.

ADMISSIONS

All applicants are expected to meet the same admission criteria. Consideration is given to the influence and impact of the students' living and learning environments. Leadership, activities, talent, research, work, and life experiences are factored into the admission decision. Recommendations and essays are required.

Additional Information

The Academic Life & Student Transitions team works with students to promote their development both inside and outside the classroom—from offering workshops and discussions about study skills and strategies to one-on-one conversations about academics and transitioning to college life.

The Lehigh-Lafayette football game has been played every year since 1897, making it one of the nation's most long-standing rivalries in college athletics and drawing sellout crowds and national media attention. One of the week's highlights is the Friday Marching 97 Campus Tour, when Lehigh's marching band weaves its way through campus buildings, dining halls, classrooms, and even the library, serenading the campus community with all the traditional Lehigh fight songs.

Lehigh University

GENERAL ADMISSIONS

Very important factors include: rigor of secondary school record, academic GPA. *Important factors include:* class rank, standardized test scores (if submitted), application essay, recommendations. High school diploma is required and GED is accepted. Institution is test-optional for entering Fall 2024. Check admissions website for updates. *Academic units required:* 4 English, 3 math, 3 science, 2 foreign language, 2 social studies, 2 academic electives. *Academic units recommended:* 4 math, 4 science, 4 social studies, 1 visual/performing arts.

FINANCIAL AID

Students should submit: Business/Farm Supplement; CSS/Financial Aid Profile; FAFSA; Noncustodial Profile. *Need-based scholarships/grants offered:* College/university scholarship or grant aid from institutional funds; Federal Pell; Private scholarships; State scholarships/grants. *Loan aid offered:* Direct PLUS loans; Direct Subsidized Loans; Direct Unsubsidized Loans. Federal Work-Study Program available. Institutional employment available.

CAMPUS LIFE

Activities: Choral groups; Concert band; Dance; Drama/theater; International Student Organization; Jazz band; Literary magazine; Marching band; Model UN; Music ensembles; Musical theater; Pep band; Radio station; Student government; Student newspaper; Student-run film society; Symphony orchestra. **Organizations:** 240 registered organizations, 18 honor societies, 12 religious organizations, 13 fraternities, 11 sororities. **Athletics (Intercollegiate):** *Men:* baseball, basketball, crew/rowing, cross-country, cycling, equestrian sports, field hockey, golf, gymnastics, ice hockey, lacrosse, martial arts, rugby, swimming, track/field (indoor), ultimate frisbee, volleyball, water polo, wrestling. *Women:* basketball, crew/rowing, cross-country, cycling, equestrian sports, field hockey, golf, gymnastics, lacrosse, martial arts, rugby, softball, swimming, track/field (indoor), ultimate frisbee, volleyball, water polo, wrestling.

CAMPUS

Type of school	Private (nonprofit)
Environment	City

STUDENTS

Undergrad enrollment	5,612
% male/female	54/46
% from out of state	73
% frosh live on campus	97

FINANCIAL FACTS

Annual tuition	$61,180
Room and board	$16,470
Required fees	$1,000

GENERAL ADMISSIONS INFO

Application fee	$70
Regular application deadline	1/15
Nonfall registration	No
Fall 2024 testing policy	Test Optional
Range SAT EBRW	660–720
Range SAT Math	680–770
Range ACT Composite	30–33

ACADEMICS

Student/faculty ratio	10:1
% students returning for sophomore year	91

Most classes have 10–19 students.

REQUESTING SERVICES FOR STUDENTS WITH LEARNING DIFFERENCES

Phone: 610-758-4152 • studentaffairs.lehigh.edu/disabilities • Email: indss@lehigh.edu

Documentation submitted to: Disability Support Services

Separate application required for Services: Yes

Documentation required for:
LD: Psychoeducational evaluation
ADHD: Psychoeducational evaluation
ASD: Psychoeducational evaluation

Mercyhurst University

501 East 38th Street, Erie, PA 16546 • Admissions: 814-824-2202 • www.mercyhurst.edu

Support: SP

ACCOMMODATIONS

Allowed in exams:

Calculators	Yes
Dictionary	Yes
Computer	Yes
Spell-checker	Yes
Extended test time	Yes
Scribe	Yes
Proctors	Yes
Oral exams	Yes
Note-takers	Yes

Support services for students with:

LD	Yes
ADHD	Yes
ASD	Yes
Distraction-reduced environment	Yes
Recording of lecture allowed	Yes
Reading technology	Yes
Audio books	Yes
Other assistive technology	Yes
Priority registration	Yes

Added costs of services:

For LD	No
For ADHD	No
For ASD	Yes
LD specialists	Yes
ADHD & ASD coaching	Yes
ASD specialists	Yes
Professional tutors	Yes
Peer tutors	Yes
Max. hours/week for services	3
How professors are notified of student approved accommodations	Learning Support Services

COLLEGE GRADUATION REQUIREMENTS

Course waivers allowed	No
Course substitutions allowed	Yes
In what courses: Math and Foreign Language	

PROGRAMS/SERVICES FOR STUDENTS WITH LEARNING DIFFERENCES

Students with current documentation of a diagnosed disability are eligible to receive academic accommodations and services free of charge. The Learning Support Services office (LSS) coordinates accommodations for students who have received approval through the ADA Committee that include extended time for tests, testing in an alternate location, notetakers, readers, scribes, course substitutions and reductions, and assistive technology. Students with disabilities who are officially enrolled at the university should submit their application for academic accommodations and supporting documentation through the academic accommodations request online portal. Mercyhurst has a summer program called Pathways to Academic Success for Students (PASS). It takes place three weeks prior to the regular move-in date and is open to any incoming Mercyhurst student with a documented learning disability. In this program, students enroll in a 3 credit college course, learn college study skills, and connect with other students before the academic year starts.

ADMISSIONS

Students should pursue a college prep curriculum, however, the admissions office will consider the totality of the student's high school curriculum when evaluating an application. The average GPA for admitted students is 3.36. Some applicants are selected for a supplemental review to provide additional information to the admission committee or just because the office periodically selects some applications as part of their efforts to improve their practices in the admission process. Students selected for supplemental review may be asked to have an interview (in person or by phone), complete an additional questionnaire, or submit a graded paper.

Additional Information

Students who use Learning Support Services may choose to enroll in the more structured Academic Advantage Program (AAP). This fee-based program includes intensive academic support to help with the transition and adjustment to college. One-on-one personalized assistance is provided, resulting in effective and efficient study skills necessary for academic success.

The first Hurst Holiday was declared in 2015 and has become a treasured day of fun and festivities. It's a surprise day off where students learn classes are canceled with the raising of the Hurst Day flag and bagpipers marching with Luke the Laker (mascot) through campus and the residence halls to wake students. By 10 A.M., over a hundred groups are participating in three rounds of a scavenger hunt to identify historical points on campus and key historical facts. The day continues with free T-shirts, food, music, giant inflatables, and a steak dinner to end the day.

Mercyhurst University

GENERAL ADMISSIONS

Very important factors include: rigor of secondary school record, class rank, academic GPA, standardized test scores (if submitted). *Important factors include:* application essay, recommendations. High school diploma is required and GED is accepted. Institution is test-optional for entering Fall 2024. Check admissions website for updates. *Academic units required:* 4 English, 3 math, 2 science (1 lab), 2 foreign language, 4 social studies. *Academic units recommended:* 3 science (2 labs).

FINANCIAL AID

Students should submit:. Need-based scholarships/grants offered: College/ university scholarship or grant aid from institutional funds; Federal Pell; Private scholarships; SEOG; State scholarships/grants. *Loan aid offered:* Direct PLUS loans; Direct Subsidized Loans; Direct Unsubsidized Loans. Federal Work-Study Program available. Institutional employment available.

CAMPUS LIFE

Activities: Campus Ministries; Choral groups; Dance; Drama/theater; International Student Organization; Jazz band; Literary magazine; Model UN; Music ensembles; Musical theater; Pep band; Radio station; Student government; Student newspaper; Television station; Yearbook. **Organizations:** 80 registered organizations, 9 honor societies, 2 religious organizations, 0 fraternities, 0 sororities. **Athletics (Intercollegiate):** *Men:* baseball, basketball, crew/rowing, cross-country, golf, ice hockey, lacrosse, water polo, wrestling. *Women:* basketball, crew/rowing, cross-country, field hockey, golf, ice hockey, lacrosse, softball, volleyball, water polo.

CAMPUS
Type of school	Private (nonprofit)
Environment	City

STUDENTS
Undergrad enrollment	2,641
% male/female	40/60
% from out of state	47
% frosh live on campus	93

FINANCIAL FACTS
Annual tuition	$41,580
Room and board	$14,025
Required fees	$2,930

GENERAL ADMISSIONS INFO
Application fee	No fee
Regular application deadline	Rolling
Nonfall registration	Yes
Fall 2024 testing policy	Test Optional

ACADEMICS
Student/faculty ratio	14:1
% students returning for sophomore year	78
Most classes have 20–29 students.	

REQUESTING SERVICES FOR STUDENTS WITH LEARNING DIFFERENCES

Phone: 814-824-2231 • www.mercyhurst.edu/academics/academic-services/learning-support-services
Email: jlong@mercyhurst.edu

Documentation submitted to: Learning Support Services
Separate application required for Services: Yes

Documentation required for:
LD: Psychoeducational evaluation
ADHD: Psychoeducational evaluation
ASD: Psychoeducational evaluation

Millersville University of Pennsylvania

P.O. Box 1002, Millersville, PA 17551-0302 • Admissions: 717-871-4625 • www.millersville.edu

(Support: CS)

ACCOMMODATIONS

Allowed in exams:

Calculators	Yes
Dictionary	Yes
Computer	Yes
Spell-checker	Yes
Extended test time	Yes
Scribe	Yes
Proctors	Yes
Oral exams	Yes
Note-takers	Yes

Support services for students with:

LD	Yes
ADHD	Yes
ASD	Yes
Distraction-reduced environment	Yes
Recording of lecture allowed	Yes
Reading technology	Yes
Audio books	Yes
Other assistive technology	Yes
Priority registration	Yes

Added costs of services:

For LD	No
For ADHD	No
For ASD	No
LD specialists	Yes
ADHD & ASD coaching	Yes
ASD specialists	No
Professional tutors	No
Peer tutors	Yes
Max. hours/week for services	3
How professors are notified of student approved accommodations	Office of Learning Services

COLLEGE GRADUATION REQUIREMENTS

Course waivers allowed	Yes

In what courses: Foreign Language and others

Course substitutions allowed	Yes

In what courses: Foreign Language and others

PROGRAMS/SERVICES FOR STUDENTS WITH LEARNING DIFFERENCES

The Office of Learning Services (OLC) creates a supportive learning environment for students through advocacy, assistive technology, collaboration, and direct services. The OLC coordinates academic accommodations and related services for students with learning disabilities who meet the eligibility criteria. Students may also be referred to the Tutoring Center, which provides students with tutors, academic resources, and educational workshops, such as succeeding with ADHD and understanding autism. Students seeking accommodations must be admitted to the school prior to requesting services. Integrated Studies is a two- to four-year initiative for students with intellectual disabilities. Students enrolled in Integrated Studies are fully immersed in the campus and enrolled as full-time, nondegree students. Credits earned become part of the student's academic record toward a degree program in the future.

ADMISSIONS

All applicants are expected to meet the same admission criteria. Students will be guaranteed admission if they have a GPA of 3.2 or greater at the end of their junior year OR if they rank in the top 25 percent of their high school class with a GPA of 3.0 or higher at the end of junior year. Students who do not qualify for guaranteed admission are evaluated for admission using a combination of factors, including GPA and rigor of coursework, PSAT scores (if available), and an interview. Students who are admitted typically have a solid B average. Millersville will consider the competitiveness of the high school, the level of courses taken, and grade trends.

Additional Information

The Tutoring Center provides individual and group peer tutoring, tutor training, and enhancing critical thinking skills to promote independent and successful learners for the future. The center's scheduled workshops focus on a variety of topics, including note-taking, study skills, skillful reading, and tools for critical thinking.

The campus is bucolic with a grass lawn, a pathway, and the scenic Millersville Pond. The pond is a certified wildlife habitat. Since 1966, the pond has been home to Miller and S'ville (well, originally Fred and Ethel), two resident swans donated to campus. Swans mate for life and won't accept a new partner, so when one of the swans die, the surviving swan is relocated to a farm. The new pair in 1987 was the first Miller and S'ville swans.

Millersville University of Pennsylvania

GENERAL ADMISSIONS

Very important factors include: rigor of secondary school record, class rank, academic GPA. *Important factors include:* application essay. *Other factors considered include:* standardized test scores (if submitted), recommendations. High school diploma is required and GED is accepted. Institution is test-optional for entering Fall 2024. Check admissions website for updates. *Academic units required:* 4 English, 3 math, 3 science (2 labs), 3 social studies.

FINANCIAL AID

Students should submit: FAFSA. *Need-based scholarships/grants offered:* College/university scholarship or grant aid from institutional funds; Federal Pell; SEOG; State scholarships/grants. *Loan aid offered:* Direct PLUS loans; Direct Subsidized Loans; Direct Unsubsidized Loans. Federal Work-Study Program available. Institutional employment available.

CAMPUS LIFE

Activities: Campus Ministries; Choral groups; Concert band; Dance; Drama/theater; International Student Organization; Jazz band; Literary magazine; Marching band; Music ensembles; Musical theater; Radio station; Student government; Student newspaper; Student-run film society; Symphony orchestra; Television station. **Organizations:** 185 registered organizations, 15 honor societies, 7 religious organizations, 9 fraternities, 8 sororities. **Athletics (Intercollegiate):** *Men:* baseball, basketball, bowling, equestrian sports, golf, ice hockey, lacrosse, martial arts, rugby, ultimate frisbee, volleyball, wrestling. *Women:* basketball, bowling, cross-country, equestrian sports, field hockey, golf, ice hockey, lacrosse, martial arts, rugby, softball, swimming, track/field (indoor), ultimate frisbee, volleyball.

CAMPUS

Type of school	Public
Environment	Village

STUDENTS

Undergrad enrollment	6,094
% male/female	41/59
% from out of state	8
% frosh live on campus	73

FINANCIAL FACTS

Annual in-state tuition	$9,570
Annual out-of-state tuition	$19,290
Room and board	$13,350
Required fees	$2,686

GENERAL ADMISSIONS INFO

Application fee	No fee
Regular application deadline	Rolling
Nonfall registration	Yes

Fall 2024 testing policy	Test Optional
Range SAT EBRW	500–620
Range SAT Math	500–600
Range ACT Composite	20–25

ACADEMICS

Student/faculty ratio	19:1
% students returning for sophomore year	75

Most classes have 20–29 students.

REQUESTING SERVICES FOR STUDENTS WITH LEARNING DIFFERENCES

Phone: 717-871-5554 • www.millersville.edu/learningservices • Email: Learning.Services@millersville.edu

Documentation submitted to: Office of Learning Services
Separate application required for Services: Yes

Documentation required for:
LD: Psychoeducational evaluation
ADHD: Psychoeducational evaluation
ASD: Psychoeducational evaluation

Misericordia University

301 Lake Street, Dallas, PA 18612 • Admissions: 570-674-6264 • www.misericordia.edu

(**Support: SP**)

ACCOMMODATIONS

Allowed in exams:

Calculators	Yes
Dictionary	Yes
Computer	Yes
Spell-checker	Yes
Extended test time	Yes
Scribe	Yes
Proctors	Yes
Oral exams	Yes
Note-takers	Yes

Support services for students with:

LD	Yes
ADHD	Yes
ASD	Yes
Distraction-reduced environment	Yes
Recording of lecture allowed	Yes
Reading technology	Yes
Audio books	Yes
Other assistive technology	Yes
Priority registration	Yes

Added costs of services:

For LD	No
For ADHD	No
For ASD	No
LD specialists	Yes
ADHD & ASD coaching	No
ASD specialists	No
Professional tutors	No
Peer tutors	Yes
Max. hours/week for services	Varies
How professors are notified of student approved accommodations	Office of Students with Disabilities

COLLEGE GRADUATION REQUIREMENTS

Course waivers allowed	No
Course substitutions allowed	No

PROGRAMS/SERVICES FOR STUDENTS WITH LEARNING DIFFERENCES

The Student Success Center provides services to students with disabilities, and the Office of Students with Disabilities (OSD) determines eligibility for accommodations. Students should fill out the request for accommodations form and submit documentation of their disability. The Alternative Learners Program (ALP) supports students with disabilities that extend beyond those accommodations required by OSD. ALP students pay a fee for participation in the program and have access to case management by academic specialists, in addition to writing support with editing and transcription, course selection, access to technology, and time management support. To apply for ALP, students submit a personally written cover letter describing their disability and indicating the wish to participate, a high school transcript, two letters of recommendation by educational professionals, and eligible documentation. Once enrolled in the program, the ALP staff notifies professors of the students served by the program and which accommodations will be needed. ALP students have the option to participate in the BRIDGE Program, which provides incoming first-year ALP students the opportunity to arrive on campus early (one week before the start of the fall semester) and participate in a series of assessments and workshops.

ADMISSIONS

The criteria for admission as a first-year student are class rank in the top 50 percent of their high school class (if provided), a rigorous high school curriculum, and a B or better average.

Additional Information

The Student Success Center offers academic support, tutoring, and writing support. The Choice Program provides workshops to help students explore majors and future career interests.

The Shakespeare Garden at Misericordia, eight years in the making, was dedicated in 2010 to the memory of Sister Regina Kelly RSM, whose love of Shakespeare and teaching influenced decades of students. Her students and admirers raised the funds to establish the garden. The garden is approximately 10,000 square feet and modeled after the style of a formal 17th-century garden, with every plant in the garden mentioned in one of Shakespeare's works.

Misericordia University

GENERAL ADMISSIONS

Very important factors include: rigor of secondary school record, academic GPA. *Important factors include:* class rank. *Other factors considered include:* application essay, recommendations. High school diploma is required and GED is accepted. Institution is test-optional for entering Fall 2024. Check admissions website for updates. *Academic units required:* 4 English, 4 math, 4 science, 4 social studies.

FINANCIAL AID

Students should submit: FAFSA. *Need-based scholarships/grants offered:* College/university scholarship or grant aid from institutional funds; Federal Pell; Private scholarships; SEOG; State scholarships/grants. *Loan aid offered:* Direct PLUS loans; Direct Subsidized Loans; Direct Unsubsidized Loans. Federal Work-Study Program available. Institutional employment available.

CAMPUS LIFE

Activities: Campus Ministries; Choral groups; Dance; Drama/theater; Jazz band; Literary magazine; Music ensembles; Radio station; Student government; Student newspaper; Television station; Yearbook. **Organizations:** 40 registered organizations, 15 honor societies, 1 religious organizations, 0 fraternities, 0 sororities. **Athletics (Intercollegiate):** *Men:* baseball, basketball, cross-country, golf, lacrosse, softball, swimming, ultimate frisbee, volleyball. *Women:* basketball, cross-country, field hockey, golf, lacrosse, softball, swimming, ultimate frisbee, volleyball.

CAMPUS
Type of school	Private (nonprofit)
Environment	Town

STUDENTS
Undergrad enrollment	1,837
% male/female	33/67
% from out of state	28
% frosh live on campus	77

FINANCIAL FACTS
Annual tuition	$36,400
Room and board	$14,520
Required fees	$1,970

GENERAL ADMISSIONS INFO
Application fee	No fee
Regular application deadline	Rolling
Nonfall registration	Yes
Fall 2024 testing policy	Test Optional
Range SAT EBRW	520–615
Range SAT Math	520–600
Range ACT Composite	22–27

ACADEMICS
Student/faculty ratio	11:1
% students returning for sophomore year	84

Most classes have 10–19 students.

REQUESTING SERVICES FOR STUDENTS WITH LEARNING DIFFERENCES

Phone: 570-674-6408 • www.misericordia.edu/life-at-mu/student-services/disability-services
Email: kricardo@misericordia.edu

Documentation submitted to: Office of Students with Disabilities
Separate application required for Services: Yes

Documentation required for:
LD: Psychoeducational evaluation
ADHD: Psychoeducational evaluation
ASD: Psychoeducational evaluation

Muhlenberg College

2400 West Chew Street, Allentown, PA 18104-5596 • Admissions: 484-664-3200 • www.muhlenberg.edu

(Support: CS)

ACCOMMODATIONS

Allowed in exams:

Calculators	Yes
Dictionary	Yes
Computer	Yes
Spell-checker	Yes
Extended test time	Yes
Scribe	Yes
Proctors	Yes
Oral exams	Yes
Note-takers	Yes

Support services for students with:

LD	Yes
ADHD	Yes
ASD	Yes
Distraction-reduced environment	Yes
Recording of lecture allowed	Yes
Reading technology	Yes
Audio books	Yes
Priority registration	Yes

Added costs of services:

For LD	No
For ADHD	No
For ASD	No
LD specialists	Yes
ADHD & ASD coaching	Yes
ASD specialists	Yes
Professional tutors	No
Peer tutors	Yes
Max. hours/week for services	12
How professors are notified of student approved accommodations	Student

COLLEGE GRADUATION REQUIREMENTS

Course waivers allowed	No
Course substitutions allowed	Yes
In what courses: Case-by-case basis	

PROGRAMS/SERVICES FOR STUDENTS WITH LEARNING DIFFERENCES

The Office of Disability Services (ODS) at Muhlenberg College provides students with reasonable accommodations and resources. Students with documented differences may schedule a pre-advising session with ODS. The office anticipates about one month to complete the process to secure accommodations; therefore, students are encouraged to contact ODS as soon as possible. Staff in the Academic Resource Center (ARC) and ODS work with students to set goals, adapt learning strategies, and work on organization and study skills.

ADMISSIONS

The average high school GPA for admitted students is 3.4. For students who submit scores, the middle 50 percent of admitted applicants have an ACT score of 27–32 or 1210–1370 on the SAT. Exceptions to academic course requirements are considered on a case-by-case basis for applicants with documented learning disabilities.

Additional Information

The Academic Resource Center provides tutoring, study skill workshops, and individual academic assistance. ARC works closely with faculty to identify, connect with, and support students. Specific workshops support a student's ability to clarify, reinforce, and deepen understanding of class material, develop the intentional habits that enable long-term success, connect with peers to understand various approaches to the work, and apply critical course concepts. There is an "early alert" system for students with a GPA at or below 2.4, and ARC works with the dean of academic life and the dean of students to support academic case management.

The 1998 HBO documentary *Frat House* was mostly filmed at the Alpha Tau Omega fraternity at Muhlenberg. Addressing fraternity hazing at its very worst, Frat House was awarded "Grand Jury Prize: Documentary" at the 1998 Sundance Film Festival. Executive director of the National Alpha Tau fraternity and a Muhlenberg spokesperson were not impressed by the film and both were confident scenes were staged and people paid to act out scenes. The film's directors and sponsor, HBO, insisted the film was real—sort of. HBO never aired the documentary.

Muhlenberg College

GENERAL ADMISSIONS

Very important factors include: rigor of secondary school record, academic GPA. *Important factors include:* standardized test scores (if submitted), application essay, recommendations. *Other factors considered include:* class rank. High school diploma is required and GED is accepted. Institution is test-optional for entering Fall 2024. Check admissions website for updates. *Academic units required:* 4 English, 3 math, 2 science (2 labs), 2 foreign language, 2 history, 1 academic elective. *Academic units recommended:* 4 math, 3 science (3 labs), 4 foreign language, 4 social studies.

FINANCIAL AID

Students should submit: FAFSA; Institution's own financial aid form. *Need-based scholarships/grants offered:* College/university scholarship or grant aid from institutional funds; Federal Pell; Private scholarships; SEOG; State scholarships/grants; United Negro College Fund. *Loan aid offered:* Direct PLUS loans; Direct Subsidized Loans; Direct Unsubsidized Loans. Federal Work-Study Program available. Institutional employment available.

CAMPUS LIFE

Activities: Campus Ministries; Choral groups; Concert band; Dance; Drama/theater; International Student Organization; Jazz band; Literary magazine; Music ensembles; Musical theater; Pep band; Radio station; Student government; Student newspaper; Student-run film society; Yearbook. **Organizations:** 123 registered organizations, 12 honor societies, 7 religious organizations, 3 fraternities, 5 sororities. **Athletics (Intercollegiate):** *Men:* baseball, basketball, cross-country, golf, lacrosse, martial arts, swimming, track/field (indoor), ultimate frisbee, volleyball, wrestling. *Women:* basketball, cross-country, field hockey, golf, lacrosse, martial arts, softball, swimming, track/field (indoor), ultimate frisbee, volleyball.

CAMPUS
Type of school	Private (nonprofit)
Environment	City

STUDENTS
Undergrad enrollment	1,933
% male/female	39/61
% from out of state	70
% frosh live on campus	96

FINANCIAL FACTS
Annual tuition	$59,505
Room and board	$13,810
Required fees	$735

GENERAL ADMISSIONS INFO
Application fee	$50
Regular application deadline	2/1
Nonfall registration	Yes

Fall 2024 testing policy	Test Optional
Range SAT EBRW	610–690
Range SAT Math	590–680
Range ACT Composite	27–32

ACADEMICS
Student/faculty ratio	9:1
% students returning for sophomore year	91

Most classes have 2–9 students.

REQUESTING SERVICES FOR STUDENTS WITH LEARNING DIFFERENCES

Phone: 484-664-3825 • www.muhlenberg.edu/offices/disabilities/ • Email: odsadmin@muhlenberg.edu

Documentation submitted to: Office of Disability Services
Separate application required for Services: Yes

Documentation required for:
LD: Psychoeducational evaluation
ADHD: Psychoeducational evaluation
ASD: Psychoeducational evaluation

Neumann University

Office of Admissions, Aston, PA 19014-1298 • Admissions: 610-558-5616 • www.neumann.edu

Support: S

ACCOMMODATIONS

Allowed in exams:

Calculators	Yes
Dictionary	No
Computer	Yes
Spell-checker	Yes
Extended test time	Yes
Scribe	Yes
Proctors	Yes
Oral exams	Yes
Note-takers	Yes

Support services for students with:

LD	Yes
ADHD	Yes
ASD	Yes
Distraction-reduced environment	Yes
Recording of lecture allowed	Yes
Reading technology	Yes
Audio books	Yes
Other assistive technology	Yes
Priority registration	Yes

Added costs of services:

For LD	No
For ADHD	No
For ASD	No
LD specialists	No
ADHD & ASD coaching	Yes
ASD specialists	No
Professional tutors	Yes
Peer tutors	Yes
Max. hours/week for services	Varies
How professors are notified of student approved accommodations	Student and Office of Disability Services

COLLEGE GRADUATION REQUIREMENTS

Course waivers allowed	Yes

In what courses: Students with certain documented disabilities, such as severe dyslexia or dyscalculia, may receive waivers for certain courses required for graduation.

Course substitutions allowed	Yes

In what courses: Math, Foreign Language, and others on a case-by-case basis

PROGRAMS/SERVICES FOR STUDENTS WITH LEARNING DIFFERENCES

The Office of Disability Services at Neumann delivers services and resources to ensure an equal experience for all students on campus. Prior to each semester, students are encouraged to submit an accommodations request form. Reasonable accommodations are discussed with the student and Disabilities Services coordinator to determine if they can be facilitated with the instructor or if they can be accommodated within the Academic Resource Center.

ADMISSIONS

The admission process is the same for all students who wish to attend. Applicants to pre-professional programs must have a minimum GPA of 3.0 for admittance.

Additional Information

There are a number of resources available across campus to all students. The Office of Academic Coaching and Tutoring provides coaching in school and life skills and focuses on the student's personal and academic development. Students also explore options beyond college. The Writing Center is the place for students to brainstorm, plan, draft, revise their writing, and obtain feedback. The tutors also support students by identifying writing strategies that meet the student's learning style. The Academic Resources Center offers the Program for Success (PFS) to help students reach their academic goals with individual coaching to determine a student's needs and develop a plan to help them become an active learner. The coaching sessions with PFS help the student develop effective study habits, structure coursework to meet deadlines, and develop accountability throughout the semester.

Each year, Neumann University recalls the Christmas at Greccio by celebrating the Festival of Lights with the lighting of the campus Christmas tree. Students and staff create a live Nativity scene complete with animals and a baby recently born to a member of the Neumann community. A community children's choir performs music for the event.

Neumann University

GENERAL ADMISSIONS

Very important factors include: rigor of secondary school record, academic GPA. *Other factors considered include:* standardized test scores (if submitted), application essay, recommendations. High school diploma is required and GED is accepted. Institution is test-optional for entering Fall 2024. Check admissions website for updates. *Academic units required:* 4 English, 2 math, 2 science (1 lab), 2 foreign language, 2 social studies, 4 academic electives. *Academic units recommended:* 3 science (2 labs).

FINANCIAL AID

Students should submit: FAFSA. *Need-based scholarships/grants offered:* College/university scholarship or grant aid from institutional funds; Federal Pell; Private scholarships; SEOG; State scholarships/grants. *Loan aid offered:* Direct PLUS loans; Direct Subsidized Loans; Direct Unsubsidized Loans. Federal Work-Study Program available. Institutional employment available.

CAMPUS LIFE

Activities: Campus Ministries; Choral groups; Dance; Drama/theater; Jazz band; Literary magazine; Music ensembles; Musical theater; Pep band; Radio station; Student government; Student newspaper; Symphony orchestra; Television station. **Organizations:** 29 registered organizations, 15 honor societies, 0 religious organizations, 0 fraternities, 0 sororities. **Athletics (Intercollegiate):** *Men:* baseball, basketball, cross-country, golf, ice hockey, lacrosse, rugby, track/field (indoor), volleyball. *Women:* basketball, cross-country, field hockey, golf, ice hockey, lacrosse, rugby, softball, track/field (indoor), volleyball.

CAMPUS

Type of school	Private (nonprofit)
Environment	Town

STUDENTS

Undergrad enrollment	1,682
% male/female	36/64
% from out of state	33
% frosh live on campus	75

FINANCIAL FACTS

Annual tuition	$35,420
Room and board	$14,700
Required fees	$1,520

GENERAL ADMISSIONS INFO

Application fee	No fee
Regular application deadline	8/15
Nonfall registration	Yes
Fall 2024 testing policy	Test Optional
Range SAT EBRW	480–600
Range SAT Math	450–560

ACADEMICS

Student/faculty ratio	15:1
% students returning for sophomore year	71

Most classes have 10–19 students.

REQUESTING SERVICES FOR STUDENTS WITH LEARNING DIFFERENCES

Phone: 610-361-5471 • www.neumann.edu/academics/ssc/disabilityservices
Email: disabilities@neumann.edu

Documentation submitted to: Office of Disability Services
Separate application required for Services: Yes

Documentation required for:
 LD: Psychoeducational evaluation
 ADHD: Psychoeducational evaluation
 ASD: Psychoeducational evaluation

Penn State University Park

201 Shields Building, University Park, PA 16802 • Admissions: 814-865-5471 • www.psu.edu

Support: CS

ACCOMMODATIONS

Allowed in exams:

Calculators	Yes
Dictionary	N/A
Computer	Yes
Spell-checker	Yes
Extended test time	Yes
Scribe	Yes
Proctors	Yes
Oral exams	Yes
Note-takers	Yes

Support services for students with:

LD	Yes
ADHD	Yes
ASD	Yes
Distraction-reduced environment	Yes
Recording of lecture allowed	Yes
Reading technology	Yes
Audio books	No
Other assistive technology	Yes
Priority registration	Yes

Added costs of services:

For LD	No
For ADHD	No
For ASD	No
LD specialists	Yes
ADHD & ASD coaching	No
ASD specialists	No
Professional tutors	No
Peer tutors	Yes
Max. hours/week for services	Varies
How professors are notified of student approved accommodations	Student

COLLEGE GRADUATION REQUIREMENTS

Course waivers allowed	No
Course substitutions allowed	Yes
In what courses: Foreign Language	

PROGRAMS/SERVICES FOR STUDENTS WITH LEARNING DIFFERENCES

The Student Disability Resources (SDR) office ensures that students with learning disabilities receive appropriate accommodations. The goal is for students to function independently while meeting the academic demands of a competitive university. Students with learning disabilities should be able to complete college-level courses with the help of support services and classroom accommodations. To receive support services, students must submit documentation regarding their learning disability to the learning disability specialist in the SDR office. Services and accommodations may include arranging course substitutions with academic departments, test accommodations, individual counseling, alternate-format textbooks, assistance with note-taking, and assistive technology.

ADMISSIONS

The application process is the same for all students. Fifty percent of admitted students have a GPA between 3.5 and 4.0. If the applicant's high school grades are low, students may submit a letter explaining why their ability to succeed in college is higher than indicated by their academic records. Students may seek admission as a provisional or nondegree student if they do not meet the criteria required for admission as a degree candidate.

Additional Information

Penn State Learning operates math, tutoring, writing, and computer learning centers. Students may receive academic help individually or in small groups for various courses. Graduate students provide individual assistance with study skills, time management, and compensatory learning strategies.

The Schwab Auditorium, completed in 1903, was the first building financed by a private gift from Charles Schwab, a Penn trustee for 30 years. The School of Communications, originally the Carnegie Library, was dedicated in 1904. Andrew Carnegie donated funds for some 200 libraries in the United States. The two steel industry tycoons were friends but also enjoyed competition and rivalry, each wanting the better building on campus; the Schwab Auditorium covers more square footage, but the Carnegie building is slightly taller.

Penn State University Park

GENERAL ADMISSIONS

Very important factors include: academic GPA. *Important factors include:* rigor of secondary school record. *Other factors considered include:* standardized test scores (if submitted). High school diploma is required and GED is accepted. Institution is test-optional for entering Fall 2024. Check admissions website for updates. *Academic units required:* 4 English, 3 math, 3 science, 2 foreign language, 3 social studies. *Academic units recommended:* 3 foreign language.

FINANCIAL AID

Students should submit: FAFSA. *Need-based scholarships/grants offered:* College/university scholarship or grant aid from institutional funds; Federal Pell; Private scholarships; SEOG; State scholarships/grants; United Negro College Fund. *Loan aid offered:* Direct PLUS loans; Direct Subsidized Loans; Direct Unsubsidized Loans. Federal Work-Study Program available. Institutional employment available.

CAMPUS LIFE

Activities: Campus Ministries; Choral groups; Concert band; Dance; Drama/theater; International Student Organization; Jazz band; Literary magazine; Marching band; Model UN; Music ensembles; Musical theater; Opera; Pep band; Radio station; Student government; Student newspaper; Student-run film society; Symphony orchestra; Television station; Yearbook. **Organizations:** 894 registered organizations, 32 honor societies, 43 religious organizations, 45 fraternities, 26 sororities. **Athletics (Intercollegiate):** *Men:* baseball, basketball, bowling, crew/rowing, cross-country, cycling, equestrian sports, field hockey, golf, gymnastics, ice hockey, lacrosse, martial arts, racquetball, rugby, softball, swimming, table tennis, track/field (indoor), ultimate frisbee, volleyball, water polo, wrestling. *Women:* baseball, basketball, bowling, crew/rowing, cross-country, cycling, equestrian sports, field hockey, golf, gymnastics, ice hockey, lacrosse, martial arts, racquetball, rugby, softball, swimming, table tennis, track/field (indoor), ultimate frisbee, volleyball, water polo, wrestling.

CAMPUS

Type of school	Public
Environment	Town

STUDENTS

Undergrad enrollment	41,745
% male/female	53/47
% from out of state	43

FINANCIAL FACTS

Annual in-state tuition	$19,286
Annual out-of-state tuition	$38,102
Room and board	$12,984
Required fees	$550

GENERAL ADMISSIONS INFO

Application fee	$65
Regular application deadline	Rolling
Nonfall registration	Yes

Fall 2024 testing policy	Test Optional
Range SAT EBRW	600–680
Range SAT Math	610–710
Range ACT Composite	26–31

ACADEMICS

Student/faculty ratio	15:1
% students returning for sophomore year	91

Most classes have 20–29 students.

REQUESTING SERVICES FOR STUDENTS WITH LEARNING DIFFERENCES

Phone: 814-863-1807 • equity.psu.edu/student-disability-resources • Email: upsdr@psu.edu

Documentation submitted to: Student Disability Resources
Separate application required for Services: Yes

Documentation required for:
LD: Psychoeducational evaluation
ADHD: Psychoeducational evaluation
ASD: Psychoeducational evaluation

Pennsylvania Western University, Edinboro

200 East Normal Street, Edinboro, PA 16444 • Admissions: 814-732-2761 • www.edinboro.edu

(Support: SP)

ACCOMMODATIONS

Allowed in exams:

Calculators	Yes
Dictionary	Yes
Computer	Yes
Spell-checker	Yes
Extended test time	Yes
Scribe	Yes
Proctors	Yes
Oral exams	Yes
Note-takers	No

Support services for students with:

LD	Yes
ADHD	Yes
ASD	Yes
Distraction-reduced environment	Yes
Recording of lecture allowed	Yes
Reading technology	Yes
Audio books	Yes
Other assistive technology	Yes
Priority registration	Yes

Added costs of services:

For LD	No
For ADHD	No
For ASD	No
LD specialists	Yes
ADHD & ASD coaching	Yes
ASD specialists	Yes
Professional tutors	No
Peer tutors	Yes
Max. hours/week for services	Varies
How professors are notified of student approved accommodations	Student

COLLEGE GRADUATION REQUIREMENTS

Course waivers allowed	No
Course substitutions allowed	Yes
In what courses: Varies	

PROGRAMS/SERVICES FOR STUDENTS WITH LEARNING DIFFERENCES

The Office for Students with Disabilities (OSD) coordinates accommodations and services for PennWest Edinboro students with documented disabilities. To receive accommodations, students must register with the OSD, and it is the student's responsibility to request services in a timely manner. OSD reviews documentation and provides an appropriate accommodation form for the student to share with the faculty. Classroom and testing accommodations may include recorded lectures, note-taking assistance, assistive listening devices, calculators, spelling aids, preferential seating, captioning, textbooks and handouts in an alternate format, extended time for various testing formats, readers, scribes, computers, and a quiet testing area with a proctor. The Boro Autism Support Initiative for Success (BASIS) is an individualized support program that works with students to identify needs and provide support. Services include social activities, weekly sessions with a transition coach, social and academic peer advising, testing and classroom accommodations, and writing specialist services. The Boro Opportunities for Organization and Study Techniques program (BOOST) pairs students registered with OSD with peer advisors to work on time management, organization, note-taking, test-taking, and study skills. The Bridge Program is a three-day experience, held before classes begin, that helps new students with disabilities transition to college life.

ADMISSIONS

All applicants are expected to meet the same admission criteria. Occasionally, OSD staff are asked for remarks on certain files, but these are not part of the admission decision. Admission decisions use a combination of high school GPA, test scores (if submitted), and choice of major.

Additional Information

The Center for Student Outreach and Success Coaching offers individual academic support to Edinboro students.

Since 1993, the PennWest campus has hosted the annual Edinboro Highland Games & Scottish Festival, including the U.S. National Scottish Fiddle Competition sanctioned by the Scottish F.I.R.E., Scottish Fiddling Revival, Ltd. The games hold sanctioned competitions in professional and amateur heavy athletics, pipe band, solo piping and drumming, highland dance, and Celtic and Scottish harp. Attendees enjoy Scottish food, vendors, games, crafts for kids, and more.

Pennsylvania Western University, Edinboro

GENERAL ADMISSIONS

Very important factors include: rigor of secondary school record, class rank, academic GPA, standardized test scores (if submitted). *Other factors considered include:* application essay, recommendations. High school diploma is required and GED is accepted. Institution is test-optional for entering Fall 2024. Check admissions website for updates. *Academic units required:* 4 English, 3 math, 3 science, 3 social studies. *Academic units recommended:* 2 foreign language, 4 social studies.

FINANCIAL AID

Students should submit: FAFSA. *Need-based scholarships/grants offered:* College/university scholarship or grant aid from institutional funds; Federal Pell; Private scholarships; SEOG; State scholarships/grants. *Loan aid offered:* Direct Subsidized Loans; Direct Unsubsidized Loans. Federal Work-Study Program available. Institutional employment available.

CAMPUS LIFE

Activities: Campus Ministries; Choral groups; Dance; Drama/theater; International Student Organization; Jazz band; Literary magazine; Marching band; Music ensembles; Opera; Radio station; Student government; Student newspaper; Student-run film society; Television station. **Organizations:** 175 registered organizations, 13 honor societies, 8 religious organizations, 7 fraternities, 7 sororities. **Athletics (Intercollegiate):** *Men:* basketball, cross-country, golf, racquetball, swimming, track/field (indoor), ultimate frisbee, volleyball, wrestling. *Women:* basketball, cross-country, golf, lacrosse, racquetball, softball, swimming, track/field (indoor), ultimate frisbee, volleyball.

CAMPUS

Type of school	Public
Environment	Rural

STUDENTS

Undergrad enrollment	2,939
% male/female	40/60
% from out of state	15
% frosh live on campus	77

FINANCIAL FACTS

Annual in-state tuition	$7,716
Annual out-of-state tuition	$11,574
Room and board	$11,660
Required fees	$2,828

GENERAL ADMISSIONS INFO

Application fee	$30
Regular application deadline	Rolling
Nonfall registration	Yes
Fall 2024 testing policy	Test Optional
Range SAT EBRW	490–600
Range SAT Math	480–570
Range ACT Composite	20–27

ACADEMICS

Student/faculty ratio	16:1
% students returning for sophomore year	71

Most classes have 20–29 students.

REQUESTING SERVICES FOR STUDENTS WITH LEARNING DIFFERENCES

Phone: 814-732-2462 • edinboro.edu/academics/support/accessibility-services
Email: osd-edn@pennwest.edu

Documentation submitted to: Office for Students with Disabilities
Separate application required for Services: Yes

Documentation required for:
 LD: Psychoeducational evaluation
 ADHD: Psychoeducational evaluation
 ASD: Psychoeducational evaluation

Saint Joseph's University

5600 City Avenue, Philadelphia, PA 19131 • Admissions: 610-660-1300 • www.sju.edu

Support: CS

ACCOMMODATIONS

Allowed in exams:

Calculators	Yes
Dictionary	Yes
Computer	Yes
Spell-checker	Yes
Extended test time	Yes
Scribe	Yes
Proctors	Yes
Oral exams	Yes
Note-takers	Yes

Support services for students with:

LD	Yes
ADHD	Yes
ASD	Yes
Distraction-reduced environment	Yes
Recording of lecture allowed	Yes
Reading technology	Yes
Audio books	Yes
Other assistive technology	Yes
Priority registration	Yes

Added costs of services:

For LD	No
For ADHD	No
For ASD	No
LD specialists	No
ADHD & ASD coaching	Yes
ASD specialists	Yes
Professional tutors	No
Peer tutors	Yes
Max. hours/week for services	1
How professors are notified of student approved accommodations	Student Disability Services

COLLEGE GRADUATION REQUIREMENTS

Course waivers allowed	Yes

In what courses: Foreign Language

Course substitutions allowed	Yes

In what courses: Foreign Language

PROGRAMS/SERVICES FOR STUDENTS WITH LEARNING DIFFERENCES

The Office of Student Disability Services (SDS) coordinates support services and determines academic accommodations for students with disabilities. Any student requesting accommodations must first submit the appropriate documentation of their disability to the Office of SDS. These academic adjustments are based on demonstrated needs as supported by documentation. The Success Center offers a variety of programs and services and advocates for students with learning disabilities.

ADMISSIONS

All applicants are expected to meet the same admission criteria. The admission process is designed to get to know the applicant holistically. The application is reviewed based on academic and personal accomplishments, with primary consideration given to the high school record and strong academic performance in college preparatory courses. Competitive applicants usually exceed the minimum academic course requirements. The admissions office also considers the personal essay, letters of academic recommendation, and extracurricular involvement when reviewing applications. Interviews are open to high school seniors to meet one-on-one with a representative from admissions. However, interviews are not required, and those unable to interview are not at a disadvantage. Students applying for direct entry to health professions need a minimum of 3 lab sciences and 3 math courses with a 3.0 GPA.

Additional Information

Services available to all students are offered by the Office of Learning Resources, including the college transition coaching program, which assists students in navigating the transition from high school to college. They help students to reach their academic goals and develop the skills to learn more effectively and efficiently. Services are offered on both the Hawk Hill and University City campuses. Peer tutoring is offered in multiple subjects, and there are Supplemental Instruction sessions in six subjects. These tutors also help to organize study groups. Learning strategy consultations are available for help with note-taking, test preparation, time management, best practices for textbook reading, and more.

Jim Brennan, an ex-Marine and SJU cheerleader, originated the Hawk as the school mascot during the 1954–55 basketball season. The student government raised the $120 needed to buy the first costume. Jim was the Hawk for the next three years. The Hawk is best known for flapping his wings through every basketball game. In 2014, SJU set a Guinness World Record for the most people "flapping" for five minutes consecutively. Since 1992, the student awarded the role of the mascot has been the recipient of an endowed scholarship and is considered a full member of the basketball team.

Saint Joseph's University

GENERAL ADMISSIONS

Very important factors include: rigor of secondary school record, class rank, academic GPA. *Important factors include:* standardized test scores (if submitted), application essay, recommendations. High school diploma is required and GED is accepted. Institution is test-optional for entering Fall 2024. Check admissions website for updates. *Academic units required:* 4 English, 3 math, 2 science (2 labs), 2 foreign language, 2 history. *Academic units recommended:* 4 math, 4 science (4 labs), 4 foreign language, 4 history.

FINANCIAL AID

Students should submit: FAFSA. *Need-based scholarships/grants offered:* College/university scholarship or grant aid from institutional funds; Federal Pell; Private scholarships; SEOG; State scholarships/grants. *Loan aid offered:* Direct PLUS loans; Direct Subsidized Loans; Direct Unsubsidized Loans. Federal Work-Study Program available. Institutional employment available.

CAMPUS LIFE

Activities: Campus Ministries; Choral groups; Dance; Drama/theater; International Student Organization; Jazz band; Literary magazine; Music ensembles; Musical theater; Pep band; Student government; Student newspaper; Student-run film society; Yearbook. **Organizations:** 90 registered organizations, 23 honor societies, 4 fraternities, 5 sororities. **Athletics (Intercollegiate):** *Men:* baseball, basketball, crew/rowing, cross-country, golf, ice hockey, lacrosse, martial arts, rugby, swimming, track/field (indoor), ultimate frisbee, volleyball, water polo. *Women:* basketball, crew/rowing, cross-country, field hockey, golf, ice hockey, lacrosse, martial arts, rugby, softball, swimming, track/field (indoor), ultimate frisbee, volleyball, water polo.

CAMPUS

Type of school	Private (nonprofit)
Environment	Metropolis

STUDENTS

Undergrad enrollment	5,073
% male/female	45/55
% from out of state	44
% frosh live on campus	89

FINANCIAL FACTS

Annual tuition	$51,140
Room and board	$15,740
Required fees	$200

GENERAL ADMISSIONS INFO

Application fee	$50
Regular application deadline	3/1
Nonfall registration	Yes
Fall 2024 testing policy	Test Optional
Range SAT EBRW	570–660
Range SAT math	560–660
Range ACT composite	26–31

ACADEMICS

Student/faculty ratio	10:1
% students returning for sophomore year	86

Most classes have 10–19 students.

REQUESTING SERVICES FOR STUDENTS WITH LEARNING DIFFERENCES

Phone: 610-660-1774 • www.sju.edu/offices/student-life/sds • Email: sds@sju.edu

Documentation submitted to: The Office of Student Disability Services
Separate application required for Services: Yes

Documentation required for:
LD: Psychoeducational evaluation
ADHD: Psychoeducational evaluation
ASD: Psychoeducational evaluation

Seton Hill University

1 Seton Hill Drive, Greensburg, PA 15601 • Admissions: 724-838-4255 • www.setonhill.edu

Support: S

ACCOMMODATIONS

Allowed in exams:

Calculators	Yes
Dictionary	Yes
Computer	Yes
Spell-checker	Yes
Extended test time	Yes
Scribe	Yes
Proctors	Yes
Oral exams	Yes
Note-takers	Yes

Support services for students with:

LD	Yes
ADHD	Yes
ASD	Yes
Distraction-reduced environment	Yes
Recording of lecture allowed	Yes
Reading technology	Yes
Audio books	Yes
Other assistive technology	Yes
Priority registration	Yes

Added costs of services:

For LD	No
For ADHD	No
For ASD	No
LD specialists	No
ADHD & ASD coaching	Yes
ASD specialists	No
Professional tutors	No
Peer tutors	Yes
Max. hours/week for services	Varies
How professors are notified of student approved accommodations	Student

COLLEGE GRADUATION REQUIREMENTS

Course waivers allowed	Yes

In what courses: Case-by-case basis

Course substitutions allowed	Yes

In what courses: Case-by-case basis

DID YOU KNOW?

Each class at Seton Hill designs and creates a banner representing its class colors and motto. In the spring, a baccalaureate mass precedes commencement, where senior class officers lead the procession and display their banner. Seton Hill displays class banners with pride during commencement ceremonies, homecoming, and various alumni events and celebrations.

PROGRAMS/SERVICES FOR STUDENTS WITH LEARNING DIFFERENCES

The Office of Disability Services (ODS) offers support to students with disabilities. ODS recommends that first-year students seeking accommodations contact the office in the summer before the fall semester begins. The director and associate director of ODS work closely with each student to determine accommodations that meet individual needs, based on the student's provided documentation and accompanying interview. Accommodations can include notetakers, learning materials in accessible formats, preferential seating in classes or at events, and extended time in a distraction-reduced testing environment.

ADMISSIONS

All students complete the same application process for general admission to SHU by submitting an official high school transcript or GED certificate. Applicants who have earned a minimum cumulative GPA of 2.5 or scored 165 in all levels of the GED may choose not to report SAT or ACT scores. Students who apply for test-optional admission are required to submit responses to essay questions. Applicants who submit their test scores have the option of including an essay on why they are choosing SHU, as well as the option of providing a letter of recommendation from a teacher, guidance counselor, or another source. Some specific programs may still require SAT or ACT scores, an interview, or an audition as part of the application. The Opportunity Program may be offered to first-year applicants as a condition of acceptance. Opportunity Program students are required to complete a free, week-long course with a minimum passing C grade to remain enrolled at SHU. They will also take Mastering College Academics I and II during their first year. Opportunity students receive an academic coach, a peer mentor, and the chance to attend events hosted by peer mentors. Students in the program are eligible for an Opportunity grant for every semester they attend SHU. For students admitted through the Collegiate, Academic & Personal Success Program (CAPS), during their first semester they will take Mastering College Academics for 1 credit and meet regularly with an academic coach. If they are in good academic standing after their first semester, they have no further requirements but are welcome to take advantage of the program's resources. If a student's grades begin to falter after their first semester, CAPS will reach out to the student to help. Students admitted through CAPS become eligible for CAPS grants each semester they attend the university.

Additional Information

The Academic Achievement Center provides study skills workshops, academic counseling, and course-specific group and individualized tutoring. Course-specific group and one-on-one tutoring sessions are also offered at the Mathematics Enrichment Center. Students may attend workshops or meet with professional staff and student writing consultants to improve their writing skills at the Writing Center.

Seton Hill University

General Admissions

Very important factors include: rigor of secondary school record, academic GPA. *Important factors include:* class rank, standardized test scores (if submitted). *Other factors considered include:* application essay, recommendations. High school diploma is required and GED is accepted. Institution is test-optional for entering Fall 2024. Check admissions website for updates. *Academic units required:* 4 English, 2 math, 1 science (1 lab), 3 social studies, 4 academic electives. *Academic units recommended:* 2 foreign language.

Financial Aid

Students should submit: FAFSA; Institution's own financial aid form; State aid form. *Need-based scholarships/grants offered:* College/university scholarship or grant aid from institutional funds; Federal Pell; Private scholarships; SEOG; State scholarships/grants. *Loan aid offered:* Direct PLUS loans; Direct Subsidized Loans; Direct Unsubsidized Loans. Federal Work-Study Program available. Institutional employment available.

Campus Life

Activities: Campus Ministries; Choral groups; Concert band; Dance; Drama/theater; International Student Organization; Jazz band; Literary magazine; Marching band; Model UN; Music ensembles; Musical theater; Pep band; Student government; Student newspaper; Symphony orchestra. **Organizations:** 40 registered organizations, 4 honor societies, 6 religious organizations, 0 fraternities, 0 sororities. **Athletics (Intercollegiate):** *Men:* baseball, basketball, cross-country, lacrosse, track/field (indoor), wrestling. *Women:* basketball, cross-country, equestrian sports, field hockey, golf, lacrosse, softball, track/field (indoor), volleyball.

CAMPUS
Type of school	Private (nonprofit)
Environment	Town

STUDENTS
Undergrad enrollment	1,653
% male/female	35/65
% from out of state	21
% frosh live on campus	78

FINANCIAL FACTS
Annual tuition	$39,674
Room and board	$13,350
Required fees	$550

GENERAL ADMISSIONS INFO
Application fee	No fee
Regular application deadline	8/15
Nonfall registration	Yes

Fall 2024 testing policy	Test Optional
Range SAT EBRW	530–630
Range SAT Math	520–610
Range ACT Composite	23–27

ACADEMICS
Student/faculty ratio	13:1
% students returning for sophomore year	82

Most classes have 10–19 students.

REQUESTING SERVICES FOR STUDENTS WITH LEARNING DIFFERENCES

Phone: 724-838-4295 • www.setonhill.edu/academics/academic-support-resources/disability-services-2/
Email: disabilityservices@setonhill.edu

Documentation submitted to: Office of Disability Services
Separate application required for Services: Yes

Documentation required for:
LD: Psychoeducational evaluation
ADHD: Psychoeducational evaluation
ASD: Psychoeducational evaluation

Temple University

1801 North Broad Street, Philadelphia, PA 19122-6096 · Admissions: 215-204-7200 · www.temple.edu

Support: S

ACCOMMODATIONS

Allowed in exams:

Calculators	Yes
Dictionary	Yes
Computer	Yes
Spell-checker	Yes
Extended test time	Yes
Scribe	Yes
Proctors	Yes
Oral exams	Yes
Note-takers	Yes

Support services for students with:

LD	Yes
ADHD	Yes
ASD	Yes
Distraction-reduced environment	Yes
Recording of lecture allowed	Yes
Reading technology	Yes
Audio books	Yes
Other assistive technology	Yes
Priority registration	Yes

Added costs of services:

For LD	No
For ADHD	No
For ASD	No
LD specialists	No
ADHD & ASD coaching	Yes
ASD specialists	No
Professional tutors	No
Peer tutors	Yes
Max. hours/week for services	20
How professors are notified of student approved accommodations	Student and Disability Resources and Services

COLLEGE GRADUATION REQUIREMENTS

Course waivers allowed	No
Course substitutions allowed	Yes
In what courses: Math and Foreign Language	

PROGRAMS/SERVICES FOR STUDENTS WITH LEARNING DIFFERENCES

Disability Resources and Services (DRS) provides accommodations for students with disabilities. Once they are registered with the university, students can access and register with DRS in their dedicated online portal. Students who do not have documentation should still register and meet with DRS to discuss accommodation needs. Once registered, students can use the DRS portal to schedule an appointment to meet with a DRS coordinator, during which they will discuss and determine reasonable accommodations. An accommodations letter will be the official document students take to their professors and use to discuss implementation in the classroom. The DRS portal can be used to access letters of accommodations, request an accommodation during placement assessments, access assistive technology, and schedule appointments and exams. Students with disabilities can come together at SHOUT (Students Helping Owls Understand Temple), a free peer support group for students with disabilities. SHOUT members meet biweekly to share stories, lend support, learn strategies, and connect with other students with disabilities. Social Xchanges is a weekly recreation program for students with social and communication challenges. The group meets to discuss social and academic challenges and successes, and then follows the meeting with a recreational activity.

ADMISSIONS

All students applying to Temple follow the same application procedures. Applicants are required to provide a copy of their high school transcript, GED, or proof of homeschooling, as defined by state law. A personal essay and up to two letters of recommendation are optional. The average high school GPA for admitted applicants is 3.42. For those submitting test scores, the average SAT score is 1273 and the average ACT score is 28.

Additional Information

The Student Success Center (SSC) offers academic coaching that helps students develop college-level learning skills. Students can also schedule appointments at SSC to practice their foreign language skills with Conversation Partners in English, Spanish, Arabic, or Japanese. Peer Assisted Study Sessions (PASS) are weekly study sessions in challenging courses like chemistry, physics, or calculus. No appointment is necessary for either of the two PASS sessions each week. Students can make appointments with the Writing Center for help at any stage of a writing project, from inspiration to final draft. The STEM Learning Lab offers one-on-one tutoring, reviews, practice tests, and pre-recorded video lessons.

In 1884, Temple founder Russell H. Conwell began teaching students who could only attend class at night. By 1888, his night school received a charter of incorporation. These "night owl" students were the inspiration for Hooter the Owl mascot, part of the Spirit Squad at games and events. Hooter's birthday in February is celebrated with mascots from all over Philadelphia at a home basketball game.

Temple University

GENERAL ADMISSIONS

Very important factors include: rigor of secondary school record, academic GPA. *Other factors considered include:* standardized test scores (if submitted), application essay, recommendations. High school diploma is required and GED is accepted. Institution is test-optional for entering Fall 2024. Check admissions website for updates. *Academic units required:* 4 English, 3 math, 2 science (1 labs), 2 foreign language, 3 social studies, 1 academic elective, 1 visual/performing arts. *Academic units recommended:* 4 math, 3 science (2 labs), 3 academic electives.

FINANCIAL AID

Students should submit: FAFSA; State aid form. *Need-based scholarships/grants offered:* College/university scholarship or grant aid from institutional funds; Federal Nursing Scholarships; Federal Pell; Private scholarships; SEOG; State scholarships/grants; United Negro College Fund. *Loan aid offered:* Direct PLUS loans; Direct Subsidized Loans; Direct Unsubsidized Loans. Federal Work-Study Program available. Institutional employment available.

CAMPUS LIFE

Activities: Campus Ministries; Choral groups; Concert band; Dance; Drama/theater; International Student Organization; Jazz band; Literary magazine; Marching band; Model UN; Music ensembles; Musical theater; Opera; Pep band; Radio station; Student government; Student newspaper; Student-run film society; Symphony orchestra; Television station; Yearbook. **Organizations:** 271 registered organizations, 29 honor societies, 32 religious organizations, 17 fraternities, 17 sororities. **Athletics (Intercollegiate):** *Men:* baseball, basketball, bowling, crew/rowing, cross-country, cycling, equestrian sports, golf, gymnastics, ice hockey, lacrosse, rugby, swimming, track/field (indoor), ultimate frisbee, volleyball, wrestling. *Women:* basketball, bowling, crew/rowing, cross-country, cycling, equestrian sports, field hockey, gymnastics, lacrosse, rugby, softball, swimming, track/field (indoor), ultimate frisbee, volleyball.

CAMPUS

Type of school	Public
Environment	Metropolis

STUDENTS

Undergrad enrollment	23,697
% male/female	44/56
% from out of state	26
% frosh live on campus	76

FINANCIAL FACTS

Annual in-state tuition	$20,171
Annual out-of-state tuition	$35,032
Room and board	$13,612
Required fees	$924

GENERAL ADMISSIONS INFO

Application fee	$55
Regular application deadline	2/1
Nonfall registration	Yes

Fall 2024 testing policy	Test Optional
Range SAT EBRW	570–690
Range SAT Math	550–680
Range ACT Composite	24–31

ACADEMICS

Student/faculty ratio	12:1
% students returning for sophomore year	84

Most classes have 10–19 students.

REQUESTING SERVICES FOR STUDENTS WITH LEARNING DIFFERENCES

Phone: 215-204-1280 • disabilityresources.temple.edu • Email: drs@temple.edu

Documentation submitted to: Disability Resources and Services

Separate application required for Services: Yes

Documentation required for:
LD: Psychoeducational evaluation
ADHD: Psychoeducational evaluation
ASD: Psychoeducational evaluation

University of Pittsburgh

4227 Fifth Avenue, Pittsburgh, PA 15260 • Admissions: 412-624-7488 • www.pitt.edu

Support: CS

ACCOMMODATIONS

Allowed in exams:

Calculators	Yes
Dictionary	No
Computer	Yes
Spell-checker	Yes
Extended test time	Yes
Scribe	Yes
Proctors	Yes
Oral exams	No
Note-takers	Yes

Support services for students with:

LD	Yes
ADHD	Yes
ASD	Yes
Distraction-reduced environment	Yes
Recording of lecture allowed	Yes
Reading technology	Yes
Audio books	Yes
Other assistive technology	Yes
Priority registration	Yes

Added costs of services:

For LD	No
For ADHD	No
For ASD	No
LD specialists	Yes
ADHD & ASD coaching	No
ASD specialists	No
Professional tutors	No
Peer tutors	Yes
Max. hours/week for services	Varies
How professors are notified of student approved accommodations	Student and Disability Resources and Services

COLLEGE GRADUATION REQUIREMENTS

Course waivers allowed	No
Course substitutions allowed	Yes
In what courses: Case-by-case basis	

PROGRAMS/SERVICES FOR STUDENTS WITH LEARNING DIFFERENCES

The University of Pittsburgh serves students with learning differences through Disability Resources and Services (DRS) under the Office for Equity, Diversity, and Inclusion. DRS offers and coordinates testing accommodations, note-taking, peer mentoring, assistive technologies, academic resources, and community resources to support students. Once admitted, students must complete an online application with DRS and submit the required documentation. Collaboration between the disability specialist, the student, the diagnosing professional, and the program director or course instructor determines reasonable accommodations. The student is responsible for requesting disability notification letters to inform faculty members of the accommodations. The DRS Peer Mentoring Program matches new students and mentors who both have disabilities. This is not intended for academic support, but to provide guidance and connection. Students are expected to participate in meetings and planned social activities to further assist in developing relationships and gaining information. On-campus student organizations exist to support students with autism and mental health challenges. There is also a local organization specific to students with autism that provides academic and organizational coaching, employment coaching, and social and self-advocacy groups.

ADMISSIONS

All applicants are expected to meet the same admission criteria. Some applicants apply to the university through the Guaranteed Admission Program for certain programs such as medicine, business, and engineering. General admission applicants must submit the application and a Self-Reported Academic Record (SRAR), which includes courses and grades. Personal statements help the university to know about the student and are required for scholarships. The average weighted GPA for accepted students is 3.9–4.4, and the average test scores (if submitted) are 29–33 ACT or 1270–1450 SAT.

Additional Information

The Stress Free Zone is a place where students can learn and regularly practice evidence-based, mind/body stress reduction skills, including mindfulness meditation and yoga.

The Men's Glee Club, founded in 1890, is the oldest non-athletic extracurricular activity on campus and has toured the U.S., Canada, Mexico, and Europe. For more than 75 years, the Heinz Chapel Choir has presented a cappella music representing a variety of time periods, cultural traditions, and languages. Founded in 1927, Pitts Women's Choral Ensemble sings the National Anthem for the Pitt women's soccer team home games, participates in the Women's Choir Festival in western Pennsylvania, and performs each semester on campus.

University of Pittsburgh

GENERAL ADMISSIONS

Very important factors include: rigor of secondary school record, academic GPA, application essay. *Other factors considered include:* class rank, standardized test scores (if submitted), recommendations. High school diploma is required and GED is accepted. Institution is test-optional for entering Fall 2024. Check admissions website for updates. *Academic units required:* 4 English, 3 math, 3 science, 2 foreign language, 2 social studies, 3 academic electives. *Academic units recommended:* 4 math, 4 science, 3 foreign language, 3 social studies, 5 academic electives.

FINANCIAL AID

Students should submit: FAFSA; State aid form. *Need-based scholarships/grants offered:* College/university scholarship or grant aid from institutional funds; Federal Pell; Private scholarships; SEOG; State scholarships/grants. *Loan aid offered:* Direct PLUS loans; Direct Subsidized Loans; Direct Unsubsidized Loans. Federal Work-Study Program available. Institutional employment available.

CAMPUS LIFE

Activities: Campus Ministries; Choral groups; Concert band; Dance; Drama/theater; International Student Organization; Jazz band; Literary magazine; Marching band; Model UN; Music ensembles; Musical theater; Pep band; Radio station; Student government; Student newspaper; Student-run film society; Symphony orchestra; Television station. **Organizations:** 694 registered organizations, 17 honor societies, 25 fraternities, 20 sororities. **Athletics (Intercollegiate):** *Men:* baseball, basketball, crew/rowing, cross-country, cycling, equestrian sports, field hockey, golf, ice hockey, lacrosse, martial arts, racquetball, rugby, swimming, ultimate frisbee, volleyball, water polo, wrestling. *Women:* basketball, crew/rowing, cross-country, cycling, equestrian sports, field hockey, golf, gymnastics, ice hockey, lacrosse, martial arts, racquetball, rugby, softball, swimming, ultimate frisbee, volleyball, water polo, wrestling.

CAMPUS

Type of school	Public
Environment	Metropolis

STUDENTS

Undergrad enrollment	19,803
% male/female	43/57
% from out of state	36
% frosh live on campus	96

FINANCIAL FACTS

Annual in-state tuition	$19,760
Annual out-of-state tuition	$36,000
Room and board	$12,360
Required fees	$1,320

GENERAL ADMISSIONS INFO

Application fee	$55
Nonfall registration	Yes
Fall 2024 testing policy	Test Optional
Range SAT EBRW	640–720
Range SAT Math	640–750
Range ACT Composite	29–33

ACADEMICS

Student/faculty ratio	14:1
% students returning for sophomore year	93
Most classes have 10–19 students.	

REQUESTING SERVICES FOR STUDENTS WITH LEARNING DIFFERENCES

Phone: 412-648-7890 • www.drs.pitt.edu • Email: drsrecep@pitt.edu

Documentation submitted to: Disability Resources and Services
Separate application required for Services: Yes

Documentation required for:
LD: Psychoeducational evaluation
ADHD: Psychoeducational evaluation
ASD: Psychoeducational evaluation

Widener University

One University Place, Chester, PA 19013 • Admissions: 610-499-4126 • www.widener.edu

(Support: CS)

ACCOMMODATIONS

Allowed in exams:

Calculators	Yes
Dictionary	Yes
Computer	Yes
Spell-checker	Yes
Extended test time	Yes
Scribe	Yes
Proctors	Yes
Oral exams	Yes
Note-takers	Yes

Support services for students with:

LD	Yes
ADHD	Yes
ASD	Yes
Distraction-reduced environment	Yes
Recording of lecture allowed	Yes
Reading technology	Yes
Audio books	Yes
Other assistive technology	Yes
Priority registration	Yes

Added costs of services:

For LD	No
For ADHD	No
For ASD	No
LD specialists	Yes
ADHD & ASD coaching	No
ASD specialists	No
Professional tutors	Yes
Peer tutors	Yes
Max. hours/week for services	Varies
How professors are notified of student approved accommodations	Student

COLLEGE GRADUATION REQUIREMENTS

Course waivers allowed	No
Course substitutions allowed	No

PROGRAMS/SERVICES FOR STUDENTS WITH LEARNING DIFFERENCES

Widener University's Office of Student Accessibility Services (SAS) provides services to students with documented learning differences. The SAS office works to create an equitable living and learning environment for all students. To request services, students must complete the request form, submit eligible documentation from either a treatment provider or evaluation provider, and meet with an SAS advocate. SAS staff ensure that accommodations are provided, and commonly requested services include extended time for test-taking, notetakers, and distraction-reduced testing spaces.

ADMISSIONS

All applicants are expected to meet the same admission criteria. Applicants who do not submit test scores must submit an essay. Test-optional applications are evaluated based on the strength of the personal essay, cumulative high school GPA, and performance in courses specific to the anticipated major. Recommendation letters are not required; however, they can be submitted to strengthen the application. Most admitted students have a minimum 2.0 GPA.

Additional Information

Academic coaches are available to all students for one-on-one help with time management, study skills, social and emotional adjustment, and academic planning. Coaches may also refer students to the Writing Center, Math Center, and peer-to-peer tutoring services. The Writing Center provides assistance with writing assignments, while the Math Center offers individual and group tutoring. Students can also meet with a career counselor to develop a career profile that includes a cover letter and résumé and receive support with interviewing and job searches.

Founded in 1821 as The Bullock School for Boys, Widener has a long and distinguished history. Under the direction of General Charles Hyatt, in 1858, it became the Pennsylvania Military College, one of the nation's senior military colleges. In 1904, PMC was recognized on the first list of distinguished institutions by the U.S. War Department. In 1923, John Philip Sousa wrote and dedicated "The Dauntless Battalion" march to PMC's president, faculty, and cadets. In 1972, with declining enrollment and anti-military sentiment surrounding the Vietnam War, Widener moved from a military college to a civilian one.

Widener University

GENERAL ADMISSIONS

Very important factors include: rigor of secondary school record, class rank, academic GPA, standardized test scores (if submitted). *Other factors considered include:* application essay, recommendations. High school diploma is required and GED is accepted. Institution is test-optional for entering Fall 2024. Check admissions website for updates. *Academic units required:* 4 English, 3 math, 3 science, 2 foreign language, 3 social studies, 3 academic electives. *Academic units recommended:* 4 math, 4 science (2 labs), 4 social studies.

FINANCIAL AID

Students should submit: FAFSA. *Need-based scholarships/grants offered:* College/university scholarship or grant aid from institutional funds; Federal Pell; Private scholarships; SEOG; State scholarships/grants. *Loan aid offered:* Direct PLUS loans; Direct Subsidized Loans; Direct Unsubsidized Loans. Federal Work-Study Program available. Institutional employment available.

CAMPUS LIFE

Activities: Campus Ministries; Choral groups; Concert band; Dance; Drama/theater; International Student Organization; Jazz band; Literary magazine; Marching band; Music ensembles; Pep band; Radio station; Student government; Student-run film society; Television station. **Organizations:** 80 registered organizations, 29 honor societies, 3 religious organizations, 5 fraternities, 6 sororities. **Athletics (Intercollegiate):** *Men:* baseball, basketball, cross-country, golf, ice hockey, lacrosse, rugby, swimming, track/field (indoor), volleyball. *Women:* basketball, cross-country, field hockey, golf, lacrosse, rugby, softball, swimming, track/field (indoor), volleyball.

CAMPUS

Type of school	Private (nonprofit)
Environment	Town

STUDENTS

Undergrad enrollment	2,766
% male/female	42/58
% from out of state	40
% frosh live on campus	87

FINANCIAL FACTS

Annual tuition	$48,724
Room and board	$14,808
Required fees	$982

GENERAL ADMISSIONS INFO

Application fee	No fee
Regular application deadline	Rolling
Nonfall registration	Yes
Fall 2024 testing policy	Test Optional
Range SAT EBRW	540–635
Range SAT Math	540–640

ACADEMICS

Student/faculty ratio	12:1
% students returning for sophomore year	85

Most classes have 10–19 students.

REQUESTING SERVICES FOR STUDENTS WITH LEARNING DIFFERENCES

Phone: 610-499-1266 • www.widener.edu/student-experience/student-success-support/student-accessibility-services • Email: rross@widener.edu

Documentation submitted to: Student Accessibility Services
Separate application required for Services: Yes

Documentation required for:
LD: Psychoeducational evaluation
ADHD: Psychoeducational evaluation
ASD: Psychoeducational evaluation

Brown University

P.O. Box 1876, Providence, RI 02912 • Admissions: 401-863-2378 • www.brown.edu

Support: S

ACCOMMODATIONS

Allowed in exams:

Calculators	Yes
Dictionary	Yes
Computer	Yes
Spell-checker	Yes
Extended test time	Yes
Scribe	Yes
Proctors	Yes
Oral exams	Yes
Note-takers	Yes

Support services for students with:

LD	Yes
ADHD	Yes
ASD	Yes
Distraction-reduced environment	Yes
Recording of lecture allowed	Yes
Reading technology	Yes
Audio books	Yes
Other assistive technology	Yes
Priority registration	No

Added costs of services:

For LD	No
For ADHD	No
For ASD	No
LD specialists	No
ADHD & ASD coaching	Yes
ASD specialists	No
Professional tutors	No
Peer tutors	Yes
Max. hours/week for services	2
How professors are notified of student approved accommodations	Student

COLLEGE GRADUATION REQUIREMENTS

Course waivers allowed	N/A
Course substitutions allowed	N/A

PROGRAMS/SERVICES FOR STUDENTS WITH LEARNING DIFFERENCES

Student Accessibility Services (SAS) offers accommodations to students with disabilities. Students register with SAS by submitting an information and release form along with disability documentation to the SAS office. Next, students will meet online or in person with a SAS staff member. At the meeting, students have their accommodations officially approved and learn how to communicate their needs with faculty. Brown provides a range of accommodations, including course material in an alternate format, use of assistive technology, notetakers, permission to record lessons, modified exam time or location, and a reduced course load with prorated tuition. Students registered with SAS may be eligible for individual tutors. There is an ADHD support group for students to discuss a variety of topics, such as medication, frustrations, study tips, relationships, and schoolwork. The group meets weekly or as needed.

ADMISSIONS

All applicants submit the same general admission application, although some programs and majors may have additional requirements. The most important considerations in the admission process are high school performance and coursework that illustrates a preparation for college learning. A high school report, personal essay, counselor recommendation, and two teacher evaluations are required. Students may submit two optional teacher evaluations and one optional evaluation from another source to be considered.

Additional Information

The college assigns each first-year student two advisors to help them navigate its open curriculum and campus resources and adjust to college life. The advisors include an academic advisor who is a Brown faculty member or administrator, and a peer advisor. The Math Resource Center provides tutors, tutoring groups, and a place for students to study. The Writing Center provides students assistance at all stages of their writing, from thesis to final edits. Small-group tutoring is available for STEM-related courses and language courses.

The Brown University Van Wickle Gates were built in 1901 with the bequest of Augustus Stout Van Wickle, class of 1876. The center gates remain closed except for two special occasions. They open inward to welcome new students to the campus at opening convocation, and open outward for the graduating students during the commencement procession.

Brown University

General Admissions

Very important factors include: rigor of secondary school record, class rank, academic GPA, application essay, recommendations. *Other factors considered include:* standardized test scores (if submitted). High school diploma is required and GED is accepted. Institution is test-optional for entering Fall 2024. Check admissions website for updates. *Academic units required:* 4 English, 4 math, 3 science (2 labs), 3 foreign language, 3 social studies. *Academic units recommended:* 4 science (3 labs), 4 foreign language, 4 social studies, 1 visual/performing arts.

Financial Aid

Students should submit: CSS/Financial Aid Profile; FAFSA; Noncustodial Profile. *Need-based scholarships/grants offered:* College/university scholarship or grant aid from institutional funds; Federal Pell; Private scholarships; SEOG; State scholarships/grants. *Loan aid offered:* Direct PLUS loans; Direct Subsidized Loans; Direct Unsubsidized Loans. Federal Work-Study Program available. Institutional employment available.

Campus Life

Activities: Campus Ministries; Choral groups; Concert band; Dance; Drama/theater; International Student Organization; Jazz band; Literary magazine; Marching band; Model UN; Music ensembles; Musical theater; Opera; Pep band; Radio station; Student government; Student newspaper; Student-run film society; Symphony orchestra; Television station; Yearbook. **Organizations:** 453 registered organizations, 4 honor societies, 18 religious organizations, 9 fraternities, 7 sororities. **Athletics (Intercollegiate):** *Men:* baseball, basketball, crew/rowing, cross-country, cycling, golf, ice hockey, lacrosse, martial arts, rugby, swimming, track/field (indoor), ultimate frisbee, volleyball, water polo, wrestling. *Women:* basketball, crew/rowing, cross-country, cycling, equestrian sports, field hockey, golf, gymnastics, ice hockey, lacrosse, martial arts, rugby, softball, swimming, track/field (indoor), ultimate frisbee, volleyball, water polo, wrestling.

Rhode Island

CAMPUS
Type of school	Private (nonprofit)
Environment	City

STUDENTS
Undergrad enrollment	7,221
% male/female	49/51
% from out of state	94
% frosh live on campus	99

FINANCIAL FACTS
Annual tuition	$65,656
Room and board	$16,598
Required fees	$2,474

GENERAL ADMISSIONS INFO
Application fee	$75
Regular application deadline	1/3
Nonfall registration	No

Fall 2024 testing policy	Test Optional
Range SAT EBRW	730–780
Range SAT Math	760–800
Range ACT Composite	34–36

ACADEMICS
Student/faculty ratio	6:1
% students returning for sophomore year	99

Most classes have 10–19 students.

REQUESTING SERVICES FOR STUDENTS WITH LEARNING DIFFERENCES

Phone: 401-863-9588 • www.brown.edu/campus-life/support/accessibility-services/
Email: sas@brown.edu

Documentation submitted to: Student Accessibility Services (SAS)
Separate application required for Services: Yes

Documentation required for:
LD: Psychoeducational evaluation
ADHD: Psychoeducational evaluation
ASD: Psychoeducational evaluation

Bryant University

1150 Douglas Pike, Smithfield, RI 02917 • Admissions: 401-232-6100 • www.bryant.edu

Support: CS

ACCOMMODATIONS

Allowed in exams:

Calculators	Yes
Dictionary	No
Computer	Yes
Spell-checker	Yes
Extended test time	Yes
Scribe	Yes
Proctors	Yes
Oral exams	Yes
Note-takers	Yes

Support services for students with:

LD	Yes
ADHD	Yes
ASD	Yes
Distraction-reduced environment	Yes
Recording of lecture allowed	Yes
Reading technology	Yes
Audio books	Yes
Other assistive technology	Yes
Priority registration	No

Added costs of services:

For LD	No
For ADHD	No
For ASD	No
LD specialists	Yes
ADHD & ASD coaching	Yes
ASD specialists	No
Professional tutors	Yes
Peer tutors	Yes
Max. hours/week for services	Varies
How professors are notified of student approved accommodations	Office of Accessibility Services

COLLEGE GRADUATION REQUIREMENTS

Course waivers allowed	No
Course substitutions allowed	Yes

In what courses: Math and Foreign Language

PROGRAMS/SERVICES FOR STUDENTS WITH LEARNING DIFFERENCES

The Office of Accessibility Services (OAS) serves the needs of students with disabilities. Upon acceptance, students may submit an online accommodation application documenting their disability. Students then meet with specialists to tailor their accommodations to their current courses. For each following semester, students will submit requests for accommodations in each of their assigned classes. The accommodation specialists provide ongoing support to students throughout the semester, as well as to prospective students and their families. Additionally, the PAWS (Promoting Access, Wellness, and Success) mentoring program helps first-year students with disabilities to ease the transition to college life. Students can find community through the Delta Alpha Pi (DAPi) honor society for students with disabilities, as well as raise awareness about disability on campus.

ADMISSIONS

All applicants are required to submit an official transcript showing senior courses and their most recent grades. Students will also include a personal statement and a recommendation from a guidance counselor. Teacher evaluations and SAT/ACT scores are optional. In lieu of test scores, admissions places an increased emphasis on transcripts and rigor of curriculum. The admission committee also looks at cocurricular activities, community involvement, writing ability, and other achievements when making final decisions. While interviews are not required, they do provide an opportunity for the students to self-advocate, elaborate on themselves, and ask questions. All applicants to Bryant are considered for merit scholarships during the review process.

Additional Information

The Academic Center for Excellence (ACE) provides learning resources for students, including subject tutoring and development of study strategies. In Learning Labs, students can pursue coursework and test preparation, either independently or with help from the labs' peer tutors. Learning Labs cover practical topics from finance and accounting to understanding the psychology of procrastination. The ACE Writing Center's peer writing consultants and professional staff are also available to help students with papers for any course.

Bryant was founded in 1863, and founding partner Ezra Mason inspired women to attend from the start. In 1865, he declared, "We have had the privilege of awarding diplomas to young ladies whose thorough attainments in all the requisites of accountantship would put to blush the pretensions of many a bearded competitor for like honors."

Bryant University

GENERAL ADMISSIONS

Very important factors include: rigor of secondary school record, academic GPA. *Important factors include:* class rank, standardized test scores (if submitted), application essay, recommendations. High school diploma is required and GED is accepted. Institution is test-optional for entering Fall 2024. Check admissions website for updates. *Academic units required:* 4 English, 4 math, 2 science (2 labs), 2 foreign language, 2 history. *Academic units recommended:* 3 science (3 labs), 3 history.

FINANCIAL AID

Students should submit: FAFSA. *Need-based scholarships/grants offered:* College/university scholarship or grant aid from institutional funds; Federal Pell; Private scholarships; SEOG; State scholarships/grants. *Loan aid offered:* Direct PLUS loans; Direct Subsidized Loans; Direct Unsubsidized Loans. Federal Work-Study Program available. Institutional employment available.

CAMPUS LIFE

Activities: Campus Ministries; Choral groups; Dance; Drama/theater; International Student Organization; Jazz band; Literary magazine; Music ensembles; Musical theater; Pep band; Radio station; Student government; Student newspaper; Television station; Yearbook. **Organizations:** 105 registered organizations, 14 honor societies, 6 religious organizations, 4 fraternities, 4 sororities. **Athletics (Intercollegiate):** *Men:* baseball, basketball, bowling, cross-country, golf, ice hockey, lacrosse, martial arts, racquetball, rugby, swimming, track/field (indoor), ultimate frisbee, volleyball. *Women:* basketball, bowling, crew/rowing, cross-country, field hockey, gymnastics, lacrosse, martial arts, racquetball, rugby, softball, swimming, track/field (indoor), ultimate frisbee, volleyball.

CAMPUS

Type of school	Private (nonprofit)
Environment	Village

STUDENTS

Undergrad enrollment	3,136
% male/female	64/36
% from out of state	88
% frosh live on campus	93

FINANCIAL FACTS

Annual tuition	$50,272
Room and board	$17,258
Required fees	$897

GENERAL ADMISSIONS INFO

Application fee	$50
Regular application deadline	2/1
Nonfall registration	Yes

Fall 2024 testing policy	Test Optional
Range SAT EBRW	580–650
Range SAT Math	583–670
Range ACT Composite	27–32

ACADEMICS

Student/faculty ratio	13:1
% students returning for sophomore year	86

Most classes have 30-39 students.

REQUESTING SERVICES FOR STUDENTS WITH LEARNING DIFFERENCES

Phone: 401-232-6830 • info.bryant.edu/accessibility-services • Email: msaddlemire@bryant.edu

Documentation submitted to: Office of Accessibility Services
Separate application required for Services: Yes

Documentation required for:
LD: Psychoeducational evaluation
ADHD: Psychoeducational evaluation
ASD: Psychoeducational evaluation

Johnson & Wales University

8 Abbott Park Place, Providence, RI 02903 • Admissions: 401-598-1000 • jwu.edu

Support: SP

ACCOMMODATIONS

Allowed in exams:

Calculators	Yes
Dictionary	Yes
Computer	Yes
Spell-checker	Yes
Extended test time	Yes
Scribe	Yes
Proctors	Yes
Oral exams	Yes
Note-takers	Yes

Support services for students with:

LD	Yes
ADHD	Yes
ASD	Yes
Distraction-reduced environment	Yes
Recording of lecture allowed	Yes
Reading technology	Yes
Audio books	Yes
Other assistive technology	Yes
Priority registration	Yes

Added costs of services:

For LD	Yes
For ADHD	Yes
For ASD	Yes
LD specialists	Yes
ADHD & ASD coaching	Yes
ASD specialists	Yes
Professional tutors	Yes
Peer tutors	Yes
Max. hours/week for services	Varies
How professors are notified of student approved accommodations	Student

COLLEGE GRADUATION REQUIREMENTS

Course waivers allowed	Yes
In what courses: Varies	
Course substitutions allowed	Yes
In what courses: Varies	

PROGRAMS/SERVICES FOR STUDENTS WITH LEARNING DIFFERENCES

The Accessibility Services office at Johnson & Wales provides reasonable accommodations for students with learning differences. Accommodative resources include notetakers, a reduced course load, audio recordings, extended test time, and more. To obtain accommodations, students will meet with an Accessibility Services advisor and submit eligible documentation. Johnson & Wales also offers the Wildcats LEAP program, a fee-based 10-month program for students with learning disabilities or ADHD. The program begins the summer prior to college, starting with a 10-day summer experience. The program continues during the school year, and through one-on-one coaching and small group sessions, students build an academic portfolio that includes identified learning strategies, and earning 3 college credits.

ADMISSIONS

Johnson & Wales University is test-optional for general admissions; however, students are encouraged to submit scores and essays that may enhance applications. The minimum GPA for admission consideration is 2.75. Applications are evaluated based on transcripts, community involvement, and other areas to gain a holistic view of the student's ability to thrive on campus.

Additional Information

To apply for LEAP, students complete an online application and upload a copy of their Individualized (IEP) or 504 Plan along with documentation from a licensed evaluator. The application process includes 13 short-answer questions that are centered on understanding the student's interests, high school experiences, learning strengths and challenges, self-perception of abilities to practice life skills, and desired accommodations. Students are also invited to complete an interview as part of the eligibility process.

J & W Business School was founded in 1914 and opened with one student and one typewriter, but soon moved to larger sites to accommodate new students. During the 1960s–1970s, as hotels and department stores moved to the suburbs, J & W expanded its downtown presence by purchasing the Crown Hotel in 1966 and the Dreyfus Hotel & Gladding's Department Store in 1975. J&W also operates hotels used as practical education facilities for the university's Hotel & Lodging Management, Food Service Management, and Culinary Arts degree programs.

Johnson & Wales University

GENERAL ADMISSIONS

Very important factors include: rigor of secondary school record, class rank, academic GPA. *Other factors considered include:* standardized test scores (if submitted), application essay, recommendations. High school diploma is required and GED is accepted. Institution is test-optional for entering Fall 2024. Check admissions website for updates. *Academic units required:* 4 English, 3 math, 3 science, 2 foreign language, 3 social studies.

FINANCIAL AID

Students should submit: FAFSA. *Need-based scholarships/grants offered:* College/university scholarship or grant aid from institutional funds; Federal Pell; Private scholarships; SEOG; State scholarships/grants. *Loan aid offered:* Direct PLUS loans; Direct Subsidized Loans; Direct Unsubsidized Loans.

CAMPUS LIFE

Activities: Campus Ministries; Choral groups; Dance; Drama/theater; International Student Organization; Music ensembles; Musical theater; Pep band; Radio station; Student government; Student newspaper; Student-run film society. **Athletics (Intercollegiate):** *Men:* baseball, basketball, cross-country, equestrian sports, golf, ice hockey, volleyball, wrestling. *Women:* basketball, cross-country, equestrian sports, golf, ice hockey, softball, volleyball.

CAMPUS

Type of school	Private (nonprofit)
Environment	City

STUDENTS

Undergrad enrollment	4,652
% male/female	40/60
% from out of state	82

FINANCIAL FACTS

Annual tuition	$39,792
Room and board	$18,760
Required fees	$200

GENERAL ADMISSIONS INFO

Application fee	No fee
Regular application deadline	Rolling
Nonfall registration	Yes
Fall 2024 testing policy	Test Optional

ACADEMICS

Student/faculty ratio	15:1
% students returning for sophomore year	71

Most classes have 20–29 students.

REQUESTING SERVICES FOR STUDENTS WITH LEARNING DIFFERENCES

Phone: 401-598-4689 • sites.jwu.edu/accessibility-services/accommodations.html#main-content
Email: accessibility.pvd@jwu.edu

Documentation submitted to: Accessibility Services
Separate application required for Services: Yes

Documentation required for:
  LD: Psychoeducational evaluation
  ADHD: Psychoeducational evaluation
  ASD: Psychoeducational evaluation

Providence College

Harkins Hall 103, Providence, RI 02918 • Admissions: 401-865-2535 • www.providence.edu

Support: CS

ACCOMMODATIONS

Allowed in exams:

Calculators	Yes
Dictionary	Yes
Computer	Yes
Spell-checker	Yes
Extended test time	Yes
Scribe	Yes
Proctors	Yes
Oral exams	Yes
Note-takers	Yes

Support services for students with:

LD	Yes
ADHD	Yes
ASD	Yes
Distraction-reduced environment	Yes
Recording of lecture allowed	Yes
Reading technology	No
Audio books	No
Other assistive technology	No
Priority registration	Yes

Added costs of services:

For LD	No
For ADHD	No
For ASD	No
LD specialists	Yes
ADHD & ASD coaching	Yes
ASD specialists	No
Professional tutors	Yes
Peer tutors	Yes
Max. hours/week for services	Varies
How professors are notified of student approved accommodations	Student

COLLEGE GRADUATION REQUIREMENTS

Course waivers allowed	Yes
In what courses: Varies	
Course substitutions allowed	Yes
In what courses: Varies	

PROGRAMS/SERVICES FOR STUDENTS WITH LEARNING DIFFERENCES

The Student Success Center (SSC) provides academic advising, support, and accommodations. First-year students requesting accommodations should register with the SSC, and Academic Support Services staff will reach out over the summer to help them begin planning for school. The staff continues to monitor and support students throughout their time at Providence. The following services and accommodations are available for students once appropriate documentation is provided: calculators and computers during exams, extended time on tests, a distraction-free testing environment, scribes, proctors, oral exams, notetakers, recording devices in class, assistive technology, and priority registration. Academic Support Services and SSC staff employ workshops and one-on-one meetings to guide students and facilitate their engagement with professors, coursework, and campus needs. There are also three different student groups on campus aimed at raising awareness and creating community for students with physical, cognitive, developmental, and learning disabilities.

ADMISSIONS

Admission requirements are the same for all students. For students with a learning disability, an interview is highly recommended, at which time individualized coursework is examined.

Additional Information

Professional staff at Academic Support Services provides academic coaching in skill building, organization, and time management. Seminars are offered in study techniques and test-taking strategies. Academic Support Services also provides specialized support for student-athletes who may need academic mentoring and supplementary programming. The Tutorial Center and Writing Center are accessible to all students. The Tutoring Center offers group, and individual, and peer tutoring. There is no foreign language requirement for any Providence College students.

Providence College sponsored baseball from 1921 to 1999. In 1924, the team gained national attention for winning the longest (mostly) scoreless game. The game lasted four hours and 17 minutes (Brown U–0, PC–1). The Friars made their first appearance in the 1929 baseball season. Six PC players went on to the major league. In 2022, the Friars entered their first full season as a club sport: NCBA Division II.

Providence College

General Admissions

Very important factors include: rigor of secondary school record, academic GPA, application essay. *Important factors include:* recommendations. *Other factors considered include:* class rank, standardized test scores (if submitted). High school diploma is required and GED is not accepted. Institution is test-optional for entering Fall 2024. Check admissions website for updates. *Academic units required:* 4 English, 4 math, 3 science (2 labs), 3 foreign language, 3 social studies. *Academic units recommended:* 4 science (2 labs), 4 foreign language, 4 social studies.

Financial Aid

Students should submit: CSS/Financial Aid Profile; FAFSA. *Need-based scholarships/grants offered:* College/university scholarship or grant aid from institutional funds; Federal Pell; Private scholarships; SEOG; State scholarships/grants; United Negro College Fund. *Loan aid offered:* Direct PLUS loans; Direct Subsidized Loans; Direct Unsubsidized Loans. Federal Work-Study Program available. Institutional employment available.

Campus Life

Activities: Campus Ministries; Choral groups; Concert band; Dance; Drama/theater; International Student Organization; Jazz band; Literary magazine; Music ensembles; Musical theater; Pep band; Radio station; Student government; Student newspaper; Student-run film society; Symphony orchestra; Television station; Yearbook. **Organizations:** 125 registered organizations, 22 honor societies, 1 religious organizations, 0 fraternities, 0 sororities. **Athletics (Intercollegiate):** *Men:* basketball, cross-country, cycling, field hockey, golf, ice hockey, lacrosse, racquetball, rugby, swimming, track/field (indoor), ultimate frisbee, volleyball, wrestling. *Women:* basketball, cross-country, cycling, field hockey, golf, ice hockey, lacrosse, racquetball, rugby, softball, swimming, track/field (indoor), ultimate frisbee, volleyball, wrestling.

Rhode Island

CAMPUS
Type of school	Private (nonprofit)
Environment	City

STUDENTS
Undergrad enrollment	4,242
% male/female	46/54
% from out of state	88
% frosh live on campus	98

FINANCIAL FACTS
Annual tuition	$59,830
Room and board	$17,150
Required fees	$880

GENERAL ADMISSIONS INFO
Application fee	$65
Regular application deadline	1/15
Nonfall registration	Yes

Fall 2024 testing policy	Test Optional
Range SAT EBRW	570–670
Range SAT Math	550–670
Range ACT Composite	25–31

ACADEMICS
Student/faculty ratio	11:1
% students returning for sophomore year	90

Most classes have 20–29 students.

REQUESTING SERVICES FOR STUDENTS WITH LEARNING DIFFERENCES

Phone: 401-865-2494 • academic-services.providence.edu/ • Email: jgomes3@providence.edu

Documentation submitted to: Student Success Center
Separate application required for Services: Yes

Documentation required for:
LD: Psychoeducational evaluation
ADHD: Psychoeducational evaluation
ASD: Psychoeducational evaluation

Rhode Island College

600 Mount Pleasant Avenue, Providence, RI 02908 • Admissions: 401-456-8234 • www.ric.edu

(Support: CS)

ACCOMMODATIONS

Allowed in exams:

Calculators	Yes
Dictionary	Yes
Computer	Yes
Spell-checker	Yes
Extended test time	Yes
Scribe	Yes
Proctors	No
Oral exams	Yes
Note-takers	Yes

Support services for students with:

LD	Yes
ADHD	Yes
ASD	Yes
Distraction-reduced environment	Yes
Recording of lecture allowed	Yes
Reading technology	Yes
Audio books	Yes
Other assistive technology	Yes
Priority registration	Yes

Added costs of services:

For LD	No
For ADHD	No
For ASD	No
LD specialists	Yes
ADHD & ASD coaching	No
ASD specialists	No
Professional tutors	No
Peer tutors	Yes
Max. hours/week for services	Varies
How professors are notified of student approved accommodations	Student and Disability Services Center

COLLEGE GRADUATION REQUIREMENTS

Course waivers allowed	Yes

In what courses: Varies

Course substitutions allowed	Yes

In what courses: Varies

PROGRAMS/SERVICES FOR STUDENTS WITH LEARNING DIFFERENCES

The Disability Services Center (DSC) determines eligibility, provides access, and coordinates accommodations for students with disabilities. Students requesting disability services should register with the DSC to determine eligibility and appropriate accommodations. Students can request and manage their accommodations through the Rhode Island College online portal, Accessible Information Management (AIM). Support services for students with disabilities may include testing accommodations, advocating for students, and assistive technology services.

ADMISSIONS

Admission requirements are the same for all applicants. Most accepted students rank in the upper 50 percent of their class. Other factors receiving admission consideration are academic potential, extracurricular activities, as well as essays and recommendations, which are both optional.

Additional Information

RIC 100 is a 1 credit, 50-minute, once-a-week class that all students must take and pass to graduate from Rhode Island College. It's designed to help students navigate RIC specifically and college in general; each section of RIC 100 has a designated instructor and peer mentor. Topics include learning online, time management, wellness, college expectations, identifying learning styles, financial literacy, cultural competency, and utilizing campus resources.

Rhode Island College is the first public institution of higher education in the state of Rhode Island. The East Campus includes the former grounds of the Rhode Island State Home and School for Dependent and Neglected Children, the first post-Civil War orphanage in the country (1885-1979). RIC acquired the property in 2002 and began a research, historical documentation, and preservation project that ran through 2010. The last remaining building, The Yellow Cottage, was restored and is on the National Registry of Historic Places.

Rhode Island College

GENERAL ADMISSIONS

Very important factors include: rigor of secondary school record, academic GPA, application essay. *Other factors considered include:* standardized test scores (if submitted), recommendations. High school diploma is required and GED is accepted. Institution is test-optional for entering Fall 2024. Check admissions website for updates. *Academic units required:* 4 English, 3 math, 2 science (2 labs), 2 foreign language, 2 social studies, 5 academic electives.

FINANCIAL AID

Students should submit: FAFSA. *Need-based scholarships/grants offered:* College/university scholarship or grant aid from institutional funds; Federal Pell; Private scholarships; SEOG; State scholarships/grants. *Loan aid offered:* Direct PLUS loans; Direct Subsidized Loans; Direct Unsubsidized Loans. Federal Work-Study Program available. Institutional employment available.

CAMPUS LIFE

Activities: Choral groups; Concert band; Dance; Drama/theater; International Student Organization; Jazz band; Literary magazine; Music ensembles; Musical theater; Opera; Radio station; Student government; Student newspaper; Student-run film society; Symphony orchestra; Television station. **Organizations:** 80 registered organizations, 14 honor societies, 2 fraternities, 3 sororities. **Athletics (Intercollegiate):** *Men:* baseball, basketball, cross-country, equestrian sports, golf, ice hockey, racquetball, rugby, track/field (indoor), ultimate frisbee, wrestling. *Women:* basketball, cross-country, equestrian sports, golf, gymnastics, lacrosse, racquetball, rugby, softball, swimming, track/field (indoor), ultimate frisbee, volleyball.

CAMPUS
Type of school	Public
Environment	City

STUDENTS
Undergrad enrollment	5,252
% male/female	31/69
% from out of state	21
% frosh live on campus	39

FINANCIAL FACTS
Annual in-state tuition	$9,481
Annual out-of-state tuition	$25,014
Room and board	$13,414
Required fees	$1,505

GENERAL ADMISSIONS INFO
Application fee	$50
Regular application deadline	3/15
Nonfall registration	Yes
Fall 2024 testing policy	Test Optional
Range SAT EBRW	450–570
Range SAT Math	420–540

ACADEMICS
Student/faculty ratio	12:1
% students returning for sophomore year	71
Most classes have 10–19 students.	

Rhode Island

REQUESTING SERVICES FOR STUDENTS WITH LEARNING DIFFERENCES

Phone: 401-456-2776 • www.ric.edu/department-directory/disability-services-center • Email: dsc@ric.edu

Documentation submitted to: Disability Services Center
Separate application required for Services: Yes

Documentation required for:
LD: Psychoeducational evaluation
ADHD: Psychoeducational evaluation
ASD: Psychoeducational evaluation

Roger Williams University

One Old Ferry Road, Bristol, RI 02809-2921 • Admissions: 401-254-3500 • www.rwu.edu

Support: CS

ACCOMMODATIONS

Allowed in exams:

Calculators	Yes
Dictionary	No
Computer	Yes
Spell-checker	Yes
Extended test time	Yes
Scribe	Yes
Proctors	Yes
Oral exams	No
Note-takers	Yes

Support services for students with:

LD	Yes
ADHD	Yes
ASD	Yes
Distraction-reduced environment	Yes
Recording of lecture allowed	Yes
Reading technology	Yes
Audio books	Yes
Other assistive technology	Yes
Priority registration	Yes

Added costs of services:

For LD	No
For ADHD	No
For ASD	No
LD specialists	Yes
ADHD & ASD coaching	No
ASD specialists	No
Professional tutors	Yes
Peer tutors	Yes
Max. hours/week for services	Varies
How professors are notified of student approved accommodations	Student

COLLEGE GRADUATION REQUIREMENTS

Course waivers allowed	No
Course substitutions allowed	No

PROGRAMS/SERVICES FOR STUDENTS WITH LEARNING DIFFERENCES

The Student Accessibility Services (SAS) office helps students with documented disabilities receive the services they need. Students must first register with the SAS office and provide documentation of a disability, which SAS will then evaluate. If needed, SAS works with the student to update documentation or provide additional information so that the student can qualify for services. Accommodations may include extended time for testing, testing in a reduced-distraction environment, and note-taking assistance. In addition, SAS helps students with problem-solving, self-advocating, and navigating a complex college environment.

ADMISSIONS

All applicants are expected to meet the same admission criteria. All students must complete the Common Application and submit at least one letter of recommendation. Submitting ACT and SAT scores is optional for all applicants except those who apply to the Department of Education. The average GPA is 3.2 for accepted applicants.

Additional Information

The Center for Student Academic Success (CSAS) offers academic advising and peer mentors who help to keep students on track with support in organizational skills and study strategies. Peer mentors are assigned to all first-year students. Professional advisors meet with students who have not declared a major or are considering changing majors.

Roger Williams University's namesake founded Rhode Island in 1663, having been banished from Massachusetts due to his threatening progressive views. In his Rhode Island Charter, he established separation of church and state, gave the vote to all heads of household, including women, and claimed Native Americans were the true owners of the land. His purchase of Providence may have been the first legal deed in North America. Two hundred years before the Emancipation Proclamation, he was part of a movement that briefly outlawed slavery in Rhode Island. Many of his radical ideals found their way into the U.S. Bill of Rights and the U.S. Constitution.

Roger Williams University

General Admissions

Very important factors include: rigor of secondary school record, academic GPA, application essay, recommendations. *Other factors considered include:* class rank, standardized test scores (if submitted). High school diploma is required and GED is accepted. Institution is test-optional for entering Fall 2024. Check admissions website for updates. *Academic units required:* 4 English, 3 math, 3 science (2 labs), 3 social studies. *Academic units recommended:* 4 math, 4 science, 2 foreign language, 4 social studies, 3 academic electives.

Financial Aid

Students should submit: FAFSA. *Need-based scholarships/grants offered:* College/university scholarship or grant aid from institutional funds; Federal Pell; Private scholarships; SEOG; State scholarships/grants. *Loan aid offered:* Direct PLUS loans; Direct Subsidized Loans; Direct Unsubsidized Loans. Federal Work-Study Program available. Institutional employment available.

Campus Life

Activities: Campus Ministries; Choral groups; Dance; Drama/theater; International Student Organization; Literary magazine; Model UN; Music ensembles; Radio station; Student government; Student newspaper; Student-run film society. **Organizations:** 74 registered organizations, 17 honor societies, 4 religious organizations, 0 fraternities, 0 sororities. **Athletics (Intercollegiate):** *Men:* baseball, basketball, cross-country, equestrian sports, golf, gymnastics, ice hockey, lacrosse, rugby, swimming, ultimate frisbee, volleyball, wrestling. *Women:* basketball, cross-country, equestrian sports, field hockey, gymnastics, ice hockey, lacrosse, rugby, softball, swimming, ultimate frisbee, volleyball.

CAMPUS

Type of school	Private (nonprofit)
Environment	Town

STUDENTS

Undergrad enrollment	4,207
% male/female	50/50
% from out of state	84
% frosh live on campus	92

FINANCIAL FACTS

Annual tuition	$42,336
Room and board	$16,690
Required fees	$330

GENERAL ADMISSIONS INFO

Application fee	$55
Regular application deadline	2/1
Nonfall registration	Yes

Fall 2024 testing policy	Test Optional
Range SAT EBRW	550–640
Range SAT Math	530–620
Range ACT Composite	23–29

ACADEMICS

Student/faculty ratio	14:1
% students returning for sophomore year	82

Most classes have 20–29 students.

REQUESTING SERVICES FOR STUDENTS WITH LEARNING DIFFERENCES

Phone: 401-254-3841 • www.rwu.edu/undergraduate/academics/student-academic-success/student-accessibility-services • Email: sas@rwu.edu

Documentation submitted to: Student Accessibility Services
Separate application required for Services: Yes

Documentation required for:
LD: Psychoeducational evaluation
ADHD: Psychoeducational evaluation
ASD: Psychoeducational evaluation

University of Rhode Island

Undergraduate Admission, Kingston, RI 2881 • Admissions: 401-874-7100 • www.uri.edu

Support: CS

ACCOMMODATIONS

Allowed in exams:

Calculators	Yes
Dictionary	Yes
Computer	Yes
Spell-checker	Yes
Extended test time	Yes
Scribe	Yes
Proctors	Yes
Oral exams	Yes
Note-takers	Yes

Support services for students with:

LD	Yes
ADHD	Yes
ASD	Yes
Distraction-reduced environment	Yes
Recording of lecture allowed	Yes
Reading technology	Yes
Audio books	Yes
Other assistive technology	Yes
Priority registration	Yes

Added costs of services:

For LD	No
For ADHD	No
For ASD	No
LD specialists	Yes
ADHD & ASD coaching	Yes
ASD specialists	Yes
Professional tutors	No
Peer tutors	Yes
Max. hours/week for services	Varies
How professors are notified of student approved accommodations	Student

COLLEGE GRADUATION REQUIREMENTS

Course waivers allowed	No
Course substitutions allowed	Yes

In what courses: Foreign Language

PROGRAMS/SERVICES FOR STUDENTS WITH LEARNING DIFFERENCES

The University of Rhode Island supports students with learning differences through the Disability, Access, and Inclusion (DAI) office. Students are required to provide documentation from a licensed or credentialed provider or evaluator, whose certification or expertise is specific to the disability or diagnosed condition. Outside of traditional accommodations and support (tutoring, note-taking, test-taking support, etc.), DAI has developed a support network and curriculum to assist students during the academic year. Students are encouraged to make accommodation requests prior to the beginning of each semester. DAI collaborates with the Academic Enhancement Center, and students can take two 1 credit courses focusing on developing effective learning strategies. The START URI Program is for students with ASD, providing workshops the week before the start of school to assist with the transition to college life. These workshops cover a variety of topics including navigating social, academic, and behavioral expectations. There is no fee for this program. During the spring semester, a weekly course focusing on the social and relational aspects of college life is offered. Following the spring semester, these students may also participate in a five-week work experience program. The MAP program provides two days of workshops before the start of the fall semester for students with ADHD, anxiety, and/or executive functioning challenges. MAP workshops focus on organizational skills and strategies, while also helping students familiarize themselves with campus resources. Students can also be assigned to student mentors who they meet with regularly throughout the academic year as accountability partners.

ADMISSIONS

All applicants are expected to meet the general admission criteria. URI expects applicants to rank in the upper 50 percent of their high school class (if rank is given). The average prospective student has a 3.5–4.0 GPA and SAT scores in the 1200–1300 range or ACT scores around 28 if submitted.

Additional Information

The Academic Skills Center offers a variety of services to all URI students, including peer tutoring, counseling services, and Student Support and Advocacy Services (SSAS).

The first copy of *The Beacon* student newspaper was published in 1908. It continued until strife caused reporters and editors to leave in 1971. *The Good 5 Cent Cigar* was born the same year and has covered everything from protests, school issues, the community, and a global pandemic. The name of the newspaper is credited to the 28th U.S. Vice President Thomas Riley Marshall but made popular by W.C. Fields: "What this country needs is a good five-cent cigar." Critics lashed out at the name; fans cherished it. The goal the time was to stimulate thought and controversy.

University of Rhode Island

GENERAL ADMISSIONS

Very important factors include: rigor of secondary school record, academic GPA. *Important factors include:* standardized test scores (if submitted), application essay, recommendations. *Other factors considered include:* class rank. High school diploma is required and GED is accepted. Institution is test-optional for entering Fall 2024. Check admissions website for updates. *Academic units required:* 4 English, 3 math, 2 science (1 lab), 2 foreign language, 2 social studies, 5 academic electives.

FINANCIAL AID

Students should submit: FAFSA. *Need-based scholarships/grants offered:* College/university scholarship or grant aid from institutional funds; Federal Pell; Private scholarships; SEOG; State scholarships/grants. *Loan aid offered:* Direct PLUS loans; Direct Subsidized Loans; Direct Unsubsidized Loans. Federal Work-Study Program available. Institutional employment available.

CAMPUS LIFE

Activities: Campus Ministries; Choral groups; Concert band; Dance; Drama/theater; International Student Organization; Jazz band; Literary magazine; Marching band; Music ensembles; Musical theater; Opera; Pep band; Radio station; Student government; Student newspaper; Student-run film society; Symphony orchestra; Television station; Yearbook. **Organizations:** 100 registered organizations, 40 honor societies, 12 religious organizations, 15 fraternities, 10 sororities. **Athletics (Intercollegiate):** *Men:* baseball, basketball, crew/rowing, cross-country, golf, ice hockey, lacrosse, rugby, swimming, track/field (indoor), ultimate frisbee, volleyball, wrestling. *Women:* basketball, crew/rowing, cross-country, equestrian sports, field hockey, gymnastics, ice hockey, lacrosse, rugby, softball, swimming, track/field (indoor), ultimate frisbee, volleyball.

CAMPUS

Type of school	Public
Environment	Village

STUDENTS

Undergrad enrollment	13,849
% male/female	43/57
% from out of state	53
% frosh live on campus	92

FINANCIAL FACTS

Annual in-state tuition	$13,586
Annual out-of-state tuition	$32,068
Room and board	$13,584
Required fees	$2,294

GENERAL ADMISSIONS INFO

Application fee	$65
Regular application deadline	2/1
Nonfall registration	Yes

Fall 2024 testing policy	Test Optional
Range SAT EBRW	530–640
Range SAT math	520–630
Range ACT Composite	25–30

ACADEMICS

Student/faculty ratio	17:1
% students returning for sophomore year	85

Most classes have 20–29 students.

REQUESTING SERVICES FOR STUDENTS WITH LEARNING DIFFERENCES

Phone: 401-874-7400 • web.uri.edu/disability/ • Email: dai@uri.edu

Documentation submitted to: Disability, Access, and Inclusion
Separate application required for Services: Yes

Documentation required for:
LD: Psychoeducational evaluation
ADHD: Psychoeducational evaluation
ASD: Psychoeducational evaluation

Clemson University

105 Sikes Hall, Clemson, SC 29634-5124 • Admissions: 864-656-2287 • www.clemson.edu

(Support: SP)

ACCOMMODATIONS

Allowed in exams:

Calculators	Yes
Dictionary	Yes
Computer	Yes
Spell-checker	Yes
Extended test time	Yes
Scribe	Yes
Proctors	Yes
Oral exams	Yes
Note-takers	Yes

Support services for students with:

LD	Yes
ADHD	Yes
ASD	Yes
Distraction-reduced environment	Yes
Recording of lecture allowed	Yes
Reading technology	Yes
Audio books	Yes
Other assistive technology	Yes
Priority registration	Yes

Added costs of services:

For LD	No
For ADHD	No
For ASD	Yes
LD specialists	No
ADHD & ASD coaching	Yes
ASD specialists	Yes
Professional tutors	No
Peer tutors	Yes
Max. hours/week for services	Varies
How professors are notified of student approved accommodations	Student

COLLEGE GRADUATION REQUIREMENTS

Course waivers allowed	No
Course substitutions allowed	No

PROGRAMS/SERVICES FOR STUDENTS WITH LEARNING DIFFERENCES

Student Accessibility Services (SAS) determines accommodations for students with disabilities on a case-by-case basis. To receive accommodations, a student must provide documentation of their disability and attend a required welcome meeting with SAS. If a student is not on the main campus, virtual or phone meetings may be available. Once students are registered with SAS, they will be able to use an online link to request formal letters so they may notify the appropriate faculty members of their accommodations. Available accommodations include e-texts, text-to-speech software, smart pens, and free or low-cost apps for note-taking, concentration, processing, and writing. Students must be granted permission to record a lecture on their own device or computer prior to the start of the class. The Spectrum Program helps students with ASD grow and find independence in their academic and professional careers, as well as develop their interpersonal communication, social, and living skills. There is a per-semester cost for this program. The University Testing and Education Center (UTEC) offers proctored testing for Clemson Students whose needs cannot be accommodated in the classroom.

ADMISSIONS

All students must meet the same admission criteria. It is recommended that students self-disclose their learning disability or other information that will help admissions to understand their challenges and explain the lack of a foreign language in their background (if applicable). Interviews are not required, but students can meet with the admissions office. Clemson University requires students to submit a Self-Reported Academic Record (SRAR) with their applications, which are not complete until the SRAR is submitted.

Additional Information

The Academic Success Center at Clemson offers peer learning support, tutoring, academic coaching, and success strategy workshops.

In 1941, Dean Ross, cadet bandmaster of the Clemson Corps band, was given the task of picking a school fight song. In Atlanta, he found a copy of "Tiger Rag" by the Dixieland Jazz Band and paid $1.50 for the band score. In 1942, the band played after every touchdown, and since 2003, the band has more than 9 variations of "Tiger Rag," including "Sock it to 'Em," "Short Rag," "Gliss Rag," "D Rag" and "First Down Cheer."

Clemson University

GENERAL ADMISSIONS

Very important factors include: rigor of secondary school record, class rank, academic GPA, standardized test scores (if submitted). *Other factors considered include:* application essay, recommendations. High school diploma is required and GED is accepted. Institution is test-optional for entering Fall 2024. Check admissions website for updates. *Academic units required:* 4 English, 3 math, 3 science (3 labs), 3 foreign language, 1 social studies, 1 history, 2 academic electives, 1 visual/performing arts.

FINANCIAL AID

Students should submit: FAFSA. *Need-based scholarships/grants offered:* College/university scholarship or grant aid from institutional funds; Federal Pell; Private scholarships; SEOG; State scholarships/grants. *Loan aid offered:* Direct PLUS loans; Direct Subsidized Loans; Direct Unsubsidized Loans. Federal Work-Study Program available. Institutional employment available.

CAMPUS LIFE

Activities: Campus Ministries; Choral groups; Concert band; Dance; Drama/theater; International Student Organization; Jazz band; Literary magazine; Marching band; Model UN; Music ensembles; Pep band; Radio station; Student government; Student newspaper; Television station; Yearbook. **Organizations:** 292 registered organizations, 23 honor societies, 24 religious organizations, 26 fraternities, 17 sororities. **Athletics (Intercollegiate):** *Men:* baseball, basketball, crew/rowing, cross-country, cycling, equestrian sports, golf, gymnastics, ice hockey, lacrosse, martial arts, racquetball, rugby, skiing (nordic/cross-country), swimming, table tennis, track/field (indoor), ultimate frisbee, volleyball. *Women:* basketball, crew/rowing, cross-country, cycling, equestrian sports, field hockey, golf, gymnastics, martial arts, racquetball, rugby, skiing (nordic/cross-country), softball, swimming, table tennis, track/field (indoor), volleyball, water polo.

South Carolina

REQUESTING SERVICES FOR STUDENTS WITH LEARNING DIFFERENCES

Phone: 864-656-6848 • www.clemson.edu/academics/studentaccess/ • Email: studentaccess@lists.clemson.edu

Documentation submitted to: Student Accessibility Services
Separate application required for Services: Yes

Documentation required for:
LD: Psychoeducational evaluation
ADHD: Psychoeducational evaluation
ASD: Psychoeducational evaluation

College of Charleston

66 George Street, Charleston, SC 29424 • Admissions: 843-953-5670 • cofc.edu

Support: SP

ACCOMMODATIONS

Allowed in exams:

Calculators	Yes
Dictionary	Yes
Computer	Yes
Spell-checker	Yes
Extended test time	Yes
Scribe	Yes
Proctors	Yes
Oral exams	No
Note-takers	Yes

Support services for students with:

LD	Yes
ADHD	Yes
ASD	Yes
Distraction-reduced environment	Yes
Recording of lecture allowed	Yes
Reading technology	Yes
Audio books	Yes
Other assistive technology	Yes
Priority registration	Yes

Added costs of services:

For LD	No
For ADHD	No
For ASD	No
LD specialists	Yes
ADHD & ASD coaching	No
ASD specialists	No
Professional tutors	No
Peer tutors	Yes
Max. hours/week for services	Varies
How professors are notified of student approved accommodations	Student

COLLEGE GRADUATION REQUIREMENTS

Course waivers allowed	No
Course substitutions allowed	Yes
In what courses: Math/Logic and Foreign Language	

PROGRAMS/SERVICES FOR STUDENTS WITH LEARNING DIFFERENCES

The Center for Disability Services (CDS) and SNAP (Students Needing Access Parity) provide reasonable accommodations for students with disabilities. Students must apply for accommodations and present supporting documentation for CDS/SNAP to determine each student's accommodations. The application reviews past accommodations, learning strategies, and academic and nonacademic strengths. Students may be permitted alternatives to foreign language and math classes under some circumstances. Those interested in math and foreign language alternatives must schedule a meeting with CDS/SNAP. Courses required for a major will not be considered for substitution. Students with mild intellectual and/or developmental disabilities may be interested in the Reach program, which focuses on academics, independent living, career development, and socialization. This four-year, fully inclusive certificate program accepts 12 students per year and includes traditional classes with support, internships, campus clubs, peer mentoring, and on-campus housing. Students applying to this program submit both student and guardian-completed questionnaires, current IEP, psycho-educational testing, neuropsychological testing, and transcript, along with three letters of recommendation.

ADMISSIONS

Admissions considers academic rigor, class rank and honors, leadership, talents, and extracurricular activities when reviewing applications. Most applicants have earned grades of A or B in the required courses, and senior-year courses in progress are also reviewed to confirm an applicant's overall academic preparedness and motivation. Some applicants can still be considered without having completed the entirety of the required courses but should submit a statement and relevant documentation explaining why certain courses are missing.

Additional Information

The Center for Student Learning offers tutoring with drop-in Labs and by-appointment sessions, academic coaching with professional staff or trained peer coaches, and Supplemental Instruction.

In 2020, the College of Charleston celebrated its 250th Anniversary. Amidst disagreements, political rivalries, and the American Revolution, CofC was founded in 1770, chartered in 1785, and held its first class in 1790 in what is now the CofC president's residence. Three of the CofC founders were signers of the Declaration of Independence and three were signers of the United States Constitution. The Main Building, Library, and Gate Lodge are all on the National Historic Registry.

College of Charleston

GENERAL ADMISSIONS

Very important factors include: rigor of secondary school record, academic GPA. *Important factors include:* class rank. *Other factors considered include:* standardized test scores (if submitted), application essay, recommendations. High school diploma is required and GED is accepted. Institution is test-optional for entering Fall 2024. Check admissions website for updates. *Academic units required:* 4 English, 4 math, 3 science (3 labs), 2 foreign language, 3 social studies, 2 academic electives, 1 visual/performing arts.

FINANCIAL AID

Students should submit: FAFSA. *Need-based scholarships/grants offered:* College/university scholarship or grant aid from institutional funds; Federal Pell; Private scholarships; SEOG; State scholarships/grants. *Loan aid offered:* Direct PLUS loans; Direct Subsidized Loans; Direct Unsubsidized Loans. Federal Work-Study Program available. Institutional employment available.

CAMPUS LIFE

Activities: Campus Ministries; Choral groups; Dance; Drama/theater; International Student Organization; Jazz band; Literary magazine; Model UN; Music ensembles; Musical theater; Opera; Pep band; Radio station; Student government; Student newspaper; Student-run film society; Symphony orchestra; Television station. **Organizations:** 225 registered organizations, 11 honor societies, 19 religious organizations, 12 fraternities, 14 sororities. **Athletics (Intercollegiate):** *Men:* baseball, basketball, crew/rowing, cross-country, golf, ice hockey, lacrosse, martial arts, rugby, swimming, ultimate frisbee, volleyball. *Women:* crew/rowing, cross-country, equestrian sports, golf, martial arts, rugby, softball, swimming, track/field (indoor), ultimate frisbee, volleyball.

CAMPUS

Type of school	Public
Environment	City

STUDENTS

Undergrad enrollment	9,770
% male/female	34/66
% from out of state	41
% frosh live on campus	86

FINANCIAL FACTS

Annual in-state tuition	$12,518
Annual out-of-state tuition	$35,338
Room and board	$12,986
Required fees	$460

GENERAL ADMISSIONS INFO

Application fee	$60
Regular application deadline	1/15
Nonfall registration	Yes

Fall 2024 testing policy	Test Optional
Range SAT EBRW	560–660
Range SAT Math	530–620
Range ACT Composite	23–29

ACADEMICS

Student/faculty ratio	16:1
% students returning for sophomore year	83

Most classes have 20–29 students.

South Carolina

REQUESTING SERVICES FOR STUDENTS WITH LEARNING DIFFERENCES

Phone: 843-953-1431 • disabilityservices.cofc.edu • Email: snap@cofc.edu

Documentation submitted to: Center for Disability Services

Separate application required for Services: Yes

Documentation required for:
LD: Psychoeducational evaluation
ADHD: Psychoeducational evaluation
ASD: Psychoeducational evaluation

Limestone University

1115 College Drive, Gaffney, SC 29340-3799 • Admissions: 864-488-4549 • www.limestone.edu

(Support: SP)

PROGRAMS/SERVICES FOR STUDENTS WITH LEARNING DIFFERENCES

The Equity and Inclusion Office (EIO) provides resources to individuals with learning differences. Students work with the Accessible Education team to determine eligibility for services. Students can also access the Learning Enrichment and Achievement Program (LEAP). LEAP is a fee-based comprehensive service supporting students with specific learning disabilities and/or ADHD. Students meet 1–2 times a week and participate in a minimum of 10 hours per week of study hall. Students work with LEAP to implement strategies in reading, writing, note-taking, time management, organization, and test-taking. To be eligible, students must be admitted to Limestone University by full or provisional acceptance, send documentation to LEAP, and arrange for an on-campus interview with the director of LEAP. Although LEAP is a fee-based program, in some cases, the Office for Vocational Rehabilitation will assist in funding the student's participation. Students needing support to adjust to difficulties in social settings, independent living skills, and daily decision-making are generally not a good fit for LEAP due to the limited training that is provided in these areas. As LEAP participants, students will participate in a 1 credit study strategies course each semester, receive secondary academic advice with attention to the student's specific learning needs, and participate in workshops on writing and studying.

ADMISSIONS

All applicants are expected to meet the same admission criteria. In addition to the academic course requirements, additional courses should be from foreign language, history, math, and natural science. Limestone will consider applicants who do not have these courses if the applicant can demonstrate evidence of success in core courses, and some applicants may be asked for an interview. Students must be admitted to Limestone to be considered for services through the Equity and Inclusion Office, including the LEAP program.

Additional Information

The Division of Student Success offers workshops each semester that are open to all students on topics like academic success strategies, career planning, and student enrichment.

Limestone University is located on the site of a former Limestone mining quarry and has been called "The Rock" for decades. The quarry dates back to the American Revolution when it supplied lime used in the production of iron. Stone placed inside the Washington Monument was mined from the quarry on LU campus. Deposits were exhausted in 1953, and the quarry was filled with water. Lake Limestone is one of the most picturesque places on campus. Ten campus buildings, Limestone Springs, and the quarry itself are on the National Register of Historic Places.

Limestone University

GENERAL ADMISSIONS

Very important factors include: rigor of secondary school record, academic GPA, standardized test scores (if submitted). *Important factors include:* class rank. *Other factors considered include:* recommendations. High school diploma is required and GED is accepted. Institution is test-optional for entering Fall 2024. Check admissions website for updates. *Academic units required:* 4 English, 3 math, 2 science (2 labs), 3 social studies.

FINANCIAL AID

Students should submit: FAFSA. *Need-based scholarships/grants offered:* College/university scholarship or grant aid from institutional funds; Federal Pell; Private scholarships; SEOG; State scholarships/grants. *Loan aid offered:* Direct PLUS loans; Direct Subsidized Loans; Direct Unsubsidized Loans. Federal Work-Study Program available. Institutional employment available.

CAMPUS LIFE

Activities: Campus Ministries; Choral groups; Concert band; Drama/theater; Jazz band; Literary magazine; Marching band; Music ensembles; Musical theater; Pep band; Student government; Yearbook. **Organizations:** 22 registered organizations, 5 honor societies, 3 religious organizations, 1 fraternities, 0 sororities. **Athletics (Intercollegiate):** *Men:* baseball, basketball, cross-country, golf, lacrosse, swimming, track/field (indoor), volleyball, wrestling. *Women:* basketball, cross-country, field hockey, golf, lacrosse, softball, swimming, track/field (indoor), volleyball.

CAMPUS

Type of school	Private (nonprofit)
Environment	Town

STUDENTS

Undergrad enrollment	1,052
% male/female	62/38
% from out of state	42
% frosh live on campus	88

FINANCIAL FACTS

Annual tuition	$26,400
Room and board	$10,645
Required fees	$1,100

GENERAL ADMISSIONS INFO

Application fee	No fee
Regular application deadline	8/25
Nonfall registration	Yes

Fall 2024 testing policy	Test Optional
Range SAT EBRW	460–570
Range SAT Math	470–570
Range ACT Composite	17–23

ACADEMICS

Student/faculty ratio	13:1
% students returning for sophomore year	67

Most classes have 10–19 students.

South Carolina

REQUESTING SERVICES FOR STUDENTS WITH LEARNING DIFFERENCES

Phone: 864-488-8377 • www.limestone.edu/equity-and-inclusion • Email: accessibility@limestone.edu

Documentation submitted to: Equity and Inclusion Office
Separate application required for Services: Yes

Documentation required for:
 LD: Psychoeducational evaluation
 ADHD: Psychoeducational evaluation
 ASD: Psychoeducational evaluation

Southern Wesleyan University

907 Wesleyan Drive, Central, SC 29630-1020 • Admissions: 864-644-5550 • www.swu.edu

Support: CS

ACCOMMODATIONS

Allowed in exams:

Calculators	Yes
Dictionary	Yes
Computer	Yes
Spell-checker	Yes
Extended test time	Yes
Scribe	Yes
Proctors	Yes
Oral exams	Yes
Note-takers	Yes

Support services for students with:

LD	Yes
ADHD	Yes
ASD	Yes
Distraction-reduced environment	Yes
Recording of lecture allowed	Yes
Reading technology	Yes
Audio books	Yes
Other assistive technology	Yes
Priority registration	No

Added costs of services:

For LD	No
For ADHD	No
For ASD	No
LD specialists	Yes
ADHD & ASD coaching	Yes
ASD specialists	No
Professional tutors	Yes
Peer tutors	Yes
Max. hours/week for services	Varies
How professors are notified of student approved accommodations	Student and SSC Coordinator

COLLEGE GRADUATION REQUIREMENTS

Course waivers allowed	No
Course substitutions allowed	No

PROGRAMS/SERVICES FOR STUDENTS WITH LEARNING DIFFERENCES

The Student Success Center provides accommodations and services for students with documented disabilities. Students should contact the Student Success manager prior to the start of classes to schedule an intake meeting and provide current and appropriate formal documentation of their disability. Once reasonable accommodations have been determined, the Student Success manager notifies the student and their instructors of any approved accommodations. It's the student's responsibility to meet with their instructors to discuss the accommodations, which may include but are not limited to alternate-format course material, copies of notes and/or PowerPoint presentations, preferential seating, the ability to record lectures using a recorder or Smartpen, extended time on tests, alternative testing locations, and having a test read aloud.

ADMISSIONS

All applicants are required to submit an official high school transcript or equivalent. Students should have a GPA of at least 2.3 or rank in the upper half of their graduating class. Applicants with an unweighted GPA of 3.0 or higher do not need to submit an essay or letter of recommendation, but an essay and letter of recommendation are required for students with an unweighted GPA of 2.99 or below. The admissions committee may review applicants with a GPA of less than 2.3 for conditional admission.

Additional Information

Peer tutoring is available in the Student Success Center by appointment or drop-in for many courses. SWU's Smarthinking online tutoring is available 24/7 in math, writing for all subjects, APA and MLA formatting, science, business, computers and technology, and Spanish. Smarthinking also offers study aids, such as math video lessons, a Writer's Handbook, and a Study Skills Handbook. At the Writing Center, peer writing coaches are available with an advance appointment, and students can submit their writing for review ahead of time. Drop-in appointments are also welcome as time allows. Success coaches, who help with academic skills and connection to the SWU community, are also available in the Student Success Center by advance appointment or drop-in as time permits.

For over a decade, SWU has been recognized as a Military Friendly® School by honoring veterans and active military for their service at graduation, military appreciation events, a military monument on campus, and the Warriors Courage, Success, Respect, and Empowerment (CARE) Center on campus, which is devoted to addressing veteran students' academic, financial, physical, and social needs.

Southern Wesleyan University

GENERAL ADMISSIONS

Very important factors include: academic GPA, standardized test scores (if submitted). *Important factors include:* rigor of secondary school record, class rank. *Other factors considered include:* recommendations. High school diploma is required and GED is accepted. Institution is test-optional for entering Fall 2024. Check admissions website for updates. *Academic units recommended:* 4 English, 2 math, 2 science, 2 social studies.

FINANCIAL AID

Students should submit: FAFSA; Institution's own financial aid form. *Need-based scholarships/grants offered:* College/university scholarship or grant aid from institutional funds; Federal Pell; Private scholarships; SEOG; State scholarships/grants. *Loan aid offered:* Direct PLUS loans; Direct Subsidized Loans; Direct Unsubsidized Loans. Federal Work-Study Program available. Institutional employment available.

CAMPUS LIFE

Activities: Campus Ministries; Choral groups; Concert band; Drama/theater; Jazz band; Literary magazine; Music ensembles; Musical theater; Student government; Yearbook. **Organizations:** 12 registered organizations, 2 honor societies, 3 religious organizations, 0 fraternities, 0 sororities. **Athletics (Intercollegiate):** *Men:* baseball, basketball, cross-country, golf. *Women:* basketball, cross-country, softball, volleyball.

CAMPUS
Type of school	Private (nonprofit)
Environment	Town

STUDENTS
Undergrad enrollment	1,444
% male/female	40/60
% from out of state	28
% frosh live on campus	71

FINANCIAL FACTS
Annual tuition	$19,950
Room and board	$8,410
Required fees	$600

GENERAL ADMISSIONS INFO
Application fee	$25
Regular application deadline	8/1
Nonfall registration	Yes

Fall 2024 testing policy	Test Optional
Range SAT EBRW	430–540
Range SAT Math	445–550
Range ACT Composite	18–22

ACADEMICS
Student/faculty ratio	18:1
% students returning for sophomore year	70
Most classes have 10–19 students.	

South Carolina

REQUESTING SERVICES FOR STUDENTS WITH LEARNING DIFFERENCES

Phone: 864-644-5137 • www.swu.edu/academics/academic-support-and-resources/student-success-center-services • Email: ctrimmierlee@swu.edu

Documentation submitted to: Student Success Center
Separate application required for Services: Yes

Documentation required for:
 LD: Psychoeducational evaluation
 ADHD: Psychoeducational evaluation
 ASD: Psychoeducational evaluation

University of South Carolina

Office of Undergraduate Admissions, Columbia, SC 29208 • Admissions: 803-777-7700 • www.sc.edu

Support: S

ACCOMMODATIONS

Allowed in exams:

Calculators	Yes
Dictionary	Yes
Computer	Yes
Spell-checker	Yes
Extended test time	Yes
Scribe	Yes
Proctors	Yes
Oral exams	No
Note-takers	Yes

Support services for students with:

LD	Yes
ADHD	Yes
ASD	Yes
Distraction-reduced environment	Yes
Recording of lecture allowed	Yes
Reading technology	Yes
Audio books	Yes
Other assistive technology	Yes
Priority registration	Yes

Added costs of services:

For LD	No
For ADHD	No
For ASD	No
LD specialists	No
ADHD & ASD coaching	No
ASD specialists	No
Professional tutors	No
Peer tutors	Yes
Max. hours/week for services	Varies
How professors are notified of student approved accommodations	Student

COLLEGE GRADUATION REQUIREMENTS

Course waivers allowed	No
Course substitutions allowed	Yes

In what courses: Foreign Language

PROGRAMS/SERVICES FOR STUDENTS WITH LEARNING DIFFERENCES

The Student Disability Resource Center (SDRC) provides educational support and assistance to students with learning differences. The university works with each student to match their needs with appropriate, tailored educational support and assistance and empowers students with the confidence to become self-reliant in their education. Some of the services students can receive are early registration, note-taking technology, alternative forms of media and other assistive technologies, traditional testing accommodations, peer tutoring, and academic coaching. To receive services through SDRC, students must complete the registration form, submit documentation from a provider, and meet with an SDRC coordinator to formulate accommodations. SDRC works with the Student Success Center to provide peer tutoring and academic coaching. While there is no specific programming for students diagnosed on the autism spectrum, the SDRC is very sensitive to their needs and assists in coordinating one-on-one coaching, housing accommodations, and dining accommodations. Students can also attend a regularly scheduled stress management group. In some cases, a reduced credit load (9–11 credits) is permitted without impacting scholarships or financial aid.

ADMISSIONS

All applicants are expected to meet the same admission criteria. Admitted students have weighted GPAs ranging from 3.8–4.5. Applicants must have a minimum cumulative C+ average in the required academic courses.

Additional Information

There is no exemption from the foreign language requirement, and the university does not offer sign language. However, if a student is receiving services through SDRC and it is deemed appropriate, arrangements can be made to take foreign language classes on a pass/fail basis, or a substitute class (such as Spanish History) may be allowed.

The statue next to the Thomas Cooper Library is of Richard T. Greener (1844-1922), the first African American professor at UofSC, who served during the Reconstruction Era. He taught philosophy, Latin, and Greek, served as the librarian, and helped reorganize and catalog the library's books and papers after the Civil War. (Confederate authorities had taken possession of UofSC buildings and converted them into a hospital). Professor Greener was the first African American to graduate from Harvard and later served as dean of Howard University.

University of South Carolina

GENERAL ADMISSIONS
Very important factors include: academic GPA. *Important factors include:* rigor of secondary school record, class rank, standardized test scores (if submitted). *Other factors considered include:* application essay, recommendations. High school diploma is required and GED is accepted. Institution is test-optional for entering Fall 2024. Check admissions website for updates. *Academic units required:* 4 English, 4 math, 3 science (3 labs), 2 foreign language, 2 social studies, 1 U.S. history, 2 academic electives, 1 visual/performing arts.

FINANCIAL AID
Students should submit: FAFSA. *Need-based scholarships/grants offered:* College/university scholarship or grant aid from institutional funds; Federal Nursing Scholarships; Federal Pell; Private scholarships; SEOG; State scholarships/grants. *Loan aid offered:* Direct PLUS loans; Direct Subsidized Loans; Direct Unsubsidized Loans. Federal Work-Study Program available. Institutional employment available.

CAMPUS LIFE
Activities: Campus Ministries; Choral groups; Concert band; Dance; Drama/theater; International Student Organization; Jazz band; Literary magazine; Marching band; Model UN; Music ensembles; Musical theater; Opera; Pep band; Radio station; Student government; Student newspaper; Student-run film society; Symphony orchestra; Television station. **Organizations:** 387 registered organizations, 28 honor societies, 31 religious organizations, 22 fraternities, 16 sororities. **Athletics (Intercollegiate):** *Men:* baseball, basketball, cycling, equestrian sports, golf, ice hockey, lacrosse, martial arts, racquetball, rugby, softball, swimming, table tennis, ultimate frisbee, volleyball, water polo, wrestling. *Women:* basketball, cross-country, cycling, equestrian sports, field hockey, golf, gymnastics, lacrosse, martial arts, racquetball, rugby, softball, swimming, table tennis, ultimate frisbee, volleyball, water polo.

CAMPUS	
Type of school	Public
Environment	City

STUDENTS	
Undergrad enrollment	26,840
% male/female	44/56
% from out of state	38
% frosh live on campus	96

FINANCIAL FACTS	
Annual in-state tuition	$12,228
Annual out-of-state tuition	$33,528
Room and board	$11,780
Required fees	$400

GENERAL ADMISSIONS INFO	
Application fee	$65
Regular application deadline	12/1
Nonfall registration	Yes

Fall 2024 testing policy	Test Optional
Range SAT EBRW	600–690
Range SAT math	580–690
Range ACT composite	27–32

ACADEMICS	
Student/faculty ratio	18:1
% students returning for sophomore year	90
Most classes have 10–19 students.	

South Carolina

REQUESTING SERVICES FOR STUDENTS WITH LEARNING DIFFERENCES

Phone: 803-777-6142 • sc.edu/about/offices_and_divisions/student_disability_resource_center
Email: sadrc@mailbox.sc.edu

Documentation submitted to: Student Disability Resource Center
Separate application required for Services: Yes

Documentation required for:
  LD: Psychoeducational evaluation
  ADHD: Psychoeducational evaluation
  ASD: Psychoeducational evaluation

South Dakota State University

Enrollment Services Center, Brookings, SD 57007 • Admissions: 605-688-4121 • www.sdstate.edu

(**Support: S**)

ACCOMMODATIONS

Allowed in exams:

Calculators	Yes
Dictionary	Yes
Computer	Yes
Spell-checker	Yes
Extended test time	Yes
Scribe	Yes
Proctors	Yes
Oral exams	Yes
Note-takers	Yes

Support services for students with:

LD	Yes
ADHD	Yes
ASD	Yes
Distraction-reduced environment	Yes
Recording of lecture allowed	Yes
Reading technology	Yes
Audio books	Yes
Other assistive technology	Yes
Priority registration	No

Added costs of services:

For LD	No
For ADHD	No
For ASD	No
LD specialists	No
ADHD & ASD coaching	No
ASD specialists	No
Professional tutors	Yes
Peer tutors	Yes
Max. hours/week for services	Varies
How professors are notified of student approved accommodations	Student

COLLEGE GRADUATION REQUIREMENTS

Course waivers allowed	No
Course substitutions allowed	No

PROGRAMS/SERVICES FOR STUDENTS WITH LEARNING DIFFERENCES

The Office of Disability Services provides assistance for students with learning disabilities. Students must contact the office and complete the online student information and disability documentation forms. When the forms have been received and reviewed the Office of Disability Services will set up an appointment to discuss services that can be provided. Disability Services may provide testing accommodations such as extended time, a reduced-distraction environment, and screen readers, in addition to other accommodations, including alternative-format books and class material, notetakers, and referrals for other resources.

ADMISSIONS

The general admission requirements are the same for all applicants. The admission committee is looking for academic achievement and applicants should have a GPA of 2.6 or higher or rank in the top 60 percent of their graduating class.

Additional Information

The Summer Bridge program is a one-week program and includes a campus resources tour, planning workshops, activities on campus or in the community, and one-on-one appointments with academic advisors. Study Hub is the SDSU web page for learning and study strategies and has links to many academic resources. Free tutoring through the Wintrode Tutoring Program has peer tutors to help students better understand course material and develop learning strategies. Tutoring sessions are small groups up to four, or students can request individual tutoring. Supplemental Instruction (SI) is available to students in historically difficult subjects as a series of weekly review sessions for students who want to improve their understanding and their grades. SDSU offers Living-Learning Communities for students who want to live and associate with like-minded individuals. There are many Living-Learning Communities, including Allied for Acceptance LLC, Engineering LLC, Performing Arts LLC, and Military Affiliation LLC, among others.

The School of American and Global Studies, began in 1927 with completion of the Lincoln Memorial Library; the first building in South Dakota constructed with funds from a cigarette tax, at a cost of $200,000 (today over $3 million). It was the first land grant building in the nation named after President Lincoln. President Calvin Coolidge attended the dedication with his wife. The gathered crowd was estimated at 15,000; Brookings's population was less than 2,500.

South Dakota State University

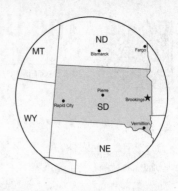

GENERAL ADMISSIONS

Very important factors include: rigor of secondary school record, class rank, academic GPA, standardized test scores (if submitted). *Other factors considered include:* application essay, recommendations. High school diploma is required and GED is accepted. Institution is test-optional for entering Fall 2024. Check admissions website for updates. *Academic units required:* 4 English, 3 math, 3 science (3 labs), 3 social studies, 1 visual/performing arts.

FINANCIAL AID

Students should submit: FAFSA. *Need-based scholarships/grants offered:* College/university scholarship or grant aid from institutional funds; Federal Nursing Scholarships; Federal Pell; Private scholarships; SEOG; State scholarships/grants. *Loan aid offered:* Direct PLUS loans; Direct Subsidized Loans; Direct Unsubsidized Loans. Federal Work-Study Program available. Institutional employment available.

CAMPUS LIFE

Activities: Campus Ministries; Choral groups; Concert band; Dance; Drama/theater; International Student Organization; Jazz band; Marching band; Musical theater; Pep band; Radio station; Student government; Student newspaper. **Organizations:** 229 registered organizations, 41 honor societies, 16 religious organizations, 8 fraternities, 4 sororities. **Athletics (Intercollegiate):** *Men:* baseball, basketball, cross-country, golf, ice hockey, lacrosse, rugby, skiing (nordic/cross-country), swimming, track/field (indoor), ultimate frisbee, volleyball, wrestling. *Women:* baseball, basketball, cross-country, equestrian sports, golf, rugby, skiing (nordic/cross-country), softball, swimming, track/field (indoor), ultimate frisbee, volleyball.

CAMPUS

Type of school	Public
Environment	Village

STUDENTS

Undergrad enrollment	9,941
% male/female	44/56
% from out of state	41
% frosh live on campus	95

FINANCIAL FACTS

Annual in-state tuition	$7,773
Annual out-of-state tuition	$11,283
Room and board	$8,054
Required fees	$1,526

GENERAL ADMISSIONS INFO

Application fee	$20
Regular application deadline	last day to add classes
Nonfall registration	Yes
Fall 2024 testing policy	Test Optional
Range SAT EBRW	500–610
Range SAT Math	520–630
Range ACT Composite	19–25

ACADEMICS

Student/faculty ratio	18:1
% students returning for sophomore year	79

Most classes have 20–29 students.

REQUESTING SERVICES FOR STUDENTS WITH LEARNING DIFFERENCES

Phone: 605-688-4504 • www.sdstate.edu/disability-services • Email: nancy.crooks@sdstate.edu

Documentation submitted to: Office of Disability Services
Separate application required for Services: Yes

Documentation required for:
LD: Psychoeducational evaluation
ADHD: Psychoeducational evaluation
ASD: Psychoeducational evaluation

The University of South Dakota

414 East Clark, Vermillion, SD 57069 • Admissions: 605-658-6200 • www.usd.edu

Support: CS

ACCOMMODATIONS

Allowed in exams:

Calculators	Yes
Dictionary	Yes
Computer	Yes
Spell-checker	Yes
Extended test time	Yes
Scribe	Yes
Proctors	Yes
Oral exams	Yes
Note-takers	Yes

Support services for students with:

LD	Yes
ADHD	Yes
ASD	Yes
Distraction-reduced environment	Yes
Recording of lecture allowed	Yes
Reading technology	Yes
Audio books	Yes
Other assistive technology	Yes
Priority registration	No

Added costs of services:

For LD	No
For ADHD	No
For ASD	No
LD specialists	Yes
ADHD & ASD coaching	No
ASD specialists	No
Professional tutors	No
Peer tutors	Yes
Max. hours/week for services	Varies
How professors are notified of student approved accommodations	Student

COLLEGE GRADUATION REQUIREMENTS

Course waivers allowed	No
Course substitutions allowed	No

PROGRAMS/SERVICES FOR STUDENTS WITH LEARNING DIFFERENCES

Disability Services provides accommodations for students with documented learning disabilities. Once admitted, students must request accommodations by completing an online application and including professional documentation of their disability. Accommodations are tailored to each student's course needs and can include alternate-format texts, notetakers, assistive technology, a distraction-free location for exams, extended time for exams, and referrals to other resources.

ADMISSIONS

All prospective students are expected to meet or exceed the minimum standards for admission. For admission to USD, applicants must have a GPA of at least 2.6 OR rank in the upper 50 percent of their graduating class OR have an ACT score of 21 or above (SAT score of 1070 or above) OR achieve a 3 or higher on the English Language Arts and Mathematics Smarter Balanced Assessments. Applicants should have a C or higher in all required high school courses. Applications from students who do not meet all admission requirements are considered on an individual basis.

Additional Information

USD 101 is a course taken during the first half of the first semester that assists first-year students transition to life at USD by connecting them to faculty, staff, students, and resources at the USD. First-Year Experience (FYE) is a program that offers a 1 credit class to help new students navigate through the first semester. These weekly seminars have small class sizes that connect students to a mentoring professor, and to other students who share the same interests. At the Academic & Career Planning Center, students can sign up for free tutoring in math, biology, chemistry, general education social sciences (criminal justice, psychology, etc.), and more. The Writing Center can help students in-person, via Zoom, or through the writing center dropbox with brainstorming ideas, organizing, revising, and polishing any homework that involves writing. The Math Emporium can help in understanding and comprehending the world of mathematics. The Presentation Center is available by appointment or drop-in to help students with presentations and get useful feedback. Supplemental Instruction (SI) includes peer-led study sessions that help with learning strategies for difficult classes and course materials.

Dakota Days is a week-long homecoming celebration of USD spirit and pride with festivities and events for all ages. The Dakota Days parade has a high school marching band parade competition that ends on campus with awards, snacks, door prizes, and a performance by the SOUND of USD Marching Band.

The University of South Dakota

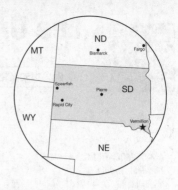

GENERAL ADMISSIONS
Very important factors include: rigor of secondary school record, class rank, academic GPA, standardized test scores (if submitted). *Other factors considered include:* application essay, recommendations. High school diploma is required and GED is accepted. Institution is test-optional for entering Fall 2024. Check admissions website for updates. *Academic units required:* 4 English, 3 math, 3 science (3 labs), 3 social studies, 1 visual/performing arts. *Academic units recommended:* 4 math, 4 science (3 labs), 2 foreign language.

FINANCIAL AID
Students should submit: FAFSA. *Need-based scholarships/grants offered:* College/university scholarship or grant aid from institutional funds; Federal Pell; Private scholarships; SEOG; State scholarships/grants; United Negro College Fund. *Loan aid offered:* Direct PLUS loans; Direct Subsidized Loans; Direct Unsubsidized Loans.

CAMPUS LIFE
Activities: Campus Ministries; Choral groups; Concert band; Dance; Drama/theater; International Student Organization; Jazz band; Literary magazine; Marching band; Music ensembles; Musical theater; Opera; Pep band; Radio station; Student government; Student newspaper; Symphony orchestra; Television station.

CAMPUS
Type of school	Public
Environment	Village

STUDENTS
Undergrad enrollment	5,265
% male/female	36/64
% from out of state	39
% frosh live on campus	87

FINANCIAL FACTS
Annual in-state tuition	$7,773
Annual out-of-state tuition	$11,283
Room and board	$8,604
Required fees	$1,659

GENERAL ADMISSIONS INFO
Application fee	$20
Regular application deadline	Rolling
Nonfall registration	Yes
Fall 2024 testing policy	Test Optional
Range SAT EBRW	500–640
Range SAT Math	520–660
Range ACT Composite	19–25

ACADEMICS
Student/faculty ratio	16:1
% students returning for sophomore year	82

Most classes have 10–19 students.

South Dakota

REQUESTING SERVICES FOR STUDENTS WITH LEARNING DIFFERENCES

Phone: 605-658-3745 • www.usd.edu/About/Departments-Offices-and-Resources/Disability-Services
Email: disabilityservices@usd.edu

Documentation submitted to: Disability Services
Separate application required for Services: Yes

Documentation required for:
  LD: Psychoeducational evaluation
  ADHD: Psychoeducational evaluation
  ASD: Psychoeducational evaluation

Lee University

P.O. Box 3450, Cleveland, TN 37320-3450 • Admissions: 423-614-8500 • www.leeuniversity.edu

Support: CS

ACCOMMODATIONS

Allowed in exams:

Calculators	Yes
Dictionary	No
Computer	Yes
Spell-checker	Yes
Extended test time	Yes
Scribe	Yes
Proctors	Yes
Oral exams	Yes
Note-takers	Yes

Support services for students with:

LD	No
ADHD	No
ASD	No
Distraction-reduced environment	Yes
Recording of lecture allowed	No
Reading technology	Yes
Audio books	Yes
Other assistive technology	Yes
Priority registration	Yes

Added costs of services:

For LD	No
For ADHD	No
For ASD	No
LD specialists	Yes
ADHD & ASD coaching	Yes
ASD specialists	Yes
Professional tutors	No
Peer tutors	Yes
Max. hours/week for services	Varies
How professors are notified of student approved accommodations	Student

COLLEGE GRADUATION REQUIREMENTS

Course waivers allowed	No
Course substitutions allowed	No

PROGRAMS/SERVICES FOR STUDENTS WITH LEARNING DIFFERENCES

The Academic Support Office (ASO) is the liaison between students with disabilities and the Lee University academic community. Students provide documentation and make an accommodations request directly to the ASO coordinator, which is followed with an initial meeting. Students may be referred to the Center for Student Success to receive academic coaching and college-to-career planning support. The Academic Support Program offers specialized services, free tutoring, and group study opportunities.

ADMISSIONS

All applicants are expected to meet the same admission criteria. Lee University requires test scores as part of the regular admissions process. To be eligible for academic scholarships, ACT or SAT scores must be submitted. Applicants must obtain a 2.0 GPA and receive a composite score of a 17 or above on the ACT, or an SAT total score of 900 or above. The average ACT score of admitted applicants is 27. The university may admit some students through academic probation and limit the number of credit hours they can take during their first semester.

Additional Information

Learning Support at Lee University provides instructional assistance and learning opportunities for students. Peer tutors offer individual tutoring online, by appointment, in a variety of courses. The Writing Center's tutors help students develop ways of thinking and reading that lead to effective writing. Every student is assigned a faculty advisor in their major area of interest. Students who do not know what they want to major in will be connected to a faculty advisor who is specifically trained to work with students who are still determining their future major.

January 1, 1918, at precisely 9:30 A.M., Nora Chambers, the first instructor, rang a small bell and called to order the first Lee (originally the Bible Training School) class of 11 students. 2018 was a full year of celebrating Lee University's centennial with the most anticipated event being the Homecoming weekend celebration. Lee produced the *Hundred Year Journey*, a full-length historical documentary about Lee's first 100 years, and published a coffee table book, *Lift High the Flame*, of historical material.

Lee University

GENERAL ADMISSIONS

Very important factors include: rigor of secondary school record, academic GPA, standardized test scores. *Important factors include:* class rank. *Other factors considered include:* application essay, recommendations. High school diploma is required and GED is accepted. Institution requires SAT/ACT scores for entering Fall 2024. Check admissions website for updates. *Academic units recommended:* 4 English, 3 math, 2 science, 1 foreign language, 2 social studies, 1 U.S. history.

FINANCIAL AID

Students should submit: FAFSA. *Need-based scholarships/grants offered:* College/university scholarship or grant aid from institutional funds; Federal Pell; Private scholarships; SEOG; State scholarships/grants. *Loan aid offered:* Direct PLUS loans; Direct Subsidized Loans; Direct Unsubsidized Loans. Federal Work-Study Program available. Institutional employment available.

CAMPUS LIFE

Activities: Campus Ministries; Choral groups; Concert band; Drama/theater; International Student Organization; Jazz band; Literary magazine; Model UN; Music ensembles; Musical theater; Opera; Pep band; Student government; Student newspaper; Symphony orchestra; Yearbook. **Organizations:** 108 registered organizations, 17 honor societies, 17 religious organizations, 5 fraternities, 5 sororities. **Athletics (Intercollegiate):** *Men:* baseball, basketball, cross-country, cycling, golf, rugby, track/field (indoor), ultimate frisbee. *Women:* basketball, cross-country, cycling, golf, lacrosse, rugby, softball, track/field (indoor), ultimate frisbee, volleyball.

CAMPUS

Type of school	Private (nonprofit)
Environment	Town

STUDENTS

Undergrad enrollment	3,405
% male/female	38/62
% from out of state	45
% frosh live on campus	82

FINANCIAL FACTS

Annual tuition	$21,000
Room and board	$8,840
Required fees	$730

GENERAL ADMISSIONS INFO

Application fee	$25
Regular application deadline	Rolling
Nonfall registration	Yes

Fall 2024 testing policy	SAT or ACT Required
Range SAT EBRW	500–630
Range SAT Math	500–600
Range ACT Composite	20–28

ACADEMICS

Student/faculty ratio	13:1
% students returning for sophomore year	81

Most classes have 10–19 students.

REQUESTING SERVICES FOR STUDENTS WITH LEARNING DIFFERENCES

Phone: 423-614-8181 • www.leeuniversity.edu/academics/academic-support
Email: academicsupport@leeuniversity.edu

Documentation submitted to: Academic Support Office
Separate application required for Services: Yes

Documentation required for:
  LD: Psychoeducational evaluation
  ADHD: Psychoeducational evaluation
  ASD: Psychoeducational evaluation

Middle Tennessee State University

1301 East Main Street, Murfreesboro, TN 37132 • Admissions: 615-898-2233 • www.mtsu.edu

Support: S

ACCOMMODATIONS

Allowed in exams:

Calculators	Yes
Dictionary	Yes
Computer	Yes
Spell-checker	Yes
Extended test time	Yes
Scribe	Yes
Proctors	Yes
Oral exams	Yes
Note-takers	Yes

Support services for students with:

LD	Yes
ADHD	Yes
ASD	Yes
Distraction-reduced environment	Yes
Recording of lecture allowed	Yes
Reading technology	Yes
Audio books	Yes
Other assistive technology	Yes
Priority registration	Yes

Added costs of services:

For LD	No
For ADHD	No
For ASD	No
LD specialists	No
ADHD & ASD coaching	No
ASD specialists	No
Professional tutors	No
Peer tutors	Yes
Max. hours/week for services	Varies
How professors are notified of student approved accommodations	Student and Disability and Access Center

COLLEGE GRADUATION REQUIREMENTS

Course waivers allowed	Yes

In what courses: Math, Foreign Language, Public Speaking on a case-by-case basis

Course substitutions allowed	Yes

In what courses: Math, Foreign Language, Public Speaking on a case-by-case basis

PROGRAMS/SERVICES FOR STUDENTS WITH LEARNING DIFFERENCES

The Disability and Access Center (DAC) is an academic support center for students. DAC staff advocates for and recommends reasonable accommodations that include extended test time, a reduced-distraction environment, readers, notetakers, and instructor notes. To request accommodations, students submit an application and formal documentation and schedule an appointment with DAC. Students determine which professors receive emails about the accommodations and what information is disclosed.

ADMISSIONS

Applicants are guaranteed admission if they have completed college prep courses and have a 3.0 GPA, or a minimum composite ACT score of 22, or a minimum SAT total score of 1100. Guaranteed admission may also be given to applicants with a minimum 2.7 GPA plus an ACT score of 19 or an SAT score of 990. Students who don't meet the requirements for guaranteed admission can still be considered for admission through a review process that assesses the student's potential for success by evaluating their personal statement, high school courses, honors or advanced placement, dual credit, and extenuating circumstances. Admission by review will also include other special interests, skills, and nonacademic factors, as explained on the personal statement form. Students who plan to apply for accommodations must be accepted to MTSU prior to beginning the DAC registration process.

Additional Information

Tutoring options are generally available by major at the Student Success Center (SSC). The SSC provides Supplemental Instruction and early arrival programs. The Scholars Academy is a first-year experience program that includes a Summer Institute, which is a two-week early arrival program for incoming first-time students that begins two weeks prior to the first day of school in August. Students must participate for the duration of the Institute, attend all Institute events, as well as, register for the Scholars Academy sections of UNIV 1010 for the fall semester. Study skills workshops, team-building exercises, leadership training, the summer reading program, and service-learning projects are integral aspects of the Scholars Academy. MTSU will cover instruction costs and room and board expenses, if applicable.

One of homecoming week's annual celebrations is the NPHC Step Show, sponsored by the National Pan-Hellenic Council. Stepping is a highly energetic art form, first developed through song and dance rituals performed by African American fraternities and sororities. The Step Show also showcases local high school steppers, musical acts, and comedians. The MTSU NPHC holds one of the premier Step Shows in the southeast region, and people from all across Tennessee attend the event.

Middle Tennessee State University

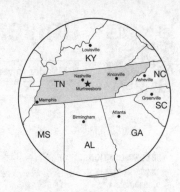

GENERAL ADMISSIONS

Very important factors include: academic GPA, standardized test scores (if submitted). *Other factors considered include:* rigor of secondary school record, application essay, recommendations. High school diploma is required and GED is accepted. Institution is test-optional for entering Fall 2024. Check admissions website for updates. *Academic units required:* 4 English, 4 math, 3 science (1 lab), 2 foreign language, 1 social studies, 1 U.S. history, 1 visual/performing arts.

FINANCIAL AID

Students should submit: FAFSA. *Need-based scholarships/grants offered:* College/university scholarship or grant aid from institutional funds; Federal Pell; Private scholarships; SEOG; State scholarships/grants. *Loan aid offered:* Direct PLUS loans; Direct Subsidized Loans; Direct Unsubsidized Loans. Federal Work-Study Program available. Institutional employment available.

CAMPUS LIFE

Activities: Campus Ministries; Choral groups; Concert band; Dance; Drama/theater; International Student Organization; Jazz band; Literary magazine; Marching band; Model UN; Music ensembles; Musical theater; Opera; Pep band; Radio station; Student government; Student newspaper; Student-run film society; Symphony orchestra; Television station. **Organizations:** 366 registered organizations, 26 honor societies, 51 religious organizations, 15 fraternities, 10 sororities. **Athletics (Intercollegiate):** *Men:* baseball, basketball, bowling, cross-country, equestrian sports, golf, ice hockey, lacrosse, martial arts, rugby, swimming, ultimate frisbee, volleyball, wrestling. *Women:* basketball, bowling, cross-country, equestrian sports, golf, ice hockey, lacrosse, martial arts, softball, swimming, ultimate frisbee, volleyball, wrestling.

CAMPUS

Type of school	Public
Environment	City

STUDENTS

Undergrad enrollment	18,005
% male/female	47/53
% from out of state	8
% frosh live on campus	31

FINANCIAL FACTS

Annual in-state tuition	$7,554
Annual out-of-state tuition	$27,168
Room and board	$9,772
Required fees	$1,870

GENERAL ADMISSIONS INFO

Application fee	$25
Regular application deadline	Rolling
Nonfall registration	Yes

Fall 2024 testing policy	Test Optional
Range SAT EBRW	500–610
Range SAT Math	490–590
Range ACT Composite	20–26

ACADEMICS

Student/faculty ratio	17:1
% students returning for sophomore year	79

Most classes have 10–19 students.

REQUESTING SERVICES FOR STUDENTS WITH LEARNING DIFFERENCES

Phone: 615-898-2783 • www.mtsu.edu/dac • Email: dacemail@mtsu.edu

Documentation submitted to: Disability & Access Center
Separate application required for Services: Yes

Documentation required for:
 LD: Psychoeducational evaluation
 ADHD: Psychoeducational evaluation
 ASD: Psychoeducational evaluation

University of Memphis

101 Wilder Tower, Memphis, TN 38152 • Admissions: 901-678-2111 • www.memphis.edu

(Support: CS)

ACCOMMODATIONS

Allowed in exams:

Calculators	Yes
Dictionary	Yes
Computer	Yes
Spell-checker	Yes
Extended test time	Yes
Scribe	Yes
Proctors	Yes
Oral exams	Yes
Note-takers	Yes

Support services for students with:

LD	Yes
ADHD	Yes
ASD	Yes
Distraction-reduced environment	Yes
Recording of lecture allowed	Yes
Reading technology	Yes
Audio books	Yes
Other assistive technology	Yes
Priority registration	Yes

Added costs of services:

For LD	No
For ADHD	No
For ASD	No
LD specialists	Yes
ADHD & ASD coaching	Yes
ASD specialists	No
Professional tutors	Yes
Peer tutors	No
Max. hours/week for services	Varies
How professors are notified of student approved accommodations	Student

COLLEGE GRADUATION REQUIREMENTS

Course waivers allowed	No
Course substitutions allowed	Yes
In what courses: Case-by-case basis	

PROGRAMS/SERVICES FOR STUDENTS WITH LEARNING DIFFERENCES

Disability Resources for Students (DRS) supports students with learning, ADHD, and autism spectrum disorders by providing resources to enhance their academic strengths and build the skills necessary to succeed in a college environment. Services available to all students registered with DRS include early registration, disability services orientation, a semester plan for accommodations and services, memos to faculty about disability needs, advocacy relating to disability access issues, information, and guidance. DRS encourages the development of lifelong learning skills and personal responsibility for academic success with a variety of programs and counseling. In coordination with the counseling center, DRS hosts a weekly social skills group and monthly organized social activity. The First HIRES (Helping Individuals Recognize Employment Skills) program helps students gain work experience and strengthen their résumés by obtaining a job or internship on campus. Students can be matched with career mentors who also have a disability.

ADMISSIONS

All applicants are expected to meet the same admission criteria. Students may substitute American Sign Language (ASL) for their foreign language requirement. Substitutions for math are permitted on a case-by-case basis, and varies by college.

Additional Information

UofM has an extensive tutoring program that is available to all students at no cost, as well as academic coaching to assist with organization and planning. First-year students are trained in college survival skills and meet regularly with the staff to improve strengths, overcome challenges, and develop their individual learning styles.

To commemorate its 100th anniversary in 2012, UofM commissioned a bronze statue of a majestic tiger in front of the University Center. The tiger appears to move upward and forward, symbolizing graduating into the world. The alumni association joined in on the fun by placing life-sized, uniquely decorated tiger statues all around Memphis. Students strive to post a selfie with all 100 tigers by the time they graduate, with the tag #tigersaroundtown.

University of Memphis

GENERAL ADMISSIONS

Very important factors include: rigor of secondary school record, class rank, academic GPA, standardized test scores (if submitted). *Other factors considered include:* application essay, recommendations. High school diploma is required and GED is accepted. Institution is test-optional for entering Fall 2024. Check admissions website for updates. *Academic units required:* 4 English, 3 math, 2 science (1 lab), 2 foreign language, 1 social studies, 1 U.S. history, 1 visual/performing arts.

FINANCIAL AID

Students should submit: FAFSA. *Need-based scholarships/grants offered:* College/university scholarship or grant aid from institutional funds; Federal Pell; Private scholarships; SEOG; State scholarships/grants. *Loan aid offered:* Direct PLUS loans; Direct Subsidized Loans; Direct Unsubsidized Loans. Federal Work-Study Program available. Institutional employment available.

CAMPUS LIFE

Activities: Campus Ministries; Choral groups; Concert band; Dance; Drama/theater; International Student Organization; Jazz band; Literary magazine; Marching band; Music ensembles; Musical theater; Opera; Pep band; Radio station; Student government; Student newspaper; Student-run film society; Symphony orchestra. **Organizations:** 186 registered organizations, 20 honor societies, 15 religious organizations, 11 fraternities, 12 sororities. **Athletics (Intercollegiate):** *Men:* baseball, basketball, cross-country, golf, track/field (indoor). *Women:* basketball, cross-country, golf, softball, track/field (indoor), volleyball.

CAMPUS

Type of school	Public
Environment	Metropolis

STUDENTS

Undergrad enrollment	16,702
% male/female	39/61
% from out of state	16
% frosh live on campus	49

FINANCIAL FACTS

Annual in-state tuition	$8,352
Annual out-of-state tuition	$12,384
Room and board	$9,354
Required fees	$1,704

GENERAL ADMISSIONS INFO

Application fee	$25
Regular application deadline	7/1
Nonfall registration	Yes
Fall 2024 testing policy	Test Optional
Range SAT EBRW	480–630
Range SAT Math	450–600
Range ACT Composite	17–24

ACADEMICS

Student/faculty ratio	16:1
% students returning for sophomore year	72

Most classes have 10–19 students.

REQUESTING SERVICES FOR STUDENTS WITH LEARNING DIFFERENCES

Phone: 901-678-2880 • www.memphis.edu/drs/ • Email: tmbchnnn@memphis.edu

Documentation submitted to: Disability Resources for Students
Separate application required for Services: Yes

Documentation required for:
LD: Psychoeducational evaluation
ADHD: Psychoeducational evaluation
ASD: Psychoeducational evaluation

Tennessee

University of Tennessee at Chattanooga

615 McCallie Avenue, Chattanooga, TN 37403 • Admissions: 423-425-4662 • www.utc.edu

Support: SP

PROGRAMS/SERVICES FOR STUDENTS WITH LEARNING DIFFERENCES

The University of Tennessee at Chattanooga supports students with learning differences through the Disability Resource Center (DRC). Once admitted to UTC, students must submit a separate application for services. Documentation may be required and is encouraged, but the university values the life experience and perspective of the student. Through a structured interview process, DRC will discuss and determine eligibility for accommodations. DRC will approve provisional accommodations for one semester to allow students time to gather more information or receive additional assessments to document the disability. Some of the accommodations offered include assistive and adaptive technology, exam accommodations, note-taking assistance, priority registration, and specialized programming for students on the autism spectrum. The Mosaic program is available to support students on the autism spectrum and help with the transition into and out of college. There is a separate application and interview process to participate in Mosaic and a fee per semester. Financial aid is available for those that qualify. The curriculum includes four components: graded courses, coaching, peer and professional mentorship, and supervised study hours. Mosaic organizes employer luncheons, mixers, and career fairs to support students transitioning out of college. A student-led events committee plans activities and volunteer opportunities to develop leadership, communication, and team skills.

ADMISSIONS

All students must meet the university's admission requirements. First-year applicants need a 2.85 GPA and a minimum 18 ACT score or 960 SAT score, or a 2.5 GPA and a 21 ACT score or 1060 SAT score.

Additional Information

The Center for Academic Support and Advisement offers peer tutoring, peer academic coaching, and Supplemental Instruction.

Homecoming Week is always memorable, with a carnival, pep rally, Yard Show, lip-sync performances, and a football game. First-year students participate in the Mocs Flock Finley and the Homecoming King and Queen selection, and high school students participate in Band Day, performing with the college band at the game.

University of Tennessee at Chattanooga

GENERAL ADMISSIONS

Very important factors include: rigor of secondary school record, academic GPA, standardized test scores. *Other factors considered include:* application essay, recommendations. High school diploma is required and GED is accepted. Institution requires SAT/ACT scores for entering Fall 2024. Check admissions website for updates. *Academic units required:* 4 English, 4 math, 3 science (3 labs), 2 foreign language, 1 social studies, 1 U.S. history, 1 visual/performing arts.

FINANCIAL AID

Students should submit: FAFSA. *Need-based scholarships/grants offered:* College/university scholarship or grant aid from institutional funds; Federal Pell; Private scholarships; SEOG; State scholarships/grants. *Loan aid offered:* Direct PLUS loans; Direct Subsidized Loans; Direct Unsubsidized Loans. Federal Work-Study Program available. Institutional employment available.

CAMPUS LIFE

Activities: Campus Ministries; Choral groups; Concert band; Dance; Drama/theater; International Student Organization; Jazz band; Literary magazine; Marching band; Model UN; Music ensembles; Musical theater; Opera; Pep band; Radio station; Student government; Student newspaper; Student-run film society; Symphony orchestra; Television station. **Organizations:** 125 registered organizations, 34 honor societies, 8 religious organizations, 14 fraternities, 11 sororities. **Athletics (Intercollegiate):** *Men:* baseball, basketball, crew/rowing, cross-country, cycling, golf, lacrosse, racquetball, rugby, swimming, ultimate frisbee, volleyball, wrestling. *Women:* basketball, crew/rowing, cross-country, cycling, golf, racquetball, rugby, softball, swimming, ultimate frisbee, volleyball.

CAMPUS
Type of school	Public
Environment	City

STUDENTS
Undergrad enrollment	10,097
% male/female	44/56
% from out of state	6
% frosh live on campus	78

FINANCIAL FACTS
Annual in-state tuition	$6,888
Annual out-of-state tuition	$23,006
Room and board	$8,786
Required fees	$1,776

GENERAL ADMISSIONS INFO
Application fee	$30
Regular application deadline	5/1
Nonfall registration	Yes
Fall 2024 testing policy	SAT or ACT Required
Range SAT EBRW	530–630
Range SAT Math	510–610
Range ACT Composite	21–26

ACADEMICS
Student/faculty ratio	14:1
% students returning for sophomore year	73

Most classes have 10–19 students.

REQUESTING SERVICES FOR STUDENTS WITH LEARNING DIFFERENCES

Phone: 423-425-4006 • www.utc.edu/disability-resource-center/ • Email: drc@utc.edu

Documentation submitted to: Disability Resource Center
Separate application required for Services: Yes

Documentation required for:
LD: Psychoeducational evaluation
ADHD: Psychoeducational evaluation
ASD: Psychoeducational evaluation

University of Tennessee, Knoxville

320 Student Service Building, Knoxville, TN 37996-0230 • Admissions: 865-974-1111 • www.utk.edu

Support: CS

ACCOMMODATIONS

Allowed in exams:

Calculators	Yes
Dictionary	Yes
Computer	Yes
Spell-checker	Yes
Extended test time	Yes
Scribe	Yes
Proctors	Yes
Oral exams	Yes
Note-takers	Yes

Support services for students with:

LD	Yes
ADHD	Yes
ASD	Yes
Distraction-reduced environment	Yes
Recording of lecture allowed	Yes
Reading technology	Yes
Audio books	Yes
Other assistive technology	Yes
Priority registration	Yes

Added costs of services:

For LD	No
For ADHD	No
For ASD	No
LD specialists	Yes
ADHD & ASD coaching	Yes
ASD specialists	Yes
Professional tutors	No
Peer tutors	Yes
Max. hours/week for services	Varies
How professors are notified of student approved accommodations	Student

COLLEGE GRADUATION REQUIREMENTS

Course waivers allowed	No
Course substitutions allowed	Yes
In what courses: Math, Foreign Language, and others	

PROGRAMS/SERVICES FOR STUDENTS WITH LEARNING DIFFERENCES

Student Disability Services (SDS) provides support and accommodations for students with documented disabilities, including testing accommodations, accessible media, note-taking in a variety of formats, assistive technology, a reduced course load, assignment extension, flexible attendance, and course substitution when appropriate. SDS also partners with the Academic Success Center to provide tutoring, academic coaching, and workshops. Students who are requesting support services are required to submit documentation from a certified professional as well as complete the online registration form prior to scheduling an initial welcome meeting with SDS. Students must also talk with professors about accommodations in the classroom, as needed, and inform SDS of barriers to a successful education. SDS offers a peer mentoring program to assist first-year students in adjusting to campus life. The program pairs students with mentees that are also registered with SDS. Advocates for Autism, a nonprofit that got its start on the UT Knoxville campus, offers an inclusive environment for students on the spectrum, serves as a group of allies, and raises awareness about individuals with autism.

ADMISSIONS

All applicants are expected to meet the same admission criteria. UT Knoxville requires students to submit either ACT or SAT scores. The middle 50 percent of admitted applicants have an ACT score of 25–31 or an SAT score of 1170–1340. Students are required to self-report their grades and test scores and upload an unofficial copy of the transcript. Once admitted, students must send official transcripts and test scores. If any course is repeated, the student must include all grades, not just the highest grade.

Additional Information

In addition to coaching and tutoring, the Academic Success Center provides numerous scheduled workshops throughout the semester that focus on study skills, stress management, time management, and test-taking skills.

The "Centaur Excavations at Volos" is an "archaeological" display in the John C. Hodges Library. The centaur display is a reminder to students not to believe everything they see or read. In reality, the centaur was created from the bones of a pony and a human skeleton.

University of Tennessee, Knoxville

General Admissions

Very important factors include: rigor of secondary school record, academic GPA. *Important factors include:* standardized test scores, application essay. *Other factors considered include:* recommendations. High school diploma is required and GED is accepted. Institution requires SAT/ACT scores for entering Fall 2024. Check admissions website for updates. *Academic units recommended:* 4 English, 4 math, 3 science (1 lab), 2 foreign language, 1 social studies, 1 U.S. history, 1 visual/performing arts.

Financial Aid

Students should submit: FAFSA. *Need-based scholarships/grants offered:* College/university scholarship or grant aid from institutional funds; Federal Pell; Private scholarships; SEOG; State scholarships/grants. *Loan aid offered:* Direct PLUS loans; Direct Subsidized Loans; Direct Unsubsidized Loans. Federal Work-Study Program available.

Campus Life

Activities: Campus Ministries; Choral groups; Concert band; Dance; Drama/theater; International Student Organization; Jazz band; Literary magazine; Marching band; Model UN; Music ensembles; Musical theater; Opera; Pep band; Radio station; Student government; Student newspaper; Student-run film society; Symphony orchestra; Television station; Yearbook. **Organizations:** 460 registered organizations, 22 honor societies, 46 religious organizations, 27 fraternities, 20 sororities. **Athletics (Intercollegiate):** *Men:* baseball, basketball, bowling, crew/rowing, cross-country, equestrian sports, golf, gymnastics, ice hockey, lacrosse, martial arts, rugby, swimming, track/field (indoor), ultimate frisbee, volleyball, water polo, wrestling. *Women:* basketball, bowling, crew/rowing, cross-country, equestrian sports, golf, gymnastics, ice hockey, lacrosse, martial arts, rugby, softball, swimming, track/field (indoor), ultimate frisbee, volleyball, water polo, wrestling.

CAMPUS

Type of school	Public
Environment	City

STUDENTS

Undergrad enrollment	26,905
% male/female	46/54
% from out of state	32
% frosh live on campus	93

FINANCIAL FACTS

Annual in-state tuition	$11,332
Annual out-of-state tuition	$29,522
Room and board	$12,150
Required fees	$1,912

GENERAL ADMISSIONS INFO

Application fee	$50
Regular application deadline	Rolling
Nonfall registration	Yes
Fall 2024 testing policy	SAT or ACT Required
Range SAT EBRW	590–660
Range SAT Math	580–670
Range ACT Composite	25–31

ACADEMICS

Student/faculty ratio	18:1
% students returning for sophomore year	89

Most classes have 20–29 students.

REQUESTING SERVICES FOR STUDENTS WITH LEARNING DIFFERENCES

Phone: 865-974-6087 • sds.utk.edu/ • Email: sds@utk.edu

Documentation submitted to: Student Disability Services
Separate application required for Services: Yes

Documentation required for:
LD: Psychoeducational evaluation
ADHD: Psychoeducational evaluation
ASD: Psychoeducational evaluation

Tennessee

University of Tennessee at Martin

201 Hall-Moody, Martin, TN 38238 • Admissions: 731-881-7020 • www.utm.edu

Support: S

ACCOMMODATIONS

Allowed in exams:

Calculators	Yes
Dictionary	Yes
Computer	Yes
Spell-checker	Yes
Extended test time	Yes
Scribe	Yes
Proctors	Yes
Oral exams	Yes
Note-takers	Yes

Support services for students with:

LD	Yes
ADHD	Yes
ASD	Yes
Distraction-reduced environment	Yes
Recording of lecture allowed	Yes
Reading technology	Yes
Audio books	Yes
Other assistive technology	Yes
Priority registration	No

Added costs of services:

For LD	No
For ADHD	No
For ASD	No
LD specialists	No
ADHD & ASD coaching	No
ASD specialists	No
Professional tutors	No
Peer tutors	Yes
Max. hours/week for services	120
How professors are notified of student approved accommodations	Student and ARC

COLLEGE GRADUATION REQUIREMENTS

Course waivers allowed	No
Course substitutions allowed	Yes

In what courses: Case-by-case basis

PROGRAMS/SERVICES FOR STUDENTS WITH LEARNING DIFFERENCES

Support and accommodations for students with disabilities are available through the Accessibility Resource Center (ARC) and may include testing accommodations, assistive technology support, note-taking services, and preferential classroom seating. Qualified students with learning disabilities should register with ARC to request accommodations and submit documentation. Students will meet with an ARC representative to review and formalize their accommodations. It can take up to 30 days to process requests for initial services or add accommodations, and students are encouraged to start the process early.

ADMISSIONS

All applicants must meet the standard admission criteria. Students may be admitted by meeting one of the following criteria: a 3.0 cumulative high school GPA and a minimum 19 ACT or 900 SAT, OR a 2.7 cumulative high school GPA and at least a 21 ACT or 980 SAT.

Additional Information

The Student Success Center offers many resources for students, including tutoring through the STEM Lab, the Mathematics Learning Center, the Writing Center, and the Reading Center. The Student Success Center also provides Supplemental Instruction support in over a dozen courses; students work in small groups and focus on exam strategies, study skills, and course materials. The Math Learning Center offers free tutoring in all math courses. The Reading Center helps students increase their reading speed or enhance their comprehension and vocabulary. The instruction in the Reading Center is geared toward first-year students who scored below 22 on the reading section of the ACT. The Writing Center is open on a drop-in basis for students to get help with writing assignments. The Writing Center also sponsors weekly writing workshops and general orientation sessions for first-year students.

For more than 50 years, UTM Rodeo has been one of the premier collegiate rodeos east of the Mississippi. The UTM rodeo team is a member of the National Intercollegiate Rodeo Association, with both men's and women's teams. In 2014, at the College National Finals Rodeo Men's National Championship, UT Martin became the first team east of the Mississippi River to win a national title in rodeo. UTM Rodeo is considered one of the biggest annual events on campus.

University of Tennessee at Martin

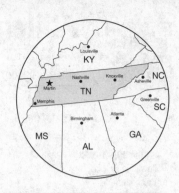

GENERAL ADMISSIONS

Very important factors include: rigor of secondary school record, academic GPA, standardized test scores. High school diploma is required and GED is accepted. Institution requires SAT/ACT scores for entering Fall 2024. Check admissions website for updates. *Academic units required:* 4 English, 4 math, 3 science (1 lab), 2 foreign language, 1 social studies, 1 U.S. history, 1 visual/performing arts.

FINANCIAL AID

Students should submit: FAFSA. *Need-based scholarships/grants offered:* College/university scholarship or grant aid from institutional funds; Federal Pell; Private scholarships; SEOG; State scholarships/grants. *Loan aid offered:* Direct PLUS loans; Direct Subsidized Loans; Direct Unsubsidized Loans. Federal Work-Study Program available. Institutional employment available.

CAMPUS LIFE

Activities: Campus Ministries; Choral groups; Concert band; Dance; Drama/theater; International Student Organization; Jazz band; Literary magazine; Marching band; Model UN; Music ensembles; Musical theater; Pep band; Radio station; Student government; Student newspaper; Student-run film society; Television station; Yearbook. **Organizations:** 153 registered organizations, 18 honor societies, 11 religious organizations, 11 fraternities, 9 sororities. **Athletics (Intercollegiate):** *Men:* baseball, basketball, cross-country, golf. *Women:* basketball, cross-country, equestrian sports, softball, volleyball.

CAMPUS

Type of school	Public
Environment	Village

STUDENTS

Undergrad enrollment	6,443
% male/female	40/60
% from out of state	11
% frosh live on campus	68

FINANCIAL FACTS

Annual in-state tuition	$9,912
Annual out-of-state tuition	$15,952
Room and board	$6,960

GENERAL ADMISSIONS INFO

Application fee	$30
Regular application deadline	Rolling
Nonfall registration	Yes
Fall 2024 testing policy	SAT or ACT Required
Range ACT Composite	19–25

ACADEMICS

Student/faculty ratio	14:1
% students returning for sophomore year	71

Most classes have 2–9 students.

REQUESTING SERVICES FOR STUDENTS WITH LEARNING DIFFERENCES

Phone: 731-881-7605 • utm.edu/offices-and-services/accessibility-resource-center
Email: DisabilityServices@utm.edu

Documentation submitted to: Accessibility Resource Center
Separate application required for Services: Yes

Documentation required for:
  LD: Psychoeducational evaluation
  ADHD: Psychoeducational evaluation
  ASD: Psychoeducational evaluation

Tennessee

Abilene Christian University

ACU Box 29000, Abilene, TX 79699 • Admissions: 325-674-2650 • www.acu.edu

Support: CS

ACCOMMODATIONS

Allowed in exams:

Calculators	Yes
Dictionary	Yes
Computer	Yes
Spell-checker	Yes
Extended test time	Yes
Scribe	Yes
Proctors	Yes
Oral exams	No
Note-takers	Yes

Support services for students with:

LD	Yes
ADHD	Yes
ASD	Yes
Distraction-reduced environment	Yes
Recording of lecture allowed	Yes
Reading technology	Yes
Audio books	Yes
Other assistive technology	Yes
Priority registration	No

Added costs of services:

For LD	No
For ADHD	No
For ASD	No
LD specialists	Yes
ADHD & ASD coaching	Yes
ASD specialists	Yes
Professional tutors	No
Peer tutors	Yes
Max. hours/week for services	20
How professors are notified of student approved accommodations	Student

COLLEGE GRADUATION REQUIREMENTS

Course waivers allowed	No
Course substitutions allowed	No

PROGRAMS/SERVICES FOR STUDENTS WITH LEARNING DIFFERENCES

University Access Programs (UAP) are designed to assist students with disabilities access the school's academic, cultural, and recreational activities and services. The Alpha Scholars Program provides academic accommodations, tutoring, academic coaching, and mentoring relationships to students with documented disabilities. Students complete the academic form and submit it with current disability documentation, then set up a meeting with Alpha staff to discuss the students' needs. Once accommodations are determined, course instructors will receive a notification of accommodations from the Alpha office. Alpha students receive an assessment of their individual learning styles and study habits, and assistance in adapting new study strategies.

ADMISSIONS

ACU requires the completion of college preparatory programs, and considers GPA and class rank. However, ACU's application is a low-stress process with no essay requirement and self-reported grades (all students must submit an official, final high school transcript with a posted graduation date). A counselor recommendation is required. ACT and SAT scores are optional but students who do not submit test scores are required to take a placement exam before enrolling in classes. Test scores can be used for placement exams and for more scholarship opportunities.

Additional Information

Excel Tutoring provides comprehensive peer tutoring to all students and is offered for most subjects. Tutors can also help with study skills areas such as time-management, organization, exam preparation, note-taking, and more. The Excel Tutors are ACU students with second-year status and a specific GPA requirement. The Academic Coaching program is designed to help students identify and address their academic barriers while increasing their academic skills and learning strategies. Students must actively participate, engage, and prepare for academic coaching sessions for them to be effective. Sessions are scheduled in 30-minute increments in-person or via Zoom, phone, or email, depending on the student's need and/or preference. Supplemental Instruction (SI) is a voluntary academic support program. SI sessions are peer-led, highly structured study sessions in traditionally difficult courses. SI leaders attend the concurrent class lecture, take class notes, and model strong study skills. SI one-hour sessions are set during the first week of each semester, and each SI leader has weekly office hours to assist students with additional support.

All first-year students get the once-in-a lifetime Once-in-an-ACU-time chance to showcase their talents and originality in the Freshman Only Lip Sync Competition during Family Weekend. Residence halls compete for the Best Hall Act, and students perform solo or small group acts. A group of first-year students is selected as the leadership team for planning, creating, and managing the show.

Abilene Christian University

General Admissions

Very important factors include: rigor of secondary school record, class rank, academic GPA, standardized test scores (if submitted). *Other factors considered include:* application essay, recommendations. High school diploma is required and GED is accepted. Institution is test-flexible for entering Fall 2024. Check admissions website for updates. *Academic units required:* 4 English, 3 math, 3 science (2 labs), 2 foreign language, 1 history.

Financial Aid

Students should submit: FAFSA. *Need-based scholarships/grants offered:* College/university scholarship or grant aid from institutional funds; Federal Pell; Private scholarships; SEOG; State scholarships/grants. *Loan aid offered:* Direct PLUS loans; Direct Subsidized Loans; Direct Unsubsidized Loans. Federal Work-Study Program available. Institutional employment available.

Campus Life

Activities: Campus Ministries; Choral groups; Concert band; Dance; Drama/theater; International Student Organization; Jazz band; Literary magazine; Marching band; Model UN; Music ensembles; Musical theater; Opera; Pep band; Radio station; Student government; Student newspaper; Symphony orchestra; Television station. **Organizations:** 103 registered organizations, 9 honor societies, 5 religious organizations, 7 fraternities, 6 sororities. **Athletics (Intercollegiate):** *Men:* baseball, basketball, cross-country, golf, lacrosse, rugby, track/field (indoor). *Women:* basketball, cross-country, golf, softball, track/field (indoor), volleyball.

CAMPUS

Type of school	Private (nonprofit)
Environment	City

STUDENTS

Undergrad enrollment	3,480
% male/female	38/62
% from out of state	12
% frosh live on campus	91

FINANCIAL FACTS

Annual tuition	$37,750
Room and board	$11,350
Required fees	$50

GENERAL ADMISSIONS INFO

Application fee	$50
Regular application deadline	2/15
Nonfall registration	Yes

Fall 2024 testing policy	Test Flexible
Range SAT EBRW	510–620
Range SAT Math	500–600
Range ACT Composite	21–27

ACADEMICS

Student/faculty ratio	13:1
% students returning for sophomore year	77

Most classes have 10–19 students.

REQUESTING SERVICES FOR STUDENTS WITH LEARNING DIFFERENCES

Phone: 325-674-2517 • acu.edu/about/uap/overview • Email: nls12a@acu.edu

Documentation submitted to: Alpha Scholars Program
Separate application required for Services: Yes

Documentation required for:
LD: Psychoeducational evaluation
ADHD: Psychoeducational evaluation
ASD: Psychoeducational evaluation

Lamar University

P.O. Box 10009, Beaumont, TX 77710 • Admissions: 409-880-8888 • www.lamar.edu

Support: CS

ACCOMMODATIONS

Allowed in exams:

Calculators	Yes
Dictionary	Yes
Computer	Yes
Spell-checker	Yes
Extended test time	Yes
Scribe	Yes
Proctors	Yes
Oral exams	Yes
Note-takers	Yes

Support services for students with:

LD	Yes
ADHD	Yes
ASD	Yes
Distraction-reduced environment	Yes
Recording of lecture allowed	Yes
Reading technology	Yes
Audio books	Yes
Other assistive technology	Yes
Priority registration	Yes

Added costs of services:

For LD	No
For ADHD	No
For ASD	No
LD specialists	Yes
ADHD & ASD coaching	No
ASD specialists	No
Professional tutors	No
Peer tutors	Yes
Max. hours/week for services	15
How professors are notified of student approved accommodations	Student

COLLEGE GRADUATION REQUIREMENTS

Course waivers allowed	No
Course substitutions allowed	Yes

In what courses: Case-by-case basis

PROGRAMS/SERVICES FOR STUDENTS WITH LEARNING DIFFERENCES

The Accessibility Resource Center (ARC) at Lamar University provides access to services for students with disabilities. To apply for services, students complete an application, submit eligible documentation, and attend an intake meeting with the director of ARC. The student works with the ARC staff to determine course-based and exam-based accommodations. General accommodations include extended test time, quiet testing rooms, note-taking, assistive technology, and priority registration.

ADMISSIONS

The admission process is the same for all students. Lamar University does not require test scores to be submitted for applicants who meet the test-optional criteria (TOC), which considers class rank, dual college credit, and non-ranking schools with transcripts that demonstrate the ability to excel in college. Students whose profile aligns to the TOC will be automatically accepted. This includes homeschooled students. All other students' applications are reviewed for academic rigor, college preparation, and test scores; the minimum scores for unranked applicants are 1040 on the SAT and 20 on the ACT.

Additional Information

Lamar University offers college-level writing help, for any course, at the University Writing Center. Students meet to obtain individualized support with understanding assignments, brainstorming, organizing, revising, editing, and interpreting graded papers. There are peer mentoring guides and collaborative group writing activities. Students are encouraged to check in at the Writing Center each semester for an assessment of writing approaches and opportunities. Additionally, students may enroll in the STARS (Student Tutoring and Retention Services) program to obtain guidance and resources for staying on track. STARS provides academic success coaching, tutoring, and support labs for complex subjects (such as physics). These services are available at no additional cost to all students.

The Lamar Spirit Bell was originally donated by the Santa Fe Railroad Company in 1966. The bell was rung by members of the cheerleading team to celebrate each football score. It was rediscovered in a storage facility, restored, and reintroduced to Cardinal Football in 2018. Carl Stockholm and Genie West, among the first to ring the bell in 1966, returned September 1, 2018, to help resurrect the tradition of ringing the bell after every LU score and passed the duty to the new generation of LU cheerleaders to celebrate success on the field.

Lamar University

GENERAL ADMISSIONS

High school diploma is required and GED is accepted; High school diploma is required and GED is not accepted. Institution is test-optional for entering Fall 2024. Check admissions website for updates. *Academic units recommended:* 4 English, 3 math, 2 science, 2 social studies, 2 academic electives.

FINANCIAL AID

Students should submit: FAFSA. *Need-based scholarships/grants offered:* College/university scholarship or grant aid from institutional funds; Federal Pell; Private scholarships; SEOG; State scholarships/grants. *Loan aid offered:* Direct PLUS loans; Direct Subsidized Loans; Direct Unsubsidized Loans. Federal Work-Study Program available. Institutional employment available.

CAMPUS LIFE

Activities: Student government; Student newspaper. **Organizations:** 145 registered organizations, 11 fraternities, 8 sororities. **Athletics (Intercollegiate):** *Men:* baseball, basketball, cross-country, golf. *Women:* basketball, cross-country, golf, volleyball.

CAMPUS	
Type of school	Public
Environment	Village

STUDENTS	
Undergrad enrollment	8,377
% male/female	41/59
% from out of state	3
% frosh live on campus	58

FINANCIAL FACTS	
Annual in-state tuition	$7,785
Annual out-of-state tuition	$20,025
Room and board	$9,884
Required fees	$2,801

GENERAL ADMISSIONS INFO	
Application fee	$25
Regular application deadline	Rolling
Nonfall registration	Yes
Fall 2024 testing policy	Test Optional
Range SAT EBRW	460–570
Range SAT Math	450–550
Range ACT Composite	16–24

ACADEMICS	
Student/faculty ratio	20:1
% students returning for sophomore year	55
Most classes have 20–29 students.	

REQUESTING SERVICES FOR STUDENTS WITH LEARNING DIFFERENCES

Phone: 409-880-8347 • www.lamar.edu/accessibility-resource-center • Email: arc@lamar.edu

Documentation submitted to: Accessibility Resource Center
Separate application required for Services: Yes

Documentation required for:
LD: Psychoeducational evaluation
ADHD: Psychoeducational evaluation
ASD: Psychoeducational evaluation

Schreiner University

2100 Memorial Boulevard, Kerrville, TX 78028-5697 • Admissions: 830-792-7217 • www.schreiner.edu

Support: SP

ACCOMMODATIONS

Allowed in exams:

Calculators	Yes
Dictionary	Yes
Computer	Yes
Spell-checker	Yes
Extended test time	Yes
Scribe	Yes
Proctors	Yes
Oral exams	Yes
Note-takers	Yes

Support services for students with:

LD	Yes
ADHD	Yes
ASD	Yes
Distraction-reduced environment	Yes
Recording of lecture allowed	Yes
Reading technology	Yes
Audio books	Yes
Other assistive technology	Yes
Priority registration	No

Added costs of services:

For LD	Yes
For ADHD	Yes
For ASD	Yes
LD specialists	Yes
ADHD & ASD coaching	Yes
ASD specialists	Yes
Professional tutors	Yes
Peer tutors	Yes
Max. hours/week for services	Varies
How professors are notified of student approved accommodations	Student and Learning Support Services

COLLEGE GRADUATION REQUIREMENTS

Course waivers allowed	No
Course substitutions allowed	No

PROGRAMS/SERVICES FOR STUDENTS WITH LEARNING DIFFERENCES

Students requesting academic accommodations must register with Learning Support Services and provide documentation of their disability. The Learning Support Services Program (LSS) is a fee-based program limited to 60–70 students each year who are diagnosed with dyslexia, attention deficit disorder, or a specific learning disability in reading, mathematics, or written expression; it also includes a limited number of students on the autism spectrum. LSS students complete the same curriculum requirements and are held to the same standard as all other degree candidates but with the flexibility to meet their needs. All LSS first-year students are enrolled in a special section of the orientation course. LSS staff help students develop independent study skills and strategies needed for college-level learning. The program includes regular tutoring sessions for all classes, progress monitoring, academic advising, and disability accommodations. LSS also works with the Center for Advising and Career Development to assist students with internships, job shadowing, and employment.

ADMISSIONS

Schreiner admission decisions are holistic and based on GPA, extracurricular activities in high school and in the community, and SAT or ACT scores, if submitted. Applicants should be taking college preparatory classes in high school; however, admission would not be denied to a qualified applicant who had some deficiencies in coursework. ACT and SAT test scores, personal essays, letters of recommendation, and résumés are all optional. Students with a GPA of less than 3.25 may receive a request from their admission advisor for some of these optional documents, and a short-answer form for the admission committee or an interview may also be requested. The admission application serves as the scholarship application.

Additional Information

The Academic Support Center has a variety of student-staffed programs and services, including the Writing Center, Peer Tutoring Center, and Supplemental Instruction. Tutoring for a variety of subjects is available free of charge on a walk-in basis for course material and skill development. The Writing Center is also available for walk-ins and can help students at any stage in the writing process. Supplemental Instruction (SI) targets historically difficult courses to provide additional resources to help students succeed. SI student leaders attend class lectures and then lead ongoing study sessions for students in the course. The Center for Teaching and Learning can help students find information on accessing any academic support services.

Schreiner's founding included military training for boys. The tradition of carrying challenge coins dates from the Civil War to today's military. Carried as reminders of experiences, the coins symbolized the bond between soldiers. The Schreiner's five Presidential Challenge Coins are earned by students throughout their stay at Schreiner and are: Entering with Hope, Leadership, Academic Excellence, the Schreiner Experience, and Graduating with Achievement.

Schreiner University

GENERAL ADMISSIONS

Very important factors include: class rank, academic GPA, standardized test scores (if submitted). *Important factors include:* rigor of secondary school record, application essay. *Other factors considered include:* recommendations. High school diploma is required and GED is accepted. Institution is test-optional for entering Fall 2024. Check admissions website for updates. *Academic units recommended:* 4 English, 3 math, 3 science (2 labs), 2 foreign language, 2 social studies, 2 history, 3.5 academic electives, 1 visual/performing arts.

FINANCIAL AID

Students should submit: FAFSA. *Need-based scholarships/grants offered:* College/university scholarship or grant aid from institutional funds; Federal Pell; Private scholarships; SEOG; State scholarships/grants. *Loan aid offered:* Direct PLUS loans; Direct Subsidized Loans; Direct Unsubsidized Loans. Federal Work-Study Program available. Institutional employment available.

CAMPUS LIFE

Activities: Campus Ministries; Choral groups; Dance; Drama/theater; Literary magazine; Music ensembles; Musical theater; Pep band; Student government; Student newspaper; Symphony orchestra. **Organizations:** 38 registered organizations, 3 honor societies, 7 religious organizations, 1 fraternities, 2 sororities. **Athletics (Intercollegiate):** *Men:* baseball, basketball, cross-country, cycling, equestrian sports, golf, racquetball, wrestling. *Women:* basketball, cross-country, cycling, equestrian sports, golf, racquetball, softball, volleyball, wrestling.

CAMPUS

Type of school	Private (nonprofit)
Environment	Town

STUDENTS

Undergrad enrollment	1,017
% male/female	44/56
% from out of state	3
% frosh live on campus	88

FINANCIAL FACTS

Annual tuition	$33,927
Room and board	$10,579

GENERAL ADMISSIONS INFO

Application fee	$25
Regular application deadline	8/1
Nonfall registration	Yes

Fall 2024 testing policy	Test Optional
Range SAT EBRW	480–590
Range SAT Math	490–570
Range ACT Composite	18–24

ACADEMICS

Student/faculty ratio	15:1
% students returning for sophomore year	64
Most classes have 10–19 students.	

REQUESTING SERVICES FOR STUDENTS WITH LEARNING DIFFERENCES

Phone: 830-792-7258 • schreiner.edu/academics/academic-resources/learning-support-services/
Email: mkwrase@schreiner.edu

Documentation submitted to: Learning Support Services
Separate application required for Services: Yes

Documentation required for:
  LD: Psychoeducational evaluation
  ADHD: Psychoeducational evaluation
  ASD: Psychoeducational evaluation

Southern Methodist University

P.O. Box 750181, Dallas, TX 75275-0181 • Admissions: 214-768-2058 • www.smu.edu

Support: CS

ACCOMMODATIONS

Allowed in exams:

Calculators	Yes
Dictionary	Yes
Computer	Yes
Spell-checker	Yes
Extended test time	Yes
Scribe	Yes
Proctors	Yes
Oral exams	Yes
Note-takers	Yes

Support services for students with:

LD	Yes
ADHD	Yes
ASD	Yes
Distraction-reduced environment	Yes
Recording of lecture allowed	Yes
Reading technology	Yes
Audio books	Yes
Other assistive technology	Yes
Priority registration	Yes

Added costs of services:

For LD	No
For ADHD	No
For ASD	No
LD specialists	Yes
ADHD & ASD coaching	Yes
ASD specialists	No
Professional tutors	Yes
Peer tutors	Yes
Max. hours/week for services	Varies
How professors are notified of student approved accommodations	Student

COLLEGE GRADUATION REQUIREMENTS

Course waivers allowed	No
Course substitutions allowed	Yes
In what courses: Foreign Language	

Former First Lady Laura Bush graduated from SMU in 1968 with a degree in education and went on to teach the second grade. Academy Award winner Kathy Bates graduated from SMU in 1969, and yes, she majored in theater. Producer Aaron Spelling majored in journalism at SMU, where he won the prestigious Harvard Award for the best original one-act play. He is the only student to direct a major play in the history of SMU.

PROGRAMS/SERVICES FOR STUDENTS WITH LEARNING DIFFERENCES

The Disability Accommodations & Success Strategies (DASS) office supports students with learning disabilities. Students are responsible for establishing eligibility by submitting their documentation and completing the accommodation request form online. DASS staff will review the request and meet with the student to discuss accommodations and finalize the process. Once accommodations are determined, students will use the DASS online system for most of their interaction with DASS: accessing letters of accommodation to share with instructors, making changes to their accommodations, or setting appointments. DASS provides Success Strategies Support for students with learning differences; this includes academic coaching and planning to help students with weekly check-ins and goal setting, accountability, and college-level learning skills. DASS HDEV 1210: Academic Success & Personal Development is a 2 credit college-level reading and study skills course. One section is reserved for students with LD/ADHD during the fall semester. This class fulfills the Oral Communication Proficiency requirement. Students for New Learning is a chartered student organization just for students with ADHD or learning differences. The group meets monthly to support each other, share tips and strategies, plan fun events, and work as a campus resource on learning differences.

ADMISSIONS

All applicants are required to meet the same general admission requirements. SMU curriculum requires all students to demonstrate proficiency in a second language. Students who are accepted with but do not meet the required second-language proficiency must improve their proficiency by two-semester levels or meet the four-semester proficiency. The admission committee reviews all elements of an application, including GPA, classroom performance, course rigor, personal essay, letters of recommendation, extracurricular activities, talents, character, and life experiences.

Additional Information

SMU has various academic opportunities and support systems across campus, including the Student Academic Success Programs (SASP), the Office of Student Success & Retention (SSR), the University Advising Center, and the University Testing Center. Through SASP, students can work with an academic counselor or learning specialist to help manage time, tests, and texts. A-LEC tutoring is a free resource meant to complement classroom coursework. Tutors are available for most first- and second-year courses, as well as many advanced courses, and no appointment is necessary. The Writing Center offers 30-minute appointments to students who need help with any type of writing or reading project. SASP also holds workshops on a wide variety of college-level study techniques. SSR helps students connect to campus resources through a mix of one-on-one student meetings, programs, outreach development, and guidance.

Southern Methodist University

GENERAL ADMISSIONS

Very important factors include: rigor of secondary school record, academic GPA, application essay, recommendations. *Important factors include:* class rank, standardized test scores (if submitted). High school diploma is required and GED is not accepted. Institution is test-optional for entering Fall 2024. Check admissions website for updates. *Academic units required:* 4 English, 3 math, 3 science (2 labs), 2 foreign language, 3 social studies. *Academic units recommended:* 4 math, 3 foreign language, 3 academic electives.

FINANCIAL AID

Students should submit: CSS/Financial Aid Profile; FAFSA; Noncustodial Profile. *Need-based scholarships/grants offered:* College/university scholarship or grant aid from institutional funds; Federal Pell; Private scholarships; SEOG; State scholarships/grants. *Loan aid offered:* Direct PLUS loans; Direct Subsidized Loans; Direct Unsubsidized Loans. Federal Work-Study Program available. Institutional employment available.

CAMPUS LIFE

Activities: Campus Ministries; Choral groups; Concert band; Dance; Drama/theater; International Student Organization; Jazz band; Literary magazine; Marching band; Model UN; Music ensembles; Musical theater; Opera; Pep band; Radio station; Student government; Student newspaper; Student-run film society; Symphony orchestra; Television station; Yearbook. **Organizations:** 180 registered organizations, 16 honor societies, 27 religious organizations, 15 fraternities, 13 sororities. **Athletics (Intercollegiate):** *Men:* baseball, basketball, cycling, golf, ice hockey, lacrosse, martial arts, racquetball, rugby, swimming, ultimate frisbee, volleyball, water polo. *Women:* basketball, crew/rowing, cross-country, cycling, equestrian sports, golf, lacrosse, swimming, volleyball, water polo.

CAMPUS
Type of school	Private (nonprofit)
Environment	Metropolis

STUDENTS
Undergrad enrollment	7,044
% male/female	49/51
% from out of state	55
% frosh live on campus	98

FINANCIAL FACTS
Annual tuition	$57,212
Room and board	$18,230
Required fees	$7,248

GENERAL ADMISSIONS INFO
Application fee	$60
Regular application deadline	7/31
Nonfall registration	Yes

Fall 2024 testing policy	Test Optional
Range SAT EBRW	680–740
Range SAT Math	690–770
Range ACT Composite	31–34

ACADEMICS
Student/faculty ratio	11:1
% students returning for sophomore year	90

Most classes have 10–19 students.

REQUESTING SERVICES FOR STUDENTS WITH LEARNING DIFFERENCES

Phone: 214-768-1470 • www.smu.edu/alec/dass • Email: dass@smu.edu

Documentation submitted to: Disability Accommodations & Success Strategies
Separate application required for Services: Yes

Documentation required for:
LD: Psychoeducational evaluation
ADHD: Psychoeducational evaluation
ASD: Psychoeducational evaluation

Texas A&M University

P.O. Box 30014, College Station, TX 77843-3014 • Admissions: 979-845-1060 • www.tamu.edu

Support: CS

ACCOMMODATIONS

Allowed in exams:

Calculators	Yes
Dictionary	Yes
Computer	Yes
Spell-checker	Yes
Extended test time	Yes
Scribe	Yes
Proctors	Yes
Oral exams	Yes
Note-takers	Yes

Support services for students with:

LD	Yes
ADHD	Yes
ASD	Yes
Distraction-reduced environment	Yes
Recording of lecture allowed	Yes
Reading technology	Yes
Audio books	Yes
Other assistive technology	Yes
Priority registration	Yes

Added costs of services:

For LD	No
For ADHD	No
For ASD	No
LD specialists	No
ADHD & ASD coaching	Yes
ASD specialists	Yes
Professional tutors	Yes
Peer tutors	Yes
Max. hours/week for services	Varies
How professors are notified of student approved accommodations	Student

COLLEGE GRADUATION REQUIREMENTS

Course waivers allowed	No
Course substitutions allowed	Yes

In what courses: Math and Foreign Language on a case-by-case basis

PROGRAMS/SERVICES FOR STUDENTS WITH LEARNING DIFFERENCES

Disability Resources (DR) offers accommodations to students with disabilities. Students must request accommodations by submitting an online new student application and supporting documentation. After the application is reviewed, an access coordinator will be assigned and meet with the student to discuss DR policies, accommodations, and potential resources. After accommodation letters have been sent to faculty, students need to meet with their instructors to discuss implementation.

ADMISSIONS

Texas A&M requires that applicants must complete the SRAR (Self-Reported Academic Record) or provide an official high school transcript. An essay is required, but up to two letters of recommendation are optional. Aggie Gateway to Success is a provisional admission program where students can gain full admission by taking summer courses and demonstrating their academic potential. During the summer program, students live on campus and complete two standard core curriculum courses assigned by the Transition Academic Programs advising staff. Successful AGS students are admitted into the university as general studies (GEST) majors.

Additional Information

The Academic Success Center offers tutoring in lower-level courses, and Supplemental Instruction (SI) is available for more challenging courses. Byrne Student Success Center has a variety of academic and student services, including a computer lab, free tutoring for math and science classes, study skills workshops, career development, and more. The Undergraduate Peer Mentor Program has mentors available for help with writing or other coursework on a first-come, first-serve basis. The Writing Center provides help in all stages of the writing process with one-on-one sessions.

Reveille, or Miss Rev, made her first appearance as Texas A&M's official mascot in 1931. Since 1960, Miss Rev has been cared for by a second-year Mascot Corporal cadet in Company E-2. She lives, attends class, socializes, and goes home for the holidays with the cadet. Wearing five silver diamonds, Miss Rev is the highest-ranking member in the Corps of Cadets (the commander only has four). If Miss Rev falls asleep in a cadet's bed, the cadet must find somewhere else to sleep since she outranks him. The current Miss Rev is a thoroughbred collie born in 2019.

Texas A&M University

GENERAL ADMISSIONS

Very important factors include: rigor of secondary school record, class rank, academic GPA, standardized test scores (if submitted). *Important factors include:* application essay. *Other factors considered include:* recommendations. High school diploma is required and GED is accepted. Institution is test-optional for entering Fall 2024. Check admissions website for updates. *Academic units required:* 4 English, 3 math, 3 science (1 lab), 2 foreign language, 3 social studies, 5 academic electives, 1 visual/performing arts. *Academic units recommended:* 4 math, 4 science (2 labs), 7 academic electives.

FINANCIAL AID

Students should submit: FAFSA. *Need-based scholarships/grants offered:* College/university scholarship or grant aid from institutional funds; Federal Pell; Private scholarships; SEOG; State scholarships/grants. *Loan aid offered:* Direct PLUS loans; Direct Subsidized Loans; Direct Unsubsidized Loans. Federal Work-Study Program available. Institutional employment available.

CAMPUS LIFE

Activities: Campus Ministries; Choral groups; Concert band; Dance; Drama/theater; International Student Organization; Jazz band; Marching band; Music ensembles; Musical theater; Pep band; Radio station; Student government; Student newspaper; Television station; Yearbook. **Organizations:** 1111 registered organizations, 36 honor societies, 86 religious organizations, 31 fraternities, 32 sororities. **Athletics (Intercollegiate):** *Men:* baseball, basketball, bowling, crew/rowing, cross-country, cycling, equestrian sports, golf, gymnastics, ice hockey, lacrosse, racquetball, rugby, swimming, table tennis, track/field (indoor), ultimate frisbee, volleyball, water polo, wrestling. *Women:* baseball, basketball, bowling, crew/rowing, cross-country, cycling, equestrian sports, golf, gymnastics, lacrosse, racquetball, rugby, softball, swimming, table tennis, track/field (indoor), ultimate frisbee, volleyball, water polo.

CAMPUS
Type of school	Public
Environment	City

STUDENTS
Undergrad enrollment	56,030
% male/female	53/47
% from out of state	4
% frosh live on campus	65

FINANCIAL FACTS
Annual in-state tuition	$9,208
Annual out-of-state tuition	$36,117
Room and board	$11,400
Required fees	$3,970

GENERAL ADMISSIONS INFO
Application fee	$75
Regular application deadline	12/1
Nonfall registration	Yes
Fall 2024 testing policy	Test Optional
Range SAT EBRW	570–680
Range SAT Math	570–700
Range ACT Composite	25–31

ACADEMICS
Student/faculty ratio	19:1
% students returning for sophomore year	93

Most classes have 20–29 students.

REQUESTING SERVICES FOR STUDENTS WITH LEARNING DIFFERENCES

Phone: 979-845-1637 • disability.tamu.edu • Email: disability@tamu.edu

Documentation submitted to: Disability Resources
Separate application required for Services: Yes

Documentation required for:
  LD: Psychoeducational evaluation
  ADHD: Psychoeducational evaluation
  ASD: Psychoeducational evaluation

Texas A&M University—Kingsville

MSC 105, Kingsville, TX 78363 • Admissions: 361-593-2315 • www.tamuk.edu

Support: S

ACCOMMODATIONS

Allowed in exams:

Calculators	Yes
Dictionary	Yes
Computer	Yes
Spell-checker	Yes
Extended test time	Yes
Scribe	Yes
Proctors	Yes
Oral exams	Yes
Note-takers	Yes

Support services for students with:

LD	Yes
ADHD	Yes
ASD	Yes
Distraction-reduced environment	Yes
Recording of lecture allowed	Yes
Reading technology	Yes
Audio books	Yes
Other assistive technology	Yes
Priority registration	Yes

Added costs of services:

For LD	No
For ADHD	No
For ASD	No
LD specialists	No
ADHD & ASD coaching	No
ASD specialists	No
Professional tutors	No
Peer tutors	Yes
Max. hours/week for services	Varies
How professors are notified of student approved accommodations	Student

COLLEGE GRADUATION REQUIREMENTS

Course waivers allowed	Yes
In what courses: Case-by-case basis	
Course substitutions allowed	Yes
In what courses: Case-by-case basis	

PROGRAMS/SERVICES FOR STUDENTS WITH LEARNING DIFFERENCES

The Disability Resources Center (DRC) ensures that students with disabilities receive appropriate accommodations. Once accepted for admission, new students should complete the new student application request and upload supporting documentation for accommodations on the DRC webpage. Students can do this before enrolling for classes; it will be processed after enrollment is complete. After the application has been reviewed and eligible accommodations approved, students attend an intake meeting with a DRC staff member. After the meeting, the DRC will email faculty notification letters to course instructors. Students must discuss their approved accommodations with their professors before they are activated.

ADMISSIONS

All applicants complete the same application for general admission to Texas A&M. Applicants may be admitted through Assured Admission if they meet at least one of the following: rank in the top 25 percent of their graduating class; have a composite ACT score of 19 or better; have a combined SAT of 1000 or better; or have a core GPA of 2.7 or higher. GPA is based on the required high school curriculum courses. Students who do not meet Assured Admission criteria can be admitted through the individual review process for academic achievements, extracurricular activities, community service, talents, awards, and other factors. These applicants should highlight their achievements on their ApplyTexas application.

Additional Information

The University Success Course is a two-semester credit course designed to assist first-year students with their academic skills and introduce them to campus life. Students can build relationships with faculty and fellow students, learn critical thinking skills, and read, discuss, and write about creative topics selected for the course. The Center for Student Success (CSS) offers tutoring, and the Peer Assisted Learning (PAL) program has support services designed to help students achieve academic success. Students can access the online list of courses and the tutoring schedule for one-on-one appointments. Sessions focus on content, learning strategies, and study skills. The CSS Mentoring Program mentors share skills, positive habits, guidance for decision-making, and resources and opportunities on campus. The University Writing Center offers free writing support through all stages of the writing process, from brainstorming and organizing to revising and polishing. Students can make in-person or online appointments.

Texas A&M-Kingsville Citrus Center opened in 1948 to support the citrus industry. The center includes a 60-acre main campus, a 250-acre research farm, and a 50-acre leased farm. It's known for citrus research and development and houses a USDA-certified diagnostic laboratory. The Citrus Center may be best known for developing several popular varieties of citrus, including the Ruby Red grapefruit.

Texas A&M University—Kingsville

GENERAL ADMISSIONS

Important factors include: rigor of secondary school record, class rank, standardized test scores (if submitted). Institution is test-optional for entering Fall 2024. Check admissions website for updates. *Academic units recommended:* 4 English, 3 math, 3 science, 2 foreign language, 3 social studies.

FINANCIAL AID

Students should submit: FAFSA. *Need-based scholarships/grants offered:* College/university scholarship or grant aid from institutional funds; Federal Pell; Private scholarships; SEOG; State scholarships/grants. *Loan aid offered:* Direct PLUS loans; Direct Subsidized Loans; Direct Unsubsidized Loans. Federal Work-Study Program available. Institutional employment available.

CAMPUS LIFE

Activities: Choral groups; Concert band; Dance; Drama/theater; Jazz band; Marching band; Music ensembles; Musical theater; Pep band; Radio station; Student government; Student newspaper; Television station.

CAMPUS

Type of school	Public
Environment	Town

STUDENTS

Undergrad enrollment	5,085
% male/female	50/50
% from out of state	1
% frosh live on campus	60

FINANCIAL FACTS

Annual in-state tuition	$5,137
Annual out-of-state tuition	$18,133
Room and board	$9,425
Required fees	$4,755

GENERAL ADMISSIONS INFO

Application fee	$25
Regular application deadline	Rolling
Nonfall registration	No

Fall 2024 testing policy	Test Optional
Range SAT EBRW	450–560
Range SAT Math	450–560
Range ACT Composite	16–21

ACADEMICS

Student/faculty ratio	17:1
% students returning for sophomore year	66

Most classes have 10–19 students.

REQUESTING SERVICES FOR STUDENTS WITH LEARNING DIFFERENCES

Phone: 361-593-3024 • www.tamuk.edu/shw/drc • Email: drc.center@tamuk.edu

Documentation submitted to: Disability Resources Center
Separate application required for Services: Yes

Documentation required for:
LD: Psychoeducational evaluation
ADHD: Psychoeducational evaluation
ASD: Psychoeducational evaluation

Texas State University

429 North Guadalupe Street, San Marcos, TX 78666 • Admissions: 512-245-2364 • www.txst.edu

Support: CS

ACCOMMODATIONS

Allowed in exams:

Calculators	Yes
Dictionary	Yes
Computer	Yes
Spell-checker	Yes
Extended test time	Yes
Scribe	Yes
Proctors	Yes
Oral exams	Yes
Note-takers	Yes

Support services for students with:

LD	Yes
ADHD	Yes
ASD	Yes
Distraction-reduced environment	Yes
Recording of lecture allowed	Yes
Reading technology	Yes
Audio books	Yes
Other assistive technology	Yes
Priority registration	Yes

Added costs of services:

For LD	No
For ADHD	No
For ASD	No
LD specialists	Yes
ADHD & ASD coaching	Yes
ASD specialists	Yes
Professional tutors	No
Peer tutors	Yes
Max. hours/week for services	Varies
How professors are notified of student approved accommodations	Student and Office of Disability Services

COLLEGE GRADUATION REQUIREMENTS

Course waivers allowed	No
Course substitutions allowed	Yes
In what courses: Math and Foreign Language	

PROGRAMS/SERVICES FOR STUDENTS WITH LEARNING DIFFERENCES

The Office of Disability Services (ODS) coordinates academic accommodations and support services for students with disabilities. Enrolled students should complete the online ODS application and provide documentation of their disability or disabilities to the office. The ODS will review the need for accommodations and schedule a meeting with the student to discuss and determine accommodations. Types of accommodations include, but are not limited to, extended time on exams, a reduced-distraction environment for testing, note-taking assistance, alternative-format texts, assistive technology, and preferential seating in the classroom.

ADMISSIONS

All applicants are expected to meet the same admission criteria. Students ranked in the bottom quarter of their class must submit ACT or SAT scores that meet the assured admission standards. The application review process considers the high school curriculum, quality and level of courses taken, grades earned, admission essay(s), extracurricular involvement, leadership, community service, work experience, and any other factors in the application. Applicants who believe their educational or personal goals have been negatively impacted due to disability-based issues may address them in the supplemental essay portion of the admission application. Applicants whose disability documentation has been reviewed by the ODS and have received a letter outlining the accommodations they would receive if admitted, should provide a copy of this letter to the Office of Undergraduate Admissions. The admissions office may consider this information during the application review.

Additional Information

The Student Learning Assistance Center (SLAC) helps students learn at the university level through a variety of academic support programs. Funded primarily through student service fees, TSU students may use all SLAC resources at no additional cost. The SLAC Lab provides peer tutoring by students specializing in accounting, science, writing, statistics, history, math, and more. Drop-in tutoring is available with course-specific schedules posted online. SLAC offers study skills assistance with online access reference sheets, subject area reference sheets, and popular online sites.

DID YOU KNOW?

The Strutters of TSU is a precision dance team, the first of its kind at a four-year U.S. institution. Founded in 1960 by Barbara Guinn Tidwell, who served as director/choreographer for 37 years, Strutters have represented TSU at state, national, and international levels in 26 countries on four continents. Performances include three presidential inaugural parades, Macy's and other Thanksgiving Day parades, NBA and NFL halftime shows, and America's Got Talent.

Texas State University

GENERAL ADMISSIONS

Very important factors include: class rank, standardized test scores (if submitted). *Other factors considered include:* rigor of secondary school record, application essay. High school diploma is required and GED is accepted. Institution is test-optional for entering Fall 2024. Check admissions website for updates. *Academic units required:* 4 English, 4 math, 4 science (2 labs), 2 foreign language, 3 social studies, 6 academic electives, 1 visual/performing arts.

FINANCIAL AID

Students should submit: FAFSA. *Need-based scholarships/grants offered:* College/university scholarship or grant aid from institutional funds; Federal Pell; Private scholarships; SEOG; State scholarships/grants. *Loan aid offered:* Direct PLUS loans; Direct Subsidized Loans; Direct Unsubsidized Loans. Federal Work-Study Program available. Institutional employment available.

CAMPUS LIFE

Activities: Campus Ministries; Choral groups; Concert band; Dance; Drama/theater; International Student Organization; Jazz band; Literary magazine; Marching band; Model UN; Music ensembles; Musical theater; Opera; Pep band; Radio station; Student government; Student newspaper; Student-run film society; Symphony orchestra; Yearbook. **Organizations:** 360 registered organizations, 18 honor societies, 35 religious organizations, 18 fraternities, 14 sororities. **Athletics (Intercollegiate):** *Men:* baseball, basketball, cross-country, cycling, equestrian sports, golf, gymnastics, ice hockey, lacrosse, racquetball, rugby, swimming, track/field (indoor), ultimate frisbee, volleyball, water polo, wrestling. *Women:* basketball, cross-country, equestrian sports, golf, gymnastics, lacrosse, racquetball, rugby, softball, swimming, track/field (indoor), ultimate frisbee, volleyball, water polo.

CAMPUS

Type of school	Public
Environment	Town

STUDENTS

Undergrad enrollment	33,405
% male/female	40/60
% from out of state	3
% frosh live on campus	86

FINANCIAL FACTS

Annual in-state tuition	$9,221
Annual out-of-state tuition	$21,461
Room and board	$11,516
Required fees	$2,986

GENERAL ADMISSIONS INFO

Application fee	$75
Regular application deadline	7/15
Nonfall registration	Yes

Fall 2024 testing policy	Test Optional
Range SAT EBRW	500–600
Range SAT Math	480–580
Range ACT Composite	19–26

ACADEMICS

Student/faculty ratio	22:1
% students returning for sophomore year	80
Most classes have 20–29 students.	

REQUESTING SERVICES FOR STUDENTS WITH LEARNING DIFFERENCES

Phone: 512-245-3451 • www.ods.txstate.edu/ • Email: ods@txstate.edu

Documentation submitted to: Office of Disability Services
Separate application required for Services: Yes

Documentation required for:
LD: Psychoeducational evaluation
ADHD: Psychoeducational evaluation
ASD: Psychoeducational evaluation

Texas Tech University

P.O. Box 45005, Lubbock, TX 79409-5005 • Admissions: 806-742-1480 • www.ttu.edu

Support: SP

ACCOMMODATIONS

Allowed in exams:

Calculators	Yes
Dictionary	No
Computer	Yes
Spell-checker	Yes
Extended test time	Yes
Scribe	Yes
Proctors	Yes
Oral exams	Yes
Note-takers	Yes

Support services for students with:

LD	Yes
ADHD	Yes
ASD	Yes
Distraction-reduced environment	Yes
Recording of lecture allowed	Yes
Reading technology	Yes
Audio books	Yes
Other assistive technology	Yes
Priority registration	Yes

Added costs of services:

For LD	Yes
For ADHD	Yes
For ASD	Yes
LD specialists	Yes
ADHD & ASD coaching	Yes
ASD specialists	Yes
Professional tutors	Yes
Peer tutors	Yes
Max. hours/week for services	7
How professors are notified of student approved accommodations	Student

COLLEGE GRADUATION REQUIREMENTS

Course waivers allowed	No
Course substitutions allowed	Yes

In what courses: Math, Foreign Language, and Physical Education.

PROGRAMS/SERVICES FOR STUDENTS WITH LEARNING DIFFERENCES

Student Disability Services (SDS) provides programs and services for students with disabilities. Once a student is accepted for admission to the university, the student is responsible for requesting accommodations and providing the appropriate documentation. After reviewing the application and documentation, a counselor will contact the student for an intake meeting. During the meeting, the counselor and student will determine the accommodations based on the type of disability, documented needs, previous accommodations, and functional limitations of the student. When accommodations have been approved, letters of accommodation are sent to the course instructors. The SDS webpage has an instructional video for students on how to discuss accommodations with instructors as well as a list of tutors, their schedules, and the courses they tutor. The tutors assist with content-specific questions, strategies on organization and time management, study skills, note-taking, goal setting, and other college-level skills needed in and out of the classroom. SDS also offers the TECHniques Center, a supplemental academic enhancement program for students with learning disabilities and ADHD. The TECHniques Center is a fee-for-service program that provides one-on-one, regularly scheduled content and study skills tutoring and weekly meetings with an academic counselor.

ADMISSIONS

All applicants must meet the same admission standards. The admission review considers how academically prepared an applicant is but also evaluates extracurricular activities, leadership experiences, community or volunteer activities, special talents or awards, and socioeconomic background. Some academic colleges and departments at Texas Tech only accept students who meet assured admission requirements.

Additional Information

All first-year students are required to sign up for and complete a Red Raider Orientation (RRO) session. Students meet with their academic advisor, register for courses, meet other new students, get advice from current students, and learn Texas Tech traditions. Additional transitional assistance includes the Texas Success Initiative (TSI), a developmental education program mandated by the state of Texas to provide additional support to students who are not college-ready in reading, writing, and mathematics. The TSI Skills Development Office creates customized plans for student development and developmental coursework. Further support services include Support Operations for Academic Retention (SOAR), a supplement to classroom and lab instruction that helps students develop lifelong learning skills. The SOAR Learning Center offers free drop-in tutoring in subjects like math, physics, chemistry, biology, accounting, engineering, and many others.

DID YOU KNOW?

Amon G. Carter, a longtime friend of Will Rogers, believed Texas Tech was the perfect setting for the Will Rogers and Soapsuds Statue. It was dedicated in 1950 and is now a well-known landmark on campus. One legend says the statue faced west so Will Rogers could ride into the sunset, but the view coming onto campus was Soapsuds backend. The statue was moved 23 degrees so that end now faces rival Texas A&M. For home games, the statue is wrapped in red crepe paper.

Texas Tech University

GENERAL ADMISSIONS

Very important factors include: rigor of secondary school record, class rank, academic GPA, standardized test scores (if submitted). *Important factors include:* application essay, recommendations. High school diploma is required and GED is accepted. Institution is test-optional for entering Fall 2024. Check admissions website for updates. *Academic units required:* 4 English, 3 math, 3 science (3 labs), 2 foreign language, 5 academic electives, 1 visual/performing arts. *Academic units recommended:* 4 math, 4 science (4 labs), 6 academic electives.

FINANCIAL AID

Students should submit: FAFSA. *Need-based scholarships/grants offered:* College/university scholarship or grant aid from institutional funds; Federal Pell; Private scholarships; SEOG; State scholarships/grants. *Loan aid offered:* Direct PLUS loans; Direct Subsidized Loans; Direct Unsubsidized Loans. Federal Work-Study Program available. Institutional employment available.

CAMPUS LIFE

Activities: Campus Ministries; Choral groups; Concert band; Dance; Drama/theater; International Student Organization; Jazz band; Literary magazine; Marching band; Model UN; Music ensembles; Musical theater; Opera; Pep band; Radio station; Student government; Student newspaper; Student-run film society; Symphony orchestra; Television station; Yearbook. **Organizations:** 562 registered organizations, 31 honor societies, 37 religious organizations, 33 fraternities, 22 sororities. **Athletics (Intercollegiate):** *Men:* baseball, basketball, bowling, cross-country, cycling, equestrian sports, golf, gymnastics, ice hockey, lacrosse, martial arts, racquetball, rugby, swimming, table tennis, track/field (indoor), ultimate frisbee, volleyball, water polo, wrestling. *Women:* basketball, bowling, cross-country, cycling, equestrian sports, golf, gymnastics, lacrosse, martial arts, racquetball, rugby, softball, swimming, table tennis, track/field (indoor), ultimate frisbee, volleyball, water polo, wrestling.

CAMPUS
Type of school	Public
Environment	City

STUDENTS
Undergrad enrollment	32,346
% male/female	51/49
% from out of state	7
% frosh live on campus	91

FINANCIAL FACTS
Annual in-state tuition	$8,934
Annual out-of-state tuition	$21,174
Room and board	$10,460
Required fees	$2,917

GENERAL ADMISSIONS INFO
Application fee	$75
Regular application deadline	8/1
Nonfall registration	Yes

Fall 2024 testing policy	Test Optional
Range SAT EBRW	550–640
Range SAT Math	540–640
Range ACT Composite	23–28

ACADEMICS
Student/faculty ratio	21:1
% students returning for sophomore year	86

Most classes have 10–19 students.

REQUESTING SERVICES FOR STUDENTS WITH LEARNING DIFFERENCES

Phone: 806-742-2405 • www.depts.ttu.edu/sds/ • Email: sds@ttu.edu

Documentation submitted to: Student Disability Services
Separate application required for Services: Yes

Documentation required for:
LD: Psychoeducational evaluation
ADHD: Psychoeducational evaluation
ASD: Psychoeducational evaluation

University of Houston

Office of Admissions, Houston, TX 77204-2023 • Admissions: 713-743-1010 • www.uh.edu

Support: CS

ACCOMMODATIONS

Allowed in exams:

Calculators	Yes
Dictionary	Yes
Computer	Yes
Spell-checker	Yes
Extended test time	Yes
Scribe	Yes
Proctors	Yes
Oral exams	Yes
Note-takers	Yes

Support services for students with:

LD	Yes
ADHD	Yes
ASD	Yes
Distraction-reduced environment	Yes
Recording of lecture allowed	Yes
Reading technology	Yes
Audio books	Yes
Other assistive technology	Yes
Priority registration	Yes

Added costs of services:

For LD	No
For ADHD	No
For ASD	No
LD specialists	No
ADHD & ASD coaching	No
ASD specialists	Yes
Professional tutors	Yes
Peer tutors	No
Max. hours/week for services	Varies
How professors are notified of student approved accommodations	Student

COLLEGE GRADUATION REQUIREMENTS

Course waivers allowed	No
Course substitutions allowed	Yes

  In what courses: Foreign Language

PROGRAMS/SERVICES FOR STUDENTS WITH LEARNING DIFFERENCES

The Justin Dart, Jr. Student Accessibility Center (the Dart Center) helps students with disabilities achieve success by providing accommodations to suit their needs. Once students have registered for classes, they may register with the Dart Center. The access coordinator then reviews documentation and meets with the student to set forth appropriate accommodations. The Dart Center offers advocacy services, computers and software, textbooks on tape, learning disability support services, and testing accommodations. It is also the resource center for campus and community services, scholarships, health care, counseling referrals, and career opportunities. UH students who identify as neurodiverse can find additional assistance through the Program for Supporting and Mentoring Students with Autism (PSMSA), which matches participants with peer mentors who provide support in organization, personal responsibility, and social engagement.

ADMISSIONS

The Texas Education Code requires that all students meet the college readiness standards to be eligible for admission. Applicants must either successfully complete the recommended or advanced high school program that is available or satisfy the College Readiness Benchmarks with SAT or ACT scores. Applicants who do not submit test scores must include a short admissions essay and their extracurricular activities in their application. A school counselor report is also required. Texas residents whose class rank is in the top 10 percent are assured admission. First-year applicants who do not meet admission requirements may request further consideration by submitting a Freshman Admissions Appeal Form. UH suggests that students appeal only if their academic credentials have changed significantly, or if they wish to further explain or document personal circumstances that may have affected their ability to meet admissions requirements.

Additional Information

LAUNCH is the UH Learning Center for students to improve their skills and comprehension. LAUNCH offers tutoring, success and psycho-educational workshops, TSI Assessment preparation help, and support groups. LAUNCH partners with participating departments to provide a number of student services. The Center for Academic Support and Assessment (CASA) provides tutoring for math students and proctored testing for students in all subject areas. The CASA Testing Centers have 120 testing stations in each of their locations for a multitude of courses. The Writing Center also offers individual, online, and in-person meetings with trained consultants to assist with general writing and discipline-specific work.

In 1958, *LIFE Magazine* called UH's spring festival, Frontier Fiesta, "the Greatest College Show on Earth." Each year, students transform a piece of campus into the fully functional town known as Fiesta City. It celebrates everything that makes the University of Houston important to the community and raises funds for scholarship opportunities.

University of Houston

GENERAL ADMISSIONS

Very important factors include: rigor of secondary school record, class rank, academic GPA. *Other factors considered include:* standardized test scores (if submitted), application essay, recommendations. High school diploma is required and GED is accepted. Institution is test-optional for entering Fall 2024. Check admissions website for updates. *Academic units required:* 4 English, 3 math, 3 science (2 labs), 3 social studies. *Academic units recommended:* 4 math, 4 science, 2 foreign language, 1 visual/performing arts.

FINANCIAL AID

Students should submit: FAFSA. *Need-based scholarships/grants offered:* College/university scholarship or grant aid from institutional funds; Federal Pell; Private scholarships; SEOG; State scholarships/grants; United Negro College Fund. *Loan aid offered:* Direct PLUS loans; Direct Subsidized Loans; Direct Unsubsidized Loans. Federal Work-Study Program available. Institutional employment available.

CAMPUS LIFE

Activities: Campus Ministries; Choral groups; Concert band; Dance; Drama/theater; International Student Organization; Jazz band; Literary magazine; Marching band; Music ensembles; Musical theater; Opera; Pep band; Radio station; Student government; Student newspaper; Student-run film society; Symphony orchestra; Television station; Yearbook. **Organizations:** 469 registered organizations, 24 honor societies, 57 religious organizations, 20 fraternities, 19 sororities. **Athletics (Intercollegiate):** *Men:* baseball, basketball, cross-country, cycling, golf, rugby, track/field (indoor), ultimate frisbee, volleyball, water polo. *Women:* basketball, cross-country, cycling, golf, softball, swimming, track/field (indoor), ultimate frisbee, volleyball, water polo.

CAMPUS
Type of school	Public
Environment	Metropolis

STUDENTS
Undergrad enrollment	37,282
% male/female	48/52
% from out of state	2
% frosh live on campus	42

FINANCIAL FACTS
Annual in-state tuition	$10,856
Annual out-of-state tuition	$26,096
Room and board	$10,418
Required fees	$1,014

GENERAL ADMISSIONS INFO
Application fee	$75
Regular application deadline	5/1
Nonfall registration	Yes
Fall 2024 testing policy	Test Optional
Range SAT EBRW	580–660
Range SAT Math	580–670
Range ACT Composite	23–29

ACADEMICS
Student/faculty ratio	21:1
% students returning for sophomore year	85

Most classes have 10–19 students.

REQUESTING SERVICES FOR STUDENTS WITH LEARNING DIFFERENCES

Phone: 713-743-5400 • uh.edu/accessibility/ • Email: JDCenter@central.uh.edu

Documentation submitted to: Justin Dart, Jr. Student Accessibility Center
Separate application required for Services: Yes

Documentation required for:
LD: Psychoeducational evaluation
ADHD: Psychoeducational evaluation
ASD: Psychoeducational evaluation

University of Texas at Austin

P.O. Box 8058, Austin, TX 78713-8058 • Admissions: 512-475-7399 • www.utexas.edu

Support: CS

ACCOMMODATIONS

Allowed in exams:

Calculators	Yes
Dictionary	Yes
Computer	Yes
Spell-checker	Yes
Extended test time	Yes
Scribe	Yes
Proctors	Yes
Oral exams	Yes
Note-takers	Yes

Support services for students with:

LD	Yes
ADHD	Yes
ASD	Yes
Distraction-reduced environment	Yes
Recording of lecture allowed	Yes
Reading technology	Yes
Audio books	Yes
Other assistive technology	Yes
Priority registration	Yes

Added costs of services:

For LD	No
For ADHD	No
For ASD	No
LD specialists	Yes
ADHD & ASD coaching	Yes
ASD specialists	Yes
Professional tutors	Yes
Peer tutors	Yes
Max. hours/week for services	Varies
How professors are notified of student approved accommodations	Student

COLLEGE GRADUATION REQUIREMENTS

Course waivers allowed	No
Course substitutions allowed	Yes
In what courses: Foreign Language	

PROGRAMS/SERVICES FOR STUDENTS WITH LEARNING DIFFERENCES

Disabilities and Access (D&A) offers support and advocacy for students with learning differences. Disability-related documentation, as well as a verification-of-disability form completed by a provider, must be emailed directly to the department. D&A will schedule an intake appointment with the student to discuss eligibility and accommodations. Some of the services offered include notetakers, scribes, readers, extended time for in-class work, flexibility with attendance, assistive technology, priority registration, course load reduction, and exam accommodations. Students can apply to the Longhorn TIES (Transition, Inclusion, Empower, Success) program, which supports neurodiverse students with advocacy, connections, and training. Specialized coaches provide individualized support and referrals for academic, social, vocational, and independent living needs. Students on the Spectrum is an on-campus group that coordinates social activities and discussion nights for students to share ideas, experiences, and resources. The Disability Advocacy Student Coalition (DASC) is the student organization associated with D&A and promotes awareness, advocacy, and education about disability and accessibility on campus and in the community.

ADMISSIONS

All applicants are expected to meet the same admission criteria. Additional classes are required for students not otherwise eligible to enter due to grades or scores, including a study skills class. Other admission factors include recommendations (although not required) and the competitiveness of the major to which the student applies. UT is test-optional, but students are encouraged to submit their scores and must indicate if they would like their scores considered. The top 6 percent of all graduates from high schools in Texas are automatically admissible. Some students can gain admission through the Path to Admission through Co-Enrollment (PACE) program. PACE students take one class per semester at UT Austin and the rest of their coursework at Austin Community College (ACC) – Rio Grande. At the end of their first year, students who successfully complete the PACE requirements continue their undergraduate studies at The University of Texas at Austin full-time.

Additional Information

The Sanger Learning Center provides all students free services, including study skills assistance, peer academic coaching, one-on-one and drop-in tutoring, and access to learning specialists.

UT Austin houses the first presidential library on a university campus. The Lyndon B Johnson (36th president) Library and Museum was dedicated on May 22, 1971, and holds 45 million pages of historical documents, 650,000 photos, and 5,000 hours of recordings. It includes a Civil Rights movement exhibition and a moving, life-size animatronic of Johnson, who wanted his library to be an honest and complete record of his time in office.

University of Texas at Austin

GENERAL ADMISSIONS

Other factors considered include: rigor of secondary school record, class rank, academic GPA, standardized test scores (if submitted), application essay, recommendations. High school diploma is required and GED is accepted. Institution is test-optional for entering Fall 2024. Check admissions website for updates. *Academic units required:* 4 English, 3 math, 2 science, 2 foreign language, 3 social studies. *Academic units recommended:* 4 math, 4 science, 4 social studies, 6 academic electives.

FINANCIAL AID

Students should submit: FAFSA; Institution's own financial aid form. *Need-based scholarships/grants offered:* College/university scholarship or grant aid from institutional funds; Federal Pell; Private scholarships; SEOG; State scholarships/grants. *Loan aid offered:* Direct PLUS loans; Direct Subsidized Loans; Direct Unsubsidized Loans. Federal Work-Study Program available. Institutional employment available.

CAMPUS LIFE

Activities: Campus Ministries; Choral groups; Concert band; Dance; Drama/theater; International Student Organization; Jazz band; Literary magazine; Marching band; Model UN; Music ensembles; Musical theater; Opera; Pep band; Radio station; Student government; Student newspaper; Student-run film society; Symphony orchestra; Television station; Yearbook. **Organizations:** 1000 registered organizations, 8 honor societies, 86 religious organizations, 33 fraternities, 31 sororities. **Athletics (Intercollegiate):** *Men:* baseball, basketball, crew/rowing, cross-country, cycling, field hockey, golf, gymnastics, ice hockey, lacrosse, martial arts, racquetball, rugby, swimming, table tennis, track/field (indoor), ultimate frisbee, volleyball, water polo, wrestling. *Women:* baseball, basketball, crew/rowing, cross-country, cycling, field hockey, golf, gymnastics, ice hockey, lacrosse, martial arts, racquetball, rugby, softball, swimming, table tennis, track/field (indoor), ultimate frisbee, volleyball, water polo, wrestling.

CAMPUS
Type of school	Public
Environment	Metropolis

STUDENTS
Undergrad enrollment	40,980
% male/female	43/57
% from out of state	5
% frosh live on campus	63

FINANCIAL FACTS
Annual in-state tuition	$11,758
Annual out-of-state tuition	$41,070
Room and board	$13,058

GENERAL ADMISSIONS INFO
Application fee	$75
Regular application deadline	12/1
Nonfall registration	Yes

Fall 2024 testing policy	Test Optional
Range SAT EBRW	620–730
Range SAT Math	610–770
Range ACT Composite	27–33

ACADEMICS
Student/faculty ratio	18:1
% students returning for sophomore year	97

Most classes have 10–19 students.

REQUESTING SERVICES FOR STUDENTS WITH LEARNING DIFFERENCES

Phone: 512-471-6259 • diversity.utexas.edu/disability • Email: access@austin.utexas.edu

Documentation submitted to: Disabilities and Access
Separate application required for Services: Yes

Documentation required for:
  LD: Psychoeducational evaluation
  ADHD: Psychoeducational evaluation
  ASD: Psychoeducational evaluation

College Profiles ■ 645

Brigham Young University

A-153 ASB, Provo, UT 84602-1110 • Admissions: 801-422-2507 • www.byu.edu

Support: CS

PROGRAMS/SERVICES FOR STUDENTS WITH LEARNING DIFFERENCES

The University Accessibility Center (UAC) provides accommodations to students with learning differences. Students should first schedule a meeting with the UAC coordinator to discuss student concerns, documentation, and academic accommodations. The coordinator can also help with petitions, assist in working with professors, and give referrals to other resources. Available services include alternative text formats, assistive technology, interpretation, note-taking, ADHD evaluations, and other resources and scholarships dedicated specifically to students with disabilities. The REACH (Reaching Educational and Career Hopes) Program is part of the Accessibility Center, and it's available to help students with disabilities transition from university life to internships, employment, or career-related endeavors. Qualified students with disabilities may join Delta Alpha Pi (DAP), an academic honor society recognizing high-achieving students with disabilities attending colleges. DAP is an opportunity to change inaccurate perceptions of students with disabilities and develop skills in leadership, advocacy, and education for participating students.

ADMISSIONS

BYU has recommendations rather than requirements and looks for applicants who demonstrate spiritual strength, strong character, intellectual curiosity, and service. The rigor of courses is considered, and applicants should be involved in extracurricular activities that are meaningful and that develop specific talents. Students should use their personal essay to provide specific examples of contributions to their community.

Additional Information

The Student Success Center provides resources to improve learning skills and workshops focusing on time management, study skills, test preparation, and motivation. Course-specific support includes free online or in-person tutoring and online/on-demand course-related help. Academic coaching and peer mentoring are available to help students set and achieve goals. The Research & Writing Center's trained consultants work with students by appointment to increase awareness, abilities, and confidence in any part of the research or writing process. Student Development Classes are credit electives for additional help building learning and study skills, career exploration/development, leadership, and improving mental health.

You'll hear ghost stories about the Maeser Building, the oldest building still in use. According to Provo Library records, it was built on top of Temple Hill Cemetery. A "Brief History of Provo City Cemetery" says 30 bodies may remain under the building, though other sources, like "Find A Grave," say all the bodies were moved before it was built.

Brigham Young University

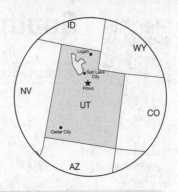

GENERAL ADMISSIONS

Very important factors include: rigor of secondary school record, academic GPA, standardized test scores (if submitted), application essay, recommendations. High school diploma is required and GED is accepted. Institution is test-optional for entering Fall 2024. Check admissions website for updates. *Academic units recommended:* 4 English, 4 math, 3 science, 2 foreign language, 2 history.

FINANCIAL AID

Students should submit: FAFSA. *Need-based scholarships/grants offered:* College/university scholarship or grant aid from institutional funds; Federal Pell; Private scholarships; State scholarships/grants. *Loan aid offered:* Direct PLUS loans; Direct Subsidized Loans; Direct Unsubsidized Loans.

CAMPUS LIFE

Activities: Choral groups; Concert band; Dance; Drama/theater; Jazz band; Literary magazine; Marching band; Music ensembles; Musical theater; Opera; Pep band; Radio station; Student government; Student newspaper; Student-run film society; Symphony orchestra; Television station. **Organizations:** 447 registered organizations, 22 honor societies, 25 religious organizations, 0 fraternities, 0 sororities. **Athletics (Intercollegiate):** *Men:* baseball, basketball, cross-country, golf, lacrosse, racquetball, rugby, swimming, track/field (indoor), volleyball. *Women:* basketball, cross-country, golf, gymnastics, racquetball, softball, swimming, track/field (indoor), volleyball.

CAMPUS

Type of school	Private (nonprofit)
Environment	City

STUDENTS

Undergrad enrollment	31,633
% male/female	49/51
% from out of state	72
% frosh live on campus	43

FINANCIAL FACTS

Annual tuition	$6,120
Room and board	$8,048
Required fees	$0

GENERAL ADMISSIONS INFO

Application fee	$35
Regular application deadline	12/15
Nonfall registration	Yes

Fall 2024 testing policy	Test Optional
Range SAT EBRW	620–720
Range SAT Math	600–720
Range ACT Composite	26–32

ACADEMICS

Student/faculty ratio	21:1
% students returning for sophomore year	89

Most classes have 10–19 students.

REQUESTING SERVICES FOR STUDENTS WITH LEARNING DIFFERENCES

Phone: 801-422-2767 • uac.byu.edu/ • Email: uacfrontdesk@byu.edu

Documentation submitted to: University Accessibility Center
Separate application required for Services: Yes

Documentation required for:
LD: Psychoeducational evaluation
ADHD: Psychoeducational evaluation
ASD: Psychoeducational evaluation

Southern Utah University

351 W. University Boulevard, Cedar City, UT 84720 • Admissions: 435-586-7740 • www.suu.edu

> **Support: S**

ACCOMMODATIONS

Allowed in exams:

Calculators	No
Dictionary	Yes
Computer	Yes
Spell-checker	Yes
Extended test time	Yes
Scribe	Yes
Proctors	Yes
Oral exams	Yes
Note-takers	Yes

Support services for students with:

LD	Yes
ADHD	Yes
ASD	Yes
Distraction-reduced environment	Yes
Recording of lecture allowed	Yes
Reading technology	Yes
Audio books	Yes
Other assistive technology	Yes
Priority registration	Yes

Added costs of services:

For LD	No
For ADHD	No
For ASD	No
LD specialists	No
ADHD & ASD coaching	No
ASD specialists	No
Professional tutors	No
Peer tutors	No
Max. hours/week for services	Varies
How professors are notified of student approved accommodations	Student and Disability Resource Center

COLLEGE GRADUATION REQUIREMENTS

Course waivers allowed	No
Course substitutions allowed	No

PROGRAMS/SERVICES FOR STUDENTS WITH LEARNING DIFFERENCES

The Disability Resource Center (DRC) offers reasonable accommodations to students with current and complete diagnostic disability documentation. Student disclosure is voluntary, and students are responsible for contacting and meeting with a DRC counselor at least two weeks prior to the needed service. DRC Support Workshops are a weekly opportunity for students to get together, learn from, and support each other. Topics cover college-level learning skills, test-taking, mindfulness, stress management, perfectionism, self-advocacy, dating, professional relationships, and self-compassion. The DRC also offers one-on-one weekly peer mentoring for help with study strategies, balancing university life, and career and job resources.

ADMISSIONS

All students are expected to meet the same standards for admission. Official high school transcripts must be submitted, showing a cumulative unweighted GPA of 2.7 or higher. First-time first-year applicants with a GPA between 2.3 and 2.69 may be provisionally admitted to SUU and to the Comprehensive Academic Support & Success (COMPASS) program. The COMPASS program helps students refine their study strategies, mindsets, and personal management skills. COMPASS students participate in a student success course and regularly meet with peer mentors; they must receive a minimum grade of C and achieve a 2.0 cumulative GPA by the end of their second semester to continue attending SUU. Students with a cumulative unweighted GPA of less than 2.3 may be admitted after a secondary review. Prospective students can register to attend a Red Riot two-day overnight event to experience the SUU campus, student life, academics, and activities.

Additional Information

Thunder U Orientation is a two-day (option of four-day) welcome program required for all new students. Students indicate their interest in an online orientation and participate in activities surrounding that interest throughout the Thunder U schedule of events. Students will connect with their assigned Assistant Coach for Excellence and Success (ACES) to learn important information to help get them started. ACES will contact their students before school begins, be with them during orientation, and plan meetings throughout the school year. ACES can help students get involved on campus, find jobs, navigate roommate conflicts and relationships, and develop effective study habits; they also host meet-ups before large campus events so that students can make new friends and have a group to attend campus events together. The Tutoring Center is available for drop-in, group, or individual sessions.

DID YOU KNOW?

A mascot is a person or thing that brings good luck. SUU's mascot also connects its history of evolving from an agricultural branch school, the Branch Aggies. In the 1946 football season, they became the Broncos. With too many other bronco herds, SUU became the Thunderbirds in 1961. Out of all schools represented by birds, only SUU can boast their Thunderbird mascot.

Southern Utah University

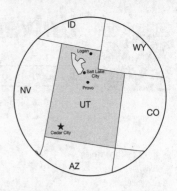

GENERAL ADMISSIONS

Very important factors include: academic GPA, standardized test scores (if submitted). High school diploma is required and GED is accepted. Institution is test-optional for entering Fall 2024. Check admissions website for updates. *Academic units recommended:* 4 English, 3 math, 3 science (1 lab), 2 foreign language, 3 social studies.

FINANCIAL AID

Students should submit: FAFSA; Institution's own financial aid form. *Need-based scholarships/grants offered:* College/university scholarship or grant aid from institutional funds; Federal Pell; Private scholarships; SEOG; State scholarships/grants. *Loan aid offered:* Direct PLUS loans; Direct Subsidized Loans; Direct Unsubsidized Loans. Federal Work-Study Program available. Institutional employment available.

CAMPUS LIFE

Activities: Campus Ministries; Choral groups; Concert band; Dance; Drama/theater; International Student Organization; Jazz band; Literary magazine; Marching band; Music ensembles; Musical theater; Opera; Pep band; Radio station; Student government; Student newspaper; Student-run film society; Symphony orchestra; Television station. **Organizations: Athletics (Intercollegiate):** *Men:* baseball, basketball, cross-country, golf, ice hockey, rugby, swimming, table tennis, volleyball. *Women:* basketball, cross-country, golf, gymnastics, ice hockey, rugby, softball, swimming, table tennis, volleyball.

CAMPUS
Type of school	Public
Environment	Village

STUDENTS
Undergrad enrollment	7,293
% male/female	45/55
% from out of state	18
% frosh live on campus	31

FINANCIAL FACTS
Annual in-state tuition	$6,006
Annual out-of-state tuition	$19,822
Room and board	$7,349
Required fees	$764

GENERAL ADMISSIONS INFO
Application fee	$50
Regular application deadline	May 1st
Nonfall registration	Yes
Fall 2024 testing policy	Test Optional
Range SAT EBRW	510–640
Range SAT Math	500–610
Range ACT Composite	21–27

ACADEMICS
Student/faculty ratio	19:1
% students returning for sophomore year	73
Most classes have 20–29 students.	

REQUESTING SERVICES FOR STUDENTS WITH LEARNING DIFFERENCES

Phone: 435-865-8042 • www.suu.edu/disabilityservices/ • Email: alldredge@suu.edu

Documentation submitted to: Disability Resource Center
Separate application required for Services: Yes

Documentation required for:
LD: Psychoeducational evaluation
ADHD: Psychoeducational evaluation
ASD: Psychoeducational evaluation

University of Utah

201 South 1460 East, Salt Lake City, UT 84112 • Admissions: 801-581-8761 • www.utah.edu

(Support: S)

ACCOMMODATIONS

Allowed in exams:

Calculators	Yes
Dictionary	Yes
Computer	Yes
Spell-checker	Yes
Extended test time	Yes
Scribe	Yes
Proctors	Yes
Oral exams	Yes
Note-takers	Yes

Support services for students with:

LD	No
ADHD	No
ASD	No
Distraction-reduced environment	Yes
Recording of lecture allowed	Yes
Reading technology	Yes
Audio books	Yes
Other assistive technology	Yes
Priority registration	Yes

Added costs of services:

For LD	No
For ADHD	No
For ASD	No
LD specialists	No
ADHD & ASD coaching	No
ASD specialists	No
Professional tutors	No
Peer tutors	Yes
Max. hours/week for services	Varies
How professors are notified of student approved accommodations	Student

COLLEGE GRADUATION REQUIREMENTS

Course waivers allowed	No
Course substitutions allowed	Yes
In what courses: Math and Foreign Language	

PROGRAMS/SERVICES FOR STUDENTS WITH LEARNING DIFFERENCES

The Center for Disability and Access (CDA) evaluates documentation, determines eligibility, and implements reasonable accommodations for enrolled students. Possible accommodations may include adaptive technology, flexibility with deadlines and due dates, alternative formats for materials, note-taking services, audio class recordings, exam accommodations, classroom assistance, classroom readers and scribes, and a reduced course load. In some instances, CDA may allow substitutions for math and foreign language courses. Additional services provided by CDA include an orientation to campus, referrals to campus and community services, general and academic advising, coordination with advisors regarding accommodations, and assistance with the procedures of admission, registration, and graduation. CDA staff, students, and faculty use the ClockWork 5 Accommodation Software System, an online portal to easily manage accommodations.

ADMISSIONS

All applicants must meet the same general admission requirements. The middle 50 percent of accepted applicants have a 3.46–3.93 GPA. Students who struggle to meet the admission requirements because of their disability may be admitted on the condition that course deficiencies are completed prior to earning 30 semester-hours at the university. Conditional admission is determined by CDA and the admissions office. While disclosure of a disability is up to the student, it is recommended for students requesting to be considered for conditional admission.

Additional Information

The Learning Center offers many free services to currently enrolled University of Utah students. The Learning Center has peer educators—students who have excelled in their academics and participate in weekly training, Supplemental Instruction—study sessions for selected courses each semester, and individual learning consultations on topics including, but not limited to, time management, study strategies, test-taking strategies, test anxiety, learning strategies, and critical thinking.

In 1905, the sophomore class painted a giant "07" on the side of Mount Van Cott, and the first-years replaced the "07" with "08." The numbers changed as often as students could climb the hill, until a giant concrete "U" replaced the numbers and became an emblem of loyalty to the whole school. After a $400,000 renovation and an official lighting ceremony in 2006, the proud symbol now flashes red and white lights and is visible from all over the Salt Lake Valley.

University of Utah

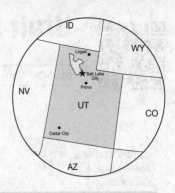

GENERAL ADMISSIONS

Very important factors include: rigor of secondary school record, academic GPA. *Other factors considered include:* class rank, standardized test scores (if submitted), application essay, recommendations. High school diploma is required and GED is accepted. Institution is test-optional for entering Fall 2024. Check admissions website for updates.

FINANCIAL AID

Students should submit: FAFSA. *Need-based scholarships/grants offered:* College/university scholarship or grant aid from institutional funds; Federal Nursing Scholarships; Federal Pell; Private scholarships; SEOG; State scholarships/grants. *Loan aid offered:* Direct PLUS loans; Direct Subsidized Loans; Direct Unsubsidized Loans. Federal Work-Study Program available. Institutional employment available.

CAMPUS LIFE

Activities: Campus Ministries; Choral groups; Concert band; Dance; Drama/theater; International Student Organization; Jazz band; Literary magazine; Marching band; Model UN; Music ensembles; Musical theater; Opera; Pep band; Radio station; Student government; Student newspaper; Student-run film society; Symphony orchestra; Television station. **Organizations:** 611 registered organizations, 27 honor societies, 19 religious organizations, 11 fraternities, 8 sororities. **Athletics (Intercollegiate):** *Men:* baseball, basketball, cycling, golf, ice hockey, lacrosse, martial arts, rugby, skiing (nordic/cross-country), swimming, track/field (indoor), ultimate frisbee, water polo. *Women:* basketball, cross-country, cycling, golf, gymnastics, ice hockey, lacrosse, martial arts, rugby, skiing (nordic/cross-country), softball, swimming, track/field (indoor), ultimate frisbee, volleyball, water polo.

CAMPUS

Type of school	Public
Environment	Metropolis

STUDENTS

Undergrad enrollment	25,392
% male/female	52/48
% from out of state	33
% frosh live on campus	59

FINANCIAL FACTS

Annual in-state tuition	$8,628
Annual out-of-state tuition	$30,201
Room and board	$10,662
Required fees	$1,188

GENERAL ADMISSIONS INFO

Application fee	$55
Regular application deadline	4/1
Nonfall registration	Yes

Fall 2024 testing policy	Test Optional
Range SAT EBRW	600–690
Range SAT Math	590–700
Range ACT Composite	22–29

ACADEMICS

Student/faculty ratio	18:1
% students returning for sophomore year	85
Most classes have 10–19 students.	

REQUESTING SERVICES FOR STUDENTS WITH LEARNING DIFFERENCES

Phone: 801-581-5020 • disability.utah.edu/ • Email: info@disability.utah.edu

Documentation submitted to: Center for Disability & Access

Separate application required for Services: Yes

Documentation required for:
LD: Psychoeducational evaluation
ADHD: Psychoeducational evaluation
ASD: Psychoeducational evaluation

Utah State University

0160 Old Main Hill, Logan, UT 84322-0160 • Admissions: 435-797-1079 • www.usu.edu

Support: CS

ACCOMMODATIONS
Allowed in exams:

Calculators	Yes
Dictionary	Yes
Computer	Yes
Spell-checker	Yes
Extended test time	Yes
Scribe	Yes
Proctors	Yes
Oral exams	Yes
Note-takers	Yes

Support services for students with:

LD	Yes
ADHD	Yes
ASD	Yes
Distraction-reduced environment	Yes
Recording of lecture allowed	Yes
Reading technology	Yes
Audio books	Yes
Other assistive technology	Yes
Priority registration	Yes

Added costs of services:

For LD	No
For ADHD	No
For ASD	No
LD specialists	Yes
ADHD & ASD coaching	No
ASD specialists	No
Professional tutors	Yes
Peer tutors	Yes
Max. hours/week for services	Varies
How professors are notified of student approved accommodations	Student and Disability Resource Center

COLLEGE GRADUATION REQUIREMENTS

Course waivers allowed	Yes

In what courses: Case-by-case basis

Course substitutions allowed	Yes

In what courses: General Education Math on a case-by-case basis

PROGRAMS/SERVICES FOR STUDENTS WITH LEARNING DIFFERENCES

The Disability Resource Center (DRC) provides services and accommodations to students with learning disabilities. Students meet with an accessibility consultant to discuss accommodation requests, which are then determined based on individual needs. Accommodations can be requested for anything related to the university experience, and may include testing accommodations, accessible text, note-taking, and course substitutions. Requests for course accommodations must be submitted for approval each semester. Aggies Elevated is a two-year certificate program for young adults with intellectual and/or developmental disabilities at both Utah State University in Logan and the Eastern campus in Price. Each participant's progress is evaluated on a regular basis, with attention to academics, independent living, social skills, and their overall adjustment to college. Some Aggie Elevated students will only experience college through this two-year program, and others will use the program as a bridge between high school and an associate or bachelor's degree. The program centers around five themes: lifelong learning, independent living, community involvement, self-advocacy, and career development. Foundational reading and writing courses are offered, as are a variety of personal and vocational electives. Coursework is for college credit and culminates with a year-end MyCLIMB presentation where students announce new goals and future plans.

ADMISSIONS

Admission criteria are the same for all students. Applicants with a 2.8 GPA or higher are automatically admissible. Applicants with a 2.79 GPA or lower may be considered for admission through the Earned Admission Path. Students on the Earned Admission Path must complete an online class before their enrollment. This course helps students develop study skills integral to academic success and can be completed at the student's own pace. Upon completion of the course, students earn 3 credits and are officially admitted to USU. Applicants to the associate degree program must apply at least two months prior to the start of the semester to be considered for admission, and the program does not have summer enrollment.

Additional Information

The university offers a number of resources for students to improve their written communication skills, including the Writing Center, Science Writing Center, Engineering Writing Center, and through communication literacy courses.

USU's first graduating class in 1894 had 15 members, eight of whom received business degrees. This makes USU the oldest continually operating business school in the West. The College of Business now offers 13 undergraduate majors, eight master's programs, and two doctorate programs.

Utah State University

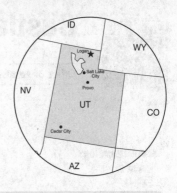

GENERAL ADMISSIONS

Very important factors include: academic GPA, standardized test scores (if submitted). *Other factors considered include:* rigor of secondary school record, class rank, recommendations. High school diploma is required and GED is accepted. Institution is test-optional for entering Fall 2024. Check admissions website for updates. *Academic units recommended:* 4 English, 4 math, 3 science (3 labs), 2 foreign language, 3.5 social studies.

FINANCIAL AID

Students should submit: FAFSA. *Need-based scholarships/grants offered:* College/university scholarship or grant aid from institutional funds; Federal Pell; Private scholarships; SEOG; State scholarships/grants. *Loan aid offered:* Direct PLUS loans; Direct Subsidized Loans; Direct Unsubsidized Loans. Federal Work-Study Program available. Institutional employment available.

CAMPUS LIFE

Activities: Campus Ministries; Choral groups; Concert band; Dance; Drama/theater; International Student Organization; Jazz band; Marching band; Music ensembles; Musical theater; Opera; Pep band; Radio station; Student government; Student newspaper; Student-run film society; Symphony orchestra; Television station. **Organizations:** 32 honor societies, 8 religious organizations, 5 fraternities, 3 sororities. **Athletics (Intercollegiate):** *Men:* baseball, basketball, cross-country, cycling, golf, ice hockey, lacrosse, racquetball, rugby, swimming, track/field (indoor), ultimate frisbee, volleyball, water polo. *Women:* basketball, cross-country, cycling, golf, gymnastics, lacrosse, racquetball, rugby, softball, swimming, track/field (indoor), ultimate frisbee, volleyball, water polo.

CAMPUS

Type of school	Public
Environment	Town

STUDENTS

Undergrad enrollment	24,255
% male/female	44/56
% from out of state	29

FINANCIAL FACTS

Annual in-state tuition	$8,042
Annual out-of-state tuition	$23,162
Room and board	$8,076
Required fees	$918

GENERAL ADMISSIONS INFO

Application fee	$50
Regular application deadline	Rolling
Nonfall registration	Yes

Fall 2024 testing policy	Test Optional
Range SAT EBRW	550–660
Range SAT Math	530–650
Range ACT Composite	21–29

ACADEMICS

Student/faculty ratio	21:1
% students returning for sophomore year	74

Most classes have 20–29 students.

REQUESTING SERVICES FOR STUDENTS WITH LEARNING DIFFERENCES

Phone: 435-797-2444 • usu.edu/drc • Email: drc@usu.edu

Documentation submitted to: Disability Resource Center
Separate application required for Services: Yes

Documentation required for:
LD: Psychoeducational evaluation
ADHD: Psychoeducational evaluation
ASD: Psychoeducational evaluation

Castleton University

Office of Admissions, Castleton, VT 05735 • Admissions: 802-468-1213 • www.castleton.edu

> **Support: CS**

ACCOMMODATIONS

Allowed in exams:	
Calculators	Yes
Dictionary	Yes
Computer	Yes
Spell-checker	Yes
Extended test time	Yes
Scribe	Yes
Proctors	Yes
Oral exams	Yes
Note-takers	Yes
Support services for students with:	
LD	Yes
ADHD	Yes
ASD	Yes
Distraction-reduced environment	Yes
Recording of lecture allowed	Yes
Reading technology	Yes
Audio books	Yes
Other assistive technology	No
Priority registration	No
Added costs of services:	
For LD	No
For ADHD	No
For ASD	No
LD specialists	No
ADHD & ASD coaching	Yes
ASD specialists	Yes
Professional tutors	Yes
Peer tutors	Yes
Max. hours/week for services	Varies
How professors are notified of student approved accommodations	Student

COLLEGE GRADUATION REQUIREMENTS

Course waivers allowed	No
Course substitutions allowed	No

PROGRAMS/SERVICES FOR STUDENTS WITH LEARNING DIFFERENCES

The Academic Support Center provides services for students with learning disabilities. Students are encouraged to set up a meeting with the coordinator of Disability Services to review documentation, discuss requested accommodations, and secure approval for appropriate accommodations. Students must meet with the coordinator each semester to secure continued accommodations, which may include text-to-speech tools, such as Natural Reader and WordTalk, or speech-to-text tools, such as Dragon or Evernote. In addition, the College STEPS Program partners with Castleton to provide the additional help and support students need, including students with ASD and learning disabilities. The on-campus College STEPS coordinator oversees a group of trained peer mentors, who provide customized academic, social, and vocational training support to College STEPS scholars. The primary goal of College STEPS is to promote autonomy and prepare students for meaningful careers after graduation. Eligible students, including those with documented disabilities, can participate in the Summer Transition Program (STP), a no-fee, five-day orientation program offered by the Academic Support Center that occurs just before first-year orientation. Students can adjust to the new environment, make friends, and start their first semester feeling confident.

ADMISSIONS

Applications for both fall and spring semesters are evaluated on a rolling basis and there is no application deadline. However, Castleton encourages students to apply early to ensure that they can be considered for financial aid, meet scholarship deadlines, and make an informed decision regarding their choice of college. Castleton arranges the Dual Enrollment and Early College Programs with the Vermont Department of Education and local school district to consider admitting students who have completed the 11th grade and wish to begin their college education.

Additional Information

The Academic Support Center offers one-on-one and group academic counseling for students who want to explore ways to manage their time and meet their goals. Castleton University joined with Northern Vermont University and Vermont Technical College to become Vermont State University on July 1, 2023.

In 1861, Professor James Hope was the first man in Castleton to volunteer for Civil War duty at age 43. But early on, Captain Hope fell ill. From sideline duties, he sketched scenes he witnessed at the Battle of Antietam. Later, he painted the images, and they became his best-known work. Hope's Gothic Revival home and studio now houses campus security. His works can be found around the state of Vermont, as well as on campus.

Castleton University

General Admissions

Very important factors include: rigor of secondary school record, class rank, academic GPA, application essay, recommendations. *Other factors considered include:* standardized test scores (if submitted). High school diploma is required and GED is accepted. Institution is test-optional for entering Fall 2024. Check admissions website for updates. *Academic units required:* 4 English, 3 math, 3 science (2 labs), 3 social studies. *Academic units recommended:* 2 foreign language.

Financial Aid

Students should submit: FAFSA. *Need-based scholarships/grants offered:* College/university scholarship or grant aid from institutional funds; Federal Pell; Private scholarships; SEOG; State scholarships/grants. *Loan aid offered:* Direct PLUS loans; Direct Subsidized Loans; Direct Unsubsidized Loans. Federal Work-Study Program available. Institutional employment available.

Campus Life

Activities: Campus Ministries; Choral groups; Concert band; Dance; Drama/theater; International Student Organization; Jazz band; Literary magazine; Marching band; Music ensembles; Musical theater; Pep band; Radio station; Student government; Student newspaper; Television station; Yearbook. **Organizations:** 40 registered organizations, 7 honor societies, 1 religious organizations, 0 fraternities, 0 sororities. **Athletics (Intercollegiate):** *Men:* baseball, basketball, cross-country, golf, ice hockey, lacrosse, rugby, track/field (indoor). *Women:* basketball, cross-country, equestrian sports, field hockey, ice hockey, lacrosse, rugby, softball, track/field (indoor), volleyball.

CAMPUS

Type of school	Public
Environment	Rural

STUDENTS

Undergrad enrollment	1,744
% male/female	44/56
% from out of state	48
% frosh live on campus	84

FINANCIAL FACTS

Annual in-state tuition	$11,832
Annual out-of-state tuition	$28,800
Room and board	$12,042
Required fees	$1,246

GENERAL ADMISSIONS INFO

Application fee	$40
Regular application deadline	Rolling
Nonfall registration	Yes

Fall 2024 testing policy	Test Optional
Range SAT EBRW	488–580
Range SAT Math	470–578
Range ACT Composite	16–22

ACADEMICS

Student/faculty ratio	14:1
% students returning for sophomore year	67

Most classes have 10–19 students.

Vermont

REQUESTING SERVICES FOR STUDENTS WITH LEARNING DIFFERENCES

Phone: 802-468-1428 • www.castleton.edu/academics/academic-support/academic-support-center/disability-services/ • Email: gerard.volpe@castleton.edu

Documentation submitted to: Disability Services
Separate application required for Services: Yes

Documentation required for:
 LD: Psychoeducational evaluation
 ADHD: Psychoeducational evaluation
 ASD: Psychoeducational evaluation

Champlain College

P.O. Box 670, Burlington, VT 05402-0670 • Admissions: 802-860-2727 • www.champlain.edu

Support: S

ACCOMMODATIONS

Allowed in exams:

Calculators	Yes
Dictionary	Yes
Computer	Yes
Spell-checker	Yes
Extended test time	Yes
Scribe	Yes
Proctors	Yes
Oral exams	Yes
Note-takers	Yes

Support services for students with:

LD	Yes
ADHD	Yes
ASD	Yes
Distraction-reduced environment	Yes
Recording of lecture allowed	Yes
Reading technology	Yes
Audio books	Yes
Other assistive technology	Yes
Priority registration	Yes

Added costs of services:

For LD	No
For ADHD	No
For ASD	No
LD specialists	No
ADHD & ASD coaching	No
ASD specialists	No
Professional tutors	Yes
Peer tutors	Yes
Max. hours/week for services	Varies
How professors are notified of student approved accommodations	Student and Office of Accessibility

COLLEGE GRADUATION REQUIREMENTS

Course waivers allowed	No
Course substitutions allowed	No

Programs/Services for Students with Learning Differences

The Office of Accessibility provides services and accommodations to students with learning disabilities. Students should complete an online form to request academic accommodations following enrollment. The Office of Accessibility requires that students seeking accommodations submit current, comprehensive, professional documentation of their disability. The office will then contact each student for an appointment at the start of the semester to discuss their documentation, needs, the process, and services. Accommodations may include tutoring, extended time for tests, readers for tests, use of computers during exams, peer notetakers, approval to record lectures, and e-books. With the student's permission, faculty members receive a letter discussing appropriate accommodations. The coordinator will act as a liaison between the student and faculty, consult with tutors, monitor the student's academic progress, and consult with faculty as needed. Students meet with the Office of Accessibility each semester to receive continued accommodations.

Admissions

The admission process is the same for all students and is fairly competitive. Application requirements include an essay and teacher and counselor recommendations. Ideal applicants have successfully completed a college preparatory curriculum with an emphasis on strong writing skills. The high school transcript is the most important part of the student's application. Applicants are evaluated based on the demands of their secondary school curriculum, grades earned, class rank, writing ability, recommendations, and academic growth; an upward grade-trend is looked upon favorably. Students are expected to continue a full, challenging course load during their senior year.

Additional Information

SMART (Study Mentors And Resource Tutors) Space provides free academic coaching, 24/7 online tutoring, and writing and tutoring centers for all Champlain students. SMART Space hosts various workshops, including the Thriving at College with ADHD workshop—a three-week coaching group for neurodiverse students.

Champlain was established in 1878, and for the first 80 years, Champlain rented classroom and office spaces in downtown Burlington. From 1911 to 1958, Champlain was located on the 3rd floor of 182-190 Main Street. Dormitories weren't built until the late 1950s, so students from out of town were hosted by area residents. Students were not permitted to smoke or drink, and chewing gum was prohibited on school premises.

Champlain College

GENERAL ADMISSIONS

Very important factors include: rigor of secondary school record, academic GPA. *Important factors include:* application essay, recommendations. *Other factors considered include:* class rank, standardized test scores (if submitted). High school diploma is required and GED is accepted. Institution is test-optional for entering Fall 2024. Check admissions website for updates. *Academic units required:* 4 English, 3 math, 3 science (2 labs), 2 foreign language, 3 history, 5 academic electives. *Academic units recommended:* 4 math, 4 science, 3 foreign language, 4 history.

FINANCIAL AID

Students should submit: FAFSA. *Need-based scholarships/grants offered:* College/university scholarship or grant aid from institutional funds; Federal Pell; Private scholarships; SEOG; State scholarships/grants. *Loan aid offered:* Direct PLUS loans; Direct Subsidized Loans; Direct Unsubsidized Loans. Federal Work-Study Program available. Institutional employment available.

CAMPUS LIFE

Activities: Choral groups; Dance; Drama/theater; International Student Organization; Literary magazine; Radio station; Student government; Student newspaper. **Organizations:** 50 registered organizations, 0 religious organizations, 0 fraternities, 0 sororities. **Athletics (Intercollegiate):** *Men:* basketball, cross-country, cycling, ice hockey, rugby, skiing (nordic/cross-country), ultimate frisbee, volleyball. *Women:* basketball, cross-country, cycling, field hockey, rugby, skiing (nordic/cross-country), ultimate frisbee, volleyball.

CAMPUS

Type of school	Private (nonprofit)
Environment	Town

STUDENTS

Undergrad enrollment	1,766
% male/female	64/36
% from out of state	77
% frosh live on campus	93

FINANCIAL FACTS

Annual tuition	$45,100
Room and board	$16,900
Required fees	$450

GENERAL ADMISSIONS INFO

Application fee	No fee
Regular application deadline	1/15
Nonfall registration	Yes

Fall 2024 testing policy	Test Optional
Range SAT EBRW	603–698
Range SAT Math	560–650
Range ACT Composite	27–31

ACADEMICS

Student/faculty ratio	11:1
% students returning for sophomore year	76

Most classes have 10–19 students.

Vermont

REQUESTING SERVICES FOR STUDENTS WITH LEARNING DIFFERENCES

Phone: 802-865-5764 • www.champlain.edu/accessibility • Email: accessibility@champlain.edu

Documentation submitted to: Office of Accessibility
Separate application required for Services: Yes

Documentation required for:
 LD: Psychoeducational evaluation
 ADHD: Psychoeducational evaluation
 ASD: Psychoeducational evaluation

Landmark College

19 River Road South, Putney, VT 05346-0820 • Admissions: 802-387-6718 • www.landmark.edu

Support: SP

ACCOMMODATIONS

Allowed in exams:

Calculators	Yes
Dictionary	Yes
Computer	Yes
Spell-checker	Yes
Extended test time	Yes
Scribe	Yes
Proctors	Yes
Oral exams	Yes
Note-takers	No

Support services for students with:

LD	Yes
ADHD	Yes
ASD	Yes
Distraction-reduced environment	Yes
Recording of lecture allowed	Yes
Reading technology	Yes
Audio books	Yes
Other assistive technology	Yes
Priority registration	N/A

Added costs of services:

For LD	No
For ADHD	No
For ASD	No
LD specialists	Yes
ADHD & ASD coaching	Yes
ASD specialists	Yes
Professional tutors	Yes
Peer tutors	No
Max. hours/week for services	Varies
How professors are notified of student approved accommodations	Director

COLLEGE GRADUATION REQUIREMENTS

Course waivers allowed	No
Course substitutions allowed	No

PROGRAMS/SERVICES FOR STUDENTS WITH LEARNING DIFFERENCES

Landmark College is an accredited college exclusively for students who learn differently. Students with dyslexia, ADHD, ASD, or other specific learning differences find academic success at Landmark. All students are evaluated through the admission process to determine which supports are needed. Landmark offers support pathways that include executive function coaching, social pragmatics, and a language-intensive curriculum. The design of Landmark's campus allows students to gain an immersive post-secondary experience with access to quality technology and services. Assisted technology is integrated into the classroom experience, and the faculty are highly trained to deliver instruction using accommodative resources.

ADMISSIONS

To be admitted to Landmark, students must have a diagnosed disability, including dyslexia, ADHD, and ASD. Students are accepted on a rolling basis for fall and spring terms. To apply for admission, students submit a completed application, documentation of diagnosis with cognitive testing reports, a personal essay, and a letter of recommendation. There is also a required interview. Students may submit test scores and a portfolio, however, neither are required.

Additional Information

Landmark's Transition at College (TaC) program is designed for students who need to develop their executive function skills, whose primary diagnosis is ADHD, and students who are unsure if college is a good fit for their immediate post-secondary next step. Through TaC, students explore academic, social, and professional interests while assessing strengths and weaknesses. TaC students take a reduced credit load within a structured academic and residential environment. They can earn up to 18 college credits while also taking developmental courses for skills strengthening and academic preparedness in a structured environment. TaC is a fee-based program. Landmark also offers three summer programs: High School Summer allows high school students to practice college-level time-management, study, and test preparation skills; College Readiness is for rising first-year college students; and Summer Bridge is for high school students needing support in social pragmatics.

Landmark is a rural campus located on the southeastern tip of Vermont, minutes away from some of the best skiing and snowboarding on the East Coast. It also offers the opportunity for kayaking, rock and ice climbing, mountain biking, hiking, and camping. The towns of Putney and Brattleboro are full of restaurants, shops, and arts events. Or when there's a need for a big city, Landmark is only two and a half hours from Boston and four hours from New York City or Montreal.

Landmark College

General Admissions

Very important factors include: recommendations. *Other factors considered include:* rigor of secondary school record, academic GPA, standardized test scores (if submitted), application essay. High school diploma is required and GED is accepted. Institution is test optional for entering Fall 2024. Check admissions website for updates. *Academic units recommended:* 4 English, 3 math, 3 science, 3 social studies.

Financial Aid

Students should submit: FAFSA. *Need-based scholarships/grants offered:* College/university scholarship or grant aid from institutional funds; Federal Pell; Private scholarships; SEOG; State scholarships/grants. *Loan aid offered:* Direct PLUS loans; Direct Subsidized Loans; Direct Unsubsidized Loans. Federal Work-Study Program available. Institutional employment available.

Campus Life

Activities: Choral groups; Drama/theater; International Student Organization; Literary magazine; Music ensembles; Radio station; Student government; Television station. **Organizations:** 14 registered organizations, 2 honor societies, 0 fraternities, 0 sororities. **Athletics (Intercollegiate):** *Men:* baseball, basketball, cross-country. *Women:* basketball, cross-country, softball.

CAMPUS
Type of school	Private (nonprofit)
Environment	Rural

STUDENTS
Undergrad enrollment	452
% male/female	65/35
% from out of state	94
% frosh live on campus	90

FINANCIAL FACTS
Annual tuition	$62,720
Room and board	$13,960

GENERAL ADMISSIONS INFO
Application fee	$75
Regular application deadline	Rolling
Nonfall registration	Yes
Fall 2024 testing policy	Test Optional

ACADEMICS
Student/faculty ratio	8:1
Most classes have 10–19 students.	

Vermont

REQUESTING SERVICES FOR STUDENTS WITH LEARNING DIFFERENCES

Phone: 802-387-4767 • www.landmark.edu • Email: admissions@landmark.edu

Documentation submitted to: Landmark College
Separate application required for Services: No

Documentation required for:
  LD: Psychoeducational evaluation
  ADHD: Psychoeducational evaluation
  ASD: Psychoeducational evaluation

Norwich University

Admissions Office, Northfield, VT 05663 • Admissions: 802-485-2001 • www.norwich.edu

Support: CS

ACCOMMODATIONS

Allowed in exams:

Calculators	Yes
Dictionary	Yes
Computer	Yes
Spell-checker	Yes
Extended test time	Yes
Scribe	Yes
Proctors	Yes
Oral exams	Yes
Note-takers	No

Support services for students with:

LD	Yes
ADHD	Yes
ASD	Yes
Distraction-reduced environment	Yes
Recording of lecture allowed	Yes
Reading technology	Yes
Audio books	Yes
Other assistive technology	Yes
Priority registration	Yes

Added costs of services:

For LD	No
For ADHD	No
For ASD	No
LD specialists	Yes
ADHD & ASD coaching	No
ASD specialists	No
Professional tutors	Yes
Peer tutors	Yes
Max. hours/week for services	Varies
How professors are notified of student approved accommodations	Student and CASA/SAR

COLLEGE GRADUATION REQUIREMENTS

Course waivers allowed	No
Course substitutions allowed	Yes
In what courses: Case-by-case basis	

PROGRAMS/SERVICES FOR STUDENTS WITH LEARNING DIFFERENCES

The Student Accessibility Resources (SAR) program at Norwich is a part of the Center for Academic Success and Achievement (CASA) and serves students with disabilities. A wide range of services are provided, including academic accommodations, assistive technology support, and individualized coaching. The CASA SAR coordinator assists students with the proper documentation necessary to qualify for accommodations and resources. The coordinator helps students access their approved academic accommodations, provides training on assistive technology, facilitates communication with staff, provides academic coaching and mentoring, and meets with students on a regular basis or as needed.

ADMISSIONS

All applicants must submit the general admission application. Admission criteria include a GPA of C or better, participation in activities, and recommendations from teachers, counselors, or coaches. There are no course waivers for admission. If grades and other indicators are problematic due to a learning disability, students should provide detailed information to give a better understanding. A small number of students not meeting general admission requirements, but showing promise, may be admitted through a minimal number of provisional admission slots. An interview is highly recommended. ACT and SAT scores are not required, except for the nursing program.

Additional Information

The online programs are structured so that students can take a single course at a time if needed. Students are put into a cohort, a small group of fellow students with whom the students stay for their entire time at Norwich. The cohort serves as both a motivational coach and an idea incubator. The goal is to not only support students while at Norwich but to create a valuable professional network for after the students leave. There will be initial correspondence upon acceptance into the program, as well as welcome calls before each class. CASA is available to provide peer tutoring. Staff assists with study, time management, organizational and learning skills and provides academic coaching services. Comprehensive one-on-one and group tutoring across the curriculum is available.

After leaving West Point, Captain Alden Partridge returned to his native state to create the American Literary, Scientific, and Military Academy, founded in 1819 in Norwich, Vermont. Norwich prepared hundreds of officers and soldiers who served with the federal armies in the American Civil War, including four recipients of the Medal of Honor. Norwich is the oldest of six senior military colleges and is recognized by the U.S. Department of Defense as the "Birthplace of ROTC" (Reserve Officers' Training Corps).

Norwich University

GENERAL ADMISSIONS

Very important factors include: rigor of secondary school record, academic GPA, standardized test scores (if submitted). *Other factors considered include:* class rank, application essay, recommendations. High school diploma is required and GED is accepted. Institution is test-optional for entering Fall 2024. Check admissions website for updates. *Academic units recommended:* 4 English, 4 math, 4 science (3 labs), 2 foreign language, 3 social studies.

FINANCIAL AID

Students should submit: FAFSA. *Need-based scholarships/grants offered:* College/university scholarship or grant aid from institutional funds; Federal Pell; Private scholarships; SEOG; State scholarships/grants. *Loan aid offered:* Direct PLUS loans; Direct Subsidized Loans; Direct Unsubsidized Loans. Federal Work-Study Program available. Institutional employment available.

CAMPUS LIFE

Activities: Campus Ministries; Dance; Drama/theater; International Student Organization; Jazz band; Marching band; Model UN; Radio station; Student government; Student newspaper; Yearbook. **Organizations:** 40 registered organizations, 8 honor societies, 4 religious organizations, 0 fraternities, 0 sororities. **Athletics (Intercollegiate):** *Men:* baseball, basketball, cross-country, ice hockey, lacrosse, rugby, swimming, volleyball, wrestling. *Women:* basketball, cross-country, ice hockey, rugby, softball, swimming, volleyball.

CAMPUS

Type of school	Private (nonprofit)
Environment	Rural

STUDENTS

Undergrad enrollment	2,201
% male/female	74/26
% from out of state	84
% frosh live on campus	94

FINANCIAL FACTS

Annual tuition	$30,048
Room and board	$10,976
Required fees	$1,734

GENERAL ADMISSIONS INFO

Application fee	$35
Regular application deadline	Rolling
Nonfall registration	Yes

Fall 2024 testing policy	Test Optional
Range SAT EBRW	480–580
Range SAT Math	500–640
Range ACT Composite	21–26

ACADEMICS

Student/faculty ratio	14:1
% students returning for sophomore year	85

Most classes have 20–29 students.

Vermont

REQUESTING SERVICES FOR STUDENTS WITH LEARNING DIFFERENCES

Phone: 802-485-2130 • www.norwich.edu/casa • Email: jhaverst@norwich.edu

Documentation submitted to: Student Accessibility Resources
Separate application required for Services: Yes

Documentation required for:
LD: Psychoeducational evaluation
ADHD: Psychoeducational evaluation
ASD: Psychoeducational evaluation

Saint Michael's College

One Winooski Park, Box 7, Colchester, VT 05439 • Admissions: 802-654-3000 • www.smcvt.edu

Support: CS

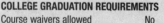
PROGRAMS/SERVICES FOR STUDENTS WITH LEARNING DIFFERENCES

Support for students with disabilities is provided through the Office of Accessibility Services. Students with learning disabilities must provide appropriate documentation to the director of Accessibility Services before the beginning of their first semester. They are then asked to meet with the director at the start of the academic semester to discuss course planning and strategies for success.

ADMISSIONS

Students admitted to Saint Michael's College are active learners prepared for a challenging college experience. Students should be committed to social justice, community, and service. Students are required to submit one to two teacher and counselor recommendations.

Additional Information

Academic support coaches are available for students seeking help with personal choices, study, skills, and time management regarding academic performance. On a fee-for-service basis, Collaborative Educational Consultants are on staff and are available for a holistic, highly focused approach to helping students define and achieve their academic goals. This one-to-one coaching model helps students identify their learning goals and find their own solutions. Students wanting individual tutors must first meet with their professors outside of class and attend at least one group or drop-in session.

DID YOU KNOW?

Since 1969, an extracurricular activity at Saint Michael's has been the entirely volunteer student-run Fire and Rescue Department serving the campus and the Chittenden County community with professional fire and emergency medical services and education. Students, alums, and staff serve 24 hours a day, year-round. The EMT program is one of seven college-run EMT programs, and the fire program is one of the only entirely volunteer student-run departments in the nation.

Saint Michael's College

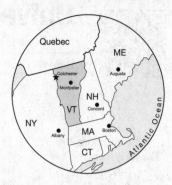

GENERAL ADMISSIONS

Very important factors include: rigor of secondary school record, class rank, academic GPA, application essay. *Important factors include:* recommendations. *Other factors considered include:* standardized test scores (if submitted). High school diploma is required and GED is accepted. Institution is test-optional for entering Fall 2024. Check admissions website for updates. *Academic units recommended:* 4 English, 3–4 math, 3–4 science (2 labs), 2–3 foreign language, 3–4 social studies.

FINANCIAL AID

Students should submit: FAFSA; State aid form. *Need-based scholarships/grants offered:* College/university scholarship or grant aid from institutional funds; Federal Pell; Private scholarships; SEOG; State scholarships/grants. *Loan aid offered:* Direct PLUS loans; Direct Subsidized Loans; Direct Unsubsidized Loans. Federal Work-Study Program available. Institutional employment available.

CAMPUS LIFE

Activities: Campus Ministries; Choral groups; Concert band; Dance; Drama/theater; International Student Organization; Jazz band; Literary magazine; Model UN; Music ensembles; Musical theater; Radio station; Student government; Student newspaper; Yearbook. **Organizations:** 40 registered organizations, 11 honor societies, 1 religious organizations, 0 fraternities, 0 sororities. **Athletics (Intercollegiate):** *Men:* baseball, basketball, cross-country, cycling, golf, ice hockey, lacrosse, rugby, skiing (nordic/cross-country), swimming, volleyball. *Women:* basketball, cross-country, cycling, field hockey, ice hockey, lacrosse, rugby, skiing (nordic/cross-country), softball, swimming, volleyball.

CAMPUS

Type of school	Private (nonprofit)
Environment	City

STUDENTS

Undergrad enrollment	1,200
% male/female	47/53
% from out of state	78
% frosh live on campus	97

FINANCIAL FACTS

Annual tuition	$47,640
Room and board	$16,495
Required fees	$2,400

GENERAL ADMISSIONS INFO

Application fee	$50
Regular application deadline	2/1
Nonfall registration	Yes

Fall 2024 testing policy	Test Optional
Range SAT EBRW	600–680
Range SAT Math	560–640
Range ACT Composite	26–30

ACADEMICS

Student/faculty ratio	10:1
% students returning for sophomore year	79

Most classes have 10–19 students.

REQUESTING SERVICES FOR STUDENTS WITH LEARNING DIFFERENCES

Phone: 802-654-2467 • smcvt.edu/academics/academic-support/accessibility-services
Email: amessuri@smcvt.edu

Documentation submitted to: Office of Accessibility Services
Separate application required for Services: Yes

Documentation required for:
 LD: Psychoeducational evaluation
 ADHD: Psychoeducational evaluation
 ASD: Psychoeducational evaluation

University of Vermont

University of Vermont, Burlington, VT 05401-3596 • Admissions: 802-656-3370 • www.uvm.edu

Support: CS

ACCOMMODATIONS

Allowed in exams:

Calculators	Yes
Dictionary	Yes
Computer	Yes
Spell-checker	Yes
Extended test time	Yes
Scribe	Yes
Proctors	Yes
Oral exams	Yes
Note-takers	Yes

Support services for students with:

LD	Yes
ADHD	Yes
ASD	Yes
Distraction-reduced environment	Yes
Recording of lecture allowed	Yes
Reading technology	Yes
Audio books	Yes
Other assistive technology	Yes
Priority registration	Yes

Added costs of services:

For LD	No
For ADHD	No
For ASD	No
LD specialists	Yes
ADHD & ASD coaching	No
ASD specialists	Yes
Professional tutors	No
Peer tutors	Yes
Max. hours/week for services	Varies
How professors are notified of student approved accommodations	Student and Student Accessibility Services

COLLEGE GRADUATION REQUIREMENTS

Course waivers allowed	No
Course substitutions allowed	No

PROGRAMS/SERVICES FOR STUDENTS WITH LEARNING DIFFERENCES

Student Accessibility Services (SAS) provides services and accommodations to all students with documented disabilities. Accommodations may include extended time on exams, note-taking services, e-books, captioning, and other adaptive technology. The Tutoring Center provides free, weekly, one-on-one tutoring in course materials and study skills, and SAS students are eligible for additional sessions per week. The online MyACCESS portal allows students to communicate directly with professors about their accommodations. Students can decide whether they want to implement their accommodations in some or all of their courses. Think College at UVM is an academic, social, and vocational transition program for students with intellectual and developmental disabilities who are interested in the college experience and career path. Participants learn independent living skills and earn a 12 credit Certificate of College Studies for nonmatriculated students.

ADMISSIONS

All applicants are expected to meet the same admission criteria. The admissions office encourages students to volunteer documentation of their disability if they believe the review committee will benefit from consulting with SAS on the impact their disability may have had on their academic record. Any submitted documentation is sent directly to SAS. Students with LD or ADHD are encouraged to submit a current educational evaluation that includes a comprehensive measure of both cognitive and academic functioning. Students may also request an assessment of their documentation to address any missing eligibility or entrance requirements, such as a foreign language, due to their disability.

Additional Information

The Center for Academic Success offers all students supplementary services, such as academic advising, sessions at the tutoring center, and peer tutoring at the writing center.

Student musicians showcase their talents on campus in Battle of the Bands. Participation and attendance are free, as long as at least one performer per act is a current student. Competitors perform 15-minute sets over three days of initial battle rounds. Students vote for four bands to advance to the finale, and the winner of Battle of the Bands goes on to perform as the opening act at SpringFest.

University of Vermont

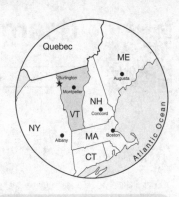

GENERAL ADMISSIONS

Very important factors include: rigor of secondary school record. *Important factors include:* academic GPA, application essay. *Other factors considered include:* standardized test scores (if submitted), recommendations. High school diploma is required and GED is accepted. Institution is test-optional for entering Fall 2024. Check admissions website for updates. *Academic units required:* 4 English, 3 math, 3 science (1 lab), 2 foreign language, 3 social studies.

FINANCIAL AID

Students should submit: FAFSA. *Need-based scholarships/grants offered:* College/university scholarship or grant aid from institutional funds; Federal Pell; Private scholarships; SEOG; State scholarships/grants. *Loan aid offered:* Direct PLUS loans; Direct Subsidized Loans; Direct Unsubsidized Loans. Federal Work-Study Program available. Institutional employment available.

CAMPUS LIFE

Activities: Campus Ministries; Choral groups; Concert band; Dance; Drama/theater; International Student Organization; Jazz band; Literary magazine; Music ensembles; Musical theater; Pep band; Radio station; Student government; Student newspaper; Student-run film society; Symphony orchestra; Television station. **Organizations:** 235 registered organizations, 29 honor societies, 8 religious organizations, 9 fraternities, 6 sororities. **Athletics (Intercollegiate):** *Men:* baseball, basketball, crew/rowing, cross-country, cycling, equestrian sports, field hockey, golf, gymnastics, ice hockey, lacrosse, martial arts, rugby, skiing (nordic/cross-country), swimming, track/field (indoor), ultimate frisbee, volleyball, water polo, wrestling. *Women:* baseball, basketball, crew/rowing, cross-country, cycling, equestrian sports, field hockey, golf, gymnastics, ice hockey, lacrosse, martial arts, rugby, skiing (nordic/cross-country), softball, swimming, track/field (indoor), ultimate frisbee, volleyball, water polo.

CAMPUS

Type of school	Public
Environment	Town

STUDENTS

Undergrad enrollment	11,081
% male/female	38/62
% from out of state	74
% frosh live on campus	99

FINANCIAL FACTS

Annual in-state tuition	$16,280
Annual out-of-state tuition	$41,280
Room and board	$13,324
Required fees	$2,610

GENERAL ADMISSIONS INFO

Application fee	$55
Regular application deadline	1/15
Nonfall registration	Yes

Fall 2024 testing policy	Test Optional
Range SAT EBRW	630–710
Range SAT Math	610–700
Range ACT Composite	29–33

ACADEMICS

Student/faculty ratio	18:1
% students returning for sophomore year	88

Most classes have 20–29 students.

REQUESTING SERVICES FOR STUDENTS WITH LEARNING DIFFERENCES

Phone: 802-656-7753 • uvm.edu/access • Email: access@uvm.edu

Documentation submitted to: Student Accessibility Services

Separate application required for Services: Yes

Documentation required for:
LD: Psychoeducational evaluation
ADHD: Psychoeducational evaluation
ASD: Psychoeducational evaluation

George Mason University

4400 University Drive, Fairfax, VA 22030-4444 • Admissions: 703-993-2400 • gmu.edu

(Support: SP)

ACCOMMODATIONS

Allowed in exams:

Calculators	Yes
Dictionary	Yes
Computer	Yes
Spell-checker	Yes
Extended test time	Yes
Scribe	Yes
Proctors	Yes
Oral exams	Yes
Note-takers	Yes

Support services for students with:

LD	Yes
ADHD	Yes
ASD	Yes
Distraction-reduced environment	Yes
Recording of lecture allowed	Yes
Reading technology	Yes
Audio books	Yes
Other assistive technology	Yes
Priority registration	Yes

Added costs of services:

For LD	Yes
For ADHD	Yes
For ASD	Yes
LD specialists	Yes
ADHD & ASD coaching	Yes
ASD specialists	Yes
Professional tutors	Yes
Peer tutors	No
Max. hours/week for services	Varies
How professors are notified of student approved accommodations	Student

COLLEGE GRADUATION REQUIREMENTS

Course waivers allowed	Yes

In what courses: Disability Services will evaluate all requests.

Course substitutions allowed	Yes

In what courses: Disability Services will evaluate all requests.

PROGRAMS/SERVICES FOR STUDENTS WITH LEARNING DIFFERENCES

Students may request accommodations from the Disability Services office by completing an intake form, submitting documentation, and meeting with a specialist. Services and accommodations may include audio recording lectures, assistive technology, a reduced-distraction environment for tests, additional time and/or breaks for tests, foreign language and quantitative reasoning exemptions, priority registration, and a reduced course load. Mason Autism Support Initiative (MASI) is a fee-based program that provides additional intensive support services to students on the autism spectrum. In addition to developing relationships with learning strategists and peer mentors, MASI students earn 0.5 credits for individualized courses that facilitate their transition to campus, social engagement, identity development, and sense of career readiness. The Executive Functioning Program (EFP) provides individualized services related to executive functioning skills for students with relevant diagnoses. Students can meet weekly with a Learning Coach to cultivate skills in time management, organization, self-advocacy, and independence. The Learning Coach may also connect students to on-campus resources and assist in communication with faculty. EFP is fee-based and offers two levels of support.

ADMISSIONS

The admission criteria are the same for all students. Academic performance is the most important factor in a student's application review. The middle 50 percent of accepted students have cumulative grade point averages of 3.3–3.9 on a weighted 4.0 scale. Students are expected to have taken a robust selection of college preparatory classes, including honors, advanced placement, and International Baccalaureate courses. George Mason seeks applicants demonstrating strong leadership, intellectual curiosity, and motivation in their extracurricular, work or service experiences.

Additional Information

There are multiple student resources at GMU, including math tutoring, individual and group counseling sessions, academic advising, a learning center, and a writing center.

In 1965, GMU was a branch campus of the University of Virginia and celebrated its founder, Thomas Jefferson, on April 13. Students couldn't resist making the following day Mason Day, and soon the celebration for Jefferson was dropped altogether. Mason Day is the university's longest tradition; by the 1970s, it had grown into a mini-Woodstock. To this day, students select the musical guests who reflect the times.

George Mason University

GENERAL ADMISSIONS

Very important factors include: rigor of secondary school record, academic GPA. *Other factors considered include:* standardized test scores (if submitted), application essay, recommendations. High school diploma is required and GED is accepted. Institution is test-optional for entering Fall 2024. Check admissions website for updates. *Academic units required:* 4 English, 3 math, 2 science (2 labs), 2 foreign language, 3 social studies, 3 academic electives. *Academic units recommended:* 4 math, 3 science (3 labs), 3 foreign language, 4 social studies, 5 academic electives.

FINANCIAL AID

Students should submit: FAFSA. *Need-based scholarships/grants offered:* Federal Pell; Private scholarships; SEOG; State scholarships/grants. *Loan aid offered:* Direct PLUS loans; Direct Subsidized Loans; Direct Unsubsidized Loans. Federal Work-Study Program available. Institutional employment available.

CAMPUS LIFE

Activities: Campus Ministries; Choral groups; Concert band; Dance; Drama/theater; International Student Organization; Jazz band; Literary magazine; Model UN; Music ensembles; Musical theater; Opera; Pep band; Radio station; Student government; Student newspaper; Student-run film society; Symphony orchestra; Television station; Yearbook. **Organizations:** 464 registered organizations, 15 honor societies, 46 religious organizations, 24 fraternities, 19 sororities. **Athletics (Intercollegiate):** *Men:* baseball, basketball, crew/rowing, cross-country, cycling, equestrian sports, field hockey, golf, ice hockey, lacrosse, martial arts, rugby, swimming, track/field (indoor), ultimate frisbee, volleyball, wrestling. *Women:* basketball, crew/rowing, cross-country, cycling, equestrian sports, field hockey, lacrosse, martial arts, rugby, softball, swimming, track/field (indoor), ultimate frisbee, volleyball.

CAMPUS

Type of school	Public
Environment	City

STUDENTS

Undergrad enrollment	26,447
% male/female	51/49
% from out of state	10
% frosh live on campus	55

FINANCIAL FACTS

Annual in-state tuition	$9,795
Annual out-of-state tuition	$33,959
Room and board	$13,120
Required fees	$3,609

GENERAL ADMISSIONS INFO

Application fee	$70
Regular application deadline	Rolling
Nonfall registration	Yes

Fall 2024 testing policy	Test Optional
Range SAT EBRW	580–670
Range SAT Math	560–680
Range ACT Composite	25–31

ACADEMICS

Student/faculty ratio	16:1
% students returning for sophomore year	85

Most classes have 20–29 students.

Virginia

REQUESTING SERVICES FOR STUDENTS WITH LEARNING DIFFERENCES

Phone: 703-993-2474 • ds.gmu.edu • Email: ods@gmu.edu

Documentation submitted to: Disability Services
Separate application required for Services: Yes

Documentation required for:
 LD: Psychoeducational evaluation
 ADHD: Psychoeducational evaluation
 ASD: Psychoeducational evaluation

Hampton University

Office of Admissions, Hampton, VA 23668 • Admissions: 757-727-5328 • www.hamptonu.edu

Support: CS

ACCOMMODATIONS

Allowed in exams:

Calculators	Yes
Dictionary	No
Computer	No
Spell-checker	No
Extended test time	Yes
Scribe	Yes
Proctors	Yes
Oral exams	Yes
Note-takers	Yes

Support services for students with:

LD	Yes
ADHD	Yes
ASD	Yes
Distraction-reduced environment	Yes
Recording of lecture allowed	Yes
Reading technology	Yes
Audio books	No
Other assistive technology	Yes
Priority registration	Yes

Added costs of services:

For LD	No
For ADHD	No
For ASD	No
LD specialists	Yes
ADHD & ASD coaching	Yes
ASD specialists	No
Professional tutors	No
Peer tutors	Yes
Max. hours/week for services	Varies
How professors are notified of student approved accommodations	Student and Office of Compliance and Disability Services

COLLEGE GRADUATION REQUIREMENTS

Course waivers allowed	Yes

In what courses: Foreign Language

Course substitutions allowed	Yes

In what courses: Foreign Language

PROGRAMS/SERVICES FOR STUDENTS WITH LEARNING DIFFERENCES

The Office of Compliance and Disability Services coordinates accommodations and support services for students with documented disabilities. Hampton recommends that students request accommodations within the first week of classes to ensure that they can take effect as soon as possible. The process for receiving services includes completion of an application form, submission of documentation, and a meeting with the director.

ADMISSIONS

Hampton University takes a holistic approach to application review, focusing on overall academic achievement, demonstration of leadership potential, and evidence of strong ethical values. Hampton recommends that candidates take the most rigorous academic program available to them, including AP, IB, and honors courses whenever possible. Students with a cumulative GPA of at least 3.3 (unweighted), or who rank in the top 10 percent of their class, may choose whether or not to submit standardized test scores.

Additional Information

The Tutoring Center offers academic coaching and Supplemental Instruction (SI), a type of peer-assisted group study that equips students to learn challenging concepts by reviewing content along with others. Hampton University offers the Pre-College/Summer Bridge Program to students who have completed their junior or senior year of high school. This five-week residential program provides academic enrichment and an opportunity to experience college life.

In 1861, during the Civil War, Union Major General Benjamin Butler decreed that any escaping slaves reaching Union lines would not be returned. Freed slaves took refuge several miles outside of Fort Monroe, at a camp that became the U.S.'s first self-contained African American community. Mary Peake, a free African American, assumed the role of teacher to freed slaves, despite it being against Virginia law at the time. She held her first class on September 17, 1861, under an oak tree. The Emancipation Oak still stands on the Hampton University campus today.

Hampton University

GENERAL ADMISSIONS

Very important factors include: rigor of secondary school record, academic GPA, application essay. *Important factors include:* class rank, recommendations. *Other factors considered include:* standardized test scores (if submitted). High school diploma is required and GED is accepted. Institution is test-optional for entering Fall 2024. Check admissions website for updates. *Academic units required:* 4 English, 3 math, 2 science, 2 social studies, 2 foreign language.

FINANCIAL AID

Students should submit: FAFSA. *Need-based scholarships/grants offered:* College/university scholarship or grant aid from institutional funds; Federal Nursing Scholarships; Federal Pell; Private scholarships; SEOG; State scholarships/grants. *Loan aid offered:* Direct PLUS loans; Direct Subsidized Loans; Direct Unsubsidized Loans. Federal Work-Study Program available.

CAMPUS LIFE

Activities: Campus Ministries; Choral groups; Concert band; Dance; Drama/theater; International Student Organization; Jazz band; Literary magazine; Marching band; Music ensembles; Musical theater; Opera; Pep band; Radio station; Student government; Student newspaper; Symphony orchestra; Television station; Yearbook. **Organizations:** 85 registered organizations, 16 honor societies, 3 religious organizations, 5 fraternities, 4 sororities. **Athletics (Intercollegiate):** *Men:* basketball, cross-country, golf, lacrosse, track/field (indoor). *Women:* basketball, bowling, cross-country, golf, softball, track/field (indoor), volleyball.

CAMPUS

Type of school	Private (nonprofit)
Environment	City

STUDENTS

Undergrad enrollment	2,863
% male/female	34/66
% from out of state	79
% frosh live on campus	99

FINANCIAL FACTS

Annual tuition	$26,198
Room and board	$12,986
Required fees	$3,114

GENERAL ADMISSIONS INFO

Application fee	$50
Regular application deadline	3/1
Nonfall registration	Yes

Fall 2024 testing policy	Test Optional
Range SAT EBRW	500–600
Range SAT Math	490–580
Range ACT Composite	19–26

ACADEMICS

Student/faculty ratio	13:1
% students returning for sophomore year	81

Virginia

REQUESTING SERVICES FOR STUDENTS WITH LEARNING DIFFERENCES

Phone: 757-727-5493 • www.hamptonu.edu/compliance • Email: disabilityservices@hamptonu.edu

Documentation submitted to: Office of Compliance and Disability Services
Separate application required for Services: Yes

Documentation required for:
LD: Psychoeducational evaluation
ADHD: Psychoeducational evaluation
ASD: Psychoeducational evaluation

James Madison University

Sonner Hall, Harrisonburg, VA 22807 • Admissions: 540-568-5681 • www.jmu.edu

Support: CS

ACCOMMODATIONS

Allowed in exams:	
Calculators	Yes
Dictionary	Yes
Computer	Yes
Spell-checker	Yes
Extended test time	Yes
Scribe	Yes
Proctors	Yes
Oral exams	Yes
Note-takers	Yes
Support services for students with:	
LD	Yes
ADHD	Yes
ASD	Yes
Distraction-reduced environment	Yes
Recording of lecture allowed	No
Reading technology	Yes
Audio books	Yes
Other assistive technology	Yes
Priority registration	Yes
Added costs of services:	
For LD	No
For ADHD	No
For ASD	No
LD specialists	No
ADHD & ASD coaching	Yes
ASD specialists	Yes
Professional tutors	Yes
Peer tutors	Yes
Max. hours/week for services	Varies
How professors are notified of student approved accommodations	Student

COLLEGE GRADUATION REQUIREMENTS

Course waivers allowed	Yes
In what courses: Case-by-case basis	
Course substitutions allowed	Yes
In what courses: Case-by-case basis	

PROGRAMS/SERVICES FOR STUDENTS WITH LEARNING DIFFERENCES

James Madison University (JMU) provides accessibility services through the Office of Disability Services (ODS). To access services through ODS, students must complete the registration process and provide eligible documentation. Students receive referrals for free academic coaching programs that offer weekly one-on-one coaching. Academic Peer Coaches use research-based methods to teach learning strategies that help students with their academics and stress levels. The ODS does not coordinate with or provide feedback to the admissions office, and learning and intellectual differences are not considered in the admissions process.

ADMISSIONS

James Madison University considers academic rigor, and students should have an A/B average. A personal essay, recommendation letters, and test scores are all optional; however, students should submit these materials if they believe they will strengthen their application. For admitted applicants who submit scores, the middle 50 percent range of the SAT is 1160–1310. Interviews are not provided.

Additional Information

In addition to the accommodative resources, the ODS team will refer students to the on-campus Learning Resource, Student Development, and Communication Resources Centers. The ODS has accessible media programs with audio and visual materials specific to students with learning differences. The audio formats are robust and have the capacity to translate to braille, produce captions, create tactile graphics, and much more. Students have the option for foreign language substitutions to meet graduation requirements.

Since 1972, the first year of JMU football, the Marching Royal Dukes (MRD) has established a strong tradition as ambassadors of the university and the community. The more than 475-member band are mostly nonmusic majors representing practically every department on campus. MRD performs at all home and away football games, marching band contests, and parades around Virginia and the Mid-Atlantic. MRD has performed at presidential inaugurations and has taken six goodwill tours abroad during school breaks. MRD is JMU's largest and most visible organization.

James Madison University

General Admissions

Very important factors include: rigor of secondary school record, academic GPA. *Other factors considered include:* standardized test scores (if submitted), application essay, recommendations. High school diploma is required and GED is accepted. Institution is test-optional for entering Fall 2024. Check admissions website for updates. *Academic units recommended:* 4 English, 4 math, 3 science (3 labs), 3 foreign language, 4 social studies.

Financial Aid

Students should submit: FAFSA. *Need-based scholarships/grants offered:* Federal Pell; Private scholarships; SEOG; State scholarships/grants. *Loan aid offered:* Direct PLUS loans; Direct Subsidized Loans; Direct Unsubsidized Loans. Federal Work-Study Program available. Institutional employment available.

Campus Life

Activities: Campus Ministries; Choral groups; Concert band; Dance; Drama/theater; International Student Organization; Jazz band; Literary magazine; Marching band; Music ensembles; Musical theater; Opera; Pep band; Radio station; Student government; Student newspaper; Student-run film society; Symphony orchestra; Television station; Yearbook. **Organizations:** 353 registered organizations, 22 honor societies, 32 religious organizations, 15 fraternities, 13 sororities. **Athletics (Intercollegiate):** *Men:* baseball, basketball, crew/rowing, cross-country, cycling, equestrian sports, golf, gymnastics, ice hockey, lacrosse, martial arts, rugby, swimming, table tennis, ultimate frisbee, volleyball, water polo, wrestling. *Women:* basketball, crew/rowing, cross-country, cycling, equestrian sports, field hockey, golf, gymnastics, ice hockey, lacrosse, martial arts, rugby, softball, swimming, table tennis, ultimate frisbee, volleyball, water polo.

CAMPUS
Type of school	Public
Environment	Town

STUDENTS
Undergrad enrollment	19,743
% male/female	42/58
% from out of state	21
% frosh live on campus	98

FINANCIAL FACTS
Annual in-state tuition	$7,684
Annual out-of-state tuition	$28,848
Room and board	$11,940
Required fees	$5,408

GENERAL ADMISSIONS INFO
Application fee	$70
Regular application deadline	1/15
Nonfall registration	Yes
Fall 2024 testing policy	Test Optional
Range SAT EBRW	580–660
Range SAT Math	560–650
Range ACT Composite	24–29

ACADEMICS
Student/faculty ratio	16:1
% students returning for sophomore year	91

Most classes have 10–19 students.

Virginia

REQUESTING SERVICES FOR STUDENTS WITH LEARNING DIFFERENCES

Phone: 540-568-6705 • www.jmu.edu/ods • Email: disability-svcs@jmu.edu

Documentation submitted to: Office of Disability Services
Separate application required for Services: Yes

Documentation required for:
LD: Psychoeducational evaluation
ADHD: Psychoeducational evaluation
ASD: Psychoeducational evaluation

Liberty University

1971 University Boulevard, Lynchburg, VA 24515 • Admissions: 434-582-2000 • www.liberty.edu

Support: CS

ACCOMMODATIONS

Allowed in exams:

Calculators	Yes
Dictionary	Yes
Computer	Yes
Spell-checker	Yes
Extended test time	Yes
Scribe	Yes
Proctors	Yes
Oral exams	Yes
Note-takers	Yes

Support services for students with:

LD	Yes
ADHD	Yes
ASD	Yes
Distraction-reduced environment	Yes
Recording of lecture allowed	Yes
Reading technology	Yes
Audio books	No
Other assistive technology	Yes
Priority registration	Yes

Added costs of services:

For LD	No
For ADHD	No
For ASD	No
LD specialists	Yes
ADHD & ASD coaching	No
ASD specialists	No
Professional tutors	No
Peer tutors	Yes
Max. hours/week for services	Varies
How professors are notified of student approved accommodations	Office of Disability Accommodation Support

COLLEGE GRADUATION REQUIREMENTS

Course waivers allowed	No
Course substitutions allowed	No

PROGRAMS/SERVICES FOR STUDENTS WITH LEARNING DIFFERENCES

Liberty University provides support and services to students with documented disabilities through the Office of Disability Accommodation Support (ODAS). Students are responsible for requesting accommodations and providing appropriate documentation. The ODAS arranges reasonable accommodations and ensures eligible students maintain a college experience that promotes living and learning success. To apply for services, students meet with the director of ODAS, complete an intake form, and provide documentation. Students must complete an academic accommodation request form every semester to continue receiving accommodations.

ADMISSIONS

Admission decisions are competitive and are based on cumulative GPA from high school, consistency, and trends of grades. Half of admitted students have mid-range high school GPAs of 3.15–3.83 and SAT scores of 1020–1220, if submitting. Applicants complete a self-certification form to prove graduation from high school.

Additional Information

The College of Applied Studies and Academic Success (CASAS) supports students through study skills help, time-management training, leading skill development, individual and group tutoring, academic advising, and academic counseling. The Academic Success Workshop series offered through CASAS helps students with procrastination, goal setting, time management, critical thinking, study skills, motivation, and academic success.

Founded in 2005, the National Civil War Chaplains Museum has an extensive collection of Union and Confederate military objects and artifacts that tell the story of religion in camps, on battlefields, and among prisoners of war. The museum raises public awareness of the role chaplains, priests, rabbis, and religious organizations played and how their commitment to faith affected the daily lives of Union and Confederate soldiers. The museum commemorates Catholic, Protestant, Jewish, and Black chaplains.

Liberty University

General Admissions

Very important factors include: rigor of secondary school record, academic GPA. *Important factors include:* standardized test scores (if submitted). *Other factors considered include:* class rank, application essay, recommendations. High school diploma is required and GED is accepted. Institution is test-optional for entering Fall 2024. Check admissions website for updates. *Academic units recommended:* 4 English, 3 math, 2 science (2 labs), 2 foreign language, 2 social studies, 4 academic electives.

Financial Aid

Students should submit: FAFSA; State aid form. *Need-based scholarships/ grants offered:* College/university scholarship or grant aid from institutional funds; Federal Pell; Private scholarships; SEOG; State scholarships/grants. *Loan aid offered:* Direct PLUS loans; Direct Subsidized Loans; Direct Unsubsidized Loans.

Campus Life

Activities: Campus Ministries; Choral groups; Concert band; Drama/theater; Literary magazine; Marching band; Music ensembles; Musical theater; Pep band; Radio station; Student government; Student newspaper; Symphony orchestra; Television station; Yearbook. **Organizations:** 25 registered organizations, 11 honor societies, 10 religious organizations. **Athletics (Intercollegiate):** *Men:* baseball, basketball, crew/rowing, cross-country, cycling, equestrian sports, golf, gymnastics, ice hockey, lacrosse, racquetball, skiing (nordic/cross-country), swimming, track/field (indoor), ultimate frisbee, volleyball, wrestling. *Women:* basketball, crew/rowing, cross-country, cycling, equestrian sports, field hockey, gymnastics, ice hockey, lacrosse, racquetball, skiing (nordic/cross-country), softball, swimming, track/field (indoor), ultimate frisbee, volleyball, wrestling.

CAMPUS

Type of school	Private (nonprofit)
Environment	Town

STUDENTS

Undergrad enrollment	15,000
% male/female	45/55
% from out of state	63
% frosh live on campus	93

FINANCIAL FACTS

Annual tuition	$23,800
Room and board	$12,350
Required fees	$1,140

GENERAL ADMISSIONS INFO

Application fee	$50
Regular application deadline	Rolling
Nonfall registration	Yes

Fall 2024 testing policy	Test Optional
Range SAT EBRW	530–650
Range SAT Math	510–630
Range ACT Composite	21–29

ACADEMICS

Student/faculty ratio	17:1
% students returning for sophomore year	79
Most classes have 20–29 students.	

Virginia

REQUESTING SERVICES FOR STUDENTS WITH LEARNING DIFFERENCES

Phone: 434-592-4016 • www.liberty.edu/disability-support/ • Email: odas@liberty.edu

Documentation submitted to: Office of Disability Accommodation Support
Separate application required for Services: Yes

Documentation required for:
LD: Psychoeducational evaluation
ADHD: Psychoeducational evaluation
ASD: Psychoeducational evaluation

Old Dominion University

1004 Rollins Hall, Norfolk, VA 23529-0050 • Admissions: 757-683-3685 • www.odu.edu

Support: S

ACCOMMODATIONS

Allowed in exams:

Calculators	Yes
Dictionary	Yes
Computer	Yes
Spell-checker	Yes
Extended test time	Yes
Scribe	Yes
Proctors	Yes
Oral exams	Yes
Note-takers	Yes

Support services for students with:

LD	Yes
ADHD	Yes
ASD	Yes
Distraction-reduced environment	Yes
Recording of lecture allowed	Yes
Reading technology	Yes
Audio books	Yes
Other assistive technology	Yes
Priority registration	Yes

Added costs of services:

For LD	No
For ADHD	No
For ASD	No
LD specialists	No
ADHD & ASD coaching	Yes
ASD specialists	No
Professional tutors	No
Peer tutors	Yes
Max. hours/week for services	Varies
How professors are notified of student approved accommodations	Student

COLLEGE GRADUATION REQUIREMENTS

Course waivers allowed	No
Course substitutions allowed	Yes

In what courses: Foreign Language

PROGRAMS/SERVICES FOR STUDENTS WITH LEARNING DIFFERENCES

The Office of Educational Accessibility offers academic support services for students with disabilities based on their individual needs, and it works collaboratively with partners across campus to ensure that all aspects of the campus are inclusive. Accommodations are based on the student's documentation and the discussion they have with the Office of Educational Accessibility. Accommodations may be adjusted during the student's academic career, and students are encouraged to reach out each semester if any of their learning needs are not being accommodated. Support services are designed to focus on a student's learning styles and special needs. There's a special section of Spanish for students with learning disabilities to meet the foreign language requirements, as well as developmental math, reading, spelling, and writing classes.

ADMISSIONS

All applicants are expected to meet the same admission criteria. Preference is given to students enrolled in Advanced Placement (AP) or International Baccalaureate (IB), honors, and college-level dual enrollment courses.

Additional Information

Counseling and advising, study skills instruction, writing, reading, and math instruction, and tutoring are all available.

ODU was one of the pioneers to offer live classes via satellite to Navy ships—the "Ships at Sea" program. First offered in 1997 on the U.S.S. George Washington, active-duty sailors were able to take classes via TELETECHNET. Classes were beamed from campus to aircraft carriers via digital satellite and televisions with two-way video connection. By 2004, ODU operated over 60 sites in five states to multiple ships. In 2014, the satellite feeds were discontinued, and courses are now taught through ODU*Online*.

Old Dominion University

GENERAL ADMISSIONS

Very important factors include: rigor of secondary school record, academic GPA, standardized test scores (if submitted). *Important factors include:* application essay, recommendations. *Other factors considered include:* class rank. High school diploma is required and GED is accepted. Institution is test-optional for entering Fall 2024. Check admissions website for updates. *Academic units recommended:* 4 English, 3 math, 3 science, 3 foreign language, 3 social studies.

FINANCIAL AID

Students should submit: FAFSA. *Need-based scholarships/grants offered:* College/university scholarship or grant aid from institutional funds; Federal Pell; Private scholarships; SEOG; State scholarships/grants; United Negro College Fund. *Loan aid offered:* Direct PLUS loans; Direct Subsidized Loans; Direct Unsubsidized Loans. Federal Work-Study Program available. Institutional employment available.

CAMPUS LIFE

Activities: Campus Ministries; Choral groups; Concert band; Dance; Drama/theater; International Student Organization; Jazz band; Literary magazine; Marching band; Model UN; Music ensembles; Musical theater; Pep band; Radio station; Student government; Student newspaper; Student-run film society; Symphony orchestra. **Organizations:** 183 registered organizations, 19 honor societies, 17 religious organizations, 13 fraternities, 10 sororities. **Athletics (Intercollegiate):** *Men:* baseball, basketball, crew/rowing, golf, ice hockey, lacrosse, rugby, swimming, volleyball. *Women:* basketball, crew/rowing, field hockey, golf, ice hockey, lacrosse, rugby, softball, swimming, volleyball.

CAMPUS

Type of school	Public
Environment	Metropolis

STUDENTS

Undergrad enrollment	18,147
% male/female	45/55
% from out of state	8
% frosh live on campus	72

FINANCIAL FACTS

Annual in-state tuition	$11,630
Annual out-of-state tuition	$31,580
Room and board	$14,166
Required fees	$360

GENERAL ADMISSIONS INFO

Application fee	$50
Regular application deadline	2/1
Nonfall registration	Yes

Fall 2024 testing policy	Test Optional
Range SAT EBRW	560–640
Range SAT Math	530–610
Range ACT Composite	22–27

ACADEMICS

Student/faculty ratio	16:1
% students returning for sophomore year	74

Most classes have 10–19 students.

Virginia

REQUESTING SERVICES FOR STUDENTS WITH LEARNING DIFFERENCES

Phone: 757-683-4655 • www.odu.edu/accessibility • Email: oea@odu.edu

Documentation submitted to: Office of Educational Accessibility
Separate application required for Services: Yes

Documentation required for:
LD: Psychoeducational evaluation
ADHD: Psychoeducational evaluation
ASD: Psychoeducational evaluation

Radford University

P.O. Box 6903, Radford, VA 24142 • Admissions: 540-831-5371 • www.radford.edu

Support: CS

ACCOMMODATIONS

Allowed in exams:	
Calculators	Yes
Dictionary	Yes
Computer	Yes
Spell-checker	Yes
Extended test time	Yes
Scribe	Yes
Proctors	Yes
Oral exams	Yes
Note-takers	Yes
Support services for students with:	
LD	Yes
ADHD	Yes
ASD	Yes
Distraction-reduced environment	Yes
Recording of lecture allowed	Yes
Reading technology	Yes
Audio books	Yes
Other assistive technology	Yes
Priority registration	Yes
Added costs of services:	
For LD	No
For ADHD	No
For ASD	No
LD specialists	Yes
ADHD & ASD coaching	Yes
ASD specialists	No
Professional tutors	Yes
Peer tutors	Yes
Max. hours/week for services	4
How professors are notified of student approved accommodations	Student

COLLEGE GRADUATION REQUIREMENTS

Course waivers allowed	No
Course substitutions allowed	Yes
In what courses: Case-by-case basis	

PROGRAMS/SERVICES FOR STUDENTS WITH LEARNING DIFFERENCES

The Center for Accessibility Services (CAS) provides equal educational opportunities for students with disabilities so that they can participate fully in the college experience. Accommodations may include alternate-format texts, reduced-distraction environments for testing, extended time for tests, dictation software, note-taking services, and reading software.

ADMISSIONS

All students have the same general admission requirements. Radford University views all materials that an applicant submits. The admissions committee looks for a 3.0 GPA.

Additional Information

The Harvey Center for Learning and Writing helps students achieve academic success. Students can access in-person or Zoom tutoring appointments, online tutoring, and paper drop-off services through NetTutor, reserve study rooms with LCD screens, and download resources and tips for learning and studying. Tutoring can be either individual or group sessions. Writing tutors are on hand to help students with writing assignments for any discipline. One-on-one consultations are available to students, as well as workshops on time management, test-taking approaches, and similar topics.

RU campus is located in the Virginia Highlands, between the Blue Ridge and Allegheny mountains at a double bend in the New River. The New River is recognized as the "second oldest river in the world" and is one of the few rivers in North America that flows northerly. The campus is in one of America's most historic regions, surrounded by Civil War trails and battle markers, the Appalachian Trail, Crooked Road (Virginia's heritage music trail), the Mary Draper Ingles Trail, and more.

Radford University

GENERAL ADMISSIONS

Very important factors include: rigor of secondary school record. *Important factors include:* academic GPA. *Other factors considered include:* class rank, standardized test scores (if submitted), application essay, recommendations. High school diploma is required and GED is accepted. Institution is test-optional for entering Fall 2024. Check admissions website for updates. *Academic units recommended:* 4 English, 4 math, 4 science (3 labs), 3–4 foreign language, 4 social studies.

FINANCIAL AID

Students should submit: FAFSA. *Need-based scholarships/grants offered:* College/university scholarship or grant aid from institutional funds; Federal Pell; Private scholarships; SEOG; State scholarships/grants. *Loan aid offered:* Direct PLUS loans; Direct Subsidized Loans; Direct Unsubsidized Loans. Federal Work-Study Program available. Institutional employment available.

CAMPUS LIFE

Activities: Campus Ministries; Choral groups; Concert band; Dance; Drama/theater; International Student Organization; Jazz band; Literary magazine; Model UN; Music ensembles; Musical theater; Pep band; Radio station; Student government; Student newspaper; Student-run film society; Television station; Yearbook. **Organizations:** 163 registered organizations, 28 honor societies, 15 religious organizations, 15 fraternities, 11 sororities. **Athletics (Intercollegiate):** *Men:* baseball, basketball, bowling, cross-country, equestrian sports, golf, ice hockey, lacrosse, rugby, swimming, table tennis, ultimate frisbee, volleyball, wrestling. *Women:* basketball, bowling, cross-country, equestrian sports, field hockey, golf, ice hockey, lacrosse, rugby, softball, swimming, table tennis, track/field (indoor), ultimate frisbee, volleyball, wrestling.

CAMPUS
Type of school	Public
Environment	Village

STUDENTS
Undergrad enrollment	5,945
% male/female	37/63
% from out of state	8
% frosh live on campus	90

FINANCIAL FACTS
Annual in-state tuition	$8,156
Annual out-of-state tuition	$20,246
Room and board	$10,424
Required fees	$3,760

GENERAL ADMISSIONS INFO
Application fee	No fee
Regular application deadline	Rolling
Nonfall registration	Yes

Fall 2024 testing policy	Test Optional
Range SAT EBRW	490–600
Range SAT Math	470–560
Range ACT Composite	19–23

ACADEMICS
Student/faculty ratio	12:1
% students returning for sophomore year	68

Most classes have 10–19 students.

Virginia

REQUESTING SERVICES FOR STUDENTS WITH LEARNING DIFFERENCES

Phone: 540-831-6350 • www.radford.edu/content/cas/home.html • Email: cas@radford.edu

Documentation submitted to: Center for Accessibility Services
Separate application required for Services: Yes

Documentation required for:
LD: Psychoeducational evaluation
ADHD: Psychoeducational evaluation
ASD: Psychoeducational evaluation

Roanoke College

221 College Lane, Salem, VA 24153-3794 • Admissions: 540-375-2270 • www.roanoke.edu

Support: CS

ACCOMMODATIONS

Allowed in exams:

Calculators	Yes
Dictionary	Yes
Computer	Yes
Spell-checker	Yes
Extended test time	Yes
Scribe	Yes
Proctors	Yes
Oral exams	Yes
Note-takers	Yes

Support services for students with:

LD	No
ADHD	No
ASD	No
Distraction-reduced environment	Yes
Recording of lecture allowed	Yes
Reading technology	Yes
Audio books	Yes
Other assistive technology	Yes
Priority registration	No

Added costs of services:

For LD	No
For ADHD	No
For ASD	No
LD specialists	No
ADHD & ASD coaching	Yes
ASD specialists	No
Professional tutors	No
Peer tutors	Yes
Max. hours/week for services	20
How professors are notified of student approved accommodations	Student and Academic Services

COLLEGE GRADUATION REQUIREMENTS

Course waivers allowed	No
Course substitutions allowed	No

PROGRAMS/SERVICES FOR STUDENTS WITH LEARNING DIFFERENCES

To obtain services at Roanoke College, students with disabilities must submit a disability registration/accommodation request as well as documentation verifying the disability. The assistant director of Academic Services for Accessible Education will review requests and documentation to determine eligibility. If the student is declared eligible, the assistant director and student will meet to discuss the process for accessing accommodations. If a student is declared not eligible, the student can accept the decision or appeal to the director of Academic Services.

ADMISSIONS

All applicants are expected to meet the same admission criteria. Admission is based on academic grades and courses, standardized test scores (if submitting), the student's interest in the college, extracurricular activities, essay, and letter of recommendation. The average GPA of students accepted to Roanoke is 3.6.

Additional Information

During orientation, academic advisors meet individually and in group settings with first-year students several times each semester. Advisors get to know students and provide guidance, especially regarding course selection and academic progress. Advisors encourage students' personal development and involvement in campus culture by suggesting co-curricular and community service activities. Students remain with their initial advisors until they declare their major, usually during the sophomore year. At that time, they are advised by faculty in their major departments. The director of Academic Services, in the Goode-Pasfield Center for Learning & Teaching, coordinates the academic advising of undeclared students.

Roanoke was one of the few Southern colleges that remained open during the Civil War. The 1861 school year ended with 17 students; most having gone to war. In August 1861, President Dr. David F. Bittle secured the college's right to stay open with only 20 students. Women were admitted but taught separately. The college company was formally mustered into the Confederate Army, Virginia Reserves, in September 1864, but did not see combat before war ended. On April 4, 1865, Dr. Bittle and two prominent citizens, carrying a white flag on a ten-foot pole, surrendered Salem to a Federal cavalry troop.

Roanoke College

General Admissions

Very important factors include: rigor of secondary school record, academic GPA. *Important factors include:* class rank. *Other factors considered include:* standardized test scores (if submitted), application essay, recommendations. High school diploma is required and GED is accepted. Institution is test-optional for entering Fall 2024. Check admissions website for updates. *Academic units required:* 4 English, 3 math, 2 science (2 labs), 2 foreign language, 2 social studies, 5 academic electives.

Financial Aid

Students should submit: FAFSA; State aid form. *Need-based scholarships/grants offered:* College/university scholarship or grant aid from institutional funds; Federal Pell; Private scholarships; SEOG; State scholarships/grants. *Loan aid offered:* Direct PLUS loans; Direct Subsidized Loans; Direct Unsubsidized Loans. Federal Work-Study Program available. Institutional employment available.

Campus Life

Activities: Campus Ministries; Choral groups; Concert band; Dance; Drama/theater; International Student Organization; Jazz band; Literary magazine; Model UN; Music ensembles; Pep band; Radio station; Student government; Student newspaper; Student-run film society. **Organizations:** 140 registered organizations, 27 honor societies, 8 religious organizations, 5 fraternities, 4 sororities. **Athletics (Intercollegiate):** *Men:* baseball, basketball, cross-country, equestrian sports, golf, ice hockey, lacrosse, rugby, swimming, track/field (indoor), ultimate frisbee, volleyball, wrestling. *Women:* basketball, cross-country, equestrian sports, field hockey, golf, lacrosse, rugby, softball, swimming, track/field (indoor), ultimate frisbee, volleyball.

CAMPUS
Type of school	Private (nonprofit)
Environment	City

STUDENTS
Undergrad enrollment	1,837
% male/female	46/54
% from out of state	45
% frosh live on campus	93

FINANCIAL FACTS
Annual tuition	$33,510
Room and board	$15,366
Required fees	$1,690

GENERAL ADMISSIONS INFO
Application fee	$30
Regular application deadline	3/15
Nonfall registration	Yes

Fall 2024 testing policy	Test Optional
Range SAT EBRW	550–630
Range SAT Math	530–600
Range ACT Composite	22–27

ACADEMICS
Student/faculty ratio	11:1
% students returning for sophomore year	76

Most classes have 10–19 students.

Virginia

REQUESTING SERVICES FOR STUDENTS WITH LEARNING DIFFERENCES

Phone: 540-375-2247 • www.roanoke.edu/inside/a-z_index/center_for_learning_and_teaching/accessible_education_services • Email: aes@roanoke.edu

Documentation submitted to: Academic Services for Accessible Education
Separate application required for Services: Yes

Documentation required for:
 LD: Psychoeducational evaluation
 ADHD: Psychoeducational evaluation
 ASD: Psychoeducational evaluation

University of Lynchburg

1501 Lakeside Drive, Lynchburg, VA 24501 • Admissions: 434-544-8300 • www.lynchburg.edu

Support: CS

ACCOMMODATIONS

Allowed in exams:

Calculators	Yes
Dictionary	Yes
Computer	Yes
Spell-checker	Yes
Extended test time	Yes
Scribe	Yes
Proctors	Yes
Oral exams	Yes
Note-takers	Yes

Support services for students with:

LD	Yes
ADHD	Yes
ASD	Yes
Distraction-reduced environment	Yes
Recording of lecture allowed	Yes
Reading technology	Yes
Audio books	Yes
Other assistive technology	Yes
Priority registration	No

Added costs of services:

For LD	No
For ADHD	No
For ASD	No
LD specialists	Yes
ADHD & ASD coaching	Yes
ASD specialists	No
Professional tutors	No
Peer tutors	Yes
Max. hours/week for services	Varies
How professors are notified of student approved accommodations	Student

COLLEGE GRADUATION REQUIREMENTS

Course waivers allowed	No
Course substitutions allowed	No

PROGRAMS/SERVICES FOR STUDENTS WITH LEARNING DIFFERENCES

The Center for Accessibility and Disability Resources (CADR) provides accommodations to students with learning differences. If students choose to disclose a disability and request accommodations, it is recommended they do so once they are admitted to the university. Intake appointments can be made at any time during a semester, but accommodations begin at the date of approval. The CADR works with students, faculty, staff, and administrators to provide or arrange for reasonable accommodations, services, training, consultation, and technical assistance based on disability. Typical accommodations may include recording devices, computers for note-taking, alternative formats for textbooks and other materials, extra time for tests, tests in a less distracting environment, changes to class location, accessible furniture, attendance allowance related to a disability, and housing and dining accommodations. The Sue and Andy Tatom Endowed Scholarship was launched in 2020 and is given to University of Lynchburg students in good academic standing who have a disability, preferably a learning disability.

ADMISSIONS

All applicants to the university must meet the same academic requirements and submit official high school transcripts. A personal essay and letters of recommendation are not required but are encouraged. The average admitted applicant has a GPA of 3.4 and an SAT score of 1120 or an ACT score of 23 if submitted.

Additional Information

The Advising and Academic Resource Center (AARC) offers various programs to assist students' academic progress and goals, including tutoring and coaching services. First-Year Initiatives offers programs and events designed to connect, inspire, and engage students throughout the year, helping build relationships with classmates, student leaders, campus administrators, and academic advisors while transitioning to the campus community. AARC's College Success Strategies (GS 104), taught by AARC staff, reinforces essential study habits by developing those skills for college-level courses. The Mathematics Engagement Center (MEC) offers undergraduate students a resource for all math courses, with many in-person and virtual tutoring options. AARC's Peer Assisted Supplemental Study (PASS) is a widely used resource and helps students improve their grades in traditionally difficult classes.

Lynchburg campus connects to 10 miles of running trails along Blackwater Creek and the James River and is walking distance to the starting line of the world-class Virginia 10 Miler.

University of Lynchburg

GENERAL ADMISSIONS
Very important factors include: rigor of secondary school record, academic GPA. *Other factors considered include:* standardized test scores (if submitted), application essay, recommendations. High school diploma is required and GED is accepted. Institution is test-optional for entering Fall 2024. Check admissions website for updates. *Academic units required:* 4 English, 3 math, 3 science (2 labs), 2 foreign language, 4 social studies. *Academic units recommended:* 4 math, 4 science (2 labs), 3 foreign language.

FINANCIAL AID
Students should submit: FAFSA; State aid form. *Need-based scholarships/grants offered:* College/university scholarship or grant aid from institutional funds; Federal Pell; SEOG. *Loan aid offered:* Direct PLUS loans; Direct Subsidized Loans; Direct Unsubsidized Loans. Federal Work-Study Program available. Institutional employment available.

CAMPUS LIFE
Activities: Campus Ministries; Choral groups; Concert band; Dance; Drama/theater; International Student Organization; Jazz band; Literary magazine; Model UN; Music ensembles; Musical theater; Opera; Pep band; Student government; Student newspaper; Symphony orchestra. **Organizations:** 70 registered organizations, 26 honor societies, 21 religious organizations, 3 fraternities, 4 sororities. **Athletics (Intercollegiate):** *Men:* baseball, basketball, cross-country, equestrian sports, golf, lacrosse, swimming, track/field (indoor), wrestling. *Women:* basketball, cross-country, equestrian sports, field hockey, golf, lacrosse, softball, swimming, track/field (indoor), volleyball.

CAMPUS
Type of school	Private (nonprofit)
Environment	City

STUDENTS
Undergrad enrollment	1,543
% male/female	37/63
% from out of state	23
% frosh live on campus	89

FINANCIAL FACTS
Annual tuition	$35,540
Room and board	$13,250

GENERAL ADMISSIONS INFO
Application fee	No fee
Regular application deadline	8/1
Nonfall registration	Yes

Fall 2024 testing policy	Test Optional
Range SAT EBRW	500–620
Range SAT Math	500–610
Range ACT Composite	21–28

ACADEMICS
Student/faculty ratio	10:1
% students returning for sophomore year	76

Most classes have 10–19 students.

Virginia

REQUESTING SERVICES FOR STUDENTS WITH LEARNING DIFFERENCES

Phone: 434-544-8339 • www.lynchburg.edu/academics/disability-services/ • Email: timmons.j@lynchburg.edu

Documentation submitted to: Center for Accessibility and Disability Resources
Separate application required for Services: Yes

Documentation required for:
LD: Psychoeducational evaluation
ADHD: Psychoeducational evaluation
ASD: Psychoeducational evaluation

University of Virginia

Office of Admission, Charlottesville, VA 22903 • Admissions: 434-982-3200 • www.virginia.edu

(Support: CS)

ACCOMMODATIONS

Allowed in exams:	
Calculators	Yes
Dictionary	Yes
Computer	Yes
Spell-checker	Yes
Extended test time	Yes
Scribe	Yes
Proctors	Yes
Oral exams	Yes
Note-takers	Yes
Support services for students with:	
LD	Yes
ADHD	Yes
ASD	Yes
Distraction-reduced environment	Yes
Recording of lecture allowed	Yes
Reading technology	Yes
Audio books	Yes
Other assistive technology	Yes
Priority registration	Yes
Added costs of services:	
For LD	No
For ADHD	No
For ASD	No
LD specialists	Yes
ADHD & ASD coaching	Yes
ASD specialists	Yes
Professional tutors	No
Peer tutors	No
Max. hours/week for services	Varies
How professors are notified of student approved accommodations	Student and Student Disability Access Center

COLLEGE GRADUATION REQUIREMENTS

Course waivers allowed	No
Course substitutions allowed	Yes
In what courses: Case-by-case basis	

PROGRAMS/SERVICES FOR STUDENTS WITH LEARNING DIFFERENCES

The Student Disability Access Center (SDAC) provides services to students with learning disabilities, ADHD, and autism spectrum disorder. Upon acceptance to the university, students must contact SDAC to receive services, and are encouraged to apply for those services online. Guidelines for documentation of a learning disorder or ADHD can be found on the Disability Services page of the UVA website. Once accommodations have been approved, SDAC provides explanatory letters to professors via email. Eligible students are offered weekly meetings with LD specialists as needed, which may include coaching. There are two psychologists on staff to conduct ADHD screenings. There is a weekly academic skills support group for students with ADHD, as well as a weekly social skills support group for students with autism spectrum disorder, run by an ASD specialist. ASD specialists are also available to meet individually with students as necessary.

ADMISSIONS

All students must meet the same criteria for admission. Eligible applicants to UVA have outstanding grades, a high rank in their high school class, excellent performance in advanced placement and honors courses, extracurricular success, special talents, and interests and goals. Letters of recommendation are required. Interviews are not required but recommended. UVA does not waive the foreign language course requirement for undergraduates.

Additional Information

Students with accommodations must make a good faith attempt to pass a foreign language at UVA. If the student cannot successfully pass a foreign language, the student may request a modification for a course substitution, which must be approved by the College of Arts and Sciences. Students in SDAC can be aided by the assistive technology program, and additional specific technology is available to all students.

Thomas Jefferson (1743–1826), author of the American Declaration of Independence and third president of the United States, was also a talented architect. He designed his ideal "academical village," which is still the heart of UVA, and he considered it one of his greatest achievements. In 1987, UNESCO named UVA, along with Jefferson's Monticello estate, a World Heritage Site, for its exhibition of innovation and representation of Jefferson's ideals of enlightenment.

University of Virginia

General Admissions

Very important factors include: rigor of secondary school record, class rank, academic GPA. *Important factors include:* application essay, recommendations. *Other factors considered include:* standardized test scores (if submitted). High school diploma is required and GED is accepted. Institution is test-optional for entering Fall 2024. Check admissions website for updates. *Academic units required:* 4 English, 4 math, 2 science, 2 foreign language, 1 social studies. *Academic units recommended:* 4 science, 4 foreign language, 3 social studies.

Financial Aid

Students should submit: CSS/Financial Aid Profile; FAFSA. *Need-based scholarships/grants offered:* College/university scholarship or grant aid from institutional funds; Federal Nursing Scholarships; Federal Pell; Private scholarships; SEOG; State scholarships/grants. *Loan aid offered:* Direct PLUS loans; Direct Subsidized Loans; Direct Unsubsidized Loans. Federal Work-Study Program available. Institutional employment available.

Campus Life

Activities: Choral groups; Concert band; Dance; Drama/theater; International Student Organization; Jazz band; Literary magazine; Marching band; Model UN; Music ensembles; Musical theater; Opera; Pep band; Radio station; Student government; Student newspaper; Student-run film society; Symphony orchestra; Television station; Yearbook. **Organizations:** 7 honor societies, 40 fraternities, 22 sororities. **Athletics (Intercollegiate):** *Men:* baseball, basketball, crew/rowing, cross-country, cycling, equestrian sports, field hockey, golf, gymnastics, ice hockey, lacrosse, martial arts, racquetball, rugby, swimming, table tennis, track/field (indoor), ultimate frisbee, volleyball, water polo, wrestling. *Women:* basketball, crew/rowing, cross-country, cycling, equestrian sports, field hockey, golf, gymnastics, ice hockey, lacrosse, martial arts, racquetball, rugby, softball, swimming, table tennis, track/field (indoor), ultimate frisbee, volleyball, water polo.

CAMPUS
Type of school	Public
Environment	City

STUDENTS
Undergrad enrollment	16,951
% male/female	43/57
% from out of state	30
% frosh live on campus	100

FINANCIAL FACTS
Annual in-state tuition	$19,023
Annual out-of-state tuition	$55,483
Room and board	$13,600
Required fees	$4,183

GENERAL ADMISSIONS INFO
Application fee	$75
Regular application deadline	1/1
Nonfall registration	No
Fall 2024 testing policy	Test Optional
Range SAT EBRW	690–750
Range SAT Math	710–738
Range ACT Composite	32–34

ACADEMICS
Student/faculty ratio	14:1
% students returning for sophomore year	97

Most classes have 10–19 students.

Virginia

REQUESTING SERVICES FOR STUDENTS WITH LEARNING DIFFERENCES

Phone: 434-243-5180 • studenthealth.virginia.edu/sdac • Email: sdac@virginia.edu

Documentation submitted to: Student Disability Access Center

Separate application required for Services: Yes

Documentation required for:
LD: Psychoeducational evaluation
ADHD: Psychoeducational evaluation
ASD: Psychoeducational evaluation

Virginia Tech

925 Prices Fork Road, Blacksburg, VA 24061 Admissions: 540-231-6267 • www.vt.edu

Support: S

ACCOMMODATIONS

Allowed in exams:

Calculators	Yes
Dictionary	Yes
Computer	Yes
Spell-checker	Yes
Extended test time	Yes
Scribe	Yes
Proctors	Yes
Oral exams	Yes
Note-takers	Yes

Support services for students with:

LD	No
ADHD	No
ASD	No
Distraction-reduced environment	Yes
Recording of lecture allowed	Yes
Reading technology	Yes
Audio books	Yes
Other assistive technology	Yes
Priority registration	No

Added costs of services:

For LD	No
For ADHD	No
For ASD	No
LD specialists	No
ADHD & ASD coaching	No
ASD specialists	No
Professional tutors	Yes
Peer tutors	Yes
Max. hours/week for services	Varies
How professors are notified of student approved accommodations	Student

COLLEGE GRADUATION REQUIREMENTS

Course waivers allowed	No
Course substitutions allowed	No

PROGRAMS/SERVICES FOR STUDENTS WITH LEARNING DIFFERENCES

Services for Students with Disabilities (SSD) works with students to provide services such as academic coaching, assistive technology, classroom accommodations, outreach, education, advocacy, and consultations. Students must complete the online form for requesting accommodations and may be required to provide documentation of their disability. Students should contact the SSD office to schedule an appointment if they have concerns or questions about the required documentation. After reviewing the documentation, the SSD staff will schedule a follow-up consultation to determine possible accommodations and next steps. Accommodations and services are determined on an individual basis.

ADMISSIONS

All applicants are expected to meet the same admission criteria. Some majors have other requirements, such as an additional year of advanced math or lab science. Most students who are selected for admission have completed more than the minimum requirements and have at least a B+ grade point average. The admission review is holistic and includes the rigor of the academic curriculum, grades, ethnicity, leadership, service, legacy, major, and personal statements.

Additional Information

The Student Success Center's Academic Services helps students become autonomous, successful learners by offering a variety of programs and services. The free, peer-led programming includes course-specific tutoring and generalized academic skill-building with topics such as overcoming procrastination, effective learning strategies, test-taking skills, and time management. Staff members are available to meet with students individually to help design a plan for success and provide academic counseling that meets individual needs.

DID YOU KNOW?

The problem of concussions in contact sports has been gaining attention since 2003. In 2009, V-Tech's Athletics equipment manager asked Stefan Duma, a professor in the Department of Biomedical Engineering and Mechanics, what helmets to buy the football team. At that time, there were no standards. Two years later, his lab published the first independent safety ratings for varsity football helmets. Ten years later, the V-Tech Helmet Lab rates protective headgear for six sports, with more to come.

Virginia Tech

GENERAL ADMISSIONS

Very important factors include: rigor of secondary school record, academic GPA, application essay. *Other factors considered include:* standardized test scores (if submitted). High school diploma is required and GED is not accepted. Institution is test-flexible for entering Fall 2024. Check admissions website for updates. *Academic units required:* 4 English, 3 math, 2 science (2 labs), 1 social studies, 1 history, 3 academic electives. *Academic units recommended:* 4 math, 3 science (3 labs), 3 foreign language.

FINANCIAL AID

Students should submit: FAFSA. *Need-based scholarships/grants offered:* College/university scholarship or grant aid from institutional funds; Federal Pell; Private scholarships; SEOG; State scholarships/grants; United Negro College Fund. *Loan aid offered:* Direct PLUS loans; Direct Subsidized Loans; Direct Unsubsidized Loans. Federal Work-Study Program available. Institutional employment available.

CAMPUS LIFE

Activities: Campus Ministries; Choral groups; Concert band; Dance; Drama/theater; International Student Organization; Jazz band; Literary magazine; Marching band; Model UN; Music ensembles; Musical theater; Opera; Pep band; Radio station; Student government; Student newspaper; Student-run film society; Symphony orchestra; Television station; Yearbook. **Organizations:** 800 registered organizations, 37 honor societies, 58 religious organizations, 27 fraternities, 20 sororities. **Athletics (Intercollegiate):** *Men:* baseball, basketball, bowling, crew/rowing, cross-country, cycling, equestrian sports, field hockey, golf, gymnastics, ice hockey, lacrosse, rugby, swimming, track/field (indoor), volleyball, water polo, wrestling. *Women:* basketball, bowling, crew/rowing, cross-country, cycling, equestrian sports, field hockey, golf, gymnastics, lacrosse, rugby, softball, swimming, track/field (indoor), volleyball, water polo.

CAMPUS	
Type of school	Public
Environment	Town

STUDENTS	
Undergrad enrollment	30,277
% male/female	57/43
% from out of state	29
% frosh live on campus	99

FINANCIAL FACTS	
Annual in-state tuition	$12,104
Annual out-of-state tuition	$31,754
Room and board	$14,490
Required fees	$2,482

GENERAL ADMISSIONS INFO	
Application fee	$60
Regular application deadline	3/15
Nonfall registration	Yes

Fall 2024 testing policy	Test Flexible
Range SAT EBRW	610–700
Range SAT Math	610–720
Range ACT Composite	26–32

ACADEMICS	
Student/faculty ratio	17:1
% students returning for sophomore year	91
Most classes have 10–19 students.	

Virginia

REQUESTING SERVICES FOR STUDENTS WITH LEARNING DIFFERENCES

Phone: 540-231-3788 • www.ssd.vt.edu • Email: ssd@vt.edu

Documentation submitted to: Services for Students with Disabilities
Separate application required for Services: Yes

Documentation required for:
LD: Psychoeducational evaluation
ADHD: Psychoeducational evaluation
ASD: Psychoeducational evaluation

William & Mary

Office of Admissions, Williamsburg, VA 23187-8795 • Admissions: 757-221-4223 • www.wm.edu

Support: CS

ACCOMMODATIONS

Allowed in exams:

Calculators	Yes
Dictionary	Yes
Computer	Yes
Spell-checker	Yes
Extended test time	Yes
Scribe	Yes
Proctors	Yes
Oral exams	Yes
Note-takers	Yes

Support services for students with:

LD	Yes
ADHD	Yes
ASD	Yes
Distraction-reduced environment	Yes
Recording of lecture allowed	Yes
Reading technology	Yes
Audio books	Yes
Other assistive technology	Yes
Priority registration	Yes

Added costs of services:

For LD	No
For ADHD	No
For ASD	No
LD specialists	No
ADHD & ASD coaching	Yes
ASD specialists	Yes
Professional tutors	Yes
Peer tutors	Yes
Max. hours/week for services	Varies
How professors are notified of student approved accommodations	Student

COLLEGE GRADUATION REQUIREMENTS

Course waivers allowed	No
Course substitutions allowed	Yes
In what courses: Case-by-case basis	

PROGRAMS/SERVICES FOR STUDENTS WITH LEARNING DIFFERENCES

William and Mary's Student Accessibility Service (SAS) provides support and accommodations to students with disabilities. Through accommodative resources and individualized support, students become self-advocates and gain the strategies for academic success. To register for accommodations, students complete the online form, submit documentation, and schedule a meeting with the SAS staff. Accommodative services and tools are available in alignment with ADA requirements.

ADMISSIONS

All students complete the regular application process to be considered for admission. For students submitting scores, the middle 50 percent have SAT scores of 1380–1520 or ACT scores of 32–34. The middle 50 percent of accepted students have a weighted GPA of 4.1–4.5. For performing arts applicants, supplemental information detailing their talent or skills is encouraged. Students may disclose their disability to provide a full perspective of academic and social challenges. The process for acquiring accommodations begins after receiving an acceptance.

Additional Information

TutorZone is a free on-campus resource available to all students at William & Mary. The purpose of TutorZone is to contribute to student retention and academic achievement, coordinate the services of well-qualified and trained peer tutors, and assist students with the development of independent learning skills. Each student receives individualized support. Other available services include academic coaching, time management tools, and consultations to review study skills.

In 1693, King William III and Queen Mary II granted a royal charter to "their majesties'" Royal College of William & Mary, the only institution of higher learning to receive its charter from the Crown and its coat of arms from the College of Heralds. The Wren Building, completed in 1699, is the oldest college building still standing in the U.S. It was used for classrooms, a library, a dining hall, and a chapel for generations and is still used for classes. Thomas Jefferson called the Wren Building a "rude misshapen pile." He had plans to improve and expand the building, but construction was halted by the advent of the Revolutionary War.

William & Mary

GENERAL ADMISSIONS
Very important factors include: rigor of secondary school record, class rank, academic GPA, standardized test scores (if submitted), application essay, recommendations. High school diploma or equivalent is not required. Institution is test optional for entering Fall 2024. Check admissions website for updates. *Academic units recommended:* 4 English, 4 math, 4 science (3 labs), 4 foreign language, 4 social studies.

FINANCIAL AID
Students should submit: CSS/Financial Aid Profile; FAFSA. *Need-based scholarships/grants offered:* College/university scholarship or grant aid from institutional funds; Federal Pell; Private scholarships; SEOG; State scholarships/grants. *Loan aid offered:* Direct PLUS loans; Direct Subsidized Loans; Direct Unsubsidized Loans. Federal Work-Study Program available. Institutional employment available.

CAMPUS LIFE
Activities: Campus Ministries; Choral groups; Concert band; Dance; Drama/theater; International Student Organization; Jazz band; Literary magazine; Model UN; Music ensembles; Musical theater; Opera; Pep band; Radio station; Student government; Student newspaper; Student-run film society; Symphony orchestra; Television station; Yearbook. **Organizations:** 485 registered organizations, 30 honor societies, 25 religious organizations, 18 fraternities, 14 sororities. **Athletics (Intercollegiate):** *Men:* baseball, basketball, crew/rowing, cross-country, cycling, equestrian sports, golf, gymnastics, ice hockey, lacrosse, racquetball, rugby, swimming, track/field (indoor), volleyball. *Women:* baseball, basketball, crew/rowing, cross-country, cycling, equestrian sports, field hockey, golf, gymnastics, ice hockey, lacrosse, martial arts, racquetball, rugby, softball, swimming, table tennis, track/field (indoor), ultimate frisbee, volleyball, water polo.

CAMPUS

Type of school	Public
Environment	Town

STUDENTS

Undergrad enrollment	6,778
% male/female	42/58
% from out of state	32
% frosh live on campus	99

FINANCIAL FACTS

Annual in-state tuition	$17,434
Annual out-of-state tuition	$40,089
Room and board	$13,534
Required fees	$6,536

GENERAL ADMISSIONS INFO

Application fee	$75
Regular application deadline	1/1
Nonfall registration	No

Fall 2024 testing policy	Test Optional
Range SAT EBRW	695–750
Range SAT Math	680–770
Range ACT Composite	32–34

ACADEMICS

Student/faculty ratio	13:1
% students returning for sophomore year	95
Most classes have 10–19 students.	

Virginia

REQUESTING SERVICES FOR STUDENTS WITH LEARNING DIFFERENCES

Phone: 757-221-2512 • www.wm.edu/sas • Email: sas@wm.edu

Documentation submitted to: Student Accessibility Services
Separate application required for Services: Yes

Documentation required for:
LD: Psychoeducational evaluation
ADHD: Psychoeducational evaluation
ASD: Psychoeducational evaluation

Bellevue College

3000 Landerholm Circle SE, Bellevue, WA 98007-6484 • Admissions: 425-564-1000 • bellevuecollege.edu

Support: CS

ACCOMMODATIONS

Allowed in exams:

Calculators	Yes
Dictionary	Yes
Computer	Yes
Spell-checker	Yes
Extended test time	Yes
Scribe	Yes
Proctors	Yes
Oral exams	Yes
Note-takers	Yes

Support services for students with:

LD	Yes
ADHD	Yes
ASD	Yes
Distraction-reduced environment	Yes
Recording of lecture allowed	Yes
Reading technology	Yes
Audio books	Yes
Other assistive technology	Yes
Priority registration	Yes

Added costs of services:

For LD	No
For ADHD	No
For ASD	No
LD specialists	Yes
ADHD & ASD coaching	Yes
ASD specialists	Yes
Professional tutors	No
Peer tutors	Yes
Max. hours/week for services	Varies
How professors are notified of student approved accommodations	Student

COLLEGE GRADUATION REQUIREMENTS

Course waivers allowed	Yes
In what courses: Varies	
Course substitutions allowed	Yes
In what courses: Varies	

PROGRAMS/SERVICES FOR STUDENTS WITH LEARNING DIFFERENCES

The Disability Resource Center (DRC) provides academic accommodations to students with disabilities. Once students are accepted and complete the New Student Orientation, they must register with DRC to begin the Disability Access Process. Registration, along with a scheduled access meeting, serves as the main source of information to determine accommodations. Additional information regarding documentation will be requested as needed. The Neurodiversity Navigators program offers advocacy, educational opportunities, and services for neurodivergent students. Bellevue College connects their students with peer mentors from nearby universities who plan to enter fields of work with neurodivergent people. Students who seek to accelerate their growth in the science, technology, engineering, and math (STEM) fields can do so via the Disabled Students Navigating STEM (DSNS) program. Both Neurodiversity Navigators and DSNS are cohort programs under the RISE Learning Institute at Bellevue College.

ADMISSIONS

All applicants are required to submit transcripts showing the completion of high school, GED certificate, or state-authorized homeschool letter of completion. Applicants can self-certify on the application. Some of Bellevue's associate degree or certificate programs may have additional entrance requirements.

Additional Information

All new students are required to take First-Year Seminar (FYS) 101, a 3 credit, first semester course as a guide to transitioning to college life. Through workshops, self-assessments, and campus engagement, students explore their strengths and interests, develop their social and academic skills, and set long-term educational and career goals. The Academic Success Center (ASC) offers free drop-in, scheduled, and e-tutoring for all students. Additional academic support is available in the form of workshops and educational resources. The Math and Writing labs offer tutoring and specialized labs, as well as reading instruction. The Reading Lab is a 1 or 2 credit lab course that supports students who find college reading challenging, and focuses on reading comprehension, speed, and vocabulary.

Art is everywhere: In 1969, John Cope gifted the beautiful fountain sculpture by well-known, contemporary northwest sculptor John Geise, that accents the central point of campus. In 1973, a Seattle 1% Ordinance for Art allowed for beautiful public art installations across campus.

Bellevue College

GENERAL ADMISSIONS
Institution is test-optional for entering Fall 2024. Check admissions website for updates. Bellevue College is an open admissions institution.

FINANCIAL AID
Students should submit: FAFSA. *Need-based scholarships/grants offered:* College/university scholarship or grant aid from institutional funds; Federal Pell; Private scholarships; SEOG; State scholarships/grants. *Loan aid offered:* Direct PLUS loans; Direct Subsidized Loans; Direct Unsubsidized Loans. Federal Work-Study Program available. Institutional employment available.

CAMPUS LIFE
Organizations: 59 registered organizations, 2 honor societies.

CAMPUS	
Type of school	Public
Environment	City

STUDENTS	
Undergrad enrollment	11,546
% male/female	43/57
% from out of state	3

FINANCIAL FACTS	
Annual in-state tuition	$4,159
Annual out-of-state tuition	$9,838
Room and board	$17,952

GENERAL ADMISSIONS INFO	
Application fee	$66
Regular application deadline	Rolling
Nonfall registration	Yes
Fall 2024 testing policy	Test Optional

ACADEMICS	
Student/faculty ratio	16:1

REQUESTING SERVICES FOR STUDENTS WITH LEARNING DIFFERENCES

Phone: 425-564-2498 • www.bellevuecollege.edu/drc/ • Email: drc@bellevuecollege.edu

Documentation submitted to: Disability Resource Center
Separate application required for Services: Yes

Documentation required for:
LD: Psychoeducational evaluation
ADHD: Psychoeducational evaluation
ASD: Psychoeducational evaluation

Washington

Eastern Washington University

304 Sutton Hall, Cheney, WA 99004 • Admissions: 509-359-6692 • www.ewu.edu

Support: S

ACCOMMODATIONS

Allowed in exams:

Calculators	Yes
Dictionary	Yes
Computer	Yes
Spell-checker	Yes
Extended test time	Yes
Scribe	Yes
Proctors	Yes
Oral exams	Yes
Note-takers	Yes

Support services for students with:

LD	Yes
ADHD	Yes
ASD	Yes
Distraction-reduced environment	Yes
Recording of lecture allowed	Yes
Reading technology	Yes
Audio books	Yes
Other assistive technology	Yes
Priority registration	No

Added costs of services:

For LD	No
For ADHD	No
For ASD	No
LD specialists	No
ADHD & ASD coaching	No
ASD specialists	No
Professional tutors	Yes
Peer tutors	Yes
Max. hours/week for services	Varies
How professors are notified of student approved accommodations	Student and SASS

COLLEGE GRADUATION REQUIREMENTS

Course waivers allowed	No
Course substitutions allowed	No

PROGRAMS/SERVICES FOR STUDENTS WITH LEARNING DIFFERENCES

Student Accommodations and Support Services (SASS) deliver services and accommodations to students with disabilities. Students must register with SASS by completing the accommodation application, submitting documentation, and scheduling an intake appointment. Services and accommodations for students with specific learning disabilities and ADHD may include alternate-format textbooks, notetakers, Kurzweil reader, access to taped lectures, testing accommodations like oral exams and extended time, informal counseling, tutoring, and referral to the learning skills center, writing center, or mathematics lab. The university encourages students to apply for funding through resource agencies that assist with specific disabilities.

ADMISSIONS

Admission criteria are the same for all students. Automatic admission is granted to applicants with a cumulative GPA of 3.0 or greater on a 4.0 scale who have also completed the required academic courses. It is also required that applicants take a math-based quantitative course in their senior year unless they have taken and passed pre-calculus, math analysis, or calculus prior to their senior year. Students with a minimum GPA of 2.0 will be considered for admission in the context of the rigor of their coursework, including the senior year course schedule.

Additional Information

First Year Experience (FYE) is a series of courses to help first-years successfully transition to university life and develop skills in time management, goal setting, and academic planning. Students meet weekly with a student success advisor, and FYE courses count toward the Breadth Area Core Requirements (BACR) at EWU.

DID YOU KNOW?

The 41,000-square-foot Jim Thorpe Fieldhouse is the star of the Sports & Recreation Center and can be configured for physical activity classes, athletic practices, intramural sports, ROTC, and special events. The Fieldhouse is named in honor of Jim Thorpe, one of the most versatile athletes of modern sports, having won Olympic gold medals in both the pentathlon and decathlon.

Eastern Washington University

GENERAL ADMISSIONS

Very important factors include: academic GPA. *Important factors include:* rigor of secondary school record, application essay. *Other factors considered include:* recommendations. High school diploma or equivalent is not required. Institution is test-free for entering Fall 2024. Check admissions website for updates. *Academic units required:* 4 English, 3 math, 3 science (3 labs), 2 foreign language, 3 social studies, 1 visual/performing arts.

FINANCIAL AID

Students should submit: FAFSA. *Need-based scholarships/grants offered:* College/university scholarship or grant aid from institutional funds; Federal Pell; Private scholarships; SEOG; State scholarships/grants. *Loan aid offered:* Direct PLUS loans; Direct Subsidized Loans; Direct Unsubsidized Loans. Federal Work-Study Program available. Institutional employment available.

CAMPUS LIFE

Activities: Campus Ministries; Choral groups; Concert band; Dance; Drama/theater; International Student Organization; Jazz band; Literary magazine; Marching band; Model UN; Music ensembles; Musical theater; Pep band; Radio station; Student government; Student newspaper; Student-run film society; Symphony orchestra. **Organizations:** 99 registered organizations, 9 honor societies, 12 religious organizations, 9 fraternities, 11 sororities. **Athletics (Intercollegiate):** *Men:* baseball, basketball, bowling, cross-country, equestrian sports, golf, ice hockey, martial arts, racquetball, rugby, softball, track/field (indoor), ultimate frisbee, volleyball, wrestling. *Women:* basketball, bowling, cross-country, equestrian sports, golf, ice hockey, martial arts, racquetball, rugby, softball, track/field (indoor), ultimate frisbee, volleyball, wrestling.

CAMPUS

Type of school	Public
Environment	Town

STUDENTS

Undergrad enrollment	8,217
% male/female	43/57
% from out of state	7
% frosh live on campus	68

FINANCIAL FACTS

Annual in-state tuition	$6,896
Annual out-of-state tuition	$24,722
Room and board	$13,060
Required fees	$1,026

GENERAL ADMISSIONS INFO

Application fee	$60
Regular application deadline	5/15, 7/1
	for Transfers
Nonfall registration	Yes
Fall 2024 testing policy	Test Free

ACADEMICS

Student/faculty ratio	20:1
% students returning for sophomore year	67

Most classes have 10–19 students.

REQUESTING SERVICES FOR STUDENTS WITH LEARNING DIFFERENCES

Phone: 509-359-6871 • inside.ewu.edu/sass • Email: sass@ewu.edu

Documentation submitted to: Student Accommodations and Support Services
Separate application required for Services: Yes

Documentation required for:
LD: Psychoeducational evaluation
ADHD: Psychoeducational evaluation
ASD: Psychoeducational evaluation

The Evergreen State College

2700 Evergreen Parkway NW, Olympia, WA 98505 • Admissions: 360-867-6170 • www.evergreen.edu

ACCOMMODATIONS

Allowed in exams:

Calculators	Yes
Dictionary	Yes
Computer	Yes
Spell-checker	Yes
Extended test time	Yes
Scribe	No
Proctors	No
Oral exams	No
Note-takers	Yes

Support services for students with:

LD	Yes
ADHD	Yes
ASD	Yes
Distraction-reduced environment	Yes
Recording of lecture allowed	Yes
Reading technology	Yes
Audio books	Yes
Other assistive technology	Yes
Priority registration	Yes

Added costs of services:

For LD	No
For ADHD	No
For ASD	No
LD specialists	Yes
ADHD & ASD coaching	Yes
ASD specialists	No
Professional tutors	No
Peer tutors	Yes
Max. hours/week for services	Varies
How professors are notified of student approved accommodations	Student and Access Services

COLLEGE GRADUATION REQUIREMENTS

Course waivers allowed	No
Course substitutions allowed	No

PROGRAMS/SERVICES FOR STUDENTS WITH LEARNING DIFFERENCES

To request accommodations and services through the Access Services office, students must complete the request for services form and upload documentation of their disability. Once the application is completed, the director will meet with students to review their information and determine reasonable and appropriate accommodations. New students are advised to start this process once they have confirmed admission to Evergreen. Accommodation requests must be updated quarterly. Accommodations for students with disabilities may include alternate media, alternative testing, access to the assistive technology lab, books on tape services, notetakers, peer support and advocacy, priority registration, and tutorial assistance through the TRiO Student Success office, where students can take advantage of free, one-on-one tutoring sessions in subject areas such as math, science, computing, or foreign languages. Types of assistive technology available include screen readers or text-to-speech software, speech recognition or speech-to-text software, executive function support software, screen magnifier software, and Daisy Reader software and hardware.

ADMISSIONS

Students entering Evergreen directly from high school must complete a college preparatory course load. Students receive a decision two weeks after applying. The Tacoma Program is a full-time course of study for students who have completed at least 90 transferable college credits.

Additional Information

TRiO Student Success offers several 2 credit courses, weekly workshops, lectures, seminars, and guest speakers throughout the academic year that help new students achieve success at Evergreen.

Speedy the Geoduck is Evergreen's Mascot. Speedy's been regularly listed and called the worst or possibly the best, the weirdest, the most baffling, ridiculous, interesting, somewhat strange but awesome mascot by multiple media outlets. Pronounced "gooey-duck", a geoduck is a clam that's too big for its shell, native to the region, and its local tribal meaning is "dig deep." Speedy the Geoduck thinks of himself as the essence of Evergreen: accessible to all who are willing to dig deep.

The Evergreen State College

GENERAL ADMISSIONS

Very important factors include: rigor of secondary school record, academic GPA. *Important factors include:* standardized test scores (if submitted). *Other factors considered include:* application essay, recommendations. High school diploma is required and GED is accepted. Institution is test-optional for entering Fall 2024. Check admissions website for updates. *Academic units required:* 4 English, 3 math, 2 science (2 labs), 2 foreign language, 3 social studies.

FINANCIAL AID

Students should submit: FAFSA. *Need-based scholarships/grants offered:* College/university scholarship or grant aid from institutional funds; Federal Pell; Private scholarships; SEOG; State scholarships/grants. *Loan aid offered:* Direct PLUS loans; Direct Subsidized Loans; Direct Unsubsidized Loans. Federal Work-Study Program available. Institutional employment available.

CAMPUS LIFE

Activities: Campus Ministries; Choral groups; Dance; Drama/theater; Jazz band; Literary magazine; Music ensembles; Radio station; Student government; Student newspaper; Student-run film society; Television station. **Athletics (Intercollegiate):** *Men:* basketball, track/field (indoor), volleyball. *Women:* basketball, volleyball.

CAMPUS
Type of school	Public
Environment	City

STUDENTS
Undergrad enrollment	1,811
% male/female	39/61
% from out of state	14
% frosh live on campus	62

FINANCIAL FACTS
Annual in-state tuition	$8,750
Annual out-of-state tuition	$30,059
Room and board	$13,806

GENERAL ADMISSIONS INFO
Application fee	$50
Regular application deadline	Rolling
Nonfall registration	Yes
Fall 2024 testing policy	Test Optional
Range SAT EBRW	510–640
Range SAT math	470–580
Range ACT composite	22–29

ACADEMICS
Student/faculty ratio	17:1
% students returning for sophomore year	65

Most classes have 20–29 students.

REQUESTING SERVICES FOR STUDENTS WITH LEARNING DIFFERENCES

Phone: 360-867-6348 • www.evergreen.edu/access/ • Email: accessservices@evergreen.edu

Documentation submitted to: Access Services
Separate application required for Services: Yes

Documentation required for:
LD: Psychoeducational evaluation
ADHD: Psychoeducational evaluation
ASD: Psychoeducational evaluation

Washington

Washington State University

P.O. Box 641067, Pullman, WA 99164-1067 • Admissions: 509-335-5586 • www.wsu.edu

Support: CS

ACCOMMODATIONS

Allowed in exams:

Calculators	Yes
Dictionary	Yes
Computer	Yes
Spell-checker	Yes
Extended test time	Yes
Scribe	Yes
Proctors	Yes
Oral exams	Yes
Note-takers	Yes

Support services for students with:

LD	Yes
ADHD	Yes
ASD	Yes
Distraction-reduced environment	Yes
Recording of lecture allowed	Yes
Reading technology	Yes
Audio books	Yes
Other assistive technology	Yes
Priority registration	Yes

Added costs of services:

For LD	No
For ADHD	No
For ASD	No
LD specialists	No
ADHD & ASD coaching	No
ASD specialists	No
Professional tutors	No
Peer tutors	Yes
Max. hours/week for services	Varies
How professors are notified of student approved accommodations	Student

COLLEGE GRADUATION REQUIREMENTS

Course waivers allowed	No
Course substitutions allowed	No

PROGRAMS/SERVICES FOR STUDENTS WITH LEARNING DIFFERENCES

The Access Center (AC) provides academic accommodations for students with disabilities. To be eligible for assistance, students must be enrolled at Washington State University and submit documentation of their disability. AC may also refer students to other service programs for academic support. The MYAccess (AIM) portal system enables students to request accommodations online and gives students direct access to professors when requesting accommodations. All academic adjustments are authorized on an individual basis. The Access Center Proctoring Office implements testing accommodations. Typical academic adjustments include notetakers, class recordings, alternative testing, extended time for exams, the use of computers with voice output, and spell-checkers. WSU offers ROAR (Responsibility Opportunity Advocacy and Respect), a two-year inclusive postsecondary education program for students with intellectual and developmental disabilities. ROAR includes individualized programs of study with social skills classes and vocational training. Students live on the Pullman campus and complete WSU audit courses with same-aged peers. ROAR is an approved Comprehensive Transition and Postsecondary (CTP) program through the U.S. Department of Education.

ADMISSIONS

Admission requirements are the same for all applicants. Students must have a 2.0 GPA for admission. Students who rank in the top 10 percent of their class or have at least a 3.6 GPA are assured admission to Washington State University. For those students who submit scores, the middle 50 percent of admitted applicants have an ACT score of 20–28 and an SAT score of 1020–1210.

Additional Information

The Academic Success and Career Center offers academic coaching and tutoring services.

Edward R. Murrow, a 1930 WSU alum, began his career broadcasting live radio from London rooftops during WWII air raids. He took listeners to places and experiences they could never imagine. Cartoonist Gary Larson graduated from WSU's Edward R. Murrow College of Communication in 1972. His The Far Side comics ran from 1980-1995 and were syndicated in over 1,900 newspapers. His cartoons were celebrated for their irreverence.

Washington State University

GENERAL ADMISSIONS

Very important factors include: academic GPA. *Important factors include:* rigor of secondary school record, class rank. *Other factors considered include:* application essay, recommendations. High school diploma is required and GED is accepted. Institution is test-free for entering Fall 2024. Check admissions website for updates. *Academic units required:* 4 English, 3 math, 2 science, 2 foreign language, 3 social studies, 1 visual/performing arts. *Academic units recommended:* 4 math.

FINANCIAL AID

Students should submit: FAFSA; State aid form. *Need-based scholarships/grants offered:* College/university scholarship or grant aid from institutional funds; Federal Pell; Private scholarships; SEOG; State scholarships/grants. *Loan aid offered:* Direct PLUS loans; Direct Subsidized Loans; Direct Unsubsidized Loans. Federal Work-Study Program available. Institutional employment available.

CAMPUS LIFE

Activities: Campus Ministries; Choral groups; Concert band; Dance; Drama/theater; International Student Organization; Jazz band; Literary magazine; Marching band; Model UN; Music ensembles; Musical theater; Opera; Pep band; Radio station; Student government; Student newspaper; Student-run film society; Symphony orchestra; Television station; Yearbook. **Organizations:** 450 registered organizations, 10 honor societies, 23 religious organizations, 24 fraternities, 14 sororities. **Athletics (Intercollegiate):** *Men:* baseball, basketball, bowling, crew/rowing, cross-country, cycling, golf, ice hockey, lacrosse, martial arts, rugby, track/field (indoor), ultimate frisbee, volleyball, wrestling. *Women:* basketball, bowling, crew/rowing, cross-country, cycling, equestrian sports, golf, ice hockey, lacrosse, martial arts, rugby, softball, swimming, track/field (indoor), ultimate frisbee, volleyball, water polo.

CAMPUS
Type of school	Public
Environment	Town

STUDENTS
Undergrad enrollment	22,256
% male/female	47/53
% from out of state	15
% frosh live on campus	81

FINANCIAL FACTS
Annual in-state tuition	$10,708
Annual out-of-state tuition	$26,392
Room and board	$12,396
Required fees	$1,993

GENERAL ADMISSIONS INFO
Application fee	$70
Regular application deadline	Rolling
Nonfall registration	Yes
Fall 2024 testing policy	Test Free

ACADEMICS
Student/faculty ratio	15:1
% students returning for sophomore year	81
Most classes have 20–29 students.	

REQUESTING SERVICES FOR STUDENTS WITH LEARNING DIFFERENCES

Phone: 509-335-3417 • accesscenter.wsu.edu/ • Email: access.center@wsu.edu

Documentation submitted to: Access Center, Division of Student Affairs
Separate application required for Services: Yes

Documentation required for:
LD: Psychoeducational evaluation
ADHD: Psychoeducational evaluation
ASD: Psychoeducational evaluation

Washington

Whitman College

345 Boyer Avenue, Walla Walla, WA 99362 • Admissions: 509-527-5176 • www.whitman.edu

Support: S

ACCOMMODATIONS

Allowed in exams:

Calculators	Yes
Dictionary	Yes
Computer	Yes
Spell-checker	Yes
Extended test time	Yes
Scribe	Yes
Proctors	Yes
Oral exams	Yes
Note-takers	Yes

Support services for students with:

LD	No
ADHD	No
ASD	No
Distraction-reduced environment	Yes
Recording of lecture allowed	Yes
Reading technology	Yes
Audio books	Yes
Other assistive technology	Yes
Priority registration	Yes

Added costs of services:

For LD	No
For ADHD	No
For ASD	No
LD specialists	No
ADHD & ASD coaching	Yes
ASD specialists	No
Professional tutors	No
Peer tutors	Yes
Max. hours/week for services	Varies
How professors are notified of student approved accommodations	Academic Resource Center

COLLEGE GRADUATION REQUIREMENTS

Course waivers allowed	Yes
In what courses: Varies	
Course substitutions allowed	Yes
In what courses: Varies	

PROGRAMS/SERVICES FOR STUDENTS WITH LEARNING DIFFERENCES

Whitman college provides services to students with learning disabilities through the Academic Resource Center (ARC). In order to receive accommodations, students must complete an application, provide documentation, and reach out to the director. Once a student is approved for accommodations, their professors are notified by email. Students who have disclosed their differences or disabilities to ARC receive formal check-ins from the center during the summer, prior to the start of classes, and a few weeks into the semester. ARC has an alert system that notifies the staff if a student is struggling; ARC and the student can then review whether modifications to accommodations or additional supports are needed. ARC has a tutoring center, which is one of the many open-access spaces where students can work, take tests, and get support. ARC also offers individualized peer tutoring and one-on-one academic coaching sessions. Sessions can cover goal setting, executive functioning support, time management, reading and study strategies, and how to overcome procrastination. DisCo (Disability & Difference Community) is a student-led group that allows students with disabilities to support and connect with one another on the topic of disability as it relates to identity.

ADMISSIONS

All applicants are expected to meet the same admission criteria. Applicants who are homeschooled or attended secondary schools with written evaluations in lieu of grades are strongly encouraged to submit ACT or SAT scores. All submitted test scores are superscored.

Additional Information

There is no foreign language requirement for Whitman undergraduates. The quantitative skills or math requirement can be fulfilled in various ways. If these ways still present an insurmountable challenge, the student can discuss the possibility of a math waiver with faculty and staff. An additional source of support for all students is the Center for Writing and Speaking (COWS). COWS offers one-on-one consultations, workshops, group writing hours, and peer-generated feedback via writing course assistants. The Whitman chapter of Eye to Eye aims to improve the educational experiences and outcomes for neurodiverse young people by bringing together middle school students and their college-aged allies in a supervised, school-based setting, and empowering each other to think and learn differently.

The Memorial Building is the oldest and tallest building on campus. The clock in the building's tower has rung ever since the building was constructed in 1899, except for a few months in 2010 for a seismic retrofitting project. The clock sounds 180 times per day. This landmark can be both heard and seen around campus; the tower is visible through the treetops.

Whitman College

GENERAL ADMISSIONS

Very important factors include: rigor of secondary school record, academic GPA, application essay. *Important factors include:* recommendations. *Other factors considered include:* class rank, standardized test scores (if submitted). High school diploma is required and GED is accepted. Institution is test-optional for entering Fall 2024. Check admissions website for updates. *Academic units recommended:* 4 English, 4 math, 3 science (3 labs), 2 foreign language, 3 social studies, 1 visual/performing arts.

FINANCIAL AID

Students should submit: CSS/Financial Aid Profile; FAFSA; Noncustodial Profile. *Need-based scholarships/grants offered:* College/university scholarship or grant aid from institutional funds; Federal Pell; Private scholarships; SEOG; State scholarships/grants. *Loan aid offered:* Direct PLUS loans; Direct Subsidized Loans; Direct Unsubsidized Loans. Federal Work-Study Program available. Institutional employment available.

CAMPUS LIFE

Activities: Campus Ministries; Choral groups; Concert band; Dance; Drama/theater; International Student Organization; Jazz band; Literary magazine; Model UN; Music ensembles; Musical theater; Radio station; Student government; Student newspaper; Student-run film society; Symphony orchestra; Yearbook. **Organizations:** 147 registered organizations, 3 honor societies, 4 religious organizations, 4 fraternities, 4 sororities. **Athletics (Intercollegiate):** *Men:* baseball, basketball, cross-country, cycling, golf, lacrosse, martial arts, rugby, skiing (nordic/cross-country), swimming, ultimate frisbee, volleyball, water polo. *Women:* basketball, cross-country, cycling, golf, lacrosse, martial arts, rugby, skiing (nordic/cross-country), softball, swimming, ultimate frisbee, volleyball, water polo.

CAMPUS
Type of school	Private (nonprofit)
Environment	Town

STUDENTS
Undergrad enrollment	1,560
% male/female	44/56
% from out of state	64
% frosh live on campus	100

FINANCIAL FACTS
Annual tuition	$55,560
Room and board	$13,800
Required fees	$422

GENERAL ADMISSIONS INFO
Application fee	$50
Regular application deadline	1/15
Nonfall registration	No

Fall 2024 testing policy	Test Optional
Range SAT EBRW	645–725
Range SAT Math	620–730
Range ACT Composite	29–33

ACADEMICS
Student/faculty ratio	9:1
% students returning for sophomore year	90

Most classes have 10–19 students.

REQUESTING SERVICES FOR STUDENTS WITH LEARNING DIFFERENCES

Phone: 509-527-5213 • www.whitman.edu/academics/academic-resource-center/disability-support-services
Email: arc@whitman.edu

Documentation submitted to: Academic Resource Center
Separate application required for Services: Yes

Documentation required for:
LD: Psychoeducational evaluation
ADHD: Psychoeducational evaluation
ASD: Psychoeducational evaluation

Whitworth University

300 W. Hawthorne Road, Spokane, WA 99251 • Admissions: 509-777-4786 • www.whitworth.edu

Support: CS

ACCOMMODATIONS

Allowed in exams:

Calculators	Yes
Dictionary	Yes
Computer	Yes
Spell-checker	Yes
Extended test time	Yes
Scribe	Yes
Proctors	Yes
Oral exams	Yes
Note-takers	Yes

Support services for students with:

LD	Yes
ADHD	Yes
ASD	Yes
Distraction-reduced environment	Yes
Recording of lecture allowed	Yes
Reading technology	Yes
Audio books	Yes
Other assistive technology	Yes
Priority registration	No

Added costs of services:

For LD	No
For ADHD	No
For ASD	No
LD specialists	No
ADHD & ASD coaching	Yes
ASD specialists	No
Professional tutors	No
Peer tutors	Yes
Max. hours/week for services	Varies
How professors are notified of student approved accommodations	Student and Educational Support Services

COLLEGE GRADUATION REQUIREMENTS

Course waivers allowed	Yes

In what courses: Case-by-case basis

Course substitutions allowed	Yes

In what courses: Case-by-case basis

PROGRAMS/SERVICES FOR STUDENTS WITH LEARNING DIFFERENCES

The Educational Support Services (ESS) office works with students one-on-one and acts as a liaison between students and Whitworth staff to determine reasonable and appropriate accommodations. Once a staff member from ESS has approved the accommodations, students are responsible for working directly with the designated faculty member, staff member, or outside agency to ensure that it is implemented. Services offered have included extended time, individually proctored exams, digital recorders, assistive technology, test-taking and study skills support, and notetakers. To apply for services, students must submit the ESS form and eligible, current documentation sent by a qualified evaluator and attend an intake meeting.

ADMISSIONS

Whitworth University considers academic rigor, quality of the student's optional writing sample, reputation of the student's high school, and participation in extracurricular, service, and leadership activities. Students with a 3.0 GPA in five or more classes from an accredited high school or college have the option to submit standardized test scores with their application. Students who have only attended non-accredited homeschool programs or who received competency-based grades with no cumulative GPA are required to submit test scores. Whitworth reviews applications on a rolling basis.

Additional Information

Students have access to additional tutoring resources through the campus Student Success Center. Success Coaches are available to help explore strategies and develop a student's academic skills. Together, they develop an academic success plan that specifically meets the needs of the student's learning style and identify resources for time management, studying, note-taking, and improving organizational skills. The ESS office recommends that students meet with Success Coaches 30 minutes per week throughout the semester.

Natsihi (not-see-hee) is a Native American Spokane word that means "among the pines," and it's also the name of Whitworth's yearbook. *Natsihi* has been in publication since 1914. All students working on *Natsihi* receive journalism credit. The yearbook has won numerous awards from the Associated Collegiate Press and the American Scholastic Press Association. Yearbooks are distributed in the spring of each year and are free to all full-time students.

Whitworth University

GENERAL ADMISSIONS

Very important factors include: academic GPA. *Important factors include:* rigor of secondary school record, application essay. *Other factors considered include:* standardized test scores (if submitted), recommendations. High school diploma is required and GED is accepted. Institution is test-optional for entering Fall 2024. Check admissions website for updates. *Academic units recommended:* 4 English, 3 math, 3 science (2 labs), 2 foreign language, 2 social studies, 2 history.

FINANCIAL AID

Students should submit: FAFSA. *Need-based scholarships/grants offered:* College/university scholarship or grant aid from institutional funds; Federal Pell; Private scholarships; SEOG; State scholarships/grants. *Loan aid offered:* Direct PLUS loans; Direct Subsidized Loans; Direct Unsubsidized Loans. Federal Work-Study Program available. Institutional employment available.

CAMPUS LIFE

Activities: Campus Ministries; Choral groups; Concert band; Dance; Drama/theater; International Student Organization; Jazz band; Literary magazine; Music ensembles; Musical theater; Pep band; Radio station; Student government; Student newspaper; Symphony orchestra; Yearbook. **Athletics (Intercollegiate):** *Men:* baseball, basketball, cross-country, golf, swimming, track/field (indoor), ultimate frisbee. *Women:* basketball, cross-country, golf, lacrosse, softball, swimming, track/field (indoor), ultimate frisbee, volleyball.

CAMPUS
Type of school	Private (nonprofit)
Environment	City

STUDENTS
Undergrad enrollment	2,033
% male/female	42/58
% from out of state	26
% frosh live on campus	87

FINANCIAL FACTS
Annual tuition	$49,600
Room and board	$13,700
Required fees	$1,320

GENERAL ADMISSIONS INFO
Application fee	No fee
Regular application deadline	8/31
Nonfall registration	Yes

Fall 2024 testing policy	Test Optional
Range SAT EBRW	570–690
Range SAT Math	540–660
Range ACT Composite	19–27

ACADEMICS
Student/faculty ratio	10:1
% students returning for sophomore year	78

Most classes have 10–19 students.

REQUESTING SERVICES FOR STUDENTS WITH LEARNING DIFFERENCES

Phone: 509-777-3380 • www.whitworth.edu/cms/administration/educational-support-services/
Email: ess@whitworth.edu

Documentation submitted to: Educational Support Services
Separate application required for Services: Yes

Documentation required for:
LD: Psychoeducational evaluation
ADHD: Psychoeducational evaluation
ASD: Psychoeducational evaluation

Davis & Elkins College

100 Campus Drive Elkins, WV 26241 • Admissions: 304-637-1230 • dewv.edu

(Support: SP)

ACCOMMODATIONS

Allowed in exams:

Calculators	Yes
Dictionary	Yes
Computer	Yes
Spell-checker	Yes
Extended test time	Yes
Scribe	Yes
Proctors	Yes
Oral exams	Yes
Note-takers	Yes

Support services for students with:

LD	Yes
ADHD	Yes
ASD	Yes
Distraction-reduced environment	Yes
Recording of lecture allowed	Yes
Reading technology	Yes
Audio books	Yes
Other assistive technology	Yes
Priority registration	Yes

Added costs of services:

For LD	Yes
For ADHD	Yes
For ASD	Yes
LD specialists	Yes
ADHD & ASD coaching	Yes
ASD specialists	Yes
Professional tutors	Yes
Peer tutors	Yes
Max. hours/week for services	Varies
How professors are notified of student approved accommodations	Student

COLLEGE GRADUATION REQUIREMENTS

Course waivers allowed	Yes
In what courses: Varies	
Course substitutions allowed	Yes
In what courses: Varies	

PROGRAMS/SERVICES FOR STUDENTS WITH LEARNING DIFFERENCES

The Naylor Learning Center houses Disability Services and related resources. Students may apply for accommodations by providing appropriate documentation, as well as register for supplemental services for added support. The Supported Learning Program (SLP) is fee-based program available to students with learning differences or other disabilities affecting academic achievement and who would benefit from increased individualized attention and structure. The combined experience of SLP staff includes special education, rehabilitation counseling, school counseling, and psychology. The SLP instructors meet weekly with students, and focus on developing skills to improve studying, time management, and communication in written, social, and interview settings. SLP has an autism program coordinator and a peer mentoring program that meets informally in various social environments to encourage students with ASD to enhance their social skills and interactions. SLP students must meet twice a semester with each of their professors to discuss progress. The professor fills out a Grade Check form for the student to review with their SLP instructor. SLP students are expected to complete 5 hours weekly at a structured study hall. Per-semester fees for SLP may decrease as a student's autonomy improves and they step down to lower-tiered support. Some students find they do not need SLP or additional levels of support and achieve success with Davis & Elkins' standard accommodations. Available assistive technology includes, but is not limited to, Read & Write, smart pens, Dragon Naturally Speaking, and alternate-format textbooks. Peer note-taking is also available.

ADMISSIONS

Interest in the SLP program does not have any bearing on a student's admission to Davis & Elkins. Students may fill out the SLP application before, during, or after admission to the college. The SLP application is separate from the admissions application, and includes a required in-person or virtual interview with the director. The minimum GPA required for admission for all students is a 2.5 on a 4.0 scale. There is no foreign language requirement at Davis & Elkins, and waivers or substitutions can be made available for math requirements.

Additional Information

All Davis & Elkins students have access to free peer tutoring, academic success coaching, and the Writing Center. The PATH Program (Preparing and Transitioning to Higher Education) is a fee-based service available in the summer for students who are hoping to ease their anxiety about college and campus life.

Davis & Elkins was founded in 1904 and named for Henry G. Davis and his son-in-law Stephen B. Elkins, both U.S. senators from West Virginia. Jennings Randolph joined D&E in 1926 and was closely identified with D&E as faculty, as a trustee, and as a member of Congress promoting the best interests of the college. In 1971, Jennings sponsored the 26th amendment to the Constitution, lowering the voting age to 18. He served D&E and Congress for over 50 years.

Davis & Elkins College

GENERAL ADMISSIONS

Very important factors include: rigor of secondary school record. *Important factors include:* class rank, academic GPA, standardized test scores (if submitted), recommendations. *Other factors considered include:* application essay. High school diploma is required and GED is accepted. Institution is test-optional for entering Fall 2024. Check admissions website for updates. *Academic units required:* 4 English, 3 math, 3 science (1 lab), 4 social studies.

FINANCIAL AID

Students should submit: FAFSA. *Need-based scholarships/grants offered:* College/university scholarship or grant aid from institutional funds; Federal Pell; Private scholarships; SEOG; State scholarships/grants. *Loan aid offered:* Direct PLUS loans; Direct Subsidized Loans; Direct Unsubsidized Loans. Federal Work-Study Program available. Institutional employment available.

CAMPUS LIFE

Activities: Choral groups; Concert band; Drama/theater; Jazz band; Literary magazine; Music ensembles; Musical theater; Radio station; Student government; Student newspaper; Yearbook. **Organizations:** 39 registered organizations, 7 honor societies, 1 religious organizations, 2 fraternities, 2 sororities. **Athletics (Intercollegiate):** *Men:* baseball, basketball, cross-country, golf. *Women:* basketball, cross-country, softball, volleyball.

CAMPUS

Type of school	Private (nonprofit)
Environment	Village

STUDENTS

Undergrad enrollment	661
% male/female	41/59
% from out of state	46
% frosh live on campus	82

FINANCIAL FACTS

Annual tuition	$30,680
Room and board	$10,125

GENERAL ADMISSIONS INFO

Application fee	No fee
Regular application deadline	Rolling
Nonfall registration	Yes

Fall 2024 testing policy	Test Optional

ACADEMICS

Student/faculty ratio	11:1
% students returning for sophomore year	67

Most classes have 2-9 students.

REQUESTING SERVICES FOR STUDENTS WITH LEARNING DIFFERENCES

Phone: 304-637-1435 • www.dewv.edu/academics/educational-support/ • Email: finchamd@dewv.edu

Documentation submitted to: Disability Services
Separate application required for Services: Yes

Documentation required for:
 LD: Psychoeducational evaluation
 ADHD: Psychoeducational evaluation
 ASD: Psychoeducational evaluation

Marshall University

Office of Admissions, Huntington, WV 25755 • Admissions: 304-696-3160 • www.marshall.edu

Support: SP

ACCOMMODATIONS

Allowed in exams:

Calculators	Yes
Dictionary	No
Computer	Yes
Spell-checker	Yes
Extended test time	Yes
Scribe	Yes
Proctors	Yes
Oral exams	Yes
Note-takers	Yes

Support services for students with:

LD	Yes
ADHD	Yes
ASD	Yes
Distraction-reduced environment	Yes
Recording of lecture allowed	Yes
Reading technology	Yes
Audio books	Yes
Other assistive technology	Yes
Priority registration	Yes

Added costs of services:

For LD	Yes
For ADHD	Yes
For ASD	Yes
LD specialists	Yes
ADHD & ASD coaching	Yes
ASD specialists	Yes
Professional tutors	Yes
Peer tutors	No
Max. hours/week for services	Varies
How professors are notified of student approved accommodations	Office of Disability Services

COLLEGE GRADUATION REQUIREMENTS

Course waivers allowed	No
Course substitutions allowed	Yes

In what courses: Math and Foreign Language

PROGRAMS/SERVICES FOR STUDENTS WITH LEARNING DIFFERENCES

The Office of Disability Services offers free services to students with a documented disability. Once the student is registered with the office, and an accommodations request has been submitted, information will be sent to their instructors concerning the services and accommodations the student will need. Accommodations or services could include test proctoring, alternative-format textbooks, early registration, extended test time, preferential seating, notetakers, readers for test questions, scribes for tests, course substitutions, quiet rooms, and tape-recorded classes. The H.E.L.P. Center (Higher Education for Learning Problems) is a fee-based comprehensive academic support program for students with documentation. Students should contact the H.E.L.P. Center to determine which particular program and division will best support their needs. The College Program for Students with Autism Spectrum Disorder uses a positive behavior support approach to assist participating students. Social, communication, academic, and personal living skills are assessed, personal goals are identified, and strategies are developed on an individual basis. This program helps students learn skills that will help them earn a college degree, work in their chosen field, and live an independent, productive, and meaningful life. Students participating in the program have met the acceptance criteria for Marshall University and have been admitted to The College Program through a separate application process.

ADMISSIONS

All applicants are expected to meet the same admission criteria. An overall GPA of at least 2.0 and a minimum ACT score of 19 or SAT of 990, or an overall GPA of 3.0 and an ACT of 16 or SAT of 880, is required for regular first-year admission. First-year applicants pursuing a four-year baccalaureate degree who meet all admission requirements will be admitted unconditionally. A small number of students are admitted conditionally and must complete all missing requirements within three semesters. Upon completion of the requirements, students may transfer into any major or college for which they are eligible.

Additional Information

Marshall offers peer tutoring, department tutors, the Writing Center, the Math Tutoring Lab, and many other academic support services for students.

A solemn, rather than fun, fact has to do with the memorial service held each year on November 14 in front of the Memorial Fountain on the Student Center Plaza. The water in the fountain is stopped during the service and remains silent until spring. The service is the anniversary of the November 14, 1970 plane crash—the greatest air tragedy in the history of collegiate athletics. Seventy-five members of the Marshall football team, coaches, staff, community members, and crew died in the crash. *We Are Marshall* is a 2006 feature film about the crash and Marshall's struggle afterward.

Marshall University

GENERAL ADMISSIONS

Very important factors include: academic GPA, standardized test scores (if submitted). *Other factors considered include:* rigor of secondary school record, recommendations. High school diploma is required and GED is accepted. Institution is test-optional for entering Fall 2024. Check admissions website for updates. *Academic units recommended:* 4 English, 4 math, 3 science (3 labs), 2 foreign language, 3 social studies, 1 visual/performing arts.

FINANCIAL AID

Students should submit: FAFSA. *Need-based scholarships/grants offered:* College/university scholarship or grant aid from institutional funds; Federal Pell; Private scholarships; SEOG; State scholarships/grants. *Loan aid offered:* Direct PLUS loans; Direct Subsidized Loans; Direct Unsubsidized Loans. Federal Work-Study Program available.

CAMPUS LIFE

Activities: Campus Ministries; Choral groups; Concert band; Dance; Drama/theater; International Student Organization; Jazz band; Literary magazine; Marching band; Model UN; Music ensembles; Musical theater; Opera; Pep band; Radio station; Student government; Student newspaper; Student-run film society; Symphony orchestra; Television station. **Organizations:** 222 registered organizations, 11 honor societies, 22 religious organizations, 15 fraternities, 6 sororities. **Athletics (Intercollegiate):** *Men:* baseball, basketball, cross-country, golf, ice hockey, lacrosse, racquetball, rugby, softball, table tennis, ultimate frisbee, volleyball. *Women:* basketball, cross-country, golf, ice hockey, racquetball, rugby, softball, swimming, table tennis, ultimate frisbee, volleyball.

CAMPUS

Type of school	Public
Environment	Town

STUDENTS

Undergrad enrollment	7,962
% male/female	42/58
% from out of state	20

FINANCIAL FACTS

Annual in-state tuition	$7,190
Annual out-of-state tuition	$18,244
Room and board	$10,336
Required fees	$1,414

GENERAL ADMISSIONS INFO

Application fee	$40
Regular application deadline	Rolling
Nonfall registration	Yes

Fall 2024 testing policy	Test Optional
Range SAT EBRW	460–600
Range SAT Math	430–550
Range ACT Composite	19–25

ACADEMICS

Student/faculty ratio	16:1
% students returning for sophomore year	74

Most classes have 20–29 students.

REQUESTING SERVICES FOR STUDENTS WITH LEARNING DIFFERENCES

Phone: 304-696-2467 • www.marshall.edu/disability • Email: wyant2@marshall.edu

Documentation submitted to: Office of Disability Services
Separate application required for Services: Yes

Documentation required for:
LD: Psychoeducational evaluation
ADHD: Psychoeducational evaluation
ASD: Psychoeducational evaluation

West Virginia University

Admissions Office, Morgantown, WV 26506-6009 • Admissions: 304-293-2121 • www.wvu.edu

Support: SP

ACCOMMODATIONS

Allowed in exams:

Calculators	Yes
Dictionary	Yes
Computer	Yes
Spell-checker	Yes
Extended test time	Yes
Scribe	Yes
Proctors	Yes
Oral exams	Yes
Note-takers	Yes

Support services for students with:

LD	Yes
ADHD	Yes
ASD	Yes
Distraction-reduced environment	Yes
Recording of lecture allowed	Yes
Reading technology	Yes
Audio books	Yes
Other assistive technology	Yes
Priority registration	Yes

Added costs of services:

For LD	Yes
For ADHD	Yes
For ASD	Yes
LD specialists	Yes
ADHD & ASD coaching	Yes
ASD specialists	Yes
Professional tutors	Yes
Peer tutors	Yes
Max. hours/week for services	Varies
How professors are notified of student approved accommodations	Student

COLLEGE GRADUATION REQUIREMENTS

Course waivers allowed	No
Course substitutions allowed	Yes
In what courses: Foreign Language	

PROGRAMS/SERVICES FOR STUDENTS WITH LEARNING DIFFERENCES

The Office of Accessibility Services (OAS) offers services to students with learning disabilities. After applying to the OAS, students have an initial meeting to discuss how to access reasonable accommodations. An accessibility specialist approves appropriate requests and emails the student and professors the notification of accommodations explaining the student's needs. Students must request accommodations each semester through the online portal SAMM. Academic accommodations are only given for lecture, online, and lab-type classes. Some accommodations include priority registration, extended testing time, note-taking, distraction-free environments, books on tape, and assistive technology. MindFit is a fee-based program for students that offers three types of services: LD/ADHD Consultation and Assessment, Academic Enhancement Services, and Cognitive Enhancement Services. MindFit offers an assessment service for students with no formal testing for LD or ADHD. MindFit's Academic Enhancement Services include an Academic Coaching option that provides academic support for students who learn differently and Learning Skill Consultations, which are available for any WVU student. The Academic Coaching tutors are trained to work with students with learning differences, and there is a per semester cost, depending on how many hours the student needs. Two forms of Cognitive Enhancement Services are offered through MindFit: cognitive training and neurofeedback. Cognitive training involves a series of mental exercises in a game-like format that helps students improve their attention span and memory. Neurofeedback uses EEG patterning to help students learn to modulate brain wave activity to help with attention and cognitive functioning. MindFit also offers learning skills development with a professional academic coach as a short-term intervention, meeting with the student one-on-one for three sessions.

ADMISSIONS

The admission process is the same for all students applying to the university. The average GPA for admitted students is 3.66, and the average ACT score is 24 and the SAT is 1132 for students submitting test scores. Students are encouraged to self-disclose a disability during the application process through their personal statement.

Additional Information

Staff members work individually with students to help them achieve academic success. There are no LD specialists on staff, but counselors are available.

WVU started playing football in 1891. Ira Errett Rodgers played football at WVU from 1915 to 1917 and in 1919 and is recognized as the school's greatest all-around athlete of the first half-century. He was the first All-American at the school and the first to rush for 200 yards in a game. He coached the football team for eight seasons and was inducted into the College Football Hall of Fame in 1953. His number, 21, has been retired by the football team.

West Virginia University

GENERAL ADMISSIONS

Very important factors include: academic GPA, standardized test scores (if submitted). *Important factors include:* rigor of secondary school record. High school diploma is required and GED is accepted. Institution is test-optional for entering Fall 2024. Check admissions website for updates. *Academic units required:* 4 English, 4 math, 3 science (3 labs), 2 foreign language, 3 social studies, 1 visual/performing arts.

FINANCIAL AID

Students should submit: FAFSA. *Need-based scholarships/grants offered:* College/university scholarship or grant aid from institutional funds; Federal Nursing Scholarships; Federal Pell; Private scholarships; SEOG. *Loan aid offered:* Direct PLUS loans; Direct Subsidized Loans; Direct Unsubsidized Loans. Federal Work-Study Program available. Institutional employment available.

CAMPUS LIFE

Activities: Campus Ministries; Choral groups; Concert band; Dance; Drama/theater; International Student Organization; Jazz band; Literary magazine; Marching band; Model UN; Music ensembles; Musical theater; Pep band; Radio station; Student government; Student newspaper; Symphony orchestra. **Organizations:** 450 registered organizations, 26 honor societies, 26 religious organizations, 9 fraternities, 8 sororities. **Athletics (Intercollegiate):** *Men:* baseball, basketball, bowling, crew/rowing, cross-country, cycling, equestrian sports, field hockey, golf, gymnastics, ice hockey, lacrosse, martial arts, racquetball, rugby, skiing (nordic/cross-country), softball, swimming, table tennis, ultimate frisbee, volleyball, water polo, wrestling. *Women:* basketball, bowling, crew/rowing, cross-country, cycling, equestrian sports, field hockey, golf, gymnastics, ice hockey, lacrosse, martial arts, racquetball, rugby, skiing (nordic/cross-country), softball, swimming, table tennis, track/field (indoor), ultimate frisbee, volleyball.

CAMPUS

Type of school	Public
Environment	Town

STUDENTS

Undergrad enrollment	20,499
% male/female	52/48
% from out of state	48
% frosh live on campus	92

FINANCIAL FACTS

Annual in-state tuition	$9,384
Annual out-of-state tuition	$26,568
Room and board	$11,618

GENERAL ADMISSIONS INFO

Application fee	$45
Regular application deadline	8/1
Nonfall registration	Yes

Fall 2024 testing policy	Test Optional
Range SAT EBRW	530–620
Range SAT Math	520–620
Range ACT Composite	21–27

ACADEMICS

Student/faculty ratio	18:1
% students returning for sophomore year	76

Most classes have 20–29 students.

REQUESTING SERVICES FOR STUDENTS WITH LEARNING DIFFERENCES

Phone: 304-293-6700 • accessibilityservices.wvu.edu/ • Email: access2@mail.wvu.edu

Documentation submitted to: Office of Accessibility Services

Separate application required for Services: Yes

Documentation required for:
LD: Psychoeducational evaluation
ADHD: Psychoeducational evaluation
ASD: Psychoeducational evaluation

West Virginia Wesleyan College

59 College Avenue, Buckhannon, WV 26201 • Admissions: 304-473-8510 • www.wvwc.edu

Support: SP

ACCOMMODATIONS

Allowed in exams:

Calculators	Yes
Dictionary	Yes
Computer	Yes
Spell-checker	Yes
Extended test time	Yes
Scribe	Yes
Proctors	Yes
Oral exams	Yes
Note-takers	Yes

Support services for students with:

LD	Yes
ADHD	Yes
ASD	Yes
Distraction-reduced environment	Yes
Recording of lecture allowed	Yes
Reading technology	Yes
Audio books	Yes
Other assistive technology	Yes
Priority registration	Yes

Added costs of services:

For LD	No
For ADHD	No
For ASD	No
LD specialists	Yes
ADHD & ASD coaching	Yes
ASD specialists	Yes
Professional tutors	Yes
Peer tutors	Yes
Max. hours/week for services	Varies
How professors are notified of student approved accommodations	Student

COLLEGE GRADUATION REQUIREMENTS

Course waivers allowed	No
Course substitutions allowed	No

PROGRAMS/SERVICES FOR STUDENTS WITH LEARNING DIFFERENCES

West Virginia Wesleyan College is committed to providing support to students with documented learning disabilities and attention difficulties with several programs available to these students through the Learning Center. The Foundational Program is free and allows students with documented disabilities to develop their accommodations plan. Students will also work with their comprehensive advisor every week to cover the following areas: transition to college, special academic advising, preferential pre-registration for the first three semesters, development of academic, organizational, and self-monitoring strategies, test analysis, setting priorities, motivational outlook, self-advocacy, social coaching, and access to an assistive technology lab with state-of-the-art software. A test-taking lab provides readers, scribes, notetakers, and word processing, as needed. The Mentor Advantage Program provides individualized support with academic challenges that occur when transitioning to college. The program is composed of several elements: one-on-one professional organizational mentoring, strategic academic content tutoring, and weekly small group discussions. Students may enroll in the program as a package or sign up for various components separately, depending on the students' needs. There is a per-hour cost; students may sign up for up to five hours per week. The Daytime and Evening Check-in Program is a study hall with tutors available and is offered as part of the Mentor Advantage Program for an additional fee.

ADMISSIONS

The Office of Admission will evaluate applications on many factors, the most important being course rigor and GPA. They will also look at the student's character, leadership, and extracurricular activities. Interviews are encouraged, and college-prep academic courses are required. If students with documented disabilities do not meet those specific admission requirements, their applications may be sent to the director of the Learning Center to determine whether the student can be successful with the appropriate accommodations.

Additional Information

The Learning Center also offers the Lindamood-Bell® Learning methods program. This fee-based, individualized clinical learning program focuses on improving reading skills and language comprehension and the Learning Center also has a walk-in peer tutoring program. There is no foreign language requirement and only one math requirement.

A 1995 rain inspired the "Mud Games," which quickly became an annual tradition. The key ingredient is, of course, mud. Fraternities and sororities, athletic teams, groups of friends, residence halls, faculty, and staff groups have competed over the years in obstacle courses, tug-of-war battles, treasure hunts, dizzy bat contests, and all manner of silly relay races using everything from sacks to sit-and-bounce balls.

West Virginia Wesleyan College

GENERAL ADMISSIONS

Very important factors include: rigor of secondary school record, academic GPA. *Important factors include:* class rank, standardized test scores (if submitted). *Other factors considered include:* application essay, recommendations. High school diploma is required and GED is accepted. Institution is test-optional for entering Fall 2024. Check admissions website for updates. *Academic units required:* 4 English, 3 math, 3 science (1 lab), 3 social studies. *Academic units recommended:* 2 foreign language.

FINANCIAL AID

Students should submit: FAFSA. *Need-based scholarships/grants offered:* College/university scholarship or grant aid from institutional funds; Federal Nursing Scholarships; Federal Pell; Private scholarships; SEOG; State scholarships/grants. *Loan aid offered:* Direct PLUS loans; Direct Subsidized Loans; Direct Unsubsidized Loans. Federal Work-Study Program available. Institutional employment available.

CAMPUS LIFE

Activities: Campus Ministries; Choral groups; Concert band; Dance; Drama/theater; International Student Organization; Jazz band; Literary magazine; Marching band; Music ensembles; Musical theater; Opera; Pep band; Radio station; Student government; Student newspaper; Yearbook. **Organizations:** 75 registered organizations, 31 honor societies, 6 religious organizations, 6 fraternities, 5 sororities. **Athletics (Intercollegiate):** *Men:* baseball, basketball, cross-country, cycling, golf, softball, swimming, track/field (indoor). *Women:* basketball, cross-country, cycling, golf, lacrosse, swimming, track/field (indoor), volleyball.

CAMPUS

Type of school	Private (nonprofit)
Environment	Village

STUDENTS

Undergrad enrollment	982
% male/female	46/54
% from out of state	38
% frosh live on campus	90

FINANCIAL FACTS

Annual tuition	$32,166
Room and board	$10,980
Required fees	$1,329

GENERAL ADMISSIONS INFO

Application fee	$35
Regular application deadline	8/15
Nonfall registration	Yes

Fall 2024 testing policy	Test Optional
Range SAT EBRW	470–590
Range SAT Math	485–580
Range ACT Composite	19–25

ACADEMICS

Student/faculty ratio	12:1
% students returning for sophomore year	65
Most classes have 10–19 students.	

REQUESTING SERVICES FOR STUDENTS WITH LEARNING DIFFERENCES

Phone: 304-473-8000 ext.8558 • www.wvwc.edu/the-learning-center/disability-support
Email: dib_a@wvwc.edu

Documentation submitted to: The Learning Center
Separate application required for Services: Yes

Documentation required for:
 LD: Psychoeducational evaluation
 ADHD: Psychoeducational evaluation
 ASD: Psychoeducational evaluation

Alverno College

3400 South 43rd Street, Milwaukee, WI 53234-3922 • Admissions: 414-382-6101 • www.alverno.edu

Support: S

ACCOMMODATIONS

Allowed in exams:	
Calculators	Yes
Dictionary	Yes
Computer	Yes
Spell-checker	Yes
Extended test time	Yes
Scribe	Yes
Proctors	Yes
Oral exams	Yes
Note-takers	Yes
Support services for students with:	
LD	Yes
ADHD	Yes
ASD	Yes
Distraction-reduced environment	Yes
Recording of lecture allowed	Yes
Reading technology	Yes
Audio books	Yes
Other assistive technology	Yes
Priority registration	No
Added costs of services:	
For LD	No
For ADHD	No
For ASD	No
LD specialists	No
ADHD & ASD coaching	No
ASD specialists	No
Professional tutors	Yes
Peer tutors	Yes
Max. hours/week for services	Varies
How professors are notified of student approved accommodations	Student and Student Accessibility Office

COLLEGE GRADUATION REQUIREMENTS

Course waivers allowed	No
Course substitutions allowed	No

PROGRAMS/SERVICES FOR STUDENTS WITH LEARNING DIFFERENCES

The Student Accessibility office provides accommodations for students with disabilities. Students should contact the office to provide documentation and accommodation requests for courses, workshops, programs, or activities as early as possible. Eligible accommodations include note-taking assistance, recording devices, adaptive technology, alternate-format textbooks, alternate testing, and classroom accommodations/modifications. Once a student's accommodations are approved, they will receive a letter and meet with each course instructor to discuss implementation.

ADMISSIONS

All applicants are expected to meet the same admission criteria and undergo the same review process. Prospective students must have graduated from an accredited high school with a minimum GPA of 2.3. Applicants should rank in the upper half of their graduating class. Students should submit two letters of recommendation that describe them as a student and as a member of the community. Applicants whose GPA falls between 2.0 and 2.3 may need to petition the admissions committee, depending on their other credentials. Students may earn college credits toward their degree through a Credit for Prior Learning (CPL) assessment by demonstrating how their learning experiences (through a variety of life, work, and educational experiences) meet the requirements of a major or support area.

Additional Information

Each summer, Alverno offers Quantitative Literacy in a Modern World, a class focused on math and algebra needed in today's world. In addition to completing a first-semester course requirement, it's a time for students to gain a good understanding of the curriculum, the campus, and faculty. Instructional Services provide a variety of academic assistance through study groups, resource centers, peer tutoring, and professional tutoring. Study groups are at the request of course instructors for course content review. Resources centers have open hours and offer course-specific assistance, such as for writing and speaking needs, science and math support, and nursing coursework support. Peer tutoring is reserved for students with accommodations and other exceptional situations, including courses not supported by study groups or resource centers. Professional tutoring is available under special circumstances identified by faculty.

Sisters Bernardin Deutsch '53 and Celestine Schall '48 first met in 1965 as part of a group helping women navigate the changing roles of women in society and the church. In 1971, Sister Celestine created and led the Off-Campus Experiential Learning (OCEL) program, while Sister Bernardin, a longtime psychology professor, was the first to videotape student work. Both helped build Alverno's abilities-based curriculum and served the school well into their nineties.

Alverno College

GENERAL ADMISSIONS

Very important factors include: academic GPA. *Important factors include:* rigor of secondary school record. *Other factors considered include:* application essay, recommendations. High school diploma is required and GED is accepted. Institution is test-optional for entering Fall 2024. Check admissions website for updates. *Academic units required:* 4 English, 3 math, 3 science, 3 social studies, 2 foreign language, 4 academic electives.

FINANCIAL AID

Students should submit: FAFSA. *Need-based scholarships/grants offered:* College/university scholarship or grant aid from institutional funds; Federal Pell; Private scholarships; SEOG; State scholarships/grants. *Loan aid offered:* Direct PLUS loans; Direct Subsidized Loans; Direct Unsubsidized Loans. Federal Work-Study Program available. Institutional employment available.

CAMPUS LIFE

Activities: Campus Ministries; Choral groups; Dance; Drama/theater; International Student Organization; Literary magazine; Model UN; Music ensembles; Radio station; Student government; Student newspaper. **Organizations:** 34 registered organizations, 1 honor societies, 2 religious organizations, 0 fraternities, 2 sororities. **Athletics (Intercollegiate):** *Women:* basketball, cross-country, golf, softball, volleyball.

CAMPUS
Type of school	Private (nonprofit)
Environment	Metropolis

STUDENTS
Undergrad enrollment	917
% male/female	3/97
% from out of state	10
% frosh live on campus	38

FINANCIAL FACTS
Annual tuition	$30,408
Room and board	$8,620
Required fees	$850

GENERAL ADMISSIONS INFO
Application fee	No fee
Regular application deadline	Rolling
Nonfall registration	Yes

Fall 2024 testing policy	Test Optional
Range ACT Composite	15–21

ACADEMICS
Student/faculty ratio	10:1
% students returning for sophomore year	69

Most classes have 2-9 students.

REQUESTING SERVICES FOR STUDENTS WITH LEARNING DIFFERENCES

Phone: 414-382-6722 • www.alverno.edu/instructional-services-accessibility
Email: studentaccessibility@alverno.edu

Documentation submitted to: Student Accessibility Office
Separate application required for Services: Yes

Documentation required for:
LD: Psychoeducational evaluation
ADHD: Psychoeducational evaluation
ASD: Psychoeducational evaluation

Beloit College

700 College Street, Beloit, WI 53511 • Admissions: 608-363-2500 • www.beloit.edu

Support: CS

ACCOMMODATIONS

Allowed in exams:

Calculators	Yes
Dictionary	No
Computer	Yes
Spell-checker	No
Extended test time	Yes
Scribe	Yes
Proctors	Yes
Oral exams	Yes
Note-takers	Yes

Support services for students with:

LD	Yes
ADHD	Yes
ASD	Yes
Distraction-reduced environment	No
Recording of lecture allowed	Yes
Audio books	Yes
Priority registration	Yes

Added costs of services:

For LD	No
For ADHD	No
For ASD	No
LD specialists	No
ADHD & ASD coaching	No
ASD specialists	Yes
Professional tutors	No
Peer tutors	Yes
Max. hours/week for services	Varies
How professors are notified of student approved accommodations	Student

COLLEGE GRADUATION REQUIREMENTS

Course waivers allowed	No
Course substitutions allowed	Yes
In what courses: Case-by-case basis	

Paul Burwell, class of 1986, was a library employee for almost 40 years. As Mister History, he expanded the archives beyond the official record of the college. In 2010, he started an online column, "Fridays with Fred." For over six years and nearly weekly episodes, his columns about student life, traditions, and history are available to read and are now part of Beloit's historical record. He retired in 2020.

PROGRAMS/SERVICES FOR STUDENTS WITH LEARNING DIFFERENCES

Learning Enrichment and Disability Services (LEADS) provides academic support, tutoring, and disability services to students with disabilities. Students who identify as such are expected to contact LEADS as soon as they know they will attend Beloit to request accommodations, provide documentation, and meet with the director to discuss accommodations, policies, and procedures. The LEADS staff verifies disabilities and determines accommodations on a case-by-case basis. Once students receive their accommodation verification letters, it is their responsibility to deliver a copy to their course instructors. Some of the most often-used accommodations include, but are not limited to, organizational tutors, print materials in an electronic or audio format or enlarged form, note-taking assistance, which may include the use of recordings, peer notetakers, access to PowerPoint, professor notes, extended time on exams and in-class assignments, use of a computer for exams, in-class assignments or note-taking, and a limited-distraction area for exams. Prospective students are encouraged to contact the director of LEADS with any questions, or, with advance notice, the director is usually able to meet with students during their campus visit.

ADMISSIONS

Beloit requires official high school transcripts of all applicants for admission but does not require a minimum GPA. The admission committee is interested in looking at overall academic records, the rigor of courses taken compared to courses offered, and academic performance over time. Most successful applicants have grades in the A- to B+ range. A personal essay is required: the admissions committee isn't just looking at writing mechanics; they're interested in the story an applicant has chosen to tell, the originality of the ideas, and a student's interests. Letters of recommendation are not required, but applicants are encouraged to submit at least one (up to three will be read). The letters usually come from teachers in core academic subjects but can come from extracurricular advisors, coaches, employers, college access counselors, clergy, family members, or peers.

Additional Information

Student Services is home to Student Success Equity and Community (SSEC), Tutoring and Academic Support, the Writing Center, and Career Works. Tutoring and Academic Support offers individual tutoring and workshops on topics from time management to support geared for students with disabilities. The Writing Center's peer tutors assist with developing ideas, final edits, writing papers, and proofreading. Students can make an appointment for individual research assistance with a librarian to discuss research papers, learn strategies to fine-tune a topic, and find the research and information needed. Once a student accepts admission to Beloit, an advisor will contact the student. The (AMP) Advanced Mentoring Program advisor will guide the student through the acceptance process, answering any questions or concerns.

Beloit College

GENERAL ADMISSIONS

Very important factors include: rigor of secondary school record, academic GPA, application essay. *Other factors considered include:* class rank, standardized test scores (if submitted), recommendations. High school diploma is required and GED is accepted. Institution is test-optional for entering Fall 2024. Check admissions website for updates. *Academic units recommended:* 4 English, 3 math, 3 science (3 labs), 2 foreign language, 3 social studies.

FINANCIAL AID

Students should submit: FAFSA. *Need-based scholarships/grants offered:* College/university scholarship or grant aid from institutional funds; Federal Pell; Private scholarships; SEOG; State scholarships/grants. *Loan aid offered:* Direct PLUS loans; Direct Subsidized Loans; Direct Unsubsidized Loans. Federal Work-Study Program available. Institutional employment available.

CAMPUS LIFE

Activities: Campus Ministries; Choral groups; Dance; Drama/theater; International Student Organization; Jazz band; Literary magazine; Model UN; Music ensembles; Musical theater; Radio station; Student government; Student newspaper; Television station. **Organizations:** 113 registered organizations, 6 honor societies, 3 religious organizations, 3 fraternities, 3 sororities. **Athletics (Intercollegiate):** *Men:* baseball, basketball, bowling, cross-country, golf, lacrosse, martial arts, swimming, track/field (indoor), ultimate frisbee. *Women:* basketball, bowling, cross-country, golf, lacrosse, martial arts, softball, swimming, track/field (indoor), ultimate frisbee, volleyball.

Wisconsin

REQUESTING SERVICES FOR STUDENTS WITH LEARNING DIFFERENCES

Phone: 608-363-2572 • www.beloit.edu/offices/leads/disability-services • Email: learning@beloit.edu

Documentation submitted to: The Learning Enrichment and Disability Services Office
Separate application required for Services: Yes

Documentation required for:
LD: Psychoeducational evaluation
ADHD: Psychoeducational evaluation
ASD: Psychoeducational evaluation

Edgewood College

1000 Edgewood College Drive, Madison, WI 53711-1997 • Admissions: 608-663-2294 • www.edgewood.edu

Support: SP

ACCOMMODATIONS

Allowed in exams:

Calculators	Yes
Dictionary	Yes
Computer	Yes
Spell-checker	Yes
Extended test time	Yes
Scribe	Yes
Proctors	Yes
Oral exams	Yes
Note-takers	Yes

Support services for students with:

LD	Yes
ADHD	Yes
ASD	Yes
Distraction-reduced environment	Yes
Recording of lecture allowed	Yes
Reading technology	Yes
Audio books	Yes
Other assistive technology	Yes
Priority registration	Yes

Added costs of services:

For LD	Yes
For ADHD	Yes
For ASD	Yes
LD specialists	Yes
ADHD & ASD coaching	Yes
ASD specialists	Yes
Professional tutors	Yes
Peer tutors	Yes
Max. hours/week for services	12
How professors are notified of student approved accommodations	Student and Disability and Accessibility Services

COLLEGE GRADUATION REQUIREMENTS

Course waivers allowed	Yes
In what courses: Foreign Language	
Course substitutions allowed	Yes
In what courses: Foreign Language	

PROGRAMS/SERVICES FOR STUDENTS WITH LEARNING DIFFERENCES

The Disability and Accessibility Services department requires students to complete the disability intake form to start the process of receiving accommodations. Students granted accommodations will be given a letter stating their accommodations, and Disability and Accessibility Services will email a copy of the support plan to the student's professors at the beginning of the semester. It is the student's responsibility to discuss with their professors how the accommodations will be carried out in the class. The Disability and Accessibility Services advisor can be included in those conversations. Common accommodations may include extra time on tests, alternate test locations, note-taking, recorded lectures, use of note-taking software, access to instructor notes, advance assignment extensions, textbooks in digital format, print materials scanned for use with text-to-speech software, and breaks during class. The Cutting-Edge program at Edgewood offers a fully integrated college experience for students with intellectual challenges and other developmental disabilities like Down syndrome, autism, traumatic brain injuries, and cerebral palsy. Through individualized advising and peer mentorship, Cutting-Edge students can take courses, live in residence halls, participate in social events, clubs, interest groups, activities, community service, internships, and employment. The program offers several degree and nondegree/certificate options. Students can enroll as traditional undergraduate students or earn a fine arts certificate, a certificate in 21st-century skills for employment, or the Para-Professional Educator Certificate.

ADMISSIONS

For students enrolling at Edgewood College, the average GPA is 3.35. Applicants should have at least 16 units of high school credit, with 12 from natural science, speech, social science, English, foreign language, history, and mathematics. Two years of the same foreign language in grades 9–12 with grades of a C or better are also recommended; if not completed in high school, the equivalent will be required at Edgewood College.

Additional Information

Incoming first-year students will be assigned their own Academic and Career Counselor who will serve as their main point of contact for all academic success and career development needs the student may have.

Jeff Erlanger graduated from Edgewood College. Spinal surgery at seven months old left him a person with quadriplegia. He received his first electric wheelchair at age four. In 1981, at 10 years old, he appeared on Mister Rogers' Neighborhood. In later speeches, Mr. Rogers told of Erlanger's example of "overcoming obstacles and feeling comfortable about yourself." Mr. Erlanger held a number of positions in Madison municipal politics, including chair of the Commission on People with Disabilities.

Edgewood College

General Admissions

Very important factors include: academic GPA. *Other factors considered include:* class rank, standardized test scores (if submitted), application essay, recommendations. High school diploma is required and GED is accepted. Institution is test-flexible for entering Fall 2024. Check admissions website for updates. *Academic units recommended:* 4 English, 3 math, 3 science, 2 foreign language, 4 social studies.

Financial Aid

Students should submit: FAFSA. *Need-based scholarships/grants offered:* College/university scholarship or grant aid from institutional funds; Federal Pell; Private scholarships; SEOG; State scholarships/grants. *Loan aid offered:* Direct PLUS loans; Direct Subsidized Loans; Direct Unsubsidized Loans. Federal Work-Study Program available. Institutional employment available.

Campus Life

Activities: Campus Ministries; Drama/theater; International Student Organization; Literary magazine; Music ensembles; Musical theater; Student government; Student newspaper; Symphony orchestra. **Organizations:** 48 registered organizations, 4 honor societies, 1 religious organizations, 0 fraternities, 0 sororities. **Athletics (Intercollegiate):** *Men:* baseball, basketball, cross-country, golf, track/field (indoor). *Women:* basketball, cross-country, golf, softball, track/field (indoor), volleyball.

CAMPUS
Type of school	Private (nonprofit)
Environment	City

STUDENTS
Undergrad enrollment	1,233
% male/female	32/68
% from out of state	10
% frosh live on campus	82

FINANCIAL FACTS
Annual tuition	$32,600
Room and board	$12,050

GENERAL ADMISSIONS INFO
Application fee	$30
Regular application deadline	8/1
Nonfall registration	Yes

Fall 2024 testing policy	Test Flexible
Range SAT EBRW	470–590
Range SAT Math	480–590
Range ACT Composite	19–25

ACADEMICS
Student/faculty ratio	12:1
% students returning for sophomore year	72

Most classes have 10–19 students.

REQUESTING SERVICES FOR STUDENTS WITH LEARNING DIFFERENCES

Phone: 608-663-2831 • www.edgewood.edu/accessibility • Email: accessdisabilityserv@edgewood.edu

Documentation submitted to: Disability and Accessibility Services
Separate application required for Services: Yes

Documentation required for:
LD: Psychoeducational evaluation
ADHD: Psychoeducational evaluation
ASD: Psychoeducational evaluation

Marian University

45 S. National Avenue, Fond du Lac, WI 54935 • Admissions: 920-923-7650 • marianuniversity.edu

(Support: CS)

ACCOMMODATIONS

Allowed in exams:

Calculators	Yes
Dictionary	No
Computer	Yes
Spell-checker	Yes
Extended test time	Yes
Scribe	Yes
Proctors	Yes
Oral exams	Yes
Note-takers	Yes

Support services for students with:

LD	Yes
ADHD	Yes
ASD	Yes
Distraction-reduced environment	Yes
Recording of lecture allowed	Yes
Reading technology	Yes
Audio books	Yes
Other assistive technology	Yes
Priority registration	Yes

Added costs of services:

For LD	No
For ADHD	No
For ASD	No
LD specialists	Yes
ADHD & ASD coaching	Yes
ASD specialists	No
Professional tutors	Yes
Peer tutors	Yes
Max. hours/week for services	Varies
How professors are notified of student approved accommodations	Student

COLLEGE GRADUATION REQUIREMENTS

Course waivers allowed	No
Course substitutions allowed	Yes
In what courses: Varies	

PROGRAMS/SERVICES FOR STUDENTS WITH LEARNING DIFFERENCES

Marian University's Accessibility Resources provides academic support, advocacy, and reasonable academic accommodations, such as extended time to complete exams, testing in a distraction-reduced environment, assistive listening devices, note-taking assistance, preferential seating, priority registration, and textbooks in alternative formats. Students are encouraged to utilize support services in the Learning and Writing Center. To request reasonable accommodations, students meet with the director of Accessibility Resources to discuss potential academic accommodations and provide appropriate documentation.

ADMISSIONS

The admission applications are reviewed individually to determine if applicants are a good fit for Marian. Admitted students have a minimum 2.0 high school GPA, an 18 on the ACT or 940 on the SAT, and rank in the top 50 percent of their high school class, if rank is provided. Applicants who do not meet the minimum admission criteria but show potential for academic success may be admitted through the EXCEL Program on a provisional basis.

Additional Information

EXCEL is a one-year program designed to support students in their transition to college. Students gain an understanding of clear expectations for academic performance, benefit from greater individualized learning and extra academic support, and learn how to navigate campus resources and services to achieve both academic and personal success. Through the EXCEL Program, students are encouraged to take responsibility for their college career by participating in orientation, attending mandatory bi-weekly meetings with their advisor, utilizing necessary campus resources and services, actively participating in the classroom, and communicating openly with their professors.

Marian University opened as Marian College of Fond du Lac, Wisconsin in 1936, with 17 full-time and 25 part-time students and eight faculty. The Congregation of Sisters of St. Agnes founded the college in response to a Wisconsin Department of Instruction decision that nuns were not allowed to teach in public schools while wearing their religious habits.

Marian University

GENERAL ADMISSIONS

Very important factors include: rigor of secondary school record, class rank, academic GPA, standardized test scores (if submitted). *Other factors considered include:* application essay, recommendations. High school diploma is required and GED is accepted. Institution is test-optional for entering Fall 2024. Check admissions website for updates. *Academic units required:* 4 English, 2 math, 1 science (1 lab), 1 history, 9 academic electives. *Academic units recommended:* 3 math, 2 science, 2 foreign language.

FINANCIAL AID

Students should submit: FAFSA; Institution's own financial aid form. *Need-based scholarships/grants offered:* College/university scholarship or grant aid from institutional funds; Federal Pell; Private scholarships; SEOG; State scholarships/grants. *Loan aid offered:* Direct PLUS loans; Direct Subsidized Loans; Direct Unsubsidized Loans. Federal Work-Study Program available. Institutional employment available.

CAMPUS LIFE

Activities: Campus Ministries; Choral groups; Concert band; Dance; Drama/theater; Jazz band; Literary magazine; Model UN; Music ensembles; Pep band; Student government; Student newspaper; Symphony orchestra. **Organizations:** 40 registered organizations, 6 honor societies, 1 religious organizations, 1 fraternities, 2 sororities. **Athletics (Intercollegiate):** *Men:* baseball, basketball, cross-country, golf, ice hockey. *Women:* basketball, cross-country, golf, ice hockey, softball, volleyball.

CAMPUS

Type of school	Private (nonprofit)
Environment	Town

STUDENTS

Undergrad enrollment	1,149
% male/female	34/66
% from out of state	34
% frosh live on campus	72

FINANCIAL FACTS

Annual tuition	$30,000
Room and board	$8,290

GENERAL ADMISSIONS INFO

Application fee	$20
Regular application deadline	Rolling
Nonfall registration	Yes

Fall 2024 testing policy	Test Optional
Range SAT EBRW	410–520
Range SAT Math	390–560
Range ACT Composite	18–23

ACADEMICS

Student/faculty ratio	12:1
% students returning for sophomore year	65

Most classes have 10–19 students.

REQUESTING SERVICES FOR STUDENTS WITH LEARNING DIFFERENCES

Phone: 920-923-8951 • my.marianuniversity.edu/Academics/case/Pages/Disability-Services.aspx
Email: lmolig65@marianuniversity.edu

Documentation submitted to: Accessibility Resources
Separate application required for Services: Yes

Documentation required for:
LD: Psychoeducational evaluation
ADHD: Psychoeducational evaluation
ASD: Psychoeducational evaluation

Marquette University

P.O. Box 1881, Milwaukee, WI 53201-1881 • Admissions: 414-288-7302 • www.marquette.edu

Support: SP

ACCOMMODATIONS

Allowed in exams:

Calculators	Yes
Dictionary	Yes
Computer	Yes
Spell-checker	Yes
Extended test time	Yes
Scribe	Yes
Proctors	Yes
Oral exams	Yes
Note-takers	Yes

Support services for students with:

LD	Yes
ADHD	Yes
ASD	Yes
Distraction-reduced environment	Yes
Recording of lecture allowed	Yes
Reading technology	Yes
Audio books	Yes
Other assistive technology	Yes
Priority registration	Yes

Added costs of services:

For LD	Yes
For ADHD	Yes
For ASD	Yes
LD specialists	No
ADHD & ASD coaching	Yes
ASD specialists	Yes
Professional tutors	No
Peer tutors	Yes
Max. hours/week for services	Varies
How professors are notified of student approved accommodations	Student

COLLEGE GRADUATION REQUIREMENTS

Course waivers allowed	No
Course substitutions allowed	Yes

In what courses: Foreign Language and Math on a case-by-case basis

PROGRAMS/SERVICES FOR STUDENTS WITH LEARNING DIFFERENCES

The Office of Disability Services (ODS) coordinates accommodations for all students with identified and documented disabilities. Based on the evaluation of the student's disability and supporting documentation, an ODS staff member determines a range of individualized accommodations. Students are responsible for delivering the written recommendations to their professors. Students can also receive as-needed guidance on multiple topics, including time management strategies, study skills, supplemental academic advising, note-taking, academic goal setting, test-taking strategies, textbook reading skills, self-advocacy, and check-in meetings. On Your Marq is a fee-based program with trained staff to support neurodivergent students at Marquette. Students receive help with academics, social skills, and independent living skills. On Your Marq (OYM) offers one-on-one coaching, tutoring, weekly seminars, and peer mentors. The program's first two years are directed toward successfully transitioning to college and identifying skills for a future career. Students enrolled in OYM are expected to be able to manage communication from professors, be open to feedback, adjust to schedule changes, and commit to follow the agreement plan signed by the student. COMPASS (Community of Marquette Peers Advising + Supporting Students) is a peer mentor program in ODS for students with disabilities. Mentors offer support, guidance, leadership, and assistance with self-advocacy skills.

ADMISSIONS

All applicants for admission must meet the same admission criteria. The middle 50 percent of accepted applicants have a GPA of 3.39–3.85. For those submitting test scores, the middle 50 percent have an ACT score of 26–31 or an SAT score of 1200–1350.

Additional Information

Student Educational Services provides free academic support services to Marquette students, including small group tutoring for classes, study skills workshops, tutoring, and academic coaching.

Raynor Memorial Libraries' Department of Special Collections is home to the original manuscripts of John Ronald Reuel Tolkien (1892-1973), professor of Old and Middle English language and literature at Oxford University, 1925-1959. The collection includes original manuscripts and working drafts of *The Hobbit* (1937), *Farmer Giles of Ham* (1949), and *The Lord of the Rings* (1954-1955).

Marquette University

General Admissions

Very important factors include: rigor of secondary school record, academic GPA. *Important factors include:* standardized test scores (if submitted), application essay. *Other factors considered include:* class rank, recommendations. High school diploma is required and GED is accepted. Institution is test-optional for entering Fall 2024. Check admissions website for updates. *Academic units required:* 4 English, 2 math, 2 science (2 labs), 2 social studies, 2 academic electives. *Academic units recommended:* 4 math, 4 science (3 labs), 2 foreign language, 3 social studies, 5 academic electives.

Financial Aid

Students should submit: FAFSA. *Need-based scholarships/grants offered:* College/university scholarship or grant aid from institutional funds; Federal Nursing Scholarships; Federal Pell; Private scholarships; SEOG; State scholarships/grants. *Loan aid offered:* Direct PLUS loans; Direct Subsidized Loans; Direct Unsubsidized Loans. Federal Work-Study Program available. Institutional employment available.

Campus Life

Activities: Campus Ministries; Choral groups; Concert band; Dance; Drama/theater; International Student Organization; Jazz band; Literary magazine; Model UN; Music ensembles; Musical theater; Pep band; Radio station; Student government; Student newspaper; Symphony orchestra; Television station; Yearbook. **Organizations:** 291 registered organizations, 16 honor societies, 13 religious organizations, 10 fraternities, 13 sororities. **Athletics (Intercollegiate):** *Men:* baseball, basketball, crew/rowing, cross-country, cycling, equestrian sports, golf, ice hockey, lacrosse, martial arts, rugby, swimming, table tennis, track/field (indoor), ultimate frisbee, volleyball, water polo. *Women:* basketball, crew/rowing, cross-country, cycling, equestrian sports, golf, lacrosse, martial arts, rugby, softball, swimming, table tennis, track/field (indoor), ultimate frisbee, volleyball, water polo.

CAMPUS	
Type of school	Private (nonprofit)
Environment	Metropolis

STUDENTS	
Undergrad enrollment	7,290
% male/female	44/56
% from out of state	64
% frosh live on campus	91

FINANCIAL FACTS	
Annual tuition	$47,690
Room and board	$15,740
Required fees	$1,010

GENERAL ADMISSIONS INFO	
Application fee	No fee
Regular application deadline	12/1
Nonfall registration	Yes

Fall 2024 testing policy	Test Optional
Range SAT EBRW	590–670
Range SAT Math	580–690
Range ACT Composite	26–31

ACADEMICS	
Student/faculty ratio	13:1
% students returning for sophomore year	90
Most classes have 10–19 students.	

REQUESTING SERVICES FOR STUDENTS WITH LEARNING DIFFERENCES

Phone: 414-288-1645 • www.marquette.edu/disability-services • Email: ods@marquette.edu

Documentation submitted to: Office of Disability Services

Separate application required for Services: Yes

Documentation required for:
LD: Psychoeducational evaluation
ADHD: Psychoeducational evaluation
ASD: Psychoeducational evaluation

Ripon College

P.O. Box 248, Ripon, WI 54971 • Admissions: 920-748-8337 • www.ripon.edu

$$\boxed{\textbf{Support: S}}$$

ACCOMMODATIONS

Allowed in exams:

Calculators	Yes
Dictionary	Yes
Computer	Yes
Spell-checker	Yes
Extended test time	Yes
Scribe	Yes
Proctors	Yes
Oral exams	Yes
Note-takers	Yes

Support services for students with:

LD	Yes
ADHD	Yes
ASD	Yes
Distraction-reduced environment	Yes
Recording of lecture allowed	Yes
Reading technology	Yes
Audio books	Yes
Other assistive technology	Yes
Priority registration	No

Added costs of services:

For LD	No
For ADHD	No
For ASD	No
LD specialists	No
ADHD & ASD coaching	No
ASD specialists	No
Professional tutors	No
Peer tutors	Yes
Max. hours/week for services	Varies
How professors are notified of student approved accommodations	Student and Student Support Services

COLLEGE GRADUATION REQUIREMENTS

Course waivers allowed	No
Course substitutions allowed	No

PROGRAMS/SERVICES FOR STUDENTS WITH LEARNING DIFFERENCES

Student Support Services (SSS) offers individualized writing support, test-taking accommodations, notetakers, and specialized computer programs. SSS provides tutoring in subject areas as well as skills classes in time management, note-taking, test-taking strategies, reading college texts, writing papers, studying for and taking exams, and setting goals. Counseling and guidance are also provided by SSS as well as intensive study groups, learning disability support, and internships. Through SSS, students are connected with peer contacts who provide them with one-on-one support in adjusting to college life and any other issues that arise. Various skill development, financial literacy, and intelligence workshops are also offered. The tutoring program helps students develop independent learning skills and improve their grades.

ADMISSIONS

All applicants are expected to meet the same admission criteria. There is no minimum GPA required for Ripon College, however, the average admitted student's GPA is 3.4. For admitted students who submit scores, the average ACT is 24 and the SAT is 1149.

Additional Information

The Franzen Center for Academic Success houses all campus academic support offerings, including one-on-one tutoring, drop-in quantitative tutoring, and writing and presentation services.

Ripon was founded in 1851, originally named Brockway College, for William S. Brockway, who presented the winning bid of $250 in an auction to name the college. Converted from a college preparatory to a four-year college, the first class of four women was held in 1863, with all four graduating in 1867. Three original buildings: East Hall constructed in 1851, Smith Hall completed in 1857, and West Hall completed in 1867, witnessed the first commencement and are still in use.

Ripon College

GENERAL ADMISSIONS

Very important factors include: rigor of secondary school record. *Important factors include:* class rank, academic GPA. *Other factors considered include:* standardized test scores (if submitted), application essay, recommendations. High school diploma is required and GED is accepted. Institution is test-optional for entering Fall 2024. Check admissions website for updates. *Academic units required:* 4 English, 2 math, 2 science, 2 social studies. *Academic units recommended:* 4 math, 4 science, 2 foreign language, 4 social studies.

FINANCIAL AID

Students should submit: FAFSA. *Need-based scholarships/grants offered:* College/university scholarship or grant aid from institutional funds; Federal Pell; Private scholarships; SEOG; State scholarships/grants. *Loan aid offered:* Direct PLUS loans; Direct Subsidized Loans; Direct Unsubsidized Loans. Federal Work-Study Program available. Institutional employment available.

CAMPUS LIFE

Activities: Campus Ministries; Choral groups; Concert band; Dance; Drama/theater; International Student Organization; Jazz band; Literary magazine; Music ensembles; Musical theater; Pep band; Radio station; Student government; Student newspaper; Student-run film society; Symphony orchestra; Yearbook. **Organizations:** 45 registered organizations, 17 honor societies, 4 religious organizations, 4 fraternities, 3 sororities. **Athletics (Intercollegiate):** *Men:* baseball, basketball, bowling, cross-country, equestrian sports, golf, ice hockey, lacrosse, martial arts, racquetball, rugby, softball, swimming, table tennis, track/field (indoor), ultimate frisbee, volleyball, water polo. *Women:* basketball, bowling, cross-country, equestrian sports, golf, ice hockey, lacrosse, martial arts, racquetball, rugby, softball, swimming, table tennis, track/field (indoor), ultimate frisbee, volleyball, water polo.

CAMPUS

Type of school	Private (nonprofit)
Environment	Village

STUDENTS

Undergrad enrollment	801
% male/female	51/49
% from out of state	27
% frosh live on campus	97

FINANCIAL FACTS

Annual tuition	$50,400
Room and board	$10,190
Required fees	$300

GENERAL ADMISSIONS INFO

Application fee	$30
Regular application deadline	Rolling
Nonfall registration	Yes

Fall 2024 testing policy	Test Optional
Range SAT EBRW	510–580
Range SAT Math	480–590
Range ACT Composite	19–23

ACADEMICS

Student/faculty ratio	14:1
% students returning for sophomore year	72
Most classes have 10–19 students.	

Wisconsin

REQUESTING SERVICES FOR STUDENTS WITH LEARNING DIFFERENCES

Phone: 920-748-8107 • ripon.edu/academics/advising/support/ • Email: krhind@ripon.edu

Documentation submitted to: Student Support Services
Separate application required for Services: Yes

Documentation required for:
LD: Psychoeducational evaluation
ADHD: Psychoeducational evaluation
ASD: Psychoeducational evaluation

University of Wisconsin—Eau Claire

105 Garfield Avenue, Eau Claire, WI 54701 • Admissions: 715-836-5415 • www.uwec.edu

Support: CS

PROGRAMS/SERVICES FOR STUDENTS WITH LEARNING DIFFERENCES

Accommodations and services for students with disabilities are determined through the Services for Students with Disabilities office. Students must fill out an application and submit documentation to request accommodations. Students will then be contacted by a staff member to schedule a meeting to discuss appropriate and reasonable accommodations.

ADMISSIONS

Admission requirements are the same for all students, and importance is placed on grade trend and rigor of courses. Students admitted to the university have a GPA of 3.4–3.9, an average class rank of 74 percent (if reported), and score between 21 to 27 on the ACT or 1120–1310 on the SAT. Students who demonstrate the potential for academic success but require extra support in their transition to college may be admitted to the university through the Student Success Program. If a student with a disability does not meet the admission requirements, it is possible to apply for an exception. Exception applications require a submission to the Services for Students with Disabilities office that includes all updated documentation, establishing both the existence of a disability and the resulting need for the exception being requested.

Additional Information

The Student Success Program is a one-year academic support program that provides small classes and structure to first-year students to support their transition to college. This program offers a study skills strategies course, tutoring, and an academic coach who provides one-on-one guidance throughout the year. The Student Success Program also includes required courses, field trips, and out-of-class activities and events. The Academic Skills Center (ASC) provides students with Supplemental Instruction, academic coaching, and peer tutoring. The peer academic coaching service includes free, hour-long meetings to teach time management, study skills, note-taking, and reading comprehension. Students can work with a coach once or weekly throughout the semester to help them stay on track. ASC's Developmental Education Program offers classes that teach college learning strategies, which may be taken for credit with permission from the ASC.

ACCOMMODATIONS

Allowed in exams:

Calculators	Yes
Dictionary	No
Computer	Yes
Spell-checker	Yes
Extended test time	Yes
Scribe	Yes
Proctors	Yes
Oral exams	No
Note-takers	Yes

Support services for students with:

LD	Yes
ADHD	Yes
ASD	Yes
Distraction-reduced environment	Yes
Recording of lecture allowed	Yes
Reading technology	Yes
Audio books	Yes
Other assistive technology	Yes
Priority registration	Yes

Added costs of services:

For LD	No
For ADHD	No
For ASD	No
LD specialists	Yes
ADHD & ASD coaching	No
ASD specialists	No
Professional tutors	Yes
Peer tutors	Yes
Max. hours/week for services	Varies
How professors are notified of student approved accommodations	Student

COLLEGE GRADUATION REQUIREMENTS

Course waivers allowed	Yes
In what courses: Case-by-case basis	
Course substitutions allowed	Yes
In what courses: Case-by-case basis	

It may not be one the coldest places in America, or even in Eau Claire, but if David Letterman says it's in the "Top 10," it sticks. The campus walking bridge over the Chippewa is beautiful in good weather, but when the winter winds are howling, it's #Bridgeface season. Students dress in as many layers as possible and take a photo of their freezing #Bridgeface on the way to class.

University of Wisconsin— Eau Claire

General Admissions

Very important factors include: rigor of secondary school record, academic GPA. *Important factors include:* class rank, application essay. *Other factors considered include:* standardized test scores (if submitted), recommendations. High school diploma is required and GED is accepted. Institution is test-optional for entering Fall 2024. Check admissions website for updates. *Academic units required:* 4 English, 3 math, 3 science, 3 social studies, 4 academic electives. *Academic units recommended:* 4 math, 4 science, 2 foreign language, 4 social studies.

Financial Aid

Students should submit: FAFSA. *Need-based scholarships/grants offered:* College/university scholarship or grant aid from institutional funds; Federal Pell; Private scholarships; SEOG; State scholarships/grants. *Loan aid offered:* Direct PLUS loans; Direct Subsidized Loans; Direct Unsubsidized Loans. Federal Work-Study Program available. Institutional employment available.

Campus Life

Activities: Campus Ministries; Choral groups; Concert band; Dance; Drama/theater; International Student Organization; Jazz band; Literary magazine; Marching band; Model UN; Music ensembles; Musical theater; Opera; Pep band; Radio station; Student government; Student newspaper; Student-run film society; Symphony orchestra; Television station. **Organizations:** 205 registered organizations, 10 honor societies, 8 religious organizations, 3 fraternities, 3 sororities. **Athletics (Intercollegiate):** *Men:* baseball, basketball, bowling, cross-country, equestrian sports, golf, ice hockey, lacrosse, martial arts, rugby, skiing (nordic/cross-country), swimming, table tennis, track/field (indoor), ultimate frisbee, volleyball, wrestling. *Women:* baseball, basketball, bowling, cross-country, equestrian sports, golf, gymnastics, ice hockey, lacrosse, martial arts, rugby, skiing (nordic/cross-country), softball, swimming, table tennis, track/field (indoor), ultimate frisbee, volleyball.

CAMPUS

Type of school	Public
Environment	City

STUDENTS

Undergrad enrollment	8,844
% male/female	40/60
% from out of state	36
% frosh live on campus	93

FINANCIAL FACTS

Annual in-state tuition	$7,361
Annual out-of-state tuition	$16,074
Room and board	$9,014
Required fees	$1,553

GENERAL ADMISSIONS INFO

Application fee	$25
Regular application deadline	8/1
Nonfall registration	Yes

Fall 2024 testing policy	Test Optional
Range SAT EBRW	550–660
Range SAT Math	550–650
Range ACT Composite	21–27

ACADEMICS

Student/faculty ratio	19:1
% students returning for sophomore year	81

Most classes have 20–29 students.

REQUESTING SERVICES FOR STUDENTS WITH LEARNING DIFFERENCES

Phone: 715-836-5800 • www.uwec.edu/ssd • Email: ssd@uwec.edu

Documentation submitted to: Services for Students with Disabilities
Separate application required for Services: Yes

Documentation required for:
  LD: Psychoeducational evaluation
  ADHD: Psychoeducational evaluation
  ASD: Psychoeducational evaluation

University of Wisconsin—Madison

702 West Johnson Street, Suite 101, Madison, WI 53715–1007 • Admissions: 608-262-3961 • www.wisc.edu

Support: CS

Allowed in exams:	
Calculators	Yes
Dictionary	Yes
Computer	Yes
Spell-checker	Yes
Extended test time	Yes
Scribe	Yes
Proctors	No
Oral exams	Yes
Note-takers	Yes
Support services for students with:	
LD	Yes
ADHD	Yes
ASD	Yes
Distraction-reduced environment	Yes
Recording of lecture allowed	Yes
Reading technology	Yes
Audio books	Yes
Other assistive technology	Yes
Priority registration	Yes
Added costs of services:	
For LD	No
For ADHD	No
For ASD	No
LD specialists	Yes
ADHD & ASD coaching	No
ASD specialists	Yes
Professional tutors	No
Peer tutors	Yes
Max. hours/week for services	Varies
How professors are notified of student approved accommodations	Student

COLLEGE GRADUATION REQUIREMENTS

Course waivers allowed	No
Course substitutions allowed	No

PROGRAMS/SERVICES FOR STUDENTS WITH LEARNING DIFFERENCES

The McBurney Disability Resource Center delivers classroom accommodation services to students with disabilities. Alternative testing accommodations are available for tests, midterms, quizzes, and final exams. Assistive technology is based on the individual's needs and may include assistive listening devices and iPads with note-taking software. With the online system McBurney Connect, students can select which approved accommodations they wish to apply to each course, and the system notifies their professors by email. The McBurney Orientation and Service Training (MOST) program helps first-year students with documented disabilities transition to the university. Topics covered in MOST include understanding faculty expectations, navigating resources, utilizing and implementing accommodations, and a course in Counseling Psychology.

ADMISSIONS

Admission is competitive and selective. The admissions department examines each applicant by reviewing coursework and grades, extracurricular involvement and leadership, essays, and letters of recommendation. There is no minimum GPA requirement, but emphasis is placed on academics and rigor of coursework. Two essays are required, but interviews are neither required nor considered. Required high school math courses cannot be satisfied by statistics, business math, or computer classes. Campus tours are encouraged so applicants can become familiar with the campus, but touring is not a factor in admission.

Additional Information

Autism Spectrum Wellbeing Education Aspiration & Relationship Empowerment (AS WE ARE) is a professionally run support group that meets weekly to discuss topics chosen by the students. DREAM (Disability Rights, Education Activism, and Mentoring) is a national organization for students with disabilities that advocates for disability culture, community, and pride. Students can connect with each other through DREAM's online disability cultural center.

DID YOU KNOW?

Camp Randall Stadium has been home to the Wisconsin Badgers football team since 1895. It was used as a Union Army training camp during the Civil War, training over 70,000 soldiers and imprisoning over 1,000 Confederate soldiers. When veterans protested plans to turn the site into building lots, the state bought the land and presented it to the university. It is the oldest and fifth-largest stadium in the Big Ten Conference.

University of Wisconsin—Madison

GENERAL ADMISSIONS
Very important factors include: rigor of secondary school record, application essay. *Important factors include:* academic GPA. *Other factors considered include:* class rank, standardized test scores (if submitted), recommendations. High school diploma is required and GED is accepted. Institution is test-optional for entering Fall 2024. Check admissions website for updates. *Academic units required:* 4 English, 4 math, 3 science, 3 foreign language, 3 social studies. *Academic units recommended:* 4 science (2 labs), 4 foreign language, 4 social studies.

FINANCIAL AID
Students should submit: FAFSA. *Need-based scholarships/grants offered:* College/university scholarship or grant aid from institutional funds; Federal Pell; Private scholarships; SEOG; State scholarships/grants. *Loan aid offered:* Direct PLUS loans; Direct Subsidized Loans; Direct Unsubsidized Loans. Federal Work-Study Program available. Institutional employment available.

CAMPUS LIFE
Activities: Choral groups; Concert band; Dance; Drama/theater; International Student Organization; Jazz band; Literary magazine; Marching band; Music ensembles; Musical theater; Opera; Pep band; Radio station; Student government; Student newspaper; Student-run film society; Symphony orchestra; Television station; Yearbook. **Organizations:** 986 registered organizations, 27 honor societies, 26 fraternities, 11 sororities. **Athletics (Intercollegiate):** *Men:* baseball, basketball, crew/rowing, cross-country, cycling, field hockey, golf, gymnastics, ice hockey, lacrosse, martial arts, racquetball, rugby, swimming, table tennis, track/field (indoor), ultimate frisbee, volleyball, water polo, wrestling. *Women:* basketball, crew/rowing, cross-country, cycling, field hockey, golf, gymnastics, ice hockey, lacrosse, martial arts, racquetball, rugby, softball, swimming, table tennis, track/field (indoor), ultimate frisbee, volleyball, water polo.

CAMPUS

Type of school	Public
Environment	City

STUDENTS

Undergrad enrollment	35,184
% male/female	47/53
% from out of state	42
% frosh live on campus	90

FINANCIAL FACTS

Annual in-state tuition	$10,722
Annual out-of-state tuition	$39,354
Room and board	$12,894

GENERAL ADMISSIONS INFO

Application fee	$60
Regular application deadline	2/1
Nonfall registration	Yes

Fall 2024 testing policy	Test Optional
Range SAT EBRW	650–730
Range SAT Math	690–780
Range ACT Composite	28–32

ACADEMICS

Student/faculty ratio	18:1
% students returning for sophomore year	95

Most classes have 10–19 students.

REQUESTING SERVICES FOR STUDENTS WITH LEARNING DIFFERENCES

Phone: 608-263-2741 • mcburney.wisc.edu/ • Email: mcburney@studentlife.wisc.edu

Documentation submitted to: McBurney Disability Resource Center
Separate application required for Services: Yes

Documentation required for:
LD: Psychoeducational evaluation
ADHD: Psychoeducational evaluation
ASD: Psychoeducational evaluation

University of Wisconsin—Milwaukee

Dept. of Admissions and Recruitment, Milwaukee, WI 53211 • Admissions: 414-229-2222 • uwm.edu

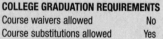

Support: CS

ACCOMMODATIONS

Allowed in exams:

Calculators	No
Dictionary	Yes
Computer	Yes
Spell-checker	Yes
Extended test time	Yes
Scribe	Yes
Proctors	Yes
Oral exams	Yes
Note-takers	Yes

Support services for students with:

LD	Yes
ADHD	Yes
ASD	Yes
Distraction-reduced environment	Yes
Recording of lecture allowed	Yes
Reading technology	Yes
Audio books	Yes
Other assistive technology	Yes
Priority registration	Yes

Added costs of services:

For LD	No
For ADHD	No
For ASD	No
LD specialists	Yes
ADHD & ASD coaching	No
ASD specialists	No
Professional tutors	No
Peer tutors	Yes
Max. hours/week for services	Varies
How professors are notified of student approved accommodations	Student

COLLEGE GRADUATION REQUIREMENTS

Course waivers allowed	No
Course substitutions allowed	Yes
In what courses: Case-by-case basis	

PROGRAMS/SERVICES FOR STUDENTS WITH LEARNING DIFFERENCES

The Accessibility Resource Center (ARC) offers academic support services to students with learning disabilities, ADHD, and ASD. Accommodations are based on need and documentation, and students can request and manage their accommodations through the online portal ARConnect. Services include note-taking assistance, exam accommodations, alternate-format textbooks, and priority registration. Students with determined needs for assistive technology can use the Computer and Assistive Technology Lab, as well as access portable, flexible technology. Training on the use of assistive technology is available. Eligible students can receive individual counseling and guidance, and ARC staff is available to meet individually with students to work on study strategies, time management issues, and organization strategies.

ADMISSIONS

All applicants are expected to meet the same admission criteria. The admission committee considers academic preparation, rigor of high school coursework, class rank (if available), overall GPA, and grades in specific courses related to the applicant's intended major at UWM. A foreign language is not required for admission to UWM, but at least two years of a foreign language in high school will help to fulfill undergraduate foreign language requirements.

Additional Information

Autism Group is a campus organization for students with ASD to meet twice a month and engage in informal conversations, activities, and events decided on by members.

DID YOU KNOW?

The American Geographical Society Library (AGSL) at UWM is a major research and reference center. Its world-renowned collection encompasses over 500,000 maps, 200,000 volumes, nearly 440,000 photographs, 12,000 atlases, and 120 globes. The library was accepted by the Board of Regents in 1976, moved from NY to UWM in 1978, and became available to the public in 1981.

University of Wisconsin— Milwaukee

General Admissions

Very important factors include: rigor of secondary school record, academic GPA, standardized test scores (if submitted). *Important factors include:* application essay. *Other factors considered include:* class rank, recommendations. High school diploma is required and GED is accepted. Institution is test-optional for entering Fall 2024. Check admissions website for updates. *Academic units required:* 4 English, 3 math, 3 science (1 lab), 3 social studies, 4 academic electives. *Academic units recommended:* 4 math, 4 science, 2 foreign language, 4 social studies.

Financial Aid

Students should submit: FAFSA. *Need-based scholarships/grants offered:* College/university scholarship or grant aid from institutional funds; Federal Pell; Private scholarships; SEOG; State scholarships/grants. *Loan aid offered:* Direct PLUS loans; Direct Subsidized Loans; Direct Unsubsidized Loans. Federal Work-Study Program available. Institutional employment available.

Campus Life

Activities: Campus Ministries; Choral groups; Concert band; Dance; Drama/theater; International Student Organization; Jazz band; Literary magazine; Model UN; Music ensembles; Musical theater; Opera; Pep band; Radio station; Student government; Student newspaper; Student-run film society; Symphony orchestra. **Organizations:** 296 registered organizations, 4 honor societies, 18 religious organizations, 10 fraternities, 7 sororities. **Athletics (Intercollegiate):** *Men:* baseball, basketball, bowling, cross-country, equestrian sports, ice hockey, lacrosse, rugby, skiing (nordic/cross-country), softball, swimming, ultimate frisbee, volleyball, wrestling. *Women:* basketball, bowling, cross-country, equestrian sports, lacrosse, rugby, skiing (nordic/cross-country), softball, swimming, ultimate frisbee, volleyball.

CAMPUS

Type of school	Public
Environment	Metropolis

STUDENTS

Undergrad enrollment	19,411
% male/female	45/55
% from out of state	11
% frosh live on campus	74

FINANCIAL FACTS

Annual in-state tuition	$9,610
Annual out-of-state tuition	$21,474
Room and board	$10,896

GENERAL ADMISSIONS INFO

Application fee	$25
Regular application deadline	8/11
Nonfall registration	Yes
Fall 2024 testing policy	Test Optional
Range ACT Composite	18–25

ACADEMICS

Student/faculty ratio	18:1
% students returning for sophomore year	76
Most classes have 20–29 students.	

REQUESTING SERVICES FOR STUDENTS WITH LEARNING DIFFERENCES

Phone: 414-229-6287 • uwm.edu/arc/ • Email: archelp@uwm.edu

Documentation submitted to: Accessibility Resource Center
Separate application required for Services: Yes

Documentation required for:
LD: Psychoeducational evaluation
ADHD: Psychoeducational evaluation
ASD: Psychoeducational evaluation

University of Wisconsin Oshkosh

Dempsey Hall 135, Oshkosh, WI 54901 • Admissions: 920-424-0202 • uwosh.edu

(Support: SP)

ACCOMMODATIONS

Allowed in exams:

Calculators	Yes
Dictionary	Yes
Computer	Yes
Spell-checker	No
Extended test time	Yes
Scribe	No
Proctors	Yes
Oral exams	No
Note-takers	Yes

Support services for students with:

LD	Yes
ADHD	Yes
ASD	Yes
Distraction-reduced environment	Yes
Recording of lecture allowed	Yes
Reading technology	Yes
Audio books	Yes
Other assistive technology	Yes
Priority registration	Yes

Added costs of services:

For LD	No
For ADHD	No
For ASD	No
LD specialists	Yes
ADHD & ASD coaching	No
ASD specialists	No
Professional tutors	Yes
Peer tutors	Yes
Max. hours/week for services	Varies
How professors are notified of student approved accommodations	Student and Accessibility Center

COLLEGE GRADUATION REQUIREMENTS

Course waivers allowed	Yes

In what courses: Foreign Language

Course substitutions allowed	Yes

In what courses: Foreign Language

PROGRAMS/SERVICES FOR STUDENTS WITH LEARNING DIFFERENCES

The Accessibility Center (AC) provides assistance and accommodations to students with disabilities. To receive accommodations, students must complete the accommodation request form and submit appropriate documentation. Once their documentation has been reviewed, students meet with the AC coordinator to discuss and determine reasonable accommodations, AC services and procedures for implementing accommodations, and connecting with course instructors. Students can utilize the online portal Accommodate to quickly and easily obtain the resources they need. Project Success is a language-remediation program for students with dyslexia and other language-based disabilities that uses a phonics-based multisensory methodology to improve reading and writing skills. The program includes remedial mathematics instruction and course support to help students ultimately become language-independent in math, spelling, reading, writing, comprehension, and study skills. Each Project Success student is assigned a case manager, or organizational tutor, who meets with the student at least weekly. The program serves over three hundred students at no additional charge.

ADMISSIONS

Admission criteria are the same for all students and includes the required core curriculum and a minimum 2.0 GPA. Students who do not meet all admission criteria may still be admitted through the Project Success Program.

Additional Information

Incoming first-year students to the Project Success program participate in a six-week summer program consisting of simultaneous multisensory instructional procedures (SMSIP). This is an opportunity for new students to gradually transition to college life, and it is mandatory for students who were granted admission to the university without having met the standard academic requirements. Students can obtain 6 college credits toward general education requirements during this summer program.

The B'Gosh Fest is a free, year-end celebration with food, inflatables, crafts, caricatures, games, and a live musical lineup of the students' choosing based on their voting results. It is the perfect way to relax and create memories prior to graduation and the start of summer.

University of Wisconsin Oshkosh

General Admissions

Very important factors include: rigor of secondary school record, class rank, academic GPA, standardized test scores (if submitted). *Important factors include:* application essay, recommendations. High school diploma is required and GED is accepted. Institution is test-optional for entering Fall 2024. Check admissions website for updates. *Academic units required:* 4 English, 3 math, 3 science (3 labs), 3 social studies, 4 academic electives. *Academic units recommended:* 4 math, 4 science (4 labs), 2 foreign language, 4 social studies, 1 visual/performing arts.

Financial Aid

Students should submit: FAFSA. *Need-based scholarships/grants offered:* College/university scholarship or grant aid from institutional funds; Federal Nursing Scholarships; Federal Pell; Private scholarships; SEOG; State scholarships/grants. *Loan aid offered:* Direct PLUS loans; Direct Subsidized Loans; Direct Unsubsidized Loans. Federal Work-Study Program available. Institutional employment available.

Campus Life

Activities: Campus Ministries; Choral groups; Concert band; Dance; Drama/theater; International Student Organization; Jazz band; Literary magazine; Model UN; Music ensembles; Musical theater; Pep band; Radio station; Student government; Student newspaper; Student-run film society; Television station. **Organizations:** 175 registered organizations, 15 honor societies, 6 religious organizations, 8 fraternities, 5 sororities. **Athletics (Intercollegiate):** *Men:* baseball, basketball, cross-country, swimming, track/field (indoor), wrestling. *Women:* basketball, cross-country, golf, gymnastics, softball, swimming, track/field (indoor), volleyball.

CAMPUS

Type of school	Public
Environment	City

STUDENTS

Undergrad enrollment	11,773
% male/female	39/61
% from out of state	10
% frosh live on campus	86

FINANCIAL FACTS

Annual in-state tuition	$7,734
Annual out-of-state tuition	$15,306
Room and board	$12,952

GENERAL ADMISSIONS INFO

Application fee	No fee
Regular application deadline	Rolling
Nonfall registration	Yes
Fall 2024 testing policy	Test Optional
Range ACT Composite	18–24

ACADEMICS

Student/faculty ratio	20:1
% students returning for sophomore year	69

Most classes have 20–29 students.

REQUESTING SERVICES FOR STUDENTS WITH LEARNING DIFFERENCES

Phone: 920-424-3100 • uwosh.edu/deanofstudents/accessibility-center/
Email: accessibilitycenter@uwosh.edu

Documentation submitted to: Accessibility Center
Separate application required for Services: Yes

Documentation required for:
 LD: Psychoeducational evaluation
 ADHD: Psychoeducational evaluation
 ASD: Psychoeducational evaluation

University of Wisconsin—Stevens Point

1108 Fremont Street, Stevens Point, WI 54481 • Admissions: 715-346-2441 • www.uwsp.edu

Support: S

ACCOMMODATIONS

Allowed in exams:

Calculators	Yes
Dictionary	No
Computer	Yes
Spell-checker	Yes
Extended test time	Yes
Scribe	Yes
Proctors	Yes
Oral exams	No
Note-takers	Yes

Support services for students with:

LD	Yes
ADHD	Yes
ASD	Yes
Distraction-reduced environment	Yes
Recording of lecture allowed	Yes
Reading technology	Yes
Audio books	Yes
Other assistive technology	Yes
Priority registration	Yes

Added costs of services:

For LD	No
For ADHD	No
For ASD	No
LD specialists	No
ADHD & ASD coaching	No
ASD specialists	No
Professional tutors	No
Peer tutors	Yes
Max. hours/week for services	Varies
How professors are notified of student approved accommodations	Student

COLLEGE GRADUATION REQUIREMENTS

Course waivers allowed	No
Course substitutions allowed	Yes
In what courses: Math, Speech, and Foreign Language	

PROGRAMS/SERVICES FOR STUDENTS WITH LEARNING DIFFERENCES

The Disability Resource Center (DRC) at the University of Wisconsin–Stevens Point provides accommodations to students with disabilities. The DRC works individually with qualified students to identify, design, and implement an accommodation plan. The DRC creates a learning environment to help maximize opportunities for students to succeed and where students will develop a good rapport with DRC staff members. The DRC staff fosters self-awareness and self-advocacy for students through their support and services. Accommodations include recorded lectures, copies of PowerPoint slides, proctored exams, assistive technology, extended time, readers, scribes, and a computer for test taking. Leading Edge is a transition program for first-year and transfer students with disabilities to learn about accommodations and academic support services at UWSP and receive assistive technology training. Students participating in the Learning Edge program take a pre-semester seminar and/or weekly class sessions and receive 1 academic credit.

ADMISSIONS

All applicants are expected to meet the same admission criteria. The university does not require letters of recommendation. However, if an academic record is not strong or has extenuating circumstances that should be considered, applicants are welcome to submit letters of recommendation for review. Students interested in the BA Dance, BA Drama, BA Music, BFA Musical Theatre, BFA Acting, and BFA Design/Technology must complete an on-campus performance audition and/or interview.

Additional Information

The Tutoring-Learning Center (TLC) offers UWSP students help with test-taking, time management, and study skills. Content tutoring is also offered.

WWSP-FM is UWSP's student-run alternative radio station. Since 1969, WWSP has hosted "The World's Largest Trivia Contest." Hundreds of teams from around the world, with as many as 12,000 players, test their knowledge, observational skills, and reflexes during the 54 hours of trivia.

University of Wisconsin— Stevens Point

GENERAL ADMISSIONS

Important factors include: rigor of secondary school record, class rank, academic GPA, standardized test scores (if submitted). *Other factors considered include:* application essay, recommendations. High school diploma is required and GED is accepted. Institution is test-optional for entering Fall 2024. Check admissions website for updates. *Academic units required:* 4 English, 3 math, 3 science, 3 social studies, 4 academic electives. *Academic units recommended:* 4 math, 4 science, 2 foreign language, 4 social studies.

FINANCIAL AID

Students should submit: FAFSA. *Need-based scholarships/grants offered:* College/university scholarship or grant aid from institutional funds; Federal Pell; Private scholarships; State scholarships/grants. *Loan aid offered:* Direct PLUS loans; Direct Subsidized Loans; Direct Unsubsidized Loans. Federal Work-Study Program available. Institutional employment available.

CAMPUS LIFE

Activities: Campus Ministries; Choral groups; Dance; Drama/theater; International Student Organization; Jazz band; Literary magazine; Model UN; Music ensembles; Musical theater; Opera; Pep band; Radio station; Student government; Student newspaper; Student-run film society; Symphony orchestra; Television station. **Organizations:** 185 registered organizations, 11 honor societies, 10 religious organizations, 5 fraternities, 3 sororities. **Athletics (Intercollegiate):** *Men:* baseball, basketball, cross-country, golf, ice hockey, lacrosse, rugby, skiing (nordic/cross-country), swimming, ultimate frisbee, volleyball, wrestling. *Women:* basketball, cross-country, golf, ice hockey, rugby, skiing (nordic/cross-country), softball, swimming, ultimate frisbee, volleyball.

CAMPUS
Type of school	Public
Environment	Town

STUDENTS
Undergrad enrollment	7,489
% male/female	43/57
% from out of state	9
% frosh live on campus	78

FINANCIAL FACTS
Annual in-state tuition	$8,884
Annual out-of-state tuition	$17,904
Room and board	$8,500

GENERAL ADMISSIONS INFO
Application fee	$25
Regular application deadline	9/1
Nonfall registration	Yes
Fall 2024 testing policy	Test Optional
Range ACT Composite	19–25

ACADEMICS
Student/faculty ratio	20:1
% students returning for sophomore year	75

Most classes have 20–29 students.

REQUESTING SERVICES FOR STUDENTS WITH LEARNING DIFFERENCES

Phone: 715-346-3365 • www.uwsp.edu/disability-resource-center • Email: drc@uwsp.edu

Documentation submitted to: Disability Resource Center
Separate application required for Services: Yes

Documentation required for:
 LD: Psychoeducational evaluation
 ADHD: Psychoeducational evaluation
 ASD: Psychoeducational evaluation

University of Wisconsin—Whitewater

800 West Main Street, Whitewater, WI 53190-1791 • Admissions: 262-472-1440 • uww.edu

Support: SP

ACCOMMODATIONS

Allowed in exams:

Calculators	Yes
Dictionary	Yes
Computer	Yes
Spell-checker	Yes
Extended test time	Yes
Scribe	Yes
Proctors	Yes
Oral exams	Yes
Note-takers	Yes

Support services for students with:

LD	Yes
ADHD	Yes
ASD	Yes
Distraction-reduced environment	Yes
Recording of lecture allowed	Yes
Reading technology	Yes
Audio books	Yes
Other assistive technology	Yes
Priority registration	Yes

Added costs of services:

For LD	No
For ADHD	No
For ASD	No
LD specialists	Yes
ADHD & ASD coaching	No
ASD specialists	No
Professional tutors	Yes
Peer tutors	Yes
Max. hours/week for services	Varies
How professors are notified of student approved accommodations	Student

COLLEGE GRADUATION REQUIREMENTS

Course waivers allowed	No
Course substitutions allowed	Yes
In what courses: Case-by-case basis	

PROGRAMS/SERVICES FOR STUDENTS WITH LEARNING DIFFERENCES

The Center for Students with Disabilities (CSD) provides programs and services for students with LD, ADHD, and ASD. Once students are admitted to UW-Whitewater, they may submit documentation of their disability to the CSD and schedule an intake appointment to determine an accommodation plan. Most services begin a few weeks after eligibility is determined. Services include alternative testing, classroom accommodations, note-taking, alternative media, and ongoing case management. CSD works directly with students on how to communicate with instructors and use their accommodations. In addition to these free services, CSD has several fee-based programs, such as Project Assist, a program that offers tutorial services to students, including drop-in, one-on-one, and organizational tutoring. Applications to Project Assist are filed after admission to UW–Whitewater. CSD also offers the Summer Transition Program, a fee-based, four-week residential transition program for incoming first-years with disabilities. Participants are mentored through the move-in process and adjustment to college life. They receive support from professional staff, access to Project ASSIST tutoring and campus and community resources, and the opportunity to enroll in the 3 credit course, Academic Study Skills, or Disability, Race, & Ethnicity in Society.

ADMISSIONS

All applicants must meet the same criteria for general admission. In addition to the core academic requirements, the four academic electives should be in art, music, foreign language, computer science, or business. Applicants are evaluated holistically, with consideration for high school community service, leadership, and talents, in conjunction with academic performance.

Additional Information

High school students, families, and teachers can learn about on- and off-campus resources through the yearly Opening Horizons program sponsored by CSD.

The Potawatomi Native Americans called it "Minneiska"(white water), named for the white sands of the Whitewater River. Approved by the Great Lakes Inter-Tribal Council, UW–Whitewater formally recognizes and honors that it exists on traditional lands of Native people with a Land Acknowledgment Statement that can be read at any event. UWW welcomes the shared duty and the opportunity of stewardship of these lands.

University of Wisconsin— Whitewater

GENERAL ADMISSIONS

Very important factors include: rigor of secondary school record, class rank, standardized test scores (if submitted). *Other factors considered include:* academic GPA, application essay, recommendations. High school diploma is required and GED is accepted. Institution is test-optional for entering Fall 2024. Check admissions website for updates. *Academic units required:* 4 English, 3 math, 3 science (1 lab), 3 social studies, 4 academic electives. *Academic units recommended:* 4 math, 4 science, 2 foreign language, 4 social studies.

FINANCIAL AID

Students should submit: FAFSA. *Need-based scholarships/grants offered:* College/university scholarship or grant aid from institutional funds; Federal Pell; Private scholarships; SEOG; State scholarships/grants. *Loan aid offered:* Direct PLUS loans; Direct Subsidized Loans; Direct Unsubsidized Loans.

CAMPUS LIFE

Activities: Choral groups; Concert band; Dance; Drama/theater; Jazz band; Literary magazine; Marching band; Music ensembles; Musical theater; Opera; Radio station; Student government; Student newspaper; Symphony orchestra; Television station. **Organizations:** 130 registered organizations, 4 honor societies, 8 religious organizations, 9 fraternities, 8 sororities. **Athletics (Intercollegiate):** *Men:* baseball, basketball, bowling, cross-country, lacrosse, racquetball, rugby, swimming, track/field (indoor), volleyball, wrestling. *Women:* basketball, bowling, cross-country, golf, gymnastics, ice hockey, racquetball, rugby, softball, swimming, track/field (indoor), volleyball, wrestling.

CAMPUS

Type of school	Public
Environment	Village

STUDENTS

Undergrad enrollment	9,375
% male/female	50/50
% from out of state	22
% frosh live on campus	90

FINANCIAL FACTS

Annual in-state tuition	$8,146
Annual out-of-state tuition	$17,688
Room and board	$7,770

GENERAL ADMISSIONS INFO

Application fee	No fee
Regular application deadline	Rolling
Nonfall registration	Yes
Fall 2024 testing policy	Test Optional
Range ACT Composite	18–24

ACADEMICS

Student/faculty ratio	19:1
% students returning for sophomore year	74
Most classes have 30–39 students.	

Wisconsin

REQUESTING SERVICES FOR STUDENTS WITH LEARNING DIFFERENCES

Phone: 262-472-4711 • www.uww.edu/csd • Email: csd@uww.edu

Documentation submitted to: Center for Students with Disabilities
Separate application required for Services: Yes

Documentation required for:
LD: Psychoeducational evaluation
ADHD: Psychoeducational evaluation
ASD: Psychoeducational evaluation

University of Wyoming

Dept 3435, Laramie, WY 82071 • Admissions: 307-766-5160 • www.uwyo.edu

Support: S

ACCOMMODATIONS

Allowed in exams:

Calculators	Yes
Dictionary	No
Computer	Yes
Spell-checker	Yes
Extended test time	Yes
Scribe	Yes
Proctors	Yes
Oral exams	No
Note-takers	Yes

Support services for students with:

LD	Yes
ADHD	Yes
ASD	Yes
Distraction-reduced environment	Yes
Recording of lecture allowed	Yes
Reading technology	Yes
Audio books	Yes
Other assistive technology	Yes
Priority registration	Yes

Added costs of services:

For LD	No
For ADHD	No
For ASD	No
LD specialists	No
ADHD & ASD coaching	No
ASD specialists	No
Professional tutors	No
Peer tutors	Yes
Max. hours/week for services	Varies
How professors are notified of student approved accommodations	Student and Disability Support Services

COLLEGE GRADUATION REQUIREMENTS

Course waivers allowed	No
Course substitutions allowed	No

PROGRAMS/SERVICES FOR STUDENTS WITH LEARNING DIFFERENCES

Disability Support Services (DSS) offers support for students with learning disabilities. In order to receive services, students must complete the intake form and request the necessary accommodations for each course in each semester. Accommodations can only be confidently implemented once faculty is officially notified by DSS. The Student Educational Opportunity (SEO) department functions within Academic Affairs to host campus-based programs and statewide outreach projects for eligible students, including those with disabilities, who can especially benefit from extra support in managing college life, achieving academic success and financial literacy, and career planning. Student Success Services (SSS) is an SEO program that provides academic support services to participating eligible students, including free tutoring for individuals and groups and study skills development. SSS offers a unique new student orientation that covers the perks and expectations of the SSS program. The Wyoming Institute for Disabilities (WIND) is an academic unit in the College of Health and Sciences and a part of the University Centers for Excellence in Developmental Disabilities (UCEDD). WIND works to assist students with developmental disabilities, as well as their families, through training, education, early intervention, and community services.

ADMISSIONS

All applicants should meet the same admission criteria, which includes a 3.0 GPA. The University of Wyoming will review applications from students who do not meet the general admission criteria. Students may apply for admission with support if they have a GPA of 2.5–2.99 and have completed the high school success curriculum with no more than two deficiencies, which cannot be in the same discipline. Students who have a GPA of 2.25–2.49 are reviewed holistically and may be required to submit an essay. Students admitted with support participate in an academic transition program, such as the UW Bridge Program. ACT or SAT scores are not required for admission but may be used for determining scholarship awards.

Additional Information

First-year students who are accepted without having met all the admission criteria are enrolled in the Bridge Program. Bridge Program students take either a first-year seminar or a seminar and an English course.

Dr. John W. Hoyt served as governor of the Wyoming Territory from 1878 to 1882, became a professor and the university's first president in 1887, and was fired in 1890 for being "too visionary and impractical." The women's dormitory Hoyt Hall was built in 1916 in his honor.

University of Wyoming

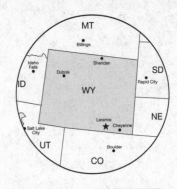

General Admissions

Very important factors include: rigor of secondary school record, academic GPA. *Other factors considered include:* application essay. High school diploma is required and GED is accepted. Institution is test-optional for entering Fall 2024. Check admissions website for updates. *Academic units required:* 4 English, 4 math, 4 science (3 labs), 3 social studies, 4 academic electives.

Financial Aid

Students should submit:. Need-based scholarships/grants offered: College/university scholarship or grant aid from institutional funds; Federal Pell; Private scholarships; SEOG; State scholarships/grants. *Loan aid offered:* Direct PLUS loans; Direct Subsidized Loans; Direct Unsubsidized Loans. Federal Work-Study Program available. Institutional employment available.

Campus Life

Activities: Campus Ministries; Choral groups; Concert band; Dance; Drama/theater; International Student Organization; Jazz band; Literary magazine; Marching band; Model UN; Music ensembles; Musical theater; Opera; Pep band; Radio station; Student government; Student newspaper; Student-run film society; Symphony orchestra; Television station. **Organizations:** 163 registered organizations, 6 honor societies, 6 religious organizations, 10 fraternities, 6 sororities. **Athletics (Intercollegiate):** *Men:* baseball, basketball, cross-country, cycling, equestrian sports, golf, ice hockey, lacrosse, racquetball, rugby, swimming, track/field (indoor), wrestling. *Women:* basketball, cross-country, cycling, equestrian sports, golf, ice hockey, lacrosse, racquetball, rugby, softball, swimming, track/field (indoor), volleyball.

CAMPUS

Type of school	Public
Environment	Town

STUDENTS

Undergrad enrollment	8,363
% male/female	47/53
% from out of state	33
% frosh live on campus	82

FINANCIAL FACTS

Annual in-state tuition	$4,800
Annual out-of-state tuition	$19,950
Room and board	$11,610
Required fees	$1,821

GENERAL ADMISSIONS INFO

Application fee	$40
Regular application deadline	8/10
Nonfall registration	Yes

Fall 2024 testing policy	Test Optional
Range SAT EBRW	510–620
Range SAT Math	520–620
Range ACT Composite	20–27

ACADEMICS

Student/faculty ratio	13:1
% students returning for sophomore year	75

Most classes have 10–19 students.

Wyoming

REQUESTING SERVICES FOR STUDENTS WITH LEARNING DIFFERENCES

Phone: 307-766-3073 • www.uwyo.edu/udss/ • Email: udss@uwyo.edu

Documentation submitted to: Disability Support Services
Separate application required for Services: Yes

Documentation required for:
LD: Psychoeducational evaluation
ADHD: Psychoeducational evaluation
ASD: Psychoeducational evaluation

Appendix

Alternative Post-Secondary Options

Alphabetical Index

Alphabetical List of Colleges by Level of Support Services

Alternative Post-Secondary Options

Program	Overview	Contact Information
29 Acres	The 29 Acres housing development is a safe and dynamic supported-living community where adults with autism (ASD) and other neurodiversities will live and be supported—enabling them to build relationships, feel value, success and happiness in their lives. 29 Acres, a registered 501(c)3, was founded in 2015 by a group of families who share a similar need: finding quality support services and safe housing for their young adults with autism and other neurodiversity in north Texas as they age out of the school system.	3000 Moseley Rd Cross Roads, TX 76227 214-550-8831 connect@29acres.org www.29acres.org
AbleLight College of Applied Learning at Concordia University *Formerly Bethesda* other areas served by Ablelight: California Colorado Illinois Kansas Michigan Minnesota Missouri New Jersey Oregon Washington	AbleLight College of Applied Learning prepares students with intellectual and developmental disabilities for independent adult living by providing them a full range of college and life experiences. AbleLight, a two-year postsecondary certificate program, is set in the safe, inclusive university environment of Concordia University Wisconsin (CUW). In addition to auditing Concordia classes of their choice, students participate in a curriculum that includes job coaching and hands-on training, financial management, transportation, and other life skills.	600 Hoffmann Dr. Watertown, WI 53094 262-243-2183/800-369-4636 ablelight.college@ablelight.org ablelight.org Concordia Wisconsin Campus 12800 N Lake Shore Drive Mequon, WI 53097
Adaptive Learning Center *Formerly Center for Adaptive Learning*	The Adaptive Learning Center (ALC) is an educational and residential 501(c)3 nonprofit California Corporation committed to facilitating growth and achievement through continuous education and therapeutic support in the lives of adults with Autism Spectrum Disorders and other neurodevelopmental disabilities. ALC provides a number of services under one umbrella, including "Day Program Services & Activities," "Vocational Support," and "Independent Community Living Services" in a supportive environment for those with a desire to do and learn what it takes to live independently.	3227 Clayton Road Concord, CA 94519 925-827-3863 info@alc-ca.org alc-ca.org
Adelphi University Bridges to Adelphi	This program is dedicated to providing the highest levels of individualized academic, social, and vocational support services to Adelphi's neurodiverse students. This includes students who self-disclose that they are on the autism spectrum, or students who have other non-verbal or neurological-social disorders.	One South Avenue Earle Hall B Lower Level Garden City, NY 11530 516-877-4181 bridges@adelphi.edu www.adelphi.edu/bridges/
Anchor to Windward, Inc.	Anchor to Windward, Inc. is a 501(c)(3) nonprofit organization dedicated to developing the full potential of adults with special needs by providing social and recreational programming, in-home support services, and daily living skills training. Since 1989, they have been helping adults with developmental disabilities lead independent and fulfilled lives.	74 Atlantic Avenue Marblehead, MA 01945 781-990-3056 www.anchortowindward.org
The Autism Program at Marian University's Ancilla College *Formerly APAC: The Autism Program at Ancilla College*	The Autism Program at Marian University's Ancilla College is a fee-based, college-level program designed to assist students diagnosed with autism spectrum disorder build academic, independent, social, and workplace skills and knowledge. The Autism program is intended for students who may struggle with communication and social interactions in an educational environment, but are also academically capable of pursuing a college-level education. The program increases the potential for career and academic success for students on the Autism Spectrum and gives faculty and staff the resources for providing a supportive campus community.	20097 9B Road Plymouth, IN 46563 1-866-Ancilla (866-262-4552) 574-936-8898 x330 www.marian.edu/ancilla/offices-services/autism

Program	Overview	Contact Information
Bancroft NeuroHealth	Bancroft is a leading regional nonprofit provider of programs and services for individuals with autism, intellectual and developmental disabilities, and those in need of neurological rehabilitation. Bancroft offers a comprehensive range of services and innovative programs supported by clinical experts. Programming includes special education, vocational training and supported employment, structured day programs, residential treatment programs, community living programs, and behavioral supports.	1-800-774-5516 Bancroft operates at various sites in New Jersey. See www.bancroft.org/locations/ for program locations
Bellevue College Neurodiversity Navigators	Bellevue College provides educational opportunities to increase successful academic outcomes in the areas of executive functioning, self-regulation, social interaction, self-advocacy, and career preparation, along with advocacy and access services for neurodivergent students; and to actively promote a campus and community environment of inclusion and understanding of students, faculty and staff with neurological differences.	3000 Landerholm Circle SE Bellevue, WA 98007 425-564-2764 asn@bellevuecollege.edu Text to 833-227-4551 www.bellevuecollege.edu/autism-spectrumnavigators/
Berkshire Hills Music Academy	Post-secondary school providing young adults with learning and developmental disabilities while living in a college setting and developing musical potential. Two-year certificate program.	48 Woodbridge Street South Hadley, MA 01075 413-540-9720 www.berkshirehills.org
Casa de Amma	Casa de Amma is a lifelong residential community for adults with special needs, including young adults who function independently but require assistance and structure in daily living. The supported living environment encourages residents to be productive, contributing members of their community and to achieve their full potential.	27231 Calle Arroyo San Juan Capistrano, CA 92675 949-496-9001 or 877-496-9001 Exec Dir: avorell@casadeamma.org casadeamma.org
Chapel Haven Schleifer Center	Chapel Haven is an award-winning, nationally accredited school and transition program serving 250-plus adults with a variety of abilities and needs. Chapel Haven provides lifelong individualized services for people with developmental and social disabilities, empowering them to live independent and self-determined lives.	1040 Whalley Avenue New Haven, CT 06151 203-397-1714 x185 admission@chapelhaven.org www.chapelhaven.org

CIP Berkeley Center
  Berkeley, CA
 	
CIP Berkshire Center
  Lee, MA
 	
CIP Bloomington Center
  Bloomington, IN
 	
CIP Brevard Center
  Melbourne, FL
 	
CIP Long Beach Center
  Long Beach, CA
	The College Internship Program (CIP) is a private young adult transition program for individuals 18–26 with autism, ADHD, and other learning differences offering comprehensive and specialized services. CIP's programs address the needs of young adults by focusing on the generalization of skills while living within a community of peers in a supported apartment living environment. Each student's unique needs are met individually as they transition to independent living, college, and employment. CIP's centers of excellence are located in areas that promote healthy living, culture, and a wide variety of social, educational, and career opportunities.	National Admissions Office:
		40 Main St, Suite 6 Lee, MA 01238
		877-566-9247 / 877-Know-CIP
		Int'l: +1 (413) 344-4019 ext 1
		admissions@cipworldwide.org
		cipworldwide.org
		
		CIP Berkshire, 413-243-2576
		CIP Brevard, 321-259-1900
		CIP Bloomington, 812-323-0600
		CIP Berkeley, 510-704-4476
		CIP Long Beach, 562-961-9250

The College Experience	The College Experience is a two-year residential noncredit certificate program hosted by The College of Saint Rose in collaboration with Living Resources. Students with intellectual disabilities practice living independently, develop social skills, intern at area businesses, and become part of a diverse campus community. The program allows students the opportunity to live away from home and attend college as a transition to independent adult living.	The College of Saint Rose 432 Western Avenue Albany, NY 12202 Colleen Dergosits, Admissions Coordinator 518-218-0000 Ext. 4625 www.thecollegeexperience.org

Program	Overview	Contact Information
College Living Experience Austin, TX Costa Mesa, CA Denver, Co Davie, FL Monterey, CA Franklin, TN Rockville, MD	College Living Experience (CLE) is a leading provider of post-secondary supports for young adults with learning differences. CLE students pursue their academic program or career of interest while also receiving services to promote independent living and social skills development. It is common for students to have a diagnosis of an autism spectrum disorder, specific learning disability, ADHD, cerebral palsy, or other types of cognitive delays.	National Admissions line: 800-486-5058 Main Office 401 N. Washington St, Suite 420 Rockville, MD 20850 info@experienceCLE.com experienceCLE.com

College Steps at Castleton University
 	
Other College Steps locations:
Kean University, NJ
Comm. College of VT,
  Montpelier & Winooski
County College of Morris, NJ
Rockland Comm. College, NY
Norwalk Comm. College, CT
American Int'l College, MA
Northern VA CC, Alexandria,
  Annadale & Loudin
Northern VT Univ,
  Johnson & Lyndon
Virtual Academy
	College Steps is a nonprofit 501(c)3 that was founded by a clinical psychologist and a special educator with a simple mission: To empower students living with learning and social challenges through structured post-secondary support. College Steps works closely with high schools, colleges and families, emphasizing peer-to-peer services that build confidence and success. They partner with colleges throughout the country who are interested in innovating their support service models to meet the needs of students living with social and learning disabilities.	Castleton University
		Castleton, VT
		802-468-1706
		patty@collegesteps.org
		www.castleton.edu/academics/
		college-steps/
		
		Business Office:
		23219 Stringtown Road #233
		Clarksburg, Maryland 20871
		888-732-1022
		contactus@collegesteps.org
		www.collegesteps.org/

Daemen College Autism Transition Support Program	The College Autism Transition Support (CATS) program offers life skills coaching and other transition support to matriculated students with autism spectrum disorder. Students involved in CATS receive weekly life skills coaching. Hours of coaching received depends on the needs of each student. Peer Life Skills Coaches are current upper-division students or recent graduates of Daemen University. Coaches have gone through training and receive continued training workshops throughout the semester.	4380 Main Street Amherst, NY 14226 800-462-7652 Director of Disability Services, Debbie Dimitrovski 716-839-8583 ddimitro@daemen.edu www.daemen.edu/student-life/ student-services/student-success- center/accessibility-services/ college-autism
Drexel University Academic and Career Program	Two-year, nondegree postsecondary experience for young adults with autism spectrum disorder (ASD). Students will receive a Certificate of Achievement upon program completion from the A.J. Drexel Autism Institute.	A.J. Drexel Autism Institute 3020 Market Street, Suite 560 Philadelphia, PA 19104-3734 215-571-3401 autisminstitute@drexel.edu drexel.edu/autisminstitute
Edgewood College Cutting Edge Program	The Cutting Edge® Program at Edgewood College offers a fully inclusive college experience for individuals with intellectual and developmental disabilities. The program offers individualized wrap-around services to support students in academics, student housing, social experiences, and practicums/internships. The program supports 28 students per academic year also and includes a Pre-College and an Alumni program. Students learn the Dominican values of justice, compassion, truth, community, and partnership, and are given the opportunity to experience civic engagement on campus and in the Madison community.	1255 Deming Way Madison, WI 53717 608-663-6869 cuttingedge@edgewood.edu www.edgewood.edu/cutting-edge
Elmhurst Learning and Success Academy *Formerly* *Life Skills Academy (ELSA)*	The Elmhurst Learning and Success Academy (ELSA) is a four-year, post-secondary certificate program for young adults, ages 18-28, with differing abilities. The program assists students with special needs in completing college and transitioning into independent adults.	Jean Koplin Memorial Hall, First Floor, 190 Prospect Avenue Elmhurst, Illinois 60126 630-617-3752 elsa@emhurst.edu admit@elmhurst.edu www.elmhurst.edu/academics/ elmhurst-learning-success-academy

Program	Overview	Contact Information
George Mason University Mason LIFE Program	The Mason Learning into Future Environments (LIFE) Program offers a four-year postsecondary curriculum of study to students with intellectual and developmental disabilities (IDD) who begin the program between the ages of 18–23. The Mason LIFE program offers programming in academics, employment, residential living, and social life to include Mason LIFE students in all aspects of the university. Apprenticeships give GMU students a hands-on opportunity to work with individuals with disabilities. This experience of learning, working, and living together mutually benefits everyone and is the basis for the Mason LIFE Program.	Division of Special Education and Disability Research 4400 University Drive, MSN 1F2 Fairfax, Virginia 22030 703-993-3905 masonlife.gmu.edu
Gersh College Experience Collaborates with: Suffolk County Community College, NY St. Josephs College, NY Five Towns College, Long Island	Gersh College Experience is a residential program for young adults on the autism spectrum designed to support maximal independence. The program teaches independent living skills, provides vocational training and work experience, skill development, and opportunities to improve socialization, and teaches coping strategies for the challenges of living independently. Academic guidance and counseling are provided and students can take college courses that align with their interests and abilities, preparing them for a career and life on their own. Gersh College Experience collaborates with local career-focused, post-secondary educational institutions.	Main NY Office 180 W Main St Patchogue, NY 11772 631-385-3342 info@gershexperience.com gershacademy.org
The Horizons School	The Horizons School provides a community-based educational program promoting successful transition to independent living for young adults with learning disabilities, autism spectrum and developmental disorders. A typical student is a young adult 18 to 26 years old with a learning disability such as ASD, developmental delay, mild CP or other similar learning difference.	2018 15th Avenue South Birmingham, AL 35205 205-322-6606 info@horizonsschool.org www.horizonsschool.org
Independence Center	Independence Center operates a nonsectarian program for adults with learning and developmental disabilities. The IC Living Program meets the needs of adults with learning differences who complete high school and need training for independent living while they work or continue their education.	3640 S. Sepulveda Blvd., Ste. 102 Los Angeles, CA 90034 310-202-7102 mgcoultas@icliving.org icliving.org
Kent State University Career and Community Studies	Career and Community Studies (CCS) is a college-based, nondegree transitional program that prepares students with intellectual and developmental disabilities for adult life through academic pursuits, peer socialization, and career discovery and preparation. The program integrates inclusive classes, a typical college experience, and a transition curriculum to assist students in achieving adult roles and a quality of life in a community of their choice. The CCS program is for students who have completed high school requirements and are at least 18 years of age.	Career & Community Studies, 218 White Hall Kent, OH 44242 330-672-0775 Dr. Vonnie Michali, Director yhale@kent.edu 330-672-0725 Cindy Kenyon, ABD Academic Faculty ckenyon@kent.edu www.kent.edu/ehhs/ccs
Lesley University Threshold Program	Threshold at Lesley University is a nondegree, post-secondary program for young adults with diverse learning, developmental, and intellectual disabilities. Students may have learning, intellectual, or developmental disabilities including (but not limited to) autism, nonverbal learning disabilities, ADHD, cerebral palsy, Down syndrome, or multiple disabilities. Students may have graduated from high school, may attend Threshold as part of their transition program as an out-of-district placement, or may have completed school at age 21 or 22 without a diploma.	29 Everett Street Cambridge, MA 02138-2790 617-349-8181 or 800-999-1959 ext. 8181 threshold@lesley.edu lesley.edu/threshold-program

Program	Overview	Contact Information
Life Development Institute	Community-based high school, summer, and young adult programs for older adolescents and adults struggling with learning disabilities, attention deficit disorders, Autism spectrum disorders, and other related-conditions. LDI programs provide students with a framework and a supportive environment while giving them enough autonomy to make decisions on their own and to gain the skills necessary for obtaining employment, living on their own, pursuing higher education or advanced job training, and developing healthy adult relationships.	5940 W. Union Hills Dr., Suite D-200 Glendale, AZ 85308 623-773-1545 discoverldi.com
LIFE Skills, Inc. Community Based Day Support programs in MA: Auburn Dudley Fitchburg Gardner Greenfield Lancaster Leominster Shrewsbury, Southbridge Webster Winchendon	Life-Skills, Inc., is an accredited nonprofit providing a wide variety of services to individuals with intellectual/developmental, physical, and emotional disabilities throughout Central and Western Massachusetts. Formerly known as Southern Worcester County Rehabilitation Center, Inc., they currently offer Residential, Day Habilitation, and Community Based Day Support programs.	Main Office Location 44 Morris Street Webster, MA 01570 508-943-0700 info@life-skillsinc.org life-skillsinc.org
Maplebrook School	Maplebrook School has a residential and day school consisting of vocational and college programs for students ages 11–21. The Academy uses a multi-sensory and individualized approach for each student with an academic environment that is supportive and adequately challenging. The Institute for Collegiate and Career Studies helps students gain skills in academics, work experience, and independent living. Students also learn the importance of good character and giving back to a community.	5142 Route 22 Amenia, NY 12501 845-373-8191 www.maplebrookschool.org
Marquette University On Your Marq	This program is designed for students with a diagnosis of Autism Spectrum Disorder, Pervasive Development Disorder (PDD), or Social Pragmatic Communication Disorder, ADHD, and all other forms of neurodivergence.	Coughlin Hall, 2nd Flr Milwaukee, WI 53233 414-288-0212 oym@marquette.edu www.marquette.edu/disability-services/on-your-marq Emily Raclaw, MS, LPC, Director 414-288-0203 emily.raclaw@marquette.ed
Minnesota Independence College and Community (MICC) *Formerly Minnesota Life College*	Apartment living, instructional program for young adults whose learning disabilities pose serious challenges to their independence. Must be 18+ and have completed K-12 education. Programs are focused on delivering curriculum and supports in the areas of independent living skills, social and emotional learning, career skills, employment, and healthy living.	7501 Logan Ave. South, Suite 2A Richfield, MN 55423 612-869-4008 info@miccommunity.org www.miccommunity.org/
Mitchell College Thames Academy	Thames at Mitchell College is a holistic college transition program for students with learning differences or students who would benefit from additional preparation to succeed in college—and it's right on the campus of Mitchell College. This unique program offers a highly individualized learning environment and a strong social network that feels safe and supportive.	Mitchell College 437 Pequot Avenue New London, CT 06320 860-701-5202 Crystal Simmons simmons_c@mitchell.edu. mitchell.edu/thames

Program	Overview	Contact Information
Northeastern University Learning Disability Services Program	The Learning Disabilities Program (LDP) is a fee-based, comprehensive academic support program for Northeastern University undergraduate day students whose primary disability is a learning disability and/or attention deficit disorder. LDP students meet with an LDP specialist in twice-weekly, hour-long sessions to promote academic growth and achievement. Areas addressed may include studying and test-taking strategies, reading, writing, executive functioning, setting and monitoring progress toward goals, and use of accommodations and campus resources.	135 Forsyth Building, 1st Floor Northeastern University 360 Huntington Avenue Boston, MA 02115 617-373-4526 j.newton@northeastern.edu www.northeastern.edu/ldp
OPTIONS Transition to Independence *Formerly OPTIONS Program at Brehm*	OPTIONS offers two different tracks: a College Transition track with John A. Logan College, and a Certificate of Completion track, which includes a variety of vocational concentrations. Both offer intensive assistance, structured supervision, and supported study hours to empower students with complex learning disabilities and differences to recognize and optimize their potential.	900 South Brehm Lane Carbondale, IL 62901 618-457-0371 618-549-4201 AdmissionsInfo@Experience OPTIONS.org www.experienceoptions.org/
P.A.C.E. Program at National Louis University	Path to Academics, Community and Employment (P.A.C.E) is a three-year, post-secondary certificate program designed to meet the transitional needs for young adults, ages 18–30, with multiple intellectual, learning and developmental disabilities. P.A.C.E. provides integrated services to empower students to become independent adults within the community.	P.A.C.E. at NLU 122 S. Michigan Avenue Chicago, IL 60603 312-261-3770 paceprogram@nl.edu nl.edu/pace
Path to Independence (P2I)	The Path to Independence is an inclusive, two-year, non-degree certificate program offering a college experience to students with intellectual disabilities. P2I is structured into three areas: Academic and Campus Activities, Employment, and Independent Living. Students must be 18–26 years, completed high school, have a minimum 3rd grade reading level, the ability to communicate, have basic safety skills in an unsupervised setting, and currently receiving, or are eligible to receive, supports through the Bureau of Vocational Rehabilitation or Aging and Disability Services.	Path to Independence at UNR NCED 664 N. Virginia Street Reno, NV 89557 775-682-9057 jkeefhaver@unr.edu www.unr.edu/nced/projects/nced-p2i
Pathway at UCLA	Two-year certificate program for students with developmental disabilities providing a blend of educational, social and vocational experiences.	UCLA Extension (dept or person) 1145 Gayley Ave. Los Angeles, CA 90024-3439 310-794-1235 pathway@uclaextension.edu www.uclaextension.edu/pathway
REACH Program at the College of Charleston	The REACH Program at the College of Charleston is a four-year, nondegree certificate program for students with mild intellectual and/or developmental disabilities. The REACH Program supports academics, socialization, independent living, and career development, and has been nationally recognized for its commitment to full-inclusion and self-determination. Students in the REACH Program can participate in all activities offered by the College of Charleston, with individualized support for success.	Reach Program Admissions College of Charleston 66 George Street Charleston, SC 29424 843-953-4849 REACHProgram@cofc.edu reach.cofc.edu
Riverview School	Riverview has a middle and high school program, a summer program, and a post high school transition program for 17–21 year olds. With a cognitive range of 70–100 and a primary diagnosis of a learning disability and/or complex language disorder, students receive structured, supportive guidance in academics, social skills, life skills, athletics, and the arts.	Admissions Office 551 Route 6A East Sandwich, MA 02537 508-888-0489 mcashdollar@riverviewschool.org riverviewschool.org/about
Shepherds College	Shepherds College is a leading post-secondary school created with the learning needs of students with intellectual and developmental disabilities in mind.	1805 15th Avenue Union Grove, Wisconsin 53182-1597 262-878-5620 262-878-6359 Admissions SCAdmissions@shepherdscollege.edu. www.shepherdscollege.edu/

Program	Overview	Contact Information
Syracuse University School of Education Inclusive U On Campus	InclusiveU is an initiative of the Taishoff Center for Inclusive Higher Education, committed to individualized and inclusive higher educational opportunities for students with intellectual and developmental disabilities. InclusiveU students complete individualized coursework, work with mentors and Peer2Peer support, and attend weekly seminars on topics like health and wellbeing, budgeting, dating and relationships, and resolution. They also have the option to pursue semester-long internships to explore their career options and gain marketable job skills, as well as on-campus jobs and a slew of social and extracurricular activities.	InclusiveU Taishoff Center for Inclusive Higher Education 300 Huntington Hall Syracuse, NY 13244-2340 315-443-4058 taishoffcenter@syr.edu taishoffcenter.syr.edu/inclusiveu
Taft College The Transition to Independent Living Program	The Transition to Independent Living Program provides students with collegiate experiences, inclusive environments, a career education, knowledge of their individual strengths, and empowerment through education. The college is a designated Hispanic Serving Institution (HSI).	Aaron Markovits Program Director 29 Cougar Court Taft, CA 93268 661-763-7773 www.taftcollege.edu/til/
Texas A & M University Aggie ACHIEVE	Aggie ACHIEVE at Texas A&M University is a comprehensive transition program (CTP) for young adults with intellectual and developmental disabilities (IDD) who have exited high school. Aggie ACHIEVE provides an inclusive and immersive college education and equips students for employment in the community. Aggie ACHIEVE aligns coursework, internship opportunities, and extracurricular activities with each student's academic interests and employment goals. Aggie ACHIEVE is designed to enroll students for up to four years.	Heather Dulas, program Director Jamie Berthold, program Coordinator 979-458-0297 aggieachieve.tamu.edu
University of Georgia Institute on Human Development and Disability Destination Dawgs	For students with intellectual disabilities between the ages of 18 -25 who have a personal desire—and support from family—to gain skills for self-determination, independent living, and career development at the University of Georgia. Completion of the program will result in a UGA Certificate in College and Career Readiness from the UGA Center on Continuing Education bearing +/– 100 continuing education units. Student competency and accomplishments will be recorded in an electronic portfolio.	River's Crossing 850 College Station Road Athens, GA 30602 706-410-7265 DestinationDawgs@uga.edu www.fcs.uga.edu/ihdd/ destination-dawgs
University of Iowa College of Education R.E.A.C.H Program (Realizing Educational and Career Hopes)	UI REACH is a comprehensive transition program for students ages 18–25 years old with intellectual, cognitive, and learning disabilities. UI REACH offers an integrated college experience in a caring and structured environment. Academics, career and transition, social growth, and campus life are areas of focus. UI REACH is a four-year program with early graduation options. There is a 2-year certificate for students with multiple learning and cognitive disabilities.	College of Education The University of Iowa Iowa City, IA 52242-1529 319-335-5359 REACH@uiowa.edu ask-education@uiowa.edu education.uiowa.edu/reach
University of the Ozarks The Jones Learning Center	The Jones Learning Center (JLC) is designed to serve students with documented learning disabilities, attention deficit/hyperactivity disorder (AD/HD), or autism spectrum disorder (ASD) with average or above average intellectual abilities. The JLC offers a comprehensive program with academic support to students who are intellectually capable of obtaining a college degree, but who also need support to accommodate for learning challenges caused by specific learning disabilities, AD/HD, or ASD.	University of the Ozarks 415 N. College Avenue Clarksville, AR 72830 800-264-8636 479-774-2962 jhughes@ozarks.edu ozarks.edu/academics/jones-learning-center
University of West Florida Argos for Autism Program	The Argos Autism Program (AAP) is a Beyond Access service offered by Student Accessibility Resources that provides academic, social, life skills, and career planning support to students with autism who attend the University of West Florida. The goal of the AAP is to enhance their college experience by providing assistance with navigating the college experience.	Student Accessibility Resources Building 21, Room 110 11000 University Parkway Pensacola, FL 32514 SAR at 850-474-2387 sar@uwf.edu uwf.edu/centers/center-for-behavior-analysis/argos-autism-program

Program	Overview	Contact Information
University of Wisconsin, White-water LIFE Program (Learning is for Everyone)	The LIFE Program provides a complete college experience for young adults between the ages of 18-25 who have an intellectual disability. With ample supports, specialized instruction, on-campus residential living, and community integration, the program provides access and opportunity for students who have historically been underrepresented in higher education. The program has two components, which includes a Basic Program (2 years) and an Advanced Program (2 years) that are designed to facilitate personal growth, independent living, and employment success.	UW-W LIFE Program Winther Hall 1002A 800 W. Main Street Whitewater, WI 53190 262-472-1905 lifeprogram@uww.edu www.uww.edu/coeps/departments/ life-program
Ursuline College FOCUS program	The FOCUS program is for students with learning disabilities and ADHD with the goal of helping students transition to Ursuline, connecting students to appropriate campus resources, improving self-advocacy skills, and developing strategies to promote academic success.	2550 Lander Rd Pepper Pike, OH 44124 Morgan Holeski, Disability Specialist 440-449-2046 morgan.weber@ursuline.edu www.ursuline.edu/academics/ academic-support-svcs/focus-program
Vista Vocational & Life Skills Center	The program is for adults 18 years and older with a wide range of disabilities and with varying educational backgrounds. It is not a requirement for a student to have graduated from high school to be accepted into the program.	Vista Vocational & Life Skills Center 1356 Old Clinton Road Westbrook, CT 06498 and 107 Bradley Road Madison, CT 06443 800-399-8080 www.vistalifeinnovations.org/
The Washington State University College of Education ROAR Program (Responsibility, Opportunity, Advocacy, and Respect)	WSU ROAR is a two-year inclusive postsecondary education program for students with intellectual and developmental disabilities (I/DD). There are individualized education programs, social skills classes, and vocational training. Students live communally on the Pullman campus. Students complete WSU audit courses with same-aged peers. WSU ROAR is an approved Comprehensive Transition Program (U.S. Department of Education).	College of Education Pullman, WA 99164-2114 509-335-4078 coe.roar@wsu.edu education.wsu.edu/ undergradprograms/wsuroar
Wellspring Foundation	Intensive residential treatment for various populations including girls 13–18 and adults. Highly structured programs are designed to treat a wide range of emotional and behavioral problems, including affective, personality, attachment, eating, and traumatic stress disorders.	The Wellspring Foundation, Inc. 21 Arch Bridge Road Bethlehem, CT 06751 203-266-8000 general 203-266-8002 admission Residential Program 203-266-8002 admission Day School info@wellspring.org www.wellspring.org
West Virginia Wesleyan Learning Center	The Learning Center promotes the academic success of students who are at risk due to diagnosed disabilities, other special needs, and insufficient preparation. In addition, all Wesleyan students are given the opportunity to be supported by instruction in college-level learning strategies and through the outreach of the Walk-In Tutoring System.	59 College Ave. Buckhannon, WV 26201 304-473-8000 admissions@wvwc.edu www.wvwc.edu/the-learning-center/

Alphabetical Index

Alphabetical List of Colleges by Level of Support Services

SP (Structured Programs): most comprehensive programs/services
CS (Coordinated Services): comprehensive programs/services
S (Services): least comprehensive programs/services
Refer to pages 8–9 for the full explanations of the levels of support.

SP: STRUCTURED PROGRAMS

College/University	State	Page
Adelphi University	New York	404
American International College	Massachusetts	280
American University	District of Columbia	114
Augsburg University	Minnesota	332
Barry University	Florida	120
Beacon College	Florida	122
Beloit College	Wisconsin	710
Bowling Green State University	Ohio	498
Castleton University	Vermont	654
Clemson University	South Carolina	600
College of Charleston	South Carolina	602
Curry College	Massachusetts	288
Davis & Elkins College	West Virginia	700
Dean College	Massachusetts	290
Drexel University	Pennsylvania	552
East Carolina University	North Carolina	466
Eastern Illinois University	Illinois	170
Eastern Michigan University	Michigan	314
Edgewood College	Wisconsin	712
Fairleigh Dickinson University—Florham	New Jersey	384
George Mason University	Virginia	666
Georgian Court University	New Jersey	386
Hofstra University	New York	418
Iona University	New York	420
Kean University	New Jersey	388
Kutztown University of Pennsylvania	Pennsylvania	558
Landmark College	Vermont	658
Lesley University	Massachusetts	300
Limestone University	South Carolina	604
Loras College	Iowa	226
Louisiana Christian University	Louisiana	252
Lynn University	Florida	134
Manhattanville College	New York	426
Marist College	New York	428

College/University	State	Page
Abilene Christian University	Texas	626
Adrian College	Michigan	310
Anderson University	Indiana	196
Appalachian State University	North Carolina	458
Arizona State University	Arizona	24
Arkansas State University	Arkansas	30
Aurora University	Illinois	164
Barnard College	New York	406
Bellevue College	Washington	688
Boston College	Massachusetts	282
Boston University	Massachusetts	284
Bradley University	Illinois	166
Brevard College	North Carolina	460
Bryant University	Rhode Island	588
Bucknell University	Pennsylvania	548
California State Polytechnic University, Pomona	California	38
California State University, Fresno	California	40
California State University, Fullerton	California	42
California State University, Long Beach	California	44
California State University, Northridge	California	46
California State University, San Bernardino	California	48
Case Western Reserve University	Ohio	500
The Catholic University of America	District of Columbia	116
Cedarville University	Ohio	502
Central Ohio Technical College	Ohio	504
Chatham University	Pennsylvania	550
Clark University	Massachusetts	286
Colby-Sawyer College	New Hampshire	372
Colgate University	New York	412
Davidson College	North Carolina	462
Defiance College	Ohio	508
DePaul University	Illinois	168
Drew University	New Jersey	382
Duke University	North Carolina	464
East Stroudsburg University of Pennsylvania	Pennsylvania	554
Eastern Kentucky University	Kentucky	242
Emerson College	Massachusetts	292
Endicott College	Massachusetts	294
Ferris State University	Michigan	316
Flagler College	Florida	126
Florida A&M University	Florida	128
Florida Atlantic University	Florida	130
The George Washington University	District of Columbia	118
Georgia Southern University	Georgia	152
Grand Valley State University	Michigan	318
Guilford College	North Carolina	470

College/University	State	Page
High Point University	North Carolina	472
Hobart and William Smith Colleges	New York	416
Illinois State University	Illinois	172
Iowa State University	Iowa	224
James Madison University	Virginia	670
Johnson & Wales University	Rhode Island	590
Kansas State University	Kansas	236
Kent State University	Ohio	510
Lasell University	Massachusetts	298
Lee University	Tennessee	614
Lehigh University	Pennsylvania	560
Long Island University Post	New York	424
Loyola Marymount University	California	50
Marian University	Wisconsin	714
Menlo College	California	52
Miami University	Ohio	512
Michigan State University	Michigan	322
Michigan Technological University	Michigan	324
Millersville University of Pennsylvania	Pennsylvania	564
Minnesota State University Moorhead	Minnesota	334
Monmouth University	New Jersey	390
Murray State University	Kentucky	244
New College of Florida	Florida	136
New England College	New Hampshire	374
New Jersey City University	New Jersey	394
New York University	New York	432
Nicholls State University	Louisiana	258
North Dakota State University	North Dakota	494
Northern Arizona University	Arizona	26
Norwich University	Vermont	660
Oberlin College	Ohio	518
Occidental College	California	54
The Ohio State University	Ohio	520
Ohio Wesleyan University	Ohio	524
Oregon State University	Oregon	542
Plymouth State University	New Hampshire	376
Providence College	Rhode Island	592
Rhode island College	Rhode Island	594
Rider University	New Jersey	396
Roanoke College	Virginia	678
Rocky Mountain College	Montana	360
Roger Williams University	Rhode Island	596
Roosevelt University	Illinois	180
Saint Joseph's University	Pennsylvania	576
Saint Michael's College	Vermont	662
San Francisco State University	California	58

College/University	State	Page
San Jose State University	California	60
Seton Hall University	New Jersey	398
Southern Connecticut State University	Connecticut	102
Southern Methodist University	Texas	632
Southern Wesleyan University	South Carolina	606
St. Ambrose University	Iowa	230
St. Catherine University	Minnesota	336
St. Thomas Aquinas College	New York	452
Stanford University	California	66
State University of New York at Albany	New York	438
State University of New York—Alfred State College	New York	440
State University of New York at Binghamton University	New York	442
State University of New York at Potsdam	New York	444
Texas A&M University	Texas	634
Texas State University	Texas	638
Towson University	Maryland	278
Tulane University	Louisiana	260
The University of Alabama	Alabama	16
University of Alaska Fairbanks	Alaska	22
University of Arkansas	Arkansas	32
University of California, Berkeley	California	68
University of California, Los Angeles	California	70
University of California, San Diego	California	72
University of California, Santa Barbara	California	74
University of Cincinnati	Ohio	526
University of Colorado Boulder	Colorado	88
University of Colorado at Colorado Springs	Colorado	90
University of Dayton	Ohio	528
University of Delaware	Delaware	112
University of Florida	Florida	142
University of Hartford	Connecticut	106
University of Illinois Springfield	Illinois	186
University of Iowa	Iowa	232
University of Kansas	Kansas	240
University of Kentucky	Kentucky	248
University of Lynchburg	Virginia	680
University of Memphis	Tennessee	618
University of Michigan	Michigan	328
University of Minnesota Morris	Minnesota	340
University of Missouri	Missouri	348
University of Nevada, Las Vegas	Nevada	370
University of New England	Maine	266
University of North Carolina at Chapel Hill	North Carolina	482
University of North Carolina Wilmington	North Carolina	488
University of Oregon	Oregon	544
University of the Pacific	California	80
University of Pittsburgh	Pennsylvania	582

College/University	State	Page
University of Rhode Island	Rhode Island	598
University of San Francisco	California	76
University of Southern California	California	78
University of Tennessee at Martin	Tennessee	624
University of Tulsa	Oklahoma	538
University of Vermont	Vermont	664
University of Virginia	Virginia	682
University of West Florida	Florida	146
University of Wisconsin—Eau Claire	Wisconsin	720
University of Wisconsin—Madison	Wisconsin	722
University of Wisconsin—Milwaukee	Wisconsin	724
University of Wyoming	Wyoming	732
Utica University	New York	456
Wake Forest University	North Carolina	490
Washington State University	Washington	694
West Virginia University	West Virginia	704
Western Carolina University	North Carolina	492
Western Colorado University	Colorado	96
Western Connecticut State University	Connecticut	110
Whittier College	California	82
Whitworth University	Washington	698
Widener University	Pennsylvania	584
William & Mary	Virginia	686
Xavier University	Ohio	534

College/University	State	Page
Montana State University Billings	Montana	356
Montana Technological University	Montana	358
Montclair State University	New Jersey	392
Morningside University	Iowa	228
Muhlenberg College	Pennsylvania	568
Neumann University	Pennsylvania	570
New Mexico Institute of Mining & Technology	New Mexico	400
New Mexico State University	New Mexico	402
North Carolina State University	North Carolina	476
Northern Michigan University	Michigan	326
Northwestern University	Illinois	178
Ohio University	Ohio	522
Oklahoma State University	Oklahoma	536
Old Dominion University	Virginia	674
Penn State University Park	Pennsylvania	572
Pittsburg State University	Kansas	238
Radford University	Virginia	676
Regis University	Colorado	86
Ripon College	Wisconsin	718
Rivier University	New Hampshire	378
Saint Louis University	Missouri	346
Salisbury University	Maryland	274
San Diego State University	California	56
Santa Clara University	California	62
Savannah College of Art and Design	Georgia	160
Seton Hill University	Pennsylvania	578
Smith College	Massachusetts	304
Sonoma State University	California	64
South Dakota State University	South Dakota	610
Southern Illinois University Edwardsville	Illinois	184
Southern Utah University	Utah	648
St. Andrews University	North Carolina	478
St. Bonaventure University	New York	448
St. Lawrence University	New York	450
St. Mary's College of Maryland	Maryland	276
St. Olaf College	Minnesota	338
State University of New York—Stony Brook University	New York	446
Stetson University	Florida	138
Temple University	Pennsylvania	580
Texas A&M University—Kingsville	Texas	636
The University of Alabama in Huntsville	Alabama	18
University of Alaska Anchorage	Alaska	20
University of Central Florida	Florida	140
University of Georgia	Georgia	162
University of Illinois at Urbana–Champaign	Illinois	188
University of Jamestown	North Dakota	496

About the Authors

Imy Wax is a Psychotherapist, Licensed Clinical Professional Counselor (LCPC), National Board Certified Counselor (NBCC), Certified Educational Planner (CEP), and a Therapeutic and Educational Consultant (EC). As a consultant, Imy travels 100,000 miles a year visiting residential programs, schools, colleges, and post-secondary options for children, adolescents, and young adults throughout the U.S. and internationally, often as a guest speaker. Imy is a frequent presenter at professional and parental conferences. She has authored and been quoted in numerous journal articles and conducts workshops for parents and school districts. She is also a wife, mother to four, and grandmother to seven. Her daughter was the inspiration for this book. Imy is often called upon by mental health professionals and attorneys to assist them in identifying appropriate education and program alternatives for their students and clients. She is the founder and president of The Aspire Group. For over 30 years, Imy and her team have been an objective voice in guiding, supporting, and empowering families to make informed decisions that will secure and enhance their child's future. Imy believes that there should never be a "closed door" to one's hopes and dreams and that today is but a stepping stone to a better tomorrow, and each child's journey is unique. For additional information or to contact Imy Wax for consultation, email or phone:

Imy Wax
847-945-0913 (office)
844-945-0913 (toll-free)
+1 224-619-3558 (Skype # -International)
Imy@TheAspireGroup.com

Marybeth Kravets, MA, is the President of Marybeth Kravets & Associates LLC, providing educational and college consulting to students with and without learning differences, and is also the Director of College Counseling at Wolcott College Prep High School in Chicago, Illinois. She received her BA in Education from the University of Michigan in Ann Arbor and her MA in Counseling from Wayne State University in Detroit, Michigan. She is a Past President of the National Association for College Admission Counseling (NACAC) and also served as the President of the Illinois Association for College Admission Counseling (IACAC). Marybeth Kravets is a recipient of the Harvard University Club of Chicago Community Service Award for her lifelong dedication to serving students who are economically challenged or challenged with learning differences. Marybeth serves on the United World College–USA Board of Trustees and the Emeritus Board of Trustees for College Bound Opportunities, Highland Park, Illinois. For additional information or to contact Marybeth Kravets for a consultation, email or call:

Marybeth Kravets
847-212-3687 (cell)
Marybeth@kravets.net